MILITARY AIRCRAFT MARKINGS 2019

MILITARY AIRCRAFT MARKINGS 2019
Howard J Curtis

Crécy Publishing Ltd

This 40th edition published by Crécy Publishing Ltd 2019

ISBN 9781910809259

Printed in Malta by Gutenberg Press Limited

Crecy Publishing Ltd
1a Ringway Trading Est
Shadowmoss Rd
Manchester
M22 5LH
Tel +44 (0)161 499 0024
www.crecy.co.uk

Front cover:
Airbus A330-MRTT Voyager ZZ330 seen
here at Fairford United Kingdom
© *Matthieu Douhaire/AirTeamImages*

CONTENTS

This 40th annual edition of *abc Military Aircraft Markings*, follows the pattern of previous years and lists in alphabetical and numerical order the aircraft that carry a United Kingdom military registration and which are normally based, or might be seen, in the UK. It also includes airworthy and current RAF/RN/Army aircraft that are based permanently or temporarily overseas. Aircraft used as targets on MoD ranges to which access is restricted, and UK military aircraft that have been permanently grounded overseas and unlikely to return to Britain have generally been omitted.

Aircraft in UK military service which carry civil registrations are listed, as are historic aircraft wearing overseas markings which are based in the UK or likely to be seen in the UK. All aircraft carrying Irish military markings are listed in a separate section. Similarly, aircraft belonging to the armed forces or governments of foreign countries are listed, including American military aircraft based in the UK and Europe.

In the main, the registrations listed are those markings presently displayed on the aircraft. Where an aircraft carries a false registration it is quoted in *italic type*. Very often these registrations are carried by replicas, which are denoted by <R> after the type. The manufacturer and aircraft type are given, together with recent alternative, previous, secondary or civil identity shown in round brackets. The operating unit and its based location, along with any known unit and code markings, in square brackets, are given as accurately as possible. Where aircraft carry special or commemorative markings, a $ indicates this. To help identification of RN bases and landing platforms on ships, a list of tail-letter codes with their appropriate name, helicopter code number, ship pennant number and type of vessel, is included; as is a helicopter code number/ship's tail-letter code grid cross-reference.

Up-to-date code changes, for example when aircraft move between units, might not be as printed here because of subsequent events, but code lists are regularly updated and uploaded to the 'Military Aircraft Markings' web site, www.militaryaircraftmarkings.co.uk, from which monthly UK updates can also be accessed. Airframes which will not appear in the next edition because of sale, accident, etc., have their fates, where known, shown in italic type in the *locations* column.

Following the significant changes made from the 2016 edition onwards, it is now possible to include fates for all aircraft listed and so this edition includes details of, for example, American aircraft going to storage at AMARG at Davis-Monthan Air Force Base. Additionally, the extra space has enabled the inclusion of previous identities and these have been further extended across the whole publication where space permits.

2018 was the centenary of the Royal Air Force, celebrated with a host of special events across the year and by a single example of each RAF type having special markings applied in the form of a 'RAF 100' sticker. As the year progressed, the Tornado GR4 fleet diminished considerably with around 16 aircraft left by February 2019 and with the whole fleet due out of service in March. Already Typhoons are being allocated to No 9 Squadron, with No 12 Squadron expected to receive examples shortly as the last handful of aircraft are delivered from Warton. Early June 2018 saw the arrival at RAF Marham of the first four F-35B Lightning IIs to No 617 Squadron, followed by a further five in October while trials continue with the first carrier for the Lightning II, HMS *Queen Elizabeth*. Turning to helicopters, the RAF's fleet of Chinooks is slowly being upgraded to HC6A status at Boscombe Down, with the prospect of 16 new build aircraft joining the service in due course. In an unusual move, 744 Naval Air Squadron reformed in October 2018 as a tri-service Test and Evaluation Squadron to operate the Chinook HC6A and the Merlin Crowsnest conversion, the Sea King ASaC7 replacement. A final fly past on 19 September saw the Sea King ASaC7 retire from Navy service with the last examples flying to Gosport eight days later, bringing to an end UK military operations of the type. The Merlin continues in Naval service, with a steady flow through Leonardo MW's plant at Yeovil for conversion to HC4 and HC4A status and repainting in the standard grey colour scheme. The Wildcat AH1 and HMA2 fleet is now well-established, unusually all based at a single location, RNAS Yeovilton in Somerset. Turning to training aircraft, the planned fleets of Prefect, Texan II and Phenom along with Juno and Jupiter helicopters have all been reached although the smaller numbers of each type make the fleets more susceptible when aircraft have accidents and currently a single Prefect and Phenom are both out of use with damage as this introduction is being put together. The Tucano continues in service at RAF Linton-on-Ouse but these will disappear during 2019 with an out of service date of October after which the base will close, as will RAF Scampton in due course. 2019 will see the delivery of the first Poseidon MRA1 to RAF Lossiemouth while Atlas C1 deliveries are near to completion with just a pair left for delivery. 2018 continued to see slow progress with the air cadet Viking fleet but also saw the retirement of the Vigilant. For QinetiQ the end of 2018 saw the complete retirement of every aircraft that it held on the UK military register and early 2019 will see its whole fleet put on the UK civil register, using the G-ETP sequence.

Across Europe types such as the F-16, Alpha Jet, Transall C-160, Tornado and even the Mirage 2000 are slowly disappearing from service as Eurofighters, Rafales, F-35 Lightnings and A400Ms continue to replace them. The Airbus H145 and H160 lines look good for many years ahead as these types, along with the NH-90 and AW101 continue to enter service. Late January 2019 saw the first KC-46A deliveries to 22 ARW at McConnell AFB and these, along with the F-35 Lightning II, C-130J Hercules II and P-8A Poseidon will replace older types and keep American production going for some considerable time.

2018 was another year in which there were few notable accidents and perhaps the most lasting memory has of the year has been the developing, and for some increasingly frustrating, political situations in both the US and Europe with considerable uncertainty ahead as this publication goes to press.

You can find 'MAM' on Facebook at www.facebook.com/MilitaryAircraftMarkings, on Twitter (@HJCurtisMAM) as well as on the 'MAM' web site, www.militaryaircraftmarkings.co.uk.

ACKNOWLEDGEMENTS

The compiler wishes to thank the many people who have taken the trouble to send comments, additions, deletions and other useful information since the publication of the previous edition of Military Aircraft Markings. In particular the following individuals: Nigel Burch, Ian Carroll, Paul Clark, Martin Condon, Glyn Coney, Oliver Curtis, Paul Duncan, Ben Dunnell, Graham Gaff, Richard Hall, Kevin Herpe, Norman Hibberd, Dave Higgins, Doug MacDonald, Peter R March, Andy Marden, Tony McCarthy, John Mellor, Martin Pole, Mark Ray, Norman Roberson, Ben Sadler, David Thompson and Paul Williamson.

The 2019 edition has also relied upon the printed publications and/or associated internet web-sites as follows: Aerodata Quantum+, 'Aeroplane' magazine, Airfields Yahoo! Group, 'Air Forces Monthly' magazine, CAA G-INFO Web Site, Coningsby Aviation Site, Delta Reflex, EGHH Google Group, Fighter Control, 'FlyPast' magazine, Joe Baugher's Home Page, Mildenhall and Lakenheath Movements Group (SMAS), Brian Pickering/'Military Aviation Review', Mil Spotters' Forum, NAMAR Yahoo! Group, The Official RAF Leeming Spotters' Group (Facebook), Planebase NG, RAF Shawbury Yahoo! Group, 'Scramble' magazine, Souairport group, South West of England Aviation Movements (Facebook), Tom McGhee/UK Serials Resource Centre, Mick Boulanger/Wolverhampton Aviation Group and 'Wrecks & Relics'.

Information shown is believed to be correct at 24 February 2019.

HJC February 2019

Note: The compiler will be pleased to receive comments, corrections and further information for inclusion in subsequent editions of *Military Aircraft Markings* and the monthly up-date of additions and amendments. Please send your information to Military Aircraft Markings, Crécy Publishing Ltd, 1a Ringway trading Estate, Shadowmoss Road, Manchester M22 5LH or by e-mail to admin@aviation-links.co.uk.

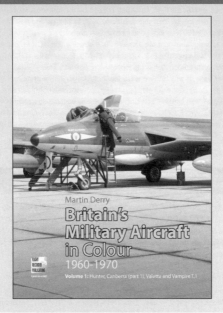

Britain's Military Aircraft in Colour 1960-1970

Martin Derry

This book offers a nostalgic selection of colour images featuring four types of aircraft in British military, or Ministry service. Full advantage has been taken of a relatively scarce photographic opportunity from a period when a roll of colour film (eight exposures) cost approximately £5 – a week's average wage in the early 1960s.

Covering the Hunter, Canberra, Valetta and Vampire T11, each type has an introduction and comprehensive captions to explain the various types in full detail. Serial numbers, units and aircraft histories are all covered and four-view artwork derived from specific photographs is included to provide in depth information for the enthusiast, historian or modeller.

ISBN: 9780955426827 **£12.95**

Available at all good book shops, enthusiast shops and pilot shops

Crecy Publishing Ltd
1a Ringway Trading Est
Shadowmoss Rd
Manchester
M22 5LH
Tel +44 (0)161 499 0024
www.crecy.co.uk

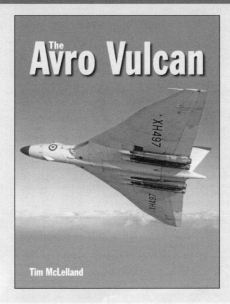

$	Aircraft in special markings
AAC	Army Air Corps
AACS	Airborne Air Control Squadron
AC	Air Cadets
ACCGS	Air Cadets Central Gliding School
ACS	Air Control Squadron
ACW	Air Control Wing
ADF	Air Defence Force
ADSU	Apache Depth Support Unit
AEF	Air Experience Flight
AESS	Air Engineering & Survival School
AEW	Airborne Early Warning
AFB	Air Force Base
AFD	Air Fleet Department
AFRC	Air Force Reserve Command
AG	Airlift Group
AGA	Academia General del Aire (General Air Academy)
AGS	Air Ground Surveillance
AK	Alaska
AL	Alabama
AMD-BA	Avions Marcel Dassault-Breguet Aviation
AMG	Aircraft Maintenance Group
AM&SU	Aircraft Maintenance & Storage Unit
AMRO	Aircraft Maintenance and Repair Organisation
AMW	Air Mobility Wing
ANG	Air National Guard
AR	Arkansas
ARS	Air Refueling Squadron
ARW	Air Refueling Wing
AS	Airlift Squadron/Air Squadron
ATC	Air Training Corps
ATCC	Air Traffic Control Centre
AVDEF	Aviation Defence Service
Avn	Aviation
AW	AgustaWestland/Airlift Wing/Armstrong Whitworth Aircraft
AWC	Air Warfare Centre
BAC	British Aircraft Corporation
BAe	British Aerospace
BAPC	British Aviation Preservation Council (now known as Aviation Heritage UK)
BATUK	British Army Training Unit Kenya
BATUS	British Army Training Unit Suffield
BBMF	Battle of Britain Memorial Flight
BDRF	Battle Damage Repair Flight
BDRT	Battle Damage Repair Training
Be	Beech
Bf	Bayerische Flugzeugwerke
BG	Bomber Group
BGA	British Gliding & Soaring Association
bk	black (squadron colours and markings)
bl	blue (squadron colours and markings)
Blt	Bojová letka (attack squadron)
BP	Boulton & Paul/Boulton Paul
br	brown (squadron colours and markings)
BS	Bomber Squadron
B-V	Boeing-Vertol
BW	Bomber Wing
CA	California
CAARP	Co-operative des Ateliers Air de la Région Parisienne
CAC	Commonwealth Aircraft Corporation
CACG	Command and Control Group
CAE	Centro Addastramento Equipaggi (Crew Training Centre)
CASA	Construcciones Aeronautics SA
CATS	Cassidian Aviation Training Services
CC	County Council
CC Air	Competence Centre Air
CCF	Combined Cadet Force/Canadian Car & Foundry Company
CEAM	Centre d'Expertise Aérienne Militaire (Centre of Military Air Expertise)

CEMAST	Centre of Excellence in Engineering & Manufacturing Advanced Skills Training
CEPA	Centre d'Expérimentation Pratique de l'Aéronautique Navale
CFAMI	Centre de Formation Aérienne Militaire Initiale de Salon
CFIA	Centre de Formation Interarmées NH.90
CFS	Central Flying School
CIEH	Centre d'Instruction des Equipages d'Hélicoptères
CHFMU	Commando Helicopter Force Maintenance Unit
CinC	Commander in Chief
CinCLANT	Commander in Chief Atlantic
CLV	Centrum Leteckeho Vycviku (Air Training Centre)
CMU	Central Maintenance Unit
Co	Company
CO	Colorado
COMALAT	Commandement de l'Aviation Légère de l'Armée de Terre
Comp	Composite with
CT	Connecticut
CV	Chance-Vought
D-BA	Daimler-Benz Aerospace
D-BD	Dassault-Breguet Dornier
D&G	Dumfries and Galloway
DCTT	Defence College of Technical Training
DE	Delaware
DE&S	Defence Equipment and Support
DEFTS	Defence Elementary Flying Training School
DEODS	Defence Explosives Ordnance Disposal School
Det	Detachment
DFTDC	Defence Fire Training and Development Centre
DGA	Délégation Générale de l'Armement
DH	de Havilland
DHC	de Havilland Canada
DHFS	Defence Helicopter Flying School
DMS	Defence Movements School
DS&TL	Defence Science & Technology Laboratory
DSAE	Defence School of Aeronautical Engineering
DSEME	Defence School of Electro-Mechanical Engineering
DSG	Defence Support Group
DSMarE	Defence School of Marine Engineering
Dvlt	Dopravná vrtul'niková letka (Helicopter Transport Squadron)
EA	Escadron Aérien (Air Squadron)
EAAT	Escadrille Avions de l'Armée de Terre
EAC	Ecole de l'Aviation de Chasse (Fighter Aviation School)
EALAT	Ecole de l'Aviation Légère de l'Armée de Terre
EAP	European Aircraft Project
EAT	Ecole de l'Aviation de Transport (Transport Aviation School)
EC	Escadre de Chasse (Fighter Wing)
E-CATS	EADS Cognac Aviation Training Services
ECG	Electronic Combat Group
ECM	Electronic Counter Measures
ECS	Electronic Countermeasures Squadron
EdC	Escadron de Convoyage
EDCA	Escadron de Détection et de Control Aéroportée (Airborne Detection & Control Sqn)
EE	English Electric/Escadrille Electronique
EEA	Escadron Electronique Aéroporté
EFA	Ecole Franco Allemande
EFTS	Elementary Flying Training School
EH	Escadron d'Helicoptères (Helicopter Squadron)
EHADT	Escadrille Helicoptères de l'Armée de Terre
EHI	European Helicopter Industries
EKW	Eidgenössiches Konstruktionswerkstätte
el	Eskadra Lotnicza (Air Sqn)
EL	Escadre de Liaison (Liaison Wing)
elt	Eskadra Lotnictwa Taktycznego (Tactical Air Squadron)
eltr	Eskadra Lotnictwa Transportowego (Air Transport Squadron)
EMA	East Midlands Airport
EMB	Ecoles Militaires de Bourges

EMVO	Elementaire Militaire Vlieg Opleiding (Elementary Flying Training)
EoN	Elliot's of Newbury
EPAA	Ecole de Pilotage Elementaire de l'Armée de l'Air (Air Force Elementary Flying School)
EPNER	Ecole du Personnel Navigant d'Essais et de Reception
ER	Escadre de Reconnaissance (Reconnaissance Wing)
ERV	Escadron de Ravitaillement en Vol (Aerial Refuelling Squadron)
ES	Escadrille de Servitude
ESAM	Ecole Supérieur d'Application du Matériel
Esc	Escuadron (Squadron)
ESHE	Ecole de Spécialisation sur Hélicoptères Embarqués (School of Specialisation on Embarked Helicopters)
Esk	Eskadrile/Eskadrille (Squadron)
Esq	Esquadra (Squadron)
ET	Escadre de Transport (Transport Wing)
ETED	Escadron de Transformation des Equipages Mirage 2000D
ETO	Escadron de Transition Operationnelle (Operational Transition Squadron)
ETPS	Empire Test Pilots' School
ETR	Escadron de Transformation Rafale
ETS	Engineering Training School/Escadron de Transport Stratégique
ETTL	Escadre de Transport Tactique et Logistique (Tactical and Logistics Transport Wing)
EVAA	Ecole de Voltige de l'Armée de l'Air (French Air Force Aerobatics School)
FAA	Fleet Air Arm (UK)/Federal Aviation Administration (USA)
FACO	Final Assembly & Check Out
FBS	Flugbereitschaftstaffel (Flight Readiness Squadron)
FBW	Fly-by-wire
FC	Forskokcentralen (Flight Centre)
FE	Further Education
FETC	Fire and Emergency Training Centre
ff	Front fuselage
FG	Fighter Group
FH	Fairchild-Hiller
FI	Falkland Islands
FJWOEU	Fast Jet & Weapons Operational Evaluation Unit
FL	Florida
FLO	Forsvarets Logistikk Organisasjon (Defence Logistics Organisation)
FISt	Fliegerstaffel (Flight Squadron)
Flt	Flight
FMA	Fabrica Militar de Aviones
FMV	Forsvarets Materielwerk (Defence Material Works)
FS	Fighter Squadron
FTS	Flying Training School
FTW	Flying Training Wing
Fw	Focke Wulf
FW	Fighter Wing/FlugWerk/Foster Wickner
FY	Fiscal Year
GA	Georgia
GAF	Government Aircraft Factory
GAL	General Aircraft Ltd
GAM	Groupe Aerien Mixte (Composite Air Group)
GAM/STAT	Groupement Aéromobile/Section Technique de l'Armée de Terre
gd	gold (squadron colours and markings)
GD	General Dynamics
GEA	Gruppo Efficienza Aeromobili (Italian AF)/Gruppo Esplorazione Aeromarittima (GdiF)
GEM	Grupo de Escuelas de Matacán (Matacán Group of Schools)
GI	Ground Instruction/Groupement d'Instruction (Instructional Group)
GMS	Glider Maintenance Section
gn	green (squadron colours and markings)
GRD	Gruppe fur Rustunggdienste (Group for Service Preparation)
GRV	Groupe de Ravitaillement en Vol (Air Refuelling Group)
GT	Grupo de Transporte (Transport Wing)
GTT	Grupo de Transporte de Tropos (Troop Carrier Wing)
gy	grey (squadron colours and markings)
HAF	Historic Aircraft Flight
HAPS	High Altitude Pseudo-Satellite
HavLLv	Hävittäjälentolaivue
HC	Helicopter Combat Support Squadron
HekoP	Helikopteripataljoona (Helicopter Battalion)

HF	Historic Flying Ltd
HI	Hawaii
HK	Helikopterikomppannia (Helicopter Company)
Hkp.Bat	Helikopter Bataljon (Helicopter Battalion)
HMA	Helicopter Maritime Attack
HMS	Her Majesty's Ship
HP	Handley-Page
HQ	Headquarters
HS	Hawker Siddeley
HSG	Hubschraubergeschwader (Helicopter Squadron)
IA	Iowa
IAF	Israeli Air Force
IAP	International Airport
IL	Illinois
IlmaStk	IlmataiStelukeskus
IN	Indiana
IntHubschr-	Internationales Hubschrauberausbildungszentrum
AusbZ	(International Helicopter Training Centre)
IOW	Isle Of Wight
IWM	Imperial War Museums
JADTEU	Joint Air Delivery Test and Evaluation Unit
JARTS	Joint Aircraft Recovery & Transportation Sqn
JFACTSU	Joint Forward Air Control Training & Standards Unit
JHC	Joint Helicopter Command
JMRC	Joint Multinational Readiness Centre
KHR	Kampfhubschrauberregiment (Combat Helicopter Regiment)
Kridlo	Wing
KS	Kansas
LA	Louisiana
lbvr	letka Bitevnich Vrtulníkú (Attack Helicopter Squadron)
Letka	Squadron
LTDB	Lufttransportdienst des Bundes (Federal Air Transport Services)
LTG	Lufttransportgeschwader (Air Transport Wing)
lTHSSta	leichte Transporthubschrauberstaffel
LTO	Letalska Transportni Oddelek (Air Transport Department)
LtSt	Lufttransport Staffel
LTV	Ling-Temco-Vought
LVG	Luftwaffen Versorgungs Geschwader (Air Force Maintenance Wing)/Luft Verkehrs Gesellschaft
LZO	Letecky Zku ební Odbor (Aviation Test Department)
m	multi-coloured (squadron colours and markings)
MA	Massachusetts
MADG	Marshall Aerospace & Defence Group
MAPK	Mira Anachestistis Pantos Kerou (All Weather Interception Sqn)
MBB	Messerschmitt Bolkow-Blohm
MCAS	Marine Corps Air Station
McD	McDonnell Douglas
MD	Maryland
MDMF	Merlin Depth Maintenance Facility
Med	Medical
MFG	Marine Flieger Geschwader (Naval Air Wing)
MFSU	Merlin Depth Forward Support Unit
MH	Max Holste
MI	Maritime Interdiction/Michigan
MIB	Military Intelligence Battalion
MiG	Mikoyan — Gurevich
MMF	(European) Multinational Multi-Role Tanker Transport Fleet
MN	Minnesota
MO	Missouri
Mod	Modified
MoD	Ministry of Defence
MPSU	Multi-Platform Support Unit
MR	Maritime Reconnaissance
MRH	Multi-role Helikopters
M&RU	Marketing & Recruitment Unit
MS	Mississippi/Morane-Saulnier
MT	Montana

MTHR	Mittlerer Transporthubschrauber Regiment (Medium Transport Helicopter Regiment)
MTM	Mira Taktikis Metaforon (Tactical Transport Sqn)
NA	North American
NACDS	Naval Air Command Driving School
NAEW&CF	NATO Airborne Early Warning & Control Force
NAF	Naval Air Facility
NAS	Naval Air Squadron (UK)/Naval Air Station (US)
NATO	North Atlantic Treaty Organisation
NAWC	Naval Air Warfare Center
NAWC-AD	Naval Air Warfare Center Aircraft Division
NBC	Nuclear, Biological and Chemical
ND	North Dakota
NDMA	Norwegian Defence Material Agency
NE	North-East/Nebraska
NFH	NATO Frigate Helicopter
NH	New Hampshire
NI	Northern Ireland
NJ	New Jersey
NM	New Mexico
NV	Nevada
NY	New York
NYARC	North Yorks Aircraft Restoration Centre
OEU	Operational Evaluation Unit
OFMC	Old Flying Machine Company
OGMA	Oficinas Gerais de Material Aeronautico
OH	Ohio
OK	Oklahoma
or	orange (squadron colours and markings)
OSAC	Operational Support Airlift Command
OSBL	Oddelek Sholskih Bojni Letal (Training & Combat School)
P2MF	Puma 2 Maintenance Flight
PA	Pennsylvania
PAS	Presidential Airlift Squadron
PAT	Priority Air Transport Detachment
PBN	Pilatus Britten-Norman
PDSH	Puma Depth Support Hub
PLM	Pulk Lotnictwa Mysliwskiego (Fighter Regiment)
pr	purple (squadron colours and markings)
PR	Puerto Rico
r	red (squadron colours and markings)
R	Replica
RAeS	Royal Aeronautical Society
RAF	Royal Aircraft Factory/Royal Air Force
RAFC	Royal Air Force College
RAFM	Royal Air Force Museum
RAFGSA	Royal Air Force Gliding and Soaring Association
RE	Royal Engineers
Regt	Regiment
REME	Royal Electrical & Mechanical Engineers
rf	Rear fuselage
RFA	Royal Fleet Auxiliary
RHC	Régiment d'Helicoptères de Combat (Combat Helicopter Regiment)
RHFS	Régiment d'Helicoptères des Forces Spéciales (Special Forces Helicopter Regiment)
RI	Rhode Island
RJAF	Royal Jordanian Air Force
RM	Royal Marines
RMB	Royal Marines Base
RN	Royal Navy
RNAS	Royal Naval Air Station
RNGSA	Royal Navy Gliding and Soaring Association
RPAS	Remotely Piloted Air System
RQS	Rescue Squadron
R-R	Rolls-Royce
RS	Reid & Sigrist/Reconnaissance Squadron
RSV	Reparto Sperimentale Volo (Experimental Flight School)
RTP	Reduction To Produce
RW	Reconnaissance Wing

SA	Scottish Aviation
SAAB	Svenska Aeroplan Aktieboleg
SAAE	School of Army Aeronautical Engineering
SAC	Strategic Airlift Capability
SAL	Scottish Aviation Limited
SAR	Search and Rescue
Saro	Saunders-Roe
SARTU	Search and Rescue Training Unit
SC	South Carolina
SCW	Strategic Communications Wing
SD	South Dakota
SEPECAT	Société Européenne de Production de l'avion Ecole de Combat et d'Appui Tactique
SFDO	School of Flight Deck Operations
SHAPE	Supreme Headquarters Allied Powers Europe
si	silver (squadron colours and markings)
SKAMG	Sea King Aircraft Maintenance Group
Skv	Skvadron (Squadron)
SLK	Stíhacie Letecké Kridlo (Fighter Air Wing)
slt	stíhací letka (Fighter Squadron)
SLV	School Licht Vliegwezen (Flying School)
Sm	Smaldeel (Squadron)
SNCAN	Société Nationale de Constructions Aéronautiques du Nord
SOG	Special Operations Group
SOS	Special Operations Squadron
SoTT	School of Technical Training
SOW	Special Operations Wing
SPAD	Société Pour les Appareils Deperdussin
SPP	Strojirny Prvni Petilesky
Sqn	Squadron
Sz.D.REB	'Szentgyörgyi Deszö' Harcászati Repülö Bázis
TA	Territorial Army
TAP	Transporten Avio Polk (Air Transport Regiment)
TASF(N)	Tornado Aircraft Servicing Flight (North)
TAZLS	Technische Ausbildungs Zentrum Luftwaffe Süd (TAubZLwSüd, Technical Training Centre South)
TES	Test and Evaluation Squadron
TFC	The Fighter Collection
TGp	Test Groep
TH	Transporthelikopter
TIARA	Tornado Integrated Avionics Research Aircraft
tl	taktická letka (Tactical Squadron)
TLG	Taktisches Luftwaffegeschwader (Air Force Tactical Squadron)
TMU	Typhoon Maintenance Unit
TN	Tennessee
Tr AB	Transport Aviation Brigade
TS	Test Squadron
ts	transportnia speciálni letka (special transport squadron)
TsAGI	Tsentral'ny Aerogidrodinamicheski Instut (Central Aero & Hydrodynamics Institute)
TSF	Tucano Servicing Flight
TsLw	Technische Schule der Luftwaffe (Luftwaffe Technical School)
TST	Tornado Support Team
TTH	Tactical Transport Helicopter
TukiLLv	Tukilentolaivue
TW	Test Wing
TX	Texas
UAS	University Air Squadron
UAV	Unmanned Air Vehicle
Überwg	Überwachungsgeschwader
UK	United Kingdom
US	United States
USAF	United States Air Force
USAFE	United States Air Forces in Europe
USAREUR	US Army Europe
USCGS	US Coast Guard Station
USEUCOM	United States European Command
USMC	United States Marine Corps
USN	United States Navy

USNWTSPM	United States Navy Test Pilots School
USW	University of South Wales
UT	Utah
VA	Virginia
VAAC	Vectored thrust Advanced Aircraft flight Control
VFW	Vereinigte Flugtechnische Werke
VGS	Volunteer Gliding Squadron
vlt	výcviková letka (training squadron)
VMGR	Marine Aerial Refuelling/Transport Squadron
VMGRT	Marine Aerial Refuelling/Transport Training Squadron
VQ	Fleet Air Reconnaissance Squadron
VR	Fleet Logistic Support Squadron
vrl	vrtulníková letka (helicopter squadron)
VS	Vickers-Supermarine
w	white (squadron colours and markings)
WA	Washington
WCM	Wildcat Contract Maintenance
Wg	Wing
WHL	Westland Helicopters Ltd
WI	Wisconsin
WLT	Weapons Loading Training
WMF	Wildcat Maintenance Facility
WR-ALC	Warner Robins Air Logistics Complex
WRS	Weather Reconnaissance Squadron
WS	Westland
WSK	Wytwornia Sprzetu Kominikacyjnego
WST	Wildcat Support Team
WTD	Wehrtechnische Dienstelle (Technical Support Unit)
WV	West Virginia
WW2	World War II
WY	Wyoming
WZM	Wildcat Maintenance
y	yellow (squadron colours and markings)
zDL	základna Dopravního Letectva (Air Transport Base)
zL	základna Letectva (Air Force Base)
zSL	základna Speciálního Letectva (Training Air Base)
zTL	základna Taktického Letectva (Tactical Air Base)
zVrL	základna Vrtulníkového Letectva (Helicopter Air Base)

A Guide to the Location of Operational Military Bases in the UK

This section is to assist the reader to locate the places in the United Kingdom where operational military aircraft (including helicopters and gliders) are based.

The alphabetical order listing gives each location in relation to its county and to its nearest classified road(s) (*by* means adjoining; *of* means close to), together with its approximate direction and mileage from the centre of a nearby major town or city. Some civil airports are included where active military units are also based, but **excluded** are MoD sites with non-operational aircraft (e.g. *gate guardians*), the bases of privately-owned civil aircraft that wear military markings and museums. For GPS users, Latitude and Longitude are also listed.

User	Base name	County/Region	Location [Lat./long.]	Distance/direction from (town)
Army	Abingdon	Oxfordshire	W by B4017, W of A34 [N51°41'16" W001°18'58"]	5m SSW of Oxford
Army	Aldergrove/Belfast Airport	Co Antrim	W by A26 [N54°39'27" W006°12'578"]	13m W of Belfast
RAF	Barkston Heath	Lincolnshire	W by B6404, S of A153 [N52°57'46" W000°33'38"]	5m NNE of Grantham
RAF	Benson	Oxfordshire	E by A423 [N51°36'55" W001°05'45"]	1m NE of Wallingford
QinetiQ/ RAF	Boscombe Down	Wiltshire	S by A303, W of A338 [N51°09'12" W001°45'04"]	6m N of Salisbury
RAF	Brize Norton	Oxfordshire	W of A4095 [N51°45'00" W001°35'01"]	5m SW of Witney

User	Base name	County/Region	Location [Lat./long.]	Distance/direction from (town)
Marshall	Cambridge Airport/ Teversham	Cambridgeshire	S by A1303 [N52°12'18" E000°10'30"]	2m E of Cambridge
RAF	Coningsby	Lincolnshire	S of A153, W by B1192 [N53°05'35" W000°10'00"]	10m NW of Boston
DCAE	Cosford	Shropshire	W of A41, N of A464 [N52°38'25" W002°18'20"]	9m WNW of Wolverhampton
RAF	Cranwell	Lincolnshire	N by A17, S by B1429 [N53°01'49" W000°29'00"]	5m WNW of Sleaford
RN	Culdrose	Cornwall	E by A3083 [N50°05'08" W005°15'17"]	1m SE of Helston
USAF	Fairford	Gloucestershire	S of A417 [N51°41'01" W001°47'24"]	9m ESE of Cirencester
Standard-Aero	Fleetlands	Hampshire	E by A32 [N50°50'06" W001°10'07"]	2m SE of Fareham
RAF	Halton	Buckinghamshire	N of A4011, S of B4544 [N51°47'28" W000°44'11"]	4m ESE of Aylesbury
RAF	Kenley	Greater London	W of A22 [N51°18'20" W000°05'37"]	1m W of Warlingham
RAF	Kirknewton	Lothian	E by B7031, N by A70 [N55°52'32" W003°24'04"]	8m SW of Edinburgh
USAF	Lakenheath	Suffolk	W by A1065 [N52°24'33" E000°33'40"]	8m W of Thetford
RAF	Leeming	North Yorkshire	E by A1 [N54°17'33" W001°32'07"]	5m SW of Northallerton
RAF	Leuchars	Fife	E of A919 [N56°22'28" W002°51'50"]	7m SE of Dundee
RAF	Linton-on-Ouse	North Yorkshire	W of A19, E of A168 [N54°02'56" W001°15'10"]	9m NW of York
RAF	Lossiemouth	Grampian	W of B9135, S of B9040 [N57°42'22" W003°20'20"]	4m N of Elgin
RAF	Marham	Norfolk	N by A1122 [N52°38'54" E000°33'02"]	6m W of Swaffham
Army	Middle Wallop	Hampshire	S by A343 [N51°08'35" W001°34'14"]	6m SW of Andover
USAF	Mildenhall	Suffolk	S by A1101 [N52°21'42" E000°29'12"]	9m NNE of Newmarket
RAF	Northolt	Greater London	N by A40 [N51°33'11" W000°25'06"]	3m E of M40 jn 1
RAF	Odiham	Hampshire	E of A32 [N51°14'03" W000°56'34"]	2m S of M3 jn 5
RN	Predannack	Cornwall	W by A3083 [N50°00'07" W005°13'54"]	7m S of Helston
RAF	Scampton	Lincolnshire	W by A15 [N53°18'28" W000°33'04"]	6m N of Lincoln
RAF	Shawbury	Shropshire	W of B5063 [N52°47'53" W002°40'05"]	7m NNE of Shrewsbury
RAF	Syerston	Nottinghamshire	W by A46 [N53°01'22" W000°54'47"]	5m SW of Newark
RAF	Ternhill	Shropshire	SW by A41 [N52°52'24" W002°31'54"]	3m SW of Market Drayton
RAF/Army	Topcliffe	North Yorkshire	E of A167, W of A168 [N54°12'20" W001°22'55"]	3m SW of Thirsk
RAF	Valley	Gwynedd	S of A5 on Anglesey [N53°14'53" W004°32'06"]	5m SE of Holyhead
RAF	Waddington	Lincolnshire	E by A607, W by A15 [N53°09'58" W000°31'26"]	5m S of Lincoln
Army	Wattisham	Suffolk	N of B1078 [N52°07'38" E000°57'21"]	5m SSW of Stowmarket
RAF	Woodvale	Merseyside	W by A565 [N53°34'56" W003°03'24"]	5m SSW of Southport
RAF	Wittering	Cambridgeshire	W by A1, N of A47 [N52°36'52" W000°27'01"]	3m S of Stamford
RN	Yeovilton	Somerset	S by B3151, S of A303 [N51°00'30" W002°38'43"]	5m N of Yeovil

The Committee of Imperial Defence through its Air Committee introduced a standardised system of numbering aircraft in November 1912. The Air Department of the Admiralty was allocated the first batch 1-200 and used these to cover aircraft already in use and those on order. The Army was issued with the next block from 201-800, which included the number 304 which was given to the Cody Biplane now preserved in the Science Museum. By the outbreak of World War I, the Royal Navy was on its second batch of registrations 801-1600 and this system continued with alternating allocations between the Army and Navy until 1916 when number 10000, a Royal Flying Corps BE2C, was reached.

It was decided not to continue with five digit numbers but instead to start again from 1, prefixing RFC aircraft with the letter A and RNAS aircraft with the prefix N. The RFC allocations commenced with A1 an FE2D and before the end of the year had reached A9999 an Armstrong Whitworth FK8. The next group commenced with B1 and continued in logical sequence through the C, D, E and F prefixes. G was used on a limited basis to identify captured German aircraft, while H was the last block of wartime-ordered aircraft. To avoid confusion I was not used, so the new post-war machines were allocated registrations in the J range. A further minor change was made in the numbering system in August 1929 when it was decided to maintain four numerals after the prefix letter, thus omitting numbers 1 to 999. The new K series therefore commenced at K1000, which was allocated to an AW Atlas.

The Naval N prefix was not used in such a logical way. Blocks of numbers were allocated for specific types of aircraft such as seaplanes or flying-boats. By the late 1920s the sequence had largely been used up and a new series using the prefix S was commenced. In 1930 separate naval allocations were stopped and subsequent registrations were issued in the 'military' range which had by this time reached the K series. A further change in the pattern of allocations came in the L range. Commencing with L7272 numbers were issued in blocks with smaller blocks of registrations between not used. These were known as 'broken blocks'. As M had already been used as a suffix for Maintenance Command instructional airframes it was not used as a prefix. Although N had previously been used for naval aircraft it was used again for registrations allocated from 1937.

With the build-up to World War II, the rate of allocations quickly accelerated and the prefix R was being used when war was declared. The letters O and Q were not allotted, nor was S, which had been used up to S1865 for naval aircraft before integration into the RAF series. By 1940 the registration Z9999 had been reached, and, as part of a broken block, with the letters U and Y not used to avoid confusion.

The option to recommence registration allocation at A1000 was not taken up; instead it was decided to use an alphabetical two-letter prefix with three numerals running from 100 to 999. Thus, AA100 was allocated to a Blenheim IV and this two-letter, three-numeral registration system which started in 1940 continues today. The letters C, I, O, Q, U and Y were, with the exception of NC, not used. For various reasons the following letter combinations were not issued: DA, DB, DH, EA, GA to GZ, HA, HT, JE, JH, JJ, KR to KT, MR, NW, NZ, SA to SK, SV, TN, TR and VE. The first post-war registrations issued were in the VP range while the end of the WZs had been reached by the Korean War.

In January 1952 a civil servant at the then Air Ministry penned a memo to his superiors alerting them to the fact that a new military aircraft registration system would soon have to be devised. With allocations accelerating to accommodate a NATO response to the Korean War and a perceived Soviet threat building, he estimated that the end of the ZZs would quickly be reached. However, more than six decades later the allocations are only in the ZKs and at the present rate are unlikely to reach ZZ999 until the end of this century!

Military aircraft registrations are allocated by MoD Head Office and Corporate Services, where the Military Aircraft Register is maintained by the Military Aviation Authority. It should be pointed out that strictly the register places a space before the last three digits of the registration and, contrary to popular opinion, refers to them as 'registrations', not serials.

A change in policy in 2003 resulted in the use of the first 99 digits in the ZK sequence (ZK001 to ZK099), following on from ZJ999. The first of these, ZK001 to ZK004, were allocated to AgustaWestland Merlins. There is also a growing trend for 'out-of-sequence' registration numbers to be issued. At first this was to a manufacturer's prototype or development aircraft. However, following the Boeing C-17 Globemasters leased and subsequently purchased from Boeing (ZZ171-ZZ178), more allocations have been noted.

Since 2002 there has also been a new official policy concerning the use of military registration numbers on some types of UAV. 'Where a UAV is of modular construction the nationality and registration mark shall be applied to the fuselage of the vehicle or on the assembly forming the main part of the fuselage. To prevent the high usage of numbers for target drones which are eventually destroyed, a single registration mark (prefix) should be issued relating to the UAV type. The agency or service operating the target drone will be responsible for the identification of each individual UAV covered by that registration mark by adding a suffix.' This has resulted in the use of the same registration on a number of UAVs (or RPASs as they are now referred to) and drones with numbers following it – hence the appearance of ZZ420/001 etc. on Banshee drones. Aircraft using this system are denoted in the text by an asterisk (*).

A serial in *italics* denotes that it is not the genuine marking for that airframe.

Serial	Type (code/other identity)	Owner/operator, location or fate	Notes
46	VS361 Spitfire LF IX <R> (*MH486*/BAPC 206) [FT-E]	*Repainted as TB288, 2018*	
168	Sopwith Tabloid Scout <R> (G-BFDE)	RAF Museum Reserve Collection, Stafford	
304	Cody Biplane (BAPC 62)	Science Museum, South Kensington	
471	RAF BE2a <R> (BAPC 321)	Montrose Air Station Heritage Centre	
687	RAF BE2c <R> (G-AWYI/*471*)	Privately owned, Sywell	
687	RAF BE2b <R> (BAPC 181)	RAF Museum, Hendon	
1264	Bristol Scout C <R> (G-FDHB)	Privately owned, Bicester	
2345	Vickers FB5 Gunbus <R> (G-ATVP)	RAF Museum, Hendon	
2699	RAF BE2c	IWM Duxford	
2783	RAF BE2b <R> (BAPC 332)	Boscombe Down Aviation Collection, Old Sarum	
3066	Caudron GIII (G-AETA/9203M)	RAF Museum, Hendon	
5191	Morane-Saulnier Type N <R> (BAPC 472)	North-East Aircraft Museum, Usworth	
5964	DH2 <R> (BAPC 112)	Privately owned, Stretton on Dunsmore	
5964	DH2 <R> (G-BFVH)	Privately owned, Wickenby	
6232	RAF BE2c <R> (BAPC 41)	*Rebuilt as 9970, 2018*	
8359	Short 184 <ff>	FAA Museum, RNAS Yeovilton	
9828	Avro 504K <R> (*H1968*/BAPC 42)	Yorkshire Air Museum, stored Elvington	
9917	Sopwith Pup (G-EBKY/N5180)	The Shuttleworth Collection, Old Warden	
9970	RAF BE2c <R> (*6232*/BAPC 41)	Yorkshire Air Museum, Elvington	
A126	Nieuport 11 <R> (G-CILI)	Privately owned,	
A301	Morane BB (frame)	RAF Museum Reserve Collection, Stafford	
A653	Sopwith Pup <R> (*A7317*/BAPC 179)	Privately owned, Stow Maries, Essex	
A1452	Vickers FB5 Gunbus <R>	Spitfire Spares, Taunton, Somerset	
A1742	Bristol Scout D <R> (BAPC 38)	Aerospace Bristol, Filton	
A2767	RAF BE2e-1 <R> (G-CJZP)	WW1 Aviation Heritage Trust, Stow Maries	
A2943	RAF BE2e-1 <R> (G-CJZO)	WW1 Aviation Heritage Trust, Bicester	
A3930	RAF RE8 <R> (ZK-TVC)	RAF Museum, Hendon	
A4850	RAF SE5a <R> (BAPC 176)	Bygone Times Antique Warehouse, Eccleston, Lancs	
A6526	RAF FE2b <R> (BAPC 400)	RAF Museum, Hendon	
A7288	Bristol F2b Fighter <R> (BAPC 386)	Aerospace Bristol, Filton	
A8226	Sopwith 1½ Strutter <R> (G-BIDW)	RAF Museum, Cosford	
A8274	Sopwith 1½ Strutter <R> (BAPC 413)	WW1 Aviation Heritage Trust, Stow Maries	
B595	RAF SE5a <R> (G-BUOD) [W]	Privately owned, Defford	
B619	Sopwith 1½ Strutter <R> (BAPC 468)	RAF Manston History Museum	
B1474	Henry Farman F.20 <R>	WW1 Aviation Heritage Trust, Stow Maries	
B5539	Sopwith F.1 Camel <R>	Privately owned, Booker	
B5577	Sopwith F.1 Camel <R> (*D3419*/BAPC 59) [W]	Montrose Air Station Heritage Centre	
B6401	Sopwith F.1 Camel <R> (G-AWYY/C1701)	FAA Museum, stored Cobham Hall, RNAS Yeovilton	
B7270	Sopwith F.1 Camel <R> (G-BFCZ)	Brooklands Museum, Weybridge	
C1096	Replica Plans SE5a <R> (G-ERFC)	Privately owned, Old Warden	
C1904	RAF SE5a <R> (G-PFAP) [Z]	Privately owned, Castle Bytham, Lincs	
C3009	Currie Wot (G-BFWD) [B]	Privately owned, Dunkeswell	
C3011	Phoenix Currie Super Wot (G-SWOT) [S]	Privately owned, Otherton, Staffs	
C3988	Sopwith 5F.1 Dolphin (BAPC 353) (comp D5329)	RAF Museum, Hendon	
C4451	Avro 504J <R> (BAPC 210)	Solent Sky, Southampton	
C4918	Bristol M1C <R> (G-BWJM)	The Shuttleworth Collection, Old Warden	
C4994	Bristol M1C <R> (G-BLWM)	RAF Museum, Cosford	
C5430	RAF SE5a <R> (G-CCXG) [V]	Privately owned, Wrexham	
C8996	RAF SE5a (G-ECAE/A2-25)	Privately owned, Milden	
C9533	RAF SE5a <R> (G-BUWE) [M]	Privately owned, Coventry	
D276	RAF SE5a <R> (BAPC 208) [A]	Prince's Mead Shopping Centre, Farnborough	
D1851	Sopwith F.1 Camel <R> (G-BZSC) [X]	The Shuttleworth Collection, Old Warden	
D3540	RAF SE5a <R> (N125QB) [K]	WW1 Aviation Heritage Trust, Old Warden	
D5649	Airco DH9	IWM Duxford	

Notes	Serial	Type (code/other identity)	Owner/operator, location or fate
	D6447	Sopwith F.1 Camel <R> (BAPC 385)	Privately owned, Knutsford, Cheshire
	D7560	Avro 504K	Science Museum, South Kensington
	D8096	Bristol F2b Fighter (G-AEPH) [D]	The Shuttleworth Collection, Old Warden
	E449	Avro 504K (G-EBJE/9205M)	RAF Museum, Hendon
	E2466	Bristol F2b Fighter (BAPC 165) [I]	RAF Museum, Hendon
	E2581	Bristol F2b Fighter [13]	IWM Duxford
	E2977	Avro 504K (G-EBHB)	Privately owned, Henlow
	E3273	Avro 504K (H5199/BK892/G-ACNB/G-ADEV/3118M)	The Shuttleworth Collection, Old Warden
	E6655	Sopwith 7F.1 Snipe <R> (BAPC 348) [B]	RAF Museum, Hendon
	E8894	Airco DH9 (G-CDLI)	Aero Vintage, Duxford
	F141	RAF SE5a <R> (G-SEVA) [G]	Privately owned, Boscombe Down
	F235	RAF SE5a <R> (G-BMDB) [B]	Privately owned, Stow Maries, Essex
	F904	RAF SE5a (G-EBIA)	The Shuttleworth Collection, Old Warden
	F904	RAF SE5a <R>	South Yorkshire Aircraft Museum, Doncaster
	F938	RAF SE5a (G-EBIC/9208M)	RAF Museum, Hendon
	F943	RAF SE5a <R> (G-BIHF) [S]	Privately owned, White Waltham
	F943	RAF SE5a <R> (G-BKDT) [S]	Yorkshire Air Museum, Elvington
	F1010	Airco DH9A [C]	RAF Museum, Hendon
	F2367	Sopwith 7F.1 Snipe <R> (ZK-SNI)	WW1 Aviation Heritage Trust, Stow Maries
	F3556	RAF RE8	IWM Duxford
	F5447	RAF SE5a <R> (G-BKER) [N]	Privately owned, Bridge of Weir
	F5459	RAF SE5a <R> (G-INNY) [Y]	Privately owned, Temple Bruer, Lincs
	F5475	RAF SE5a <R> (BAPC 250)	Brooklands Museum, Weybridge
	F6314	Sopwith F.1 Camel (9206M) [B]	RAF Museum, Hendon
	F8010	RAF SE5a <R> (G-BDWJ) [Z]	Privately owned, Langport, Somerset
	F8614	Vickers FB27A Vimy IV <R> (G-AWAU)	RAF Museum, Hendon
	J7326	DH53 Humming Bird (G-EBQP)	de Havilland Aircraft Museum, London Colney
	J7904	Gloster Gamecock (BAPC 259) <R>	Jet Age Museum, Gloucester
	J8067	Westland Pterodactyl 1a	Science Museum, South Kensington
	J9941	Hawker Hart 2 (G-ABMR)	RAF Museum, Hendon
	K1786	Hawker Tomtit (G-AFTA)	The Shuttleworth Collection, Old Warden
	K1926	Hawker Fury I	Cambs Fighter & Bomber Society, Little Gransden
	K2048	Isaacs Fury II (G-BZNW)	Privately owned, Linton-on-Ouse
	K2050	Isaacs Fury II (G-ASCM)	Privately owned, Enstone
	K2059	Isaacs Fury II (G-PFAR)	Privately owned, Netherthorpe
	K2060	Isaacs Fury II (G-BKZM)	Privately owned stored, Limetree, Ireland
	K2065	Isaacs Fury II (G-AYJY/K2046)	Privately owned, Henstridge
	K2075	Isaacs Fury II (G-BEER)	Privately owned, Combrook, Warks
	K2227	Bristol 105 Bulldog IIA (G-ABBB)	RAF Museum, Hendon
	K2567	DH82A Tiger Moth (DE306/G-MOTH/7035M)	Privately owned, Tadlow
	K2572	DH82A Tiger Moth (NM129/G-AOZH)	Privately owned, Frensham, Surrey
	K2585	DH82A Tiger Moth II (T6818/G-ANKT)	The Shuttleworth Collection, Old Warden
	K2587	DH82A Tiger Moth <R> (G-BJAP)	Privately owned, Shobdon
	K3241	Avro 621 Tutor (K3215/G-AHSA)	The Shuttleworth Collection, Old Warden
	K3661	Hawker Nimrod II (G-BURZ) [562]	Aero Vintage, Duxford
	K3731	Isaacs Fury (G-RODI)	Privately owned, RAF Waddington
	K4232	Avro 671 Rota I (SE-AZB)	RAF Museum, Hendon
	K4259	DH82A Tiger Moth (G-ANMO) [71]	Privately owned, Headcorn
	K4556	Boulton & Paul Overstrand <R> (BAPC 358) [F-101]	Norfolk & Suffolk Avn Museum, Flixton
	K4972	Hawker Hart Trainer IIA (1764M)	RAF Museum, Cosford
	K5054	Supermarine Spitfire <R> (EN398/BAPC 190)	Privately owned, Hawkinge
	K5054	Supermarine Spitfire <R> (BAPC 214)	Tangmere Military Aviation Museum
	K5054	Supermarine Spitfire <R> (G-BRDV)	Privately owned, Kent
	K5054	Supermarine Spitfire <R> (BAPC 297)	Kent Battle of Britain Museum, Hawkinge
	K5054	Supermarine Spitfire <R>	Southampton Airport, on display
	K5409	Hawker Hind	Currently not known
	K5414	Hawker Hind (G-AENP/BAPC 78) [XV]	The Shuttleworth Collection, Old Warden
	K5462	Hawker Hind	Currently not known

Serial	Type (code/other identity)	Owner/operator, location or fate	Notes
K5554	Hawker Hind	*Currently not known*	
K5600	Hawker Audax I (G-BVVI/2015M)	Aero Vintage, Westfield, Sussex	
K5673	Isaacs Fury II (G-BZAS)	Privately owned, Morpeth	
K5673	Hawker Fury I <R> (BAPC 249)	Brooklands Museum, Weybridge	
K5674	Hawker Fury I (G-CBZP)	Historic Aircraft Collection Ltd, Duxford	
K5682	Isaacs Fury II (S1579/G-BBVO) [6]	Privately owned, Felthorpe (wreck)	
K6035	Westland Wallace II (2361M)	RAF Museum Reserve Collection, Stafford	
K6618	Hawker Hind	*Currently not known*	
K6833	Hawker Hind	*Currently not known*	
K7271	Hawker Fury II <R> (BAPC 148)	Shropshire Wartime Aircraft Recovery Grp Mus, Sleap	
K7271	Isaacs Fury II <R> (G-CCKV)	Privately owned, Dunkeswell	
K7985	Gloster Gladiator I (L8032/G-AMRK)	The Shuttleworth Collection, Old Warden	
K8042	Gloster Gladiator II (8372M)	RAF Museum, Cosford	
K8203	Hawker Demon I (G-BTVE/2292M)	Demon Displays, Old Warden	
K8303	Isaacs Fury II (G-BWWN) [D]	Privately owned, RAF Henlow	
K9926	VS300 Spitfire I <R> (BAPC 217) [JH-C]	Privately owned, Newquay	
K9942	VS300 Spitfire I (8383M) [SD-D]	RAF Museum, Cosford	
K9998	VS300 Spitfire I (BAPC 431) <R> [QJ-K]	RAF Biggin Hill, on display	
L1019	VS300 Spitfire I <R> (BAPC 308) [LO-S]	Privately owned, Currie, Lothian	
L1035	VS300 Spitfire I <R> (BAPC 500) [SH-D]	Battle of Britain Bunker, Uxbridge	
L1067	VS300 Spitfire I <R> (BAPC 227) [XT-D]	Edinburgh Airport, on display	
L1592	Hawker Hurricane I [KW-Z]	Science Museum, South Kensington	
L1639	Hawker Hurricane I (BAPC 362)	Cambridge Fighter & Bomber Society, Little Gransden	
L1679	Hawker Hurricane I <R> (BAPC 241) [JX-G]	Tangmere Military Aviation Museum	
L1684	Hawker Hurricane I <R> (BAPC 219)	RAF Northolt, on display	
L2005	Hawker Hurricane I	Hawker Restorations, Milden	
L2301	VS Walrus I (G-AIZG)	FAA Museum, RNAS Yeovilton	
L2940	Blackburn Skua I	FAA Museum, RNAS Yeovilton	
L5343	Fairey Battle I	RAF Museum, Hendon	
L6739	Bristol 149 Bolingbroke IVT (G-BPIV/R3821) [YP-Q]	Blenheim(Duxford) Ltd, Duxford	
L6906	Miles M14A Magister I (G-AKKY/T9841/BAPC 44)	Museum of Berkshire Aviation, Woodley	
L7005	Boulton Paul P82 Defiant I <R> [PS-B]	Kent Battle of Britain Museum, Hawkinge	
L7181	Hawker Hind (G-CBLK)	Aero Vintage, Duxford	
L7191	Hawker Hind	*Currently not known*	
L7775	Vickers Wellington B Ic <ff>	Lincolnshire Avn Heritage Centre, E Kirkby	
L8756	Bristol 149 Bolingbroke IVT (RCAF 10001) [XD-E]	RAF Museum, Hendon	
N248	Supermarine S6A (S1596)	Solent Sky, Southampton	
N500	Sopwith LC-1T Triplane <R> (G-PENY/G-BWRA)	Privately owned, Yarcombe, Devon/RNAS Yeovilton	
N540	Port Victoria PV8 Eastchurch Kitten <R>	Yorkshire Air Museum, Elvington	
N546	Wright Quadruplane 1 <R> (BAPC 164)	Solent Sky, Southampton	
N1671	Boulton Paul P82 Defiant I (8370M) [EW-D]	RAF Museum, Cosford	
N1854	Fairey Fulmar II (G-AIBE)	FAA Museum, RNAS Yeovilton	
N2078	Sopwith Baby (8214/8215/BAPC 442)	FAA Museum, RNAS Yeovilton	
N2532	Hawker Hurricane I <R> (BAPC 272) [GZ-H]	Kent Battle of Britain Museum, Hawkinge	
N2980	Vickers Wellington Ia [R]	Brooklands Museum, Weybridge	
N3200	VS300 Spitfire IA (G-CFGJ) [QV]	IWM Duxford	
N3289	VS300 Spitfire I <R> (BAPC 65) [DW-K]	Kent Battle of Britain Museum, Hawkinge	
N3290	VS300 Spitfire I <R> [AI-H]	Privately owned, St Mawgan	
N3310	VS361 Spitfire IX <R> (BAPC 393) [A]	Privately owned, Abingdon	
N3313	VS300 Spitfire I <R> (MH314/BAPC 69) [KL-B]	Kent Battle of Britain Museum, Hawkinge	
N3317	VS329 Spitfire II <R> (P8140/BAPC 71) [BO-U]	Norfolk & Suffolk Avn Museum, Flixton	
N3378	Boulton Paul P82 Defiant I (wreck)	RAF Museum, Cosford	
N3549	DH82A Tiger Moth II (PG645/N3549)	Privately owned, Netherthorpe	
N3788	Miles M14A Magister I (V1075/G-AKPF)	Privately owned, Old Warden	
N4389	Fairey Albacore (N4172) [4M]	FAA Museum, stored Cobham Hall, RNAS Yeovilton	
N4877	Avro 652A Anson I (G-AMDA) [MK-V]	IWM Duxford	
N5137	DH82A Tiger Moth (N6638/G-BNDW)	Caernarfon Air World	
N5177	Sopwith 1½ Strutter (BAPC 452) <R>	Privately owned, stored Mersham, Surrey	
N5182	Sopwith Pup <R> (G-APUP/9213M)	RAF Museum, Cosford	
N5195	Sopwith Pup (G-ABOX)	Army Flying Museum, Middle Wallop	

Notes	Serial	Type (code/other identity)	Owner/operator, location or fate
	N5199	Sopwith Pup <R> (G-BZND)	Privately owned, Yarcombe, Devon
	N5459	Sopwith Triplane <R> (BAPC 111)	FAA Museum, stored Cobham Hall, RNAS Yeovilton
	N5518	Gloster Sea Gladiator (N5579)	FAA Museum, stored Cobham Hall, RNAS Yeovilton
	N5628	Gloster Gladiator II	RAF Museum, Cosford
	N5719	Gloster Gladiator II (G-CBHO)	Privately owned, Dursley, Glos
	N5903	Gloster Gladiator II (N2276/G-GLAD)	The Fighter Collection, Duxford
	N5912	Sopwith Triplane (8385M)	RAF Museum, Hendon
	N5914	Gloster Gladiator II (frame)	Jet Age Museum, Gloucester
	N6161	Sopwith Pup (G-ELRT)	Privately owned, Turweston
	N6290	Sopwith Triplane <R> (G-BOCK)	The Shuttleworth Collection, Old Warden
	N6377	Sopwith F.1 Camel <R> (G-BPOB/B2458)	Privately owned, Stow Maries
	N6452	Sopwith Pup <R> (G-BIAU)	FAA Museum, stored Cobham Hall, RNAS Yeovilton
	N6466	DH82A Tiger Moth (G-ANKZ)	Privately owned, Compton Abbas
	N6473	DH82A Tiger Moth (F-GTBO)	Privately owned, Orbigny, France
	N6537	DH82A Tiger Moth (G-AOHY)	Privately owned, Wickenby
	N6635	DH82A Tiger Moth (comp G-APAO & G-APAP) [25]	IWM Duxford
	N6720	DH82A Tiger Moth (G-BYTN/7014M) [VX]	Privately owned, stored Darley Moor, Derbyshire
	N6797	DH82A Tiger Moth (G-ANEH)	Privately owned, Swyncombe
	N6812	Sopwith 2F.1 Camel	IWM London, Lambeth
	N6847	DH82A Tiger Moth (G-APAL)	Privately owned, Braceborough, Lincs
	N6965	DH82A Tiger Moth (G-AJTW) [FL-J]	Privately owned, Tibenham
	N7033	Noorduyn AT-16 Harvard IIb (FX442)	Kent Battle of Britain Museum, Hawkinge
	N9191	DH82A Tiger Moth (G-ALND)	Privately owned, Pontypool
	N9192	DH82A Tiger Moth (G-DHZF) [RCO-N]	Privately owned, Sywell
	N9328	DH82A Tiger Moth (G-ALWS) [69]	Privately owned, Henstridge
	N9372	DH82A Tiger Moth (G-ANHK)	Privately owned, Sturgate
	N9389	DH82A Tiger Moth (G-ANJA)	Privately owned, Thruxton
	N9899	Supermarine Southampton I (fuselage)	RAF Museum, Hendon
	P1344	HP52 Hampden I (9175M) [PL-K]	Michael Beetham Conservation Centre, RAFM Cosford
	P2617	Hawker Hurricane I (8373M) [AF-F]	RAF Museum, Hendon
	P2725	Hawker Hurricane I (wreck)	IWM London, Lambeth
	P2725	Hawker Hurricane I <R> (BAPC 68) [TM-B]	Privately owned, Delabole, Cornwall
	P2725	Hawker Hurricane I <R> (Z3427/BAPC 205) [TM-B]	RAF Museum, Hendon
	P2793	Hawker Hurricane I <R> (BAPC 236) [SD-M]	Eden Camp Theme Park, stored Malton, North Yorkshire
	P2793	Hawker Hurricane I <R> (BAPC 399) [SD-M]	Eden Camp Theme Park, Malton, North Yorkshire
	P2902	Hawker Hurricane I (G-ROBT) [DX-R]	Privately owned, Duxford
	P2921	Hawker Hurricane I <R> (BAPC 273) [GZ-L]	Kent Battle of Britain Museum, Hawkinge
	P2921	Hawker Hurricane I <R> (BAPC 477) [GZ-L]	RAF Biggin Hill, on display
	P2921	Hawker Sea Hurricane X (AE977/G-CHTK) [GZ-L]	Privately owned, Biggin Hill
	P2954	Hawker Hurricane I <R> (BAPC 267) [WX-E]	Repainted as V7467
	P2970	Hawker Hurricane I <R> (BAPC 291) [US-X]	Battle of Britain Memorial, Capel le Ferne, Kent
	P3059	Hawker Hurricane I <R> (BAPC 64) [SD-N]	Kent Battle of Britain Museum, Hawkinge
	P3175	Hawker Hurricane I (wreck)	RAF Museum Reserve Collection, Stafford
	P3179	Hawker Hurricane I <ff>	Tangmere Military Aviation Museum
	P3208	Hawker Hurricane I <R> (BAPC 63/L1592) [SD-T]	Kent Battle of Britain Museum, Hawkinge
	P3351	Hawker Hurricane IIa (DR393/F-AZXR) [K]	Privately owned, Cannes, France
	P3386	Hawker Hurricane I <R> (BAPC 218) [FT-A]	RAF Bentley Priory, on display
	P3395	Hawker Hurricane IV (KX829)[JX-B]	Thinktank, Birmingham
	P3554	Hawker Hurricane I (composite)	The Air Defence Collection, Salisbury
	P3679	Hawker Hurricane I <R> (BAPC 278) [GZ-K]	Kent Battle of Britain Museum, Hawkinge
	P3700	Hawker Hurricane XIIa (Z5140/G-HURI) [RF-E]	Historic Aircraft Collection, Duxford
	P3708	Hawker Hurricane I	Norfolk & Suffolk Avn Museum, Flixton (on rebuild)
	P3717	Hawker Hurricane I (composite) (DR348/G-HITT) [SW-P]	Privately owned, Old Warden
	P3873	Hawker Hurricane I <R> (BAPC 499) [YO-H]	Battle of Britain Bunker, Uxbridge
	P3873	Hawker Hurricane I <R> [YO-H]	Battle of Britain Bunker, Uxbridge
	P3901	Hawker Hurricane I <R> (BAPC 475) [RF-E]	Battle of Britain Bunker, Uxbridge
	P4139	Fairey Swordfish II (HS618) [5H]	FAA Museum, RNAS Yeovilton
	P6382	Miles M14A Hawk Trainer 3 (G-AJRS) [C]	The Shuttleworth Collection, Old Warden
	P7308	VS300 Spitfire IA (AR213/R9632/G-AIST) [XR-D]	Privately owned, Duxford

Serial	Type (code/other identity)	Owner/operator, location or fate	Notes
P7350	VS329 Spitfire IIa (G-AWIJ) [QJ-G,QV-E]	RAF BBMF, Biggin Hill (servicing)	
P7370	VS329 Spitfire II <R> (BAPC 410) [ZP-A]	Battle of Britain Experience, Canterbury	
P7540	VS329 Spitfire IIa [DU-W]	Dumfries & Galloway Avn Mus, Dumfries	
P7666	VS329 Spitfire II <R> (BAPC 335) [EB-Z]	RAF High Wycombe, on display	
P7819	VS329 Spitfire IIa (G-TCHZ)	Privately owned, Exeter	
P7923	VS329 Spitfire IIa <R> (BAPC 369) [TM-F]	Ulster Aviation Society, Long Kesh	
P7966	VS329 Spitfire II <R> [D-B]	Manx Aviation & Military Museum, Ronaldsway	
P8088	VS329 Spitfire IIa (G-CGRM) [NK-K]	Privately owned, Knutsford, Cheshire	
P8208	VS329 Spitfire IIb (G-RRFF)	Privately owned, Durley, Glos	
P8448	VS329 Spitfire II <R> (BAPC 225) [UM-D]	RAF Cranwell, on display	
P9398	Supermarine Aircraft Spitfire 26 (G-CEPL) [KL-B]	Privately owned, Rochester	
P9444	VS300 Spitfire Ia [RN-D]	Science Museum, South Kensington	
P9637	Supermarine Aircraft Spitfire 26 (G-RORB) [GR-B]	Privately owned, Perth	
R1914	Miles M14A Magister (G-AHUJ)	Privately owned, Gloucester	
R4118	Hawker Hurricane I (G-HUPW) [UP-W]	Privately owned, Duxford	
R4229	Hawker Hurricane I <R> (BAPC 334) [GN-J]	Alexandra Park, Windsor	
R4922	DH82A Tiger Moth II (G-APAO)	Privately owned, Henlow	
R4959	DH82A Tiger Moth II (G-ARAZ) [59]	Privately owned, Temple Bruer, Lincs	
R5136	DH82A Tiger Moth II (G-APAP)	Privately owned, Darley Moor, Derbyshire	
R5172	DH82A Tiger Moth II (G-AOIS) [FIJE]	Privately owned, Sywell	
R5246	DH82A Tiger Moth II (D-EDHA) [40]	Privately owned, Heringsdorf, Germany	
R5868	Avro 683 Lancaster I (7325M) [PO-S]	RAF Museum, Hendon	
R5868	Avro 683 Lancaster I <R> (BAPC 471) [PO-S] <ff>	Avro Heritage Museum, Woodford	
R6690	VS300 Spitfire I <R> (BAPC 254) [PR-A]	Yorkshire Air Museum, Elvington	
R6775	VS300 Spitfire I <R> (BAPC 299) [YT-J]	Battle of Britain Memorial, Capel le Ferne, Kent	
R6904	VS300 Spitfire I <R> [BT-K]	Privately owned, Cornwall	
R6915	VS300 Spitfire I	IWM London, Lambeth	
R9125	Westland Lysander III (8377M)[LX-L]	Michael Beetham Conservation Centre, RAFM Cosford	
R9612	VS300 Spitfire I <R> [LC]	Privately owned, Duxford	
S1287	Fairey Flycatcher <R> (G-BEYB) [5]	FAA Museum, stored Cobham Hall, RNAS Yeovilton	
S1581	Hawker Nimrod I (G-BWWK) [573]	The Fighter Collection, Duxford	
S1595	Supermarine S6B [1]	Science Museum, South Kensington	
S1615	Isaacs Fury II (G-BMEU)	Privately owned, stored Netherthorpe	
T5298	Bristol 156 Beaufighter I (4552M) <ff>	Midland Air Museum, Coventry	
T5424	DH82A Tiger Moth II (G-AJOA)	Privately owned, Swindon	
T5854	DH82A Tiger Moth II (G-ANKK)	Privately owned, Baxterley	
T5879	DH82A Tiger Moth II (G-AXBW) [RUC-W]	Privately owned, Frensham	
T6296	DH82A Tiger Moth II (8387M)	RAF Museum, Cosford	
T6953	DH82A Tiger Moth II (G-ANNI)	Privately owned, Tisted, Hants	
T6991	DH82A Tiger Moth II (DE694/HB-UPY)	Privately owned, Lausanne, Switzerland	
T7109	DH82A Tiger Moth II (G-AOIM)	Privately owned, Bicester	
T7230	DH82A Tiger Moth II (G-AFVE)	Privately owned, Mazowiecke, Poland	
T7281	DH82A Tiger Moth II (G-ARTL)	Privately owned, Egton, nr Whitby	
T7290	DH82A Tiger Moth II (G-ANNK) [14]	Privately owned, Sywell	
T7793	DH82A Tiger Moth II (G-ANKV)	Privately owned, Wickenby	
T7794	DH82A Tiger Moth II (G-ASPV)	Privately owned, Bagby	
T7842	DH82A Tiger Moth II (G-AMTF)	Privately owned, Westfield, Surrey	
T7909	DH82A Tiger Moth II (G-ANON)	Privately owned, Sherburn-in-Elmet	
T7997	DH82A Tiger Moth II (NL750/G-AHUF)	Privately owned, Breighton	
T8191	DH82A Tiger Moth II (G-BWMK)	Privately owned, Henstridge	
T9707	Miles M14A Magister I (G-AKKR/8378M/T9708)	RAF Museum Reserve Collection, Stafford	
T9738	Miles M14A Magister I (G-AKAT)	Privately owned, Breighton	
V3388	Airspeed AS10 Oxford I (G-AHTW)	IWM Duxford	
V6028	Bristol 149 Bolingbroke IVT (G-MKIV) [GB-D] <rf>	The Aircraft Restoration Co, stored Duxford	
V6555	Hawker Hurricane I (BAPC 411/P3144) <R> [DT-A]	Battle of Britain Experience, Canterbury	
V6799	Hawker Hurricane I <R> (BAPC 72/V7767) [SD-X]	Jet Age Museum, Gloucester	
V7313	Hawker Hurricane I <R> (BAPC 346) [US-F]	Privately owned, North Weald, on display	

Notes	Serial	Type (code/other identity)	Owner/operator, location or fate
	V7350	Hawker Hurricane I <ff>	Romney Marsh Wartime Collection
	V7467	Hawker Hurricane I <R> (BAPC 223) [ZJ-L]	Spitfire Visitor Centre, Blackpool
	V7467	Hawker Hurricane I <R> (P2954/BAPC 267) [LE-D]	IWM Duxford
	V7467	Hawker Hurricane I <R> (BAPC 288) [LE-D]	Wonderland Pleasure Park, Farnsfield, Notts
	V7467	Hawker Hurricane I <R> (BAPC 378) [LE-D]	RAF High Wycombe, on display
	V7497	Hawker Hurricane I (G-HRLI) [SD-X]	Privately owned, Elmsett
	V9312	Westland Lysander IIIa (G-CCOM) [LX-E]	The Aircraft Restoration Co, Duxford
	V9367	Westland Lysander IIIa (G-AZWT) [MA-B]	The Shuttleworth Collection, Old Warden
	V9673	Westland Lysander IIIa (V9300/G-LIZY) [MA-J]	IWM Duxford
	V9723	Westland Lysander IIIa (V9546/OO-SOT) [MA-D]	SABENA Old Timers, Brussels, Belgium
	V9875	Westland Lysander IIIa <R> (BAPC 371) [MA-J]	Tangmere Military Aviation Museum
	W1048	HP59 Halifax II (8465M) [TL-S]	RAF Museum, Hendon
	W2068	Avro 652A Anson I (9261M/VH-ASM) [68]	RAF Museum, Hendon
	W2718	VS Walrus I (G-RNLI)	Privately owned, Duxford
	W3644	VS349 Spitfire V <R> (BAPC 323) [QV-J]	Privately owned, Lake Fairhaven, Lancs
	W3850	VS349 Spitfire V <R> (BAPC 304) [PR-A]	Privately owned, Knutsford, Cheshire
	W4041	Gloster E28/39	Science Museum, South Kensington
	W4041	Gloster E28/39 <R> (BAPC 331)	Jet Age Museum, Gloucester
	W4050	DH98 Mosquito	de Havilland Aircraft Museum, London Colney
	W5856	Fairey Swordfish I (G-BMGC) [4A]	RN Historic Flight, Yeovilton
	W9385	DH87B Hornet Moth (G-ADND) [YG-L,3]	Privately owned, Oaksey Park
	X4178	VS300 Spitfire I <R> (BAPC 394) [EB-K]	Repainted as X4474, 2018
	X4253	VS300 Spitfire I <R> (BAPC 326) [FY-N]	Spitfire Visitor Centre, Blackpool
	X4276	VS300 Spitfire I (G-CDGU)	Privately owned, Sandown
	X4474	VS300 Spitfire I <R> (X4178/BAPC 394) [QV-I]	IWM Duxford
	X4590	VS300 Spitfire I (8384M) [PR-F]	RAF Museum, Hendon
	X4650	VS300 Spitfire I (R9612/G-CGUK) [KL-A]	Privately owned, Duxford
	X4683	Jurca MJ10 Spitfire (G-MUTS) [EB-N]	Privately owned, Fishburn
	X4859	VS300 Spitfire I <R> (BAPC 319) [PQ-N]	Grangemouth Spitfire Memorial Trust
	X9407	Percival P.16A Q6 (G-AFFD)	Privately owned, Seething (on rebuild)
	Z1206	Vickers Wellington IV (fuselage)	Privately owned, Kenilworth
	Z2033	Fairey Firefly I (G-ASTL) [275/N]	FAA Museum, stored Cobham Hall, RNAS Yeovilton
	Z2315	Hawker Hurricane IIa [JU-E]	IWM Duxford
	Z2389	Hawker Hurricane IIa [XR-T]	Brooklands Museum, Weybridge
	Z3427	Hawker Hurricane IIc <R> (BAPC 205) [AV-R]	Repainted as P2725, 2018
	Z5207	Hawker Hurricane IIb (G-BYDL)	Privately owned, Thruxton
	Z7015	Hawker Sea Hurricane Ib (G-BKTH) [7-L]	The Shuttleworth Collection, Old Warden
	Z7197	Percival P30 Proctor III (G-AKZN/8380M)	RAF Museum Reserve Collection, Stafford
	Z7258	DH89A Dragon Rapide (NR786/G-AHGD)	Privately owned, Membury (wreck)
	AA810	VS353 Spitfire F IV (wreck)	Airframe Assemblies, Sandown
	AB196	Supermarine Aircraft Spitfire 26 (G-CCGH)	Privately owned, Enstone
	AB910	VS349 Spitfire Vb (G-AISU) [SH-F]	RAF BBMF, Coningsby
	AD189	VS349 Spitfire Vb (G-CHVJ)	Privately owned, Raglan, Monmouthshire
	AD370	Jurca Spitfire (G-CHBW) [PJ-C]	Privately owned, Perranporth
	AD540	VS349 Spitfire Vb (wreck)	Privately owned, Launceston (on rebuild)
	AE436	HP52 Hampden I [PL-J] (parts)	Lincolnshire Avn Heritage Centre, E Kirkby
	AG244	Hawker Hurricane XII (RCAF 5487/G-CBOE)	Privately owned, Aalen, Germany
	AJ841	CCF T-6J Texan (MM53795/G-BJST/KF729)	Privately owned, Duxford
	AL246	Grumman Martlet I	FAA Museum, RNAS Yeovilton
	AP506	Cierva C30A (G-ACWM) (wreck)	The Helicopter Museum, Weston-super-Mare
	AP507	Cierva C30A (G-ACWP) [KX-P]	Science Museum, South Kensington
	AR501	VS349 Spitfire LF Vc (G-AWII/AR4474) [DU-E]	The Shuttleworth Collection, Old Warden
	AV511	EHI-101 Merlin <R> [511]	SFDO, RNAS Culdrose
	AW101	AgustaWestland AW101 Mk.510 (G-17-510)	AgustaWestland, Yeovil
	BB803	DH82A Tiger Moth (G-ADWJ) [75]	Privately owned, Henstridge
	BB807	DH82A Tiger Moth (G-ADWO)	Solent Sky, Southampton
	BD713	Hawker Hurricane IIb	Currently not known

Serial	Type (code/other identity)	Owner/operator, location or fate	Notes
BE505	Hawker Hurricane IIb (RCAF 5403/G-HHII) [XP-L]	Privately owned, Elmsett	
BH238	Hawker Hurricane IIb	Airframe Assemblies, stored Sandown	
BL614	VS349 Spitfire Vb (4354M) [ZD-F]	RAF Museum, Hendon	
BL655	VS349 Spitfire Vb (wreck)	Lincolnshire Avn Heritage Centre, East Kirkby	
BL688	VS349 Spitfire LF Vb (G-CJWO)	Privately owned, Launceston	
BL735	Supermarine Aircraft Spitfire 26 (G-HABT) [BT-A]	Privately owned, Hohenems, Austria	
BL924	VS349 Spitfire Vb <R> (BAPC 242) [AZ-G]	Beale Park, Pangbourne, Berks	
BL927	Supermarine Aircraft Spitfire 26 (G-CGWI) [JH-I]	Privately owned, Perth	
BM361	VS349 Spitfire Vb <R> (BAPC 269) [XR-C]	RAF Lakenheath, on display	
BM481	VS349 Spitfire Vb <R> (BAPC 301) [YO-T] (also wears PK651/RAO-B)	Thornaby Aerodrome Memorial	
BM539	VS349 Spitfire LF Vb (G-SSVB)	Privately owned, Hastings	
BM597	VS349 Spitfire LF Vb (G-MKVB/5718M) [JH-C]	Historic Aircraft Collection, Duxford	
BN230	Hawker Hurricane IIc (LF751/5466M) [FT-A]	RAF Manston, Memorial Pavilion	
BP926	VS353 Spitfire PR IV (G-PRIV)	Privately owned, Newport Pagnell	
BR954	VS353 Spitfire PR IV <R> (N3194/BAPC 220) [JP-A]	Merlin ERD, Perth	
BS239	VS361 Spitfire IX <R> (BAPC 222) [5R-E]	Battle of Britain Bunker, Uxbridge	
BS410	VS361 Spitfire IXc (G-TCHI)	Privately owned, Biggin Hill	
BS435	VS361 Spitfire IX <R> (BAPC 324) [FY-F]	Privately owned, Lytham St Annes	
BW853	Hawker Hurricane XIIa (G-BRKE) (fuselage)	Currently not known	
DD931	Bristol 152 Beaufort VIII (9131M/BAPC 436) [L]	RAF Museum, Hendon	
DE208	DH82A Tiger Moth II (G-AGYU)	Privately owned, Treswell, Notts	
DE470	DH82A Tiger Moth II (G-ANMY) [16]	Privately owned, Garford, Oxon (rebuild)	
DE623	DH82A Tiger Moth II (G-ANFI)	Privately owned, Cardiff	
DE673	DH82A Tiger Moth II (G-ADNZ/6948M)	Privately owned, Tibenham	
DE971	DH82A Tiger Moth II (G-OOSY)	Privately owned, Bicester	
DE974	DH82A Tiger Moth II (G-ANZZ)	Privately owned, Clacton/Duxford	
DE992	DH82A Tiger Moth II (G-AXXV)	Privately owned, Membury, Berks	
DF112	DH82A Tiger Moth II (G-ANRM)	Privately owned, Clacton/Duxford	
DF128	DH82A Tiger Moth II (G-AOJJ) [RCO-U]	Privately owned, White Waltham	
DF198	DH82A Tiger Moth II (G-BBRB)	Privately owned, stored West Wickham, Kent	
DG202	Gloster F9/40 (5758M)	RAF Museum, stored Cosford	
DG590	Miles M2H Hawk Major (G-ADMW/8379M)	Montrose Air Station Heritage Centre	
DP872	Fairey Barracuda II <ff>	FAA Museum, stored Cobham Hall, RNAS Yeovilton	
DP872	Fairey Barracuda II <rf>	FAA Museum, RNAS Yeovilton	
DV372	Avro 683 Lancaster I <ff>	IWM London, Lambeth	
DZ313	DH98 Mosquito B IV <R>	Privately owned, Little Rissington	
EB518	Airspeed AS10 Oxford V	Privately owned, Kenilworth	
EE416	Gloster Meteor F3 <ff>	Martin Baker Aircraft, Chalgrove, fire section	
EE425	Gloster Meteor F3 <ff>	Jet Age Museum, Gloucester	
EE531	Gloster Meteor F4 (7090M)	Midland Air Museum, Coventry	
EE549	Gloster Meteor F4 (7008M) [A]	Tangmere Military Aviation Museum	
EE602	VS349 Spitfire LF Vc (G-IBSY) [DV-V]	Privately owned, Biggin Hill	
EF545	VS349 Spitfire LF Vc (G-CDGY)	Aero Vintage, Rye	
EJ922	Hawker Typhoon Ib <ff>	Privately owned, Booker	
EM720	DH82A Tiger Moth II (G-AXAN)	Privately owned, Duxford	
EM726	DH82A Tiger Moth II (G-ANDE) [FY]	Privately owned, Headcorn	
EM840	DH82A Tiger Moth II (G-ANBY)	Privately owned, Middle Wallop	
EM973	DH82A Tiger Moth II (T6774/G-ALNA) [OY]	Privately owned, Darley Moor, Derbys	
EN130	Supermarine Aircraft Spitfire 26B (G-ENAA) [FN-A]	Privately owned, Enstone	
EN179	VS361 Spitfire F IX (G-TCHO)	Privately owned, Exeter	
EN224	VS366 Spitfire F XII (G-FXII)	Privately owned, Sywell	
EN398	VS361 Spitfire F IX <R> [JE-J]	AMSS, Pyle, Bridgend	
EN398	VS361 Spitfire F IX <R> [JE-J]	RAF Coningsby, on display	
EN398	VS361 Spitfire F IX <R> (BAPC 184) [JE-J]	Northern 40s Re-enactment Group, Belper	
EN398	VS361 Spitfire F IX <R> [JE-J]	Spitfire Spares, Taunton, Somerset	
EN570	VS361 Spitfire F IX (G-CISP/LN-AOA)	Airframe Assemblies, Sandown	
EN961	Isaacs Spitfire <R> (G-CGIK) [SD-X]	Privately owned, Stoulton, Worcs	
EP120	VS349 Spitfire LF Vb (G-LFVB/5377M/8070M) [AE-A]	The Fighter Collection, Duxford	
EP121	VS349 Spitfire LF Vb <R> (BAPC 320) [LO-D]	Montrose Air Station Heritage Centre	

Notes	Serial	Type (code/other identity)	Owner/operator, location or fate
	EV771	Fairchild UC-61 Argus <R> (BAPC 294)	Thorpe Camp Preservation Group, Lincs
	EX976	NA AT-6D Harvard III (FAP 1657)	FAA Museum, RNAS Yeovilton
	FE511	Noorduyn AT-16 Harvard IIb (G-CIUW)	Privately owned, Old Warden
	FE695	Noorduyn AT-16 Harvard IIb (G-BTXI) [94]	The Fighter Collection, Duxford
	FE788	CCF Harvard IV (MM54137/G-CTKL)	Privately owned, Biggin Hill
	FE905	Noorduyn AT-16 Harvard IIb (LN-BNM)	RAF Museum, Hendon
	FE992	Noorduyn AT-16 Harvard IIb (G-BDAM)	*Repainted in Canadian markings, 2018*
	FJ801	Boeing-Stearman PT-27 Kaydet (N62842/BAPC 375)	Norfolk & Suffolk Avn Museum, Flixton
	FJ992	Boeing-Stearman PT-17 Kaydet (OO-JEH) [44]	Privately owned, Wevelgem, Belgium
	FK338	Fairchild 24W-41 Argus I (G-AJOZ)	Yorkshire Air Museum, Elvington
	FL586	Douglas C-47B Dakota (OO-SMA) [AI-N] (fuselage)	WWII Remembrance Museum, Handcross, W Sussex
	FR886	Piper L-4J Grasshopper (G-BDMS)	Privately owned, Old Sarum
	FS628	Fairchild Argus 2 (43-14601/G-AIZE)	RAF Museum, Cosford
	FS728	Noorduyn AT-16 Harvard IIb (D-FRCP)	Privately owned, Gelnhausen, Germany
	FT118	Noorduyn AT-16 Harvard IIb (G-BZHL) [TM-13]	Privately owned, Hibaldstow
	FT323	NA AT-6D Harvard III (FAP 1513/G-CCOY)	Privately owned, France
	FT391	Noorduyn AT-16 Harvard IIb (G-AZBN)	Privately owned, White Waltham
	FX322	Noorduyn AT-16 Harvard IIb <ff>	Privately owned, Doncaster
	FX760	Curtiss P-40N Kittyhawk IV (A29-556/9150M) [GA-?]	RAF Museum, Hendon
	FZ626	Douglas Dakota III (KN566/G-AMPO) [YS-DH]	RAF Brize Norton, for display
	GZ100	AgustaWestland AW109SP Grand New (G-ZIOO)	RAF No 32(The Royal) Sqn, Northolt
	HB737	Fairchild Argus III (G-BCBH)	Privately owned, Spanhoe
	HB751	Fairchild Argus III (G-BCBL)	Privately owned, Woolsery, Devon
	HG691	DH89A Dragon Rapide (G-AIYR)	Privately owned, Clacton/Duxford
	HH268	GAL48 Hotspur II (HH379/BAPC 261) [H]	Army Flying Museum, Middle Wallop
	HJ711	DH98 Mosquito NF II (BAPC 434) [VI-C]	Lincolnshire Avn Heritage Centre, E Kirkby
	HM580	Cierva C-30A (G-ACUU) [KX-K]	IWM Duxford
	HS503	Fairey Swordfish IV (BAPC 108)	RAF Museum Reserve Collection, Stafford
	IR206	Eurofighter Typhoon <R> (BAPC 360) [IR]	RAF M&RU, Bottesford
	IR808	B-V Chinook <R> (BAPC 361)	RAF M&RU, Bottesford
	JG241	Supermarine Aircraft Spitfire 26B (G-SMSP) [ZX-J]	Privately owned, Blackbushe
	JG668	VS359 Spitfire T8 (A58-441/G-CFGA)	Privately owned, Haverfordwest
	JG891	VS349 Spitfire F Vc (N5TF/G-LFVC) [T-B]	Privately owned, Duxford
	JN768	Hawker Tempest V (4887M/G-TMPV)	Privately owned, Bentwaters
	JP843	Hawker Typhoon Ib [Y]	Privately owned, Shrewsbury
	JR505	Hawker Typhoon Ib <ff>	Midland Air Museum, Coventry
	JV482	Grumman Wildcat V	Ulster Aviation Society, Long Kesh
	JV579	Grumman FM-2 Wildcat (N4845V/G-RUMW) [F]	The Fighter Collection, Duxford
	KB889	Avro 683 Lancaster B X (G-LANC) [NA-I]	IWM Duxford
	KB976	Avro 683 Lancaster B X <ff>	Lincolnshire Avn Heritage Centre, E Kirkby
	KB976	Avro 683 Lancaster B X (G-BCOH) <rf>	South Yorkshire Aircraft Museum, Doncaster
	KD345	Goodyear FG-1D Corsair (88297/G-FGID) [130-A]	The Fighter Collection, Duxford
	KD431	CV Corsair IV [E2-M]	FAA Museum, RNAS Yeovilton
	KE209	Grumman Hellcat II	FAA Museum, RNAS Yeovilton
	KE418	Hawker Tempest <rf>	*Currently not known*
	KF183	Noorduyn AT-16 Harvard IIb (G-CORS) [3]	Privately owned, Duxford
	KF388	Noorduyn AT-16 Harvard IIb (composite)	Bournemouth Aviation Museum
	KF402	NA T-6G Texan (49-3072/G-TEXN) [HT-Y]	Boultbee Flight Academy, Goodwood
	KF532	Noorduyn AT-16 Harvard IIb <ff>	Privately owned, Bruntingthorpe
	KF584	CCF T-6J Texan (G-RAIX) [RAI-X]	Sold to Poland, April 2018
	KF650	Noorduyn AT-16 Harvard IIb <ff>	Sywell Aviation Museum
	KF741	Noorduyn AT-16 Harvard IIb <ff>	Privately owned, Kenilworth
	KG374	Douglas Dakota IV (KP208) [YS-DM]	Merville Barracks, Colchester, on display
	KG651	Douglas Dakota III (G-AMHJ)	Metheringham Airfield Visitor Centre, Lincs
	KH570	Titan T-51B Mustang (G-CIXK) [5J-X]	*Crashed, Oakham, 24 November 2017*
	KH774	NA P-51D Mustang IV (44-73877/G-SHWN) [GA-S]	Privately owned, Goodwood

Serial	Type (code/other identity)	Owner/operator, location or fate	Notes
KJ351	Airspeed AS58 Horsa II (TL659/BAPC 80) [23]	Army Flying Museum, Middle Wallop	
KJ994	Douglas Dakota III (F-AZTE)	Dakota et Cie, La Ferté Alais, France	
KK116	Douglas Dakota IV (G-AMPY)	Privately owned, Coventry	
KK527	Fairchild 24R Argus III (44-83184/G-RGUS)	Privately owned, Sibson	
KK995	Sikorsky Hoverfly I [E]	RAF Museum, Hendon	
KL216	Republic P-47D Thunderbolt (45-49295/9212M) [RS-L]	RAF Museum, Hendon	
KN353	Douglas Dakota IV (G-AMYJ)	Yorkshire Air Museum, Elvington	
KN645	Douglas Dakota IV (KG374/8355M)	RAF Museum, Cosford	
KN751	Consolidated Liberator C VI (IAF HE807) [F]	RAF Museum, Hendon	
KZ191	Hawker Hurricane IV (frame only)	Privately owned, East Garston, Bucks	
LA198	VS356 Spitfire F21 (7118M) [RAI-G]	Kelvingrove Art Gallery & Museum, Glasgow	
LA226	VS356 Spitfire F21 (7119M)	RAF Museum Reserve Collection, Stafford	
LA255	VS356 Spitfire F21 (6490M)	RAF Lossiemouth, preserved	
LA543	VS474 Seafire F46 <ff>	The Air Defence Collection, Salisbury	
LA546	VS474 Seafire F46 (G-CFZJ)	Privately owned, Colchester	
LA564	VS474 Seafire F46 (G-FRSX)	Kennet Aviation, Old Warden	
LB264	Taylorcraft Plus D (G-AIXA)	RAF Museum, Hendon	
LB294	Taylorcraft Plus D (G-AHWJ)	Saywell Heritage Centre, Worthing	
LB312	Taylorcraft Plus D (HH982/G-AHXE)	Privately owned, Netheravon	
LB314	Taylorcraft Plus D (OY-DSZ)	South Yorkshire Aircraft Museum, Doncaster	
LB323	Taylorcraft Plus D (G-AHSD)	Privately owned, Spanhoe	
LB352	Taylorcraft Plus D (G-AHCR)	Privately owned, Dunkeswell	
LB367	Taylorcraft Plus D (G-AHGZ)	Privately owned, Melksham	
LB375	Taylorcraft Plus D (G-AHGW)	Privately owned, Spanhoe	
LF363	Hawker Hurricane IIc [GN-F,SD-A]	RAF BBMF, Coningsby	
LF738	Hawker Hurricane IIc (5405M) [UH-A]	RAF Museum, Cosford	
LF789	DH82 Queen Bee (K3584/BAPC 186) [R2-K]	de Havilland Aircraft Museum, London Colney	
LF858	DH82 Queen Bee (G-BLUZ)	Privately owned, Henlow	
LH291	Airspeed AS51 Horsa I <R> (BAPC 279)	RAF Museum, stored Cosford	
LS326	Fairey Swordfish II (G-AJVH) [L2]	RN Historic Flight, Yeovilton	
LV907	HP59 Halifax III (HR792/BAPC 449) [NP-F] (marked NP763 [H7-N] on port side)	Yorkshire Air Museum, Elvington	
LZ551	DH100 Vampire	FAA Museum, RNAS Yeovilton	
LZ766	Percival P34 Proctor III (G-ALCK)	IWM Duxford	
LZ842	VS361 Spitfire F IX (G-CGZU) [EF-F]	Privately owned, Biggin Hill	
LZ844	VS349 Spitfire F Vc [UP-X]	Currently not known	
MA764	VS361 Spitfire F IX (G-MCDB)	Privately owned, Biggin Hill	
MD338	VS359 Spitfire LF VIII	Privately owned, Sandown	
MF628	Vickers Wellington T10 (9210M)	Michael Beetham Conservation Centre, RAFM Cosford	
MH314	VS361 Spitfire IX <R> (EN526/BAPC 221) [SZ-G]	RAF Northolt, on display	
MH415	VS361 Spitfire IX <R> (MJ751/BAPC 209) [DU-V]	The Aircraft Restoration Co, Duxford	
MH434	VS361 Spitfire LF IXb (G-ASJV) [ZD-B]	The Old Flying Machine Company, Duxford	
MH526	Supermarine Aircraft Spitfire 26 (G-CJWW) [LO-D]	Privately owned, Wethersfield, Essex	
MJ627	VS509 Spitfire T9 (G-BMSB) [9G-P]	Privately owned, Biggin Hill	
MJ755	VS361 Spitfire LF IXe	Privately owned, Biggin Hill	
MJ772	VS509 Spitfire T9 (G-AVAV) [NL-R]	Privately owned, Biggin Hill	
MJ832	VS361 Spitfire IX <R> (L1096/BAPC 229) [DN-Y]	RAF Digby, on display	
MK356	VS361 Spitfire LF IXe (5690M) [QJ-3]	RAF BBMF, Coningsby	
MK356	VS361 Spitfire LF IXc <R> [2I-V]	Kent Battle of Britain Museum, Hawkinge	
MK356	VS361 Spitfire LF IXc (BAPC 298) <R>	RAF Cosford, on display	
MK392	VS361 Spitfire LF IXc <R> [JE-J]	Boultbee Flight Academy, Goodwood	
MK805	VS361 Spitfire IX (BAPC 426) <R> [SH-B]	Simply Spitfire, Oulton Broad, Suffolk	
MK912	VS361 Spitfire LF IXc (G-BRRA) [SH-L]	Privately owned, Biggin Hill	
ML135	VS361 Spitfire IX <R> (BAPC 513)	Essex Memorial Spitfire Monument	
ML295	VS361 Spitfire LF IXe (NH341/G-CICK)	Privately owned, Duxford	
ML407	VS509 Spitfire T9 (G-LFIX) [OU-V]	Privately owned, Sywell	
ML411	VS361 Spitfire LF IXe (G-CBNU)	Privately owned, Ashford, Kent	
ML427	VS361 Spitfire IX (6457M) [HK-A]	Thinktank, Birmingham	
ML796	Short S25 Sunderland V [NS-F]	IWM Duxford	

Notes	Serial	Type (code/other identity)	Owner/operator, location or fate
	ML824	Short S25 Sunderland V [NS-Z]	RAF Museum, Hendon
	MN235	Hawker Typhoon Ib [I8-T]	RAF Museum, Hendon
	MP425	Airspeed AS10 Oxford I (G-AITB) [G]	RAF Museum, Hendon
	MS902	Miles M25 Martinet TT1 (TF-SHC)	Museum of Berkshire Aviation, Woodley
	MS968	Auster AOP5 (G-ALYG)	Privately owned, Old Sarum
	MT182	Auster J/1 Autocrat (G-AJDY)	Privately owned, Spanhoe
	MT197	Auster IV (G-ANHS)	Privately owned, Spanhoe
	MT438	Auster III (G-AREI)	Privately owned, Eggesford
	MT818	VS502 Spitfire T8 (G-AIDN)	Privately owned, Biggin Hill
	MT928	VS359 Spitfire HF VIIIc (D-FEUR/MV154/AR654) [ZX-M]	Privately owned, Bremgarten, Germany
	MV268	VS379 Spitfire FR XIVe (MV293/G-SPIT) [JE-J]	Privately owned, Duxford
	MW401	Hawker Tempest II (IAF HA604/G-PEST)	Privately owned, Great Dunmow, Essex
	MW763	Hawker Tempest II (IAF HA586/G-TEMT) [HF-A]	North Weald Heritage Aviation, North Weald
	MW810	Hawker Tempest II (IAF HA591) <ff>	Privately owned, Bentwaters
	NF314	GEC Phoenix (BAPC 408)	Army, Larkhill, on display
	NF370	Fairey Swordfish III [NH-L]	IWM Duxford
	NF389	Fairey Swordfish III	RN Historic Flight, Yeovilton
	NH238	VS361 Spitfire LF IXe (G-MKIX) [D-A]	Privately owned, stored Greenham Common
	NH341	VS509 Spitfire T9 (G-CICK) [DB-E]	Privately owned, Headcorn
	NJ633	Auster 5D (G-AKXP)	Privately owned, Old Sarum
	NJ673	Auster 5D (G-AOCR)	Privately owned, Shenington, Oxon
	NJ689	Auster AOP5 (G-ALXZ)	Privately owned, Breighton
	NJ695	Auster AOP5 (G-AJXV)	Privately owned, Newark
	NJ703	Auster AOP5 (TJ207/G-AKPI) [P]	Privately owned, Wickenby
	NJ719	Auster AOP5 (TW385/G-ANFU)	South Yorkshire Aircraft Museum, Doncaster
	NJ728	Auster AOP5 (G-AIKE)	Privately owned, Little Gransden
	NJ889	Auster AOP3 (G-AHLK)	Privately owned, Ledbury, Herefordshire
	NL750	DH82A Tiger Moth II (T7997/G-AOBH)	Privately owned, Eaglescott
	NL985	DH82A Tiger Moth I (G-BWIK/7015M)	Privately owned, Oaksey Park
	NM138	DH82A Tiger Moth I (G-ANEW) [41]	Privately owned, Henstridge
	NM181	DH82A Tiger Moth I (G-AZGZ)	Privately owned, Rush Green
	NP294	Percival P31 Proctor IV [TB-M]	Lincolnshire Avn Heritage Centre, E Kirkby
	NV778	Hawker Tempest TT5 (8386M)	RAF Museum, Hendon
	NS710	DH98 Mosquito TT35 (TJ118) <ff>	Victoria and Albert Museum, Knightsbridge, London
	NX534	Auster III (G-BUDL)	Privately owned, Spanhoe
	NX611	Avro 683 Lancaster B VII (G-ASXX/8375M) [DX-F,LE-H]	Lincolnshire Avn Heritage Centre, E Kirkby
	PA474	Avro 683 Lancaster B I [AR-L,VN-T]	RAF BBMF, Coningsby
	PD685	Slingsby T7 Cadet TX1 (BAPC 355)	Tettenhall Transport Heritage Centre
	PF179	HS Gnat T1 (XR541/8602M)	Privately owned, North Weald
	PG657	DH82A Tiger Moth II (G-AGPK)	Privately owned, Clacton/Duxford
	PG712	DH82A Tiger Moth II (PH-CSL) [2]	Privately owned, Hilversum, The Netherlands
	PK519	VS356 Spitfire F22 [G-SPXX]	Privately owned, Newport Pagnell
	PK624	VS356 Spitfire F22 (8072M)	The Fighter Collection, Duxford
	PK664	VS356 Spitfire F22 (7759M) [V6-B]	Kennet Aviation, Old Warden
	PK683	VS356 Spitfire F24 (7150M)	Solent Sky, Southampton
	PK724	VS356 Spitfire F24 (7288M)	RAF Museum, Hendon
	PL256	VS361 Spitfire IX <R> (BAPC 325) [AI-L]	Privately owned, Leicester
	PL279	VS361 Spitfire IX <R> (N3317/BAPC 268) [ZF-Z]	Privately owned, St Mawgan
	PL788	Supermarine Aircraft Spitfire 26 (G-CIEN)	Privately owned, Perth
	PL793	Supermarine Aircraft Spitfire 26 (G-CIXM)	Privately owned, Enstone
	PL904	VS365 Spitfire PR XI <R> (EN343/BAPC 226)	RAF Benson, on display
	PL965	VS365 Spitfire PR XI (G-MKXI) [R]	Hangar 11 Collection, North Weald
	PL983	VS365 Spitfire PR XI (G-PRXI)	Privately owned, Duxford
	PM631	VS390 Spitfire PR XIX	RAF BBMF, Coningsby
	PM651	VS390 Spitfire PR XIX (7758M) [X]	RAF Museum Reserve Collection, Stafford
	PN323	HP Halifax VII <ff>	IWM Duxford
	PP566	Fairey Firefly I <rf>	Privately owned, Newton Abbott, Devon
	PP972	VS358 Seafire LF IIIc (G-BUAR) [11-5/N]	Privately owned, Sywell

Serial	Type (code/other identity)	Owner/operator, location or fate	Notes
PR478	Supermarine Aircraft Spitfire 26 [S]	Privately owned, Dunkeswell	
PR536	Hawker Tempest II (IAF HA457)[OQ-H]	RAF Museum, Hendon	
PS004	Airbus Zephyr 8B	For MoD	
PS853	VS390 Spitfire PR XIX (G-RRGN) [C]	Rolls-Royce, East Midlands	
PS890	VS390 Spitfire PR XIX (F-AZJS) [UM-E]	Privately owned, Dijon, France	
PS915	VS390 Spitfire PR XIX (7548M/7711M)	RAF BBMF, Coningsby	
PT462	VS509 Spitfire T9 (G-CTIX/N462JC) [SW-A]	Privately owned, Caernarfon/Duxford	
PT462	VS361 Spitfire IX <R> (BAPC 318) [SW-A]	Privately owned, Moffat, Dumfries & Galloway	
PT879	VS361 Spitfire F IX (G-BYDE/G-PTIX)	Hangar 11 Collection, North Weald	
PV202	VS509 Spitfire T9 (H-98/W3632/G-CCCA) [5R-H]	Historic Flying Ltd, Duxford	
PV303	Supermarine Aircraft Spitfire 26 (G-CCJL) [ON-B]	Privately owned, Enstone	
PZ460	BBC Mosquito (F-PMOZ) [NE-K]	Privately owned, Fontenay-le-Comte, France	
PZ865	Hawker Hurricane IIc (G-AMAU) [EG-S]	RAF BBMF, Coningsby	
QQ100	Agusta A109E Power Elite (G-CFVB)	MoD/ETPS, Boscombe Down	
QQ101	BAe RJ.100 (G-BZAY)	*Registered as G-ETPL, 28 September 2018*	
QQ102	BAe RJ.70ER (G-BVRJ)	*Registered as G-ETPK, 23 January 2019*	
QQ103	Diamond DA.42M-NG Twin Star (G-LTPA)	*Registered as G-ETPM, 19 September 2018*	
RA848	Slingsby T7 Cadet TX1 <ff>	Privately owned, Leeds	
RA854	Slingsby T7 Cadet TX1	Yorkshire Air Museum, Elvington	
RA897	Slingsby T7 Cadet TX1	Newark Air Museum, Winthorpe	
RA905	Slingsby T7 Cadet TX1 (BGA1143)	Trenchard Museum, RAF Halton	
RB142	Supermarine Aircraft Spitfire 26 (G-CEFC) [DW-B]	Privately owned, Lee-on-Solent	
RB159	VS379 Spitfire F XIV <R> [DW-D]	Privately owned, Delabole, Cornwall	
RB396	Hawker Typhoon IB (fuselage)	Privately owned, Goodwood	
RD220	Bristol 156 Beaufighter TF X	National Museum of Flight, stored E Fortune	
RD253	Bristol 156 Beaufighter TF X (7931M)	RAF Museum, Hendon	
RF398	Avro 694 Lincoln B II (8376M)	RAF Museum, Cosford	
RG333	Miles M38 Messenger IIA (G-AIEK)	Privately owned, North Coates	
RG904	VS Spitfire <R> (BAPC 333) [BT-K]	RAF Museum, Cosford	
RG907	Miles M25 Martinet <ff> (BAPC 514)	Tettenhall Transport Heritage Centre	
RH746	Bristol 164 Brigand TF1 (fuselage)	RAF Museum, stored Cosford	
RK838	VS349 Spitfire Vb <R> (BAPC 230/AB550) [GE-P]	Eden Camp Theme Park, Malton, North Yorkshire	
RK855	Supermarine Aircraft Spitfire 26 (G-PIXY) [FT-C]	Privately owned, Henstridge	
RL962	DH89A Dominie II (G-AHED)	RAF Museum Reserve Collection, Stafford	
RM169	Percival P31 Proctor IV (G-ANVY) [4-47]	Privately owned, Great Oakley, Essex	
RM221	Percival P31 Proctor IV (G-ANXR)	Privately owned, Headcorn	
RM689	VS379 Spitfire F XIV (G-ALGT)	Rolls-Royce, stored East Midlands Airport	
RM694	VS379 Spitfire F XIV (G-DBKL/6640M)	Privately owned, Booker	
RM927	VS379 Spitfire F XIV (G-JNMA)	Privately owned, Biggin Hill	
RN218	Isaacs Spitfire <R> (G-BBJI) [N]	Privately owned, Builth Wells	
RP001	AeroVironment Puma AE Micro UAV	MoD	
RP002	AeroVironment Wasp AE Micro UAV	MoD	
RP003	AeroVironment Shrike Mk1 Micro UAV	MoD	
RR232	VS361 Spitfire HF IXc (PV181/G-BRSF)	Privately owned, Goodwood	
RT486	Auster 5 (G-AJGJ)	RAF Manston History Museum	
RT520	Auster 5 (G-ALYB)	South Yorkshire Aircraft Museum, Doncaster	
RT610	Auster 5A-160 (G-AKWS)	Privately owned, Shobdon	
RW382	VS361 Spitfire LF XVIe (G-PBIX/7245M/8075M) [3W-P]	Privately owned, Biggin Hill	
RW386	VS361 Spitfire LF XVIe (SE-BIR/6944M) [NG-D]	Privately owned, Angelholm, Sweden	
RW388	VS361 Spitfire LF XVIe (6946M) [U4-U]	Stoke-on-Trent City Museum, Rochester (restoration)	
RX168	VS358 Seafire L IIIc (IAC 157/G-BWEM)	Privately owned, Launceston	
SE001*	Boeing Scan Eagle RM1 RPAS	*Withdrawn from use*	
SL611	VS361 Spitfire LF XVIe (G-SAEA)	Supermarine Aero Engineering, Stoke-on-Trent	
SL674	VS361 Spitfire LF IX (8392M) [RAS-H]	RAF Museum Reserve Collection, Stafford	
SL721	VS361 Spitfire LF XVIe (OO-XVI) [AU-J]	Privately owned, Brasschaat, Belgium	
SM520	VS509 Spitfire T9 (H-99/G-ILDA) [KJ-I]	Boultbee Flight Academy, Goodwood	
SM639	VS361 Spitfire LF IXe (G-CKYM)	Privately owned, Godalming	
SM845	VS394 Spitfire FR XVIII (G-BUOS) [R]	Spitfire Ltd, Humberside	

Notes	Serial	Type (code/other identity)	Owner/operator, location or fate
	SN280	Hawker Tempest V <ff>	South Yorkshire Aircraft Museum, Doncaster
	SR462	VS377 Seafire F XV (UB415/G-TGVP)	Airframe Assemblies, Sandown
SR661	Hawker Fury ISS (G-CBEL)	Privately owned, Sywell
	SX137	VS384 Seafire F XVII	FAA Museum, RNAS Yeovilton
	SX300	VS384 Seafire F XVII (G-RIPH)	Kennet Aviation, Old Warden
	SX336	VS384 Seafire F XVII (G-KASX) [105/VL]	Kennet Aviation, Old Warden
	TA122	DH98 Mosquito FB VI [UP-G]	de Havilland Aircraft Museum, London Colney
	TA634	DH98 Mosquito TT35 (G-AWJV) [8K-K]	de Havilland Aircraft Museum, London Colney
	TA639	DH98 Mosquito TT35 (7806M) [AZ-E]	RAF Museum, Cosford
	TA719	DH98 Mosquito TT35 (G-ASKC) [56]	IWM Duxford
	TA805	VS361 Spitfire HF IX (G-PMNF) [FX-M]	Privately owned, Biggin Hill
TB288	VS361 Spitfire LF IX <R> (MH486/46/BAPC 206) [HT-H]	RAF Museum, Hendon
	TB382	VS361 Spitfire LF XVIe (X4277/MK673)	Airframe Assemblies, Sandown
TB675	VS361 Spitfire LF XVIe (RW393/7293M) [4D-V]	RAF Museum, Hendon
	TB752	VS361 Spitfire LF XVIe (8086M) [KH-Z]	RAF Manston, Memorial Pavilion
	TB885	VS361 Spitfire LF XVIe (G-CKUE) [3W-V]	Privately owned, Biggin Hill
	TD248	VS361 Spitfire LF XVIe (G-OXVI/7246M) [CR-S]	Spitfire Ltd, Humberside
	TD248	VS361 Spitfire LF XVIe (BAPC 368) [8Q-T] (fuselage)	Norfolk & Suffolk Avn Mus'm, Flixton
	TD314	VS361 Spitfire LF IX (G-CGYJ) [FX-P]	Privately owned, Duxford
	TE184	VS361 Spitfire LF XVIe (G-MXVI/6850M) [9N-B]	Privately owned, Biggin Hill/Bremgarten, Germany
	TE311	VS361 Spitfire LF XVIe (MK178/7241M) [SZ-G]	RAF BBMF, Biggin Hill (on overhaul)
	TE356	VS361 Spitfire LF XVIe (N356TE) [DD-E]	Privately owned, Biggin Hill
	TE462	VS361 Spitfire LF XVIe (7243M)	National Museum of Flight, E Fortune
	TE517	VS361 Spitfire LF IXe (G-JGCA) [HL-K]	Privately owned, Biggin Hill
	TE566	VS509 Spitfire T9 (VH-IXT)	Vintage Flyers, Cotswold Airport (rebuild)
	TG263	Saro SR A1 (G-12-1)	Solent Sky, Southampton
	TG511	HP67 Hastings T5 (8554M) [511]	RAF Museum, Cosford
	TG517	HP67 Hastings T5 [517]	Newark Air Museum, Winthorpe
	TG528	HP67 Hastings C1A [528,T]	IWM Duxford
	TJ138	DH98 Mosquito B35 (7607M) [VO-L]	RAF Museum, Hendon
TJ207	Auster AOP5 (NJ703/G-AKPI) [P]	Repainted as NJ703, 2018
	TJ343	Auster AOP5 (G-AJXC)	Privately owned, White Waltham
TJ518	Auster J/1 Autocrat (G-AJIH)	Privately owned, Gloucester
	TJ534	Auster AOP5 (G-AKSY)	Privately owned, Dunsfold
	TJ569	Auster AOP5 (G-AKOW)	Army Flying Museum, Middle Wallop
TJ652	Auster AOP5 (TJ565/G-AMVD)	Privately owned, Hardwick, Norfolk
	TJ672	Auster 5D (G-ANIJ) [TS-D]	Privately owned, Netheravon
	TK718	GAL59 Hamilcar I (fuselage)	The Tank Museum, Bovington
	TK777	GAL59 Hamilcar I (fuselage)	Army Flying Museum, Middle Wallop
	TP280	VS394 Spitfire FR XVIIIe (D-FSPT)	Hangar 10 Collection, Heringsdorf, Germany
	TP298	VS394 Spitfire FR XVIII [UM-T]	Airframe Assemblies, Sandown
	TS291	Slingsby T7 Cadet TX1 (BGA852)	Royal Scottish Mus'm of Flight, stored Granton
	TS798	Avro 685 York C1 (G-AGNV/MW100)	RAF Museum, Cosford
	TW439	Auster AOP5 (G-ANRP)	Privately owned, Breighton
	TW467	Auster AOP5 (G-ANIE)	Privately owned, Elmsett
	TW477	Auster AOP5 (OY-EFI)	Privately owned, Ringsted, Denmark
	TW501	Auster AOP5 (G-ALBJ)	Privately owned, Dunkeswell
TW511	Auster AOP5 (G-APAF)	Privately owned, Chisledon, Wilts
	TW519	Auster AOP5 (G-ANHX) [ROA-V]	Privately owned, Newark
	TW536	Auster AOP6 (G-BNGE/7704M)	Privately owned, Netheravon
	TW591	Auster 6A (G-ARIH)	Privately owned, Eggesford
	TW641	Beagle A61 Terrier 2 (G-ATDN)	Privately owned, Biggin Hill
TX176	Avro XIX Anson Series 2 (G-AHKX)	BAE Systems, Old Warden
	TX213	Avro 652A Anson C19 (G-AWRS)	North-East Aircraft Museum, Usworth
	TX214	Avro 652A Anson C19 (7817M)	RAF Museum, Cosford
	TX226	Avro 652A Anson C19 (7865M)	Montrose Air Station Heritage Centre
	TX235	Avro 652A Anson C19	Privately owned, stored Compton Verney
	TX310	DH89A Dragon Rapide 6 (G-AIDL)	Privately owned, Duxford
TZ164	Isaacs Spitfire (G-ISAC) [01-A]	Privately owned, Hampstead Norreys, Berks

Serial	Type (code/other identity)	Owner/operator, location or fate	Notes
VF301	DH100 Vampire F1 (7060M) [RAL-G]	Midland Air Museum, Coventry	
VF512	Auster 6A (G-ARRX) [PF-M]	Privately owned, Popham	
VF516	Beagle A61 Terrier 2 (G-ASMZ)	Privately owned, Eshott	
VF519	Auster AOP6 (G-ASYN)	Privately owned, Doncaster	
VF526	Auster 6A (G-ARXU) [T]	Privately owned, Netheravon	
VF557	Auster 6A (G-ARHM) [H]	Privately owned, Headcorn	
VF560	Auster 6A (frame)	South Yorkshire Aircraft Museum, stored Doncaster	
VF581	Beagle A61 Terrier 1 (G-ARSL) [G]	National Museum of Scotland, Edinburgh	
VF631	Auster AOP6 (G-ASDK)	Privately owned, Hibaldstow	
VH127	Fairey Firefly TT4 [200/R]	FAA Museum, stored Cobham Hall, RNAS Yeovilton	
VL348	Avro 652A Anson C19 (G-AVVO)	Newark Air Museum, Winthorpe	
VL349	Avro 652A Anson C19 (G-AWSA) [V7-Q]	Norfolk & Suffolk Avn Museum, Flixton	
VM325	Avro 652A Anson C19	Privately owned, Carew Cheriton, Pembrokeshire	
VM360	Avro 652A Anson C19 (G-APHV)	National Museum of Flight, E Fortune	
VM657	Slingsby T8 Tutor TX2 (IGA-6)	Privately owned, stored Ashbourne, Eire	
VM687	Slingsby T8 Tutor (BGA794)	Privately owned, Lee-on-Solent	
VM791	Slingsby Cadet TX3 (XA312/8876M)	RAF Manston History Museum	
VN485	VS356 Spitfire F24 (7326M)	IWM Duxford	
VN799	EE Canberra T4 (WJ874/G-CDSX)	Aerohub, Newquay	
VP293	Avro 696 Shackleton T4 [X] <ff>	Shackleton Preservation Trust, Coventry	
VP519	Avro 652A Anson C19 (G-AVVR) <ff>	South Yorkshire Aircraft Museum, Doncaster	
VP952	DH104 Devon C2 (8820M)	RAF Museum, Cosford	
VP955	DH104 Devon C2 (G-DVON)	Privately owned, Cricklade, Wilts	
VP957	DH104 Devon C2 (8822M) <ff>	No 1137 Sqn ATC, Long Kesh	
VP967	DH104 Devon C2 (G-KOOL)	Yorkshire Air Museum, Elvington	
VP975	DH104 Devon C2 [M]	Science Museum, stored Wroughton	
VP981	DH104 Devon C2 (G-DHDV)	Aero Legends, Headcorn/Duxford	
VR137	Westland Wyvern TF1	FAA Museum, stored Cobham Hall, RNAS Yeovilton	
VR192	Percival P40 Prentice T1 (G-APIT)	Romney Marsh Wartime Collection	
VR249	Percival P40 Prentice T1 (G-APIY) [FA-EL]	Newark Air Museum, Winthorpe	
VR259	Percival P40 Prentice T1 (G-APJB) [M]	Privately owned, Headcorn	
VR930	Hawker Sea Fury FB11 (8382M) [110/Q]	RN Historic Flight, Yeovilton	
VS356	Percival P40 Prentice T1 (G-AOLU)	Privately owned, Fordoun, Aberdeenshire	
VS562	Avro 652A Anson T21 (8012M) <ff>	Shannon Aviation Museum, Eire	
VS610	Percival P40 Prentice T1 (G-AOKL)[K-L]	Privately owned, Fordoun, Aberdeenshire	
VS618	Percival P40 Prentice T1 (G-AOLK)	RAF Museum Reserve Collection, Stafford	
VS623	Percival P40 Prentice T1 (G-AOKZ)[KQ-F]	Midland Air Museum, Coventry	
VT812	DH100 Vampire F3 (7200M) [N]	RAF Museum, Hendon	
VT935	Boulton Paul P111A (VT769)	Midland Air Museum, Coventry	
VT987	Auster AOP6 (G-BKXP)	Privately owned, Thruxton	
VV106	Supermarine 510 (7175M)	FAA Museum, stored Cobham Hall, RNAS Yeovilton	
VV217	DH100 Vampire FB5 (7323M)	de Havilland Aircraft Museum, stored London Colney	
VV400	EoN Olympia 2 (BGA1697)	Privately owned, Aston Down	
VV401	EoN Olympia 2 (BGA1125) [99]	Privately owned, Ringmer, E Sussex	
VV901	Avro 652A Anson T21	Yorkshire Air Museum, Elvington	
VW453	Gloster Meteor T7 (8703M)	Jet Age Museum, Gloucester	
VW957	DH103 Sea Hornet NF21 <rf>	Privately owned, Chelmsford	
VW993	Beagle A61 Terrier 2 (G-ASCD)	Yorkshire Air Museum, Elvington	
VX113	Auster AOP6 (G-ARNO) [36]	Privately owned, Stow Maries, Essex	
VX185	EE Canberra B(I)8 (7631M) <ff>	National Museum of Flight, E Fortune	
VX250	DH103 Sea Hornet NF21 [48] <rf>	de Havilland Aircraft Museum, London Colney	
VX272	Hawker P.1052 (7174M)	FAA Museum, stored RNAS Yeovilton	
VX275	Slingsby T21B Sedbergh TX1 (BGA572/8884M)	RAF Museum Reserve Collection, Stafford	
VX281	Hawker Sea Fury T20S (G-RNHF) [120/VL]	Naval Aviation Ltd, RNAS Yeovilton	
VX573	Vickers Valetta C2 (8389M)	RAF Museum, stored Cosford	
VX580	Vickers Valetta C2 [580]	Norfolk & Suffolk Avn Museum, Flixton	
VX595	WS51 Dragonfly HR1	FAA Museum, RNAS Yeovilton	
VX665	Hawker Sea Fury FB11 <rf>	RN Historic Flight, at BAE Systems Brough	
VX924	Beagle A61 Terrier 2 (G-NTVE)	Privately owned, Fenland	
VX926	Auster T7 (G-ASKJ)	Privately owned, Gamlingay, Cambs	
VX927	Auster T7 (G-ASYG)	Privately owned, RAF Scampton	
VZ193	DH100 Vampire FB5 <ff>	Privately owned, Warrington	

Notes	Serial	Type (code/other identity)	Owner/operator, location or fate
	VZ305	DH100 Vampire FB6 (J-1196/PX-K/LN-DHY) [N]	Norwegian AF Historical Sqn, Rygge, Norway
	VZ440	Gloster Meteor F8 (WA984) [X]	Tangmere Military Aviation Museum
	VZ477	Gloster Meteor F8 (7741M) <ff>	Midland Air Museum, Coventry
	VZ608	Gloster Meteor FR9	Newark Air Museum, Winthorpe
	VZ634	Gloster Meteor T7 (8657M)	Newark Air Museum, Winthorpe
	VZ638	Gloster Meteor T7 (G-JETM) [HF]	Gatwick Aviation Museum, Charlwood, Surrey
	VZ728	RS4 Desford Trainer (G-AGOS)	Privately owned, Spanhoe
	WA346	DH100 Vampire FB5	RAF Museum, stored Cosford
	WA473	VS Attacker F1 [102/J]	FAA Museum, RNAS Yeovilton
	WA576	Bristol 171 Sycamore 3 (G-ALSS/7900M)	Dumfries & Galloway Avn Mus, Dumfries
	WA577	Bristol 171 Sycamore 3 (G-ALST/7718M)	North-East Aircraft Museum, Usworth
	WA630	Gloster Meteor T7 [69] <ff>	Robertsbridge Aviation Society, Newhaven
	WA634	Gloster Meteor T7/8	RAF Museum, Cosford
	WA638	Gloster Meteor T7(mod) (G-JWMA)	Martin-Baker Aircraft, Chalgrove
	WA662	Gloster Meteor T7	South Yorkshire Aircraft Museum, Doncaster
	WB188	Hawker Hunter F3 (7154M)	Tangmere Military Aviation Museum
	WB188	Hawker Hunter GA11 (XF300/G-BZPC)	Privately owned, Melksham, Wilts
	WB440	Fairey Firefly AS6 <ff>	Privately owned, Newton Abbott, Devon
	WB491	Avro 706 Ashton 2 (TS897/G-AJJW) <ff>	Newark Air Museum, Winthorpe
	WB549	DHC1 Chipmunk 22A (G-BAPB))	Privately owned, Old Buckenham
	WB555	DHC1 Chipmunk T10 <ff>	Privately owned, Ellerton
	WB560	DHC1 Chipmunk T10 (comp WG403) <ff>	Privately owned, Norwich
	WB565	DHC1 Chipmunk 22 (G-PVET) [X]	Privately owned, Rendcomb
	WB569	DHC1 Chipmunk 22 (G-BYSJ)	Privately owned, Duxford
	WB571	DHC1 Chipmunk 22 (D-EOSF) [34]	Privately owned, Porta Westfalica, Germany
	WB584	DHC1 Chipmunk T10 (comp WG303/7706M)	Solway Aviation Society, stored Carlisle
	WB585	DHC1 Chipmunk 22 (G-AOSY) [28]	Privately owned, Audley End
	WB588	DHC1 Chipmunk 22 (G-AOTD) [D]	Privately owned, Old Sarum
	WB615	DHC1 Chipmunk 22 (G-BXIA) [E]	Privately owned, Blackpool
	WB624	DHC1 Chipmunk T10	Newark Air Museum, Winthorpe
	WB626	DHC1 Chipmunk T10 [19] <ff>	Trenchard Museum, RAF Halton
	WB627	DHC1 Chipmunk T10 (9248M) (fuselage) [N]	Dulwich College CCF
	WB645	DHC1 Chipmunk T10 (8218M) <rf>	Privately owned, Norwich
	WB654	DHC1 Chipmunk 22 (G-BXGO) [U]	Privately owned, Finmere
	WB657	DHC1 Chipmunk T10 [908]	RN Historic Flight, Yeovilton
	WB670	DHC1 Chipmunk T10 (comp WG303)(8361M)	Privately owned, Carlisle
	WB671	DHC1 Chipmunk 22 (G-BWTG) [910]	Privately owned, Teuge, The Netherlands
	WB685	DHC1 Chipmunk T10 (comp WP969/G-ATHC)	de Havilland Aircraft Museum, London Colney
	WB685	DHC1 Chipmunk T10 <rf>	North-East Aircraft Museum, stored Usworth
	WB697	DHC1 Chipmunk 22 (G-BXCT) [95]	Privately owned, Wickenby
	WB702	DHC1 Chipmunk 22A (G-AOFE)	Privately owned, Audley End
	WB703	DHC1 Chipmunk 22A (G-ARMC)	Privately owned, Compton Abbas
	WB711	DHC1 Chipmunk 22 (G-APPM)	Privately owned, Sywell
	WB726	DHC1 Chipmunk 22A (G-AOSK) [E]	Privately owned, Turweston
	WB733	DHC1 Chipmunk T10 (comp WG422)	South Yorkshire Aircraft Museum, Doncaster
	WB758	DHC1 Chipmunk T10 (7729M) [P]	Privately owned, Torquay
	WB763	DHC1 Chipmunk 22 (G-BBMR) [K]	Privately owned, Turweston
	WB922	Slingsby T21B Sedbergh TX1 (BGA4366)	Privately owned, Shrivenham
	WB924	Slingsby T21B Sedbergh TX1 (BGA3901)	Privately owned, Dunstable
	WB944	Slingsby T21B Sedbergh TX1 (BGA3160)	Privately owned, Bicester
	WB945	Slingsby T21B Sedbergh TX1 (BGA1254)	Privately owned, stored RAF Halton
	WB971	Slingsby T21B Sedbergh TX1 (BGA3324)	Privately owned, Eaglescott
	WB975	Slingsby T21B Sedbergh TX1 (BGA3288) [FJB]	Privately owned, Shipdham
	WB980	Slingsby T21B Sedbergh TX1 (BGA3290)	Privately owned, Husbands Bosworth
	WB981	Slingsby T21B Sedbergh TX1 (BGA3238)	Privately owned, Eaglescott
	WD286	DHC1 Chipmunk 22 (G-BBND)	Privately owned, Old Warden
	WD292	DHC1 Chipmunk 22 (G-BCRX)	Privately owned, White Waltham
	WD293	DHC1 Chipmunk T10 (7645M) <ff>	South Wales Aviation Museum, St Athan
	WD310	DHC1 Chipmunk 22 (G-BWUN) [B]	Privately owned, Jersey

Serial	Type (code/other identity)	Owner/operator, location or fate	Notes
WD319	DHC1 Chipmunk 22 (OY-ATF)	Privately owned, Stauning, Denmark	
WD321	DHC1 Chipmunk 22 (G-BDCC)	Boscombe Down Aviation Collection, Old Sarum	
WD325	DHC1 Chipmunk T10 [N]	AAC, stored Middle Wallop	
WD331	DHC1 Chipmunk 22 (G-BXDH)	Privately owned, Farnborough	
WD355	DHC1 Chipmunk T10 (WD335/G-CBAJ)	Privately owned, Eastleigh	
WD363	DHC1 Chipmunk 22 (G-BCIH) [5]	Privately owned, Netheravon	
WD370	DHC1 Chipmunk T10 <ff>	No 225 Sqn ATC, Brighton	
WD373	DHC1 Chipmunk 22 (G-BXDI) [12]	Privately owned, Turweston	
WD377	DHC1 Chipmunk T10 <ff>	Wings Museum, Balcombe, W Sussex	
WD386	DHC1 Chipmunk T10 (comp WD377)	Ulster Aviation Soc, stored Upper Ballinderry, NI	
WD388	DHC1 Chipmunk 22 (D-EPAK) [68]	Quax Flieger, Hamm, Germany	
WD390	DHC1 Chipmunk 22 (G-BWNK) [68]	Privately owned, Compton Abbas	
WD413	Avro 652A Anson T21 (7881M/G-VROE)	Privately owned, Sleap	
WD615	Gloster Meteor TT20 (WD646/8189M) [R]	RAF Manston History Museum	
WD686	Gloster Meteor NF11 <ff>	Boscombe Down Aviation Collection, Old Sarum	
WD790	Gloster Meteor NF11 (8743M) <ff>	Boscombe Down Aviation Collection, Old Sarum	
WD889	Fairey Firefly AS5 (comp VT809)	Privately owned, Newton Abbot, Devon	
WD935	EE Canberra B2 (8440M) <ff>	South Yorkshire Aircraft Museum, Doncaster	
WD954	EE Canberra B2 <ff>	Privately owned, St Mawgan	
WD956	EE Canberra B2 <ff>	RAF Defford Museum, Croome Park	
WE113	EE Canberra B2 <ff>	Privately owned, Tangmere	
WE122	EE Canberra TT18 [845] <ff>	Blyth Valley Aviation Collection, Walpole, Suffolk	
WE139	EE Canberra PR3 (8369M)	RAF Museum, Hendon	
WE168	EE Canberra PR3 (8049M) <ff>	Norfolk & Suffolk Avn Museum, Flixton	
WE173	EE Canberra PR3 (8740M) <ff>	Robertsbridge Aviation Society, Mayfield	
WE188	EE Canberra T4	Solway Aviation Society, Carlisle	
WE192	EE Canberra T4 <ff>	Blyth Valley Aviation Collection, Walpole, Suffolk	
WE275	DH112 Venom FB50 (J-1601/G-VIDI)	BAE Systems Hawarden, Fire Section	
WE558	Auster T7 (frame)	East Midlands Airport Aeropark	
WE569	Auster T7 (G-ASAJ)	Privately owned, Defford	
WE570	Auster T7 (G-ASBU)	Privately owned, Stonehaven	
WE591	Auster T7 (F-AZTJ)	Privately owned, Toussus-le-Noble, France	
WE600	Auster T7 Antarctic (7602M)	RAF Museum, Cosford	
WE724	Hawker Sea Fury FB11 (VX653/G-BUCM) [062]	The Fighter Collection, Duxford	
WE982	Slingsby T30B Prefect TX1 (8781M)	RAF Museum, stored Cosford	
WE987	Slingsby T30B Prefect TX1 (BGA2517)	South Yorkshire Aircraft Museum, Doncaster	
WE990	Slingsby T30B Prefect TX1 (BGA2583)	Privately owned, Tibenham	
WE992	Slingsby T30B Prefect TX1 (BGA2692)	Privately owned, Little Rissington	
WF118	Percival P57 Sea Prince T1 (G-DACA) [569/CU]	Privately owned, St Athan	
WF122	Percival P57 Sea Prince T1 [575/CU]	Ulster Aviation Society, Long Kesh	
WF128	Percival P57 Sea Prince T1 (8611M)	Norfolk & Suffolk Avn Museum, Flixton	
WF145	Hawker Sea Hawk F1 <ff>	Privately owned, Newton Abbot, Devon	
WF219	Hawker Sea Hawk F1 <rf>	FAA Museum, stored Cobham Hall, RNAS Yeovilton	
WF225	Hawker Sea Hawk F1 [CU]	RNAS Culdrose, at main gate	
WF259	Hawker Sea Hawk F2 [171/A]	National Museum of Flight, E Fortune	
WF369	Vickers Varsity T1 [F]	Newark Air Museum, Winthorpe	
WF372	Vickers Varsity T1	Brooklands Museum, Weybridge	
WF408	Vickers Varsity T1 (8395M) <ff>	Privately owned, Ashford, Kent	
WF643	Gloster Meteor F8 [F]	Norfolk & Suffolk Avn Museum, Flixton	
WF784	Gloster Meteor T7 (7895M)	Jet Age Museum, Gloucester	
WF825	Gloster Meteor T7 (8359M) [A]	Montrose Air Station Heritage Centre	
WF877	Gloster Meteor T7 (G-BPOA)	Sold to the USA, 2018	
WF911	EE Canberra B2 [CO] <ff>	Ulster Aviation Society, Long Kesh	
WF922	EE Canberra PR3	Midland Air Museum, Coventry	
WG303	DHC1 Chipmunk T10 (8208M) <ff> [83]	Privately owned, Hooton Park	
WG308	DHC1 Chipmunk 22 (G-BYHL) [8]	Privately owned, Averham, Notts	
WG316	DHC1 Chipmunk 22 (G-BCAH)	Privately owned, Gamston	
WG319	DHC1 Chipmunk T10 <ff>	Privately owned, Blandford Forum, Dorset	
WG321	DHC1 Chipmunk 22 (G-DHCC)	Privately owned, Wevelgem, Belgium	

Notes	Serial	Type (code/other identity)	Owner/operator, location or fate
	WG322	DHC1 Chipmunk 22A (G-ARMF) [H]	Privately owned, Spanhoe
	WG348	DHC1 Chipmunk 22 (G-BBMV)	Boultbee Flight Academy, Goodwood
	WG350	DHC1 Chipmunk 22 (G-BPAL)	Privately owned, Popham
	WG362	DHC1 Chipmunk T10 (8437M/8630M/*WX643*) <ff>	No 1094 Sqn ATC, Ely
	WG407	DHC1 Chipmunk 22 (G-BWMX) [67]	Privately owned, Fen End Farm, Cambs
	WG418	DHC1 Chipmunk T10 (8209M/G-ATDY) <ff>	No 1940 Sqn ATC, Levenshulme, Gr Manchester
	WG419	DHC1 Chipmunk T10 (8206M) <ff>	Sywell Aviation Museum
	WG422	DHC1 Chipmunk 22 (8394M/G-BFAX) [16]	Privately owned, Eggesford
	WG432	DHC1 Chipmunk T10 [L]	Army Flying Museum, Middle Wallop
	WG458	DHC1 Chipmunk 22 (N458BG) [2]	Privately owned, Breighton
	WG465	DHC1 Chipmunk 22 (G-BCEY)	Privately owned, White Waltham
	WG469	DHC1 Chipmunk 22 (G-BWJY) [72]	*Sold to France, January 2019*
	WG471	DHC1 Chipmunk T10 (8210M) <ff>	*Currently not known*
	WG472	DHC1 Chipmunk 22A (G-AOTY)	Privately owned, Bryngwyn Bach, Clwyd
	WG477	DHC1 Chipmunk T10 (8362M/G-ATDP) <ff>	RAF Scampton Heritage Centre
	WG486	DHC1 Chipmunk T10 [E]	RAF BBMF, Coningsby
	WG498	Slingsby T21B Sedbergh TX1 (BGA3245)	Privately owned, Aston Down
	WG511	Avro 696 Shackleton T4 (fuselage)	Flambards Village Theme Park, Helston
	WG599	Hawker Sea Fury FB11 (G-SEAF) [161/R]	The Fighter Collection, Reno, Nevada, USA
	WG655	Hawker Sea Fury T20 (G-INVN) [910/GN]	Privately owned, Duxford
	WG719	WS51 Dragonfly HR5 (G-BRMA)	The Helicopter Museum, Weston-super-Mare
	WG724	WS51 Dragonfly HR5 [932]	North-East Aircraft Museum, Usworth
	WG751	WS51 Dragonfly HR5 [710/GJ]	World Naval Base, Chatham
	WG760	EE P1A (7755M)	RAF Museum, Cosford
	WG763	EE P1A (7816M)	Museum of Science & Industry, Manchester
	WG768	Short SB5 (8005M)	RAF Museum, Cosford
	WG724	WS51 Dragonfly HR5 [932/LM]	North-East Aircraft Museum, Usworth
	WG774	BAC 221	Science Museum, at FAA Museum, RNAS Yeovilton
	WG777	Fairey FD2 (7986M)	RAF Museum, Cosford
	WG789	EE Canberra B2/6 <ff>	Norfolk & Suffolk Avn Museum, Flixton
	WH132	Gloster Meteor T7 (7906M) [J]	Privately owned, Hooton Park
	WH166	Gloster Meteor T7 (8052M) [A]	Privately owned, Birlingham, Worcs
	WH291	Gloster Meteor F8	Privately owned, Liverpool Airport
	WH301	Gloster Meteor F8 (7930M) [T]	RAF Museum, Hendon
	WH364	Gloster Meteor F8 (8169M)	Jet Age Museum, Gloucester
	WH453	Gloster Meteor F8	Bentwaters Cold War Air Museum
	WH646	EE Canberra T17A <ff>	Midland Air Museum, Coventry
	WH657	EE Canberra B2 <ff>	Romney Marsh Wartime Collection
	WH725	EE Canberra B2	IWM Duxford
	WH734	EE Canberra B2(mod) <ff>	Privately owned, Pershore
	WH739	EE Canberra B2 <ff>	No 2475 Sqn ATC, Ammanford, Dyfed
	WH740	EE Canberra T17 (8762M) [K]	East Midlands Airport Aeropark
	WH775	EE Canberra PR7 (8128M/8868M) <ff>	Privately owned, Welshpool
	WH779	EE Canberra PR7 <ff>	South Yorkshire Aircraft Museum, Doncaster
	WH779	EE Canberra PR7 [BP] <rf>	RAF AM&SU, stored Shawbury
	WH792	EE Canberra PR7 (WH791/8165M/8176M/8187M)	Newark Air Museum, Winthorpe
	WH798	EE Canberra PR7 (8130M) <ff>	Suffolk Aviation Heritage Centre, Foxhall Heath
	WH840	EE Canberra T4 (8350M)	Privately owned, Flixton
	WH846	EE Canberra T4	Yorkshire Air Museum, Elvington
	WH850	EE Canberra T4 <ff>	RAF Marham Aviation Heritage Centre
	WH863	EE Canberra T17 (8693M) <ff>	Newark Air Museum, Winthorpe
	WH876	EE Canberra B2(mod) <ff>	Boscombe Down Aviation Collection, Old Sarum
	WH887	EE Canberra TT18 [847] <ff>	Sywell Aviation Museum
	WH903	EE Canberra B2 <ff>	Yorkshire Air Museum, Elvington
	WH904	EE Canberra T19	Newark Air Museum, Winthorpe
	WH953	EE Canberra B6(mod) <ff>	Blyth Valley Aviation Collection, Walpole, Suffolk
	WH957	EE Canberra E15 (8869M) <ff>	Lincolnshire Avn Heritage Centre, East Kirkby
	WH960	EE Canberra B15 (8344M) <ff>	Rolls-Royce Heritage Trust, Derby
	WH964	EE Canberra E15 (8870M) <ff>	Privately owned, Lewes
	WH984	EE Canberra B15 (8101M) <ff>	City of Norwich Aviation Museum
	WH991	WS51 Dragonfly HR3	Yorkshire Helicopter Preservation Group, Elvington

Serial	Type (code/other identity)	Owner/operator, location or fate	Notes
WJ231	Hawker Sea Fury FB11 (WE726) [115/O]	FAA Museum, RNAS Yeovilton	
WJ306	Slingsby T21B Sedbergh TX1 (BGA3240)	Privately owned, Weston-on-the-Green	
WJ306	Slingsby T21B Sedbergh TX1 (WB957/BGA2720)	Privately owned, Parham Park, Sussex	
WJ358	Auster AOP6 (G-ARYD)	Army Flying Museum, Middle Wallop	
WJ368	Auster AOP6 (G-ASZX)	Privately owned, Eggesford	
WJ404	Auster AOP6 (G-ASOI)	Privately owned, Bidford-on-Avon, Warks	
WJ476	Vickers Valetta T3 <ff>	South Yorkshire Aircraft Museum, Doncaster	
WJ565	EE Canberra T17 (8871M) <ff>	South Yorkshire Aircraft Museum, Doncaster	
WJ567	EE Canberra B2 <ff>	Privately owned, Houghton, Cambs	
WJ576	EE Canberra T17 <ff>	Tettenhall Transport Heritage Centre	
WJ633	EE Canberra T17 <ff>	City of Norwich Aviation Museum	
WJ639	EE Canberra TT18 [39]	North-East Aircraft Museum, Usworth	
WJ677	EE Canberra B2 <ff>	Privately owned, Redruth	
WJ717	EE Canberra TT18 (9052M) <ff>	Currently not known	
WJ721	EE Canberra TT18 [21] <ff>	Morayvia, Kinloss	
WJ731	EE Canberra B2T [BK] <ff>	Privately owned, Golders Green	
WJ775	EE Canberra B6 (8581M) <ff>	Privately owned, stored Farnborough	
WJ865	EE Canberra T4 <ff>	Boscombe Down Aviation Collection, Old Sarum	
WJ880	EE Canberra T4 (8491M) <ff>	Dumfries & Galloway Avn Mus, Dumfries	
WJ903	Vickers Varsity T1 <ff>	South Yorkshire Aircraft Museum, Doncaster	
WJ945	Vickers Varsity T1 (G-BEDV)	Aerohub, Newquay	
WJ975	EE Canberra T19 <ff>	South Yorkshire Aircraft Museum, Doncaster	
WJ992	EE Canberra T4	Bournemouth Airport (derelict)	
WK001	Thales Watchkeeper 450 RPAS (4X-USC)	Army 47 Regt Royal Artillery, Boscombe Down	
WK002	Thales Watchkeeper 450 RPAS (4X-USD)	Army 47 Regt Royal Artillery, Boscombe Down	
WK003	Thales Watchkeeper 450 RPAS	Army 47 Regt Royal Artillery, Boscombe Down	
WK004	Thales Watchkeeper 450 RPAS	Army 47 Regt Royal Artillery, Boscombe Down	
WK005	Thales Watchkeeper 450 RPAS	Crashed 15 June 2018, Llandegfan Common	
WK007	Thales Watchkeeper 450 RPAS	Army 47 Regt Royal Artillery, Boscombe Down	
WK008	Thales Watchkeeper 450 RPAS	Army 47 Regt Royal Artillery, Boscombe Down	
WK009	Thales Watchkeeper 450 RPAS	Army 47 Regt Royal Artillery, Boscombe Down	
WK010	Thales Watchkeeper 450 RPAS	Army 47 Regt Royal Artillery, Boscombe Down	
WK011	Thales Watchkeeper 450 RPAS	Army 47 Regt Royal Artillery, Boscombe Down	
WK012	Thales Watchkeeper 450 RPAS	Army 47 Regt Royal Artillery, Boscombe Down	
WK013	Thales Watchkeeper 450 RPAS	Army 47 Regt Royal Artillery, Boscombe Down	
WK014	Thales Watchkeeper 450 RPAS	Army 47 Regt Royal Artillery, Boscombe Down	
WK015	Thales Watchkeeper 450 RPAS	Army 47 Regt Royal Artillery, Boscombe Down	
WK016	Thales Watchkeeper 450 RPAS	Army 47 Regt Royal Artillery, Boscombe Down	
WK017	Thales Watchkeeper 450 RPAS	Army 47 Regt Royal Artillery, Boscombe Down	
WK018	Thales Watchkeeper 450 RPAS	Army 47 Regt Royal Artillery, Boscombe Down	
WK019	Thales Watchkeeper 450 RPAS	Army 47 Regt Royal Artillery, Boscombe Down	
WK020	Thales Watchkeeper 450 RPAS	Army 47 Regt Royal Artillery, Boscombe Down	
WK021	Thales Watchkeeper 450 RPAS	Army 47 Regt Royal Artillery, Boscombe Down	
WK022	Thales Watchkeeper 450 RPAS	Army 47 Regt Royal Artillery, Boscombe Down	
WK023	Thales Watchkeeper 450 RPAS	Army 47 Regt Royal Artillery, Boscombe Down	
WK024	Thales Watchkeeper 450 RPAS	Army 47 Regt Royal Artillery, Boscombe Down	
WK025	Thales Watchkeeper 450 RPAS	Army 47 Regt Royal Artillery, Boscombe Down	
WK026	Thales Watchkeeper 450 RPAS	Army 47 Regt Royal Artillery, Boscombe Down	
WK027	Thales Watchkeeper 450 RPAS	Army 47 Regt Royal Artillery, Boscombe Down	
WK028	Thales Watchkeeper 450 RPAS	Army 47 Regt Royal Artillery, Boscombe Down	
WK029	Thales Watchkeeper 450 RPAS	Army 47 Regt Royal Artillery, Boscombe Down	
WK030	Thales Watchkeeper 450 RPAS	Army 47 Regt Royal Artillery, Boscombe Down	
WK032	Thales Watchkeeper 450 RPAS	Army 47 Regt Royal Artillery, Boscombe Down	
WK033	Thales Watchkeeper 450 RPAS	Army 47 Regt Royal Artillery, Boscombe Down	
WK034	Thales Watchkeeper 450 RPAS	Army 47 Regt Royal Artillery, Boscombe Down	
WK035	Thales Watchkeeper 450 RPAS	Army 47 Regt Royal Artillery, Boscombe Down	
WK036	Thales Watchkeeper 450 RPAS	Army 47 Regt Royal Artillery, Boscombe Down	
WK037	Thales Watchkeeper 450 RPAS	Army 47 Regt Royal Artillery, Boscombe Down	
WK038	Thales Watchkeeper 450 RPAS	Army 47 Regt Royal Artillery, Boscombe Down	
WK039	Thales Watchkeeper 450 RPAS	Army 47 Regt Royal Artillery, Boscombe Down	
WK040	Thales Watchkeeper 450 RPAS	Army 47 Regt Royal Artillery, Boscombe Down	

Notes	Serial	Type (code/other identity)	Owner/operator, location or fate
	WK041	Thales Watchkeeper 450 RPAS	Army 47 Regt Royal Artillery, Boscombe Down
	WK044	Thales Watchkeeper 450 RPAS	Army 47 Regt Royal Artillery, Boscombe Down
	WK045	Thales Watchkeeper 450 RPAS	Army 47 Regt Royal Artillery, Boscombe Down
	WK046	Thales Watchkeeper 450 RPAS	Army 47 Regt Royal Artillery, Boscombe Down
	WK047	Thales Watchkeeper 450 RPAS	Army 47 Regt Royal Artillery, Boscombe Down
	WK048	Thales Watchkeeper 450 RPAS	Army 47 Regt Royal Artillery, Boscombe Down
	WK049	Thales Watchkeeper 450 RPAS	Army 47 Regt Royal Artillery, Boscombe Down
	WK050	Thales Watchkeeper 450 RPAS	Army 47 Regt Royal Artillery, Boscombe Down
	WK051	Thales Watchkeeper 450 RPAS	Army 47 Regt Royal Artillery, Boscombe Down
	WK052	Thales Watchkeeper 450 RPAS	Army 47 Regt Royal Artillery, Boscombe Down
	WK053	Thales Watchkeeper 450 RPAS	Army 47 Regt Royal Artillery, Boscombe Down
	WK054	Thales Watchkeeper 450 RPAS	Army 47 Regt Royal Artillery, Boscombe Down
	WK060	Thales Watchkeeper 450 RPAS	MoD/Thales, Aberporth
	WK102	EE Canberra T17 (8780M) <ff>	Privately owned, Welshpool
	WK118	EE Canberra TT18 [CQ] <ff>	Avro Heritage Museum, Woodford
	WK122	EE Canberra TT18 <ff>	Privately owned, Wesham, Lancs
	WK124	EE Canberra TT18 (9093M) [CR]	Privately owned, Gilberdyke, E Yorks
	WK126	EE Canberra TT18 (N2138J) [843]	Jet Age Museum, stored Gloucester
	WK127	EE Canberra TT18 (8985M) <ff>	Privately owned, stored Handcross, W Sussex
	WK146	EE Canberra B2 <ff>	Gatwick Aviation Museum, Charlwood, Surrey
	WK163	EE Canberra B2/6 (G-BVWC/G-CTTS)	Vulcan To The Sky Trust, Doncaster Sheffield Airport
	WK198	VS Swift F4 (7428M) (fuselage)	Brooklands Museum, Weybridge
	WK275	VS Swift F4	Privately owned, Doncaster Sheffield Airport
	WK277	VS Swift FR5 (7719M) [N]	Newark Air Museum, Winthorpe
	WK281	VS Swift FR5 (7712M) [S]	Tangmere Military Aviation Museum
	WK393	DH112 Venom FB1 <ff>	Privately owned, Lavendon, Bucks
	WK436	DH112 Venom FB50 (J-1614/G-VENM)	Sold to the USA, August 2018
	WK512	DHC1 Chipmunk 22 (G-BXIM) [A]	Privately owned, RAF Halton
	WK514	DHC1 Chipmunk 22 (G-BBMO)	Privately owned, Wellesbourne Mountford
	WK517	DHC1 Chipmunk 22 (G-ULAS)	Privately owned, Goodwood
	WK518	DHC1 Chipmunk T10 [C]	RAF BBMF, Coningsby
	WK522	DHC1 Chipmunk 22 (G-BCOU)	Privately owned, Duxford
	WK549	DHC1 Chipmunk 22 (G-BTWF)	Privately owned, Breighton
	WK558	DHC1 Chipmunk 22A (G-ARMG) [DH]	Privately owned, Shenington, Oxon
	WK562	DHC1 Chipmunk 22 (F-AZUR) [91]	Privately owned, La Baule, France
	WK570	DHC1 Chipmunk T10 (8211M) <ff>	No 424 Sqn ATC, Solent Sky, Southampton
	WK576	DHC1 Chipmunk T10 (8357M) <ff>	Tettenhall Transport Heritage Centre
	WK577	DHC1 Chipmunk 22 (G-BCYM)	Privately owned, Oaksey Park
	WK584	DHC1 Chipmunk T10 (7556M) <ff>	No 511 Sqn ATC, Ramsey, Cambs
	WK585	DHC1 Chipmunk 22 (9265M/G-BZGA)	Privately owned, Compton Abbas
	WK586	DHC1 Chipmunk 22 (G-BXGX) [V]	Privately owned, Shoreham
	WK590	DHC1 Chipmunk 22 (G-BWVZ) [69]	Privately owned, Grimbergen, Belgium
	WK608	DHC1 Chipmunk T10 [906]	RN Historic Flight, Yeovilton
	WK609	DHC1 Chipmunk 22 (G-BXDN) [93]	Privately owned, Booker
	WK611	DHC1 Chipmunk 22 (G-ARWB)	Privately owned, Thruxton
	WK620	DHC1 Chipmunk T10 [T] (fuselage)	Privately owned, Enstone
	WK622	DHC1 Chipmunk 22 (G-BCZH)	Privately owned, Horsford
	WK624	DHC1 Chipmunk 22A (G-BWHI)	Privately owned, Blackpool
	WK626	DHC1 Chipmunk T10 (8213M) <ff>	South Yorkshire Aircraft Museum, Doncaster
	WK628	DHC1 Chipmunk 22 (G-BBMW)	Privately owned, Goodwood
	WK630	DHC1 Chipmunk 22 (G-BXDG)	Privately owned, Felthorpe
	WK633	DHC1 Chipmunk 22 (G-BXEC) [A]	Privately owned, Duxford
	WK634	DHC1 Chipmunk T10 (G-CIGE) [902]	Privately owned, Dunkeswell
	WK635	DHC1 Chipmunk 22 (G-HFRH)	Privately owned, Hawarden
	WK638	DHC1 Chipmunk 22 (G-BWJZ) (fuselage)	Privately owned, South Marston, Swindon
	WK640	DHC1 Chipmunk 22A (G-BWUV) [C]	Privately owned, Hooton Park (wreck)
	WK640	OGMA/DHC1 Chipmunk T20 (G-CERD)	Privately owned, Spanhoe
	WK642	DHC1 Chipmunk 22 (EI-AFZ) [94]	Privately owned, Kilrush, Eire
	WK654	Gloster Meteor F8 (8092M)	City of Norwich Aviation Museum
	WK800	Gloster Meteor D16 [Z]	Boscombe Down Aviation Collection, Old Sarum
	WK864	Gloster Meteor F8 (WL168/7750M) [C]	Yorkshire Air Museum, Elvington

Serial	Type (code/other identity)	Owner/operator, location or fate	Notes
WK935	Gloster Meteor Prone Pilot (7869M)	RAF Museum, Cosford	
WK991	Gloster Meteor F8 (7825M)	IWM Duxford	
WL131	Gloster Meteor F8 (7751M) <ff>	South Yorkshire Aircraft Museum, Doncaster	
WL181	Gloster Meteor F8 [X]	North-East Aircraft Museum, Usworth	
WL332	Gloster Meteor T7 [888]	Privately owned, Long Marston	
WL345	Gloster Meteor T7 (comp WL360)	Privately owned, Booker	
WL349	Gloster Meteor T7	Jet Age Museum, Gloucester	
WL375	Gloster Meteor T7(mod)	Dumfries & Galloway Avn Mus, Dumfries	
WL405	Gloster Meteor T7 <ff>	Privately owned, Parbold, Lancs	
WL419	Gloster Meteor T7(mod) (G-JSMA)	Martin-Baker Aircraft, Chalgrove	
WL505	DH100 Vampire FB9 (7705M/G-FBIX)	Privately owned, Mendlesham	
WL626	Vickers Varsity T1 (G-BHDD) [P]	East Midlands Airport Aeropark	
WL627	Vickers Varsity T1 (8488M) [D] <ff>	Privately owned, Preston, E Yorkshire	
WL679	Vickers Varsity T1 (9155M)	RAF Museum, Cosford	
WL732	BP P108 Sea Balliol T21	RAF Museum, Cosford	
WL795	Avro 696 Shackleton MR2C (8753M) [T]	Privately owned, Newquay	
WL798	Avro 696 Shackleton MR2C (8114M) <ff>	Privately owned, Elgin	
WM145	AW Meteor NF11 <ff>	Morayvia, Kinloss	
WM167	AW Meteor NF11 (G-LOSM)	Privately owned, Bruntingthorpe	
WM224	AW Meteor TT20 (WM311/8177M) [X]	East Midlands Airport Aeropark	
WM267	AW Meteor NF11 <ff>	City of Norwich Aviation Museum	
WM292	AW Meteor TT20 [841]	FAA Museum, stored Cobham Hall, RNAS Yeovilton	
WM366	AW Meteor NF13 (4X-FNA) (comp VZ462)	Jet Age Museum, Gloucester	
WM367	AW Meteor NF13 <ff>	East Midlands Airport Aeropark	
WM571	DH112 Sea Venom FAW21 [VL]	Solent Sky, stored Romsey	
WM729	DH113 Vampire NF10 <ff>	de Havilland Aircraft Mus'm, stored London Colney	
WM913	Hawker Sea Hawk FB5 (8162M) [456/J]	Newark Air Museum, Winthorpe	
WM961	Hawker Sea Hawk FB5 [J]	Caernarfon Air World	
WM969	Hawker Sea Hawk FB5 [10/Z]	IWM Duxford	
WN105	Hawker Sea Hawk FB3 (WF299/8164M)	Privately owned, Birlingham, Worcs	
WN108	Hawker Sea Hawk FB5 [033]	Ulster Aviation Society, Long Kesh	
WN149	BP P108 Balliol T2 [AT]	RAF Museum, stored Cosford	
WN411	Fairey Gannet AS1 (fuselage)	Privately owned, Sholing, Hants	
WN493	WS51 Dragonfly HR5	FAA Museum, RNAS Yeovilton	
WN499	WS51 Dragonfly HR5	South Yorkshire Aircraft Museum, stored Doncaster	
WN516	BP P108 Balliol T2 <ff>	Tettenhall Transport Heritage Centre	
WN534	BP P108 Balliol T2 <ff>	Tettenhall Transport Heritage Centre	
WN890	Hawker Hunter F2 <ff>	Boscombe Down Aviation Collection, Old Sarum	
WN904	Hawker Hunter F2 (7544M)	Sywell Aviation Museum	
WN907	Hawker Hunter F2 (7416M) <ff>	Robertsbridge Aviation Society, Newhaven	
WN957	Hawker Hunter F5 <ff>	Morayvia, Kinloss	
WP185	Hawker Hunter F5 (7583M)	Privately owned, Great Dunmow, Essex	
WP190	Hawker Hunter F5 (7582M/8473M/WP180) [K]	Tangmere Military Aviation Museum	
WP255	DH113 Vampire NF10 <ff>	South Yorkshire Aircraft Museum, stored Doncaster	
WP266	EoN AP.5 Primary (BAPC 423)	Privately owned, Fishburn	
WP269	EoN Eton TX1 (BGA3214)	Privately owned, Little Rissington	
WP270	EoN Eton TX1 (8598M)	Gliding Heritage Centre, Lasham	
WP308	Percival P57 Sea Prince T1 (G-GACA) [572/CU]	Gatwick Aviation Museum, Charlwood, Surrey	
WP313	Percival P57 Sea Prince T1 [568/CU]	FAA Museum, stored Cobham Hall, RNAS Yeovilton	
WP314	Percival P57 Sea Prince T1 (8634M) [573/CU]	Privately owned, Carlisle Airport	
WP321	Percival P57 Sea Prince T1 (G-BRFC) [750/CU]	South Wales Aviation Museum, St Athan	
WP772	DHC1 Chipmunk T10 (WK518) [4]	RAF Manston History Museum	
WP784	DHC1 Chipmunk T10 (comp WZ876) [RCY-E]	East Midlands Airport Aeropark	
WP788	DHC1 Chipmunk 22A (G-BCHL)	Privately owned, Sleap	
WP790	DHC1 Chipmunk T10 (G-BBNC) [T]	de Havilland Aircraft Museum, London Colney	
WP795	DHC1 Chipmunk 22 (G-BVZZ) [901]	Privately owned, Lee-on-Solent	
WP800	DHC1 Chipmunk 22 (G-BCXN) [2]	Privately owned, RAF Halton	
WP803	DHC1 Chipmunk 22 (G-HAPY) [G]	Privately owned, Booker	

Notes	Serial	Type (code/other identity)	Owner/operator, location or fate
	WP805	DHC1 Chipmunk 22 (G-MAJR) [D]	Privately owned, Lee-on-Solent
	WP809	DHC1 Chipmunk 22A (G-BVTX) [78]	Privately owned, Husbands Bosworth
	WP811	DHC1 Chipmunk 22 (G-BCKN)	Privately owned, Husbands Bosworth
	WP835	DHC1 Chipmunk 22 (D-ERTY)	Privately owned, Porta Westfalica, Germany
	WP840	DHC1 Chipmunk 22 (F-AZQM) [9]	Privately owned, Reims, France
	WP844	DHC1 Chipmunk 22 (G-BWOX) [85]	Privately owned, Adriers, France
	WP848	DHC1 Chipmunk 22 (8342M/G-BFAW)	Privately owned, Old Buckenham
	WP859	DHC1 Chipmunk 22 (G-BXCP) [E] (wreck)	Privately owned, Fishburn
	WP860	DHC1 Chipmunk 22 (G-BXDA) [6]	Privately owned, Kirknewton
	WP863	DHC1 Chipmunk T10 (8360M/G-ATJI) <ff>	No 1011 Sqn ATC, Boscombe Down
	WP869	DHC1 Chipmunk T10 (8215M) <ff>	de Havilland Aircraft Museum, London Colney
	WP870	DHC1 Chipmunk 22 (G-BCOI) [12]	Privately owned, Rayne Hall Farm, Essex
	WP896	DHC1 Chipmunk 22 (G-BWVY)	Privately owned, RAF Halton
	WP901	DHC1 Chipmunk 22 (G-BWNT) [B]	Privately owned, Biggin Hill
	WP903	DHC1 Chipmunk 22 (G-BCGC)	Privately owned, Henlow
	WP912	DHC1 Chipmunk T10 (8467M)	RAF Museum, Cosford
	WP921	DHC1 Chipmunk T10 (G-ATJJ) <ff>	Privately owned, Brooklands
	WP925	DHC1 Chipmunk 22 (G-BXHA) [C]	Privately owned, Meppershall
	WP927	DHC1 Chipmunk T10 (8216M/G-ATJK) <ff>	Privately owned, Wyton
	WP928	DHC1 Chipmunk 22 (G-BXGM) [D]	Privately owned, Goodwood
	WP929	DHC1 Chipmunk 22 (G-BXCV) [F]	Privately owned, Duxford
	WP930	DHC1 Chipmunk 22 (G-BXHF) [J]	Privately owned, Redhill
	WP962	DHC1 Chipmunk T10 (9287M) [C]	RAF Museum, Hendon
	WP964	DHC1 Chipmunk T20 (G-HDAE)	Privately owned, Wellesbourne Mountford
	WP971	DHC1 Chipmunk 22 (G-ATHD)	Privately owned, Denham
	WP973	DHC1 Chipmunk 22 (G-BCPU)	Privately owned, Turweston
	WP977	DHC1 Chipmunk 22 (G-BHRD) <ff>	Privately owned, South Molton, Devon
	WP983	DHC1 Chipmunk 22 (G-BXNN) [B]	Privately owned, Eggesford
	WP984	DHC1 Chipmunk 22 (G-BWTO) [H]	Privately owned, Little Gransden
	WR410	DH112 Venom FB50 (J-1539/G-DHUU)	Shannon Aviation Museum, Eire
	WR470	DH112 Venom FB50 (J-1542/G-DHVM)	Privately owned, Bruntingthorpe
	WR539	DH112 Venom FB4 (8399M) <ff>	Privately owned, Cantley, Norfolk
	WR960	Avro 696 Shackleton AEW2 (8772M)	Museum of Science & Industry, Manchester
	WR963	Avro 696 Shackleton AEW2 (G-SKTN) [B-M]	Shackleton Preservation Trust, Coventry
	WR971	Avro 696 Shackleton MR3/3 (8119M) [Q] (fuselage)	Fenland & W Norfolk Aviation Museum, Wisbech
	WR974	Avro 696 Shackleton MR3/3 (8117M) [K]	Privately owned, Bruntingthorpe
	WR977	Avro 696 Shackleton MR3/3 (8186M) [B]	Newark Air Museum, Winthorpe
	WR982	Avro 696 Shackleton MR3/3 (8106M) [J]	Gatwick Aviation Museum, Charlwood, Surrey
	WR985	Avro 696 Shackleton MR3/3 (8103M) [H]	Privately owned, Long Marston
	WS103	Gloster Meteor T7 [709]	FAA Museum, stored Cobham Hall, RNAS Yeovilton
	WS692	Gloster Meteor NF12 (7605M) [C]	Newark Air Museum, Winthorpe
	WS726	Gloster Meteor NF14 (7960M) [H]	No 1855 Sqn ATC, Royton, Gr Manchester
	WS739	Gloster Meteor NF14 (7961M)	Newark Air Museum, Winthorpe
	WS760	Gloster Meteor NF14 (7964M)	East Midlands Airport Aeropark, stored
	WS776	Gloster Meteor NF14 (7716M) [K]	Bournemouth Aviation Museum
	WS788	Gloster Meteor NF14 (7967M) [Z]	Yorkshire Air Museum, Elvington
	WS792	Gloster Meteor NF14 (7965M) [K]	Brighouse Bay Caravan Park, Borgue, D&G
	WS807	Gloster Meteor NF14 (7973M) [N]	Jet Age Museum, Gloucester
	WS832	Gloster Meteor NF14 [W]	Solway Aviation Society, Carlisle
	WS838	Gloster Meteor NF14 [D]	Midland Air Museum, Coventry
	WS840	Gloster Meteor NF14 (7969M) [N] <rf>	Privately owned, Upper Ballinderry, NI
	WS843	Gloster Meteor NF14 (7937M) [J]	RAF Museum, Cosford
	WT121	Douglas Skyraider AEW1 [415/CU]	FAA Museum, stored Cobham Hall, RNAS Yeovilton
	WT205	EE Canberra B15 <ff>	RAF Manston History Museum
	WT308	EE Canberra B(I)6	RN, Predannack Fire School
	WT309	EE Canberra B(I)6 <ff>	Farnborough Air Sciences Trust, Farnborough
	WT319	EE Canberra B(I)6 <ff>	Privately owned, Lavendon, Bucks
	WT333	EE Canberra B6(mod) (G-BVXC)	Privately owned, Bruntingthorpe
	WT339	EE Canberra B(I)8 (8198M)	RAF Barkston Heath Fire Section

Serial	Type (code/other identity)	Owner/operator, location or fate	Notes
WT482	EE Canberra T4 <ff>	Privately owned, Marske by the Sea, Durham	
WT486	EE Canberra T4 (8102M)	Privately owned, Newtownards	
WT507	EE Canberra PR7 (8131M/8548M) [44] <ff>	No 384 Sqn ATC, Mansfield	
WT520	EE Canberra PR7 (8094M/8184M) <ff>	Rays-Tek Surplus Ltd, Biddulph, Staffs	
WT525	EE Canberra T22 [855] <ff>	Cornwall College, Newquay Airport	
WT532	EE Canberra PR7 (8728M/8890M) <ff>	Bournemouth Aviation Museum	
WT534	EE Canberra PR7 (8549M) [43] <ff>	South Yorkshire Aircraft Museum, Doncaster	
WT536	EE Canberra PR7 (8063M) <ff>	South Yorkshire Aircraft Museum, Doncaster	
WT555	Hawker Hunter F1 (7499M)	Vanguard Haulage, Greenford, London	
WT569	Hawker Hunter F1 (7491M)	No 2117 Sqn ATC, Kenfig Hill, Mid-Glamorgan	
WT612	Hawker Hunter F1 (7496M)	RAF Henlow, on display	
WT619	Hawker Hunter F1 (7525M)	RAF Museum Reserve Collection, Stafford	
WT648	Hawker Hunter F1 (7530M) <ff>	Boscombe Down Aviation Collection, Old Sarum	
WT651	Hawker Hunter F1 (7532M) [C]	Newark Air Museum, Winthorpe	
WT660	Hawker Hunter F1 (7421M) [C]	Highland Aviation Museum, Inverness	
WT680	Hawker Hunter F1 (7533M) [J]	Privately owned, Holbeach, Lincs	
WT684	Hawker Hunter F1 (7422M) <ff>	Privately owned, Lavendon, Bucks	
WT694	Hawker Hunter F1 (7510M)	Caernarfon Air World	
WT711	Hawker Hunter GA11 [833/DD]	Lakes Lightnings, Spark Bridge, Cumbria	
WT720	Hawker Hunter F51 (RDAF E-408/8565M) [B]	Privately owned, Lee-on-Solent	
WT722	Hawker Hunter T8C (G-BWGN) [873]	Aerohub, Newquay	
WT723	Hawker Hunter PR11 (XG194/G-PRII) [692/LM]	Hunter Flight Academy, St Athan	
WT741	Hawker Hunter GA11 [791] <ff>	Privately owned, South Yorks Air Mus'm, Doncaster	
WT744	Hawker Hunter GA11 [868/VL]	Privately owned, Braunton, Devon	
WT746	Hawker Hunter F4 (XF506/7770M) [A]	Dumfries & Galloway Avn Mus, Dumfries	
WT799	Hawker Hunter T8C [879]	Blue Lagoon Diving Centre, Womersley, N Yorks	
WT804	Hawker Hunter GA11 [831/DD]	Privately owned, Todenham, Glos	
WT806	Hawker Hunter GA11	Privately owned, Bruntingthorpe	
WT859	Supermarine 544 <ff>	Boscombe Down Aviation Collection, Old Sarum	
WT867	Slingsby T31B Cadet TX3	Privately owned, Eaglescott	
WT874	Slingsby T31B Cadet TX3 (BGA1255)	Privately owned,	
WT877	Slingsby T31B Cadet TX3	Tettenhall Transport Heritage Centre	
WT905	Slingsby T31B Cadet TX3	Privately owned, Keevil	
WT908	Slingsby T31B Cadet TX3 (BGA3487)	Privately owned, Dunstable	
WT910	Slingsby T31B Cadet TX3 (BGA3953)	Privately owned, Llandegla, Denbighshire	
WT914	Slingsby T31B Cadet TX3 (BGA3194) (fuselage)	East Midlands Airport Aeropark	
WT933	Bristol 171 Sycamore 3 (G-ALSW/7709M)	Newark Air Museum, Winthorpe	
WV106	Douglas Skyraider AEW1 [427/C]	FAA Museum, stored Cobham Hall, RNAS Yeovilton	
WV198	Sikorsky S55 Whirlwind HAR21 (G-BJWY) [K]	Solway Aviation Society, Carlisle	
WV256	Hawker Hunter GA11 (WB188/G-BZPB)	Aerohub, Newquay	
WV314	Hawker Hunter F51 (G-9-445/E-424) [B]	South Yorkshire Aircraft Museum, Doncaster	
WV318	Hawker Hunter T7A (9236M/G-FFOX)	To Sweden, 2019	
WV322	Hawker Hunter T8C (G-BZSE/9096M) [22/VL]	Privately owned, North Weald	
WV332	Hawker Hunter F4 (7673M) <ff>	Tangmere Military Aircraft Museum	
WV381	Hawker Hunter GA11 (732) <ff>	Hovercraft Museum, Lee-on-Solent	
WV382	Hawker Hunter GA11 [830/VL]	East Midlands Airport Aeropark	
WV383	Hawker Hunter T7	Farnborough Air Sciences Trust, Farnborough	
WV396	Hawker Hunter T8C (9249M) [91]	Tacla Taid Museum, Newborough, Anglesey	
WV493	Percival P56 Provost T1 (G-BDYG/7696M) [29]	National Museum of Flight, stored E Fortune	
WV499	Percival P56 Provost T1 (G-BZRF/7698M) [P-G]	Privately owned, Westonzoyland, Somerset	
WV514	Percival P56 Provost T51 (G-BLIW) [N-C]	Privately owned, Shoreham	
WV562	Percival P56 Provost T1 (XF688/7606M) [P-C]	RAF Museum, Cosford	
WV605	Percival P56 Provost T1 [T-B]	Norfolk & Suffolk Avn Museum, Flixton	
WV606	Percival P56 Provost T1 (7622M)[P-B]	Newark Air Museum, Winthorpe	
WV679	Percival P56 Provost T1 (7615M) [O-J]	Wellesbourne Wartime Museum	
WV705	Percival P66 Pembroke C1 <ff>	Privately owned, Awbridge, Hants	
WV740	Percival P66 Pembroke C1 (G-BNPH)	Privately owned, St Athan	
WV746	Percival P66 Pembroke C1 (8938M)	RAF Museum, Cosford	
WV781	Bristol 171 Sycamore HR12 (G-ALTD/7839M) <ff>	Caernarfon Air World	
WV783	Bristol 171 Sycamore HR12 (G-ALSP/7841M)	RAF Museum, Hendon	
WV787	EE Canberra B2/8 (8799M)	Newark Air Museum, Winthorpe	

Notes	Serial	Type (code/other identity)	Owner/operator, location or fate
	WV795	Hawker Sea Hawk FGA6 (8151M)	Privately owned, Dunsfold
	WV797	Hawker Sea Hawk FGA6 (8155M) [491/J]	Midland Air Museum, Coventry
	WV798	Hawker Sea Hawk FGA6 [026/CU]	Privately owned, Newquay
	WV838	Hawker Sea Hawk FGA4 [182] <ff>	Norfolk & Suffolk Avn Museum, Flixton
	WV856	Hawker Sea Hawk FGA6 [163]	FAA Museum, RNAS Yeovilton
	WV903	Hawker Sea Hawk FGA6 (8153M) [128] <ff>	Privately owned, Stranraer
	WV908	Hawker Sea Hawk FGA6 (8154M) [188/A]	RN Historic Flight, stored Shawbury
	WV910	Hawker Sea Hawk FGA6 <ff>	Boscombe Down Aviation Collection, Old Sarum
	WV911	Hawker Sea Hawk FGA4 [115/C]	RNAS Yeovilton, Fire Section
	WW138	DH112 Sea Venom FAW22 [227/Z]	FAA Museum, RNAS Yeovilton
	WW145	DH112 Sea Venom FAW22 [680/LM]	National Museum of Flight, E Fortune
	WW217	DH112 Sea Venom FAW22 [351]	Newark Air Museum, Winthorpe
	WW388	Percival P56 Provost T1 (7616M) [O-F]	Privately owned, Cambridge
	WW421	Percival P56 Provost T1 (WW450/G-BZRE/7689M)	Bournemouth Aviation Museum
	WW442	Percival P56 Provost T1 (7618M) [N]	East Midlands Airport Aeropark
	WW444	Percival P56 Provost T1 [D]	Privately owned, Brownhills, Staffs
	WW447	Percival P56 Provost T1 [F]	Privately owned, Shoreham
	WW453	Percival P56 Provost T1 (G-TMKI) [W-S]	Privately owned, Westonzoyland, Somerset
	WW654	Hawker Hunter GA11 [834/DD]	Privately owned, Ford, W Sussex
	WW664	Hawker Hunter F4 <ff>	Privately owned, Norfolk
	WX788	DH112 Venom NF3 <ff>	South Yorkshire Aircraft Museum, stored Doncaster
	WX853	DH112 Venom NF3 (7443M)	de Havilland Aircraft Mus'm, stored London Colney
	WX905	DH112 Venom NF3 (7458M)	Newark Air Museum, Winthorpe
	WZ425	DH115 Vampire T11	Privately owned, Birlingham, Worcs
	WZ447	DH115 Vampire T55 (U-1230/PX-M/LN-DHZ) [M]	Norwegian AF Historical Sqn, Rygge, Norway
	WZ450	DH115 Vampire T11 <ff>	Privately owned, Corscombe, Dorset
	WZ507	DH115 Vampire T11 (G-VTII) [74]	Privately owned, North Weald
	WZ515	DH115 Vampire T11 [60]	Solway Aviation Society, Carlisle
	WZ518	DH115 Vampire T11 [B]	North-East Aircraft Museum, Usworth
	WZ549	DH115 Vampire T11 (8118M) [F]	Ulster Aviation Society, Long Kesh
	WZ553	DH115 Vampire T11 (G-DHYY) <ff>	Privately owned, Stockton, Warks
	WZ557	DH115 Vampire T11	Morayvia, Kinloss
	WZ572	DH115 Vampire T11 (8124M) [65] <ff>	Privately owned, Sholing, Hants
	WZ581	DH115 Vampire T11 <ff>	The Vampire Collection, Hemel Hempstead
	WZ584	DH115 Vampire T11 (G-BZRC) [K]	Privately owned, Binbrook
	WZ589	DH115 Vampire T11 [19]	Privately owned, Wigmore, Kent
	WZ590	DH115 Vampire T11 [49]	IWM Duxford
	WZ662	Auster AOP9 (G-BKVK)	Privately owned, Liverpool
	WZ679	Auster AOP9 (7863M/*XP248*/G-CIUX)	Privately owned, Whittlesford, Cambs
	WZ706	Auster AOP9 (7851M/G-BURR)	Privately owned, Darley Moor, Derbys
	WZ711	Auster AOP9/Beagle E3 (G-AVHT)	South Yorkshire Aircraft Museum, stored Doncaster
	WZ721	Auster AOP9	Army Flying Museum, Middle Wallop
	WZ724	Auster AOP9 (7432M) (frame)	Army Flying Museum, Middle Wallop
	WZ736	Avro 707A (7868M)	Museum of Science & Industry, Manchester
	WZ744	Avro 707C (7932M)	RAF Museum, stored Cosford
	WZ753	Slingsby T38 Grasshopper TX1	Solent Sky, stored Romsey
	WZ755	Slingsby T38 Grasshopper TX1 (BGA3481)	Tettenhall Transport Heritage Centre
	WZ757	Slingsby T38 Grasshopper TX1 (comp XK820)	Privately owned, Saltby, Lincs
	WZ767	Slingsby T38 Grasshopper TX1	North-East Aircraft Museum, Usworth
	WZ772	Slingsby T38 Grasshopper TX1	Trenchard Museum, RAF Halton
	WZ773	Slingsby T38 Grasshopper TX1	Edinburgh Academy
	WZ784	Slingsby T38 Grasshopper TX1 (comp WZ824)	Solway Aviation Society, stored Carlisle
	WZ784	Slingsby T38 Grasshopper TX1	Privately owned, stored Felixstowe
	WZ791	Slingsby T38 Grasshopper TX1 (8944M)	RAF Museum, Hendon
	WZ793	Slingsby T38 Grasshopper TX1	Privately owned, Keevil
	WZ796	Slingsby T38 Grasshopper TX1	Privately owned, stored Aston Down
	WZ798	Slingsby T38 Grasshopper TX1	Privately owned, Eaglescott
	WZ816	Slingsby T38 Grasshopper TX1 (BGA3979)	Privately owned, Redhill
	WZ818	Slingsby T38 Grasshopper TX1 (BGA4361)	Privately owned, Nympsfield

Serial	Type (code/other identity)	Owner/operator, location or fate	Notes
WZ819	Slingsby T38 Grasshopper TX1 (BGA3498)	Privately owned, Halton	
WZ820	Slingsby T38 Grasshopper TX1 <ff>	Sywell Aviation Museum, stored	
WZ822	Slingsby T38 Grasshopper TX1	South Yorkshire Aircraft Museum, stored Doncaster	
WZ824	Slingsby T38 Grasshopper TX1	Privately owned, Bridge of Weir, Renfrewshire	
WZ826	Vickers Valiant B(K)1 (XD826/7872M) <ff>	Privately owned, Rayleigh, Essex	
WZ828	Slingsby T38 Grasshopper TX1 (BGA4421)	Privately owned, Little Rissington	
WZ831	Slingsby T38 Grasshopper TX1	Privately owned, stored Nympsfield, Glos	
WZ846	DHC1 Chipmunk 22 (G-BCSC/8439M)	No 2427 Sqn ATC, Biggin Hill	
WZ847	DHC1 Chipmunk 22 (G-CPMK) [F]	Privately owned, Sleap	
WZ868	DHC1 Chipmunk 22 (WG322/G-ARMF)	Privately owned, stored St Athan	
WZ869	DHC1 Chipmunk T10 (8019M) <ff> [6]	South Yorkshire Aircraft Museum, Doncaster	
WZ872	DHC1 Chipmunk 22 (G-BZGB) [E]	Privately owned, Blackpool	
WZ876	DHC1 Chipmunk 22 (G-BBWN) <ff>	Tangmere Military Aviation Museum	
WZ879	DHC1 Chipmunk 22 (G-BWUT) [X]	Privately owned, Audley End	
WZ882	DHC1 Chipmunk 22 (G-BXGP) [K]	Privately owned, Hurstbourne Tarrant	
XA109	DH115 Sea Vampire T22	Montrose Air Station Heritage Centre	
XA127	DH115 Sea Vampire T22 <ff>	FAA Museum, RNAS Yeovilton	
XA129	DH115 Sea Vampire T22	FAA Museum, stored Cobham Hall, RNAS Yeovilton	
XA225	Slingsby T38 Grasshopper TX1	Gliding Heritage Centre, Lasham	
XA226	Slingsby T38 Grasshopper TX1	Norfolk & Suffolk Avn Museum, Flixton	
XA228	Slingsby T38 Grasshopper TX1	National Museum of Flight, East Fortune	
XA230	Slingsby T38 Grasshopper TX1 (BGA4098)	Privately owned, Henlow	
XA231	Slingsby T38 Grasshopper TX1 (8888M)	RAF Manston History Museum	
XA240	Slingsby T38 Grasshopper TX1 (BGA4556)	Privately owned, Portmoak, Perth & Kinross	
XA241	Slingsby T38 Grasshopper TX1	Shuttleworth Collection, stored Old Warden	
XA243	Slingsby T38 Grasshopper TX1 (8886M)	Privately owned, Gransden Lodge, Cambs	
XA244	Slingsby T38 Grasshopper TX1	Privately owned, Brent Tor, Devon	
XA282	Slingsby T31B Cadet TX3	Caernarfon Air World	
XA289	Slingsby T31B Cadet TX3 (BGA5804)	Sold to Germany, 2018	
XA290	Slingsby T31B Cadet TX3	Privately owned, Portmoak, Perth & Kinross	
XA293	Slingsby T31B Cadet TX3 <ff>	Privately owned, Breighton	
XA295	Slingsby T31B Cadet TX3 (BGA3336)	Privately owned, Eaglescott	
XA302	Slingsby T31B Cadet TX3 (BGA3786)	RAF Museum, Hendon	
XA310	Slingsby T31B Cadet TX3 (BGA4963)	Privately owned, Shrivenham	
XA459	Fairey Gannet ECM6 [E]	Privately owned, White Waltham	
XA460	Fairey Gannet ECM6 [768/BY]	Ulster Aviation Society, Long Kesh	
XA466	Fairey Gannet COD4 [777/LM]	FAA Museum, RNAS Yeovilton	
XA508	Fairey Gannet T2 [627/GN]	FAA Museum, at Midland Air Museum, Coventry	
XA564	Gloster Javelin FAW1 (7464M)	RAF Museum, Cosford	
XA634	Gloster Javelin FAW4 (7641M)	Jet Age Museum, stored Gloucester	
XA699	Gloster Javelin FAW5 (7809M)	Midland Air Museum, Coventry	
XA847	EE P1B (8371M)	Privately owned, Stowmarket, Suffolk	
XA862	WS55 Whirlwind HAR1 (G-AMJT) [704] <ff>	South Yorkshire Aircraft Museum, Doncaster	
XA864	WS55 Whirlwind HAR1	FAA Museum, stored Cobham Hall, RNAS Yeovilton	
XA870	WS55 Whirlwind HAR1 [911]	South Yorkshire Aircraft Museum, Doncaster	
XA880	DH104 Devon C2 (G-BVXR) <ff>	Privately owned, Elstree Studios	
XA893	Avro 698 Vulcan B1 (8591M) <ff>	RAF Museum, stored Cosford	
XA903	Avro 698 Vulcan B1 <ff>	Privately owned, Stoneykirk, D&G	
XA917	HP80 Victor B1 (7827M) <ff>	Privately owned, Cupar, Fife	
XB259	Blackburn B101 Beverley C1 (G-AOAI)	Fort Paull Armoury	
XB261	Blackburn B101 Beverley C1 <ff>	Newark Air Museum, Winthorpe	
XB446	Grumman TBM-3 Avenger ECM6B	FAA Museum, Yeovilton	
XB480	Hiller HT1 [537]	FAA Museum, stored Cobham Hall, RNAS Yeovilton	
XB812	Canadair CL-13 Sabre F4 (9227M) [U]	RAF Museum, Cosford	
XD145	Saro SR53	RAF Museum, Cosford	
XD163	WS55 Whirlwind HAR10 (8645M) [X]	The Helicopter Museum, Weston-super-Mare	
XD165	WS55 Whirlwind HAR10 (8673M)	Caernarfon Airfield Fire Section	
XD215	VS Scimitar F1 <ff>	Privately owned, Cheltenham	
XD235	VS Scimitar F1 <ff>	Privately owned, Lavendon, Bucks	

Notes	Serial	Type (code/other identity)	Owner/operator, location or fate
	XD317	VS Scimitar F1 [112/R]	FAA Museum, RNAS Yeovilton
	XD332	VS Scimitar F1 [194/C]	Solent Sky, stored Romsey
	XD375	DH115 Vampire T11 (7887M)	Privately owned, Elland, W Yorks
	XD377	DH115 Vampire T11 (8203M) <ff>	South Yorkshire Aircraft Museum, stored Doncaster
	XD382	DH115 Vampire T11 (comp XD534) [41]	East Midlands Airport Aeropark
	XD425	DH115 Vampire T11 <ff>	Morayvia, Kinloss
	XD434	DH115 Vampire T11 [25]	Fenland & W Norfolk Aviation Museum, Wisbech
	XD445	DH115 Vampire T11 [51]	Tettenhall Transport Heritage Centre
	XD447	DH115 Vampire T11 [50]	East Midlands Airport Aeropark
	XD452	DH115 Vampire T11 (7990M) [66] <ff>	Privately owned, Dursley, Glos
	XD459	DH115 Vampire T11 (comp XE872) [57]	*Sold to France, January 2019*
	XD506	DH115 Vampire T11 (7983M)	Suffolk Aviation Heritage Centre, Foxhall Heath
	XD515	DH115 Vampire T11 (7998M/*XM515*)	RAF Museum, stored Cosford
	XD525	DH115 Vampire T11 (7882M) <ff>	Privately owned, Templepatrick, NI
	XD542	DH115 Vampire T11 (7604M) [N]	Privately owned, Patrington, E Yorks
	XD547	DH115 Vampire T11 (composite) [Z]	Privately owned, Cantley, Norfolk
	XD593	DH115 Vampire T11	Newark Air Museum, Winthorpe
	XD595	DH115 Vampire T11 <ff>	Privately owned, Glentham, Lincs
	XD596	DH115 Vampire T11 (7939M)	Solent Sky, stored Timsbury, Hants
	XD599	DH115 Vampire T11 [A] <ff>	Sywell Aviation Museum
	XD616	DH115 Vampire T11 [56]	Suffolk Aviation Heritage Centre, Foxhall Heath
	XD624	DH115 Vampire T11	Privately owned, Hooton Park
	XD626	DH115 Vampire T11 [Q]	Midland Air Museum, stored Coventry
	XD674	Hunting Jet Provost T1 (7570M)	RAF Museum, Cosford
XD693	XD693	Hunting Jet Provost T1 (XM129/G-AOBU) [Z-Q]	Kennet Aviation, North Weald
	XD816	Vickers Valiant B(K)1 <ff>	Brooklands Museum, Weybridge
	XD818	Vickers Valiant B(K)1 (7894M)	RAF Museum, Cosford
	XD857	Vickers Valiant B(K)1 <ff>	RAF Marham Aviation Heritage Centre
	XD875	Vickers Valiant B(K)1 <ff>	Morayvia, Kinloss
	XE317	Bristol 171 Sycamore HR14 (G-AMWO)	South Yorkshire Aircraft Museum, Doncaster
	XE339	Hawker Sea Hawk FGA6 (8156M) [149] <ff>	Privately owned, Glos
	XE339	Hawker Sea Hawk FGA6 (8156M) [E] <rf>	Privately owned, Booker
	XE340	Hawker Sea Hawk FGA6 [131/Z]	FAA Museum, stored Cobham Hall, RNAS Yeovilton
XE364	XE364	Hawker Sea Hawk FGA6 (G-JETH) (comp WM983) [485/J]	Gatwick Aviation Museum, Charlwood, Surrey
	XE368	Hawker Sea Hawk FGA6 [200/J]	Privately owned, Barrow-in-Furness
	XE521	Fairey Rotodyne Y (parts)	The Helicopter Museum, Weston-super-Mare
	XE584	Hawker Hunter FGA9 <ff>	Privately owned, Hooton Park
	XE597	Hawker Hunter FGA9 (8874M) <ff>	Privately owned, Bromsgrove
XE620	XE620	Hawker Hunter F6A (XE606/8841M) [B]	RAF Waddington, on display
	XE624	Hawker Hunter FGA9 (8875M) [G]	Privately owned, Wickenby
	XE627	Hawker Hunter F6A [T]	IWM Duxford
	XE643	Hawker Hunter FGA9 (8586M) <ff>	No 1137 Sqn ATC, Aldergrove
	XE650	Hawker Hunter FGA9 (G-9-449) <ff>	Farnborough Air Sciences Trust, Farnborough
	XE664	Hawker Hunter F4 <ff>	Jet Age Museum, Gloucester
	XE665	Hawker Hunter T8C (G-BWGM)	Privately owned, stored Cotswold Airport
	XE668	Hawker Hunter GA11 [832/DD]	Hamburger Hill Paintball, Marksbury, Somerset
	XE670	Hawker Hunter F4 (7762M/8585M) <ff>	RAF Museum, Cosford
XE683	XE683	Hawker Hunter F51 (RDAF E-409) [G]	City of Norwich Aviation Museum
	XE685	Hawker Hunter GA11 (G-GAII) [861/VL]	RAF Scampton Heritage Centre
	XE689	Hawker Hunter GA11 (G-BWGK) <ff>	Privately owned, Cotswold Airport
	XE707	Hawker Hunter GA11 (N707XE) [865]	Bentwaters Cold War Museum
	XE762	Slingsby T8 Cadet TX2 (VM594)	Gliding Heritage Centre, Lasham
	XE786	Slingsby T31B Cadet TX3 (BGA4033)	Privately owned, Arbroath
	XE793	Slingsby T31B Cadet TX3 (8666M)	Privately owned, Tamworth
	XE797	Slingsby T31B Cadet TX3	South Yorkshire Aviation Museum, Doncaster
	XE799	Slingsby T31B Cadet TX3 (8943M) [R]	Privately owned, stored Lasham
	XE802	Slingsby T31B Cadet TX3 (BGA5283)	Privately owned, North Hill, Devon
	XE852	DH115 Vampire T11 [58]	No 2247 Sqn ATC, Hawarden
	XE855	DH115 Vampire T11 <ff>	Midland Air Museum, stored Coventry (wreck)
	XE856	DH115 Vampire T11 (G-DUSK) [V]	Bournemouth Aviation Museum

Serial	Type (code/other identity)	Owner/operator, location or fate	Notes
XE864	DH115 Vampire T11(comp XD435) <ff>	Privately owned, Ingatstone, Essex	
XE872	DH115 Vampire T11 [62]	Midland Air Museum, Coventry	
XE874	DH115 Vampire T11 (8582M)	Paintball Commando, Birkin, W Yorks	
XE897	DH115 Vampire T11 (XD403)	Privately owned, Errol, Tayside	
XE921	DH115 Vampire T11 [VR] <ff>	Privately owned, Stoneykirk, D&G	
XE935	DH115 Vampire T11	South Yorkshire Aircraft Museum, Doncaster	
XE946	DH115 Vampire T11 (7473M) <ff>	RAF Cranwell Aviation Heritage Centre	
XE956	DH115 Vampire T11 (G-OBLN)	South Wales Aviation Museum, St Athan	
XE979	DH115 Vampire T11 [54]	Privately owned, Cantley, Norfolk	
XE982	DH115 Vampire T11 (7564M) (fuselage)	Privately owned, Glos	
XE985	DH115 Vampire T11 (WZ476)	Privately owned, New Inn, Torfaen	
XF113	VS Swift F7 [19] <ff>	Boscombe Down Aviation Collection, Old Sarum	
XF114	VS Swift F7 (G-SWIF)	Solent Sky, Southampton	
XF321	Hawker Hunter T7 <rf>	Phoenix Aviation, Bruntingthorpe	
XF368	Hawker Hunter F51 (RDAF E-412/XF314)	Brooklands Museum, Weybridge	
XF375	Hawker Hunter F6A (8736M/G-BUEZ) [6]	Boscombe Down Aviation Collection, Old Sarum	
XF382	Hawker Hunter F6A [15]	Midland Air Museum, Coventry	
XF383	Hawker Hunter F6 (8706M) <ff>	Gloster Aviation Club, Gloucester	
XF418	Hawker Hunter F51 (RDAF E-430)	Gatwick Aviation Museum, Charlwood, Surrey	
XF509	Hawker Hunter F6 (8708M)	Fort Paull Armoury	
XF522	Hawker Hunter F6 <ff>	Herts & Bucks ATC Wing, RAF Halton	
XF526	Hawker Hunter F6 (8679M) [78/E]	Privately owned, Birlingham, Worcs	
XF527	Hawker Hunter F6 (8680M)	RAF Halton, on display	
XF545	Percival P56 Provost T1 (7957M) [O-K]	Privately owned, Bucklebury, Berks	
XF597	Percival P56 Provost T1 (G-BKFW) [AH]	Privately owned, Audley End	
XF603	Percival P56 Provost T1 (G-KAPW)	Shuttleworth Collection, Old Warden	
XF690	Percival P56 Provost T1 (8041M/G-MOOS)	Kennet Aviation, Yeovilton	
XF708	Avro 716 Shackleton MR3/3 [C]	IWM Duxford	
XF785	Bristol 173 (7648M/G-ALBN)	Aerospace Bristol, Filton	
XF836	Percival P56 Provost T1 (8043M/G-AWRY) [JG]	Privately owned stored, Cambs	
XF840	Percival P56 Provost T1 <ff>	Tangmere Military Aviation Museum	
XF926	Bristol 188 (8368M)	RAF Museum, Cosford	
XF940	Hawker Hunter F4 <ff>	Privately owned, Kew Stoke, Somerset	
XF994	Hawker Hunter T8C (G-CGHU) [873/VL]	Hawker Hunter Aviation, Scampton	
XF995	Hawker Hunter T8B (G-BZSF/9237M) [K]	Hawker Hunter Aviation, Scampton	
XG154	Hawker Hunter FGA9 (8863M)	RAF Museum, Hendon	
XG160	Hawker Hunter F6A (8831M/G-BWAF) [U]	Bournemouth Aviation Museum	
XG164	Hawker Hunter F6 (8681M)	Davidstow Airfield & Cornwall At War Museum	
XG168	Hawker Hunter F6A (XG172/8832M) [10]	City of Norwich Aviation Museum	
XG190	Hawker Hunter F51 (RDAF E-425) [C]	Solway Aviation Society, Carlisle	
XG193	Hawker Hunter FGA9 (XG297) (comp with WT741) <ff>	South Yorkshire Aircraft Museum, Doncaster	
XG194	Hawker Hunter FGA9 (8839M)	Wattisham Station Heritage Museum	
XG195	Hawker Hunter FGA9 <ff>	Privately owned, Lewes	
XG196	Hawker Hunter F6A (8702M) [31]	Privately owned, Bentwaters	
XG209	Hawker Hunter F6 (8709M) <ff>	Privately owned, Kingston-on-Thames	
XG210	Hawker Hunter F6	Privately owned, Beck Row, Suffolk	
XG225	Hawker Hunter F6A (8713M)	DSAE Cosford, at main gate	
XG226	Hawker Hunter F6A (8800M) <ff>	RAF Manston History Museum	
XG254	Hawker Hunter FGA9 (8881M) [A]	Norfolk & Suffolk Avn Museum, Flixton	
XG274	Hawker Hunter F6 (8710M) [71]	Privately owned, Newmarket	
XG290	Hawker Hunter F6 (8711M) <ff>	Boscombe Down Aviation Collection, Old Sarum	
XG297	Hawker Hunter FGA9 [Y] <ff>	South Yorkshire Aircraft Museum, Doncaster	
XG325	EE Lightning F1 <ff>	Privately owned, Norfolk	
XG329	EE Lightning F1 (8050M)	Privately owned, Flixton	
XG331	EE Lightning F1 <ff>	Privately owned, Glos	
XG337	EE Lightning F1 (8056M) [M]	RAF Museum, Cosford	
XG452	Bristol 192 Belvedere HC1 (7997M/G-BRMB)	The Helicopter Museum, Weston-super-Mare	
XG454	Bristol 192 Belvedere HC1 (8366M)	Museum of Science & Industry, Manchester	

Notes	Serial	Type (code/other identity)	Owner/operator, location or fate
	XG462	Bristol 192 Belvedere HC1 <ff>	The Helicopter Museum, Weston-super-Mare
	XG474	Bristol 192 Belvedere HC1 (8367M) [O]	RAF Museum, Hendon
	XG502	Bristol 171 Sycamore HR14	Army Flying Museum, Middle Wallop
	XG518	Bristol 171 Sycamore HR14 (8009M) [S-E]	Norfolk & Suffolk Avn Museum, Flixton
	XG523	Bristol 171 Sycamore HR14 <ff> [V]	Norfolk & Suffolk Avn Museum, Flixton
	XG545	Bristol 171 Sycamore HR52 (OE-XSY)	Flying Bulls, Salzburg, Austria
	XG574	WS55 Whirlwind HAR3 [752/PO]	FAA Museum, stored Cobham Hall, RNAS Yeovilton
	XG588	WS55 Whirlwind HAR3 (G-BAMH/VR-BEP)	East Midlands Airport Aeropark
	XG592	WS55 Whirlwind HAS7 [54]	Task Force Adventure Park, Cowbridge, S Glam
	XG594	WS55 Whirlwind HAS7 [517]	FAA Museum, stored Cobham Hall, RNAS Yeovilton
	XG596	WS55 Whirlwind HAS7 [66]	The Helicopter Museum, stored Weston-super-Mare
	XG629	DH112 Sea Venom FAW22	Privately owned, Stone, Staffs
	XG680	DH112 Sea Venom FAW22 [438]	North-East Aircraft Museum, Usworth
	XG692	DH112 Sea Venom FAW22 [668/LM]	Privately owned, Stockport
	XG730	DH112 Sea Venom FAW22	de Havilland Aircraft Museum, London Colney
	XG736	DH112 Sea Venom FAW22	Privately owned, East Midlands
	XG737	DH112 Sea Venom FAW22 [220/Z]	East Midlands Airport Aeropark
	XG743	DH115 Sea Vampire T22 [798/BY]	Fishburn Historic Aviation Centre
	XG797	Fairey Gannet ECM6 [277]	IWM Duxford
	XG831	Fairey Gannet ECM6 [396]	Davidstow Airfield & Cornwall At War Museum
	XG882	Fairey Gannet T5 (8754M) [771/LM]	Privately owned, Errol, Tayside
	XG883	Fairey Gannet T5 [773/BY]	FAA Museum, at Museum of Berkshire Aviation, Woodley
	XG900	Short SC1	Science Museum, South Kensington
	XG905	Short SC1	Ulster Folk & Transport Mus, Holywood, Co Down
	XH131	EE Canberra PR9	Ulster Aviation Society, Long Kesh
	XH134	EE Canberra PR9 (G-OMHD)	Privately owned, stored Cotswold Airport
	XH135	EE Canberra PR9	Privately owned, Cotswold Airport
	XH136	EE Canberra PR9 (8782M) [W] <ff>	Romney Marsh Wartime Collection
	XH165	EE Canberra PR9 <ff>	Blyth Valley Aviation Collection, Walpole
	XH169	EE Canberra PR9	RAF Marham, on display
	XH170	EE Canberra PR9 (8739M)	RAF Wyton, on display
	XH171	EE Canberra PR9 (8746M) [U]	RAF Museum, Cosford
	XH174	EE Canberra PR9 <ff>	Privately owned, Leicester
	XH175	EE Canberra PR9 <ff>	Privately owned, Bewdley, Worcs
	XH177	EE Canberra PR9 <ff>	Newark Air Museum, Winthorpe
	XH278	DH115 Vampire T11 (8595M/7866M) [42]	Yorkshire Air Museum, Elvington
	XH312	DH115 Vampire T11	Privately owned, Dodleston, Cheshire
	XH313	DH115 Vampire T11 (G-BZRD) [E]	Tangmere Military Aviation Museum
	XH318	DH115 Vampire T11 (7761M) [64]	Privately owned, Sholing, Hants
	XH328	DH115 Vampire T11 <ff>	Privately owned, Cantley, Norfolk
	XH330	DH115 Vampire T11 [73]	Privately owned, Milton Keynes
	XH537	Avro 698 Vulcan B2MRR (8749M) <ff>	Bournemouth Aviation Museum
	XH558	Avro 698 Vulcan B2 (G-VLCN)	Vulcan To The Sky Trust, Doncaster Sheffield Airport
	XH560	Avro 698 Vulcan K2 <ff>	Privately owned, Foulness
	XH563	Avro 698 Vulcan B2MRR <ff>	Morayvia, Kinloss
	XH584	EE Canberra T4 (G-27-374) <ff>	South Yorkshire Aircraft Museum, Doncaster
	XH592	HP80 Victor B1A (8429M) <ff>	Midland Air Museum, Coventry
	XH648	HP80 Victor K1A	IWM Duxford
	XH669	HP80 Victor K2 (9092M) <ff>	Privately owned, Foulness
	XH670	HP80 Victor SR2 <ff>	Privately owned, Foulness
	XH672	HP80 Victor K2 (9242M)	RAF Museum, Cosford
	XH673	HP80 Victor K2 (8911M)	RAF Marham, on display
	XH767	Gloster Javelin FAW9 (7955M) [L]	Yorkshire Air Museum, Elvington
	XH783	Gloster Javelin FAW7 (7798M) <ff>	Privately owned, Catford
	XH837	Gloster Javelin FAW7 (8032M) <ff>	Caernarfon Air World
	XH892	Gloster Javelin FAW9R (7982M) [J]	Norfolk & Suffolk Avn Museum, Flixton
	XH897	Gloster Javelin FAW9	IWM Duxford
	XH903	Gloster Javelin FAW9 (7938M) [G]	Jet Age Museum, Gloucester
	XH992	Gloster Javelin FAW8 (7829M) [P]	Newark Air Museum, Winthorpe

Serial	Type (code/other identity)	Owner/operator, location or fate	Notes
XJ314	RR Thrust Measuring Rig	Science Museum, South Kensington	
XJ380	Bristol 171 Sycamore HR14 (8628M)	Boscombe Down Aviation Collection, Old Sarum	
XJ389	Fairey Jet Gyrodyne (XD759/G-AJJP)	Museum of Berkshire Aviation, Woodley	
XJ398	WS55 Whirlwind HAR10 (XD768/G-BDBZ)	South Yorkshire Aircraft Museum, Doncaster	
XJ407	WS55 Whirlwind HAR10 (N7013H)	Privately owned, Tattershall Thorpe	
XJ435	WS55 Whirlwind HAR10 (XD804/8671M) [V]	RAF Manston History Museum, spares use	
XJ476	DH110 Sea Vixen FAW1 <ff>	Boscombe Down Aviation Collection, Old Sarum	
XJ481	DH110 Sea Vixen FAW1 [VL]	FAA Museum, stored Cobham Hall, RNAS Yeovilton	
XJ482	DH110 Sea Vixen FAW1 [713/VL]	Norfolk & Suffolk Avn Museum, Flixton	
XJ488	DH110 Sea Vixen FAW1 <ff>	Robertsbridge Aviation Society, Mayfield	
XJ494	DH110 Sea Vixen FAW2 [121/E]	Privately owned, Bruntingthorpe	
XJ560	DH110 Sea Vixen FAW2 (8142M) [243/H]	Newark Air Museum, Winthorpe	
XJ565	DH110 Sea Vixen FAW2 [127/E]	de Havilland Aircraft Museum, London Colney	
XJ571	DH110 Sea Vixen FAW2 (8140M) [242]	Solent Sky, Southampton	
XJ575	DH110 Sea Vixen FAW2 <ff> [SAH-13]	Wellesbourne Wartime Museum	
XJ579	DH110 Sea Vixen FAW2 <ff>	Midland Air Museum, stored Coventry	
XJ580	DH110 Sea Vixen FAW2 [131/E]	Tangmere Military Aviation Museum	
XJ714	Hawker Hunter FR10 (comp XG226)	East Midlands Airport Aeropark	
XJ723	WS55 Whirlwind HAR10	Morayvia, Kinloss	
XJ726	WS55 Whirlwind HAR10	Caernarfon Air World	
XJ727	WS55 Whirlwind HAR10 (8661M)	Combat Paintball Park, Thetford	
XJ729	WS55 Whirlwind HAR10 (8732M/G-BVGE)	Privately owned, Chard, Somerset	
XJ758	WS55 Whirlwind HAR10 (8464M) <ff>	Privately owned, Welshpool	
XJ772	DH115 Vampire T11 [H]	de Havilland Aircraft Museum, London Colney	
XJ823	Avro 698 Vulcan B2A	Solway Aviation Society, Carlisle	
XJ824	Avro 698 Vulcan B2A	IWM Duxford	
XJ917	Bristol 171 Sycamore HR14 [H-S]	Aerospace Bristol, stored Filton	
XJ918	Bristol 171 Sycamore HR14 (8190M)	RAF Museum, Cosford	
XK416	Auster AOP9 (7855M/G-AYUA)	Privately owned, Widmerpool	
XK417	Auster AOP9 (G-AVXY)	Privately owned, Messingham, Lincs	
XK418	Auster AOP9 (7976M)	93rd Bomb Group Museum, Hardwick, Norfolk	
XK421	Auster AOP9 (8365M) (frame)	South Yorkshire Aircraft Museum, stored Doncaster	
XK488	Blackburn NA39 Buccaneer S1	FAA Museum, stored Cobham Hall, RNAS Yeovilton	
XK526	Blackburn NA39 Buccaneer S2 (8648M)	RAF Honington, at main gate	
XK527	Blackburn NA39 Buccaneer S2D (8818M) <ff>	Privately owned, North Wales	
XK532	Blackburn NA39 Buccaneer S1 (8867M) [632/LM]	Highland Aviation Museum, Inverness	
XK533	Blackburn NA39 Buccaneer S1 <ff>	Royal Scottish Mus'm of Flight, stored Granton	
XK590	DH115 Vampire T11 [V]	Wellesbourne Wartime Museum	
XK623	DH115 Vampire T11 (G-VAMP) [56]	Caernarfon Air World	
XK624	DH115 Vampire T11 [32]	Norfolk & Suffolk Avn Museum, Flixton	
XK625	DH115 Vampire T11 [14]	Romney Marsh Wartime Collection	
XK627	DH115 Vampire T11 <ff>	Davidstow Airfield & Cornwall At War Museum	
XK632	DH115 Vampire T11 <ff>	Privately owned, Greenford, London	
XK637	DH115 Vampire T11 [56]	Top Gun Flight Simulation Centre, Stalybridge	
XK695	DH106 Comet C2(RC) (G-AMXH/9164M) <ff>	de Havilland Aircraft Museum, London Colney	
XK699	DH106 Comet C2 (7971M) <ff>	Boscombe Down Aviation Collection, Old Sarum	
XK724	Folland Gnat F1 (7715M)	RAF Museum, stored Cosford	
XK740	Folland Gnat F1 (8396M)	Solent Sky, Southampton	
XK776	ML Utility 1	Army Flying Museum, Middle Wallop	
XK789	Slingsby T38 Grasshopper TX1	Midland Air Museum, Coventry	
XK790	Slingsby T38 Grasshopper TX1	Privately owned, stored Husbands Bosworth	
XK819	Slingsby T38 Grasshopper TX1	Privately owned, stored Rufforth	
XK819	Slingsby T38 Grasshopper TX1	Privately owned, stored Rufforth	
XK820	Slingsby T38 Grasshopper TX1 (comp WZ754/WZ778)	Privately owned, Bridge of Weir, Renfrewshire	
XK885	Percival P66 Pembroke C1 (8452M/N46EA)	Privately owned, St Athan	
XK895	DH104 Sea Devon C20 (G-SDEV) [19/CU]	South Wales Aviation Museum, St Athan	
XK907	WS55 Whirlwind HAS7	Midland Air Museum, stored Coventry	
XK911	WS55 Whirlwind HAS7(mod)	Privately owned, Dagenham	
XK936	WS55 Whirlwind HAS7 [62]	IWM Duxford	
XK940	WS55 Whirlwind HAS7 (G-AYXT) [911]	The Helicopter Museum, Weston-super-Mare	

Notes	Serial	Type (code/other identity)	Owner/operator, location or fate
	XK970	WS55 Whirlwind HAR10 (8789M)	Army, Bramley, Hants (for disposal)
	XL149	Blackburn B101 Beverley C1 (7988M) <ff>	South Yorkshire Aircraft Museum, Doncaster
	XL160	HP80 Victor K2 (8910M) <ff>	RAF Marham Aviation Heritage Centre
	XL164	HP80 Victor K2 (9215M) <ff>	Bournemouth Aviation Museum
	XL190	HP80 Victor K2 (9216M) <ff>	RAF Manston History Museum
	XL231	HP80 Victor K2	Yorkshire Air Museum, Elvington
	XL318	Avro 698 Vulcan B2 (8733M)	RAF Museum, Hendon
	XL319	Avro 698 Vulcan B2	North-East Aircraft Museum, Usworth
	XL360	Avro 698 Vulcan B2A	Midland Air Museum, Coventry
	XL388	Avro 698 Vulcan B2 <ff>	South Yorkshire Aircraft Museum, Doncaster
	XL426	Avro 698 Vulcan B2 (G-VJET)	Vulcan Restoration Trust, Southend
	XL445	Avro 698 Vulcan K2 (8811M) <ff>	Norfolk & Suffolk Avn Museum, Flixton
	XL449	Fairey Gannet AEW3 <ff>	Privately owned, Booker
	XL472	Fairey Gannet AEW3 [044/R]	South Wales Aviation Museum, St Athan
	XL497	Fairey Gannet AEW3 [041/R]	Dumfries & Galloway Avn Mus, Dumfries
	XL500	Fairey Gannet AEW3 (G-KAEW) [CU]	South Wales Aviation Museum, St Athan
	XL502	Fairey Gannet AEW3 (8610M/G-BMYP)	Yorkshire Air Museum, Elvington
	XL503	Fairey Gannet AEW3 [070/E]	FAA Museum, stored Cobham Hall, RNAS Yeovilton
	XL563	Hawker Hunter T7 (9218M)	Farnborough Air Sciences Trust, stored Farnborough
	XL564	Hawker Hunter T7 <ff>	City of Norwich Aviation Museum
	XL565	Hawker Hunter T7 (parts of WT745) [Y]	Privately owned, Bruntingthorpe
	XL568	Hawker Hunter T7A (9224M) [X]	RAF Museum, Cosford
	XL569	Hawker Hunter T7 (8833M)	East Midlands Airport Aeropark
	XL572	Hawker Hunter T7 (8834M/XL571/G-HNTR) [V]	Yorkshire Air Museum, Elvington
	XL573	Hawker Hunter T7 (G-BVGH)	South Wales Aviation Museum, St Athan
	XL580	Hawker Hunter T8M [723]	FAA Museum, stored Cobham Hall, RNAS Yeovilton
	XL586	Hawker Hunter T7 (comp XL578)	Action Park, Wickford, Essex
	XL587	Hawker Hunter T7 (8807M/G-HPUX)	Hawker Hunter Aviation, stored Scampton
	XL591	Hawker Hunter T7	Gatwick Aviation Museum, Charlwood, Surrey
	XL592	Hawker Hunter T7 (8836M) [Y]	Maidenhead Heritage Centre
	XL601	Hawker Hunter T7 (G-BZSR) [874/VL]	Withdrawn from use, 2018
	XL602	Hawker Hunter T8M (G-BWFT)	Hunter Flying Ltd, St Athan
	XL609	Hawker Hunter T7 <ff>	Privately owned, South Molton, Devon
	XL621	Hawker Hunter T7 (G-BNCX)	Privately owned, Dunsfold
	XL623	Hawker Hunter T7 (8770M)	Privately owned, Dunsfold
	XL629	EE Lightning T4	MoD/QinetiQ Boscombe Down, at main gate
	XL714	DH82A Tiger Moth II (T6099/G-AOGR)	Privately owned, Boughton, Lincs
	XL736	Saro Skeeter AOP12	The Helicopter Museum stored, Weston-super-Mare
	XL738	Saro Skeeter AOP12 (XM565/7861M)	Privately owned, Storwood, Yorkshire
	XL739	Saro Skeeter AOP12	Norfolk Tank Museum, Forncett St Peter
	XL762	Saro Skeeter AOP12 (8017M)	National Museum of Flight, E Fortune
	XL763	Saro Skeeter AOP12	Privately owned, Storwood, Yorkshire
	XL764	Saro Skeeter AOP12 (7940M) [J]	Newark Air Museum, Winthorpe
	XL765	Saro Skeeter AOP12	Privately owned, Melksham, Wilts
	XL770	Saro Skeeter AOP12 (8046M)	Solent Sky, Southampton
	XL809	Saro Skeeter AOP12 (G-BLIX)	Privately owned, Wilden, Beds
	XL811	Saro Skeeter AOP12	The Helicopter Museum, Weston-super-Mare
	XL812	Saro Skeeter AOP12 (G-SARO)	AAC Historic Aircraft Flight, stored Middle Wallop
	XL813	Saro Skeeter AOP12	Army Flying Museum, Middle Wallop
	XL814	Saro Skeeter AOP12	Army Flying Museum, stored Middle Wallop
	XL824	Bristol 171 Sycamore HR14 (8021M)	Aerospace Bristol, Filton
	XL829	Bristol 171 Sycamore HR14	The Helicopter Museum, Weston-super-Mare
	XL840	WS55 Whirlwind HAS7	Privately owned, Bawtry
	XL853	WS55 Whirlwind HAS7 [PO]	FAA Museum, stored Cobham Hall, RNAS Yeovilton
	XL875	WS55 Whirlwind HAR9	Perth Technical College
	XL929	Percival P66 Pembroke C1 (G-BNPU)	Privately owned, stored Compton Verney
	XL954	Percival P66 Pembroke C1 (9042M/N4234C/G-BXES)	Privately owned, Weston, Ireland
	XL993	SAL Twin Pioneer CC2 (8388M)	RAF Museum, Cosford
	XM135	BAC Lightning F1 [B]	IWM Duxford

Serial	Type (code/other identity)	Owner/operator, location or fate	Notes
XM144	BAC Lightning F1 (8417M) <ff>	Shannon Aviation Museum, Eire	
XM169	BAC Lightning F1A (8422M) <ff>	Morayvia, Kinloss	
XM172	BAC Lightning F1A (8427M)	Lakes Lightnings, Spark Bridge, Cumbria	
XM173	BAC Lightning F1A (8414M) [A]	Privately owned, Malmesbury, Glos	
XM191	BAC Lightning F1A (7854M/8590M) <ff>	Privately owned, Thorpe Wood, N Yorks	
XM192	BAC Lightning F1A (8413M) [K]	Thorpe Camp Preservation Group, Lincs	
XM223	DH104 Devon C2 (G-BWWC) [J]	Privately owned, stored Compton Verney	
XM279	EE Canberra B(I)8 <ff>	Privately owned, Flixton	
XM300	WS58 Wessex HAS1	Privately owned, Nantgarw, Rhondda	
XM328	WS58 Wessex HAS3 [653/PO]	The Helicopter Museum, Weston-super-Mare	
XM330	WS58 Wessex HAS1	The Helicopter Museum, Weston-super-Mare	
XM350	Hunting Jet Provost T3A (9036M)	South Yorkshire Aircraft Museum, Doncaster	
XM351	Hunting Jet Provost T3 (8078M) [Y]	RAF Museum, Cosford	
XM355	Hunting Jet Provost T3 (8229M)	Newcastle Aviation Academy	
XM358	Hunting Jet Provost T3A (8987M) [53]	Privately owned, Newbridge, Powys	
XM362	Hunting Jet Provost T3 (8230M)	DSAE No 1 SoTT, Cosford	
XM365	Hunting Jet Provost T3 (G-BXBH)	Privately owned, Bruntingthorpe	
XM373	Hunting Jet Provost T3A (7726M) [2] <ff>	Yorkshire Air Museum, Elvington	
XM383	Hunting Jet Provost T3A [90]	Newark Air Museum, Winthorpe	
XM402	Hunting Jet Provost T3 (8055AM) [18]	Fenland & W Norfolk Aviation Museum, Wisbech	
XM404	Hunting Jet Provost T3 (8055BM) <ff>	Bournemouth Aviation Museum	
XM409	Hunting Jet Provost T3 (8082M) <ff>	Air Scouts, Guernsey Airport	
XM410	Hunting Jet Provost T3 (8054AM) [B]	Privately owned, Gillingham, Kent	
XM411	Hunting Jet Provost T3 (8434M) <ff>	South Yorkshire Aircraft Museum, Doncaster	
XM412	Hunting Jet Provost T3A (9011M) [41]	Privately owned, Balado Bridge, Scotland	
XM414	Hunting Jet Provost T3 (8996M)	Ulster Aviation Society, Long Kesh	
XM417	Hunting Jet Provost T3 (8054BM) [D] <ff>	Privately owned, Bracknell	
XM419	Hunting Jet Provost T3 (8990M) [102]	Newcastle Aviation Academy	
XM424	Hunting Jet Provost T3 (G-BWDS)	Privately owned, Coventry	
XM425	Hunting Jet Provost T3A (8995M) [88]	Privately owned, Longton, Staffs	
XM463	Hunting Jet Provost T3A [38] (fuselage)	RAF Museum, Hendon	
XM468	Hunting Jet Provost T3 (8081M) <ff>	Wings Museum, Balcombe, W Sussex	
XM473	Hunting Jet Provost T3A (8974M/G-TINY)	Privately owned, Wethersfield	
XM474	Hunting Jet Provost T3 (8121M) <ff>	No 247 Sqn ATC, Ashton-under-Lyne, Gr Manchester	
XM479	Hunting Jet Provost T3A (G-BVEZ) [U]	Privately owned, Newcastle	
XM480	Hunting Jet Provost T3 (8080M)	4x4 Car Centre, Chesterfield	
XM496	Bristol 253 Britannia C1 (EL-WXA) [496]	Britannia Preservation Society, Cotswold Airport	
XM497	Bristol 175 Britannia 312F (G-AOVF) [497]	RAF Museum, Cosford	
XM529	Saro Skeeter AOP12 (7979M/G-BDNS)	Privately owned, Handforth	
XM553	Saro Skeeter AOP12 (G-AWSV)	Yorkshire Air Museum, Elvington	
XM555	Saro Skeeter AOP12 (8027M)	North-East Aircraft Museum, Usworth	
XM557	Saro Skeeter AOP12 <ff>	The Helicopter Museum, stored Weston-super-Mare	
XM564	Saro Skeeter AOP12	The Tank Museum, stored Bovington	
XM569	Avro 698 Vulcan B2 <ff>	Jet Age Museum, Gloucester	
XM575	Avro 698 Vulcan B2A (G-BLMC)	East Midlands Airport Aeropark	
XM594	Avro 698 Vulcan B2	Newark Air Museum, Winthorpe	
XM597	Avro 698 Vulcan B2	National Museum of Flight, E Fortune	
XM598	Avro 698 Vulcan B2 (8778M)	RAF Museum, Cosford	
XM602	Avro 698 Vulcan B2 (8771M) <ff>	Avro Heritage Museum, Woodford	
XM603	Avro 698 Vulcan B2	Avro Heritage Museum, Woodford	
XM607	Avro 698 Vulcan B2 (8779M)	RAF Waddington, on display	
XM612	Avro 698 Vulcan B2	City of Norwich Aviation Museum	
XM651	Saro Skeeter AOP12 (XM561/7980M)	South Yorkshire Aircraft Museum, Doncaster	
XM652	Avro 698 Vulcan B2 <ff>	Privately owned, Welshpool	
XM655	Avro 698 Vulcan B2 (G-VULC)	Privately owned, Wellesbourne Mountford	
XM685	WS55 Whirlwind HAS7 (G-AYZJ) [513/PO]	Newark Air Museum, Winthorpe	
XM692	HS Gnat T1 <ff>	Privately owned, Dunkeswell	
XM693	HS Gnat T1 (7891M)	GE Aviation Hamble, on display	
XM697	HS Gnat T1 (G-NAAT)	Reynard Garden Centre, Carluke, S Lanarkshire	
XM708	HS Gnat T1 (8573M)	Privately owned, Lytham St Annes	
XM715	HP80 Victor K2	Cold War Jets Collection, Bruntingthorpe	
XM717	HP80 Victor K2 <ff>	RAF Museum, Hendon	

Notes	Serial	Type (code/other identity)	Owner/operator, location or fate
	XM819	Lancashire EP9 Prospector (G-APXW)	Army Flying Museum, stored Middle Wallop
	XM833	WS58 Wessex HAS3	North-East Aircraft Museum, Usworth
	XN126	WS55 Whirlwind HAR10 (8655M) [S]	Pinewood Studios, Elstree
	XN137	Hunting Jet Provost T3 <ff>	Privately owned, Little Addington, Northants
	XN149	Slingsby T21B (BGA1085/9G-ABD)	Boscombe Down Aviation Collection, Old Sarum
	XN156	Slingsby T21B Sedbergh TX1 (BGA3250)	Privately owned, Portmoak, Perth & Kinross
	XN157	Slingsby T21B Sedbergh TX1 (BGA3255)	Privately owned, Long Mynd
	XN185	Slingsby T21B Sedbergh TX1 (8942M/BGA4077)	Privately owned, Scampton
	XN186	Slingsby T21B Sedbergh TX1 (BGA3905) [HFG]	Privately owned, Wethersfield
	XN187	Slingsby T21B Sedbergh TX1 (BGA3903)	Privately owned, RAF Halton
	XN198	Slingsby T31B Cadet TX3	Privately owned, Bodmin
	XN238	Slingsby T31B Cadet TX3 <ff>	South Yorkshire Aircraft Museum, Doncaster
	XN239	Slingsby T31B Cadet TX3 (8889M) [G]	IWM Duxford, stored
	XN246	Slingsby T31B Cadet TX3	Solent Sky, stored Southampton
	XN258	WS55 Whirlwind HAR9 [589/CU]	North-East Aircraft Museum, Usworth
	XN297	WS55 Whirlwind HAR9 (XN311) [12]	Privately owned, Hull
	XN298	WS55 Whirlwind HAR9 [810/LS]	Privately owned
	XN304	WS55 Whirlwind HAS7 [WW/B]	Norfolk & Suffolk Avn Museum, Flixton
	XN332	Saro P531 (G-APNV) [759]	FAA Museum, stored Cobham Hall, RNAS Yeovilton
	XN334	Saro P531	FAA Museum, stored Cobham Hall, RNAS Yeovilton
	XN344	Saro Skeeter AOP12 (8018M)	Science Museum, South Kensington
	XN345	Saro Skeeter AOP12 <ff>	The Helicopter Museum, stored Weston-super-Mare
	XN351	Saro Skeeter AOP12 (G-BKSC)	Privately owned, Norwich
	XN380	WS55 Whirlwind HAS7	RAF Manston History Museum
	XN385	WS55 Whirlwind HAS7	Battleground Paintball, Yarm, Cleveland
	XN386	WS55 Whirlwind HAR9 [435/ED]	South Yorkshire Aircraft Museum, Doncaster
	XN412	Auster AOP9	Auster 9 Group, Melton Mowbray
	XN437	Auster AOP9 (G-AXWA)	Privately owned, Rush Green
	XN441	Auster AOP9 (G-BGKT)	Privately owned, Exeter
	XN458	Hunting Jet Provost T3 (8234M/XN594) [19]	Privately owned, Northallerton
	XN459	Hunting Jet Provost T3A (G-BWOT) [59]	Kennet Aviation, North Weald
	XN462	Hunting Jet Provost T3A [17]	FAA Museum, stored Cobham Hall, RNAS Yeovilton
	XN466	Hunting Jet Provost T3A [29] <ff>	No 247 Sqn ATC, Ashton-under-Lyne, Gr Manchester
	XN492	Hunting Jet Provost T3A (8079M) <ff>	East Midlands Airport Aeropark
	XN494	Hunting Jet Provost T3A (9012M) [43]	Cornwall College, Newquay
	XN500	Hunting Jet Provost T3A	Norfolk & Suffolk Avn Museum, Flixton
	XN503	Hunting Jet Provost T3 <ff>	North-East Aircraft Museum, Usworth
	XN511	Hunting Jet Provost T3 [12] <ff>	South Yorkshire Aircraft Museum, Doncaster
	XN549	Hunting Jet Provost T3A (8235M) <ff>	Privately owned, Warrington
	XN551	Hunting Jet Provost T3A (8984M)	Privately owned, Felton Common, Bristol
	XN554	Hunting Jet Provost T3 (8436M) [K]	Gunsmoke Paintball, Colchester, Essex
	XN573	Hunting Jet Provost T3 [E] <ff>	Newark Air Museum, Winthorpe
	XN579	Hunting Jet Provost T3A (9137M) [14]	Gunsmoke Paintball, Colchester, Essex
	XN582	Hunting Jet Provost T3A (8957M) [95,H]	Privately owned, Bruntingthorpe
	XN584	Hunting Jet Provost T3A (9014M) [E]	USW Aerospace Centre, Treforest, Glamorgan
	XN586	Hunting Jet Provost T3A (9039M) [91]	Brooklands Museum, Weybridge
	XN589	Hunting Jet Provost T3A (9143M) [46]	RAF Linton-on-Ouse, on display
	XN597	Hunting Jet Provost T3 (7984M) <ff>	Privately owned, Market Drayton, Shrops
	XN607	Hunting Jet Provost T3 <ff>	Morayvia, Kinloss
	XN623	Hunting Jet Provost T3 (XN632/8352M)	Privately owned, Birlingham, Worcs
	XN629	Hunting Jet Provost T3A (G-BVEG/G-KNOT) [49]	Suffolk Aviation Heritage Centre, Foxhall Heath
	XN634	Hunting Jet Provost T3A <ff>	Privately owned, Blackpool
	XN634	Hunting Jet Provost T3A [53] <rf>	BAE Systems Warton Fire Section
	XN637	Hunting Jet Provost T3 (G-BKOU) [03]	Privately owned, North Weald
	XN647	DH110 Sea Vixen FAW2 <ff>	Privately owned, Steventon, Oxon
	XN650	DH110 Sea Vixen FAW2 [456] <ff>	Privately owned, Norfolk
	XN651	DH110 Sea Vixen FAW2 <ff>	Privately owned, Lavendon, Bucks
	XN685	DH110 Sea Vixen FAW2 (8173M) [703/VL]	Midland Air Museum, Coventry
	XN696	DH110 Sea Vixen FAW2 [751] <ff>	North-East Aircraft Museum, Usworth
	XN714	Hunting H126	RAF Museum, Cosford
	XN726	EE Lightning F2A (8545M) <ff>	Boscombe Down Aviation Collection, Old Sarum

Serial	Type (code/other identity)	Owner/operator, location or fate	Notes
XN728	EE Lightning F2A (8546M) <ff>	Privately owned, Binbrook	
XN774	EE Lightning F2A (8551M) <ff>	Privately owned, Boston	
XN776	EE Lightning F2A (8535M) [C]	National Museum of Flight, E Fortune	
XN795	EE Lightning F2A <ff>	Privately owned, Rayleigh, Essex	
XN819	AW660 Argosy C1 (8205M) <ff>	Newark Air Museum, Winthorpe	
XN923	HS Buccaneer S1 [13]	Gatwick Aviation Museum, Charlwood, Surrey	
XN928	HS Buccaneer S1 (8179M) <ff>	Privately owned, Gravesend	
XN957	HS Buccaneer S1 [630/LM]	FAA Museum, RNAS Yeovilton	
XN964	HS Buccaneer S1 [118/V]	Newark Air Museum, Winthorpe	
XN967	HS Buccaneer S1 [233] <ff>	City of Norwich Aviation Museum	
XN972	HS Buccaneer S1 (8183M/XN962) <ff>	RAF Museum, Cosford	
XN974	HS Buccaneer S2A	Yorkshire Air Museum, Elvington	
XN981	HS Buccaneer S2B (fuselage)	Privately owned, Errol	
XN983	HS Buccaneer S2B <ff>	Fenland & W Norfolk Aviation Museum, Wisbech	
XP110	WS58 Wessex HAS3 (A2636)	DSAE RNAESS, HMS Sultan, Gosport	
XP137	WS58 Wessex HAS3 [11/DD]	Currently not known	
XP142	WS58 Wessex HAS3	FAA Museum, stored Cobham Hall, RNAS Yeovilton	
XP150	WS58 Wessex HAS3 [LS]	FETC, Moreton-in-Marsh, Glos	
XP165	WS Scout AH1	The Helicopter Museum, Weston-super-Mare	
XP190	WS Scout AH1	South Yorkshire Aircraft Museum, Doncaster	
XP191	WS Scout AH1	Privately owned, Prenton, The Wirral	
XP226	Fairey Gannet AEW3	Newark Air Museum, Winthorpe	
XP241	Auster AOP9 (G-CEHR)	Privately owned, Spanhoe	
XP242	Auster AOP9 (G-BUCI)	AAC Historic Aircraft Flight, Middle Wallop	
XP244	Auster AOP9 (7864M/M7922)	Privately owned, Stretton on Dunsmore	
XP254	Auster AOP11 (G-ASCC)	Privately owned, Whittlesford, Cambs	
XP279	Auster AOP9 (G-BWKK)	Privately owned, stored Winchester	
XP280	Auster AOP9	Privately owned, stored Leics	
XP281	Auster AOP9	IWM, stored Duxford	
XP282	Auster AOP9 (G-BGTC)	Privately owned, Scampton	
XP286	Auster AOP9	Privately owned, South Molton, Devon	
XP299	WS55 Whirlwind HAR10 (8726M)	RAF Museum, Hendon	
XP328	WS55 Whirlwind HAR10 (G-BKHC)	Privately owned, Tattershall Thorpe (wreck)	
XP329	WS55 Whirlwind HAR10 (8791M) [V]	Privately owned, Tattershall Thorpe (wreck)	
XP330	WS55 Whirlwind HAR10	CAA Fire School, Durham/Tees Valley	
XP344	WS55 Whirlwind HAR10 (8764M) [H723]	RAF North Luffenham Training Area	
XP345	WS55 Whirlwind HAR10 (8792M) [UN]	Yorkshire Helicopter Preservation Group, Doncaster	
XP346	WS55 Whirlwind HAR10 (8793M)	Privately owned, Honeybourne, Worcs	
XP350	WS55 Whirlwind HAR10	Privately owned, Bassetts Pole, Staffs	
XP351	WS55 Whirlwind HAR10 (8672M) [Z]	Currently not known	
XP354	WS55 Whirlwind HAR10 (8721M)	Privately owned, Mullingar, Eire	
XP355	WS55 Whirlwind HAR10 (8463M/G-BEBC)	City of Norwich Aviation Museum	
XP360	WS55 Whirlwind HAR10 [V]	Privately owned, Bicton, nr Leominster	
XP398	WS55 Whirlwind HAR10 (8794M)	Currently not known	
XP404	WS55 Whirlwind HAR10 (8682M)	The Helicopter Museum, stored Weston-super-Mare	
XP411	AW660 Argosy C1 (8442M) [C]	RAF Museum, Cosford	
XP454	Slingsby T38 Grasshopper TX1	Privately owned, Sywell	
XP459	Slingsby T38 Grasshopper TX1	Privately owned, stored Nayland, Suffolk	
XP463	Slingsby T38 Grasshopper TX1 (frame)	Privately owned, Rufforth	
XP463	Slingsby T38 Grasshopper TX1 (BGA4372)	Privately owned, Lasham	
XP488	Slingsby T38 Grasshopper TX1	Privately owned, Keevil	
XP490	Slingsby T38 Grasshopper TX1 (BGA4552)	Privately owned, stored Watton	
XP492	Slingsby T38 Grasshopper TX1 (BGA3480)	Currently not known	
XP493	Slingsby T38 Grasshopper TX1	Privately owned, stored Aston Down	
XP494	Slingsby T38 Grasshopper TX1	Privately owned, stored Baxterley	
XP505	HS Gnat T1	Science Museum, stored Wroughton	
XP513	HS Gnat T1 (N513X)	Privately owned, North Weald	
XP516	HS Gnat T1 (8580M) [16]	Farnborough Air Sciences Trust, Farnborough	
XP540	HS Gnat T1 (8608M) [62]	Privately owned, Bruntingthorpe	
XP542	HS Gnat T1 (8575M)	No 424 Sqn ATC, Southampton	
XP556	Hunting Jet Provost T4 (9027M) [B]	RAF Cranwell Aviation Heritage Centre	

Notes	Serial	Type (code/other identity)	Owner/operator, location or fate
	XP557	Hunting Jet Provost T4 (8494M) [72]	Dumfries & Galloway Avn Mus, Dumfries
	XP558	Hunting Jet Provost T4 (8627M) <ff>	Privately owned, Stoneykirk, D&G
	XP558	Hunting Jet Provost T4 (8627M)[20] <rf>	Privately owned, Sproughton
	XP568	Hunting Jet Provost T4	East Midlands Airport Aeropark
	XP573	Hunting Jet Provost T4 (8236M) [19]	Jersey Airport Fire Section
	XP585	Hunting Jet Provost T4 (8407M) [24]	NE Wales Institute, Wrexham
	XP627	Hunting Jet Provost T4	North-East Aircraft Museum, stored Usworth
	XP629	Hunting Jet Provost T4 (9026M) [P]	Gunsmoke Paintball, Colchester, Essex
	XP640	Hunting Jet Provost T4 (8501M) [M]	Yorkshire Air Museum, Elvington
	XP642	Hunting Jet Provost T4 <ff>	Aerohub, Newquay
	XP672	Hunting Jet Provost T4 (8458M/G-RAFI) [03]	South Wales Aviation Museum, St Athan
	XP680	Hunting Jet Provost T4 (8460M)	FETC, Moreton-in-Marsh, Glos
	XP686	Hunting Jet Provost T4 (8401M/8502M) [G]	Gunsmoke Paintball, Colchester, Essex
	XP701	BAC Lightning F3 (8924M) <ff>	Robertsbridge Aviation Society, Mayfield
	XP703	BAC Lightning F3 <ff>	Lightning Preservation Group, Bruntingthorpe
	XP706	BAC Lightning F3 (8925M)	South Yorkshire Aircraft Museum, Doncaster
	XP743	BAC Lightning F3 <ff>	Wattisham Station Heritage Museum
	XP745	BAC Lightning F3 (8453M) <ff>	Vanguard Haulage, Greenford, London
	XP757	BAC Lightning F3 <ff>	Privately owned, Boston, Lincs
	XP765	BAC Lightning F6 (XS897) [A]	Lakes Lightnings, RAF Coningsby
	XP820	DHC2 Beaver AL1 (G-CICP)	Army Historic Aircraft Flight, Middle Wallop
	XP821	DHC2 Beaver AL1 [MCO]	Army Flying Museum, Middle Wallop
	XP822	DHC2 Beaver AL1	Army Flying Museum, Middle Wallop
	XP831	Hawker P.1127 (8406M)	Science Museum, South Kensington
	XP841	Handley-Page HP115	FAA Museum, RNAS Yeovilton
	XP847	WS Scout AH1	Army Flying Museum, Middle Wallop
	XP848	WS Scout AH1	Farnborough Air Sciences Trust, Farnborough
	XP849	WS Scout AH1 (XP895)	Museum of Berkshire Aviation, Woodley, Berks
	XP853	WS Scout AH1	Privately owned, Sutton, Surrey
	XP854	WS Scout AH1 (7898M/TAD 043)	Mayhem Paintball, Abridge, Essex
	XP855	WS Scout AH1	Privately owned, Arncott, Oxon
	XP883	WS Scout AH1	Currently not known
	XP883	WS Scout AH1 (XW281/G-BYNZ) [T]	Privately owned, Dungannon, NI
	XP884	WS Scout AH1	AAC, stored Middle Wallop
	XP885	WS Scout AH1	AAC Wattisham, instructional use
	XP886	WS Scout AH1	The Helicopter Museum, stored Weston-super-Mare
	XP888	WS Scout AH1	Privately owned, Sproughton
	XP890	WS Scout AH1 [G] (fuselage)	Privately owned, Ipswich
	XP899	WS Scout AH1	Boscombe Down Aviation Collection, Old Sarum
	XP900	WS Scout AH1	AAC Wattisham, instructional use
	XP902	WS Scout AH1 <ff>	South Yorkshire Aircraft Museum, Doncaster
	XP905	WS Scout AH1	Privately owned, stored Sproughton
	XP907	WS Scout AH1 (G-SROE)	Privately owned, Wattisham
	XP910	WS Scout AH1	Army Flying Museum, Middle Wallop
	XP924	DH110 Sea Vixen D3 (G-CVIX) [134/E]	Fly Navy Heritage Trust, Yeovilton
	XP925	DH110 Sea Vixen FAW2 [752] <ff>	Privately owned, Stoneykirk, D&G
	XP980	Hawker P.1127	FAA Museum, RNAS Yeovilton
	XP984	Hawker P.1127	Brooklands Museum, Weybridge
	XR220	BAC TSR2 (7933M)	RAF Museum, Cosford
	XR222	BAC TSR2	IWM Duxford
	XR232	Sud Alouette AH2 (F-WEIP)	Army Flying Museum, Middle Wallop
	XR239	Auster AOP9	Privately owned, Stretton on Dunsmore
	XR240	Auster AOP9 (G-BDFH)	Privately owned, Eggesford
	XR241	Auster AOP9 (G-AXRR)	Privately owned, Eggesford
	XR244	Auster AOP9 (G-CICR)	Army Historic Aircraft Flight, Middle Wallop
	XR246	Auster AOP9 (7862M/G-AZBU)	Privately owned, Melton Mowbray
	XR267	Auster AOP9 (G-BJXR)	Privately owned, Hucknall
	XR271	Auster AOP9	Privately owned, stored Wroughton
	XR346	Northrop Shelduck D1 (comp XW578)	Bournemouth Aviation Museum
	XR371	SC5 Belfast C1	RAF Museum, Cosford
	XR379	Sud Alouette AH2 (2-ALOU)	Repainted as 2-ALOU

Serial	Type (code/other identity)	Owner/operator, location or fate	Notes
XR447	Northrop Shelduck D1 (wreck)	Morayvia, Kinloss	
XR453	WS55 Whirlwind HAR10 (8873M) [A]	RAF Odiham, on gate	
XR458	WS55 Whirlwind HAR10 (8662M) [H]	*Scrapped at Irthlingborough, 22 February 2019*	
XR485	WS55 Whirlwind HAR10 [Q]	Norfolk & Suffolk Avn Museum, Flixton	
XR486	WS55 Whirlwind HCC12 (8727M/G-RWWW)	The Helicopter Museum, Weston-super-Mare	
XR498	WS58 Wessex HC2 (9342M)	DSAE Cosford, on display	
XR503	WS58 Wessex HC2	MoD DFTDC, Manston	
XR506	WS58 Wessex HC2 (9343M) [V]	Privately owned, Corley Moor, Warks	
XR516	WS58 Wessex HC2 (9319M) [V]	RAF Shawbury, on display	
XR517	WS58 Wessex HC2 [N]	Ulster Aviation Society, Long Kesh	
XR523	WS58 Wessex HC2 [M]	MoD Pembrey Sands Air Weapons Range, GI use	
XR525	WS58 Wessex HC2 [G]	RAF Museum, Cosford	
XR526	WS58 Wessex HC2 (8147M)	The Helicopter Museum, stored Weston-super-Mare	
XR528	WS58 Wessex HC2	Morayvia, Kinloss	
XR529	WS58 Wessex HC2 (9268M) [E]	Ulster Aviation Society, Long Kesh	
XR534	HS Gnat T1 (8578M) [65]	Newark Air Museum, Winthorpe	
XR537	HS Gnat T1 (8642M/G-NATY)	Privately owned, North Weald	
XR538	HS Gnat T1 (8621M/G-RORI) [01]	Heritage Aircraft Trust, North Weald	
XR540	HS Gnat T1 (XP502/8576M) [2]	Privately owned, Cotswold Airport	
XR571	HS Gnat T1 (8493M)	RAF Scampton Heritage Centre	
XR574	HS Gnat T1 (8631M) [72]	Trenchard Museum, Halton	
XR595	WS Scout AH1 (G-BWHU) [M]	Privately owned, North Weald	
XR601	WS Scout AH1	Privately owned, Sproughton	
XR627	WS Scout AH1 [X]	Privately owned, Storwood, Yorkshire	
XR628	WS Scout AH1	Privately owned, Ipswich	
XR629	WS Scout AH1 (fuselage)	Privately owned, Ipswich	
XR635	WS Scout AH1	Midland Air Museum, Coventry	
XR650	Hunting Jet Provost T4 (8459M) [28]	Boscombe Down Aviation Collection, Old Sarum	
XR654	Hunting Jet Provost T4 <ff>	Privately owned, Chester	
XR658	Hunting Jet Provost T4 (8192M)	RAF Manston History Museum	
XR662	Hunting Jet Provost T4 (8410M) [25]	Privately owned, Gilberdyke, E Yorks	
XR673	Hunting Jet Provost T4 (G-BXLO/9032M) [L]	Privately owned, Gamston	
XR681	Hunting Jet Provost T4 (8588M) <ff>	Robertsbridge Aviation Society, Mayfield	
XR700	Hunting Jet Provost T4 (8589M) <ff>	No 1137 Sqn ATC, Aldergrove	
XR713	BAC Lightning F3 (8935M) [C]	Lightning Preservation Grp, Bruntingthorpe	
	(wears *XR718* on starboard side)		
XR718	BAC Lightning F6 (8932M) [DA]	Privately owned, Over Dinsdale, N Yorks	
XR724	BAC Lightning F6 (G-BTSY)	The Lightning Association, Binbrook	
XR725	BAC Lightning F6	Privately owned, Binbrook	
XR726	BAC Lightning F6 <ff>	Privately owned, Harrogate	
XR728	BAC Lightning F6 [JS]	Lightning Preservation Grp, Bruntingthorpe	
XR747	BAC Lightning F6 <ff>	No 20 Sqn ATC, Bideford, Devon	
XR749	BAC Lightning F3 (8934M) [DA]	Privately owned, Peterhead	
XR751	BAC Lightning F3 <ff>	Privately owned, Thorpe Wood, N Yorks	
XR753	BAC Lightning F6 (8969M) [XI]	RAF Coningsby on display	
XR753	BAC Lightning F53 (ZF578) [A]	Tangmere Military Aviation Museum	
XR754	BAC Lightning F6 (8972M) <ff>	Privately owned, Upwood, Cambs	
XR755	BAC Lightning F6	Privately owned, Callington, Cornwall	
XR757	BAC Lightning F6 <ff>	Newark Air Museum, Winthorpe	
XR759	BAC Lightning F6 <ff>	Privately owned, Haxey, Lincs	
XR768	BAC Lightning F53 (53-672/204/ZF580) [A]	Aerohub, Newquay	
XR770	BAC Lightning F6 [AA]	RAF Manston History Museum	
XR771	BAC Lightning F6 [BF]	Midland Air Museum, Coventry	
XR806	BAC VC10 C1K (9285M) <ff>	RAF Brize Norton, BDRT	
XR808	BAC VC10 C1K [R] $	RAF Museum, Cosford	
XR810	BAC VC10 C1K <ff>	Privately owned, Crondall, Hants	
XR944	Wallis WA116 (G-ATTB)	Privately owned, Old Buckenham	
XR977	HS Gnat T1 (8640M)	RAF Museum, Hendon	
XR992	HS Gnat T1 (8624M/XS102/G-MOUR)	Heritage Aircraft Trust, North Weald	
XR993	HS Gnat T1 (8620M/XP534/G-BVPP)	Privately owned, Bruntingthorpe	
XS100	HS Gnat T1 (8561M) <ff>	Privately owned, stored Wimbledon	

Notes	Serial	Type (code/other identity)	Owner/operator, location or fate
	XS100	HS Gnat T1 (8561M) <rf>	Privately owned, North Weald
	XS104	HS Gnat T1 (8604M/G-FRCE)	Privately owned, North Weald
	XS149	WS58 Wessex HAS3 [661/GL]	The Helicopter Museum, Weston-super-Mare
	XS176	Hunting Jet Provost T4 (8514M) <ff>	Privately owned, Kinloss
	XS177	Hunting Jet Provost T4 (9044M) [N]	Privately owned, Gilberdyke, E Yorks
	XS179	Hunting Jet Provost T4 (8237M) [20]	Secret Nuclear Bunker, Hack Green, Cheshire
	XS180	Hunting Jet Provost T4 (8238M/8338M) [21]	MoD JARTS, Boscombe Down
	XS181	Hunting Jet Provost T4 (9033M) <ff>	Lakes Lightnings, Spark Bridge, Cumbria
	XS183	Hunting Jet Provost T4 <ff>	Privately owned, Plymouth
	XS186	Hunting Jet Provost T4 (8408M) [M]	Metheringham Airfield Visitors Centre
	XS209	Hunting Jet Provost T4 (8409M)	Solway Aviation Society, Carlisle
	XS216	Hunting Jet Provost T4 <ff>	South Yorkshire Aircraft Museum, Doncaster
	XS218	Hunting Jet Provost T4 (8508M) <ff>	No 447 Sqn ATC, Henley-on-Thames, Berks
	XS231	BAC Jet Provost T5 (G-ATAJ)	Boscombe Down Aviation Collection, Old Sarum
	XS235	DH106 Comet 4C (G-CPDA)	Cold War Jets Collection, Bruntingthorpe
	XS238	Auster AOP9 (TAD 200)	Newark Air Museum, Winthorpe
	XS416	BAC Lightning T5	Privately owned, New York, Lincs
	XS417	BAC Lightning T5 [DZ]	Newark Air Museum, Winthorpe
	XS420	BAC Lightning T5	Privately owned, FAST, Farnborough
	XS421	BAC Lightning T5 <ff>	Privately owned, Foulness
	XS456	BAC Lightning T5 [DX]	Skegness Water Leisure Park
	XS457	BAC Lightning T5 <ff>	Privately owned, Binbrook
	XS458	BAC Lightning T5 [T]	T5 Projects, Cranfield
	XS459	BAC Lightning T5 [AW]	Fenland & W Norfolk Aviation Museum, Wisbech
	XS481	WS58 Wessex HU5	South Yorkshire Aircraft Museum, Doncaster
	XS482	WS58 Wessex HU5	RAF Manston History Museum
	XS486	WS58 Wessex HU5 (9272M) [524/CU,F]	The Helicopter Museum, Weston-super-Mare
	XS488	WS58 Wessex HU5 (9056M) [F]	Privately owned, Tiptree, Essex
	XS489	WS58 Wessex HU5 [R]	Privately owned, Westerham, Kent
	XS493	WS58 Wessex HU5	StandardAero, stored Fleetlands
	XS507	WS58 Wessex HU5	RAF Benson, for display
	XS508	WS58 Wessex HU5	FAA Museum, RNAS Yeovilton
	XS510	WS58 Wessex HU5 [626/PO]	No 1414 Sqn ATC, Crowborough, Sussex
	XS511	WS58 Wessex HU5 [M]	Tangmere Military Aircraft Museum
	XS513	WS58 Wessex HU5	RNAS Yeovilton Fire Section
	XS515	WS58 Wessex HU5 [N]	Army, Keogh Barracks, Aldershot, instructional use
	XS516	WS58 Wessex HU5 [Q]	Privately owned, Redruth, Cornwall
	XS520	WS58 Wessex HU5 [F]	*Currently not known*
	XS522	WS58 Wessex HU5 [ZL]	Blackball Paintball, Truro, Cornwall
	XS527	WS Wasp HAS1	FAA Museum, stored Cobham Hall, RNAS Yeovilton
	XS529	WS Wasp HAS1	Privately owned, Redruth, Cornwall
	XS539	WS Wasp HAS1 [435]	StandardAero Fleetlands Apprentice School
	XS567	WS Wasp HAS1 [434/E]	IWM Duxford
	XS568	WS Wasp HAS1 (A2715) [441]	DSAE RNAESS, *HMS Sultan*, Gosport
	XS574	Northrop Shelduck D1 <R>	FAA Museum, stored Cobham Hall, RNAS Yeovilton
	XS576	DH110 Sea Vixen FAW2 [125/E]	IWM Duxford
	XS587	DH110 Sea Vixen FAW(TT)2 (8828M/G-VIXN)	Gatwick Aviation Museum, Charlwood, Surrey
	XS590	DH110 Sea Vixen FAW2 [131/E]	FAA Museum, RNAS Yeovilton
	XS639	HS Andover E3A (9241M)	RAF Museum, Cosford
	XS641	HS Andover C1PR (9198M) (fuselage)	Privately owned, Sandbach, Cheshire
	XS643	HS Andover E3A (9278M) <ff>	Privately owned, Dudley, W Mids
	XS646	HS Andover C1(mod) (fuselage)	MoD JARTS, Boscombe Down
	XS651	Slingsby T45 Swallow TX1 (BGA1211) [BYB]	Privately owned, Lasham
	XS652	Slingsby T45 Swallow TX1 (BGA1107)	Privately owned, Chipping, Lancs
	XS674	WS58 Wessex HC2 [R]	Privately owned, Biggin Hill
	XS695	HS Kestrel FGA1 [5]	RAF Museum, Cosford
	XS709	HS125 Dominie T1 [M]	RAF Museum, Cosford
	XS710	HS125 Dominie T1 (9259M) [O]	RAF Cranwell Fire Section
	XS713	HS125 Dominie T1 [C]	RAF Shawbury Fire Section
	XS714	HS125 Dominie T1 (9246M) [P]	MoD DFTDC, Manston
	XS726	HS125 Dominie T1 (9273M) [T]	Newark Air Museum, Winthorpe
	XS727	HS125 Dominie T1 [D]	RAF Cranwell, on display

Serial	Type (code/other identity)	Owner/operator, location or fate	Notes
XS731	HS125 Dominie T1 (N19XY) (fuselage)	Privately owned, Marlborough, Wilts	
XS734	HS125 Dominie T1 (9260M) [N]	Privately owned, Sproughton	
XS735	HS125 Dominie T1 (9264M) [R]	South Yorkshire Aircraft Museum, Doncaster	
XS736	HS125 Dominie T1 [S]	MoD Winterbourne Gunner, Wilts	
XS738	HS125 Dominie T1 (9274M) [U]	RN, Predannack Fire School	
XS743	Beagle B206Z	QinetiQ Apprentice Training School, Boscombe Down	
XS765	Beagle B206 Basset CC1 (G-BSET)	QinetiQ Apprentice Training School, Boscombe Down	
XS770	Beagle B206 Basset CC1 (G-HRHI)	*Currently not known*	
XS790	HS748 Andover CC2 <ff>	Boscombe Down Aviation Collection, Old Sarum	
XS791	HS748 Andover CC2 (fuselage)	Privately owned, Stock, Essex	
XS859	Slingsby T45 Swallow TX1 (BGA1136) [859]	Privately owned, stored Felthorpe	
XS863	WS58 Wessex HAS1 [304/R]	IWM Duxford	
XS865	WS58 Wessex HAS1 (A2694)	Privately owned, Ballygowan, NI	
XS885	WS58 Wessex HAS1 [512/DD]	Delta Force Paintball, Burnley	
XS886	WS58 Wessex HAS1 [527/CU]	Privately owned, Ditchling, E Sussex	
XS887	WS58 Wessex HAS1 [403/FI]	South Yorkshire Aircraft Museum, Doncaster	
XS888	WS58 Wessex HAS1 [521]	*Scrapped at Guernsey, 2018*	
XS898	BAC Lightning F6 <ff>	Privately owned, Lavendon, Bucks	
XS899	BAC Lightning F6 <ff>	Privately owned, Binbrook	
XS903	BAC Lightning F6 [BA]	Yorkshire Air Museum, Elvington	
XS904	BAC Lightning F6 [BQ]	Lightning Preservation Grp, Bruntingthorpe	
XS919	BAC Lightning F6	Privately owned,	
XS921	BAC Lightning F6 <R> [BA]	BAE Systems, Samlesbury, on display	
XS922	BAC Lightning F6 (8973M) <ff>	Lakes Lightnings, Spark Bridge, Cumbria	
XS923	BAC Lightning F6 <ff>	Privately owned, Welshpool	
XS925	BAC Lightning F6 (8961M) [BA]	RAF Museum, Hendon	
XS928	BAC Lightning F6 [AD]	BAE Systems Warton, on display	
XS932	BAC Lightning F6 <ff>	Privately owned, Walcott, Lincs	
XS933	BAC Lightning F6 <ff>	Privately owned, Farnham	
XS933	BAC Lightning F53 (ZF594) [BE]	North-East Aircraft Museum, Usworth	
XS936	BAC Lightning F6	Castle Motors, Liskeard, Cornwall	
XT005	Northrop Shelduck D1 (XR898)	Boscombe Down Aviation Collection, Old Sarum	
XT108	Agusta-Bell 47G-3 Sioux AH1 [U]	Army Flying Museum, Middle Wallop	
XT123	WS Sioux AH1 (XT827) [D]	AAC Middle Wallop, at main gate	
XT131	Agusta-Bell 47G-3 Sioux AH1 (G-CICN) [B]	Army Historic Aircraft Flight, Middle Wallop	
XT140	Agusta-Bell 47G-3 Sioux AH1	Privately owned, Malmesbury	
XT148	Agusta-Bell 47G-3 Sioux AH1	North-East Aircraft Museum, Usworth	
XT150	Agusta-Bell 47G-3 Sioux AH1 (7883M) [R]	South Yorkshire Aircraft Museum, stored Doncaster	
XT151	WS Sioux AH1	Army Flying Museum, stored Middle Wallop	
XT176	WS Sioux AH1 [U]	FAA Museum, stored Cobham Hall, RNAS Yeovilton	
XT190	WS Sioux AH1	The Helicopter Museum, Weston-super-Mare	
XT200	WS Sioux AH1 [F]	Newark Air Museum, Winthorpe	
XT208	WS Sioux AH1 (wreck)	Privately owned, Fivemiletown, Co Tyrone, NI	
XT236	WS Sioux AH1 (frame only)	Privately owned, Cheshire	
XT242	WS Sioux AH1 (composite) [12]	South Yorkshire Aircraft Museum, Doncaster	
XT257	WS58 Wessex HAS3 (8719M)	Bournemouth Aviation Museum	
XT277	HS Buccaneer S2A (8853M) <ff>	Privately owned, Welshpool	
XT280	HS Buccaneer S2A <ff>	Dumfries & Galloway Avn Mus, Dumfries	
XT284	HS Buccaneer S2A (8855M) <ff>	Privately owned, Felixstowe	
XT288	HS Buccaneer S2B (9134M)	National Museum of Flight, E Fortune	
XT420	WS Wasp HAS1 (G-CBUI) [606]	Privately owned, Yeovilton	
XT427	WS Wasp HAS1 [606]	FAA Museum, stored Cobham Hall, RNAS Yeovilton	
XT431	WS Wasp HAS1 (comp XS463) [462]	Bournemouth Aviation Museum	
XT434	WS Wasp HAS1 (G-CGGK) [455]	Privately owned, Breighton	
XT435	WS Wasp HAS1 (NZ3907/G-RIMM) [430]	Privately owned, Badwell Green, Suffolk	
XT437	WS Wasp HAS1 [423]	Boscombe Down Aviation Collection, Old Sarum	
XT439	WS Wasp HAS1 [605]	Privately owned, Hemel Hempstead	
XT443	WS Wasp HAS1 [422/AU]	The Helicopter Museum, Weston-super-Mare	
XT453	WS58 Wessex HU5 (A2756) [B/PO]	DSAE, stored *HMS Sultan*, Gosport	
XT455	WS58 Wessex HU5 (A2654) [U]	Mayhem Paintball, Abridge, Essex	
XT456	WS58 Wessex HU5 (8941M) [XZ]	Belfast Airport Fire Section	

Notes	Serial	Type (code/other identity)	Owner/operator, location or fate
	XT466	WS58 Wessex HU5 (A2617/8921M) [528/CU]	Morayvia, Kinloss
	XT467	WS58 Wessex HU5 (8922M) [BF]	Gunsmoke Paintball, Hadleigh, Suffolk
	XT469	WS58 Wessex HU5 (8920M)	Privately owned, Clatterford, Isle of Wight
	XT472	WS58 Wessex HU5 [XC]	The Helicopter Museum, stored Weston-super-Mare
	XT480	WS58 Wessex HU5 [468/RG]	Rednal Paintball, Shropshire
	XT482	WS58 Wessex HU5 [ZM/VL]	FAA Museum, RNAS Yeovilton
	XT486	WS58 Wessex HU5 (8919M)	Dumfries & Galloway Avn Mus, Dumfries
	XT550	WS Sioux AH1 [D]	Currently not known
	XT575	Vickers Viscount 837 <ff>	Brooklands Museum, Weybridge
	XT581	Northrop Shelduck D1	Muckleburgh Collection, Weybourne, Norfolk
	XT583	Northrop Shelduck D1	Privately owned, stored Wroughton
	XT596	McD F-4K Phantom FG1	FAA Museum, RNAS Yeovilton
	XT597	McD F-4K Phantom FG1	Privately owned, Bentwaters
	XT601	WS58 Wessex HC2 (9277M) (composite)	RAF Odiham, BDRT
	XT604	WS58 Wessex HC2	East Midlands Airport Aeropark
	XT617	WS Scout AH1	Wattisham Station Heritage Museum
	XT621	WS Scout AH1	Defence Academy of the UK, Shrivenham
	XT623	WS Scout AH1	DSAE SAAE, Lyneham
	XT626	WS Scout AH1 (G-CIBW) [Q]	Army Historic Aircraft Flt, Middle Wallop
	XT630	WS Scout AH1 (G-BXRL) [X]	Privately owned, Rough Close, Staffs
	XT631	WS Scout AH1 [D]	Privately owned, Ipswich
	XT633	WS Scout AH1	Privately owned, Barton Ashes, Hants
	XT634	WS Scout AH1 (G-BYRX) [T]	Privately owned, North Weald
	XT638	WS Scout AH1 [N]	AAC Middle Wallop, at main gate
	XT640	WS Scout AH1	Privately owned, Sproughton
	XT643	WS Scout AH1	Army, Thorpe Camp, East Wretham (wreck)
	XT653	Slingsby T45 Swallow TX1 (BGA3469)	Privately owned, Oakhill, Somerset
	XT672	WS58 Wessex HC2 [WE]	RAF Stafford, on display
	XT681	WS58 Wessex HC2 (9279M) [U] <ff>	Privately owned, Wallingford, Oxon
	XT761	WS58 Wessex HU5 (G-WSEX)	Privately owned, Chard, Somerset
	XT762	WS58 Wessex HU5	Hamburger Hill Paintball, Marksbury, Somerset
	XT765	WS58 Wessex HU5 [J]	FAA Museum, stored Cobham Hall, RNAS Yeovilton
	XT765	WS58 Wessex HU5 (XT458/A2768) [P/VL]	RNAS Yeovilton, on display
	XT769	WS58 Wessex HU5 [823]	FAA Museum, RNAS Yeovilton
	XT771	WS58 Wessex HU5 [620/PO]	Privately owned, Chard, Somerset
	XT773	WS58 Wessex HU5 (9123M)	RAF Shawbury Fire Section
	XT778	WS Wasp HAS1 [430]	FAA Museum, stored Cobham Hall, RNAS Yeovilton
	XT780	WS Wasp HAS1 [636]	CEMAST, Fareham College, Lee-on-Solent
	XT787	WS Wasp HAS1 (NZ3905/G-KAXT)	Westland Wasp Historic Flt, Barton Ashes, Hants
	XT788	WS Wasp HAS1 (G-BMIR) [474]	Privately owned, Storwood, Yorkshire
	XT793	WS Wasp HAS1 (G-BZPP) [456] <ff>	Boscombe Down Aviation Collection, Old Sarum (spares use)
	XT863	McD F-4K Phantom FG1 <ff>	Privately owned, Cowes, IOW
	XT864	McD F-4K Phantom FG1 (8998M/XT684) [007/R]	Ulster Aviation Society, Long Kesh
	XT891	McD F-4M Phantom FGR2 (9136M)	RAF Coningsby, at main gate
	XT903	McD F-4M Phantom FGR2 <ff>	RAF Museum, stored Cosford
	XT905	McD F-4M Phantom FGR2 (9286M) [P]	Privately owned, Bentwaters
	XT907	McD F-4M Phantom FGR2 (9151M) [W]	Privately owned, Bentwaters
	XT914	McD F-4M Phantom FGR2 (9269M) [Z]	Wattisham Station Heritage Museum
	XV104	BAC VC10 C1K <ff>	South Wales Aviation Museum, St Athan
	XV106	BAC VC10 C1K <ff>	Avro Heritage Museum, Woodford
	XV108	BAC VC10 C1K <ff>	East Midlands Airport Aeropark
	XV109	BAC VC10 C1K <ff>	South Wales Aviation Museum, St Athan
	XV118	WS Scout AH1 (9141M) <ff>	Kennet Aviation, North Weald
	XV122	WS Scout AH1 [D]	Defence Academy of the UK, Shrivenham
	XV123	WS Scout AH1	Privately owned, Sproughton
	XV124	WS Scout AH1 [W]	Privately owned, Godstone, Surrey
	XV127	WS Scout AH1	Army Flying Museum, Middle Wallop
	XV130	WS Scout AH1 (G-BWJW) [R]	Privately owned, North Weald
	XV136	WS Scout AH1 [X]	Ulster Aviation Society, Long Kesh
	XV137	WS Scout AH1 (G-CRUM)	Privately owned, Chiseldon, Wilts

Serial	Type (code/other identity)	Owner/operator, location or fate	Notes
XV137	WS Scout AH1 (XV139)	South Yorkshire Aircraft Museum, stored Doncaster	
XV138	WS Scout AH1 (G-SASM) [S]	Privately owned, North Weald	
XV139	WS Scout AH1 (comp XP886)	South Yorkshire Aircraft Museum, Doncaster	
XV141	WS Scout AH1	REME Museum, Lyneham	
XV148	HS Nimrod MR1(mod) <ff>	Privately owned, Malmesbury	
XV161	HS Buccaneer S2B (9117M) <ff>	Dundonald Aviation Centre	
XV165	HS Buccaneer S2B <ff>	Privately owned, Ashford, Kent	
XV168	HS Buccaneer S2B [AF]	Yorkshire Air Museum, Elvington	
XV177	Lockheed C-130K Hercules C3A [177]	RAF, St Athan (wfu)	
XV188	Lockheed C-130K Hercules C3A [188]	RAF, St Athan (wfu)	
XV200	Lockheed C-130K Hercules C1 [200]	RAF, St Athan (wfu)	
XV201	Lockheed C-130K Hercules C1K <ff>	Marshalls, Cambridge	
XV202	Lockheed C-130K Hercules C3 [202]	RAF Museum, Cosford	
XV208	Lockheed C-130K Hercules W2 <ff>	Marshalls, Cambridge	
XV209	Lockheed C-130K Hercules C3A [209]	RAF, St Athan (wfu)	
XV221	Lockheed C-130K Hercules C3 <ff>	Privately owned, White Waltham	
XV226	HS Nimrod MR2 $	Cold War Jets Collection, Bruntingthorpe	
XV229	HS Nimrod MR2 [29]	MoD DFTDC, Manston	
XV231	HS Nimrod MR2 [31]	Aviation Viewing Park, Manchester	
XV232	HS Nimrod MR2 [32]	Privately owned, Coventry	
XV235	HS Nimrod MR2 [35] <ff>	Avro Heritage Museum, Woodford	
XV240	HS Nimrod MR2 [40] <ff>	Morayvia, Kinloss	
XV241	HS Nimrod MR2 [41] <ff>	National Museum of Flight, E Fortune	
XV244	HS Nimrod MR2 [44]	Morayvia, RAF Kinloss	
XV249	HS Nimrod R1 $	RAF Museum, Cosford	
XV250	HS Nimrod MR2 [50]	Yorkshire Air Museum, Elvington	
XV252	HS Nimrod MR2 [52] <ff>	Privately owned, Cullen, Moray	
XV254	HS Nimrod MR2 [54] <ff>	Highland Aviation Museum, Inverness	
XV255	HS Nimrod MR2 [55]	City of Norwich Aviation Museum	
XV259	BAe Nimrod AEW3 <ff>	Privately owned, Wales	
XV263	BAe Nimrod AEW3P (8967M) <ff>	BAE Systems, Brough	
XV263	BAe Nimrod AEW3P (8967M) <rf>	MoD/BAE Systems, Woodford	
XV268	DHC2 Beaver AL1 (G-BVER)	Privately owned, Cumbernauld	
XV277	HS P.1127(RAF)	National Museum of Flight, E Fortune	
XV279	HS P.1127(RAF) (8566M)	Harrier Heritage Centre, RAF Wittering	
XV280	HS P.1127(RAF) <ff>	South Yorkshire Aviation Museum, Doncaster	
XV281	HS P.1127(RAF) (BAPC 484)	South Yorkshire Aviation Museum, Doncaster	
XV302	Lockheed C-130K Hercules C3 [302]	Marshalls, Cambridge, fatigue test airframe	
XV304	Lockheed C-130K Hercules C3A	RAF JADTEU, Brize Norton, instructional use	
XV328	BAC Lightning T5 <ff>	Lightning Preservation Group, Bruntingthorpe	
XV333	HS Buccaneer S2B [234/H]	FAA Museum, RNAS Yeovilton	
XV344	HS Buccaneer S2C	QinetiQ Farnborough, on display	
XV350	HS Buccaneer S2B	East Midlands Airport Aeropark	
XV352	HS Buccaneer S2B <ff>	RAF Manston History Museum	
XV359	HS Buccaneer S2B [035/R]	Privately owned, Topsham, Devon	
XV361	HS Buccaneer S2B	Ulster Aviation Society, Long Kesh	
XV370	Sikorsky SH-3D (A2682) [260]	DSAE RNAESS, *HMS Sultan*, Gosport	
XV371	WS61 Sea King HAS1(DB) [61/DD]	RN, Predannack Fire School	
XV372	WS61 Sea King HAS1	MoD Pembrey Sands Air Weapons Range, GI use	
XV383	Northrop MQM-57A/3 (fuselage)	Privately owned, Wimborne, Dorset	
XV401	McD F-4M Phantom FGR2 [I]	Privately owned, Bentwaters	
XV402	McD F-4M Phantom FGR2 <ff>	Privately owned, Kent	
XV406	McD F-4M Phantom FGR2 (9098M) [CK]	Solway Aviation Society, Carlisle	
XV408	McD F-4M Phantom FGR2 (9165M) [Z]	Tangmere Military Aviation Museum	
XV411	McD F-4M Phantom FGR2 (9103M) [L]	MoD DFTDC, Manston	
XV415	McD F-4M Phantom FGR2 (9163M) [E]	RAF Boulmer, on display	
XV424	McD F-4M Phantom FGR2 (9152M) [I]	RAF Museum, Hendon	
XV426	McD F-4M Phantom FGR2 <ff>	City of Norwich Aviation Museum	
XV426	McD F-4M Phantom FGR2 [P] <rf>	RAF Coningsby, BDRT	
XV460	McD F-4M Phantom FGR2 <ff>	Privately owned, Bentwaters	
XV474	McD F-4M Phantom FGR2 [T]	The Old Flying Machine Company, Duxford	
XV490	McD F-4M Phantom FGR2 [R] <ff>	Newark Air Museum, Winthorpe	

Notes	Serial	Type (code/other identity)	Owner/operator, location or fate
	XV497	McD F-4M Phantom FGR2 (9295M) [D]	Privately owned, Bentwaters
	XV499	McD F-4M Phantom FGR2 <ff>	South Wales Aviation Museum, St Athan
	XV581	McD F-4K Phantom FG1 (9070M) <ff>	Staffordshire Wing ATC Aerospace & Technology Centre
	XV582	McD F-4K Phantom FG1 (9066M) [M]	South Wales Aviation Museum, St Athan
	XV586	McD F-4K Phantom FG1 (9067M) [010-R]	Privately owned, RNAS Yeovilton
	XV591	McD F-4K Phantom FG1 [013] <ff>	RAF Museum, Cosford
	XV631	WS Wasp HAS1 (fuselage)	Farnborough Air Sciences Trust, stored Farnborough
	XV642	WS61 Sea King HAS2A (A2614) [259]	DSAE RNAESS, HMS Sultan, Gosport
	XV643	WS61 Sea King HAS6 [262]	DSAE RNAESS, HMS Sultan, Gosport
	XV647	WS61 Sea King HU5 [28]	DSAE RNAESS, HMS Sultan, Gosport
	XV648	WS61 Sea King HU5 [18/CU]	Privately owned, Acharacle, Argyll
	XV649	WS61 Sea King ASaC7 [180]	DSAE, stored HMS Sultan, Gosport
	XV651	WS61 Sea King HU5	Mini Moos Farm, Edmondsley, Durham
	XV653	WS61 Sea King HAS6 (9326M) [63/CU]	DSAE No 1 SoTT, Cosford
	XV654	WS61 Sea King HAS6 [705/DD] (wreck)	RN, Predannack Fire School
	XV655	WS61 Sea King HAS6 [270/N]	DSAE RNAESS, HMS Sultan, Gosport
	XV656	WS61 Sea King ASaC7 [185]	DSAE, stored HMS Sultan, Gosport
	XV657	WS61 Sea King HAS5 (ZA135) [32/DD]	RN, Predannack Fire School
	XV659	WS61 Sea King HAS6 (9324M) [62/CU]	DSAE No 1 SoTT, Cosford
	XV660	WS61 Sea King HAS6 [269/N]	DSAE RNAESS, HMS Sultan, Gosport
	XV661	WS61 Sea King HU5 [26]	Privately owned, Colsterworth
	XV663	WS61 Sea King HAS6 [18]	FAA Museum, RNAS Yeovilton
	XV664	WS61 Sea King ASaC7 [190]	DSAE, stored HMS Sultan, Gosport
	XV665	WS61 Sea King HAS6 [507/CU]	DSAE RNAESS, HMS Sultan, Gosport
	XV666	WS61 Sea King HU5	HeliOperations Ltd, Portland
	XV670	WS61 Sea King HU5 [17]	DSAE, stored HMS Sultan, Gosport
	XV671	WS61 Sea King ASaC7 [183/CU]	DSAE, stored HMS Sultan, Gosport
	XV672	WS61 Sea King ASaC7 [187]	DSAE, stored HMS Sultan, Gosport
	XV673	WS61 Sea King HU5 [827/CU]	RN Culdrose, on display
	XV674	WS61 Sea King HAS6	Privately owned, Horsham
	XV675	WS61 Sea King HAS6 [701/PW]	DSAE RNAESS, HMS Sultan, Gosport
	XV676	WS61 Sea King HC6 [ZE]	DSAE RNAESS, HMS Sultan, Gosport
	XV677	WS61 Sea King HAS6 [269]	South Yorkshire Aircraft Museum, Doncaster
	XV696	WS61 Sea King HAS6 [267/L]	SFDO, RNAS Culdrose
	XV697	WS61 Sea King ASaC7 [181/CU]	DSAE, stored HMS Sultan, Gosport
	XV699	WS61 Sea King HU5 [823/PW]	DSAE RNAESS, HMS Sultan, Gosport
	XV700	WS61 Sea King HC6 [ZC]	RAF St Mawgan, instructional use
	XV701	WS61 Sea King HAS6 [268/N,64]	DSAE RNAESS, HMS Sultan, Gosport
	XV703	WS61 Sea King HC6 [ZD]	DSAE RNAESS, HMS Sultan, Gosport
	XV705	WS61 Sea King HU5 [29]	Privately owned, Colsterworth, Leics
	XV706	WS61 Sea King HAS6 (9344M) [017/L]	DSAE RNAESS, HMS Sultan, Gosport
	XV707	WS61 Sea King ASaC7 [184]	DSAE, stored HMS Sultan, Gosport
	XV708	WS61 Sea King HAS6 [501/CU]	DSAE RNAESS, HMS Sultan, Gosport
	XV709	WS61 Sea King HAS6 (9303M)	MoD/QinetiQ, Boscombe Down
	XV711	WS61 Sea King HAS6 [15/CW]	DSAE, stored HMS Sultan, Gosport
	XV712	WS61 Sea King HAS6 [66]	IWM Duxford
	XV713	WS61 Sea King HAS6 (A2646) [018/L]	DSAE RNAESS, HMS Sultan, Gosport
	XV714	WS61 Sea King ASaC7 [188]	DSAE, stored HMS Sultan, Gosport
	XV720	WS58 Wessex HC2 (A2701)	Privately owned, Culham, Oxon
	XV722	WS58 Wessex HC2 (8805M) [WH]	Privately owned, Badgers Mount, Kent
	XV724	WS58 Wessex HC2	DSAE RNAESS, HMS Sultan, Gosport
	XV725	WS58 Wessex HC2 [C]	MoD DFTDC, Manston
	XV726	WS58 Wessex HC2 [J]	Privately owned, Biggin Hill
	XV728	WS58 Wessex HC2 [A]	Newark Air Museum, Winthorpe
	XV731	WS58 Wessex HC2 [Y]	Privately owned, Badgers Mount, Kent
	XV732	WS58 Wessex HCC4	RAF Museum, Hendon
	XV733	WS58 Wessex HCC4	The Helicopter Museum, Weston-super-Mare
	XV741	HS Harrier GR3 (A2608)	Privately owned, Thorpe Wood, N Yorks
	XV744	HS Harrier GR3 (9167M) [3K]	Tangmere Military Aviation Museum
	XV748	HS Harrier GR3 [3D]	Yorkshire Air Museum, Elvington
	XV751	HS Harrier GR3 [AU]	Gatwick Aviation Museum, Charlwood, Surrey

Serial	Type (code/other identity)	Owner/operator, location or fate	Notes
XV752	HS Harrier GR3 (9075M) [B]	South Yorkshire Aircraft Museum, Doncaster	
XV753	HS Harrier GR3 (9078M) [53/DD]	Aerohub, Newquay	
XV759	HS Harrier GR3 [O] <ff>	Privately owned, Hitchin, Herts	
XV760	HS Harrier GR3 <ff>	Solent Sky, Southampton	
XV779	HS Harrier GR3 (8931M)	Harrier Heritage Centre, RAF Wittering	
XV783	HS Harrier GR3 [83/DD]	Privately owned, Corley Moor, Warks	
XV784	HS Harrier GR3 (8909M) <ff>	Boscombe Down Aviation Collection, Old Sarum	
XV786	HS Harrier GR3 [123] <ff>	RNAS Culdrose Fire Section	
XV786	HS Harrier GR3 [S] <rf>	RN, Predannack Fire School	
XV798	HS Harrier GR1(mod) (BAPC 450)	The Helicopter Museum, Weston-super-Mare	
XV806	HS Harrier GR3 <ff>	Privately owned, Worksop, Notts	
XV808	HS Harrier GR3 (9076M/A2687) [08/DD]	Privately owned, Chetton, Shrops	
XV810	HS Harrier GR3 (9038M) [K]	Privately owned, Walcott, Lincs	
XV814	DH106 Comet 4 (G-APDF) <ff>	Privately owned, Chipping Campden	
XV863	HS Buccaneer S2B (9115M/9139M/9145M) [S]	Privately owned, Weston, Eire	
XV864	HS Buccaneer S2B (9234M)	MoD DFTDC, Manston	
XV865	HS Buccaneer S2B (9226M)	IWM Duxford	
XV867	HS Buccaneer S2B <ff>	Morayvia, Kinloss	
XW175	HS Harrier T4(VAAC)	DSAE No 1 SoTT, Cosford	
XW198	WS Puma HC1	RAF AM&SU, stored Shawbury	
XW199	WS Puma HC2	RAF No 28 Sqn/No 33 Sqn/No 230 Sqn, Benson	
XW202	WS Puma HC1	Army, Stensall Barracks, York	
XW204	WS Puma HC2	RAF No 28 Sqn/No 33 Sqn/No 230 Sqn, Benson	
XW208	WS Puma HC1	Newark Air Museum, Winthorpe	
XW209	WS Puma HC2	RAF No 28 Sqn/No 33 Sqn/No 230 Sqn, Benson	
XW210	WS Puma HC1 (comp XW215)	RAF AM&SU, stored Shawbury	
XW212	WS Puma HC2	RAF No 28 Sqn/No 33 Sqn/No 230 Sqn, Benson	
XW213	WS Puma HC2	RAF No 28 Sqn/No 33 Sqn/No 230 Sqn, Benson	
XW214	WS Puma HC2	RAF No 28 Sqn/No 33 Sqn/No 230 Sqn, Benson	
XW216	WS Puma HC2 (F-ZWDD) [G]	RAF No 28 Sqn/No 33 Sqn/No 230 Sqn, Benson	
XW217	WS Puma HC2	RAF No 28 Sqn/No 33 Sqn/No 230 Sqn, Benson	
XW219	WS Puma HC2	RAF No 28 Sqn/No 33 Sqn/No 230 Sqn, Benson	
XW220	WS Puma HC2	RAF No 28 Sqn/No 33 Sqn/No 230 Sqn, Benson	
XW222	WS Puma HC1	Ulster Aviation Society, Long Kesh	
XW223	WS Puma HC1	RAF AM&SU, stored Shawbury	
XW224	WS Puma HC2 $	RAF No 28 Sqn/No 33 Sqn/No 230 Sqn, Benson	
XW226	WS Puma HC1	RAF AM&SU, stored Shawbury	
XW231	WS Puma HC2	RAF No 28 Sqn/No 33 Sqn/No 230 Sqn, Benson	
XW232	WS Puma HC2 (F-ZWDE)	RAF No 28 Sqn/No 33 Sqn/No 230 Sqn, Benson	
XW235	WS Puma HC2 (F-ZWBI)	RAF/Airbus, Marignane	
XW236	WS Puma HC1	RAF Defence Movements School, Brize Norton	
XW237	WS Puma HC2	RAF No 28 Sqn/No 33 Sqn/No 230 Sqn, Benson	
XW241	Sud SA330E Puma	Farnborough Air Sciences Trust, Farnborough	
XW264	HS Harrier T2 <ff>	Jet Age Museum, Gloucester	
XW265	HS Harrier T4A (9258M) <ff>	No 2345 Sqn ATC, RAF Leuchars	
XW267	HS Harrier T4 (9263M)	Privately owned, Bentwaters	
XW268	HS Harrier T4N	City of Norwich Aviation Museum	
XW269	HS Harrier T4 [TB]	Caernarfon Air World	
XW270	HS Harrier T4 [T]	Coventry University, instructional use	
XW276	Aérospatiale SA341 Gazelle (F-ZWRI)	Newark Air Museum, Winthorpe	
XW283	WS Scout AH1 (G-CIMX) [U]	Kennet Aviation, North Weald	
XW289	BAC Jet Provost T5A (G-BVXT/G-JPVA) [73]	Kennet Aviation, Yeovilton	
XW290	BAC Jet Provost T5A (9199M) [41,MA]	Privately owned, Bruntingthorpe	
XW293	BAC Jet Provost T5 (G-BWCS) [Z]	Privately owned, Bournemouth	
XW299	BAC Jet Provost T5A (9146M) [60,MB]	QinetiQ Apprentice Training School, Boscombe Down	
XW303	BAC Jet Provost T5A (9119M) [127]	RAF Halton	
XW304	BAC Jet Provost T5 (9172M) [MD]	Privately owned, Eye, Suffolk	
XW309	BAC Jet Provost T5 (9179M) [V,ME]	Hartlepool College of Further Education	
XW311	BAC Jet Provost T5 (9180M) [W,MF]	Privately owned, North Weald	
XW315	BAC Jet Provost T5A <ff>	Privately owned, Preston	
XW320	BAC Jet Provost T5A (9015M) [71]	DSAE No 1 SoTT, Cosford	

Notes	Serial	Type (code/other identity)	Owner/operator, location or fate
	XW321	BAC Jet Provost T5A (9154M) [62,MH]	Privately owned, Bentwaters
	XW323	BAC Jet Provost T5A (9166M) [86]	RAF Museum, Hendon
	XW324	BAC Jet Provost T5 (G-BWSG) [U]	Privately owned, East Midlands
	XW325	BAC Jet Provost T5B (G-BWGF) [E]	Privately owned, Coventry
	XW327	BAC Jet Provost T5A (9130M) [62]	DSAE No 1 SoTT, Cosford
	XW330	BAC Jet Provost T5A (9195M) [82,MJ]	Privately owned, Knutsford, Cheshire
	XW333	BAC Jet Provost T5A (G-BVTC)	Global Aviation, Humberside
	XW353	BAC Jet Provost T5A (9090M) [3]	RAF Cranwell, on display
	XW354	*BAC Jet Provost T5A (XW355/G-JPTV)*	*Sold to Italy, August 2018*
	XW358	BAC Jet Provost T5A (9181M) [59,MK]	CEMAST, Fareham College, Lee-on-Solent
	XW360	BAC Jet Provost T5A (9153M) [61,ML]	Privately owned, Thorpe Wood, N Yorks
	XW363	BAC Jet Provost T5A [36]	Dumfries & Galloway Avn Mus, stored Dumfries
	XW364	BAC Jet Provost T5A (9188M) [35,MN]	RAF Halton, GI use
	XW370	BAC Jet Provost T5A (9196M) [72,MP]	Privately owned, Sproughton
	XW375	BAC Jet Provost T5A (9149M) [52]	DSAE No 1 SoTT, Cosford
	XW404	BAC Jet Provost T5A (9049M) [77]	Hartlepool FE College
	XW405	BAC Jet Provost T5A (9187M)	Hartlepool FE College, on display
	XW409	BAC Jet Provost T5A (9047M)	Privately owned, Hawarden
	XW410	BAC Jet Provost T5A (9125M) [80] <ff>	Privately owned, Conington
	XW416	*BAC Jet Provost T5A (9191M) [84,MS]*	*Sold to China, 2018*
	XW418	BAC Jet Provost T5A (9173M) [MT]	RAF Museum, Cosford
	XW419	BAC Jet Provost T5A (9120M) [125]	Highland Aviation Museum, Inverness
	XW420	BAC Jet Provost T5A (9194M) [83,MU]	South Wales Aviation Museum, St Athan
	XW422	BAC Jet Provost T5A (G-BWEB) [3]	Privately owned, Cotswold Airport
	XW423	BAC Jet Provost T5A (G-BWUW) [14]	Deeside College, Connah's Quay, Clwyd
	XW430	BAC Jet Provost T5A (9176M) [77,MW]	Privately owned, Arncott, Oxon
	XW432	BAC Jet Provost T5A (9127M) [76,MX]	Privately owned, Thame
	XW433	BAC Jet Provost T5A (G-JPRO)	Privately owned, Inverness Airport
	XW434	BAC Jet Provost T5A (9091M) [78,MY]	Halfpenny Green Airport, on display
	XW436	BAC Jet Provost T5A (9148M) [68]	DSAE No 1 SoTT, Cosford
	XW530	HS Buccaneer S2B [530]	Buccaneer Service Station, Elgin
	XW541	HS Buccaneer S2B (8858M) <ff>	Privately owned, Lavendon, Bucks
	XW544	HS Buccaneer S2B (8857M) [O]	The Buccaneer Aviation Group, Bruntingthorpe
	XW547	HS Buccaneer S2B (9095M/9169M) [R]	RAF Museum, Hendon
	XW550	HS Buccaneer S2B <ff>	Privately owned, Bruntingthorpe
	XW560	SEPECAT Jaguar S <ff>	Boscombe Down Aviation Collection, Old Sarum
	XW563	SEPECAT Jaguar S (XX822/8563M)	County Hall, Norwich, on display
	XW566	SEPECAT Jaguar B	Farnborough Air Sciences Trust, Farnborough
	XW612	WS Scout AH1 (G-KAXW)	Privately owned, Old Warden
	XW613	WS Scout AH1 (G-BXRS)	Privately owned, North Weald
	XW616	WS Scout AH1	AAC Dishforth, instructional use
	XW630	HS Harrier GR3	RNAS Yeovilton, Fire Section
	XW635	Beagle D5/180 (G-AWSW)	Privately owned, Spanhoe
	XW664	HS Nimrod R1	East Midlands Airport Aeropark
	XW666	HS Nimrod R1 <ff>	South Yorkshire Aircraft Museum, Doncaster
	XW763	HS Harrier GR3 (9002M/9041M) <ff>	Privately owned, Wigston, Leics
	XW768	HS Harrier GR3 (9072M) [N]	MoD DFTDC, Manston
	XW784	Mitchell-Procter Kittiwake I (G-BBRN) [VL]	Privately owned, RNAS Yeovilton
	XW795	WS Scout AH1	Privately owned, Fivemiletown, Co Tyrone, NI
	XW796	WS Scout AH1	Gunsmoke Paintball, Colchester, Essex
	XW838	WS Lynx (TAD009)	DSAE SAAE, Lyneham
	XW839	WS Lynx	The Helicopter Museum, Weston-super-Mare
	XW844	WS Gazelle AH1	StandardAero Fleetlands, preserved
	XW846	WS Gazelle AH1	AAC 7 Regiment Conversion Flt, Middle Wallop
	XW847	WS Gazelle AH1	AAC No 665 Sqn/5 Regt, Aldergrove
	XW848	WS Gazelle AH1 [D]	Privately owned, Stapleford Tawney
	XW849	WS Gazelle AH1	Privately owned, Hurstbourne Tarrant, Hants
	XW852	WS Gazelle HCC4 (9331M)	DSAE, stored HMS Sultan, Gosport
	XW855	WS Gazelle HCC4	RAF Museum, Hendon
	XW858	WS Gazelle HT3 (G-ONNE) [C]	Privately owned, Steeple Bumstead, Cambs
	XW860	WS Gazelle HT2 (TAD 021)	DSAE SAAE, Lyneham
	XW863	WS Gazelle HT2 (TAD 022)	Privately owned, Middle Wallop

Serial	Type (code/other identity)	Owner/operator, location or fate	Notes
XW864	WS Gazelle HT2 [54/CU]	FAA Museum, stored Cobham Hall, RNAS Yeovilton	
XW865	WS Gazelle AH1	AAC No 29 Flt, BATUS, Suffield, Canada	
XW870	WS Gazelle HT3 (9299M) [F]	MoD DFTDC, Manston	
XW888	WS Gazelle AH1 (TAD 017)	DSAE SAAE, Lyneham	
XW889	WS Gazelle AH1 (TAD 018)	*Currently not known*	
XW890	WS Gazelle HT2	RNAS Yeovilton, on display	
XW892	WS Gazelle AH1 (G-CGJX/9292M)	Privately owned, Hurstbourne Tarrant, Hants	
XW897	WS Gazelle AH1	DSAE No 1 SoTT, Cosford	
XW899	WS Gazelle AH1 [Z]	DSAE No 1 SoTT, Cosford	
XW900	WS Gazelle AH1 (TAD 900)	Army, Bramley, Hants	
XW904	WS Gazelle AH1 [H]	AAC, stored Middle Wallop	
XW906	WS Gazelle HT3 [J]	QinetiQ Apprentice Training School, Boscombe Down	
XW908	WS Gazelle AH1 [A]	QinetiQ, Boscombe Down (spares use)	
XW909	WS Gazelle AH1	Privately owned, Stapleford Tawney	
XW912	WS Gazelle AH1 (TAD 019)	DSAE SAAE, Lyneham	
XW913	WS Gazelle AH1	Privately owned, Stapleford Tawney	
XW917	HS Harrier GR3 (8975M)	NATS Air Traffic Control Centre, Swanwick	
XW922	HS Harrier GR3 (8885M)	MoD DFTDC, Manston	
XW923	HS Harrier GR3 (8724M) <ff>	Harrier Heritage Centre, RAF Wittering	
XW924	HS Harrier GR3 (9073M) [G]	RAF Coningsby, preserved	
XW927	HS Harrier T4 <ff>	Privately owned, South Molton, Devon	
XW934	HS Harrier T4 [Y]	Farnborough Air Sciences Trust, Farnborough	
XW994	Northrop Chukar D1	FAA Museum, stored Cobham Hall, RNAS Yeovilton	
XW999	Northrop Chukar D1	Davidstow Airfield & Cornwall At War Museum	
XX108	SEPECAT Jaguar GR1(mod)	IWM Duxford	
XX109	SEPECAT Jaguar GR1 (8918M) [GH]	City of Norwich Aviation Museum	
XX110	SEPECAT Jaguar GR1 (8955M) [EP]	RAF Cosford, on display	
XX110	SEPECAT Jaguar GR1 <R> (BAPC 169)	DSAE No 1 SoTT, Cosford	
XX112	SEPECAT Jaguar GR3A [EA]	DSAE No 1 SoTT, Cosford	
XX115	SEPECAT Jaguar GR1 (8821M) (fuselage)	DSAE No 1 SoTT, Cosford	
XX116	SEPECAT Jaguar GR3A [EO]	MoD DFTDC, Manston	
XX117	SEPECAT Jaguar GR3A [ES]	DSAE No 1 SoTT, Cosford	
XX119	SEPECAT Jaguar GR3A (8898M) [AI]\$	DSAE No 1 SoTT, Cosford	
XX121	SEPECAT Jaguar GR1 [EQ]	Privately owned, Selby, N Yorks	
XX139	SEPECAT Jaguar T4 [PT]	Privately owned, Sproughton	
XX140	SEPECAT Jaguar T2 (9008M) <ff>	Privately owned, Selby, N Yorks	
XX141	SEPECAT Jaguar T2A (9297M) [T]	DSAE No 1 SoTT, Cosford	
XX144	SEPECAT Jaguar T2A [U]	Privately owned, Sproughton	
XX145	SEPECAT Jaguar T2A	Privately owned, Bruntingthorpe	
XX146	SEPECAT Jaguar T4 [GT]	Bradwell Bay Military & Science Museum, Essex	
XX153	WS Lynx AH1 (9320M)	Army Flying Museum, Middle Wallop	
XX154	HS Hawk T1	QinetiQ, Boscombe Down (wfu)	
XX156	HS Hawk T1 [156]	RAF Valley, on display	
XX157	HS Hawk T1A [CU]	RAF AM&SU, stored Shawbury	
XX158	HS Hawk T1A [158]	RAF AM&SU, stored Shawbury	
XX159	HS Hawk T1A [159]	RAF AM&SU, stored Shawbury	
XX160	HS Hawk T1 [160]	RAF AM&SU, stored Shawbury	
XX161	HS Hawk T1 [161]	RN No 736 NAS, Culdrose	
XX162	HS Hawk T1	RAF Centre of Aviation Medicine, Boscombe Down	
XX165	HS Hawk T1 [165] (fuselage)	QinetiQ, Boscombe Down, spares use	
XX167	HS Hawk T1 [167]	RAF AM&SU, stored Shawbury	
XX168	HS Hawk T1 [168]	RAF AM&SU, stored Shawbury	
XX169	HS Hawk T1W [169]	RAF AM&SU, stored Shawbury	
XX170	HS Hawk T1 [CH]	RAF AM&SU, stored Shawbury	
XX171	HS Hawk T1 [171]	RAF AM&SU, stored Shawbury	
XX172	HS Hawk T1 [172] (fuselage)	QinetiQ Boscombe Down, GI use	
XX173	HS Hawk T1	RAF AM&SU, stored Shawbury	
XX174	HS Hawk T1 [174]	RAF AM&SU, stored Shawbury	
XX175	HS Hawk T1 [175]	Privately owned, St Athan	
XX176	HS Hawk T1W [176]	RAF AM&SU, stored Shawbury	
XX177	HS Hawk T1	RAF *Red Arrows*, Scampton	

Notes	Serial	Type (code/other identity)	Owner/operator, location or fate
	XX178	HS Hawk T1W [178]	RAF AM&SU, stored Shawbury
	XX181	HS Hawk T1 [181]	RAF AM&SU, stored Shawbury
	XX184	HS Hawk T1 [CQ]	RN No 1710 NAS, Portsmouth
	XX185	HS Hawk T1 [185]	RAF AM&SU, stored Shawbury
	XX187	HS Hawk T1A [CN]	RAF No 100 Sqn, Leeming
	XX188	HS Hawk T1A	RAF *Red Arrows*, Scampton
	XX189	HS Hawk T1A [CR]	RN No 736 NAS, Culdrose
	XX190	HS Hawk T1A [CN]	RAF AM&SU, stored Shawbury
	XX191	HS Hawk T1A [CC]	RAF No 100 Sqn, Leeming
	XX194	HS Hawk T1A [CP]	RAF AM&SU, stored Shawbury
	XX195	HS Hawk T1W [195]	RAF AM&SU, stored Shawbury
	XX198	HS Hawk T1A [CH]	RAF No 100 Sqn, Leeming
	XX199	HS Hawk T1A [199]	RAF AM&SU, stored Shawbury
	XX200	HS Hawk T1A [CO]	RN No 736 NAS, Culdrose
	XX201	HS Hawk T1A [CQ]	RAF AM&SU, Shawbury
	XX202	HS Hawk T1A [CS]	RAF No 100 Sqn, Leeming
	XX203	HS Hawk T1A [CF]	RAF No 100 Sqn, Leeming
	XX204	HS Hawk T1A	*Crashed Valley, 20 March 2018*
	XX205	HS Hawk T1A [CK]	RAF No 100 Sqn, Leeming
	XX217	HS Hawk T1A [217]	RAF AM&SU, stored Shawbury
	XX218	HS Hawk T1A [218]	RAF AM&SU, stored Shawbury
	XX219	HS Hawk T1A	RAF *Red Arrows*, Scampton
	XX220	HS Hawk T1A [220]	RAF AM&SU, stored Shawbury
	XX221	HS Hawk T1A [CO]	RAF No 100 Sqn, Leeming
	XX222	HS Hawk T1A [CI]	RAF AM&SU, stored Shawbury
	XX224	HS Hawk T1 [224]	RAF AM&SU, stored Shawbury
	XX225	HS Hawk T1 [322]	RAF AM&SU, stored Shawbury
	XX226	HS Hawk T1 [226]	Privately owned, St Athan
	XX227	HS Hawk T1 <R> (*XX226*/BAPC 152)	RAF Scampton Heritage Centre
	XX227	HS Hawk T1A	RAF AM&SU, stored Shawbury
	XX228	HS Hawk T1 [CG]	RAF AM&SU, stored Shawbury
	XX230	HS Hawk T1A [CM]	RAF AM&SU, stored Shawbury
	XX231	HS Hawk T1W [213]	RAF AM&SU, stored Shawbury
	XX232	HS Hawk T1	RAF *Red Arrows*, Scampton
	XX234	HS Hawk T1 [234]	RAF AM&SU, stored Shawbury
	XX235	HS Hawk T1 [235]	RAF AM&SU, stored Shawbury
	XX236	HS Hawk T1W [236]	RAF AM&SU, stored Shawbury
	XX237	HS Hawk T1	Bournemouth Airport, on display
	XX238	HS Hawk T1 [238]	RAF AM&SU, stored Shawbury
	XX239	HS Hawk T1W [842/CU]	RN No 736 NAS, Culdrose
	XX240	HS Hawk T1 [840/CU]	RAF AM&SU, stored Shawbury
	XX242	HS Hawk T1	RAF *Red Arrows*, Scampton
	XX244	HS Hawk T1	RAF *Red Arrows*, Scampton
	XX245	HS Hawk T1	RAF *Red Arrows*, Scampton
	XX246	HS Hawk T1A [CA] $	RAF No 100 Sqn, Leeming
	XX247	HS Hawk T1A [247]	RAF Woodvale, at main gate
	XX248	HS Hawk T1A [CJ]	RAF AM&SU, stored Shawbury
	XX250	HS Hawk T1W [250]	RAF AM&SU, stored Shawbury
	XX253	HS Hawk T1A	RAF Scampton, on display
	XX254	HS Hawk T1A <R>	Privately owned, Marlow, Bucks
	XX255	HS Hawk T1A [CB]	RAF No 100 Sqn, Leeming
	XX256	HS Hawk T1A [846/CU]	RN No 736 NAS, Culdrose
	XX257	HS Hawk T1A (fuselage)	*Currently not known*
	XX258	HS Hawk T1A [CE]	RAF No 100 Sqn, Leeming
	XX260	HS Hawk T1A	RAF AM&SU, stored Shawbury
	XX261	HS Hawk T1A $	RAF AMRO, Valley
	XX263	HS Hawk T1A	Cardiff University, GI use
	XX264	HS Hawk T1A $	RAF AM&SU, stored Shawbury
	XX265	HS Hawk T1A [CP]	RAF AM&SU, stored Shawbury
	XX266	HS Hawk T1A	RAF Scampton, instructional use
	XX278	HS Hawk T1A	RAF *Red Arrows*, Scampton
	XX280	HS Hawk T1A [280]	RN No 736 NAS, Culdrose

Serial	Type (code/other identity)	Owner/operator, location or fate	Notes
XX281	HS Hawk T1A	RAF AMRO, Valley	
XX283	HS Hawk T1W [283]	RAF AM&SU, stored Shawbury	
XX284	HS Hawk T1A [CN]	RAF AM&SU, stored Shawbury	
XX285	HS Hawk T1A $	RN No 736 NAS, Culdrose	
XX286	HS Hawk T1A [286]	RAF AM&SU, stored Shawbury	
XX287	HS Hawk T1A [287]	RAF AM&SU, stored Shawbury	
XX289	HS Hawk T1A [CO]	RAF AM&SU, stored Shawbury	
XX290	HS Hawk T1W	Privately owned, St Athan	
XX292	HS Hawk T1	Privately owned, Bentwaters	
XX294	HS Hawk T1	RAF AM&SU, stored Shawbury	
XX295	HS Hawk T1 [295]	RAF AM&SU, Shawbury	
XX296	HS Hawk T1 [296]	RAF AM&SU, stored Shawbury	
XX299	HS Hawk T1W [299]	RAF AM&SU, stored Shawbury	
XX301	HS Hawk T1A $	RAF AM&SU, stored Shawbury	
XX303	HS Hawk T1A [CR]	RAF No 100 Sqn, Leeming	
XX304	HS Hawk T1A <rf>	Scrapped	
XX306	HS Hawk T1A	RAF Scampton, on display	
XX307	HS Hawk T1 [307]	RAF AM&SU, stored Shawbury	
XX308	HS Hawk T1	National Museum of Flight, E Fortune	
XX308	HS Hawk T1 <R> (XX263/BAPC 171)	RAF M&RU, Bottesford	
XX309	HS Hawk T1	RAF AM&SU, stored Shawbury	
XX310	HS Hawk T1	RAF Red Arrows, Scampton	
XX311	HS Hawk T1	RAF Red Arrows, Scampton	
XX312	HS Hawk T1W	Norwich Airport, on display	
XX313	HS Hawk T1W [313]	RAF AM&SU, stored Shawbury	
XX314	HS Hawk T1W [314]	RAF AM&SU, stored Shawbury	
XX315	HS Hawk T1A [315]	RAF AM&SU, stored Shawbury	
XX316	HS Hawk T1A [849/CU]	RAF No 100 Sqn, Leeming	
XX317	HS Hawk T1A [849/CU]	RN No 736 NAS, Culdrose	
XX318	HS Hawk T1A [CG]	RAF No 100 Sqn, Leeming	
XX319	HS Hawk T1A	RAF Red Arrows, Scampton	
XX320	HS Hawk T1A <ff>	RAF Scampton Heritage Centre	
XX321	HS Hawk T1A [CI]	RAF No 100 Sqn, Leeming	
XX322	HS Hawk T1A	RAF Red Arrows, Scampton	
XX323	HS Hawk T1A	RAF Red Arrows, Scampton	
XX324	HS Hawk T1A [324]	RN No 736 NAS, Culdrose	
XX325	HS Hawk T1	RAF Red Arrows, Scampton	
XX327	HS Hawk T1	RAF Centre of Aviation Medicine, Boscombe Down	
XX329	HS Hawk T1A [844/CU]	RN No 736 NAS, Culdrose	
XX330	HS Hawk T1A [330]	RAF AM&SU, stored Shawbury	
XX331	HS Hawk T1A [331]	RAF AM&SU, stored Shawbury	
XX332	HS Hawk T1A [CD]	RAF No 100 Sqn, Leeming	
XX335	HS Hawk T1A [335]	DSAE No 1 SoTT, Cosford	
XX337	HS Hawk T1A [CM]	RAF No 100 Sqn, Leeming	
XX338	HS Hawk T1W	RAF AM&SU, stored Shawbury	
XX339	HS Hawk T1A [CL]	RAF No 100 Sqn, Leeming	
XX341	HS Hawk T1 ASTRA	MoD, stored Boscombe Down	
XX342	HS Hawk T1 [2]	MoD, stored Boscombe Down	
XX343	HS Hawk T1 [3] (fuselage)	Boscombe Down Aviation Collection, Old Sarum	
XX345	HS Hawk T1A [CB]	RAF AM&SU, stored Shawbury	
XX346	HS Hawk T1A [CP]	RAF No 100 Sqn, Leeming	
XX348	HS Hawk T1A [CQ]	RAF No 100 Sqn, Leeming	
XX349	HS Hawk T1W <ff>	RAF Scampton Fire Section	
XX350	HS Hawk T1A [D] $	RAF AM&SU, stored Shawbury	
XX351	HS Hawk T1A	RAF No 71(IR) Sqn, Wittering, GI use	
XX372	WS Gazelle AH1 <ff>	Privately owned, Hurstbourne Tarrant, Hants	
XX375	WS Gazelle AH1	Privately owned,	
XX378	WS Gazelle AH1 [Q]	AAC, stored Middle Wallop	
XX379	WS Gazelle AH1 [Y]	MoD Boscombe Down, GI use	
XX380	WS Gazelle AH1 [A]	AAC Wattisham, on display	
XX381	WS Gazelle AH1	Privately owned, Welbeck	
XX386	WS Gazelle AH1	Privately owned, Stapleford Tawney	

Notes	Serial	Type (code/other identity)	Owner/operator, location or fate
	XX387	WS Gazelle AH1 (TAD 014)	Privately owned, stored Cranfield
	XX392	WS Gazelle AH1	Army, Middle Wallop, preserved
	XX394	WS Gazelle AH1 [X]	Privately owned, Stapleford Tawney
	XX396	WS Gazelle HT3 (8718M) [N]	Privately owned, Arncott, Oxon
	XX398	WS Gazelle AH1	Privately owned, Stapleford Tawney
	XX399	WS Gazelle AH1 <ff>	Privately owned, Hurstbourne Tarrant, Hants
	XX403	WS Gazelle AH1 [U]	AAC, stored Middle Wallop
	XX405	WS Gazelle AH1	AAC 7 Regiment Conversion Flt, Middle Wallop
	XX406	WS Gazelle HT3 (G-CBSH) [P]	Privately owned, Hurstbourne Tarrant, Hants
	XX411	WS Gazelle AH1 [X]	South Yorkshire Aircraft Museum, Doncaster
	XX411	WS Gazelle AH1 <rf>	FAA Museum, RNAS Yeovilton
	XX412	WS Gazelle AH1 [B]	DSAE RNAESS, *HMS Sultan*, Gosport
	XX414	WS Gazelle AH1 [V]	Privately owned, Biggin Hill
	XX416	WS Gazelle AH1	Privately owned, Stapleford Tawney
	XX418	WS Gazelle AH1 <ff>	Privately owned, Hurstbourne Tarrant, Hants
	XX419	WS Gazelle AH1	AAC, stored Middle Wallop
	XX431	WS Gazelle HT2 (9300M) [43/CU]	DSAE, stored *HMS Sultan*, Gosport
	XX433	WS Gazelle AH1 <ff>	Privately owned, Hurstbourne Tarrant, Hants
	XX435	WS Gazelle AH1 (fuselage)	QinetiQ, Boscombe Down (spares use)
	XX436	WS Gazelle HT2 (G-ZZLE) [39/CU]	Privately owned, Hurstbourne Tarrant, Hants
	XX437	WS Gazelle AH1	Privately owned, Stapleford Tawney
	XX438	WS Gazelle AH1 [F]	Privately owned, Stapleford Tawney
	XX442	WS Gazelle AH1 [E]	AAC, stored Middle Wallop
	XX443	WS Gazelle AH1 [Y]	Army, Aldergrove, on display
	XX444	WS Gazelle AH1	Wattisham Station Heritage Museum
	XX445	WS Gazelle AH1 [T]	Privately owned, Stapleford Tawney
	XX447	WS Gazelle AH1 [D1]	AAC, stored Middle Wallop
	XX449	WS Gazelle AH1	QinetiQ, Boscombe Down (wfu)
	XX450	WS Gazelle AH1 [D]	Privately owned, Hurstbourne Tarrant, Hants
	XX453	WS Gazelle AH1	QinetiQ, Boscombe Down (wfu)
	XX454	WS Gazelle AH1 (TAD 023)	DSAE SAAE, Lyneham
	XX455	WS Gazelle AH1	Privately owned, Stapleford Tawney
	XX456	WS Gazelle AH1	Privately owned, Stapleford Tawney
	XX457	WS Gazelle AH1 (TAD 001)	East Midlands Airport Aeropark
	XX460	WS Gazelle AH1	AAC AM&SU, stored Shawbury
	XX462	WS Gazelle AH1 [W]	Privately owned, Stapleford Tawney
	XX466	HS Hunter T66B/T7 [830] <ff>	Privately owned, Glos
	XX467	HS Hunter T66B/T7 (XL605/G-TVII) [86]	Newark Air Museum, Winthorpe
	XX477	HP137 Jetstream T1 (G-AXXS/8462M) <ff>	South Yorkshire Aircraft Museum, Doncaster
	XX478	HP137 Jetstream T2 (G-AXXT) [564/CU]	Solihull College, Woodlands Campus
	XX479	HP137 Jetstream T2 (G-AXUR)	RN, Predannack Fire School
	XX482	SA Jetstream T1 [J]	*Scrapped at Hixon*
	XX483	SA Jetstream T2 [562] <ff>	Dumfries & Galloway Avn Mus, Dumfries
	XX487	SA Jetstream T2 [568/CU]	Barry Technical College, instructional use
	XX491	SA Jetstream T1 [K]	Northbrook College, Shoreham, instructional use
	XX492	SA Jetstream T1 [A]	Newark Air Museum, Winthorpe
	XX494	SA Jetstream T1 [B]	East Midlands Airport Aeropark
	XX495	SA Jetstream T1 [C]	South Yorkshire Aircraft Museum, Doncaster
	XX496	SA Jetstream T1 [D]	RAF Museum, Cosford
	XX499	SA Jetstream T1 [G]	Brooklands Museum, Weybridge
	XX510	WS Lynx HAS2 [69/DD]	SFDO, RNAS Culdrose
	XX513	SA Bulldog T1 (G-KKKK) [10]	Privately owned, Bagby
	XX515	SA Bulldog T1 (G-CBBC) [4]	Privately owned, Blackbushe
	XX518	SA Bulldog T1 (G-UDOG) [S]	Privately owned, Ursel, Belgium
	XX520	SA Bulldog T1 (9288M) [A]	No 172 Sqn ATC, Haywards Heath
	XX521	SA Bulldog T1 (G-CBEH) [H]	Privately owned, Charney Bassett, Oxon
	XX522	SA Bulldog T1 (G-DAWG) [06]	Privately owned, Blackpool
	XX524	SA Bulldog T1 (G-DDOG) [04]	Privately owned, Malaga, Spain
	XX528	SA Bulldog T1 (G-BZON) [D]	Privately owned, Earls Colne
	XX530	SA Bulldog T1 (XX637/9197M) [F]	No 2175 Sqn ATC, RAF Kinloss
	XX534	SA Bulldog T1 (G-EDAV) [B]	Privately owned, Tollerton
	XX537	SA Bulldog T1 (G-CBCB) [C]	Privately owned, RAF Halton

Serial	Type (code/other identity)	Owner/operator, location or fate	Notes
XX538	SA Bulldog T1 (G-TDOG) [O]	Privately owned, Shobdon	
XX539	SA Bulldog T1 [L]	Privately owned, Derbyshire	
XX546	SA Bulldog T1 (G-WINI) [03]	Privately owned, Conington	
XX549	SA Bulldog T1 (G-CBID) [6]	Privately owned, White Waltham	
XX550	SA Bulldog T1 (G-CBBL) [Z]	Privately owned, Abbeyshrule, Eire	
XX551	SA Bulldog T1 (G-BZDP) [E]	Privately owned, Boscombe Down	
XX554	SA Bulldog T1 (G-BZMD) [09]	Privately owned, Wellesbourne Mountford	
XX557	SA Bulldog T1	Privately owned, stored Fort Paull, Yorks	
XX561	SA Bulldog T1 (G-BZEP) [7]	Privately owned, Eggesford	
XX611	SA Bulldog T1 (G-CBDK) [7]	Privately owned, Coventry	
XX612	SA Bulldog T1 (G-BZXC) [A,03]	Ayr College, instructional use	
XX614	SA Bulldog T1 (G-GGRR) [1]	Privately owned, Cotswold Airport	
XX619	SA Bulldog T1 (G-CBBW) [T]	Privately owned, Coventry	
XX621	SA Bulldog T1 (G-CBEF) [H]	Privately owned, Leicester	
XX622	SA Bulldog T1 (G-CBGX) [B]	Privately owned, Shoreham	
XX623	SA Bulldog T1 [M]	Privately owned, Hurstbourne Tarrant, Hants	
XX624	SA Bulldog T1 (G-KDOG) [E]	Privately owned, Hurstbourne Tarrant, Hants	
XX625	SA Bulldog T1 (XX543/G-UWAS) [U]	Privately owned, Tain	
XX626	SA Bulldog T1 (G-CDVV/9290M) [W,02]	Privately owned, Abbots Bromley, Staffs	
XX628	SA Bulldog T1 (G-CBFU) [9]	Privately owned, Faversham	
XX629	SA Bulldog T1 (G-BZXZ)	Privately owned, Wellesbourne Mountford	
XX630	SA Bulldog T1 (G-SIJW) [5]	Privately owned, Audley End	
XX631	SA Bulldog T1 (G-BZXS) [W]	Privately owned, Sligo, Eire	
XX634	SA Bulldog T1 [T]	Newark Air Museum, Winthorpe	
XX636	SA Bulldog T1 (G-CBFP) [Y]	Privately owned, Netherthorpe	
XX638	SA Bulldog T1 (G-DOGG)	Privately owned, Hurstbourne Tarrant, Hants	
XX639	SA Bulldog T1 (F-AZTF) [D]	Privately owned, La Baule, France	
XX654	SA Bulldog T1 [3]	RAF Museum, Cosford	
XX655	SA Bulldog T1 (9294M) [V] <ff>	Privately owned, Stockport	
XX656	SA Bulldog T1 [C]	Privately owned, Derbyshire	
XX658	SA Bulldog T1 (G-BZPS) [07]	Privately owned, Wellesbourne Mountford	
XX659	SA Bulldog T1 [E]	Privately owned, Derbyshire	
XX664	SA Bulldog T1 (F-AZTV) [04]	Privately owned, Pontoise, France	
XX665	SA Bulldog T1 (9289M) [V]	Privately owned, Evesham, Worcs	
XX667	SA Bulldog T1 (G-BZFN) [16]	Privately owned, Ronaldsway, IoM	
XX668	SA Bulldog T1 (G-CBAN) [1]	Privately owned, St Athan	
XX669	SA Bulldog T1 (8997M) [B]	South Yorkshire Aircraft Museum, Doncaster	
XX687	SA Bulldog T1 [F]	Barry Technical College, Cardiff Airport	
XX690	SA Bulldog T1 [A]	Privately owned, Strathaven, S Lanarks	
XX692	SA Bulldog T1 (G-BZMH) [A]	Privately owned, Wellesbourne Mountford	
XX693	SA Bulldog T1 (G-BZML) [07]	Privately owned, Elmsett	
XX694	SA Bulldog T1 (G-CBBS) [E]	Privately owned, Turweston	
XX695	SA Bulldog T1 (G-CBBT)	Privately owned, Perth	
XX698	SA Bulldog T1 (G-BZME) [9]	Privately owned, Sleap	
XX700	SA Bulldog T1 (G-CBEK) [17]	Privately owned, Thruxton	
XX702	SA Bulldog T1 (G-CBCR) [m]	Privately owned, Egginton	
XX704	SA122 Bulldog (G-BCUV/G-112)	Privately owned, Bournemouth	
XX705	SA Bulldog T1 [5]	Privately owned, Norfolk	
XX707	SA Bulldog T1 (G-CBDS) [4]	Privately owned, stored Caernarfon	
XX711	SA Bulldog T1 (G-CBBU) [X]	Privately owned, stored Perth	
XX720	SEPECAT Jaguar GR3A [FL]	Privately owned, Sproughton	
XX722	SEPECAT Jaguar GR1 (9252M) <ff>	Currently not known	
XX723	SEPECAT Jaguar GR3A [EU]	DSAE No 1 SoTT, Cosford	
XX724	SEPECAT Jaguar GR3A [C]	DSAE No 1 SoTT, Cosford	
XX725	SEPECAT Jaguar GR3A [KC-F,T]	DSAE No 1 SoTT, Cosford	
XX726	SEPECAT Jaguar GR1 (8947M) [EB]	DSAE No 1 SoTT, Cosford	
XX727	SEPECAT Jaguar GR1 (8951M) [ER]	DSAE No 1 SoTT, Cosford	
XX729	SEPECAT Jaguar GR1 [EL]	DSAE No 1 SoTT, Cosford	
XX734	SEPECAT Jaguar GR1 (8816M)	Boscombe Down Aviation Collection, Old Sarum	
XX736	SEPECAT Jaguar GR1 (9110M) <ff>	South Yorkshire Aircraft Museum, Doncaster	
XX738	SEPECAT Jaguar GR3A [ED]	DSAE No 1 SoTT, Cosford	
XX739	SEPECAT Jaguar GR1 (8902M) [I]	Delta Force Paintball, Birmingham	

Notes	Serial	Type (code/other identity)	Owner/operator, location or fate
	XX741	SEPECAT Jaguar GR1A [EJ]	Bentwaters Cold War Museum
	XX743	SEPECAT Jaguar GR1 (8949M) [EG]	DSAE No 1 SoTT, Cosford
	XX744	SEPECAT Jaguar GR1 (9251M)	Mayhem Paintball, Abridge, Essex
	XX745	SEPECAT Jaguar GR1A <ff>	No 1350 Sqn ATC, Fareham
	XX746	SEPECAT Jaguar GR1 (8895M) [S]	DSAE No 1 SoTT, Cosford
	XX747	SEPECAT Jaguar GR1 (8903M)	QinetiQ Boscombe Down, GI use
	XX748	SEPECAT Jaguar GR3A [L]	DSAE No 1 SoTT, Cosford
	XX751	SEPECAT Jaguar GR1 (8937M) [10]	Privately owned, Aldershot, Hants
	XX752	SEPECAT Jaguar GR3A [EK]	DSAE No 1 SoTT, Cosford
	XX753	SEPECAT Jaguar GR1 (9087M) <ff>	Newark Air Museum, Winthorpe
	XX756	SEPECAT Jaguar GR1 (8899M) [W]	DSAE No 1 SoTT, Cosford
	XX761	SEPECAT Jaguar GR1 (8600M) <ff>	Boscombe Down Aviation Collection, Old Sarum
	XX763	SEPECAT Jaguar GR1 (9009M) [24]	Bournemouth Aviation Museum
	XX764	SEPECAT Jaguar GR1 (9010M)	Privately owned, Enstone
	XX765	SEPECAT Jaguar ACT	RAF Museum, Cosford
	XX766	SEPECAT Jaguar GR3A [EF]	DSAE No 1 SoTT, Cosford
	XX767	SEPECAT Jaguar GR3A [Z]	DSAE No 1 SoTT, Cosford
	XX818	SEPECAT Jaguar GR1 (8945M) [DE]	DSAE No 1 SoTT, Cosford
	XX819	SEPECAT Jaguar GR1 (8923M) [CE]	DSAE No 1 SoTT, Cosford
	XX821	SEPECAT Jaguar GR1 (8896M) [P]	DSAE No 1 SoTT, Cosford
	XX824	SEPECAT Jaguar GR1 (9019M) [AD]	RAF Museum, Hendon
	XX825	SEPECAT Jaguar GR1 (9020M) [BN]	DSAE No 1 SoTT, Cosford
	XX826	SEPECAT Jaguar GR1 (9021M) [34] <ff>	Shannon Aviation Museum, Eire
	XX829	SEPECAT Jaguar T2A [GZ]	Newark Air Museum, Winthorpe
	XX830	SEPECAT Jaguar T2 <ff>	City of Norwich Aviation Museum
	XX833	SEPECAT Jaguar T2B	DSAE No 1 SoTT, Cosford
	XX835	SEPECAT Jaguar T4 [P]	DSAE No 1 SoTT, Cosford
	XX836	SEPECAT Jaguar T2A [X]	Privately owned, Sproughton
	XX837	SEPECAT Jaguar T2 (8978M) [Z]	DSAE No 1 SoTT, Cosford
	XX838	SEPECAT Jaguar T4 [FZ]	Privately owned, Bentwaters
	XX840	SEPECAT Jaguar T4 [T]	DSAE No 1 SoTT, Cosford
	XX841	SEPECAT Jaguar T4	Privately owned, North Weald
	XX842	SEPECAT Jaguar T2A [FX]	Privately owned, Bentwaters
	XX845	SEPECAT Jaguar T4 [EV]	RN, Predannack Fire School
	XX847	SEPECAT Jaguar T4 [EZ]	DSAE No 1 SoTT, Cosford
	XX885	HS Buccaneer S2B (9225M/G-HHAA)	Hawker Hunter Aviation, Scampton
	XX888	HS Buccaneer S2B <ff>	Privately owned, Barnstaple
	XX889	HS Buccaneer S2B [T]	Privately owned, Bruntingthorpe
	XX892	HS Buccaneer S2B <ff>	Blue Sky Experiences, Methven, Perth & Kinross
	XX894	HS Buccaneer S2B [020/R]	The Buccaneer Aviation Group, Bruntingthorpe
	XX895	HS Buccaneer S2B <ff>	Privately owned, Tattershall Thorpe
	XX897	HS Buccaneer S2B(mod)	Shannon Aviation Museum, Eire
	XX899	HS Buccaneer S2B <ff>	Newark Air Museum, Winthorpe
	XX900	HS Buccaneer S2B [900]	Cold War Jets Collection, Bruntingthorpe
	XX901	HS Buccaneer S2B	Yorkshire Air Museum, Elvington
	XX910	WS Lynx HAS2	The Helicopter Museum, Weston-super-Mare
	XX919	BAC 1-11/402AP (PI-C1121) <ff>	Boscombe Down Aviation Collection, Old Sarum
	XX946	Panavia Tornado (P02) (8883M)	RAF Museum, stored Cosford
	XX958	SEPECAT Jaguar GR1 (9022M) [BK]	DSAE No 1 SoTT, Cosford
	XX959	SEPECAT Jaguar GR1 (8953M) [CJ]	DSAE No 1 SoTT, Cosford
	XX965	SEPECAT Jaguar GR1A (9254M) [C]	DSAE No 1 SoTT, Cosford
	XX967	SEPECAT Jaguar GR1 (9006M) [AC]	DSAE No 1 SoTT, Cosford
	XX968	SEPECAT Jaguar GR1 (9007M) [AJ]	DSAE No 1 SoTT, Cosford
	XX969	SEPECAT Jaguar GR1 (8897M) [01]	DSAE No 1 SoTT, Cosford
	XX970	SEPECAT Jaguar GR3A [EH]	DSAE No 1 SoTT, Cosford
	XX975	SEPECAT Jaguar GR1 (8905M) [07]	DSAE No 1 SoTT, Cosford
	XX976	SEPECAT Jaguar GR1 (8906M) [BD]	DSAE No 1 SoTT, Cosford
	XX977	SEPECAT Jaguar GR1 (9132M) [DL,05] <rf>	Privately owned, Sproughton
	XX979	SEPECAT Jaguar GR1A (9306M) <ff>	RAF Air Defence Radar Museum, Neatishead
	XZ103	SEPECAT Jaguar GR3A [EF]	DSAE No 1 SoTT, Cosford
	XZ104	SEPECAT Jaguar GR3A [FM]	DSAE No 1 SoTT, Cosford

Serial	Type (code/other identity)	Owner/operator, location or fate	Notes
XZ106	SEPECAT Jaguar GR3A [FR]	RAF Manston History Museum	
XZ107	SEPECAT Jaguar GR3A [FH]	Privately owned, Bentwaters	
XZ109	SEPECAT Jaguar GR3A [EN]	DSAE No 1 SoTT, Cosford	
XZ112	SEPECAT Jaguar GR3A [GW]	DSAE No 1 SoTT, Cosford	
XZ113	SEPECAT Jaguar GR3 [FD,FG]	Morayvia, Kinloss	
XZ114	SEPECAT Jaguar GR3 [EO]	DSAE No 1 SoTT, Cosford	
XZ115	SEPECAT Jaguar GR3 [ER]	DSAE No 1 SoTT, Cosford	
XZ117	SEPECAT Jaguar GR3 [ES]	DSAE No 1 SoTT, Cosford	
XZ119	SEPECAT Jaguar GR1A (9266M) [FG]	National Museum of Flight, E Fortune	
XZ130	HS Harrier GR3 (9079M) [A]	Privately owned, Thorpe Wood, N Yorks	
XZ131	HS Harrier GR3 (9174M) <ff>	Privately owned, Spark Bridge, Cumbria	
XZ132	HS Harrier GR3 (9168M) [C]	Privately owned, Thorpe Wood, N Yorks	
XZ133	HS Harrier GR3 [10]	IWM Duxford	
XZ138	HS Harrier GR3 (9040M) <ff>	RAFC Cranwell, Trenchard Hall	
XZ146	HS Harrier T4 (9281M) [S]	Harrier Heritage Centre, RAF Wittering	
XZ166	WS Lynx HAS2 <ff>	Farnborough Air Sciences Trust, stored Farnborough	
XZ170	WS Lynx AH9	DSAE SAAE, Lyneham	
XZ171	WS Lynx AH7	Army, Salisbury Plain	
XZ172	WS Lynx AH7	DSAE SAAE, Lyneham	
XZ173	WS Lynx AH7 [6] <ff>	Privately owned, Weeton, Lancs	
XZ174	WS Lynx AH7 <ff>	Defence Coll of Policing, Gosport, instructional use	
XZ175	WS Lynx AH7	Privately owned, Barby, Northants	
XZ177	Aérospatiale SA341G Gazelle (G-SFTA/XZ345) [T]	North-East Aircraft Museum, Usworth	
XZ177	WS Lynx AH7	Delta Force, Kegworth	
XZ178	WS Lynx AH7 <ff>	Bilsthorpe Paintball Park, Notts	
XZ179	WS Lynx AH7 <ff>	Privately owned, Sproughton	
XZ180	WS Lynx AH7 [C]	DSAE SAAE, Lyneham	
XZ181	WS Lynx AH1	AAC Middle Wallop Fire Section	
XZ183	WS Lynx AH7 <ff>	RAF Wittering, instructional use	
XZ184	WS Lynx AH7 [B]	AAC Middle Wallop, at main gate	
XZ187	WS Lynx AH7	DSAE SAAE, Lyneham	
XZ188	WS Lynx AH7	DSAE SAAE, Lyneham	
XZ190	WS Lynx AH7 <ff>	Army, Longmoor Camp, Hants, GI use	
XZ191	WS Lynx AH7 [R]	DSAE SAAE, Lyneham	
XZ192	WS Lynx AH7 [H]	AAC, stored St Athan	
XZ193	WS Lynx AH7 [4] <ff>	Kidderminster Paintball	
XZ194	WS Lynx AH7 [V]	IWM Duxford	
XZ195	WS Lynx AH7 <ff>	Privately owned, Mildenhall	
XZ198	WS Lynx AH7 <ff>	Destroyed at Faldingworth, Lincs, 2018	
XZ203	WS Lynx AH7 [F]	Army, Salisbury Plain	
XZ206	WS Lynx AH7 <ff>	Privately owned, Hixon, Staffs	
XZ207	WS Lynx AH7 <rf>	DSAE SAAE, Lyneham	
XZ208	WS Lynx AH7	Privately owned, Sproughton	
XZ209	WS Lynx AH7 <ff>	MoD JARTS, Boscombe Down	
XZ211	WS Lynx AH7	Bawtry Paintball Park, S Yorks	
XZ212	WS Lynx AH7 [X]	AAC Middle Wallop, GI use	
XZ213	WS Lynx AH1 (TAD 213)	StandardAero Fleetlands Apprentice School	
XZ214	WS Lynx AH7 <ff>	DSAE SAAE, Lyneham	
XZ216	WS Lynx AH7 <ff>	MoD DFTDC, Manston	
XZ217	WS Lynx AH7	Privately owned, Guildford	
XZ218	WS Lynx AH7	Warfighters R6 Centre, Barby, Northants	
XZ219	WS Lynx AH7 <ff>	Army, Bramley, Hants	
XZ220	WS Lynx AH7 <ff>	Privately owned, South Clifton, Notts	
XZ222	WS Lynx AH7	DSAE SAAE, Lyneham	
XZ228	WS Lynx HAS3GMS [313]	AAC, stored Middle Wallop	
XZ229	WS Lynx HAS3GMS [360/MC]	Privately owned, Hixon, Staffs	
XZ232	WS Lynx HAS3GMS	Falck Nutec UK, Aberdeen, GI use	
XZ233	WS Lynx HAS3S [635] $	AAC, stored Middle Wallop	
XZ234	WS Lynx HAS3S	Privately owned, Sproughton	
XZ235	WS Lynx HAS3S(ICE) [630]	Wild Park Derbyshire, Brailsford	
XZ236	WS Lynx HMA8 [LST-1]	RN, stored St Athan	
XZ237	WS Lynx HAS3S [631]	Privately owned, Wild Park, Derbyshire	

Notes	Serial	Type (code/other identity)	Owner/operator, location or fate
	XZ239	WS Lynx HAS3GMS [633]	Privately owned, Hixon, Staffs
	XZ246	WS Lynx HAS3S(ICE) [434/EE]	South Yorkshire Aircraft Museum, Doncaster
	XZ248	WS Lynx HAS3S	SFDO, RNAS Culdrose
	XZ250	WS Lynx HAS3S [426/PO] $	RN, Portland, on display
	XZ252	WS Lynx HAS3S	Privately owned, Hixon, Staffs
	XZ254	WS Lynx HAS3S	Privately owned, Hixon, Staffs
	XZ255	WS Lynx HMA8SRU [454/DF]	RN, stored St Athan
	XZ257	WS Lynx HAS3S	RN Yeovilton, GI use (Wildcat ground trainer)
	XZ287	BAe Nimrod AEW3 (9140M) (fuselage)	RAF TSW, Stafford
	XZ290	WS Gazelle AH1	AAC No 665 Sqn/5 Regt, Aldergrove
	XZ292	WS Gazelle AH1	Privately owned, Stapleford Tawney
	XZ294	WS Gazelle AH1 [X]	AAC AM&SU, stored Shawbury
	XZ295	WS Gazelle AH1	MoD/ETPS, Boscombe Down
	XZ298	WS Gazelle AH1 <ff>	AAC Middle Wallop, GI use
	XZ300	WS Gazelle AH1	Army, Bramley, Hants
	XZ303	WS Gazelle AH1	AAC, stored Middle Wallop
	XZ304	WS Gazelle AH1	Privately owned, Stapleford Tawney
	XZ305	WS Gazelle AH1 (TAD 020)	DSAE, stored HMS Sultan, Gosport
	XZ308	WS Gazelle AH1	QinetiQ, Boscombe Down (spares use)
	XZ311	WS Gazelle AH1 [U]	AAC, stored Middle Wallop
	XZ312	WS Gazelle AH1	RAF Henlow, instructional use
	XZ313	WS Gazelle AH1 <ff>	Privately owned, Shotton, Durham
	XZ314	WS Gazelle AH1 [A]	Privately owned, Stapleford Tawney
	XZ315	WS Gazelle AH1 <ff>	Privately owned, Babcary, Somerset
	XZ316	WS Gazelle AH1 [B]	DSAE SAAE, Lyneham
	XZ318	WS Gazelle AH1 (fuselage)	Tong Paintball Park, Shropshire
	XZ320	WS Gazelle AH1	MoD/StandardAero, Fleetlands
	XZ321	WS Gazelle AH1 (G-CDNS) [D]	Privately owned, Hurstbourne Tarrant, Hants
	XZ322	WS Gazelle AH1 (9283M) [N]	DSAE SAAE, Lyneham
	XZ323	WS Gazelle AH1 [J]	MoD, stored Boscombe Down
	XZ324	WS Gazelle AH1	Privately owned, Stapleford Tawney
	XZ325	WS Gazelle AH1	DSAE SAAE, Lyneham
	XZ326	WS Gazelle AH1	AAC No 665 Sqn/5 Regt, Aldergrove
	XZ327	WS Gazelle AH1	AAC Middle Wallop (recruiting aid)
	XZ328	WS Gazelle AH1 [C]	AAC AM&SU, stored Shawbury
	XZ329	WS Gazelle AH1 (G-BZYD) [J]	Privately owned, Lewes, Sussex
	XZ330	WS Gazelle AH1 [Y]	AAC Wattisham, instructional use
	XZ331	WS Gazelle AH1 [D]	Currently not known
	XZ332	WS Gazelle AH1	DSAE SAAE, Lyneham
	XZ333	WS Gazelle AH1	DSAE SAAE, Lyneham
	XZ334	WS Gazelle AH1	AAC No 665 Sqn/5 Regt, Aldergrove
	XZ335	WS Gazelle AH1 <ff>	South Yorkshire Aviation Museum, Doncaster
	XZ337	WS Gazelle AH1 [Z]	AAC, stored Middle Wallop
	XZ340	WS Gazelle AH1	MoD/StandardAero, stored Fleetlands
	XZ341	WS Gazelle AH1	AAC AM&SU, stored Shawbury
	XZ342	WS Gazelle AH1	Currently not known
	XZ343	WS Gazelle AH1	AAC AM&SU, stored Shawbury
	XZ334	WS Gazelle AH1	AAC No 667 Sqn/7 Regt, Middle Wallop
	XZ345	WS Gazelle AH1 [M]	AAC, stored Middle Wallop
	XZ346	WS Gazelle AH1	AAC Middle Wallop, at main gate
	XZ356	SEPECAT Jaguar GR3A [FU]	Privately owned, Welshpool
	XZ358	SEPECAT Jaguar GR1A (9262M) [L]	DSAE No 1 SoTT, Cosford
	XZ360	SEPECAT Jaguar GR3 [FN]	Privately owned, Bentwaters
	XZ363	SEPECAT Jaguar GR1A <R> (XX824/BAPC 151) [A]	RAF M&RU, Bottesford
	XZ364	SEPECAT Jaguar GR3A <ff>	Privately owned, Thorpe Wood, N Yorks
	XZ366	SEPECAT Jaguar GR3A [FC]	Privately owned, Bentwaters
	XZ367	SEPECAT Jaguar GR3 [EE]	DSAE No 1 SoTT, Cosford
	XZ368	SEPECAT Jaguar GR1 [8900M] [E]	DSAE No 1 SoTT, Cosford
	XZ369	SEPECAT Jaguar GR3A [EU]	Delta Force Paintball, Rugby
	XZ370	SEPECAT Jaguar GR1 (9004M) [JB]	DSAE No 1 SoTT, Cosford
	XZ371	SEPECAT Jaguar GR1 (8907M) [AP]	DSAE No 1 SoTT, Cosford
	XZ372	SEPECAT Jaguar GR3 [FV]	Aberdeen Airport Fire Section

Serial	Type (code/other identity)	Owner/operator, location or fate	Notes
XZ374	SEPECAT Jaguar GR1 (9005M) [JC]	DSAE, stored Cosford	
XZ375	SEPECAT Jaguar GR1 (9255M) <ff>	City of Norwich Aviation Museum	
XZ377	SEPECAT Jaguar GR3A [P]	DSAE No 1 SoTT, Cosford	
XZ378	SEPECAT Jaguar GR1A [EP]	Privately owned, Topsham, Devon	
XZ382	SEPECAT Jaguar GR1 (8908M)	Cold War Jets Collection, Bruntingthorpe	
XZ383	SEPECAT Jaguar GR1 (8901M) [AF]	DSAE No 1 SoTT, Cosford	
XZ384	SEPECAT Jaguar GR1 (8954M) [BC]	DSAE No 1 SoTT, Cosford	
XZ385	SEPECAT Jaguar GR3A [FT]	Privately owned, Bentwaters	
XZ389	SEPECAT Jaguar GR1 (8946M) [BL]	DSAE No 1 SoTT, Cosford	
XZ390	SEPECAT Jaguar GR1 (9003M) [DM]	DSAE No 1 SoTT, Cosford	
XZ391	SEPECAT Jaguar GR3A [ET]	DSAE No 1 SoTT, Cosford	
XZ392	SEPECAT Jaguar GR3A [EM]	DSAE No 1 SoTT, Cosford	
XZ394	SEPECAT Jaguar GR3	Shoreham Airport, on display	
XZ398	SEPECAT Jaguar GR3A [EQ]	DSAE No 1 SoTT, Cosford	
XZ399	SEPECAT Jaguar GR3A [EJ]	DSAE No 1 SoTT, Cosford	
XZ400	SEPECAT Jaguar GR3A [FQ]	Privately owned, Bentwaters	
XZ431	HS Buccaneer S2B (9233M) <ff>	South Yorkshire Aviation Museum, stored Doncaster	
XZ440	BAe Sea Harrier FA2 [40/DD]	SFDO, RNAS Culdrose	
XZ455	BAe Sea Harrier FA2 [001] (wreck)	Privately owned, Thorpe Wood, N Yorks	
XZ457	BAe Sea Harrier FA2 [104/VL]	Boscombe Down Aviation Collection, Old Sarum	
XZ459	BAe Sea Harrier FA2 [126]	Privately owned, Sussex	
XZ493	BAe Sea Harrier FRS1 (comp XV760) [001/N]	FAA Museum, RNAS Yeovilton	
XZ493	BAe Sea Harrier FRS1 <ff>	RN Yeovilton, Fire Section	
XZ494	BAe Sea Harrier FA2 [128]	Privately owned, Wedmore, Somerset	
XZ497	BAe Sea Harrier FA2 [126]	Privately owned, Charlwood	
XZ499	BAe Sea Harrier FA2 [003]	FAA Museum, stored Cobham Hall, RNAS Yeovilton	
XZ559	Slingsby T61F Venture T2 (G-BUEK)	Privately owned, Tibenham	
XZ570	WS61 Sea King HAS5(mod)	RN, Predannack Fire School	
XZ574	WS61 Sea King HAS6	FAA Museum, stored Cobham Hall, RNAS Yeovilton	
XZ575	WS61 Sea King HU5	Privately owned, Charlwood	
XZ576	WS61 Sea King HAS6	DSAE RNAESS, HMS Sultan, Gosport	
XZ578	WS61 Sea King HU5 [30]	Privately owned, Brynrefail, Gwynedd	
XZ579	WS61 Sea King HAS6 [707/PW]	DSAE RNAESS, HMS Sultan, Gosport	
XZ580	WS61 Sea King HC6 [ZB]	DSAE RNAESS, HMS Sultan, Gosport	
XZ581	WS61 Sea King HAS6 [69/CU]	DSAE RNAESS, HMS Sultan, Gosport	
XZ585	WS61 Sea King HAR3 [A]	RAF Museum, Hendon	
XZ586	WS61 Sea King HAR3 [B]	DSAE, stored HMS Sultan, Gosport	
XZ587	WS61 Sea King HAR3 [C]	RAF St Mawgan, on display	
XZ588	WS61 Sea King HAR3 [D]	StandardAero Fleetlands Apprentice School	
XZ589	WS61 Sea King HAR3 [E] $	DSAE RNAESS, HMS Sultan, Gosport	
XZ590	WS61 Sea King HAR3 [F]	DSAE, stored HMS Sultan, Gosport	
XZ592	WS61 Sea King HAR3 [H]	Morayvia, Kinloss	
XZ594	WS61 Sea King HAR3	DSAE, stored HMS Sultan, Gosport	
XZ595	WS61 Sea King HAR3 [K]	Privately owned, Charlwood	
XZ596	WS61 Sea King HAR3 [L]	DSAE, stored HMS Sultan, Gosport	
XZ597	WS61 Sea King HAR3 [M]	Privately owned, Chard, Somerset	
XZ598	WS61 Sea King HAR3 [N]	Privately owned, Scarborough	
XZ605	WS Lynx AH7	Wattisham Station Heritage Museum	
XZ606	WS Lynx AH7 [O]	Delta Force Paintball, Billericay, Essex	
XZ607	WS Lynx AH7 <ff>	MoD DFTDC, Manston	
XZ607	WS Lynx AH7 (comp XZ215)	MoD DFTDC, Manston	
XZ608	WS Lynx AH7 (fuselage)	Army Bury St Edmunds, GI use	
XZ609	WS Lynx AH7	Army Bury St Edmunds, GI use	
XZ611	WS Lynx AH7 <ff>	Bilsthorpe Paintball Park, Notts	
XZ612	WS Lynx AH7	Delta Force Paintball, Bovingdon	
XZ613	WS Lynx AH7 [F]	Privately owned, Belstead, Suffolk	
XZ615	WS Lynx AH7 <ff>	Currently not known	
XZ616	WS Lynx AH7	MoD/StandardAero, stored Fleetlands	
XZ617	WS Lynx AH7 <ff>	DSAE SAAE, Lyneham	
XZ630	Panavia Tornado (P12) (8976M)	RAF Halton, on display	
XZ631	Panavia Tornado (P15)	Yorkshire Air Museum, Elvington	
XZ642	WS Lynx AH7	DSAE SAAE, Lyneham	

Notes	Serial	Type (code/other identity)	Owner/operator, location or fate
	XZ643	WS Lynx AH7 [C]	Privately owned, Culham, Oxon
	XZ645	WS Lynx AH7	Delta Force Paintball, Romsey, Hants
	XZ646	WS Lynx AH7 <ff>	MoD JARTS, Boscombe Down
	XZ646	WS Lynx AH7 (really XZ649)	Bristol University, instructional use
	XZ647	WS Lynx AH7 <ff>	Aberdeen Airport Fire Section
	XZ648	WS Lynx AH7 <ff>	Privately owned, Weeton, Lancs
	XZ651	WS Lynx AH7 [O]	AAC, stored Middle Wallop
	XZ652	WS Lynx AH7	IFTC, Durham/Tees Valley
	XZ653	WS Lynx AH7	DSAE SAAE, Lyneham
	XZ654	WS Lynx AH7	Shannon Aviation Museum, Eire
	XZ655	WS Lynx AH7 [3] <ff>	Privately owned, Weeton, Lancs
	XZ661	WS Lynx AH7 [V]	Army, Bramley, Hants
	XZ663	WS Lynx AH7 <ff>	Privately owned, Hixon, Staffs
	XZ664	WS Lynx AH7	Warfighters R6 Centre, Barby, Northants
	XZ665	WS Lynx AH7	Privately owned, Barby, Northants
	XZ666	WS Lynx AH7	DSAE SAAE, Lyneham
	XZ668	WS Lynx AH7 [UN] <ff>	Privately owned, stored Cranfield
	XZ670	WS Lynx AH7 [A]	RNAS Yeovilton, on display
	XZ671	WS Lynx AH7 <ff>	Leonardo MW, Yeovil, instructional use
	XZ672	WS Lynx AH7 <ff>	AAC Middle Wallop Fire Section
	XZ673	WS Lynx AH7 [5]	Privately owned, Weeton, Lancs
	XZ674	WS Lynx AH7 [T]	RNAS Yeovilton Fire Section
	XZ675	WS Lynx AH7 [H]	Army Flying Museum, Middle Wallop
	XZ676	WS Lynx AH7 [N]	Privately owned, Weeton, Lancs
	XZ677	WS Lynx AH7 <ff>	Army, Longmoor Camp, Hants, GI use
	XZ678	WS Lynx AH7 <ff>	Privately owned, Sproughton
	XZ679	WS Lynx AH7 [W]	DSAE SAAE, Lyneham
	XZ680	WS Lynx AH7 <ff>	*Currently not known*
	XZ689	WS Lynx HMA8SRU [314]	RN, stored Middle Wallop
	XZ690	WS Lynx HMA8SRU [640]	Delta Force Paintball, West Glasgow
	XZ691	WS Lynx HMA8SRU [310]	RN, stored St Athan
	XZ692	WS Lynx HMA8SRU [764/SN] $	DSAE RNAESS, *HMS Sultan*, Gosport
	XZ693	WS Lynx HAS3S [311]	Wild Park Derbyshire, Brailsford
	XZ694	WS Lynx HAS3GMS [434]	Privately owned, South Clifton, Notts
	XZ696	WS Lynx HAS3GMS [633]	Privately owned, Hixon, Staffs
	XZ697	WS Lynx HMA8SRU [313]	MoD/StandardAero, Fleetlands
	XZ699	WS Lynx HAS2	FAA Museum, RNAS Yeovilton
	XZ719	WS Lynx HMA8SRU [64]	RNAS Yeovilton Fire Section
	XZ720	WS Lynx HAS3GMS [410/GC]	FAA Museum, RNAS Yeovilton
	XZ721	WS Lynx HAS3GMS [322]	East Midlands Airport Aeropark
	XZ723	WS Lynx HMA8SRU [672]	Delta Force Paintball, Thornbury, Glos
	XZ725	WS Lynx HMA8SRU [415/MM]	RN, stored St Athan
	XZ726	WS Lynx HMA8SRU [316]	School of Maritime Survival *HMS Raleigh*, Plymouth
	XZ727	WS Lynx HAS3S [634]	Delta Force Paintball, Romsey, Hants
	XZ728	WS Lynx HMA8 [326/AW]	RNAS Yeovilton, on display
	XZ729	WS Lynx HMA8SRU [425/DT]	RN, stored Middle Wallop
	XZ730	WS Lynx HAS3S	Privately owned, Hixon, Staffs
	XZ731	WS Lynx HMA8SRU [311/VL]	AAC, stored Middle Wallop
	XZ732	WS Lynx HMA8SRU [315/VL]	DSAE SAAE, Lyneham
	XZ735	WS Lynx HAS3GMS <ff>	Privately owned, Sproughton
	XZ736	WS Lynx HMA8SRU [815]	RN Yeovilton, GI use
	XZ791	Northrop Shelduck D1	Davidstow Airfield & Cornwall at War Museum
	XZ795	Northrop Shelduck D1	Army Flying Museum, Middle Wallop
	XZ920	WS61 Sea King HU5 [24]	DSAE, stored *HMS Sultan*, Gosport
	XZ921	WS61 Sea King HAS6 [269/N]	Mini Moos Farm, Edmondsley, Durham
	XZ922	WS61 Sea King HC6 [ZA]	DSAE RNAESS, *HMS Sultan*, Gosport
	XZ930	WS Gazelle HT3 (A2713) [SN]	DSAE, *HMS Sultan*, Gosport, on display
	XZ933	WS Gazelle HT3 (XZ936/G-CGJZ)	Privately owned, Hurstbourne Tarrant, Hants
	XZ934	WS Gazelle HT3 (G-CBSI)	Privately owned, Hurstbourne Tarrant, Hants
	XZ935	WS Gazelle HCC4 (9332M)	DSAE SAAE, Lyneham
	XZ936	WS Gazelle HT3 [6]	MoD, stored Boscombe Down (damaged)
	XZ939	WS Gazelle HT3	QinetiQ, Boscombe Down (wfu)

Serial	Type (code/other identity)	Owner/operator, location or fate	Notes
XZ941	WS Gazelle HT3 (9301M) [B]	*Currently not known*	
XZ964	BAe Harrier GR3 [D]	Royal Engineers Museum, Chatham	
XZ966	BAe Harrier GR3 (9221M) [G]	MoD DFTDC, Manston	
XZ968	BAe Harrier GR3 (9222M) [3G]	Muckleborough Collection, Weybourne	
XZ969	BAe Harrier GR3 [69/DD]	RN, Predannack Fire School	
XZ971	BAe Harrier GR3 (9219M)	HQ DSDA, Donnington, Shropshire, on display	
XZ987	BAe Harrier GR3 (9185M) [C]	RAF Stafford, at main gate	
XZ990	BAe Harrier GR3 <ff>	*Currently not known*	
XZ990	BAe Harrier GR3 <rf>	RAF Wittering, derelict	
XZ991	BAe Harrier GR3 (9162M)	DSAE Cosford, on display	
XZ993	BAe Harrier GR3 (9240M) <ff>	Privately owned, Upwood, Cambs	
XZ994	BAe Harrier GR3 (9170M) [U]	*Sold to Estonia, 2018*	
XZ995	BAe Harrier GR3 (9220M/G-CBGK) [3G]	Privately owned, Dolly's Grove, Co Dublin, Eire	
XZ996	BAe Harrier GR3 [96/DD]	Privately owned, Bentwaters	
XZ997	BAe Harrier GR3 (9122M) [V]	RAF Museum, Cosford Privately owned,	
ZA101	BAe Hawk 100 (G-HAWK)	Brooklands Museum, Weybridge	
ZA105	WS61 Sea King HAR3 [Q]	DSAE, stored *HMS Sultan*, Gosport	
ZA110	BAe Jetstream T2 (F-BTMI) [563/CU]	Aberdeen Airport Fire Section	
ZA111	BAe Jetstream T2 (9Q-CTC) [565/CU]	RN, Predannack Fire School	
ZA126	WS61 Sea King ASaC7 [91]	DSAE, stored *HMS Sultan*, Gosport	
ZA127	WS61 Sea King HAS6 [509/CU]	Privately owned, Thornhill, Stirlingshire	
ZA128	WS61 Sea King HAS6 [010]	DSAE No 1 SoTT, Cosford	
ZA130	WS61 Sea King HU5 [19]	Privately owned, Charlwood	
ZA131	WS61 Sea King HAS6 [271/N]	DSAE RNAESS, *HMS Sultan*, Gosport	
ZA133	WS61 Sea King HAS6 [831/CU]	DSAE RNAESS, *HMS Sultan*, Gosport	
ZA134	WS61 Sea King HU5 [25]	DSAE, stored *HMS Sultan*, Gosport	
ZA135	WS61 Sea King HAS6	Privately owned, Woodperry, Oxon	
ZA136	WS61 Sea King HAS6 [018]	Mayhem Paintball, Abridge, Essex	
ZA137	WS61 Sea King HU5 [20]	DSAE, stored *HMS Sultan*, Gosport	
ZA147	BAe VC10 K3 (5H-MMT) [F]	Privately owned, Bruntingthorpe	
ZA148	BAe VC10 K3 (5Y-ADA) [G]	Aerohub, Newquay	
ZA150	BAe VC10 K3 (5H-MOG) [J]	Brooklands Museum, Dunsfold	
ZA166	WS61 Sea King HU5	HeliOperations Ltd, Portland	
ZA167	WS61 Sea King HU5 [22/CU]	DSAE RNAESS, *HMS Sultan*, Gosport	
ZA168	WS61 Sea King HAS6 [830/CU]	DSAE RNAESS, *HMS Sultan*, Gosport	
ZA169	WS61 Sea King HAS6 [515/CW]	DSAE No 1 SoTT, Cosford	
ZA170	WS61 Sea King HAS5	*Currently not known*	
ZA175	BAe Sea Harrier FA2	Norfolk & Suffolk Avn Museum, Flixton	
ZA176	BAe Sea Harrier FA2 [126/R]	Newark Air Museum, Winthorpe	
ZA195	BAe Sea Harrier FA2	Tangmere Military Aviation Museum	
ZA209	Short MATS-B	Army Flying Museum, Middle Wallop	
ZA220	Short MATS-B (ZA242)	Boscombe Down Aviation Collection, Old Sarum	
ZA250	BAe Harrier T52 (G-VTOL)	Brooklands Museum, Weybridge	
ZA267	Panavia Tornado F2 (9284M) [FA]	Privately owned, RAF Syerston	
ZA291	WS61 Sea King HC4 [N]	Mini Moos Farm, Edmondsley, Durham	
ZA296	WS61 Sea King HC4 [Q]	*Dismantled at Fleetlands, 2017*	
ZA298	WS61 Sea King HC4 (G-BJNM) [Y]	FAA Museum, RNAS Yeovilton	
ZA312	WS61 Sea King HC4 [E]	Privately owned, Charlwood	
ZA313	WS61 Sea King HC4 [M]	Mini Moos Farm, Edmondsley, Durham	
ZA314	WS61 Sea King HC4 [WT]	DSAE, stored *HMS Sultan*, Gosport	
ZA319	Panavia Tornado GR1 (9315M)	DSDA, Arncott, Oxon, on display	
ZA320	Panavia Tornado GR1 (9314M) [TAW]	DSAE No 1 SoTT, Cosford	
ZA323	Panavia Tornado GR1 [TAZ]	DSAE No 1 SoTT, Cosford	
ZA325	Panavia Tornado GR1 <ff>	RAF Manston History Museum	
ZA325	Panavia Tornado GR1 [TAX] <rf>	RAF AM&SU, stored Shawbury	
ZA326	Panavia Tornado GR1P	South Wales Aviation Museum, St Athan	
ZA327	Panavia Tornado GR1 <ff>	Privately owned, Spark Bridge, Cumbria	
ZA328	Panavia Tornado GR1	BAE Systems, Samlesbury	
ZA353	Panavia Tornado GR1 [B-53]	Privately owned, Thorpe Wood, N Yorks	
ZA354	Panavia Tornado GR1	Yorkshire Air Museum, Elvington	
ZA355	Panavia Tornado GR1 (9310M) [TAA]	Privately owned, White Waltham	
ZA356	Panavia Tornado GR1 <ff>	RAF Tornado Maintenance School, Marham	

Notes	Serial	Type (code/other identity)	Owner/operator, location or fate
	ZA357	Panavia Tornado GR1 [TTV]	DSAE No 1 SoTT, Cosford
	ZA359	Panavia Tornado GR1	Privately owned, Thorpe Wood, N Yorks
	ZA360	Panavia Tornado GR1 (9318M) <ff>	RAF Marham, instructional use
	ZA362	Panavia Tornado GR1 [TR]	Highland Aviation Museum, Inverness
	ZA369	Panavia Tornado GR4A [003]	Scrapped at Leeming, December 2018
	ZA370	Panavia Tornado GR4A [004]	Scrapped at Leeming, August 2018
	ZA398	Panavia Tornado GR4A [087]	Aerohub, Newquay
	ZA399	Panavia Tornado GR1 (9316M) [AJ-C]	Privately owned, Knutsford, Cheshire
	ZA406	Panavia Tornado GR4 [015]	Scrapped at Leeming, February 2018
	ZA407	Panavia Tornado GR1 (9336M) [AJ-N]	RAF Marham, on display
	ZA447	Panavia Tornado GR4 [019]	DSAE No 1 SoTT, Cosford
	ZA449	Panavia Tornado GR4 [020]	RAF Marham, RTP
	ZA450	Panavia Tornado GR1 (9317M) [TH]	DSAE No 1 SoTT, Cosford
	ZA452	Panavia Tornado GR4 [021]	Midland Air Museum, Coventry
	ZA453	Panavia Tornado GR4 [022]	Scrapped at Leeming, May 2018
	ZA457	Panavia Tornado GR1 [AJ-J]	RAF Museum, Hendon
	ZA458	Panavia Tornado GR4 [024]	Scrapped at Leeming, January 2018
	ZA459	Panavia Tornado GR4 [025]	DSAE No 1 SoTT, Cosford
	ZA462	Panavia Tornado GR4 [027]	Scrapped at Leeming, January 2019
	ZA463	Panavia Tornado GR4 [028]	RAF Marham, RTP
	ZA465	Panavia Tornado GR1 [FF]	IWM Duxford
	ZA469	Panavia Tornado GR4 [029]	IWM Duxford
	ZA472	Panavia Tornado GR4 [031]	RAF Marham (wfu)
	ZA473	Panavia Tornado GR4 [032]	Scrapped at RAF Marham, 2018
	ZA475	Panavia Tornado GR1 (9311M) [AJ-G]	RAF Lossiemouth, on display
	ZA542	Panavia Tornado GR4 [035]	RAF Marham, RTP
	ZA543	Panavia Tornado GR4 [036]	Scrapped at Leeming, February 2019
	ZA546	Panavia Tornado GR4 [038]	Scrapped at RAF Marham, 2018
	ZA548	Panavia Tornado GR4 [040] $	Scrapped at Leeming, December 2017
	ZA549	Panavia Tornado GR4 [041]	BAE Systems Aircraft Maintenance Academy, Humberside
	ZA550	Panavia Tornado GR4 [042]	Scrapped at Leeming, 2018
	ZA551	Panavia Tornado GR4 [043]	Scrapped
	ZA553	Panavia Tornado GR4 [045]	RAF Marham, RTP
	ZA554	Panavia Tornado GR4 [046]	RAF Marham, RTP
	ZA556	Panavia Tornado GR4 [047]	Scrapped at RAF Marham, 2018
	ZA556	Panavia Tornado GR1 <R> (ZA368/BAPC 155) [Z]	RAF M&RU, Bottesford
	ZA559	Panavia Tornado GR4 [049]	RAF Leeming, RTP
	ZA560	Panavia Tornado GR4 [EB-Q]	RAF Wittering, GI use
	ZA585	Panavia Tornado GR4 [054]	DSAE No 1 SoTT, Cosford
	ZA587	Panavia Tornado GR4 [055]	RAF Marham, RTP
	ZA588	Panavia Tornado GR4 [056]	RAF TST, Marham
	ZA591	Panavia Tornado GR4 [058]	Scrapped at RAF Marham, 2018
	ZA597	Panavia Tornado GR4 [063]	RAF Marham, RTP
	ZA601	Panavia Tornado GR4 [066]	RAF Marham, RTP
	ZA607	Panavia Tornado GR4 [EB-X]	RAF Sealand, on display
	ZA611	Panavia Tornado GR4 [073]	RAF Marham (wfu)
	ZA612	Panavia Tornado GR4 [074]	RAF Marham, RTP
	ZA613	Panavia Tornado GR4 [075]	RAF Marham, RTP
	ZA614	Panavia Tornado GR4 [076]	RAF Marham (wfu)
	ZA630	Slingsby T61F Venture T2 (G-BUGL)	Privately owned, Tibenham
	ZA634	Slingsby T61F Venture T2 (G-BUHA) [C]	Privately owned, Saltby, Leics
	ZA652	Slingsby T61F Venture T2 (G-BUDC)	Privately owned, Enstone
	ZA656	Slingsby T61F Venture T2 (G-BTWC)	Privately owned, Nympsfield
	ZA665	Slingsby T61F Venture T2 (G-BVKK)	Privately owned, Saltby, Leics
	ZA670	B-V Chinook HC6A (N37010)	MoD/Boeing/QinetiQ, Boscombe Down (conversion)
	ZA671	B-V Chinook HC4 (N37011) [AB]	MoD/StandardAero, Fleetlands
	ZA674	B-V Chinook HC6A (N37019)	MoD/StandardAero, Fleetlands
	ZA675	B-V Chinook HC6A (N37020)	RAF No 28 Sqn, Benson
	ZA677	B-V Chinook HC6A (N37022) [AF]	RAF No 28 Sqn, Benson
	ZA678	B-V Chinook HC1 (N37023/9229M) [EZ] (wreck)	RAF Odiham, BDRT
	ZA679	B-V Chinook HC6A (N37025) [AG]	MoD/StandardAero, Fleetlands
	ZA680	B-V Chinook HC6A (N37026) [AH]	MoD/Boeing/QinetiQ, Boscombe Down (conversion)

Serial	Type (code/other identity)	Owner/operator, location or fate	Notes
ZA681	B-V Chinook HC6A (N37027)	RAF No 18 Sqn, Odiham	
ZA682	B-V Chinook HC6A (N37029) [AJ]	RAF No 28 Sqn, Benson	
ZA683	B-V Chinook HC6A (N37030)	RAF No 18 Sqn, Odiham	
ZA684	B-V Chinook HC6A (N37031)	RAF No 7 Sqn, Odiham	
ZA704	B-V Chinook HC4 (N37033)	RAF No 28 Sqn, Benson	
ZA705	B-V Chinook HC4 (N37035) [AN]	MoD/StandardAero, Fleetlands	
ZA707	B-V Chinook HC6A (N37040) [AO]	MoD/Boeing/QinetiQ, Boscombe Down (conversion)	
ZA708	B-V Chinook HC6A (N37042) [AP]	MoD/Boeing/QinetiQ, Boscombe Down (conversion)	
ZA710	B-V Chinook HC6A (N37044)	MoD/Boeing/QinetiQ, Boscombe Down (conversion)	
ZA711	B-V Chinook HC4 (N37046)	MoD/StandardAero, Fleetlands	
ZA712	B-V Chinook HC6A (N37047) [W] $	MoD/Boeing/QinetiQ, Boscombe Down (conversion)	
ZA713	B-V Chinook HC4 (N37048)	MoD/StandardAero, Fleetlands	
ZA714	B-V Chinook HC6A (N37051)	MoD/Boeing/QinetiQ, Boscombe Down (conversion)	
ZA717	B-V Chinook HC1 (N37056/9238M) (wreck)	Newark Air Museum, Winthorpe	
ZA718	B-V Chinook HC4 (N37058) [BN]	MoD/StandardAero, Fleetlands	
ZA720	B-V Chinook HC6A (N37060)	MoD/Boeing/QinetiQ, Boscombe Down (conversion)	
ZA726	WS Gazelle AH1 [F1]	Privately owned, Stapleford Tawney	
ZA726	WS Gazelle AH1 (XW851/G-CIEY)	Privately owned, Escrick, N Yorks	
ZA728	WS Gazelle AH1 [E]	Privately owned, Stapleford Tawney	
ZA729	WS Gazelle AH1	AAC Wattisham, BDRT	
ZA730	WS Gazelle AH1 (G-FUKM) <ff>	Privately owned, Hurstbourne Tarrant, Hants	
ZA731	WS Gazelle AH1	AAC No 29 Flt, BATUS, Suffield, Canada	
ZA735	WS Gazelle AH1	DSAE SAAE, Lyneham	
ZA736	WS Gazelle AH1	AAC No 29 Flt, BATUS, Suffield, Canada	
ZA737	WS Gazelle AH1	Army Flying Museum, Middle Wallop	
ZA766	WS Gazelle AH1	AAC 7 Regiment Conversion Flt, Middle Wallop	
ZA769	WS Gazelle AH1 [K]	DSAE SAAE, Lyneham	
ZA771	WS Gazelle AH1	DSAE No 1 SoTT, Cosford	
ZA772	WS Gazelle AH1	AAC No 665 Sqn/5 Regt, Aldergrove	
ZA773	WS Gazelle AH1 [F]	AAC AM&SU, stored Shawbury	
ZA774	WS Gazelle AH1	Privately owned, Babcary, Somerset	
ZA775	WS Gazelle AH1	MoD/StandardAero, Fleetlands	
ZA776	WS Gazelle AH1 [F]	Privately owned, Stapleford Tawney	
ZA804	WS Gazelle HT3	Privately owned, Solstice Park, Amesbury, Wilts	
ZA935	WS Puma HC2	RAF No 28 Sqn/No 33 Sqn/No 230 Sqn, Benson	
ZA936	WS Puma HC2	RAF No 28 Sqn/No 33 Sqn/No 230 Sqn, Benson	
ZA937	WS Puma HC1	RAF Benson (wfu)	
ZA939	WS Puma HC2	RAF No 28 Sqn/No 33 Sqn/No 230 Sqn, Benson	
ZA940	WS Puma HC2 (F-ZWBZ)	RAF No 28 Sqn/No 33 Sqn/No 230 Sqn, Benson	
ZA947	Douglas Dakota C3	RAF BBMF, Coningsby	
ZB500	WS Lynx 800 (G-LYNX/ZA500)	The Helicopter Museum, Weston-super-Mare	
ZB506	WS61 Sea King Mk 4X	Privately owned, Charlwood	
ZB507	WS61 Sea King HC4 [F]	Currently not known	
ZB601	BAe Harrier T4 (fuselage)	Privately owned, Selby, N Yorks	
ZB603	BAe Harrier T8 [T03/DD]	SFDO, RNAS Culdrose	
ZB604	BAe Harrier T8 [722]	FAA Museum, stored Cobham Hall, RNAS Yeovilton	
ZB615	SEPECAT Jaguar T2A	DSAE No 1 SoTT, Cosford	
ZB625	WS Gazelle HT3	QinetiQ, Boscombe Down (wfu)	
ZB627	WS Gazelle HT3 (G-CBSK) [A]	Privately owned, Hurstbourne Tarrant, Hants	
ZB646	WS Gazelle HT2 (G-CBGZ) [59/CU]	Privately owned, Knebworth	
ZB647	WS Gazelle HT2 (G-CBSF) [40]	Privately owned, Hurstbourne Tarrant, Hants	
ZB665	WS Gazelle AH1	MoD/StandardAero, Fleetlands	
ZB667	WS Gazelle AH1	AAC AM&SU, stored Shawbury	
ZB668	WS Gazelle AH1 (TAD 015)	DSAE SAAE, Lyneham	
ZB669	WS Gazelle AH1	AAC No 665 Sqn/5 Regt, Aldergrove	
ZB670	WS Gazelle AH1	Territorial Army Centre, Taunton, on display	
ZB671	WS Gazelle AH1	AAC No 29 Flt, BATUS, Suffield, Canada	
ZB672	WS Gazelle AH1	Army Training Regiment, Winchester	
ZB673	WS Gazelle AH1 [P]	Privately owned, Stapleford Tawney	
ZB674	WS Gazelle AH1	MoD/StandardAero, Fleetlands	
ZB677	WS Gazelle AH1 [5B]	AAC No 29 Flt, BATUS, Suffield, Canada	

Notes	Serial	Type (code/other identity)	Owner/operator, location or fate
	ZB678	WS Gazelle AH1	MoD/StandardAero, Fleetlands
	ZB679	WS Gazelle AH1	AAC No 665 Sqn/5 Regt, Aldergrove
	ZB683	WS Gazelle AH1	AAC No 665 Sqn/5 Regt, Aldergrove
	ZB684	WS Gazelle AH1	RAF JADTEU, Brize Norton, instructional use
	ZB686	WS Gazelle AH1 <ff>	The Helicopter Museum, Weston-super-Mare
	ZB689	WS Gazelle AH1	AAC No 665 Sqn/5 Regt, Aldergrove
	ZB690	WS Gazelle AH1	MoD/StandardAero, Fleetlands
	ZB691	WS Gazelle AH1 [S]	AAC 7 Regt Conversion Flt, Middle Wallop
	ZB692	WS Gazelle AH1 [Y]	MoD/StandardAero, Fleetlands
	ZB693	WS Gazelle AH1	AAC No 665 Sqn/5 Regt, Aldergrove
	ZD230	BAC Super VC10 K4 (G-ASGA) <ff>	Privately owned, Crondall, Hants
	ZD240	BAC Super VC10 K4 (G-ASGL) <ff>	Privately owned, Crondall, Hants
	ZD241	BAC Super VC10 K4 (G-ASGM) [N]	Privately owned, Bruntingthorpe
	ZD242	BAC Super VC10 K4 (G-ASGP) <ff>	JARTS, Boscombe Down
	ZD249	WS Lynx HMA8SRU (XZ698) (comp ZD249) [316]	Delta Force Paintball, Edinburgh
	ZD250	WS Lynx HAS3S [636]	RAF Henlow, instructional use
	ZD251	WS Lynx HAS3S	Privately owned, Hixon, Staffs
	ZD252	WS Lynx HMA8SRU [312/VL]	RN Yeovilton, GI use
	ZD254	WS Lynx HAS3S [305]	DSAE AESS, HMS Sultan, Gosport
	ZD255	WS Lynx HAS3GMS [635]	Bawtry Paintball Park, S Yorks
	ZD257	WS Lynx HMA8SRU [302/VL]	AAC, stored Middle Wallop
	ZD258	WS Lynx HMA8SRU [365]	Privately owned, Bentwaters
	ZD259	WS Lynx HMA8SRU [474/RM]	RN, stored St Athan
	ZD260	WS Lynx HMA8SRU [313/VL]	AAC, stored Middle Wallop
	ZD261	WS Lynx HMA8SRU [314]	RN, stored St Athan
	ZD262	WS Lynx HMA8SRU [316]	AAC MPSU, Middle Wallop
	ZD263	WS Lynx HAS3S [632]	Bawtry Paintball Park, S Yorks
	ZD264	WS Lynx HAS3GMS [407] (fuselage)	Air Defence Collection, Wilts
	ZD265	WS Lynx HMA8SRU [302]	AAC Middle Wallop, GI use
	ZD266	WS Lynx HMA8SRU [673]	Bradwell Bay Military & Science Museum, Essex
	ZD267	WS Lynx HMA8 (comp XZ672) [LST-2]	RN, stored St Athan
	ZD268	WS Lynx HMA8SRU [366/YB]	RN, stored St Athan
	ZD273	WS Lynx AH7 [E]	Sold to The Netherlands
	ZD274	WS Lynx AH7 [M]	Privately owned, Sproughton
	ZD276	WS Lynx AH7	Mayhem Paintball, Abridge, Essex
	ZD278	WS Lynx AH7 [F]	Delta Force, Liverpool
	ZD279	WS Lynx AH7 <ff>	Privately owned, Hixon, Staffs
	ZD280	WS Lynx AH7	Farnborough Air Sciences Trust, Farnborough
	ZD281	WS Lynx AH7 [K]	Privately owned, Willenhall, Staffs
	ZD283	WS Lynx AH7 <ff>	Privately owned, Stoke-on-Trent
	ZD284	WS Lynx AH7 [K]	Privately owned, Corley Moor, Warks
	ZD285	WS Lynx AH7	QinetiQ Apprentice Training School, Boscombe Down
	ZD318	BAe Harrier GR7A	Harrier Heritage Centre, RAF Wittering
	ZD412	BAe Harrier GR5 (fuselage)	Scrapped
	ZD433	BAe Harrier GR9A [45A]	FAA Museum, RNAS Yeovilton
	ZD461	BAe Harrier GR9A [51A]	IWM London, Lambeth
	ZD462	BAe Harrier GR7 (9302M) [52]	Privately owned, Malmesbury, Glos
	ZD465	BAe Harrier GR9 [55]	RAF Cosford
	ZD469	BAe Harrier GR7A [59A]	RAF Wittering, on display
	ZD476	WS61 Sea King HC4 [WZ]	Privately owned, Charlwood
	ZD477	WS61 Sea King HC4 [E]	East Midlands Airport Aeropark
	ZD478	WS61 Sea King HC4 [J]	Privately owned, Hixon, Staffs
	ZD479	WS61 Sea King HC4 [WQ]	DSAE, stored HMS Sultan, Gosport
	ZD480	WS61 Sea King HC4 [J]	StandardAero, Fleetlands, on display
	ZD559	WS Lynx AH5X	QinetiQ Apprentice Training School, Boscombe Down
	ZD560	WS Lynx AH7	Privately owned, Hants
	ZD565	WS Lynx HMA8SRU [404/IR]	Delta Force Paintball, Cardiff
	ZD566	WS Lynx HMA8SRU [305]	Privately owned,
	ZD574	B-V Chinook HC6A (N37077) [DB]	MoD/StandardAero, Fleetlands
	ZD575	B-V Chinook HC6A (N37078)	RAF No 28 Sqn, Benson
	ZD578	BAe Sea Harrier FA2 [000,122]	RNAS Yeovilton, at main gate

Serial	Type (code/other identity)	Owner/operator, location or fate	Notes
ZD579	BAe Sea Harrier FA2 [79/DD]	SFDO, RNAS Culdrose	
ZD581	BAe Sea Harrier FA2 [124]	RN, Predannack Fire School	
ZD582	BAe Sea Harrier FA2 [002/N]	Privately owned, Banbury, Oxon	
ZD607	BAe Sea Harrier FA2	DSDA, Arncott, Oxon, preserved	
ZD610	BAe Sea Harrier FA2 [714,002/N]	Aerospace Bristol, Filton	
ZD611	BAe Sea Harrier FA2 [001]	RN, Portsmouth, preserved	
ZD612	BAe Sea Harrier FA2 [724]	Privately owned, Topsham, Devon	
ZD613	BAe Sea Harrier FA2 [127/R]	Privately owned, Cross Green, Leeds	
ZD614	BAe Sea Harrier FA2	Privately owned, Walcott, Lincs	
ZD620	BAe 125 CC3	Bournemouth Aviation Museum	
ZD621	BAe 125 CC3	RAF Northolt, on display	
ZD625	WS61 Sea King HC4 [P]	Mini Moos Farm, Edmondsley, Durham	
ZD626	WS61 Sea King HC4 (fuselage)	Scrapped at Fleetlands, 2016	
ZD627	WS61 Sea King HC4 <ff>	South Wales Aviation Museum, St Athan	
ZD630	WS61 Sea King HAS6 [012/L]	DSAE RNAESS, HMS Sultan, Gosport	
ZD631	WS61 Sea King HAS6 [66] (fuselage)	Privately owned, St Agnes, Cornwall	
ZD634	WS61 Sea King HAS6 [503]	SFDO, RNAS Culdrose	
ZD636	WS61 Sea King ASaC7 [182/CU]	DSAE, stored HMS Sultan, Gosport	
ZD637	WS61 Sea King HAS6 [700/PW]	DSAE RNAESS, HMS Sultan, Gosport	
ZD667	BAe Harrier GR3 (9201M) [U]	Bentwaters Cold War Museum	
ZD703	BAe 125 CC3	Privately owned, Shepton Mallet	
ZD704	BAe 125 CC3	Aerohub, Newquay	
ZD710	Panavia Tornado GR1 <ff>	Privately owned, Hawarden	
ZD711	Panavia Tornado GR4 [079]	RAF Honington, GI use	
ZD713	Panavia Tornado GR4 [081]	RAF Leeming, RTP	
ZD715	Panavia Tornado GR4 [083]	RAF Cosford, GI use	
ZD716	Panavia Tornado GR4 [DH] $	RAF Marham, RTP	
ZD739	Panavia Tornado GR4 [087]	Scrapped at Leeming, May 2018	
ZD741	Panavia Tornado GR4 [LS-F] $	Scrapped at Leeming, October 2018	
ZD742	Panavia Tornado GR4 [090]	Scrapped at Leeming, 2018	
ZD744	Panavia Tornado GR4 [092]	RAF Marham, RTP	
ZD792	Panavia Tornado GR4 [100]	Scrapped at RAF Marham, 2018	
ZD793	Panavia Tornado GR4	DSAE No 1 SoTT, Cosford	
ZD848	Panavia Tornado GR4 [109]	RAF Marham, RTP	
ZD849	Panavia Tornado GR4 [110]	DSAE No 1 SoTT, Cosford	
ZD890	Panavia Tornado GR4 [113]	Scrapped at Leeming, May 2018	
ZD899	Panavia Tornado F2	Gr Manchester Fire & Rescue Training Centre, Bury	
ZD902	Panavia Tornado F2A(TIARA)	Privately owned, Church Fenton	
ZD932	Panavia Tornado F2 (comp ZE255) (9308M) (fuselage)	Privately owned, Thorpe Wood, N Yorks	
ZD936	Panavia Tornado F2 (comp ZE251) <ff>	Boscombe Down Aviation Collection, Old Sarum	
ZD938	Panavia Tornado F2 (comp ZE295) <ff>	South Yorkshire Aircraft Museum, Doncaster	
ZD939	Panavia Tornado F2 (comp ZE292) <ff>	DSAE No 1 SoTT, Cosford, instructional use	
ZD948	Lockheed TriStar KC1 (G-BFCA/N304CS)	Privately owned, Bruntingthorpe	
ZD951	Lockheed TriStar K1 (G-BFCD/N309CS) $	Privately owned, Bruntingthorpe	
ZD980	B-V Chinook HC6A (N37082) [DD]	MoD/Boeing/QinetiQ, Boscombe Down (conversion)	
ZD981	B-V Chinook HC6A (N37083)	MoD/Boeing/QinetiQ, Boscombe Down (conversion)	
ZD982	B-V Chinook HC6A (N37085)	MoD/StandardAero, Fleetlands	
ZD983	B-V Chinook HC6A (N37086)	MoD/StandardAero, Fleetlands	
ZD984	B-V Chinook HC6A (N37088) [DH]	MoD/Boeing/QinetiQ, Boscombe Down (conversion)	
ZD990	BAe Harrier T8 [T90/DD]	Privately owned, St Athan	
ZD992	BAe Harrier T8 [724]	Privately owned, Knutsford, Cheshire	
ZE114	Panavia Tornado IDS (RSAF 703)	BAE Systems, Warton	
ZE119	Panavia Tornado IDS (RSAF 760)	BAE Systems, Warton	
ZE165	Panavia Tornado F3 [GE]	MoD DFTDC, Manston	
ZE168	Panavia Tornado F3 <ff>	Privately owned, Thorpe Wood, N Yorks	
ZE204	Panavia Tornado F3 [FC]	MoD DFTDC, Manston	
ZE256	Panavia Tornado F3 [DZ] (wears ZE343 on port side)	Privately owned, Thorpe Wood, N Yorks	
ZE340	Panavia Tornado F3 (ZE758/9298M) [GO]	DSAE No 1 SoTT, Cosford	
ZE342	Panavia Tornado F3 [HP]	Rolls Royce, RAF Leeming	
ZE352	McD F-4J(UK) Phantom (9086M) <ff>	Currently not known	

Notes	Serial	Type (code/other identity)	Owner/operator, location or fate
	ZE360	McD F-4J(UK) Phantom (9059M) [O]	MoD DFTDC, Manston
	ZE368	WS61 Sea King HAR3 [R]	Mini Moos Farm, Edmondsley, Durham
	ZE369	WS61 Sea King HAR3 [S]	Privately owned, Charlwood
	ZE370	WS61 Sea King HAR3 [T]	DSAE, stored HMS Sultan, Gosport
	ZE375	WS Lynx AH9A	Privately owned, Bentwaters
	ZE376	WS Lynx AH9A	AAC, stored Middle Wallop
	ZE378	WS Lynx AH7	AAC, stored Middle Wallop
	ZE379	WS Lynx AH7 <ff>	QinetiQ, Boscombe Down
	ZE380	WS Lynx AH9A	AAC, stored Middle Wallop
	ZE381	WS Lynx AH7 [X]	DSAE SAAE, Lyneham
	ZE395	BAe 125 CC3	Privately owned, Dunsfold
	ZE410	Agusta A109A (AE-334)	Army Flying Museum, Middle Wallop
	ZE412	Agusta A109A	Army, Credenhill
	ZE413	Agusta A109A	Perth Technical College
	ZE416	Agusta A109E Power Elite (G-ESLH)	MoD/ETPS, Boscombe Down
	ZE418	WS61 Sea King ASaC7 [186]	DSAE, stored HMS Sultan, Gosport
	ZE420	WS61 Sea King ASaC7 [189]	DSAE, stored HMS Sultan, Gosport
	ZE422	WS61 Sea King ASaC7 [192]	DSAE, stored HMS Sultan, Gosport
	ZE425	WS61 Sea King HC4 [WR]	Mini Moos Farm, Edmondsley, Durham
	ZE426	WS61 Sea King HC4 [WX]	DSAE RNAESS, HMS Sultan, Gosport
	ZE427	WS61 Sea King HC4 [K]	To Norway, December 2017
	ZE428	WS61 Sea King HC4 [H]	Mini Moos Farm, Edmondsley, Durham
	ZE432	BAC 1-11/479FU (DQ-FBV) <ff>	Bournemouth Aviation Museum
	ZE449	SA330L Puma HC1 (9017M/PA-12)	Army Whittington Barracks, Lichfield, on display
	ZE477	WS Lynx 3	The Helicopter Museum, Weston-super-Mare
	ZE495	Grob G103 Viking T1 (BGA3000) [VA]	RAF ACCGS/No 644 VGS, Syerston
	ZE496	Grob G103 Viking T1 (BGA3001) [VB]	RAF/Serco GMS, Syerston
	ZE498	Grob G103 Viking T1 (BGA3003) [VC]	RAF, stored Little Rissington
	ZE499	Grob G103 Viking T1 (BGA3004) [VD]	RAF/Serco GMS, Syerston
	ZE500	Grob G103 Viking T1 (BGA3005) <ff>	Privately owned, Gransden Lodge
	ZE502	Grob G103 Viking T1 (BGA3007) [VF]	RAF/Serco, stored Syerston
	ZE503	Grob G103 Viking T1 (BGA3008) [VG]	MoD/MADG, Cambridge (spares use)
	ZE504	Grob G103 Viking T1 (BGA3009) [VH]	RAF/Serco, stored Syerston
	ZE520	Grob G103 Viking T1 (BGA3010) [VJ]	RAF/Serco GMS, Syerston
	ZE521	Grob G103 Viking T1 (BGA3011) [VK]	RAF/Serco GMS, Syerston
	ZE522	Grob G103 Viking T1 (BGA3012) [VL]	RAF ACCGS/No 644 VGS, Syerston
	ZE524	Grob G103 Viking T1 (BGA3014) [VM]	RAF No 637 VGS, Little Rissington, GI use
	ZE526	Grob G103 Viking T1 (BGA3016) [VN]	RAF/Serco GMS, Syerston
	ZE527	Grob G103 Viking T1 (BGA3017) [VP]	RAF ACCGS/No 644 VGS, Syerston
	ZE528	Grob G103 Viking T1 (BGA3018) [VQ]	RAF/Serco GMS, Syerston
	ZE529	Grob G103 Viking T1 (BGA3019) (comp ZE655) [VR]	RAF/Serco GMS, Syerston
	ZE530	Grob G103 Viking T1 (BGA3020) [VS]	RAF, stored Little Rissington
	ZE531	Grob G103 Viking T1 (BGA3021) [VT]	RAF, stored Little Rissington
	ZE532	Grob G103 Viking T1 (BGA3022) [VU]	RAF/Serco GMS, Syerston
	ZE533	Grob G103 Viking T1 (BGA3023) [VV]	RAF/Serco GMS, Syerston
	ZE550	Grob G103 Viking T1 (BGA3025) [VX]	MoD/MADG, Cambridge (spares use)
	ZE551	Grob G103 Viking T1 (BGA3026) [VY]	RAF/Serco GMS, Syerston
	ZE552	Grob G103 Viking T1 (BGA3027) [VZ]	RAF, stored Little Rissington
	ZE553	Grob G103 Viking T1 (BGA3028) [WA]	RAF No 632 VGS, Ternhill
	ZE554	Grob G103 Viking T1 (BGA3029) [WB]	RAF, stored Little Rissington
	ZE555	Grob G103 Viking T1 (BGA3030) [WC]	RAF/Serco GMS, Syerston
	ZE556	Grob G103 Viking T1 (BGA3031) <ff>	No 308 Sqn ATC, Colchester
	ZE557	Grob G103 Viking T1 (BGA3032) [WE]	RAF/Serco GMS, Syerston
	ZE558	Grob G103 Viking T1 (BGA3033) [WF]	RAF, stored Little Rissington
	ZE559	Grob G103 Viking T1 (BGA3034) [WG]	RAF No 661 VGS, Kirknewton
	ZE560	Grob G103 Viking T1 (BGA3035) [WH]	RAF No 661 VGS, Kirknewton
	ZE561	Grob G103 Viking T1 (BGA3036) [WJ]	RAF, stored Little Rissington
	ZE562	Grob G103 Viking T1 (BGA3037) [WK]	RAF/Serco, stored Syerston
	ZE563	Grob G103 Viking T1 (BGA3038) [WL]	RAF/Serco GMS, Syerston
	ZE564	Grob G103 Viking T1 (BGA3039) [WN]	MoD/Southern Sailplanes, Membury
	ZE584	Grob G103 Viking T1 (BGA3040) [WP]	RAF ACCGS/No 644 VGS, Syerston
	ZE585	Grob G103 Viking T1 (BGA3041) [WQ]	RAF/Serco GMS, Syerston

Serial	Type (code/other identity)	Owner/operator, location or fate	Notes
ZE586	Grob G103 Viking T1 (BGA3042) [WR]	RAF/Serco, stored Syerston	
ZE587	Grob G103 Viking T1 (BGA3043) [WS]	RAF No 622 VGS, Upavon	
ZE590	Grob G103 Viking T1 (BGA3046) [WT]	RAF/Serco GMS, Syerston	
ZE591	Grob G103 Viking T1 (BGA3047) [WU]	RAF, stored Little Rissington	
ZE592	Grob G103 Viking T1 (BGA3048) <ff>	RAF, Upavon, GI use	
ZE593	Grob G103 Viking T1 (BGA3049) [WW]	RAF, stored Little Rissington	
ZE594	Grob G103 Viking T1 (BGA3050) [WX]	RAF/Serco GMS, Syerston	
ZE595	Grob G103 Viking T1 (BGA3051) [WY]	RAF/Serco GMS, Syerston	
ZE600	Grob G103 Viking T1 (BGA3052) [WZ]	MoD/Southern Sailplanes, Membury	
ZE601	Grob G103 Viking T1 (BGA3053) [XA]	RAF No 622 VGS, Upavon	
ZE602	Grob G103 Viking T1 (BGA3054) [XB]	RAF ACCGS/No 644 VGS, Syerston	
ZE603	Grob G103 Viking T1 (BGA3055) [XC]	RAF, stored Little Rissington	
ZE604	Grob G103 Viking T1 (BGA3056) [XD]	RAF, stored Little Rissington	
ZE605	Grob G103 Viking T1 (BGA3057) [XE]	RAF ACCGS/No 644 VGS, Syerston	
ZE606	Grob G103 Viking T1 (BGA3058) [XF]	RAF/Serco GMS, Syerston	
ZE607	Grob G103 Viking T1 (BGA3059) [XG]	RAF, stored Little Rissington	
ZE608	Grob G103 Viking T1 (BGA3060) [XH]	RAF/Serco GMS, Syerston	
ZE609	Grob G103 Viking T1 (BGA3061) [XJ]	RAF/Serco GMS, Syerston	
ZE610	Grob G103 Viking T1 (BGA3062) [XK]	RAF, stored Little Rissington	
ZE611	Grob G103 Viking T1 (BGA3063) [XL]	RAF, stored Little Rissington	
ZE613	Grob G103 Viking T1 (BGA3065) [XM]	RAF/Serco GMS, Syerston	
ZE614	Grob G103 Viking T1 (BGA3066) [XN]	RAF No 621 VGS/No 637 VGS, Little Rissington	
ZE625	Grob G103 Viking T1 (BGA3067) [XP]	RAF/Serco GMS, Syerston	
ZE626	Grob G103 Viking T1 (BGA3068) [XQ]	RAF/Serco GMS, Syerston	
ZE627	Grob G103 Viking T1 (BGA3069) [XR]	RAF, stored Little Rissington	
ZE628	Grob G103 Viking T1 (BGA3070) [XS]	RAF No 621 VGS/No 637 VGS, Little Rissington	
ZE629	Grob G103 Viking T1 (BGA3071) [XT]	RAF/Serco GMS, Syerston	
ZE630	Grob G103 Viking T1 (BGA3072) [XU]	RAF/Serco GMS, Syerston	
ZE631	Grob G103 Viking T1 (BGA3073) [XV]	RAF ACCGS/No 644 VGS, Syerston	
ZE632	Grob G103 Viking T1 (BGA3074) [XW]	RAF No 621 VGS/No 637 VGS, Little Rissington	
ZE633	Grob G103 Viking T1 (BGA3075) [XX]	RAF/Serco GMS, Syerston	
ZE636	Grob G103 Viking T1 (BGA3078) [XZ]	MoD/Southern Sailplanes, Membury	
ZE637	Grob G103 Viking T1 (BGA3079) [YA]	RAF No 632 VGS, Ternhill	
ZE650	Grob G103 Viking T1 (BGA3080) [YB]	RAF/Serco GMS, Syerston	
ZE651	Grob G103 Viking T1 (BGA3081) [YC]	RAF/Serco GMS, Syerston	
ZE652	Grob G103 Viking T1 (BGA3082) [YD]	RAF/Serco, stored Syerston	
ZE653	Grob G103 Viking T1 (BGA3083) [YE]	RAF/Serco GMS, Syerston	
ZE656	Grob G103 Viking T1 (BGA3086) [YH]	RAF, stored Little Rissington	
ZE657	Grob G103 Viking T1 (BGA3087) [YJ]	RAF, stored Little Rissington	
ZE658	Grob G103 Viking T1 (BGA3088) [YK]	RAF/Serco, stored Syerston	
ZE677	Grob G103 Viking T1 (BGA3090) [YM]	RAF, stored Little Rissington	
ZE678	Grob G103 Viking T1 (BGA3091) [YN]	RAF/Serco, stored Syerston	
ZE679	Grob G103 Viking T1 (BGA3092) [YP]	RAF, stored Little Rissington	
ZE680	Grob G103 Viking T1 (BGA3093) [YQ]	RAF/Serco GMS, Syerston	
ZE681	Grob G103 Viking T1 (BGA3094) <ff>	Privately owned, Frampton Cotterell, Glos, GI use	
ZE682	Grob G103 Viking T1 (BGA3095) [YS]	RAF/Serco GMS, Syerston	
ZE683	Grob G103 Viking T1 (BGA3096) [YT]	RAF, stored Little Rissington	
ZE684	Grob G103 Viking T1 (BGA3097) [YU]	RAF, stored Little Rissington	
ZE685	Grob G103 Viking T1 (BGA3098) [YV]	RAF ACCGS/No 644 VGS, Syerston	
ZE686	Grob G103 Viking T1 (BGA3099) <ff>	RAF Museum, Hendon	
ZE690	BAe Sea Harrier FA2 [90/DD]	SFDO, RNAS Culdrose	
ZE691	BAe Sea Harrier FA2 [710]	Classic Autos, Winsford, Cheshire	
ZE692	BAe Sea Harrier FA2 [92/DD]	SFDO, RNAS Culdrose	
ZE694	BAe Sea Harrier FA2 [004]	Midland Air Museum, Coventry	
ZE697	BAe Sea Harrier FA2 [006]	Privately owned, Binbrook	
ZE698	BAe Sea Harrier FA2 [001]	Privately owned, Charlwood	
ZE700	BAe 146 CC2 (G-6-021) $	RAF No 32(The Royal) Sqn, Northolt	
ZE701	BAe 146 CC2 (G-6-029)	RAF No 32(The Royal) Sqn, Northolt	
ZE704	Lockheed TriStar C2 (N508PA/N507CS)	Privately owned, Bruntingthorpe	
ZE705	Lockheed TriStar C2 (N509PA/N703CS)	Privately owned, Bruntingthorpe	
ZE707	BAe 146 C3 (OO-TAZ)	RAF No 32(The Royal) Sqn, Northolt	
ZE708	BAe 146 C3 (OO-TAY)	RAF No 32(The Royal) Sqn, Northolt	

Notes	Serial	Type (code/other identity)	Owner/operator, location or fate
	ZE760	Panavia Tornado F3 (MM7206) [AP]	RAF Coningsby, on display
	ZE887	Panavia Tornado F3 [GF] $	RAF Museum, Hendon
	ZE934	Panavia Tornado F3 [TA]	National Museum of Flight, E Fortune
	ZE936	Panavia Tornado F3 <ff>	RAF Air Defence Radar Museum, Neatishead
	ZE965	Panavia Tornado F3 <ff>	Privately owned,
	ZE966	Panavia Tornado F3 [VT]	Tornado Heritage Centre, Hawarden
	ZE967	Panavia Tornado F3 [UT]	RAF Leuchars, at main gate
	ZF115	WS61 Sea King HC4 [R,WV]	DSAE, stored HMS Sultan, Gosport
	ZF116	WS61 Sea King HC4 [WP]	Privately owned, Charlwood
	ZF118	WS61 Sea King HC4 [O]	School of Maritime Survival HMS Raleigh, Plymouth
	ZF119	WS61 Sea King HC4 [WY]	DSAE, stored HMS Sultan, Gosport
	ZF120	WS61 Sea King HC4 [Z]	Privately owned, Colsterworth, Leics
	ZF121	WS61 Sea King HC4 [T]	Mini Moos Farm, Edmondsley, Durham
	ZF122	WS61 Sea King HC4 [V]	Privately owned, Chard, Somerset
	ZF135	Shorts Tucano T1 [135]	RAF No 1 FTS, Linton-on-Ouse
	ZF137	Shorts Tucano T1 [137]	RAF, stored Linton-on-Ouse
	ZF139	Shorts Tucano T1 [139]	RAF No 1 FTS, Linton-on-Ouse
	ZF140	Shorts Tucano T1 [140] $	RAF No 1 FTS/72 Sqn, Linton-on-Ouse
	ZF142	Shorts Tucano T1 [142]	RAF No 1 FTS, Linton-on-Ouse
	ZF143	Shorts Tucano T1 [143]	RAF No 1 FTS, Linton-on-Ouse
	ZF144	Shorts Tucano T1 [144]	RAF TSF, Linton-on-Ouse
	ZF145	Shorts Tucano T1 [145]	RAF No 1 FTS, Linton-on-Ouse
	ZF160	Shorts Tucano T1 [160]	Privately owned, Bentwaters
	ZF163	Shorts Tucano T1 [163]	RAF AM&SU, stored Shawbury
	ZF166	Shorts Tucano T1 [166]	Privately owned, Bentwaters
	ZF167	Shorts Tucano T1 (fuselage)	Ulster Aviation Society, Long Kesh
	ZF169	Shorts Tucano T1 [169]	RAF, stored Linton-on-Ouse
	ZF170	Shorts Tucano T1 [MP-A]	RAF, stored Linton-on-Ouse
	ZF171	Shorts Tucano T1 [171]	RAF No 1 FTS, Linton-on-Ouse
	ZF172	Shorts Tucano T1 [172]	RAF No 1 FTS, Linton-on-Ouse
	ZF202	Shorts Tucano T1 [202]	RAF Linton-on-Ouse, on display
	ZF204	Shorts Tucano T1 [204]	RAF No 1 FTS, Linton-on-Ouse
	ZF205	Shorts Tucano T1 [205]	RAF No 1 FTS/72 Sqn, Linton-on-Ouse
	ZF210	Shorts Tucano T1 [210]	RAF, stored Linton-on-Ouse
	ZF211	Shorts Tucano T1 [211]	Privately owned, Bentwaters
	ZF239	Shorts Tucano T1 [239]	RAF No 1 FTS, Linton-on-Ouse
	ZF240	Shorts Tucano T1 [240]	RAF TSF, Linton-on-Ouse
	ZF243	Shorts Tucano T1 [243]	RAF No 1 FTS, Linton-on-Ouse
	ZF244	Shorts Tucano T1 [244]	RAF No 1 FTS/72 Sqn, Linton-on-Ouse
	ZF263	Shorts Tucano T1 [263]	RAF AM&SU, stored Shawbury
	ZF264	Shorts Tucano T1 [264]	RAF No 1 FTS, Linton-on-Ouse
	ZF268	Shorts Tucano T1 [268]	RAF AM&SU, stored Shawbury
	ZF269	Shorts Tucano T1 [269]	RAF No 1 FTS, Linton-on-Ouse
	ZF286	Shorts Tucano T1 [286]	RAF AM&SU, stored Shawbury
	ZF287	Shorts Tucano T1 [287]	RAF No 1 FTS/72 Sqn, Linton-on-Ouse
	ZF288	Shorts Tucano T1 [288]	RAF AM&SU, stored Shawbury
	ZF289	Shorts Tucano T1 [289]	Bombardier, Belfast
	ZF290	Shorts Tucano T1 [290] $	RAF No 1 FTS/72 Sqn, Linton-on-Ouse
	ZF291	Shorts Tucano T1 [291]	RAF No 1 FTS, Linton-on-Ouse
	ZF292	Shorts Tucano T1 [292]	RAF, stored Linton-on-Ouse
	ZF293	Shorts Tucano T1 [293] $	RAF No 1 FTS/72 Sqn, Linton-on-Ouse
	ZF294	Shorts Tucano T1 [294]	RAF, stored Linton-on-Ouse
	ZF295	Shorts Tucano T1 [295] $	Bombardier, Belfast
	ZF315	Shorts Tucano T1 [315]	RAF AM&SU, stored Shawbury
	ZF317	Shorts Tucano T1 [317]	RAF No 1 FTS, Linton-on-Ouse
	ZF318	Shorts Tucano T1 [318] $	RAF AM&SU, stored Shawbury
	ZF319	Shorts Tucano T1 [319]	RAF, stored Linton-on-Ouse
	ZF338	Shorts Tucano T1 [338]	RAF No 1 FTS, Linton-on-Ouse
	ZF341	Shorts Tucano T1 [341]	RAF, stored Linton-on-Ouse
	ZF342	Shorts Tucano T1 [342]	RAF No 1 FTS, Linton-on-Ouse
	ZF343	Shorts Tucano T1 [343]	RAF No 1 FTS/72 Sqn, Linton-on-Ouse

Serial	Type (code/other identity)	Owner/operator, location or fate	Notes
ZF347	Shorts Tucano T1 [347]	RAF TSF, Linton-on-Ouse	
ZF348	Shorts Tucano T1 [348]	RAF No 1 FTS, Linton-on-Ouse	
ZF349	Shorts Tucano T1 [349] (fuselage)	RAF, stored Linton-on-Ouse (wreck)	
ZF350	Shorts Tucano T1 [350]	RAF AM&SU, stored Shawbury	
ZF355	WS Lynx HAS3S(ICE) (XZ238) [633]	Privately owned, White Waltham	
ZF372	Shorts Tucano T1 [372]	RAF AM&SU, stored Shawbury	
ZF374	Shorts Tucano T1 [374]	RAF No 1 FTS, Linton-on-Ouse	
ZF376	Shorts Tucano T1 [376]	RAF AM&SU, stored Shawbury	
ZF377	Shorts Tucano T1 [377]	RAF No 1 FTS, Linton-on-Ouse	
ZF378	Shorts Tucano T1 [RN-S] $	RAF No 1 FTS/72 Sqn, Linton-on-Ouse	
ZF379	Shorts Tucano T1 [379]	RAF No 1 FTS, Linton-on-Ouse	
ZF380	Shorts Tucano T1 [380]	Privately owned, Bentwaters	
ZF405	Shorts Tucano T1 [405]	RAF AM&SU, stored Shawbury	
ZF406	Shorts Tucano T1 [406]	RAF, stored Linton-on-Ouse	
ZF407	Shorts Tucano T1 [407]	RAF No 1 FTS, Linton-on-Ouse	
ZF408	Shorts Tucano T1 [408]	RAF AM&SU, stored Shawbury	
ZF412	Shorts Tucano T1 [412]	Privately owned, Bentwaters	
ZF414	Shorts Tucano T1 [414]	RAF AM&SU, stored Shawbury	
ZF416	Shorts Tucano T1 [416]	RAF AM&SU, stored Shawbury	
ZF417	Shorts Tucano T1 [417]	RAF No 1 FTS, Linton-on-Ouse	
ZF418	Shorts Tucano T1 [418]	RAF AM&SU, stored Shawbury	
ZF446	Shorts Tucano T1 [446]	RAF AM&SU, stored Shawbury	
ZF448	Shorts Tucano T1 [448]	RAF No 1 FTS, Linton-on-Ouse	
ZF449	Shorts Tucano T1 [449]	RAF AM&SU, stored Shawbury	
ZF485	Shorts Tucano T1 (G-BULU) [485]	RAF No 1 FTS, Linton-on-Ouse	
ZF486	Shorts Tucano T1 [486]	RAF AM&SU, stored Shawbury	
ZF487	Shorts Tucano T1 [487]	RAF AM&SU, stored Shawbury	
ZF488	Shorts Tucano T1 [488]	RAF AM&SU, stored Shawbury	
ZF489	Shorts Tucano T1 [489]	RAF No 1 FTS, Linton-on-Ouse	
ZF490	Shorts Tucano T1 [490]	RAF AM&SU, stored Shawbury	
ZF491	Shorts Tucano T1 [491]	RAF No 1 FTS, Linton-on-Ouse	
ZF492	Shorts Tucano T1 [492]	RAF AM&SU, stored Shawbury	
ZF510	Shorts Tucano T1 [510]	QinetiQ, Boscombe Down (wfu)	
ZF511	Shorts Tucano T1 [511]	QinetiQ, Boscombe Down (wfu)	
ZF512	Shorts Tucano T1 [512]	RAF CFS, Cranwell	
ZF513	Shorts Tucano T1 [513]	RAF AM&SU, stored Shawbury	
ZF515	Shorts Tucano T1 [515]	RAF No 1 FTS/72 Sqn, Linton-on-Ouse	
ZF516	Shorts Tucano T1 [516]	Privately owned, Bentwaters	
ZF534	BAe EAP	RAF Museum, Cosford	
ZF537	WS Lynx AH9A	AAC Middle Wallop, RTP	
ZF538	WS Lynx AH9A	AAC Middle Wallop, RTP	
ZF539	WS Lynx AH9A	Privately owned, Sproughton	
ZF557	WS Lynx HMA8SRU [426/PD]	AAC, stored Middle Wallop	
ZF558	WS Lynx HMA8SRU [336/WK]	AAC, stored Middle Wallop	
ZF560	WS Lynx HMA8SRU [456]	RN, stored St Athan	
ZF562	WS Lynx HMA8SRU [353/MB]	AAC, stored Middle Wallop	
ZF563	WS Lynx HMA8SRU [312/VL]	AAC, stored Middle Wallop	
ZF580	BAC Lightning F53 (53-672/204)	Repainted as XR768, April 2018	
ZF581	BAC Lightning F53 (53-675/206)	Bentwaters Cold War Museum	
ZF582	BAC Lightning F53 (53-676/210/207) <ff>	Bournemouth Aviation Museum	
ZF583	BAC Lightning F53 (53-681/306/210)	Solway Aviation Society, Carlisle	
ZF584	BAC Lightning F53 (53-682/307/211)	Dumfries & Galloway Avn Mus, Dumfries	
ZF587	BAC Lightning F53 (53-691/215) <ff>	Lashenden Air Warfare Museum, Headcorn	
ZF587	BAC Lightning F53 (53-691/215) <rf>	Privately owned, Stowmarket, Suffolk	
ZF588	BAC Lightning F53 (53-693/216) [L]	East Midlands Airport Aeropark	
ZF589	BAC Lightning F53 (53-700/218) <ff>	Gatwick Aviation Museum, stored Charlwood	
ZF590	BAC Lightning F53 (53-679/206/1302/220) <ff>	Privately owned, stored Bruntingthorpe	
ZF595	BAC Lightning T55 (55-714/212/1317/231) (fuselage)	Privately owned, Binbrook	
ZF596	BAC Lightning T55 (55-715/305/205/220/233) <ff>	Lakes Lightnings, Spark Bridge, Cumbria	
ZF622	Piper PA-31 Navajo Chieftain 350 (N3548Y)	Aerohub, Newquay	
ZF641	EHI-101 [PP1]	SFDO, RNAS Culdrose	
ZF649	EHI-101 Merlin (A2714) [PP5]	DSAE AESS, HMS Sultan, Gosport	

Notes	Serial	Type (code/other identity)	Owner/operator, location or fate
	ZG101	EHI-101 (mock-up) [GB]	*Currently not known*
	ZG347	Northrop Chukar D2	Davidstow Airfield & Cornwall At War Museum
	ZG477	BAe Harrier GR9 $	RAF Museum, Hendon
	ZG478	BAe Harrier GR9 (fuselage)	Privately owned, Sproughton
	ZG509	BAe Harrier GR7 [80]	Privately owned, Petersfield, Hants
	ZG631	Northrop Chukar D2	Farnborough Air Sciences Trust, stored Farnborough
	ZG705	Panavia Tornado GR4A [118]	*Scrapped at Leeming, November 2017*
	ZG707	Panavia Tornado GR4A [119]	*Scrapped at Leeming, February 2018*
	ZG750	Panavia Tornado GR4 [128] $	*Scrapped at Leeming, January 2018*
	ZG751	Panavia Tornado F3 (fuselage)	MoD JARTS, Boscombe Down
	ZG752	Panavia Tornado GR4 $	RAF Marham, RTP
	ZG771	Panavia Tornado GR4 $	RAF Marham, RTP
	ZG773	Panavia Tornado GR4	RAF
	ZG775	Panavia Tornado GR4 [AF] $	RAF Marham, RTP
	ZG777	Panavia Tornado GR4 [135]	*Scrapped at Leeming, August 2018*
	ZG779	Panavia Tornado GR4 [136]	*Scrapped at Leeming, March 2018*
	ZG791	Panavia Tornado GR4 [137]	RAF No 9 Sqn, Marham
	ZG816	WS61 Sea King HAS6 [014/L]	DSAE, stored *HMS Sultan*, Gosport
	ZG817	WS61 Sea King HAS6 [702/PW]	DSAE RNAESS, *HMS Sultan*, Gosport
	ZG818	WS61 Sea King HAS6 [707/PW]	DSAE RNAESS, *HMS Sultan*, Gosport
	ZG819	WS61 Sea King HAS6 [265/N]	DSAE RNAESS, *HMS Sultan*, Gosport
	ZG822	WS61 Sea King HC4 [WS]	South Wales Aviation Museum, St Athan
	ZG844	PBN 2T Islander AL1 (G-BLNE)	AAC AM&SU, stored Shawbury
	ZG845	PBN 2T Islander AL1 (G-BLNT)	AAC No 651 Sqn/5 Regt, Aldergrove
	ZG846	PBN 2T Islander AL1 (G-BLNU)	AAC No 651 Sqn/5 Regt, Aldergrove
	ZG847	PBN 2T Islander AL1 (G-BLNV)	AAC AM&SU, stored Shawbury
	ZG848	PBN 2T Islander AL1 (G-BLNY)	AAC No 651 Sqn/5 Regt, Aldergrove
	ZG875	WS61 Sea King HAS6 [013] <ff>	Privately owned, Crewe
	ZG875	WS61 Sea King HAS6 <rf>	Mayhem Paintball, Aybridge, Essex
	ZG884	WS Lynx AH9A	Privately owned, Bentwaters
	ZG885	WS Lynx AH9A	AAC Middle Wallop, RTP
	ZG886	WS Lynx AH9A	Privately owned, Bentwaters
	ZG887	WS Lynx AH9A	Privately owned, Sproughton
	ZG888	WS Lynx AH9A	Privately owned, Sproughton
	ZG889	WS Lynx AH9A	Privately owned, Bentwaters
	ZG914	WS Lynx AH9A	Privately owned, Wainfleet, Lincs
	ZG915	WS Lynx AH9A	RN, Predannack Fire School
	ZG916	WS Lynx AH9A	Pennant Training Systems, Staverton
	ZG917	WS Lynx AH9A $	AAC, stored Middle Wallop
	ZG918	WS Lynx AH9A	AAC Middle Wallop, RTP
	ZG919	WS Lynx AH9A	RN, Predannack Fire School
	ZG920	WS Lynx AH9A	AAC, stored Middle Wallop
	ZG921	WS Lynx AH9A	AAC, stored Middle Wallop
	ZG922	WS Lynx AH9	Privately owned, Staverton, instructional use
	ZG923	WS Lynx AH9A	AAC Middle Wallop, RTP
	ZG969	Pilatus PC-9 (HB-HQE)	BAE Systems, Warton, GI use
	ZG993	PBN 2T Islander AL1 (G-BOMD)	Army Flying Museum, Middle Wallop
	ZG994	PBN 2T Islander AL1 (G-BPLN) (fuselage)	Britten-Norman, stored Bembridge
	ZG995	PBN 2T Defender AL1 (G-SURV)	AAC No 651 Sqn/5 Regt, Aldergrove
	ZG996	PBN 2T Defender AL1 (G-BWPR)	AAC No 651 Sqn/5 Regt, Aldergrove
	ZG997	PBN 2T Defender AL2 (G-BWPV)	AAC No 651 Sqn/5 Regt, Aldergrove
	ZG998	PBN 2T Defender AL2 (G-BWPX)	AAC No 651 Sqn/5 Regt, Aldergrove
	ZH001	PBN 2T Defender AL2 (G-CEIO)	AAC No 651 Sqn/5 Regt, Aldergrove
	ZH002	PBN 2T Defender AL2 (G-CEIP)	AAC No 651 Sqn/5 Regt, Aldergrove
	ZH003	PBN 2T Defender AL2 (G-CEIR)	AAC No 651 Sqn/5 Regt, Aldergrove
	ZH004	PBN 2T Defender T3 (G-BWPO)	AAC No 651 Sqn/5 Regt, Aldergrove
	ZH005	PBN 2T Defender AL2 (G-CGVB)	AAC No 651 Sqn/5 Regt, Aldergrove
	ZH101	Boeing E-3D Sentry AEW1 [01]	RAF No 8 Sqn/No 54 Sqn, Waddington
	ZH102	Boeing E-3D Sentry AEW1 [02]	RAF No 8 Sqn/No 54 Sqn, Waddington
	ZH103	Boeing E-3D Sentry AEW1 [03]	RAF No 8 Sqn/No 54 Sqn, Waddington
	ZH104	Boeing E-3D Sentry AEW1 [04]	RAF No 8 Sqn/No 54 Sqn, Waddington

Serial	Type (code/other identity)	Owner/operator, location or fate	Notes
ZH105	Boeing E-3D Sentry AEW1 [05]	RAF, stored Waddington	
ZH106	Boeing E-3D Sentry AEW1 [06]	RAF No 8 Sqn/No 54 Sqn, Waddington	
ZH107	Boeing E-3D Sentry AEW1 [07] $	RAF, stored Waddington	
ZH115	Grob G109B Vigilant T1 [TA]	RAF, stored Little Rissington	
ZH116	Grob G109B Vigilant T1 [TB]	RAF, stored Watton	
ZH117	Grob G109B Vigilant T1 [TC]	RAF, stored Little Rissington	
ZH118	Grob G109B Vigilant T1 [TD]	RAF, stored Watton	
ZH119	Grob G109B Vigilant T1 (fuselage)	RAF, stored Little Rissington	
ZH120	Grob G109B Vigilant T1 [TF]	RAF, stored Little Rissington	
ZH121	Grob G109B Vigilant T1 [TG]	RAF, stored Little Rissington	
ZH122	Grob G109B Vigilant T1 [TH]	RAF, stored Little Rissington	
ZH123	Grob G109B Vigilant T1 [TJ]	RAF/Serco, stored Syerston	
ZH124	Grob G109B Vigilant T1 [TK]	RAF, stored Little Rissington	
ZH125	Grob G109B Vigilant T1 [TL]	RAF, stored Little Rissington	
ZH126	Grob G109B Vigilant T1 (D-KGRA) [TM]	RAF/Serco, stored Syerston	
ZH127	Grob G109B Vigilant T1 (D-KEEC) [TN]	RAF/Serco, stored Syerston	
ZH128	Grob G109B Vigilant T1 [TP]	RAF/Serco, stored Syerston	
ZH129	Grob G109B Vigilant T1 [TQ]	RAF/Serco, stored Syerston	
ZH139	BAe Harrier GR7 <R> (BAPC 191/ZD472)	Currently not known	
ZH144	Grob G109B Vigilant T1 [TR]	Grob Aircraft, Tussenhausen, Germany (for disposal)	
ZH145	Grob G109B Vigilant T1 [TS]	RAF, stored Little Rissington	
ZH146	Grob G109B Vigilant T1 [TT]	RAF, stored Linton-on-Ouse	
ZH147	Grob G109B Vigilant T1 [TU]	RAF, stored Little Rissington	
ZH148	Grob G109B Vigilant T1 [TV]	RAF, stored Little Rissington	
ZH184	Grob G109B Vigilant T1 [TW]	RAF, stored Little Rissington	
ZH185	Grob G109B Vigilant T1 [TX]	RAF/Serco, stored Syerston	
ZH186	Grob G109B Vigilant T1 [TY]	RAF/Serco, stored Syerston	
ZH187	Grob G109B Vigilant T1 [TZ]	RAF, stored Little Rissington	
ZH188	Grob G109B Vigilant T1 [UA]	RAF, stored Little Rissington	
ZH189	Grob G109B Vigilant T1 [UB]	RAF, stored Little Rissington	
ZH190	Grob G109B Vigilant T1 [UC]	RAF, stored Little Rissington	
ZH191	Grob G109B Vigilant T1 [UD]	RAF, stored Abingdon	
ZH192	Grob G109B Vigilant T1 [UE]	RAF, stored Little Rissington	
ZH193	Grob G109B Vigilant T1 [UF]	RAF, stored Woodvale	
ZH194	Grob G109B Vigilant T1 [UG]	RAF, stored Little Rissington	
ZH195	Grob G109B Vigilant T1 [UH]	RAF, stored Little Rissington	
ZH196	Grob G109B Vigilant T1 [UJ]	RAF, stored Little Rissington	
ZH197	Grob G109B Vigilant T1 [UK]	RAF/Serco, stored Syerston	
ZH200	BAe Hawk 200	Loughborough University	
ZH205	Grob G109B Vigilant T1 [UL]	RAF, stored Linton-on-Ouse	
ZH206	Grob G109B Vigilant T1 [UM]	RAF/Serco, stored Syerston	
ZH207	Grob G109B Vigilant T1 [UN]	RAF/Serco, stored Syerston	
ZH208	Grob G109B Vigilant T1 [UP]	RAF, stored Little Rissington	
ZH209	Grob G109B Vigilant T1 [UQ]	RAF, stored Little Rissington	
ZH211	Grob G109B Vigilant T1 [UR]	RAF, stored Little Rissington	
ZH247	Grob G109B Vigilant T1 [US]	RAF, stored Little Rissington	
ZH248	Grob G109B Vigilant T1 [UT]	RAF, stored Little Rissington	
ZH249	Grob G109B Vigilant T1 [UU]	RAF/Serco, stored Syerston	
ZH257	B-V CH-47C Chinook (9217M) (fuselage)	RAF Odiham, BDRT	
ZH263	Grob G109B Vigilant T1 [UV]	RAF, stored Little Rissington	
ZH264	Grob G109B Vigilant T1 [UW]	RAF, stored Little Rissington	
ZH265	Grob G109B Vigilant T1 [UX]	RAF, stored Little Rissington	
ZH266	Grob G109B Vigilant T1 [UY]	RAF, stored Abingdon	
ZH267	Grob G109B Vigilant T1 [UZ]	RAF, stored Little Rissington	
ZH268	Grob G109B Vigilant T1 [SA]	RAF, stored Little Rissington	
ZH269	Grob G109B Vigilant T1 [SB]	RAF, stored Little Rissington	
ZH270	Grob G109B Vigilant T1 [SC]	RAF, stored Little Rissington	
ZH271	Grob G109B Vigilant T1 [SD]	RAF/Serco, stored Syerston	
ZH278	Grob G109B Vigilant T1 (D-KAIS) [SF]	RAF, stored Little Rissington	
ZH279	Grob G109B Vigilant T1 (D-KNPS) [SG]	RAF, stored Little Rissington	
ZH545	WS61 Sea King HAR3A [Z]	Broken up at Fleetlands	
ZH552	Panavia Tornado F3	RAF Leeming, at main gate	

Notes	Serial	Type (code/other identity)	Owner/operator, location or fate
	ZH553	Panavia Tornado F3 [RT]	Aerohub, Newquay
	ZH588	Eurofighter Typhoon (DA2)	RAF Museum, Hendon
	ZH590	Eurofighter Typhoon (DA4)	IWM Duxford
	ZH654	BAe Harrier T10 <ff>	*Currently not known*
	ZH655	BAe Harrier T10 <ff>	Privately owned, Worksop, Notts
	ZH658	BAe Harrier T10 (fuselage)	Privately owned, Sproughton
	ZH763	BAC 1-11/539GL (G-BGKE)	Aerohub, Newquay
	ZH775	B-V Chinook HC6A (N7424J)	RAF No 18 Sqn, Odiham
	ZH776	B-V Chinook HC6A (N7424L)	MoD/StandardAero, Fleetlands
	ZH777	B-V Chinook HC6A (N7424M)	RAF No 18 Sqn, Odiham
	ZH796	BAe Sea Harrier FA2 [001/L]	DSAE No 1 SoTT, stored Cosford
	ZH797	BAe Sea Harrier FA2 [97/DD]	SFDO, RNAS Culdrose
	ZH798	BAe Sea Harrier FA2 [98/DD]	SFDO, RNAS Culdrose
	ZH800	BAe Sea Harrier FA2 (ZH801) [123]	*RNAS Yeovilton, stored*
	ZH801	BAe Sea Harrier FA2 (ZH800) [001]	*RNAS Yeovilton, stored*
	ZH802	BAe Sea Harrier FA2 [02/DD]	SFDO, RNAS Culdrose
	ZH803	BAe Sea Harrier FA2 [03/DD]	Privately owned, St Athan
	ZH804	BAe Sea Harrier FA2 [003/L]	RN, stored Culdrose
	ZH806	BAe Sea Harrier FA2 [007]	Privately owned, Bentwaters
	ZH807	BAe Sea Harrier FA2 <ff>	Privately owned, Thorpe Wood, N Yorks
	ZH810	BAe Sea Harrier FA2 [125]	*Sold to the USA, 2018*
	ZH811	BAe Sea Harrier FA2 [002/L]	RN, stored Culdrose
	ZH812	BAe Sea Harrier FA2 [005/L]	Privately owned, Bentwaters
	ZH813	BAe Sea Harrier FA2 [13/DD]	SFDO, RNAS Culdrose
	ZH814	Bell 212HP AH1 (G-BGMH) [X]	AAC No 7 Flt, Brunei
	ZH815	Bell 212HP AH1 (G-BGCZ) [Y]	AAC No 7 Flt, Brunei
	ZH816	Bell 212HP AH1 (G-BGMG)	AAC No 7 Flt, Brunei
	ZH821	EHI-101 Merlin HM1	RN AM&SU, stored Shawbury
	ZH822	EHI-101 Merlin HM1	RN AM&SU, stored Shawbury
	ZH823	EHI-101 Merlin HM1	RN AM&SU, stored Shawbury
	ZH824	EHI-101 Merlin HM2 [83]	RN No 824 NAS, Culdrose
	ZH825	EHI-101 Merlin HM1 [583]	RN AM&SU, stored Shawbury
	ZH826	EHI-101 Merlin HM2 [68/CU]	MoD/AFD/QinetiQ, Boscombe Down
	ZH827	EHI-101 Merlin HM2 [10]	RN No 820 NAS, Culdrose
	ZH828	EHI-101 Merlin HM2 [62]	RN No 814 NAS, Culdrose
	ZH829	EHI-101 Merlin HM2 [NL]	MoD/Leonardo MW, Yeovil
	ZH830	EHI-101 Merlin HM1 [88]	QinetiQ, stored Boscombe Down
	ZH831	EHI-101 Merlin HM2	MoD/Leonardo MW, Yeovil (conversion)
	ZH832	EHI-101 Merlin HM2 [81]	RN No 824 NAS, Culdrose
	ZH833	EHI-101 Merlin HM2 [82]	RN MDMF, Culdrose
	ZH834	EHI-101 Merlin HM2 [87]	RN No 814 NAS, Culdrose
	ZH835	EHI-101 Merlin HM2 [13/CU]	RN No 820 NAS, Culdrose
	ZH836	EHI-101 Merlin HM2 [80]	RN No 824 NAS, Culdrose
	ZH837	EHI-101 Merlin HM2 [14]	RN No 820 NAS, Culdrose
	ZH838	EHI-101 Merlin HM1 [70]	QinetiQ, stored Boscombe Down
	ZH839	EHI-101 Merlin HM2 [69]	RN No 814 NAS, Culdrose
	ZH840	EHI-101 Merlin HM2 [81]	RN No 824 NAS, Culdrose
	ZH841	EHI-101 Merlin HM2 [61]	RN MDMF, Culdrose
	ZH842	EHI-101 Merlin HM2 [82]	RN No 824 NAS, Culdrose
	ZH843	EHI-101 Merlin HM2 [88]	RN MDMF, Culdrose
	ZH845	EHI-101 Merlin HM2	RN No 814 NAS, Culdrose
	ZH846	EHI-101 Merlin HM2 [12/CU]	RN No 820 NAS, Culdrose
	ZH847	EHI-101 Merlin HM2 [66/CU]	RN No 814 NAS, Culdrose
	ZH848	EHI-101 Merlin HM1	QinetiQ, stored Boscombe Down
	ZH849	EHI-101 Merlin HM1 [67]	QinetiQ, stored Boscombe Down
	ZH850	EHI-101 Merlin HM2 [67]	RN No 814 NAS, Culdrose
	ZH851	EHI-101 Merlin HM2 [84]	RN MDMF, Culdrose
	ZH852	EHI-101 Merlin HM1(mod)	QinetiQ, stored Boscombe Down
	ZH853	EHI-101 Merlin HM2 [68]	RN No 814 NAS, Culdrose
	ZH854	EHI-101 Merlin HM2 [14]	RN No 814 NAS, Culdrose
	ZH855	EHI-101 Merlin HM1 [68]	QinetiQ, stored Boscombe Down
	ZH856	EHI-101 Merlin HM2 [11]	RN No 820 NAS, Culdrose

Serial	Type (code/other identity)	Owner/operator, location or fate	Notes
ZH857	EHI-101 Merlin HM2 [86]	RN No 814 NAS, Culdrose	
ZH858	EHI-101 Merlin HM1 [17]	QinetiQ, stored Boscombe Down	
ZH860	EHI-101 Merlin HM2 [66]	RN MDMF, Culdrose	
ZH861	EHI-101 Merlin HM2 [85]	RN No 824 NAS, Culdrose	
ZH862	EHI-101 Merlin HM2 [86]	RN No 824 NAS, Culdrose	
ZH863	EHI-101 Merlin HM1 [80]	RN stored, QinetiQ Boscombe Down	
ZH864	EHI-101 Merlin HM2 [85]	MoD/Leonardo MW, Yeovil	
ZH865	Lockheed C-130J-30 Hercules C4 (N130JA) [865]	RAF No 24 Sqn/No 30 Sqn/No 47 Sqn, Brize Norton	
ZH866	Lockheed C-130J-30 Hercules C4 (N130JE) [866] $	MoD/AFD/QinetiQ, Boscombe Down	
ZH867	Lockheed C-130J-30 Hercules C4 (N130JJ) [867]	RAF No 24 Sqn/No 30 Sqn/No 47 Sqn, Brize Norton	
ZH868	Lockheed C-130J-30 Hercules C4 (N130JN) [868]	RAF No 24 Sqn/No 30 Sqn/No 47 Sqn, Brize Norton	
ZH869	Lockheed C-130J-30 Hercules C4 (N130JV) [869]	RAF No 24 Sqn/No 30 Sqn/No 47 Sqn, Brize Norton	
ZH870	Lockheed C-130J-30 Hercules C4 (N78235) [870]	RAF No 24 Sqn/No 30 Sqn/No 47 Sqn, Brize Norton	
ZH871	Lockheed C-130J-30 Hercules C4 (N73238) [871]	RAF No 24 Sqn/No 30 Sqn/No 47 Sqn, Brize Norton	
ZH872	Lockheed C-130J-30 Hercules C4 (N4249Y) [872]	RAF No 24 Sqn/No 30 Sqn/No 47 Sqn, Brize Norton	
ZH873	Lockheed C-130J-30 Hercules C4 (N4242N) [873]	*Damaged beyond repair, Erbil, Iraq, 25 August 2017*	
ZH874	Lockheed C-130J-30 Hercules C4 (N41030) [874]	RAF No 24 Sqn/No 30 Sqn/No 47 Sqn, Brize Norton	
ZH875	Lockheed C-130J-30 Hercules C4 (N4099R) [875]	RAF No 24 Sqn/No 30 Sqn/No 47 Sqn, Brize Norton	
ZH877	Lockheed C-130J-30 Hercules C4 (N4081M) [877]	RAF No 24 Sqn/No 30 Sqn/No 47 Sqn, Brize Norton	
ZH878	Lockheed C-130J-30 Hercules C4 (N73232) [878]	RAF No 24 Sqn/No 30 Sqn/No 47 Sqn, Brize Norton	
ZH879	Lockheed C-130J-30 Hercules C4 (N4080M) [879]	RAF No 24 Sqn/No 30 Sqn/No 47 Sqn, Brize Norton	
ZH880	Lockheed C-130J Hercules C5 (N73238) [880]	MADG, Cambridge, for R Bahraini AF as 701	
ZH881	Lockheed C-130J Hercules C5 (N4081M) [881]	MADG, Cambridge, for Bangladesh AF as 99-5479	
ZH882	Lockheed C-130J Hercules C5 (N4099R) [882]	MoD/MADG, Cambridge (wfu)	
ZH883	Lockheed C-130J Hercules C5 (N4242N) [883] $	RAF No 24 Sqn/No 30 Sqn/No 47 Sqn, Brize Norton	
ZH884	Lockheed C-130J Hercules C5 (N4249Y) [884]	MoD/MADG, Cambridge (wfu)	
ZH885	Lockheed C-130J Hercules C5 (N41030) [885]	MoD/MADG, Cambridge (wfu)	
ZH886	Lockheed C-130J Hercules C5 (N73235) [886]	*To Royal Bahraini AF as 702, 10 November 2018*	
ZH887	Lockheed C-130J Hercules C5 (N4187W) [887] $	RAF No 24 Sqn/No 30 Sqn/No 47 Sqn, Brize Norton	
ZH888	Lockheed C-130J Hercules C5 (N4187) [888]	RAF No 24 Sqn/No 30 Sqn/No 47 Sqn, Brize Norton	
ZH889	Lockheed C-130J Hercules C5 (N4099R) [889]	RAF No 24 Sqn/No 30 Sqn/No 47 Sqn, Brize Norton	
ZH890	Grob G109B Vigilant T1 [SE]	RAF/Serco, stored Syerston	
ZH891	B-V Chinook HC6A (N20075) [HF]	RAF No 27 Sqn, Odiham	
ZH892	B-V Chinook HC6A (N2019V) [HG]	RAF No 27 Sqn, Odiham	
ZH893	B-V Chinook HC6A (N2025L)	RAF No 27 Sqn, Odiham	
ZH894	B-V Chinook HC6A (N2026E) [HI]	RAF No 27 Sqn, Odiham	
ZH895	B-V Chinook HC6A (N2034K) [HJ]	RAF No 27 Sqn, Odiham	
ZH896	B-V Chinook HC6A (N2038G) [HK]	RAF No 27 Sqn, Odiham	
ZH897	B-V Chinook HC5 (N2045G)	RAF No 18 Sqn, Odiham	
ZH898	B-V Chinook HC5 (N2057Q)	RAF No 27 Sqn, Odiham	
ZH899	B-V Chinook HC5 (N2057R)	RAF No 18 Sqn, Odiham	
ZH900	B-V Chinook HC5 (N2060H)	RAF No 27 Sqn, Odiham	
ZH901	B-V Chinook HC5 (N2060M)	RAF No 18 Sqn, Odiham	
ZH902	B-V Chinook HC5 (N2064W)	MoD/AFD/QinetiQ, Boscombe Down	
ZH903	B-V Chinook HC5 (N20671) [HR]	RAF No 27 Sqn, Odiham	
ZH904	B-V Chinook HC5 (N2083K)	RAF No 27 Sqn, Odiham	
ZH962	Westland Lynx Mk.21A (AH-11B) (N-4001)	*To Brazilian Navy as N4001, February 2019*	
ZH965	Westland Lynx Mk.21A (AH-11B) (N-4004)	*To Brazilian Navy as N4004, February 2019*	
ZH966	Westland Lynx Mk.21A (AH-11B) (N-4005)	Leonardo MW, Yeovil	
ZJ100	BAe Hawk 102D	BAE Systems National Training Academy, Humberside	
ZJ117	EHI-101 Merlin HC3 [A]	QinetiQ, stored Boscombe Down	
ZJ118	EHI-101 Merlin HC4 [B]	MoD/Leonardo MW, Yeovil (conversion)	
ZJ119	EHI-101 Merlin HC4 [C]	MoD/Leonardo MW, Yeovil (conversion)	
ZJ120	EHI-101 Merlin HC4 [D]	RN No 845 NAS, Yeovilton	
ZJ121	EHI-101 Merlin HC4 [E]	RN No 845 NAS, Yeovilton	
ZJ122	EHI-101 Merlin HC4 [F]	RN MDMF, Culdrose	
ZJ123	EHI-101 Merlin HC4 [G]	MoD/Leonardo MW, Yeovil (conversion)	
ZJ124	EHI-101 Merlin HC4 [H]	MoD/Leonardo MW, Yeovil (conversion)	
ZJ125	EHI-101 Merlin HC4 [J]	MoD/Leonardo MW, Yeovil	
ZJ126	EHI-101 Merlin HC3i [K]	RN No 846 NAS, Yeovilton	
ZJ127	EHI-101 Merlin HC4 [L]	RN MDMF, Culdrose	

Notes	Serial	Type (code/other identity)	Owner/operator, location or fate
	ZJ128	EHI-101 Merlin HC4 [M]	MoD/Leonardo MW, Yeovil (conversion)
	ZJ129	EHI-101 Merlin HC4 [N]	RN No 845 NAS, Yeovilton
	ZJ130	EHI-101 Merlin HC3i [O]	RN No 846 NAS, Yeovilton
	ZJ131	EHI-101 Merlin HC4 [P]	RN No 845 NAS, Yeovilton
	ZJ132	EHI-101 Merlin HC3i [Q]	RN No 846 NAS, Yeovilton
	ZJ133	EHI-101 Merlin HC3 [R]	QinetiQ, stored Boscombe Down
	ZJ134	EHI-101 Merlin HC4 [S]	RN No 845 NAS, Yeovilton
	ZJ135	EHI-101 Merlin HC3i [T]	RN No 846 NAS, Yeovilton
	ZJ136	EHI-101 Merlin HC3i [U]	RN No 846 NAS, Yeovilton
	ZJ137	EHI-101 Merlin HC3i [W]	RN No 846 NAS, Yeovilton
	ZJ138	EHI-101 Merlin HC3 [X]	QinetiQ, stored Boscombe Down
	ZJ164	AS365N-2 Dauphin 2 (G-BTLC)	RN/Bond Helicopters, Newquay
	ZJ165	AS365N-2 Dauphin 2 (G-NTOO)	RN/Bond Helicopters, Newquay
	ZJ166	WAH-64 Apache AH1 (N9219G)	MoD/Boeing, Mesa, USA
	ZJ167	WAH-64 Apache AH1 (N3266B)	MoD/Boeing, Mesa, USA
	ZJ168	WAH-64 Apache AH1 (N3123T)	MoD/Boeing, Mesa, USA
	ZJ169	WAH-64 Apache AH1 (N3114H)	MoD/Boeing, Mesa, USA
	ZJ170	WAH-64 Apache AH1 (N3065U)	MoD/Boeing, Mesa, USA
	ZJ171	WAH-64 Apache AH1 (N3266T)	AAC ADSU, stored Wattisham
	ZJ172	WAH-64 Apache AH1	MoD/Boeing, Mesa, USA
	ZJ173	WAH-64 Apache AH1 (N3266W)	MoD/Boeing, Mesa, USA
	ZJ174	WAH-64 Apache AH1	MoD/Boeing, Mesa, USA
	ZJ175	WAH-64 Apache AH1 (N3218V)	MoD/Boeing, Mesa, USA
	ZJ176	WAH-64 Apache AH1	MoD/Boeing, Mesa, USA
	ZJ177	WAH-64 Apache AH1	AAC, Wattisham (wreck)
	ZJ178	WAH-64 Apache AH1	AAC No 673 Sqn/7 Regt, Middle Wallop
	ZJ179	WAH-64 Apache AH1	AAC No 3 Regt, Wattisham
	ZJ180	WAH-64 Apache AH1	AAC No 673 Sqn/7 Regt, Middle Wallop
	ZJ181	WAH-64 Apache AH1	AAC No 3 Regt, Wattisham
	ZJ182	WAH-64 Apache AH1	AAC No 3 Regt, Wattisham
	ZJ183	WAH-64 Apache AH1	AAC No 4 Regt, Wattisham
	ZJ184	WAH-64 Apache AH1	AAC No 3 Regt, Wattisham
	ZJ185	WAH-64 Apache AH1	AAC No 4 Regt, Wattisham
	ZJ186	WAH-64 Apache AH1	AAC No 3 Regt, Wattisham
	ZJ187	WAH-64 Apache AH1	AAC ADSU, Wattisham
	ZJ188	WAH-64 Apache AH1	AAC No 673 Sqn/7 Regt, Middle Wallop
	ZJ189	WAH-64 Apache AH1	AAC No 4 Regt, Wattisham
	ZJ190	WAH-64 Apache AH1	AAC No 3 Regt, Wattisham
	ZJ191	WAH-64 Apache AH1	AAC No 3 Regt, Wattisham
	ZJ192	WAH-64 Apache AH1	AAC No 4 Regt, Wattisham
	ZJ193	WAH-64 Apache AH1	AAC No 3 Regt, Wattisham
	ZJ194	WAH-64 Apache AH1	AAC ADSU, Wattisham
	ZJ195	WAH-64 Apache AH1	AAC ADSU, Wattisham
	ZJ196	WAH-64 Apache AH1	AAC No 673 Sqn/7 Regt, Middle Wallop
	ZJ197	WAH-64 Apache AH1	AAC No 4 Regt, Wattisham
	ZJ198	WAH-64 Apache AH1	AAC No 4 Regt, Wattisham
	ZJ199	WAH-64 Apache AH1	AAC No 3 Regt, Wattisham
	ZJ200	WAH-64 Apache AH1	AAC No 3 Regt, Wattisham
	ZJ202	WAH-64 Apache AH1	MoD/Boeing, Mesa, USA
	ZJ203	WAH-64 Apache AH1	AAC No 3 Regt, Wattisham
	ZJ204	WAH-64 Apache AH1	AAC No 673 Sqn/7 Regt, Middle Wallop
	ZJ205	WAH-64 Apache AH1	AAC No 3 Regt, Wattisham
	ZJ206	WAH-64 Apache AH1	MoD/Boeing, Mesa, USA
	ZJ207	WAH-64 Apache AH1	AAC ADSU, Wattisham
	ZJ208	WAH-64 Apache AH1	AAC No 4 Regt, Wattisham
	ZJ209	WAH-64 Apache AH1	AAC No 673 Sqn/7 Regt, Middle Wallop
	ZJ210	WAH-64 Apache AH1	AAC No 4 Regt, Wattisham
	ZJ211	WAH-64 Apache AH1	AAC No 3 Regt, Wattisham
	ZJ212	WAH-64 Apache AH1	MoD/Boeing, Mesa, USA
	ZJ213	WAH-64 Apache AH1	AAC No 3 Regt, Wattisham
	ZJ214	WAH-64 Apache AH1	MoD/Boeing, Mesa, USA
	ZJ215	WAH-64 Apache AH1	AAC No 4 Regt, Wattisham

Serial	Type (code/other identity)	Owner/operator, location or fate	Notes
ZJ216	WAH-64 Apache AH1	AAC No 673 Sqn/7 Regt, Middle Wallop	
ZJ217	WAH-64 Apache AH1	AAC ADSU, Wattisham	
ZJ218	WAH-64 Apache AH1	AAC No 4 Regt, Wattisham	
ZJ219	WAH-64 Apache AH1	MoD/Boeing, Mesa, USA	
ZJ220	WAH-64 Apache AH1	AAC No 4 Regt, Wattisham	
ZJ221	WAH-64 Apache AH1	AAC No 4 Regt, Wattisham	
ZJ222	WAH-64 Apache AH1	AAC ADSU, Wattisham	
ZJ223	WAH-64 Apache AH1	AAC No 4 Regt, Wattisham	
ZJ224	WAH-64 Apache AH1	AAC No 4 Regt, Wattisham	
ZJ225	WAH-64 Apache AH1	AAC No 3 Regt, Wattisham	
ZJ226	WAH-64 Apache AH1	AAC No 4 Regt, Wattisham	
ZJ227	WAH-64 Apache AH1	AAC No 673 Sqn/7 Regt, Middle Wallop	
ZJ228	WAH-64 Apache AH1	AAC No 3 Regt, Wattisham	
ZJ229	WAH-64 Apache AH1	AAC No 3 Regt, Wattisham	
ZJ230	WAH-64 Apache AH1	AAC ADSU, Wattisham	
ZJ231	WAH-64 Apache AH1	AAC No 3 Regt, Wattisham	
ZJ232	WAH-64 Apache AH1	AAC No 673 Sqn/7 Regt, Middle Wallop	
ZJ233	WAH-64 Apache AH1	AAC No 673 Sqn/7 Regt, Middle Wallop	
ZJ234	Bell 412EP Griffin HT1 (G-BWZR) [S]	*Sold as G-BWZR, 2 November 2018*	
ZJ235	Bell 412EP Griffin HT1 (G-BXBF) [I]	*Sold as G-BXBF, 5 April 2018*	
ZJ236	Bell 412EP Griffin HT1 (G-BXBE) [X]	*Sold as G-BXBE, 2 November 2018*	
ZJ237	Bell 412EP Griffin HT1 (G-BXFF) [T]	*Sold as G-BXFF, 2 November 2018*	
ZJ238	Bell 412EP Griffin HT1 (G-BXHC) [Y]	*Sold as G-BXHC, 2 November 2018*	
ZJ239	Bell 412EP Griffin HT1 (G-BXFH) [R]	*Sold as G-BXFH, 2 November 2018*	
ZJ240	Bell 412EP Griffin HT1 (G-BXIR) [U]	MoD/Cobham Helicopter Academy, Newquay	
ZJ242	Bell 412EP Griffin HT1 (G-BXDK) [E]	*Sold as G-BXDK, 26 April 2018*	
ZJ243	AS350BB Squirrel HT2 (G-BWZS) [43]	MoD/Cobham Helicopter Academy, Newquay	
ZJ244	AS350BB Squirrel HT2 (G-BXMD) [44]	MoD/Cobham Helicopter Academy, Newquay	
ZJ245	AS350BB Squirrel HT2 (G-BXME) [45]	*Sold as G-BXME, 2 November 2018*	
ZJ246	AS350BB Squirrel HT2 (G-BXMJ) [46]	MoD/Cobham Helicopter Academy, Newquay	
ZJ248	AS350BB Squirrel HT2 (G-BXNE) [48]	MoD/Cobham Helicopter Academy, Newquay	
ZJ249	AS350BB Squirrel HT2 (G-BXNJ) [49]	MoD/Cobham, Bournemouth	
ZJ250	AS350BB Squirrel HT2 (G-BXNY) [50]	MoD/Cobham, Bournemouth	
ZJ251	AS350BB Squirrel HT2 (G-BXOG) [51]	MoD/Cobham, Bournemouth	
ZJ252	AS350BB Squirrel HT2 (G-BXOK) [52]	MoD/Cobham Helicopter Academy, Newquay	
ZJ253	AS350BB Squirrel HT2 (G-BXPG) [53]	MoD/Cobham, Bournemouth	
ZJ254	AS350BB Squirrel HT2 (G-BXPJ) [54]	MoD/Cobham, Bournemouth	
ZJ257	AS350BB Squirrel HT1 (G-BXDJ) [57]	*Sold as G-BXDJ, 16 March 2018*	
ZJ261	AS350BB Squirrel HT1 (G-BXGJ) [61]	*Sold as G-BXGJ, 16 March 2018*	
ZJ264	AS350BB Squirrel HT1 (G-BXHW) [64]	MoD/Cobham, Bournemouth	
ZJ265	AS350BB Squirrel HT1 (G-BXHX) [65]	*Sold as G-BXHX, 20 March 2018*	
ZJ267	AS350BB Squirrel HT1 (G-BXIP) [67]	MoD/Cobham, Bournemouth	
ZJ268	AS350BB Squirrel HT1 (G-BXJE) [68]	MoD/Cobham, Bournemouth	
ZJ271	AS350BB Squirrel HT1 (G-BXKE) [71]	MoD/Cobham, Bournemouth	
ZJ272	AS350BB Squirrel HT1 (G-BXKN) [72]	MoD/Cobham, Bournemouth	
ZJ273	AS350BB Squirrel HT1 (G-BXKP) [73]	MoD/Cobham, Bournemouth	
ZJ276	AS350BB Squirrel HT1 (G-BXLE) [76]	*Sold as G-BXLE, 16 March 2018*	
ZJ277	AS350BB Squirrel HT1 (G-BXLH) [77]	MoD/Cobham, Bournemouth	
ZJ279	AS350BB Squirrel HT1 (G-BXMC) [79]	MoD/Cobham, Bournemouth	
ZJ280	AS350BB Squirrel HT1 (G-BXMI) [80]	*Sold as G-BXMI, 3 April 2018*	
ZJ369	GEC Phoenix RPAS	Defence Academy of the UK, Shrivenham	
ZJ385	GEC Phoenix RPAS	Muckleburgh Collection, Weybourne, Norfolk	
ZJ392	GEC Phoenix RPAS	Privately owned, Holt Heath, Worcs	
ZJ449	GEC Phoenix RPAS	REME Museum, Lyneham	
ZJ452	GEC Phoenix RPAS	Science Museum, stored Wroughton	
ZJ469	GEC Phoenix RPAS	Army, Larkhill, on display	
ZJ481	Northrop MQM-74C Chukar D2	RNAS Culdrose, preserved	
ZJ493	GAF Jindivik 104AL (A92-814)	RAF Museum Reserve Collection, Stafford	
ZJ496	GAF Jindivik 104AL (A92-901)	Farnborough Air Sciences Trust, Farnborough	
ZJ515	BAE Systems Nimrod MRA4 (XV258) <ff>	Cranfield University, instructional use	
ZJ620	AgustaWestland Merlin Simulator	RN No 824 NAS, Culdrose	
ZJ621	AgustaWestland Merlin Simulator	RN No 824 NAS, Culdrose	

Notes	Serial	Type (code/other identity)	Owner/operator, location or fate
	ZJ622	AgustaWestland Merlin Simulator	RN No 824 NAS, Culdrose
	ZJ623	AgustaWestland Merlin Simulator	RN No 824 NAS, Culdrose
	ZJ624	AgustaWestland Merlin Simulator	RN No 824 NAS, Culdrose
	ZJ625	AgustaWestland Merlin Simulator	RN No 824 NAS, Culdrose
	ZJ626	AgustaWestland Merlin Simulator	RN No 824 NAS, Culdrose
	ZJ645	D-BD Alpha Jet (98+62) [45]	MoD/QinetiQ, stored Boscombe Down
	ZJ646	D-BD Alpha Jet (98+55) [46]	MoD/QinetiQ, stored Boscombe Down
	ZJ647	D-BD Alpha Jet (98+71) [47]	MoD/QinetiQ, stored Boscombe Down
	ZJ648	D-BD Alpha Jet (98+09) [48]	MoD/QinetiQ Boscombe Down, spares use
	ZJ649	D-BD Alpha Jet (98+73) [49]	MoD/QinetiQ, stored Boscombe Down
	ZJ650	D-BD Alpha Jet (98+35)	MoD/QinetiQ, stored Boscombe Down
	ZJ651	D-BD Alpha Jet (41+42) [51]	MoD/QinetiQ, stored Boscombe Down
	ZJ652	D-BD Alpha Jet (41+09)	MoD/QinetiQ Boscombe Down, spares use
	ZJ653	D-BD Alpha Jet (40+22)	MoD/QinetiQ Boscombe Down, spares use
	ZJ654	D-BD Alpha Jet (41+02)	MoD/QinetiQ Boscombe Down, spares use
	ZJ655	D-BD Alpha Jet (41+19)	MoD/QinetiQ Boscombe Down, spares use
	ZJ656	D-BD Alpha Jet (41+40)	MoD/QinetiQ Boscombe Down, spares use
	ZJ690	Bombardier Sentinel R1 (C-GJRG)	RAF No 5 Sqn, Waddington
	ZJ691	Bombardier Sentinel R1 (C-FZVM)	RAF No 5 Sqn, Waddington
	ZJ692	Bombardier Sentinel R1 (C-FZWW)	RAF No 5 Sqn, Waddington
	ZJ693	Bombardier Sentinel R1 (C-FZXC)	MoD/Raytheon, stored Hawarden
	ZJ694	Bombardier Sentinel R1 (C-FZYL)	RAF No 5 Sqn, Waddington
	ZJ699	Eurofighter Typhoon (PT001)	MoD/BAE Systems, Warton
	ZJ700	Eurofighter Typhoon (PS002)	MoD/BAE Systems, Warton
	ZJ703	Bell 412EP Griffin HAR2 (G-CBST) [Spades,3]	RAF No 84 Sqn, Akrotiri
	ZJ704	Bell 412EP Griffin HAR2 (G-CBWT) [Clubs,4]	RAF No 84 Sqn, Akrotiri
	ZJ705	Bell 412EP Griffin HAR2 (G-CBXL) [Hearts,5]	MoD/AFD/QinetiQ, Boscombe Down
	ZJ706	Bell 412EP Griffin HAR2 (G-CBYR) [Diamonds,6]	RAF No 84 Sqn, Akrotiri
	ZJ707	Bell 412EP Griffin HT1 (G-CBUB) [O]	Sold as G-CBUB, 2 November 2018
	ZJ708	Bell 412EP Griffin HT1 (G-CBVP) [K]	Sold as G-CBVP, 2 November 2018
	ZJ765	Meteor Mirach 100/5	QinetiQ Apprentice Training School, Boscombe Down
	ZJ780	AS365N-3 Dauphin AH1 (G-CEXT)	AAC No 658 Sqn, Credenhill
	ZJ781	AS365N-3 Dauphin AH1 (G-CEXU)	AAC No 658 Sqn, Credenhill
	ZJ782	AS365N-3 Dauphin AH1 (G-CEXV)	AAC No 658 Sqn, Credenhill
	ZJ783	AS365N-3 Dauphin AH1 (G-CEXW)	AAC No 658 Sqn, Credenhill
	ZJ785	AS365N-3 Dauphin AH1 (G-CFFW)	AAC No 658 Sqn, Credenhill
	ZJ787	AS365N-3 Dauphin AH1 (G-CHNJ)	AAC No 658 Sqn, Credenhill
	ZJ800	Eurofighter Typhoon T3 [BC]	BAE Systems Aircraft Maintenance Academy, Humberside
	ZJ801	Eurofighter Typhoon T3 [BJ]	RAF, stored Coningsby
	ZJ802	Eurofighter Typhoon T3 [802]	RAF Coningsby, RTP
	ZJ803	Eurofighter Typhoon T3 (fuselage)	RAF, stored Coningsby
	ZJ804	Eurofighter Typhoon T3 (fuselage)	RAF, stored Coningsby
	ZJ805	Eurofighter Typhoon T3 [BD]	RAF, stored Coningsby
	ZJ806	Eurofighter Typhoon T3 (fuselage)	RAF, stored Coningsby
	ZJ807	Eurofighter Typhoon T3 [807]	RAF No 1 Sqn, Lossiemouth
	ZJ808	Eurofighter Typhoon T3 (fuselage)	RAF, stored Coningsby
	ZJ809	Eurofighter Typhoon T3 (fuselage)	Currently not known
	ZJ810	Eurofighter Typhoon T3 (fuselage)	Scrapped, February 2019
	ZJ811	Eurofighter Typhoon T3 (fuselage)	RAF, stored Coningsby
	ZJ812	Eurofighter Typhoon T3 [812]	RAF Coningsby, RTP
	ZJ813	Eurofighter Typhoon T3 [BL]	RAF, stored Coningsby
	ZJ814	Eurofighter Typhoon T3 (fuselage)	RAF, stored Coningsby
	ZJ815	Eurofighter Typhoon T3 (fuselage)	Currently not known
	ZJ910	Eurofighter Typhoon FGR4 [DO]	RAF AM&SU, stored Shawbury
	ZJ911	Eurofighter Typhoon FGR4 [QO-Z]	RAF AM&SU, stored Shawbury
	ZJ912	Eurofighter Typhoon FGR4 [912]	RAF AM&SU, stored Shawbury
	ZJ913	Eurofighter Typhoon FGR4 [913]	RAF No 9 Sqn, Lossiemouth
	ZJ914	Eurofighter Typhoon FGR4 [914]	RAF No 29 Sqn, Coningsby
	ZJ915	Eurofighter Typhoon FGR4 [F]	RAF No 1435 Flt, Mount Pleasant, Fl
	ZJ916	Eurofighter Typhoon FGR4 [916]	RAF No 29 Sqn, Coningsby
	ZJ917	Eurofighter Typhoon FGR4 [917]	RAF No 3 Sqn, Coningsby

Serial	Type (code/other identity)	Owner/operator, location or fate	Notes
ZJ918	Eurofighter Typhoon FGR4	RAF AM&SU, stored Shawbury	
ZJ919	Eurofighter Typhoon FGR4 [919]	RAF No 6 Sqn, Lossiemouth	
ZJ920	Eurofighter Typhoon FGR4 [920]	RAF No 29 Sqn, Coningsby	
ZJ921	Eurofighter Typhoon FGR4 [921]	RAF No 9 Sqn, Lossiemouth	
ZJ922	Eurofighter Typhoon FGR4 [QO-C]	MoD/BAE Systems, Warton	
ZJ923	Eurofighter Typhoon FGR4 [923]	RAF No 1 Sqn, Lossiemouth	
ZJ924	Eurofighter Typhoon FGR4 [924]	RAF No 9 Sqn, Lossiemouth	
ZJ925	Eurofighter Typhoon FGR4 [DXI] $	RAF AM&SU, stored Shawbury	
ZJ926	Eurofighter Typhoon FGR4 [H]	RAF No 1435 Flt, Mount Pleasant, FI	
ZJ927	Eurofighter Typhoon FGR4 [927]	RAF AM&SU, stored Shawbury	
ZJ928	Eurofighter Typhoon FGR4 [928]	RAF No 29 Sqn, Coningsby	
ZJ929	Eurofighter Typhoon FGR4 [929]	RAF No 29 Sqn, Coningsby	
ZJ930	Eurofighter Typhoon FGR4 [930]	RAF AM&SU, stored Shawbury	
ZJ931	Eurofighter Typhoon FGR4 [931]	RAF No 29 Sqn, Coningsby	
ZJ932	Eurofighter Typhoon FGR4 [DB]	RAF AM&SU, stored Shawbury	
ZJ933	Eurofighter Typhoon FGR4 [C]	RAF No 1435 Flt, Mount Pleasant, FI	
ZJ934	Eurofighter Typhoon FGR4 [934]	RAF AM&SU, stored Shawbury	
ZJ935	Eurofighter Typhoon FGR4 [935]	RAF No 9 Sqn, Lossiemouth	
ZJ936	Eurofighter Typhoon FGR4 [QO-C]	RAF AM&SU, stored Shawbury	
ZJ937	Eurofighter Typhoon FGR4 [937]	RAF TMF, Coningsby	
ZJ938	Eurofighter Typhoon FGR4	MoD/BAE Systems, Warton	
ZJ939	Eurofighter Typhoon FGR4 [939]	RAF No 29 Sqn, Coningsby	
ZJ940	Eurofighter Typhoon FGR4 [DJ666]	RAF, stored Coningsby	
ZJ941	Eurofighter Typhoon FGR4 [D]	RAF No 1435 Flt, Mount Pleasant, FI	
ZJ942	Eurofighter Typhoon FGR4 [942]	RAF Coningsby, WLT	
ZJ943	Eurofighter Typhoon FGR4 (fuselage)	RAF AM&SU, stored Shawbury (wreck)	
ZJ944	Eurofighter Typhoon FGR4	RAF, stored Coningsby	
ZJ945	Eurofighter Typhoon FGR4	RAF, stored Coningsby	
ZJ946	Eurofighter Typhoon FGR4 [946]	RAF No 11 Sqn, Coningsby	
ZJ947	Eurofighter Typhoon FGR4 [947]	RAF No 1 Sqn, Lossiemouth	
ZJ948	Eurofighter Typhoon FGR4	RAF, stored Coningsby	
ZJ949	Eurofighter Typhoon FGR4 [949]	RAF No 3 Sqn, Coningsby	
ZJ950	Eurofighter Typhoon FGR4 [950]	RAF TMF, Coningsby	
ZJ951	BAE Systems Advanced Hawk 120D	MoD/BAE Systems, Warton	
ZJ954	SA330H Puma HC2 (SAAF 144)	RAF No 28 Sqn/No 33 Sqn/No 230 Sqn, Benson	
ZJ955	SA330H Puma HC2 (SAAF 148) [X]	RAF No 28 Sqn/No 33 Sqn/No 230 Sqn, Benson	
ZJ956	SA330H Puma HC2 (SAAF 172/F-ZWCC)	RAF No 28 Sqn/No 33 Sqn/No 230 Sqn, Benson	
ZJ957	SA330H Puma HC2 (SAAF 169)	RAF No 28 Sqn/No 33 Sqn/No 230 Sqn, Benson	
ZJ960	Grob G109B Vigilant T1 (D-KSMU) [SH]	RAF, stored Little Rissington	
ZJ961	Grob G109B Vigilant T1 (D-KLCW) [SJ]	RAF, stored Little Rissington	
ZJ962	Grob G109B Vigilant T1 (D-KBEU) [SK]	RAF, stored Little Rissington	
ZJ963	Grob G109B Vigilant T1 (D-KMSN) [SL]	RAF/Serco, stored Syerston	
ZJ967	Grob G109B Vigilant T1 (G-DEWS) [SM]	RAF/Serco, stored Syerston	
ZJ968	Grob G109B Vigilant T1 (N109BT) [SN]	RAF, stored Woodvale	
ZJ969	Bell 212HP AH1 (G-BGLJ) [K]	AAC JHC/No 7 Regt, Middle Wallop	
ZJ990	EHI-101 Merlin HC3A (M-501) [AA]	RN No 845 NAS, Yeovilton	
ZJ992	EHI-101 Merlin HC3A (M-503) [AB]	RN MDMF, Culdrose	
ZJ994	EHI-101 Merlin HC3A (M-505) [AC]	RN MDMF, Culdrose	
ZJ995	EHI-101 Merlin HC4A (M-506) [AD]	MoD/Leonardo MW, Yeovil (conversion)	
ZJ998	EHI-101 Merlin HC3A (M-509) [AE]	RN No 845 NAS, Yeovilton	
ZK001	EHI-101 Merlin HC3A (M-511) [AF]	RN No 845 NAS, Yeovilton	
ZK005	Grob G109B Vigilant T1 (OH-797) [SP]	RAF, stored Little Rissington	
ZK010	BAE Systems Hawk T2 [A]	RAF No 4 FTS/4 Sqn, Valley	
ZK011	BAE Systems Hawk T2 [B]	RAF No 4 FTS/4 Sqn, Valley	
ZK012	BAE Systems Hawk T2 [C]	RAF HSF, stored Valley	
ZK013	BAE Systems Hawk T2 [D]	RAF No 4 FTS/4 Sqn, Valley	
ZK014	BAE Systems Hawk T2 [E]	RAF No 4 FTS/4 Sqn, Valley	
ZK015	BAE Systems Hawk T2 [F]	RAF No 4 FTS/4 Sqn, Valley	
ZK016	BAE Systems Hawk T2 [G]	RAF No 4 FTS/4 Sqn, Valley	
ZK017	BAE Systems Hawk T2 [H]	RAF No 4 FTS/4 Sqn, Valley	
ZK018	BAE Systems Hawk T2 [I] $	RAF No 4 FTS/4 Sqn, Valley	

Notes	Serial	Type (code/other identity)	Owner/operator, location or fate
	ZK019	BAE Systems Hawk T2 [J]	RAF No 4 FTS/4 Sqn, Valley
	ZK020	BAE Systems Hawk T2 [K] $	RAF No 4 FTS/4 Sqn, Valley
	ZK021	BAE Systems Hawk T2 [L]	RAF No 4 FTS/4 Sqn, Valley
	ZK022	BAE Systems Hawk T2 [M]	RAF No 4 FTS/4 Sqn, Valley
	ZK023	BAE Systems Hawk T2 [N]	RAF No 4 FTS/4 Sqn, Valley
	ZK024	BAE Systems Hawk T2 [O]	RAF No 4 FTS/4 Sqn, Valley
	ZK025	BAE Systems Hawk T2 [P]	RAF No 4 FTS/25 Sqn, Valley
	ZK026	BAE Systems Hawk T2 [FB]	RAF No 4 FTS/25 Sqn, Valley
	ZK027	BAE Systems Hawk T2 [R]	RAF No 4 FTS/25 Sqn, Valley
	ZK028	BAE Systems Hawk T2 [S]	RAF No 4 FTS/25 Sqn, Valley
	ZK029	BAE Systems Hawk T2 [FE]	RAF No 4 FTS/25 Sqn, Valley
	ZK030	BAE Systems Hawk T2 [U]	RAF No 4 FTS/25 Sqn, Valley
	ZK031	BAE Systems Hawk T2 [FG]	RAF No 4 FTS/25 Sqn, Valley
	ZK032	BAE Systems Hawk T2 [FH]	RAF No 4 FTS/25 Sqn, Valley
	ZK033	BAE Systems Hawk T2 [X]	RAF, stored Valley
	ZK034	BAE Systems Hawk T2 [Y]	RAF No 4 FTS/25 Sqn, Valley
	ZK035	BAE Systems Hawk T2 [Z]	RAF No 4 FTS/25 Sqn, Valley
	ZK036	BAE Systems Hawk T2	RAF No 4 FTS/25 Sqn, Valley
	ZK037	BAE Systems Hawk T2 [AB]	RAF No 4 FTS/25 Sqn, Valley
	ZK067	Bell 212HP AH3 (G-BFER) [B]	AAC, Middle Wallop
	ZK114	M2370 RPAS	QinetiQ
	ZK150*	Lockheed Martin Desert Hawk 3 RPAS	Army 47 Regt Royal Artillery, Thorney Island
	ZK150	Lockheed Martin Desert Hawk 3 RPAS (ZK150/617)	Imperial War Museum, Lambeth
	ZK155*	Honeywell T-Hawk RPAS	Army 32 Regt Royal Artillery, Larkhill
	ZK205	Grob G109B Vigilant T1 (D-KBRU) [SS]	RAF/Serco, stored Syerston
	ZK210	BAE Systems Mantis RPAS	MoD/BAE Systems, Warton
	ZK300	Eurofighter Typhoon FGR4 [300]	RAF TMF, Coningsby
	ZK301	Eurofighter Typhoon FGR4 [301]	RAF No 11 Sqn, Coningsby
	ZK302	Eurofighter Typhoon FGR4 [302]	RAF TMF, Coningsby
	ZK303	Eurofighter Typhoon T3 [AX]	MoD/BAE Systems, Warton
	ZK304	Eurofighter Typhoon FGR4 [304]	RAF No 11 Sqn, Coningsby
	ZK305	Eurofighter Typhoon FGR4 [305]	RAF, stored Coningsby
	ZK306	Eurofighter Typhoon FGR4 [306]	RAF No 1 Sqn, Lossiemouth
	ZK307	Eurofighter Typhoon FGR4 [307]	RAF No 3 Sqn, Coningsby
	ZK308	Eurofighter Typhoon FGR4 [308]	RAF No 3 Sqn, Coningsby
	ZK309	Eurofighter Typhoon FGR4 [309]	RAF TMF, Coningsby
	ZK310	Eurofighter Typhoon FGR4 [310]	RAF No 1 Sqn, Lossiemouth
	ZK311	Eurofighter Typhoon FGR4	RAF No 3 Sqn, Coningsby
	ZK312	Eurofighter Typhoon FGR4 [312]	RAF No 6 Sqn, Lossiemouth
	ZK313	Eurofighter Typhoon FGR4 [313]	RAF No 2 Sqn, Lossiemouth
	ZK314	Eurofighter Typhoon FGR4 [314]	RAF No 2 Sqn, Lossiemouth
	ZK315	Eurofighter Typhoon FGR4 [315]	RAF No 6 Sqn, Lossiemouth
	ZK316	Eurofighter Typhoon FGR4 [316]	RAF No 11 Sqn, Coningsby
	ZK317	Eurofighter Typhoon FGR4 [317]	RAF No 3 Sqn, Coningsby
	ZK318	Eurofighter Typhoon FGR4 $	RAF TMF, Coningsby
	ZK319	Eurofighter Typhoon FGR4 [319]	RAF No 29 Sqn, Coningsby
	ZK320	Eurofighter Typhoon FGR4 [320]	RAF No 1 Sqn, Lossiemouth
	ZK321	Eurofighter Typhoon FGR4 [321]	RAF No 1 Sqn, Lossiemouth
	ZK322	Eurofighter Typhoon FGR4 [322]	RAF TMF, Coningsby
	ZK323	Eurofighter Typhoon FGR4 [323]	RAF No 1 Sqn, Lossiemouth
	ZK324	Eurofighter Typhoon FGR4 [324]	RAF No 2 Sqn, Lossiemouth
	ZK325	Eurofighter Typhoon FGR4 [325]	RAF No 11 Sqn, Coningsby
	ZK326	Eurofighter Typhoon FGR4 [FB]	RAF, stored Coningsby
	ZK327	Eurofighter Typhoon FGR4 [327]	RAF No 29 Sqn, Coningsby
	ZK328	Eurofighter Typhoon FGR4 [328]	RAF No 2 Sqn, Lossiemouth
	ZK329	Eurofighter Typhoon FGR4 [329]	RAF TMF, Coningsby
	ZK330	Eurofighter Typhoon FGR4 [330]	RAF No 1 Sqn, Lossiemouth
	ZK331	Eurofighter Typhoon FGR4 [331]	RAF No 11 Sqn, Coningsby
	ZK332	Eurofighter Typhoon FGR4 [332]	RAF No 1 Sqn, Lossiemouth
	ZK333	Eurofighter Typhoon FGR4 [333]	RAF TMF, Coningsby
	ZK334	Eurofighter Typhoon FGR4 [334]	RAF No 6 Sqn, Lossiemouth
	ZK335	Eurofighter Typhoon FGR4 [335]	RAF AWC/FJWOEU/No 41 Sqn, Coningsby

Serial	Type (code/other identity)	Owner/operator, location or fate	Notes
ZK336	Eurofighter Typhoon FGR4 [336]	RAF No 1 Sqn, Lossiemouth	
ZK337	Eurofighter Typhoon FGR4 [337]	RAF No 6 Sqn, Lossiemouth	
ZK338	Eurofighter Typhoon FGR4 [338]	RAF No 2 Sqn, Lossiemouth	
ZK339	Eurofighter Typhoon FGR4 [EB-E]	RAF AWC/FJWOEU/No 41 Sqn, Coningsby	
ZK340	Eurofighter Typhoon FGR4 [340]	RAF No 3 Sqn, Coningsby	
ZK341	Eurofighter Typhoon FGR4 [341]	RAF No 11 Sqn, Coningsby	
ZK342	Eurofighter Typhoon FGR4 [342]	RAF No 11 Sqn, Coningsby	
ZK343	Eurofighter Typhoon FGR4 [343]	RAF No 1 Sqn, Lossiemouth	
ZK344	Eurofighter Typhoon FGR4 [344]	RAF No 1 Sqn, Lossiemouth	
ZK345	Eurofighter Typhoon FGR4 [345]	RAF No 1 Sqn, Lossiemouth	
ZK346	Eurofighter Typhoon FGR4 [346]	RAF No 3 Sqn, Coningsby	
ZK347	Eurofighter Typhoon FGR4 [347]	RAF No 11 Sqn, Coningsby	
ZK348	Eurofighter Typhoon FGR4 [348]	RAF TMF, Coningsby	
ZK349	Eurofighter Typhoon FGR4 [349]	RAF TMF, Coningsby	
ZK350	Eurofighter Typhoon FGR4	MoD/BAE Systems, Warton	
ZK351	Eurofighter Typhoon FGR4 [351]	RAF No 29 Sqn, Coningsby	
ZK352	Eurofighter Typhoon FGR4 [352]	RAF No 3 Sqn, Coningsby	
ZK353	Eurofighter Typhoon FGR4 [353]	RAF No 11 Sqn, Coningsby	
ZK354	Eurofighter Typhoon FGR4 [354]	RAF No 11 Sqn, Coningsby	
ZK355	Eurofighter Typhoon FGR4	MoD/BAE Systems, Warton	
ZK356	Eurofighter Typhoon FGR4	MoD/BAE Systems, Warton	
ZK357	Eurofighter Typhoon FGR4 [357]	RAF No 11 Sqn, Coningsby	
ZK358	Eurofighter Typhoon FGR4 [358]	RAF No 11 Sqn, Coningsby	
ZK359	Eurofighter Typhoon FGR4	RAF TMF, Coningsby	
ZK360	Eurofighter Typhoon FGR4 [360]	RAF No 1 Sqn, Lossiemouth	
ZK361	Eurofighter Typhoon FGR4 [361]	RAF No 11 Sqn, Coningsby	
ZK362	Eurofighter Typhoon FGR4 [362]	RAF No 3 Sqn, Coningsby	
ZK363	Eurofighter Typhoon FGR4 [363]	RAF No 29 Sqn, Coningsby	
ZK364	Eurofighter Typhoon FGR4 [364]	RAF No 6 Sqn, Lossiemouth	
ZK365	Eurofighter Typhoon FGR4 [365]	RAF AWC/FJWOEU/No 41 Sqn, Coningsby	
ZK366	Eurofighter Typhoon FGR4 [366]	RAF No 11 Sqn, Coningsby	
ZK367	Eurofighter Typhoon FGR4 [EB-R]	RAF AWC/FJWOEU/No 41 Sqn, Coningsby	
ZK368	Eurofighter Typhoon FGR4 [368]	RAF Lossiemouth, WLT	
ZK369	Eurofighter Typhoon FGR4 [369]	RAF No 3 Sqn, Coningsby	
ZK370	Eurofighter Typhoon FGR4	MoD/BAE Systems, Warton	
ZK371	Eurofighter Typhoon FGR4	RAF No 29 Sqn, Coningsby	
ZK372	Eurofighter Typhoon FGR4 [372]	RAF No 3 Sqn, Coningsby	
ZK373	Eurofighter Typhoon FGR4 [373]	RAF Coningsby, WLT	
ZK374	Eurofighter Typhoon FGR4 [374]	RAF No 2 Sqn, Lossiemouth	
ZK375	Eurofighter Typhoon FGR4 [375]	RAF AWC/FJWOEU/No 41 Sqn, Coningsby	
ZK376	Eurofighter Typhoon FGR4 [376]	RAF AWC/FJWOEU/No 41 Sqn, Coningsby	
ZK377	Eurofighter Typhoon FGR4 [377]	RAF No 3 Sqn, Coningsby	
ZK378	Eurofighter Typhoon FGR4 [378]	RAF No 2 Sqn, Lossiemouth	
ZK379	Eurofighter Typhoon T3 [379]	RAF AWC/FJWOEU/No 41 Sqn, Coningsby	
ZK380	Eurofighter Typhoon T3 [380]	RAF No 29 Sqn, Coningsby	
ZK381	Eurofighter Typhoon T3 [381]	RAF No 29 Sqn, Coningsby	
ZK382	Eurofighter Typhoon T3 [382]	RAF No 29 Sqn, Coningsby	
ZK383	Eurofighter Typhoon T3 [383]	RAF No 29 Sqn, Coningsby	
ZK424	Eurofighter Typhoon FGR4 [424]	RAF No 6 Sqn, Lossiemouth	
ZK425	Eurofighter Typhoon FGR4 [425]	RAF No 2 Sqn, Lossiemouth	
ZK426	Eurofighter Typhoon FGR4 [426]	RAF No 2 Sqn, Lossiemouth	
ZK427	Eurofighter Typhoon FGR4	RAF No 11 Sqn, Coningsby	
ZK428	Eurofighter Typhoon FGR4	RAF TMF, stored Coningsby	
ZK429	Eurofighter Typhoon FGR4 [429]	RAF TMF, stored Coningsby	
ZK430	Eurofighter Typhoon FGR4 [430]	RAF No 3 Sqn, Coningsby	
ZK431	Eurofighter Typhoon FGR4 [431]	RAF TMF, Coningsby	
ZK432	Eurofighter Typhoon FGR4 [432]	RAF No 29 Sqn, Coningsby	
ZK433	Eurofighter Typhoon FGR4 [433]	RAF AWC/FJWOEU/No 41 Sqn, Coningsby	
ZK434	Eurofighter Typhoon FGR4 [434] $	RAF No 29 Sqn, Coningsby	
ZK435	Eurofighter Typhoon FGR4	RAF TMF, Coningsby	
ZK436	Eurofighter Typhoon FGR4	RAF TMF, Coningsby	
ZK437	Eurofighter Typhoon FGR4	DE&S/BAE Systems, Warton	

Notes	Serial	Type (code/other identity)	Owner/operator, location or fate
	ZK438	Eurofighter Typhoon FGR4	DE&S/BAE Systems, Warton
	ZK439	Eurofighter Typhoon FGR4	DE&S/BAE Systems, Warton
	ZK451	Beech King Air B200 (G-RAFK) [K]	*Sold as G-RAFK, 21 March 2018*
	ZK452	Beech King Air B200 (G-RAFL) [L]	*Sold as G-RAFL, 21 March 2018*
	ZK455	Beech King Air B200 (G-RAFO) [O]	*Sold as G-RAFO, 27 March 2018*
	ZK456	Beech King Air B200 (G-RAFP) [P]	*Sold as G-RAFP, 27 March 2018*
	ZK458	Hawker Beechcraft King Air B200GT (G-RAFD) [D]	*Sold as G-RAFD, 23 March 2018*
	ZK459	Hawker Beechcraft King Air B200GT (G-RAFX) [X]	*Sold as G-RAFX, 28 March 2018*
	ZK460	Hawker Beechcraft King Air B200GT (G-RAFU) [U] $	*Sold as G-RAFU, 11 March 2018*
	ZK531	BAe Hawk T53 (LL-5306)	Humberside Airport, on display
	ZK532	BAe Hawk T53 (LL-5315)	MoD/BAE Systems, Warton
	ZK533	BAe Hawk T53 (LL-5317)	MoD/BAE Systems, Samlesbury, GI use
	ZK534	BAe Hawk T53 (LL-5319)	Horizon Aircraft Services, St Athan
	ZK535	BAe Hawk T53 (LL-5320)	BAE Systems Aircraft Maintenance Academy, Humberside
	ZK550	Boeing Chinook HC6 (N701UK)	RAF No 7 Sqn, Odiham
	ZK551	Boeing Chinook HC6 (N702UK)	RAF No 7 Sqn, Odiham
	ZK552	Boeing Chinook HC6 (N703UK)	RAF No 7 Sqn, Odiham
	ZK553	Boeing Chinook HC6 (N700UK)	RAF No 7 Sqn, Odiham
	ZK554	Boeing Chinook HC6 (N705UK)	RAF No 7 Sqn, Odiham
	ZK555	Boeing Chinook HC6 (N706UK)	RAF No 7 Sqn, Odiham
	ZK556	Boeing Chinook HC6 (N707UK)	RAF No 7 Sqn, Odiham
	ZK557	Boeing Chinook HC6 (N708UK)	RAF No 7 Sqn, Odiham
	ZK558	Boeing Chinook HC6 (N709UK)	MoD/StandardAero, Fleetlands
	ZK559	Boeing Chinook HC6 (N710UK)	MoD/StandardAero, Fleetlands
	ZK560	Boeing Chinook HC6 (N711UK)	MoD/StandardAero, Fleetlands
	ZK561	Boeing Chinook HC6 (N712UK)	MoD/StandardAero, Fleetlands
	ZK562	Boeing Chinook HC6 (N713UK)	RAF No 7 Sqn, Odiham
	ZK563	Boeing Chinook HC6 (N714UK)	RAF No 7 Sqn, Odiham
	ZK848	McD F-4F Phantom II (38+48)	For Hawker Hunter Aviation
	ZM135	Lockheed Martin F-35B Lightning II (168315/BK-1)	RAF No 17 Sqn, Edwards AFB, California
	ZM136	Lockheed Martin F-35B Lightning II (168316/BK-2)	RAF No 17 Sqn, Edwards AFB, California
	ZM137	Lockheed Martin F-35B Lightning II (168737/BK-3)	RAF No 617 Sqn, MCAS Beaufort, South Carolina
	ZM138	Lockheed Martin F-35B Lightning II (169170/BK-4)	RAF No 17 Sqn, Edwards AFB, California
	ZM139	Lockheed Martin F-35B Lightning II (169298/BK-5)	RAF No 617 Sqn, MCAS Beaufort, South Carolina
	ZM140	Lockheed Martin F-35B Lightning II (169299/BK-6)	RAF No 617 Sqn, Marham
	ZM141	Lockheed Martin F-35B Lightning II (169300/BK-7)	RAF No 617 Sqn, Marham
	ZM142	Lockheed Martin F-35B Lightning II (169301/BK-8)	RAF No 617 Sqn, Marham
	ZM143	Lockheed Martin F-35B Lightning II (169417/BK-9)	RAF No 617 Sqn, Marham
	ZM144	Lockheed Martin F-35B Lightning II (169418/BK-10)	RAF No 617 Sqn, Marham
	ZM145	Lockheed Martin F-35B Lightning II (169419/BK-11)	RAF No 617 Sqn, Marham
	ZM146	Lockheed Martin F-35B Lightning II (169420/BK-12)	RAF No 617 Sqn, Marham
	ZM147	Lockheed Martin F-35B Lightning II (169421/BK-13)	RAF No 617 Sqn, Marham
	ZM148	Lockheed Martin F-35B Lightning II (169422/BK-14)	RAF No 617 Sqn, Marham
	ZM149	Lockheed Martin F-35B Lightning II (169596/BK-15)	RAF No 617 Sqn, MCAS Beaufort, South Carolina
	ZM150	Lockheed Martin F-35B Lightning II (169597/BK-16)	LMTAS, Fort Worth, USA, for RAF/RN
	ZM151	Lockheed Martin F-35B Lightning II (169598/BK-17)	RAF No 617 Sqn, MCAS Beaufort, South Carolina
	ZM152	Lockheed Martin F-35B Lightning II (BK-18)	LMTAS, Fort Worth, USA, for RAF/RN
	ZM153	Lockheed Martin F-35B Lightning II	Reservation for RAF/RN
	ZM154	Lockheed Martin F-35B Lightning II	Reservation for RAF/RN
	ZM155	Lockheed Martin F-35B Lightning II	Reservation for RAF/RN
	ZM156	Lockheed Martin F-35B Lightning II	Reservation for RAF/RN
	ZM157	Lockheed Martin F-35B Lightning II	Reservation for RAF/RN
	ZM158	Lockheed Martin F-35B Lightning II	Reservation for RAF/RN
	ZM159	Lockheed Martin F-35B Lightning II	Reservation for RAF/RN
	ZM160	Lockheed Martin F-35B Lightning II	Reservation for RAF/RN
	ZM161	Lockheed Martin F-35B Lightning II	Reservation for RAF/RN
	ZM162	Lockheed Martin F-35B Lightning II	Reservation for RAF/RN
	ZM163	Lockheed Martin F-35B Lightning II	Reservation for RAF/RN
	ZM164	Lockheed Martin F-35B Lightning II	Reservation for RAF/RN
	ZM165	Lockheed Martin F-35B Lightning II	Reservation for RAF/RN

Serial	Type (code/other identity)	Owner/operator, location or fate	Notes
ZM166	Lockheed Martin F-35B Lightning II	Reservation for RAF/RN	
ZM167	Lockheed Martin F-35B Lightning II	Reservation for RAF/RN	
ZM168	Lockheed Martin F-35B Lightning II	Reservation for RAF/RN	
ZM169	Lockheed Martin F-35B Lightning II	Reservation for RAF/RN	
ZM170	Lockheed Martin F-35B Lightning II	Reservation for RAF/RN	
ZM171	Lockheed Martin F-35B Lightning II	Reservation for RAF/RN	
ZM172	Lockheed Martin F-35B Lightning II	Reservation for RAF/RN	
ZM173	Lockheed Martin F-35B Lightning II	Reservation for RAF/RN	
ZM174	Lockheed Martin F-35B Lightning II	Reservation for RAF/RN	
ZM175	Lockheed Martin F-35B Lightning II	Reservation for RAF/RN	
ZM176	Lockheed Martin F-35B Lightning II	Reservation for RAF/RN	
ZM177	Lockheed Martin F-35B Lightning II	Reservation for RAF/RN	
ZM178	Lockheed Martin F-35B Lightning II	Reservation for RAF/RN	
ZM179	Lockheed Martin F-35B Lightning II	Reservation for RAF/RN	
ZM180	Lockheed Martin F-35B Lightning II	Reservation for RAF/RN	
ZM181	Lockheed Martin F-35B Lightning II	Reservation for RAF/RN	
ZM182	Lockheed Martin F-35B Lightning II	Reservation for RAF/RN	
ZM183	Lockheed Martin F-35 Lightning II	Reservation for RAF/RN	
ZM184	Lockheed Martin F-35 Lightning II	Reservation for RAF/RN	
ZM185	Lockheed Martin F-35 Lightning II	Reservation for RAF/RN	
ZM186	Lockheed Martin F-35 Lightning II	Reservation for RAF/RN	
ZM187	Lockheed Martin F-35 Lightning II	Reservation for RAF/RN	
ZM188	Lockheed Martin F-35 Lightning II	Reservation for RAF/RN	
ZM189	Lockheed Martin F-35 Lightning II	Reservation for RAF/RN	
ZM190	Lockheed Martin F-35 Lightning II	Reservation for RAF/RN	
ZM191	Lockheed Martin F-35 Lightning II	Reservation for RAF/RN	
ZM192	Lockheed Martin F-35 Lightning II	Reservation for RAF/RN	
ZM193	Lockheed Martin F-35 Lightning II	Reservation for RAF/RN	
ZM194	Lockheed Martin F-35 Lightning II	Reservation for RAF/RN	
ZM195	Lockheed Martin F-35 Lightning II	Reservation for RAF/RN	
ZM196	Lockheed Martin F-35 Lightning II	Reservation for RAF/RN	
ZM197	Lockheed Martin F-35 Lightning II	Reservation for RAF/RN	
ZM198	Lockheed Martin F-35 Lightning II	Reservation for RAF/RN	
ZM199	Lockheed Martin F-35 Lightning II	Reservation for RAF/RN	
ZM200	Lockheed Martin F-35 Lightning II	Reservation for RAF/RN	
ZM300	Grob G120TP-A Prefect T1 (D-ETPJ/G-MFTS)	Affinity/RAF No 3 FTS/No 57 Sqn, Cranwell	
ZM301	Grob G120TP-A Prefect T1 (D-EGUX/G-MEFT)	Affinity/RAF No 3 FTS/No 57 Sqn, Cranwell	
ZM302	Grob G120TP-A Prefect T1 (D-ETPT/G-CJYB)	Affinity/RAF No 3 FTS/No 57 Sqn, Barkston Heath	
ZM303	Grob G120TP-A Prefect T1 (G-CJYG)	Affinity/RAF No 3 FTS/No 57 Sqn, Cranwell	
ZM304	Grob G120TP-A Prefect T1 (G-CJYH)	Affinity/RAF No 3 FTS/No 57 Sqn, Barkston Heath	
ZM305	Grob G120TP-A Prefect T1 (G-CJZR)	Affinity/RAF No 3 FTS/No 57 Sqn, Barkston Heath	
ZM306	Grob G120TP-A Prefect T1 (G-CJZJ)	Affinity/RAF No 3 FTS/No 57 Sqn, Cranwell	
ZM307	Grob G120TP-A Prefect T1 (G-CJZI)	Affinity/RAF No 3 FTS/No 57 Sqn, Barkston Heath	
ZM308	Grob G120TP-A Prefect T1 (G-CJZF)	Affinity/RAF No 3 FTS/No 57 Sqn, Barkston Heath	
ZM309	Grob G120TP-A Prefect T1 (G-CKCO)	Affinity/RAF No 3 FTS/No 57 Sqn, Barkston Heath	
ZM310	Grob G120TP-A Prefect T1 (G-CKCS)	Affinity/RAF No 3 FTS/No 57 Sqn, Cranwell	
ZM311	Grob G120TP-A Prefect T1 (G-CKIA)	Affinity/RAF No 3 FTS/No 57 Sqn, Barkston Heath	
ZM312	Grob G120TP-A Prefect T1 (G-CKIB)	Affinity/RAF No 3 FTS/No 57 Sqn, Cranwell	
ZM313	Grob G120TP-A Prefect T1 (G-CKIC)	Affinity/RAF No 3 FTS/No 57 Sqn, Cranwell	
ZM314	Grob G120TP-A Prefect T1 (G-CKID)	Affinity/RAF, stored Barkston Heath (damaged)	
ZM315	Grob G120TP-A Prefect T1 (G-CKIV)	Affinity/RAF No 3 FTS/No 57 Sqn, Cranwell	
ZM316	Grob G120TP-A Prefect T1 (G-CKIW)	Affinity/RAF No 3 FTS/No 57 Sqn, Barkston Heath	
ZM317	Grob G120TP-A Prefect T1 (G-CKLJ)	Affinity/RAF No 3 FTS/No 57 Sqn, Barkston Heath	
ZM318	Grob G120TP-A Prefect T1 (G-CKLO)	Affinity/RAF No 3 FTS/No 57 Sqn, Cranwell	
ZM319	Grob G120TP-A Prefect T1 (G-CKRY)	Affinity/RAF No 3 FTS/No 57 Sqn, Barkston Heath	
ZM320	Grob G120TP-A Prefect T1 (G-CKRP) $	Affinity/RAF No 3 FTS/No 57 Sqn, Barkston Heath	
ZM321	Grob G120TP-A Prefect T1 (G-CKSJ)	Affinity/RAF No 3 FTS/No 57 Sqn, Cranwell	
ZM322	Grob G120TP-A Prefect T1 (G-CKSI)	Affinity/RAF No 3 FTS/No 57 Sqn, Barkston Heath	
ZM323	Beechcraft T-6C Texan T1 (N2824B/G-TBFT) [323]	Affinity/RAF No 4 FTS, Valley	
ZM324	Beechcraft T-6C Texan T1 (N2826B/G-CKGO) [324]	Affinity/RAF No 4 FTS, Valley	
ZM325	Beechcraft T-6C Texan T1 (N2843B/G-CKGP) [325]	Affinity/RAF No 4 FTS, Valley	

Notes	Serial	Type (code/other identity)	Owner/operator, location or fate
	ZM326	Beechcraft T-6C Texan T1 (N2770B/G-CKGW) [326] $	Affinity/RAF No 4 FTS, Valley
	ZM327	Beechcraft T-6C Texan T1 (N2856B/G-CKVL) [327]	Affinity/RAF No 4 FTS, Valley
	ZM328	Beechcraft T-6C Texan T1 (N2857B/G-CKVN) [328]	Affinity/RAF No 4 FTS, Valley
	ZM329	Beechcraft T-6C Texan T1 (N2858B/G-CKVO) [329]	Affinity/RAF No 4 FTS, Valley
	ZM330	Beechcraft T-6C Texan T1 (N2859B/G-CKVR) [330]	Affinity/RAF No 4 FTS, Valley
	ZM331	Beechcraft T-6C Texan T1 (N2860B/G-CKVS) [331]	Affinity/RAF No 4 FTS, Valley
	ZM332	Beechcraft T-6C Texan T1 (N2872B/G-CKVU) [332]	Affinity/RAF No 4 FTS, Valley
	ZM333	Embraer EMB-500 Phenom 100 (PR-PHK/G-MEPT)	Affinity/RAF No 3 FTS/No 45 Sqn, Cranwell
	ZM334	Embraer EMB-500 Phenom 100 (PR-ING/G-MEPS)	Affinity/RAF No 3 FTS/No 45 Sqn, Cranwell
	ZM335	Embraer EMB-500 Phenom 100 (PR-LTE/G-CJXH)	Affinity/RAF No 3 FTS/No 45 Sqn, Cranwell
	ZM336	Embraer EMB-500 Phenom 100 (PR-LTF/G-CKCU)	Affinity/RAF, stored Waddington (damaged)
	ZM337	Embraer EMB-500 Phenom 100 (PR-LTJ/G-CKEF) $	Affinity/RAF No 3 FTS/No 45 Sqn, Cranwell
	ZM398	Airbus A400M Atlas Full Flight Simulator	RAF Brize Norton
	ZM399	Airbus A400M Atlas Full Flight Simulator	RAF Brize Norton
	ZM400	Airbus A400M Atlas C1 (A4M015/EC-405)	RAF No 1312 Flt, Mount Pleasant, FI
	ZM401	Airbus A400M Atlas C1 (A4M016/EC-406)	RAF No 24 Sqn/No 70 Sqn, Brize Norton
	ZM402	Airbus A400M Atlas C1 (A4M017/EC-407)	MoD/Airbus Defence & Space, Getafe
	ZM403	Airbus A400M Atlas C1 (A4M020)	MoD/Airbus Defence & Space, Getafe
	ZM404	Airbus A400M Atlas C1 (A4M021/EC-401)	MoD/Airbus Defence & Space, Getafe
	ZM405	Airbus A400M Atlas C1 (A4M024)	MoD/Airbus Defence & Space, Getafe
	ZM406	Airbus A400M Atlas C1 (A4M025/EC-405) $	RAF No 24 Sqn/No 70 Sqn, Brize Norton
	ZM407	Airbus A400M Atlas C1 (A4M026)	RAF No 24 Sqn/No 70 Sqn, Brize Norton
	ZM408	Airbus A400M Atlas C1 (A4M027)	MoD/Airbus Defence & Space, Getafe
	ZM409	Airbus A400M Atlas C1 (A4M034) $	RAF No 24 Sqn/No 70 Sqn, Brize Norton
	ZM410	Airbus A400M Atlas C1 (A4M038)	RAF No 24 Sqn/No 70 Sqn, Brize Norton
	ZM411	Airbus A400M Atlas C1 (A4M039)	RAF No 24 Sqn/No 70 Sqn, Brize Norton
	ZM412	Airbus A400M Atlas C1 (A4M042)	RAF No 24 Sqn/No 70 Sqn, Brize Norton
	ZM413	Airbus A400M Atlas C1 (A4M045)	MoD/Airbus Defence & Space, Getafe
	ZM414	Airbus A400M Atlas C1 (A4M047)	RAF No 24 Sqn/No 70 Sqn, Brize Norton
	ZM415	Airbus A400M Atlas C1 (A4M052)	RAF No 24 Sqn/No 70 Sqn, Brize Norton
	ZM416	Airbus A400M Atlas C1 (A4M058)	RAF No 24 Sqn/No 70 Sqn, Brize Norton
	ZM417	Airbus A400M Atlas C1 (A4M060)	RAF No 24 Sqn/No 70 Sqn, Brize Norton
	ZM418	Airbus A400M Atlas C1 (A4M072)	RAF No 24 Sqn/No 70 Sqn, Brize Norton
	ZM419	Airbus A400M Atlas C1 (A4M077)	RAF No 24 Sqn/No 70 Sqn, Brize Norton
	ZM420	Airbus A400M Atlas C1 (A4M095)	Airbus Defence & Space, Seville, for RAF
	ZM421	Airbus A400M Atlas C1 (A4M056/EC-400)	Airbus Defence & Space, Seville, for RAF
	ZM500	Airbus H145 Jupiter HT1 (D-HADT/G-CJIV) [00] $	DHFS No 202 Sqn, RAF Valley
	ZM501	Airbus H145 Jupiter HT1 (D-HADM/G-CJIZ/G-CKGE) [01]	DHFS No 202 Sqn, RAF Valley
	ZM502	Airbus H145 Jupiter HT1 (D-HADQ/G-CJRW) [02]	DHFS No 202 Sqn, RAF Valley
	ZM503	Airbus H145 Jupiter HT1	Reservation for MoD
	ZM504	Airbus H135 Juno HT1 (D-HECZ/G-CJJG) [04]	DHFS, RAF Shawbury
	ZM505	Airbus H135 Juno HT1 (D-HECV/G-CJIW) [05]	DHFS, RAF Shawbury
	ZM506	Airbus H135 Juno HT1 (D-HECW/G-CJIY) [06]	DHFS, RAF Shawbury
	ZM507	Airbus H135 Juno HT1 (D-HECX/G-CJRP) [07]	DHFS, RAF Shawbury
	ZM508	Airbus H135 Juno HT1 (D-HECD/G-CJRY) [08]	DHFS, RAF Shawbury
	ZM509	Airbus H135 Juno HT1 (D-HECB/G-CJTZ) [09]	DHFS, RAF Shawbury
	ZM510	Airbus H135 Juno HT1 (D-HECG/G-CJUA) [10]	DHFS, RAF Shawbury
	ZM511	Airbus H135 Juno HT1 (D-HECJ/G-CJUC) [11]	DHFS, RAF Shawbury
	ZM512	Airbus H135 Juno HT1 (D-HECQ/G-CJXS) [12]	DHFS, RAF Shawbury
	ZM513	Airbus H135 Juno HT1 (D-HECP/G-CJXU) [13]	DHFS, RAF Shawbury
	ZM514	Airbus H135 Juno HT1 (D-HECV/G-CJXV) [14]	DHFS, RAF Shawbury
	ZM515	Airbus H135 Juno HT1 (D-HECT/G-CJSO) [15]	DHFS, RAF Shawbury
	ZM516	Airbus H135 Juno HT1 (D-HECY/G-CJZS) [16]	DHFS, RAF Shawbury
	ZM517	Airbus H135 Juno HT1 (D-HECL/G-CJZT) [17]	DHFS, RAF Shawbury
	ZM518	Airbus H135 Juno HT1 (D-HCBA/G-CKEO) [18]	DHFS, RAF Shawbury
	ZM519	Airbus H135 Juno HT1 (D-HCBC/G-CKEU) [19]	DHFS, RAF Shawbury
	ZM520	Airbus H135 Juno HT1 (D-HCBD/G-CKEW) [20]	DHFS, RAF Shawbury
	ZM521	Airbus H135 Juno HT1 (D-HECJ/G-CKIK) [21]	DHFS, RAF Shawbury
	ZM522	Airbus H135 Juno HT1 (D-HCBB/G-CKIM) [22]	DHFS, RAF Shawbury
	ZM523	Airbus H135 Juno HT1 (G-CKJW) [23]	DHFS, RAF Shawbury

Serial	Type (code/other identity)	Owner/operator, location or fate	Notes
ZM524	Airbus H135 Juno HT1 (D-HECK/G-CKJU) [24]	DHFS, RAF Shawbury	
ZM525	Airbus H135 Juno HT1 (D-HECQ/G-CKJX) [25]	DHFS, RAF Shawbury	
ZM526	Airbus H135 Juno HT1 (D-HECU/G-CKOC) [26]	DHFS, RAF Shawbury	
ZM527	Airbus H135 Juno HT1 (D-HECX/G-CKOB) [27]	DHFS, RAF Shawbury	
ZM528	Airbus H135 Juno HT1 (G-CKOA) [28]	DHFS, RAF Shawbury	
ZM529	Airbus H135 Juno HT1 (D-HECW/G-CKPT) [29]	DHFS, RAF Shawbury	
ZM530	Airbus H135 Juno HT1 (D-HECD/G-CKRA) [30]	DHFS, RAF Shawbury	
ZM531	Airbus H135 Juno HT1 (D-HECA/G-CKSB) [31]	DHFS, RAF Shawbury	
ZM532	Airbus H135 Juno HT1 (D-HECY/G-CKSA) [32]	DHFS, RAF Shawbury	
ZM533	Airbus H135 Juno HT1	Reservation for MoD	
ZM534	Airbus H135 Juno HT1	Reservation for MoD	
ZM700	Boeing AH-64E Apache	For AAC	
ZM701	Boeing AH-64E Apache	For AAC	
ZM702	Boeing AH-64E Apache	For AAC	
ZM703	Boeing AH-64E Apache	For AAC	
ZM704	Boeing AH-64E Apache	For AAC	
ZM705	Boeing AH-64E Apache	For AAC	
ZM706	Boeing AH-64E Apache	For AAC	
ZM707	Boeing AH-64E Apache	For AAC	
ZM708	Boeing AH-64E Apache	For AAC	
ZM709	Boeing AH-64E Apache	For AAC	
ZM710	Boeing AH-64E Apache	For AAC	
ZM711	Boeing AH-64E Apache	For AAC	
ZM712	Boeing AH-64E Apache	For AAC	
ZM713	Boeing AH-64E Apache	For AAC	
ZM714	Boeing AH-64E Apache	For AAC	
ZM715	Boeing AH-64E Apache	For AAC	
ZM716	Boeing AH-64E Apache	For AAC	
ZM717	Boeing AH-64E Apache	For AAC	
ZM718	Boeing AH-64E Apache	For AAC	
ZM719	Boeing AH-64E Apache	For AAC	
ZM720	Boeing AH-64E Apache	For AAC	
ZM721	Boeing AH-64E Apache	For AAC	
ZM722	Boeing AH-64E Apache	For AAC	
ZM723	Boeing AH-64E Apache	For AAC	
ZM724	Boeing AH-64E Apache	For AAC	
ZM725	Boeing AH-64E Apache	For AAC	
ZM726	Boeing AH-64E Apache	For AAC	
ZM727	Boeing AH-64E Apache	For AAC	
ZM728	Boeing AH-64E Apache	For AAC	
ZM729	Boeing AH-64E Apache	For AAC	
ZM730	Boeing AH-64E Apache	For AAC	
ZM731	Boeing AH-64E Apache	For AAC	
ZM732	Boeing AH-64E Apache	For AAC	
ZM733	Boeing AH-64E Apache	For AAC	
ZM734	Boeing AH-64E Apache	For AAC	
ZM735	Boeing AH-64E Apache	For AAC	
ZM736	Boeing AH-64E Apache	For AAC	
ZM737	Boeing AH-64E Apache	For AAC	
ZM738	Boeing AH-64E Apache	For AAC	
ZM739	Boeing AH-64E Apache	For AAC	
ZM740	Boeing AH-64E Apache	For AAC	
ZM741	Boeing AH-64E Apache	For AAC	
ZM742	Boeing AH-64E Apache	For AAC	
ZM743	Boeing AH-64E Apache	For AAC	
ZM744	Boeing AH-64E Apache	For AAC	
ZM745	Boeing AH-64E Apache	For AAC	
ZM746	Boeing AH-64E Apache	For AAC	
ZM747	Boeing AH-64E Apache	For AAC	
ZM748	Boeing AH-64E Apache	For AAC	
ZM749	Boeing AH-64E Apache	For AAC	

Notes	Serial	Type (code/other identity)	Owner/operator, location or fate
	ZP801	Boeing P-8A Poseidon MRA1	For RAF
	ZP802	Boeing P-8A Poseidon MRA1	For RAF
	ZP803	Boeing P-8A Poseidon MRA1	For RAF
	ZP804	Boeing P-8A Poseidon MRA1	For RAF
	ZP805	Boeing P-8A Poseidon MRA1	For RAF
	ZP806	Boeing P-8A Poseidon MRA1	For RAF
	ZP807	Boeing P-8A Poseidon MRA1	For RAF
	ZP808	Boeing P-8A Poseidon MRA1	For RAF
	ZP809	Boeing P-8A Poseidon MRA1	For RAF
	ZP810	Boeing P-8A Poseidon MRA1	Reservation for RAF
	ZP811	Boeing P-8A Poseidon MRA1	Reservation for RAF
	ZP812	Boeing P-8A Poseidon MRA1	Reservation for RAF
	ZP813	Boeing P-8A Poseidon MRA1	Reservation for RAF
	ZP814	Boeing P-8A Poseidon MRA1	Reservation for RAF
	ZP815	Boeing P-8A Poseidon MRA1	Reservation for RAF
	ZR283	AgustaWestland AW139 (G-FBHA)	MoD/Cobham Helicopter Academy, Newquay
	ZR324	Agusta A109E Power (G-EMHB)	MoD/Cobham Helicopter Academy, Newquay
	ZR325	Agusta A109E Power (G-BZEI)	MoD/Cobham Helicopter Academy, Newquay
	ZR339	AgustaWestland AW101 Mk.641 (ZW-4302)	Leonardo MW, Yeovil
	ZR342	AgustaWestland AW101 Mk.641 (ZW-4305)	Leonardo MW, Yeovil
	ZR346	AgustaWestland AW101 Mk.641 (ZW-4309)	Leonardo MW, Yeovil
	ZR347	AgustaWestland AW101 Mk.641 (ZW-4310)	Leonardo MW, Yeovil, for Azerbaijan as 4K-Ai010
	ZR348	AgustaWestland AW101 Mk.641 (ZW-4311)	Leonardo MW, Yeovil
	ZR349	AgustaWestland AW101 Mk.641 (ZW-4312)	Leonardo MW, Yeovil
	ZR358	AgustaWestland AW101 Mk.611 [15-07]	Leonardo MW, Yeovil, for Italian AF as MM81870
	ZR359	AgustaWestland AW101 Mk.611	Leonardo MW, Yeovil, for Italian AF as MM81871
	ZR360	AgustaWestland AW101 Mk.611	Leonardo MW, Yeovil, for Italian AF as MM81872
	ZR361	AgustaWestland AW101 Mk.611	Leonardo MW, Yeovil, for Italian AF as MM81873
	ZR362	AgustaWestland AW101 Mk.611	Leonardo MW, Yeovil, for Italian AF as MM81874
	ZR363	AgustaWestland AW101 Mk.611	Leonardo MW, Yeovil, for Italian AF as MM81875
	ZR408	Eurofighter Typhoon	*To RAFO as 217, 4 June 2018*
	ZR409	Eurofighter Typhoon	*To RAFO as 218, 4 June 2018*
	ZS782	WS WG25 Sharpeye	The Helicopter Museum, Weston-super-Mare
	ZT800	WS Super Lynx Mk 300	Yeovil College, instructional use
	ZZ100	AgustaWestland AW101 Mk.612	Leonardo MW, Yeovil, for Norway as 0262
	ZZ101	AgustaWestland AW101 Mk.612	*To Norway as 0264, 5 July 2018*
	ZZ103	AgustaWestland AW101 Mk.612	Leonardo MW, Yeovil, for Norway as 0268
	ZZ104	AgustaWestland AW101 Mk.612	*To Norway as 0270, 25 May 2018*
	ZZ105	AgustaWestland AW101 Mk.612	Leonardo MW, Yeovil, for Norway as 0273
	ZZ106	AgustaWestland AW101 Mk.612	Leonardo MW, Yeovil, for Norway as 0275
	ZZ107	AgustaWestland AW101 Mk.612	Leonardo MW, Yeovil, for Norway as 0276
	ZZ108	AgustaWestland AW101 Mk.612	Leonardo MW, Yeovil, for Norway as 0277
	ZZ109	AgustaWestland AW101 Mk.612	Leonardo MW, Yeovil, for Norway as 0278
	ZZ110	AgustaWestland AW101 Mk.612	Leonardo MW, Yeovil, for Norway as 0279
	ZZ111	AgustaWestland AW101 Mk.612	Leonardo MW, Yeovil, for Norway as 0280
	ZZ112	AgustaWestland AW101 Mk.612	Leonardo MW, Yeovil, for Norway as 0281
	ZZ113	AgustaWestland AW101 Mk.612	Leonardo MW, Yeovil, for Norway as 0282
	ZZ114	AgustaWestland AW101 Mk.612	Leonardo MW, Yeovil, for Norway as 0283
	ZZ115	AgustaWestland AW101 Mk.612	Leonardo MW, Yeovil, for Norway as 0284
	ZZ171	Boeing C-17A Globemaster III (00-201/N171UK)	RAF No 99 Sqn, Brize Norton
	ZZ172	Boeing C-17A Globemaster III (00-202/N172UK)	RAF No 99 Sqn, Brize Norton
	ZZ173	Boeing C-17A Globemaster III (00-203/N173UK)	RAF No 99 Sqn, Brize Norton
	ZZ174	Boeing C-17A Globemaster III (00-204/N174UK)	RAF/Boeing, San Antonio, Texas, USA
	ZZ175	Boeing C-17A Globemaster III (06-0205/N9500Z)	RAF No 99 Sqn, Brize Norton
	ZZ176	Boeing C-17A Globemaster III (08-0206/N9500B) $	RAF No 99 Sqn, Brize Norton
	ZZ177	Boeing C-17A Globemaster III (09-8207/N9500B)	RAF No 99 Sqn, Brize Norton
	ZZ178	Boeing C-17A Globemaster III (12-0208/N9500N)	RAF No 99 Sqn, Brize Norton
	ZZ190	Hawker Hunter F58 (J-4066/G-HHAE)	Hawker Hunter Aviation, Scampton

Serial	Type (code/other identity)	Owner/operator, location or fate	Notes
ZZ191	Hawker Hunter F58 (J-4058/G-HHAD)	Hawker Hunter Aviation, Scampton	
ZZ192	Grob G109B Vigilant T1 (D-KLVI) [SQ]	RAF, stored Little Rissington	
ZZ193	Grob G109B Vigilant T1 (D-KBLO) [SR]	RAF, stored Little Rissington	
ZZ194	Hawker Hunter F58 (J-4021/G-HHAC)	Hawker Hunter Aviation, Scampton	
ZZ201	General Atomics Reaper RPAS (07-0111)	RAF No 13 Sqn/No 39 Sqn, Creech AFB, Nevada, USA	
ZZ202	General Atomics Reaper RPAS (07-0117)	RAF No 13 Sqn/No 39 Sqn, Creech AFB, Nevada, USA	
ZZ203	General Atomics Reaper RPAS (08-0113)	RAF No 13 Sqn/No 39 Sqn, Creech AFB, Nevada, USA	
ZZ204	General Atomics Reaper RPAS (10-0157)	RAF No 13 Sqn/No 39 Sqn, Creech AFB, Nevada, USA	
ZZ206	General Atomics Reaper RPAS (12-0707)	RAF No 13 Sqn/No 39 Sqn, Creech AFB, Nevada, USA	
ZZ207	General Atomics Reaper RPAS (12-0708)	RAF No 13 Sqn/No 39 Sqn, Creech AFB, Nevada, USA	
ZZ208	General Atomics Reaper RPAS (12-0709)	RAF No 13 Sqn/No 39 Sqn, Creech AFB, Nevada, USA	
ZZ209	General Atomics Reaper RPAS (12-0710)	RAF No 13 Sqn/No 39 Sqn, Creech AFB, Nevada, USA	
ZZ210	General Atomics Reaper RPAS (12-0711)	RAF No 13 Sqn/No 39 Sqn, Creech AFB, Nevada, USA	
ZZ211	General Atomics Reaper RPAS	General Atomics, for RAF	
ZZ212	General Atomics Reaper RPAS	General Atomics, for RAF	
ZZ213	General Atomics Reaper RPAS	General Atomics, for RAF	
ZZ250	BAE Systems Taranis RPAS	BAE Systems, Warton	
ZZ251	BAE Systems HERTI RPAS	BAE Systems, Warton	
ZZ252	BAE Systems HERTI RPAS	BAE Systems, Woomera, Australia	
ZZ253	BAE Systems HERTI RPAS	BAE Systems, Woomera, Australia	
ZZ254	BAE Systems HERTI RPAS	BAE Systems, Woomera, Australia	
ZZ330	Airbus A330 Voyager KC2 (MRTT017/EC-337/G-VYGA) $	RAF No 10 Sqn/No 101 Sqn, Brize Norton	
ZZ331	Airbus A330 Voyager KC2 (MRTT018/EC-331/G-VYGB)	RAF No 10 Sqn/No 101 Sqn, Brize Norton	
ZZ332	Airbus A330 Voyager KC3 (MRTT019/EC-330/G-VYGC)	RAF No 1312 Flt, Mount Pleasant, FI	
ZZ333	Airbus A330 Voyager KC3 (MRTT020/EC-337/G-VYGD)	RAF No 10 Sqn/No 101 Sqn, Brize Norton	
ZZ334	Airbus A330 Voyager KC3 (MRTT016/EC-335/G-VYGE)	RAF No 10 Sqn/No 101 Sqn, Brize Norton	
ZZ335	Airbus A330 Voyager KC3 (MRTT021/EC-338/G-VYGF)	RAF No 10 Sqn/No 101 Sqn, Brize Norton	
ZZ336	Airbus A330 Voyager KC3 (MRTT022/EC-333/G-VYGG)	RAF No 10 Sqn/No 101 Sqn, Brize Norton	
ZZ337	Airbus A330 Voyager KC3 (MRTT023/EC-336/G-VYGH)	RAF No 10 Sqn/No 101 Sqn, Brize Norton	
ZZ338	Airbus A330 Voyager KC3 (MRTT024/EC-331/G-VYGI)	RAF No 10 Sqn/No 101 Sqn, Brize Norton	
ZZ339	Airbus A330-243 (MRTT025/EC-333/G-VYGJ)	Airtanker Ltd, Brize Norton [flies as G-VYGJ]	
ZZ340	Airbus A330-243 (MRTT026/EC-330/G-VYGK) [flies as G-VYGK]	Airtanker Ltd/Thomas Cook Airlines, Manchester	
ZZ341	Airbus A330-243 (MRTT027/EC-336/G-VYGL)	Airtanker Ltd, Brize Norton [flies as G-VYGL]	
ZZ342	Airbus A330-243 (MRTT028/EC-332/G-VYGM) [flies as G-VYGM]	Airtanker Ltd/Eurowings, Munich, Germany	
ZZ343	Airbus A330 Voyager KC2 (MRTT029/EC-331/G-VYGN)	RAF No 10 Sqn/No 101 Sqn, Brize Norton	
ZZ375	AgustaWestland AW159 Wildcat HMA2	RN No 815 NAS, 206 Flt, Yeovilton	
ZZ376	AgustaWestland AW159 Wildcat HMA2	MoD/Leonardo MW, Yeovil	
ZZ377	AgustaWestland AW159 Wildcat HMA2	RN No 825 NAS, Yeovilton	
ZZ378	AgustaWestland AW159 Wildcat HMA2	RN No 825 NAS, Yeovilton	
ZZ379	AgustaWestland AW159 Wildcat HMA2	RN No 815 NAS, MI Flt Yeovilton	
ZZ380	AgustaWestland AW159 Wildcat HMA2	RN No 815 NAS, 209 Flt, Yeovilton	
ZZ381	AgustaWestland AW159 Wildcat HMA2	RN No 815 NAS, Yeovilton	
ZZ382	AgustaWestland AW159 Wildcat AH1	MoD/Leonardo MW, Yeovil	
ZZ383	AgustaWestland AW159 Wildcat AH1	AAC No 1 Regiment, Yeovilton	
ZZ384	AgustaWestland AW159 Wildcat AH1	RN No 847 NAS, Yeovilton	
ZZ385	AgustaWestland AW159 Wildcat AH1	AAC No 1 Regiment, Yeovilton	
ZZ386	AgustaWestland AW159 Wildcat AH1	RN No 847 NAS, Yeovilton	
ZZ387	AgustaWestland AW159 Wildcat AH1	AAC WCM, Yeovilton	
ZZ388	AgustaWestland AW159 Wildcat AH1	MoD/Leonardo MW, Yeovil	
ZZ389	AgustaWestland AW159 Wildcat AH1	RN No 847 NAS, Yeovilton	

Notes	Serial	Type (code/other identity)	Owner/operator, location or fate
	ZZ390	AgustaWestland AW159 Wildcat AH1	AAC WST, stored Yeovilton
	ZZ391	AgustaWestland AW159 Wildcat AH1	AAC WCM, Yeovilton
	ZZ392	AgustaWestland AW159 Wildcat AH1	AAC No 1 Regiment, Yeovilton
	ZZ393	AgustaWestland AW159 Wildcat AH1	AAC No 1 Regiment, Yeovilton
	ZZ394	AgustaWestland AW159 Wildcat AH1	AAC WCM, Yeovilton
	ZZ395	AgustaWestland AW159 Wildcat AH1	AAC WCM, Yeovilton
	ZZ396	AgustaWestland AW159 Wildcat HMA2	RN No 815 NAS, 202 Flt, Yeovilton
	ZZ397	AgustaWestland AW159 Wildcat HMA2	RN No 815 NAS, 207 Flt, Yeovilton
	ZZ398	AgustaWestland AW159 Wildcat AH1	AAC No 1 Regiment, Yeovilton
	ZZ399	AgustaWestland AW159 Wildcat AH1	RN No 847 NAS, Yeovilton
	ZZ400	AgustaWestland AW159 Wildcat (TI01)	Yeovil College, instructional use
	ZZ401	AgustaWestland AW159 Wildcat (TI02)	RNAS Yeovilton, instructional use
	ZZ402	AgustaWestland AW159 Wildcat (TI03)	DSAE RNAESS, *HMS Sultan*, Gosport
	ZZ403	AgustaWestland AW159 Wildcat AH1	AAC No 1 Regiment, Yeovilton
	ZZ404	AgustaWestland AW159 Wildcat AH1	AAC No 1 Regiment, Yeovilton
	ZZ405	AgustaWestland AW159 Wildcat AH1	AAC No 1 Regiment, Yeovilton
	ZZ406	AgustaWestland AW159 Wildcat AH1	AAC No 1 Regiment, Yeovilton
	ZZ407	AgustaWestland AW159 Wildcat AH1	AAC No 1 Regiment, Yeovilton
	ZZ408	AgustaWestland AW159 Wildcat AH1	MoD/Leonardo MW, Yeovil
	ZZ409	AgustaWestland AW159 Wildcat AH1	AAC WST, stored Yeovilton
	ZZ410	AgustaWestland AW159 Wildcat AH1	MoD/Leonardo MW, Yeovil
	ZZ413	AgustaWestland AW159 Wildcat HMA2	RN No 815 NAS, MI Flt, Yeovilton
	ZZ414	AgustaWestland AW159 Wildcat HMA2	RN No 815 NAS, 202 Flt, Yeovilton
	ZZ415	AgustaWestland AW159 Wildcat HMA2	MoD/Leonardo MW, Yeovil
	ZZ416	Hawker Beechcraft Shadow R1 (G-JENC)	RAF No 14 Sqn, Waddington
	ZZ417	Hawker Beechcraft Shadow R1+ (G-NICY)	RAF No 14 Sqn, Waddington
	ZZ418	Hawker Beechcraft Shadow R1 (G-JIMG)	RAF No 14 Sqn, Waddington
	ZZ419	Hawker Beechcraft Shadow R1+ (G-OTCS)	RAF No 14 Sqn, Waddington
	ZZ500	Hawker Beechcraft Avenger T1 (G-MFTA)	RN No 750 NAS, Culdrose
	ZZ501	Hawker Beechcraft Avenger T1 (G-MFTB)	RN No 750 NAS, Culdrose
	ZZ502	Hawker Beechcraft Avenger T1 (G-MFTC)	RN No 750 NAS, Culdrose
	ZZ503	Hawker Beechcraft Avenger T1 (G-MFTD)	RN No 750 NAS, Culdrose
	ZZ504	Hawker Beechcraft Shadow R1 (G-CGUM)	RAF No 14 Sqn, Waddington
	ZZ505	Hawker Beechcraft Shadow R2 (G-DAYP)	RAF, on order
	ZZ506	Hawker Beechcraft Shadow R2 (G-GMAD)	RAF, on order
	ZZ507	Hawker Beechcraft Shadow R1+ (G-LBSB)	MoD/Raytheon, Hawarden (conversion)
	ZZ510	AgustaWestland AW159 Wildcat AH1	AAC WCM, Yeovilton
	ZZ511	AgustaWestland AW159 Wildcat AH1	AAC No 1 Regiment, Yeovilton
	ZZ512	AgustaWestland AW159 Wildcat AH1	RN No 847 NAS, Yeovilton
	ZZ513	AgustaWestland AW159 Wildcat HMA2	MoD/Leonardo MW, Yeovil
	ZZ514	AgustaWestland AW159 Wildcat HMA2	RN No 825 NAS, Yeovilton
	ZZ515	AgustaWestland AW159 Wildcat HMA2	RN No 815 NAS, 203 Flt, Yeovilton
	ZZ516	AgustaWestland AW159 Wildcat HMA2	RN No 815 NAS, 212 Flt, Yeovilton
	ZZ517	AgustaWestland AW159 Wildcat HMA2	RN WST, stored Yeovilton
	ZZ518	AgustaWestland AW159 Wildcat HMA2	RN WST, stored Yeovilton
	ZZ519	AgustaWestland AW159 Wildcat HMA2	RN No 825 NAS, Yeovilton
	ZZ520	AgustaWestland AW159 Wildcat AH1	AAC WCM, Yeovilton
	ZZ521	AgustaWestland AW159 Wildcat AH1	MoD/Leonardo MW, Yeovil
	ZZ522	AgustaWestland AW159 Wildcat HMA2	MoD/Leonardo MW, Yeovil
	ZZ523	AgustaWestland AW159 Wildcat AH1	RN No 847 NAS, Yeovilton
	ZZ524	AgustaWestland AW159 Wildcat AH1	AAC No 1 Regiment, Yeovilton
	ZZ525	AgustaWestland AW159 Wildcat AH1	AAC WCM, Yeovilton
	ZZ526	AgustaWestland AW159 Wildcat AH1	AAC WCM, Yeovilton
	ZZ527	AgustaWestland AW159 Wildcat AH1	RN No 847 NAS, Yeovilton
	ZZ528	AgustaWestland AW159 Wildcat HMA2	RN No 825 NAS, Yeovilton
	ZZ529	AgustaWestland AW159 Wildcat HMA2	RN No 815 NAS, 213 Flt, Yeovilton
	ZZ530	AgustaWestland AW159 Wildcat HMA2	RN No 815 NAS, 205 Flt, Yeovilton
	ZZ531	AgustaWestland AW159 Wildcat HMA2	RN No 825 NAS, Yeovilton
	ZZ532	AgustaWestland AW159 Wildcat HMA2	RN No 815 NAS, 214 Flt, Yeovilton
	ZZ533	AgustaWestland AW159 Wildcat HMA2	RN No 815 NAS, MI Flt, Yeovilton
	ZZ534	AgustaWestland AW159 Wildcat HMA2	RN No 825 NAS, Yeovilton
	ZZ535	AgustaWestland AW159 Wildcat HMA2	RN No 825 NAS, Yeovilton

Serial	Type (code/other identity)	Owner/operator, location or fate	Notes
ZZ549	AgustaWestland AW159 Mk.220 [44]	Leonardo MW, for Philippine Navy	
ZZ550	AgustaWestland AW159 Mk.220 [45]	Leonardo MW, for Philippine Navy	
ZZ664	Boeing RC-135W (64-14833) $	RAF/Northrop Grumman, Greenville, SC, USA	
ZZ665	Boeing RC-135W (64-14838)	RAF No 51 Sqn, Waddington	
ZZ666	Boeing RC-135W (64-14830)	RAF No 51 Sqn, Waddington	

Aircraft in UK Military Service with Civil Registrations   G-BYUB-G-BYVI

Serial	Type (code/other identity)	Owner/operator, location or fate	Notes
G-BYUB	Grob G.115E Tutor T1	Babcock/Cambridge UAS/East Midlands Universities AS/University of London AS/No 115 Sqn, Wittering	
G-BYUC	Grob G.115E Tutor T1	Babcock/No 3 FTS/No 16 Sqn, Cranwell	
G-BYUD	Grob G.115E Tutor T1	Babcock/Yorkshire Universities AS, Linton-on-Ouse	
G-BYUE	Grob G.115E Tutor T1	Babcock/Cambridge UAS/East Midlands Universities AS/University of London AS/No 115 Sqn, Wittering	
G-BYUF	Grob G.115E Tutor T1	Babcock/Northumbrian Universities AS, Leeming	
G-BYUH	Grob G.115E Tutor T1	Babcock/Cambridge UAS/East Midlands Universities AS/University of London AS/No 115 Sqn, Wittering	
G-BYUI	Grob G.115E Tutor T1	Babcock/Liverpool UAS/Manchester and Salford Universities AS, Woodvale	
G-BYUJ	Grob G.115E Tutor T1	Babcock/East of Scotland UAS, Leuchars	
G-BYUK	Grob G.115E Tutor T1	Babcock/Cambridge UAS/East Midlands Universities AS/University of London AS/No 115 Sqn, Wittering	
G-BYUL	Grob G.115E Tutor T1	Babcock/Cambridge UAS/East Midlands Universities AS/University of London AS/No 115 Sqn, Wittering	
G-BYUM	Grob G.115E Tutor T1	Babcock/Cambridge UAS/East Midlands Universities AS/University of London AS/No 115 Sqn, Wittering	
G-BYUN	Grob G.115E Tutor T1	Babcock/No 3 FTS/No 16 Sqn, Cranwell	
G-BYUO	Grob G.115E Tutor T1	Babcock/No 3 FTS/No 16 Sqn, Cranwell	
G-BYUR	Grob G.115E Tutor T1	Babcock/East of Scotland UAS, Leuchars	
G-BYUS	Grob G.115E Tutor T1	Babcock/East of Scotland UAS, Leuchars	
G-BYUU	Grob G.115E Tutor T1	Babcock/Cambridge UAS/East Midlands Universities AS/University of London AS/No 115 Sqn, Wittering	
G-BYUV	Grob G.115E Tutor T1	Babcock/Bristol UAS/Southampton UAS, Boscombe Down	
G-BYUW	Grob G.115E Tutor T1	Babcock/No 3 FTS/No 16 Sqn, Cranwell	
G-BYUX	Grob G.115E Tutor T1	Babcock/No 3 FTS/No 16 Sqn, Cranwell	
G-BYUY	Grob G.115E Tutor T1	Babcock/Liverpool UAS/Manchester and Salford Universities AS, Woodvale	
G-BYUZ	Grob G.115E Tutor T1	Babcock/No 3 FTS/No 16 Sqn, Cranwell	
G-BYVA	Grob G.115E Tutor T1	Babcock/Bristol UAS/Southampton UAS, Boscombe Down	
G-BYVB	Grob G.115E Tutor T1	Babcock/University of Wales AS, St Athan	
G-BYVC	Grob G.115E Tutor T1	Babcock/Cambridge UAS/East Midlands Universities AS/University of London AS/No 115 Sqn, Wittering	
G-BYVD	Grob G.115E Tutor T1	Babcock/Bristol UAS/Southampton UAS, Boscombe Down	
G-BYVE	Grob G.115E Tutor T1	Babcock/Cambridge UAS/East Midlands Universities AS/University of London AS/No 115 Sqn, Wittering	
G-BYVF	Grob G.115E Tutor T1	Babcock/RN No 727 NAS, Yeovilton	
G-BYVG	Grob G.115E Tutor T1	Babcock/Cambridge UAS/East Midlands Universities AS/University of London AS/No 115 Sqn, Wittering	
G-BYVH	Grob G.115E Tutor T1	Babcock/Cambridge UAS/East Midlands Universities AS/University of London AS/No 115 Sqn, Wittering	
G-BYVI	Grob G.115E Tutor T1	Babcock/Liverpool UAS/Manchester and Salford Universities AS, Woodvale	

Notes	Serial	Type (code/other identity)	Owner/operator, location or fate
	G-BYVK	Grob G.115E Tutor T1	Babcock/RN No 727 NAS, Yeovilton
	G-BYVL	Grob G.115E Tutor T1	Babcock/University of Birmingham AS, Cosford
	G-BYVM	Grob G.115E Tutor T1	Babcock/No 3 FTS/No 16 Sqn, Cranwell
	G-BYVO	Grob G.115E Tutor T1	Babcock/University of Wales AS, St Athan
	G-BYVP	Grob G.115E Tutor T1	Babcock/Liverpool UAS/Manchester and Salford Universities AS, Woodvale
	G-BYVR	Grob G.115E Tutor T1	Babcock/Cambridge UAS/East Midlands Universities AS/ University of London AS/No 115 Sqn, Wittering
	G-BYVU	Grob G.115E Tutor T1	Babcock/No 1 EFTS/676 Sqn, Middle Wallop
	G-BYVW	Grob G.115E Tutor T1	Babcock/University of Wales AS, St Athan
	G-BYVY	Grob G.115E Tutor T1	Babcock/No 1 EFTS/676 Sqn, Middle Wallop
	G-BYVZ	Grob G.115E Tutor T1	Babcock/University of Birmingham AS, Cosford
	G-BYWA	Grob G.115E Tutor T1	Babcock/Yorkshire Universities AS, Linton-on-Ouse
	G-BYWB	Grob G.115E Tutor T1	Babcock/Bristol UAS/Southampton UAS, Boscombe Down
	G-BYWD	Grob G.115E Tutor T1	Babcock/University of Birmingham AS, Cosford
	G-BYWF	Grob G.115E Tutor T1	Babcock/Cambridge UAS/East Midlands Universities AS/ University of London AS/No 115 Sqn, Wittering
	G-BYWG	Grob G.115E Tutor T1	Babcock/University of Birmingham AS, Cosford
	G-BYWH	Grob G.115E Tutor T1	Babcock/Cambridge UAS/East Midlands Universities AS/ University of London AS/No 115 Sqn, Wittering
	G-BYWI	Grob G.115E Tutor T1	Babcock/No 3 FTS/No 16 Sqn, Cranwell
	G-BYWK	Grob G.115E Tutor T1	Babcock/Northumbrian Universities AS, Leeming
	G-BYWL	Grob G.115E Tutor T1	Babcock/Bristol UAS/Southampton UAS, Boscombe Down
	G-BYWM	Grob G.115E Tutor T1	Babcock/RN No 727 NAS, Yeovilton
	G-BYWO	Grob G.115E Tutor T1	Babcock/Cambridge UAS/East Midlands Universities AS/ University of London AS/No 115 Sqn, Wittering
	G-BYWR	Grob G.115E Tutor T1	Babcock/No 3 FTS/No 16 Sqn, Cranwell
	G-BYWS	Grob G.115E Tutor T1	Babcock/Cambridge UAS/East Midlands Universities AS/ University of London AS/No 115 Sqn, Wittering
	G-BYWU	Grob G.115E Tutor T1	Babcock/University of Birmingham AS, Cosford
	G-BYWV	Grob G.115E Tutor T1	Babcock/Yorkshire Universities AS, Linton-on-Ouse
	G-BYWW	Grob G.115E Tutor T1	Babcock/Bristol UAS/Southampton UAS, Boscombe Down
	G-BYWX	Grob G.115E Tutor T1	Babcock/Cambridge UAS/East Midlands Universities AS/ University of London AS/No 115 Sqn, Wittering
	G-BYWY	Grob G.115E Tutor T1	Babcock/No 3 FTS/No 16 Sqn, Cranwell
	G-BYWZ	Grob G.115E Tutor T1	Babcock/Cambridge UAS/East Midlands Universities AS/ University of London AS/No 115 Sqn, Wittering
	G-BYXA	Grob G.115E Tutor T1	Babcock/University of Birmingham AS, Cosford
	G-BYXC	Grob G.115E Tutor T1	Babcock/Cambridge UAS/East Midlands Universities AS/ University of London AS/No 115 Sqn, Wittering
	G-BYXD	Grob G.115E Tutor T1	Babcock/Cambridge UAS/East Midlands Universities AS/ University of London AS/No 115 Sqn, Wittering
	G-BYXE	Grob G.115E Tutor T1	Babcock/Cambridge UAS/East Midlands Universities AS/ University of London AS/No 115 Sqn, Wittering
	G-BYXF	Grob G.115E Tutor T1	Babcock/No 1 EFTS/676 Sqn, Middle Wallop
	G-BYXG	Grob G.115E Tutor T1	Babcock/Bristol UAS/Southampton UAS, Boscombe Down
	G-BYXH	Grob G.115E Tutor T1	Babcock/Cambridge UAS/East Midlands Universities AS/ University of London AS/No 115 Sqn, Wittering
	G-BYXI	Grob G.115E Tutor T1	Babcock/No 1 EFTS/676 Sqn, Middle Wallop
	G-BYXJ	Grob G.115E Tutor T1	Babcock/Northumbrian Universities AS, Leeming
	G-BYXK	Grob G.115E Tutor T1	Babcock/RN No 727 NAS, Yeovilton
	G-BYXL	Grob G.115E Tutor T1	Babcock/East of Scotland UAS, Leuchars
	G-BYXM	Grob G.115E Tutor T1 $	Babcock/Cambridge UAS/East Midlands Universities AS/ University of London AS/No 115 Sqn, Wittering
	G-BYXO	Grob G.115E Tutor T1	Babcock/East of Scotland UAS, Leuchars
	G-BYXP	Grob G.115E Tutor T1	Babcock/Cambridge UAS/East Midlands Universities AS/ University of London AS/No 115 Sqn, Wittering
	G-BYXS	Grob G.115E Tutor T1	Babcock/RN No 727 NAS, Yeovilton

Serial	Type (code/other identity)	Owner/operator, location or fate	Notes
G-BYXT	Grob G.115E Tutor T1	Babcock/Yorkshire Universities AS, Linton-on-Ouse	
G-BYXX	Grob G.115E Tutor T1	Babcock/East of Scotland UAS, Leuchars	
G-BYXZ	Grob G.115E Tutor T1 $	Babcock/Cambridge UAS/East Midlands Universities AS/ University of London AS/No 115 Sqn, Wittering	
G-BYYA	Grob G.115E Tutor T1	Babcock/Northumbrian Universities AS, Leeming	
G-BYYB	Grob G.115E Tutor T1	Babcock/Yorkshire Universities AS, Linton-on-Ouse	
G-CGKD	Grob G.115E Tutor T1EA	Babcock/Oxford UAS, Benson	
G-CGKE	Grob G.115E Tutor T1EA	Babcock/Universities of Glasgow & Strathclyde AS, Glasgow	
G-CGKG	Grob G.115E Tutor T1EA	Babcock/Oxford UAS, Benson	
G-CGKH	Grob G.115E Tutor T1EA	Babcock/Oxford UAS, Benson	
G-CGKK	Grob G.115E Tutor T1EA	Babcock/Oxford UAS, Benson	
G-CGKL	Grob G.115E Tutor T1EA	Babcock/Oxford UAS, Benson	
G-CGKM	Grob G.115E Tutor T1EA	*Sold to Finland, 14 March 2018*	
G-CGKN	Grob G.115E Tutor T1EA	Babcock/Oxford UAS, Benson	
G-CGKO	Grob G.115E Tutor T1EA	*Sold to Finland, 14 March 2018*	
G-CGKP	Grob G.115E Tutor T1EA	Babcock/Oxford UAS, Benson	
G-CGKR	Grob G.115E Tutor T1EA	Babcock/Universities of Glasgow & Strathclyde AS, Glasgow	
G-CGKS	Grob G.115E Tutor T1EA	Babcock/Universities of Glasgow & Strathclyde AS, Glasgow	
G-CGKT	Grob G.115E Tutor T1EA	*Sold to Finland, 14 March 2018*	
G-CGKU	Grob G.115E Tutor T1EA	Babcock/No 3 FTS/No 16 Sqn, Cranwell	
G-CGKW	Grob G.115E Tutor T1EA	Babcock/Oxford UAS, Benson	
G-CGKX	Grob G.115E Tutor T1EA	*Sold to Finland, 14 March 2018*	
G-DAYP	Hawker Beechcraft Super King Air 350C	MoD/Raytheon, Hawarden (for conversion to Shadow R2 ZZ505)	
G-ETPA	Pilatus PC-21 (HB-HYX)	QinetiQ/ETPS, MoD Boscombe Down	
G-ETPB	Pilatus PC-21 (HB-HYY)	QinetiQ/ETPS, MoD Boscombe Down	
G-ETPC	Grob G.120TP-A (D-ETQI)	QinetiQ/ETPS, MoD Boscombe Down	
G-ETPD	Grob G.120TP-A (D-ETIQ)	QinetiQ/ETPS, MoD Boscombe Down	
G-ETPE	Airbus Helicopters H.125	QinetiQ/ETPS, MoD Boscombe Down	
G-ETPF	Airbus Helicopters H.125	QinetiQ/ETPS, MoD Boscombe Down	
G-ETPG	Airbus Helicopters H.125	QinetiQ/ETPS, MoD Boscombe Down	
G-ETPH	Airbus Helicopters H.125	QinetiQ/ETPS, MoD Boscombe Down	
G-ETPI	Agusta A109E Power Elite (G-CFVB/QQ100)	QinetiQ (reservation)	
G-ETPJ	Agusta A109E Power Elite (G-ESLH/ZE416)	QinetiQ (reservation)	
G-ETPK	BAe RJ.70ER (G-BVRJ/QQ102)	QinetiQ/ETPS, MoD Boscombe Down	
G-ETPL	BAe RJ.100 (G-BZAY/QQ101)	QinetiQ/ETPS, MoD Boscombe Down	
G-ETPM	Diamond DA.42M-NG Twin Star (G-LTPA/QQ103)	QinetiQ/ETPS, MoD Boscombe Down	
G-FFRA	Dassault Falcon 20DC (N902FR)	Cobham Leasing Ltd, Durham/Tees Valley	
G-FRAD	Dassault Falcon 20E (9M-BDK)	Cobham Leasing Ltd, Bournemouth	
G-FRAF	Dassault Falcon 20E (N911FR)	Cobham Leasing Ltd, Durham/Tees Valley	
G-FRAH	Dassault Falcon 20DC (N900FR)	Cobham Leasing Ltd, Bournemouth	
G-FRAI	Dassault Falcon 20E (N901FR)	Cobham Leasing Ltd, Durham/Tees Valley	
G-FRAJ	Dassault Falcon 20E (N903FR)	Cobham Leasing Ltd, Durham/Tees Valley	
G-FRAK	Dassault Falcon 20DC (N905FR)	Cobham Leasing Ltd, Bournemouth	
G-FRAL	Dassault Falcon 20DC (N904FR)	Cobham Leasing Ltd, Bournemouth	
G-FRAP	Dassault Falcon 20DC (N908FR)	Cobham Leasing Ltd, Bournemouth	
G-FRAR	Dassault Falcon 20DC (N909FR)	Cobham Leasing Ltd, Durham/Tees Valley	
G-FRAS	Dassault Falcon 20C (117501)	Cobham Leasing Ltd, Bournemouth	
G-FRAT	Dassault Falcon 20C (117502)	Cobham Leasing Ltd, Durham/Tees Valley	
G-FRAU	Dassault Falcon 20C (117504)	Cobham Leasing Ltd, Durham/Tees Valley	
G-FRAW	Dassault Falcon 20ECM (117507)	Cobham Leasing Ltd, Durham/Tees Valley	
G-GMAD	Hawker Beechcraft Super King Air 350C	GAMA Aviation, Bournemouth (for conversion to Shadow R2 ZZ506)	
G-LBSB	Hawker Beechcraft Shadow R2	*To Shadow R1+ ZZ507, May 2018*	

1764M/K4972	7491M/WT569	7829M/XH992	8018M/XN344
2015M/K5600	7496M/WT612	7839M/WV781	8019M/WZ869
2292M/K8203	7499M/WT555	7841M/WV783	8021M/XL824
2361M/K6035	7510M/WT694	7851M/WZ706	8027M/XM555
3118M/H5199/(BK892)	7525M/WT619	7854M/XM191	8032M/XH837
3858M/X7688	7530M/WT648	7855M/XK416	8034M/*XL554*/ (XL703)
4354M/BL614	7532M/WT651	7859M/XP283	8041M/XF690
4552M/T5298	7533M/WT680	7861M/*XL738*/(XM565)	8043M/XF836
4887M/JN768	7544M/WN904	7862M/XR246	8046M/XL770
5377M/EP120	7548M/PS915	7863M/*XP248*	8049M/WE168
5405M/LF738	7556M/WK584	7864M/XP244	8050M/XG329
5466M/*BN230*/(LF751)	7564M/XE982	7865M/TX226	8052M/WH166
5690M/MK356	7570M/XD674	7866M/XH278	8054AM/XM410
5718M/BM597	7582M/WP190	7868M/WZ736	8054BM/XM417
5758M/DG202	7583M/WP185	7869M/WK935	8055AM/XM402
6457M/ML427	7602M/WE600	7872M/*WZ826*/(XD826)	8055BM/XM404
6490M/LA255	7605M/WS692	7881M/WD413	8056M/XG337
6640M/RM694	7606M/*XF688*/ (WV562)	7882M/XD525	8057M/XR243
6850M/TE184	7607M/TJ138	7883M/XT150	8063M/WT536
6946M/RW388	7615M/WV679	7887M/XD375	8070M/EP120
6948M/DE673	7616M/WW388	7891M/XM693	8072M/PK624
6960M/MT847	7618M/WW442	7894M/XD818	8073M/TB252
7008M/EE549	7622M/WV606	7895M/WF784	8075M/RW382
7014M/N6720	7631M/VX185	7898M/XP854	8078M/XM351
7015M/NL985	7641M/XA634	7900M/WA576	8080M/XM480
7035M/*K2567*/(DE306)	7645M/WD293	7906M/WH132	8081M/XM468
7060M/VF301	7648M/XF785	7917M/WA591	8082M/XM409
7090M/EE531	7673M/WV332	7930M/WH301	8086M/TB752
7118M/LA198	7689M/*WW421*/(WW450)	7931M/RD253	8092M/WK654
7119M/LA226	7696M/WV493	7932M/WZ744	8094M/WT520
7150M/PK683	7698M/WV499	7933M/XR220	8097M/XN492
7154M/WB188	7704M/TW536	7937M/WS843	8101M/WH984
7174M/VX272	7705M/WL505	7938M/XH903	8102M/WT486
7175M/VV106	7706M/WB584	7939M/XD596	8103M/WR985
7200M/VT812	7709M/WT933	7940M/XL764	8106M/WR982
7241M/TE311/(*MK178*)	7711M/PS915	7955M/XH767	8114M/WL798
7243M/TE462	7712M/WK281	7957M/XF545	8117M/WR974
7245M/RW382	7715M/XK724	7960M/WS726	8118M/WZ549
7246M/TD248	7716M/WS776	7961M/WS739	8119M/WR971
7256M/TB752	7718M/WA577	7964M/WS760	8121M/XM474
7257M/TB252	7719M/WK277	7965M/WS792	8124M/WZ572
7279M/TB752	7726M/XM373	7967M/WS788	8128M/WH775
7281M/TB252	7729M/WB758	7969M/WS840	8130M/WH798
7288M/PK724	7741M/VZ477	7971M/XK699	8131M/WT507
7293M/*TB675*/(RW393)	7750M/*WK864*/(WL168)	7973M/WS807	8140M/XJ571
7323M/VV217	7751M/WL131	7979M/XM529	8142M/XJ560
7325M/R5868	7755M/WG760	7980M/XM561	8147M/XR526
7326M/VN485	7759M/PK664	7982M/XH892	8151M/WV795
7362M/475081/(VP546)	7761M/XH318	7983M/XD506	8153M/WV903
7416M/WN907	7762M/XE670	7984M/XN597	8154M/WV908
7421M/WT660	7764M/XH318	7986M/WG777	8155M/WV797
7422M/WT684	7770M/*XF506*/(WT746)	7988M/XL149	8156M/XE339
7428M/WK198	7793M/XG523	7990M/XD452	8158M/XE369
7432M/WZ724	7798M/XH783	7997M/XG452	8162M/WM913
7438M/*18671*/(WP905)	7806M/TA639	7998M/*XM515*/(XD515)	8164M/*WN105*/(WF299)
7443M/WX853	7809M/XA699	8005M/WG768	8165M/WH791
7458M/WX905	7816M/WG763	8009M/XG518	8169M/WH364
7464M/XA564	7817M/TX214	8010M/XG547	8173M/XN685
7470M/XA553	7825M/WK991	8012M/VS562	8176M/WH791
7473M/XE946	7827M/XA917	8017M/XL762	8177M/WM224

8179M/XN928	8392M/SL674	8535M/XN776	8703M/VW453
8183M/*XN972*/(XN962)	8394M/WG422	8538M/XN781	8706M/XF383
8184M/WT520	8395M/WF408	8545M/XN726	8708M/XF509
8186M/WR977	8396M/XK740	8546M/XN728	8709M/XG209
8187M/WH791	8399M/WR539	8548M/WT507	8710M/XG274
8189M/*WD615* (WD646)	8401M/XP686	8549M/WT534	8711M/XG290
8190M/XJ918	8406M/XP831	8554M/TG511	8713M/XG225
8192M/XR658	8407M/XP585	8561M/XS100	8718M/XX396
8198M/WT339	8408M/XS186	8563M/*XX822*/(XW563)	8719M/XT257
8203M/XD377	8409M/XS209	8565M/*WT720*/(E-408)	8721M/XP354
8205M/XN819	8410M/XR662	8566M/XV279	8724M/XW923
8206M/WG419	8413M/XM192	8573M/XM708	8726M/XP299
8208M/WG303	8414M/XM173	8575M/XP542	8727M/XR486
8209M/WG418	8417M/XM144	8576M/XP502	8728M/WT532
8210M/WG471	8422M/XM169	8578M/XR534	8729M/WJ815
8211M/WK570	8427M/XM172	8581M/WJ775	8732M/XJ729
8213M/WK626	8429M/XH592	8582M/XE874	8733M/XL318
8215M/WP869	8434M/XM411	8583M/BAPC 94	8736M/XF375
8216M/WP927	8436M/XN554	8585M/XE670	8739M/XH170
8218M/WB645	8437M/WG362	8586M/XE643	8740M/WE173
8229M/XM355	8439M/WZ846	8588M/XR681	8741M/XW329
8230M/XM362	8440M/WD935	8589M/XR700	8743M/WD790
8234M/XN458	8442M/XP411	8590M/XM191	8746M/XH171
8235M/XN549	8452M/XK885	8591M/XA813	8749M/XH537
8236M/XP573	8453M/XP745	8595M/XH278	8751M/XT255
8237M/XS179	8458M/XP672	8598M/WP270	8753M/WL795
8238M/XS180	8459M/XR650	8600M/XX761	8762M/WH740
8338M/XS180	8460M/XP680	8602M/*PF179*/(XR541)	8764M/XP344
8342M/WP848	8462M/XX477	8604M/XS104	8768M/A-522
8344M/WH960	8463M/XP355	8606M/XP530	8769M/A-528
8350M/WH840	8464M/XJ758	8608M/XP540	8770M/XL623
8352M/XN632	8465M/W1048	8610M/XL502	8771M/XM602
8355M/KN645	8466M/L-866	8611M/WF128	8772M/WR960
8357M/WK576	8467M/WP912	8620M/XP534	8778M/XM598
8359M/WF825	8468M/MM5701/(BT474)	8621M/XR538	8779M/XM607
8361M/WB670	8469M/100503	8624M/*XR991*/(XS102)	8780M/WK102
8362M/WG477	8470M/584219	8627M/XP558	8781M/WE982
8364M/WG464	8471M/701152	8628M/XJ380	8782M/XH136
8365M/XK421	8472M/120227/(VN679)	8630M/WG362	8785M/XS642
8366M/XG454	8473M/WP190	8631M/XR574	8789M/XK970
8367M/XG474	8474M/494083	8633M/3W-17/MK732	8791M/XP329
8368M/XF926	8475M/360043/(PJ876)	8634M/WP314	8792M/XP345
8369M/WE139	8476M/24	8640M/XR977	8793M/XP346
8370M/N1671	8477M/4101/(DG200)	8642M/XR537	8794M/XP398
8371M/XA847	8478M/10639	8645M/XD163	8796M/XK943
8372M/K8042	8479M/730301	8648M/XK526	8799M/WV787
8373M/P2617	8481M/191614	8653M/XS120	8800M/XG226
8375M/NX611	8482M/112372/(VK893)	8655M/XN126	8805M/XV722
8376M/RF398	8483M/420430	8656M/XP405	8807M/XL587
8377M/R9125	8484M/5439	8657M/VZ634	8810M/XJ825
8378M/*T9707*	8485M/997	8661M/XJ727	8816M/XX734
8379M/DG590	8486M/BAPC 99	8666M/XE793	8818M/XK527
8380M/Z7197	8487M/J-1172	8671M/XJ435	8820M/VP952
8382M/VR930	8488M/WL627	8672M/XP351	8821M/XX115
8383M/K9942	8491M/WJ880	8673M/XD165	8822M/WP957
8384M/X4590	8493M/XR571	8676M/XL577	8828M/XS587
8385M/N5912	8494M/XP557	8679M/XF526	8830M/*N-294*/(XF515)
8386M/NV778	8501M/XP640	8680M/XF527	8831M/XG160
8387M/T6296	8502M/XP686	8681M/XG164	8832M/*XG168*/(XG172)
8388M/XL993	8508M/XS218	8682M/XP404	8833M/XL569
8389M/VX573	8509M/XT141	8693M/WH863	8834M/XL572
8390M/SL542	8514M/XS176	8702M/XG196	8836M/XL592

8838M/*34037*/(429356)	8947M/XX726	9070M/XV581	9180M/XW311
8839M/XG194	8949M/XX743	9072M/XW768	9181M/XW358
8841M/XE606	8951M/XX727	9073M/XW924	9185M/XZ987
8853M/XT277	8953M/XX959	9075M/XV752	9187M/XW405
8855M/XT284	8954M/XZ384	9076M/XV808	9188M/XW364
8857M/XW544	8955M/XX110	9078M/XV753	9194M/XW420
8858M/XW541	8957M/XN582	9079M/XZ130	9195M/XW330
8863M/XG154	8961M/XS925	9080M/ZE350	9196M/XW370
8867M/XK532	8967M/XV263	9086M/ZE352	9197M/*XX530*/(XX637)
8868M/WH775	8969M/XR753	9087M/XX753	9198M/XS641
8869M/WH957	8972M/XR754	9090M/XW353	9199M/XW290
8870M/WH964	8973M/XS922	9091M/XW434	9201M/ZD667
8871M/WJ565	8974M/XM473	9092M/XH669	9203M/*3066*
8873M/XR453	8975M/XW917	9093M/WK124	9205M/*E449*
8874M/XE597	8976M/XZ630	9095M/XW547	9206M/F6314
8875M/XE624	8978M/XX837	9096M/WV322	9207M/*8417/18*
8876M/*VM791*/(XA312)	8984M/XN551	9098M/XV406	9208M/F938
8880M/XF435	8985M/WK127	9103M/XV411	9210M/MF628
8881M/XG254	8986M/XV261	9110M/XX736	9211M/*733682*
8883M/XX946	8987M/XM358	9111M/XW421	9212M/*KL216*/(45-49295)
8884M/VX275	8990M/XM419	9115M/XV863	9213M/N5182
8885M/XW922	8995M/XM425	9117M/XV161	9215M/XL164
8886M/XA243	8996M/XM414	9119M/XW303	9216M/XL190
8888M/XA231	8997M/XX669	9120M/XW419	9217M/ZH257
8889M/XN239	8998M/XT864	9122M/XZ997	9218M/XL563
8890M/WT532	9002M/XW763	9123M/XT773	9219M/XZ971
8895M/XX746	9003M/XZ390	9125M/XW410	9221M/XZ966
8896M/XX821	9004M/XZ370	9127M/XW432	9222M/XZ968
8897M/XX969	9005M/XZ374	9130M/XW327	9224M/XL568
8898M/XX119	9006M/XX967	9131M/*DD931*	9225M/XX885
8899M/XX756	9007M/XX968	9132M/XX977	9226M/XV865
8900M/XZ368	9008M/XX140	9133M/*413573*	9227M/XB812
8901M/XZ383	9009M/XX763	9134M/XT288	9229M/ZA678
8902M/XX739	9010M/XX764	9136M/XT891	9233M/XZ431
8903M/XX747	9011M/XM412	9137M/XN579	9234M/XV864
8905M/XX975	9012M/XN494	9139M/XV863	9236M/WV318
8906M/XX976	9014M/XN584	9140M/XZ287	9237M/XF445
8907M/XZ371	9015M/XW320	9141M/XV118	9238M/ZA717
8908M/XZ382	9017M/ZE449	9143M/XN589	9239M/*7198/18*
8909M/XV784	9019M/XX824	9145M/XV863	9241M/XS639
8910M/XL160	9020M/XX825	9146M/XW299	9242M/XH672
8911M/XH673	9021M/XX826	9148M/XW436	9246M/XS714
8918M/XX109	9022M/XX958	9149M/XW375	9248M/WB627
8919M/XT486	9026M/XP629	9150M/*FX760*	9249M/WV396
8920M/XT469	9027M/XP556	9151M/XT907	9251M/XX744
8921M/XT466	9032M/XR673	9152M/XV424	9252M/XX722
8922M/XT467	9033M/XS181	9153M/XW360	9254M/XX965
8923M/XX819	9036M/XM350	9154M/XW321	9255M/XZ375
8924M/XP701	9038M/XV810	9155M/WL679	9257M/XX962
8925M/XP706	9039M/XN586	9162M/XZ991	9258M/XW265
8931M/XV779	9040M/XZ138	9163M/XV415	9259M/XS710
8932M/XR718	9041M/XW763	9166M/XW323	9260M/XS734
8934M/XR749	9042M/XL954	9167M/XV744	9261M/*W2068*
8935M/XR713	9044M/XS177	9168M/XZ132	9262M/XZ358
8937M/XX751	9047M/XW409	9169M/XW547	9263M/XW267
8938M/WV746	9048M/XM403	9170M/XZ994	9264M/XS735
8941M/XT456	9049M/XW404	9172M/XW304	9265M/WK585
8942M/XN185	9052M/WJ717	9173M/XW418	9266M/XZ119
8943M/XE799	9056M/XS488	9174M/XZ131	9267M/XW269
8944M/WZ791	9059M/ZE360	9175M/P1344	9268M/XR529
8945M/XX818	9066M/XV582	9176M/XW430	9269M/XT914
8946M/XZ389	9067M/XV586	9179M/XW309	9270M/XZ145

9272M/XS486	9289M/XX665	9310M/ZA355	9328M/ZD607
9273M/XS726	9290M/XX626	9311M/ZA475	9329M/ZD578
9274M/XS738	9292M/XW892	9314M/ZA320	9330M/ZB684
9275M/XS729	9293M/XX830	9315M/ZA319	9331M/XW852
9277M/XT601	9294M/XX655	9316M/ZA399	9332M/XZ935
9278M/XS643	9295M/XV497	9317M/ZA450	9336M/ZA407
9279M/XT681	9298M/ZE340	9318M/ZA360	9337M/ZA774
9281M/XZ146	9299M/XW870	9319M/XR516	9338M/ZA325
9283M/XZ322	9300M/XX431	9320M/XX153	9339M/ZA323
9284M/ZA267	9301M/XZ941	9321M/XZ367	9340M/XX745
9285M/XR806	9302M/ZD462	9322M/ZB686	9341M/ZA357
9286M/XT905	9303M/XV709	9323M/XV643	9342M/XR498
9287M/WP962	9306M/XX979	9324M/XV659	9343M/XR506
9288M/XX520	9308M/ZD932	9326M/XV653	9344M/XV706

Jaguar GR1 XZ383/AF is one of a fleet of the type still in use with No 1 SoTT at RAF Cosford. It wears the markings of 41 Sqn.

Tornado F3 ZE340/GO wears 43 Sqn markings and is usually kept inside at No 1 SoTT at Cosford so it was nice to see it outside for an airing in June at the air show.

Deck Letters	Vessel Name and Pennant No.	Vessel Type and Unit
AB	HMS *Albion* (L14)	Assault
AS	RFA *Argus* (A135)	Aviation Training ship
AY	HMS *Argyll* (F231)	Type 23
BK	HMS *Bulwark* (L15)	Assault
BV	RFA *Black Rover* (A273)	Fleet tanker
CB	RFA *Cardigan Bay* (L3009)	Landing ship
CU	RNAS Culdrose (HMS *Seahawk*)	
DA	HMS *Daring* (D32)	Type 45
DF	HMS *Defender* (D36)	Type 45
DG	RFA *Diligence* (A132)	Maintenance
DM	HMS *Diamond* (D34)	Type 45
DN	HMS *Dragon* (D35)	Type 45
DT	HMS *Dauntless* (D33)	Type 45
DU	HMS *Duncan* (D37)	Type 45
FA	RFA *Fort Austin* (A386)	Support ship
FE	RFA *Fort Rosalie* (A385)	Support ship
FV	RFA *Fort Victoria* (A387)	Auxiliary Oiler
IR	HMS *Iron Duke* (F234)	Type 23
KT	HMS *Kent* (F78)	Type 23
LA	HMS *Lancaster* (F229)	Type 23
MB	RFA *Mounts Bay* (L3008)	Landing ship
MM	HMS *Monmouth* (F235)	Type 23
MR	HMS *Montrose* (F236)	Type 23
NL	HMS *Northumberland* (F238)	Type 23
O	HMS *Ocean* (L12)	Helicopter carrier
P	HMS *Prince of Wales* (R09)	Aircraft carrier
Q	HMS *Queen Elizabeth* (R08)	Aircraft carrier
PD	HMS *Portland* (F79)	Type 23
RM	HMS *Richmond* (F239)	Type 23
SB	HMS *St Albans* (F83)	Type 23
SM	HMS *Somerset* (F82)	Type 23
SU	HMS *Sutherland* (F81)	Type 23
VL	RNAS Yeovilton (HMS *Heron*)	
WK	RFA *Wave Knight* (A389)	Fleet tanker
WM	HMS *Westminster* (F237)	Type 23
YB	RFA *Lyme Bay* (L3007)	Landing ship
–	HMS *Protector* (A173)	Ice patrol
–	RFA *Wave Ruler* (A390)	Fleet tanker

RN CODE – SQUADRON – BASE – AIRCRAFT CROSS-CHECK

Deck/Base Code Numbers	Letters	Unit	Location	Aircraft Type(s)
010 — 015	CU	820 NAS	Culdrose	Merlin HM2
264 — 274	CU	814 NAS	Culdrose	Merlin HM2
500 — 515	CU	829 NAS	Culdrose	Merlin HM2
580 — 588	CU	824 NAS	Culdrose	Merlin HM2

Note that only the 'last two' digits of the Code are worn by some aircraft types, especially helicopters.

This table gives brief details of the markings worn by aircraft of RAF squadrons. While this may help to identify the operator of a particular machine, it may not always give the true picture. For example, from time to time aircraft are loaned to other units while others wear squadron marks but are actually operated on a pool basis. Squadron badges are usually located on the front fuselage.

Squadron	Type(s) operated	Base(s)	Distinguishing marks & other comments
No 1(F) Sqn	Typhoon T3/FGR4	RAF Lossiemouth	Badge (on tail): A red 1 with yellow wings on a white background, flanked in red. Roundel is flanked by two white chevrons, edged in red.
No 2(AC) Sqn/ II(AC) Sqn	Typhoon T3/FGR4	RAF Lossiemouth	Badge: A wake knot on a white circular background flanked on either side by black and white triangles. Tail fin has a black stripe with white triangles and the badge repeated on it.
No 3(F) Sqn	Typhoon T3/FGR4	RAF Coningsby	Badge: A blue cockatrice on a white circular background flanked by two green bars edged with yellow. Tail fin as a green stripe edged with yellow.
No 4 Sqn/ IV Sqn	Hawk T2	RAF Valley	Badge (on nose): A yellow lightning flash on a red background with IV superimposed. Aircraft carry a yellow lightning flash on a red and black background on the tail and this is repeated in bars either side of the roundel on the fuselage. Part of No 4 FTS.
No 5(AC) Sqn/ V(AC) Sqn	Sentinel R1	RAF Waddington	Badge (on tail): A green maple leaf on a white circle over a red horizontal band.
No 6 Sqn	Typhoon T3/FGR4	RAF Lossiemouth	Badge (on tail): A red, winged can opener on a blue shield, edged in red. The roundel is flanked by a red zigzag on a blue background.
No 7 Sqn	Chinook HC6	RAF Odiham	Badge (on tail): A blue badge containing the seven stars of Ursa Major ('The Plough') in yellow.
No 8 Sqn	Sentry AEW1	RAF Waddington	Badge (on tail): A grey, sheathed, Arabian dagger. Aircraft pooled with No 54 Sqn.
No 9 Sqn/IX Sqn	Typhoon T3/FGR4	RAF Lossiemouth	Badge: A green bat on a black circular background, flanked by yellow and green horizontal stripes. The green bat also appears on the tail, edged in yellow.
No 10 Sqn	Voyager KC2/KC3	RAF Brize Norton	No markings worn.
No 11 Sqn	Typhoon T3/FGR4	RAF Coningsby	Badge (on tail): Two eagles in flight on a white shield. The roundel is flanked by yellow and black triangles.
No 12 Sqn	Typhoon T3/FGR4	RAF Coningsby	Badge: Not known.
No 13 Sqn	Reaper	RAF Waddington	No markings worn.
No 14 Sqn	Shadow R1	RAF Waddington	No markings worn.
No 16 Sqn	Tutor T1	RAF Cranwell	No markings carried. Part of No 1 EFTS.
No 17 Test & Evaluation Sqn	Lightning II	Edwards AFB, USA	No markings worn

Squadron	Type(s) operated	Base(s)	Distinguishing marks & other comments
No 18(B) Sqn	Chinook HC4/ HC5/HC6/HC6A	RAF Odiham	Badge (on tail): A red winged horse on a black circle. Aircraft pooled with No 27 Sqn.
No 24 Sqn/ XXIV Sqn	Hercules C4/C5/ Atlas C1	RAF Brize Norton	No squadron markings carried. Aircraft pooled with No 30 Sqn, No 47 Sqn and No 70 Sqn.
No 25 Sqn/ XXV Sqn	Hawk T2	RAF Valley	Badge (on tail): A hawk on a gauntlet. Aircraft have XXV on the tail and silver and grey bars either side of the roundel on the fuselage. Part of No 4 FTS. Aircraft are coded F*.
No 27 Sqn	Chinook HC4/ HC5/HC6	RAF Odiham	Badge (on tail): A dark green elephant on a green circle, flanked by green and dark green stripes. Aircraft pooled with No 18 Sqn.
No 28 Sqn	Chinook HC4/ Puma HC2	RAF Benson	Badge: A winged horse above two white crosses on a red shield.
No 29 Sqn	Typhoon T3/FGR4	RAF Coningsby	Badge (on tail): An eagle in flight, preying on a buzzard, with three red Xs across the top. The roundel is flanked by two white bars outlined by a red line, each containing three red Xs.
No 30 Sqn	Hercules C4/C5	RAF Brize Norton	No squadron markings carried. Aircraft pooled with No 24 Sqn and No 47 Sqn.
No 32(The Royal) Sqn	BAe 146 CC2/146 C3/ Agusta 109	RAF Northolt	No squadron markings carried but aircraft carry a distinctive livery with a red stripe, edged in blue along the middle of the fuselage and a red tail.
No 33 Sqn	Puma HC2	RAF Benson	Badge: A stag's head.
No 39 Sqn	Predator/ Reaper	Nellis AFB Creech AFB	No markings worn.
No 41 Test & Evaluation Sqn [FJWOEU]	Typhoon T3/FGR4	RAF Coningsby	Badge: A red, double armed cross on the tail with a gold crown above. White and red horizontal bars flanking the roundel on the fuselage. Aircraft are coded EB-*.
No 45 Sqn	Phenom/Tutor T1EA	RAF Cranwell	The Phenoms carry a dark blue stripe on the tail superimposed with red diamonds. Part of No 3 FTS.
No 47 Sqn	Hercules C4/C5	RAF Brize Norton	No squadron markings usually carried. Aircraft pooled with No 24 Sqn and No 30 Sqn.
No 51 Sqn	RC-135W	RAF Waddington	Badge (on tail): A red goose in flight.
No 54 Sqn [ISTAR OCU]	Sentry AEW1	RAF Waddington	Based aircraft as required.
No 56 Sqn [ISTAR Test & Evaluation Sqn]	Shadow R1/ Sentry AEW1/ Sentinel R1	RAF Waddington	Based aircraft as required.
No 57 Sqn	Prefect T1	RAF Barkston Heath/ RAF Cranwell	No markings carried. Part of No 1 EFTS.
No 60 Sqn	Juno HT1	RAF Shawbury [DHFS]	No squadron markings usually carried.

Squadron	Type(s) operated	Base(s)	Distinguishing marks & other comments
No 70 Sqn Fixed Wing Air Mobility OCU/LXX Sqn	Atlas C1	RAF Brize Norton	No squadron markings usually carried. Aircraft pooled with No 24 Sqn.
No 72 Sqn	Tucano T1	RAF Linton-on-Ouse	Badge: A black swift in flight on a red disk, flanked by blue bars edged with red. The blue bars edged with red also flank the roundel on the fuselage; part of No 1 FTS
No 84 Sqn	Griffin HAR2	RAF Akrotiri	Badge (on tail): A scorpion on a playing card symbol (diamonds, clubs etc.). Aircraft carry a vertical light blue stripe through the roundel on the fuselage.
No 99 Sqn	Globemaster III	RAF Brize Norton	Badge (on tail): A black puma leaping.
No 100 Sqn	Hawk T1A	RAF Leeming	Badge (on tail): A skull in front of two bones crossed. Aircraft are usually coded C*. Incorporates the Joint Forward Air Control Training and Standards Unit (JFACTSU)
No 101 Sqn	Voyager KC2/KC3	RAF Brize Norton	No markings worn.
No 115 Sqn	Tutor T1	Wittering	No markings carried. Part of the CFS.
No 202 Sqn	Jupiter HT1	RAF Valley	Badge: A mallard alighting on a white circle.
No 206 Sqn [HAT&ES]	Hercules C4/C5	RAF Brize Norton/ Boscombe Down	No squadron markings usually carried.
No 230 Sqn	Puma HC2	RAF Benson	Badge: A tiger in front of a palm tree on a black pentagon.
No 617 Sqn	Lightning II	MCAS Beaufort, USA	No markings worn
No 1310 Flt	Chinook HC4	Mount Pleasant, FI	No markings worn
No 1312 Flt	Hercules C5/ Voyager KC2/KC3	Mount Pleasant, FI	Badge (on tail): A red Maltese cross on a white circle, flanked by red and white horizontal bars.
No 1435 Flt	Typhoon FGR4	Mount Pleasant, FI	Badge (on tail): A red Maltese cross on a white circle, flanked by red and white horizontal bars.

As from 7 September 2015 all UAS flights and AEFs are commanded and managed by No 6 FTS RAF. Some UAS aircraft carry squadron badges and markings, usually on the tail. Squadron crests all consist of a white circle surrounded by a blue circle, topped with a red crown and having a yellow scroll beneath. Each differs by the motto on the scroll, the UAS name running around the blue circle & by the contents at the centre and it is the latter which are described below.

* All AEFs come under the administration of local UASs and these are listed here.

UAS	Base	Marks
Bristol UAS/ No 3 AEF	Boscombe Down	A sailing ship on water.
Cambridge UAS/ No 5 AEF	Wittering	A heraldic lion in front of a red badge. Aircraft pooled with University of London AS.
East Midlands Universities AS/ No 7 AEF	Wittering	A yellow quiver, full of arrows.
East of Scotland UAS/ No 12 AEF	RAF Leuchars	An open book in front of a white diagonal cross edged in blue.
Liverpool UAS	RAF Woodvale	A bird atop an open book, holding a branch in its beak. Aircraft pooled with Manchester and Salford Universities AS
Manchester and Salford Universities AS/ No 10 AEF	RAF Woodvale	A bird of prey with a green snake in its beak. Aircraft pooled with Liverpool UAS
Northern Ireland Universities AS/ No 14 AEF	JHFS Aldergrove	(Currently not known)
Northumbrian Universities AS/ No 11 AEF	RAF Leeming	A white cross on a blue background.
Oxford UAS/ No 6 AEF	RAF Benson	An open book in front of crossed swords.
Southampton UAS/ No 2 AEF	Boscombe Down	A red stag in front of a stone pillar.
Universities of Glasgow and Strathclyde AS/ No 4 AEF	Glasgow	A bird of prey in flight, holding a branch in its beak, in front of an upright sword.
University of Birmingham AS/ No 8 AEF	DCAE Cosford	A blue griffon with two heads.
University of London AS	Wittering	A globe superimposed over an open book. Aircraft pooled with Cambridge UAS.
University of Wales AS/ No 1 AEF	MoD St Athan	A red Welsh dragon in front of an open book, clasping a sword. Some aircraft have the dragon in front of white and green squares.
Yorkshire Universities AS/ No 9 AEF	RAF Linton-on-Ouse	An open book in front of a Yorkshire rose with leaves.

This table gives brief details of the markings worn by aircraft of FAA squadrons. Squadron badges, when worn, are usually located on the front fuselage. All FAA squadron badges comprise a crown atop a circle edged in gold braid and so the badge details below list only what appears in the circular part.

Squadron	Type(s) operated	Base(s)	Distinguishing marks & other comments
No 700X NAS	Scan Eagle RM1	RNAS Culdrose	Badge: No markings carried.
No 727 NAS	Tutor T1	RNAS Yeovilton	Badge: The head of Britannia wearing a gold helmet on a background of blue and white waves.
No 736 NAS	Hawk T1A	RNAS Culdrose & RNAS Yeovilton	A white lightning bolt on the tail.
No 744 NAS	Chinook HC6A/ Merlin (Crowsnest)	MoD Boscombe Down	Badge: No details
No 750 NAS	Avenger T1	RNAS Culdrose	Badge: A Greek runner bearing a torch & sword on a background of blue and white waves.
No 814 NAS	Merlin HM2	RNAS Culdrose	Badge: A winged tiger mask on a background of dark blue and white waves.
No 815 NAS	Wildcat HMA2	RNAS Yeovilton	Badge: A winged, gold harpoon on a background of blue and white waves.
No 820 NAS	Merlin HM2	RNAS Culdrose	Badge: A flying fish on a background of blue and white waves.
No 824 NAS	Merlin HM2	RNAS Culdrose	Badge: A heron on a background of blue and white waves.
No 825 NAS	Wildcat HMA2	RNAS Yeovilton	Badge: An eagle over a Maltese cross.
No 845 NAS	Merlin HC3i/HC4	RNAS Yeovilton	Badge: A dragonfly on a background of blue and white waves.
No 846 NAS	Merlin HC3/HC3A	RNAS Yeovilton	Badge: A swordsman riding a winged horse whilst attacking a serpent on a background of blue and white waves.
No 847 NAS	Wildcat AH1	RNAS Yeovilton	Badge (not currently worn): A gold sea lion on a blue background.

This section lists the codes worn by some UK military aircraft and, alongside, the Registration of the aircraft currently wearing this code. It should be pointed out that in some cases more than one aircraft wears the same code but the aircraft listed is the one believed to be in service with the unit concerned at the time of going to press. This list will be updated regularly and those with Internet access can download the latest version via the 'Military Aircraft Markings' Web Site, www.militaryaircraftmarkings.co.uk.

ROYAL AIR FORCE

BAE Hawk T1/T2

Code	Registration
A	ZK010
B	ZK011
C	ZK012
D	ZK013
E	ZK014
F	ZK015
G	ZK016
H	ZK017
I	ZK018
J	ZK019
K	ZK020
L	ZK021
M	ZK022
N	ZK023
O	ZK024
P	ZK025
R	ZK027
S	ZK028
U	ZK030
X	ZK033
Y	ZK034
Z	ZK035
AB	ZK037
CA	XX246
CB	XX255
CC	XX191
CD	XX332
CE	XX258
CF	XX203
CG	XX318
CH	XX198
CI	XX321
CK	XX205
CL	XX339
CM	XX337
CN	XX187
CO	XX200 & XX221
CP	XX346
CQ	XX348
CR	XX189 & XX303
CS	XX202
CU	XX329
FB	ZK026
FD	ZK208
FE	ZK029
FG	ZK031
FH	ZK032

B-V Chinook

Code	Registration
W	ZA712
AA	ZA670
AB	ZA671
AD	ZA674
AE	ZA675
AF	ZA677
AG	ZA679
AH	ZA680
AI	ZA681
AJ	ZA682
AN	ZA705
AO	ZA707
AP	ZA708
AR	ZA710
AV	ZA714
AW	ZA720
BN	ZA718
DB	ZD574
DD	ZD980
DG	ZD983
DH	ZD984
HB	ZH775
HC	ZH776
HF	ZH891
HG	ZH892
HH	ZH893
HI	ZH894
HJ	ZH895
HK	ZH896
HR	ZH903

Eurofighter Typhoon

Code	Registration
C	ZJ935
D	ZJ941
F	ZJ915
H	ZJ926
AX	ZK303
EB-E	ZK339
EB-R	ZK367

Shorts Tucano T1

Code	Registration
MP-A	ZF170
RN-S	ZF378

WS Puma HC2

Code	Registration
G	XW216
X	ZJ955

ROYAL NAVY

BAE Hawk T1

Code	Registration
842	XX239
844	XX329
846	XX256
849	XX317

EHI-101 Merlin

Code	Registration
10	ZH827
11	ZH856
12	ZH846
13	ZH835
14	ZH837
61	ZH841
62	ZH828
66	ZH847
67	ZH850
68	ZH826 & ZH853
69	ZH839
70	ZH847
80	ZH836
81	ZH840
82	ZH842
83	ZH824
85	ZH861 & ZH864
86	ZH862
87	ZH834
88	ZH843
A	ZJ117
B	ZJ118
C	ZJ119
D	ZJ120
E	ZJ121
F	ZJ122
G	ZJ123
H	ZJ124
J	ZJ125
K	ZJ126
L	ZJ127
M	ZJ128
N	ZJ129
O	ZJ130
P	ZJ131
Q	ZJ132
R	ZJ133
S	ZJ134
T	ZJ135
U	ZJ136
W	ZJ137
X	ZJ138
AA	ZJ990
AB	ZJ992
AC	ZJ994
AD	ZJ995
AE	ZJ998
AF	ZK001

ARMY AIR CORPS

Bell 212

Code	Registration
B	ZK067
K	ZJ969
X	ZH814
Y	ZH815

WS Gazelle AH1

Code	Registration
S	ZB691

Some *historic, classic and warbird* aircraft carry the markings of overseas air arms and can be seen in the UK, mainly preserved in museums and collections or taking part in air shows.

Serial	Type (code/other identity)	Owner/operator, location or fate	Notes
AFGHANISTAN			
-	Hawker Afghan Hind (K4672/BAPC 82)	RAF Museum Reserve Collection, Stafford	
ARGENTINA			
-	Bell UH-1H Iroquois (AE-406/*998-8888*) [Z]	South Yorkshire Aircraft Museum, Doncaster	
0729	Beech T-34C Turbo Mentor	FAA Museum, stored Cobham Hall, RNAS Yeovilton	
0767	Aermacchi MB339AA	South Yorkshire Aircraft Museum, Doncaster	
A-515	FMA IA58 Pucará (ZD485)	RAF Museum, stored Cosford	
A-517	FMA IA58 Pucará (G-BLRP)	Privately owned, Channel Islands	
A-522	FMA IA58 Pucará (8768M)	FAA Museum, at NE Aircraft Museum, Usworth	
A-528	FMA IA58 Pucará (8769M)	Norfolk & Suffolk Avn Museum, Flixton	
A-533	FMA IA58 Pucará (ZD486) <ff>	Privately owned, Chelmsford	
A-549	FMA IA58 Pucará (ZD487)	IWM Duxford	
AE-331	Agusta A109A (ZE411)	FAA Museum, stored Cobham Hall, RNAS Yeovilton	
AE-409	Bell UH-1H Iroquois [656]	Army Flying Museum, Middle Wallop	
AE-422	Bell UH-1H Iroquois	FAA Museum, stored Cobham Hall, RNAS Yeovilton	
AUSTRALIA			
369	Hawker Fury ISS (F-AZXL) [D]	Privately owned, Cannes, France	
A2-4	Supermarine Seagull V (VH-ALB)	RAF Museum Reserve Collection, Stafford	
A11-301	Auster J/5G (G-ARKG) [931-NW]	Privately owned, Spanhoe	
A16-199	Lockheed Hudson IIIA (G-BEOX) [SF-R]	RAF Museum, Hendon	
A17-48	DH82A Tiger Moth (G-BPHR)	Privately owned, Wanborough, Wilts	
A17-376	DH82A Tiger Moth (T6830/G-ANJI) [376]	Privately owned, Gloucester	
A19-144	Bristol 156 Beaufighter XIc (JM135/A8-324)	The Fighter Collection, Duxford	
A92-255	GAF Jindivik 102	QinetiQ Apprentice Training School, Boscombe Down	
A92-664	GAF Jindivik 103A	Boscombe Down Aviation Collection, Old Sarum	
A92-708	GAF Jindivik 103BL	Aerospace Bristol, stored Filton	
A92-908	GAF Jindivik 104AL (ZJ503)	Privately owned, Llanbedr	
N16-114	WS61 Sea King Mk.50A [05]	Privately owned, Horsham	
N16-125	WS61 Sea King Mk.50A [10]	Privately owned, Horsham	
N16-238	WS61 Sea King Mk.50A [20]	Privately owned, Horsham	
N16-239	WS61 Sea King Mk.50A [21]	Privately owned, Horsham	
N16-918	WS61 Sea King Mk.50B (XZ918) [22]	Privately owned, Horsham	
WH589	Hawker Fury ISS (F-AZXJ) [115-NW]	Privately owned, Dijon, France	
AUSTRIA			
5S-TC	Short SC.7 Skyvan 3 Variant 100 (G-BEOL)	Invicta Aviation, Rotterdam, The Netherlands	
BELGIUM			
A-41	SA318C Alouette II	The Helicopter Museum, Weston-super-Mare	
FT-36	Lockheed T-33A Shooting Star	Dumfries & Galloway Avn Mus, Dumfries	
H-02	Agusta A109HO (N504TS)	Privately owned, Cotswold Airport	
H-05	Agusta A109HO (N504WG)	Currently not known	
H-50	Noorduyn AT-16 Harvard IIb (OO-DAF)	Privately owned, Brasschaat, Belgium	
IF-68	Hawker Hunter F6 <ff>	Privately owned, Kings Lynn	
L-44	Piper L-18C Super Cub (OO-SPQ)	Royal Aéro Para Club de Spa, Belgium	
L-47	Piper L-18C Super Cub (OO-SPG)	Aeroclub Brasschaat VZW, Brasschaat, Belgium	
OL-L49	Piper L-18C Super Cub (L-156/OO-LGB)	Aeroclub Brasschaat VZW, Brasschaat, Belgium	
V-4	SNCAN Stampe SV-4B (OO-EIR)	Antwerp Stampe Centre, Antwerp-Deurne, Belgium	
V-18	SNCAN Stampe SV-4B (OO-GWD)	Antwerp Stampe Centre, Antwerp-Deurne, Belgium	

Notes	Serial	Type (code/other identity)	Owner/operator, location or fate
	V-29	SNCAN Stampe SV-4B (OO-GWB)	Antwerp Stampe Centre, Antwerp-Deurne, Belgium
	V-66	SNCAN Stampe SV-4C (OO-GWA)	Antwerp Stampe Centre, Antwerp-Deurne, Belgium
	BOLIVIA		
	FAB-108	BAe RJ.70	Privately owned, Southend
	BRAZIL		
	1317	Embraer T-27 Tucano	Shorts, Belfast (engine test bed)
	BURKINA FASO		
	BF8431	SIAI-Marchetti SF.260 (G-NRRA) [31]	Privately owned, Lydd
	CANADA		
	-	Lockheed T-33A Shooting Star (17473)	Repainted in US marks as 117529
	622	Piasecki HUP-3 Retriever (51-16622/N6699D)	The Helicopter Museum, Weston-super-Mare
	920	VS Stranraer (CF-BXO) [Q-N]	RAF Museum, Hendon
	3091	NA81 Harvard II (3019/G-CPPM)	Beech Restorations, Bruntingthorpe
	3349	NA64 Yale (G-BYNF)	Privately owned, Duxford
	5084	DH82C Tiger Moth (G-FCTK)	Privately owned, Hailsham
	9041	Bristol 149 Bolingbroke IV <ff>	Manx Aviation Museum, Ronaldsway
	9048	Bristol 149 Bolingbroke IV	Aerospace Bristol, Filton
	9893	Bristol 149 Bolingbroke IVT <ff>	Kent Battle of Britain Museum, Hawkinge
	9893	Bristol 149 Bolingbroke IVT <rf>	IWM, stored Duxford
	9940	Bristol 149 Bolingbroke IVT	National Museum of Flight, E Fortune
	15252	Fairchild PT-19A Cornell (comp 15195)	RAF Museum Reserve Collection, Stafford
	16693	Auster J/1N Alpha (G-BLPG) [693]	Privately owned, Dunkeswell
	17447	McD F-101F Voodoo (56-0312)	Midland Air Museum, Coventry
	18393	Avro Canada CF-100 Canuck 4B (G-BCYK)	IWM Duxford
	18671	DHC1 Chipmunk 22 (WP905/7438M/G-BNZC) [671]	The Shuttleworth Collection, Old Warden
	20249	Noorduyn AT-16 Harvard IIb (PH-KLU) [XS-249]	Privately owned, Texel, The Netherlands
	21417	Canadair CT-133 Silver Star	Yorkshire Air Museum, Elvington
	23140	Canadair CL-13A Sabre 5 [AX] <rf>	Midland Air Museum, Coventry
	23380	Canadair CL-13B Sabre 6 <rf>	Privately owned, Haverigg
	FE992	Noorduyn AT-16 Harvard IIb (G-BDAM) [ER-992]	Privately owned, Duxford
	KN448	Douglas Dakota IV <ff>	Science Museum, South Kensington
	CHILE		
	H-255	Aérospatiale SA330H Puma	Ultimate Activity, Faygate
	CHINA		
	68 r	Nanchang CJ-6A Chujiao (2751219/G-BVVG)	Privately owned, White Waltham
	61367	Nanchang CJ-6A Chujiao (4532009/G-CGHB) [37]	Privately owned, Redhill
	CZECH REPUBLIC		
	3677	Letov S-103 (MiG-15bisSB) (613677)	National Museum of Flight, E Fortune
	3794	Letov S-102 (MiG-15) (623794)	Norfolk & Suffolk Avn Museum, Flixton
		(starboard side only, painted in Polish marks as 1972 on port side)	
	9147	Mil Mi-4	The Helicopter Museum, Weston-super-Mare
	DENMARK		
	A-011	SAAB A-35XD Draken	Privately owned, Westhoughton, Lancs
	AR-107	SAAB S-35XD Draken	Newark Air Museum, Winthorpe
	E-419	Hawker Hunter F51 (G-9-441)	North-East Aircraft Museum, Usworth
	E-420	Hawker Hunter F51 (G-9-442) <ff>	Privately owned, Walton-on-Thames
	E-421	Hawker Hunter F51 (G-9-443)	Brooklands Museum, Weybridge
	ET-272	Hawker Hunter T53 <ff>	Norfolk & Suffolk Avn Museum, Flixton
	K-682	Douglas C-47A Skytrain (OY-BPB)	Foreningen For Flyvende Mus, Vaerløse, Denmark
	L-866	Consolidated PBY-6A Catalina (8466M)	RAF Museum, Cosford
	P-129	DHC-1 Chipmunk 22 (OY-ATO)	Privately owned, Roskilde, Denmark

Serial	Type (code/other identity)	Owner/operator, location or fate	Notes
P-139	DHC-1 Chipmunk 22 (OY-AVF)	Privately owned, Roskilde, Denmark	
R-756	Lockheed F-104G Starfighter	Midland Air Museum, Coventry	
S-881	Sikorsky S-55C	The Helicopter Museum, Weston-super-Mare	
S-882	Sikorsky S-55C	Skirmish Paintball, Portishead	
S-886	Sikorsky S-55C	Hamburger Hill Paintball, Marksbury, Somerset	
S-887	Sikorsky S-55C	The Helicopter Museum, Weston-super-Mare	
EGYPT			
356	Heliopolis Gomhouria Mk 6	Privately owned, stored Ellerton, E Yorks	
764	Mikoyan MiG-21SPS <ff>	Privately owned, Northampton	
771	WS61 Sea King Mk.47 (WA.826)	DSTO Shoeburyness, Essex, GI use	
773	WS61 Sea King Mk.47 (WA.823)	RNAS Yeovilton Fire Section	
774	WS61 Sea King Mk.47 (WA.822)	*Scrapped*	
775	WS61 Sea King Mk.47 (WA.824)	*Scrapped*	
776	WS61 Sea King Mk.47 (WA.825) <ff>	Mayhem Paintball, Aybridge, Essex	
0446	Mikoyan MiG-21UM <ff>	*Currently not known*	
7907	Sukhoi Su-7 <ff>	Robertsbridge Aviation Society, Mayfield	
FINLAND			
GA-43	Gloster Gamecock II (G-CGYF)	Privately owned, Dursley, Glos	
GN-101	Folland Gnat F1 (XK741)	Midland Air Museum, Coventry	
SZ-12	Focke-Wulf Fw44J Stieglitz (D-EXWO)	Privately owned, Bienenfarm, Germany	
VI-3	Valtion Viima 2 (OO-EBL)	Privately owned, Brasschaat, Belgium	
FRANCE			
1/4513	Spad XIII <R> (G-BFYO/*S3398*)	American Air Museum, Duxford	
7	Nord NC854 (G-NORD)	Privately owned, English Bicknor, Glos	
28	Fouga CM175 Zéphyr [F-AZPF]	Association Zéphyr 28, Nîmes, France	
32	Morane-Saulnier MS760 Paris (F-AZLT)	Armor Aéro Passion, Morlaix, France	
37	Nord 3400 (G-ZARA) [MAB]	Privately owned, Swanton Morley	
45	Dassault Mirage IVP [BR]	Yorkshire Air Museum, Elvington	
54	SNCAN NC856A Norvigie (G-CGWR) [AOM]	Privately owned, Spanhoe	
67	SNCAN 1101 Noralpha (F-GMCY) [CY]	Privately owned, la Ferté-Alais, France	
70	Dassault Mystère IVA [8-NV]	Midland Air Museum, Coventry	
78	Nord 3202B-1 (G-BIZK)	Privately owned, Swaffham, Norfolk	
79	Dassault Mystère IVA [2-EG]	Norfolk & Suffolk Avn Museum, Flixton	
82	Curtiss H75-C1 Hawk (G-CCVH) [X-881]	The Fighter Collection, Duxford	
82	NA T-28D Fennec (F-AZKG)	Privately owned, Strasbourg, France	
83	Dassault Mystère IVA [8-MS]	Newark Air Museum, Winthorpe	
83	Morane-Saulnier MS733 Alcyon (F-AZKS)	Privately owned, Montlucon, France	
85	Dassault Mystère IVA [8-MV]	Cold War Jets Collection, Bruntingthorpe	
104	MH1521M Broussard (F-GHFG) [307-FG]	Privately owned, Monteau-les-Mines, France	
105	Nord N2501F Noratlas (F-AZVM) [62-SI]	Le Noratlas de Provence, Marseilles, France	
106	MH1521M Broussard (F-GKJT) [33-JT]	Privately owned, Montceau-les-Mines, France	
108	MH1521M Broussard (F-BNEX) [50S9]	Privately owned, Lelystad, The Netherlands	
108	SO1221 Djinn (FR108) [CDL]	The Helicopter Museum, Weston-super-Mare	
121	Dassault Mystère IVA [8-MY]	City of Norwich Aviation Museum	
128	Morane-Saulnier MS733 Alcyon (F-BMMY)	Privately owned, St Cyr, France	
143	Morane-Saulnier MS733 Alcyon (G-MSAL)	Privately owned, Spanhoe	
146	Dassault Mystère IVA [8-MC]	North-East Aircraft Museum, Usworth	
154	MH1521M Broussard (F-GKRO) [315-SM]	Privately owned, Damyns Hall, Essex	
156	SNCAN Stampe SV-4B (G-NIFE)	Privately owned, Gloucester	
158	Dassault MD312 Flamant (F-AZGE) [12-XA]	Privately owned, Albert, France	
160	Dassault MD312 Flamant (F-AZDR) [V]	Privately owned, Alençon, France	
189	Dassault MD312 Flamant (F-AZVG) [G]	Ailes Anciennes de Corbas, Lyon, France	
208	MH1521C1 Broussard (G-YYYY) [IR]	Privately owned, Eggesford	
226	Dassault MD312 Flamant (F-AZES) [319-CG]	Privately owned, Montbeliard, France	
237	Dassault MD312 Flamant (F-AZFE) [319-DM]	Privately owned, Alençon, France	
255	MH1521M Broussard (G-CIGH) [5-ML]	Privately owned, Breighton	
260	Dassault MD311 Flamant (F-AZKT) [316-KT]	Privately owned, Albert, France	
261	MH1521M Broussard (F-GIBN) [30-QA]	Privately owned, Walldürn, Germany	
276	Dassault MD311 Flamant (F-AZER)	Privately owned, Alençon, France	

Notes	Serial	Type (code/other identity)	Owner/operator, location or fate
	290	Dewoitine D27 (F-AZJD)	Les Casques de Cuir, la Ferté-Alais, France
	316	MH1521M Broussard (F-GGKR) [315-SN]	Privately owned, Lognes, France
	318	Dassault Mystère IVA [8-NY]	Dumfries & Galloway Avn Mus, Dumfries
	319	Dassault Mystère IVA [8-ND]	Rebel Air Museum, Andrewsfield
	351	Morane-Saulnier MS317 (G-MOSA) [HY22]	Privately owned, Barton
	354	Morane-Saulnier MS315E-D2 (G-BZNK)	Privately owned, Wickenby
	538	Dassault Mirage IIIE [3-QH]	Yorkshire Air Museum, Elvington
	569	Fouga CM170R Magister [F-AZZP]	Privately owned, Le Havre, France
	24541	Cessna L-19E Bird Dog (G-JDOG) [BMG]	Privately owned, Cotswold Airport
	24545	Cessna L-19E Bird Dog (F-AZTA) [BYA]	Privately owned, Chavenay, France
	42157	NA F-100D Super Sabre [11-ER]	North-East Aircraft Museum, Usworth
	54439	Lockheed T-33A Shooting Star (55-4439) [WI]	North-East Aircraft Museum, Usworth
	125716	Douglas AD-4N Skyraider (F-AZFN) [22-DG]	Privately owned, Mélun, France
	127002	Douglas AD-4NA Skyraider (F-AZHK) [20-LN]	Privately owned, Avignon, France
	18-5395	Piper L-18C Super Cub (52-2436/G-CUBJ) [CDG]	Privately owned, Old Warden
	C850	Salmson 2A2 <R>	Barton Aviation Heritage Society, Barton
	FR41	Piasecki H-21C	The Helicopter Museum, Weston-super-Mare
	MS824	Morane-Saulnier Type N <R> (G-AWBU)	Privately owned, Stow Maries
	N856	SNCAN NC856 (G-CDWE)	Privately owned, Wickenby
	N1977	Nieuport Scout 17/23 <R> (N1723/G-BWMJ) [8]	Privately owned, Stow Maries
	XC	Piper L-4J Grasshopper (44-80513/G-BSYO)	Privately owned, Postling, Kent
	GERMANY		
	-	Fieseler Fi103R-IV (V-1) (BAPC 91)	Lashenden Air Warfare Museum, Headcorn
	-	Fokker Dr1 Dreidekker <R> (BAPC 88)	FAA Museum, stored Cobham Hall, RNAS Yeovilton
	-	Messerschmitt Bf109 <R> (6357/BAPC 74) [6]	Kent Battle of Britain Museum, Hawkinge
	-	Messerschmitt Bf109 <R> [<-]	Battle of Britain Experience, Canterbury
	Green 1	Messerschmitt Bf109G <R> (BAPC 240)	Yorkshire Air Museum, Elvington
	White 1	Focke-Wulf Fw190 <R> (G-WULF)	Privately owned, Halfpenny Green
	3	SNCAN 1101 Noralpha (G-BAYV) (fuselage)	Privately owned, Newquay
	Yellow 3	Hispano HA 1.112M1L Buchón (C.4K-40/D-FDME)	Messerschmitt Stiftung, Manching, Germany
	Red 7	Hispano HA 1.112M1L Buchón (C.4K-75/D-FWME)	Messerschmitt Stiftung, Manching, Germany
	Yellow 7	Hispano HA 1.112M1L Buchón (C.4K-99/G-AWHM)	Privately owned, Sywell
	Black 8	Hispano HA 1.112M1L Buchón (C.4K-102/G-AWHK)	Historic Flying Ltd, Duxford
	White 9	Focke-Wulf Fw190 <R> (G-CCFW)	Privately owned, Oaksey Park
	White 9	Hispano HA 1.112M1L Buchón (C.4K-105/G-AWHH)	Privately owned, Sywell
	Red 11	Hispano HA 1.112K1L Buchón (C.4K-112/G-AWHC)	Privately owned, Sywell
	White 14	Messerschmitt Bf109 <R> (BAPC 67)	Kent Battle of Britain Museum, Hawkinge
	Yellow 14	Nord 1002 (G-ETME)	Privately owned, White Waltham
	Yellow 27	Hispano HA 1.112K1L Buchón (D-FMGZ)	Air Fighter Academy, Heringsdorf, Germany
	33/15	Fokker EIII <R> (G-CHAW)	Privately owned, Membury
	87	Heinkel He111 <R> <ff>	Privately owned, East Kirkby
	105/15	Fokker EIII <R> (G-UDET)	Privately owned, Horsham
	152/17	Fokker Dr1 Dreidekker <R> (F-AZPQ)	Les Casques de Cuir, la Ferté-Alais, France
	152/17	Fokker Dr1 Dreidekker <R> (G-BVGZ)	Privately owned, Breighton
	157/18	Fokker D.VIII <R> (BAPC 239)	Norfolk & Suffolk Air Museum, Flixton
	210/16	Fokker EIII (BAPC 56)	Science Museum, South Kensington
	403/17	Fokker Dr1 Dreidekker <R> (G-CDXR)	Privately owned, Popham
	416/15	Fokker EIII <R> (G-GSAL)	Privately owned, Aston Down
	422/15	Fokker EIII <R> (G-AVJO)	Privately owned, Stow Maries
	422/15	Fokker EIII <R> (G-FOKR)	Privately owned, Eshott
	425/17	Fokker Dr1 Dreidekker <R> (BAPC 133)	Kent Battle of Britain Museum, Hawkinge
	425/17	Fokker Dr1 Dreidekker <R> (G-DREI)	Privately owned, Felthorpe
	477/17	Fokker Dr1 Dreidekker <R> (G-FOKK)	Privately owned, Sywell
	556/17	Fokker Dr1 Dreidekker <R> (G-CFHY)	Privately owned, Tibenham
	626/8	Fokker DVII <R> (N6268)	Privately owned, Booker
	764	Mikoyan MiG-21SPS <ff>	Privately owned, Norfolk
	959	Mikoyan MiG-21SPS	Midland Air Museum, Coventry
	1160	Dornier Do17Z-2	Michael Beetham Conservation Centre, Cosford
	1190	Messerschmitt Bf109E-3 [White 4]	IWM Duxford
	1480	Messerschmitt Bf109 <R> (BAPC 66) [6]	Kent Battle of Britain Museum, Hawkinge

Serial	Type (code/other identity)	Owner/operator, location or fate	Notes
1801/18	Bowers Fly Baby 1A (G-BNPV)	Privately owned, Chessington	
1803/18	Bowers Fly Baby 1A (G-BUYU)	Privately owned, Chessington	
1983	Messerschmitt Bf109E-3 (G-EMIL)	Privately owned, Colchester	
3579	Messerschmitt Bf109E-7 (G-CIPB) [White 14]	Privately owned, Biggin Hill	
4101	Messerschmitt Bf109E-3 (DG200/8477M) [Black 12]	RAF Museum, Hendon	
4477	CASA 1.131E Jungmann (G-RETA) [GD+EG]	The Shuttleworth Collection, Old Warden	
7198/18	LVG CVI (G-AANJ/9239M)	Michael Beetham Conservation Centre, Cosford	
8417/18	Fokker DVII (9207M)	RAF Museum, Hendon	
10639	Messerschmitt Bf109G-2/Trop (8478M/G-USTV) [Black 6]	RAF Museum, Cosford	
12802	Antonov An-2T (D-FOFM)	Historische Flugzeuge, Grossenhain, Germany	
13605	Messerschmitt Bf109G-2(G-JIMP) [Yellow 12]	Privately owned, Knutsford	
100143	Focke-Achgelis Fa330A-1 Bachstelze	IWM Duxford	
100502	Focke-Achgelis Fa330A-1 Bachstelze	Privately owned, Millom	
100503	Focke-Achgelis Fa330A-1 Bachstelze (8469M)	RAF Museum, Cosford	
100509	Focke-Achgelis Fa330A-1 Bachstelze	Science Museum, stored Wroughton	
100545	Focke-Achgelis Fa330A-1 Bachstelze	FAA Museum, RNAS Yeovilton	
100549	Focke-Achgelis Fa330A-1 Bachstelze	Lashenden Air Warfare Museum, Headcorn	
112372	Messerschmitt Me262A-2a (VK893/8482M) [Yellow 4]	RAF Museum, Cosford	
120227	Heinkel He162A-2 Salamander (VN679/8472M) [Red 2]	RAF Museum, Hendon	
120235	Heinkel He162A-1 Salamander (AM.68) [Yellow 6]	IWM Duxford	
191316	Messerschmitt Me163B Komet	Science Museum, South Kensington	
191454	Messerschmitt Me163B Komet <R> (BAPC 271)	The Shuttleworth Collection, Old Warden	
191461	Messerschmitt Me163B Komet (191614/8481M) [Yellow 14]	RAF Museum, Cosford	
191659	Messerschmitt Me163B Komet (8480M) [Yellow 15]	National Museum of Flight, E Fortune	
280020	Flettner Fl282/B-V20 Kolibri (frame only)	Midland Air Museum, Coventry	
360043	Junkers Ju88R-1 (PJ876/8475M) [D5+EV]	RAF Museum, Cosford	
420430	Messerschmitt Me410A-1/U2 (AM.72/8483M) [3U+CC]	RAF Museum, Cosford	
475081	Fieseler Fi156C-7 Storch (VP546/AM.101/7362M)[GM+AK]	RAF Museum, Cosford	
494083	Junkers Ju87D-3 (8474M) [RI+JK]	RAF Museum, Hendon	
502074	Heliopolis Gomhouria Mk 6 (158/G-CGEV) [CG+EV]	Privately owned, Breighton	
584219	Focke-Wulf Fw190F-8/U1 (AM.29/8470M) [Black 38]	RAF Museum, Hendon	
701152	Heinkel He111H-23 (8471M) [NT+SL]	RAF Museum, Hendon	
730301	Messerschmitt Bf110G-4 (AM.34/8479M) [D5+RL]	RAF Museum, Hendon	
733682	Focke-Wulf Fw190A-8/R7 (AM.75/9211M)	RAF Museum, Cosford	
980554	Flug Werk FW190A-8/N (D-FMWW)	Meier Motors, Bremgarten, Germany	
2+1	Focke-Wulf Fw190 <R> (G-SYFW) [7334]	Privately owned, Empingham, Rutland	
20+45	Mikoyan MiG-23BN	Privately owned, Danbury, Essex	
22+35	Lockheed F-104G Starfighter	Privately owned, Bruntingthorpe	
28+08	Aero L-39ZO Albatros (142/28+04)	Pinewood Studios, Bucks	
2E+RA	Fieseler Fi-156C-3 Storch (F-AZRA)	Amicale J-B Salis, la Ferté-Alais, France	
4+1	Focke-Wulf Fw190 <R> (G-BSLX)	Privately owned, Norwich	
6G+ED	Slepcev Storch (G-BZOB) [5447]	Privately owned, Breighton	
37+86	McD F-4F Phantom II <ff>	Privately owned,	
37+89	McD F-4F Phantom II	Hawker Hunter Aviation Ltd, Scampton (spares)	
58+89	Dornier Do28D-2 Skyservant (D-ICDY)	Privately owned, Uetersen, Germany	
72+59	Dornier UH-1D Iroquois (comp 73+01)	Privately owned, Dunsfold	
80+55	MBB Bo.105M	Lufthansa Resource Technical Training, Cotswold Airport	
80+77	MBB Bo.105M	Lufthansa Resource Technical Training, Cotswold Airport	
81+00	MBB Bo.105M (D-HZYR)	The Helicopter Museum, Weston-super-Mare	
96+26	Mil Mi-24D (421)	The Helicopter Museum, Weston-super-Mare	
98+14	Sukhoi Su-22M-4	Hawker Hunter Aviation Ltd, stored Scampton	
99+18	NA OV-10B Bronco (G-ONAA)	Bronco Demo Team, Wevelgem, Belgium	
99+26	NA OV-10B Bronco (G-BZGL)	Bronco Demo Team, Wevelgem, Belgium	
AZ+JU	CASA 3.52L (F-AZJU)	Amicale J-B Salis, la Ferté-Alais, France	
BB+103	Canadair CL-13B Sabre 6 (1730/JB+114)	Privately owned,	
BF+070	CCF T-6J Texan (G-CHYN)	Privately owned, Dunkeswell	
BG+KM	Nord 1002 Pingouin (G-ASTG)	Privately owned, Peterborough	
BU+CC	CASA 1.131E Jungmann (G-BUCC)	Privately owned, Deanland	
CX+HI	CASA 1.131E Jungmann (E.3B-379/G-CDJU)	Privately owned, Sleap	
D2263	Albatros DVA-1 <R> (ZK-ALB/G-WAHT)	Privately owned, Old Warden	

Notes	Serial	Type (code/other identity)	Owner/operator, location or fate
	D7343/17	Albatros DVA <R> (ZK-TVD)	RAF Museum, Hendon
	DG+BE	CASA 1.131E Jungmann (E.3B-350/G-BHPL)	Privately owned, Henstridge
	DM+BK	Morane-Saulnier MS505 (G-BPHZ)	Aero Vintage, Westfield, E Sussex
	E37/15	Fokker EIII <R> (G-CGJF)	Privately owned, Herts
	ES+BH	Messerschmitt Bf108B-2 (D-ESBH)	Messerschmitt Stiftung, Manching, Germany
	FI+S	Morane-Saulnier MS505 (G-BIRW)	National Museum of Flight, E Fortune
	FM+BB	Messerschmitt Bf109G-6 (D-FMBB)	Messerschmitt Stiftung, Manching, Germany
	KG+GB	CASA 1.131E Jungmann (G-BHSL)	Privately owned, Old Warden
	LG+01	CASA 1.133L Jungmeister (ES.1-16/G-CIJV)	Privately owned, Sleap
	LG+03	Bücker Bü133C Jungmeister (G-AEZX)	Privately owned, Milden
	NJ+C11	Nord 1002 (G-ATBG)	Privately owned, Duxford
	NM+AA	CASA 1.131E Jungmann 1000 (G-BZJV)	Privately owned, Sleap
	NQ+NR	Klemm Kl35D (D-EQXD)	Quax Flieger, Paderborn, Germany
	NV+KG	Focke-Wulf Fw44J Stieglitz (D-ENAY)	Quax Flieger, Paderborn, Germany
	S4-A07	CASA 1.131E Jungmann (G-BWHP)	Privately owned, Yarcombe, Devon
	TP+WX	Heliopolis Gomhouria Mk 6 (G-TPWX)	Privately owned, Swanborough
	GHANA		
	G360	PBN 2T Islander (G-BRSR)	Privately owned, Biggin Hill
	G361	PBN 2T Islander (G-BRPB)	Privately owned, Biggin Hill
	G362	PBN 2T Islander (G-BRPC)	Privately owned, Biggin Hill
	G363	PBN 2T Islander (G-BRSV)	Privately owned, Biggin Hill
	GREECE		
	26541	Republic F-84F Thunderflash (52-6541) [541]	North-East Aircraft Museum, Usworth
	HONG KONG		
	HKG-5	SA128 Bulldog (G-BULL)	Privately owned, Cotswold Airport
	HKG-6	SA128 Bulldog (G-BPCL)	Privately owned, North Weald
	HKG-11	Slingsby T.67M Firefly 200 (G-BYRY)	Privately owned, Wellesbourne Mountford
	HKG-13	Slingsby T.67M Firefly 200 (G-BXKW)	Privately owned, St Ghislain, Belgium
	HUNGARY		
	125	Aero L-39ZO Albatros (831125/G-JMGP)	Privately owned, France
	335	Mil Mi-24D (3532461715415)	Privately owned, Dunsfold
	501	Mikoyan MiG-21PF	IWM Duxford
	503	Mikoyan MiG-21SMT (G-BRAM)	RAF Museum, Cosford
	INDIA		
	E296	Hindustan Gnat F1 (G-SLYR)	Privately owned, North Weald
	Q497	EE Canberra T4 (WE191) <ff>	Privately owned, Stoneykirk, D&G
	HA561	Hawker Tempest II (MW743)	Privately owned, stored Wickenby
	VP905	Douglas C-47B Skytrain (KN397/G-AMSV)	*To India, April 2018*
	INDONESIA		
	LL-5313	BAe Hawk T53	BAE Systems, Brough, on display
	IRAQ		
	333	DH115 Vampire T55 <ff>	South Yorkshire Aircraft Mus'm, stored Doncaster
	ITALY		
	MM5701	Fiat CR42 (BT474/8468M) [13-95]	RAF Museum, Hendon
	MM6976	Fiat CR42 (2542/G-CBLS) [85-16]	The Fighter Collection, Duxford
	MM53211	Fiat G46-1B (MM52799) [ZI-4]	Privately owned, Shipdham
	MM53692	CCF T-6G Texan	RAeS Medway Branch, Rochester
	MM53774	Fiat G59-4B (I-MRSV) [181]	Privately owned, Parma, Italy
	MM54099	NA T-6G Texan (G-BRBC) [RR-56]	Privately owned, Chigwell
	MM54532	SIAI-Marchetti SF.260AM (G-ITAF) [70-42]	Privately owned, Leicester
	MM80270	Agusta-Bell AB204B (MM80279)	*Repainted in US markings as 18, 2018*
	MM80927	Agusta-Bell AB206A-1 JetRanger [CC-49]	The Helicopter Museum, Weston-super-Mare
	MM81205	Agusta A109A-2 SEM [GF-128]	The Helicopter Museum, Weston-super-Mare
	MM52-2392	Piper L-21B Super Cub (G-HELN) [E.I.69]	Privately owned, White Waltham

Serial	Type (code/other identity)	Owner/operator, location or fate	Notes
MM54-2372	Piper L-21B Super Cub	Privately owned, Foxhall Heath, Suffolk	
JAPAN			
-	Kawasaki Ki100-1B (16336/8476M/BAPC 83)	RAF Museum, Cosford	
-	Mitsubishi A6M5-52 Zero (196) [CI-05] <ff>	IWM Duxford	
-	Yokosuka MXY 7 Ohka II (BAPC 159)	IWM Duxford, stored	
997	Yokosuka MXY 7 Ohka II (8485M/BAPC 98)	Museum of Science & Industry, Manchester	
3443	NA T-6 Texan Zero (F-AZRO)	Privately owned, St Rambert d'Albon, France	
5439	Mitsubishi Ki46-III (8484M/BAPC 84)	RAF Museum, Cosford	
15-1585	Yokosuka MXY 7 Ohka II (BAPC 58)	Science Museum, stored Cobham Hall, RNAS Yeovilton	
I-13	Yokosuka MXY 7 Ohka II (8486M/BAPC 99)	RAF Museum, Cosford	
Y2-176	Mitsubishi A6M3-2 Zero (3685) [76]	IWM London, Lambeth	
JORDAN			
408	SA125 Bulldog (G-BDIN)	*Currently not known*	
KENYA			
115	Dornier Do28D-2 Skyservant	Privately owned, stored Hibaldstow	
117	Dornier Do28D-2 Skyservant	Privately owned, stored Hibaldstow	
MALAYSIA			
M25-04	SA102 Bulldog (FM1224) (fuselage)	Privately owned, Cotswold Airport	
MYANMAR			
UB441	VS361 Spitfire IX (ML119/G-SDNI)	Privately owned, Sandown	
THE NETHERLANDS			
16-218	Consolidated PBY-5A Catalina (2459/PH-PBY)	Neptune Association, Lelystad, The Netherlands	
174	Fokker S-11 Instructor (E-31/G-BEPV) [K]	Privately owned, Spanhoe	
179	Fokker S-11 Instructor (PH-ACG) [K]	Privately owned, Lelystad, The Netherlands	
197	Fokker S-11 Instructor (PH-GRY) [K]	KLu Historic Flt, Gilze-Rijen, The Netherlands	
204	Lockheed SP-2H Neptune [V]	RAF Museum, Cosford	
A-57	DH82A Tiger Moth (PH-TYG)	KLu Historic Flt, Gilze-Rijen, The Netherlands	
B-64	Noorduyn AT-16 Harvard IIb (PH-LSK)	KLu Historic Flt, Gilze-Rijen, The Netherlands	
B-71	Noorduyn AT-16 Harvard IIb (PH-MLM)	KLu Historic Flt, Gilze-Rijen, The Netherlands	
B-118	Noorduyn AT-16 Harvard IIb (PH-IIB)	KLu Historic Flt, Gilze-Rijen, The Netherlands	
B-182	Noorduyn AT-16 Harvard IIb (PH-TBR)	KLu Historic Flt, Gilze-Rijen, The Netherlands	
E-14	Fokker S-11 Instructor (PH-AFS)	Privately owned, Lelystad, The Netherlands	
E-15	Fokker S-11 Instructor (G-BIYU)	Privately owned, RAF Linton-on-Ouse	
E-20	Fokker S-11 Instructor (PH-GRB)	Privately owned, Gilze-Rijen, The Netherlands	
E-27	Fokker S-11 Instructor (PH-HOL)	Privately owned, Lelystad, The Netherlands	
E-29	Fokker S-11 Instructor (PH-HOK)	Privately owned, Lelystad, The Netherlands	
E-32	Fokker S-11 Instructor (PH-HOI)	Privately owned, Gilze-Rijen, The Netherlands	
E-39	Fokker S-11 Instructor (PH-HOG)	Privately owned, Lelystad, The Netherlands	
G-29	Beech D18S (PH-KHV)	KLu Historic Flt, Gilze-Rijen, The Netherlands	
MH424	VS361 Spitfire LF IXc (MJ271/H-53/G-IRTY)	*Repainted as G-IRTY, 2018*	
MK732	VS361 Spitfire LF IXc (8633M/PH-OUQ) [3W-17]	KLu Historic Flt, Gilze-Rijen, The Netherlands	
N-202	Hawker Hunter F6 [10] <ff>	Privately owned, Stockport	
N-250	Hawker Hunter F6 (G-9-185) <ff>	IWM Duxford	
N-294	Hawker Hunter F6A (XF515/G-KAXF)	Stichting Hawker Hunter Foundation, Leeuwarden, The Netherlands	
N-302	Hawker Hunter T7 (ET-273/G-9-431) <ff>	South Yorkshire Aircraft Museum, Doncaster	
N-315	Hawker Hunter T7 (comp XM121)	Privately owned, Netherley, Aberdeenshire	
N-321	Hawker Hunter T8C (G-BWGL)	Stichting Hawker Hunter Foundation, Leeuwarden, The Netherlands	
N5-149	NA B-25J Mitchell (44-29507/HD346/PH-XXV) [232511]	KLu Historic Flt, Gilze-Rijen, The Netherlands	
R-18	Auster III (PH-NGK)	KLu Historic Flt, Gilze-Rijen, The Netherlands	
R-55	Piper L-18C Super Cub (52-2466/G-BLMI)	Privately owned, Antwerp, Belgium	
R-109	Piper L-21B Super Cub (54-2337/PH-GAZ)	KLu Historic Flt, Gilze-Rijen, The Netherlands	
R-122	Piper L-21B Super Cub (54-2412/PH-PPW)	KLu Historic Flt, Gilze-Rijen, The Netherlands	
R-124	Piper L-21B Super Cub (54-2414/PH-APA)	Privately owned, Eindhoven, The Netherlands	

Notes	Serial	Type (code/other identity)	Owner/operator, location or fate
	R-137	Piper L-21B Super Cub (54-2427/PH-PSC)	Privately owned, Gilze-Rijen, The Netherlands
	R-151	Piper L-21B Super Cub (54-2441/G-BIYR)	Privately owned, Yarcombe, Devon
	R-156	Piper L-21B Super Cub (54-2446/G-ROVE)	Privately owned, Damyn's Hall
	R-167	Piper L-21B Super Cub (54-2457/G-LION)	Privately owned,
	R-170	Piper L-21B Super Cub (52-6222/PH-ENJ)	Privately owned, Seppe, The Netherlands
	R-177	Piper L-21B Super Cub (54-2467/PH-KNR)	KLu Historic Flt, Gilze-Rijen, The Netherlands
	R-181	Piper L-21B Super Cub (54-2471/PH-GAU)	Privately owned, Gilze-Rijen, The Netherlands
	R-213	Piper L-21A Super Cub (51-15682/PH-RED)	Privately owned, Seppe, The Netherlands
	R-345	Piper L-4J Grasshopper (PH-UCS)	Privately owned, Hilversum, The Netherlands
	S-9	DHC2 L-20A Beaver (55-4585/PH-DHC)	KLu Historic Flt, Gilze-Rijen, The Netherlands

NEW ZEALAND

| | NZ3909 | WS Wasp HAS1 (XT782/G-KANZ) | Privately owned, Thruxton |
| | NZ5911 | Bristol 170 Freighter 31M (ZK-EPG) | Aerospace Bristol, stored Filton |

NORTH KOREA

| | - | WSK Lim-2 (MiG-15) (01420/G-BMZF) | FAA Museum, RNAS Yeovilton |

NORTH VIETNAM

| | 1211 | WSK Lim-5 (MiG-17F) (G-MIGG) | Privately owned, North Weald |

NORWAY

	145	DH82A Tiger Moth II (DE248/LN-BDM)	Privately owned, Kjeller, Norway
	163	Fairchild PT-19A Cornell (42-83641/LN-BIF)	Privately owned, Kjeller, Norway
	171	DH82A Tiger Moth II (T6168/LN-KAY)	Privately owned, Kjeller, Norway
	599	Canadair CT-133AUP Silver Star Mk.3 (133599/NX865SA)	Norwegian AF Historical Sqn, Ørland, Norway
	848	Piper L-18C Super Cub (LN-ACL) [FA-N]	Privately owned, Norway
	56321	SAAB S91B Safir (G-BKPY)	Newark Air Museum, Winthorpe

OMAN

	417	BAC Strikemaster Mk.80A (G-RSAF)	Privately owned, Hawarden
	425	BAC Strikemaster Mk.82A (G-SOAF)	Privately owned, Hawarden
	801	Hawker Hunter T66B <ff>	Privately owned, St Athan
	801	Hawker Hunter T66B <rf>	Privately owned, Hawarden
	853	Hawker Hunter FR10 (XF426)	RAF Museum, stored Cosford
	XF688	Percival P56 Provost T1 (WV562/7606M)	Repainted as WV562, 2018
	XL554	SAL Pioneer CC1 (XL703/8034M)	Michael Beetham Conservation Centre, Cosford

POLAND

	05	WSK SM-2 (Mi-2) (S2-03006)	The Helicopter Museum, Weston-super-Mare
	309	WSK SBLim-2A (MiG-15UTI) <ff>	R Scottish Mus'm of Flight, stored Granton
	458	Mikoyan MiG-23ML (04 red/024003607)	Newark Air Museum, Winthorpe
	618	Mil Mi-8P (10618)	The Helicopter Museum, Weston-super-Mare
	1018	WSK-PZL Mielec TS-11 Iskra (1H-1018/G-ISKA)	Cold War Jets Collection, Bruntingthorpe
	1120	WSK Lim-2 (MiG-15bis)	RAF Museum, Cosford
	1706	WSK-PZL Mielec TS-11 Iskra (1H-0408)	Midland Air Museum, Coventry
	1972	Letov S-102 (MiG-15) (623794)	Norfolk & Suffolk Avn Museum, Flixton
		(port side only, painted in Czech marks as 3794 on starboard side)	

PORTUGAL

	1350	OGMA/DHC1 Chipmunk T20 (G-CGAO)	Privately owned, Spanhoe
	1365	OGMA/DHC1 Chipmunk T20 (G-DHPM)	Privately owned, Sywell
	1367	OGMA/DHC1 Chipmunk T20 (G-UANO)	Privately owned, Sherburn-in-Elmet
	1372	OGMA/DHC1 Chipmunk T20 (HB-TUM)	Privately owned, Switzerland
	1373	OGMA/DHC1 Chipmunk T20 (G-CBJG)	Privately owned, Winwick, Cambs
	1375	OGMA/DHC1 Chipmunk T20 (F-AZJV)	Privately owned, Valenciennes, France
	1377	DHC1 Chipmunk 22 (WK520/G-BARS)	Privately owned, Yeovilton
	1741	CCF T-6J Texan (G-HRVD)	Privately owned, Bruntingthorpe
	1747	CCF T-6J Texan (20385/G-BGPB)	The Aircraft Restoration Co, Duxford
	3303	MH1521M Broussard (G-CBGL)	Privately owned, Rochester

Serial	Type (code/other identity)	Owner/operator, location or fate	Notes
QATAR			
QA10	Hawker Hunter FGA78	Yorkshire Air Museum, Elvington	
QA12	Hawker Hunter FGA78 <ff>	Privately owned, New Inn, Torfaen	
QP30	WS Lynx Mk.28 (G-BFDV/TAD013)	DSAE SAAE, Lyneham	
QP31	WS Lynx Mk.28	Newark Air Museum, Winthorpe	
QP32	WS Lynx Mk.28 (TD 016) [A]	DSAE SAAE, Lyneham	
ROMANIA			
29	LET L-29 Delfin	Privately owned, Pocklington	
42	LET L-29 Delfin <ff>	Privately owned, Catshill, Worcs	
42	LET L-29 Delfin <rf>	Privately owned, Hinstock, Shrops	
47	LET L-29 Delfin <ff>	Top Gun Flight Simulator Centre, Stalybridge	
53	LET L-29 Delfin [66654]	Privately owned, Bruntingthorpe	
RUSSIA (& FORMER SOVIET UNION)			
-	Mil Mi-24D (3532464505029)	Midland Air Museum, Coventry	
00 w	Yakovlev Yak-3M (0470202/G-OLEG)	Privately owned, Goodwood	
1 w	SPP Yak C-11 (171314/G-BZMY)	Privately owned, Booker	
01 y	Yakovlev Yak-52 (9311709/G-YKSZ)	Privately owned, White Waltham	
03 bl	Yakovlev Yak-55M (910103/RA-01274)	Privately owned, Halfpenny Green	
03 w	Yakovlev Yak-18A (1160403/G-CEIB)	Privately owned, Breighton	
5 w	Yakovlev Yak-3UA (0470204/D-FYGJ)	Privately owned, Bremgarten, Germany	
06 y	Yakovlev Yak-9UM (HB-RYA)	Flying Fighter Association, Bex, Switzerland	
07 y	WSK SM-1 (Mi-1) (Polish AF 2007)	The Helicopter Museum, Weston-super-Mare	
07 y	Yakovlev Yak-18M (G-BMJY)	Privately owned, Membury, Bucks	
9 w	SPP Yak C-11 (1701139/G-OYAK)	Privately owned, Little Gransden	
10 r	Yakovlev Yak-50 (877610/G-YAKE)	Privately owned, Henstridge	
12 r	LET L-29 Delfin (194555/ES-YLM/G-DELF)	To Hungary, April 2018	
14 r	WSK-PZL An-2R (HA-MKE)	Morayvia, Kinloss	
15 w	SPP Yak C-11 (170103/D-FYAK)	Classic Aviation Company, Hannover, Germany	
18 r	LET L-29 Delfin (591771/YL-PAF)	Privately owned, Hawarden	
18 r	WSK SBLim-2 (MiG-15UTI) (1A01004/N104CJ)	Norwegian AF Historical Sqn, Rygge, Norway	
18 r	Yakovlev Yak-50 (801810/G-BTZB)	Privately owned, Henstridge	
20 r	Yakovlev Yak-50 (812003/G-YAAK)	Privately owned, Henstridge	
20 w	Lavochkin La-11	The Fighter Collection, Duxford	
21 w	Yakovlev Yak-3UA (0470203/G-CDBJ)	Privately owned, Folkestone	
21 w	Yakovlev Yak-9UM (0470403/D-FENK)	Privately owned, Magdeburg, Germany	
23 y	Bell P-39Q Airacobra (44-2911)	Privately owned, Sussex	
23 r	Mikoyan MiG-27D (83712515040)	Privately owned, Hawarden	
26 bl	Yakovlev Yak-52 (9111306/G-BVXK)	Privately owned, White Waltham	
27 w	Yakovlev Yak-3UTI-PW (9/04623/F-AZIM)	Privately owned, la Ferté-Alais, France	
27 r	Yakovlev Yak-52 (9111307/G-YAKX)	Privately owned, Popham	
28 w	Polikarpov Po-2 (0094/G-BSSY)	The Shuttleworth Collection, Old Warden	
33 r	Yakovlev Yak-50 (853206/G-YAKZ)	Privately owned, Henstridge	
33 w	Yakovlev Yak-52 (899915/G-YAKH)	Privately owned, White Waltham	
35 r	Sukhoi Su-17M-3 (25102)	Privately owned, Hawarden	
36 w	LET/Yak C-11 (171101/G-KYAK)	Privately owned, North Weald	
36 r	Yakovlev Yak-52 (9111604/G-IUII)	Privately owned, St Athan	
43 bl	Yakovlev Yak-52 (877601/G-BWSV)	Privately owned, Elstree	
48 w	Yakovlev Yak-3UPW <R> (F-AZZK)	Privately owned, Lelystad, The Netherlands	
49 r	Yakovlev Yak-50 (822305/G-YAKU)	Privately owned, Henstridge	
50 gy	Yakovlev Yak-52 (9111415/G-CBRW)	Meier Motors, Bremgarten, Germany	
51 r	LET L-29S Delfin (491273/YL-PAG)	Privately owned, Breighton	
51 y	Yakovlev Yak-50 (812004/G-BWYK)	Privately owned, West Meon, Hants	
52 bk	Yakovlev Yak-52 (877409/G-FLSH)	Privately owned, North Weald	
52 w	Yakovlev Yak-52 (9612001/G-CCJK)	Privately owned, White Waltham	
52 y	Yakovlev Yak-52 (878202/G-BWVR)	Privately owned, Eshott	
54 r	Sukhoi Su-17M (69004)	Privately owned, Hawarden	
61 r	Yakovlev Yak-50 (842710/G-YAKM)	Privately owned, Henstridge	
66 r	Yakovlev Yak-50 (855905/G-YAKN)	Privately owned, Henstridge	
67 r	Yakovlev Yak-52 (822013/G-CBSL)	Sold to Belgium, 5 November 2018	
71 r	Mikoyan MiG-27K (61912507006)	Newark Air Museum, Winthorpe	

Notes	Serial	Type (code/other identity)	Owner/operator, location or fate
	74 w	Yakovlev Yak-52 (877404/G-OUGH) [JA-74, IV-62]	Privately owned, Swansea
	86 r	Yakovlev Yak-52 (867212/G-YAKC)	Privately owned, Henstridge
	93 w	Yakovlev Yak-50 (853001/G-JYAK) [R]	*Sold as N11YK, 2017*
	100 bl	Yakovlev Yak-52 (866904/G-YAKI)	Privately owned, Popham
	100 w	Yakovlev Yak-3M (0470107/G-CGXG)	Privately owned, Bentwaters
	139 y	Yakovlev Yak-52 (833810/G-BWOD)	Privately owned, Sywell
	526 bk	Mikoyan MiG-29 (2960725887) <ff>	Fenland & West Norfolk Aviation Museum, Wisbech
	1342	Yakovlev Yak-1 (G-BTZD)	Privately owned, Westfield, Sussex
	1870710	Ilyushin Il-2 (G-BZVW)	Privately owned, Wickenby
	1878576	Ilyushin Il-2 (G-BZVX)	Privately owned, Wickenby
	(RK858)	VS361 Spitfire LF IX (G-CGJE)	The Fighter Collection, Duxford
	(SM639)	VS361 Spitfire LF IX	Privately owned, Catfield

SAUDI ARABIA
Notes	Serial	Type (code/other identity)	Owner/operator, location or fate
	1115	BAC Strikemaster Mk.80A	Global Aviation, Humberside
	1129	BAC Strikemaster Mk.80A	Humberside Airport, on display
	1133	BAC Strikemaster Mk.80A (G-BESY)	IWM Duxford
	53-671	BAC Lightning F53 (203/ZF579)	Gatwick Aviation Museum, Charlwood
	53-686	BAC Lightning F53 (G-AWON/201/1305/223/ZF592)	City of Norwich Aviation Museum
	55-713	BAC Lightning T55 (206/1316/235/ZF598) [C]	Midland Air Museum, Coventry

SIERRA LEONE
Notes	Serial	Type (code/other identity)	Owner/operator, location or fate
	SL-01	Westland Commando Mk.2C	Privately owned, Dunsfold

SINGAPORE
Notes	Serial	Type (code/other identity)	Owner/operator, location or fate
	311	BAC Strikemaster Mk.84 (G-MXPH)	Privately owned, Leeds East
	323	BAC Strikemaster Mk.81 (N21419)	Privately owned, stored Hawarden

SOUTH AFRICA
Notes	Serial	Type (code/other identity)	Owner/operator, location or fate
	91	Westland Wasp HAS1 (pod)	Privately owned, Oaksey Park
	92	Westland Wasp HAS1 (G-BYCX)	Privately owned, Thruxton
	6130	Lockheed Ventura II (AJ469)	RAF Museum, stored Cosford
	7429	NA AT-6D Harvard III (D-FASS)	Privately owned, Aachen, Germany

SOUTH ARABIA
Notes	Serial	Type (code/other identity)	Owner/operator, location or fate
	104	BAC Jet Provost T52A (G-PROV)	Privately owned, North Weald

SOUTH VIETNAM
Notes	Serial	Type (code/other identity)	Owner/operator, location or fate
	24550	Cessna L-19E Bird Dog (G-PDOG) [GP]	Privately owned, Fenland

SPAIN
Notes	Serial	Type (code/other identity)	Owner/operator, location or fate
	B.2I-27	CASA 2.111B (He111H-16) (B.2I-103)	IWM Duxford, stored
	C.4K-30	Hispano HA 1.112M1L Buchón [471-26]	Privately owned, Sywell
	C.4K-111	Hispano HA 1.112M1L Buchón (G-HISP) [471-15]	Privately owned, Sywell
	C.4K-152	Hispano HA 1.112M1L Buchón (G-AWHR/N4109G)	Privately owned, Sywell
	E.3B-143	CASA 1.131E Jungmann (G-JUNG)	Privately owned, White Waltham
	E.3B-153	CASA 1.131E Jungmann (G-BPTS) [781-75]	Privately owned, Egginton
	E.3B-494	CASA 1.131E Jungmann (G-CDLC) [81-47]	Privately owned, Chiseldon
	E.3B-521	CASA 1.131E Jungmann [781-3]	RAF Museum Reserve Collection, Stafford
	E.3B-599	CASA 1.131E Jungmann (G-CGTX) [31]	Privately owned, Archerfield, Lothian
	E.18-2	Piper PA-31P Navajo 425 [42-71]	High Harthay Outdoor Pursuits, Huntingdon

SRI LANKA
Notes	Serial	Type (code/other identity)	Owner/operator, location or fate
	CT180	Nanchang CJ-6A Chujiao (2632016/G-BXZB)	Privately owned, White Waltham

SWEDEN
Notes	Serial	Type (code/other identity)	Owner/operator, location or fate
	-	Thulin A/Bleriot XI (SE-XMC)	Privately owned, Loberod, Sweden
	087	CFM 01 Tummelisa <R> (SE-XIL)	Privately owned, Loberod, Sweden
	2542	Fiat CR42 (G-CBLS)	*Rebuilt as MM6976, 2018*
	5033	Klemm KI35D (SE-BPT) [78]	Privately owned, Barkaby, Sweden
	5060	Klemm KI35D (SE-BPU) [174]	Privately owned, Barkaby, Sweden

Serial	Type (code/other identity)	Owner/operator, location or fate	Notes
05108	DH60 Moth	Privately owned, Langham	
17239	SAAB B 17A (SE-BYH) [7-J]	Flygvapenmuseum, Linköping, Sweden	
29640	SAAB J 29F [20-08]	Midland Air Museum, Coventry	
29670	SAAB J 29F (SE-DXB) [10-R]	Swedish Air Force Historic Flt, Såtenäs, Sweden	
32028	SAAB 32A Lansen (G-BMSG) <ff>	Privately owned, Willenhall, Staffs	
32542	SAAB J 32B Lansen (SE-RMD) [23]	Swedish Air Force Historic Flt, Såtenäs, Sweden	
35075	SAAB J 35A Draken [40]	Dumfries & Galloway Aviation Museum	
35515	SAAB J 35F Draken [49]	Airborne Systems, Llangeinor	
35810	SAAB Sk 35C Draken (SE-DXP) [79]	Swedish Air Force Historic Flt, Såtenäs, Sweden	
37098	SAAB AJSF 37 Viggen (SE-DXN) [52]	Swedish Air Force Historic Flt, Såtenäs, Sweden	
37809	SAAB Sk 37E Viggen (SE-DXO) [61]	Swedish Air Force Historic Flt, Såtenäs, Sweden	
37918	SAAB AJSH 37 Viggen [57]	Newark Air Museum, Winthorpe	
60140	SAAB Sk 60E (SE-DXG) [140-5]	Swedish Air Force Historic Flt, Såtenäs, Sweden	
91130	SAAB S91A Safir (SE-BNN) [10-30]	Privately owned, Barkaby, Sweden	

SWITZERLAND

Serial	Type (code/other identity)	Owner/operator, location or fate	Notes
-	DH112 Venom FB54 (J-1758/N203DM)	Grove Technology Park, Wantage, Oxon	
A-10	CASA 1.131E Jungmann (G-BECW)	Privately owned, Rochester	
A-44	CASA 1.131E Jungmann 2000 (G-CIUE)	Privately owned, Breighton	
A-57	CASA 1.131E Jungmann (G-BECT)	Privately owned, Goodwood	
A-125	Pilatus P2-05 (G-BLKZ) (fuselage)	Privately owned, Newquay	
A-806	Pilatus P3-03 (G-BTLL)	Privately owned, Guist, Norfolk	
A-815	Pilatus P3-03 (HB-RCQ)	Privately owned, Locarno, Switzerland	
A-818	Pilatus P3-03 (HB-RCH)	Privately owned, Ambri, Switzerland	
A-829	Pilatus P3-03 (HB-RCJ)	Privately owned, Altenrhein, Switzerland	
A-873	Pilatus P3-03 (HB-RCL)	Privately owned, Locarno, Switzerland	
C-509	EKW C-3605 (HB-RDH)	46 Aviation, Sion, Switzerland	
C-552	EKW C-3605 (G-DORN)	Privately owned, Little Gransden (dismantled)	
C-558	EKW C-3605 (G-CCYZ)	Privately owned, Wickenby	
J-143	F+W D-3801 (MS406) (HB-RCF)	Privately owned, Bex, Switzerland	
J-1008	DH100 Vampire FB6	de Havilland Aircraft Museum, London Colney	
J-1169	DH100 Vampire FB6	Privately owned, Henley-on-Thames	
J-1172	DH100 Vampire FB6 (8487M)	RAF Museum Reserve Collection, Stafford	
J-1573	DH112 Venom FB50 (G-VICI) <ff>	Privately owned, Glos	
J-1605	DH112 Venom FB50 (G-BLID)	Gatwick Aviation Museum, Charlwood, Surrey	
J-1629	DH112 Venom FB50	Privately owned, Shropshire	
J-1632	DH112 Venom FB50 (G-VNOM) <ff>	Privately owned, Cantley, Norfolk	
J-1649	DH112 Venom FB50 <ff>	Aerohub, Newquay	
J-1704	DH112 Venom FB54	RAF Museum, stored Cosford	
J-1790	DH112 Venom FB54 (G-BLKA/*WR410*)	Historic Aviation Centre, Fishburn	
J-4015	Hawker Hunter F58 (J-4040/HB-RVS)	Privately owned, St Stephan, Switzerland	
J-4064	Hawker Hunter F58 (HB-RVQ)	Fliegermuseum Altenrhein, Switzerland	
J-4086	Hawker Hunter F58 (HB-RVU)	Privately owned, Altenrhein, Switzerland	
J-4110	Hawker Hunter F58A (XF318/G-CJWL)	Hawker Hunter Aviation Ltd, Scampton	
J-4201	Hawker Hunter T68 (HB-RVR)	Amici dell'Hunter, Sion, Switzerland	
J-4205	Hawker Hunter T68 (HB-RVP)	Fliegermuseum Altenrhein, Switzerland	
J-4206	Hawker Hunter T68 (HB-RVV)	Fliegermuseum Altenrhein, Switzerland	
U-80	Bücker Bü133D Jungmeister (G-BUKK)	Privately owned, Kirdford, W Sussex	
U-95	Bücker Bü133C Jungmeister (G-BVGP)	Privately owned, Turweston	
U-99	Bücker Bü133C Jungmeister (G-AXMT)	Privately owned, Breighton	
U-1215	DH115 Vampire T11 (XE998)	Solent Sky, Southampton	
U-1229	DH115 Vampire T55 (G-HATD)	*Sold to the USA, January 2019*	
V-54	SE3130 Alouette II (G-BVSD)	Privately owned, Glos	

UNITED ARAB EMIRATES

Serial	Type (code/other identity)	Owner/operator, location or fate	Notes
DU-103	Bell 206B JetRanger II	Privately owned, Coney Park, Leeds	

USA

Serial	Type (code/other identity)	Owner/operator, location or fate	Notes
-	Noorduyn AT-16 Harvard IIB (KLu B-168)	American Air Museum, Duxford	
001	Ryan ST-3KR Recruit (G-BYPY)	Privately owned, Goodwood	
07	Boeing-Stearman PT-17 Kaydet (N62658)	Privately owned, Hurstbourne Tarrant, Hants	
14	Boeing-Stearman A75N-1 Kaydet (3486/G-ISDN)	Privately owned, Oaksey Park	

Notes	Serial	Type (code/other identity)	Owner/operator, location or fate
	18	Agusta-Bell AB204B (MM80279/*MM80270*)	MAG36-UK, Kent
	23	Fairchild PT-23 (N49272)	Privately owned, Sleap
	26	Boeing-Stearman A75N-1 Kaydet (G-BAVO)	Privately owned, Enstone
	27	Boeing-Stearman N2S-3 Kaydet (4304/G-CJYK)	Privately owned, Enstone
	27	NA SNJ-7 Texan (90678/G-BRVG)	Privately owned, Rochester
	28	Boeing-Stearman PT-27 Kaydet (42-15666/G-CKSR)	Privately owned, Enstone
	31	Boeing-Stearman A75N-1 Kaydet (42-16338/G-KAYD)	Privately owned, Enstone
	43	Noorduyn AT-16 Harvard IIB (43-13064/G-AZSC) [SC]	Privately owned, Goodwood
	44	Boeing-Stearman D75N-1 Kaydet (42-15852/G-DINS)	Privately owned, Duxford
	72	NA SNJ-5 Texan (42-85897/*431917*/G-DHHF) [JF]	DH Heritage Flights Ltd, Compton Abbas
	85	WAR P-47 Thunderbolt <R> (G-BTBI)	Privately owned, Perth
	104	Boeing-Stearman PT-13D Kaydet (42-16931/N4712V) [W]	Privately owned, Hardwick, Norfolk
	107	Boeing-Stearman PT-17 Kaydet (42-16107/N62658)	Privately owned, Hurstbourne Tarrant, Hants
	112	Boeing-Stearman PT-13D Kaydet (42-17397/G-BSWC)	Privately owned, Gloucester
	131	Boeing-Stearman PT-17 Kaydet (38254/N74677)	Privately owned, Enstone
	164	Boeing-Stearman PT-13B Kaydet (41-0823/N60320)	Privately owned, Fenland
	286	Boeing-Stearman N2S-4 Kaydet (55749/N10053)	Privately owned, Streethay, Staffs
	317	Boeing-Stearman PT-18 Kaydet (41-61042/G-CIJN)	Privately owned, Goodwood
	379	Boeing-Stearman PT-13D Kaydet (42-14865/G-ILLE)	Privately owned, Hohenems, Austria
	399	Boeing-Stearman N2S-5 Kaydet (38495/N67193)	Privately owned, Gelnhausen, Germany
	408	Boeing-Stearman A75 Kaydet (4280/G-FRDM)	Privately owned, Enstone
	441	Boeing-Stearman N2S-4 Kaydet (30010/G-BTFG)	Privately owned, Postling, Kent
	443	Boeing-Stearman E75 Kaydet (N43YP) [6018]	Privately owned, Bicester
	466	Boeing-Stearman PT-13A Kaydet (37-0089/G-PTBA)	Privately owned, Gloucester
	540	Piper L-4H Grasshopper (43-29877/G-BCNX)	Privately owned, Monewden
	560	Bell UH-1H Iroquois (73-22077/G-HUEY)	Privately owned, North Weald
	578	Boeing-Stearman N2S-5 Kaydet (N1364V)	Privately owned, North Weald
	586	Boeing-Stearman N2S-3 Kaydet (07874/N74650)	Privately owned, Seppe, The Netherlands
	628	Beech D17S (44-67761/N18V)	Privately owned, stored East Garston, Bucks
	669	Boeing-Stearman A75N-1 Kaydet (37869/G-CCXA)	Privately owned, Old Buckenham
	671	Boeing-Stearman PT-13D Kaydet (61181/G-CGPY)	Privately owned, Gloucester
	699	Boeing-Stearman N2S-3 Kaydet (38233/G-CCXB)	Privately owned, Goodwood
	716	Boeing-Stearman PT-13D Kaydet (42-17553/N1731B)	Privately owned, Compton Abbas
	718	Boeing-Stearman PT-13D Kaydet (42-17555/N5345N)	Privately owned, Tibenham
	744	Boeing-Stearman A75N-1 Kaydet (42-16532/OO-USN)	Privately owned, Wevelgem, Belgium
	805	Boeing-Stearman PT-17 Kaydet (42-17642/N3922B)	Privately owned, Tibenham
	854	Ryan PT-22 Recruit (41-20854/G-BTBH)	Privately owned, Goodwood
	855	Ryan PT-22 Recruit (41-15510/N56421)	Privately owned, Sleap
	897	Aeronca 11AC Chief (G-BJEV) [E]	Privately owned, English Bicknor, Glos
	985	Boeing-Stearman PT-13D Kaydet (42-16930/OO-OPS)	Privately owned, Brasschaat, Belgium
	1102	Boeing-Stearman N2S-5 Kaydet (43449/G-AZLE) [102]	DH Heritage Flights Ltd, Compton Abbas
	1164	Beech D18S (G-BKGL)	Privately owned, Leicester
	3072	NA T-6G Texan (49-3072/G-TEXN) [72]	*Repainted as KF402, May 2018*
	3397	Boeing-Stearman N2S-3 Kaydet (G-OBEE) [174]	Privately owned, Old Buckenham
	3403	Boeing-Stearman N2S-3 Kaydet (N75TQ) [180]	Privately owned, Tibenham
	3583	Piper L-4B Grasshopper (45-0583/G-FINT) [44-D]	Privately owned, Eggesford
	3681	Piper L-4J Grasshopper (44-80248/G-AXGP)	Privately owned, Bentwaters
	4406	Naval Aircraft Factory N3N-3 (G-ONAF) [12]	Privately owned, Sandown
	4826	Boeing-Stearman PT-17 Kaydet (42-16663/G-CJIN) [582]	Privately owned, Enstone
	6136	Boeing-Stearman A75N-1 Kaydet(42-16136/G-BRUJ) [205]	Privately owned, Liverpool
	6771	Republic F-84F Thunderstreak (BAF FU-6)	RAF Museum, stored Cosford
	7797	Aeronca L-16A Grasshopper (47-0797/G-BFAF)	Privately owned, Finmere
	8242	NA F-86A Sabre (48-0242) [FU-242]	Midland Air Museum, Coventry
	01532	Northrop F-5E Tiger II <R> (BAPC 336)	RAF Alconbury on display
	02538	Fairchild PT-19B (N33870)	Privately owned, Mendlesham, Suffolk
	07539	Boeing-Stearman N2S-3 Kaydet (N63590) [143]	Privately owned, North Weald
	14286	Lockheed T-33A Shooting Star (51-4286)	IWM, stored Duxford
	O-14419	Lockheed T-33A Shooting Star (51-4419)	Midland Air Museum, Coventry
	14863	NA AT-6D Harvard III (41-33908/G-BGOR)	Privately owned, Rednal
	15372	Piper L-18C Super Cub (51-15372/N123SA) [372-A]	Privately owned, Crowfield
	15979	Hughes OH-6A Cayuse (69-15979)	RAF Mildenhall, instructional use
	15990	Bell AH-1F Hueycobra (70-15990)	Army Flying Museum, Middle Wallop

Serial	Type (code/other identity)	Owner/operator, location or fate	Notes
16011	Hughes OH-6A Cayuse (69-16011/G-OHGA)	Privately owned, Wesham, Lancs	
16037	Piper J-3C-65 Cub (G-BSFD)	Privately owned, Sleap	
16171	NA F-86D Sabre (51-6171)	North-East Aircraft Museum, Usworth	
16445	Bell AH-1F Hueycobra (69-16445)	Defence Academy of the UK, Shrivenham	
16506	Hughes OH-6A Cayuse (67-16506)	The Helicopter Museum, Weston-super-Mare	
16544	NA AT-6A Texan (41-16544/N13FY) [FY]	Privately owned, Hilversum, The Netherlands	
16579	Bell UH-1H Iroquois (66-16579)	The Helicopter Museum, Weston-super-Mare	
16718	Lockheed T-33A Shooting Star (51-6718) [TR-999]	City of Norwich Aviation Museum	
O-16957	Cessna L-19A Bird Dog (N51-16957/N5308G)	Privately owned, Sleap	
17692	NA T-28S Fennec (51-7692/G-TROY) [TL-692]	Privately owned, Duxford	
17962	Lockheed SR-71A Blackbird (61-7962)	American Air Museum, Duxford	
18263	Boeing-Stearman PT-17 Kaydet (41-8263/N38940) [822]	Privately owned, Tibenham	
19252	Lockheed T-33A Shooting Star (51-9252)	Bentwaters Cold War Museum	
21300	Cessna O-2A Super Skymaster (67-21300/N590D)	Privately owned, Lelystad, The Netherlands	
21509	Bell UH-1H Iroquois (72-21509/G-UHIH)	Privately owned, Wesham, Lancs	
21605	Bell UH-1H Iroquois (72-21605)	American Air Museum, Duxford	
24538	Kaman HH-43F Huskie (62-4535)	Midland Air Museum, Coventry	
24568	Cessna L-19E Bird Dog (LN-WNO)	Army Aviation Norway, Kjeller, Norway	
24582	Cessna L-19E Bird Dog (G-VDOG)	Privately owned, Dundee	
28521	CCF T-6J Texan(52-8521/G-TVIJ) [TA-521]	Privately owned, Woodchurch, Kent	
28562	CCF T-6J Texan (52-8562/20310/G-BSBG) [TA-562]	Privately owned, Liverpool	
30274	Piper AE-1 Cub Cruiser (N203SA)	Privately owned, Nangis, France	
30861	NA TB-25J Mitchell (44-30861/N9089Z)	Privately owned,	
31145	Piper L-4B Grasshopper (43-1145/G-BBLH) [26-G]	Privately owned, Biggin Hill	
31430	Piper L-4B Grasshopper (43-1430/G-BHVV)	Privately owned, Perranporth	
31952	Aeronca O-58B Defender (G-BRPR)	Privately owned, Belchamp Water	
34037	NA TB-25N Mitchell (44-29366/N9115Z/8838M)	RAF Museum, Hendon	
34064	NA B-25J Mitchell (44-31171/N7614C) [8U]	American Air Museum, Duxford	
36922	Titan T-51 Mustang (G-CMPC) [WD-Y]	Privately owned, Benwick, Cambs	
37414	McD F-4C Phantom II (63-7414)	Midland Air Museum, stored Coventry	
39624	Wag Aero Sport Trainer (EI-GMH) [39-D]	Privately owned, Abbeyshrule, Eire	
41386	Thomas-Morse S4 Scout <R> (G-MJTD)	Privately owned, Lutterworth	
42165	NA F-100D Super Sabre (54-2165) [VM]	IWM, stored Duxford	
42196	NA F-100D Super Sabre (54-2196)	Norfolk & Suffolk Avn Museum, Flixton	
43517	Boeing-Stearman N2S-5 Kaydet (G-NZSS) [227]	Privately owned, Woodchurch, Kent	
46214	Grumman TBM-3E Avenger (69327/CF-KCG) [X-3]	IWM, Duxford	
51809	NA AT-6D Texan (41-33888/G-TXAN) [V-970]	Privately owned, Aalen, Germany	
53319	Grumman TBM-3E Avenger (HB-RDG) [19]	Privately owned, Lausanne, Switzerland	
54433	Lockheed T-33A Shooting Star (55-4433) [TR-433]	Norfolk & Suffolk Avn Museum, Flixton	
54884	Piper L-4J Grasshopper (45-4884/N61787) [57-D]	Privately owned, Sywell	
55771	Boeing-Stearman N2S-4 Kaydet (N68427) [427]	Privately owned, Bodmin	
56498	Douglas C-54Q Skymaster (N44914)	Privately owned, stored North Weald	
60312	McD F-101F Voodoo (56-0312)	Repainted in Canadian markings as 17447, 2018	
60344	Ryan Navion (N4956C)	Privately owned, Earls Colne	
60689	Boeing B-52D Stratofortress (56-0689)	American Air Museum, Duxford	
63319	NA F-100D Super Sabre (54-2269) [FW-319]	RAF Lakenheath, on display	
66692	Lockheed U-2CT (56-6692)	American Air Museum, Duxford	
70270	McD F-101B Voodoo (57-270) (fuselage)	Midland Air Museum, stored Coventry	
80105	Replica SE5a <R> (PH-WWI/G-CCBN) [19]	Privately owned, White Waltham	
82062	DHC U-6A Beaver (58-2062)	Midland Air Museum, Coventry	
82127	Cessna 310 (G-APNJ)	Newark Air Museum, Winthorpe	
85061	NA SNJ-5 Texan (G-CHIA) [7F]	Privately owned, White Waltham	
86690	Grumman FM-2 Wildcat (G-KINL) [F-2]	Privately owned, Duxford	
96995	CV F4U-4 Corsair (OE-EAS) [BR-37]	Flying Bulls, Salzburg, Austria	
111836	NA AT-6C Harvard IIa (41-33262/G-TSIX) [JZ-6]	Privately owned, Gamston	
111989	Cessna L-19A Bird Dog (51-11989/N33600)	Army Flying Museum, Middle Wallop	
114700	NA T-6G Texan (51-14700/G-TOMC)	Privately owned, Netherthorpe	
115042	NA T-6G Texan (51-15042/G-BGHU) [TA-042]	Privately owned, Postling, Kent	
115227	NA T-6G Texan (51-15227/G-BKRA)	Privately owned, Gloucester	
115302	Piper L-18C Super Cub (51-15302/G-BJTP) [TP]	Privately owned, Defford	
115373	Piper L-18C Super Cub (51-15373/G-AYPM) [A-373]	Privately owned, Leicester	
115684	Piper L-21A Super Cub (51-15684/G-BKVM) [849-DC]	Privately owned, Dunkeswell	

Notes	Serial	Type (code/other identity)	Owner/operator, location or fate
	117415	Canadair CT-133 Silver Star (G-BYOY) [TR-415]	RAF Manston History Museum
	117529	Lockheed T-33A Shooting Star (17473) [TR-529]	Midland Air Museum, Coventry
	121714	Grumman F8F-2P Bearcat (G-RUMM) [201-B]	The Fighter Collection, Duxford
	123716	CV F4U-5NL Corsair (124541/D-FCOR) [19-WF]	Meier Motors, Bremgarten, Germany
	124143	Douglas AD-4NA Skyraider (F-AZDP) [205-RM]	Amicale J-B Salis, la Ferté-Alais, France
	124485	Boeing B-17G Flying Fortress (44-85784/G-BEDF)[DF-A]	B-17 Preservation Ltd, Duxford
	124724	CV F4U-5NL Corsair (F-AZEG) [22-NP]	Les Casques de Cuir, la Ferté-Alais, France
	126922	Douglas AD-4NA Skyraider (G-RADR) [503-H]	Kennet Aviation, North Weald
	134076	NA AT-6D Texan (41-34671/F-AZSC) [TA076]	Privately owned, Yvetot, France
	138179	NA T-28A Trojan (OE-ESA) [BA]	The Flying Bulls, Salzburg, Austria
	138266	NA T-28B Trojan (HB-RCT) [266-CT]	Jet Alpine Fighter, Sion, Switzerland
	138343	NA T-28B Trojan (N343NA) [212]	Privately owned, Siegerland, Germany
	140547	NA T-28C Trojan (F-AZHN) [IF-28]	Privately owned, Toussus le Noble, France
	140566	NA T-28C Trojan (N556EB) [252]	Privately owned, la Ferté-Alais, France
	146289	NA T-28C Trojan (N99153) [2W]	Norfolk & Suffolk Avn Museum, Flixton
	150225	WS58 Wessex 60 (G-AWOX) [123]	Privately owned, Lulsgate
	155454	NA OV-10B Bronco (158300/99+24/F-AZKM) [26]	Privately owned, Montelimar, France
	155529	McD F-4J(UK) Phantom II (ZE359) [AJ-114]	American Air Museum, Duxford
	155848	McD F-4S Phantom II [WT-11]	National Museum of Flight, E Fortune
	159233	HS AV-8A Harrier [CG-33]	IWM North, Salford Quays
	162068	McD AV-8B Harrier II <ff>	Privately owned, Thorpe Wood, N Yorks
	162071	McD AV-8B Harrier II (fuselage)	Rolls-Royce, Filton
	162074	McD AV-8B Harrier II <ff>	Privately owned, South Molton, Devon
	162730	McD AV-8B Harrier II <ff>	Privately owned, Liverpool
	162737	McD AV-8B Harrier II (fuselage) [38]	MoD/JARTS, Boscombe Down
	162958	McD AV-8B Harrier II <ff>	QinetiQ, Farnborough
	162964	McD AV-8B Harrier II <ff>	Harrier Heritage Centre, RAF Wittering
	162964	McD AV-8B Harrier II <rf>	Privately owned, Charlwood, Surrey
	163205	McD AV-8B Harrier II (fuselage)	Privately owned, Thorpe Wood, N Yorks
	163423	McD AV-8B Harrier II <ff>	QinetiQ, Boscombe Down
	163423	McD AV-8B Harrier II <rf>	Privately owned, Sproughton
	210766	Douglas C-47B Skytrain (composite) (K-1) [4U]	Wings Museum, Balcombe, W Sussex
	217786	Boeing-Stearman PT-17 Kaydet (41-8169/CF-EQS) [25]	American Air Museum, Duxford
	224319	Douglas C-47B Skytrain (44-77047/G-AMSN) <ff>	Privately owned, Sussex
	226413	Republic P-47D Thunderbolt (45-49192/N47DD) [UN-Z]	American Air Museum, Duxford
	234539	Fairchild PT-19B Cornell (42-34539/N50429) [63]	Privately owned, Dunkeswell
	236657	Piper L-4A Grasshopper (42-36657/G-BGSJ) [72-D]	Privately owned, Langport, Somerset
	237123	Waco CG-4A Hadrian <R> (fuselage)	Yorkshire Air Museum, Elvington
	238133	Boeing B-17G Flying Fortress (44-83735/F-BDRS) [C]	American Air Museum, Duxford
	238410	Piper L-4A Grasshopper (42-38410/G-BHPK) [44-A]	Privately owned, Tibenham
	241079	Waco CG-4A Hadrian <R> (BAPC 370)	RAF Museum, stored Cosford
	243809	Waco CG-4A Hadrian (BAPC 185)	Army Flying Museum, Middle Wallop
	252983	Schweizer TG-3A (42-52983/N66630)	IWM Duxford, stored
	285068	NA AT-6D Texan (42-85068/G-KAMY)	Kennet Aviation, North Weald/Yeovilton
	298177	Stinson L-5A Sentinel (42-98177/N6438C) [8-R]	Privately owned, Tibenham
	313048	NA AT-6D Texan (44-81506/G-TDJN)	Privately owned, Gloucester
	314887	Fairchild Argus III (43-14887/G-AJPI)	Privately owned, Eelde, The Netherlands
	315509	Douglas C-47A Skytrain (43-15509/G-BHUB) [W7-S]	American Air Museum, Duxford
	319764	Waco CG-4A Hadrian (237123/BAPC 157) (fuselage)	Yorkshire Air Museum, Elvington
	329282	Piper J-3C-65 Cub (N46779)	Privately owned, Abbots Bromley
	329405	Piper L-4H Grasshopper (43-29405/G-BCOB) [23-A]	Privately owned, Bicester
	329417	Piper L-4A Grasshopper (42-38400/G-BDHK)	Privately owned, English Bicknor, Glos
	329471	Piper L-4H Grasshopper (43-29471/G-BGXA) [44-F]	Privately owned, Martley, Worcs
	329601	Piper L-4H Grasshopper (43-29601/G-AXHR) [44-D]	Privately owned, Nayland
	329707	Piper L-4H Grasshopper (43-29707/G-BFBY) [44-S]	Privately owned, Old Buckenham
	329854	Piper L-4H Grasshopper (43-29854/G-BMKC) [44-R]	Privately owned, Biggin Hill
	329934	Piper L-4H Grasshopper (43-29934/G-BCPH) [72-B]	Privately owned, Garford, Oxon
	330238	Piper L-4H Grasshopper (43-30238/G-LIVH) [24-A]	Privately owned, Yarcombe, Devon
	330244	Piper L-4H Grasshopper (43-30244/G-CGIY) [46-C]	Privately owned, Church Fenton
	330314	Piper L-4H Grasshopper (43-30314/G-BAET)	Privately owned, Winwick, Cambs
	330372	Piper L-4H Grasshopper (43-30372/G-AISX)	Privately owned, Booker
	330426	Piper L-4J Grasshopper (45-4884/N61787) [53-K]	Privately owned, Sywell

Serial	Type (code/other identity)	Owner/operator, location or fate	Notes
330485	Piper L-4H Grasshopper (43-30485/G-AJES) [44-C]	Privately owned, Shifnal	
379994	Piper J-3L-65 Cub (G-BPUR) [52-J]	Privately owned, Popham	
411622	NA P-51D Mustang (44-74427/F-AZSB) [G4-C]	Privately owned, Melun, France	
411631	NA P-51D Mustang (44-73979/472218) [MX-V]	American Air Museum, Duxford	
413317	NA P-51D Mustang (44-74409/N51RT) [VF-B]	RAF Museum, Hendon	
413357	NA P-51D Mustang <R> [B7-R]	Privately owned, Byfleet, Surrey	
413573	NA P-51D Mustang (44-73415/9133M/N6526D) [B6-V]	RAF Museum, stored Cosford	
413578	NA P-51D Mustang (44-74923/PH-JAT) [C5-W]	Privately owned, Lelystad, The Netherlands	
413926	Stewart S-51 Mustang (G-CGOI) [E2-S]	Privately owned, Benwick, Cambs	
414237	NA P-51D Mustang (44-73656/F-AZXS) [HO-W]	Sold to the USA, 2018	
414251	NA TF-51D Mustang (44-84847/G-TFSI) [WZ-I]	Privately owned, Duxford	
414673	Bonsall Replica Mustang (G-BDWM) [LH-I]	Privately owned, Gamston	
414907	Titan T-51 Mustang (G-DHYS) [CY-S]	Privately owned, Pershore	
431212	Douglas C-47A Skytrain (42-100884/N147DC) [D]	Privately owned, North Weald	
431917	NA SNJ-5 Texan (42-85897/N6972C/G-DHHF)	Repainted as 72, September 2018	
433915	Consolidated PBV-1A Canso A (RCAF 11005/G-PBYA)	Privately owned, Duxford	
434602	Douglas A-26B Invader (44-34602/LN-IVA) [B]	Nordic Warbirds, Västerås, Sweden	
436021	Piper J-3C-65 Cub (G-BWEZ)	Privately owned, Archerfield, Lothian	
441968	Titan T-51 Mustang (G-FION) [VF-E]	Privately owned, Netherthorpe	
442268	Noorduyn AT-16 Harvard IIb (KF568/LN-TEX) [TA-268]	Privately owned, Kjeller, Norway	
454467	Piper L-4J Grasshopper (45-4467/G-BILI) [44-J]	Privately owned, RAF Halton	
454537	Piper L-4J Grasshopper (45-4537/G-BFDL) [04-J]	Privately owned, Shempston Farm, Lossiemouth	
461748	Boeing B-29A Superfortress (44-61748/G-BHDK) [Y]	American Air Museum, Duxford	
463209	NA P-51D Mustang <R> (BAPC 255) [WZ-S]	IWM Duxford	
464005	NA P-51D Mustang (44-64005/N51CK) [E9-Z]	Privately owned, Sywell	
472216	NA P-51D Mustang (44-72216/G-BIXL) [HO-M]	Privately owned, Goodwood	
472218	Titan T-51 Mustang (G-MUZY) [WZ-I]	Privately owned, Tibenham	
472773	NA P-51D Mustang (44-72773/D-FPSI) [QP-M]	Meier Motors, Bremgarten, Germany	
472922	NA TF-51D Mustang (44-72922/OO-RYL) [L2-W]	Privately owned, Antwerp, Belgium	
473871	NA TF-51D Mustang (44-73871/D-FTSI) [TF-871]	Meier Motors, Bremgarten, Germany	
474008	Jurca MJ77 Gnatsum (G-PSIR) [VF-R]	Privately owned, Fishburn	
474425	NA P-51D Mustang (44-74425/PH-PSI) [OC-G]	Privately owned, Lelystad, The Netherlands	
479712	Piper L-4H Grasshopper (44-79826/G-AHIP) [8-R]	Privately owned, Coleford	
479744	Piper L-4H Grasshopper (44-79744/G-BGPD) [49-M]	Privately owned, Marsh, Bucks	
479766	Piper L-4H Grasshopper (44-79766/G-BKHG) [63-D]	Privately owned, Frogland Cross	
479781	Piper L-4H Grasshopper (44-79781/G-AISS)	Privately owned, Insch (under restoration)	
479878	Piper L-4H Grasshopper (44-79878/G-BEUI) [MF-D]	Privately owned, Blackpool	
479897	Piper L-4H Grasshopper (44-79897/G-BOXJ) [JD]	Privately owned, Rochester	
480015	Piper L-4H Grasshopper (44-80015/G-AKIB) [44-M]	Privately owned, Perranporth	
480133	Piper L-4J Grasshopper (44-80133/G-BDCD) [44-B]	Privately owned, Slinfold	
480173	Piper L-4J Grasshopper (44-80609/G-RRSR) [57-H]	Privately owned, Shotteswell	
480321	Piper L-4J Grasshopper (44-80321/G-FRAN) [44-H]	Privately owned, Rayne, Essex	
480480	Piper L-4J Grasshopper (44-80480/G-BECN) [44-E]	Privately owned, Rayne, Essex	
480636	Piper L-4J Grasshopper (44-80636/G-AXHP) [58-A]	Privately owned, Spanhoe	
480723	Piper L-4J Grasshopper (44-80723/G-BFZB) [E5-J]	Privately owned, Egginton	
480752	Piper L-4J Grasshopper (44-80752/G-BCXJ) [39-E]	Privately owned, Melksham	
481273	CCF T-6J Harvard IV (20306/G-CJWE)	Privately owned, Leicester	
483868	Boeing B-17G Flying Fortress (44-83868/N5237V) [A-N]	RAF Museum, Hendon	
484786	NA F-6D Mustang (44-84786/N51BS) [5M-K]	Privately owned, Duxford (damaged)	
493209	NA T-6G Texan (49-3209/G-DDMV/41)	Privately owned, Headcorn	
549192	Republic P-47D Thunderbolt (45-49192/G-THUN) [F4-J]	Privately owned, Duxford	
779465	Hiller UH-12C (N5315V)	Privately owned, Lower Upham, Hants	
2106638	Titan T-51 Mustang (G-CIFD) [E9-R]	Privately owned, Shobdon	
2100882	Douglas C-47A Skytrain (42-100882/N473DC) [3X-P]	Privately owned, East Kirkby	
2100884	Douglas C-47A Skytrain (42-100884/N147DC) [L4-D]	Repainted as 431212, 2018	
2105915	Curtiss P-40N Kittyhawk (42-105915/F-AZKU)	France's Flying Warbirds, Melun, France	
03-08003	B-V CH-47F Chinook [DT]	RAF Odiham, at main gate	
03-33119	General Atomics MQ-1B Predator [CH]	RAF Museum, Hendon	
03-33119	General Atomics MQ-1B Predator [CH]	IWM, Duxford	
3-1923	Aeronca O-58B Defender (43-1923/G-BRHP)	Privately owned, Chiseldon	
18-2001	Piper L-18C Super Cub (52-2401/G-BIZV)	Privately owned, Wicklow, Ireland	
22-296	Eberhardt SE5E Replica (G-BLXT)	Privately owned, Sywell	

Notes	Serial	Type (code/other identity)	Owner/operator, location or fate
	39-139	Beech YC-43 Traveler (N295BS)	Duke of Brabant AF, Eindhoven, The Netherlands
	39-0285	Curtiss P-40B Warhawk	The Fighter Collection, stored Duxford (wreck)
	39-0287	Curtiss P-40B Warhawk	The Fighter Collection, stored Duxford (wreck)
	40-2538	Fairchild PT-19A Cornell (N33870)	Privately owned, Mendlesham
	41-8689	Boeing-Stearman PT-17D Kaydet (G-BIXN) (frame)	Privately owned, Rendcomb
	41-13357	Curtiss P-40C Warhawk (G-CIIO) [160,10AB]	The Fighter Collection, Duxford
	41-19393	Douglas A-20C Havoc (wreck)	Wings Museum, Balcombe, W Sussex
	41-33275	NA AT-6C Texan (G-BICE) [CE]	Privately owned, Great Oakley, Essex
	41-35253	Martin B-26C Marauder <rf>	Boxted Airfield Museum
	42-66841	Lockheed P-38H Lightning [153]	Privately owned, Bentwaters
	42-12417	Noorduyn AT-16 Harvard IIb (KLu. B-163)	Newark Air Museum, Winthorpe
	42-35870	Taylorcraft DCO-65 (G-BWLJ) [129]	Privately owned, Nayland
	42-46703	Stinson AT-19 Reliant (FK877/N69745)	Privately owned, Birmingham
	42-58678	Taylorcraft DF-65 (G-BRIY) [IY]	Privately owned, Carlisle
	42-78044	Aeronca 11AC Chief (G-BRXL)	Privately owned, Andrewsfield
	42-84555	NA AT-6D Harvard III (FAP.1662/G-ELMH) [EP-H]	Privately owned, Hardwick, Norfolk
	42-93510	Douglas C-47A Skytrain [CM] <ff>	Privately owned, Kew
	43-9628	Douglas A-20G Havoc <ff>	Privately owned, Hinckley, Leics
	43-11137	Bell P-63C Kingcobra (wreck)	Wings Museum, Balcombe, W Sussex
	43-21664	Douglas A-20G Havoc (wreck)	Wings Museum, Balcombe, W Sussex
	43-35943	Beech 3N (G-BKRN) [943]	Beech Restorations, Bruntingthorpe
	43-36140	NA B-25J Mitchell <ff>	Wings Museum, Balcombe, W Sussex
	44-4315	Bell P-63C Kingcobra	Wings Museum, Balcombe, W Sussex
	44-4368	Bell P-63C Kingcobra	Privately owned, Surrey
	44-13954	NA P-51D Mustang (G-UAKE)	Mustang Restoration Co Ltd, Coventry
	44-14574	NA P-51D Mustang (fuselage)	East Essex Aviation Museum, Clacton
	44-42914	Douglas DC-4 (N31356) <ff>	Privately owned, Burtonwood
	44-51228	Consolidated B-24M Liberator [EC-493]	American Air Museum, Duxford
	44-79609	Piper L-4H Grasshopper (G-BHXY) [PR]	Privately owned, Bealbury, Cornwall
	44-79649	Piper L-4H Grasshopper (G-AIIH)	Privately owned, Stonesfield, Oxon
	44-80594	Piper L-4J Grasshopper (G-BEDJ)	Privately owned, White Waltham
	44-80647	Piper L-4J Grasshopper (D-EGAF)	Privately owned, Donauwörth, Germany
	45-5772	Piper J-5A Cub Cruiser (G-BSXT)	Privately owned, Norwich
	51-9036	Lockheed T-33A Shooting Star	Newark Air Museum, Winthorpe
	51-15319	Piper L-18C Super Cub (G-FUZZ) [A-319]	Privately owned, Elvington
	51-15555	Piper L-18C Super Cub (G-OSPS) [A-555]	Privately owned, Andrewsfield
	52-8543	CCF T-6J Texan (G-BUKY) [66]	*Sold to Germany, 29 January 2019*
	54-005	NA F-100D Super Sabre (54-2163) [HA]	Dumfries & Galloway Avn Mus, Dumfries
	54-174	NA F-100D Super Sabre (54-2174) [SM]	Midland Air Museum, Coventry
	54-2223	NA F-100D Super Sabre	Newark Air Museum, Winthorpe
	54-2445	Piper L-21B Super Cub (G-OTAN) [A-445]	Privately owned, Hawarden
	54-2447	Piper L-21B Super Cub (G-SCUB)	Privately owned, Anwick
	55-138354	NA T-28B Trojan (138354/N1328B) [TL-354]	Privately owned, Antwerp, Belgium
	63-699	McD F-4C Phantom II (63-7699) [CG]	Midland Air Museum, Coventry
	64-0553	Lockheed WC-130E Hercules <ff>	RAF Museum, Hendon
	64-17657	Douglas B-26K Counter Invader (N99218) <ff>	WWII Remembrance Museum, Handcross, W Sussex
	65-777	McD F-4C Phantom II (63-7419) [SA]	RAF Lakenheath, on display
	66-374	Helio H.295 Super Courier (G-BAGT) [EO]	Privately owned, Spanhoe
	67-120	GD F-111E Aardvark (67-0120) [UH]	American Air Museum, Duxford
	68-0060	GD F-111E Aardvark <ff>	Dumfries & Galloway Avn Mus, Dumfries
	68-8284	Sikorsky MH-53M Pave Low IV	RAF Museum, Cosford
	70-0389	GD F-111E Aardvark (68-0011) [LN]	RAF Lakenheath, on display
	72-1447	GD F-111F Aardvark <ff>	American Air Museum, Duxford
	74-0177	GD F-111F Aardvark [FN]	RAF Museum, Cosford
	76-020	McD F-15A Eagle (76-0020) [BT]	American Air Museum, Duxford
	76-124	McD F-15B Eagle (76-0124) [LN]	RAF Lakenheath, instructional use
	77-259	Fairchild A-10A Thunderbolt (77-0259) [AR]	American Air Museum, Duxford
	80-219	Fairchild GA-10A Thunderbolt (80-0219) [WR]	Bentwaters Cold War Museum
	82-23762	B-V CH-47D Chinook <ff>	RAF Odiham, instructional use
	83-24104	B-V CH-47D Chinook [BN] <ff>	RAF Museum, Hendon

Serial	Type (code/other identity)	Owner/operator, location or fate	Notes
86-180	McD F-15A Eagle (74-0131) [LN]	RAF Lakenheath, on display	
	(starboard side only, painted as 86-169 on port side)		
86-01677	B-V CH-47D Chinook	RAF, stored Odiham	
89-00159	B-V CH-47D Chinook	RAF, stored Odiham	
108-1601	Stinson 108-1 Voyager (G-CFGE) [H]	Privately owned, Spanhoe	
146-11042	Wolf W-11 Boredom Fighter (G-BMZX) [7]	Privately owned, Popham	
146-11083	Wolf W-11 Boredom Fighter (G-BNAI) [5]	Privately owned, Haverfordwest	
A3-3	NA P-51D Mustang (44-72035/G-SIJJ)	Hangar 11 Collection, North Weald	
S666	Noorduyn AT-16 Harvard IIb (KF435) [BS]	Maidenhead Heritage Centre	
X-17	Curtiss P-40F Warhawk (41-19841/G-CGZP)	The Fighter Collection, Duxford	
CY-D	NA TF-51D Mustang (44-84847/G-TFSI)	*Repainted as 414251, July 2018*	
CY-G	Titan T-51 Mustang (G-TSIM)	Privately owned, Shobdon	
PA50	Curtiss P-36C Hawk (38-0210/G-CIXJ)	The Fighter Collection, Duxford	

YUGOSLAVIA

30131	Soko P-2 Kraguj [131]	Privately owned, stored Minskip, N Yorks	
30140	Soko P-2 Kraguj (G-RADA) [140]	Privately owned, Fishburn	
30146	Soko P-2 Kraguj (G-BSXD) [146]	Privately owned, Fishburn	
30149	Soko P-2 Kraguj (G-SOKO) [149]	Privately owned, Fenland	
51109	UTVA-66 (YU-DLG)	Privately owned, Morpeth	

66 DHC-1 Chipmunks were licence-built by OGMA (Oficinas Gerais de Material Aeronáutico) in Portugal and several of these have now appeared in UK skies. 1365 is an OGMA-built Chipmunk T20, on the UK civil register as G-DHPM and based at Sywell.

Notes	Serial	Type (code/other identity)	Owner/operator, location or fate
	C7	Avro 631 Cadet (EI-AGO)	IAC Museum, Baldonnel
	34	Miles M14A Magister I (N5392)	National Museum of Ireland, Dublin
	141	Avro 652A Anson C19	IAC Museum, Baldonnel
	164	DHC1 Chipmunk T20	IAC Museum, Baldonnel
	168	DHC1 Chipmunk T20 (EI-HFA)	Irish Historic Flight, Ballyboy
	169	DHC1 Chipmunk 22 (WD305/EI-HFB)	Irish Historic Flight, Ballyboy
	170	DHC1 Chipmunk 22 (WP857/EI-HFC)	Irish Historic Flight, Ballyboy
	172	DHC1 Chipmunk T20	IAC, stored Baldonnel
	173	DHC1 Chipmunk T20	South East Aviation Enthusiasts, Dromod
	176	DH104 Dove 4 (VP-YKF)	South East Aviation Enthusiasts, Waterford
	183	Percival P56 Provost T51	IAC Museum, Baldonnel
	184	Percival P56 Provost T51	South East Aviation Enthusiasts, Dromod
	187	DH115 Vampire T55 <ff>	South East Aviation Enthusiasts, Dromod
	191	DH115 Vampire T55	IAC Museum, Baldonnel
	192	DH115 Vampire T55 <ff>	South East Aviation Enthusiasts, Dromod
	195	Sud SA316 Alouette III (F-WJDH)	IAC Museum, stored Baldonnel
	198	DH115 Vampire T11 (XE977)	National Museum of Ireland, Dublin
	199	DHC1 Chipmunk T20	IAC, stored Baldonnel
	202	Sud SA316 Alouette III	Ulster Aviation Society, Long Kesh
	203	Reims-Cessna FR172H	IAC No 104 Sqn/1 Operations Wing, Baldonnel
	205	Reims-Cessna FR172H	IAC No 104 Sqn/1 Operations Wing, Baldonnel
	206	Reims-Cessna FR172H	IAC No 104 Sqn/1 Operations Wing, Baldonnel
	207	Reims-Cessna FR172H	IAC, stored Waterford
	208	Reims-Cessna FR172H	IAC No 104 Sqn/1 Operations Wing, Baldonnel
	210	Reims-Cessna FR172H	IAC No 104 Sqn/1 Operations Wing, Baldonnel
	215	Fouga CM170R Super Magister	Dublin Institute of Technology
	216	Fouga CM170R Super Magister	IAC Museum, Baldonnel
	218	Fouga CM170R Super Magister	IAC, stored Baldonnel
	219	Fouga CM170R Super Magister	IAC Museum, Baldonnel
	220	Fouga CM170R Super Magister	Cork University, instructional use
	221	Fouga CM170R Super Magister [3-KE]	IAC Museum, stored Baldonnel
	231	SIAI SF-260WE Warrior	IAC Museum, Baldonnel
	240	Beech Super King Air 200MR	IAC No 102 Sqn/1 Operations Wing, Baldonnel
	251	Grumman G1159C Gulfstream IV (N17584)	IAC No 102 Sqn/1 Operations Wing, Baldonnel
	252	Airtech CN.235 MPA Persuader	IAC No 101 Sqn/1 Operations Wing, Baldonnel
	253	Airtech CN.235 MPA Persuader	IAC No 101 Sqn/1 Operations Wing, Baldonnel
	254	PBN-2T Defender 4000 (G-BWPN)	IAC No 106 Sqn/1 Operations Wing, Baldonnel
	256	Eurocopter EC135T-1 (G-BZRM)	IAC No 106 Sqn/1 Operations Wing, Baldonnel
	258	Gates Learjet 45 (N5009T)	IAC No 102 Sqn/1 Operations Wing, Baldonnel
	260	Pilatus PC-9M (HB-HQS)	IAC Flying Training School, Baldonnel
	261	Pilatus PC-9M (HB-HQT)	IAC Flying Training School, Baldonnel
	262	Pilatus PC-9M (HB-HQU)	IAC Flying Training School, Baldonnel
	263	Pilatus PC-9M (HB-HQV)	IAC Flying Training School, Baldonnel
	264	Pilatus PC-9M (HB-HQW)	IAC Flying Training School, Baldonnel
	266	Pilatus PC-9M (HB-HQY)	IAC Flying Training School, Baldonnel
	267	Pilatus PC-9M (HB-HQZ)	IAC Flying Training School, Baldonnel
	269	Pilatus PC-9M (HB-HXI)	IAC Flying Training School, Baldonnel
	270	Eurocopter EC135P-2 (D-HECF)	IAC No 302 Sqn/3 Operations Wing, Baldonnel
	271	Eurocopter EC135P-2 (D-HECB)	IAC No 302 Sqn/3 Operations Wing, Baldonnel
	272	Eurocopter EC135T-2 (G-CECT)	IAC No 106 Sqn/1 Operations Wing, Baldonnel
	274	AgustaWestland AW139	IAC No 301 Sqn/3 Operations Wing, Baldonnel
	275	AgustaWestland AW139	IAC No 301 Sqn/3 Operations Wing, Baldonnel
	276	AgustaWestland AW139	IAC No 301 Sqn/3 Operations Wing, Baldonnel
	277	AgustaWestland AW139	IAC No 301 Sqn/3 Operations Wing, Baldonnel
	278	AgustaWestland AW139	IAC No 301 Sqn/3 Operations Wing, Baldonnel
	279	AgustaWestland AW139	IAC No 301 Sqn/3 Operations Wing, Baldonnel
	2..	Pilatus PC.XII/47 (HB-FSF)	IAC (on order)
	2..	Pilatus PC.XII/47	IAC (on order)
	2..	Pilatus PC.XII/47	IAC (on order)

Serial	Type (code/other identity)	Owner/operator, location or fate	Notes

Aircraft included in this section include those likely to be seen visiting UK civil and military airfields on transport flights, exchange visits, exercises and for air shows. It is not a comprehensive list of *all* aircraft operated by the air arms concerned.

ALGERIA
Ministry of Defence

7T-VPC	Grumman G.1159C Gulfstream IVSP (1418)	Ministry of Defence, Boufarik	
7T-VPG	Gulfstream Aerospace Gulfstream V (617)	Ministry of Defence, Boufarik	
7T-VPM	Grumman G.1159C Gulfstream IVSP (1421)	Ministry of Defence, Boufarik	
7T-VPP	Airbus A.340-541	Ministry of Defence, Boufarik	
7T-VPR	Grumman G.1159C Gulfstream IVSP (1288)	Ministry of Defence, Boufarik	
7T-VPS	Grumman G.1159C Gulfstream IVSP (1291)	Ministry of Defence, Boufarik	

Force Aérienne Algérienne (FAA)/Al Quwwat al Jawwiya al Jaza'eriya

7T-WHA	Lockheed C-130H-30 Hercules (4997)	FAA 2 ETTL, Boufarik	
7T-WHB	Lockheed C-130H-30 Hercules (5224)	FAA 2 ETTL, Boufarik	
7T-WHD	Lockheed C-130H-30 Hercules (4987)	FAA 2 ETTL, Boufarik	
7T-WHE	Lockheed C-130H Hercules (4935)	FAA 2 ETTL, Boufarik	
7T-WHF	Lockheed C-130H Hercules (4934)	FAA 2 ETTL, Boufarik	
7T-WHI	Lockheed C-130H Hercules (4930)	FAA 2 ETTL, Boufarik	
7T-WHJ	Lockheed C-130H Hercules (4928)	FAA 2 ETTL, Boufarik	
7T-WHL	Lockheed C-130H-30 Hercules (4989)	FAA 2 ETTL, Boufarik	
7T-WHN	Lockheed C-130H-30 Hercules (4894)	FAA 2 ETTL, Boufarik	
7T-WHO	Lockheed C-130H-30 Hercules (4897)	FAA 2 ETTL, Boufarik	
7T-WHP	Lockheed C-130H-30 Hercules (4921)	FAA 2 ETTL, Boufarik	
7T-WHQ	Lockheed C-130H Hercules (4926)	FAA 2 ETTL, Boufarik	
7T-WHR	Lockheed C-130H Hercules (4924)	FAA 2 ETTL, Boufarik	
7T-WHS	Lockheed C-130H Hercules (4912)	FAA 2 ETTL, Boufarik	
7T-WHT	Lockheed C-130H Hercules (4911)	*Crashed Biskra, 3 June 2018*	
7T-WHY	Lockheed C-130H Hercules (4913)	FAA 2 ETTL, Boufarik	
7T-WHZ	Lockheed C-130H Hercules (4914)	FAA 2 ETTL, Boufarik	
7T-WIA	Ilyushin Il-76MD	FAA 347 ETS, Boufarik	
7T-WIB	Ilyushin Il-76MD	FAA 347 ETS, Boufarik	
7T-WIC	Ilyushin Il-76MD	FAA 347 ETS, Boufarik	
7T-WID	Ilyushin Il-76TD	FAA 347 ETS, Boufarik	
7T-WIE	Ilyushin Il-76TD	FAA 347 ETS, Boufarik	
7T-WIF	Ilyushin Il-78	FAA 357 ERV, Boufarik	
7T-WIG	Ilyushin Il-76TD	FAA 347 ETS, Boufarik	
7T-WIL	Ilyushin Il-78	FAA 357 ERV, Boufarik	
7T-WIM	Ilyushin Il-76TD	FAA 347 ETS, Boufarik	
7T-WIN	Ilyushin Il-78	FAA 357 ERV, Boufarik	
7T-WIP	Ilyushin Il-76TD	FAA 347 ETS, Boufarik	
7T-WIQ	Ilyushin Il-78	FAA 357 ERV, Boufarik	
7T-WIR	Ilyushin Il-76TD	FAA 347 ETS, Boufarik	
7T-WIS	Ilyushin Il-78	FAA 357 ERV, Boufarik	
7T-WIT	Ilyushin Il-76TD	FAA 347 ETS, Boufarik	
7T-WIU	Ilyushin Il-76TD	FAA 347 ETS, Boufarik	
7T-WIV	Ilyushin Il-76TD	*Crashed 11 April 2018, Boufarik*	

ANGOLA

D2-ANG	Bombardier Global Express XRS	Angola Government, Luanda	
D2-ANH	Bombardier Global Express	Angola Government, Luanda	

ARMENIA

701	Airbus A.319CJ-132	Armenian Government, Yerevan	

AUSTRALIA
Royal Australian Air Force (RAAF)

A9-656	Lockheed AP-3C Orion	*Sold as N656T, September 2018*	
A9-657	Lockheed EAP-3C Orion	RAAF 10 Sqn/92 Wing, Edinburgh, South Australia	
A9-659	Lockheed AP-3C Orion	RAAF 10 Sqn/92 Wing, Edinburgh, South Australia	
A9-660	Lockheed EAP-3C Orion	RAAF 10 Sqn/92 Wing, Edinburgh, South Australia	
A9-661	Lockheed AP-3C Orion	*Sold as N661MK, November 2018*	
A9-662	Lockheed AP-3C Orion	*Sold as N662JD, November 2018*	

Notes	Serial	Type (code/other identity)	Owner/operator, location or fate
	A9-664	Lockheed AP-3C Orion $	*Sold as N664SD, November 2018*
	A9-665	Lockheed AP-3C Orion	*Sold as N665BD, December 2018*
	A9-752	Lockheed AP-3C Orion	RAAF 10 Sqn/92 Wing, Edinburgh, South Australia
	A9-757	Lockheed AP-3C Orion	*Withdrawn from use and preserved at Darwin, 2019*
	A9-759	Lockheed AP-3C Orion	RAAF 10 Sqn/92 Wing, Edinburgh, South Australia
	A9-760	Lockheed AP-3C Orion	RAAF 10 Sqn/92 Wing, Edinburgh, South Australia
	A30-001	Boeing E-7A Wedgetail (737-7ES)	RAAF 2 Sqn/41 Wing, Canberra, ACT
	A30-002	Boeing E-7A Wedgetail (737-7ES)	RAAF 2 Sqn/41 Wing, Canberra, ACT
	A30-003	Boeing E-7A Wedgetail (737-7ES)	RAAF 2 Sqn/41 Wing, Canberra, ACT
	A30-004	Boeing E-7A Wedgetail (737-7ES)	RAAF 2 Sqn/41 Wing, Canberra, ACT
	A30-005	Boeing E-7A Wedgetail (737-7ES)	RAAF 2 Sqn/41 Wing, Canberra, ACT
	A30-006	Boeing E-7A Wedgetail (737-7ES)	RAAF 2 Sqn/41 Wing, Canberra, ACT
	A36-001	Boeing 737-7DT	RAAF 34 Sqn/84 Wing, Canberra, ACT
	A36-002	Boeing 737-7DF	RAAF 34 Sqn/84 Wing, Canberra, ACT
	A37-001	Canadair CL.604 Challenger	RAAF 34 Sqn/84 Wing, Canberra, ACT
	A37-002	Canadair CL.604 Challenger	RAAF 34 Sqn/84 Wing, Canberra, ACT
	A37-003	Canadair CL.604 Challenger	RAAF 34 Sqn/84 Wing, Canberra, ACT
	A39-001	Airbus KC-30A (A.330-203 MRTT)	RAAF 33 Sqn/84 Wing, Amberley, Queensland
	A39-002	Airbus KC-30A (A.330-203 MRTT)	RAAF 33 Sqn/84 Wing, Amberley, Queensland
	A39-003	Airbus KC-30A (A.330-203 MRTT)	RAAF 33 Sqn/84 Wing, Amberley, Queensland
	A39-004	Airbus KC-30A (A.330-203 MRTT)	RAAF 33 Sqn/84 Wing, Amberley, Queensland
	A39-005	Airbus KC-30A (A.330-203 MRTT)	RAAF 33 Sqn/84 Wing, Amberley, Queensland
	A39-006	Airbus KC-30A (A.330-203 MRTT) (VH-EBH)	RAAF 33 Sqn/84 Wing, Amberley, Queensland
	A39-007	Airbus KC-30A (A.330-203 MRTT) (VH-EBI)	Airbus, Getafe (on order)
	A41-206	Boeing C-17A Globemaster III (06-0206)	RAAF 36 Sqn/86 Wing, Amberley, Queensland
	A41-207	Boeing C-17A Globemaster III (06-0207)	RAAF 36 Sqn/86 Wing, Amberley, Queensland
	A41-208	Boeing C-17A Globemaster III (06-0208)	RAAF 36 Sqn/86 Wing, Amberley, Queensland
	A41-209	Boeing C-17A Globemaster III (06-0209)	RAAF 36 Sqn/86 Wing, Amberley, Queensland
	A41-210	Boeing C-17A Globemaster III (11-0210)	RAAF 36 Sqn/86 Wing, Amberley, Queensland
	A41-211	Boeing C-17A Globemaster III (12-0211)	RAAF 36 Sqn/86 Wing, Amberley, Queensland
	A41-212	Boeing C-17A Globemaster III (14-0001)	RAAF 36 Sqn/86 Wing, Amberley, Queensland
	A41-213	Boeing C-17A Globemaster III (14-0002)	RAAF 36 Sqn/86 Wing, Amberley, Queensland
	A47-001	Boeing P-8A Poseidon (N940DS)	RAAF 11 Sqn/92 Wing, Edinburgh, South Australia
	A47-002	Boeing P-8A Poseidon (N956DS)	RAAF 11 Sqn/92 Wing, Edinburgh, South Australia
	A47-003	Boeing P-8A Poseidon (N959DS)	RAAF 11 Sqn/92 Wing, Edinburgh, South Australia
	A47-004	Boeing P-8A Poseidon (N974DS)	RAAF 11 Sqn/92 Wing, Edinburgh, South Australia
	A47-005	Boeing P-8A Poseidon (N832DS)	RAAF 11 Sqn/92 Wing, Edinburgh, South Australia
	A47-006	Boeing P-8A Poseidon (N849DS)	RAAF 11 Sqn/92 Wing, Edinburgh, South Australia
	A47-007	Boeing P-8A Poseidon (N862DS)	RAAF 11 Sqn/92 Wing, Edinburgh, South Australia
	A47-008	Boeing P-8A Poseidon (N872DS)	RAAF (on order)
	A47-009	Boeing P-8A Poseidon	RAAF (on order)
	A47-010	Boeing P-8A Poseidon	RAAF (on order)
	A47-011	Boeing P-8A Poseidon	RAAF (on order)
	A47-012	Boeing P-8A Poseidon	RAAF (on order)
	A97-440	Lockheed C-130J-30 Hercules II	RAAF 37 Sqn/86 Wing, Richmond, NSW
	A97-441	Lockheed C-130J-30 Hercules II	RAAF 37 Sqn/86 Wing, Richmond, NSW
	A97-442	Lockheed C-130J-30 Hercules II	RAAF 37 Sqn/86 Wing, Richmond, NSW
	A97-447	Lockheed C-130J-30 Hercules II	RAAF 37 Sqn/86 Wing, Richmond, NSW
	A97-448	Lockheed C-130J-30 Hercules II	RAAF 37 Sqn/86 Wing, Richmond, NSW
	A97-449	Lockheed C-130J-30 Hercules II	RAAF 37 Sqn/86 Wing, Richmond, NSW
	A97-450	Lockheed C-130J-30 Hercules II	RAAF 37 Sqn/86 Wing, Richmond, NSW
	A97-464	Lockheed C-130J-30 Hercules II	RAAF 37 Sqn/86 Wing, Richmond, NSW
	A97-465	Lockheed C-130J-30 Hercules II	RAAF 37 Sqn/86 Wing, Richmond, NSW
	A97-466	Lockheed C-130J-30 Hercules II	RAAF 37 Sqn/86 Wing, Richmond, NSW
	A97-467	Lockheed C-130J-30 Hercules II	RAAF 37 Sqn/86 Wing, Richmond, NSW
	A97-468	Lockheed C-130J-30 Hercules II	RAAF 37 Sqn/86 Wing, Richmond, NSW

AUSTRIA
Öesterreichische Luftstreitkräfte (OL)

Notes	Serial	Type (code/other identity)	Owner/operator, location or fate
	3C-OA	Bell OH-58B Kiowa	OL Mehrzweckhubschrauberstaffel, Tulln
	3C-OB	Bell OH-58B Kiowa	OL Mehrzweckhubschrauberstaffel, Tulln
	3C-OC	Bell OH-58B Kiowa	OL Mehrzweckhubschrauberstaffel, Tulln

Serial	Type (code/other identity)	Owner/operator, location or fate	Notes
3C-OD	Bell OH-58B Kiowa	OL Mehrzweckhubschrauberstaffel, Tulln	
3C-OE	Bell OH-58B Kiowa	OL Mehrzweckhubschrauberstaffel, Tulln	
3C-OH	Bell OH-58B Kiowa	OL Mehrzweckhubschrauberstaffel, Tulln	
3C-OI	Bell OH-58B Kiowa	OL Mehrzweckhubschrauberstaffel, Tulln	
3C-OJ	Bell OH-58B Kiowa	OL Mehrzweckhubschrauberstaffel, Tulln	
3C-OK	Bell OH-58B Kiowa $	OL Mehrzweckhubschrauberstaffel, Tulln	
3C-OL	Bell OH-58B Kiowa	OL Mehrzweckhubschrauberstaffel, Tulln	
3G-EB	Pilatus PC-6B/B2-H2 Turbo Porter	OL leichte Lufttransportstaffel, Tulln	
3G-ED	Pilatus PC-6B/B2-H2 Turbo Porter	OL leichte Lufttransportstaffel, Tulln	
3G-EE	Pilatus PC-6B/B2-H2 Turbo Porter	OL leichte Lufttransportstaffel, Tulln	
3G-EF	Pilatus PC-6B/B2-H2 Turbo Porter	OL leichte Lufttransportstaffel, Tulln	
3G-EG	Pilatus PC-6B/B2-H2 Turbo Porter	OL leichte Lufttransportstaffel, Tulln	
3G-EH	Pilatus PC-6B/B2-H2 Turbo Porter	OL leichte Lufttransportstaffel, Tulln	
3G-EL	Pilatus PC-6B/B2-H2 Turbo Porter	OL leichte Lufttransportstaffel, Tulln	
3G-EN	Pilatus PC-6B/B2-H4 Turbo Porter $	OL leichte Lufttransportstaffel, Tulln	
3H-FA	Pilatus PC-7 Turbo Trainer	OL Lehrabteilung Fläche, Zeltweg	
3H-FB	Pilatus PC-7 Turbo Trainer	OL Lehrabteilung Fläche, Zeltweg	
3H-FC	Pilatus PC-7 Turbo Trainer $	OL Lehrabteilung Fläche, Zeltweg	
3H-FD	Pilatus PC-7 Turbo Trainer	OL Lehrabteilung Fläche, Zeltweg	
3H-FE	Pilatus PC-7 Turbo Trainer	OL Lehrabteilung Fläche, Zeltweg	
3H-FF	Pilatus PC-7 Turbo Trainer	OL Lehrabteilung Fläche, Zeltweg	
3H-FG	Pilatus PC-7 Turbo Trainer $	OL Lehrabteilung Fläche, Zeltweg	
3H-FH	Pilatus PC-7 Turbo Trainer	OL Lehrabteilung Fläche, Zeltweg	
3H-FJ	Pilatus PC-7 Turbo Trainer	OL Lehrabteilung Fläche, Zeltweg	
3H-FK	Pilatus PC-7 Turbo Trainer	OL Lehrabteilung Fläche, Zeltweg	
3H-FL	Pilatus PC-7 Turbo Trainer	OL Lehrabteilung Fläche, Zeltweg	
3H-FM	Pilatus PC-7 Turbo Trainer	OL Lehrabteilung Fläche, Zeltweg	
3H-FO	Pilatus PC-7 Turbo Trainer	OL Lehrabteilung Fläche, Zeltweg	
5D-HB	Agusta-Bell AB.212	OL 1 Staffel/2 Staffel ITHSSta, Linz	
5D-HC	Agusta-Bell AB.212	OL 1 Staffel/2 Staffel ITHSSta, Linz	
5D-HD	Agusta-Bell AB.212	OL 1 Staffel/2 Staffel ITHSSta, Linz	
5D-HF	Agusta-Bell AB.212	OL 1 Staffel/2 Staffel ITHSSta, Linz	
5D-HG	Agusta-Bell AB.212	OL 1 Staffel/2 Staffel ITHSSta, Linz	
5D-HH	Agusta-Bell AB.212	OL 1 Staffel/2 Staffel ITHSSta, Linz	
5D-HI	Agusta-Bell AB.212	OL 1 Staffel/2 Staffel ITHSSta, Linz	
5D-HJ	Agusta-Bell AB.212	OL 1 Staffel/2 Staffel ITHSSta, Linz	
5D-HK	Agusta-Bell AB.212	OL 1 Staffel/2 Staffel ITHSSta, Linz	
5D-HL	Agusta-Bell AB.212	OL 1 Staffel/2 Staffel ITHSSta, Linz	
5D-HN	Agusta-Bell AB.212	OL 1 Staffel/2 Staffel ITHSSta, Linz	
5D-HO	Agusta-Bell AB.212	OL 1 Staffel/2 Staffel ITHSSta, Linz	
5D-HP	Agusta-Bell AB.212	OL 1 Staffel/2 Staffel ITHSSta, Linz	
5D-HQ	Agusta-Bell AB.212	OL 1 Staffel/2 Staffel ITHSSta, Linz	
5D-HR	Agusta-Bell AB.212	OL 1 Staffel/2 Staffel ITHSSta, Linz	
5D-HS	Agusta-Bell AB.212	OL 1 Staffel/2 Staffel ITHSSta, Linz	
5D-HT	Agusta-Bell AB.212	OL 1 Staffel/2 Staffel ITHSSta, Linz	
5D-HU	Agusta-Bell AB.212	OL 1 Staffel/2 Staffel ITHSSta, Linz	
5D-HV	Agusta-Bell AB.212	OL 1 Staffel/2 Staffel ITHSSta, Linz	
5D-HW	Agusta-Bell AB.212	OL 1 Staffel/2 Staffel ITHSSta, Linz	
5D-HX	Agusta-Bell AB.212	OL 1 Staffel/2 Staffel ITHSSta, Linz	
5D-HY	Bell 212	OL 1 Staffel/2 Staffel ITHSSta, Linz	
5D-HZ	Agusta-Bell AB.212 $	OL 1 Staffel/2 Staffel ITHSSta, Linz	
6M-BA	Sikorsky S-70A	OL mittlere Transporthubschrauberstaffel, Tulln	
6M-BB	Sikorsky S-70A	OL mittlere Transporthubschrauberstaffel, Tulln	
6M-BC	Sikorsky S-70A	OL mittlere Transporthubschrauberstaffel, Tulln	
6M-BD	Sikorsky S-70A	OL mittlere Transporthubschrauberstaffel, Tulln	
6M-BE	Sikorsky S-70A	OL mittlere Transporthubschrauberstaffel, Tulln	
6M-BF	Sikorsky S-70A	OL mittlere Transporthubschrauberstaffel, Tulln	
6M-BG	Sikorsky S-70A	OL mittlere Transporthubschrauberstaffel, Tulln	
6M-BH	Sikorsky S-70A	OL mittlere Transporthubschrauberstaffel, Tulln	
6M-BI	Sikorsky S-70A	OL mittlere Transporthubschrauberstaffel, Tulln	
7L-WA	Eurofighter EF.2000	OL 1 Staffel/2 Staffel Überwg, Zeltweg	
7L-WB	Eurofighter EF.2000	OL 1 Staffel/2 Staffel Überwg, Zeltweg	

Notes	Serial	Type (code/other identity)	Owner/operator, location or fate
	7L-WC	Eurofighter EF.2000 $	OL 1 Staffel/2 Staffel Überwg, Zeltweg
	7L-WD	Eurofighter EF.2000	OL 1 Staffel/2 Staffel Überwg, Zeltweg
	7L-WE	Eurofighter EF.2000	OL 1 Staffel/2 Staffel Überwg, Zeltweg
	7L-WF	Eurofighter EF.2000	OL 1 Staffel/2 Staffel Überwg, Zeltweg
	7L-WG	Eurofighter EF.2000	OL 1 Staffel/2 Staffel Überwg, Zeltweg
	7L-WH	Eurofighter EF.2000	OL 1 Staffel/2 Staffel Überwg, Zeltweg
	7L-WI	Eurofighter EF.2000	OL 1 Staffel/2 Staffel Überwg, Zeltweg
	7L-WJ	Eurofighter EF.2000	OL 1 Staffel/2 Staffel Überwg, Zeltweg
	7L-WK	Eurofighter EF.2000	OL 1 Staffel/2 Staffel Überwg, Zeltweg
	7L-WL	Eurofighter EF.2000	OL 1 Staffel/2 Staffel Überwg, Zeltweg
	7L-WM	Eurofighter EF.2000	OL 1 Staffel/2 Staffel Überwg, Zeltweg
	7L-WN	Eurofighter EF.2000	OL 1 Staffel/2 Staffel Überwg, Zeltweg
	7L-WO	Eurofighter EF.2000	OL 1 Staffel/2 Staffel Überwg, Zeltweg
	8T-CA	Lockheed C-130K Hercules	OL Lufttransportstaffel, Linz
	8T-CB	Lockheed C-130K Hercules	OL Lufttransportstaffel, Linz
	8T-CC	Lockheed C-130K Hercules	OL Lufttransportstaffel, Linz
	BA-31	SAAB 105ÖE [blue A]	OL Düsentrainerstaffel Überwg, Linz
	BE-35	SAAB 105ÖE [blue E]	OL Düsentrainerstaffel Überwg, Linz
	BF-36	SAAB 105ÖE [blue F]	OL Düsentrainerstaffel Überwg, Linz
	BG-37	SAAB 105ÖE [blue G]	OL Düsentrainerstaffel Überwg, Linz
	BI-39	SAAB 105ÖE [blue I]	OL, stored Linz
	BJ-40	SAAB 105ÖE [blue J]	OL Düsentrainerstaffel Überwg, Linz
	GD-14	SAAB 105ÖE [green D] $	OL Düsentrainerstaffel Überwg, Linz
	GG-17	SAAB 105ÖE [green G]	OL Düsentrainerstaffel Überwg, Linz
	RB-22	SAAB 105ÖE [red B]	OL Düsentrainerstaffel Überwg, Linz
	RC-23	SAAB 105ÖE [red C]	OL Düsentrainerstaffel Überwg, Linz
	RD-24	SAAB 105ÖE [red D]	OL Düsentrainerstaffel Überwg, Linz
	RE-25	SAAB 105ÖE [red E] $	OL Düsentrainerstaffel Überwg, Linz
	RF-26	SAAB 105ÖE [red F] $	OL Düsentrainerstaffel Überwg, Linz
	RG-27	SAAB 105ÖE [red G]	OL Düsentrainerstaffel Überwg, Linz
	RH-28	SAAB 105ÖE [red H]	OL Düsentrainerstaffel Überwg, Linz
	RI-29	SAAB 105ÖE [red I]	OL Düsentrainerstaffel Überwg, Linz
	RJ-30	SAAB 105ÖE [red J]	OL Düsentrainerstaffel Überwg, Linz
	YI-09	SAAB 105ÖE [yellow I]	OL Düsentrainerstaffel Überwg, Linz
	YJ-10	SAAB 105ÖE [yellow J]	OL Düsentrainerstaffel Überwg, Linz

AZERBAIJAN

	4K-AI01	Boeing 767-32LER	Azerbaijan Government, Baku
	4K-AI02	Airbus A.319-115LR	Azerbaijan Government, Baku
	4K-AI88	Gulfstream Aerospace G.650	Azerbaijan Government, Baku

BAHRAIN

	A9C-AWL	BAE RJ.100	Royal Bahraini Air Force
	A9C-BAH	Gulfstream Aerospace G.650	Bahrain Royal Flight
	A9C-BDF	BAE RJ.100	Royal Bahraini Air Force
	A9C-BG	Grumman G.1159 Gulfstream IITT	Bahrain Royal Flight
	A9C-BHR	Gulfstream Aerospace G.450	Bahrain Royal Flight
	A9C-BRF	Grumman G.1159C Gulfstream IV-SP	Bahrain Royal Flight
	A9C-BRN	Gulfstream Aerospace G.550	Bahrain Royal Flight
	A9C-HAK	Boeing 747-4F6	Bahrain Royal Flight
	A9C-HAK	Boeing 747SP-Z5	*Withdrawn from use*
	A9C-HMH	Boeing 767-4FSER	Bahrain Royal Flight
	A9C-HMK	Boeing 747-4P8	Bahrain Royal Flight
	A9C-HWR	BAE RJ.85	Royal Bahraini Air Force
	A9C-ISA	Boeing 737-86J	Bahrain Royal Flight

BELGIUM

Force Aérienne Belge (FAB)/Belgische Luchtmacht: Composante Aérienne Belge/Belgische Luchtcomponent

	AT-01	D-BD Alpha Jet 1B+	FAB 11 Sm (1 Wg), Cazaux, France (ET 02.008)
	AT-02	D-BD Alpha Jet 1B+	FAB 11 Sm (1 Wg), Cazaux, France (ET 02.008)
	AT-03	D-BD Alpha Jet 1B+	FAB 11 Sm (1 Wg), Cazaux, France (ET 02.008)
	AT-05	D-BD Alpha Jet 1B+	FAB 11 Sm (1 Wg), Cazaux, France (ET 02.008)

Serial	Type (code/other identity)	Owner/operator, location or fate	Notes
AT-06	D-BD Alpha Jet 1B+	FAB 11 Sm (1 Wg), Cazaux, France (ET 02.008)	
AT-08	D-BD Alpha Jet 1B+	FAB 11 Sm (1 Wg), Cazaux, France (ET 02.008)	
AT-10	D-BD Alpha Jet 1B+	FAB 11 Sm (1 Wg), Cazaux, France (ET 02.008)	
AT-11	D-BD Alpha Jet 1B+	FAB 11 Sm (1 Wg), Cazaux, France (ET 02.008)	
AT-12	D-BD Alpha Jet 1B+	FAB 11 Sm (1 Wg), Cazaux, France (ET 02.008)	
AT-13	D-BD Alpha Jet 1B+	FAB 11 Sm (1 Wg), Cazaux, France (ET 02.008)	
AT-14	D-BD Alpha Jet 1B+	FAB 11 Sm (1 Wg), Cazaux, France (ET 02.008)	
AT-15	D-BD Alpha Jet 1B+	FAB 11 Sm (1 Wg), Cazaux, France (ET 02.008)	
AT-17	D-BD Alpha Jet 1B+	FAB 11 Sm (1 Wg), Cazaux, France (ET 02.008)	
AT-18	D-BD Alpha Jet 1B+	FAB 11 Sm (1 Wg), Cazaux, France (ET 02.008)	
AT-19	D-BD Alpha Jet 1B+	FAB 11 Sm (1 Wg), Cazaux, France (ET 02.008)	
AT-20	D-BD Alpha Jet 1B+	FAB 11 Sm (1 Wg), Cazaux, France (ET 02.008)	
AT-21	D-BD Alpha Jet 1B+	*Withdrawn from use, October 2016*	
AT-22	D-BD Alpha Jet 1B+	FAB 11 Sm (1 Wg), Cazaux, France (ET 02.008)	
AT-23	D-BD Alpha Jet 1B+	FAB 11 Sm (1 Wg), Cazaux, France (ET 02.008)	
AT-24	D-BD Alpha Jet 1B+ $	FAB 11 Sm (1 Wg), Cazaux, France (ET 02.008)	
AT-25	D-BD Alpha Jet 1B+	FAB 11 Sm (1 Wg), Cazaux, France (ET 02.008)	
AT-26	D-BD Alpha Jet 1B+	FAB 11 Sm (1 Wg), Cazaux, France (ET 02.008)	
AT-27	D-BD Alpha Jet 1B+	FAB 11 Sm (1 Wg), Cazaux, France (ET 02.008)	
AT-28	D-BD Alpha Jet 1B+	FAB 11 Sm (1 Wg), Cazaux, France (ET 02.008)	
AT-29	D-BD Alpha Jet 1B+ $	FAB 11 Sm (1 Wg), Cazaux, France (ET 02.008)	
AT-30	D-BD Alpha Jet 1B+	FAB 11 Sm (1 Wg), Cazaux, France (ET 02.008)	
AT-31	D-BD Alpha Jet 1B+	*Withdrawn from use, July 2018*	
AT-32	D-BD Alpha Jet 1B+ $	FAB 11 Sm (1 Wg), Cazaux, France (ET 02.008)	
AT-33	D-BD Alpha Jet 1B+ $	FAB 11 Sm (1 Wg), Cazaux, France (ET 02.008)	
CD-01	Dassault Falcon 900B	FAB 21 Smaldeel (15 Wg), Brussels/Melsbroek	
CE-01	Embraer ERJ.135LR	FAB 21 Smaldeel (15 Wg), Brussels/Melsbroek	
CE-02	Embraer ERJ.135LR $	FAB 21 Smaldeel (15 Wg), Brussels/Melsbroek	
CE-03	Embraer ERJ.145LR $	FAB 21 Smaldeel (15 Wg), Brussels/Melsbroek	
CE-04	Embraer ERJ.145LR $	*Withdrawn from use, 2018*	
CH-01	Lockheed C-130H Hercules	FAB 20 Smaldeel (15 Wg), Brussels/Melsbroek	
CH-03	Lockheed C-130H Hercules	FAB 20 Smaldeel (15 Wg), Brussels/Melsbroek	
CH-04	Lockheed C-130H Hercules	FAB 20 Smaldeel (15 Wg), Brussels/Melsbroek	
CH-05	Lockheed C-130H Hercules	FAB 20 Smaldeel (15 Wg), Brussels/Melsbroek	
CH-07	Lockheed C-130H Hercules $	FAB 20 Smaldeel (15 Wg), Brussels/Melsbroek	
CH-09	Lockheed C-130H Hercules	FAB 20 Smaldeel (15 Wg), Brussels/Melsbroek	
CH-10	Lockheed C-130H Hercules $	*Withdrawn from use, December 2018*	
CH-11	Lockheed C-130H Hercules	FAB 20 Smaldeel (15 Wg), Brussels/Melsbroek	
CH-12	Lockheed C-130H Hercules	FAB 20 Smaldeel (15 Wg), Brussels/Melsbroek	
CH-13	Lockheed C-130H Hercules $	FAB 20 Smaldeel (15 Wg), Brussels/Melsbroek	
FA-56	SABCA (GD) F-16A MLU Fighting Falcon	FAB 31 Sm/349 Sm/OCU (10 Wg), Kleine-Brogel	
FA-57	SABCA (GD) F-16A MLU Fighting Falcon	FAB 1 Sm/350 Sm (2 Wg), Florennes	
FA-67	SABCA (GD) F-16A MLU Fighting Falcon	FAB 1 Sm/350 Sm (2 Wg), Florennes	
FA-68	SABCA (GD) F-16A MLU Fighting Falcon $	FAB 1 Sm/350 Sm (2 Wg), Florennes	
FA-69	SABCA (GD) F-16A MLU Fighting Falcon	FAB 1 Sm/350 Sm (2 Wg), Florennes	
FA-70	SABCA (GD) F-16A MLU Fighting Falcon	FAB 31 Sm/349 Sm/OCU (10 Wg), Kleine-Brogel	
FA-71	SABCA (GD) F-16A MLU Fighting Falcon	FAB 1 Sm/350 Sm (2 Wg), Florennes	
FA-72	SABCA (GD) F-16A MLU Fighting Falcon	FAB 1 Sm/350 Sm (2 Wg), Florennes	
FA-77	SABCA (GD) F-16A MLU Fighting Falcon $	FAB 31 Sm/349 Sm/OCU (10 Wg), Kleine-Brogel	
FA-81	SABCA (GD) F-16A MLU Fighting Falcon	FAB 31 Sm/349 Sm/OCU (10 Wg), Kleine-Brogel	
FA-82	SABCA (GD) F-16A MLU Fighting Falcon	FAB 31 Sm/349 Sm/OCU (10 Wg), Kleine-Brogel	
FA-83	SABCA (GD) F-16A MLU Fighting Falcon	FAB 1 Sm/350 Sm (2 Wg), Florennes	
FA-84	SABCA (GD) F-16A MLU Fighting Falcon $	FAB 1 Sm/350 Sm (2 Wg), Florennes	
FA-86	SABCA (GD) F-16A MLU Fighting Falcon	FAB 31 Sm/349 Sm/OCU (10 Wg), Kleine-Brogel	
FA-87	SABCA (GD) F-16A MLU Fighting Falcon	FAB 31 Sm/349 Sm/OCU (10 Wg), Kleine-Brogel	
FA-89	SABCA (GD) F-16A MLU Fighting Falcon	FAB 1 Sm/350 Sm (2 Wg), Florennes	
FA-91	SABCA (GD) F-16A MLU Fighting Falcon	FAB 31 Sm/349 Sm/OCU (10 Wg), Kleine-Brogel	
FA-92	SABCA (GD) F-16A MLU Fighting Falcon	FAB 1 Sm/350 Sm (2 Wg), Florennes	
FA-94	SABCA (GD) F-16A MLU Fighting Falcon	FAB 31 Sm/349 Sm/OCU (10 Wg), Kleine-Brogel	
FA-95	SABCA (GD) F-16A MLU Fighting Falcon	FAB 31 Sm/349 Sm/OCU (10 Wg), Kleine-Brogel	
FA-97	SABCA (GD) F-16A MLU Fighting Falcon	FAB 31 Sm/349 Sm/OCU (10 Wg), Kleine-Brogel	
FA-98	SABCA (GD) F-16A MLU Fighting Falcon	FAB 1 Sm/350 Sm (2 Wg), Florennes	

Notes	Serial	Type (code/other identity)	Owner/operator, location or fate
	FA-101	SABCA (GD) F-16A MLU Fighting Falcon $	FAB 31 Sm/349 Sm/OCU (10 Wg), Kleine-Brogel
	FA-102	SABCA (GD) F-16A MLU Fighting Falcon	FAB 31 Sm/349 Sm/OCU (10 Wg), Kleine-Brogel
	FA-103	SABCA (GD) F-16A MLU Fighting Falcon	FAB 31 Sm/349 Sm/OCU (10 Wg), Kleine-Brogel
	FA-104	SABCA (GD) F-16A MLU Fighting Falcon	FAB 31 Sm/349 Sm/OCU (10 Wg), Kleine-Brogel
	FA-106	SABCA (GD) F-16A MLU Fighting Falcon	FAB 31 Sm/349 Sm/OCU (10 Wg), Kleine-Brogel
	FA-107	SABCA (GD) F-16A MLU Fighting Falcon	FAB 31 Sm/349 Sm/OCU (10 Wg), Kleine-Brogel
	FA-109	SABCA (GD) F-16A MLU Fighting Falcon	FAB 1 Sm/350 Sm (2 Wg), Florennes
	FA-110	SABCA (GD) F-16A MLU Fighting Falcon	FAB 31 Sm/349 Sm/OCU (10 Wg), Kleine-Brogel
	FA-114	SABCA (GD) F-16A MLU Fighting Falcon	FAB 31 Sm/349 Sm/OCU (10 Wg), Kleine-Brogel
	FA-116	SABCA (GD) F-16A MLU Fighting Falcon $	FAB 31 Sm/349 Sm/OCU (10 Wg), Kleine-Brogel
	FA-117	SABCA (GD) F-16A MLU Fighting Falcon	FAB 1 Sm/350 Sm (2 Wg), Florennes
	FA-118	SABCA (GD) F-16A MLU Fighting Falcon	FAB 31 Sm/349 Sm/OCU (10 Wg), Kleine-Brogel
	FA-119	SABCA (GD) F-16A MLU Fighting Falcon	FAB 31 Sm/349 Sm/OCU (10 Wg), Kleine-Brogel
	FA-121	SABCA (GD) F-16A MLU Fighting Falcon	FAB 1 Sm/350 Sm (2 Wg), Florennes
	FA-123	SABCA (GD) F-16A MLU Fighting Falcon	FAB 31 Sm/349 Sm/OCU (10 Wg), Kleine-Brogel
	FA-124	SABCA (GD) F-16A MLU Fighting Falcon	FAB 31 Sm/349 Sm/OCU (10 Wg), Kleine-Brogel
	FA-126	SABCA (GD) F-16A MLU Fighting Falcon	FAB 1 Sm/350 Sm (2 Wg), Florennes
	FA-127	SABCA (GD) F-16A MLU Fighting Falcon	FAB 1 Sm/350 Sm (2 Wg), Florennes
	FA-128	SABCA (GD) F-16A MLU Fighting Falcon	*Destroyed by fire at Florennes, 11 October 2018*
	FA-129	SABCA (GD) F-16A MLU Fighting Falcon	FAB 1 Sm/350 Sm (2 Wg), Florennes
	FA-130	SABCA (GD) F-16A MLU Fighting Falcon	FAB 1 Sm/350 Sm (2 Wg), Florennes
	FA-131	SABCA (GD) F-16A MLU Fighting Falcon	FAB 31 Sm/349 Sm/OCU (10 Wg), Kleine-Brogel
	FA-132	SABCA (GD) F-16A MLU Fighting Falcon $	FAB 1 Sm/350 Sm (2 Wg), Florennes
	FA-133	SABCA (GD) F-16A MLU Fighting Falcon	FAB 1 Sm/350 Sm (2 Wg), Florennes
	FA-134	SABCA (GD) F-16A MLU Fighting Falcon	FAB 31 Sm/349 Sm/OCU (10 Wg), Kleine-Brogel
	FA-135	SABCA (GD) F-16A MLU Fighting Falcon $	FAB 1 Sm/350 Sm (2 Wg), Florennes
	FA-136	SABCA (GD) F-16A MLU Fighting Falcon	FAB 31 Sm/349 Sm/OCU (10 Wg), Kleine-Brogel
	FB-12	SABCA (GD) F-16B MLU Fighting Falcon	FAB 1 Sm/350 Sm (2 Wg), Florennes
	FB-14	SABCA (GD) F-16B MLU Fighting Falcon	FAB 31 Sm/349 Sm/OCU (10 Wg), Kleine-Brogel
	FB-15	SABCA (GD) F-16B MLU Fighting Falcon	FAB 31 Sm/349 Sm/OCU (10 Wg), Kleine-Brogel
	FB-17	SABCA (GD) F-16B MLU Fighting Falcon	FAB 31 Sm/349 Sm/OCU (10 Wg), Kleine-Brogel
	FB-18	SABCA (GD) F-16B MLU Fighting Falcon	FAB 31 Sm/349 Sm/OCU (10 Wg), Kleine-Brogel
	FB-20	SABCA (GD) F-16B MLU Fighting Falcon	FAB 31 Sm/349 Sm/OCU (10 Wg), Kleine-Brogel
	FB-21	SABCA (GD) F-16B MLU Fighting Falcon	FAB 1 Sm/350 Sm (2 Wg), Florennes
	FB-22	SABCA (GD) F-16B MLU Fighting Falcon	FAB 1 Sm/350 Sm (2 Wg), Florennes
	FB-23	SABCA (GD) F-16B MLU Fighting Falcon	FAB 31 Sm/349 Sm/OCU (10 Wg), Kleine-Brogel
	FB-24	SABCA (GD) F-16B MLU Fighting Falcon $	FAB 31 Sm/349 Sm/OCU (10 Wg), Kleine-Brogel
	G-01	Cessna 182Q Skylane	FAB Federal Police, Brussels/Melsbroek
	G-04	Cessna 182R Skylane	FAB Federal Police, Brussels/Melsbroek
	G-10	MDH MD.902 Explorer	FAB Federal Police, Brussels/Melsbroek
	G-11	MDH MD.902 Explorer	FAB Federal Police, Brussels/Melsbroek
	G-12	MDH MD.902 Explorer	FAB Federal Police, Brussels/Melsbroek
	G-14	MDH MD.520N	FAB Federal Police, Brussels/Melsbroek
	G-15	MDH MD.520N	FAB Federal Police, Brussels/Melsbroek
	G-16	MDH MD.902 Explorer	FAB Federal Police, Brussels/Melsbroek
	G-17	MDH MD.902 Explorer	FAB Federal Police (on order)
	H-20	Agusta A109HA	FAB, stored Beauvechain
	H-21	Agusta A109HA	FAB 17 Smaldeel MRH (1 Wg), Beauvechain
	H-22	Agusta A109HA	FAB 17 Smaldeel MRH (1 Wg), Beauvechain
	H-24	Agusta A109HA $	FAB 17 Smaldeel MRH (1 Wg), Beauvechain
	H-25	Agusta A109HA	FAB, stored Beauvechain
	H-26	Agusta A109HA	FAB 17 Smaldeel MRH (1 Wg), Beauvechain
	H-27	Agusta A109HA	FAB 17 Smaldeel MRH (1 Wg), Beauvechain
	H-28	Agusta A109HA	FAB 17 Smaldeel MRH (1 Wg), Beauvechain
	H-29	Agusta A109HA $	FAB 17 Smaldeel MRH (1 Wg), Beauvechain
	H-30	Agusta A109HA	FAB, stored Beauvechain
	H-31	Agusta A109HA	FAB 17 Smaldeel MRH (1 Wg), Beauvechain
	H-33	Agusta A109HA	FAB, stored Beauvechain
	H-35	Agusta A109HA	FAB 17 Smaldeel MRH (1 Wg), Beauvechain
	H-36	Agusta A109HA	FAB 17 Smaldeel MRH (1 Wg), Beauvechain
	H-38	Agusta A109HA	FAB 17 Smaldeel MRH (1 Wg), Beauvechain
	H-40	Agusta A109HA	FAB, stored Beauvechain

Serial	Type (code/other identity)	Owner/operator, location or fate	Notes
H-41	Agusta A109HA	FAB, stored Beauvechain	
H-42	Agusta A109HA	FAB SLV (1 Wg), Beauvechain	
H-44	Agusta A109HA	FAB 17 Smaldeel MRH (1 Wg), Beauvechain	
H-45	Agusta A109HA	FAB 17 Smaldeel MRH (1 Wg), Beauvechain	
H-46	Agusta A109HA	FAB 17 Smaldeel MRH (1 Wg), Beauvechain	
LB-01	Piper L-21B Super Cub	FAB Air Cadets, Florennes/Goetsenhoeven/Zoersel	
LB-02	Piper L-21B Super Cub	FAB Air Cadets, Florennes/Goetsenhoeven/Zoersel	
LB-03	Piper L-21B Super Cub	FAB Air Cadets, Florennes/Goetsenhoeven/Zoersel	
LB-05	Piper L-21B Super Cub	FAB Air Cadets, Florennes/Goetsenhoeven/Zoersel	
M-1	Sud SA.316B Alouette III	FAB 40 Smaldeel, Koksijde	
M-2	Sud SA.316B Alouette III	FAB 40 Smaldeel, Koksijde	
M-3	Sud SA.316B Alouette III	FAB 40 Smaldeel, Koksijde	
RN-01	NH Industries NH.90-NFH	FAB 40 Smaldeel (1 Wg), Koksijde	
RN-02	NH Industries NH.90-NFH	FAB 40 Smaldeel (1 Wg), Koksijde	
RN-03	NH Industries NH.90-NFH	FAB 40 Smaldeel (1 Wg), Koksijde	
RN-04	NH Industries NH.90-NFH	FAB 40 Smaldeel (1 Wg), Koksijde	
RN-05	NH Industries NH.90-TTH	FAB 18 Smaldeel MRH (1 Wg), Beauvechain	
RN-06	NH Industries NH.90-TTH	FAB 18 Smaldeel MRH (1 Wg), Beauvechain	
RN-07	NH Industries NH.90-TTH	FAB 18 Smaldeel MRH (1 Wg), Beauvechain	
RN-08	NH Industries NH.90-TTH	FAB 18 Smaldeel MRH (1 Wg), Beauvechain	
RS-02	Westland Sea King Mk.48	*Withdrawn from use, January 2019*	
RS-04	Westland Sea King Mk.48	*Withdrawn from use, February 2019*	
RS-05	Westland Sea King Mk.48 $	*Withdrawn from use, March 2019*	
ST-02	SIAI Marchetti SF260M+	FAB 5 Smaldeel/9 Smaldeel, CC Air, Beauvechain	
ST-03	SIAI Marchetti SF260M+	FAB 5 Smaldeel/9 Smaldeel, CC Air, Beauvechain	
ST-04	SIAI Marchetti SF260M+	FAB 5 Smaldeel/9 Smaldeel, CC Air, Beauvechain	
ST-06	SIAI Marchetti SF260M+	FAB *Red Devils*, CC Air, Beauvechain	
ST-12	SIAI Marchetti SF260M+	FAB 5 Smaldeel/9 Smaldeel, CC Air, Beauvechain	
ST-15	SIAI Marchetti SF260M+	FAB *Red Devils*, CC Air, Beauvechain	
ST-16	SIAI Marchetti SF260M+	FAB 5 Smaldeel/9 Smaldeel, CC Air, Beauvechain	
ST-17	SIAI Marchetti SF260M+	FAB 5 Smaldeel/9 Smaldeel, CC Air, Beauvechain	
ST-18	SIAI Marchetti SF260M+	FAB 5 Smaldeel/9 Smaldeel, CC Air, Beauvechain	
ST-19	SIAI Marchetti SF260M+	FAB 5 Smaldeel/9 Smaldeel, CC Air, Beauvechain	
ST-20	SIAI Marchetti SF260M+	FAB 5 Smaldeel/9 Smaldeel, CC Air, Beauvechain	
ST-22	SIAI Marchetti SF260M+	FAB *Red Devils*, CC Air, Beauvechain	
ST-23	SIAI Marchetti SF260M+	FAB *Red Devils*, CC Air, Beauvechain	
ST-24	SIAI Marchetti SF260M+	FAB 5 Smaldeel/9 Smaldeel, CC Air, Beauvechain	
ST-25	SIAI Marchetti SF260M+	FAB 5 Smaldeel/9 Smaldeel, CC Air, Beauvechain	
ST-26	SIAI Marchetti SF260M+	FAB 5 Smaldeel/9 Smaldeel, CC Air, Beauvechain	
ST-27	SIAI Marchetti SF260M+	FAB *Red Devils*, CC Air, Beauvechain	
ST-30	SIAI Marchetti SF260M+ $	FAB 5 Smaldeel/9 Smaldeel, CC Air, Beauvechain	
ST-31	SIAI Marchetti SF260M+	FAB *Red Devils*, CC Air, Beauvechain	
ST-32	SIAI Marchetti SF260M+	FAB 5 Smaldeel/9 Smaldeel, CC Air, Beauvechain	
ST-34	SIAI Marchetti SF260M+	FAB *Red Devils*, CC Air, Beauvechain	
ST-35	SIAI Marchetti SF260M+	FAB *Red Devils*, CC Air, Beauvechain	
ST-36	SIAI Marchetti SF260M+	FAB *Red Devils*, CC Air, Beauvechain	
ST-40	SIAI Marchetti SF260D	FAB 5 Smaldeel/9 Smaldeel, CC Air, Beauvechain	
ST-41	SIAI Marchetti SF260D	FAB 5 Smaldeel/9 Smaldeel, CC Air, Beauvechain	
ST-42	SIAI Marchetti SF260D	FAB 5 Smaldeel/9 Smaldeel, CC Air, Beauvechain	
ST-43	SIAI Marchetti SF260D	FAB 5 Smaldeel/9 Smaldeel, CC Air, Beauvechain	
ST-44	SIAI Marchetti SF260D	FAB 5 Smaldeel/9 Smaldeel, CC Air, Beauvechain	
ST-45	SIAI Marchetti SF260D	FAB 5 Smaldeel/9 Smaldeel, CC Air, Beauvechain	
ST-46	SIAI Marchetti SF260D	FAB 5 Smaldeel/9 Smaldeel, CC Air, Beauvechain	
ST-47	SIAI Marchetti SF260D	FAB 5 Smaldeel/9 Smaldeel, CC Air, Beauvechain	
ST-48	SIAI Marchetti SF260D	FAB 5 Smaldeel/9 Smaldeel, CC Air, Beauvechain	
CS-TRJ	Airbus A.321-231	FAB 21 Smaldeel (15 Wg), Brussels/Melsbroek	

BOTSWANA

Botswana Defence Force (BDF)

OK1	Bombardier Global Express	BDF VIP Sqn, Sir Seretse Kharma IAP, Gaborone	
OM-1	Lockheed C-130B Hercules	BDF Z10 Sqn, Thebephatshwa	
OM-2	Lockheed C-130B Hercules	BDF Z10 Sqn, Thebephatshwa	

Notes	Serial	Type (code/other identity)	Owner/operator, location or fate
	OM-3	Lockheed C-130B Hercules	BDF Z10 Sqn, Thebephatshwa

BRAZIL
Força Aérea Brasileira (FAB)

Notes	Serial	Type (code/other identity)	Owner/operator, location or fate
	2101	Airbus A.319-133CJ (VC-1A)	FAB 1º GT Especial, 1º Esq, Brasília
	2454	Lockheed C-130E Hercules	Withdrawn from use
	2459	Lockheed SC-130E Hercules	Scrapped
	2461	Lockheed KC-130M Hercules	FAB 1º GT, 1º Esq, Galeão
	2462	Lockheed KC-130H Hercules	FAB 1º GT, 1º Esq, Galeão
	2463	Lockheed C-130H Hercules	Withdrawn from use
	2464	Lockheed C-130H Hercules	Scrapped
	2465	Lockheed C-130M Hercules	Scrapped
	2466	Lockheed C-130M Hercules	FAB 1º GT, 1º Esq, Galeão
	2467	Lockheed C-130M Hercules	FAB 1º GT, 1º Esq, Galeão
	2471	Lockheed C-130H Hercules	FAB 1º GT, 1º Esq, Galeão
	2472	Lockheed C-130H Hercules	FAB 1º GT, 1º Esq, Galeão
	2473	Lockheed C-130M Hercules	FAB 1º GT, 1º Esq, Galeão
	2474	Lockheed C-130M Hercules	FAB 1º GT, 1º Esq, Galeão
	2475	Lockheed C-130H Hercules	FAB 1º GT, 1º Esq, Galeão
	2476	Lockheed C-130M Hercules	FAB 1º GTT, 1º Esq, Afonsos
	2477	Lockheed C-130H Hercules	FAB 1º GT, 1º Esq, Galeão
	2479	Lockheed C-130M Hercules	FAB 1º GT, 1º Esq, Galeão
	2550	Embraer VC-99A Legacy	FAB 2º GT Especial, 1º Esq, Brasília
	2560	Embraer VC-99C Legacy	FAB 2º GT Especial, 1º Esq, Brasília
	2561	Embraer VC-99C Legacy	FAB 2º GT Especial, 1º Esq, Brasília
	2580	Embraer VC-99B Legacy	FAB 2º GT Especial, 1º Esq, Brasília
	2581	Embraer VC-99B Legacy	FAB 2º GT Especial, 1º Esq, Brasília
	2582	Embraer VC-99B Legacy	FAB 2º GT Especial, 1º Esq, Brasília
	2583	Embraer VC-99B Legacy	FAB 2º GT Especial, 1º Esq, Brasília
	2584	Embraer VC-99B Legacy	FAB 2º GT Especial, 1º Esq, Brasília
	2585	Embraer VC-99B Legacy	FAB 2º GT Especial, 1º Esq, Brasília
	2586	Embraer VC-99B Legacy	FAB 2º GT Especial, 1º Esq, Brasília
	2590	Embraer EMB.190-190IGW (VC-2)	FAB 1º GT Especial, 1º Esq, Brasília
	2591	Embraer EMB.190-190IGW (VC-2)	FAB 1º GT Especial, 1º Esq, Brasília
	2900	Boeing 767-31AER (C-767)	FAB 2º GT, 2º Esq, Galeão
	6700	Embraer E-99	FAB 2º Esq, 6º GAv, Anapolis
	6701	Embraer R-99A	FAB 2º Esq, 6º GAv, Anapolis
	6702	Embraer R-99A	FAB 2º Esq, 6º GAv, Anapolis
	6703	Embraer E-99	FAB 2º Esq, 6º GAv, Anapolis
	6704	Embraer R-99A	FAB 2º Esq, 6º GAv, Anapolis
	6750	Embraer R-99B	FAB 2º Esq, 6º GAv, Anapolis
	6751	Embraer R-99B	FAB 2º Esq, 6º GAv, Anapolis
	6752	Embraer R-99B	FAB 2º Esq, 6º GAv, Anapolis

BRUNEI

Notes	Serial	Type (code/other identity)	Owner/operator, location or fate
	V8-001	Airbus A.340-212 (V8-BKH)	Brunei Government, Bandar Seri Bergawan
	V8-BKH	Boeing 747-8LQ	Brunei Government, Bandar Seri Bergawan
	V8-MHB	Boeing 767-27GER	Brunei Government, Bandar Seri Bergawan

BULGARIA
Bulgarsky Voenno-Vazdushni Sily (BVVS)

Notes	Serial	Type (code/other identity)	Owner/operator, location or fate
	020	Pilatus PC.XII/45	BVVS 16 TAP, Sofia/Dobroslavtzi
	055	Antonov An-30	BVVS 16 TAP, Sofia/Dobroslavtzi
	071	Aeritalia C-27J Spartan	BVVS 16 TAB, Sofia/Vrazhdebna
	072	Aeritalia C-27J Spartan	BVVS 16 TAB, Sofia/Vrazhdebna
	073	Aeritalia C-27J Spartan	BVVS 16 TAB, Sofia/Vrazhdebna

Bulgarian Government

Notes	Serial	Type (code/other identity)	Owner/operator, location or fate
	LZ-AOB	Airbus A.319-112	Bulgarian Government/BH Air, Sofia
	LZ-OOI	Dassault Falcon 2000	Bulgarian Government, Sofia

BURKINA FASO

Notes	Serial	Type (code/other identity)	Owner/operator, location or fate
	XT-BFA	Boeing 727-282	Government of Burkina Faso, Ouagadougou

Serial	Type (code/other identity)	Owner/operator, location or fate	Notes
CAMEROON			
TJ-AAW	Grumman G.1159A Gulfstream III	Government of Cameroon, Yaounde	
CANADA			
Royal Canadian Air Force (RCAF)			
15001	Airbus CC-150 Polaris (A.310-304) [991]	RCAF 437 Sqn (8 Wing), Trenton	
15002	Airbus CC-150 Polaris (A.310-304F) [992]	RCAF 437 Sqn (8 Wing), Trenton	
15003	Airbus CC-150 Polaris (A.310-304F) [993] $	RCAF 437 Sqn (8 Wing), Trenton	
15004	Airbus CC-150 Polaris (A.310-304F) [994]	RCAF 437 Sqn (8 Wing), Trenton	
15005	Airbus CC-150 Polaris (A.310-304F) [995]	RCAF 437 Sqn (8 Wing), Trenton	
130332	Lockheed CC-130H(SAR) Hercules	RCAF 413 Sqn (14 Wing), Greenwood	
130334	Lockheed CC-130H(SAR) Hercules	RCAF 413 Sqn (14 Wing), Greenwood	
130335	Lockheed CC-130H Hercules	RCAF 426 Sqn (8 Wing), Trenton	
130336	Lockheed CC-130H Hercules	RCAF 426 Sqn (8 Wing), Trenton	
130337	Lockheed CC-130H Hercules	RCAF 426 Sqn (8 Wing), Trenton	
130338	Lockheed CC-130H(T) Hercules	RCAF 435 Sqn (17 Wing), Winnipeg	
130339	Lockheed CC-130H(T) Hercules	RCAF 435 Sqn (17 Wing), Winnipeg	
130340	Lockheed CC-130H(T) Hercules	RCAF 435 Sqn (17 Wing), Winnipeg	
130341	Lockheed CC-130H(T) Hercules	RCAF 435 Sqn (17 Wing), Winnipeg	
130343	Lockheed CC-130H-30 Hercules	RCAF 426 Sqn (8 Wing), Trenton	
130344	Lockheed CC-130H-30 Hercules	RCAF 426 Sqn (8 Wing), Trenton	
130601	Lockheed CC-130J Hercules II	RCAF 436 Sqn (8 Wing), Trenton	
130602	Lockheed CC-130J Hercules II	RCAF 436 Sqn (8 Wing), Trenton	
130603	Lockheed CC-130J Hercules II	RCAF 436 Sqn (8 Wing), Trenton	
130604	Lockheed CC-130J Hercules II	RCAF 436 Sqn (8 Wing), Trenton	
130605	Lockheed CC-130J Hercules II	RCAF 436 Sqn (8 Wing), Trenton	
130606	Lockheed CC-130J Hercules II	RCAF 436 Sqn (8 Wing), Trenton	
130607	Lockheed CC-130J Hercules II	RCAF 436 Sqn (8 Wing), Trenton	
130608	Lockheed CC-130J Hercules II	RCAF 436 Sqn (8 Wing), Trenton	
130609	Lockheed CC-130J Hercules II	RCAF 436 Sqn (8 Wing), Trenton	
130610	Lockheed CC-130J Hercules II	RCAF 436 Sqn (8 Wing), Trenton	
130611	Lockheed CC-130J Hercules II	RCAF 436 Sqn (8 Wing), Trenton	
130612	Lockheed CC-130J Hercules II	RCAF 436 Sqn (8 Wing), Trenton	
130613	Lockheed CC-130J Hercules II	RCAF 436 Sqn (8 Wing), Trenton	
130614	Lockheed CC-130J Hercules II $	RCAF 436 Sqn (8 Wing), Trenton	
130615	Lockheed CC-130J Hercules II	RCAF 436 Sqn (8 Wing), Trenton	
130616	Lockheed CC-130J Hercules II	RCAF 436 Sqn (8 Wing), Trenton	
130617	Lockheed CC-130J Hercules II	RCAF 436 Sqn (8 Wing), Trenton	
140101	Lockheed CP-140 Aurora	RCAF 404 Sqn/405 Sqn (14 Wing), Greenwood	
140102	Lockheed CP-140 Aurora	*Withdrawn from use, 2018*	
140103	Lockheed CP-140M Aurora	RCAF 404 Sqn/405 Sqn (14 Wing), Greenwood	
140104	Lockheed CP-140M Aurora	RCAF 404 Sqn/405 Sqn (14 Wing), Greenwood	
140105	Lockheed CP-140M Aurora	RCAF 407 Sqn (19 Wing), Comox	
140106	Lockheed CP-140 Aurora	RCAF 404 Sqn/405 Sqn (14 Wing), Greenwood	
140107	Lockheed CP-140 Aurora	*Withdrawn from use, 2018*	
140108	Lockheed CP-140M Aurora	RCAF 404 Sqn/405 Sqn (14 Wing), Greenwood	
140109	Lockheed CP-140 Aurora	RCAF 404 Sqn/405 Sqn (14 Wing), Greenwood	
140110	Lockheed CP-140 Aurora	RCAF 407 Sqn (19 Wing), Comox	
140111	Lockheed CP-140M Aurora	RCAF 404 Sqn/405 Sqn (14 Wing), Greenwood	
140112	Lockheed CP-140M Aurora	RCAF 404 Sqn/405 Sqn (14 Wing), Greenwood	
140113	Lockheed CP-140 Aurora	RCAF 407 Sqn (19 Wing), Comox	
140114	Lockheed CP-140M Aurora	RCAF 404 Sqn/405 Sqn (14 Wing), Greenwood	
140115	Lockheed CP-140M Aurora	RCAF 407 Sqn (19 Wing), Comox	
140116	Lockheed CP-140M Aurora	RCAF 407 Sqn (19 Wing), Comox	
140117	Lockheed CP-140M Aurora	RCAF 407 Sqn (19 Wing), Comox	
140118	Lockheed CP-140M Aurora	RCAF 407 Sqn (19 Wing), Comox	
142803	De Havilland Canada CT-142	RCAF 402 Sqn (17 Wing), Winnipeg	
142804	De Havilland Canada CT-142	RCAF 402 Sqn (17 Wing), Winnipeg	
142805	De Havilland Canada CT-142	RCAF 402 Sqn (17 Wing), Winnipeg	
142806	De Havilland Canada CT-142	RCAF 402 Sqn (17 Wing), Winnipeg	
144614	Canadair CC-144B Challenger (C-GCUP)	RCAF 412 Sqn (8 Wing), Ottawa	
144615	Canadair CC-144B Challenger (C-GCUR)	RCAF 412 Sqn (8 Wing), Ottawa	

Notes	Serial	Type (code/other identity)	Owner/operator, location or fate
	144617	Canadair CC-144C Challenger (C-GKGR)	RCAF 412 Sqn (8 Wing), Ottawa
	144618	Canadair CC-144C Challenger (C-GKGS)	RCAF 412 Sqn (8 Wing), Ottawa
	177701	Boeing CC-177 Globemaster III (07-7701/N9500B)	RCAF 429 Sqn (8 Wing), Trenton
	177702	Boeing CC-177 Globemaster III (07-7702/N9500H)	RCAF 429 Sqn (8 Wing), Trenton
	177703	Boeing CC-177 Globemaster III (07-7703/N9500N)	RCAF 429 Sqn (8 Wing), Trenton
	177704	Boeing CC-177 Globemaster III (07-7704/N9500R) $	RCAF 429 Sqn (8 Wing), Trenton
	177705	Boeing CC-177 Globemaster III (14-0004/N273ZD)	RCAF 429 Sqn (8 Wing), Trenton

CHAD

	TT-ABD	Boeing 737-74Q	Chad Government, N'djamena

CHILE
Fuerza Aérea de Chile (FACh)

	145	Extra EA-300L [5]	FACh Los Halcones, Santiago
	146	Extra EA-300L [4]	FACh Los Halcones, Santiago
	147	Extra EA-300L [2]	FACh Los Halcones, Santiago
	902	Boeing 707-351C	FACh, Grupo de Aviación 10, Santiago
	904	Boeing 707-358C	FACh, Grupo de Aviación 10, Santiago
	911	Grumman G.1159C Gulfstream IV	FACh, Grupo de Aviación 10, Santiago
	912	Grumman G.1159C Gulfstream IV	FACh, Grupo de Aviación 10, Santiago
	921	Boeing 737-58N	FACh, Grupo de Aviación 10, Santiago
	922	Boeing 737-330	FACh, Grupo de Aviación 10, Santiago
	982	Boeing KC-135E Stratotanker	FACh, Grupo de Aviación 10, Santiago
	983	Boeing KC-135E Stratotanker	FACh, Grupo de Aviación 10, Santiago
	985	Boeing 767-3Y0ER	FACh, Grupo de Aviación 10, Santiago
	990	Lockheed KC-130R Hercules	FACh, Grupo de Aviación 10, Santiago
	991	Lockheed C-130H Hercules	FACh, Grupo de Aviación 10, Santiago
	992	Lockheed KC-130R Hercules	FACh, Grupo de Aviación 10, Santiago
	995	Lockheed C-130H Hercules	FACh, Grupo de Aviación 10, Santiago
	996	Lockheed C-130H Hercules	FACh, Grupo de Aviación 10, Santiago
	999	Lockheed KC-130R Hercules	FACh, Grupo de Aviación 10, Santiago
	1304	Extra EA-300L [3]	FACh Los Halcones, Santiago
	1325	Extra EA-300L [1]	FACh Los Halcones, Santiago

COLOMBIA
Fuerza Aérea Colombiana (FAC)

	FAC-0001	Boeing 737-74V	FAC Escuadrón de Transporte Especial, Bogotà

CROATIA
Hrvatske Zračne Snage (HZS)

	054	Pilatus PC-9M	HZS 93 Zakroplova Baza, Zadar
	055	Pilatus PC-9M	HZS 93 Zakroplova Baza, Zadar
	056	Pilatus PC-9M	HZS 93 Zakroplova Baza, Zadar
	057	Pilatus PC-9M	HZS 93 Zakroplova Baza, Zadar
	059	Pilatus PC-9M $	HZS 93 Zakroplova Baza, Zadar
	061	Pilatus PC-9M	HZS 93 Zakroplova Baza, Zadar
	062	Pilatus PC-9M	HZS 93 Zakroplova Baza, Zadar
	063	Pilatus PC-9M	HZS 93 Zakroplova Baza, Zadar
	064	Pilatus PC-9M	HZS 93 Zakroplova Baza, Zadar
	066	Pilatus PC-9M	HZS 93 Zakroplova Baza, Zadar
	067	Pilatus PC-9M	HZS 93 Zakroplova Baza, Zadar
	068	Pilatus PC-9M	HZS 93 Zakroplova Baza, Zadar
	069	Pilatus PC-9M	HZS 93 Zakroplova Baza, Zadar
	070	Pilatus PC-9M	HZS 93 Zakroplova Baza, Zadar

Croatian Government

	9A-CRO	Canadair CL.601 Challenger	Croatian Government, Zagreb
	9A-CRT	Canadair CL.601 Challenger	Croatian Government, Zagreb

CZECH REPUBLIC
Vzdušné Síly Armády (Czech Air Force)

	0103	Aero L-39C Albatros	Preserved at Vyskov
	0106	Aero L-39C Albatros	Withdrawn from use

Serial	Type (code/other identity)	Owner/operator, location or fate	Notes
0107	Aero L-39C Albatros	Czech AF CLV, Pardubice	
0108	Aero L-39C Albatros	Czech AF CLV, Pardubice	
0113	Aero L-39C Albatros	Czech AF CLV, Pardubice	
0115	Aero L-39C Albatros	Czech AF CLV, Pardubice	
0260	Yakovlev Yak-40	Czech 241.dlt/24.zDL, Praha/Kbely	
0441	Aero L-39C Albatros	Czech AF CLV, Pardubice	
0444	Aero L-39C Albatros	Czech AF CLV, Pardubice	
0445	Aero L-39C Albatros	Czech AF CLV, Pardubice	
0452	CASA C-295M	Czech 242.tsl/24.zDL, Praha/Kbely	
0453	CASA C-295M	Czech 242.tsl/24.zDL, Praha/Kbely	
0454	CASA C-295M	Czech 242.tsl/24.zDL, Praha/Kbely	
0455	CASA C-295M	Czech 242.tsl/24.zDL, Praha/Kbely	
0458	Evektor EV-55M Outback	Evektor, Kunovice	
0475	Aero L-39NG Albatros (7001)	Aero, Vodochody	
0731	LET L-410UVP-E Turbolet	Czech AF CLV, Pardubice	
0803	Mil Mi-17	*Withdrawn from use*	
0811	Mil Mi-17	*Withdrawn from use*	
0825	Mil Mi-17	Czech AF CLV, Pardubice	
0828	Mil Mi-17	Czech AF CLV, Pardubice	
0832	Mil Mi-17	Czech AF CLV, Pardubice	
0834	Mil Mi-17	Czech AF 243.vrl/24.zDL, Praha/Kbely	
0835	Mil Mi-17	Czech AF CLV, Pardubice	
0836	Mil Mi-17	Czech AF CLV, Pardubice	
0837	Mil Mi-17	Czech AF CLV, Pardubice	
0839	Mil Mi-17	Czech AF 243.vrl/24.zDL, Praha/Kbely	
0840	Mil Mi-17	*Withdrawn from use*	
0848	Mil Mi-17	Czech AF 243.vrl/24.zDL, Praha/Kbely	
0849	Mil Mi-17	Czech AF 243.vrl/24.zDL, Praha/Kbely	
0850	Mil Mi-17	Czech AF 243.vrl/24.zDL, Praha/Kbely	
0928	LET L-410UVP-T Turbolet	Czech AF CLV, Pardubice	
0981	Mil Mi-24V2	Czech AF 221.lbvr/22.zL, Náměšt	
1257	Yakovlev Yak-40K	Czech 241.dlt/24.zDL, Praha/Kbely	
1526	LET L-410FG Turbolet	Czech 242.tsl/24.zDL, Praha/Kbely	
2344	Aero L-39ZA Albatros	*Withdrawn from use*	
2415	Aero L-39ZA Albatros	Czech AF 213.vlt/21.zTL, Čáslav	
2421	Aero L-39ZA Albatros	Czech AF 213.vlt/21.zTL, Čáslav	
2433	Aero L-39ZA Albatros $	*Withdrawn from use*	
2436	Aero L-39ZA Albatros	*Withdrawn from use*	
2601	LET L-410UVP-E Turbolet	Czech 242.tsl/24.zDL, Praha/Kbely	
2602	LET L-410UVP-E Turbolet	Czech 242.tsl/24.zDL, Praha/Kbely	
2626	Aero L-39CW Albatros	Aero, Vodochody	
2801	Airbus A.319CJ-115X	Czech 241.dlt/24.zDL, Praha/Kbely	
3085	Airbus A.319CJ-115X	Czech 241.dlt/24.zDL, Praha/Kbely	
3361	Mil Mi-35	Czech AF 221.lbvr/22.zL, Náměšt	
3362	Mil Mi-35	Czech AF 221.lbvr/22.zL, Náměšt	
3365	Mil Mi-35	Czech AF 221.lbvr/22.zL, Náměšt	
3366	Mil Mi-35 $	Czech AF 221.lbvr/22.zL, Náměšt	
3367	Mil Mi-35	Czech AF 221.lbvr/22.zL, Náměšt	
3368	Mil Mi-35	Czech AF 221.lbvr/22.zL, Náměšt	
3369	Mil Mi-35	Czech AF 221.lbvr/22.zL, Náměšt	
3370	Mil Mi-35 $	Czech AF 221.lbvr/22.zL, Náměšt	
3371	Mil Mi-35	Czech AF 221.lbvr/22.zL, Náměšt	
3903	Aero L-39ZA Albatros	Czech AF 213.vlt/21.zTL, Čáslav	
5015	Aero L-39ZA Albatros	Czech AF 213.vlt/21.zTL, Čáslav	
5017	Aero L-39ZA Albatros	Czech AF 213.vlt/21.zTL, Čáslav	
5019	Aero L-39ZA Albatros $	Czech AF 213.vlt/21.zTL, Čáslav	
5105	Canadair CL.601-3A Challenger	Czech 241.dlt/24.zDL, Praha/Kbely	
5832	Aero L-159B ALCA	Czech AF LZO, Praha/Kbely	
6028	Aero L-159T-2 ALCA	Aero, Vodochody (for Czech AF)	
6046	Aero L-159T-1 ALCA	Czech AF 213.vlt/21.zTL, Čáslav	
6047	Aero L-159T-1 ALCA	Czech AF 213.vlt/21.zTL, Čáslav	
6048	Aero L-159A ALCA	Czech AF 212.tl/21.zTL, Čáslav	

Notes	Serial	Type (code/other identity)	Owner/operator, location or fate
	6050	Aero L-159A ALCA	Czech AF 212.tl/21.zTL, Cáslav
	6051	Aero L-159A ALCA	Czech AF 212.tl/21.zTL, Cáslav
	6052	Aero L-159A ALCA	Czech AF 212.tl/21.zTL, Cáslav
	6053	Aero L-159A ALCA (AD572/DU-C) $	Czech AF 212.tl/21.zTL, Cáslav
	6054	Aero L-159A ALCA	Czech AF 212.tl/21.zTL, Cáslav
	6057	Aero L-159A ALCA	Czech AF 212.tl/21.zTL, Cáslav
	6058	Aero L-159A ALCA	Czech AF 212.tl/21.zTL, Cáslav
	6059	Aero L-159A ALCA	Czech AF 212.tl/21.zTL, Cáslav
	6060	Aero L-159A ALCA	Czech AF 212.tl/21.zTL, Cáslav
	6062	Aero L-159A ALCA	Czech AF 212.tl/21.zTL, Cáslav
	6063	Aero L-159A ALCA	Czech AF 212.tl/21.zTL, Cáslav
	6064	Aero L-159A ALCA	Czech AF 212.tl/21.zTL, Cáslav
	6066	Aero L-159A ALCA $	Czech AF 212.tl/21.zTL, Cáslav
	6069	Aero L-159B ALCA	*Sold to Iraq, 2018*
	6070	Aero L-159A ALCA	Czech AF 212.tl/21.zTL, Cáslav
	6073	Aero L-159T-2X ALCA	Aero, Vodochody
	6075	Aero L-159T-1 ALCA	Czech AF 213.vlt/21.zTL, Cáslav
	6078	Aero L-159T-1 ALCA	Czech AF 213.vlt/21.zTL, Cáslav
	6079	Aero L-159T-1 ALCA	Czech AF 213.vlt/21.zTL, Cáslav
	7004	Aero L-39NG Albatros	Aero, Vodochody
	7005	Aero L-39NG Albatros	Aero, Vodochody
	7353	Mil Mi-24V $	Czech AF 221.lbvr/22.zL, Náměšt
	7354	Mil Mi-24V	Czech AF 221.lbvr/22.zL, Náměšt
	7355	Mil Mi-24V	Czech AF 221.lbvr/22.zL, Náměšt
	7356	Mil Mi-24V	Czech AF 221.lbvr/22.zL, Náměšt
	7357	Mil Mi-24V	Czech AF 221.lbvr/22.zL, Náměšt
	7360	Mil Mi-24V	Czech AF 221.lbvr/22.zL, Náměšt
	9234	SAAB JAS 39C Gripen $	Czech AF 211.tl/21.zTL, Cáslav
	9235	SAAB JAS 39C Gripen $	Czech AF 211.tl/21.zTL, Cáslav
	9236	SAAB JAS 39C Gripen $	Czech AF 211.tl/21.zTL, Cáslav
	9237	SAAB JAS 39C Gripen	Czech AF 211.tl/21.zTL, Cáslav
	9238	SAAB JAS 39C Gripen	Czech AF 211.tl/21.zTL, Cáslav
	9239	SAAB JAS 39C Gripen	Czech AF 211.tl/21.zTL, Cáslav
	9240	SAAB JAS 39C Gripen $	Czech AF 211.tl/21.zTL, Cáslav
	9241	SAAB JAS 39C Gripen $	Czech AF 211.tl/21.zTL, Cáslav
	9242	SAAB JAS 39C Gripen	Czech AF 211.tl/21.zTL, Cáslav
	9243	SAAB JAS 39C Gripen	Czech AF 211.tl/21.zTL, Cáslav
	9244	SAAB JAS 39C Gripen	Czech AF 211.tl/21.zTL, Cáslav
	9245	SAAB JAS 39C Gripen	Czech AF 211.tl/21.zTL, Cáslav
	9767	Mil Mi-171Sh	Czech AF 221.lbvr & 222.vrlt/22.zVrL, Náměšt
	9774	Mil Mi-171Sh	Czech AF 221.lbvr & 222.vrlt/22.zVrL, Náměšt
	9781	Mil Mi-171Sh	Czech AF 221.lbvr & 222.vrlt/22.zVrL, Náměšt
	9799	Mil Mi-171Sh	Czech AF 221.lbvr & 222.vrlt/22.zVrL, Náměšt
	9806	Mil Mi-171Sh	Czech AF 221.lbvr & 222.vrlt/22.zVrL, Náměšt
	9813	Mil Mi-171Sh	Czech AF 221.lbvr & 222.vrlt/22.zVrL, Náměšt
	9819	SAAB JAS 39D Gripen $	Czech AF 211.tl/21.zTL, Cáslav
	9820	SAAB JAS 39D Gripen	Czech AF 211.tl/21.zTL, Cáslav
	9825	Mil Mi-171Sh	Czech AF 221.lbvr & 222.vrlt/22.zVrL, Náměšt
	9837	Mil Mi-171Sh	Czech AF 221.lbvr & 222.vrlt/22.zVrL, Náměšt
	9844	Mil Mi-171Sh	Czech AF 221.lbvr & 222.vrlt/22.zVrL, Náměšt
	9868	Mil Mi-171Sh	Czech AF 221.lbvr & 222.vrlt/22.zVrL, Náměšt
	9873	Mil Mi-171Sh	Czech AF 221.lbvr & 222.vrlt/22.zVrL, Náměšt
	9887	Mil Mi-171Sh	Czech AF 221.lbvr & 222.vrlt/22.zVrL, Náměšt
	9892	Mil Mi-171Sh	Czech AF 221.lbvr & 222.vrlt/22.zVrL, Náměšt
	9904	Mil Mi-171Sh	Czech AF 221.lbvr & 222.vrlt/22.zVrL, Náměšt
	9915	Mil Mi-171Sh	Czech AF 221.lbvr & 222.vrlt/22.zVrL, Náměšt
	9926	Mil Mi-171Sh	Czech AF 221.lbvr & 222.vrlt/22.zVrL, Náměšt
	....	CASA C-295M	Czech AF (on order)
	....	CASA C-295M	Czech AF (on order)

Serial	Type (code/other identity)	Owner/operator, location or fate	Notes
DENMARK			
Kongelige Danske Flyvevåben (KDF)			
B-536	Lockheed C-130J-30 Hercules II	KDF Eskadrille 721, Aalborg	
B-537	Lockheed C-130J-30 Hercules II	KDF Eskadrille 721, Aalborg	
B-538	Lockheed C-130J-30 Hercules II	KDF Eskadrille 721, Aalborg	
B-583	Lockheed C-130J-30 Hercules II	KDF Eskadrille 721, Aalborg	
C-080	Canadair CL.604 Challenger	KDF Eskadrille 721, Aalborg	
C-168	Canadair CL.604 Challenger $	KDF Eskadrille 721, Aalborg	
C-172	Canadair CL.604 Challenger	KDF Eskadrille 721, Aalborg	
C-215	Canadair CL.604 Challenger	KDF Eskadrille 721, Aalborg	
E-004	SABCA (GD) F-16A MLU Fighting Falcon	KDF Eskadrille 727, Skrydstrup	
E-005	SABCA (GD) F-16A MLU Fighting Falcon	KDF Eskadrille 727, Skrydstrup	
E-006	SABCA (GD) F-16A MLU Fighting Falcon	KDF Eskadrille 730, Skrydstrup	
E-007	SABCA (GD) F-16A MLU Fighting Falcon	KDF Eskadrille 727, Skrydstrup	
E-008	SABCA (GD) F-16A MLU Fighting Falcon $	KDF Eskadrille 727, Skrydstrup	
E-011	GD F-16A MLU Fighting Falcon	KDF Eskadrille 727, Skrydstrup	
E-016	GD F-16A MLU Fighting Falcon	KDF Eskadrille 727, Skrydstrup	
E-017	SABCA (GD) F-16A MLU Fighting Falcon	KDF Eskadrille 727, Skrydstrup	
E-018	SABCA (GD) F-16A MLU Fighting Falcon	KDF Eskadrille 730, Skrydstrup	
E-024	GD F-16A MLU Fighting Falcon	KDF Eskadrille 727, Skrydstrup	
E-074	GD F-16A MLU Fighting Falcon	KDF Eskadrille 730, Skrydstrup	
E-075	GD F-16A MLU Fighting Falcon	KDF Eskadrille 727, Skrydstrup	
E-107	GD F-16A MLU Fighting Falcon	KDF Eskadrille 727, Skrydstrup	
E-189	SABCA (GD) F-16A MLU Fighting Falcon	KDF Eskadrille 730, Skrydstrup	
E-190	SABCA (GD) F-16A MLU Fighting Falcon	KDF Eskadrille 730, Skrydstrup	
E-191	SABCA (GD) F-16A MLU Fighting Falcon	KDF Eskadrille 730, Skrydstrup	
E-194	SABCA (GD) F-16A MLU Fighting Falcon $	KDF Eskadrille 730, Skrydstrup	
E-596	SABCA (GD) F-16A MLU Fighting Falcon	KDF Eskadrille 730, Skrydstrup	
E-597	SABCA (GD) F-16A MLU Fighting Falcon	KDF Eskadrille 730, Skrydstrup	
E-598	SABCA (GD) F-16A MLU Fighting Falcon	KDF Eskadrille 727, Skrydstrup	
E-599	SABCA (GD) F-16A MLU Fighting Falcon	KDF, stored Skrydstrup	
E-600	SABCA (GD) F-16A MLU Fighting Falcon	KDF Eskadrille 730, Skrydstrup	
E-601	SABCA (GD) F-16A MLU Fighting Falcon $	KDF Eskadrille 730, Skrydstrup	
E-602	SABCA (GD) F-16A MLU Fighting Falcon	KDF Eskadrille 730, Skrydstrup	
E-603	SABCA (GD) F-16A MLU Fighting Falcon	KDF Eskadrille 730, Skrydstrup	
E-604	SABCA (GD) F-16A MLU Fighting Falcon	KDF Eskadrille 727, Skrydstrup	
E-605	SABCA (GD) F-16A MLU Fighting Falcon	KDF Eskadrille 730, Skrydstrup	
E-606	SABCA (GD) F-16A MLU Fighting Falcon	KDF Eskadrille 730, Skrydstrup	
E-607	SABCA (GD) F-16A MLU Fighting Falcon $	KDF Eskadrille 727, Skrydstrup	
E-608	SABCA (GD) F-16A MLU Fighting Falcon	KDF Eskadrille 730, Skrydstrup	
E-609	SABCA (GD) F-16A MLU Fighting Falcon	KDF Eskadrille 727, Skrydstrup	
E-610	SABCA (GD) F-16A MLU Fighting Falcon	KDF Eskadrille 730, Skrydstrup	
E-611	SABCA (GD) F-16A MLU Fighting Falcon	KDF Eskadrille 727, Skrydstrup	
ET-022	Fokker (GD) F-16B MLU Fighting Falcon	KDF Eskadrille 730, Skrydstrup	
ET-197	Fokker (GD) F-16B MLU Fighting Falcon	KDF Eskadrille 727, Skrydstrup	
ET-198	Fokker (GD) F-16B MLU Fighting Falcon	KDF Eskadrille 727, Skrydstrup	
ET-199	Fokker (GD) F-16B MLU Fighting Falcon	KDF Eskadrille 730, Skrydstrup	
ET-207	SABCA (GD) F-16B MLU Fighting Falcon	KDF Eskadrille 727, Skrydstrup	
ET-208	SABCA (GD) F-16B MLU Fighting Falcon	KDF Eskadrille 730, Skrydstrup	
ET-210	SABCA (GD) F-16B MLU Fighting Falcon	KDF Eskadrille 727/730, Skrydstrup	
ET-612	SABCA (GD) F-16B MLU Fighting Falcon	KDF Eskadrille 727, Skrydstrup	
ET-613	SABCA (GD) F-16B MLU Fighting Falcon	KDF Eskadrille 727, Skrydstrup	
ET-614	SABCA (GD) F-16B MLU Fighting Falcon	KDF Eskadrille 727, Skrydstrup	
ET-615	SABCA (GD) F-16B MLU Fighting Falcon	KDF Eskadrille 727, Skrydstrup	
M-502	AgustaWestland EH.101 Mk.512 (ZJ991)	KDF Eskadrille 722, Karup	
M-504	AgustaWestland EH.101 Mk.512 (ZJ993)	KDF Eskadrille 722, Karup	
M-507	AgustaWestland EH.101 Mk.512 (ZJ996)	KDF Eskadrille 722, Karup	
M-508	AgustaWestland EH.101 Mk.512 (ZJ997)	KDF Eskadrille 722, Karup	
M-510	AgustaWestland EH.101 Mk.512 (ZJ999)	KDF Eskadrille 722, Karup	
M-512	AgustaWestland EH.101 Mk.512 (ZK002)	KDF Eskadrille 722, Karup	
M-513	AgustaWestland EH.101 Mk.512 (ZK003)	KDF Eskadrille 722, Karup	
M-514	AgustaWestland EH.101 Mk.512 (ZK004)	KDF Eskadrille 722, Karup	

Notes	Serial	Type (code/other identity)	Owner/operator, location or fate
	M-515	AgustaWestland EH.101 Mk.512 (ZK160)	KDF Eskadrille 722, Karup
	M-516	AgustaWestland EH.101 Mk.512 (ZK161)	KDF Eskadrille 722, Karup
	M-517	AgustaWestland EH.101 Mk.512 (ZK162)	KDF Eskadrille 722, Karup
	M-518	AgustaWestland EH.101 Mk.512 (ZK163)	KDF Eskadrille 722, Karup
	M-519	AgustaWestland EH.101 Mk.512 (ZK164)	KDF Eskadrille 722, Karup
	M-520	AgustaWestland EH.101 Mk.512	KDF Eskadrille 722, Karup
	N-971	Sikorsky MH-60R Sea Hawk	KDF Eskadrille 723, Karup
	N-972	Sikorsky MH-60R Sea Hawk	KDF Eskadrille 723, Karup
	N-973	Sikorsky MH-60R Sea Hawk	KDF Eskadrille 723, Karup
	N-974	Sikorsky MH-60R Sea Hawk	KDF Eskadrille 723, Karup
	N-975	Sikorsky MH-60R Sea Hawk	KDF Eskadrille 723, Karup
	N-976	Sikorsky MH-60R Sea Hawk	KDF Eskadrille 723, Karup
	N-977	Sikorsky MH-60R Sea Hawk	KDF Eskadrille 723, Karup
	N-978	Sikorsky MH-60R Sea Hawk	KDF Eskadrille 723, Karup
	N-979	Sikorsky MH-60R Sea Hawk	KDF Eskadrille 723, Karup
	P-090	Aérospatiale AS.550C-2 Fennec	KDF Eskadrille 724, Karup
	P-234	Aérospatiale AS.550C-2 Fennec	KDF Eskadrille 724, Karup
	P-254	Aérospatiale AS.550C-2 Fennec	KDF Eskadrille 724, Karup
	P-275	Aérospatiale AS.550C-2 Fennec	KDF Eskadrille 724, Karup
	P-276	Aérospatiale AS.550C-2 Fennec	KDF Eskadrille 724, Karup
	P-287	Aérospatiale AS.550C-2 Fennec	KDF Eskadrille 724, Karup
	P-288	Aérospatiale AS.550C-2 Fennec	KDF Eskadrille 724, Karup
	P-319	Aérospatiale AS.550C-2 Fennec	KDF Eskadrille 724, Karup
	P-320	Aérospatiale AS.550C-2 Fennec	KDF Eskadrille 724, Karup
	P-339	Aérospatiale AS.550C-2 Fennec	KDF Eskadrille 724, Karup
	P-352	Aérospatiale AS.550C-2 Fennec	KDF Eskadrille 724, Karup
	P-369	Aérospatiale AS.550C-2 Fennec	KDF Eskadrille 724, Karup
	T-401	SAAB T-17 Supporter	KDF Flyveskolen, Karup
	T-402	SAAB T-17 Supporter	KDF Flyveskolen, Karup
	T-403	SAAB T-17 Supporter	KDF Flyveskolen, Karup
	T-404	SAAB T-17 Supporter	KDF Flyveskolen, Karup
	T-405	SAAB T-17 Supporter	KDF Skrydstrup Station Flight
	T-407	SAAB T-17 Supporter	KDF Eskadrille 721, Aalborg
	T-409	SAAB T-17 Supporter	KDF Flyveskolen, Karup
	T-410	SAAB T-17 Supporter	KDF Flyveskolen, Karup
	T-411	SAAB T-17 Supporter	KDF Skrydstrup Station Flight
	T-412	SAAB T-17 Supporter	KDF Flyveskolen, Karup
	T-413	SAAB T-17 Supporter	KDF Flyveskolen, Karup
	T-414	SAAB T-17 Supporter	KDF Eskadrille 721, Aalborg
	T-415	SAAB T-17 Supporter	KDF Flyveskolen, Karup
	T-417	SAAB T-17 Supporter	KDF Flyveskolen, Karup
	T-418	SAAB T-17 Supporter	KDF Skrydstrup Station Flight
	T-419	SAAB T-17 Supporter	KDF Flyveskolen, Karup
	T-420	SAAB T-17 Supporter	KDF Skrydstrup Station Flight
	T-421	SAAB T-17 Supporter	KDF Flyveskolen, Karup
	T-423	SAAB T-17 Supporter	KDF Flyveskolen, Karup
	T-425	SAAB T-17 Supporter	KDF Flyveskolen, Karup
	T-426	SAAB T-17 Supporter	KDF Flyveskolen, Karup
	T-427	SAAB T-17 Supporter	KDF Flyveskolen, Karup
	T-428	SAAB T-17 Supporter	KDF Flyveskolen, Karup
	T-429	SAAB T-17 Supporter	KDF Flyveskolen, Karup
	T-430	SAAB T-17 Supporter	KDF Flyveskolen, Karup
	T-431	SAAB T-17 Supporter	KDF Eskadrille 721, Aalborg
	T-432	SAAB T-17 Supporter	KDF Flyveskolen, Karup

ECUADOR
Fuerza Aérea Ecuatoriana (FAE)

Notes	Serial	Type (code/other identity)	Owner/operator, location or fate
	FAE-051	Embraer ERJ.135 Legacy 600	FAE Escuadrón de Transporte 1114, Quito
	FAE-052	Dassault Falcon 7X	FAE Escuadrón de Transporte 1114, Quito

Serial	Type (code/other identity)	Owner/operator, location or fate	Notes
EGYPT			
Al Quwwat al-Jawwiya il Misriya (Egyptian Air Force)			
1271	Lockheed C-130H Hercules (SU-BAB)	Egyptian AF 16 Sqn, Cairo West	
1273	Lockheed C-130H Hercules (SU-BAD)	Egyptian AF 16 Sqn, Cairo West	
1274	Lockheed C-130H Hercules (SU-BAE)	Egyptian AF 16 Sqn, Cairo West	
1275	Lockheed C-130H Hercules (SU-BAF)	Egyptian AF 16 Sqn, Cairo West	
1277	Lockheed C-130H Hercules (SU-BAI)	Egyptian AF 16 Sqn, Cairo West	
1278	Lockheed C-130H Hercules (SU-BAJ)	Egyptian AF 16 Sqn, Cairo West	
1279	Lockheed C-130H Hercules (SU-BAK)	Egyptian AF 16 Sqn, Cairo West	
1280	Lockheed C-130H Hercules (SU-BAL)	Egyptian AF 16 Sqn, Cairo West	
1281	Lockheed C-130H Hercules (SU-BAM)	Egyptian AF 16 Sqn, Cairo West	
1282	Lockheed C-130H Hercules (SU-BAN)	Egyptian AF 16 Sqn, Cairo West	
1283	Lockheed C-130H Hercules (SU-BAP)	Egyptian AF 16 Sqn, Cairo West	
1284	Lockheed C-130H Hercules (SU-BAQ)	Egyptian AF 16 Sqn, Cairo West	
1285	Lockheed C-130H Hercules (SU-BAR)	Egyptian AF 16 Sqn, Cairo West	
1286	Lockheed C-130H Hercules (SU-BAS)	Egyptian AF 16 Sqn, Cairo West	
1287	Lockheed C-130H Hercules (SU-BAT)	Egyptian AF 16 Sqn, Cairo West	
1288	Lockheed C-130H Hercules (SU-BAU)	Egyptian AF 16 Sqn, Cairo West	
1289	Lockheed C-130H Hercules (SU-BAV)	Egyptian AF 16 Sqn, Cairo West	
1290	Lockheed C-130H Hercules (SU-BEW)	Egyptian AF 16 Sqn, Cairo West	
1291	Lockheed C-130H Hercules (SU-BEX)	Egyptian AF 16 Sqn, Cairo West	
1292	Lockheed C-130H Hercules (SU-BEY)	Egyptian AF 16 Sqn, Cairo West	
1293	Lockheed C-130H-30 Hercules (SU-BKS)	Egyptian AF 16 Sqn, Cairo West	
1294	Lockheed C-130H-30 Hercules (SU-BKT)	Egyptian AF 16 Sqn, Cairo West	
1295	Lockheed C-130H-30 Hercules (SU-BKU)	Egyptian AF 16 Sqn, Cairo West	
1296	Lockheed C-130H Hercules (SU-BPJ)	Egyptian AF 16 Sqn, Cairo West	
1297	Lockheed C-130H Hercules (SU-BPK)	Egyptian AF 16 Sqn, Cairo West	
1298	Lockheed C-130H Hercules (SU-BPL)	Egyptian AF 16 Sqn, Cairo West	
....	Lockheed C-130J Hercules II	Egyptian AF (on order)	
....	Lockheed C-130J Hercules II	Egyptian AF (on order)	
Egyptian Government			
SU-BGV	Grumman G.1159A Gulfstream III	Egyptian AF/Government, Cairo	
SU-BNC	Grumman G.1159C Gulfstream IV	Egyptian AF/Government, Cairo	
SU-BND	Grumman G.1159C Gulfstream IV	Egyptian AF/Government, Cairo	
SU-BNO	Grumman G.1159C Gulfstream IV-SP	Egyptian AF/Government, Cairo	
SU-BNP	Grumman G.1159C Gulfstream IV-SP	Egyptian AF/Government, Cairo	
SU-BPE	Gulfstream Aerospace G.400	Egyptian AF/Government, Cairo	
SU-BPF	Gulfstream Aerospace G.400	Egyptian AF/Government, Cairo	
SU-BRF	Cessna 680 Citation Sovereign	Egyptian Government, Cairo	
SU-BRG	Cessna 680 Citation Sovereign	Egyptian Government, Cairo	
SU-BTU	Dassault Falcon 7X	Egyptian AF/Government, Cairo	
SU-BTV	Dassault Falcon 7X	Egyptian AF/Government, Cairo	
SU-BTW	Dassault Falcon 8X	Egyptian AF/Government, Cairo	
SU-GGG	Airbus A.340-211	Egyptian Government, Cairo	
ESTONIA			
Estonian Air Force			
10	Aero L-39C Albatros (ES-RAZ)	Estonian AF Fixed Wing Squadron, Ämari	
11	Aero L-39C Albatros (ES-TLH)	Estonian AF Fixed Wing Squadron, Ämari	
20 y	WSK-PZL An-2T	*Withdrawn from use*	
40 y	WSK-PZL An-2T	Estonian AF Fixed Wing Squadron, Ämari	
41 y	Antonov An-2	Estonian AF Fixed Wing Squadron, Ämari	
FINLAND			
Suomen Ilmavoimat (Finnish Air Force) & Suomen Maavoimat (Finnish Army)			
CC-1	CASA C-295M	Ilmavoimat TukiLLv, Tampere/Pirkkala	
CC-2	CASA C-295M	Ilmavoimat TukiLLv, Tampere/Pirkkala	
CC-3	CASA C-295M	Ilmavoimat TukiLLv, Tampere/Pirkkala	
FF-1	Fokker F.27-100 Friendship	*Withdrawn from use*	
HN-401	McDonnell Douglas F-18C Hornet	Ilmavoimat HävLLv 31, Kuopio/Rissala	
HN-402	McDonnell Douglas F-18C Hornet	Ilmavoimat HävLLv 11, Roveniemi	
HN-403	McDonnell Douglas F-18C Hornet	Ilmavoimat HävLLv 31, Kuopio/Rissala	

Notes	Serial	Type (code/other identity)	Owner/operator, location or fate
	HN-404	McDonnell Douglas F-18C Hornet	Ilmavoimat HävLLv 31, Kuopio/Rissala
	HN-405	McDonnell Douglas F-18C Hornet	Ilmavoimat HävLLv 31, Kuopio/Rissala
	HN-406	McDonnell Douglas F-18C Hornet	Ilmavoimat HävLLv 31, Kuopio/Rissala
	HN-407	McDonnell Douglas F-18C Hornet	Ilmavoimat HävLLv 31, Kuopio/Rissala
	HN-408	McDonnell Douglas F-18C Hornet	Ilmavoimat HävLLv 31, Kuopio/Rissala
	HN-409	McDonnell Douglas F-18C Hornet	Ilmavoimat HävLLv 11, Roveniemi
	HN-410	McDonnell Douglas F-18C Hornet	Ilmavoimat IlmaStk, Tampere/Pirkkala
	HN-411	McDonnell Douglas F-18C Hornet	Ilmavoimat HävLLv 11, Roveniemi
	HN-412	McDonnell Douglas F-18C Hornet	Ilmavoimat HävLLv 11, Roveniemi
	HN-414	McDonnell Douglas F-18C Hornet	Ilmavoimat HävLLv 31, Kuopio/Rissala
	HN-415	McDonnell Douglas F-18C Hornet	Ilmavoimat HävLLv 31, Kuopio/Rissala
	HN-416	McDonnell Douglas F-18C Hornet	Ilmavoimat HävLLv 11, Roveniemi
	HN-417	McDonnell Douglas F-18C Hornet	Ilmavoimat HävLLv 31, Kuopio/Rissala
	HN-418	McDonnell Douglas F-18C Hornet	Ilmavoimat HävLLv 11, Roveniemi
	HN-419	McDonnell Douglas F-18C Hornet	Ilmavoimat IlmaStk, Tampere/Pirkkala
	HN-420	McDonnell Douglas F-18C Hornet	Ilmavoimat HävLLv 31, Kuopio/Rissala
	HN-421	McDonnell Douglas F-18C Hornet	Ilmavoimat HävLLv 11, Roveniemi
	HN-422	McDonnell Douglas F-18C Hornet	Ilmavoimat HävLLv 11, Roveniemi
	HN-423	McDonnell Douglas F-18C Hornet	Ilmavoimat HävLLv 31, Kuopio/Rissala
	HN-424	McDonnell Douglas F-18C Hornet	Ilmavoimat HävLLv 31, Kuopio/Rissala
	HN-425	McDonnell Douglas F-18C Hornet	Ilmavoimat HävLLv 31, Kuopio/Rissala
	HN-426	McDonnell Douglas F-18C Hornet	Ilmavoimat HävLLv 31, Kuopio/Rissala
	HN-427	McDonnell Douglas F-18C Hornet	Ilmavoimat HävLLv 11, Roveniemi
	HN-428	McDonnell Douglas F-18C Hornet	Ilmavoimat HävLLv 11, Roveniemi
	HN-429	McDonnell Douglas F-18C Hornet	Ilmavoimat HävLLv 11, Roveniemi
	HN-431	McDonnell Douglas F-18C Hornet	Ilmavoimat HävLLv 31, Kuopio/Rissala
	HN-432	McDonnell Douglas F-18C Hornet	Ilmavoimat HävLLv 31, Kuopio/Rissala
	HN-433	McDonnell Douglas F-18C Hornet	Ilmavoimat HävLLv 31, Kuopio/Rissala
	HN-434	McDonnell Douglas F-18C Hornet	Ilmavoimat HävLLv 11, Roveniemi
	HN-435	McDonnell Douglas F-18C Hornet	Ilmavoimat HävLLv 31, Kuopio/Rissala
	HN-436	McDonnell Douglas F-18C Hornet	Ilmavoimat HävLLv 31, Kuopio/Rissala
	HN-437	McDonnell Douglas F-18C Hornet	Ilmavoimat HävLLv 31, Kuopio/Rissala
	HN-438	McDonnell Douglas F-18C Hornet	Ilmavoimat HävLLv 11, Roveniemi
	HN-439	McDonnell Douglas F-18C Hornet	Ilmavoimat HävLLv 31, Kuopio/Rissala
	HN-440	McDonnell Douglas F-18C Hornet	Ilmavoimat HävLLv 11, Roveniemi
	HN-441	McDonnell Douglas F-18C Hornet	Ilmavoimat HävLLv 11, Roveniemi
	HN-442	McDonnell Douglas F-18C Hornet	Ilmavoimat HävLLv 11, Roveniemi
	HN-443	McDonnell Douglas F-18C Hornet	Ilmavoimat HävLLv 31, Kuopio/Rissala
	HN-444	McDonnell Douglas F-18C Hornet	Ilmavoimat HävLLv 11, Roveniemi
	HN-445	McDonnell Douglas F-18C Hornet	Ilmavoimat HävLLv 11, Roveniemi
	HN-446	McDonnell Douglas F-18C Hornet	Ilmavoimat HävLLv 11, Roveniemi
	HN-447	McDonnell Douglas F-18C Hornet	Ilmavoimat HävLLv 11, Roveniemi
	HN-448	McDonnell Douglas F-18C Hornet	Ilmavoimat HävLLv 31, Kuopio/Rissala
	HN-449	McDonnell Douglas F-18C Hornet	Ilmavoimat HävLLv 11, Roveniemi
	HN-450	McDonnell Douglas F-18C Hornet	Ilmavoimat HävLLv 11, Roveniemi
	HN-451	McDonnell Douglas F-18C Hornet	Ilmavoimat HävLLv 31, Kuopio/Rissala
	HN-452	McDonnell Douglas F-18C Hornet	Ilmavoimat HävLLv 11, Roveniemi
	HN-453	McDonnell Douglas F-18C Hornet	Ilmavoimat HävLLv 31, Kuopio/Rissala
	HN-454	McDonnell Douglas F-18C Hornet	Ilmavoimat HävLLv 31, Kuopio/Rissala
	HN-455	McDonnell Douglas F-18C Hornet	Ilmavoimat HävLLv 31, Kuopio/Rissala
	HN-456	McDonnell Douglas F-18C Hornet	Ilmavoimat HävLLv 31, Kuopio/Rissala
	HN-457	McDonnell Douglas F-18C Hornet	Ilmavoimat HävLLv 11, Roveniemi
	HN-461	McDonnell Douglas F-18D Hornet	Ilmavoimat HävLLv 31, Kuopio/Rissala
	HN-462	McDonnell Douglas F-18D Hornet	Ilmavoimat HävLLv 11, Roveniemi
	HN-463	McDonnell Douglas F-18D Hornet	Ilmavoimat HävLLv 11, Roveniemi
	HN-464	McDonnell Douglas F-18D Hornet	Ilmavoimat HävLLv 11, Roveniemi
	HN-465	McDonnell Douglas F-18D Hornet	Ilmavoimat HävLLv 31, Kuopio/Rissala
	HN-466	McDonnell Douglas F-18D Hornet	Ilmavoimat HävLLv 31, Kuopio/Rissala
	HN-467	McDonnell Douglas F-18D Hornet	Ilmavoimat HävLLv 31, Kuopio/Rissala
	HW-307	BAe Hawk 51	Ilmavoimat HävLLv 41, Jyväskylä/Tikkakoski
	HW-320	BAe Hawk 51	Ilmavoimat HävLLv 41, Jyväskylä/Tikkakoski
	HW-321	BAe Hawk 51	Ilmavoimat HävLLv 41, Jyväskylä/Tikkakoski

Serial	Type (code/other identity)	Owner/operator, location or fate	Notes
HW-327	BAe Hawk 51	Ilmavoimat HävLLv 41, Jyväskylä/Tikkakoski	
HW-330	BAe Hawk 51	Ilmavoimat, stored Halli (for upgrade)	
HW-333	BAe Hawk 51	*Withdrawn from use*	
HW-334	BAe Hawk 51	Ilmavoimat HävLLv 41, Jyväskylä/Tikkakoski	
HW-336	BAe Hawk 51	Ilmavoimat, stored Halli (for upgrade)	
HW-338	BAe Hawk 51	Ilmavoimat HävLLv 41, Jyväskylä/Tikkakoski	
HW-339	BAe Hawk 51	Ilmavoimat HävLLv 41, Jyväskylä/Tikkakoski	
HW-340	BAe Hawk 51	Ilmavoimat HävLLv 41, Jyväskylä/Tikkakoski	
HW-341	BAe Hawk 51 [1]	Ilmavoimat HävLLv 41, Jyväskylä/Tikkakoski	
HW-343	BAe Hawk 51	Ilmavoimat HävLLv 41, Jyväskylä/Tikkakoski	
HW-344	BAe Hawk 51	Ilmavoimat, stored Halli (for upgrade)	
HW-345	BAe Hawk 51 [4]	Ilmavoimat HävLLv 41, Jyväskylä/Tikkakoski	
HW-348	BAe Hawk 51	Ilmavoimat, stored Halli (for upgrade)	
HW-349	BAe Hawk 51	Ilmavoimat, stored Halli (for upgrade)	
HW-350	BAe Hawk 51	Ilmavoimat, stored Halli (for upgrade)	
HW-351	BAe Hawk 51A	Ilmavoimat HävLLv 41, Jyväskylä/Tikkakoski	
HW-352	BAe Hawk 51A [7]	Ilmavoimat HävLLv 41, Jyväskylä/Tikkakoski	
HW-353	BAe Hawk 51A	Ilmavoimat HävLLv 41, Jyväskylä/Tikkakoski	
HW-354	BAe Hawk 51A [3]	Ilmavoimat HävLLv 41, Jyväskylä/Tikkakoski	
HW-355	BAe Hawk 51A	Ilmavoimat HävLLv 41, Jyväskylä/Tikkakoski	
HW-356	BAe Hawk 51A	Ilmavoimat HävLLv 41, Jyväskylä/Tikkakoski	
HW-357	BAe Hawk 51A [2]	Ilmavoimat HävLLv 41, Jyväskylä/Tikkakoski	
HW-360	BAe Hawk 66	Ilmavoimat HävLLv 41, Jyväskylä/Tikkakoski	
HW-361	BAe Hawk 66	Ilmavoimat HävLLv 41, Jyväskylä/Tikkakoski	
HW-362	BAe Hawk 66	Ilmavoimat HävLLv 41, Jyväskylä/Tikkakoski	
HW-363	BAe Hawk 66	Ilmavoimat HävLLv 41, Jyväskylä/Tikkakoski	
HW-364	BAe Hawk 66	Ilmavoimat HävLLv 41, Jyväskylä/Tikkakoski	
HW-365	BAe Hawk 66	Ilmavoimat HävLLv 41, Jyväskylä/Tikkakoski	
HW-366	BAe Hawk 66	Ilmavoimat HävLLv 41, Jyväskylä/Tikkakoski	
HW-367	BAe Hawk 66	Ilmavoimat HävLLv 41, Jyväskylä/Tikkakoski	
HW-368	BAe Hawk 66	Ilmavoimat HävLLv 41, Jyväskylä/Tikkakoski	
HW-370	BAe Hawk 66	Ilmavoimat HävLLv 41, Jyväskylä/Tikkakoski	
HW-371	BAe Hawk 66	Ilmavoimat HävLLv 41, Jyväskylä/Tikkakoski	
HW-373	BAe Hawk 66	Ilmavoimat HävLLv 41, Jyväskylä/Tikkakoski	
HW-374	BAe Hawk 66	Ilmavoimat HävLLv 41, Jyväskylä/Tikkakoski	
HW-375	BAe Hawk 66	Ilmavoimat HävLLv 41, Jyväskylä/Tikkakoski	
HW-376	BAe Hawk 66	Ilmavoimat HävLLv 41, Jyväskylä/Tikkakoski	
HW-377	BAe Hawk 66	Ilmavoimat HävLLv 41, Jyväskylä/Tikkakoski	
LJ-1	Gates Learjet 35A	Ilmavoimat TukiLLv (Det.), Kuopio/Rissala	
LJ-2	Gates Learjet 35A	Ilmavoimat TukiLLv, Tampere/Pirkkala	
LJ-3	Gates Learjet 35A	Ilmavoimat TukiLLv, Tampere/Pirkkala	
NH-202	NH Industries NH.90-TTH	Maavoimat 1.HK/HekoP, Utti	
NH-203	NH Industries NH.90-TTH	Maavoimat 1.HK/HekoP, Utti	
NH-204	NH Industries NH.90-TTH	Maavoimat 1.HK/HekoP, Utti	
NH-205	NH Industries NH.90-TTH	Maavoimat 1.HK/HekoP, Utti	
NH-206	NH Industries NH.90-TTH	Maavoimat 1.HK/HekoP, Utti	
NH-207	NH Industries NH.90-TTH	Maavoimat 1.HK/HekoP, Utti	
NH-208	NH Industries NH.90-TTH	Maavoimat 1.HK/HekoP, Utti	
NH-209	NH Industries NH.90-TTH	Maavoimat 1.HK/HekoP, Utti	
NH-210	NH Industries NH.90-TTH	Maavoimat 1.HK/HekoP, Utti	
NH-211	NH Industries NH.90-TTH	Maavoimat 1.HK/HekoP, Utti	
NH-212	NH Industries NH.90-TTH	Maavoimat 1.HK/HekoP, Utti	
NH-213	NH Industries NH.90-TTH	Maavoimat 1.HK/HekoP, Utti	
NH-214	NH Industries NH.90-TTH	Maavoimat 1.HK/HekoP, Utti	
NH-215	NH Industries NH.90-TTH	Maavoimat 1.HK/HekoP, Utti	
NH-216	NH Industries NH.90-TTH	Maavoimat 1.HK/HekoP, Utti	
NH-217	NH Industries NH.90-TTH	Maavoimat 1.HK/HekoP, Utti	
NH-218	NH Industries NH.90-TTH	Maavoimat 1.HK/HekoP, Utti	
NH-219	NH Industries NH.90-TTH	Maavoimat 1.HK/HekoP, Utti	
NH-220	NH Industries NH.90-TTH	Maavoimat 1.HK/HekoP, Utti	
NH-221	NH Industries NH.90-TTH	Maavoimat 1.HK/HekoP, Utti	
PI-01	Pilatus PC-12/47E	Ilmavoimat TukiLLv, Tampere/Pirkkala	

Notes	Serial	Type (code/other identity)	Owner/operator, location or fate
	PI-02	Pilatus PC-12/47E	Ilmavoimat TukiLLv, Tampere/Pirkkala
	PI-03	Pilatus PC-12/47E	Ilmavoimat TukiLLv, Tampere/Pirkkala
	PI-04	Pilatus PC-12/47E	Ilmavoimat TukiLLv, Tampere/Pirkkala
	PI-05	Pilatus PC-12/47E	Ilmavoimat TukiLLv, Tampere/Pirkkala
	PI-06	Pilatus PC-12/47E	Ilmavoimat TukiLLv, Tampere/Pirkkala

FRANCE

NB: Due to the way in which French military aircraft serials are issued, this section is sorted by type

Armée de l'Air (AA)

Notes	Serial	Type (code/other identity)	Owner/operator, location or fate
	418	Airbus A.310-304 (F-RADC)	AA ET 03.060 *Esterel*, Paris/Charles de Gaulle
	421	Airbus A.310-304 (F-RADA)	AA ET 03.060 *Esterel*, Paris/Charles de Gaulle
	422	Airbus A.310-304 (F-RADB)	AA ET 03.060 *Esterel*, Paris/Charles de Gaulle
	240	Airbus A.330-223 (F-RARF)	AA ET 00.060, Evreux
	041	Airbus A.330-243 MRTT Phénix (MRTT041) [F-UJCG]	AA GRV 02.091 *Bretagne*, Istres
	042	Airbus A.330-243 MRTT Phénix (EC-338) [F-UJCH]	AA GRV 02.091 *Bretagne*, Istres (on order)
	043	Airbus A.330-243 MRTT Phénix [F-UJCI]	AA GRV 02.091 *Bretagne*, Istres (on order)
	...	Airbus A.330-243 MRTT Phénix	AA GRV 02.091 *Bretagne*, Istres (on order)
	...	Airbus A.330-243 MRTT Phénix	AA GRV 02.091 *Bretagne*, Istres (on order)
	...	Airbus A.330-243 MRTT Phénix	AA GRV 02.091 *Bretagne*, Istres (on order)
	...	Airbus A.330-243 MRTT Phénix	AA GRV 02.091 *Bretagne*, Istres (on order)
	...	Airbus A.330-243 MRTT Phénix	AA GRV 02.091 *Bretagne*, Istres (on order)
	...	Airbus A.330-243 MRTT Phénix	AA GRV 02.091 *Bretagne*, Istres (on order)
	...	Airbus A.330-243 MRTT Phénix	AA GRV 02.091 *Bretagne*, Istres (on order)
	...	Airbus A.330-243 MRTT Phénix	AA GRV 02.091 *Bretagne*, Istres (on order)
	...	Airbus A.330-243 MRTT Phénix	AA GRV 02.091 *Bretagne*, Istres (on order)
	...	Airbus A.330-243 MRTT Phénix	AA GRV 02.091 *Bretagne*, Istres (on order)
	...	Airbus A.330-243 MRTT Phénix	AA GRV 02.091 *Bretagne*, Istres (on order)
	075	Airbus A.340-212 (F-RAJA)	AA ET 03.060 *Esterel*, Paris/Charles de Gaulle
	081	Airbus A.340-212 (F-RAJB)	AA ET 03.060 *Esterel*, Paris/Charles de Gaulle
	0007	Airbus Military A.400M (F-RBAA)	AA ET 01.061 *Touraine*, Orléans
	0008	Airbus Military A.400M (F-RBAB)	AA ET 01.061 *Touraine*, Orléans
	0010	Airbus Military A.400M (F-RBAC)	AA ET 01.061 *Touraine*, Orléans
	0011	Airbus Military A.400M (F-RBAD)	AA ET 01.061 *Touraine*, Orléans
	0012	Airbus Military A.400M (F-RBAE)	AA ET 01.061 *Touraine*, Orléans
	0014	Airbus Military A.400M (F-RBAF)	AA ET 01.061 *Touraine*, Orléans
	0019	Airbus Military A.400M (F-RBAG)	AA ET 01.061 *Touraine*, Orléans
	0031	Airbus Military A.400M (F-RBAH)	AA ET 01.061 *Touraine*, Orléans
	0033	Airbus Military A.400M (F-RBAI)	AA ET 01.061 *Touraine*, Orléans
	0037	Airbus Military A.400M (F-RBAJ)	AA ET 01.061 *Touraine*, Orléans
	0053	Airbus Military A.400M (F-RBAK)	AA ET 01.061 *Touraine*, Orléans
	0062	Airbus Military A.400M (F-RBAL) $	AA ET 01.061 *Touraine*, Orléans
	0065	Airbus Military A.400M (F-RBAM)	AA ET 01.061 *Touraine*, Orléans
	0073	Airbus Military A.400M (F-RBAN)	AA ET 01.061 *Touraine*, Orléans
	0089	Airbus Military A.400M (F-RBAO)	AA (on order)
	0095	Airbus Military A.400M (F-RBAP)	AA (on order)
	0...	Airbus Military A.400M (F-RBAQ)	AA (on order)
	0...	Airbus Military A.400M (F-RBAR)	AA (on order)
	0...	Airbus Military A.400M (F-RBAS)	AA (on order)
	045	Airtech CN-235M-200 [62-IB]	AA ET 01.062 *Vercours*, Evreux
	065	Airtech CN-235M-200 [52-IC]	AA ET 00.052 *La Tontouta*, Nouméa
	066	Airtech CN-235M-200 [52-ID]	AA ET 00.052 *La Tontouta*, Nouméa
	071	Airtech CN-235M-200 [62-IE]	AA ET 01.062 *Vercours*, Evreux
	072	Airtech CN-235M-200 [52-IF]	AA ET 00.052 *La Tontouta*, Nouméa
	105	Airtech CN-235M-200 [52-IG]	AA ET 00.052 *La Tontouta*, Nouméa
	107	Airtech CN-235M-200 [52-IH]	AA ET 00.052 *La Tontouta*, Nouméa
	111	Airtech CN-235M-200 [64-II]	AA ET 01.062 *Vercours*, Evreux
	114	Airtech CN-235M-200 [62-IJ]	AA ET 01.062 *Vercours*, Evreux
	123	Airtech CN-235M-200 [62-IM]	AA ET 01.062 *Vercours*, Evreux
	128	Airtech CN-235M-200 [62-IK]	AA ET 01.062 *Vercours*, Evreux
	129	Airtech CN-235M-200 [62-IL]	AA ET 01.062 *Vercours*, Evreux
	137	Airtech CN-235M-200 [62-IN]	AA ET 01.062 *Vercours*, Evreux

Serial	Type (code/other identity)	Owner/operator, location or fate	Notes
141	Airtech CN-235M-200 [62-IO]	AA ET 00.058 *Antilles*, Fort-de-France	
152	Airtech CN-235M-200 [62-IP]	AA ET 01.062 *Vercors*, Evreux	
156	Airtech CN-235M-200 [62-IQ]	AA ET 01.062 *Vercors*, Evreux	
158	Airtech CN-235M-200 [62-IR]	AA ET 01.062 *Vercors*, Evreux	
160	Airtech CN-235M-200 [62-IS]	AA ET 01.062 *Vercors*, Evreux	
165	Airtech CN-235M-200 [62-IT]	AA ET 01.062 *Vercors*, Evreux	
193	Airtech CN-235M-300 [62-HA]	AA ET 03.062 *Ventoux*, Evreux	
194	Airtech CN-235M-300 [62-HB]	AA ET 03.062 *Ventoux*, Evreux	
195	Airtech CN-235M-300 [62-HC]	AA ET 03.062 *Ventoux*, Evreux	
196	Airtech CN-235M-300 [62-HD]	AA ET 03.062 *Ventoux*, Evreux	
197	Airtech CN-235M-300 [62-HE]	AA ET 03.062 *Ventoux*, Evreux	
198	Airtech CN-235M-300 [62-HF]	AA ET 03.062 *Ventoux*, Evreux	
199	Airtech CN-235M-300 [62-HG]	AA ET 03.062 *Ventoux*, Evreux	
200	Airtech CN-235M-300 [62-HH]	AA ET 03.062 *Ventoux*, Evreux	
....	Beechcraft King Air 350 (F-WTAO)	AA (on order)	
....	Beechcraft King Air 350 (F-WTAP)	AA (on order)	
470	Boeing C-135FR Stratotanker [31-CA]	AA GRV 02.091 *Bretagne*, Istres	
471	Boeing C-135FR Stratotanker [31-CB]	AA GRV 02.091 *Bretagne*, Istres	
472	Boeing C-135FR Stratotanker [31-CC]	AA GRV 02.091 *Bretagne*, Istres	
474	Boeing C-135FR Stratotanker [31-CE]	AA GRV 02.091 *Bretagne*, Istres	
475	Boeing C-135FR Stratotanker [31-CF]	AA GRV 02.091 *Bretagne*, Istres	
497	Boeing C-135FR Stratotanker [31-CM]$	AA GRV 02.091 *Bretagne*, Istres	
525	Boeing C-135FR Stratotanker [31-CN]	AA GRV 02.091 *Bretagne*, Istres	
574	Boeing KC-135RG Stratotanker [31-CP]	AA GRV 02.091 *Bretagne*, Istres	
735	Boeing C-135FR Stratotanker [31-CG]	AA GRV 02.091 *Bretagne*, Istres	
736	Boeing C-135FR Stratotanker [93-CH]	AA GRV 02.091 *Bretagne*, Istres	
737	Boeing C-135FR Stratotanker [31-CI]	AA GRV 02.091 *Bretagne*, Istres	
738	Boeing C-135FR Stratotanker [31-CJ]	AA GRV 02.091 *Bretagne*, Istres	
739	Boeing C-135FR Stratotanker [93-CK]	AA GRV 02.091 *Bretagne*, Istres	
740	Boeing C-135FR Stratotanker [31-CL]	AA GRV 02.091 *Bretagne*, Istres	
201	Boeing E-3F Sentry [36-CA]	AA EDCA 00.036, Avord	
202	Boeing E-3F Sentry [36-CB]	AA EDCA 00.036, Avord	
203	Boeing E-3F Sentry [36-CC]	AA EDCA 00.036, Avord	
204	Boeing E-3F Sentry [36-CD] $	AA EDCA 00.036, Avord	
377	CASA 212-300 Aviocar (F-ZAEA)	AA DGA EV, Cazaux & Istres	
378	CASA 212-300 Aviocar [MP]	AA DGA EV, Cazaux & Istres	
386	CASA 212-300 Aviocar [MQ]	AA DGA EV, Cazaux & Istres	
820	Cessna 310Q [CL]	AA DGA EV, Cazaux & Istres	
981	Cessna 310Q [BF]	AA DGA EV, Cazaux & Istres	
E4	D-BD Alpha Jet E	AA DGA EV, Cazaux & Istres	
E7	D-BD Alpha Jet E [705-TU]	AA EAC 00.314, Tours	
E8	D-BD Alpha Jet E	AA DGA EV, Cazaux & Istres	
E11	D-BD Alpha Jet E [8-UB]	AA EE 03.008 *Côte d'Or*, Cazaux	
E12	D-BD Alpha Jet E	AA DGA EV, Cazaux & Istres	
E13	D-BD Alpha Jet E [8-MM]	AA, stored Châteaudun	
E17	D-BD Alpha Jet E [705-AA]	AA, stored Châteaudun	
E18	D-BD Alpha Jet E	AA	
E20	D-BD Alpha Jet E [705-MS]	AA EAC 00.314, Tours	
E22	D-BD Alpha Jet E [8-LS] $	AA EE 03.008 *Côte d'Or*, Cazaux	
E25	D-BD Alpha Jet E [8-TJ]	AA EE 03.008 *Côte d'Or*, Cazaux	
E26	D-BD Alpha Jet E [705-ND] $	AA EAC 00.314, Tours	
E28	D-BD Alpha Jet E [705-AB]	AA EAC 00.314, Tours	
E29	D-BD Alpha Jet E [102-NB]	AA EE 03.008 *Côte d'Or*, Cazaux	
E30	D-BD Alpha Jet E [705-MD]	AA, stored Châteaudun	
E31	D-BD Alpha Jet E [705-RK]	AA EAC 00.314, Tours	
E32	D-BD Alpha Jet E [102-FI]	AA EE 03.008 *Côte d'Or*, Cazaux	
E33	D-BD Alpha Jet E [705-FJ] $	AA EAC 00.314, Tours	
E35	D-BD Alpha Jet E [705-MA]	AA EAC 00.314, Tours	
E37	D-BD Alpha Jet E [705-NL]	AA EAC 00.314, Tours	
E38	D-BD Alpha Jet E $	AA ETO 01.008 *Saintonge*, Cazaux	
E41	D-BD Alpha Jet E [8-RA]	*Preserved at Cazaux, 2018*	
E42	D-BD Alpha Jet E [705-TA] $	AA EAC 00.314, Tours	

Notes	Serial	Type (code/other identity)	Owner/operator, location or fate
	E44	D-BD Alpha Jet E [F-UHRE,1]	AA *Patrouille de France*, Salon de Provence
	E45	D-BD Alpha Jet E [F-TETF,2]	AA *Patrouille de France*, Salon de Provence
	E46	D-BD Alpha Jet E [F-UHRF]	AA *Patrouille de France*, Salon de Provence
	E48	D-BD Alpha Jet E [8-MH]	AA EE 03.008 *Côte d'Or*, Cazaux
	E51	D-BD Alpha Jet E [705-AD]	AA EAC 00.314, Tours
	E53	D-BD Alpha Jet E [102-LI]	AA EE 03.008 *Côte d'Or*, Cazaux
	E58	D-BD Alpha Jet E [705-TK]	AA, stored Châteaudun
	E60	D-BD Alpha Jet E	AA EPNER, Istres
	E67	D-BD Alpha Jet E [705-TB]	AA EAC 00.314, Tours
	E68	D-BD Alpha Jet E [F-TEMO,9]	AA *Patrouille de France*, Salon de Provence
	E72	D-BD Alpha Jet E [705-LA]	AA, stored Châteaudun
	E73	D-BD Alpha Jet E [F-TENE]	AA *Patrouille de France*, Salon de Provence
	E74	D-BD Alpha Jet E	AA
	E75	D-BD Alpha Jet E [8-AE]	AA EE 03.008 *Côte d'Or*, Cazaux
	E76	D-BD Alpha Jet E [102-RJ]	AA EE 03.008 *Côte d'Or*, Cazaux
	E79	D-BD Alpha Jet E [F-TENA]	AA *Patrouille de France*, Salon de Provence
	E80	D-BD Alpha Jet E	AA DGA EV, Cazaux & Istres
	E81	D-BD Alpha Jet E [8-FO]	AA ETO 01.008 *Saintonge*, Cazaux
	E82	D-BD Alpha Jet E [8-LW]	AA ETO 01.008 *Saintonge*, Cazaux
	E83	D-BD Alpha Jet E [705-TZ]	AA EAC 00.314, Tours
	E85	D-BD Alpha Jet E [F-UGFF,3]	AA *Patrouille de France*, Salon de Provence
	E86	D-BD Alpha Jet E [102-FB]	AA EE 03.008 *Côte d'Or*, Cazaux
	E87	D-BD Alpha Jet E [F-TELC]	AA *Patrouille de France*, Salon de Provence
	E88	D-BD Alpha Jet E [F-TELL]	AA, stored Châteaudun
	E89	D-BD Alpha Jet E [120-LX]	AA ETO 01.008 *Saintonge*, Cazaux
	E90	D-BD Alpha Jet E [8-TH]	AA ETO 01.008 *Saintonge*, Cazaux
	E93	D-BD Alpha Jet E [8-TX]	AA ETO 01.008 *Saintonge*, Cazaux
	E94	D-BD Alpha Jet E [705-RH]	AA EAC 00.314, Tours
	E95	D-BD Alpha Jet E [F-TERQ]	AA, stored Châteaudun
	E97	D-BD Alpha Jet E [102-MB]	AA EE 03.008 *Côte d'Or*, Cazaux
	E98	D-BD Alpha Jet E [F-TEMF]	AA *Patrouille de France*, Salon de Provence
	E99	D-BD Alpha Jet E [120-AH]	AA, stored Châteaudun
	E100	D-BD Alpha Jet E $	AA EPNER, Istres
	E101	D-BD Alpha Jet E [120-TT]	AA ETO 01.008 *Saintonge*, Cazaux
	E102	D-BD Alpha Jet E [120-LM]	AA, stored Châteaudun
	E104	D-BD Alpha Jet E [705-TG]	AA EAC 00.314, Tours
	E105	D-BD Alpha Jet E [8-FM]	AA EE 03.008 *Côte d'Or*, Cazaux
	E107	D-BD Alpha Jet E [705-UD]	AA EAC 00.314, Tours
	E108	D-BD Alpha Jet E [8-AF]	AA ETO 01.008 *Saintonge*, Cazaux
	E109	D-BD Alpha Jet E [8-AG]	AA ETO 01.008 *Saintonge*, Cazaux
	E110	D-BD Alpha Jet E [705-AH]	AA, stored Châteaudun
	E112	D-BD Alpha Jet E [8-AO]	AA EE 03.008 *Côte d'Or*, Cazaux
	E113	D-BD Alpha Jet E [F-TETD,7]	AA *Patrouille de France*, Salon de Provence
	E114	D-BD Alpha Jet E [705-RR]	AA EAC 00.314, Tours
	E115	D-BD Alpha Jet E [705-MR]	AA EAC 00.314, Tours
	E116	D-BD Alpha Jet E [8-FN]	AA ETO 01.008 *Saintonge*, Cazaux
	E117	D-BD Alpha Jet E [705-RI]	AA EAC 00.314, Tours
	E118	D-BD Alpha Jet E [8-LN]	AA ETO 01.008 *Saintonge*, Cazaux
	E119	D-BD Alpha Jet E [F-UGFE]	AA *Patrouille de France*, Salon de Provence
	E120	D-BD Alpha Jet E [705-LG]	AA EAC 00.314, Tours
	E123	D-BD Alpha Jet E [8-RM]	AA EE 03.008 *Côte d'Or*, Cazaux
	E124	D-BD Alpha Jet E [8-RN]	AA ETO 01.008 *Saintonge*, Cazaux
	E125	D-BD Alpha Jet E [705-LK]	AA EAC 00.314, Tours
	E127	D-BD Alpha Jet E [F-UGFK,8]	AA *Patrouille de France*, Salon de Provence
	E128	D-BD Alpha Jet E [705-TM]	AA EAC 00.314, Tours
	E129	D-BD Alpha Jet E [705-LP]	AA EAC 00.314, Tours
	E130	D-BD Alpha Jet E [8-RP]	AA EE 03.008 *Côte d'Or*, Cazaux
	E131	D-BD Alpha Jet E [120-RO]	AA ETO 01.008 *Saintonge*, Cazaux
	E134	D-BD Alpha Jet E [705-RM]	AA EAC 00.314, Tours
	E135	D-BD Alpha Jet E [8-RX]	AA EE 03.008 *Côte d'Or*, Cazaux
	E136	D-BD Alpha Jet E [8-RP]	AA, stored Châteaudun
	E137	D-BD Alpha Jet E [705-LJ]	AA EAC 00.314, Tours

Serial	Type (code/other identity)	Owner/operator, location or fate	Notes
E138	D-BD Alpha Jet E [8-RQ]	AA EE 03.008 *Côte d'Or*, Cazaux	
E139	D-BD Alpha Jet E [F-UGFC,6]	AA *Patrouille de France*, Salon de Provence	
E140	D-BD Alpha Jet E [102-FA]	AA, stored Châteaudun	
E141	D-BD Alpha Jet E [8-NF]	AA EE 03.008 *Côte d'Or*, Cazaux	
E142	D-BD Alpha Jet E [8-LO]	AA ETO 01.008 *Saintonge*, Cazaux	
E143	D-BD Alpha Jet E	AA	
E144	D-BD Alpha Jet E [8-AK]	AA ETO 01.008 *Saintonge*, Cazaux	
E145	D-BD Alpha Jet E	AA	
E146	D-BD Alpha Jet E [F-UHRR,5]	AA *Patrouille de France*, Salon de Provence	
E147	D-BD Alpha Jet E [120-LT]	AA ETO 01.008 *Saintonge*, Cazaux	
E148	D-BD Alpha Jet E [705-LU]	AA EAC 00.314, Tours	
E149	D-BD Alpha Jet E [705-RS]	AA EAC 00.314, Tours	
E151	D-BD Alpha Jet E [8-FD]	AA EE 03.008 *Côte d'Or*, Cazaux	
E152	D-BD Alpha Jet E [F-UHRT,4]	AA *Patrouille de France*, Salon de Provence	
E153	D-BD Alpha Jet E [705-RU]	AA EAC 00.314, Tours	
E154	D-BD Alpha Jet E [120-AL]	AA ETO 01.008 *Saintonge*, Cazaux	
E156	D-BD Alpha Jet E [30-TI]	AA, stored Châteaudun	
E157	D-BD Alpha Jet E [8-UC]	AA ETO 01.008 *Saintonge*, Cazaux	
E158	D-BD Alpha Jet E [705-RF]	AA EAC 00.314, Tours	
E160	D-BD Alpha Jet E [8-UH]	AA ETO 01.008 *Saintonge*, Cazaux	
E162	D-BD Alpha Jet E [F-TERJ]	AA *Patrouille de France*, Salon de Provence	
E163	D-BD Alpha Jet E [705-RB]	AA EAC 00.314, Tours	
E164	D-BD Alpha Jet E [120-RV]	AA ETO 01.008 *Saintonge*, Cazaux	
E165	D-BD Alpha Jet E [8-RE]	AA, stored Châteaudun	
E166	D-BD Alpha Jet E [705-RW]	AA EAC 00.314, Tours	
E167	D-BD Alpha Jet E [705-MN]	AA EAC 00.314, Tours	
E168	D-BD Alpha Jet E [8-FP]	AA EE 03.008 *Côte d'Or*, Cazaux	
E169	D-BD Alpha Jet E [30-RX]	AA, stored Châteaudun	
E170	D-BD Alpha Jet E [705-RY]	AA EAC 00.314, Tours	
E171	D-BD Alpha Jet E [705-RZ]	AA EAC 00.314, Tours	
E173	D-BD Alpha Jet E [8-MA]	AA EE 03.008 *Côte d'Or*, Cazaux	
E176	D-BD Alpha Jet E [120-MB]	AA, stored Châteaudun	
68	Dassault Falcon 7X (F-RAFA)	AA ET 00.060, Villacoublay	
86	Dassault Falcon 7X (F-RAFB)	AA ET 00.060, Villacoublay	
79	Dassault Falcon 20C [CT]	AA DGA EV, Cazaux & Istres	
104	Dassault Falcon 20C [CW]	AA DGA EV, Cazaux & Istres	
138	Dassault Falcon 20C [CR]	AA, stored Cazaux	
252	Dassault Falcon 20E [CA]	AA DGA EV, Cazaux & Istres	
288	Dassault Falcon 20E [CV]	AA DGA EV, Cazaux & Istres	
342	Dassault Falcon 20F [CU]	AA DGA EV, Cazaux & Istres	
375	Dassault Falcon 20F [CZ]	AA DGA EV, Cazaux & Istres	
02	Dassault Falcon 900 (F-RAFP)	AA ET 00.060, Villacoublay	
004	Dassault Falcon 900 (F-RAFQ)	AA ET 00.060, Villacoublay	
...	Dassault Falcon 900	(on order)	
...	Dassault Falcon 900	(on order)	
...	Dassault Falcon 900	(on order)	
231	Dassault Falcon 2000LX (F-RAFC)	AA ET 00.060, Villacoublay	
237	Dassault Falcon 2000LX (F-RAFD)	AA ET 00.060, Villacoublay	
501	Dassault Mirage 2000B (BX1)	AA DGA EV, Cazaux & Istres	
523	Dassault Mirage 2000B [115-KJ]	AA EC 02.005 *Ile de France*, Orange	
524	Dassault Mirage 2000B [115-OA]	AA EC 02.005 *Ile de France*, Orange	
525	Dassault Mirage 2000B [115-AM]	AA EC 02.005 *Ile de France*, Orange	
527	Dassault Mirage 2000B [115-OR]	AA EC 02.005 *Ile de France*, Orange	
528	Dassault Mirage 2000B [115-KS]	AA EC 02.005 *Ile de France*, Orange	
529	Dassault Mirage 2000B [115-OC]	AA EC 02.005 *Ile de France*, Orange	
530	Dassault Mirage 2000B [115-OL]	AA EC 02.005 *Ile de France*, Orange	
01	Dassault Mirage 2000-5F	AA DGA EV, Istres	
2	Dassault Mirage 2000C	AA, stored Châteaudun	
38	Dassault Mirage 2000-5F [116-EI]	AA GC 01.002 *Cigognes*, Luxeuil	
40	Dassault Mirage 2000-5F [2-EX]	AA GC 01.002 *Cigognes*, Luxeuil	
41	Dassault Mirage 2000-5F [2-FZ]	AA GC 01.002 *Cigognes*, Luxeuil	
42	Dassault Mirage 2000-5F [2-EY]	AA GC 01.002 *Cigognes*, Luxeuil	

Notes	Serial	Type (code/other identity)	Owner/operator, location or fate
	43	Dassault Mirage 2000-5F [116-EJ] $	AA GC 01.002 Cigognes, Luxeuil
	44	Dassault Mirage 2000-5F [2-EQ]	AA GC 01.002 Cigognes, Luxeuil
	45	Dassault Mirage 2000-5F [2-EF]	AA GC 01.002 Cigognes, Luxeuil
	46	Dassault Mirage 2000-5F [2-EN]	AA GC 01.002 Cigognes, Luxeuil
	47	Dassault Mirage 2000-5F [2-EP]	AA GC 01.002 Cigognes, Luxeuil
	48	Dassault Mirage 2000-5F [2-EW]	AA GC 01.002 Cigognes, Luxeuil
	49	Dassault Mirage 2000-5F [2-EA]	AA GC 01.002 Cigognes, Luxeuil
	51	Dassault Mirage 2000-5F	AA DGA EV, Istres
	52	Dassault Mirage 2000-5F [2-EH]	AA GC 01.002 Cigognes, Luxeuil
	54	Dassault Mirage 2000-5F [2-EZ]	AA GC 01.002 Cigognes, Luxeuil
	55	Dassault Mirage 2000-5F [2-EU]	AA GC 01.002 Cigognes, Luxeuil
	56	Dassault Mirage 2000-5F [2-EG]	AA GC 01.002 Cigognes, Luxeuil
	57	Dassault Mirage 2000-5F [2-ET]	AA GC 01.002 Cigognes, Luxeuil
	58	Dassault Mirage 2000-5F [2-EL]	AA GC 01.002 Cigognes, Luxeuil
	59	Dassault Mirage 2000-5F [2-EV]	AA GC 01.002 Cigognes, Luxeuil
	61	Dassault Mirage 2000-5F [2-ME]	AA GC 01.002 Cigognes, Luxeuil
	62	Dassault Mirage 2000-5F [2-ED]	AA GC 01.002 Cigognes, Luxeuil
	63	Dassault Mirage 2000-5F [2-EM]	AA GC 01.002 Cigognes, Luxeuil
	64	Dassault Mirage 2000C	AA DGA EV, Istres
	65	Dassault Mirage 2000-5F [2-MG]	AA GC 01.002 Cigognes, Luxeuil
	66	Dassault Mirage 2000-5F [2-EO]	AA GC 01.002 Cigognes, Luxeuil
	67	Dassault Mirage 2000-5F [2-MH]	AA GC 01.002 Cigognes, Luxeuil
	71	Dassault Mirage 2000-5F [116-EE]	AA GC 01.002 Cigognes, Luxeuil
	74	Dassault Mirage 2000-5F [2-MK]	AA GC 01.002 Cigognes, Luxeuil
	77	Dassault Mirage 2000-5F [2-AX]	AA GC 01.002 Cigognes, Luxeuil
	78	Dassault Mirage 2000-5F [2-EC]	AA GC 01.002 Cigognes, Luxeuil
	82	Dassault Mirage 2000C [115-YL]	AA EC 02.005 Ile de France, Orange
	83	Dassault Mirage 2000C [115-YC]	AA EC 02.005 Ile de France, Orange
	85	Dassault Mirage 2000C [115-LK]	AA EC 02.005 Ile de France, Orange
	88	Dassault Mirage 2000C [115-KV]	AA EC 02.005 Ile de France, Orange
	93	Dassault Mirage 2000C [115-YA]	AA EC 02.005 Ile de France, Orange
	94	Dassault Mirage 2000C [115-KB]	AA, stored Châteaudun
	96	Dassault Mirage 2000C [115-KI]	AA EC 02.005 Ile de France, Orange
	99	Dassault Mirage 2000C [115-YB]	AA EC 02.005 Ile de France, Orange
	100	Dassault Mirage 2000C [115-YF]	AA EC 02.005 Ile de France, Orange
	101	Dassault Mirage 2000C [115-KE] $	AA EC 02.005 Ile de France, Orange
	102	Dassault Mirage 2000C [115-KR]	AA EC 02.005 Ile de France, Orange
	104	Dassault Mirage 2000C [115-KG]	AA EC 02.005 Ile de France, Orange
	105	Dassault Mirage 2000C [115-LJ]	AA EC 02.005 Ile de France, Orange
	106	Dassault Mirage 2000C [115-KL]	AA EC 02.005 Ile de France, Orange
	107	Dassault Mirage 2000C [115-YD]	AA EC 02.005 Ile de France, Orange
	108	Dassault Mirage 2000C [115-LC]	AA EC 02.005 Ile de France, Orange
	109	Dassault Mirage 2000C [115-YH]	AA EC 02.005 Ile de France, Orange
	111	Dassault Mirage 2000C [115-KF]	AA EC 02.005 Ile de France, Orange
	113	Dassault Mirage 2000C [115-YO]	AA EC 02.005 Ile de France, Orange
	115	Dassault Mirage 2000C [115-YM]	AA, stored Châteaudun
	117	Dassault Mirage 2000C [115-LD]	AA, stored Châteaudun
	118	Dassault Mirage 2000C [115-YG]	AA EC 02.005 Ile de France, Orange
	120	Dassault Mirage 2000C [115-KC] $	AA EC 02.005 Ile de France, Orange
	121	Dassault Mirage 2000C [115-KN]	AA EC 02.005 Ile de France, Orange
	122	Dassault Mirage 2000C [115-YE]	AA EC 02.005 Ile de France, Orange
	123	Dassault Mirage 2000C [115-KD]	AA EC 02.005 Ile de France, Orange
	124	Dassault Mirage 2000C [115-YT]	AA EC 02.005 Ile de France, Orange
	601	Dassault Mirage 2000D [133-JG]	AA EC 01.003 Navarre, Nancy
	602	Dassault Mirage 2000D [3-XJ] $	AA EC 03.003 Ardennes, Nancy
	603	Dassault Mirage 2000D [3-XL]	AA EC 03.003 Ardennes, Nancy
	604	Dassault Mirage 2000D [30-IP]	AA CEAM/ECE 01.030 Côte d'Argent, Mont-de-Marsan
	605	Dassault Mirage 2000D [133-LF]	AA EC 02.003 Champagne, Nancy
	606	Dassault Mirage 2000D [3-JC]	AA EC 02.003 Champagne, Nancy
	607	Dassault Mirage 2000D	AA DGA EV, Istres
	609	Dassault Mirage 2000D [3-IF]	AA EC 03.003 Ardennes, Nancy

Serial	Type (code/other identity)	Owner/operator, location or fate	Notes
610	Dassault Mirage 2000D [133-XX]	AA EC 03.003 *Ardennes*, Nancy	
611	Dassault Mirage 2000D [3-JP]	AA EC 02.003 *Champagne*, Nancy	
613	Dassault Mirage 2000D [3-MO]	AA EC 03.003 *Ardennes*, Nancy	
614	Dassault Mirage 2000D [3-JU]	AA EC 02.003 *Champagne*, Nancy	
615	Dassault Mirage 2000D [3-JY]	AA EC 02.003 *Champagne*, Nancy	
616	Dassault Mirage 2000D [118-XH]	AA CEAM/ECE 01.030 *Côte d'Argent*, Mont-de-Marsan	
617	Dassault Mirage 2000D [3-IS]	AA EC 01.003 *Navarre*, Nancy	
618	Dassault Mirage 2000D [3-XC] $	AA EC 03.003 *Ardennes*, Nancy	
620	Dassault Mirage 2000D [3-IU]	AA EC 01.003 *Navarre*, Nancy	
622	Dassault Mirage 2000D [3-IL]	AA EC 01.003 *Navarre*, Nancy	
623	Dassault Mirage 2000D [133-MP]	AA EC 02.003 *Champagne*, Nancy	
624	Dassault Mirage 2000D [3-IT] $	AA EC 01.003 *Navarre*, Nancy	
625	Dassault Mirage 2000D [3-XG]	AA EC 03.003 *Ardennes*, Nancy	
626	Dassault Mirage 2000D [133-IC]	AA EC 01.003 *Navarre*, Nancy	
627	Dassault Mirage 2000D [30-JO]	AA CEAM/ECE 01.030 *Côte d'Argent*, Mont-de-Marsan	
628	Dassault Mirage 2000D [133-JL]	AA EC 02.003 *Champagne*, Nancy	
629	Dassault Mirage 2000D [3-XO]	AA EC 03.003 *Ardennes*, Nancy	
630	Dassault Mirage 2000D [3-XD] $	AA EC 03.003 *Ardennes*, Nancy	
631	Dassault Mirage 2000D [133-IH]	AA EC 01.003 *Navarre*, Nancy	
632	Dassault Mirage 2000D [133-XE]	AA EC 01.003 *Navarre*, Nancy	
634	Dassault Mirage 2000D [133-JE]	AA EC 01.003 *Navarre*, Nancy	
635	Dassault Mirage 2000D [3-AS]	AA EC 01.003 *Navarre*, Nancy	
636	Dassault Mirage 2000D [133-JV]	AA EC 02.003 *Champagne*, Nancy	
637	Dassault Mirage 2000D [30-XQ]	AA CEAM/ECE 01.030 *Côte d'Argent*, Mont-de-Marsan	
638	Dassault Mirage 2000D [3-IJ]	AA EC 03.003 *Ardennes*, Nancy	
639	Dassault Mirage 2000D [3-JJ]	AA EC 02.003 *Champagne*, Nancy	
640	Dassault Mirage 2000D [3-IN]	AA EC 01.003 *Navarre*, Nancy	
641	Dassault Mirage 2000D [3-JW]	AA EC 02.003 *Champagne*, Nancy	
642	Dassault Mirage 2000D [30-IE]	AA CEAM/ECE 01.030 *Côte d'Argent*, Mont-de-Marsan	
643	Dassault Mirage 2000D [3-JD]	AA EC 02.003 *Champagne*, Nancy	
644	Dassault Mirage 2000D $	AA DGA EV, Istres	
645	Dassault Mirage 2000D [3-XP]	AA EC 03.003 *Ardennes*, Nancy	
646	Dassault Mirage 2000D [3-MQ]	AA EC 01.003 *Navarre*, Nancy	
647	Dassault Mirage 2000D [3-IO]	AA EC 01.003 *Navarre*, Nancy	
648	Dassault Mirage 2000D [3-XT] $	AA EC 03.003 *Ardennes*, Nancy	
649	Dassault Mirage 2000D [3-XY]	AA EC 03.003 *Ardennes*, Nancy	
650	Dassault Mirage 2000D [3-IA]	AA EC 01.003 *Navarre*, Nancy	
652	Dassault Mirage 2000D [3-XN] $	AA EC 03.003 *Ardennes*, Nancy	
653	Dassault Mirage 2000D [3-AU]	AA ETD 04.003 *Argonne*, Nancy	
654	Dassault Mirage 2000D [3-ID]	AA EC 01.003 *Navarre*, Nancy	
655	Dassault Mirage 2000D [3-LH]	AA EC 01.003 *Navarre*, Nancy	
657	Dassault Mirage 2000D [3-JM]	AA EC 03.003 *Ardennes*, Nancy	
658	Dassault Mirage 2000D [3-JN]	AA EC 02.003 *Champagne*, Nancy	
659	Dassault Mirage 2000D [133-XR]	AA EC 03.003 *Ardennes*, Nancy	
660	Dassault Mirage 2000D [3-JF]	AA ETD 04.003 *Argonne*, Nancy	
661	Dassault Mirage 2000D [133-XI]	AA EC 03.003 *Ardennes*, Nancy	
662	Dassault Mirage 2000D [3-XA]	AA EC 03.003 *Ardennes*, Nancy	
664	Dassault Mirage 2000D [133-IW]	AA EC 01.003 *Navarre*, Nancy	
666	Dassault Mirage 2000D [133-IQ]	AA EC 01.003 *Navarre*, Nancy	
667	Dassault Mirage 2000D [3-JZ]	*Crashed 9 January 2019, Mignovillard*	
668	Dassault Mirage 2000D [3-IG]	AA EC 03.003 *Ardennes*, Nancy	
669	Dassault Mirage 2000D [133-AL]	AA ETD 04.003 *Argonne*, Nancy	
670	Dassault Mirage 2000D [3-XF]	AA EC 03.003 *Ardennes*, Nancy	
671	Dassault Mirage 2000D [3-XK]	AA EC 03.003 *Ardennes*, Nancy	
672	Dassault Mirage 2000D [3-XV]	AA EC 03.003 *Ardennes*, Nancy	
673	Dassault Mirage 2000D	AA DGA EV, Istres	
674	Dassault Mirage 2000D [30-IR]	AA CEAM/ECE 01.030 *Côte d'Argent*, Mont-de-Marsan	

Notes	Serial	Type (code/other identity)	Owner/operator, location or fate
	675	Dassault Mirage 2000D [3-JI] $	AA EC 01.003 *Navarre*, Nancy
	676	Dassault Mirage 2000D $	AA DGA EV, Istres
	677	Dassault Mirage 2000D [3-JT]	AA EC 02.003 *Champagne*, Nancy
	678	Dassault Mirage 2000D [133-JB]	AA EC 02.003 *Champagne*, Nancy
	679	Dassault Mirage 2000D [3-JX]	AA EC 01.003 *Navarre*, Nancy
	680	Dassault Mirage 2000D [3-XM]	AA EC 03.003 *Ardennes*, Nancy
	681	Dassault Mirage 2000D [3-AG]	AA EC 01.003 *Navarre*, Nancy
	682	Dassault Mirage 2000D [3-JR]	AA EC 02.003 *Champagne*, Nancy
	683	Dassault Mirage 2000D [3-IV]	AA EC 01.003 *Navarre*, Nancy
	684	Dassault Mirage 2000D	AA
	685	Dassault Mirage 2000D [3-XZ]	AA EC 01.003 *Navarre*, Nancy
	686	Dassault Mirage 2000D [133-JH]	AA EC 02.003 *Champagne*, Nancy
	D02	Dassault Mirage 2000D	AA DGA EV, Istres
	301	Dassault Mirage 2000N	AA DGA EV, Istres
	306	Dassault Mirage 2000N [116-BL]	*Withdrawn from use, June 2018*
	316	Dassault Mirage 2000N [116-AU] $	*Withdrawn from use, June 2018*
	319	Dassault Mirage 2000N	*Withdrawn from use*
	333	Dassault Mirage 2000N	*Withdrawn from use*
	334	Dassault Mirage 2000N	AA DGA EV, Istres
	335	Dassault Mirage 2000N [125-CI]	*Withdrawn from use, June 2018*
	338	Dassault Mirage 2000N [125-CG]	*Withdrawn from use, June 2018*
	342	Dassault Mirage 2000N [125-BA]	*Withdrawn from use, June 2018*
	345	Dassault Mirage 2000N [125-BU]	*Withdrawn from use, June 2018*
	348	Dassault Mirage 2000N [125-AL]	*Withdrawn from use, June 2018*
	350	Dassault Mirage 2000N [125-AJ]	*Withdrawn from use, June 2018*
	351	Dassault Mirage 2000N [125-AQ]	*Withdrawn from use, March 2018*
	354	Dassault Mirage 2000N [125-BJ]	*Withdrawn from use, June 2018*
	355	Dassault Mirage 2000N [125-AE]	*Withdrawn from use, June 2018*
	356	Dassault Mirage 2000N [125-BX]	AA DGA EV, Istres
	357	Dassault Mirage 2000N [125-CO] $	*Withdrawn from use, June 2018*
	358	Dassault Mirage 2000N [125-BQ]	*Withdrawn from use, June 2018*
	359	Dassault Mirage 2000N [125-AK] $	*Withdrawn from use, June 2017*
	361	Dassault Mirage 2000N [125-CK]	*Withdrawn from use, June 2018*
	362	Dassault Mirage 2000N [125-CU]	*Withdrawn from use, June 2018*
	364	Dassault Mirage 2000N [125-BB]	*Withdrawn from use, June 2018*
	365	Dassault Mirage 2000N [4-AI]	*Withdrawn from use*
	366	Dassault Mirage 2000N [125-BC]	*Withdrawn from use, June 2018*
	367	Dassault Mirage 2000N [125-AW]	*Withdrawn from use, June 2018*
	368	Dassault Mirage 2000N [125-AR]	*Withdrawn from use, June 2018*
	369	Dassault Mirage 2000N [125-AG]	AA DGA EV, Istres
	370	Dassault Mirage 2000N [125-CQ]	*Withdrawn from use, June 2018*
	371	Dassault Mirage 2000N [125-BD]	*Withdrawn from use, June 2018*
	372	Dassault Mirage 2000N [125-CM]	*Withdrawn from use, June 2018*
	373	Dassault Mirage 2000N [125-CF]	*Withdrawn from use, June 2018*
	374	Dassault Mirage 2000N [125-BS]	*Withdrawn from use, June 2018*
	375	Dassault Mirage 2000N [125-CL]	*Withdrawn from use, June 2018*
	301	Dassault Rafale B	AA DGA EV, Istres
	302	Dassault Rafale B	AA DGA EV, Istres
	303	Dassault Rafale B [4-EA]	AA ETR 03.004 *Aquitaine*, St Dizier
	304	Dassault Rafale B [4-EB]	AA ETR 03.004 *Aquitaine*, St Dizier
	305	Dassault Rafale B [4-EC]	AA ETR 03.004 *Aquitaine*, St Dizier
	306	Dassault Rafale B [30-IB]	AA CEAM/ECE 01.030 *Côte d'Argent*, Mont-de-Marsan
	307	Dassault Rafale B [4-IA]	AA ETR 03.004 *Aquitaine*, St Dizier
	308	Dassault Rafale B [4-HA]	AA EC 01.004 *Gascogne*, St Dizier
	309	Dassault Rafale B [4-HB]	AA EC 01.004 *Gascogne*, St Dizier
	310	Dassault Rafale B [4-HC]	AA ETR 03.004 *Aquitaine*, St Dizier
	311	Dassault Rafale B [4-HD]	AA EC 01.004 *Gascogne*, St Dizier
	312	Dassault Rafale B [4-HF]	AA EC 01.004 *Gascogne*, St Dizier
	313	Dassault Rafale B [4-HI]	AA ETR 03.004 *Aquitaine*, St Dizier
	314	Dassault Rafale B [4-HP]	AA EC 01.004 *Gascogne*, St Dizier

Serial	Type (code/other identity)	Owner/operator, location or fate	Notes
315	Dassault Rafale B [30-HK]	AA CEAM/ECE 01.030 Côte d'Argent, Mont-de-Marsan	
317	Dassault Rafale B [4-HO]	AA ETR 03.004 Aquitaine, St Dizier	
318	Dassault Rafale B [30-HM]	AA EC 02.030 Normandie-Niémen, Mont-de-Marsan	
319	Dassault Rafale B [4-HN]	AA EC 01.004 Gascogne, St Dizier	
320	Dassault Rafale B [4-HV]	AA EC 01.004 Gascogne, St Dizier	
321	Dassault Rafale B [4-HQ]	AA EC 03.030 Lorraine, St Dizier	
322	Dassault Rafale B [4-HU]	AA EC 01.004 Gascogne, St Dizier	
323	Dassault Rafale B [30-HT]	AA CEAM/ECE 01.030 Côte d'Argent, Mont-de-Marsan	
324	Dassault Rafale B [30-HW] $	AA CEAM/ECE 01.030 Côte d'Argent, Mont-de-Marsan	
325	Dassault Rafale B [4-HX]	AA ETR 03.004 Aquitaine, St Dizier	
326	Dassault Rafale B [113-HY]	AA EC 01.004 Gascogne, St Dizier	
327	Dassault Rafale B [4-HZ]	AA ETR 03.004 Aquitaine, St Dizier	
328	Dassault Rafale B [4-IC]	AA EC 01.004 Gascogne, St Dizier	
329	Dassault Rafale B [4-ID]	AA ETR 03.004 Aquitaine, St Dizier	
330	Dassault Rafale B [4-IE]	AA EC 01.004 Gascogne, St Dizier	
331	Dassault Rafale B [30-IF]	AA EC 02.030 Normandie-Niémen, Mont-de-Marsan	
332	Dassault Rafale B [4-IG]	AA EC 01.004 Gascogne, St Dizier	
333	Dassault Rafale B [4-IH]	AA ETR 03.004 Aquitaine, St Dizier	
334	Dassault Rafale B [4-II]	AA ETR 03.004 Aquitaine, St Dizier	
335	Dassault Rafale B [4-IJ]	AA EC 01.004 Gascogne, St Dizier	
336	Dassault Rafale B [4-IK] $	AA EC 01.004 Gascogne, St Dizier	
337	Dassault Rafale B [4-IL]	AA EC 01.004 Gascogne, St Dizier	
338	Dassault Rafale B [4-IO]	AA EC 01.004 Gascogne, St Dizier	
339	Dassault Rafale B [4-FF]	AA ETR 03.004 Aquitaine, St Dizier	
340	Dassault Rafale B [4-FG]	AA EC 01.004 Gascogne, St Dizier	
341	Dassault Rafale B [4-FH]	AA EC 01.004 Gascogne, St Dizier	
342	Dassault Rafale B [4-FI]	AA EC 01.004 Gascogne, St Dizier	
343	Dassault Rafale B [4-FJ]	AA EC 01.004 Gascogne, St Dizier	
344	Dassault Rafale B [4-FK]	AA EC 01.004 Gascogne, St Dizier	
345	Dassault Rafale B [4-FL]	AA EC 01.004 Gascogne, St Dizier	
346	Dassault Rafale B [4-FM]	AA ETR 03.004 Aquitaine, St Dizier	
347	Dassault Rafale B [4-FN]	AA ETR 03.004 Aquitaine, St Dizier	
348	Dassault Rafale B [4-FO]	AA ETR 03.004 Aquitaine, St Dizier	
349	Dassault Rafale B [4-FP] $	AA ETR 03.004 Aquitaine, St Dizier	
350	Dassault Rafale B [113-FQ]	AA ETR 03.004 Aquitaine, St Dizier	
351	Dassault Rafale B [4-FR]	AA EC 02.004 La Fayette, St Dizier	
352	Dassault Rafale B [4-FS]	AA ETR 03.004 Aquitaine, St Dizier	
353	Dassault Rafale B [4-FT]	AA EC 02.004 La Fayette, St Dizier	
354	Dassault Rafale B [4-FU]	AA EC 02.004 La Fayette, St Dizier	
355	Dassault Rafale B [4-FV]	AA EC 02.004 La Fayette, St Dizier	
356	Dassault Rafale B [4-FW]	AA EC 02.004 La Fayette, St Dizier	
357	Dassault Rafale B [4-FX]	AA EC 02.004 La Fayette, St Dizier	
358	Dassault Rafale B	AA (on order)	
101	Dassault Rafale C	AA DGA EV, Istres	
102	Dassault Rafale C [30-EF]	AA CEAM/ECE 01.030 Côte d'Argent, Mont-de-Marsan	
103	Dassault Rafale C [30-HR]	AA EC 03.030 Lorraine, St Dizier	
104	Dassault Rafale C [30-HH]	AA EC 03.030 Lorraine, St Dizier	
105	Dassault Rafale C [30-HE]	AA CEAM/ECE 01.030 Côte d'Argent, Mont-de-Marsan	
106	Dassault Rafale C [113-HG]	AA EC 03.030 Lorraine, St Dizier	
107	Dassault Rafale C [113-HJ] $	AA EC 03.030 Lorraine, St Dizier	
108	Dassault Rafale C [113-HS]	AA EC 03.030 Lorraine, St Dizier	
109	Dassault Rafale C [30-IM]	AA EC 02.030 Normandie-Niémen, Mont-de-Marsan	
110	Dassault Rafale C [30-IN]	AA EC 03.030 Lorraine, St Dizier	

Notes	Serial	Type (code/other identity)	Owner/operator, location or fate
	111	Dassault Rafale C [30-IP]	AA EC 02.030 *Normandie-Niémen*, Mont-de-Marsan
	112	Dassault Rafale C [30-IQ]	AA EC 02.030 *Normandie-Niémen*, Mont-de-Marsan
	113	Dassault Rafale C [30-IR]	AA EC 02.030 *Normandie-Niémen*, Mont-de-Marsan
	114	Dassault Rafale C [30-IS]	AA EC 02.030 *Normandie-Niémen*, Mont-de-Marsan
	115	Dassault Rafale C [30-IT]	AA EC 03.030 *Lorraine*, St Dizier
	116	Dassault Rafale C [30-IU]	AA EC 02.030 *Normandie-Niémen*, Mont-de-Marsan
	117	Dassault Rafale C [113-IV]	AA EC 03.030 *Lorraine*, St Dizier
	118	Dassault Rafale C [30-IW]	AA EC 02.030 *Normandie-Niémen*, Mont-de-Marsan
	119	Dassault Rafale C [30-IX]	AA EC 03.030 *Lorraine*, St Dizier
	120	Dassault Rafale C [30-IY] $	AA EC 03.030 *Lorraine*, St Dizier
	121	Dassault Rafale C [113-IZ]	AA EC 01.004 *Gascogne*, St Dizier
	122	Dassault Rafale C [4-GA]	AA ETR 03.004 *Aquitaine*, St Dizier
	123	Dassault Rafale C [30-GB]	AA EC 02.030 *Normandie-Niémen*, Mont-de-Marsan
	124	Dassault Rafale C [104-GC]	AA EC 01.007 *Provence*, Al Dhafra, UAE
	125	Dassault Rafale C [30-GD]	AA EC 02.030 *Normandie-Niémen*, Mont-de-Marsan
	126	Dassault Rafale C [30-GE]	AA EC 02.030 *Normandie-Niémen*, Mont-de-Marsan
	127	Dassault Rafale C [30-GF]	AA EC 02.030 *Normandie-Niémen*, Mont-de-Marsan
	128	Dassault Rafale C [30-GG]	AA EC 02.030 *Normandie-Niémen*, Mont-de-Marsan
	129	Dassault Rafale C [30-GH]	AA EC 02.030 *Normandie-Niémen*, Mont-de-Marsan
	130	Dassault Rafale C [4-GI] $	AN ETR 03.004 *Aquitaine*, St Dizier
	131	Dassault Rafale C [4-GJ]	AN ETR 03.004 *Aquitaine*, St Dizier
	132	Dassault Rafale C [30-GK]	AA EC 02.030 *Normandie-Niémen*, Mont-de-Marsan
	133	Dassault Rafale C [4-GL] $	AN ETR 03.004 *Aquitaine*, St Dizier
	134	Dassault Rafale C [30-GM]	AA EC 02.030 *Normandie-Niémen*, Mont-de-Marsan
	135	Dassault Rafale C [30-GN]	AA EC 03.030 *Lorraine*, St Dizier
	136	Dassault Rafale C [104-GO]	AA EC 01.007 *Provence*, Al Dhafra, UAE
	137	Dassault Rafale C [104-GP]	AA EC 01.007 *Provence*, Al Dhafra, UAE
	138	Dassault Rafale C [30-GQ]	AA EC 02.030 *Normandie-Niémen*, Mont-de-Marsan
	139	Dassault Rafale C [30-GR]	AA EC 02.030 *Normandie-Niémen*, Mont-de-Marsan
	140	Dassault Rafale C [30-GS]	AA EC 02.030 *Normandie-Niémen*, Mont-de-Marsan
	141	Dassault Rafale C [30-GT]	AA EC 02.030 *Normandie-Niémen*, Mont-de-Marsan
	142	Dassault Rafale C [4-GU]	AA ETR 03.004 *Aquitaine*, St Dizier
	143	Dassault Rafale C [30-GV] $	AA EC 03.030 *Lorraine*, St Dizier
	144	Dassault Rafale C [30-GW]	AA EC 03.030 *Lorraine*, St Dizier
	145	Dassault Rafale C [30-GX]	AA EC 03.030 *Lorraine*, St Dizier
	146	Dassault Rafale C [30-GY]	AA EC 03.030 *Lorraine*, St Dizier
	147	Dassault Rafale C [30-GZ]	AA EC 02.030 *Normandie-Niémen*, Mont-de-Marsan
	148	Dassault Rafale C [30-VA] $	AA EC 02.030 *Normandie-Niémen*, Mont-de-Marsan
	149	Dassault Rafale C	AA (on order)
	150	Dassault Rafale C	AA (on order)
	151	Dassault Rafale C	AA (on order)
	152	Dassault Rafale C	AA (on order)

Serial	Type (code/other identity)	Owner/operator, location or fate	Notes
153	Dassault Rafale C	AA (on order)	
154	Dassault Rafale C	AA (on order)	
155	Dassault Rafale C	AA (on order)	
156	Dassault Rafale C	AA (on order)	
157	Dassault Rafale C	AA (on order)	
158	Dassault Rafale C	AA (on order)	
159	Dassault Rafale C	AA (on order)	
160	Dassault Rafale C	AA (on order)	
292	DHC-6 Twin Otter 200 [F-RACC]	AA GAM 00.056 *Vaucluse*, Evreux	
298	DHC-6 Twin Otter 200 [F-RACD]	AA GAM 00.056 *Vaucluse*, Evreux	
300	DHC-6 Twin Otter 200 [F-RACE]	AA GAM 00.056 *Vaucluse*, Evreux	
730	DHC-6 Twin Otter 300 [F-RACA]	AA ET 03.061 *Poitou*, Orléans	
745	DHC-6 Twin Otter 300 [CV]	AA ET 03.061 *Poitou*, Orléans	
054	Embraer EMB.121AA Xingu [YX]	AA EAT 00.319 *Capitaine Dartigues*, Avord	
064	Embraer EMB.121AA Xingu [YY]	AA EAT 00.319 *Capitaine Dartigues*, Avord	
066	Embraer EMB.121AN Xingu [ZA]	AA EAT 00.319 *Capitaine Dartigues*, Avord	
072	Embraer EMB.121AA Xingu [YA]	AA EAT 00.319 *Capitaine Dartigues*, Avord	
075	Embraer EMB.121AA Xingu [YC]	AA EAT 00.319 *Capitaine Dartigues*, Avord	
078	Embraer EMB.121AA Xingu [YE]	AA EAT 00.319 *Capitaine Dartigues*, Avord	
082	Embraer EMB.121AA Xingu [YG] $	AA EAT 00.319 *Capitaine Dartigues*, Avord	
083	Embraer EMB.121AN Xingu [ZE]	AA EAT 00.319 *Capitaine Dartigues*, Avord	
084	Embraer EMB.121AA Xingu [YH]	AA EAT 00.319 *Capitaine Dartigues*, Avord	
086	Embraer EMB.121AA Xingu [YI]	AA EAT 00.319 *Capitaine Dartigues*, Avord	
089	Embraer EMB.121AA Xingu [YJ]	AA EAT 00.319 *Capitaine Dartigues*, Avord	
090	Embraer EMB.121AN Xingu [ZF]	AA EAT 00.319 *Capitaine Dartigues*, Avord	
091	Embraer EMB.121AA Xingu [YK]	AA EAT 00.319 *Capitaine Dartigues*, Avord	
092	Embraer EMB.121AA Xingu [YL]	AA EAT 00.319 *Capitaine Dartigues*, Avord	
096	Embraer EMB.121AA Xingu [YN]	AA EAT 00.319 *Capitaine Dartigues*, Avord	
098	Embraer EMB.121AA Xingu [YO]	AA EAT 00.319 *Capitaine Dartigues*, Avord	
099	Embraer EMB.121AA Xingu [YP]	AA EAT 00.319 *Capitaine Dartigues*, Avord	
102	Embraer EMB.121AA Xingu [YS]	AA EAT 00.319 *Capitaine Dartigues*, Avord	
103	Embraer EMB.121AA Xingu [YT]	AA EAT 00.319 *Capitaine Dartigues*, Avord	
105	Embraer EMB.121AA Xingu [YU]	AA EAT 00.319 *Capitaine Dartigues*, Avord	
107	Embraer EMB.121AA Xingu [YV]	AA EAT 00.319 *Capitaine Dartigues*, Avord	
108	Embraer EMB.121AA Xingu [YW]	AA EAT 00.319 *Capitaine Dartigues*, Avord	
2233	Eurocopter AS.332L-1 Super Puma [FY]	AA GAM 00.056 *Vaucluse*, Evreux	
2235	Eurocopter AS.332L-1 Super Puma [FZ]	AA EH 03.067 *Parisis*, Villacoublay	
2244	Eurocopter AS.332L-1 Super Puma [PM]	*Sold to Spain, 2018*	
2377	Eurocopter AS.332L-1 Super Puma [FU]	AA EH 03.067 *Parisis*, Villacoublay	
2461	Eurocopter EC.725AP Caracal [SA]	AA EH 01.067 *Pyrénées*, Cazaux	
2549	Eurocopter EC.725AP Caracal [SB]	AA EH 01.067 *Pyrénées*, Cazaux	
2552	Eurocopter EC.725AP Caracal [SE]	AA EH 01.067 *Pyrénées*, Cazaux	
2619	Eurocopter EC.725AP Caracal [SC]	AA EH 05.067 *Alpilles*, Aix-en-Provence	
2626	Eurocopter EC.725AP Caracal [SD]	AA EH 01.067 *Pyrénées*, Cazaux	
2741	Eurocopter EC.225LP Caracal [SY]	AA GAM 00.056 *Vaucluse*, Evreux	
2752	Eurocopter EC.225LP Caracal [SZ]	AA GAM 00.056 *Vaucluse*, Evreux	
2770	Eurocopter EC.725R-2 Caracal [SG]	AA EH 01.067 *Pyrénées*, Cazaux	
2772	Eurocopter EC.725R-2 Caracal [SH]	AA EH 01.067 *Pyrénées*, Cazaux	
2778	Eurocopter EC.725R-2 Caracal [SI]	AA EH 01.067 *Pyrénées*, Cazaux	
2789	Eurocopter EC.725R-2 Caracal [SJ]	AA EH 01.067 *Pyrénées*, Cazaux	
2802	Eurocopter EC.725R-2 Caracal [SK]	AA EH 01.067 *Pyrénées*, Cazaux	
5361	Eurocopter AS.555AN Fennec [UT]	AA EH 05.067 *Alpilles*, Orange	
5382	Eurocopter AS.555AN Fennec [UV]	AA EH 05.067 *Alpilles*, Orange	
5386	Eurocopter AS.555AN Fennec [UX]	AA EH 05.067 *Alpilles*, Orange	
5387	Eurocopter AS.555AN Fennec [UY]	AA EH 05.067 *Alpilles*, Orange	
5390	Eurocopter AS.555AN Fennec [UZ]	AA EH 03.067 *Parisis*, Villacoublay	
5391	Eurocopter AS.555AN Fennec [VA]	AA EH 05.067 *Alpilles*, Orange	
5392	Eurocopter AS.555AN Fennec [VB]	AA EH 05.067 *Alpilles*, Orange	
5393	Eurocopter AS.555AN Fennec [VC]	AA EH 05.067 *Alpilles*, Orange	
5396	Eurocopter AS.555AN Fennec [VD]	AA EH 05.067 *Alpilles*, Orange	
5397	Eurocopter AS.555AN Fennec [VE]	AA ET 00.068 *Antilles-Guyane*, Cayenne	
5398	Eurocopter AS.555AN Fennec [VF]	AA EH 03.067 *Parisis*, Villacoublay	

Notes	Serial	Type (code/other identity)	Owner/operator, location or fate
	5399	Eurocopter AS.555AN Fennec [VG] $	AA
	5400	Eurocopter AS.555AN Fennec [VH]	AA EH 05.067 *Alpilles*, Orange
	5412	Eurocopter AS.555AN Fennec [VI]	AA EH 05.067 *Alpilles*, Orange
	5427	Eurocopter AS.555AN Fennec [VJ]	AA EH 03.067 *Parisis*, Villacoublay
	5430	Eurocopter AS.555AN Fennec [VL]	AA EH 03.067 *Parisis*, Villacoublay
	5431	Eurocopter AS.555AN Fennec [VM] $	AA EH 05.067 *Alpilles*, Orange
	5440	Eurocopter AS.555AN Fennec [VN]	AA, stored Creil
	5441	Eurocopter AS.555AN Fennec [VO]	AA EH 03.067 *Parisis*, Villacoublay
	5444	Eurocopter AS.555AN Fennec [VP]	AA EH 03.067 *Parisis*, Villacoublay
	5445	Eurocopter AS.555AN Fennec [VQ]	AA EH 05.067 *Alpilles*, Orange
	5448	Eurocopter AS.555AN Fennec [VR]	AA EH 03.067 *Parisis*, Villacoublay
	5452	Eurocopter AS.555AN Fennec [VS]	AA EH 05.067 *Alpilles*, Orange
	5455	Eurocopter AS.555AN Fennec [VT]	AA EH 03.067 *Parisis*, Villacoublay
	5457	Eurocopter AS.555AN Fennec [VU]	AA ET 00.068 *Antilles-Guyane*, Cayenne
	5458	Eurocopter AS.555AN Fennec [VV]	AA EH 05.067 *Alpilles*, Orange
	5466	Eurocopter AS.555AN Fennec [VW]	AA ET 00.068 *Antilles-Guyane*, Cayenne
	5468	Eurocopter AS.555AN Fennec [VX]	AA EH 03.067 *Parisis*, Villacoublay
	5490	Eurocopter AS.555AN Fennec [VY]	AA EH 05.067 *Alpilles*, Orange
	5506	Eurocopter AS.555AN Fennec [WA]	AA EH 05.067 *Alpilles*, Orange
	5509	Eurocopter AS.555AN Fennec [WB]	AA EH 05.067 *Alpilles*, Orange
	5511	Eurocopter AS.555AN Fennec [WC] $	AA EH 03.067 *Parisis*, Villacoublay
	5516	Eurocopter AS.555AN Fennec [WD]	AA EH 03.067 *Parisis*, Villacoublay
	5520	Eurocopter AS.555AN Fennec [WE]	AA EH 03.067 *Parisis*, Villacoublay
	5523	Eurocopter AS.555AN Fennec [WF]	AA EH 05.067 *Alpilles*, Orange
	5526	Eurocopter AS.555AN Fennec [WG]	AA EH 03.067 *Parisis*, Villacoublay
	5530	Eurocopter AS.555AN Fennec [WH]	AA EH 05.067 *Alpilles*, Orange
	5532	Eurocopter AS.555AN Fennec [WI]	AA EH 05.067 *Alpilles*, Orange
	5534	Eurocopter AS.555AN Fennec [WJ]	AA EH 05.067 *Alpilles*, Orange
	5536	Eurocopter AS.555AN Fennec [WK]	AA EH 03.067 *Parisis*, Villacoublay
	5559	Eurocopter AS.555AN Fennec [WL]	AA EH 05.067 *Alpilles*, Orange
	03	Extra EA-330LC [F-TGCH]	AA EVAA, Salon de Provence
	04	Extra EA-330SC [F-TGCI]	AA EVAA, Salon de Provence
	05	Extra EA-330SC [F-TGCJ]	AA EVAA, Salon de Provence
	290	Fokker 100 [F-ZAFT]	AA DGA EV, Istres
	...	Fokker 100	AA DGA EV, Istres (on order)
	4588	Lockheed C-130H Hercules [61-PM] $	AA ET 02.061 *Franche-Comté*, Orléans
	4589	Lockheed C-130H Hercules [61-PN]	AA ET 02.061 *Franche-Comté*, Orléans
	5114	Lockheed C-130H Hercules [61-PA]	AA ET 02.061 *Franche-Comté*, Orléans
	5116	Lockheed C-130H Hercules [61-PB]	AA ET 02.061 *Franche-Comté*, Orléans
	5119	Lockheed C-130H Hercules [61-PC]	AA ET 02.061 *Franche-Comté*, Orléans
	5140	Lockheed C-130H Hercules [61-PD]	AA ET 02.061 *Franche-Comté*, Orléans
	5142	Lockheed C-130H-30 Hercules [61-PE]	AA ET 02.061 *Franche-Comté*, Orléans
	5144	Lockheed C-130H-30 Hercules [61-PF] $	AA ET 02.061 *Franche-Comté*, Orléans
	5150	Lockheed C-130H-30 Hercules [61-PG]	AA ET 02.061 *Franche-Comté*, Orléans
	5151	Lockheed C-130H-30 Hercules [61-PH]	AA ET 02.061 *Franche-Comté*, Orléans
	5152	Lockheed C-130H-30 Hercules [61-PI]	AA ET 02.061 *Franche-Comté*, Orléans
	5153	Lockheed C-130H-30 Hercules [61-PJ]	AA ET 02.061 *Franche-Comté*, Orléans
	5226	Lockheed C-130H-30 Hercules [61-PK]	AA ET 02.061 *Franche-Comté*, Orléans
	5227	Lockheed C-130H-30 Hercules [61-PL]	AA ET 02.061 *Franche-Comté*, Orléans
	5836	Lockheed C-130J Hercules II [61-PO]	AA ET 02.061 *Franche-Comté*, Orléans
	5847	Lockheed C-130J Hercules II [61-PP]	AA ET 02.061 *Franche-Comté*, Orléans
	....	Lockheed KC-130J Hercules II	AA (on order)
	....	Lockheed KC-130J Hercules II	AA (on order)
	01	Pilatus PC-21 (HB-HVA) [709-FC]	AA EPAA 00.315, Cognac
	02	Pilatus PC-21 (HB-HVB) [709-FD]	AA EPAA 00.315, Cognac
	03	Pilatus PC-21 (HB-HVC/F-ZXAC) [709-FE]	AA EPAA 00.315, Cognac
	04	Pilatus PC-21 (HB-HVD) [709-FF]	AA EPAA 00.315, Cognac
	05	Pilatus PC-21 (HB-HVE) [709-FG]	AA EPAA 00.315, Cognac
	06	Pilatus PC-21 (HB-HVF) [709-FH]	AA EPAA 00.315, Cognac
	07	Pilatus PC-21 (HB-HVG) [709-FI]	AA EPAA 00.315, Cognac
	08	Pilatus PC-21 (HB-HVH) [709-FJ]	AA EPAA 00.315, Cognac
	09	Pilatus PC-21 (HB-HVI) [709-FK]	AA EPAA 00.315, Cognac

Serial	Type (code/other identity)	Owner/operator, location or fate	Notes
10	Pilatus PC-21 (HB-HVJ) [709-FL]	AA EPAA 00.315, Cognac	
11	Pilatus PC-21 (HB-HVK) [709-FM]	AA EPAA 00.315, Cognac	
12	Pilatus PC-21 (HB-HVL) [709-FN]	AA EPAA 00.315, Cognac	
13	Pilatus PC-21 (HB-HVM) [709-FO]	AA EPAA 00.315, Cognac	
14	Pilatus PC-21 (HB-HVN) [709-FP]	AA EPAA 00.315, Cognac	
15	Pilatus PC-21 (HB-HVO) [709-FQ]	AA EPAA 00.315, Cognac	
16	Pilatus PC-21 (HB-HVP) [709-FR]	AA EPAA 00.315, Cognac	
17	Pilatus PC-21 (HB-HVQ) [709-FS]	AA EPAA 00.315, Cognac	
7	SOCATA TB-30 Epsilon [315-UF]	AA EPAA 00.315, Cognac	
26	SOCATA TB-30 Epsilon [315-UY]	AA EPAA 00.315, Cognac	
27	SOCATA TB-30 Epsilon [315-UZ]	AA EPAA 00.315, Cognac	
30	SOCATA TB-30 Epsilon [315-VC]	AA EPAA 00.315, Cognac	
64	SOCATA TB-30 Epsilon [315-WG]	AA EPAA 00.315, Cognac	
65	SOCATA TB-30 Epsilon [315-WH]	AA EPAA 00.315, Cognac	
66	SOCATA TB-30 Epsilon [315-WI]	AA EPAA 00.315, Cognac	
67	SOCATA TB-30 Epsilon [315-WJ] $	AA EPAA 00.315, Cognac	
69	SOCATA TB-30 Epsilon [F-SEWL]	AA *Cartouche Dorée* (EPAA 00.315), Cognac	
73	SOCATA TB-30 Epsilon [315-WP]	AA EPAA 00.315, Cognac	
78	SOCATA TB-30 Epsilon [315-WU]	AA EPAA 00.315, Cognac	
82	SOCATA TB-30 Epsilon [315-WY]	AA EPAA 00.315, Cognac	
83	SOCATA TB-30 Epsilon [315-WZ]	AA EPAA 00.315, Cognac	
84	SOCATA TB-30 Epsilon [315-XA]	AA EPAA 00.315, Cognac	
90	SOCATA TB-30 Epsilon [F-SEXG]	AA *Cartouche Dorée* (EPAA 00.315), Cognac	
91	SOCATA TB-30 Epsilon [315-XH]	AA EPAA 00.315, Cognac	
92	SOCATA TB-30 Epsilon [315-XI]	AA EPAA 00.315, Cognac	
95	SOCATA TB-30 Epsilon [315-XL]	AA EPAA 00.315, Cognac	
96	SOCATA TB-30 Epsilon [315-XM]	AA EPAA 00.315, Cognac	
97	SOCATA TB-30 Epsilon [315-XN]	AA EPAA 00.315, Cognac	
99	SOCATA TB-30 Epsilon [F-SEXP]	AA *Cartouche Dorée* (EPAA 00.315), Cognac	
101	SOCATA TB-30 Epsilon [315-XR] $	AA EPAA 00.315, Cognac	
102	SOCATA TB-30 Epsilon [F-SEXS,2]	AA *Cartouche Dorée* (EPAA 00.315), Cognac	
103	SOCATA TB-30 Epsilon [315-XT]	AA EPAA 00.315, Cognac	
104	SOCATA TB-30 Epsilon [315-XU]	AA EPAA 00.315, Cognac	
113	SOCATA TB-30 Epsilon [F-SEYD]	AA *Cartouche Dorée* (EPAA 00.315), Cognac	
116	SOCATA TB-30 Epsilon [F-SEYG]	AA *Cartouche Dorée* (EPAA 00.315), Cognac	
117	SOCATA TB-30 Epsilon [315-YH]	AA EPAA 00.315, Cognac	
118	SOCATA TB-30 Epsilon [315-YI]	AA EPAA 00.315, Cognac	
121	SOCATA TB-30 Epsilon [315-YL]	AA EPAA 00.315, Cognac	
127	SOCATA TB-30 Epsilon [315-YR]	AA EPAA 00.315, Cognac	
131	SOCATA TB-30 Epsilon [315-YV]	AA EPAA 00.315, Cognac	
133	SOCATA TB-30 Epsilon [315-YX]	AA EPAA 00.315, Cognac	
136	SOCATA TB-30 Epsilon [315-ZA]	AA EPAA 00.315, Cognac	
141	SOCATA TB-30 Epsilon [F-SEZF]	AA *Cartouche Dorée* (EPAA 00.315), Cognac	
142	SOCATA TB-30 Epsilon [315-ZG]	AA EPAA 00.315, Cognac	
144	SOCATA TB-30 Epsilon [315-ZI]	AA EPAA 00.315, Cognac	
146	SOCATA TB-30 Epsilon [315-ZK]	AA EPAA 00.315, Cognac	
149	SOCATA TB-30 Epsilon [315-ZM] $	AA EPAA 00.315, Cognac	
150	SOCATA TB-30 Epsilon [315-ZN] $	AA EPAA 00.315, Cognac	
33	SOCATA TBM 700A [XA]	AA ET 00.043 *Médoc*, Bordeaux	
35	SOCATA TBM 700A [BW]	AA DGA EV, Cazaux & Istres	
77	SOCATA TBM 700A [XD]	AA ET 00.043 *Médoc*, Bordeaux	
78	SOCATA TBM 700A [XE]	AA CEAM, Mont-de-Marsan	
80	SOCATA TBM 700A [BY]	AA DGA EV, Cazaux & Istres	
93	SOCATA TBM 700A [XL]	AA ET 00.041 *Verdun*, Villacoublay	
94	SOCATA TBM 700A [BZ]	AA DGA EV, Cazaux & Istres	
95	SOCATA TBM 700A [XH]	AA CEAM, Mont-de-Marsan	
103	SOCATA TBM 700A [XI]	AA ET 00.041 *Verdun*, Villacoublay	
104	SOCATA TBM 700A [XJ]	AA ET 00.043 *Médoc*, Bordeaux	
105	SOCATA TBM 700A [XK] $	AA ET 00.043 *Médoc*, Bordeaux	
106	SOCATA TBM 700A [BX]	AA DGA EV, Cazaux & Istres	

Notes	Serial	Type (code/other identity)	Owner/operator, location or fate
	110	SOCATA TBM 700A [XP]	AA ET 00.041 *Verdun*, Villacoublay
	111	SOCATA TBM 700A [XM]	AA ET 00.041 *Verdun*, Villacoublay
	115	SOCATA TBM 700A [BQ]	AA DGA EV, Cazaux & Istres
	117	SOCATA TBM 700A [XN]	AA ET 00.043 *Médoc*, Bordeaux
	125	SOCATA TBM 700A [XO]	AA ET 00.043 *Médoc*, Bordeaux
	131	SOCATA TBM 700A [XQ]	AA ET 00.041 *Verdun*, Villacoublay
	146	SOCATA TBM 700A [XR]	AA ET 00.041 *Verdun*, Villacoublay
	147	SOCATA TBM 700A [XS]	AA ET 00.041 *Verdun*, Villacoublay
	R93	Transall C-160R [61-ZK]	*Withdrawn from use, 2018*
	R97	Transall C-160R [61-ZA]	*Withdrawn from use, 2018*
	R160	Transall C-160R [61-ZZ]	*Withdrawn from use, 2018*
	R201	Transall C-160R [64-GA]	AA ET 02.064 *Anjou*, Evreux
	R202	Transall C-160R [64-GB]	AA ET 02.064 *Anjou*, Evreux
	R203	Transall C-160R [64-GC] $	AA ET 02.064 *Anjou*, Evreux
	R206	Transall C-160R [64-GF]	AA ET 02.064 *Anjou*, Evreux
	R208	Transall C-160R [64-GH] $	AA ET 02.064 *Anjou*, Evreux
	R210	Transall C-160R [64-GJ]	AA ET 02.064 *Anjou*, Evreux
	R212	Transall C-160R [64-GL]	AA ET 02.064 *Anjou*, Evreux
	R213	Transall C-160R [64-GM]	AA ET 02.064 *Anjou*, Evreux
	R214	Transall C-160R [64-GN]	AA ET 02.064 *Anjou*, Evreux
	F216	Transall C-160NG GABRIEL [GT]	AA EEA 00.054 *Dunkerque*, Evreux
	R217	Transall C-160R [64-GQ]	AA ET 02.064 *Anjou*, Evreux
	R218	Transall C-160R [64-GR]	AA ET 02.064 *Anjou*, Evreux
	F221	Transall C-160NG GABRIEL [GS] $	AA EEA 00.054 *Dunkerque*, Evreux
	R223	Transall C-160R [64-GW]	AA ET 02.064 *Anjou*, Evreux
	R224	Transall C-160R [64-GX]	AA ET 02.064 *Anjou*, Evreux
	R225	Transall C-160R [64-GY]	AA ET 02.064 *Anjou*, Evreux
	R226	Transall C-160R [64-GZ]	AA ET 02.064 *Anjou*, Evreux
	Aéronautique Navale/Marine (AN)		
	2	Dassault-Breguet Atlantique 2	AN 21 Flottille, Lorient/Lann Bihoué
	3	Dassault-Breguet Atlantique 2	AN 23 Flottille, Lorient/Lann Bihoué
	4	Dassault-Breguet Atlantique 2	AN 23 Flottille, Lorient/Lann Bihoué
	5	Dassault-Breguet Atlantique 2	AN 21 Flottille, Lorient/Lann Bihoué
	9	Dassault-Breguet Atlantique 2	AN 23 Flottille, Lorient/Lann Bihoué
	12	Dassault-Breguet Atlantique 2	AN 23 Flottille, Lorient/Lann Bihoué
	13	Dassault-Breguet Atlantique 2	AN 21 Flottille, Lorient/Lann Bihoué
	14	Dassault-Breguet Atlantique 2	AN 23 Flottille, Lorient/Lann Bihoué
	15	Dassault-Breguet Atlantique 2	AN 21 Flottille, Lorient/Lann Bihoué
	16	Dassault-Breguet Atlantique 2	AN 21 Flottille, Lorient/Lann Bihoué
	17	Dassault-Breguet Atlantique 2 $	AN 21 Flottille, Lorient/Lann Bihoué
	18	Dassault-Breguet Atlantique 2	AN 21 Flottille, Lorient/Lann Bihoué
	19	Dassault-Breguet Atlantique 2	AN 23 Flottille, Lorient/Lann Bihoué
	20	Dassault-Breguet Atlantique 2	AN 23 Flottille, Lorient/Lann Bihoué
	21	Dassault-Breguet Atlantique 2	AN 21 Flottille, Lorient/Lann Bihoué
	22	Dassault-Breguet Atlantique 2	AN 21 Flottille, Lorient/Lann Bihoué
	23	Dassault-Breguet Atlantique 2	AN 21 Flottille, Lorient/Lann Bihoué
	24	Dassault-Breguet Atlantique 2	AN 21 Flottille, Lorient/Lann Bihoué
	26	Dassault-Breguet Atlantique 2	AN 21 Flottille, Lorient/Lann Bihoué
	27	Dassault-Breguet Atlantique 2	AN 21 Flottille, Lorient/Lann Bihoué
	32	Dassault Falcon 10(MER)	AN 57 Escadrille, Landivisiau
	101	Dassault Falcon 10(MER)	AN 57 Escadrille, Landivisiau
	129	Dassault Falcon 10(MER)	AN 57 Escadrille, Landivisiau
	133	Dassault Falcon 10(MER)	AN 57 Escadrille, Landivisiau
	143	Dassault Falcon 10(MER)	AN 57 Escadrille, Landivisiau
	185	Dassault Falcon 10(MER) $	AN 57 Escadrille, Landivisiau
	48	Dassault Falcon 20G Guardian	AN 25 Flottille, Papeete & Tontouta
	65	Dassault Falcon 20G Guardian	AN 25 Flottille, Papeete & Tontouta
	72	Dassault Falcon 20G Guardian	AN 25 Flottille, Papeete & Tontouta
	77	Dassault Falcon 20G Guardian	AN 25 Flottille, Papeete & Tontouta
	80	Dassault Falcon 20G Guardian	AN 25 Flottille, Papeete & Tontouta
	5	Dassault Falcon 50MS SURMAR	AN 24 Flottille, Lorient/Lann Bihoué
	7	Dassault Falcon 50MI SURMAR	AN 24 Flottille, Lorient/Lann Bihoué

Serial	Type (code/other identity)	Owner/operator, location or fate	Notes
27	Dassault Falcon 50MS SURMAR	AN 24 Flottille, Lorient/Lann Bihoué	
30	Dassault Falcon 50MI SURMAR	AN 24 Flottille, Lorient/Lann Bihoué	
34	Dassault Falcon 50MS SURMAR	AN 24 Flottille, Lorient/Lann Bihoué	
36	Dassault Falcon 50MI SURMAR	AN 24 Flottille, Lorient/Lann Bihoué	
78	Dassault Falcon 50MS SURMAR	AN 24 Flottille, Lorient/Lann Bihoué	
132	Dassault Falcon 50MI SURMAR	AN 24 Flottille, Lorient/Lann Bihoué	
2	Dassault Rafale M	AN 17 Flottille, Landivisiau	
5	Dassault Rafale M $	AN 12 Flottille, Landivisiau	
6	Dassault Rafale M	AN 12 Flottille, Landivisiau	
7	Dassault Rafale M	AN 11 Flottille, Landivisiau	
8	Dassault Rafale M	AN 12 Flottille, Landivisiau	
9	Dassault Rafale M	AN 12 Flottille, Landivisiau	
10	Dassault Rafale M	AN 12 Flottille, Landivisiau	
11	Dassault Rafale M	AN 11 Flottille, Landivisiau	
12	Dassault Rafale M	AN ETR 03.004 *Aquitaine*, St Dizier	
13	Dassault Rafale M	AN 11 Flottille, Landivisiau	
14	Dassault Rafale M	AN 11 Flottille, Landivisiau	
15	Dassault Rafale M	AN 12 Flottille, Landivisiau	
16	Dassault Rafale M	AN 12 Flottille, Landivisiau	
17	Dassault Rafale M	AN 12 Flottille, Landivisiau	
19	Dassault Rafale M	AN 11 Flottille, Landivisiau	
20	Dassault Rafale M	AN 17 Flottille, Landivisiau	
21	Dassault Rafale M	AN 12 Flottille, Landivisiau	
23	Dassault Rafale M	AN 12 Flottille, Landivisiau	
26	Dassault Rafale M	AN 12 Flottille, Landivisiau	
27	Dassault Rafale M $	AN ETR 03.004 *Aquitaine*, St Dizier	
28	Dassault Rafale M	AN ETR 03.004 *Aquitaine*, St Dizier	
29	Dassault Rafale M	AN 12 Flottille, Landivisiau	
30	Dassault Rafale M	AN CEPA/10 Escadrille, Landivisiau	
31	Dassault Rafale M	AN 11 Flottille, Landivisiau	
32	Dassault Rafale M	AN 11 Flottille, Landivisiau	
33	Dassault Rafale M	AN ETR 03.004 *Aquitaine*, St Dizier	
34	Dassault Rafale M	AN 11 Flottille, Landivisiau	
35	Dassault Rafale M	AN 12 Flottille, Landivisiau	
36	Dassault Rafale M $	AN 11 Flottille, Landivisiau	
37	Dassault Rafale M	AN ETR 03.004 *Aquitaine*, St Dizier	
38	Dassault Rafale M	AN 12 Flottille, Landivisiau	
39	Dassault Rafale M	AN 11 Flottille, Landivisiau	
40	Dassault Rafale M	AN 11 Flottille, Landivisiau	
41	Dassault Rafale M	AN	
42	Dassault Rafale M	AN 11 Flottille, Landivisiau	
43	Dassault Rafale M	AN 11 Flottille, Landivisiau	
44	Dassault Rafale M $	AN 11 Flottille, Landivisiau	
45	Dassault Rafale M	AN 11 Flottille, Landivisiau	
46	Dassault Rafale M	AN 17 Flottille, Landivisiau	
47	Dassault Rafale M	AN (on order)	
48	Dassault Rafale M	AN (on order)	
49	Dassault Rafale M	AN (on order)	
50	Dassault Rafale M	AN (on order)	
M02	Dassault Rafale M	AN DGA EV, Istres	
65	Embraer EMB.121AN Xingu	AN 28 Flottille, Hyères	
67	Embraer EMB.121AN Xingu $	AN 28 Flottille, Hyères	
68	Embraer EMB.121AN Xingu	AN 28 Flottille, Hyères	
69	Embraer EMB.121AN Xingu	AN 28 Flottille, Hyères	
71	Embraer EMB.121AN Xingu	AN 28 Flottille, Hyères	
74	Embraer EMB.121AN Xingu $	AN 28 Flottille, Hyères	
77	Embraer EMB.121AN Xingu	AN 28 Flottille, Hyères	
81	Embraer EMB.121AN Xingu	AN 24 Flottille, Lorient/Lann Bihoué	
85	Embraer EMB.121AN Xingu	AN 24 Flottille, Lorient/Lann Bihoué	
87	Embraer EMB.121AN Xingu	AN 28 Flottille, Hyères	
17	Eurocopter AS.365N Dauphin	AN 35 Flottille, Le Touquet	
19	Eurocopter AS.365N Dauphin	AN 35 Flottille, Hyères	

Notes	Serial	Type (code/other identity)	Owner/operator, location or fate
	24	Eurocopter AS.365N Dauphin	AN 35 Flottille, Hyères
	57	Eurocopter AS.365N Dauphin	AN 35 Flottille, Hyères
	81	Eurocopter AS.365N Dauphin	AN 35 Flottille, Hyères
	91	Eurocopter AS.365N Dauphin	AN 35 Flottille, Hyères
	157	Eurocopter AS.365N Dauphin	AN 35 Flottille, Hyères
	313	Eurocopter SA.365F-1 Dauphin II	AN 35 Flottille, Hyères
	318	Eurocopter SA.365F-1 Dauphin II	AN 35 Flottille, Hyères
	322	Eurocopter SA.365F-1 Dauphin II	AN 35 Flottille, Hyères
	355	Eurocopter AS.565MA Panther	AN 36 Flottille, Hyères
	362	Eurocopter AS.565MA Panther	AN 36 Flottille, Hyères
	403	Eurocopter AS.565MA Panther	AN 36 Flottille, Hyères
	436	Eurocopter AS.565MA Panther	AN 36 Flottille, Hyères
	452	Eurocopter AS.565MA Panther	AN 36 Flottille, Hyères
	453	Eurocopter AS.565MA Panther	AN 36 Flottille, Hyères
	466	Eurocopter AS.565MA Panther	AN 36 Flottille, Hyères
	482	Eurocopter AS.565MA Panther	AN 36 Flottille, Hyères
	486	Eurocopter AS.565MA Panther	AN 36 Flottille, Hyères
	488	Eurocopter AS.565MA Panther	AN 36 Flottille, Hyères
	503	Eurocopter AS.565MA Panther	AN 36 Flottille, Hyères
	505	Eurocopter AS.565MA Panther	AN 36 Flottille, Hyères
	506	Eurocopter AS.565MA Panther	AN 36 Flottille, Hyères
	507	Eurocopter AS.565MA Panther $	AN 36 Flottille, Hyères
	511	Eurocopter AS.565MA Panther	AN 36 Flottille, Hyères
	519	Eurocopter AS.565MA Panther	AN 36 Flottille, Hyères
	522	Eurocopter AS.565MA Panther $	AN 36 Flottille, Hyères
	524	Eurocopter AS.565MA Panther	AN 36 Flottille, Hyères
	542	Eurocopter AS.565MA Panther	AN 36 Flottille, Hyères
	6872	Eurocopter AS.365N-3 Dauphin	AN 35 Flottille, Tahiti
	6928	Eurocopter AS.365N-3 Dauphin	AN 35 Flottille, Tahiti
	1	NH Industries NH.90-NFH Caïman (F-ZWTO)	AN 33 Flottille, Lanvéoc/Poulmic
	2	NH Industries NH.90-NFH Caïman	AN CEPA/10 Escadrille, Hyères
	3	NH Industries NH.90-NFH Caïman	AN 31 Flottille, Hyères
	4	NH Industries NH.90-NFH Caïman	AN 33 Flottille, Lanvéoc/Poulmic
	5	NH Industries NH.90-NFH Caïman	AN 33 Flottille, Lanvéoc/Poulmic
	6	NH Industries NH.90-NFH Caïman	AN 33 Flottille, Lanvéoc/Poulmic
	7	NH Industries NH.90-NFH Caïman	AN 33 Flottille, Lanvéoc/Poulmic
	8	NH Industries NH.90-NFH Caïman	AN 31 Flottille, Hyères
	9	NH Industries NH.90-NFH Caïman	AN 31 Flottille, Hyères
	10	NH Industries NH.90-NFH Caïman	AN 31 Flottille, Hyères
	11	NH Industries NH.90-NFH Caïman	AN 33 Flottille, Lanvéoc/Poulmic
	12	NH Industries NH.90-NFH Caïman	AN 31 Flottille, Hyères
	13	NH Industries NH.90-NFH Caïman	AN 31 Flottille, Hyères
	14	NH Industries NH.90-NFH Caïman	AN 33 Flottille, Lanvéoc/Poulmic
	15	NH Industries NH.90-NFH Caïman	AN CEPA/10 Escadrille, Hyères
	16	NH Industries NH.90-NFH Caïman	AN 31 Flottille, Hyères
	17	NH Industries NH.90-NFH Caïman	AN
	18	NH Industries NH.90-NFH Caïman	AN 31 Flottille, Hyères
	19	NH Industries NH.90-NFH Caïman	AN
	20	NH Industries NH.90-NFH Caïman	AN 33 Flottille, Lanvéoc/Poulmic
	21	NH Industries NH.90-NFH Caïman	AN
	22	NH Industries NH.90-NFH Caïman	AN (on order)
	23	NH Industries NH.90-NFH Caïman	AN (on order)
	24	NH Industries NH.90-NFH Caïman	AN (on order)
	25	NH Industries NH.90-NFH Caïman	AN (on order)
	26	NH Industries NH.90-NFH Caïman	AN (on order)
	27	NH Industries NH.90-NFH Caïman	AN (on order)
	1	Northrop Grumman E-2C Hawkeye (165455)	AN 4 Flottille, Lorient/Lann Bihoué
	2	Northrop Grumman E-2C Hawkeye (165456)	AN 4 Flottille, Lorient/Lann Bihoué
	3	Northrop Grumman E-2C Hawkeye (166417)	AN 4 Flottille, Lorient/Lann Bihoué
	4	Northrop Grumman E-2C Hawkeye	AN (on order)
	13	Sud Aviation SE.3160 Alouette III	AN 35 Flottille, Hyères
	14	Sud Aviation SE.3160 Alouette III	AN 22 Escadrille/ESHE, Lanvéoc/Poulmic

Serial	Type (code/other identity)	Owner/operator, location or fate	Notes
41	Sud Aviation SE.3160 Alouette III	AN 35 Flottille, Hyères	
100	Sud Aviation SA.319B Alouette III	AN 22 Escadrille/ESHE, Lanvéoc/Poulmic	
106	Sud Aviation SA.319B Alouette III	AN 22 Escadrille/ESHE, Lanvéoc/Poulmic	
114	Sud Aviation SA.319B Alouette III	AN 22 Escadrille/ESHE, Lanvéoc/Poulmic	
160	Sud Aviation SA.319B Alouette III	AN 22 Escadrille/ESHE, Lanvéoc/Poulmic	
161	Sud Aviation SA.319B Alouette III	AN 22 Escadrille/ESHE, Lanvéoc/Poulmic	
219	Sud Aviation SE.3160 Alouette III	AN 35 Flottille, Hyères	
237	Sud Aviation SA.319B Alouette III	AN 35 Flottille, Hyères	
244	Sud Aviation SE.3160 Alouette III	AN 22 Escadrille/ESHE, Lanvéoc/Poulmic	
245	Sud Aviation SE.3160 Alouette III	AN 22 Escadrille/ESHE, Lanvéoc/Poulmic	
262	Sud Aviation SA.319B Alouette III	AN 22 Escadrille/ESHE, Lanvéoc/Poulmic	
268	Sud Aviation SA.319B Alouette III	AN 22 Escadrille/ESHE, Lanvéoc/Poulmic	
279	Sud Aviation SE.3160 Alouette III	AN 22 Escadrille/ESHE, Lanvéoc/Poulmic	
302	Sud Aviation SA.319B Alouette III	AN 22 Escadrille/ESHE, Lanvéoc/Poulmic	
303	Sud Aviation SA.319B Alouette III	AN 22 Escadrille/ESHE, Lanvéoc/Poulmic	
309	Sud Aviation SA.319B Alouette III	AN 22 Escadrille/ESHE, Lanvéoc/Poulmic	
314	Sud Aviation SA.319B Alouette III	*Crashed 31 December 2017, Nouméa*	
347	Sud Aviation SA.319B Alouette III	AN 22 Escadrille/ESHE, Lanvéoc/Poulmic	
358	Sud Aviation SA.319B Alouette III	AN 22 Escadrille/ESHE, Lanvéoc/Poulmic	
444	Sud Aviation SE.3160 Alouette III	AN 22 Escadrille/ESHE, Lanvéoc/Poulmic	
731	Sud Aviation SA.316B Alouette III	AN 22 Escadrille/ESHE, Lanvéoc/Poulmic	
806	Sud Aviation SA.316B Alouette III	AN 22 Escadrille/ESHE, Lanvéoc/Poulmic	
809	Sud Aviation SA.316B Alouette III	AN 22 Escadrille/ESHE, Lanvéoc/Poulmic	
997	Sud Aviation SA.319B Alouette III	AN 22 Escadrille/ESHE, Lanvéoc/Poulmic	
263	Westland Lynx HAS2(FN)	AN 34 Flottille, Lanvéoc/Poulmic	
264	Westland Lynx HAS2(FN)	AN 34 Flottille, Lanvéoc/Poulmic	
265	Westland Lynx HAS2(FN)	AN 34 Flottille, Lanvéoc/Poulmic	
267	Westland Lynx HAS2(FN)	AN 34 Flottille, Lanvéoc/Poulmic	
270	Westland Lynx HAS2(FN)	AN 34 Flottille, Lanvéoc/Poulmic	
272	Westland Lynx HAS2(FN) $	AN 34 Flottille, Lanvéoc/Poulmic	
273	Westland Lynx HAS2(FN)	AN 34 Flottille, Lanvéoc/Poulmic	
276	Westland Lynx HAS2(FN)	AN 34 Flottille, Lanvéoc/Poulmic	
621	Westland Lynx HAS2(FN)	AN 34 Flottille, Lanvéoc/Poulmic	
622	Westland Lynx HAS2(FN)	AN 34 Flottille, Lanvéoc/Poulmic	
624	Westland Lynx HAS2(FN)	AN 34 Flottille, Lanvéoc/Poulmic	
802	Westland Lynx HAS4(FN)	AN 34 Flottille, Lanvéoc/Poulmic	
804	Westland Lynx HAS4(FN)	AN 34 Flottille, Lanvéoc/Poulmic	
806	Westland Lynx HAS4(FN)	AN 34 Flottille, Lanvéoc/Poulmic	
807	Westland Lynx HAS4(FN)	AN 34 Flottille, Lanvéoc/Poulmic	
808	Westland Lynx HAS4(FN)	AN 34 Flottille, Lanvéoc/Poulmic	
810	Westland Lynx HAS4(FN)	AN 34 Flottille, Lanvéoc/Poulmic	
811	Westland Lynx HAS4(FN)	AN 34 Flottille, Lanvéoc/Poulmic	
814	Westland Lynx HAS4(FN)	AN 34 Flottille, Lanvéoc/Poulmic	
Aviation Legére de l'Armée de Terre (ALAT)			
1005	Aérospatiale SA.330Ba Puma [DCA]	ALAT ESAM, Bourges	
1020	Aérospatiale SA.330Ba Puma [DAB]	ALAT 5 RHC, Pau	
1036	Aérospatiale SA.330Ba Puma [DAC]	ALAT 3 RHC, Etain	
1037	Aérospatiale SA.330Ba Puma [DAD]	ALAT 5 RHC, Pau	
1049	Aérospatiale SA.330Ba Puma [DAE]	ALAT 5 RHC, Pau	
1052	Aérospatiale SA.330Ba Puma [DCB]	ALAT EALAT, Le Luc	
1055	Aérospatiale SA.330Ba Puma [DAF]	ALAT GIH, Cazaux	
1056	Aérospatiale SA.330Ba Puma [DCC]	ALAT GAM/STAT, Valence	
1057	Aérospatiale SA.330Ba Puma [DCD]	ALAT EALAT, Le Luc	
1069	Aérospatiale SA.330Ba Puma [DAG]	ALAT	
1071	Aérospatiale SA.330Ba Puma [DCE]	ALAT EALAT, Le Luc	
1073	Aérospatiale SA.330Ba Puma [DCF]	ALAT EALAT, Le Luc	
1078	Aérospatiale SA.330Ba Puma [DAH]	ALAT 3 RHC, Etain	
1092	Aérospatiale SA.330Ba Puma [DAI]	ALAT	
1093	Aérospatiale SA.330Ba Puma [DCG]	ALAT 3 RHC, Etain	
1100	Aérospatiale SA.330Ba Puma [DAJ]	ALAT 3 RHC, Etain	
1102	Aérospatiale SA.330Ba Puma [DAK]	ALAT	
1107	Aérospatiale SA.330Ba Puma [DAL]	ALAT	

Notes	Serial	Type (code/other identity)	Owner/operator, location or fate
	1109	Aérospatiale SA.330Ba Puma [DAM]	ALAT 5 RHC, Pau
	1114	Aérospatiale SA.330Ba Puma [DCH]	ALAT 3 RHC, Etain
	1122	Aérospatiale SA.330Ba Puma [DCI]	ALAT 5 RHC, Pau
	1123	Aérospatiale SA.330Ba Puma [DCJ]	ALAT 5 RHC, Pau
	1128	Aérospatiale SA.330Ba Puma [DAN]	ALAT 3 RHC, Etain
	1130	Aérospatiale SA.330Ba Puma [DCK]	ALAT 3 RHC, Etain
	1135	Aérospatiale SA.330Ba Puma [DCL]	ALAT
	1136	Aérospatiale SA.330Ba Puma [DCM]	ALAT
	1142	Aérospatiale SA.330Ba Puma [DCN]	ALAT EALAT, Le Luc
	1143	Aérospatiale SA.330Ba Puma [DAO]	ALAT
	1145	Aérospatiale SA.330Ba Puma [DCO]	ALAT 3 RHC, Etain
	1149	Aérospatiale SA.330Ba Puma [DAP]	ALAT 5 RHC, Pau
	1150	Aérospatiale SA.330Ba Puma [DCP]	ALAT 3 RHC, Etain
	1155	Aérospatiale SA.330Ba Puma [DCQ]	ALAT 4 RHFS, Pau
	1156	Aérospatiale SA.330Ba Puma [DAQ]	ALAT
	1163	Aérospatiale SA.330Ba Puma [DCR]	ALAT EALAT, Le Luc
	1164	Aérospatiale SA.330Ba Puma [DCS]	ALAT
	1165	Aérospatiale SA.330Ba Puma [DCT]	ALAT
	1171	Aérospatiale SA.330Ba Puma [DCU]	ALAT
	1172	Aérospatiale SA.330Ba Puma [DCV]	ALAT EALAT, Le Luc
	1173	Aérospatiale SA.330Ba Puma [DAR]	ALAT 3 RHC, Etain
	1176	Aérospatiale SA.330Ba Puma [DAS]	ALAT 3 RHC, Etain
	1177	Aérospatiale SA.330Ba Puma [DCW]	ALAT 3 RHC, Etain
	1179	Aérospatiale SA.330Ba Puma [DCX]	ALAT
	1182	Aérospatiale SA.330Ba Puma [DCY]	ALAT
	1186	Aérospatiale SA.330Ba Puma [DCZ]	ALAT 5 RHC, Pau
	1189	Aérospatiale SA.330Ba Puma [DAT]	*Withdrawn from use and preserved at Etain, 2019*
	1190	Aérospatiale SA.330Ba Puma [DDA]	ALAT 5 RHC, Pau
	1192	Aérospatiale SA.330Ba Puma [DDB]	ALAT
	1196	Aérospatiale SA.330Ba Puma [DDC]	ALAT EALAT, Le Luc
	1197	Aérospatiale SA.330Ba Puma [DAU]	ALAT 5 RHC, Pau
	1198	Aérospatiale SA.330Ba Puma [DDD]	ALAT
	1204	Aérospatiale SA.330Ba Puma [DAV]	ALAT 3 RHC, Etain
	1206	Aérospatiale SA.330Ba Puma [DDE]	ALAT 3 RHC, Etain
	1211	Aérospatiale SA.330Ba Puma [DAW]	ALAT
	1213	Aérospatiale SA.330Ba Puma [DDF]	ALAT
	1214	Aérospatiale SA.330Ba Puma [DAX]	ALAT 3 RHC, Etain
	1217	Aérospatiale SA.330Ba Puma [DAY]	ALAT
	1219	Aérospatiale SA.330Ba Puma [DAZ]	ALAT 3 RHC, Etain
	1222	Aérospatiale SA.330Ba Puma [DDG]	ALAT 3 RHC, Etain
	1223	Aérospatiale SA.330Ba Puma [DDH]	ALAT EALAT, Le Luc
	1229	Aérospatiale SA.330Ba Puma [DDJ]	ALAT EALAT, Le Luc
	1231	Aérospatiale SA.330Ba Puma [DDK]	ALAT 3 RHC, Etain
	1232	Aérospatiale SA.330Ba Puma [DBA]	ALAT 5 RHC, Pau
	1235	Aérospatiale SA.330Ba Puma [DDL]	ALAT 5 RHC, Pau
	1236	Aérospatiale SA.330Ba Puma [DDM]	ALAT EALAT, Le Luc
	1239	Aérospatiale SA.330Ba Puma [DDN]	ALAT 5 RHC, Pau
	1243	Aérospatiale SA.330Ba Puma [DBB]	ALAT 5 RHC, Pau
	1244	Aérospatiale SA.330Ba Puma [DDO]	ALAT 5 RHC, Pau
	1248	Aérospatiale SA.330Ba Puma [DBC]	ALAT 3 RHC, Etain
	1252	Aérospatiale SA.330Ba Puma [DDP]	ALAT EALAT, Le Luc
	1255	Aérospatiale SA.330Ba Puma [DDQ]	ALAT
	1256	Aérospatiale SA.330Ba Puma [DDR]	ALAT GAM/STAT, Valence
	1260	Aérospatiale SA.330Ba Puma [DDS]	ALAT EALAT, Le Luc
	1262	Aérospatiale SA.330Ba Puma [DBD]	ALAT 5 RHC, Pau
	1269	Aérospatiale SA.330Ba Puma [DDT]	ALAT 3 RHC, Etain
	1277	Aérospatiale SA.330Ba Puma [DBE]	ALAT
	1411	Aérospatiale SA.330Ba Puma [DDU]	ALAT 3 RHC, Etain
	1417	Aérospatiale SA.330Ba Puma [DBF]	ALAT 3 RHC, Etain
	1419	Aérospatiale SA.330Ba Puma [DDV]	ALAT
	1438	Aérospatiale SA.330Ba Puma [DBG]	ALAT GAM/STAT, Valence
	1447	Aérospatiale SA.330Ba Puma [DDW]	ALAT 3 RHC, Etain

Serial	Type (code/other identity)	Owner/operator, location or fate	Notes
1451	Aérospatiale SA.330Ba Puma [DBH]	ALAT	
1507	Aérospatiale SA.330Ba Puma [DBI]	ALAT EALAT, Le Luc	
1510	Aérospatiale SA.330Ba Puma [DBJ]	ALAT 3 RHC, Etain	
1512	Aérospatiale SA.330Ba Puma [DBK]	ALAT	
1519	Aérospatiale SA.330Ba Puma [DBL]	ALAT 3 RHC, Etain	
1617	Aérospatiale SA.330Ba Puma [DBM]	ALAT	
1632	Aérospatiale SA.330Ba Puma [DBN]	ALAT 5 RHC, Pau	
1634	Aérospatiale SA.330Ba Puma [DBO]	ALAT 3 RHC, Etain	
1654	Aérospatiale SA.330Ba Puma [DBP]	ALAT 3 RHC, Etain	
1662	Aérospatiale SA.330Ba Puma [DDX]	ALAT EALAT, Le Luc	
1663	Aérospatiale SA.330Ba Puma [DBQ]	ALAT 3 RHC, Etain	
5682	Aérospatiale SA.330Ba Puma [DBR]	ALAT 4 RHFS, Pau	
1732	Aérospatiale SA.342M Gazelle [GJA]	ALAT EALAT, Le Luc	
3458	Aérospatiale SA.342M Gazelle [GNA]	ALAT EALAT, Le Luc	
3459	Aérospatiale SA.342M Gazelle [GAA]	ALAT 1 RHC, Phalsbourg	
3476	Aérospatiale SA.342M Gazelle [GAB]	ALAT 3 RHC, Etain	
3511	Aérospatiale SA.342M Gazelle [GJC]	ALAT EALAT, Le Luc	
3512	Aérospatiale SA.342M Gazelle [GAC]	ALAT 1 RHC, Phalsbourg	
3513	Aérospatiale SA.342M Gazelle [GNB]	ALAT 1 RHC, Phalsbourg	
3529	Aérospatiale SA.342M Gazelle [GJD]	ALAT EALAT, Le Luc	
3530	Aérospatiale SA.342M Gazelle [GAD]	ALAT 4 RHFS, Pau	
3546	Aérospatiale SA.342M Gazelle [GJF]	ALAT EALAT, Le Luc	
3548	Aérospatiale SA.342M Gazelle [GAE]	ALAT 1 RHC, Phalsbourg	
3549	Aérospatiale SA.342M Gazelle [GNC]	ALAT EALAT, Le Luc	
3567	Aérospatiale SA.342M Gazelle [GMA]	ALAT EALAT, Le Luc	
3615	Aérospatiale SA.342M Gazelle [GJH]	*Sold as G-CLBC, September 2018*	
3617	Aérospatiale SA.342M Gazelle [GND]	ALAT GAM/STAT, Valence	
3664	Aérospatiale SA.342M Gazelle [GAF]	ALAT 1 RHC, Phalsbourg	
3848	Aérospatiale SA.342M Gazelle [GAG]	ALAT 5 RHC, Pau	
3849	Aérospatiale SA.342M Gazelle [GAH]	ALAT 5 RHC, Pau	
3850	Aérospatiale SA.342M Gazelle [GAI]	ALAT 3 RHC, Etain	
3851	Aérospatiale SA.342M Gazelle [GJI]	ALAT EALAT, Le Luc	
3852	Aérospatiale SA.342M Gazelle [GNE]	ALAT 1 RHC, Phalsbourg	
3853	Aérospatiale SA.342M Gazelle [GNF]	ALAT EALAT, Le Luc	
3855	Aérospatiale SA.342M Gazelle [GJJ]	ALAT EALAT, Le Luc	
3856	Aérospatiale SA.342M Gazelle [GAJ]	ALAT 5 RHC, Pau	
3857	Aérospatiale SA.342M Gazelle [GJK]	ALAT EALAT, Le Luc	
3858	Aérospatiale SA.342M Gazelle [GNG]	ALAT	
3859	Aérospatiale SA.342M Gazelle [GAK]	ALAT 5 RHC, Pau	
3862	Aérospatiale SA.342M Gazelle [GAL] $	ALAT 1 RHC, Phalsbourg	
3863	Aérospatiale SA.342M Gazelle [GAM]	ALAT 3 RHC, Etain	
3864	Aérospatiale SA.342M Gazelle [GJL]	ALAT	
3865	Aérospatiale SA.342M Gazelle [GAN]	ALAT EALAT, Le Luc	
3866	Aérospatiale SA.342M Gazelle [GNI]	*Crashed 10 July 2018, Modeste, Ivory Coast*	
3867	Aérospatiale SA.342M Gazelle [GJM]	ALAT EALAT, Le Luc	
3868	Aérospatiale SA.342M Gazelle [GAO]	ALAT 1 RHC, Phalsbourg	
3870	Aérospatiale SA.342M Gazelle [GME]	ALAT	
3896	Aérospatiale SA.342M Gazelle [GNJ]	ALAT	
3911	Aérospatiale SA.342M Gazelle [GAP]	ALAT 1 RHC, Phalsbourg	
3921	Aérospatiale SA.342M Gazelle [GAQ]	ALAT EALAT, Le Luc	
3929	Aérospatiale SA.342M Gazelle [GJN]	ALAT EALAT, Le Luc	
3930	Aérospatiale SA.342M Gazelle [GMF]	ALAT	
3938	Aérospatiale SA.342M Gazelle [GAR]	ALAT EALAT, Le Luc	
3939	Aérospatiale SA.342M Gazelle [GMG]	ALAT	
3947	Aérospatiale SA.342M Gazelle [GAS]	ALAT 5 RHC, Pau	
3948	Aérospatiale SA.342M Gazelle [GAT]	ALAT 1 RHC, Phalsbourg	
3956	Aérospatiale SA.342M Gazelle [GNK]	ALAT	
3957	Aérospatiale SA.342M Gazelle [GAU]	ALAT 5 RHC, Pau	
3964	Aérospatiale SA.342M Gazelle [GAV]	ALAT 3 RHC, Etain	
3965	Aérospatiale SA.342M Gazelle [GJO]	ALAT EALAT, Le Luc	
3992	Aérospatiale SA.342M Gazelle [GNM]	ALAT EALAT, Le Luc	
3996	Aérospatiale SA.342M Gazelle [GAW]	ALAT 5 RHC, Pau	

Notes	Serial	Type (code/other identity)	Owner/operator, location or fate
	4008	Aérospatiale SA.342M Gazelle [GNN]	ALAT
	4014	Aérospatiale SA.342M Gazelle [GJP]	ALAT GAM/STAT, Valence
	4018	Aérospatiale SA.342M Gazelle [GAX]	ALAT 3 RHC, Etain
	4020	Aérospatiale SA.342M Gazelle [GAZ]	ALAT 1 RHC, Phalsbourg
	4022	Aérospatiale SA.342M Gazelle [GJQ]	ALAT EALAT, Le Luc
	4023	Aérospatiale SA.342M Gazelle [GMH]	ALAT ESAM, Bourges
	4026	Aérospatiale SA.342M Gazelle [GBA]	ALAT 1 RHC, Phalsbourg
	4032	Aérospatiale SA.342M Gazelle [GNO]	ALAT EALAT, Le Luc
	4034	Aérospatiale SA.342M Gazelle [GBB]	ALAT 1 RHC, Phalsbourg
	4038	Aérospatiale SA.342M Gazelle [GJR]	ALAT EALAT, Le Luc
	4039	Aérospatiale SA.342M Gazelle [GBC]	ALAT 1 RHC, Phalsbourg
	4042	Aérospatiale SA.342M Gazelle [GMB]	ALAT EALAT, Le Luc
	4047	Aérospatiale SA.342M Gazelle [GJS]	ALAT EALAT, Le Luc
	4048	Aérospatiale SA.342M Gazelle [GBD]	ALAT EALAT, Le Luc
	4049	Aérospatiale SA.342M Gazelle [GNP]	ALAT EALAT, Le Luc
	4053	Aérospatiale SA.342M Gazelle [GBE]	ALAT 3 RHC, Etain
	4059	Aérospatiale SA.342M Gazelle [GBF]	ALAT 1 RHC, Phalsbourg
	4060	Aérospatiale SA.342M Gazelle [GNQ]	ALAT EALAT, Le Luc
	4061	Aérospatiale SA.342M Gazelle [GBG]	ALAT GAM/STAT, Valence
	4065	Aérospatiale SA.342M Gazelle [GNR]	ALAT EALAT, Le Luc
	4066	Aérospatiale SA.342M Gazelle [GBH]	ALAT 3 RHC, Etain
	4067	Aérospatiale SA.342M Gazelle [GJU]	ALAT EALAT, Le Luc
	4071	Aérospatiale SA.342M Gazelle [GNS]	ALAT EHADT, Etain
	4072	Aérospatiale SA.342M Gazelle [GBI]	ALAT 3 RHC, Etain
	4078	Aérospatiale SA.342M Gazelle [GJV]	ALAT EALAT, Le Luc
	4079	Aérospatiale SA.342M Gazelle [GMC]	ALAT EALAT, Le Luc
	4083	Aérospatiale SA.342M Gazelle [GNT]	ALAT EALAT, Le Luc
	4084	Aérospatiale SA.342M Gazelle [GBJ] $	ALAT 3 RHC, Etain
	4095	Aérospatiale SA.342M Gazelle [GBL]	ALAT 5 RHC, Pau
	4096	Aérospatiale SA.342M Gazelle [GNU]	ALAT EALAT, Le Luc
	4102	Aérospatiale SA.342M Gazelle [GJW]	ALAT EALAT, Le Luc
	4103	Aérospatiale SA.342M Gazelle [GJX]	ALAT EALAT, Le Luc
	4108	Aérospatiale SA.342M Gazelle [GBM]	ALAT GAM/STAT, Valence
	4109	Aérospatiale SA.342M Gazelle [GBN]	ALAT 5 RHC, Pau
	4114	Aérospatiale SA.342M Gazelle [GBO]	ALAT EALAT, Le Luc
	4115	Aérospatiale SA.342M Gazelle [GBP]	ALAT 5 RHC, Pau
	4118	Aérospatiale SA.342M Gazelle [GNV]	ALAT EALAT, Le Luc
	4119	Aérospatiale SA.342M Gazelle [GBQ]	ALAT 5 RHC, Pau
	4120	Aérospatiale SA.342M Gazelle [GBR]	ALAT EALAT, Le Luc
	4123	Aérospatiale SA.342M Gazelle [GJY]	ALAT EALAT, Le Luc
	4124	Aérospatiale SA.342M Gazelle [GBS]	ALAT 1 RHC, Phalsbourg
	4135	Aérospatiale SA.342M Gazelle [GNW]	ALAT
	4136	Aérospatiale SA.342M Gazelle [GBT]	ALAT 1 RHC, Phalsbourg
	4140	Aérospatiale SA.342M Gazelle [GBU]	ALAT 1 RHC, Phalsbourg
	4141	Aérospatiale SA.342M Gazelle [GBV]	ALAT
	4142	Aérospatiale SA.342M Gazelle [GBW]	ALAT 5 RHC, Pau
	4143	Aérospatiale SA.342M Gazelle [GNX]	ALAT EALAT, Le Luc
	4144	Aérospatiale SA.342M Gazelle [GBX]	ALAT 3 RHC, Etain
	4145	Aérospatiale SA.342M Gazelle [GBY] $	ALAT 3 RHC, Etain
	4146	Aérospatiale SA.342M Gazelle [GNY]	ALAT EALAT, Le Luc
	4151	Aérospatiale SA.342M Gazelle [GBZ]	ALAT 3 RHC, Etain
	4159	Aérospatiale SA.342M Gazelle [GNZ]	ALAT EALAT, Le Luc
	4160	Aérospatiale SA.342M Gazelle [GCC]	ALAT 1 RHC, Phalsbourg
	4161	Aérospatiale SA.342M Gazelle [GCD]	ALAT 1 RHC, Phalsbourg
	4162	Aérospatiale SA.342M Gazelle [GCE]	ALAT 5 RHC, Pau
	4164	Aérospatiale SA.342M Gazelle [GCF]	ALAT 3 RHC, Etain
	4166	Aérospatiale SA.342M Gazelle [GJZ]	ALAT EALAT, Le Luc
	4168	Aérospatiale SA.342M Gazelle [GCG]	ALAT 5 RHC, Pau
	4171	Aérospatiale SA.342M Gazelle [GMI]	ALAT EALAT, Le Luc
	4175	Aérospatiale SA.342M Gazelle [GCI]	ALAT 4 RHFS, Pau
	4176	Aérospatiale SA.342M Gazelle [GKA]	ALAT EALAT, Le Luc
	4177	Aérospatiale SA.342M Gazelle [GKB]	ALAT 1 RHC, Phalsbourg

Serial	Type (code/other identity)	Owner/operator, location or fate	Notes
4178	Aérospatiale SA.342M Gazelle [GOA]	ALAT EALAT, Le Luc	
4179	Aérospatiale SA.342M Gazelle [GCJ]	ALAT 3 RHC, Etain	
4180	Aérospatiale SA.342M Gazelle [GCK]	ALAT GAM/STAT, Valence	
4181	Aérospatiale SA.342M Gazelle [GCL]	ALAT 3 RHC, Etain	
4182	Aérospatiale SA.342M Gazelle [GKC]	ALAT EALAT, Le Luc	
4183	Aérospatiale SA.342M Gazelle [GOB]	ALAT EALAT, Le Luc	
4184	Aérospatiale SA.342M Gazelle [GOC]	ALAT 1 RHC, Phalsbourg	
4185	Aérospatiale SA.342M Gazelle [GKD]	ALAT 3 RHC, Etain	
4186	Aérospatiale SA.342M Gazelle [GCM]	ALAT 1 RHC, Phalsbourg	
4187	Aérospatiale SA.342M Gazelle [GKE]	ALAT EALAT, Le Luc	
4189	Aérospatiale SA.342M Gazelle [GCN]	ALAT 4 RHFS, Pau	
4190	Aérospatiale SA.342M Gazelle [GMJ]	ALAT EALAT, Le Luc	
4191	Aérospatiale SA.342M Gazelle [GCO]	ALAT 4 RHFS, Pau	
4192	Aérospatiale SA.342M Gazelle [GOD]	ALAT	
4194	Aérospatiale SA.342M Gazelle [GMD]	ALAT EALAT, Le Luc	
4195	Aérospatiale SA.342M Gazelle [GCP]	ALAT 3 RHC, Etain	
4198	Aérospatiale SA.342M Gazelle [GCQ]	ALAT 3 RHC, Etain	
4201	Aérospatiale SA.342M Gazelle [GMK]	ALAT EALAT, Le Luc	
4205	Aérospatiale SA.342L-1 Gazelle [GEA]	ALAT 1 RHC, Phalsbourg	
4206	Aérospatiale SA.342L-1 Gazelle [GEB]	ALAT EALAT, Le Luc	
4207	Aérospatiale SA.342L-1 Gazelle [GEC]	ALAT 3 RHC, Etain	
4208	Aérospatiale SA.342L-1 Gazelle [GED]	ALAT GAM/STAT, Valence	
4210	Aérospatiale SA.342L-1 Gazelle [GEF]	ALAT 1 RHC, Phalsbourg	
4211	Aérospatiale SA.342L-1 Gazelle [GEG]	ALAT 5 RHC, Pau	
4214	Aérospatiale SA.342L-1 Gazelle [GEI]	ALAT EALAT, Le Luc	
4215	Aérospatiale SA.342L-1 Gazelle [GEJ]	ALAT 5 RHC, Pau	
4216	Aérospatiale SA.342L-1 Gazelle [GEK]	ALAT GAM/STAT, Valence	
4217	Aérospatiale SA.342L-1 Gazelle [GEL]	ALAT 3 RHC, Etain	
4218	Aérospatiale SA.342L-1 Gazelle [GEM]	ALAT 1 RHC, Phalsbourg	
4219	Aérospatiale SA.342L-1 Gazelle [GEN]	ALAT 4 RHFS, Pau	
4220	Aérospatiale SA.342L-1 Gazelle [GEO]	ALAT 3 RHC, Etain	
4221	Aérospatiale SA.342L-1 Gazelle [GEP]	ALAT EALAT, Le Luc	
4222	Aérospatiale SA.342L-1 Gazelle [GEQ]	ALAT EALAT, Le Luc	
4223	Aérospatiale SA.342L-1 Gazelle [GER]	ALAT GAM/STAT, Valence	
4224	Aérospatiale SA.342L-1 Gazelle [GES]	ALAT 1 RHC, Phalsbourg	
4225	Aérospatiale SA.342L-1 Gazelle [GET]	ALAT GAM/STAT, Valence	
4226	Aérospatiale SA.342L-1 Gazelle [GEU]	ALAT GAM/STAT, Valence	
4227	Aérospatiale SA.342L-1 Gazelle [GEV]	ALAT 1 RHC, Phalsbourg	
4228	Aérospatiale SA.342L-1 Gazelle [GEW]	ALAT 1 RHC, Phalsbourg	
4229	Aérospatiale SA.342L-1 Gazelle [GEX]	ALAT 4 RHFS, Pau	
4230	Aérospatiale SA.342L-1 Gazelle [GEY]	ALAT GAM/STAT, Valence	
4231	Aérospatiale SA.342L-1 Gazelle [GEZ]	ALAT 5 RHC, Pau	
4232	Aérospatiale SA.342L-1 Gazelle [GFA]	ALAT EALAT, Le Luc	
4233	Aérospatiale SA.342L-1 Gazelle [GFB]	ALAT 3 RHC, Etain	
4234	Aérospatiale SA.342L-1 Gazelle [GFC]	ALAT	
2252	Aérospatiale AS.532UL Cougar [CGA]	ALAT GAM/STAT, Valence	
2266	Aérospatiale AS.532UL Cougar [CGB]	ALAT 5 RHC, Pau	
2267	Aérospatiale AS.532UL Cougar [CGC]	ALAT 4 RHFS, Pau	
2271	Aérospatiale AS.532UL Cougar [CGD]	ALAT 4 RHFS, Pau	
2272	Aérospatiale AS.532UL Cougar [CGE]	ALAT GAM/STAT, Valence	
2273	Aérospatiale AS.532UL Cougar [CGF]	ALAT 1 RHC, Phalsbourg	
2282	Aérospatiale AS.532UL Cougar [CGG]	ALAT	
2285	Aérospatiale AS.532UL Cougar [CGH]	ALAT	
2290	Aérospatiale AS.532UL Cougar [CGI]	ALAT 4 RHFS, Pau	
2293	Aérospatiale AS.532UL Cougar [CGJ]	ALAT 4 RHFS, Pau	
2299	Aérospatiale AS.532UL Cougar [CGK]	ALAT 4 RHFS, Pau	
2300	Aérospatiale AS.532UL Cougar [CGL]	ALAT 1 RHC, Phalsbourg	
2301	Aérospatiale AS.532UL Cougar [CGM]	ALAT 1 RHC, Phalsbourg	
2303	Aérospatiale AS.532UL Cougar [CGN]	ALAT 1 RHC, Phalsbourg	
2316	Aérospatiale AS.532UL Cougar [CGO]	ALAT 4 RHFS, Pau	
2323	Aérospatiale AS.532UL Cougar [CGQ]	ALAT 4 RHFS, Pau	
2324	Aérospatiale AS.532UL Cougar [CGR]	ALAT 4 RHFS, Pau	

Notes	Serial	Type (code/other identity)	Owner/operator, location or fate
	2325	Aérospatiale AS.532UL Cougar [CGS]	ALAT
	2327	Aérospatiale AS.532UL Cougar [CGT]	ALAT
	2331	Aérospatiale AS.532UL Cougar [CGU]	ALAT GAM/STAT, Valence
	2336	Aérospatiale AS.532UL Cougar [CGV]	ALAT 4 RHFS, Pau
	2342	Aérospatiale AS.532UL Cougar [CHA]	ALAT
	2369	Aérospatiale AS.532UL Cougar [CHB]	ALAT
	2375	Aérospatiale AS.532UL Cougar [CHC]	ALAT
	2443	Aérospatiale AS.532UL Cougar [CGW]	ALAT
	2446	Aérospatiale AS.532UL Cougar [CGX]	ALAT 1 RHC, Phalsbourg
	2001	Eurocopter EC.665 Tigre HAP [BHH]	ALAT EFA, Le Luc
	2002	Eurocopter EC.665 Tigre HAP [BHI]	ALAT EFA, Le Luc
	2003	Eurocopter EC.665 Tigre HAP [BHJ]	ALAT 5 RHC, Pau
	2004	Eurocopter EC.665 Tigre HAP [BHK]	ALAT EFA, Le Luc
	2006	Eurocopter EC.665 Tigre HAP [BHL]	ALAT EFA, Le Luc
	2009	Eurocopter EC.665 Tigre HAP [BHB]	ALAT EFA, Le Luc
	2010	Eurocopter EC.665 Tigre HAP [BHA]	ALAT EFA, Le Luc
	2011	Eurocopter EC.665 Tigre HAP [BHM]	ALAT 5 RHC, Pau
	2012	Eurocopter EC.665 Tigre HAP [BHT]	ALAT GAM/STAT, Valence
	2013	Eurocopter EC.665 Tigre HAP [BHC]	ALAT GAM/STAT, Valence
	2015	Eurocopter EC.665 Tigre HAP [BHD]	ALAT 5 RHC, Pau
	2016	Eurocopter EC.665 Tigre HAP [BIA]	Airbus Helicopters, Marseille
	2018	Eurocopter EC.665 Tigre HAP [BHE]	ALAT 5 RHC, Pau
	2019	Eurocopter EC.665 Tigre HAP [BHF]	ALAT 5 RHC, Pau
	2021	Eurocopter EC.665 Tigre HAP [BHN] $	ALAT EFA, Le Luc
	2022	Eurocopter EC.665 Tigre HAP [BHG]	ALAT 5 RHC, Pau
	2023	Eurocopter EC.665 Tigre HAP [BHP]	ALAT 5 RHC, Pau
	2024	Eurocopter EC.665 Tigre HAP [BHO]	ALAT 3 RHC, Etain
	2025	Eurocopter EC.665 Tigre HAP [BHQ]	ALAT 5 RHC, Pau
	2026	Eurocopter EC.665 Tigre HAP [BHR]	ALAT GAM/STAT, Valence
	2027	Eurocopter EC.665 Tigre HAP [BHS]	ALAT 5 RHC, Pau
	2028	Eurocopter EC.665 Tigre HAP [BHU]	ALAT 5 RHC, Pau
	2029	Eurocopter EC.665 Tigre HAP [BHV]	ALAT 5 RHC, Pau
	2030	Eurocopter EC.665 Tigre HAP [BHW]	ALAT
	2031	Eurocopter EC.665 Tigre HAP [BHX]	ALAT EFA, Le Luc
	2033	Eurocopter EC.665 Tigre HAP [BHZ]	ALAT 5 RHC, Pau
	2034	Eurocopter EC.665 Tigre HAP [BIB]	ALAT EFA, Le Luc
	2035	Eurocopter EC.665 Tigre HAP [BIC]	ALAT 4 RHFS, Pau
	2037	Eurocopter EC.665 Tigre HAP [BIE]	ALAT 5 RHC, Pau
	2038	Eurocopter EC.665 Tigre HAP	Airbus Helicopters, Marseille
	2039	Eurocopter EC.665 Tigre HAP [BIG]	ALAT
	2040	Eurocopter EC.665 Tigre HAP [BIH]	ALAT 5 RHC, Pau
	2041	Eurocopter EC.665 Tigre HAP [BII]	ALAT
	2042	Eurocopter EC.665 Tigre HAP [BIJ]	ALAT 5 RHC, Pau
	2043	Eurocopter EC.665 Tigre HAP [BIK]	ALAT 5 RHC, Pau
	2044	Eurocopter EC.665 Tigre HAP [BIL]	ALAT GAM/STAT, Valence
	2045	Eurocopter EC.665 Tigre HAP [BIM]	ALAT EFA, Le Luc
	2046	Eurocopter EC.665 Tigre HAP [BIN]	ALAT EFA, Le Luc
	2047	Eurocopter EC.665 Tigre HAP [BIO]	ALAT (on order)
	2048	Eurocopter EC.665 Tigre HAP [BIP]	ALAT (on order)
	2049	Eurocopter EC.665 Tigre HAP [BIQ]	ALAT (on order)
	2050	Eurocopter EC.665 Tigre HAP [BIR]	ALAT (on order)
	2051	Eurocopter EC.665 Tigre HAP [BIS]	ALAT (on order)
	2052	Eurocopter EC.665 Tigre HAP [BIT]	ALAT (on order)
	6001	Eurocopter EC.665 Tigre HAD [BJA]	ALAT 1 RHC, Phalsbourg
	6002	Eurocopter EC.665 Tigre HAD [BJB]	ALAT EFA, Le Luc
	6003	Eurocopter EC.665 Tigre HAD [BJC]	ALAT EFA, Le Luc
	6004	Eurocopter EC.665 Tigre HAD [BJD]	ALAT EFA, Le Luc
	6005	Eurocopter EC.665 Tigre HAD [BJE]	ALAT EFA, Le Luc
	6006	Eurocopter EC.665 Tigre HAD [BJF]	ALAT 1 RHC, Phalsbourg
	6007	Eurocopter EC.665 Tigre HAD [BJG]	ALAT EFA, Le Luc
	6008	Eurocopter EC.665 Tigre HAD [BJH]	ALAT
	6009	Eurocopter EC.665 Tigre HAD [BJI]	ALAT 1 RHC, Phalsbourg

Serial	Type (code/other identity)	Owner/operator, location or fate	Notes
6010	Eurocopter EC.665 Tigre HAD [BJJ]	ALAT GAM/STAT, Valence	
6011	Eurocopter EC.665 Tigre HAD [BJK]	ALAT	
6012	Eurocopter EC.665 Tigre HAD [BJL]	ALAT 1 RHC, Phalsbourg	
6013	Eurocopter EC.665 Tigre HAD [BJM]	ALAT 1 RHC, Phalsbourg	
6014	Eurocopter EC.665 Tigre HAD [BJN]	ALAT EALAT, Le Luc	
6015	Eurocopter EC.665 Tigre HAD [BJO]	ALAT 1 RHC, Phalsbourg	
6016	Eurocopter EC.665 Tigre HAD [BJP]	ALAT 1 RHC, Phalsbourg	
6017	Eurocopter EC.665 Tigre HAD [BJQ]	ALAT 1 RHC, Phalsbourg	
6018	Eurocopter EC.665 Tigre HAD [BJR]	ALAT	
6019	Eurocopter EC.665 Tigre HAD [BJS]	ALAT	
6020	Eurocopter EC.665 Tigre HAD [BJT]	ALAT 1 RHC, Phalsbourg	
6021	Eurocopter EC.665 Tigre HAD [BJU]	ALAT EALAT, Le Luc	
6022	Eurocopter EC.665 Tigre HAD [BJV]	ALAT	
6023	Eurocopter EC.665 Tigre HAD [BJW]	ALAT	
6024	Eurocopter EC.665 Tigre HAD [BJX]	ALAT	
6025	Eurocopter EC.665 Tigre HAD [BJY]	ALAT	
6026	Eurocopter EC.665 Tigre HAD [BJZ]	ALAT	
6027	Eurocopter EC.665 Tigre HAD [BKA]	ALAT (on order)	
6028	Eurocopter EC.665 Tigre HAD [BKB]	ALAT (on order)	
6029	Eurocopter EC.665 Tigre HAD [BKC]	ALAT (on order)	
6030	Eurocopter EC.665 Tigre HAD [BKD]	ALAT (on order)	
6031	Eurocopter EC.665 Tigre HAD [BKE]	ALAT (on order)	
2611	Eurocopter EC.725AP Caracal [CAA]	ALAT 4 RHFS, Pau	
2628	Eurocopter EC.725AP Caracal [CAB]	ALAT GIH, Cazaux	
2630	Eurocopter EC.725AP Caracal [CAC]	ALAT 4 RHFS, Pau	
2631	Eurocopter EC.725AP Caracal [CAD]	ALAT 4 RHFS, Pau	
2633	Eurocopter EC.725AP Caracal [CAE]	ALAT 4 RHFS, Pau	
2638	Eurocopter EC.725AP Caracal [CAF]	ALAT GIH, Cazaux	
2640	Eurocopter EC.725AP Caracal [CAG]	ALAT GIH, Cazaux	
2642	Eurocopter EC.725AP Caracal [CAH]	ALAT GIH, Cazaux	
1239	NH Industries NH.90-TTH Caïman [EAA]	ALAT CFIA NH.90, Le Luc	
1256	NH Industries NH.90-TTH Caïman [EAB]	ALAT GAM/STAT, Valence	
1271	NH Industries NH.90-TTH Caïman [EAC]	ALAT CFIA NH.90, Le Luc	
1273	NH Industries NH.90-TTH Caïman [EAD]	ALAT 1 RHC, Phalsbourg	
1290	NH Industries NH.90-TTH Caïman [EAE]	ALAT CFIA NH.90, Le Luc	
1291	NH Industries NH.90-TTH Caïman [EAF]	ALAT CFIA NH.90, Le Luc	
1292	NH Industries NH.90-TTH Caïman [EAG]	ALAT 1 RHC, Phalsbourg	
1293	NH Industries NH.90-TTH Caïman [EAH]	ALAT CFIA NH.90, Le Luc	
1294	NH Industries NH.90-TTH Caïman [EAI]	ALAT 1 RHC, Phalsbourg	
1295	NH Industries NH.90-TTH Caïman [EAJ]	ALAT 1 RHC, Phalsbourg	
1306	NH Industries NH.90-TTH Caïman [EAK]	ALAT	
1307	NH Industries NH.90-TTH Caïman [EAL]	ALAT 1 RHC, Phalsbourg	
1308	NH Industries NH.90-TTH Caïman [EAM]	ALAT	
1309	NH Industries NH.90-TTH Caïman [EAN]	ALAT	
1310	NH Industries NH.90-TTH Caïman [EAO]	ALAT 1 RHC, Phalsbourg	
1311	NH Industries NH.90-TTH Caïman [EAP]	ALAT 1 RHC, Phalsbourg	
1312	NH Industries NH.90-TTH Caïman [EAQ]	ALAT 1 RHC, Phalsbourg	
1313	NH Industries NH.90-TTH Caïman [EAR]	ALAT 1 RHC, Phalsbourg	
1332	NH Industries NH.90-TTH Caïman [EAS]	ALAT 1 RHC, Phalsbourg (damaged)	
1333	NH Industries NH.90-TTH Caïman [EAT]	ALAT	
1334	NH Industries NH.90-TTH Caïman [EAU]	ALAT 1 RHC, Phalsbourg	
1335	NH Industries NH.90-TTH Caïman [EAV]	ALAT 1 RHC, Phalsbourg	
1336	NH Industries NH.90-TTH Caïman [EAW]	ALAT 1 RHC, Phalsbourg	
1337	NH Industries NH.90-TTH Caïman [EAX]	ALAT 1 RHC, Phalsbourg	
1338	NH Industries NH.90-TTH Caïman [EAY]	ALAT 1 RHC, Phalsbourg	
1386	NH Industries NH.90-TTH Caïman [EAZ]	ALAT 1 RHC, Phalsbourg	
1390	NH Industries NH.90-TTH Caïman [EBA]	ALAT 1 RHC, Phalsbourg	
1391	NH Industries NH.90-TTH Caïman [EBB]	ALAT 1 RHC, Phalsbourg	
1387	NH Industries NH.90-TTH Caïman [EBC]	ALAT 1 RHC, Phalsbourg	
1392	NH Industries NH.90-TTH Caïman [EBD]	ALAT 1 RHC, Phalsbourg	
1...	NH Industries NH.90-TTH Caïman [EBE]	ALAT 5 RHC, Pau	
1...	NH Industries NH.90-TTH Caïman [EBF]	ALAT (on order)	

Notes	Serial	Type (code/other identity)	Owner/operator, location or fate
	1...	NH Industries NH.90-TTH Caïman [EBG]	ALAT (on order)
	1404	NH Industries NH.90-TTH Caïman [EBH]	ALAT (on order)
	1405	NH Industries NH.90-TTH Caïman [EBI]	ALAT (on order)
	1432	NH Industries NH.90-TTH Caïman [EBJ]	ALAT (on order)
	887	Pilatus PC-6B/B2-H4 Turbo Porter [MCA]	ALAT 1 GSALAT, Montauban
	888	Pilatus PC-6B/B2-H4 Turbo Porter [MCB]	ALAT 1 GSALAT, Montauban
	889	Pilatus PC-6B/B2-H4 Turbo Porter [MCC]	ALAT 1 GSALAT, Montauban
	890	Pilatus PC-6B/B2-H4 Turbo Porter [MCD]	ALAT 1 GSALAT, Montauban
	891	Pilatus PC-6B/B2-H4 Turbo Porter [MCE]	ALAT 1 GSALAT, Montauban
	99	SOCATA TBM 700A [ABO]	ALAT EAAT, Rennes
	100	SOCATA TBM 700A [ABP]	ALAT EAAT, Rennes
	136	SOCATA TBM 700A [ABR]	ALAT EAAT, Rennes
	139	SOCATA TBM 700A [ABS]	ALAT EAAT, Rennes
	156	SOCATA TBM 700B [ABT]	ALAT EAAT, Rennes
	159	SOCATA TBM 700B [ABU]	ALAT EAAT, Rennes
	160	SOCATA TBM 700B [ABV]	ALAT EAAT, Rennes
French Government			
	JBA	Eurocopter EC.145C-1 (9008)	Gendarmerie
	JBC	Eurocopter EC.145C-1 (9018)	Gendarmerie
	JBD	Eurocopter EC.145C-1 (9019)	Gendarmerie
	JBE	Eurocopter EC.145C-1 (9025)	Gendarmerie
	JBF	Eurocopter EC.145C-2 (9035)	Gendarmerie
	JBG	Eurocopter EC.145C-2 (9036)	Gendarmerie
	JBH	Eurocopter EC.145C-2 (9037)	Gendarmerie
	JBI	Eurocopter EC.145C-2 (9127)	Gendarmerie
	JBJ	Eurocopter EC.145C-2 (9140)	Gendarmerie, Briançon
	JBK	Eurocopter EC.145C-2 (9162)	Gendarmerie
	JBM	Eurocopter EC.145C-2 (9113)	Gendarmerie
	JBN	Eurocopter EC.145C-2 (9173)	Gendarmerie
	JBO	Eurocopter EC.145C-2 (9124)	Gendarmerie
	JBR	Eurocopter EC.145C-2 (9169)	Gendarmerie
	JBT	Eurocopter EC.145C-2 (9173)	Gendarmerie
	JBU	Eurocopter EC.145C-2 (9700)	Gendarmerie, Villacoublay
	JCA	Aérospatiale AS.350BA Ecureuil (1028)	Gendarmerie, St Nazaire
	JCB	Aérospatiale AS.350BA Ecureuil (1574)	Gendarmerie, Bayonne
	JCD	Aérospatiale AS.350BA Ecureuil (1576)	Gendarmerie, Hyères
	JCE	Aérospatiale AS.350B-2 Ecureuil (1812)	Gendarmerie, Saint-Denis, Réunion
	JCF	Aérospatiale AS.350B-2 Ecureuil (1691)	Gendarmerie, Mayotte
	JCI	Aérospatiale AS.350B-2 Ecureuil (2222)	Gendarmerie, Pointe-à-Pitre
	JCK	Aérospatiale AS.350BA Ecureuil (1953)	Gendarmerie, Egletons
	JCL	Aérospatiale AS.350B-2 Ecureuil (1811)	Gendarmerie, Fort-de-France
	JCM	Aérospatiale AS.350BA Ecureuil (1952)	Gendarmerie, Rennes
	JCN	Aérospatiale AS.350BA Ecureuil (2044)	Gendarmerie, Bordeaux
	JCO	Aérospatiale AS.350BA Ecureuil (1917)	Gendarmerie, Metz
	JCP	Aérospatiale AS.350BA Ecureuil (2045)	Gendarmerie, stored Orléans
	JCQ	Aérospatiale AS.350BA Ecureuil (2057)	Gendarmerie, Dijon
	JCR	Aérospatiale AS.350BA Ecureuil (2088)	Gendarmerie, stored Orléans
	JCS	Aérospatiale AS.350B-2 Ecureuil (1575)	Gendarmerie, Cayenne
	JCT	Aérospatiale AS.350BA Ecureuil (2104)	Gendarmerie, Amiens
	JCU	Aérospatiale AS.350BA Ecureuil (2117)	Gendarmerie, Orléans
	JCV	Aérospatiale AS.350BA Ecureuil (2118)	Gendarmerie, Orléans
	JCW	Aérospatiale AS.350BA Ecureuil (2218)	Gendarmerie, Cazaux
	JCX	Aérospatiale AS.350BA Ecureuil (2219)	Gendarmerie, Tours
	JCY	Aérospatiale AS.350BA Ecureuil (2221)	Gendarmerie, Limoges
	JCZ	Aérospatiale AS.350BA Ecureuil (1467) $	Gendarmerie, Lyon
	JDA	Eurocopter EC.135T-2 (0642)	Gendarmerie
	JDB	Eurocopter EC.135T-2 (0654)	Gendarmerie
	JDC	Eurocopter EC.135T-2 (0717)	Gendarmerie, Lyon
	JDD	Eurocopter EC.135T-2 (0727)	Gendarmerie, Lille/Lesquin
	JDE	Eurocopter EC.135T-2 (0747)	Gendarmerie
	JDF	Eurocopter EC.135T-2 (0757)	Gendarmerie, Brest/Guipavas
	JDG	Eurocopter EC.135T-2 (0772)	Gendarmerie

Serial	Type (code/other identity)	Owner/operator, location or fate	Notes
JDH	Eurocopter EC.135T-2 (0787)	Gendarmerie	
JDI	Eurocopter EC.135T-2 (0797)	Gendarmerie	
JDJ	Eurocopter EC.135T-2 (0806)	Gendarmerie	
JDK	Eurocopter EC.135T-2 (0857)	Gendarmerie, Toulouse/Francazal	
JDL	Eurocopter EC.135T-2 (0867)	Gendarmerie	
JDM	Eurocopter EC.135T-2 (1055)	Gendarmerie	
JDN	Eurocopter EC.135T-2 (1058)	Gendarmerie	
JDO	Eurocopter EC.135T-2 (1086)	Gendarmerie, Bordeaux/Merignac	
JED	Aérospatiale AS.350B-2 Ecureuil (2096)	Gendarmerie, St Nazaire	
JEE	Aérospatiale AS.350B-2 Ecureuil (2423)	Gendarmerie, Nouméa	
JEF	Aérospatiale AS.350B-2 Ecureuil (2225)	Gendarmerie, Nouméa	
F-ZBAA	Conair Turbo Firecat [22]	Sécurité Civile, Nîmes/Garons	
F-ZBAB	Cessna F.406 Caravan II (0025)	Douanes Françaises, stored Bordeaux/Merignac	
F-ZBAD	Aérospatiale AS.355F-2 Twin Ecureuil	Douanes Françaises	
F-ZBAP	Conair Turbo Firecat [12]	Sécurité Civile, Nîmes/Garons	
F-ZBAZ	Conair Turbo Firecat [01]	Sécurité Civile, Nîmes/Garons	
F-ZBBN	Aérospatiale AS.350B-2 Ecureuil	Sécurité Civile, Nîmes/Garons	
F-ZBCE	Cessna F.406 Caravan II (0042)	Douanes Françaises	
F-ZBCF	Cessna F.406 Caravan II (0077)	Douanes Françaises, stored Lorient/Lann Bihoué	
F-ZBCG	Cessna F.406 Caravan II (0066)	Douanes Françaises	
F-ZBCH	Cessna F.406 Caravan II (0075)	Douanes Françaises, stored Lorient/Lann Bihoué	
F-ZBCI	Cessna F.406 Caravan II (0070)	Douanes Françaises, stored Hyères	
F-ZBCJ	Cessna F.406 Caravan II (0074)	Douanes Françaises	
F-ZBCZ	Conair Turbo Firecat [23]	Sécurité Civile, Nîmes/Garons	
F-ZBEA	Aérospatiale AS.350B-2 Ecureuil	Sécurité Civile, Nîmes/Garons	
F-ZBEF	Aérospatiale AS.355F-1 Twin Ecureuil	Douanes Françaises	
F-ZBEG	Canadair CL-415 [39]	Sécurité Civile, Nîmes/Garons	
F-ZBEH	Conair Turbo Firecat [20]	Sécurité Civile, Nîmes/Garons	
F-ZBEK	Aérospatiale AS.355F-1 Twin Ecureuil	Douanes Françaises	
F-ZBEL	Aérospatiale AS.355F-1 Twin Ecureuil	Douanes Françaises	
F-ZBES	Cessna F.406 Caravan II (0017)	Douanes Françaises	
F-ZBET	Conair Turbo Firecat [15]	Sécurité Civile, Nîmes/Garons	
F-ZBEU	Canadair CL-415 [42]	Sécurité Civile, Nîmes/Garons	
F-ZBEW	Conair Turbo Firecat [11] $	Sécurité Civile, Nîmes/Garons	
F-ZBEY	Conair Turbo Firecat [07]	Sécurité Civile, Nîmes/Garons	
F-ZBFC	Aérospatiale AS.350B-2 Ecureuil	Sécurité Civile, Nîmes/Garons	
F-ZBFD	Aérospatiale AS.350B-2 Ecureuil	Sécurité Civile, Nîmes/Garons	
F-ZBFJ	Beech Super King Air B200 [98]	Sécurité Civile, Nîmes/Garons	
F-ZBFK	Beech Super King Air B200 [96]	Sécurité Civile, Nîmes/Garons	
F-ZBFN	Canadair CL-415 [33]	Sécurité Civile, Nîmes/Garons	
F-ZBFP	Canadair CL-415 [31]	Sécurité Civile, Nîmes/Garons	
F-ZBFS	Canadair CL-415 [32] $	Sécurité Civile, Nîmes/Garons	
F-ZBFV	Canadair CL-415 [37]	Sécurité Civile, Nîmes/Garons	
F-ZBFW	Canadair CL-415 [38]	Sécurité Civile, Nîmes/Garons	
F-ZBFX	Canadair CL-415 [34]	Sécurité Civile, Nîmes/Garons	
F-ZBFY	Canadair CL-415 [35]	Sécurité Civile, Nîmes/Garons	
F-ZBGA	Cessna F.406 Caravan II (0086)	Douanes Françaises	
F-ZBGD	Cessna F.406 Caravan II (0090)	Douanes Françaises	
F-ZBGE	Cessna F.406 Caravan II (0061)	Douanes Françaises	
F-ZBGF	Eurocopter EC.135T-2	Douanes Françaises	
F-ZBGG	Eurocopter EC.135T-2	Douanes Françaises, Calais	
F-ZBGH	Eurocopter EC.135T-2	Douanes Françaises	
F-ZBGI	Eurocopter EC.135T-2	Douanes Françaises	
F-ZBGJ	Eurocopter EC.135T-2	Douanes Françaises	
F-ZBGK	Hawker Beechcraft King Air B350ER (FL-682)	Douanes Françaises	
F-ZBGL	Hawker Beechcraft King Air B350ER (FL-746)	Douanes Françaises	
F-ZBGM	Hawker Beechcraft King Air B350ER (FL-752)	Douanes Françaises	
F-ZBGN	Hawker Beechcraft King Air B350ER (FL-781)	Douanes Françaises	
F-ZBGO	Hawker Beechcraft King Air B350ER (FL-800)	Douanes Françaises	
F-ZBGP	Hawker Beechcraft King Air B350ER (FL-802)	Douanes Françaises	
F-ZBGQ	Hawker Beechcraft King Air B350ER (FL-777)	Douanes Françaises	
F-ZBGR	Hawker Beechcraft King Air B350ER	Douanes Françaises (on order)	

Notes	Serial	Type (code/other identity)	Owner/operator, location or fate
	F-ZBMA	Conair Turbo Firecat [24]	Sécurité Civile, Nîmes/Garons
	F-ZBMB	Beech Super King Air B200 [97]	Sécurité Civile, Nîmes/Garons
	F-ZBMC	De Havilland Canada DHC-8Q-402MR [73] $	Sécurité Civile, Nîmes/Garons
	F-ZBMD	De Havilland Canada DHC-8Q-402MR [74]	Sécurité Civile, Nîmes/Garons
	F-ZBME	Canadair CL-415 [44]	Sécurité Civile, Nîmes/Garons
	F-ZBMF	Canadair CL-415 [45]	Sécurité Civile, Nîmes/Garons
	F-ZBMG	Canadair CL-415 [48]	Sécurité Civile, Nîmes/Garons
	F-ZBPA	Eurocopter EC.145C-1	Sécurité Civile, Perpignan
	F-ZBPD	Eurocopter EC.145C-1	Sécurité Civile, Granville
	F-ZBPE	Eurocopter EC.145C-1	Sécurité Civile, Clermont-Ferrand
	F-ZBPF	Eurocopter EC.145C-1	Sécurité Civile, Cannes/Mandelieu
	F-ZBPG	Eurocopter EC.145C-1	Sécurité Civile, Strasbourg/Entzheim
	F-ZBPH	Eurocopter EC.145C-1	Sécurité Civile, Le Luc
	F-ZBPI	Eurocopter EC.145C-1	Sécurité Civile, Quimper
	F-ZBPJ	Eurocopter EC.145C-1	Sécurité Civile, La Rochelle
	F-ZBPK	Eurocopter EC.145C-1	Sécurité Civile, Ajaccio
	F-ZBPL	Eurocopter EC.145C-1	Sécurité Civile, Le Havre/Octeville
	F-ZBPM	Eurocopter EC.145C-1	Sécurité Civile, Bordeaux/Merignac
	F-ZBPN	Eurocopter EC.145C-1	Sécurité Civile, Courchevel
	F-ZBPO	Eurocopter EC.145C-1	Sécurité Civile, Paris/Issy-les-Molineaux
	F-ZBPP	Eurocopter EC.145C-2	Sécurité Civile, Fort-de-France, Martinique
	F-ZBPQ	Eurocopter EC.145C-2	Sécurité Civile, Chamonix
	F-ZBPS	Eurocopter EC.145C-2	Sécurité Civile, Nîmes/Garons
	F-ZBPT	Eurocopter EC.145C-2	Sécurité Civile, L'Alpe du Huez
	F-ZBPU	Eurocopter EC.145C-2	Sécurité Civile, Lorient
	F-ZBPV	Eurocopter EC.145C-2	Sécurité Civile, Besançon/La Veze
	F-ZBPW	Eurocopter EC.145C-2	Sécurité Civile, Lyon/Bron
	F-ZBPX	Eurocopter EC.145C-2	Sécurité Civile, Paris/Issy-les-Molineaux
	F-ZBPY	Eurocopter EC.145C-2	Sécurité Civile, Montpellier
	F-ZBPZ	Eurocopter EC.145C-2	Sécurité Civile, Mende-Brenoux
	F-ZBQA	Eurocopter EC.145C-2	Sécurité Civile, Perpignan
	F-ZBQB	Eurocopter EC.145C-2	Sécurité Civile, Nîmes/Garons
	F-ZBQC	Eurocopter EC.145C-2	Sécurité Civile, Strasbourg/Entzheim
	F-ZBQD	Eurocopter EC.145C-2	Sécurité Civile, Le Raizet, Guadeloupe
	F-ZBQE	Eurocopter EC.145C-2	Sécurité Civile, Guyane
	F-ZBQF	Eurocopter EC.145C-2	Sécurité Civile, Marseille/Provence
	F-ZBQG	Eurocopter EC.145C-2	Sécurité Civile, Nîmes/Garons
	F-ZBQH	Eurocopter EC.145C-2	Sécurité Civile, Nîmes/Garons
	F-ZBQI	Eurocopter EC.145C-2	Sécurité Civile, Grenoble/Le Versoud
	F-ZBQJ	Eurocopter EC.145C-2	Sécurité Civile, Bastia
	F-ZBQK	Eurocopter EC.145C-2	Sécurité Civile, Pau
	F-ZBQL	Eurocopter EC.145C-2	Sécurité Civile, Lacanau/le Huga
	Civil operated aircraft in military use		
	F-GJDB	Dassault Falcon 20C	AVDEF, Nîmes/Garons
	F-GKCI	Cirrus SR.22	CATS/CFAMI 05.312, Salon de Provence
	F-GPAA	Dassault Falcon 20ECM	AVDEF, Nîmes/Garons
	F-GPAD	Dassault Falcon 20E	AVDEF, Nîmes/Garons
	F-GUKA	Grob G120A-F	CATS/EPAA 00.315, Cognac
	F-GUKB	Grob G120A-F	CATS/EPAA 00.315, Cognac
	F-GUKC	Grob G120A-F	CATS/EPAA 00.315, Cognac
	F-GUKD	Grob G120A-F	CATS/EPAA 00.315, Cognac
	F-GUKE	Grob G120A-F	CATS/EPAA 00.315, Cognac
	F-GUKF	Grob G120A-F	CATS/EPAA 00.315, Cognac
	F-GUKG	Grob G120A-F	CATS/EPAA 00.315, Cognac
	F-GUKH	Grob G120A-F	CATS/EPAA 00.315, Cognac
	F-GUKI	Grob G120A-F	CATS/EPAA 00.315, Cognac
	F-GUKJ	Grob G120A-F	CATS/EPAA 00.315, Cognac
	F-GUKK	Grob G120A-F	CATS/EPAA 00.315, Cognac
	F-GUKL	Grob G120A-F	CATS/EPAA 00.315, Cognac
	F-GUKM	Grob G120A-F	CATS/EPAA 00.315, Cognac
	F-GUKN	Grob G120A-F	CATS/EPAA 00.315, Cognac
	F-GUKO	Grob G120A-F	CATS/EPAA 00.315, Cognac

BE2c replica 687 is registered as G-AWYI and based at Sywell. It regularly flies with the Great War Display Team. This aircraft was commissioned in 1969 by the makers of the film Biggles Sweeps the Skies. After being stored for 25 years in the USA, it was restored to fly again by co-owners Matthew Boddington, son of the original builder, and Steve Slater.

K5674 is a Hawker Fury I of the Historic Aircraft Collection at Duxford. Registered as G-CBZP, the aircraft wears the 1937 colours of the mount of Flying Officer F.E. Rosier of 43 Sqn at RAF Tangmere.

N1671 is the sole remaining complete example of the Boulton-Paul Defiant night fighter. Painted in themarkings of 307(Polish) Sqn, it normally resides in the RAF Museum at Cosford.

Spitfire PR XI PL965/R is registered as G-MKXI and has been displayed superbly by Peter Teichman over the years, before he retired from air show flying in 2018. PL965 is the only airworthy example of this Spitfire variant and is based at North Weald with the Hangar 11 Collection.

TW536 is an Auster AOP6. Civil-registered as G-BNGE, it is based at the Army airfield at Netheravon.

Avro XIX Anson 2 G-AHKX is owned by BAe Systems and based at Old Warden. For the centenary of the RAF it was painted in the markings of TX176, an Anson based at RAF Coningsby in the late 1950s/early 1960s.

Vampire FB6 LN-DHY of the Norwegian Air Force Historical Squadron was repainted as VZ305/N in 72 Sqn markings for the RAF 100 celebrations.

XP345 is a Whirlwind HAR10 and belongs to the Yorkshire Helicopter Preservation Group at Doncaster. In the RAF's centenary year, it was one of a number of airframes brought to Cosford in June 2018 for the air show. It is painted in the markings it wore while in use with 84 Sqn 'B' Flt based at Nicosia in Cyprus in the early 1970s.

Wessex HC2 XR498 is now resplendent in 22 Sqn markings and is due to be placed on the gate at Newquay/RAF St Mawgan.

Hawk T1A XX335 is painted in 207 Sqn markings and was moved to RAF Cosford by road from Shawbury in late 2018.

Buccaneer S2B XX889/T wears Gulf War markings and is seen here at Cosford, having been brought in by road from its Bruntingthorpe base.

By the start of 2019 around 20 Tornado GR4s (of an original fleet of more than 130) were left flying, operated by 9 Sqn and 31 Sqn, based at RAF Marham. ZA588/056 is one such example and by 31 March 2019 they will all be out of service. The end of an era.

The RAF's latest Chinook upgrade will see its HC4 fleet converted to HC6A status and ZA683 is one of those which has already undergone this modification, which includes the replacement of the analogue flight control systems with the Boeing Digital Automatic Flight Control System. Future plans include the need for even more of this type, so it will be flying in UK skies for many years to come.

Tornado GR4 ZD793 got a nice repaint in time for the RAF100 celebrations at RAF Cosford, by which point it was wearing Gulf War style markings and '100 not out' on the nose.

With the retirement of the Vigilant T1, Air Cadet gliding now relies solely on the Viking T1 fleet which itself is going through some considerable change and reduction in size. ZE636, wearing RAF 100 markings, was used as a mobile display during 2018 but by the end of the year had gone to Membury so in due course should be back in the air again.

2018 was the RAF's centenary year and a single example of every type operated received 'RAF 100' stickers. BAe 146 CC2 ZE700 of No 32 (The Royal) Sqn based at RAF Northolt is seen here at the Royal International Air Tattoo at Fairford, adorned with its 'RAF 100' markings.

Wearing the distinctive 8 Sqn dagger on its tail, ZH103 is one of five Sentry AEW1s currently flying from RAF Waddington.

Coded 'O', Merlin ZJ130 is one of a handful of HC3i variants operated by 846 NAS at RNAS Yeovilton in Somerset. Ahead of the introduction of the Merlin HC4, seven were modified to interim status with a folding main rotor head, revised undercarriage and deck lashing rings to allow for operations from naval vessels. The first HC3i to be converted to full HC4 status, ZJ118, was on the line at Yeovil by the end of 2018.

The Typhoon FGR4 selected to receive 'RAF 100' markings was FGR4 ZK318, also wearing 29 Sqn bars either side of the roundel on the fuselage and based at RAF Coningsby.

ZK379 is a Typhoon T3, based at RAF Coningsby, one of just five two-seaters to be left in RAF service once the Reduce To Produce (RTP) programme is complete. 41 Sqn normally has aircraft which don't use numerical codes, but this one seems to reflect the inevitable trend that the whole fleet may end up with these.

2018 saw the first deliveries of the F-35B Lightning II to RAF Marham, with 617 Sqn initially operating the type from the base. The distinctive 'barn door' intake on top of the fuselage, along with the exhaust nozzle turned vertically are both part of its pure hover mode configuration.

ZM320 is a Grob 120 Prefect T1, operating with No 3 FTS. It was also the one chosen to wear 'RAF 100' markings to celebrate the centenary of the RAF in 2018.

ZM506/06 is an Airbus H135 Juno HT1, operated by the Defence Helicopter Flying School at RAF Shawbury. The type took over these duties from the Squirrel HT1, completing the transition in 2018.

When it arrived for the static display at the Royal International Air Tattoo in July 2018, Hunter F58 ZZ191 caught a few people out with its newly painted and rather fetching colour scheme. It operates with Hawker Hunter Aviation (HHA) from RAF Scampton.

ZZ528 is a Wildcat HMA2, operated by 825 NAS from RNAS Yeovilton. With the retirement of the Lynx it also appears that the Navy has retired the use of squadron codes, deck letters and other markings, making most of these machines look very similar.

By mid-December 2018 QinetiQ at Boscombe Down had effectively removed its whole fleet from the UK military register while also acquiring new types during the year which went directly onto the UK civil register. Two brand new Pilatus PC-21s have been acquired and both keep the tradition of magnificent paint schemes alive!

G-ETPD is one of a pair of Grob G.120TP-As now operated by QinetiQ from Boscombe Down in rather stunning paint schemes.

Four Airbus H.125s have been acquired by QinetiQ for operations from Boscombe Down, alongside its two Agusta 109Es. H.125 G-ETPH is one of the new quartet.

For those unable to identify it, much of the information is helpfully on its fuselage! 28 is a Fouga CM175 ZÈphyr, the naval version of the Magister, complete with tail hook. Now operated from the French Register as F-AZPF, this one belongs to the appropriately titled Association ZÈphyr 28, based at NÔmes.

CCF T-6J Texan G-CHYN wears these rather distinctive German markings and is based at Dunkeswell in Devon.

Aeronca 11AC Chief G-BJEV is painted in false US Navy markings as 897/E which appear to relate to its previous identity, when it was on the US civil register as N85897.

Kaydet G-AZLE wears false US Navy markings as 1102 and is based at the delightful Dorset hilltop airfield at Compton Abbas, from which it is possible to take joyrides in this very machine.

Piper L-4A Grasshopper G-BGSJ wears its original US markings from World War II, when it flew with the US Army as 42-36657.

Fans of the film 'Catch 22' will be waiting eagerly for the new version. For the filming several aircraft were used, including Compton Abbas' SNJ-5 Texan, G-DHHF, which wore this temporary colour scheme during 2018.

260 is one of ten Pilatus PC-9Ms used by the Flying Training School of the Irish Air Corps at Baldonnel.

271 is a Eurocopter EC135P-2 operated by 302 Sqn of 3 Operations Wing, Irish Air Corps, Baldonnel

F-16A MLU FA-101 of the Belgian Air Force currently wears these special markings, titled 'Dark Falcon' for air show use. In a nice touch, one horizontal stabiliser was marked in the flag of the country where it was being displayed, or in this case, RAF 100 markings added, probably the only overseas aircraft to carry these markings.

M-3 is a SA.316B Alouette III operated by 40 Smaldeel of the Belgian Air Force, based at Koksijde. It has been in service since April 1971.

The Czech Air Force operates a dozen single-seat JAS 39C Gripens and a pair of two-seat JAS 39D Gripens, including this one, 9239, operated by 211.taktick· letka (Tactical Squadron) of 21 z·kladna TaktickÈho Letectva (Tactical Air Base) at C·slav.

E-607 is an F-16A MLU of the Danish Air Force, operated by Eskadrille 727 at Skrydstrup. It wears special markings for air displays.

19 is a Dassault Rafale M of the French Navy's 11 Flottille, based at Landivisiau in Western Brittany.

The Embraer Xingu is a type very rarely seen nowadays and one of the last operators is the French Navy, which flies this example, EMB.121AN 77, from 28 Flottille, at HyËres.

The French Navy operates eight Dassault Falcon 50 SURMAR aircraft, including this one, Falcon 50MS 5, flow by 24 Flottille, based at Lorient/Lann BihouÈ in Southern Brittany.

30+94 is a single-seat Eurofighter EF.2000GS, operated by TLG 74 'Molders' of the Luftwaffe, based at Neuburg/Donau.

Very few Air Forces operate the Boeing 757, but the Royal New Zealand Air Force has two, operated by 40 Sqn at Whenuapai, including this one, Boeing 757-2K2 NZ7571. They are surprisingly agile, being popular air show performers.

With the C-130J Hercules II in full production, the sight and sound of the older C-130H model is slowly becoming a thing of the past. Here 501 of the Royal Oman Air Force's 16 Sqn from Al Musana creates some impressive vortices as it departs in the damp English weather.

The Swiss Air Force operates a dwindling fleet of F-5E and F-5F Tigers. F-5F Tiger J-3210 is a special aircraft because it has been converted into an Electronic Countermeasures platform, carrying several underwing pods for this purpose. © *Oliver Curtis*

As part of the RAF 100 celebrations, nine Typhoons, a mix of FGR4s and T3s, were put up in this rather nice formation for the Royal International Air Tattoo at Fairford in July 2018.

Serial	Type (code/other identity)	Owner/operator, location or fate	Notes
F-GUKP	Grob G120A-F	CATS/EPAA 00.315, Cognac	
F-GUKR	Grob G120A-F	CATS/EPAA 00.315, Cognac	
F-GUKS	Grob G120A-F	CATS/EPAA 00.315, Cognac	
F-HAVD	BAE Jetstream 41	AVDEF, Nîmes/Garons	
F-HAVF	BAE Jetstream 41	AVDEF, Nîmes/Garons	
F-HGDU	Cirrus SR.20	CATS/CFAMI 05.312, Salon de Provence	
F-HKCA	Cirrus SR.22	CATS/CFAMI 05.312, Salon de Provence	
F-HKCB	Cirrus SR.20	CATS/CFAMI 05.312, Salon de Provence	
F-HKCC	Cirrus SR.22	CATS/CFAMI 05.312, Salon de Provence	
F-HKCD	Cirrus SR.20	CATS/CFAMI 05.312, Salon de Provence	
F-HKCE	Cirrus SR.20	CATS/CFAMI 05.312, Salon de Provence	
F-HKCF	Cirrus SR.22	CATS/CFAMI 05.312, Salon de Provence	
F-HKCG	Cirrus SR.20	CATS/CFAMI 05.312, Salon de Provence	
F-HKCH	Cirrus SR.20	CATS/CFAMI 05.312, Salon de Provence	
F-HKCI	Cirrus SR.22	CATS/CFAMI 05.312, Salon de Provence	
F-HKCJ	Cirrus SR.20	CATS/CFAMI 05.312, Salon de Provence	
F-HKCK	Cirrus SR.20	CATS/CFAMI 05.312, Salon de Provence	
F-HKCL	Cirrus SR.22	CATS/CFAMI 05.312, Salon de Provence	
F-HKCN	Cirrus SR.20	CATS/CFAMI 05.312, Salon de Provence	
F-HKCO	Cirrus SR.22	CATS/CFAMI 05.312, Salon de Provence	
F-HKCP	Cirrus SR.20	CATS/CFAMI 05.312, Salon de Provence	
F-HKCQ	Cirrus SR.20	CATS/CFAMI 05.312, Salon de Provence	
F-HKCR	Cirrus SR.22	*Crashed 7 April 2015, Salon de Provence*	
F-HKCS	Cirrus SR.22	CATS/CFAMI 05.312, Salon de Provence	
F-HKCT	Cirrus SR.20	CATS/CFAMI 05.312, Salon de Provence	
F-HKCU	Cirrus SR.20	CATS/CFAMI 05.312, Salon de Provence	
F-HKCV	Cirrus SR.20	CATS/CFAMI 05.312, Salon de Provence	
F-HKCX	Cirrus SR.20	CATS/CFAMI 05.312, Salon de Provence	
F-HKCY	Cirrus SR.22	CATS/CFAMI 05.312, Salon de Provence	
F-HKCZ	Cirrus SR.22	CATS/CFAMI 05.312, Salon de Provence	
OO-NHD	Eurocopter AS.365N-3 Dauphin	22 Escadrille/ESHE, Lanvéoc/Poulmic	
OO-NHN	Eurocopter AS.365N-3 Dauphin	22 Escadrille/ESHE, Lanvéoc/Poulmic	
OO-NHO	Eurocopter AS.365N-3 Dauphin	22 Escadrille/ESHE, Lanvéoc/Poulmic	

GABON

TR-KGM	Gulfstream Aerospace G.650ER	Gabonese Government, Libreville	
TR-KPR	Boeing 777-236	Gabonese Government, Libreville	
TR-KSP	Grumman G.1159C Gulfstream IVSP	Gabonese Government, Libreville	
TR-LEX	Dassault Falcon 900EX	Gabonese Government, Libreville	

GERMANY

Please note that German serials do not officially include the '+' part in them but aircraft wearing German markings are often painted with a cross in the middle, which is why it is included here.

Luftwaffe, Marineflieger & Heeresfliegertruppe (Heer)

10+23	Airbus A.310-304	Luftwaffe 1/FBS, Köln-Bonn	
10+24	Airbus A.310-304/MRTT	Luftwaffe 1/FBS, Köln-Bonn	
10+25	Airbus A.310-304/MRTT	Luftwaffe 1/FBS, Köln-Bonn	
10+26	Airbus A.310-304/MRTT	Luftwaffe 1/FBS, Köln-Bonn	
10+27	Airbus A.310-304/MRTT	Luftwaffe 1/FBS, Köln-Bonn	
14+01	Bombardier Global 5000	Luftwaffe 3/FBS, Köln-Bonn	
14+02	Bombardier Global 5000	Luftwaffe 3/FBS, Köln-Bonn	
14+03	Bombardier Global 5000	Luftwaffe 3/FBS, Köln-Bonn	
14+04	Bombardier Global 5000	Luftwaffe 3/FBS, Köln-Bonn	
15+01	Airbus A.319CJ-115X	Luftwaffe 3/FBS, Köln-Bonn	
15+02	Airbus A.319CJ-115X	Luftwaffe 3/FBS, Köln-Bonn	
15+04	Airbus A.321-231 (D-AISE/98+10)	Luftwaffe 3/FBS, Köln-Bonn	
16+01	Airbus A.340-313X	Luftwaffe 3/FBS, Köln-Bonn	
16+02	Airbus A.340-313X	Luftwaffe 3/FBS, Köln-Bonn	
30+01	Eurofighter EF.2000GT	Luftwaffe TLG 73 *Steinhoff*, Laage	
30+02	Eurofighter EF.2000GT	Luftwaffe TLG 71 *Richthofen*, Wittmund	
30+03	Eurofighter EF.2000GT	Luftwaffe TLG 74 *Molders*, Neuburg/Donau	
30+04	Eurofighter EF.2000GT	Luftwaffe TLG 71 *Richthofen*, Wittmund	
30+05	Eurofighter EF.2000GT	Luftwaffe TLG 31 *Boelcke*, Nörvenich	

Notes	Serial	Type (code/other identity)	Owner/operator, location or fate
	30+06	Eurofighter EF.2000GS	Luftwaffe TLG 71 *Richthofen*, Wittmund
	30+07	Eurofighter EF.2000GS	Luftwaffe TLG 74 *Molders*, Neuburg/Donau
	30+09	Eurofighter EF.2000GS	Luftwaffe TAubZLwSüd, Kaufbeuren
	30+10	Eurofighter EF.2000GT	Luftwaffe TLG 74 *Molders*, Neuburg/Donau
	30+11	Eurofighter EF.2000GS	Luftwaffe TLG 74 *Molders*, Neuburg/Donau
	30+12	Eurofighter EF.2000GS	Luftwaffe TLG 71 *Richthofen*, Wittmund
	30+14	Eurofighter EF.2000GT	Luftwaffe TLG 71 *Richthofen*, Wittmund
	30+15	Eurofighter EF.2000GS	Luftwaffe TLG 74 *Molders*, Neuburg/Donau
	30+17	Eurofighter EF.2000GT	Luftwaffe TLG 73 *Steinhoff*, Laage
	30+20	Eurofighter EF.2000GT	Luftwaffe TLG 73 *Steinhoff*, Laage
	30+22	Eurofighter EF.2000GS	Luftwaffe TLG 74 *Molders*, Neuburg/Donau
	30+23	Eurofighter EF.2000GS	Luftwaffe TLG 71 *Richthofen*, Wittmund
	30+24	Eurofighter EF.2000GT	Luftwaffe TLG 73 *Steinhoff*, Laage
	30+25	Eurofighter EF.2000GS	Luftwaffe TLG 74 *Molders*, Neuburg/Donau
	30+26	Eurofighter EF.2000GS $	Luftwaffe TLG 74 *Molders*, Neuburg/Donau
	30+27	Eurofighter EF.2000GT	Luftwaffe TLG 73 *Steinhoff*, Laage
	30+28	Eurofighter EF.2000GS	Luftwaffe TLG 71 *Richthofen*, Wittmund
	30+29	Eurofighter EF.2000GS $	Luftwaffe TLG 74 *Molders*, Neuburg/Donau
	30+30	Eurofighter EF.2000GS	Luftwaffe TLG 74 *Molders*, Neuburg/Donau
	30+31	Eurofighter EF.2000GT	Luftwaffe TLG 31 *Boelcke*, Nörvenich
	30+32	Eurofighter EF.2000GT	Luftwaffe TLG 71 *Richthofen*, Wittmund
	30+33	Eurofighter EF.2000GS	Luftwaffe TLG 71 *Richthofen*, Wittmund
	30+35	Eurofighter EF.2000GT	Luftwaffe TLG 73 *Steinhoff*, Laage
	30+38	Eurofighter EF.2000GT	Luftwaffe TLG 73 *Steinhoff*, Laage
	30+39	Eurofighter EF.2000GS	Luftwaffe TLG 74 *Molders*, Neuburg/Donau
	30+40	Eurofighter EF.2000GS	Luftwaffe TLG 74 *Molders*, Neuburg/Donau
	30+42	Eurofighter EF.2000GT	Luftwaffe TLG 74 *Molders*, Neuburg/Donau
	30+45	Eurofighter EF.2000GS $	Luftwaffe TLG 73 *Steinhoff*, Laage
	30+46	Eurofighter EF.2000GS	Luftwaffe TLG 73 *Steinhoff*, Laage
	30+47	Eurofighter EF.2000GS	Luftwaffe TLG 71 *Richthofen*, Wittmund
	30+48	Eurofighter EF.2000GS $	Luftwaffe TLG 73 *Steinhoff*, Laage
	30+49	Eurofighter EF.2000GS	Luftwaffe TLG 73 *Steinhoff*, Laage
	30+50	Eurofighter EF.2000GS	Luftwaffe TLG 73 *Steinhoff*, Laage
	30+51	Eurofighter EF.2000GS	Luftwaffe TLG 73 *Steinhoff*, Laage
	30+52	Eurofighter EF.2000GS	Luftwaffe TLG 31 *Boelcke*, Nörvenich
	30+53	Eurofighter EF.2000GS	Luftwaffe TLG 74 *Molders*, Neuburg/Donau
	30+54	Eurofighter EF.2000GT	Luftwaffe TLG 31 *Boelcke*, Nörvenich
	30+55	Eurofighter EF.2000GS	Luftwaffe TLG 73 *Steinhoff*, Laage
	30+56	Eurofighter EF.2000GS	Luftwaffe TLG 73 *Steinhoff*, Laage
	30+57	Eurofighter EF.2000GS	Luftwaffe TLG 71 *Richthofen*, Wittmund
	30+58	Eurofighter EF.2000GS	Luftwaffe TLG 71 *Richthofen*, Wittmund
	30+59	Eurofighter EF.2000GT	Luftwaffe TLG 73 *Steinhoff*, Laage
	30+60	Eurofighter EF.2000GS	Luftwaffe TLG 73 *Steinhoff*, Laage
	30+61	Eurofighter EF.2000GS	Luftwaffe TLG 73 *Steinhoff*, Laage
	30+62	Eurofighter EF.2000GS	Luftwaffe TLG 73 *Steinhoff*, Laage
	30+63	Eurofighter EF.2000GS	Luftwaffe TLG 74 *Molders*, Neuburg/Donau
	30+64	Eurofighter EF.2000GS	Luftwaffe TLG 73 *Steinhoff*, Laage
	30+65	Eurofighter EF.2000GS	Luftwaffe TLG 73 *Steinhoff*, Laage
	30+66	Eurofighter EF.2000GS	Luftwaffe TLG 71 *Richthofen*, Wittmund
	30+67	Eurofighter EF.2000GT	Luftwaffe TLG 73 *Steinhoff*, Laage
	30+68	Eurofighter EF.2000GS $	Luftwaffe TLG 74 *Molders*, Neuburg/Donau
	30+69	Eurofighter EF.2000GS	Luftwaffe TLG 74 *Molders*, Neuburg/Donau
	30+70	Eurofighter EF.2000GS	Luftwaffe TLG 74 *Molders*, Neuburg/Donau
	30+71	Eurofighter EF.2000GT	Luftwaffe TLG 71 *Richthofen*, Wittmund
	30+72	Eurofighter EF.2000GS	Luftwaffe TLG 74 *Molders*, Neuburg/Donau
	30+73	Eurofighter EF.2000GS $	Luftwaffe TLG 73 *Steinhoff*, Laage
	30+74	Eurofighter EF.2000GS	Luftwaffe TLG 74 *Molders*, Neuburg/Donau
	30+75	Eurofighter EF.2000GS $	Luftwaffe TLG 71 *Richthofen*, Wittmund
	30+76	Eurofighter EF.2000GS	Luftwaffe TLG 74 *Molders*, Neuburg/Donau
	30+77	Eurofighter EF.2000GT	Luftwaffe TLG 73 *Steinhoff*, Laage
	30+78	Eurofighter EF.2000GS	Luftwaffe TLG 71 *Richthofen*, Wittmund
	30+79	Eurofighter EF.2000GS	Luftwaffe TLG 73 *Steinhoff*, Laage

Serial	Type (code/other identity)	Owner/operator, location or fate	Notes
30+80	Eurofighter EF.2000GS	Luftwaffe TLG 74 *Molders*, Neuburg/Donau	
30+81	Eurofighter EF.2000GS	Luftwaffe TLG 73 *Steinhoff*, Laage	
30+82	Eurofighter EF.2000GS	Luftwaffe TLG 31 *Boelcke*, Nörvenich	
30+83	Eurofighter EF.2000GS	Luftwaffe TLG 31 *Boelcke*, Nörvenich	
30+84	Eurofighter EF.2000GT	Luftwaffe TLG 31 *Boelcke*, Nörvenich	
30+85	Eurofighter EF.2000GS	Luftwaffe TLG 71 *Richthofen*, Wittmund	
30+86	Eurofighter EF.2000GS	Luftwaffe TLG 71 *Richthofen*, Wittmund	
30+87	Eurofighter EF.2000GS $	Luftwaffe TLG 71 *Richthofen*, Wittmund	
30+88	Eurofighter EF.2000GS	Luftwaffe TLG 74 *Molders*, Neuburg/Donau	
30+89	Eurofighter EF.2000GS	Luftwaffe TLG 71 *Richthofen*, Wittmund	
30+90	Eurofighter EF.2000GS $	Luftwaffe TLG 71 *Richthofen*, Wittmund	
30+91	Eurofighter EF.2000GS	Luftwaffe TLG 31 *Boelcke*, Nörvenich	
30+92	Eurofighter EF.2000GS	Luftwaffe TLG 73 *Steinhoff*, Laage	
30+93	Eurofighter EF.2000GS	Luftwaffe TLG 74 *Molders*, Neuburg/Donau	
30+94	Eurofighter EF.2000GS	Luftwaffe TLG 74 *Molders*, Neuburg/Donau	
30+95	Eurofighter EF.2000GT	Luftwaffe TLG 74 *Molders*, Neuburg/Donau	
30+96	Eurofighter EF.2000GS	Luftwaffe TLG 31 *Boelcke*, Nörvenich	
30+97	Eurofighter EF.2000GS	Luftwaffe TLG 31 *Boelcke*, Nörvenich	
30+98	Eurofighter EF.2000GS	Luftwaffe TLG 31 *Boelcke*, Nörvenich	
30+99	Eurofighter EF.2000GT	Luftwaffe TLG 31 *Boelcke*, Nörvenich	
31+00	Eurofighter EF.2000GS	Luftwaffe TLG 74 *Molders*, Neuburg/Donau	
31+01	Eurofighter EF.2000GS	Luftwaffe TLG 71 *Richthofen*, Wittmund	
31+02	Eurofighter EF.2000GS	Luftwaffe TLG 74 *Molders*, Neuburg/Donau	
31+03	Eurofighter EF.2000GT	Airbus Defence & Space, Manching	
31+04	Eurofighter EF.2000GS	Luftwaffe TLG 71 *Richthofen*, Wittmund	
31+05	Eurofighter EF.2000GS	Luftwaffe TLG 31 *Boelcke*, Nörvenich	
31+06	Eurofighter EF.2000GS $	Luftwaffe TLG 31 *Boelcke*, Nörvenich	
31+07	Eurofighter EF.2000GS	Luftwaffe TLG 71 *Richthofen*, Wittmund	
31+08	Eurofighter EF.2000GS	Luftwaffe TLG 71 *Richthofen*, Wittmund	
31+09	Eurofighter EF.2000GS	Luftwaffe TLG 31 *Boelcke*, Nörvenich	
31+10	Eurofighter EF.2000GS	Luftwaffe TLG 31 *Boelcke*, Nörvenich	
31+11	Eurofighter EF.2000GS	Luftwaffe TLG 74 *Molders*, Neuburg/Donau	
31+12	Eurofighter EF.2000GS	Luftwaffe TLG 71 *Richthofen*, Wittmund	
31+13	Eurofighter EF.2000GT	Luftwaffe TLG 73 *Steinhoff*, Laage	
31+14	Eurofighter EF.2000GS	Luftwaffe TAubZLwSüd, Kaufbeuren	
31+15	Eurofighter EF.2000GS	Luftwaffe TAubZLwSüd, Kaufbeuren	
31+16	Eurofighter EF.2000GS	Luftwaffe TLG 31 *Boelcke*, Nörvenich	
31+17	Eurofighter EF.2000GS	Luftwaffe TLG 73 *Steinhoff*, Laage	
31+18	Eurofighter EF.2000GS	Luftwaffe TLG 73 *Steinhoff*, Laage	
31+19	Eurofighter EF.2000GS	Luftwaffe TLG 74 *Molders*, Neuburg/Donau	
31+20	Eurofighter EF.2000GS	Luftwaffe TLG 73 *Steinhoff*, Laage	
31+21	Eurofighter EF.2000GS	Luftwaffe TLG 73 *Steinhoff*, Laage	
31+22	Eurofighter EF.2000GS	Luftwaffe TLG 73 *Steinhoff*, Laage	
31+24	Eurofighter EF.2000GT	Luftwaffe TLG 73 *Steinhoff*, Laage	
31+25	Eurofighter EF.2000GT	Luftwaffe TLG 74 *Molders*, Neuburg/Donau	
31+26	Eurofighter EF.2000GT	Luftwaffe TLG 73 *Steinhoff*, Laage	
31+27	Eurofighter EF.2000GT	Luftwaffe	
31+28	Eurofighter EF.2000GT	Airbus Defence & Space, Manching	
31+29	Eurofighter EF.2000GS	Luftwaffe TLG 31 *Boelcke*, Nörvenich	
31+30	Eurofighter EF.2000GS	Luftwaffe TLG 31 *Boelcke*, Nörvenich	
31+31	Eurofighter EF.2000GS $	Luftwaffe TLG 31 *Boelcke*, Nörvenich	
31+32	Eurofighter EF.2000GS $	Luftwaffe TLG 31 *Boelcke*, Nörvenich	
31+33	Eurofighter EF.2000GS	Luftwaffe TLG 31 *Boelcke*, Nörvenich	
31+34	Eurofighter EF.2000GS	Luftwaffe TLG 31 *Boelcke*, Nörvenich	
31+35	Eurofighter EF.2000GS	Luftwaffe TLG 31 *Boelcke*, Nörvenich	
31+36	Eurofighter EF.2000GS	Luftwaffe TLG 31 *Boelcke*, Nörvenich	
31+37	Eurofighter EF.2000GS	Luftwaffe TLG 31 *Boelcke*, Nörvenich	
31+38	Eurofighter EF.2000GS	Luftwaffe TLG 31 *Boelcke*, Nörvenich	
31+39	Eurofighter EF.2000GS	Luftwaffe TLG 31 *Boelcke*, Nörvenich	
31+40	Eurofighter EF.2000GS	Luftwaffe TLG 31 *Boelcke*, Nörvenich	
31+41	Eurofighter EF.2000GS	Airbus Defence & Space, Manching	
31+42	Eurofighter EF.2000GS	Airbus Defence & Space, Manching	

Notes	Serial	Type (code/other identity)	Owner/operator, location or fate
	31+43	Eurofighter EF.2000GS	Airbus Defence & Space, Manching
	31+44	Eurofighter EF.2000GS	Luftwaffe TLG 71 *Richthofen*, Wittmund
	31+45	Eurofighter EF.2000GS	Luftwaffe TLG 31 *Boelcke*, Nörvenich
	31+46	Eurofighter EF.2000GS	Airbus Defence & Space, Manching
	31+47	Eurofighter EF.2000GS	Airbus Defence & Space, Manching
	31+48	Eurofighter EF.2000GS	Airbus Defence & Space, Manching
	31+49	Eurofighter EF.2000GS	Luftwaffe TLG 31 *Boelcke*, Nörvenich
	31+50	Eurofighter EF.2000GS	Luftwaffe (on order)
	31+51	Eurofighter EF.2000GS	Luftwaffe (on order)
	31+52	Eurofighter EF.2000GS	Luftwaffe (on order)
	31+53	Eurofighter EF.2000GS	Luftwaffe (on order)
	43+01	Panavia Tornado IDS(T) $	Luftwaffe TLG 33, Büchel
	43+07	Panavia Tornado IDS(T)	Luftwaffe TLG 51 *Immelmann*, Schleswig/Jagel
	43+10	Panavia Tornado IDS(T)	Luftwaffe TLG 33, Büchel
	43+25	Panavia Tornado IDS	Luftwaffe TLG 33, Büchel
	43+29	Panavia Tornado IDS(T)	Luftwaffe TLG 33, Büchel
	43+34	Panavia Tornado IDS	Luftwaffe TAubZLwSüd, Kaufbeuren
	43+38	Panavia Tornado IDS	Luftwaffe TLG 33, Büchel
	43+42	Panavia Tornado IDS(T)	Luftwaffe
	43+45	Panavia Tornado IDS(T)	Luftwaffe TLG 51 *Immelmann*, Schleswig/Jagel
	43+46	Panavia Tornado IDS	Luftwaffe TLG 33, Büchel
	43+48	Panavia Tornado IDS	Luftwaffe TLG 33, Büchel
	43+50	Panavia Tornado IDS	Luftwaffe TLG 33, Büchel
	43+52	Panavia Tornado IDS	Luftwaffe TLG 33, Büchel
	43+54	Panavia Tornado IDS	Luftwaffe TAubZLwSüd, Kaufbeuren
	43+59	Panavia Tornado IDS	Luftwaffe TAubZLwSüd, Kaufbeuren
	43+92	Panavia Tornado IDS(T)	Luftwaffe
	43+94	Panavia Tornado IDS(T)	*Withdrawn from use*
	43+97	Panavia Tornado IDS(T)	Luftwaffe TLG 51 *Immelmann*, Schleswig/Jagel
	43+98	Panavia Tornado IDS	Luftwaffe TLG 33, Büchel
	44+06	Panavia Tornado IDS	*Withdrawn from use*
	44+16	Panavia Tornado IDS(T)	Luftwaffe TLG 33, Büchel
	44+17	Panavia Tornado IDS	Luftwaffe TLG 51 *Immelmann*, Schleswig/Jagel
	44+21	Panavia Tornado IDS	Luftwaffe TLG 51 *Immelmann*, Schleswig/Jagel
	44+23	Panavia Tornado IDS	Luftwaffe TLG 33, Büchel
	44+29	Panavia Tornado IDS	Luftwaffe
	44+30	Panavia Tornado IDS	Luftwaffe TLG 51 *Immelmann*, Schleswig/Jagel
	44+33	Panavia Tornado IDS	Luftwaffe TLG 33, Büchel
	44+34	Panavia Tornado IDS	Luftwaffe TLG 33, Büchel
	44+58	Panavia Tornado IDS	Luftwaffe TLG 33, Büchel
	44+61	Panavia Tornado IDS $	Luftwaffe TLG 33, Büchel
	44+64	Panavia Tornado IDS	Luftwaffe TLG 33, Büchel
	44+65	Panavia Tornado IDS	Luftwaffe TLG 51 *Immelmann*, Schleswig/Jagel
	44+69	Panavia Tornado IDS	Luftwaffe TLG 51 *Immelmann*, Schleswig/Jagel
	44+70	Panavia Tornado IDS	Luftwaffe TLG 33, Büchel
	44+72	Panavia Tornado IDS(T)	Luftwaffe TLG 33, Büchel
	44+73	Panavia Tornado IDS(T)	Luftwaffe WTD 61, Ingolstadt
	44+75	Panavia Tornado IDS(T)	Luftwaffe TLG 51 *Immelmann*, Schleswig/Jagel
	44+78	Panavia Tornado IDS	Luftwaffe TLG 33, Büchel
	44+79	Panavia Tornado IDS	Luftwaffe TLG 33, Büchel
	44+90	Panavia Tornado IDS	Luftwaffe TLG 51 *Immelmann*, Schleswig/Jagel
	45+00	Panavia Tornado IDS	Luftwaffe TLG 33, Büchel
	45+08	Panavia Tornado IDS	*Withdrawn from use*
	45+09	Panavia Tornado IDS	Luftwaffe TLG 33, Büchel
	45+13	Panavia Tornado IDS(T)	Luftwaffe TLG 51 *Immelmann*, Schleswig/Jagel
	45+14	Panavia Tornado IDS(T)	Luftwaffe
	45+16	Panavia Tornado IDS(T)	Luftwaffe TLG 51 *Immelmann*, Schleswig/Jagel
	45+19	Panavia Tornado IDS	Luftwaffe TLG 33, Büchel
	45+20	Panavia Tornado IDS	Luftwaffe TLG 33, Büchel
	45+22	Panavia Tornado IDS	Luftwaffe TLG 51 *Immelmann*, Schleswig/Jagel
	45+23	Panavia Tornado IDS	Luftwaffe TLG 33, Büchel
	45+28	Panavia Tornado IDS	Luftwaffe TLG 33, Büchel

Serial	Type (code/other identity)	Owner/operator, location or fate	Notes
45+35	Panavia Tornado IDS	Luftwaffe TLG 33, Büchel	
45+39	Panavia Tornado IDS	Luftwaffe TLG 51 *Immelmann*, Schleswig/Jagel	
45+50	Panavia Tornado IDS	Luftwaffe TLG 51 *Immelmann*, Schleswig/Jagel	
45+53	Panavia Tornado IDS	Luftwaffe TAubZLwSüd, Kaufbeuren	
45+54	Panavia Tornado IDS	*Withdrawn from use*	
45+57	Panavia Tornado IDS	Luftwaffe TLG 33, Büchel	
45+59	Panavia Tornado IDS	Luftwaffe TLG 51 *Immelmann*, Schleswig/Jagel	
45+61	Panavia Tornado IDS(T)	Luftwaffe TLG 51 *Immelmann*, Schleswig/Jagel	
45+64	Panavia Tornado IDS	Luftwaffe TLG 33, Büchel	
45+66	Panavia Tornado IDS	Luftwaffe TLG 33, Büchel	
45+67	Panavia Tornado IDS	Luftwaffe TLG 33, Büchel	
45+68	Panavia Tornado IDS	Luftwaffe TLG 33, Büchel	
45+69	Panavia Tornado IDS	Luftwaffe TLG 33, Büchel	
45+70	Panavia Tornado IDS(T)	Luftwaffe TLG 51 *Immelmann*, Schleswig/Jagel	
45+71	Panavia Tornado IDS	Luftwaffe TLG 33, Büchel	
45+72	Panavia Tornado IDS	*Withdrawn from use*	
45+74	Panavia Tornado IDS	Luftwaffe TAubZLwSüd, Kaufbeuren	
45+76	Panavia Tornado IDS	Luftwaffe TLG 33, Büchel	
45+77	Panavia Tornado IDS(T)	Luftwaffe TLG 51 *Immelmann*, Schleswig/Jagel	
45+84	Panavia Tornado IDS	Luftwaffe TLG 33, Büchel	
45+85	Panavia Tornado IDS	Luftwaffe TLG 33, Büchel	
45+88	Panavia Tornado IDS	Luftwaffe TLG 33, Büchel	
45+90	Panavia Tornado IDS	Luftwaffe TLG 33, Büchel	
45+92	Panavia Tornado IDS	Luftwaffe TLG 33, Büchel	
45+93	Panavia Tornado IDS	Luftwaffe TLG 33, Büchel	
45+94	Panavia Tornado IDS	Luftwaffe TLG 33, Büchel	
46+00	Panavia Tornado IDS(T)	*Withdrawn from use*	
46+02	Panavia Tornado IDS $	Luftwaffe TLG 33, Büchel	
46+05	Panavia Tornado IDS(T)	Luftwaffe TLG 33, Büchel	
46+07	Panavia Tornado IDS(T)	Luftwaffe TLG 33, Büchel	
46+09	Panavia Tornado IDS(T)	*Withdrawn from use*	
46+10	Panavia Tornado IDS	Luftwaffe TLG 33, Büchel	
46+11	Panavia Tornado IDS	Luftwaffe TLG 33, Büchel	
46+15	Panavia Tornado IDS	Luftwaffe TLG 33, Büchel	
46+18	Panavia Tornado IDS	Luftwaffe TLG 33, Büchel	
46+20	Panavia Tornado IDS	Luftwaffe TLG 51 *Immelmann*, Schleswig/Jagel	
46+21	Panavia Tornado IDS	Luftwaffe TLG 33, Büchel	
46+22	Panavia Tornado IDS	Luftwaffe TLG 33, Büchel	
46+23	Panavia Tornado ECR $	Luftwaffe TLG 51 *Immelmann*, Schleswig/Jagel	
46+24	Panavia Tornado ECR	Luftwaffe TLG 51 *Immelmann*, Schleswig/Jagel	
46+25	Panavia Tornado ECR	Luftwaffe TLG 51 *Immelmann*, Schleswig/Jagel	
46+26	Panavia Tornado ECR	*Withdrawn from use*	
46+28	Panavia Tornado ECR $	Luftwaffe TLG 51 *Immelmann*, Schleswig/Jagel	
46+29	Panavia Tornado ECR	*Withdrawn from use*	
46+30	Panavia Tornado ECR	*Withdrawn from use*	
46+32	Panavia Tornado ECR	Luftwaffe TLG 51 *Immelmann*, Schleswig/Jagel	
46+33	Panavia Tornado ECR	*Withdrawn from use*	
46+34	Panavia Tornado ECR	*Withdrawn from use*	
46+35	Panavia Tornado ECR	Luftwaffe TLG 51 *Immelmann*, Schleswig/Jagel	
46+36	Panavia Tornado ECR	Luftwaffe TLG 51 *Immelmann*, Schleswig/Jagel	
46+37	Panavia Tornado ECR	*Withdrawn from use*	
46+38	Panavia Tornado ECR	Luftwaffe WTD 61, Ingolstadt	
46+39	Panavia Tornado ECR	Luftwaffe TAubZLwSüd, Kaufbeuren	
46+40	Panavia Tornado ECR	Luftwaffe TLG 51 *Immelmann*, Schleswig/Jagel	
46+41	Panavia Tornado ECR	*Withdrawn from use*	
46+43	Panavia Tornado ECR	*Withdrawn from use*	
46+44	Panavia Tornado ECR	Luftwaffe TLG 51 *Immelmann*, Schleswig/Jagel	
46+45	Panavia Tornado ECR	Luftwaffe TLG 51 *Immelmann*, Schleswig/Jagel	
46+46	Panavia Tornado ECR	Luftwaffe TLG 51 *Immelmann*, Schleswig/Jagel	
46+48	Panavia Tornado ECR	Luftwaffe TLG 51 *Immelmann*, Schleswig/Jagel	
46+49	Panavia Tornado ECR	Luftwaffe TLG 51 *Immelmann*, Schleswig/Jagel	
46+50	Panavia Tornado ECR	Luftwaffe TLG 51 *Immelmann*, Schleswig/Jagel	

Notes	Serial	Type (code/other identity)	Owner/operator, location or fate
	46+51	Panavia Tornado ECR	Luftwaffe TLG 51 *Immelmann*, Schleswig/Jagel
	46+52	Panavia Tornado ECR	Luftwaffe TLG 51 *Immelmann*, Schleswig/Jagel
	46+53	Panavia Tornado ECR	*Withdrawn from use*
	46+54	Panavia Tornado ECR $	Luftwaffe TLG 51 *Immelmann*, Schleswig/Jagel
	46+55	Panavia Tornado ECR	Luftwaffe TLG 51 *Immelmann*, Schleswig/Jagel
	46+56	Panavia Tornado ECR	Luftwaffe TLG 51 *Immelmann*, Schleswig/Jagel
	46+57	Panavia Tornado ECR $	Luftwaffe TLG 51 *Immelmann*, Schleswig/Jagel
	50+08	Transall C-160D	*Withdrawn from use*
	50+09	Transall C-160D	*Withdrawn from use*
	50+10	Transall C-160D	*Withdrawn from use*
	50+17	Transall C-160D	Luftwaffe LTG 63 (4.LwDiv), Hohn
	50+29	Transall C-160D	Luftwaffe
	50+33	Transall C-160D	Luftwaffe LTG 63 (4.LwDiv), Hohn
	50+36	Transall C-160D	Luftwaffe LTG 63 (4.LwDiv), Hohn
	50+38	Transall C-160D	Luftwaffe LTG 63 (4.LwDiv), Hohn
	50+40	Transall C-160D	Luftwaffe LTG 63 (4.LwDiv), Hohn
	50+41	Transall C-160D $	*Withdrawn from use, 2018*
	50+42	Transall C-160D	*Scrapped, 2018*
	50+44	Transall C-160D	Luftwaffe
	50+45	Transall C-160D	Luftwaffe
	50+46	Transall C-160D	*Withdrawn from use*
	50+47	Transall C-160D	*Withdrawn from use, 2018*
	50+48	Transall C-160D $	Luftwaffe
	50+49	Transall C-160D	Luftwaffe LTG 63 (4.LwDiv), Hohn
	50+51	Transall C-160D	Luftwaffe LTG 63 (4.LwDiv), Hohn
	50+53	Transall C-160D	Luftwaffe LTG 63 (4.LwDiv), Hohn
	50+54	Transall C-160D	Luftwaffe LTG 63 (4.LwDiv), Hohn
	50+55	Transall C-160D	Luftwaffe LTG 63 (4.LwDiv), Hohn
	50+57	Transall C-160D	Luftwaffe LTG 63 (4.LwDiv), Hohn
	50+58	Transall C-160D	Luftwaffe LTG 63 (4.LwDiv), Hohn
	50+59	Transall C-160D	Luftwaffe LTG 63 (4.LwDiv), Hohn
	50+61	Transall C-160D	Luftwaffe LTG 63 (4.LwDiv), Hohn
	50+64	Transall C-160D $	*Withdrawn from use, 2018*
	50+65	Transall C-160D $	Luftwaffe
	50+66	Transall C-160D	Luftwaffe/Airbus, Manching
	50+67	Transall C-160D	Luftwaffe LTG 63 (4.LwDiv), Hohn
	50+69	Transall C-160D	Luftwaffe LTG 63 (4.LwDiv), Hohn
	50+70	Transall C-160D	*Withdrawn from use, 2018*
	50+71	Transall C-160D	Luftwaffe LTG 63 (4.LwDiv), Hohn
	50+72	Transall C-160D	Luftwaffe LTG 63 (4.LwDiv), Hohn
	50+73	Transall C-160D	Luftwaffe LTG 63 (4.LwDiv), Hohn
	50+74	Transall C-160D	Luftwaffe
	50+75	Transall C-160D	Luftwaffe LTG 63 (4.LwDiv), Hohn
	50+76	Transall C-160D	Luftwaffe LTG 63 (4.LwDiv), Hohn
	50+77	Transall C-160D	Luftwaffe LTG 63 (4.LwDiv), Hohn
	50+78	Transall C-160D	Luftwaffe LTG 63 (4.LwDiv), Hohn
	50+79	Transall C-160D	Luftwaffe LTG 63 (4.LwDiv), Hohn
	50+81	Transall C-160D	Luftwaffe LTG 63 (4.LwDiv), Hohn
	50+82	Transall C-160D $	Luftwaffe LTG 63 (4.LwDiv), Hohn
	50+83	Transall C-160D	Luftwaffe LTG 63 (4.LwDiv), Hohn
	50+84	Transall C-160D	*Scrapped*
	50+86	Transall C-160D	Luftwaffe WTD 61, Ingolstadt
	50+87	Transall C-160D	Luftwaffe LTG 63 (4.LwDiv), Hohn
	50+88	Transall C-160D	Luftwaffe LTG 63 (4.LwDiv), Hohn
	50+89	Transall C-160D	*Withdrawn from use*
	50+91	Transall C-160D	Luftwaffe LTG 63 (4.LwDiv), Hohn
	50+92	Transall C-160D	Luftwaffe
	50+93	Transall C-160D $	Luftwaffe LTG 63 (4.LwDiv), Hohn
	50+96	Transall C-160D	Luftwaffe
	50+97	Transall C-160D	Luftwaffe LTG 63 (4.LwDiv), Hohn
	51+03	Transall C-160D	Luftwaffe LTG 63 (4.LwDiv), Hohn
	51+04	Transall C-160D	Luftwaffe LTG 63 (4.LwDiv), Hohn

Serial	Type (code/other identity)	Owner/operator, location or fate	Notes
51+05	Transall C-160D	Luftwaffe LTG 63 (4.LwDiv), Hohn	
51+06	Transall C-160D	*Preserved at Hohn, 2018*	
51+08	Transall C-160D	Luftwaffe WTD 61, Ingolstadt	
51+10	Transall C-160D	Luftwaffe	
51+12	Transall C-160D	Luftwaffe LTG 63 (4.LwDiv), Hohn	
51+13	Transall C-160D	*Withdrawn from use*	
51+14	Transall C-160D	Luftwaffe LTG 63 (4.LwDiv), Hohn	
51+15	Transall C-160D	*Withdrawn from use, 2016*	
54+01	Airbus Military A.400M	Luftwaffe LTG 62, Wunstorf	
54+02	Airbus Military A.400M	Luftwaffe LTG 62, Wunstorf	
54+03	Airbus Military A.400M $	Luftwaffe LTG 62, Wunstorf	
54+04	Airbus Military A.400M	Luftwaffe LTG 62, Wunstorf	
54+05	Airbus Military A.400M	Luftwaffe LTG 62, Wunstorf	
54+06	Airbus Military A.400M	Luftwaffe LTG 62, Wunstorf	
54+07	Airbus Military A.400M	Luftwaffe LTG 62, Wunstorf	
54+08	Airbus Military A.400M	Luftwaffe LTG 62, Wunstorf	
54+09	Airbus Military A.400M	Luftwaffe LTG 62, Wunstorf	
54+10	Airbus Military A.400M	Luftwaffe LTG 62, Wunstorf	
54+11	Airbus Military A.400M	Luftwaffe LTG 62, Wunstorf	
54+12	Airbus Military A.400M	Luftwaffe LTG 62, Wunstorf	
54+13	Airbus Military A.400M	Luftwaffe LTG 62, Wunstorf	
54+14	Airbus Military A.400M	Luftwaffe LTG 62, Wunstorf	
54+15	Airbus Military A.400M	Luftwaffe LTG 62, Wunstorf	
54+16	Airbus Military A.400M	Luftwaffe LTG 62, Wunstorf	
54+17	Airbus Military A.400M	Luftwaffe LTG 62, Wunstorf	
54+18	Airbus Military A.400M	Luftwaffe LTG 62, Wunstorf	
54+19	Airbus Military A.400M	Luftwaffe LTG 62, Wunstorf	
54+20	Airbus Military A.400M	Luftwaffe LTG 62, Wunstorf	
54+21	Airbus Military A.400M	Luftwaffe LTG 62, Wunstorf	
54+22	Airbus Military A.400M	Luftwaffe LTG 62, Wunstorf	
54+23	Airbus Military A.400M	Luftwaffe LTG 62, Wunstorf	
54+24	Airbus Military A.400M	Luftwaffe (on order)	
54+25	Airbus Military A.400M	Luftwaffe LTG 62, Wunstorf	
54+26	Airbus Military A.400M	Luftwaffe (on order)	
54+27	Airbus Military A.400M	Luftwaffe (on order)	
54+28	Airbus Military A.400M	Luftwaffe (on order)	
54+29	Airbus Military A.400M	Luftwaffe (on order)	
54+30	Airbus Military A.400M	Luftwaffe (on order)	
57+04	Dornier Do.228LM	Marineflieger MFG 3, Nordholz	
57+05	Dornier Do.228NG	Marineflieger MFG 3, Nordholz	
5.+..	Lockheed C-130J Hercules II	Luftwaffe (on order)	
5.+..	Lockheed C-130J Hercules II	Luftwaffe (on order)	
5.+..	Lockheed C-130J Hercules II	Luftwaffe (on order)	
5.+..	Lockheed C-130J Hercules II	Luftwaffe (on order)	
5.+..	Lockheed C-130J Hercules II	Luftwaffe (on order)	
5.+..	Lockheed C-130J Hercules II	Luftwaffe (on order)	
60+01	Lockheed P-3C CUP Orion $	Marineflieger MFG 3, Nordholz	
60+02	Lockheed P-3C CUP Orion	Marineflieger MFG 3, Nordholz	
60+03	Lockheed P-3C CUP Orion	Marineflieger MFG 3, Nordholz	
60+04	Lockheed P-3C CUP Orion	Marineflieger MFG 3, Nordholz	
60+05	Lockheed P-3C CUP Orion $	Marineflieger MFG 3, Nordholz	
60+06	Lockheed P-3C CUP Orion	Marineflieger MFG 3, Nordholz	
60+07	Lockheed P-3C CUP Orion	Marineflieger MFG 3, Nordholz	
60+08	Lockheed P-3C CUP Orion	Marineflieger MFG 3, Nordholz	
74+01	Eurocopter EC.665 Tiger UHT	Luftwaffe WTD 61, Ingolstadt	
74+02	Eurocopter EC.665 Tiger UHT	Heer KHR 36, Fritzlar	
74+03	Eurocopter EC.665 Tiger UHT	Luftwaffe TsLw 3, Fassberg	
74+05	Eurocopter EC.665 Tiger UHT	Heer IntHubschrAusbZ, Le Luc, France	
74+06	Eurocopter EC.665 Tiger UHT	Heer KHR 36, Fritzlar	
74+07	Eurocopter EC.665 Tiger UHT	Heer IntHubschrAusbZ, Le Luc, France	
74+08	Eurocopter EC.665 Tiger UHT	Luftwaffe TsLw 3, Fassberg	
74+09	Eurocopter EC.665 Tiger UHT	Heer IntHubschrAusbZ, Le Luc, France	

Notes	Serial	Type (code/other identity)	Owner/operator, location or fate
	74+10	Eurocopter EC.665 Tiger UHT	Heer KHR 36, Fritzlar
	74+11	Eurocopter EC.665 Tiger UHT	Heer IntHubschrAusbZ, Le Luc, France
	74+13	Eurocopter EC.665 Tiger UHT	Heer IntHubschrAusbZ, Le Luc, France
	74+14	Eurocopter EC.665 Tiger UHT	Heer IntHubschrAusbZ, Le Luc, France
	74+15	Eurocopter EC.665 Tiger UHT	Heer IntHubschrAusbZ, Le Luc, France
	74+16	Eurocopter EC.665 Tiger UHT	Heer KHR 36, Fritzlar
	74+17	Eurocopter EC.665 Tiger UHT	Heer KHR 36, Fritzlar
	74+18	Eurocopter EC.665 Tiger UHT	Heer KHR 36, Fritzlar
	74+19	Eurocopter EC.665 Tiger UHT	Heer KHR 36, Fritzlar
	74+20	Eurocopter EC.665 Tiger UHT	Heer KHR 36, Fritzlar
	74+21	Eurocopter EC.665 Tiger UHT	Heer KHR 36, Fritzlar
	74+22	Eurocopter EC.665 Tiger UHT	Heer KHR 36, Fritzlar
	74+23	Eurocopter EC.665 Tiger UHT	Heer KHR 36, Fritzlar
	74+24	Eurocopter EC.665 Tiger UHT	Heer KHR 36, Fritzlar
	74+25	Eurocopter EC.665 Tiger UHT	Heer KHR 36, Fritzlar
	74+26	Eurocopter EC.665 Tiger UHT	Heer KHR 36, Fritzlar
	74+28	Eurocopter EC.665 Tiger UHT	Heer KHR 36, Fritzlar
	74+29	Eurocopter EC.665 Tiger UHT	Heer KHR 36, Fritzlar
	74+30	Eurocopter EC.665 Tiger UHT	Heer KHR 36, Fritzlar
	74+31	Eurocopter EC.665 Tiger UHT	Heer KHR 36, Fritzlar
	74+32	Eurocopter EC.665 Tiger UHT	Heer KHR 36, Fritzlar
	74+34	Eurocopter EC.665 Tiger UHT	Heer KHR 36, Fritzlar
	74+35	Eurocopter EC.665 Tiger UHT	Heer KHR 36, Fritzlar
	74+36	Eurocopter EC.665 Tiger UHT	Heer KHR 36, Fritzlar
	74+37	Eurocopter EC.665 Tiger UHT	Heer IntHubschrAusbZ, Le Luc, France
	74+38	Eurocopter EC.665 Tiger UHT	Heer KHR 36, Fritzlar
	74+39	Eurocopter EC.665 Tiger UHT	Heer
	74+40	Eurocopter EC.665 Tiger UHT	Heer KHR 36, Fritzlar
	74+41	Eurocopter EC.665 Tiger UHT	Heer
	74+42	Eurocopter EC.665 Tiger UHT	Heer KHR 36, Fritzlar
	74+43	Eurocopter EC.665 Tiger UHT	Heer
	74+44	Eurocopter EC.665 Tiger UHT	Heer
	74+45	Eurocopter EC.665 Tiger UHT	Heer KHR 36, Fritzlar
	74+46	Eurocopter EC.665 Tiger UHT	Heer KHR 36, Fritzlar
	74+47	Eurocopter EC.665 Tiger UHT	Luftwaffe WTD 61, Ingolstadt
	74+48	Eurocopter EC.665 Tiger UHT	Heer KHR 26, Roth
	74+50	Eurocopter EC.665 Tiger UHT	Heer KHR 36, Fritzlar
	74+51	Eurocopter EC.665 Tiger UHT	Heer IntHubschrAusbZ, Le Luc, France
	74+52	Eurocopter EC.665 Tiger UHT	Airbus Helicopters, stored Donauwörth
	74+53	Eurocopter EC.665 Tiger UHT	Heer KHR 36, Fritzlar
	74+54	Eurocopter EC.665 Tiger UHT	Heer KHR 36, Fritzlar
	74+55	Eurocopter EC.665 Tiger UHT	Heer
	74+56	Eurocopter EC.665 Tiger UHT	Heer KHR 36, Fritzlar
	74+57	Eurocopter EC.665 Tiger UHT	Heer KHR 36, Fritzlar
	74+58	Eurocopter EC.665 Tiger UHT	Heer
	74+59	Eurocopter EC.665 Tiger UHT	Heer
	74+61	Eurocopter EC.665 Tiger UHT	Heer KHR 36, Fritzlar
	74+62	Eurocopter EC.665 Tiger UHT	Airbus Helicopters, Donauwörth
	74+63	Eurocopter EC.665 Tiger UHT	Heer KHR 36, Fritzlar
	74+64	Eurocopter EC.665 Tiger UHT	Heer (on order)
	74+65	Eurocopter EC.665 Tiger UHT	Heer (on order)
	74+66	Eurocopter EC.665 Tiger UHT	Airbus Helicopters, Donauwörth
	74+67	Eurocopter EC.665 Tiger UHT	Heer KHR 36, Fritzlar
	74+68	Eurocopter EC.665 Tiger UHT	Airbus Helicopters, Donauwörth
	74+69	Eurocopter EC.665 Tiger UHT	Heer
	74+70	Eurocopter EC.665 Tiger UHT	Heer KHR 36, Fritzlar
	76+01	Airbus Helicopters H.145M	Luftwaffe HSG 64, Laupheim
	76+02	Airbus Helicopters H.145M	Luftwaffe HSG 64, Laupheim
	76+03	Airbus Helicopters H.145M	Luftwaffe HSG 64, Laupheim
	76+04	Airbus Helicopters H.145M	Luftwaffe HSG 64, Laupheim
	76+05	Airbus Helicopters H.145M	Luftwaffe HSG 64, Laupheim
	76+06	Airbus Helicopters H.145M	Luftwaffe HSG 64, Laupheim

Serial	Type (code/other identity)	Owner/operator, location or fate	Notes
76+07	Airbus Helicopters H.145M	Luftwaffe HSG 64, Laupheim	
76+08	Airbus Helicopters H.145M	Luftwaffe HSG 64, Laupheim	
76+09	Airbus Helicopters H.145M	Luftwaffe HSG 64, Laupheim	
76+10	Airbus Helicopters H.145M	Luftwaffe HSG 64, Laupheim	
76+11	Airbus Helicopters H.145M	Luftwaffe HSG 64, Laupheim	
76+12	Airbus Helicopters H.145M	Luftwaffe HSG 64, Laupheim	
76+13	Airbus Helicopters H.145M	Luftwaffe HSG 64, Laupheim	
76+14	Airbus Helicopters H.145M	Luftwaffe HSG 64, Laupheim	
76+15	Airbus Helicopters H.145M	Luftwaffe HSG 64, Laupheim	
78+01	NH Industries NH.90-TTH (98+91)	Heer IntHubschrAusbZ, Bückeburg	
78+02	NH Industries NH.90-TTH	Heer IntHubschrAusbZ, Bückeburg	
78+03	NH Industries NH.90-TTH (98+93)	Heer IntHubschrAusbZ, Bückeburg	
78+04	NH Industries NH.90-TTH	Luftwaffe TsLw 3, Fassberg	
78+05	NH Industries NH.90-TTH	Luftwaffe TsLw 3, Fassberg	
78+06	NH Industries NH.90-TTH	Heer IntHubschrAusbZ, Bückeburg	
78+07	NH Industries NH.90-TTH	Heer IntHubschrAusbZ, Bückeburg	
78+08	NH Industries NH.90-TTH	Heer IntHubschrAusbZ, Bückeburg	
78+09	NH Industries NH.90-TTH (98+92)	Heer THR 30, Niederstetten	
78+10	NH Industries NH.90-TTH (98+94)	Luftwaffe TsLw 3, Fassberg	
78+11	NH Industries NH.90-TTH (98+95)	Heer THR 10, Fassberg	
78+12	NH Industries NH.90-TTH (98+96)	Heer THR 30, Niederstetten	
78+13	NH Industries NH.90-TTH	Heer IntHubschrAusbZ, Bückeburg	
78+14	NH Industries NH.90-TTH	Heer THR 10, Fassberg	
78+15	NH Industries NH.90-TTH	Heer THR 10, Fassberg	
78+16	NH Industries NH.90-TTH	Airbus Helicopters, Donauwörth	
78+17	NH Industries NH.90-TTH	Heer IntHubschrAusbZ, Bückeburg	
78+18	NH Industries NH.90-TTH	Heer THR 10, Fassberg	
78+19	NH Industries NH.90-TTH	Heer IntHubschrAusbZ, Bückeburg	
78+20	NH Industries NH.90-TTH (98+52)	Heer IntHubschrAusbZ, Bückeburg	
78+21	NH Industries NH.90-TTH	Heer IntHubschrAusbZ, Bückeburg	
78+22	NH Industries NH.90-TTH	Heer IntHubschrAusbZ, Bückeburg	
78+23	NH Industries NH.90-TTH	Heer THR 10, Fassberg	
78+24	NH Industries NH.90-TTH	Heer THR 30, Niederstetten	
78+25	NH Industries NH.90-TTH	Heer THR 30, Niederstetten	
78+26	NH Industries NH.90-TTH	Heer IntHubschrAusbZ, Bückeburg	
78+27	NH Industries NH.90-TTH	Heer IntHubschrAusbZ, Bückeburg	
78+28	NH Industries NH.90-TTH	Heer THR 10, Fassberg	
78+29	NH Industries NH.90-TTH	Heer IntHubschrAusbZ, Bückeburg	
78+30	NH Industries NH.90-TTH	Heer THR 10, Fassberg	
78+31	NH Industries NH.90-TTH	Heer THR 10, Fassberg	
78+32	NH Industries NH.90-TTH	Heer THR 10, Fassberg	
78+33	NH Industries NH.90-TTH	Heer THR 10, Fassberg	
78+34	NH Industries NH.90-TTH	Heer THR 30, Niederstetten	
78+35	NH Industries NH.90-TTH	Heer THR 30, Niederstetten	
78+36	NH Industries NH.90-TTH	Heer THR 30, Niederstetten	
78+37	NH Industries NH.90-TTH	Heer THR 30, Niederstetten	
78+38	NH Industries NH.90-TTH	Heer IntHubschrAusbZ, Bückeburg	
78+39	NH Industries NH.90-TTH	Heer THR 30, Niederstetten	
78+40	NH Industries NH.90-TTH	Heer THR 30, Niederstetten	
78+41	NH Industries NH.90-TTH	Heer	
78+42	NH Industries NH.90-TTH	Heer	
78+43	NH Industries NH.90-TTH	Heer	
78+44	NH Industries NH.90-TTH	Heer	
78+45	NH Industries NH.90-TTH	Heer	
78+46	NH Industries NH.90-TTH	Heer	
78+47	NH Industries NH.90-TTH	Heer	
78+48	NH Industries NH.90-TTH	Heer	
78+49	NH Industries NH.90-TTH	Heer	
78+50	NH Industries NH.90-TTH	Heer	
79+01	NH Industries NH.90-TTH	Heer IntHubschrAusbZ, Bückeburg	
79+02	NH Industries NH.90-TTH	Heer THR 30, Niederstetten	
79+03	NH Industries NH.90-TTH	Heer THR 10, Fassberg	

Notes	Serial	Type (code/other identity)	Owner/operator, location or fate
	79+04	NH Industries NH.90-TTH	Heer THR 10, Fassberg
	79+05	NH Industries NH.90-TTH	Heer THR 10, Fassberg
	79+06	NH Industries NH.90-TTH	Heer THR 10, Fassberg
	79+07	NH Industries NH.90-TTH	Heer IntHubschrAusbZ, Bückeburg
	79+08	NH Industries NH.90-TTH	Heer IntHubschrAusbZ, Bückeburg
	79+09	NH Industries NH.90-TTH	Heer IntHubschrAusbZ, Bückeburg
	79+10	NH Industries NH.90-TTH	Heer
	79+11	NH Industries NH.90-TTH	Heer THR 30, Niederstetten
	79+12	NH Industries NH.90-TTH	Heer
	79+13	NH Industries NH.90-TTH	Heer THR 30, Niederstetten
	79+14	NH Industries NH.90-TTH	Heer
	79+15	NH Industries NH.90-TTH	Heer THR 30, Niederstetten
	79+16	NH Industries NH.90-TTH	Heer
	79+17	NH Industries NH.90-TTH	Heer IntHubschrAusbZ, Bückeburg
	79+18	NH Industries NH.90-TTH	Heer IntHubschrAusbZ, Bückeburg
	79+19	NH Industries NH.90-TTH	Heer IntHubschrAusbZ, Bückeburg
	79+20	NH Industries NH.90-TTH	Heer IntHubschrAusbZ, Bückeburg
	79+21	NH Industries NH.90-TTH	Heer IntHubschrAusbZ, Bückeburg
	79+23	NH Industries NH.90-TTH	Airbus Helicopters, Donauwörth
	79+24	NH Industries NH.90-TTH (98+93)	Heer THR 30, Niederstetten
	79+25	NH Industries NH.90-TTH	Heer IntHubschrAusbZ, Bückeburg
	79+26	NH Industries NH.90-TTH	Heer THR 30, Niederstetten
	79+27	NH Industries NH.90-TTH	Heer (on order)
	79+28	NH Industries NH.90-TTH	Heer IntHubschrAusbZ, Bückeburg
	79+29	NH Industries NH.90-TTH	Heer (on order)
	79+30	NH Industries NH.90-TTH	Heer (on order)
	79+31	NH Industries NH.90-TTH	Airbus Helicopters, Donauwörth
	79+32	NH Industries NH.90-TTH	Heer (on order)
	79+33	NH Industries NH.90-TTH	Heer (on order)
	79+34	NH Industries NH.90-TTH	Heer (on order)
	79+35	NH Industries NH.90-TTH	Heer (on order)
	79+36	NH Industries NH.90-TTH	Heer (on order)
	79+37	NH Industries NH.90-TTH	Heer (on order)
	79+38	NH Industries NH.90-TTH	Heer (on order)
	79+39	NH Industries NH.90-TTH	Heer (on order)
	79+40	NH Industries NH.90-TTH	Heer (on order)
	79+51	NH Industries NH.90-NFH Sea Lion	Marineflieger/Heer THR 10, Fassberg
	79+52	NH Industries NH.90-NFH Sea Lion	Airbus Helicopters, Donauwörth
	79+54	NH Industries NH.90-NFH Sea Lion	Marineflieger (on order)
	79+55	NH Industries NH.90-NFH Sea Lion	Marineflieger (on order)
	79+56	NH Industries NH.90-NFH Sea Lion	Marineflieger (on order)
	79+57	NH Industries NH.90-NFH Sea Lion	Marineflieger (on order)
	79+58	NH Industries NH.90-NFH Sea Lion	Marineflieger (on order)
	79+59	NH Industries NH.90-NFH Sea Lion	Marineflieger (on order)
	79+60	NH Industries NH.90-NFH Sea Lion	Marineflieger (on order)
	79+61	NH Industries NH.90-NFH Sea Lion	Marineflieger (on order)
	79+62	NH Industries NH.90-NFH Sea Lion	Marineflieger (on order)
	79+63	NH Industries NH.90-NFH Sea Lion	Marineflieger (on order)
	79+64	NH Industries NH.90-NFH Sea Lion	Marineflieger (on order)
	79+65	NH Industries NH.90-NFH Sea Lion	Marineflieger (on order)
	79+66	NH Industries NH.90-NFH Sea Lion	Marineflieger (on order)
	79+67	NH Industries NH.90-NFH Sea Lion	Marineflieger (on order)
	79+68	NH Industries NH.90-NFH Sea Lion	Marineflieger (on order)
	82+01	Eurocopter AS.532U-2 Cougar	Luftwaffe 3/FBS, Berlin-Tegel
	82+02	Eurocopter AS.532U-2 Cougar	Luftwaffe 3/FBS, Berlin-Tegel
	82+03	Eurocopter AS.532U-2 Cougar	Luftwaffe 3/FBS, Berlin-Tegel
	82+51	Eurocopter EC.135P-1	Heer IntHubschrAusbZ, Bückeburg
	82+52	Eurocopter EC.135P-1	Heer IntHubschrAusbZ, Bückeburg
	82+53	Eurocopter EC.135P-1	Heer IntHubschrAusbZ, Bückeburg
	82+54	Eurocopter EC.135P-1	Heer IntHubschrAusbZ, Bückeburg
	82+55	Eurocopter EC.135P-1	Heer IntHubschrAusbZ, Bückeburg
	82+56	Eurocopter EC.135P-1	Heer IntHubschrAusbZ, Bückeburg

Serial	Type (code/other identity)	Owner/operator, location or fate	Notes
82+57	Eurocopter EC.135P-1	Heer IntHubschrAusbZ, Bückeburg	
82+59	Eurocopter EC.135P-1	Heer IntHubschrAusbZ, Bückeburg	
82+60	Eurocopter EC.135P-1	Heer IntHubschrAusbZ, Bückeburg	
82+61	Eurocopter EC.135P-1	Heer IntHubschrAusbZ, Bückeburg	
82+62	Eurocopter EC.135P-1	Heer IntHubschrAusbZ, Bückeburg	
82+63	Eurocopter EC.135P-1	Heer IntHubschrAusbZ, Bückeburg	
82+64	Eurocopter EC.135P-1	Heer IntHubschrAusbZ, Bückeburg	
82+65	Eurocopter EC.135P-1	Heer IntHubschrAusbZ, Bückeburg	
83+02	Westland Sea Lynx Mk88A	Marineflieger MFG 5, Nordholz	
83+03	Westland Sea Lynx Mk88A	Marineflieger MFG 5, Nordholz	
83+04	Westland Sea Lynx Mk88A	Marineflieger MFG 5, Nordholz	
83+05	Westland Sea Lynx Mk88A	Marineflieger MFG 5, Nordholz	
83+06	Westland Sea Lynx Mk88A	Marineflieger MFG 5, Nordholz	
83+07	Westland Sea Lynx Mk88A	Luftwaffe WTD 61, Ingolstadt	
83+09	Westland Sea Lynx Mk88A	Marineflieger MFG 5, Nordholz	
83+10	Westland Sea Lynx Mk88A	Marineflieger MFG 5, Nordholz	
83+11	Westland Sea Lynx Mk88A $	Marineflieger MFG 5, Nordholz	
83+12	Westland Sea Lynx Mk88A	Marineflieger MFG 5, Nordholz	
83+13	Westland Sea Lynx Mk88A	Marineflieger MFG 5, Nordholz	
83+15	Westland Sea Lynx Mk88A	Marineflieger MFG 5, Nordholz	
83+17	Westland Sea Lynx Mk88A	Marineflieger MFG 5, Nordholz	
83+18	Westland Sea Lynx Mk88A	Marineflieger MFG 5, Nordholz	
83+19	Westland Sea Lynx Mk88A	Marineflieger MFG 5, Nordholz	
83+20	Westland Sea Lynx Mk88A $	Marineflieger MFG 5, Nordholz	
83+21	Westland Sea Lynx Mk88A	Marineflieger MFG 5, Nordholz	
83+22	Westland Sea Lynx Mk88A	Marineflieger MFG 5, Nordholz	
83+23	Westland Sea Lynx Mk88A	Marineflieger MFG 5, Nordholz	
83+24	Westland Sea Lynx Mk88A	Marineflieger MFG 5, Nordholz	
83+25	Westland Sea Lynx Mk88A	Marineflieger MFG 5, Nordholz	
84+05	Sikorsky/VFW CH-53G	Luftwaffe HSG 64, Laupheim & Rheine-Bentlage	
84+09	Sikorsky/VFW CH-53G	Luftwaffe TsLw 3, Fassberg	
84+10	Sikorsky/VFW CH-53G	Luftwaffe TsLw 3, Fassberg	
84+12	Sikorsky/VFW CH-53G	Luftwaffe HSG 64, Laupheim & Rheine-Bentlage	
84+13	Sikorsky/VFW CH-53GA	Luftwaffe HSG 64, Laupheim & Rheine-Bentlage	
84+14	Sikorsky/VFW CH-53GE	Luftwaffe HSG 64, Laupheim & Rheine-Bentlage	
84+15	Sikorsky/VFW CH-53GS	Luftwaffe HSG 64, Laupheim & Rheine-Bentlage	
84+16	Sikorsky/VFW CH-53G	Luftwaffe	
84+18	Sikorsky/VFW CH-53G	Luftwaffe HSG 64, Laupheim & Rheine-Bentlage	
84+19	Sikorsky/VFW CH-53G	Luftwaffe TsLw 3, Fassberg	
84+24	Sikorsky/VFW CH-53GA	Luftwaffe HSG 64, Laupheim & Rheine-Bentlage	
84+25	Sikorsky/VFW CH-53GS	Luftwaffe HSG 64, Laupheim & Rheine-Bentlage	
84+26	Sikorsky/VFW CH-53GE	Luftwaffe WTD 61, Ingolstadt	
84+27	Sikorsky/VFW CH-53G	Luftwaffe	
84+28	Sikorsky/VFW CH-53GA	Luftwaffe HSG 64, Laupheim & Rheine-Bentlage	
84+29	Sikorsky/VFW CH-53G	Luftwaffe HSG 64, Laupheim & Rheine-Bentlage	
84+30	Sikorsky/VFW CH-53GS	Luftwaffe HSG 64, Laupheim & Rheine-Bentlage	
84+31	Sikorsky/VFW CH-53GA	Luftwaffe HSG 64, Laupheim & Rheine-Bentlage	
84+32	Sikorsky/VFW CH-53G	Luftwaffe HSG 64, Laupheim & Rheine-Bentlage	
84+33	Sikorsky/VFW CH-53GA	Luftwaffe HSG 64, Laupheim & Rheine-Bentlage	
84+34	Sikorsky/VFW CH-53G	Luftwaffe HSG 64, Laupheim & Rheine-Bentlage	
84+35	Sikorsky/VFW CH-53GA	Luftwaffe HSG 64, Laupheim & Rheine-Bentlage	
84+37	Sikorsky/VFW CH-53GA	Luftwaffe HSG 64, Laupheim & Rheine-Bentlage	
84+38	Sikorsky/VFW CH-53G	Luftwaffe HSG 64, Laupheim & Rheine-Bentlage	
84+39	Sikorsky/VFW CH-53GA	Luftwaffe HSG 64, Laupheim & Rheine-Bentlage	
84+40	Sikorsky/VFW CH-53G	Luftwaffe HSG 64, Laupheim & Rheine-Bentlage	
84+42	Sikorsky/VFW CH-53GS	Luftwaffe HSG 64, Laupheim & Rheine-Bentlage	
84+43	Sikorsky/VFW CH-53G	Luftwaffe HSG 64, Laupheim & Rheine-Bentlage	
84+44	Sikorsky/VFW CH-53G	Luftwaffe HSG 64, Laupheim & Rheine-Bentlage	
84+45	Sikorsky/VFW CH-53GS	Luftwaffe HSG 64, Laupheim & Rheine-Bentlage	
84+46	Sikorsky/VFW CH-53G	Luftwaffe HSG 64, Laupheim & Rheine-Bentlage	
84+47	Sikorsky/VFW CH-53GA	Luftwaffe HSG 64, Laupheim & Rheine-Bentlage	
84+48	Sikorsky/VFW CH-53G	Luftwaffe HSG 64, Laupheim & Rheine-Bentlage	

Notes	Serial	Type (code/other identity)	Owner/operator, location or fate
	84+49	Sikorsky/VFW CH-53GA	Luftwaffe HSG 64, Laupheim & Rheine-Bentlage
	84+50	Sikorsky/VFW CH-53GA	Luftwaffe HSG 64, Laupheim & Rheine-Bentlage
	84+51	Sikorsky/VFW CH-53GS	Luftwaffe HSG 64, Laupheim & Rheine-Bentlage
	84+52	Sikorsky/VFW CH-53GS	Luftwaffe HSG 64, Laupheim & Rheine-Bentlage
	84+53	Sikorsky/VFW CH-53GE	Luftwaffe HSG 64, Laupheim & Rheine-Bentlage
	84+54	Sikorsky/VFW CH-53G	Luftwaffe HSG 64, Laupheim & Rheine-Bentlage
	84+55	Sikorsky/VFW CH-53G	Airbus Helicopters, Donauwörth
	84+57	Sikorsky/VFW CH-53G	Luftwaffe HSG 64, Laupheim & Rheine-Bentlage
	84+58	Sikorsky/VFW CH-53G	Luftwaffe HSG 64, Laupheim & Rheine-Bentlage
	84+59	Sikorsky/VFW CH-53GS	Luftwaffe HSG 64, Laupheim & Rheine-Bentlage
	84+60	Sikorsky/VFW CH-53G	Luftwaffe HSG 64, Laupheim & Rheine-Bentlage
	84+62	Sikorsky/VFW CH-53GS	Luftwaffe HSG 64, Laupheim & Rheine-Bentlage
	84+63	Sikorsky/VFW CH-53G	Luftwaffe HSG 64, Laupheim & Rheine-Bentlage
	84+64	Sikorsky/VFW CH-53GS	Luftwaffe HSG 64, Laupheim & Rheine-Bentlage
	84+65	Sikorsky/VFW CH-53GA	Luftwaffe HSG 64, Laupheim & Rheine-Bentlage
	84+66	Sikorsky/VFW CH-53GS	Luftwaffe HSG 64, Laupheim & Rheine-Bentlage
	84+67	Sikorsky/VFW CH-53GS	Luftwaffe HSG 64, Laupheim & Rheine-Bentlage
	84+68	Sikorsky/VFW CH-53GS	Luftwaffe HSG 64, Laupheim & Rheine-Bentlage
	84+70	Sikorsky/VFW CH-53GA	Luftwaffe TsLw 3, Fassberg
	84+71	Sikorsky/VFW CH-53G	Luftwaffe HSG 64, Laupheim & Rheine-Bentlage
	84+72	Sikorsky/VFW CH-53G	Luftwaffe HSG 64, Laupheim & Rheine-Bentlage
	84+73	Sikorsky/VFW CH-53GS	Luftwaffe HSG 64, Laupheim & Rheine-Bentlage
	84+74	Sikorsky/VFW CH-53G	Luftwaffe HSG 64, Laupheim & Rheine-Bentlage
	84+75	Sikorsky/VFW CH-53G	Luftwaffe HSG 64, Laupheim & Rheine-Bentlage
	84+76	Sikorsky/VFW CH-53G	Luftwaffe HSG 64, Laupheim & Rheine-Bentlage
	84+77	Sikorsky/VFW CH-53G	Luftwaffe HSG 64, Laupheim & Rheine-Bentlage
	84+78	Sikorsky/VFW CH-53GS	Luftwaffe TsLw 3, Fassberg
	84+79	Sikorsky/VFW CH-53GS	Luftwaffe HSG 64, Laupheim & Rheine-Bentlage
	84+80	Sikorsky/VFW CH-53G	Luftwaffe HSG 64, Laupheim & Rheine-Bentlage
	84+82	Sikorsky/VFW CH-53GE	Luftwaffe HSG 64, Laupheim & Rheine-Bentlage
	84+83	Sikorsky/VFW CH-53G	Luftwaffe TsLw 3, Fassberg
	84+84	Sikorsky/VFW CH-53G	Luftwaffe HSG 64, Laupheim & Rheine-Bentlage
	84+85	Sikorsky/VFW CH-53GS	Luftwaffe HSG 64, Laupheim & Rheine-Bentlage
	84+86	Sikorsky/VFW CH-53GA	Luftwaffe HSG 64, Laupheim & Rheine-Bentlage
	84+87	Sikorsky/VFW CH-53GS	Luftwaffe HSG 64, Laupheim & Rheine-Bentlage
	84+88	Sikorsky/VFW CH-53G	Luftwaffe HSG 64, Laupheim & Rheine-Bentlage
	84+89	Sikorsky/VFW CH-53GA	Luftwaffe HSG 64, Laupheim & Rheine-Bentlage
	84+90	Sikorsky/VFW CH-53G	Luftwaffe HSG 64, Laupheim & Rheine-Bentlage
	84+91	Sikorsky/VFW CH-53GS	Luftwaffe HSG 64, Laupheim & Rheine-Bentlage
	84+92	Sikorsky/VFW CH-53GS	Luftwaffe HSG 64, Laupheim & Rheine-Bentlage
	84+94	Sikorsky/VFW CH-53G	Luftwaffe WTD 61, Ingolstadt
	84+95	Sikorsky/VFW CH-53GA	Luftwaffe HSG 64, Laupheim & Rheine-Bentlage
	84+96	Sikorsky/VFW CH-53GE	Luftwaffe HSG 64, Laupheim & Rheine-Bentlage
	84+97	Sikorsky/VFW CH-53G	Luftwaffe HSG 64, Laupheim & Rheine-Bentlage
	84+98	Sikorsky/VFW CH-53GS	Luftwaffe HSG 64, Laupheim & Rheine-Bentlage
	84+99	Sikorsky/VFW CH-53GA	Luftwaffe HSG 64, Laupheim & Rheine-Bentlage
	85+00	Sikorsky/VFW CH-53GS	Luftwaffe HSG 64, Laupheim & Rheine-Bentlage
	85+01	Sikorsky/VFW CH-53GS	Luftwaffe HSG 64, Laupheim & Rheine-Bentlage
	85+02	Sikorsky/VFW CH-53G	Luftwaffe HSG 64, Laupheim & Rheine-Bentlage
	85+03	Sikorsky/VFW CH-53G	Luftwaffe HSG 64, Laupheim & Rheine-Bentlage
	85+04	Sikorsky/VFW CH-53GA	Luftwaffe HSG 64, Laupheim & Rheine-Bentlage
	85+05	Sikorsky/VFW CH-53GS	Luftwaffe HSG 64, Laupheim & Rheine-Bentlage
	85+06	Sikorsky/VFW CH-53GA	Luftwaffe HSG 64, Laupheim & Rheine-Bentlage
	85+07	Sikorsky/VFW CH-53GS	Luftwaffe HSG 64, Laupheim & Rheine-Bentlage
	85+08	Sikorsky/VFW CH-53G	Luftwaffe HSG 64, Laupheim & Rheine-Bentlage
	85+10	Sikorsky/VFW CH-53GS	Luftwaffe HSG 64, Laupheim & Rheine-Bentlage
	85+11	Sikorsky/VFW CH-53G	Luftwaffe HSG 64, Laupheim & Rheine-Bentlage
	85+12	Sikorsky/VFW CH-53GS	Luftwaffe HSG 64, Laupheim & Rheine-Bentlage
	89+50	Westland Sea King Mk.41	Marineflieger MFG 5, Nordholz
	89+51	Westland Sea King Mk.41	Marineflieger MFG 5, Nordholz
	89+52	Westland Sea King Mk.41	Marineflieger MFG 5, Nordholz
	89+53	Westland Sea King Mk.41	Marineflieger MFG 5, Nordholz

Serial	Type (code/other identity)	Owner/operator, location or fate	Notes
89+54	Westland Sea King Mk.41	Marineflieger MFG 5, Nordholz	
89+55	Westland Sea King Mk.41 $	Marineflieger MFG 5, Nordholz	
89+56	Westland Sea King Mk.41	Marineflieger MFG 5, Nordholz	
89+57	Westland Sea King Mk.41	Marineflieger MFG 5, Nordholz	
89+58	Westland Sea King Mk.41 $	Marineflieger MFG 5, Nordholz	
89+60	Westland Sea King Mk.41	Marineflieger MFG 5, Nordholz	
89+61	Westland Sea King Mk.41	Marineflieger MFG 5, Nordholz	
89+62	Westland Sea King Mk.41	Marineflieger MFG 5, Nordholz	
89+63	Westland Sea King Mk.41	Marineflieger MFG 5, Nordholz	
89+64	Westland Sea King Mk.41 $	Marineflieger MFG 5, Nordholz	
89+65	Westland Sea King Mk.41	Marineflieger MFG 5, Nordholz	
89+66	Westland Sea King Mk.41	Marineflieger MFG 5, Nordholz	
89+67	Westland Sea King Mk.41	Marineflieger MFG 5, Nordholz	
89+68	Westland Sea King Mk.41	Marineflieger MFG 5, Nordholz	
89+69	Westland Sea King Mk.41	Marineflieger MFG 5, Nordholz	
89+70	Westland Sea King Mk.41	Marineflieger MFG 5, Nordholz	
89+71	Westland Sea King Mk.41	Marineflieger MFG 5, Nordholz	
98+03	Eurofighter EF.2000(T) (IPA3)	Luftwaffe WTD 61, Ingolstadt	
98+07	Eurofighter EF.2000 (IPA7)	Luftwaffe WTD 61, Ingolstadt	
98+08	Eurofighter EF.2000GT (IPA8)	Airbus Defence & Space, Manching	
98+16	Eurocopter EC.665 Tiger UHT	Luftwaffe TsLw 3, Fassberg	
98+18	Eurocopter EC.665 Tiger UHT	Airbus Helicopters, Donauwörth	
98+49	Eurocopter EC.665 Tiger UHT (74+49)	Airbus Helicopters, Donauwörth	
98+50	NH Industries NH.90-TTH	Airbus Helicopters, Donauwörth	
98+53	NH Industries NH.90-NFH Sea Lion (79+53)	Airbus Helicopters, Donauwörth	
98+56	NH Industries NH.90-NFH Sea Lion	Airbus Helicopters, Donauwörth	
98+59	Panavia Tornado IDS(T)	Luftwaffe WTD 61, Ingolstadt	
98+60	Panavia Tornado IDS	Luftwaffe WTD 61, Ingolstadt	
98+77	Panavia Tornado IDS $	Luftwaffe WTD 61, Ingolstadt	
98+79	Panavia Tornado ECR	Luftwaffe WTD 61, Ingolstadt	
98+90	NH Industries NH.90-TTH	Airbus Helicopters, Donauwörth	
99+01	Northrop Grumman RQ-4E Euro Hawk	Luftwaffe WTD 61, Manching	
Civil operated aircraft in military use			
D-HCDL	Eurocopter EC.135P-2+	Marineflieger MFG 5, Nordholz	
D-HDDL	Eurocopter EC.135P-2+	Marineflieger MFG 5, Nordholz	
GHANA			
9G-EXE	Dassault Falcon 900EASy	Ghana Air Force VIP Flight, Accra	
GREECE			
Elliniki Polemiki Aeroporía/Hellenic Air Force (HAF)			
001	Lockheed Martin F-16C-52 Fighting Falcon	HAF 335 Mira/116 PM, Áraxos	
002	Lockheed Martin F-16C-52 Fighting Falcon	HAF 335 Mira/116 PM, Áraxos	
003	Lockheed Martin F-16C-52 Fighting Falcon	HAF 335 Mira/116 PM, Áraxos	
004	Lockheed Martin F-16C-52 Fighting Falcon	HAF 335 Mira/116 PM, Áraxos	
005	Lockheed Martin F-16C-52 Fighting Falcon $	HAF 335 Mira/116 PM, Áraxos	
006	Lockheed Martin F-16C-52 Fighting Falcon	HAF 335 Mira/116 PM, Áraxos	
007	Lockheed Martin F-16C-52 Fighting Falcon	HAF 335 Mira/116 PM, Áraxos	
008	Lockheed Martin F-16C-52 Fighting Falcon	HAF 335 Mira/116 PM, Áraxos	
009	Lockheed Martin F-16C-52 Fighting Falcon	HAF 335 Mira/116 PM, Áraxos	
010	Lockheed Martin F-16C-52 Fighting Falcon	HAF 335 Mira/116 PM, Áraxos	
011	Lockheed Martin F-16C-52 Fighting Falcon	HAF 335 Mira/116 PM, Áraxos	
012	Lockheed Martin F-16C-52 Fighting Falcon	HAF 335 Mira/116 PM, Áraxos	
013	Lockheed Martin F-16C-52 Fighting Falcon	HAF 335 Mira/116 PM, Áraxos	
014	Lockheed Martin F-16C-52 Fighting Falcon	HAF 335 Mira/116 PM, Áraxos	
015	Lockheed Martin F-16C-52 Fighting Falcon	HAF 335 Mira/116 PM, Áraxos	
016	Lockheed Martin F-16C-52 Fighting Falcon	HAF 335 Mira/116 PM, Áraxos	
017	Lockheed Martin F-16C-52 Fighting Falcon	HAF 335 Mira/116 PM, Áraxos	
018	Lockheed Martin F-16C-52 Fighting Falcon	HAF 335 Mira/116 PM, Áraxos	
019	Lockheed Martin F-16C-52 Fighting Falcon	HAF 335 Mira/116 PM, Áraxos	
020	Lockheed Martin F-16C-52 Fighting Falcon	HAF 335 Mira/116 PM, Áraxos	
021	Lockheed Martin F-16D-52 Fighting Falcon	HAF 335 Mira/116 PM, Áraxos	

Notes	Serial	Type (code/other identity)	Owner/operator, location or fate
	022	Lockheed Martin F-16D-52 Fighting Falcon	HAF 335 Mira/116 PM, Áraxos
	023	Lockheed Martin F-16D-52 Fighting Falcon $	HAF 335 Mira/116 PM, Áraxos
	024	Lockheed Martin F-16D-52 Fighting Falcon	HAF 335 Mira/116 PM, Áraxos
	025	Lockheed Martin F-16D-52 Fighting Falcon	HAF 335 Mira/116 PM, Áraxos
	026	Lockheed Martin F-16D-52 Fighting Falcon	HAF 335 Mira/116 PM, Áraxos
	027	Lockheed Martin F-16D-52 Fighting Falcon	HAF 335 Mira/116 PM, Áraxos
	028	Lockheed Martin F-16D-52 Fighting Falcon	HAF 335 Mira/116 PM, Áraxos
	029	Lockheed Martin F-16D-52 Fighting Falcon	HAF 335 Mira/116 PM, Áraxos
	030	Lockheed Martin F-16D-52 Fighting Falcon	HAF 335 Mira/116 PM, Áraxos
	045	Lockheed Martin F-16C-50 Fighting Falcon	HAF 347 Mira/111 PM, Nea Ankhialos
	046	Lockheed Martin F-16C-50 Fighting Falcon	HAF 341 Mira/111 PM, Nea Ankhialos
	047	Lockheed Martin F-16C-50 Fighting Falcon	HAF 347 Mira/111 PM, Nea Ankhialos
	048	Lockheed Martin F-16C-50 Fighting Falcon	HAF 341 Mira/111 PM, Nea Ankhialos
	049	Lockheed Martin F-16C-50 Fighting Falcon	HAF 347 Mira/111 PM, Nea Ankhialos
	050	Lockheed Martin F-16C-50 Fighting Falcon	HAF 341 Mira/111 PM, Nea Ankhialos
	051	Lockheed Martin F-16C-50 Fighting Falcon	HAF 347 Mira/111 PM, Nea Ankhialos
	052	Lockheed Martin F-16C-50 Fighting Falcon	HAF 341 Mira/111 PM, Nea Ankhialos
	053	Lockheed Martin F-16C-50 Fighting Falcon	HAF 347 Mira/111 PM, Nea Ankhialos
	054	Lockheed Martin F-16C-50 Fighting Falcon	HAF 341 Mira/111 PM, Nea Ankhialos
	055	Lockheed Martin F-16C-50 Fighting Falcon	HAF 347 Mira/111 PM, Nea Ankhialos
	056	Lockheed Martin F-16C-50 Fighting Falcon	HAF 341 Mira/111 PM, Nea Ankhialos
	057	Lockheed Martin F-16C-50 Fighting Falcon	HAF 347 Mira/111 PM, Nea Ankhialos
	058	Lockheed Martin F-16C-50 Fighting Falcon	HAF 341 Mira/111 PM, Nea Ankhialos
	060	Lockheed Martin F-16C-50 Fighting Falcon	HAF 347 Mira/111 PM, Nea Ankhialos
	061	Lockheed Martin F-16C-50 Fighting Falcon	HAF 347 Mira/111 PM, Nea Ankhialos
	062	Lockheed Martin F-16C-50 Fighting Falcon $	HAF 341 Mira/111 PM, Nea Ankhialos
	063	Lockheed Martin F-16C-50 Fighting Falcon	HAF 347 Mira/111 PM, Nea Ankhialos
	064	Lockheed Martin F-16C-50 Fighting Falcon	HAF 341 Mira/111 PM, Nea Ankhialos
	065	Lockheed Martin F-16C-50 Fighting Falcon	HAF 347 Mira/111 PM, Nea Ankhialos
	066	Lockheed Martin F-16C-50 Fighting Falcon	HAF 341 Mira/111 PM, Nea Ankhialos
	067	Lockheed Martin F-16C-50 Fighting Falcon	HAF 347 Mira/111 PM, Nea Ankhialos
	068	Lockheed Martin F-16C-50 Fighting Falcon	HAF 341 Mira/111 PM, Nea Ankhialos
	069	Lockheed Martin F-16C-50 Fighting Falcon	HAF 347 Mira/111 PM, Nea Ankhialos
	070	Lockheed Martin F-16C-50 Fighting Falcon	HAF 341 Mira/111 PM, Nea Ankhialos
	071	Lockheed Martin F-16C-50 Fighting Falcon	HAF 347 Mira/111 PM, Nea Ankhialos
	072	Lockheed Martin F-16C-50 Fighting Falcon	HAF 341 Mira/111 PM, Nea Ankhialos
	073	Lockheed Martin F-16C-50 Fighting Falcon	HAF 347 Mira/111 PM, Nea Ankhialos
	074	Lockheed Martin F-16C-50 Fighting Falcon	HAF 341 Mira/111 PM, Nea Ankhialos
	075	Lockheed Martin F-16C-50 Fighting Falcon	HAF 347 Mira/111 PM, Nea Ankhialos
	076	Lockheed Martin F-16C-50 Fighting Falcon $	HAF 341 Mira/111 PM, Nea Ankhialos
	077	Lockheed Martin F-16D-50 Fighting Falcon	HAF 341 Mira/111 PM, Nea Ankhialos
	078	Lockheed Martin F-16D-50 Fighting Falcon	HAF 347 Mira/111 PM, Nea Ankhialos
	079	Lockheed Martin F-16D-50 Fighting Falcon	HAF 347 Mira/111 PM, Nea Ankhialos
	080	Lockheed Martin F-16D-50 Fighting Falcon	HAF 341 Mira/111 PM, Nea Ankhialos
	081	Lockheed Martin F-16D-50 Fighting Falcon	HAF 347 Mira/111 PM, Nea Ankhialos
	082	Lockheed Martin F-16D-50 Fighting Falcon	HAF 341 Mira/111 PM, Nea Ankhialos
	083	Lockheed Martin F-16D-50 Fighting Falcon	HAF 347 Mira/111 PM, Nea Ankhialos
	110	Lockheed Martin F-16C-30 Fighting Falcon	HAF 330 Mira/111 PM, Nea Ankhialos
	111	Lockheed Martin F-16C-30 Fighting Falcon	HAF 330 Mira/111 PM, Nea Ankhialos
	112	Lockheed Martin F-16C-30 Fighting Falcon	HAF
	113	Lockheed Martin F-16C-30 Fighting Falcon	HAF 330 Mira/111 PM, Nea Ankhialos
	114	Lockheed Martin F-16C-30 Fighting Falcon	HAF 330 Mira/111 PM, Nea Ankhialos
	115	Lockheed Martin F-16C-30 Fighting Falcon	HAF 330 Mira/111 PM, Nea Ankhialos
	116	Lockheed Martin F-16C-30 Fighting Falcon	HAF 330 Mira/111 PM, Nea Ankhialos
	117	Lockheed Martin F-16C-30 Fighting Falcon	HAF 330 Mira/111 PM, Nea Ankhialos
	118	Lockheed Martin F-16C-30 Fighting Falcon	HAF
	119	Lockheed Martin F-16C-30 Fighting Falcon	HAF 330 Mira/111 PM, Nea Ankhialos
	120	Lockheed Martin F-16C-30 Fighting Falcon	HAF
	121	Lockheed Martin F-16C-30 Fighting Falcon	HAF 341 Mira/111 PM, Nea Ankhialos
	122	Lockheed Martin F-16C-30 Fighting Falcon	HAF 330 Mira/111 PM, Nea Ankhialos
	124	Lockheed Martin F-16C-30 Fighting Falcon	HAF
	125	Lockheed Martin F-16C-30 Fighting Falcon	HAF 330 Mira/111 PM, Nea Ankhialos

Serial	Type (code/other identity)	Owner/operator, location or fate	Notes
126	Lockheed Martin F-16C-30 Fighting Falcon	HAF 330 Mira/111 PM, Nea Ankhialos	
127	Lockheed Martin F-16C-30 Fighting Falcon	HAF 330 Mira/111 PM, Nea Ankhialos	
128	Lockheed Martin F-16C-30 Fighting Falcon	HAF 330 Mira/111 PM, Nea Ankhialos	
129	Lockheed Martin F-16C-30 Fighting Falcon	HAF 330 Mira/111 PM, Nea Ankhialos	
130	Lockheed Martin F-16C-30 Fighting Falcon	HAF 330 Mira/111 PM, Nea Ankhialos	
132	Lockheed Martin F-16C-30 Fighting Falcon	HAF	
133	Lockheed Martin F-16C-30 Fighting Falcon	HAF 330 Mira/111 PM, Nea Ankhialos	
134	Lockheed Martin F-16C-30 Fighting Falcon	HAF 330 Mira/111 PM, Nea Ankhialos	
136	Lockheed Martin F-16C-30 Fighting Falcon	HAF 330 Mira/111 PM, Nea Ankhialos	
138	Lockheed Martin F-16C-30 Fighting Falcon	HAF	
139	Lockheed Martin F-16C-30 Fighting Falcon	HAF 330 Mira/111 PM, Nea Ankhialos	
140	Lockheed Martin F-16C-30 Fighting Falcon	HAF 330 Mira/111 PM, Nea Ankhialos	
141	Lockheed Martin F-16C-30 Fighting Falcon	HAF 330 Mira/111 PM, Nea Ankhialos	
143	Lockheed Martin F-16C-30 Fighting Falcon	HAF 330 Mira/111 PM, Nea Ankhialos	
144	Lockheed Martin F-16D-30 Fighting Falcon	HAF 330 Mira/111 PM, Nea Ankhialos	
145	Lockheed Martin F-16D-30 Fighting Falcon	HAF 330 Mira/111 PM, Nea Ankhialos	
146	Lockheed Martin F-16D-30 Fighting Falcon	HAF	
147	Lockheed Martin F-16D-30 Fighting Falcon	HAF 330 Mira/111 PM, Nea Ankhialos	
148	Lockheed Martin F-16D-30 Fighting Falcon	HAF 330 Mira/111 PM, Nea Ankhialos	
149	Lockheed Martin F-16D-30 Fighting Falcon	HAF 330 Mira/111 PM, Nea Ankhialos	
201	Dassault Mirage 2000-BG	HAF 332 MAPK/114 PM, Tanagra	
202	Dassault Mirage 2000-BG	HAF 332 MAPK/114 PM, Tanagra	
210	Dassault Mirage 2000-EG	HAF 332 MAPK/114 PM, Tanagra	
212	Dassault Mirage 2000-EG	HAF 332 MAPK/114 PM, Tanagra	
213	Dassault Mirage 2000-EG	HAF 332 MAPK/114 PM, Tanagra	
215	Dassault Mirage 2000-EG	HAF 332 MAPK/114 PM, Tanagra	
216	Dassault Mirage 2000-EG	HAF 332 MAPK/114 PM, Tanagra	
217	Dassault Mirage 2000-EG	HAF 332 MAPK/114 PM, Tanagra	
218	Dassault Mirage 2000-EG	HAF 332 MAPK/114 PM, Tanagra	
219	Dassault Mirage 2000-EG	HAF 332 MAPK/114 PM, Tanagra	
220	Dassault Mirage 2000-EG	HAF 332 MAPK/114 PM, Tanagra	
221	Dassault Mirage 2000-EG	HAF 332 MAPK/114 PM, Tanagra	
226	Dassault Mirage 2000-EG	HAF 332 MAPK/114 PM, Tanagra	
231	Dassault Mirage 2000-EG	HAF 332 MAPK/114 PM, Tanagra	
232	Dassault Mirage 2000-EG	HAF 332 MAPK/114 PM, Tanagra	
233	Dassault Mirage 2000-EG	HAF 332 MAPK/114 PM, Tanagra	
237	Dassault Mirage 2000-EG	HAF 332 MAPK/114 PM, Tanagra	
241	Dassault Mirage 2000-EG	HAF 332 MAPK/114 PM, Tanagra	
242	Dassault Mirage 2000-EG	HAF 332 MAPK/114 PM, Tanagra	
374	Embraer ERJ.145H AEW&C	HAF 380 Mira/112 PM, Elefsís	
500	Lockheed Martin F-16C-52 Fighting Falcon	HAF 343 Mira/115 PM, Souda	
501	Lockheed Martin F-16C-52 Fighting Falcon	HAF 337 Mira/110 PM, Larissa	
502	Lockheed Martin F-16C-52 Fighting Falcon	HAF 337 Mira/110 PM, Larissa	
503	Lockheed Martin F-16C-52 Fighting Falcon	HAF 343 Mira/115 PM, Souda	
504	Lockheed Martin F-16C-52 Fighting Falcon	HAF 343 Mira/115 PM, Souda	
505	Dassault Mirage 2000-5BG	HAF 331 MAPK/114 PM, Tanagra	
505	Lockheed Martin F-16C-52 Fighting Falcon $	HAF 343 Mira/115 PM, Souda	
506	Dassault Mirage 2000-5BG	HAF 331 MAPK/114 PM, Tanagra	
506	Lockheed Martin F-16C-52 Fighting Falcon	HAF 340 Mira/115 PM, Souda	
507	Dassault Mirage 2000-5BG	HAF 331 MAPK/114 PM, Tanagra	
507	Lockheed Martin F-16C-52 Fighting Falcon	HAF 337 Mira/110 PM, Larissa	
508	Dassault Mirage 2000-5BG	HAF 331 MAPK/114 PM, Tanagra	
508	Lockheed Martin F-16C-52 Fighting Falcon	HAF 337 Mira/110 PM, Larissa	
509	Dassault Mirage 2000-5BG	HAF 331 MAPK/114 PM, Tanagra	
509	Lockheed Martin F-16C-52 Fighting Falcon	HAF 343 Mira/115 PM, Souda	
510	Lockheed Martin F-16C-52 Fighting Falcon	HAF 343 Mira/115 PM, Souda	
511	Dassault Mirage 2000-5BG	HAF 331 MAPK/114 PM, Tanagra	
511	Lockheed Martin F-16C-52 Fighting Falcon	HAF 343 Mira/115 PM, Souda	
513	Lockheed Martin F-16C-52 Fighting Falcon	HAF 343 Mira/115 PM, Souda	
514	Dassault Mirage 2000-5BG	HAF 331 MAPK/114 PM, Tanagra	
515	Lockheed Martin F-16C-52 Fighting Falcon	HAF 343 Mira/115 PM, Souda	
517	Lockheed Martin F-16C-52 Fighting Falcon	HAF 337 Mira/110 PM, Larissa	

Notes	Serial	Type (code/other identity)	Owner/operator, location or fate
	518	Lockheed Martin F-16C-52 Fighting Falcon	HAF 340 Mira/115 PM, Souda
	519	Lockheed Martin F-16C-52 Fighting Falcon	HAF 340 Mira/115 PM, Souda
	520	Lockheed Martin F-16C-52 Fighting Falcon	HAF 343 Mira/115 PM, Souda
	521	Lockheed Martin F-16C-52 Fighting Falcon	HAF 340 Mira/115 PM, Souda
	523	Lockheed Martin F-16C-52 Fighting Falcon $	HAF 340 Mira/115 PM, Souda
	524	Lockheed Martin F-16C-52 Fighting Falcon	HAF 337 Mira/110 PM, Larissa
	525	Lockheed Martin F-16C-52 Fighting Falcon	HAF 340 Mira/115 PM, Souda
	526	Lockheed Martin F-16C-52 Fighting Falcon	HAF 343 Mira/115 PM, Souda
	527	Dassault Mirage 2000-5BG	HAF 331 MAPK/114 PM, Tanagra
	527	Lockheed Martin F-16C-52 Fighting Falcon	HAF 343 Mira/115 PM, Souda
	528	Lockheed Martin F-16C-52 Fighting Falcon	HAF 337 Mira/110 PM, Larissa
	529	Lockheed Martin F-16C-52 Fighting Falcon	HAF 343 Mira/115 PM, Souda
	530	Dassault Mirage 2000-5BG	HAF 331 MAPK/114 PM, Tanagra
	530	Lockheed Martin F-16C-52 Fighting Falcon	HAF 337 Mira/110 PM, Larissa
	531	Lockheed Martin F-16C-52 Fighting Falcon $	HAF 337 Mira/110 PM, Larissa
	532	Lockheed Martin F-16C-52 Fighting Falcon	HAF 337 Mira/110 PM, Larissa
	533	Lockheed Martin F-16C-52 Fighting Falcon	HAF 340 Mira/115 PM, Souda
	534	Dassault Mirage 2000-5BG	HAF 331 MAPK/114 PM, Tanagra
	534	Lockheed Martin F-16C-52 Fighting Falcon	HAF 340 Mira/115 PM, Souda
	535	Dassault Mirage 2000-5BG	HAF 331 MAPK/114 PM, Tanagra
	535	Lockheed Martin F-16C-52 Fighting Falcon	HAF 340 Mira/115 PM, Souda
	536	Dassault Mirage 2000-5BG	HAF 331 MAPK/114 PM, Tanagra
	536	Lockheed Martin F-16C-52 Fighting Falcon	HAF 340 Mira/115 PM, Souda
	537	Lockheed Martin F-16C-52 Fighting Falcon	HAF 340 Mira/115 PM, Souda
	538	Lockheed Martin F-16C-52 Fighting Falcon	HAF 340 Mira/115 PM, Souda
	539	Lockheed Martin F-16C-52 Fighting Falcon	HAF 337 Mira/110 PM, Larissa
	540	Dassault Mirage 2000-5BG	HAF 331 MAPK/114 PM, Tanagra
	543	Dassault Mirage 2000-5BG	HAF 331 MAPK/114 PM, Tanagra
	545	Dassault Mirage 2000-5BG	HAF 331 MAPK/114 PM, Tanagra
	546	Dassault Mirage 2000-5BG	*Crashed 12 April 2018, off Skyros*
	547	Dassault Mirage 2000-5BG	HAF 331 MAPK/114 PM, Tanagra
	548	Dassault Mirage 2000-5BG	HAF 331 MAPK/114 PM, Tanagra
	549	Dassault Mirage 2000-5BG	HAF 331 MAPK/114 PM, Tanagra
	550	Dassault Mirage 2000-5BG	HAF 331 MAPK/114 PM, Tanagra
	551	Dassault Mirage 2000-5BG	HAF 331 MAPK/114 PM, Tanagra
	552	Dassault Mirage 2000-5BG	HAF 331 MAPK/114 PM, Tanagra
	553	Dassault Mirage 2000-5BG	HAF 331 MAPK/114 PM, Tanagra
	554	Dassault Mirage 2000-5BG	HAF 331 MAPK/114 PM, Tanagra
	555	Dassault Mirage 2000-5BG	HAF 331 MAPK/114 PM, Tanagra
	600	Lockheed Martin F-16D-52 Fighting Falcon	HAF 337 Mira/110 PM, Larissa
	601	Lockheed Martin F-16D-52 Fighting Falcon	HAF 340 Mira/115 PM, Souda
	602	Lockheed Martin F-16D-52 Fighting Falcon	HAF 340 Mira/115 PM, Souda
	603	Lockheed Martin F-16D-52 Fighting Falcon	HAF 340 Mira/115 PM, Souda
	605	Lockheed Martin F-16D-52 Fighting Falcon	HAF 340 Mira/115 PM, Souda
	606	Lockheed Martin F-16D-52 Fighting Falcon	HAF 337 Mira/110 PM, Larissa
	607	Lockheed Martin F-16D-52 Fighting Falcon	HAF 343 Mira/115 PM, Souda
	608	Lockheed Martin F-16D-52 Fighting Falcon	HAF 340 Mira/115 PM, Souda
	609	Lockheed Martin F-16D-52 Fighting Falcon	HAF 337 Mira/110 PM, Larissa
	610	Lockheed Martin F-16D-52 Fighting Falcon	HAF 340 Mira/115 PM, Souda
	611	Lockheed Martin F-16D-52 Fighting Falcon	HAF 337 Mira/110 PM, Larissa
	612	Lockheed Martin F-16D-52 Fighting Falcon	HAF 337 Mira/110 PM, Larissa
	613	Lockheed Martin F-16D-52 Fighting Falcon	HAF 343 Mira/115 PM, Souda
	615	Lockheed Martin F-16D-52 Fighting Falcon	HAF 343 Mira/115 PM, Souda
	616	Lockheed Martin F-16D-52 Fighting Falcon	HAF 343 Mira/115 PM, Souda
	617	Lockheed Martin F-16D-52 Fighting Falcon	HAF 343 Mira/115 PM, Souda
	618	Lockheed Martin F-16D-52 Fighting Falcon	HAF 343 Mira/115 PM, Souda
	619	Lockheed Martin F-16D-52 Fighting Falcon $	HAF 337 Mira/110 PM, Larissa
	671	Embraer ERJ.145H AEW&C	HAF 380 Mira/112 PM, Elefsis
	678	Gulfstream Aerospace Gulfstream V	HAF 352 MMYP/112 PM, Elefsis
	729	Embraer ERJ.145H AEW&C	HAF 380 Mira/112 PM, Elefsis
	741	Lockheed C-130H Hercules (ECM)	HAF 356 MTM/112 PM, Elefsis
	742	Lockheed C-130H Hercules	HAF 356 MTM/112 PM, Elefsis

Serial	Type (code/other identity)	Owner/operator, location or fate	Notes
743	Lockheed C-130H Hercules	HAF 356 MTM/112 PM, Elefsís	
744	Lockheed C-130H Hercules	HAF 356 MTM/112 PM, Elefsís	
745	Lockheed C-130H Hercules $	HAF 356 MTM/112 PM, Elefsís	
746	Lockheed C-130H Hercules	HAF 356 MTM/112 PM, Elefsís	
747	Lockheed C-130H Hercules (ECM)	HAF 356 MTM/112 PM, Elefsís	
749	Lockheed C-130H Hercules	HAF 356 MTM/112 PM, Elefsís	
751	Lockheed C-130H Hercules	HAF 356 MTM/112 PM, Elefsís	
752	Lockheed C-130H Hercules $	HAF 356 MTM/112 PM, Elefsís	
757	Embraer ERJ.145H AEW&C	HAF 380 Mira/112 PM, Elefsís	
4117	Aeritalia C-27J Spartan	HAF 354 Mira, Elefsís	
4118	Aeritalia C-27J Spartan	HAF 354 Mira, Elefsís	
4120	Aeritalia C-27J Spartan	HAF 354 Mira, Elefsís	
4121	Aeritalia C-27J Spartan	HAF 354 Mira, Elefsís	
4122	Aeritalia C-27J Spartan	HAF 354 Mira, Elefsís	
4123	Aeritalia C-27J Spartan	HAF 354 Mira, Elefsís	
4124	Aeritalia C-27J Spartan	HAF 354 Mira, Elefsís	
4125	Aeritalia C-27J Spartan	HAF 354 Mira, Elefsís	
135L-484	Embraer ERJ.135BJ Legacy	HAF 352 MMYP/112 PM, Elefsís	
145-209	Embraer ERJ.135LR	HAF 352 MMYP/112 PM, Elefsís	

HONDURAS
Fuerza Aérea Hondureña (FAH)/Honduran Air Force

FAH-001	Embraer ERJ.135BJ Legacy 600	FAH, Tegucigalpa	

HUNGARY
Magyar Légierö/Hungarian Air Force

01	Boeing C-17A Globemaster III (08-0001)	NATO SAC, Heavy Airlift Wing, Pápa	
02	Boeing C-17A Globemaster III (08-0002)	NATO SAC, Heavy Airlift Wing, Pápa	
03	Boeing C-17A Globemaster III (08-0003)	NATO SAC, Heavy Airlift Wing, Pápa	
30	SAAB 39C Gripen	Hungarian AF 59 Sz.D.REB, Kecskemét	
31	SAAB 39C Gripen	Hungarian AF 59 Sz.D.REB, Kecskemét	
32	SAAB 39C Gripen	Hungarian AF 59 Sz.D.REB, Kecskemét	
33	SAAB 39C Gripen	Hungarian AF 59 Sz.D.REB, Kecskemét	
34	SAAB 39C Gripen	Hungarian AF 59 Sz.D.REB, Kecskemét	
35	SAAB 39C Gripen	Hungarian AF 59 Sz.D.REB, Kecskemét	
36	SAAB 39C Gripen	Hungarian AF 59 Sz.D.REB, Kecskemét	
37	SAAB 39C Gripen	Hungarian AF 59 Sz.D.REB, Kecskemét	
38	SAAB 39C Gripen	Hungarian AF 59 Sz.D.REB, Kecskemét	
39	SAAB 39C Gripen	Hungarian AF 59 Sz.D.REB, Kecskemét	
40	SAAB 39C Gripen $	Hungarian AF 59 Sz.D.REB, Kecskemét	
41	SAAB 39C Gripen	Hungarian AF 59 Sz.D.REB, Kecskemét	
43	SAAB 39D Gripen	Hungarian AF 59 Sz.D.REB, Kecskemét	
44	SAAB 39D Gripen (39842)	Hungarian AF 59 Sz.D.REB, Kecskemét	
110	Antonov An-26	Hungarian AF 59 Sz.D.REB, Kecskemét	
405	Antonov An-26	Hungarian AF 59 Sz.D.REB, Kecskemét	
406	Antonov An-26	Hungarian AF 59 Sz.D.REB, Kecskemét	
407	Antonov An-26	Hungarian AF 59 Sz.D.REB, Kecskemét	
603	Antonov An-26	Hungarian AF 59 Sz.D.REB, Kecskemét	
604	Airbus A.319-112 (9H-AGM)	Hungarian AF 59 Sz.D.REB, Kecskemét	
605	Airbus A.319-112 (9H-AGN)	Hungarian AF 59 Sz.D.REB, Kecskemét	
606	Dassault Falcon 7X (9H-AGO)	Hungarian AF 59 Sz.D.REB, Kecskemét	

INDIA
Bharatiya Vayu Sena/Indian Air Force (IAF)

CB-8001	Boeing C-17A Globemaster III (11-0101)	IAF 81 Sqn, Hindon AB	
CB-8002	Boeing C-17A Globemaster III (11-0102)	IAF 81 Sqn, Hindon AB	
CB-8003	Boeing C-17A Globemaster III (11-0103)	IAF 81 Sqn, Hindon AB	
CB-8004	Boeing C-17A Globemaster III (11-0104)	IAF 81 Sqn, Hindon AB	
CB-8005	Boeing C-17A Globemaster III (11-0105)	IAF 81 Sqn, Hindon AB	
CB-8006	Boeing C-17A Globemaster III (11-0106)	IAF 81 Sqn, Hindon AB	
CB-8007	Boeing C-17A Globemaster III (11-0107)	IAF 81 Sqn, Hindon AB	
CB-8008	Boeing C-17A Globemaster III (11-0108)	IAF 81 Sqn, Hindon AB	

Notes	Serial	Type (code/other identity)	Owner/operator, location or fate
	CB-8009	Boeing C-17A Globemaster III (11-0109)	IAF 81 Sqn, Hindon AB
	CB-8010	Boeing C-17A Globemaster III (11-0110)	IAF 81 Sqn, Hindon AB
	CB-8011	Boeing C-17A Globemaster III (14-0003)	IAF 81 Sqn, Hindon AB
	KC-3801	Lockheed C-130J-30 Hercules II	IAF 77 Sqn, Hindon AB
	KC-3802	Lockheed C-130J-30 Hercules II	IAF 77 Sqn, Hindon AB
	KC-3804	Lockheed C-130J-30 Hercules II	IAF 77 Sqn, Hindon AB
	KC-3805	Lockheed C-130J-30 Hercules II	IAF 77 Sqn, Hindon AB
	KC-3806	Lockheed C-130J-30 Hercules II	IAF 77 Sqn, Hindon AB
	KC-3807	Lockheed C-130J-30 Hercules II	IAF 87 Sqn, Arjan Singh AB
	KC-3808	Lockheed C-130J-30 Hercules II	IAF 87 Sqn, Arjan Singh AB
	KC-3809	Lockheed C-130J-30 Hercules II	IAF 87 Sqn, Arjan Singh AB
	KC-3810	Lockheed C-130J-30 Hercules II	IAF 87 Sqn, Arjan Singh AB
	KC-3811	Lockheed C-130J-30 Hercules II	IAF 87 Sqn, Arjan Singh AB
	KC-3812	Lockheed C-130J-30 Hercules II	IAF 87 Sqn, Arjan Singh AB
	KC-3813	Lockheed C-130J-30 Hercules II	IAF (on order)

INDONESIA
Indonesian Government

| | A-001 | Boeing 737-8U3 | Government of Indonesia, Jakarta |

ISRAEL
Heyl ha'Avir/Israeli Air Force

	102	Lockheed C-130H Karnaf	Israeli AF 131 Sqn, Nevatim
	140	Boeing KC-707 Re'em	Israeli AF 120 Sqn, Nevatim
	208	Lockheed C-130E Karnaf	Israeli AF 131 Sqn, Nevatim
	248	Boeing KC-707 Re'em	Israeli AF 120 Sqn, Nevatim
	250	Boeing KC-707 Re'em	Israeli AF 120 Sqn, Nevatim
	260	Boeing KC-707 Re'em	Israeli AF 120 Sqn, Nevatim
	264	Boeing KC-707 Re'em	Israeli AF 120 Sqn, Nevatim
	272	Boeing KC-707 Re'em	Israeli AF 120 Sqn, Nevatim
	275	Boeing KC-707 Re'em	Israeli AF 120 Sqn, Nevatim
	290	Boeing KC-707 Re'em	Israeli AF 120 Sqn, Nevatim
	295	Boeing KC-707 Re'em	Israeli AF 120 Sqn, Nevatim
	305	Lockheed C-130E Karnaf	Israeli AF 131 Sqn, Nevatim
	309	Lockheed C-130E Karnaf	Israeli AF 131 Sqn, Nevatim
	310	Lockheed C-130E Karnaf	Israeli AF 131 Sqn, Nevatim
	314	Lockheed C-130E Karnaf	Israeli AF 131 Sqn, Nevatim
	316	Lockheed C-130E Karnaf	Withdrawn from use, 2018
	318	Lockheed C-130E Karnaf	Israeli AF 131 Sqn, Nevatim
	420	Lockheed KC-130H Karnaf	Israeli AF 131 Sqn, Nevatim
	427	Lockheed C-130H Karnaf	Israeli AF 131 Sqn, Nevatim
	428	Lockheed C-130H Karnaf	Israeli AF 131 Sqn, Nevatim
	435	Lockheed C-130H Karnaf	Israeli AF 131 Sqn, Nevatim
	436	Lockheed KC-130H Karnaf	Israeli AF 131 Sqn, Nevatim
	522	Lockheed KC-130H Karnaf	Israeli AF 131 Sqn, Nevatim
	545	Lockheed KC-130H Karnaf	Israeli AF 131 Sqn, Nevatim
	661	Lockheed C-130J-30 Shimshon	Israeli AF 103 Sqn, Nevatim
	662	Lockheed C-130J-30 Shimshon	Israeli AF 103 Sqn, Nevatim
	663	Lockheed C-130J-30 Shimshon	Israeli AF 103 Sqn, Nevatim
	664	Lockheed C-130J-30 Shimshon	(on order)
	665	Lockheed C-130J-30 Shimshon	Israeli AF 103 Sqn, Nevatim
	667	Lockheed C-130J-30 Shimshon	Israeli AF 103 Sqn, Nevatim
	668	Lockheed C-130J-30 Shimshon	Israeli AF 103 Sqn, Nevatim
	669	Lockheed C-130J-30 Shimshon	Israeli AF 103 Sqn, Nevatim

ITALY
Aeronautica Militare Italiana (AMI), Aviazione dell'Esercito, Guardia di Finanza (GdiF) & Marina Militare Italiana (MMI)

	MMX602	Eurofighter F-2000A Typhoon $	Preserved at Torino/Caselle
	MMX614	Eurofighter TF-2000A Typhoon	Alenia, Torino/Caselle
	CPX616	Aermacchi M-346 Master	Aermacchi, Venegono
	CPX619	Aermacchi M-345HET [1]	Withdrawn from use, October 2018

Serial	Type (code/other identity)	Owner/operator, location or fate	Notes
CPX622	Aermacchi M-346FA	Aermacchi, Venegono	
CPX624	Aermacchi M-345HET	Aermacchi, Venegono	
MM7004	Panavia A-200C Tornado (IDS (MLU)) [6-55]	AMI GEA 6° Stormo, Ghedi	
MM7006	Panavia A-200C Tornado (IDS (MLU)) [6-31] $	AMI GEA 6° Stormo, Ghedi	
MM7007	Panavia A-200A Tornado (IDS) [6-01] $	AMI GEA 6° Stormo, Ghedi	
MM7008	Panavia A-200C Tornado (IDS (MLU)) [50-53]	AMI GEA 6° Stormo, Ghedi	
MM7013	Panavia A-200C Tornado (IDS (MLU)) [6-75]	AMI GEA 6° Stormo, Ghedi	
MM7014	Panavia A-200C Tornado (IDS (MLU)) [6-13]	AMI GEA 6° Stormo, Ghedi	
MM7015	Panavia A-200C Tornado (IDS (MLU)) [6-32]	AMI GEA 6° Stormo, Ghedi	
MM7019	Panavia EA-200B Tornado (ECR) [6-02]	AMI GEA 6° Stormo, Ghedi	
MM7020	Panavia EA-200C Tornado (ECR (MLU)) [6-77]	AMI GEA 6° Stormo, Ghedi	
MM7021	Panavia EA-200B Tornado (ECR) [6-20]	AMI GEA 6° Stormo, Ghedi	
MM7023	Panavia A-200A Tornado (IDS) [6-63]	AMI GEA 6° Stormo, Ghedi	
MM7024	Panavia A-200C Tornado (IDS (MLU)) [6-50]	AMI GEA 6° Stormo, Ghedi	
MM7025	Panavia A-200A Tornado (IDS) [6-05]	AMI GEA 6° Stormo, Ghedi	
MM7026	Panavia A-200C Tornado (IDS (MLU)) [6-35]	AMI GEA 6° Stormo, Ghedi	
MM7029	Panavia A-200A Tornado (IDS) [6-22]	AMI GEA 6° Stormo, Ghedi	
CSX7030	Panavia EA-200C Tornado (ECR (MLU))	Leonardo, Turin	
MM7034	Panavia EA-200B Tornado (ECR)	AMI, stored Gioia del Colle	
MM7035	Panavia A-200C Tornado (IDS (MLU)) [6-27]	AMI GEA 6° Stormo, Ghedi	
MM7036	Panavia EA-200B Tornado (ECR) [6-06]	AMI GEA 6° Stormo, Ghedi	
MM7037	Panavia A-200A Tornado (IDS) [6-16]	AMI GEA 6° Stormo, Ghedi	
MM7038	Panavia A-200C Tornado (IDS (MLU)) [6-37]	AMI GEA 6° Stormo, Ghedi	
MM7039	Panavia EA-200C Tornado (ECR (MLU)) [6-33]	AMI GEA 6° Stormo, Ghedi	
MM7040	Panavia A-200A Tornado (IDS) [6-21]	AMI GEA 6° Stormo, Ghedi	
CSX7041	Panavia A-200C Tornado (IDS (MLU)) [RS-01] $	AMI RSV, Pratica di Mare	
MM7043	Panavia A-200A Tornado (IDS) [6-25]	AMI GEA 6° Stormo, Ghedi	
MM7044	Panavia A-200C Tornado (IDS (MLU))	Leonardo, Turin	
MM7047	Panavia EA-200C Tornado (ECR (MLU)) [6-61]	AMI GEA 6° Stormo, Ghedi	
MM7051	Panavia EA-200B Tornado (ECR) [6-72]	AMI GEA 6° Stormo, Ghedi	
MM7052	Panavia EA-200C Tornado (ECR (MLU)) [6-64]	AMI GEA 6° Stormo, Ghedi	
MM7053	Panavia EA-200B Tornado (ECR (MLU)) [6-101]	AMI GEA 6° Stormo, Ghedi	
MM7054	Panavia EA-200C Tornado (ECR (MLU)) [6-100] $	AMI GEA 6° Stormo, Ghedi	
MM7055	Panavia A-200A Tornado (ECR (MLU)) [6-65]	AMI GEA 6° Stormo, Ghedi	
MM7056	Panavia A-200A Tornado (IDS)	AMI GEA 6° Stormo, Ghedi	
MM7057	Panavia A-200A Tornado (IDS) [6-04]	AMI GEA 6° Stormo, Ghedi	
MM7058	Panavia A-200C Tornado (IDS (MLU)) [6-11]	AMI GEA 6° Stormo, Ghedi	
MM7059	Panavia A-200A Tornado (IDS) [6-66]	AMI GEA 6° Stormo, Ghedi	
MM7062	Panavia EA-200C Tornado (ECR (MLU)) [6-74]	AMI GEA 6° Stormo, Ghedi	
MM7063	Panavia A-200C Tornado (IDS (MLU)) [6-26]	AMI GEA 6° Stormo, Ghedi	
MM7066	Panavia A-200A Tornado (ECR (MLU))	AMI GEA 6° Stormo, Ghedi	
MM7067	Panavia EA-200C Tornado (ECR (MLU)) [6-41]	AMI GEA 6° Stormo, Ghedi	
MM7068	Panavia EA-200B Tornado (ECR) [6-67]	AMI GEA 6° Stormo, Ghedi	
MM7070	Panavia EA-200C Tornado (ECR (MLU)) [6-71]	AMI GEA 6° Stormo, Ghedi	
MM7071	Panavia A-200C Tornado (IDS (MLU)) [6-12]	AMI GEA 6° Stormo, Ghedi	
MM7072	Panavia A-200C Tornado (IDS (MLU)) [6-30]	AMI GEA 6° Stormo, Ghedi	
MM7073	Panavia EA-200B Tornado (ECR) [6-34]	AMI GEA 6° Stormo, Ghedi	
MM7075	Panavia A-200A Tornado (IDS) [6-07]	AMI GEA 6° Stormo, Ghedi	
CMX7079	Panavia EA-200B Tornado (ECR)	Alenia, Torino/Caselle	
MM7081	Panavia EA-200C Tornado (ECR (MLU)) [6-57]	AMI GEA 6° Stormo, Ghedi	
MM7082	Panavia EA-200C Tornado (ECR (MLU)) [6-62]	AMI GEA 6° Stormo, Ghedi	
MM7083	Panavia A-200A Tornado (IDS)	AMI GEA 6° Stormo, Ghedi	
MM7084	Panavia EA-200C Tornado (ECR (MLU)) [6-03]	AMI GEA 6° Stormo, Ghedi	
CMX7085	Panavia A-200A Tornado (IDS) [36-50]	Alenia, Torino/Caselle	
MM7086	Panavia A-200A Tornado (IDS) [6-60]	AMI GEA 6° Stormo, Ghedi	
MM7088	Panavia A-200A Tornado (IDS) [6-10]	AMI GEA 6° Stormo, Ghedi	
MM7114	Aeritalia-EMB A-11B (AMX-ACOL) [51-27]	AMI GEA 51° Stormo, Istrana	
MM7126	Aeritalia-EMB A-11B (AMX-ACOL) [51-61]	AMI GEA 51° Stormo, Istrana	
MM7129	Aeritalia-EMB A-11B (AMX-ACOL) [32-15]	AMI, stored Amendola	
MM7148	Aeritalia-EMB A-11B (AMX-ACOL)	AMI, stored Amendola	
MM7149	Aeritalia-EMB A-11B (AMX-ACOL) [51-26]	AMI GEA 51° Stormo, Istrana	
MM7151	Aeritalia-EMB A-11B (AMX-ACOL) [51-51]	AMI GEA 51° Stormo, Istrana	

Notes	Serial	Type (code/other identity)	Owner/operator, location or fate
	MM7159	Aeritalia-EMB A-11A (AMX) [51-10] $	*Withdrawn from use*
	MM7160	Aeritalia-EMB A-11B (AMX-ACOL)	AMI, stored Amendola
	MM7161	Aeritalia-EMB A-11B (AMX-ACOL) [51-31]	AMI GEA 51° Stormo, Istrana
	MM7162	Aeritalia-EMB A-11B (AMX-ACOL) [51-33]	AMI GEA 51° Stormo, Istrana
	MM7163	Aeritalia-EMB A-11B (AMX-ACOL) [51-72]	AMI GEA 51° Stormo, Istrana
	MM7164	Aeritalia-EMB A-11B (AMX-ACOL)	AMI
	MM7165	Aeritalia-EMB A-11B (AMX-ACOL) [32-16]	AMI, stored Amendola
	MM7166	Aeritalia-EMB A-11B (AMX-ACOL) [51-32]	AMI GEA 51° Stormo, Istrana
	MM7167	Aeritalia-EMB A-11B (AMX-ACOL) [51-56]	AMI GEA 51° Stormo, Istrana
	MM7168	Aeritalia-EMB A-11B (AMX-ACOL) [51-55]	AMI GEA 51° Stormo, Istrana
	MM7169	Aeritalia-EMB A-11B (AMX-ACOL) [51-66]	AMI GEA 51° Stormo, Istrana
	MM7170	Aeritalia-EMB A-11B (AMX-ACOL) [51-30]	AMI GEA 51° Stormo, Istrana
	MM7171	Aeritalia-EMB A-11B (AMX-ACOL) [51-52]	AMI GEA 51° Stormo, Istrana
	MM7172	Aeritalia-EMB A-11B (AMX-ACOL) [51-67]	AMI, stored Istrana
	MM7173	Aeritalia-EMB A-11B (AMX-ACOL) [51-63]	AMI, stored Istrana
	MM7174	Aeritalia-EMB A-11B (AMX-ACOL) [51-60]	AMI GEA 51° Stormo, Istrana
	MM7175	Aeritalia-EMB A-11B (AMX-ACOL) [51-45]	AMI GEA 51° Stormo, Istrana
	MM7176	Aeritalia-EMB A-11B (AMX-ACOL)	AMI GEA 51° Stormo, Istrana
	MM7177	Aeritalia-EMB A-11B (AMX-ACOL) [51-42]	AMI GEA 51° Stormo, Istrana
	MM7178	Aeritalia-EMB A-11B (AMX-ACOL) [51-43]	AMI GEA 51° Stormo, Istrana
	MM7179	Aeritalia-EMB A-11B (AMX-ACOL) [51-64]	AMI GEA 51° Stormo, Istrana
	MM7180	Aeritalia-EMB A-11B (AMX-ACOL) [51-53]	AMI GEA 51° Stormo, Istrana
	MM7182	Aeritalia-EMB A-11B (AMX-ACOL) [51-62]	AMI GEA 51° Stormo, Istrana
	MM7183	Aeritalia-EMB A-11B (AMX-ACOL) [51-41]	AMI GEA 51° Stormo, Istrana
	MM7184	Aeritalia-EMB A-11B (AMX-ACOL) [51-65]	AMI GEA 51° Stormo, Istrana
	MM7185	Aeritalia-EMB A-11B (AMX-ACOL) [51-36]	AMI GEA 51° Stormo, Istrana
	MM7186	Aeritalia-EMB A-11B (AMX-ACOL) [51-50]	AMI GEA 51° Stormo, Istrana
	MM7189	Aeritalia-EMB A-11B (AMX-ACOL) [51-71]	AMI GEA 51° Stormo, Istrana
	MM7190	Aeritalia-EMB A-11B (AMX-ACOL) [51-57]	AMI GEA 51° Stormo, Istrana
	MM7191	Aeritalia-EMB A-11B (AMX-ACOL) [51-34]	AMI GEA 51° Stormo, Istrana
	MM7192	Aeritalia-EMB A-11B (AMX-ACOL) [51-70]	AMI GEA 51° Stormo, Istrana
	MM7194	Aeritalia-EMB A-11B (AMX-ACOL) [51-67]	AMI GEA 51° Stormo, Istrana
	MM7196	Aeritalia-EMB A-11B (AMX-ACOL) [51-35]	AMI GEA 51° Stormo, Istrana
	MM7197	Aeritalia-EMB A-11B (AMX-ACOL) [51-46]	AMI GEA 51° Stormo, Istrana
	MM7198	Aeritalia-EMB A-11B (AMX-ACOL) [51-44] $	AMI GEA 51° Stormo, Istrana
	MM7199	McDonnell Douglas AV-8B Harrier II+ [1-03]	MMI Gruppo Aerei Imbarcati, Taranto/Grottaglie
	MM7200	McDonnell Douglas AV-8B Harrier II+ [1-04]	MMI Gruppo Aerei Imbarcati, Taranto/Grottaglie
	MM7201	McDonnell Douglas AV-8B Harrier II+ [1-05]	MMI Gruppo Aerei Imbarcati, Taranto/Grottaglie
	MM7212	McDonnell Douglas AV-8B Harrier II+ [1-06]	MMI Gruppo Aerei Imbarcati, Taranto/Grottaglie
	MM7213	McDonnell Douglas AV-8B Harrier II+ [1-07]	MMI Gruppo Aerei Imbarcati, Taranto/Grottaglie
	MM7214	McDonnell Douglas AV-8B Harrier II+ [1-08]	MMI Gruppo Aerei Imbarcati, Taranto/Grottaglie
	MM7215	McDonnell Douglas AV-8B Harrier II+ [1-09]	MMI Gruppo Aerei Imbarcati, Taranto/Grottaglie
	MM7217	McDonnell Douglas AV-8B Harrier II+ [1-11]	MMI Gruppo Aerei Imbarcati, Taranto/Grottaglie
	MM7218	McDonnell Douglas AV-8B Harrier II+ [1-12]	MMI Gruppo Aerei Imbarcati, Taranto/Grottaglie
	MM7219	McDonnell Douglas AV-8B Harrier II+ [1-13] $	MMI Gruppo Aerei Imbarcati, Taranto/Grottaglie
	MM7220	McDonnell Douglas AV-8B Harrier II+ [1-14]	MMI Gruppo Aerei Imbarcati, Taranto/Grottaglie
	MM7222	McDonnell Douglas AV-8B Harrier II+ [1-16]	MMI Gruppo Aerei Imbarcati, Taranto/Grottaglie
	MM7223	McDonnell Douglas AV-8B Harrier II+ [1-18]	MMI Gruppo Aerei Imbarcati, Taranto/Grottaglie
	MM7224	McDonnell Douglas AV-8B Harrier II+ [1-19] $	MMI Gruppo Aerei Imbarcati, Taranto/Grottaglie
	MM7235	Eurofighter F-2000A Typhoon [4-13]	AMI 904° GEA, Grosseto
	MM7270	Eurofighter F-2000A Typhoon [4-1]	AMI 904° GEA, Grosseto
	MM7271	Eurofighter F-2000A Typhoon [4-15]	AMI 904° GEA, Grosseto
	MM7272	Eurofighter F-2000A Typhoon [4-18]	AMI 904° GEA, Grosseto
	MM7273	Eurofighter F-2000A Typhoon [4-10]	AMI 904° GEA, Grosseto
	MM7274	Eurofighter F-2000A Typhoon [4-4]	AMI 904° GEA, Grosseto
	MM7275	Eurofighter F-2000A Typhoon	AMI RSV, Pratica di Mare
	MM7276	Eurofighter F-2000A Typhoon [36-05]	AMI 936° GEA, Gioia del Colle
	MM7277	Eurofighter F-2000A Typhoon [36-14]	AMI 936° GEA, Gioia del Colle
	MM7279	Eurofighter F-2000A Typhoon [4-20]	AMI 904° GEA, Grosseto
	MM7280	Eurofighter F-2000A Typhoon [36-30]	AMI 936° GEA, Gioia del Colle
	MM7281	Eurofighter F-2000A Typhoon [36-03]	AMI 936° GEA, Gioia del Colle
	MM7282	Eurofighter F-2000A Typhoon [36-15]	AMI 936° GEA, Gioia del Colle

Serial	Type (code/other identity)	Owner/operator, location or fate	Notes
MM7284	Eurofighter F-2000A Typhoon [4-12]	AMI 904° GEA, Grosseto	
MM7285	Eurofighter F-2000A Typhoon	AMI 904° GEA, Grosseto	
MM7286	Eurofighter F-2000A Typhoon [36-02]	AMI 936° GEA, Gioia del Colle	
MM7287	Eurofighter F-2000A Typhoon [4-3]	AMI 904° GEA, Grosseto	
MM7288	Eurofighter F-2000A Typhoon [36-42]	AMI 936° GEA, Gioia del Colle	
MM7289	Eurofighter F-2000A Typhoon [4-5]	AMI 904° GEA, Grosseto	
MM7290	Eurofighter F-2000A Typhoon [4-7]	AMI 904° GEA, Grosseto	
MM7291	Eurofighter F-2000A Typhoon [4-11]	AMI 904° GEA, Grosseto	
MM7292	Eurofighter F-2000A Typhoon [36-21]	AMI 936° GEA, Gioia del Colle	
MM7293	Eurofighter F-2000A Typhoon [37-22]	AMI 18° Gruppo/37° Stormo, Trapani/Birgi	
MM7294	Eurofighter F-2000A Typhoon [37-11]	AMI 18° Gruppo/37° Stormo, Trapani/Birgi	
MM7295	Eurofighter F-2000A Typhoon [4-51]	AMI 904° GEA, Grosseto	
MM7296	Eurofighter F-2000A Typhoon [36-22]	AMI 936° GEA, Gioia del Colle	
MM7297	Eurofighter F-2000A Typhoon [36-23] $	AMI 936° GEA, Gioia del Colle	
MM7298	Eurofighter F-2000A Typhoon [36-24]	AMI 936° GEA, Gioia del Colle	
MM7299	Eurofighter F-2000A Typhoon [4-41]	AMI 904° GEA, Grosseto	
MM7300	Eurofighter F-2000A Typhoon [4-44]	AMI 904° GEA, Grosseto	
MM7301	Eurofighter F-2000A Typhoon	AMI	
MM7302	Eurofighter F-2000A Typhoon [36-25]	AMI 936° GEA, Gioia del Colle	
MM7303	Eurofighter F-2000A Typhoon [4-2]	AMI 904° GEA, Grosseto	
MM7304	Eurofighter F-2000A Typhoon [4-21]	AMI 904° GEA, Grosseto	
CSX7305	Eurofighter F-2000A Typhoon	AMI RSV, Pratica di Mare	
MM7306	Eurofighter F-2000A Typhoon [4-50]	AMI 904° GEA, Grosseto	
MM7307	Eurofighter F-2000A Typhoon [37-01]	AMI 18° Gruppo/37° Stormo, Trapani/Birgi	
MM7308	Eurofighter F-2000A Typhoon [36-31]	AMI 936° GEA, Gioia del Colle	
MM7309	Eurofighter F-2000A Typhoon [4-22]	AMI 904° GEA, Grosseto	
MM7310	Eurofighter F-2000A Typhoon [36-32]	AMI 936° GEA, Gioia del Colle	
MM7311	Eurofighter F-2000A Typhoon [37-10]	AMI 18° Gruppo/37° Stormo, Trapani/Birgi	
MM7312	Eurofighter F-2000A Typhoon [36-34]	AMI 936° GEA, Gioia del Colle	
MM7313	Eurofighter F-2000A Typhoon [36-35]	AMI 936° GEA, Gioia del Colle	
MM7314	Eurofighter F-2000A Typhoon [36-37]	AMI 936° GEA, Gioia del Colle	
MM7315	Eurofighter F-2000A Typhoon [36-46]	AMI 936° GEA, Gioia del Colle	
MM7316	Eurofighter F-2000A Typhoon [37-07]	AMI 18° Gruppo/37° Stormo, Trapani/Birgi	
MM7317	Eurofighter F-2000A Typhoon [4-43]	AMI 904° GEA, Grosseto	
MM7318	Eurofighter F-2000A Typhoon [36-12] $	AMI 936° GEA, Gioia del Colle	
MM7319	Eurofighter F-2000A Typhoon [36-45]	AMI 936° GEA, Gioia del Colle	
MM7320	Eurofighter F-2000A Typhoon [4-45]	AMI 904° GEA, Grosseto	
MM7321	Eurofighter F-2000A Typhoon [37-12]	AMI 18° Gruppo/37° Stormo, Trapani/Birgi	
MM7322	Eurofighter F-2000A Typhoon [36-40] $	AMI 936° GEA, Gioia del Colle	
MM7323	Eurofighter F-2000A Typhoon [4-6]	AMI 904° GEA, Grosseto	
MM7324	Eurofighter F-2000A Typhoon [36-41]	AMI 936° GEA, Gioia del Colle	
MM7325	Eurofighter F-2000A Typhoon [36-44]	AMI 936° GEA, Gioia del Colle	
MM7326	Eurofighter F-2000A Typhoon [4-46] $	AMI 904° GEA, Grosseto	
MM7327	Eurofighter F-2000A Typhoon [4-47]	AMI 904° GEA, Grosseto	
MM7328	Eurofighter F-2000A Typhoon [37-14]	AMI 18° Gruppo/37° Stormo, Trapani/Birgi	
MM7329	Eurofighter F-2000A Typhoon [37-15]	AMI 18° Gruppo/37° Stormo, Trapani/Birgi	
MM7330	Eurofighter F-2000A Typhoon [37-21]	AMI 18° Gruppo/37° Stormo, Trapani/Birgi	
MM7331	Eurofighter F-2000A Typhoon [37-16]	AMI 18° Gruppo/37° Stormo, Trapani/Birgi	
MM7332	Lockheed Martin F-35A Lightning II [32-01]	AMI 62nd FS/56th FW, Luke AFB, AZ, USA	
MM7333	Lockheed Martin F-35A Lightning II [32-02]	AMI 62nd FS/56th FW, Luke AFB, AZ, USA	
MM7334	Lockheed Martin F-35A Lightning II [32-03]	AMI 13° Gruppo/32° Stormo, Cameri	
MM7335	Lockheed Martin F-35A Lightning II [32-04]	AMI 13° Gruppo/32° Stormo, Cameri	
MM7336	Lockheed Martin F-35A Lightning II [32-05]	AMI 13° Gruppo/32° Stormo, Cameri	
MM7337	Lockheed Martin F-35A Lightning II [32-13]	AMI 13° Gruppo/32° Stormo, Cameri	
MM7338	Eurofighter F-2000A Typhoon [4-60]	AMI 904° GEA, Grosseto	
MM7339	Eurofighter F-2000A Typhoon [4-61]	AMI 904° GEA, Grosseto	
MM7340	Eurofighter F-2000A Typhoon	AMI	
MM7341	Eurofighter F-2000A Typhoon [36-10] $	AMI 936° GEA, Gioia del Colle	
MM7342	Eurofighter F-2000A Typhoon [36-51]	AMI 936° GEA, Gioia del Colle	
MM7343	Eurofighter F-2000A Typhoon [36-52]	AMI 936° GEA, Gioia del Colle	
CSX7344	Eurofighter F-2000A Typhoon	AMI	
MM7345	Eurofighter F-2000A Typhoon [37-45]	AMI 18° Gruppo/37° Stormo, Trapani/Birgi	

Notes	Serial	Type (code/other identity)	Owner/operator, location or fate
	MM7346	Eurofighter F-2000A Typhoon [37-37]	AMI 18° Gruppo/37° Stormo, Trapani/Birgi
	MM7347	Eurofighter F-2000A Typhoon [36-53]	AMI 936° GEA, Gioia del Colle
	MM7348	Eurofighter F-2000A Typhoon [37-24]	AMI 18° Gruppo/37° Stormo, Trapani/Birgi
	MM7349	Eurofighter F-2000A Typhoon [36-54]	AMI 936° GEA, Gioia del Colle
	MM7350	Eurofighter F-2000A Typhoon [36-55] $	AMI 936° GEA, Gioia del Colle
	MM7351	Eurofighter F-2000A Typhoon [4-9]	AMI 904° GEA, Grosseto
	MM7352	Eurofighter F-2000A Typhoon	AMI (on order)
	MM7353	Eurofighter F-2000A Typhoon	AMI (on order)
	MM7354	Eurofighter F-2000A Typhoon	AMI (on order)
	MM7355	Eurofighter F-2000A Typhoon	AMI (on order)
	MM7356	Eurofighter F-2000A Typhoon	AMI (on order)
	MM7357	Lockheed Martin F-35A Lightning II [32-07] $	AMI 13° Gruppo/32° Stormo, Cameri
	MM7358	Lockheed Martin F-35A Lightning II [32-08]	AMI 13° Gruppo/32° Stormo, Cameri
	MM7359	Lockheed Martin F-35A Lightning II [32-09]	AMI 13° Gruppo/32° Stormo, Cameri
	MM7360	Lockheed Martin F-35A Lightning II [32-10]	AMI 13° Gruppo/32° Stormo, Cameri
	MM7361	Lockheed Martin F-35A Lightning II [32-11]	MMI FACO, Cameri
	MM7451	Lockheed Martin F-35B Lightning II [4-01]	MMI FACO, Cameri
	MM7452	Lockheed Martin F-35B Lightning II	MMI FACO, Cameri
	MM54456	Aermacchi T-339A (MB339A) [61-10]	AMI, stored Lecce
	MM54457	Aermacchi T-339A (MB339A(MLU)) [61-11]	AMI 61° Stormo, Lecce
	MM54458	Aermacchi T-339A (MB339A(MLU)) [61-121]	AMI 61° Stormo, Lecce
	MM54465	Aermacchi T-339A (MB339A(MLU)) [61-21]	AMI 61° Stormo, Lecce
	MM54468	Aermacchi T-339A (MB339A(MLU)) [61-24]	AMI 61° Stormo, Lecce
	MM54473	Aermacchi AT-339A (MB339PAN)	AMI *Frecce Tricolori* (313° Gruppo), Rivolto
	MM54477	Aermacchi AT-339A (MB339PAN)	AMI *Frecce Tricolori* (313° Gruppo), Rivolto
	MM54479	Aermacchi AT-339A (MB339PAN)	AMI 632ª SC/32° Stormo, Amendola
	MM54480	Aermacchi AT-339A (MB339PAN)	AMI *Frecce Tricolori* (313° Gruppo), Rivolto
	MM54482	Aermacchi AT-339A (MB339PAN)	AMI *Frecce Tricolori* (313° Gruppo), Rivolto
	MM54487	Aermacchi AT-339A (MB339PAN)	AMI *Frecce Tricolori* (313° Gruppo), Rivolto
	MM54488	Aermacchi T-339A (MB339A(MLU)) [61-32]	AMI 61° Stormo, Lecce
	MM54492	Aermacchi T-339A (MB339A(MLU)) [61-36]	AMI 61° Stormo, Lecce
	MM54493	Aermacchi T-339A (MB339A(MLU)) [61-37]	AMI 61° Stormo, Lecce
	MM54496	Aermacchi T-339A (MB339A(MLU)) [61-42]	AMI 61° Stormo, Lecce
	MM54499	Aermacchi T-339A (MB339A(MLU)) [61-45]	AMI 61° Stormo, Lecce
	MM54500	Aermacchi AT-339A (MB339PAN)	AMI *Frecce Tricolori* (313° Gruppo), Rivolto
	MM54504	Aermacchi T-339A (MB339A(MLU)) [61-52]	AMI 61° Stormo, Lecce
	MM54505	Aermacchi AT-339A (MB339PAN) [10]	AMI *Frecce Tricolori* (313° Gruppo), Rivolto
	MM54507	Aermacchi T-339A (MB339A(MLU)) [61-55]	AMI 61° Stormo, Lecce
	MM54509	Aermacchi T-339A (MB339A(MLU)) [61-57]	AMI 61° Stormo, Lecce
	MM54510	Aermacchi AT-339A (MB339PAN)	AMI *Frecce Tricolori* (313° Gruppo), Rivolto
	MM54511	Aermacchi T-339A (MB339A(MLU)) [61-61]	AMI 61° Stormo, Lecce
	MM54512	Aermacchi T-339A (MB339A(MLU)) [61-62]	AMI 61° Stormo, Lecce
	MM54514	Aermacchi AT-339A (MB339PAN) [8]	AMI *Frecce Tricolori* (313° Gruppo), Rivolto
	MM54515	Aermacchi T-339A (MB339A(MLU)) [61-65]	AMI 61° Stormo, Lecce
	MM54516	Aermacchi T-339A (MB339A(MLU)) [61-66]	AMI 61° Stormo, Lecce
	MM54517	Aermacchi AT-339A (MB339PAN) [2]	AMI *Frecce Tricolori* (313° Gruppo), Rivolto
	MM54518	Aermacchi AT-339A (MB339PAN) [5]	AMI *Frecce Tricolori* (313° Gruppo), Rivolto
	MM54533	Aermacchi T-339A (MB339A(MLU)) [61-72]	AMI 61° Stormo, Lecce
	MM54534	Aermacchi AT-339A (MB339PAN) [0]	AMI *Frecce Tricolori* (313° Gruppo), Rivolto
	MM54535	Aermacchi T-339A (MB339A(MLU)) [61-74]	AMI 61° Stormo, Lecce
	MM54538	Aermacchi AT-339A (MB339PAN) [6]	AMI *Frecce Tricolori* (313° Gruppo), Rivolto
	MM54539	Aermacchi AT-339A (MB339PAN) [9]	AMI *Frecce Tricolori* (313° Gruppo), Rivolto
	MM54547	Aermacchi AT-339A (MB339PAN)	AMI *Frecce Tricolori* (313° Gruppo), Rivolto
	MM54548	Aermacchi T-339A (MB339A(MLU)) [61-106]	AMI 61° Stormo, Lecce
	MM54549	Aermacchi T-339A (MB339A(MLU)) [61-107]	AMI 61° Stormo, Lecce
	MM54551	Aermacchi AT-339A (MB339PAN) [12]	AMI *Frecce Tricolori* (313° Gruppo), Rivolto
	MM55002	Panavia TA-200A Tornado (IDS Trainer) [6-52] $	AMI GEA 6° Stormo, Ghedi
	MM55003	Panavia TA-200A Tornado (IDS Trainer)	AMI
	MM55004	Panavia TA-200A Tornado (IDS Trainer) [6-53]	AMI GEA 6° Stormo, Ghedi
	MM55006	Panavia TA-200C Tornado (IDS Trainer (MLU)) [6-15]	AMI GEA 6° Stormo, Ghedi
	MM55007	Panavia TA-200A Tornado (IDS Trainer) [6-51]	AMI GEA 6° Stormo, Ghedi
	MM55008	Panavia TA-200A Tornado (IDS Trainer) [6-45]	AMI GEA 6° Stormo, Ghedi

Serial	Type (code/other identity)	Owner/operator, location or fate	Notes
MM55009	Panavia TA-200A Tornado (IDS Trainer) [6-44]	AMI GEA 6° Stormo, Ghedi	
MM55010	Panavia TA-200A Tornado (IDS Trainer) [6-42]	AMI GEA 6° Stormo, Ghedi	
MM55029	Aeritalia-EMB TA-11A (AMX-T) [32-50] $]	*Withdrawn from use*	
MM55030	Aeritalia-EMB TA-11A (AMX-T) [32-41]	*Withdrawn from use*	
MM55032	McDonnell Douglas TAV-8B Harrier II+ [1-01]	MMI Gruppo Aerei Imbarcarti, Taranto/Grottaglie	
MM55033	McDonnell Douglas TAV-8B Harrier II+ [1-02]	MMI, stored Taranto/Grottaglie	
MM55034	Aeritalia-EMB TA-11B (AMX-T-ACOL) [RS-20]	AMI RSV, Pratica di Mare	
MM55036	Aeritalia-EMB TA-11B (AMX-T-ACOL) [32-51]	AMI, stored Amendola	
MM55037	Aeritalia-EMB TA-11B (AMX-T-ACOL) [51-80]	AMI GEA 51° Stormo, Istrana	
MM55042	Aeritalia-EMB TA-11B (AMX-T-ACOL) [32-56]	AMI, stored Amendola	
MM55043	Aeritalia-EMB TA-11B (AMX-T-ACOL) [51-81]	AMI GEA 51° Stormo, Istrana	
MM55044	Aeritalia-EMB TA-11B (AMX-T-ACOL) [51-82]	AMI GEA 51° Stormo, Istrana	
MM55046	Aeritalia-EMB TA-11B (AMX-T-ACOL) [32-47]	AMI, stored Amendola	
MM55047	Aeritalia-EMB TA-11B (AMX-T-ACOL) [32-53]	AMI, stored Amendola	
MM55049	Aeritalia-EMB TA-11B (AMX-T-ACOL) [51-83]	AMI GEA 51° Stormo, Istrana	
MM55051	Aeritalia-EMB TA-11B (AMX-T-ACOL) [51-84]	AMI GEA 51° Stormo, Istrana	
MM55052	Aermacchi AT-339A (MB339PAN) [11	AMI *Frecce Tricolori* (313° Gruppo), Rivolto	
MM55053	Aermacchi AT-339A (MB339PAN) [4]	AMI *Frecce Tricolori* (313° Gruppo), Rivolto	
MM55054	Aermacchi AT-339A (MB339PAN)	AMI *Frecce Tricolori* (313° Gruppo), Rivolto	
MM55055	Aermacchi AT-339A (MB339PAN)	AMI *Frecce Tricolori* (313° Gruppo), Rivolto	
MM55058	Aermacchi AT-339A (MB339PAN) [3]	AMI *Frecce Tricolori* (313° Gruppo), Rivolto	
MM55059	Aermacchi AT-339A (MB339PAN)	AMI *Frecce Tricolori* (313° Gruppo), Rivolto	
MM55062	Aermacchi FT-339 (MB339CD) [61-126]	AMI 61° Stormo, Lecce	
MM55063	Aermacchi FT-339 (MB339CD) [61-127]	AMI 61° Stormo, Lecce	
MM55064	Aermacchi FT-339 (MB339CD) [61-130]	AMI 61° Stormo, Lecce	
MM55065	Aermacchi FT-339 (MB339CD) [61-131]	AMI 61° Stormo, Lecce	
MM55066	Aermacchi FT-339 (MB339CD) [61-132]	AMI 632ª SC/32° Stormo, Amendola	
MM55067	Aermacchi FT-339 (MB339CD) [61-133]	AMI 61° Stormo, Lecce	
MM55068	Aermacchi FT-339 (MB339CD) [RS-33]	AMI RSV, Pratica di Mare	
MM55069	Aermacchi FT-339 (MB339CD) [61-135]	AMI 61° Stormo, Lecce	
MM55070	Aermacchi FT-339 (MB339CD) [61-136]	AMI 61° Stormo, Lecce	
MM55072	Aermacchi FT-339 (MB339CD) [61-140]	AMI 61° Stormo, Lecce	
MM55073	Aermacchi FT-339 (MB339CD) [61-141]	AMI 61° Stormo, Lecce	
MM55074	Aermacchi FT-339 (MB339CD) [36-06]	AMI 12° Gruppo/36° Stormo, Gioia del Colle	
MM55075	Aermacchi FT-339 (MB339CD) [61-143]	AMI 61° Stormo, Lecce	
MM55076	Aermacchi FT-339 (MB339CD) [61-144]	AMI 61° Stormo, Lecce	
MM55077	Aermacchi FT-339 (MB339CD) [61-145]	AMI 61° Stormo, Lecce	
MM55078	Aermacchi FT-339 (MB339CD) [61-146]	AMI 61° Stormo, Lecce	
MM55079	Aermacchi FT-339 (MB339CD) [61-147]	AMI 61° Stormo, Lecce	
MM55080	Aermacchi FT-339 (MB339CD) [61-150]	AMI 61° Stormo, Lecce	
MM55081	Aermacchi FT-339 (MB339CD) [61-151]	AMI 61° Stormo, Lecce	
MM55082	Aermacchi FT-339 (MB339CD) [61-152]	AMI 61° Stormo, Lecce	
MM55084	Aermacchi FT-339 (MB339CD) [61-154]	AMI 61° Stormo, Lecce	
MM55085	Aermacchi FT-339 (MB339CD) [61-155]	AMI 61° Stormo, Lecce	
MM55086	Aermacchi FT-339 (MB339CD) [61-156]	AMI 61° Stormo, Lecce	
MM55087	Aermacchi FT-339 (MB339CD) [61-167]	AMI 61° Stormo, Lecce	
MM55088	Aermacchi FT-339 (MB339CD) [61-160]	AMI 61° Stormo, Lecce	
MM55089	Aermacchi FT-339 (MB339CD) [32-161]	AMI 632ª SC/32° Stormo, Amendola	
MM55090	Aermacchi FT-339 (MB339CD) [61-162]	AMI 61° Stormo, Lecce	
MM55091	Aermacchi FT-339 (MB339CD) [RS-32]	AMI RSV, Pratica di Mare	
MM55092	Eurofighter TF-2000A Typhoon [36-62]	AMI 936° GEA, Gioia del Colle	
MM55093	Eurofighter TF-2000A Typhoon [4-31]	AMI 904° GEA, Grosseto	
MM55094	Eurofighter TF-2000A Typhoon [36-60]	AMI 936° GEA, Gioia del Colle	
MM55095	Eurofighter TF-2000A Typhoon [36-63]	AMI 936° GEA, Gioia del Colle	
MM55096	Eurofighter TF-2000A Typhoon [4-30]	AMI 904° GEA, Grosseto	
MM55097	Eurofighter TF-2000A Typhoon [4-27]	AMI 904° GEA, Grosseto	
MM55128	Eurofighter TF-2000A Typhoon [4-26]	AMI 904° GEA, Grosseto	
MM55129	Eurofighter TF-2000A Typhoon [4-32]	AMI 904° GEA, Grosseto	
MM55130	Eurofighter TF-2000A Typhoon [4-33]	AMI 904° GEA, Grosseto	
MM55131	Eurofighter TF-2000A Typhoon [4-34]	AMI 904° GEA, Grosseto	
MM55132	Eurofighter TF-2000A Typhoon [4-35]	AMI 904° GEA, Grosseto	
MM55133	Eurofighter TF-2000A Typhoon [4-36]	Leonardo, Turin	

Notes	Serial	Type (code/other identity)	Owner/operator, location or fate
	MM55144	Aermacchi T-346A Master [61-02]	AMI 61° Stormo, Lecce
	CSX55145	Aermacchi T-346A Master	Leonardo, Turin
	MT55152	Aermacchi M-346FT [61-11]	Leonardo, Turin
	MM55153	Aermacchi T-346A Master [61-05]	AMI 61° Stormo, Lecce
	MM55154	Aermacchi T-346A Master [61-01]	AMI 61° Stormo, Lecce
	MM55155	Aermacchi T-346A Master [61-04]	AMI 61° Stormo, Lecce
	MM55168	Eurofighter TF-2000A Typhoon [4-37] $	AMI 904° GEA, Grosseto
	CSX55169	Eurofighter TF-2000A Typhoon	Leonardo, Turin
	MM55213	Aermacchi T-346A Master [61-06]	AMI 61° Stormo, Lecce
	MM55214	Aermacchi T-346A Master [61-07]	AMI 61° Stormo, Lecce
	MM55215	Aermacchi T-346A Master [61-10]	AMI 61° Stormo, Lecce
	MM55216	Aermacchi T-346A Master [61-12]	AMI 61° Stormo, Lecce
	MM55217	Aermacchi T-346A Master [61-13]	AMI 61° Stormo, Lecce
	MM55218	Aermacchi T-346A Master [61-14]	AMI 61° Stormo, Lecce
	MT55219	Aermacchi T-346A Master [61-20]	AMI 61° Stormo, Lecce
	MM55220	Aermacchi T-346A Master [61-16]	AMI 61° Stormo, Lecce
	MM55221	Aermacchi T-346A Master [61-15]	AMI 61° Stormo, Lecce
	MT55222	Aermacchi T-346A Master [61-21]	AMI 61° Stormo, Lecce
	MT55223	Aermacchi T-346A Master [61-22]	AMI 61° Stormo, Lecce
	MM55224	Aermacchi T-346A Master [61-23]	AMI 61° Stormo, Lecce
	MT55229	Aermacchi T-346FA	Leonardo, Turin
	MM62026	Dassault VC-50A (Falcon 50)	AMI 93° Gruppo/31° Stormo, Roma-Ciampino
	MM62029	Dassault VC-50A (Falcon 50)	AMI 93° Gruppo/31° Stormo, Roma-Ciampino
	CSX62127	Aeritalia MC-27J Pretorian	Alenia, Turin
	MM62156	Dornier UC-228 (Do.228-212) [E.I.101]	Esercito 28° Gruppo Squadroni, Viterbo
	MM62157	Dornier UC-228 (Do.228-212) [E.I.102]	Esercito 28° Gruppo Squadroni, Viterbo
	MM62158	Dornier UC-228 (Do.228-212) [E.I.103]	Esercito 28° Gruppo Squadroni, Viterbo
	MM62159	Piaggio VC-180A (P-180AM) Avanti	AMI RSV, Pratica di Mare
	MM62160	Piaggio RC-180A (P-180RM) Avanti	AMI 71° Gruppo/14° Stormo, Pratica di Mare
	MM62161	Piaggio VC-180A (P-180AM) Avanti	AMI RSV, Pratica di Mare
	MM62162	Piaggio RC-180A (P-180RM) Avanti	AMI 71° Gruppo/14° Stormo, Pratica di Mare
	MM62163	Piaggio RC-180A (P-180RM) Avanti	AMI 71° Gruppo/14° Stormo, Pratica di Mare
	MM62164	Piaggio RC-180A (P-180RM) Avanti	AMI 71° Gruppo/14° Stormo, Pratica di Mare
	MM62165	Aérospatiale P-42A (ATR.42-400MP) [GF-13]	GdiF GEA, Pratica di Mare
	MM62166	Aérospatiale P-42A (ATR.42-400MP) [GF-14]	GdiF GEA, Pratica di Mare
	MM62167	Piaggio VC-180A (P-180AM) Avanti	Esercito 28° Gruppo Sqd Det, Roma/Ciampino
	MM62168	Piaggio VC-180A (P-180AM) Avanti	Esercito 28° Gruppo Sqd Det, Roma/Ciampino
	MM62169	Piaggio VC-180A (P-180AM) Avanti	Esercito 28° Gruppo Sqd Det, Roma/Ciampino
	MM62170	Aérospatiale P-42A (ATR.42-400MP) [10-01]	Guardia Costiera 3° Nucleo, Pescara
	MM62171	Dassault VC-900A (Falcon 900EX) $	AMI 93° Gruppo/31° Stormo, Roma-Ciampino
	MM62174	Airbus VC-319A (A.319CJ-115X)	AMI 306° Gruppo/31° Stormo, Roma-Ciampino
	MM62175	Lockheed C-130J Hercules II [46-40]	AMI, stored Pisa
	MM62177	Lockheed C-130J Hercules II [46-42]	AMI 46ª Brigata Aerea, Pisa
	MM62178	Lockheed C-130J Hercules II [46-43]	AMI 46ª Brigata Aerea, Pisa
	MM62179	Lockheed C-130J Hercules II [46-44]	AMI 46ª Brigata Aerea, Pisa
	MM62180	Lockheed C-130J Hercules II [46-45]	AMI 46ª Brigata Aerea, Pisa
	MM62181	Lockheed KC-130J Hercules II [46-46]	AMI 46ª Brigata Aerea, Pisa
	MM62182	Lockheed C-130J Hercules II [46-47]	AMI, stored Pisa
	MM62183	Lockheed KC-130J Hercules II [46-48]	AMI 46ª Brigata Aerea, Pisa
	MM62184	Lockheed KC-130J Hercules II [46-49]	AMI, stored Pisa
	MM62185	Lockheed C-130J Hercules II [46-50]	AMI 46ª Brigata Aerea, Pisa
	MM62186	Lockheed C-130J Hercules II [46-51]	AMI 46ª Brigata Aerea, Pisa
	MM62187	Lockheed C-130J-30 Hercules II [46-53]	AMI 46ª Brigata Aerea, Pisa
	MM62188	Lockheed C-130J-30 Hercules II [46-54]	AMI 46ª Brigata Aerea, Pisa
	MM62189	Lockheed C-130J-30 Hercules II [46-55]	AMI 46ª Brigata Aerea, Pisa
	MM62190	Lockheed C-130J-30 Hercules II [46-56]	AMI 46ª Brigata Aerea, Pisa
	MM62191	Lockheed C-130J-30 Hercules II [46-57]	AMI, stored Pisa
	MM62192	Lockheed C-130J-30 Hercules II [46-58]	AMI, stored Pisa
	MM62193	Lockheed C-130J-30 Hercules II [46-59]	AMI 46ª Brigata Aerea, Pisa
	MM62194	Lockheed C-130J-30 Hercules II [46-60]	AMI 46ª Brigata Aerea, Pisa
	MM62195	Lockheed C-130J-30 Hercules II [46-61]	AMI 46ª Brigata Aerea, Pisa
	MM62196	Lockheed C-130J-30 Hercules II [46-62]	AMI 46ª Brigata Aerea, Pisa

Serial	Type (code/other identity)	Owner/operator, location or fate	Notes
MM62199	Piaggio VC-180A (P-180AM) Avanti	AMI CAE Multicrew, Pratica di Mare	
MM62200	Piaggio VC-180A (P-180AM) Avanti	AMI 71º Gruppo/14º Stormo, Pratica di Mare	
MM62201	Piaggio VC-180A (P-180AM) Avanti	AMI CAE Multicrew, Pratica di Mare	
MM62202	Piaggio VC-180A (P-180AM) Avanti	AMI 71º Gruppo/14º Stormo, Pratica di Mare	
MM62203	Piaggio VC-180A (P-180AM) Avanti	AMI CAE Multicrew, Pratica di Mare	
MM62204	Piaggio VC-180A (P-180AM) Avanti	AMI 71º Gruppo/14º Stormo, Pratica di Mare	
MM62205	Piaggio VC-180A (P-180AM) Avanti	AMI CAE Multicrew, Pratica di Mare	
MM62206	Piaggio VC-180A (P-180AM) Avanti	AMI CAE Multicrew, Pratica di Mare	
MM62207	Piaggio VC-180A (P-180AM) Avanti	AMI CAE Multicrew, Pratica di Mare	
MM62208	Aérospatiale P-42A (ATR.42-400MP) [10-02]	Guardia Costiera 2º Nucleo, Catania	
MM62209	Airbus VC-319A (A.319CJ-115X)	AMI 306º Gruppo/31º Stormo, Roma-Ciampino	
MM62210	Dassault VC-900A (Falcon 900EX)	AMI 93º Gruppo/31º Stormo, Roma-Ciampino	
MM62211	Piaggio VC-180A (P-180AM) Avanti [9-02]	MMI 9ª Brigata Aerea, Pratica di Mare	
MM62212	Piaggio VC-180A (P-180AM) Avanti [9-01]	MMI 9ª Brigata Aerea, Pratica di Mare	
MM62213	Piaggio VC-180A (P-180AM) Avanti [9-03]	MMI 9ª Brigata Aerea, Pratica di Mare	
MM62214	Aeritalia C-27J Spartan [46-84]	AMI, stored Pisa	
MM62215	Aeritalia C-27J Spartan [46-80]	AMI 98º Gruppo/46ª Brigata Aerea, Pisa	
MM62217	Aeritalia C-27J Spartan [46-81]	AMI, stored Pisa	
MM62218	Aeritalia C-27J Spartan [46-82]	AMI 98º Gruppo/46ª Brigata Aerea, Pisa	
CSX62219	Aeritalia C-27J Spartan [RS-50]	AMI RSV, Pratica di Mare	
MM62220	Aeritalia MC-27J Pretorian [46-83]	AMI 98º Gruppo/46ª Brigata Aerea, Pisa	
MM62221	Aeritalia EC-27J JEDI [46-85]	AMI 98º Gruppo/46ª Brigata Aerea, Pisa	
MM62222	Aeritalia C-27J Spartan [46-86]	AMI 98º Gruppo/46ª Brigata Aerea, Pisa	
MM62223	Aeritalia C-27J Spartan [46-88]	AMI 98º Gruppo/46ª Brigata Aerea, Pisa	
MM62224	Aeritalia EC-27J JEDI [46-89]	AMI 98º Gruppo/46ª Brigata Aerea, Pisa	
MM62225	Aeritalia C-27J Spartan [46-90]	AMI 98º Gruppo/46ª Brigata Aerea, Pisa	
MM62226	Boeing KC-767A (767-2EYER) [14-01] $	AMI 8º Gruppo/14º Stormo, Pratica di Mare	
MM62227	Boeing KC-767A (767-2EYER) [14-02]	AMI 8º Gruppo/14º Stormo, Pratica di Mare	
MM62228	Boeing KC-767A (767-2EYER) [14-03]	AMI 8º Gruppo/14º Stormo, Pratica di Mare	
MM62229	Boeing KC-767A (767-2EYER) [14-04]	AMI 8º Gruppo/14º Stormo, Pratica di Mare	
MM62230	Aérospatiale P-42A (ATR.42-400MP) [GF-15]	GdiF GEA, Pratica di Mare	
MM62243	Airbus VC-319A (A.319CJ-115X)	AMI 306º Gruppo/31º Stormo, Roma-Ciampino	
MM62244	Dassault VC-900B (Falcon 900EX EASy)	AMI 93º Gruppo/31º Stormo, Roma-Ciampino	
MM62245	Dassault VC-900B (Falcon 900EX EASy)	AMI 93º Gruppo/31º Stormo, Roma-Ciampino	
MM62248	Piaggio VC-180A (P-180AM) Avanti [GF-18]	GdiF GEA, Pratica di Mare	
MM62249	Piaggio VC-180B (P-180AM) Avanti II [GF-19]	GdiF GEA, Pratica di Mare	
MM62250	Aeritalia C-27J Spartan [46-91]	AMI 98º Gruppo/46ª Brigata Aerea, Pisa	
MM62251	Aérospatiale P-42A (ATR.42-400MP) [GF-16]	GdiF GEA, Pratica di Mare	
MM62270	Aérospatiale P-42B (ATR.42-500MP) [10-03]	Guardia Costiera 2º Nucleo, Catania	
CSX62279	Aérospatiale P-72A (ATR.72-600MP) [41-01]	Alenia	
CSX62280	Aérospatiale P-72A (ATR.72-600MP) [41-02]	Alenia	
MM62281	Aérospatiale P-72A (ATR.72-600MP) [41-04]	AMI 88º Gruppo/41º Stormo, Catania	
CSX62282	Aérospatiale P-72A (ATR.72-600MP) [41-05]	(on order)	
MM62286	Piaggio VC-180A (P-180AM) Avanti	AMI 93º Gruppo/31º Stormo, Roma-Ciampino	
MM62287	Piaggio VC-180A (P-180AM) Avanti	AMI 93º Gruppo/31º Stormo, Roma-Ciampino	
MM62293	Gulfstream Aerospace E-550A (N849GA) [14-11]	AMI 71º Gruppo/14º Stormo, Pratica di Mare	
MM62298	Aérospatiale P-72A (ATR.72-600MP) [41-03]	AMI 71º Gruppo/14º Stormo, Pratica di Mare	
MM62300	Beechcraft King Air 350ER	AMI 71º Gruppo/14º Stormo, Pratica di Mare	
MM62303	Gulfstream Aerospace E-550A (N554GA) [14-12]	AMI 71º Gruppo/14º Stormo, Pratica di Mare	
MM81480	AgustaWestland SH-101A (EH-101 Mk110 ASW) [2-01]	MMI 3º Grupelicot, Catania	
MM81481	AgustaWestland SH-101A (EH-101 Mk110 ASW) [2-02]	MMI 3º Grupelicot, Catania	
MM81482	AgustaWestland SH-101A (EH-101 Mk110 ASW) [2-03]	MMI 3º Grupelicot, Catania	
MM81483	AgustaWestland SH-101A (EH-101 Mk110 ASW) [2-04]	MMI 3º Grupelicot, Catania	
MM81484	AgustaWestland SH-101A (EH-101 Mk110 ASW) [2-05]	MMI 3º Grupelicot, Catania	
MM81485	AgustaWestland SH-101A (EH-101 Mk110 ASW) [2-06]	MMI 3º Grupelicot, Catania	
MM81486	AgustaWestland SH-101A (EH-101 Mk110 ASW) [2-07]	MMI 3º Grupelicot, Catania	
MM81487	AgustaWestland SH-101A (EH-101 Mk110 ASW) [2-08]	MMI 3º Grupelicot, Catania	
MM81488	AgustaWestland EH-101A (EH-101 Mk112 AEW) [2-09]	MMI 1º Grupelicot, La Spezia/Luni	
MM81489	AgustaWestland EH-101A (EH-101 Mk112 AEW) [2-10]	MMI 3º Grupelicot, Catania	
MM81490	AgustaWestland EH-101A (EH-101 Mk112 AEW) [2-11]	MMI 3º Grupelicot, Catania	
MM81491	AgustaWestland EH-101A (EH-101 Mk112 AEW) [2-12]	MMI 1º Grupelicot, La Spezia/Luni	
MM81492	AgustaWestland UH-101A (EH-101 Mk410 UTY) [2-13]	MMI 1º Grupelicot, La Spezia/Luni	

Notes	Serial	Type (code/other identity)	Owner/operator, location or fate
	MM81493	AgustaWestland UH-101A (EH-101 Mk410 UTY) [2-14]	MMI 1° Grupelicot, La Spezia/Luni
	MM81494	AgustaWestland UH-101A (EH-101 Mk410 UTY) [2-15]	MMI 1° Grupelicot, La Spezia/Luni
	MM81495	AgustaWestland UH-101A (EH-101 Mk410 UTY) [2-16]	MMI 1° Grupelicot, La Spezia/Luni
	MM81633	AgustaWestland UH-101A (EH-101 Mk410 UTY) [2-18]	MMI 1° Grupelicot, La Spezia/Luni
	MM81634	AgustaWestland UH-101A (EH-101 Mk410 UTY) [2-19]	MMI 1° Grupelicot, La Spezia/Luni
	MM81635	AgustaWestland UH-101A (EH-101 Mk410 UTY) [2-20]	MMI 1° Grupelicot, La Spezia/Luni
	MM81636	AgustaWestland UH-101A (EH-101 Mk410 UTY) [2-21]	MMI 1° Grupelicot, La Spezia/Luni
	MM81719	AgustaWestland SH-101A (EH-101 Mk110 ASW) [2-22]	MMI 1° Grupelicot, La Spezia/Luni
	MM81726	AgustaWestland SH-101A (EH-101 Mk110 ASW) [2-23]	MMI 1° Grupelicot, La Spezia/Luni
	MM81796	AgustaWestland HH-139A [15-40]	AMI 83° Gruppo SAR/15° Stormo, Cervia
	MM81797	AgustaWestland HH-139A [15-41]	AMI 82° Centro SAR/15° Stormo, Trapani/Birgi
	MM81798	AgustaWestland HH-139A [15-42]	AMI 82° Centro SAR/15° Stormo, Trapani/Birgi
	MM81799	AgustaWestland HH-139A [15-43]	AMI 81° Centro/15° Stormo, Cervia
	MM81800	AgustaWestland HH-139A [15-44]	AMI 82° Centro SAR/15° Stormo, Trapani/Birgi
	MM81801	AgustaWestland HH-139A [15-45]	AMI 85° Centro SAR/15° Stormo, Gioia del Colle
	MM81802	AgustaWestland HH-139A [15-46]	AMI 85° Centro SAR/15° Stormo, Gioia del Colle
	MM81803	AgustaWestland HH-139A [15-47]	AMI 81° Centro/15° Stormo, Cervia
	MM81804	AgustaWestland HH-139A [15-48]	AMI 83° Gruppo SAR/15° Stormo, Cervia
	MM81805	AgustaWestland HH-139A [15-49]	AMI 82° Centro SAR/15° Stormo, Trapani/Birgi
	MM81806	AgustaWestland VH-139A	AMI 93° Gruppo/31° Stormo, Roma-Ciampino
	MM81807	AgustaWestland VH-139A	AMI 93° Gruppo/31° Stormo, Roma-Ciampino
	MM81811	AgustaWestland VH-139A	AMI 93° Gruppo/31° Stormo, Roma-Ciampino
	MM81812	AgustaWestland VH-139A	AMI 93° Gruppo/31° Stormo, Roma-Ciampino
	MM81822	AgustaWestland HH-139A [15-50]	AMI 85° Centro SAR/15° Stormo, Gioia del Colle
	MM81823	AgustaWestland HH-139A [15-51]	AMI 81° Centro/15° Stormo, Cervia
	MM81824	AgustaWestland HH-139A [15-52]	AMI 85° Centro SAR/15° Stormo, Gioia del Colle
	CSX81848	AgustaWestland AW149 [1-49]	Leonardo
	MM81864	AgustaWestland HH-101A Caesar [15-01]	AMI 81° Centro/15° Stormo, Cervia
	MM81865	AgustaWestland HH-101A Caesar [15-02]	AMI 81° Centro/15° Stormo, Cervia
	MM81866	AgustaWestland HH-101A Caesar [15-03]	AMI 85° Centro SAR/15° Stormo, Pratica di Mare
	MM81867	AgustaWestland HH-101A Caesar [15-04]	AMI 23° Gruppo/15° Stormo, Cervia
	MM81868	AgustaWestland HH-101A Caesar [15-05]	AMI 81° Centro/15° Stormo, Cervia
	MM81869	AgustaWestland HH-101A Caesar [15-06]	AMI 81° Centro/15° Stormo, Cervia
	MM81870	AgustaWestland HH-101A Caesar [15-07]	AMI (on order)
	MM81871	AgustaWestland HH-101A Caesar	AMI (on order)
	MM81872	AgustaWestland HH-101A Caesar	AMI (on order)
	MM81873	AgustaWestland HH-101A Caesar	AMI (on order)
	MM81874	AgustaWestland HH-101A Caesar	AMI (on order)
	MM81875	AgustaWestland HH-101A Caesar	AMI (on order)
	CSX81890	AgustaWestland AW149	Leonardo

Italian Government

	I-CAEX	Dassault Falcon 900	Italian Government/Soc. CAI, Roma/Ciampino
	I-DIES	Dassault Falcon 900	Italian Government/Soc. CAI, Roma/Ciampino
	I-TALY	Airbus A.340-541 (A6-EHA)	*Withdrawn from use, 2018*
	I-TARH	Dassault Falcon 900EX (MM62172)	Italian Government/Soc. CAI, Roma/Ciampino

IVORY COAST

	TU-VAD	Grumman G.1159C Gulfstream IV	Ivory Coast Government, Abidjan
	TU-VAE	Gulfstream Aerospace G.550	Ivory Coast Government, Abidjan
	TU-VAF	Grumman G.1159A Gulfstream III	Ivory Coast Government, Abidjan
	TU-VAS	Airbus A.319CJ-133	Ivory Coast Government, Abidjan

JAPAN
Japan Air Self Defence Force (JASDF)

	07-3604	Boeing KC-767J	JASDF 404th Hikotai, Nagoya
	20-1101	Boeing 747-47C	JASDF 701st Flight Sqn, Chitose
	20-1102	Boeing 747-47C	JASDF 701st Flight Sqn, Chitose
	80-1111	Boeing 777-3SB(ER) (N509BJ)	JASDF 701st Flight Sqn, Chitose
	80-1112	Boeing 777-3SB(ER) (N511BJ)	JASDF 701st Flight Sqn, Chitose
	87-3601	Boeing KC-767J	JASDF 404th Hikotai, Nagoya
	87-3602	Boeing KC-767J	JASDF 404th Hikotai, Nagoya

Serial	Type (code/other identity)	Owner/operator, location or fate	Notes
97-3603	Boeing KC-767J	JASDF 404th Hikotai, Nagoya	
..-....	Boeing KC-46A	JASDF (on order)	
..-....	Boeing KC-46A	JASDF (on order)	
JORDAN			
Al Quwwat al Jawwiya al Malakiya al Urduniya/Jordanian Air Force			
344	Lockheed C-130H Hercules	Jordanian AF 3 Sqn, Amman/Marka	
345	Lockheed C-130H Hercules $	Jordanian AF 3 Sqn, Amman/Marka	
346	Lockheed C-130H Hercules	Jordanian AF 3 Sqn, Amman/Marka	
347	Lockheed C-130H Hercules $	Jordanian AF 3 Sqn, Amman/Marka	
360	Ilyushin Il-76MF (JY-JIC)	Jordanian AF 3 Sqn, Amman/Marka	
361	Ilyushin Il-76MF (JY-JID)	Jordanian AF 3 Sqn, Amman/Marka	
JY-RFA	Extra EA-300LP	*Sold as N251RF, January 2018*	
JY-RFB	Extra EA-300LP	*Sold as N252RF, January 2018*	
JY-RFC	Extra EA-300LP	*Sold as N253RF, January 2018*	
JY-RFD	Extra EA-300LP	*Sold as N255RF, January 2018*	
JY-RFE	Extra EA-300LP	*Sold as N254RF, January 2018*	
JY-RFA	Extra EA-330LX [RJF 01]	Jordanian AF *Royal Jordanian Falcons*, Amman	
JY-RFB	Extra EA-330LX [RJF 02]	Jordanian AF *Royal Jordanian Falcons*, Amman	
JY-RFC	Extra EA-330LX [RJF 03]	Jordanian AF *Royal Jordanian Falcons*, Amman	
JY-RFD	Extra EA-330LX [RJF 04]	Jordanian AF *Royal Jordanian Falcons*, Amman	
JY-RFE	Extra EA-330LX [RJF 05]	Jordanian AF *Royal Jordanian Falcons*, Amman	
Jordanian Government			
VQ-BDD	Airbus A.318-112	Jordanian Government, Amman	
VQ-BMZ	Gulfstream Aerospace G.650	Jordanian Government, Amman	
VQ-BNZ	Gulfstream Aerospace G.650ER	Jordanian Government, Amman	
KAZAKHSTAN			
01 r	CASA C-295M	Kazakstan ADF 18th Air Transport Sqn, Almaty	
02 r	CASA C-295M	Kazakstan ADF 18th Air Transport Sqn, Almaty	
03 r	CASA C-295M	Kazakstan ADF 18th Air Transport Sqn, Almaty	
04 r	CASA C-295M	Kazakstan ADF 18th Air Transport Sqn, Almaty	
05 r	CASA C-295M	Kazakstan ADF 18th Air Transport Sqn, Almaty	
06 r	CASA C-295M	Kazakstan ADF 18th Air Transport Sqn, Almaty	
07 r	Antonov An-72	Kazakstan ADF 18th Air Transport Sqn, Almaty	
07 r	CASA C-295M	Kazakstan ADF 18th Air Transport Sqn, Almaty	
08 r	Antonov An-72	Kazakstan ADF 18th Air Transport Sqn, Almaty	
08 r	CASA C-295M	Kazakstan ADF 18th Air Transport Sqn, Almaty	
UP-A3001	Airbus A.330-223	Government of Kazakhstan, Almaty	
UP-B5701	Boeing 757-2M6	Government of Kazakhstan, Almaty	
UP-T5401	Tupolev Tu-154M	Government of Kazakhstan, Almaty	
KENYA			
KAF 308	Fokker 70ER	Kenyan Government, Nairobi	
KUWAIT			
Al Quwwat al Jawwiya al Kuwaitiya/Kuwaiti Air Force			
KAF 323	Lockheed L100-30 Hercules	Kuwaiti AF 41 Sqn, Kuwait International	
KAF 324	Lockheed L100-30 Hercules	Kuwaiti AF 41 Sqn, Kuwait International	
KAF 325	Lockheed L100-30 Hercules	Kuwaiti AF 41 Sqn, Kuwait International	
KAF 326	Lockheed KC-130J Hercules II	Kuwaiti AF 41 Sqn, Kuwait International	
KAF 327	Lockheed KC-130J Hercules II	Kuwaiti AF 41 Sqn, Kuwait International	
KAF 328	Lockheed KC-130J Hercules II	Kuwaiti AF 41 Sqn, Kuwait International	
KAF 342	Boeing C-17A Globemaster III (13-0001)	Kuwaiti AF 41 Sqn, Kuwait International	
KAF 343	Boeing C-17A Globemaster III (13-0002)	Kuwaiti AF 41 Sqn, Kuwait International	
Kuwaiti Government			
9K-AKD	Airbus A.320-212	Kuwaiti Government, Safat	
9K-GAA	Boeing 747-8JK	Kuwaiti Government, Safat	
9K-GBA	Airbus A.340-542	Kuwaiti Government, Safat	
9K-GBB	Airbus A.340-542	Kuwaiti Government, Safat	
9K-GCC	Boeing 737-9BQER	Kuwaiti Government, Safat	
9K-GEA	Airbus A.319CJ-115X	Kuwaiti Government, Safat	

Notes	Serial	Type (code/other identity)	Owner/operator, location or fate
	9K-GFA	Gulfstream Aerospace G.550	Kuwaiti Government, Safat
	9K-GGA	Gulfstream Aerospace G.650	Kuwaiti Government, Safat
	9K-GGB	Gulfstream Aerospace G.650	Kuwaiti Government, Safat
	9K-GGC	Gulfstream Aerospace G.650	Kuwaiti Government, Safat
	9K-GGD	Gulfstream Aerospace G.650	Kuwaiti Government, Safat

KYRGYZSTAN

	EX-00001	Tupolev Tu-154M	Government of Kyrgyzstan, Bishkek

LITHUANIA
Karines Oro Pajegos (KOP)

	01 bl	LET 410UVP Turbolet	KOP Transporto Esk, Siauliai/Zokniai
	06 bl	Aeritalia C-27J Spartan	KOP Transporto Esk, Siauliai/Zokniai
	07 bl	Aeritalia C-27J Spartan	KOP Transporto Esk, Siauliai/Zokniai
	08 bl	Aeritalia C-27J Spartan	KOP Transporto Esk, Siauliai/Zokniai
	21 bl	Mil Mi-8MTV-1	KOP Sraigtasparniu Esk, Siauliai/Zokniai
	22 bl	Mil Mi-8T	*Withdrawn from use, 2018*
	23 bl	Mil Mi-8T	KOP Sraigtasparniu Esk, Siauliai/Zokniai
	25 bl	Mil Mi-8T (10 bl)	KOP Sraigtasparniu Esk, Siauliai/Zokniai
	26 bl	Mil Mi-8T (09 bl)	KOP Sraigtasparniu Esk, Siauliai/Zokniai
	28 bl	Mil Mi-8T	KOP Sraigtasparniu Esk, Siauliai/Zokniai

LUXEMBOURG
NATO

	LX-N90442	Boeing E-3A Sentry	NATO NAEW&CF, Geilenkirchen, Germany
	LX-N90443	Boeing E-3A Sentry $	NATO NAEW&CF, Geilenkirchen, Germany $
	LX-N90444	Boeing E-3A Sentry	NATO NAEW&CF, Geilenkirchen, Germany
	LX-N90445	Boeing E-3A Sentry	NATO NAEW&CF, Geilenkirchen, Germany
	LX-N90446	Boeing E-3A Sentry	NATO NAEW&CF, Geilenkirchen, Germany
	LX-N90447	Boeing E-3A Sentry	NATO NAEW&CF, Geilenkirchen, Germany
	LX-N90448	Boeing E-3A Sentry	NATO NAEW&CF, Geilenkirchen, Germany
	LX-N90450	Boeing E-3A Sentry $	NATO NAEW&CF, Geilenkirchen, Germany
	LX-N90451	Boeing E-3A Sentry	NATO NAEW&CF, Geilenkirchen, Germany
	LX-N90452	Boeing E-3A Sentry	NATO NAEW&CF, Geilenkirchen, Germany
	LX-N90453	Boeing E-3A Sentry	NATO NAEW&CF, Geilenkirchen, Germany
	LX-N90454	Boeing E-3A Sentry	Airbus, Manching, Germany (on upgrade)
	LX-N90456	Boeing E-3A Sentry	NATO NAEW&CF, Geilenkirchen, Germany
	LX-N90458	Boeing E-3A Sentry $	*To 309th AMARG, 11 September 2018*
	LX-N90459	Boeing E-3A Sentry	NATO NAEW&CF, Geilenkirchen, Germany
	OO-TFA	Boeing 757-28A	NATO, Geilenkirchen, Germany

MACEDONIA

	Z3-MKD	Bombardier Lear 60	Macedonian Government, Skopje

MALI

	TZ-PRM	Boeing 737-7DW	Government of Mali, Bamako

MALAYSIA
Tentera Udara Diraja Malaysia/Royal Malaysian Air Force (RMAF)

	M30-01	Lockheed C-130T Hercules	RMAF 20 Sqn, Subang
	M30-02	Lockheed C-130H Hercules	RMAF 20 Sqn, Subang
	M30-03	Lockheed C-130H Hercules	RMAF 14 Sqn, Labuan
	M30-04	Lockheed C-130H-30 Hercules	RMAF 20 Sqn, Subang
	M30-05	Lockheed C-130H-30 Hercules	RMAF 14 Sqn, Labuan
	M30-06	Lockheed C-130H-30 Hercules	RMAF 14 Sqn, Labuan
	M30-07	Lockheed C-130T Hercules	RMAF 20 Sqn, Subang
	M30-08	Lockheed C-130H(MP) Hercules	RMAF 20 Sqn, Subang
	M30-09	Lockheed C-130H(MP) Hercules	RMAF 20 Sqn, Subang
	M30-10	Lockheed C-130H-30 Hercules	RMAF 20 Sqn, Subang
	M30-11	Lockheed C-130H-30 Hercules	RMAF 20 Sqn, Subang
	M30-12	Lockheed C-130H-30 Hercules	RMAF 20 Sqn, Subang
	M30-14	Lockheed C-130H-30 Hercules	RMAF 14 Sqn, Labuan

Serial	Type (code/other identity)	Owner/operator, location or fate	Notes
M30-15	Lockheed C-130H-30 Hercules	RMAF 20 Sqn, Subang	
M30-16	Lockheed C-130H-30 Hercules	RMAF 20 Sqn, Subang	
M37-01	Dassault Falcon 900	RMAF 2 Sqn, Simpang	
M48-02	Bombardier BD.700-1A10 Global Express	RMAF 2 Sqn, Simpang	
M53–01	Boeing 737-7H6	RMAF 2 Sqn, Simpang	
M54-01	Airbus Military A.400M	RMAF 22 Sqn, Subang	
M54-02	Airbus Military A.400M	RMAF 22 Sqn, Subang	
M54-03	Airbus Military A.400M	RMAF 22 Sqn, Subang	
M54-04	Airbus Military A.400M	RMAF 22 Sqn, Subang	
9M-NAA	Airbus A.319CJ-115X	RMAF, Subang	
9M-NAB	Airbus A.320CJ-214 (M37-07)	RMAF, Subang	

MALTA

9H-AFK	Bombardier Learjet 60	Government of Malta, Luqa	

MEXICO

Fuerza Aérea Mexicana (FAM)/Mexican Air Force

TP-01	Boeing 787-8 (XC-MEX/3523)	*Withdrawn from use, December 2018*	
TP-02	Boeing 757-225 (XC-UJM)	FAM 8° Grupo Aéreo, Mexico City	

Armada de Mexico/Mexican Navy

ANX-1201	Gulfstream Aerospace G.550	Armada PRIESCAERTRANS, Mexico City	
XC-LMF	Gulfstream Aerospace G.450	Armada PRIESCAERTRANS, Mexico City	

MOROCCO

Al Quwwat al Jawwiya al Malakiya Marakishiya/Force Aérienne Royaume Marocaine/Royal Moroccan Air Force (RMAF) & Moroccan Government

CN-ABP	CAP-232 (28) [6]	RMAF *Marche Verte*, Marrakech/Ménara	
CN-ABQ	CAP-232 (29) [7]	RMAF *Marche Verte*, Marrakech/Ménara	
CN-ABR	CAP-232 (31) [2]	RMAF *Marche Verte*, Marrakech/Ménara	
CN-ABS	CAP-232 (36) [3]	RMAF *Marche Verte*, Marrakech/Ménara	
CN-ABT	CAP-232 (37) [1]	RMAF *Marche Verte*, Marrakech/Ménara	
CN-ABU	CAP-232 (41) [5]	RMAF *Marche Verte*, Marrakech/Ménara	
CN-ABV	CAP-232 (42) [4]	RMAF *Marche Verte*, Marrakech/Ménara	
CN-ABW	CAP-232 (43) [8]	RMAF *Marche Verte*, Marrakech/Ménara	
CN-ABX	CAP-232 (44) [7]	RMAF *Marche Verte*, Marrakech/Ménara	
CN-AMA	Airtech CN.235M-100 (023)	RMAF Escadrille de Transport 3, Kenitra	
CN-AMB	Airtech CN.235M-100 (024)	RMAF Escadrille de Transport 3, Kenitra	
CN-AMC	Airtech CN.235M-100 (025)	RMAF Escadrille de Transport 3, Kenitra	
CN-AMD	Airtech CN.235M-100 (026)	RMAF Escadrille de Transport 3, Kenitra	
CN-AME	Airtech CN.235M-100 (027)	*Withdrawn from use at Kenitra*	
CN-AMF	Airtech CN.235M-100 (028)	*Withdrawn from use at Kenitra*	
CN-AMG	Airtech CN.235M-100 (031)	RMAF Escadrille de Transport 3, Kenitra	
CN-AMH	Gulfstream Aerospace G.650	Government of Morocco, Rabat	
CN-AMJ	Cessna 560XLS+ Citation Excel	Government of Morocco, Rabat	
CN-AMK	Cessna 560XLS+ Citation Excel	Government of Morocco, Rabat	
CN-AMN	Aeritalia C-27J Spartan	RMAF Escadrille de Transport 3, Kenitra	
CN-AMO	Aeritalia C-27J Spartan	RMAF Escadrille de Transport 3, Kenitra	
CN-AMP	Aeritalia C-27J Spartan	RMAF Escadrille de Transport 3, Kenitra	
CN-AMQ	Aeritalia C-27J Spartan	RMAF Escadrille de Transport 3, Kenitra	
CN-AMR	Gulfstream Aerospace G.550	Government of Morocco, Rabat	
CN-AMS	Gulfstream Aerospace G.550	Government of Morocco, Rabat	
CN-AMY	Cessna 560XLS+ Citation Excel	Government of Morocco, Rabat	
CN-ANL	Grumman G.1159 Gulfstream IITT	Government of Morocco, Rabat	
CN-ANO	Dassault Falcon 50	Government of Morocco, Rabat	
CN-ANU	Grumman G.1159A Gulfstream III	Government of Morocco, Rabat	
CNA-NV	Cessna 560 Citation V	Government of Morocco, Rabat	
CNA-NW	Cessna 560 Citation V	Government of Morocco, Rabat	
CN-AOA	Lockheed C-130H Hercules (4535)	RMAF Escadrille de Transport 3, Kenitra	
CNA-OC	Lockheed C-130H Hercules (4551)	RMAF Escadrille de Transport 3, Kenitra	
CN-AOD	Lockheed C-130H Hercules (4575)	RMAF Escadrille de Transport 3, Kenitra	
CN-AOE	Lockheed C-130H Hercules (4581)	RMAF Escadrille de Transport 3, Kenitra	
CN-AOF	Lockheed C-130H Hercules (4583)	RMAF Escadrille de Transport 3, Kenitra	

Notes	Serial	Type (code/other identity)	Owner/operator, location or fate
	CN-AOG	Lockheed C-130H Hercules (4713)	RMAF Escadrille de Transport 3, Kenitra
	CN-AOI	Lockheed C-130H Hercules (4733)	RMAF Escadrille de Transport 3, Kenitra
	CNA-OJ	Lockheed C-130H Hercules (4738)	RMAF Escadrille de Transport 3, Kenitra
	CN-AOK	Lockheed C-130H Hercules (4739)	RMAF Escadrille de Transport 3, Kenitra
	CN-AOL	Lockheed C-130H Hercules (4742)	RMAF Escadrille de Transport 3, Kenitra
	CN-AOM	Lockheed C-130H Hercules (4875)	RMAF Escadrille de Transport 3, Kenitra
	CN-AON	Lockheed C-130H Hercules (4876)	RMAF Escadrille de Transport 3, Kenitra
	CN-AOO	Lockheed EC-130H Hercules (4877)	RMAF Escadron Electronique, Kenitra
	CN-AOP	Lockheed C-130H Hercules (4888)	RMAF Escadrille de Transport 3, Kenitra
	CN-AOR	Lockheed KC-130H Hercules (4907)	RMAF Escadrille de Transport 3, Kenitra
	CN-AOS	Lockheed KC-130H Hercules (4909)	RMAF Escadrille de Transport 3, Kenitra
	CNA-SM	BAE RJ100	Government of Morocco, Rabat
	CN-MBH	Boeing 747-8Z5 (A6-PFA)	Government of Morocco, Rabat
	CN-MVI	Boeing 737-8KB	Government of Morocco, Rabat

NAMIBIA

| | V5-GON | Dassault Falcon 7X | Government of Namibia, Eros |
| | V5-NAM | Dassault Falcon 900B | Government of Namibia, Eros |

NETHERLANDS
Koninklijke Luchtmacht (KLu)

	D-101	Boeing-Vertol CH-47D Chinook	KLu 298 Sqn, Gilze-Rijen
	D-102	Boeing-Vertol CH-47D Chinook	KLu 298 Sqn, Gilze-Rijen
	D-103	Boeing-Vertol CH-47D Chinook	KLu 298 Sqn, Gilze-Rijen
	D-106	Boeing-Vertol CH-47D Chinook	KLu 298 Sqn, Gilze-Rijen
	D-661	Boeing-Vertol CH-47D Chinook	KLu 298 Sqn, Gilze-Rijen
	D-662	Boeing-Vertol CH-47D Chinook	KLu 298 Sqn, Gilze-Rijen
	D-663	Boeing-Vertol CH-47D Chinook	KLu 298 Sqn, Gilze-Rijen
	D-664	Boeing-Vertol CH-47D Chinook	KLu 298 Sqn, Gilze-Rijen
	D-665	Boeing-Vertol CH-47D Chinook	KLu 298 Sqn, Gilze-Rijen
	D-666	Boeing-Vertol CH-47D Chinook	KLu 298 Sqn, Gilze-Rijen
	D-667	Boeing-Vertol CH-47D Chinook	KLu 298 Sqn, Gilze-Rijen
	D-890	Boeing-Vertol CH-47F Chinook	KLu 298 Sqn, Gilze-Rijen
	D-891	Boeing-Vertol CH-47F Chinook	KLu 302 Sqn, Fort Hood, Texas, USA
	D-892	Boeing-Vertol CH-47F Chinook	KLu 298 Sqn, Gilze-Rijen
	D-893	Boeing-Vertol CH-47F Chinook	KLu 302 Sqn, Fort Hood, Texas, USA
	D-894	Boeing-Vertol CH-47F Chinook	KLu 302 Sqn, Fort Hood, Texas, USA
	D-895	Boeing-Vertol CH-47F Chinook	KLu 302 Sqn, Fort Hood, Texas, USA
	F-001	Lockheed Martin F-35A Lightning II [OT]	KLu 323 Sqn, Edwards AFB California, USA
	F-002	Lockheed Martin F-35A Lightning II $	KLu 308th FS/56th FW, Luke AFB, Arizona, USA
	F-003	Lockheed Martin F-35A Lightning II	KLu 308th FS/56th FW, Luke AFB, Arizona, USA
	F-004	Lockheed Martin F-35A Lightning II	KLu 308th FS/56th FW, Luke AFB, Arizona, USA
	F-005	Lockheed Martin F-35A Lightning II	KLu 308th FS/56th FW, Luke AFB, Arizona, USA
	F-006	Lockheed Martin F-35A Lightning II	KLu 308th FS/56th FW, Luke AFB, Arizona, USA
	F-007	Lockheed Martin F-35A Lightning II	KLu (on order)
	F-008	Lockheed Martin F-35A Lightning II	KLu (on order)
	G-273	Lockheed C-130H-30 Hercules	KLu 336 Sqn, Eindhoven
	G-275	Lockheed C-130H-30 Hercules	KLu 336 Sqn, Eindhoven
	G-781	Lockheed C-130H Hercules	KLu 336 Sqn, Eindhoven
	G-988	Lockheed C-130H Hercules	KLu 336 Sqn, Eindhoven
	J-001	Fokker (GD) F-16AM Fighting Falcon [AZ]	KLu 148th FS/162th FW, Tucson IAP, Arizona, USA
	J-002	Fokker (GD) F-16AM Fighting Falcon $	KLu 322 Sqn, Leeuwarden
	J-003	Fokker (GD) F-16AM Fighting Falcon	KLu 313 Sqn, Volkel
	J-004	Fokker (GD) F-16AM Fighting Falcon [AZ]	KLu 148th FS/162th FW, Tucson IAP, Arizona, USA
	J-005	Fokker (GD) F-16AM Fighting Falcon	KLu 313 Sqn, Volkel
	J-006	Fokker (GD) F-16AM Fighting Falcon $	KLu, stored Leeuwarden
	J-008	Fokker (GD) F-16AM Fighting Falcon $	KLu 313 Sqn, Volkel
	J-009	Fokker (GD) F-16AM Fighting Falcon	KLu 322 Sqn, Leeuwarden
	J-010	Fokker (GD) F-16AM Fighting Falcon [AZ]	KLu 148th FS/162th FW, Tucson IAP, Arizona, USA
	J-011	Fokker (GD) F-16AM Fighting Falcon	KLu 322 Sqn, Leeuwarden
	J-013	Fokker (GD) F-16AM Fighting Falcon	KLu 312 Sqn/313 Sqn, Volkel
	J-014	Fokker (GD) F-16AM Fighting Falcon	KLu 313 Sqn, Volkel

Serial	Type (code/other identity)	Owner/operator, location or fate	Notes
J-015	Fokker (GD) F-16AM Fighting Falcon	KLu 312 Sqn/313 Sqn, Volkel	
J-016	Fokker (GD) F-16AM Fighting Falcon	KLu 313 Sqn, Volkel	
J-017	Fokker (GD) F-16AM Fighting Falcon	KLu 312 Sqn, Volkel	
J-018	Fokker (GD) F-16AM Fighting Falcon [AZ]	KLu 148th FS/162th FW, Tucson IAP, Arizona, USA	
J-019	Fokker (GD) F-16AM Fighting Falcon [AZ]	KLu 148th FS/162th FW, Tucson IAP, Arizona, USA	
J-020	Fokker (GD) F-16AM Fighting Falcon	KLu 312 Sqn, Volkel	
J-021	Fokker (GD) F-16AM Fighting Falcon	KLu 322 Sqn, Leeuwarden	
J-055	Fokker (GD) F-16AM Fighting Falcon	KLu 313 Sqn, Volkel	
J-060	Fokker (GD) F-16AM Fighting Falcon	KLu 322 Sqn, Leeuwarden	
J-061	Fokker (GD) F-16AM Fighting Falcon	KLu 322 Sqn, Leeuwarden	
J-062	Fokker (GD) F-16AM Fighting Falcon	KLu 313 Sqn, Volkel	
J-063	Fokker (GD) F-16AM Fighting Falcon	KLu 313 Sqn, Volkel	
J-064	Fokker (GD) F-16BM Fighting Falcon [AZ]	KLu 148th FS/162th FW, Tucson IAP, Arizona, USA	
J-065	Fokker (GD) F-16BM Fighting Falcon	KLu 322 Sqn, Leeuwarden	
J-066	Fokker (GD) F-16BM Fighting Falcon	KLu Test Flt, Leeuwarden	
J-067	Fokker (GD) F-16BM Fighting Falcon [AZ]	KLu 148th FS/162th FW, Tucson IAP, Arizona, USA	
J-135	Fokker (GD) F-16AM Fighting Falcon	KLu 322 Sqn, Leeuwarden	
J-136	Fokker (GD) F-16AM Fighting Falcon	KLu 312 Sqn/313 Sqn, Volkel	
J-142	Fokker (GD) F-16AM Fighting Falcon	KLu 322 Sqn, Leeuwarden	
J-144	Fokker (GD) F-16AM Fighting Falcon	KLu 312 Sqn/313 Sqn, Volkel	
J-146	Fokker (GD) F-16AM Fighting Falcon	KLu 323 Sqn, Leeuwarden	
J-196	Fokker (GD) F-16AM Fighting Falcon $	KLu 312 Sqn/313 Sqn, Volkel	
J-197	Fokker (GD) F-16AM Fighting Falcon	KLu 312 Sqn/313 Sqn, Volkel	
J-201	Fokker (GD) F-16AM Fighting Falcon	KLu 322 Sqn, Leeuwarden	
J-202	Fokker (GD) F-16AM Fighting Falcon	KLu, stored Volkel	
J-209	Fokker (GD) F-16BM Fighting Falcon [AZ]	KLu 148th FS/162th FW, Tucson IAP, Arizona, USA	
J-210	Fokker (GD) F-16BM Fighting Falcon [AZ]	KLu 148th FS/162th FW, Tucson IAP, Arizona, USA	
J-362	Fokker (GD) F-16AM Fighting Falcon	KLu 322 Sqn, Leeuwarden	
J-366	Fokker (GD) F-16AM Fighting Falcon [AZ]	KLu 148th FS/162th FW, Tucson IAP, Arizona, USA	
J-367	Fokker (GD) F-16AM Fighting Falcon	KLu 322 Sqn, Leeuwarden	
J-368	Fokker (GD) F-16BM Fighting Falcon	KLu 313 Sqn, Volkel	
J-369	Fokker (GD) F-16BM Fighting Falcon [AZ]	KLu 148th FS/162th FW, Tucson IAP, Arizona, USA	
J-508	Fokker (GD) F-16AM Fighting Falcon	KLu 313 Sqn, Volkel	
J-509	Fokker (GD) F-16AM Fighting Falcon	KLu 322 Sqn, Leeuwarden	
J-511	Fokker (GD) F-16AM Fighting Falcon	KLu 322 Sqn, Leeuwarden	
J-512	Fokker (GD) F-16AM Fighting Falcon	KLu 313 Sqn, Volkel	
J-513	Fokker (GD) F-16AM Fighting Falcon	KLu 323 Sqn, Volkel	
J-514	Fokker (GD) F-16AM Fighting Falcon	KLu 313 Sqn, Volkel	
J-515	Fokker (GD) F-16AM Fighting Falcon	KLu 312 Sqn/313 Sqn, Volkel	
J-516	Fokker (GD) F-16AM Fighting Falcon	KLu 322 Sqn, Leeuwarden	
J-616	Fokker (GD) F-16AM Fighting Falcon	KLu 312 Sqn, Volkel	
J-624	Fokker (GD) F-16AM Fighting Falcon	KLu 322 Sqn, Leeuwarden	
J-628	Fokker (GD) F-16AM Fighting Falcon	KLu 322 Sqn, Leeuwarden	
J-630	Fokker (GD) F-16AM Fighting Falcon	KLu 312 Sqn/313 Sqn, Volkel	
J-631	Fokker (GD) F-16AM Fighting Falcon $	KLu 322 Sqn, Leeuwarden	
J-632	Fokker (GD) F-16AM Fighting Falcon	KLu 322 Sqn, Leeuwarden	
J-635	Fokker (GD) F-16AM Fighting Falcon	*Crashed 8 May 2018, Volkel*	
J-641	Fokker (GD) F-16AM Fighting Falcon	KLu 312 Sqn, Volkel	
J-642	Fokker (GD) F-16AM Fighting Falcon	KLu 322 Sqn, Leeuwarden	
J-643	Fokker (GD) F-16AM Fighting Falcon	KLu 313 Sqn, Volkel	
J-644	Fokker (GD) F-16AM Fighting Falcon	KLu 322 Sqn, Leeuwarden	
J-646	Fokker (GD) F-16AM Fighting Falcon	KLu 313 Sqn, Volkel	
J-647	Fokker (GD) F-16AM Fighting Falcon	KLu, stored Volkel	
J-866	Fokker (GD) F-16AM Fighting Falcon	KLu 312 Sqn, Volkel	
J-871	Fokker (GD) F-16AM Fighting Falcon	KLu 322 Sqn, Leeuwarden	
J-877	Fokker (GD) F-16AM Fighting Falcon	KLu 322 Sqn, Leeuwarden	
J-879	Fokker (GD) F-16AM Fighting Falcon $	KLu 322 Sqn, Leeuwarden	
J-881	Fokker (GD) F-16AM Fighting Falcon	KLu 322 Sqn, Leeuwarden	
J-882	Fokker (GD) F-16BM Fighting Falcon $	KLu 312 Sqn/313 Sqn, Volkel	
L-01	Pilatus PC-7 Turbo Trainer	KLu 131 EMVO Sqn, Woensdrecht	
L-02	Pilatus PC-7 Turbo Trainer $	KLu 131 EMVO Sqn, Woensdrecht	
L-03	Pilatus PC-7 Turbo Trainer	KLu 131 EMVO Sqn, Woensdrecht	

Notes	Serial	Type (code/other identity)	Owner/operator, location or fate
	L-04	Pilatus PC-7 Turbo Trainer	KLu 131 EMVO Sqn, Woensdrecht
	L-05	Pilatus PC-7 Turbo Trainer	KLu 131 EMVO Sqn, Woensdrecht
	L-06	Pilatus PC-7 Turbo Trainer	KLu 131 EMVO Sqn, Woensdrecht
	L-07	Pilatus PC-7 Turbo Trainer	KLu 131 EMVO Sqn, Woensdrecht
	L-08	Pilatus PC-7 Turbo Trainer	KLu 131 EMVO Sqn, Woensdrecht
	L-09	Pilatus PC-7 Turbo Trainer	KLu 131 EMVO Sqn, Woensdrecht
	L-10	Pilatus PC-7 Turbo Trainer	KLu 131 EMVO Sqn, Woensdrecht
	L-11	Pilatus PC-7 Turbo Trainer	KLu 131 EMVO Sqn, Woensdrecht
	L-12	Pilatus PC-7 Turbo Trainer	KLu 131 EMVO Sqn, Woensdrecht
	L-13	Pilatus PC-7 Turbo Trainer $	KLu 131 EMVO Sqn, Woensdrecht
	M-001	Airbus A.330-243 MRTT (KC-30) (F-WWKR/EC-340)	KLu/MMF (or order)
	M-002	Airbus A.330-243 MRTT (KC-30)	KLu/MMF (or order)
	M-003	Airbus A.330-243 MRTT (KC-30)	KLu/MMF (or order)
	M-004	Airbus A.330-243 MRTT (KC-30)	KLu/MMF (or order)
	M-005	Airbus A.330-243 MRTT (KC-30)	KLu/MMF (or order)
	M-006	Airbus A.330-243 MRTT (KC-30)	KLu/MMF (or order)
	M-007	Airbus A.330-243 MRTT (KC-30)	KLu/MMF (or order)
	M-008	Airbus A.330-243 MRTT (KC-30)	KLu/MMF (or order)
	N-088	NH Industries NH.90-NFH	KLu 860 Sqn, De Kooij
	N-102	NH Industries NH.90-NFH	KLu 860 Sqn, De Kooij
	N-110	NH Industries NH.90-NFH	KLu 860 Sqn, De Kooij
	N-164	NH Industries NH.90-NFH	KLu 860 Sqn, De Kooij
	N-175	NH Industries NH.90-NFH	KLu 860 Sqn, De Kooij
	N-195	NH Industries NH.90-NFH	KLu 860 Sqn, De Kooij
	N-227	NH Industries NH.90-NFH	KLu 860 Sqn, De Kooij
	N-228	NH Industries NH.90-NFH	KLu 860 Sqn, De Kooij
	N-233	NH Industries NH.90-NFH	KLu 860 Sqn, De Kooij
	N-234	NH Industries NH.90-NFH	KLu 860 Sqn, De Kooij
	N-258	NH Industries NH.90-NFH	KLu 860 Sqn, De Kooij
	N-277	NH Industries NH.90-NFH	KLu 860 Sqn, De Kooij
	N-316	NH Industries NH.90-NFH	KLu 860 Sqn, De Kooij
	N-317	NH Industries NH.90-NFH	KLu 860 Sqn, De Kooij
	N-318	NH Industries NH.90-NFH	KLu 860 Sqn, De Kooij
	N-319	NH Industries NH.90-NFH	KLu 860 Sqn, De Kooij
	N-324	NH Industries NH.90-NFH	KLu 860 Sqn, De Kooij
	N-325	NH Industries NH.90-NFH	KLu 860 Sqn, De Kooij
	N-326	NH Industries NH.90-NFH	KLu 860 Sqn, De Kooij
	N-327	NH Industries NH.90-NFH	KLu 860 Sqn, De Kooij
	Q-01	MDH AH-64D Apache Longbow	KLu 301 Sqn, Gilze-Rijen
	Q-02	MDH AH-64D Apache Longbow	KLu 302 Sqn, Fort Hood, Texas, USA
	Q-03	MDH AH-64D Apache Longbow	KLu 302 Sqn, Fort Hood, Texas, USA
	Q-04	MDH AH-64D Apache Longbow	KLu 301 Sqn, Gilze-Rijen
	Q-05	MDH AH-64D Apache Longbow	KLu 301 Sqn, Gilze-Rijen
	Q-06	MDH AH-64D Apache Longbow	KLu 302 Sqn, Fort Hood, Texas, USA
	Q-07	MDH AH-64D Apache Longbow	KLu 302 Sqn, Fort Hood, Texas, USA
	Q-08	MDH AH-64D Apache Longbow	KLu 301 Sqn, Gilze-Rijen
	Q-09	MDH AH-64D Apache Longbow	KLu 301 Sqn, Gilze-Rijen
	Q-10	MDH AH-64D Apache Longbow	KLu 301 Sqn, Gilze-Rijen
	Q-11	MDH AH-64D Apache Longbow	KLu 302 Sqn, Fort Hood, Texas, USA
	Q-12	MDH AH-64D Apache Longbow	KLu 302 Sqn, Fort Hood, Texas, USA
	Q-13	MDH AH-64D Apache Longbow	KLu 301 Sqn, Gilze-Rijen
	Q-14	MDH AH-64D Apache Longbow	KLu 301 Sqn, Gilze-Rijen
	Q-16	MDH AH-64D Apache Longbow	KLu 301 Sqn, Gilze-Rijen
	Q-17	MDH AH-64D Apache Longbow	KLu 301 Sqn, Gilze-Rijen
	Q-18	MDH AH-64D Apache Longbow	KLu 301 Sqn, Gilze-Rijen
	Q-19	MDH AH-64D Apache Longbow	KLu 301 Sqn, Gilze-Rijen
	Q-21	MDH AH-64D Apache Longbow	KLu 301 Sqn, Gilze-Rijen
	Q-22	MDH AH-64D Apache Longbow	KLu 301 Sqn, Gilze-Rijen
	Q-23	MDH AH-64D Apache Longbow	KLu 301 Sqn, Gilze-Rijen
	Q-24	MDH AH-64D Apache Longbow	KLu 301 Sqn, Gilze-Rijen
	Q-25	MDH AH-64D Apache Longbow	KLu 301 Sqn, Gilze-Rijen
	Q-26	MDH AH-64D Apache Longbow	KLu 301 Sqn, Gilze-Rijen

Serial	Type (code/other identity)	Owner/operator, location or fate	Notes
Q-27	MDH AH-64D Apache Longbow	KLu 302 Sqn, Fort Hood, Texas, USA	
Q-28	MDH AH-64D Apache Longbow	KLu 302 Sqn, Fort Hood, Texas, USA	
Q-29	MDH AH-64D Apache Longbow	KLu 301 Sqn, Gilze-Rijen	
Q-30	MDH AH-64D Apache Longbow	KLu 301 Sqn, Gilze-Rijen	
S-419	Eurocopter AS.532U-2 Cougar	KLu 300 Sqn, Gilze-Rijen	
S-440	Eurocopter AS.532U-2 Cougar	KLu 300 Sqn, Gilze-Rijen	
S-441	Eurocopter AS.532U-2 Cougar	KLu 300 Sqn, Gilze-Rijen	
S-442	Eurocopter AS.532U-2 Cougar	KLu 300 Sqn, Gilze-Rijen	
S-444	Eurocopter AS.532U-2 Cougar	KLu 300 Sqn, Gilze-Rijen	
S-445	Eurocopter AS.532U-2 Cougar	KLu 300 Sqn, Gilze-Rijen	
S-447	Eurocopter AS.532U-2 Cougar	KLu 300 Sqn, Gilze-Rijen	
S-453	Eurocopter AS.532U-2 Cougar	KLu 300 Sqn, Gilze-Rijen	
S-454	Eurocopter AS.532U-2 Cougar	KLu 300 Sqn, Gilze-Rijen	
S-456	Eurocopter AS.532U-2 Cougar	KLu 300 Sqn, Gilze-Rijen	
S-457	Eurocopter AS.532U-2 Cougar	KLu, Woensdrecht (wfu)	
S-458	Eurocopter AS.532U-2 Cougar	KLu 300 Sqn, Gilze-Rijen	
S-459	Eurocopter AS.532U-2 Cougar	KLu 300 Sqn, Gilze-Rijen	
T-235	McDonnell Douglas KDC-10	KLu 334 Sqn, Eindhoven	
T-264	McDonnell Douglas KDC-10	KLu 334 Sqn, Eindhoven	
V-11	Grumman G.1159C Gulfstream IV	KLu 334 Sqn, Eindhoven	
Kustwacht & Netherlands Government			
PH-CGC	Dornier Do.228-212	Kustwacht, Amsterdam/Schiphol	
PH-CGN	Dornier Do.228-212	Kustwacht, Amsterdam/Schiphol	
PH-GOV	Boeing 737-700(BBJ) (N513BJ)	Dutch Royal Flight, Amsterdam/Schiphol	
PH-KBX	Fokker 70	Dutch Royal Flight, Amsterdam/Schiphol	
NEW ZEALAND			
Royal New Zealand Air Force (RNZAF)			
NZ4201	Lockheed P-3K2 Orion	RNZAF 5 Sqn, Whenuapai	
NZ4202	Lockheed P-3K2 Orion	RNZAF 5 Sqn, Whenuapai	
NZ4203	Lockheed P-3K2 Orion	RNZAF 5 Sqn, Whenuapai	
NZ4204	Lockheed P-3K2 Orion	RNZAF 5 Sqn, Whenuapai	
NZ4205	Lockheed P-3K2 Orion	RNZAF 5 Sqn, Whenuapai	
NZ4206	Lockheed P-3K2 Orion	RNZAF 5 Sqn, Whenuapai	
NZ7001	Lockheed C-130H(NZ) Hercules $	RNZAF 40 Sqn, Whenuapai	
NZ7002	Lockheed C-130H(NZ) Hercules	RNZAF 40 Sqn, Whenuapai	
NZ7003	Lockheed C-130H(NZ) Hercules	RNZAF 40 Sqn, Whenuapai	
NZ7004	Lockheed C-130H(NZ) Hercules	RNZAF 40 Sqn, Whenuapai	
NZ7005	Lockheed C-130H(NZ) Hercules	RNZAF 40 Sqn, Whenuapai	
NZ7571	Boeing 757-2K2	RNZAF 40 Sqn, Whenuapai	
NZ7572	Boeing 757-2K2	RNZAF 40 Sqn, Whenuapai	
NIGER			
5U-GRN	Boeing 737-75U	Government of Niger, Niamey	
NIGERIA			
Nigerian Air Force (NAF)			
NAF-910	Lockheed C-130H Hercules	Withdrawn from use	
NAF-912	Lockheed C-130H Hercules	Withdrawn from use	
NAF-913	Lockheed C-130H Hercules	NAF 301 HAG, Ikeja	
NAF-917	Lockheed C-130H-30 Hercules	NAF 301 HAG, Ikeja	
NAF-918	Lockheed C-130H-30 Hercules	NAF 301 HAG, Ikeja	
NAF-961	Dassault Falcon 900	NAF 307 HAG, Minna	
Nigerian Government			
5N-FGS	Gulfstream Aerospace Gulfstream V	Federal Government of Nigeria, Abuja	
5N-FGT	Boeing 737-7N6 [001]	Federal Government of Nigeria, Abuja	
5N-FGU	Dassault Falcon 7X	Federal Government of Nigeria, Abuja	
5N-FGV	Dassault Falcon 7X	Federal Government of Nigeria, Abuja	
5N-FGW	Gulfstream Aerospace G.550	Federal Government of Nigeria, Abuja	
5N-FGX	Hawker 4000 Horizon	Federal Government of Nigeria, Abuja	

Notes	Serial	Type (code/other identity)	Owner/operator, location or fate
	NORWAY		
	Luftforsvaret/Royal Norwegian Air Force (RNoAF)		
	013	NH Industries NH.90-NFH	RNoAF (on order)
	027	NH Industries NH.90-NFH	RNoAF (on order)
	041	Dassault Falcon 20 ECM	RNoAF 717 Skv, Gardermoen
	049	NH Industries NH.90-NFH	RNoAF 337 Skv, Bardufoss
	053	Dassault Falcon 20 ECM	RNoAF 717 Skv, Gardermoen
	057	NH Industries NH.90-NFH	RNoAF 337 Skv, Bardufoss
	058	NH Industries NH.90-NFH	RNoAF 337 Skv, Bardufoss
	060	Westland Sea King Mk.43B	RNoAF 330 Skv Bodø/Banak/Ørland & Sola
	062	Westland Sea King Mk.43B	RNoAF 330 Skv Bodø/Banak/Ørland & Sola
	066	Westland Sea King Mk.43B	RNoAF 330 Skv Bodø/Banak/Ørland & Sola
	069	Westland Sea King Mk.43B	RNoAF 330 Skv Bodø/Banak/Ørland & Sola
	070	Westland Sea King Mk.43B	RNoAF 330 Skv Bodø/Banak/Ørland & Sola
	071	Westland Sea King Mk.43B	RNoAF 330 Skv Bodø/Banak/Ørland & Sola
	073	Westland Sea King Mk.43B	RNoAF 330 Skv Bodø/Banak/Ørland & Sola
	074	Westland Sea King Mk.43B	RNoAF 330 Skv Bodø/Banak/Ørland & Sola
	087	NH Industries NH.90-NFH	RNoAF 337 Skv, Bardufoss
	139	Bell 412HP	RNoAF 339 Skv, Bardufoss
	140	Bell 412HP	RNoAF 339 Skv, Bardufoss
	141	Bell 412HP	RNoAF 339 Skv, Bardufoss
	142	Bell 412HP	RNoAF 339 Skv, Bardufoss
	143	Bell 412HP	RNoAF 339 Skv, Bardufoss
	144	Bell 412HP	RNoAF 339 Skv, Bardufoss
	145	Bell 412HP	RNoAF 339 Skv, Bardufoss
	146	Bell 412HP	RNoAF 339 Skv, Bardufoss
	147	Bell 412HP	RNoAF 339 Skv, Bardufoss
	148	Bell 412HP	RNoAF 339 Skv, Bardufoss
	149	Bell 412HP	RNoAF 339 Skv, Bardufoss
	161	Bell 412HP	RNoAF 339 Skv, Bardufoss
	162	Bell 412HP	RNoAF 339 Skv, Bardufoss
	163	Bell 412HP	RNoAF 339 Skv, Bardufoss
	164	Bell 412HP	RNoAF 339 Skv, Bardufoss
	165	Bell 412HP	RNoAF 339 Skv, Bardufoss
	166	Bell 412HP	RNoAF 339 Skv, Bardufoss
	167	Bell 412HP	RNoAF 339 Skv, Bardufoss
	171	NH Industries NH.90-NFH	RNoAF 337 Skv, Bardufoss
	189	Westland Sea King Mk.43B	RNoAF 330 Skv Bodø/Banak/Ørland & Sola
	194	Bell 412SP	RNoAF 339 Skv, Bardufoss
	217	NH Industries NH.90-ASW	RNoAF (on order)
	0262	AgustaWestland AW101 Mk.612 (ZZ100)	RNoAF (on order)
	0264	AgustaWestland AW101 Mk.612 (ZZ101)	RNoAF 330 Skv Sola
	0265	AgustaWestland AW101 Mk.612 (ZZ102)	RNoAF 330 Skv Sola
	0268	AgustaWestland AW101 Mk.612 (ZZ103)	RNoAF/Leonardo MW, Yeovil (rebuild)
	0270	AgustaWestland AW101 Mk.612 (ZZ104)	RNoAF 330 Skv Sola
	272	Fokker (GD) F-16A MLU Fighting Falcon $	RNoAF FLO 331 Skv, Bodø/338 Skv, Ørland
	273	Fokker (GD) F-16A MLU Fighting Falcon	RNoAF FLO 331 Skv, Bodø/338 Skv, Ørland
	0273	AgustaWestland AW101 Mk.612 (ZZ105)	RNoAF (on order)
	275	Fokker (GD) F-16A MLU Fighting Falcon	RNoAF FLO 331 Skv, Bodø/338 Skv, Ørland
	0275	AgustaWestland AW101 Mk.612 (ZZ106)	RNoAF (on order)
	276	Fokker (GD) F-16A MLU Fighting Falcon	RNoAF FLO 331 Skv, Bodø/338 Skv, Ørland
	0276	AgustaWestland AW101 Mk.612 (ZZ107)	RNoAF (on order)
	277	Fokker (GD) F-16A MLU Fighting Falcon	RNoAF FLO 331 Skv, Bodø/338 Skv, Ørland
	0277	AgustaWestland AW101 Mk.612 (ZZ108)	RNoAF (on order)
	0278	AgustaWestland AW101 Mk.612 (ZZ109)	RNoAF (on order)
	279	Fokker (GD) F-16A MLU Fighting Falcon	RNoAF FLO 331 Skv, Bodø/338 Skv, Ørland
	0279	AgustaWestland AW101 Mk.612 (ZZ110)	RNoAF (on order)
	0280	AgustaWestland AW101 Mk.612 (ZZ111)	RNoAF (on order)
	281	Fokker (GD) F-16A MLU Fighting Falcon	RNoAF FLO 331 Skv, Bodø/338 Skv, Ørland
	0281	AgustaWestland AW101 Mk.612 (ZZ112)	RNoAF (on order)
	282	Fokker (GD) F-16A MLU Fighting Falcon	RNoAF FLO 331 Skv, Bodø/338 Skv, Ørland
	0282	AgustaWestland AW101 Mk.612 (ZZ113)	RNoAF (on order)

Serial	Type (code/other identity)	Owner/operator, location or fate	Notes
0283	AgustaWestland AW101 Mk.612 (ZZ114)	RNoAF (on order)	
284	Fokker (GD) F-16A MLU Fighting Falcon	RNoAF FLO 331 Skv, Bodø/338 Skv, Ørland	
0284	AgustaWestland AW101 Mk.612 (ZZ115)	RNoAF (on order)	
285	Fokker (GD) F-16A MLU Fighting Falcon	RNoAF FLO 331 Skv, Bodø/338 Skv, Ørland	
286	Fokker (GD) F-16A MLU Fighting Falcon	RNoAF FLO 331 Skv, Bodø/338 Skv, Ørland	
288	Fokker (GD) F-16A MLU Fighting Falcon	RNoAF FLO 331 Skv, Bodø/338 Skv, Ørland	
289	Fokker (GD) F-16A MLU Fighting Falcon	RNoAF FLO 331 Skv, Bodø/338 Skv, Ørland	
291	Fokker (GD) F-16A MLU Fighting Falcon	RNoAF FLO 331 Skv, Bodø/338 Skv, Ørland	
292	Fokker (GD) F-16A MLU Fighting Falcon	RNoAF FLO 331 Skv, Bodø/338 Skv, Ørland	
293	Fokker (GD) F-16A MLU Fighting Falcon	RNoAF FLO 331 Skv, Bodø/338 Skv, Ørland	
295	Fokker (GD) F-16A MLU Fighting Falcon	RNoAF FLO 331 Skv, Bodø/338 Skv, Ørland	
297	Fokker (GD) F-16A MLU Fighting Falcon	RNoAF FLO 331 Skv, Bodø/338 Skv, Ørland	
298	Fokker (GD) F-16A MLU Fighting Falcon $	RNoAF FLO 331 Skv, Bodø/338 Skv, Ørland	
299	Fokker (GD) F-16A MLU Fighting Falcon	RNoAF FLO 331 Skv, Bodø/338 Skv, Ørland	
302	Fokker (GD) F-16B MLU Fighting Falcon	RNoAF FLO 331 Skv, Bodø/338 Skv, Ørland	
304	Fokker (GD) F-16B MLU Fighting Falcon	RNoAF FLO 331 Skv, Bodø/338 Skv, Ørland	
305	Fokker (GD) F-16B MLU Fighting Falcon	RNoAF FLO 331 Skv, Bodø/338 Skv, Ørland	
306	Fokker (GD) F-16B MLU Fighting Falcon	RNoAF FLO 331 Skv, Bodø/338 Skv, Ørland	
322	Westland Sea King Mk.43B	RNoAF 330 Skv Bodø/Banak/Ørland & Sola	
329	Westland Sea King Mk.43B	RNoAF 330 Skv Bodø/Banak/Ørland & Sola	
330	Westland Sea King Mk.43B	RNoAF 330 Skv Bodø/Banak/Ørland & Sola	
352	NH Industries NH.90-ASW	RNoAF 334 Skv, Haakonsvern	
353	NH Industries NH.90-ASW	RNoAF 334 Skv, Haakonsvern	
658	Fokker (GD) F-16A MLU Fighting Falcon	RNoAF FLO 331 Skv, Bodø/338 Skv, Ørland	
659	Fokker (GD) F-16A MLU Fighting Falcon	RNoAF FLO 331 Skv, Bodø/338 Skv, Ørland	
660	Fokker (GD) F-16A MLU Fighting Falcon	RNoAF FLO 331 Skv, Bodø/338 Skv, Ørland	
661	Fokker (GD) F-16A MLU Fighting Falcon	RNoAF FLO 331 Skv, Bodø/338 Skv, Ørland	
662	Fokker (GD) F-16A MLU Fighting Falcon	RNoAF FLO 331 Skv, Bodø/338 Skv, Ørland	
663	Fokker (GD) F-16A MLU Fighting Falcon	RNoAF FLO 331 Skv, Bodø/338 Skv, Ørland	
664	Fokker (GD) F-16A MLU Fighting Falcon $	RNoAF FLO 331 Skv, Bodø/338 Skv, Ørland	
665	Fokker (GD) F-16A MLU Fighting Falcon	RNoAF FLO 331 Skv, Bodø/338 Skv, Ørland	
666	Fokker (GD) F-16A MLU Fighting Falcon	RNoAF/USAF 416th FTS/412th TW, Edwards AFB, USA	
667	Fokker (GD) F-16A MLU Fighting Falcon	RNoAF FLO 331 Skv, Bodø/338 Skv, Ørland	
668	Fokker (GD) F-16A MLU Fighting Falcon	RNoAF FLO 331 Skv, Bodø/338 Skv, Ørland	
670	Fokker (GD) F-16A MLU Fighting Falcon	RNoAF FLO 331 Skv, Bodø/338 Skv, Ørland	
671	Fokker (GD) F-16A MLU Fighting Falcon $	RNoAF FLO 331 Skv, Bodø/338 Skv, Ørland	
672	Fokker (GD) F-16A MLU Fighting Falcon	RNoAF FLO 331 Skv, Bodø/338 Skv, Ørland	
673	Fokker (GD) F-16A MLU Fighting Falcon	RNoAF FLO 331 Skv, Bodø/338 Skv, Ørland	
674	Fokker (GD) F-16A MLU Fighting Falcon	RNoAF FLO 331 Skv, Bodø/338 Skv, Ørland	
675	Fokker (GD) F-16A MLU Fighting Falcon	RNoAF FLO 331 Skv, Bodø/338 Skv, Ørland	
677	Fokker (GD) F-16A MLU Fighting Falcon	RNoAF FLO 331 Skv, Bodø/338 Skv, Ørland	
678	Fokker (GD) F-16A MLU Fighting Falcon	RNoAF FLO 331 Skv, Bodø/338 Skv, Ørland	
680	Fokker (GD) F-16A MLU Fighting Falcon	RNoAF FLO 331 Skv, Bodø/338 Skv, Ørland	
681	Fokker (GD) F-16A MLU Fighting Falcon	RNoAF FLO 331 Skv, Bodø/338 Skv, Ørland	
682	Fokker (GD) F-16A MLU Fighting Falcon	RNoAF FLO 331 Skv, Bodø/338 Skv, Ørland	
683	Fokker (GD) F-16A MLU Fighting Falcon	RNoAF FLO 331 Skv, Bodø/338 Skv, Ørland	
686	Fokker (GD) F-16A MLU Fighting Falcon $	RNoAF FLO 331 Skv, Bodø/338 Skv, Ørland	
687	Fokker (GD) F-16A MLU Fighting Falcon	RNoAF FLO 331 Skv, Bodø/338 Skv, Ørland	
688	Fokker (GD) F-16A MLU Fighting Falcon	RNoAF FLO 331 Skv, Bodø/338 Skv, Ørland	
689	Fokker (GD) F-16B MLU Fighting Falcon	RNoAF FLO 331 Skv, Bodø/338 Skv, Ørland	
691	Fokker (GD) F-16B MLU Fighting Falcon	RNoAF FLO 331 Skv, Bodø/338 Skv, Ørland	
692	Fokker (GD) F-16B MLU Fighting Falcon $	RNoAF FLO 331 Skv, Bodø/338 Skv, Ørland	
693	Fokker (GD) F-16B MLU Fighting Falcon	RNoAF FLO 331 Skv, Bodø/338 Skv, Ørland	
711	GD F-16B MLU Fighting Falcon	RNoAF FLO 331 Skv, Bodø/338 Skv, Ørland	
1216	NH Industries NH.90-NFH	RNoAF 337 Skv, Bardufoss	
3296	Lockheed P-3C UIP Orion	RNoAF 333 Skv, Andøya	
3297	Lockheed P-3C UIP Orion	RNoAF 333 Skv, Andøya	
3298	Lockheed P-3C UIP Orion	RNoAF 333 Skv, Andøya	
3299	Lockheed P-3C UIP Orion	RNoAF 333 Skv, Andøya	
4576	Lockheed P-3N Orion	RNoAF 333 Skv, Andøya	
5087	Lockheed Martin F-35A Lightning II	RNoAF 62nd FS/56th FW, Luke AFB, AZ, USA	

Notes	Serial	Type (code/other identity)	Owner/operator, location or fate
	5088	Lockheed Martin F-35A Lightning II	RNoAF 62nd FS/56th FW, Luke AFB, AZ, USA
	5110	Lockheed Martin F-35A Lightning II	RNoAF 62nd FS/56th FW, Luke AFB, AZ, USA
	5111	Lockheed Martin F-35A Lightning II	RNoAF 62nd FS/56th FW, Luke AFB, AZ, USA
	5145	Lockheed Martin F-35A Lightning II	RNoAF 62nd FS/56th FW, Luke AFB, AZ, USA
	5146	Lockheed Martin F-35A Lightning II	RNoAF 62nd FS/56th FW, Luke AFB, AZ, USA
	5147	Lockheed Martin F-35A Lightning II	RNoAF 62nd FS/56th FW, Luke AFB, AZ, USA
	5148	Lockheed Martin F-35A Lightning II	RNoAF, NDMA Ørland (for FLO/332 Skv)
	5149	Lockheed Martin F-35A Lightning II	RNoAF, NDMA Ørland (for FLO/332 Skv)
	5150	Lockheed Martin F-35A Lightning II	RNoAF, NDMA Ørland (for FLO/332 Skv)
	5205	Lockheed Martin F-35A Lightning II	RNoAF, NDMA Ørland (for FLO/332 Skv)
	5206	Lockheed Martin F-35A Lightning II	RNoAF, NDMA Ørland (for FLO/332 Skv)
	5207	Lockheed Martin F-35A Lightning II	RNoAF, NDMA Ørland (for FLO/332 Skv)
	5208	Lockheed Martin F-35A Lightning II	RNoAF, NDMA Ørland (for FLO/332 Skv)
	5209	Lockheed Martin F-35A Lightning II	RNoAF, NDMA Ørland (for FLO/332 Skv)
	5210	Lockheed Martin F-35A Lightning II	RNoAF, NDMA Ørland (for FLO/332 Skv)
	5601	Lockheed C-130J-30 Hercules II	RNoAF 335 Skv, Gardermoen
	5607	Lockheed C-130J-30 Hercules II	RNoAF 335 Skv, Gardermoen
	5629	Lockheed C-130J-30 Hercules II	RNoAF 335 Skv, Gardermoen
	5699	Lockheed C-130J-30 Hercules II	RNoAF 335 Skv, Gardermoen
	6603	Lockheed P-3N Orion	RNoAF 333 Skv, Andøya
	...	NH Industries NH.90-ASW	RNoAF (on order)
	...	NH Industries NH.90-ASW	RNoAF (on order)
	...	NH Industries NH.90-ASW	RNoAF (on order)

OMAN
Royal Air Force of Oman (RAFO)

Notes	Serial	Type (code/other identity)	Owner/operator, location or fate
	501	Lockheed C-130H Hercules	RAFO 16 Sqn, Al Musana
	502	Lockheed C-130H Hercules	RAFO 16 Sqn, Al Musana
	503	Lockheed C-130H Hercules	RAFO 16 Sqn, Al Musana
	505	Lockheed C-130J Hercules II	RAFO 16 Sqn, Al Musana
	506	Lockheed C-130J Hercules II	RAFO 16 Sqn, Al Musana
	507	Lockheed C-130J-30 Hercules II	RAFO (on order)
	508	Lockheed C-130J-30 Hercules II	RAFO (on order)
	525	Lockheed C-130J-30 Hercules II	RAFO Royal Flt, Seeb
	554	Airbus A.320-214X	RAFO 4 Sqn, Seeb
	555	Airbus A.320-214X	RAFO 4 Sqn, Seeb
	556	Airbus A.320-214X	RAFO 4 Sqn, Seeb
	557	Grumman G.1159C Gulfstream IV	RAFO 4 Sqn, Seeb
	558	Grumman G.1159C Gulfstream IV	RAFO 4 Sqn, Seeb
	901	CASA C-295M	RAFO 5 Sqn, Salalah
	902	CASA C-295M	RAFO 5 Sqn, Salalah
	903	CASA C-295M	RAFO 5 Sqn, Salalah
	904	CASA C-295M	RAFO 5 Sqn, Salalah
	905	CASA C-295M	RAFO (on order)
	906	CASA C-295M	RAFO (on order)
	907	CASA C-295M	RAFO (on order)
	908	CASA C-295M	RAFO (on order)
	909	CASA C-295M	RAFO (on order)
	910	CASA C-295MPA Persuader	RAFO 2 Sqn, Al Musana
	911	CASA C-295MPA Persuader	RAFO 2 Sqn, Al Musana
	912	CASA C-295MPA Persuader	RAFO 2 Sqn, Al Musana
	913	CASA C-295MPA Persuader	RAFO 2 Sqn, Al Musana
	914	CASA C-295MPA Persuader	RAFO (on order)
	915	CASA C-295MPA Persuader	RAFO (on order)
	916	CASA C-295MPA Persuader	RAFO (on order)

Omani Government

Notes	Serial	Type (code/other identity)	Owner/operator, location or fate
	A4O-AA	Airbus A.320-233	Government of Oman, Seeb
	A4O-AD	Gulfstream Aerospace G.550	Government of Oman, Seeb
	A4O-AE	Gulfstream Aerospace G.550	Government of Oman, Seeb
	A4O-AJ	Airbus A.319-115CJ	Government of Oman, Seeb
	A4O-SO	Boeing 747SP-27	Government of Oman, Seeb
	A4O-HMS	Boeing 747-8H0	Government of Oman, Seeb

Serial	Type (code/other identity)	Owner/operator, location or fate	Notes
A4O-OMN	Boeing 747-430	Government of Oman, Seeb	
PAKISTAN			
Pakistan Air Force (PAF)/Pakistani Army			
4119	Lockheed C-130E Hercules [119]	PAF 21 Sqn, Karachi	
4144	Lockheed L.100 Hercules [144]	PAF 6 Sqn, Islamabad	
4148	Lockheed C-130E Hercules [148]	PAF 6 Sqn, Islamabad	
4153	Lockheed C-130E Hercules [153] $	PAF 21 Sqn, Karachi	
4159	Lockheed C-130E Hercules [159]	PAF 21 Sqn, Karachi	
4171	Lockheed C-130E Hercules [171]	PAF 6 Sqn, Islamabad	
4177	Lockheed C-130E Hercules [177]	PAF 6 Sqn, Islamabad	
4178	Lockheed C-130E Hercules [178]	PAF 21 Sqn, Karachi	
4180	Lockheed C-130E Hercules [180]	Crashed 9 November 2018, Islamabad	
4189	Lockheed C-130E Hercules [189]	PAF 6 Sqn, Islamabad	
4270	Gulfstream Aerospace G.450	Pakistani Army, Rawalpindi	
4282	Lockheed C-130E Hercules [282]	PAF 6 Sqn, Islamabad	
EYE77	Bombardier Challenger 605	Pakistani Army, Rawalpindi	
J-754	Cessna 560 Citation VI	PAF 12 VIP Communications Sqn, Islamabad	
J-755	Gulfstream Aerospace G.1159C Gulfstream IV-SP	PAF 12 VIP Communications Sqn, Islamabad	
J-756	Gulfstream Aerospace G.450	PAF 12 VIP Communications Sqn, Islamabad	
POLAND			
Sily Powietrzne (SP)/Polish Air Force & Lotnictwo Marynarki Wojennej (LMW)/Polish Navy			
0001	Gulfstream Aerospace G.550 (N547GA)	SP 1.BLTr, Warszawa	
0002	Gulfstream Aerospace G.550 (N554GD)	SP 1.BLTr, Warszawa	
011	CASA C-295M	SP 13.eltr/8.BLTr, Kraków/Balice	
012	CASA C-295M $	SP 13.eltr/8.BLTr, Kraków/Balice	
013	CASA C-295M	SP 13.eltr/8.BLTr, Kraków/Balice	
014	CASA C-295M	SP 13.eltr/8.BLTr, Kraków/Balice	
015	CASA C-295M	SP 13.eltr/8.BLTr, Kraków/Balice	
15	Mikoyan MiG-29UBM $	SP 1.elt/23.BLT, Minsk/Mazowiecki	
016	CASA C-295M	SP 13.eltr/8.BLTr, Kraków/Balice	
016	PZL 130TC-I Orlik	SP 2.OSzL/42.BLSz, Radom	
017	CASA C-295M	SP 13.eltr/8.BLTr, Kraków/Balice	
018	CASA C-295M	SP 13.eltr/8.BLTr, Kraków/Balice	
020	CASA C-295M	SP 13.eltr/8.BLTr, Kraków/Balice	
021	CASA C-295M	SP 13.eltr/8.BLTr, Kraków/Balice	
022	CASA C-295M	SP 13.eltr/8.BLTr, Kraków/Balice	
023	CASA C-295M	SP 13.eltr/8.BLTr, Kraków/Balice	
024	CASA C-295M	SP 13.eltr/8.BLTr, Kraków/Balice	
025	CASA C-295M	SP 13.eltr/8.BLTr, Kraków/Balice	
026	CASA C-295M	SP 13.eltr/8.BLTr, Kraków/Balice	
027	CASA C-295M	SP 13.eltr/8.BLTr, Kraków/Balice	
28	Mikoyan MiG-29UBM	SP 1.elt/23.BLT, Minsk/Mazowiecki	
029	PZL 130TC-II Orlik	SP 2.OSzL/42.BLSz, Radom	
030	PZL 130TC-II Orlik	SP 2.OSzL/42.BLSz, Radom	
031	PZL 130TC-II Orlik	SP 2.OSzL/42.BLSz, Radom	
032	PZL 130TC-II Orlik	SP 2.OSzL/42.BLSz, Radom	
037	PZL 130TC-II Orlik	SP 2.OSzL/42.BLSz, Radom	
38	Mikoyan MiG-29M	SP 1.elt/23.BLT, Minsk/Mazowiecki	
038	PZL 130TC-II Orlik	SP 2.OSzL/42.BLSz, Radom	
40	Mikoyan MiG-29M	SP 1.elt/23.BLT, Minsk/Mazowiecki	
40	Mikoyan MiG-29M	Crashed 4 March 2019, Stoczek, Poland	
041	PZL 130TC-II Orlik	SP 2.OSzL/42.BLSz, Radom	
42	Mikoyan MiG-29UBM	SP 1.elt/23.BLT, Minsk/Mazowiecki	
042	PZL 130TC-II Orlik	SP 2.OSzL/42.BLSz, Radom	
043	PZL 130TC-II Orlik	SP 2.OSzL/42.BLSz, Radom	
045	PZL 130TC-I Orlik	SP 2.OSzL/42.BLSz, Radom	
047	PZL 130TC-II Orlik	SP 2.OSzL/42.BLSz, Radom	
048	PZL 130TC-II Orlik	SP 2.OSzL/42.BLSz, Radom	
049	PZL 130TC-II Orlik	SP 2.OSzL/42.BLSz, Radom	
050	PZL 130TC-II Orlik	SP 2.OSzL/42.BLSz, Radom	

Notes	Serial	Type (code/other identity)	Owner/operator, location or fate
	051	PZL 130TC-II Orlik	SP 2.OSzL/42.BLSz, Radom
	052	PZL 130TC-II Orlik	SP 2.OSzL/42.BLSz, Radom
	54	Mikoyan MiG-29M	SP 1.elt/23.BLT, Minsk/Mazowiecki
	56	Mikoyan MiG-29M	SP 1.elt/23.BLT, Minsk/Mazowiecki
	59	Mikoyan MiG-29M	SP 1.elt/23.BLT, Minsk/Mazowiecki
	64	Mikoyan MiG-29UB	SP
	65	Mikoyan MiG-29A	SP 41.elt/22.BLT, Malbork
	66	Mikoyan MiG-29A	SP 41.elt/22.BLT, Malbork
	70	Mikoyan MiG-29A	SP 41.elt/22.BLT, Malbork
	83	Mikoyan MiG-29M	SP 1.elt/23.BLT, Minsk/Mazowiecki
	89	Mikoyan MiG-29M	SP 1.elt/23.BLT, Minsk/Mazowiecki
	92	Mikoyan MiG-29A	SP 41.elt/22.BLT, Malbork
	105	Mikoyan MiG-29M	SP 1.elt/23.BLT, Minsk/Mazowiecki
	108	Mikoyan MiG-29M	SP 1.elt/23.BLT, Minsk/Mazowiecki
	0110	Boeing 737-800 (N893BA)	SP 1.BLTr, Warszawa
	111	Mikoyan MiG-29M	SP 1.elt/23.BLT, Minsk/Mazowiecki
	114	Mikoyan MiG-29M	SP 1.elt/23.BLT, Minsk/Mazowiecki
	115	Mikoyan MiG-29AM	SP 1.elt/23.BLT, Minsk/Mazowiecki
	0204	PZL M28B-TD Bryza	SP 1.OSzL/41.BLSz, Deblin
	0205	PZL M28B-TD Bryza	SP 1.OSzL/41.BLSz, Deblin
	0206	PZL M28B-TD Bryza	SP 14.eltr/33.BLTr, Powidz
	0207	PZL M28B-TD Bryza	SP 13.eltr/8.BLTr, Kraków/Balice
	0208	PZL M28B-TD Bryza	SP 14.eltr/33.BLTr, Powidz
	0209	PZL M28B-TD Bryza	SP 14.eltr/33.BLTr, Powidz
	0210	PZL M28B-TD Bryza	SP 14.eltr/33.BLTr, Powidz
	0211	PZL M28B-TD Bryza	SP 14.eltr/33.BLTr, Powidz
	0212	PZL M28B-TD Bryza	SP 13.eltr/8.BLTr, Kraków/Balice
	0213	PZL M28B/PT Bryza	SP 13.eltr/8.BLTr, Kraków/Balice
	0214	PZL M28B/PT Bryza	SP 13.eltr/8.BLTr, Kraków/Balice
	0215	PZL M28B/PT Bryza	SP 13.eltr/8.BLTr, Kraków/Balice
	0216	PZL M28B/PT Bryza	SP 13.eltr/8.BLTr, Kraków/Balice
	0217	PZL M28B/PT Bryza	SP 13.eltr/8.BLTr, Kraków/Balice
	0218	PZL M28B/PT Bryza	SP 13.eltr/8.BLTr, Kraków/Balice
	0219	PZL M28B/PT Bryza	SP 13.eltr/8.BLTr, Kraków/Balice
	0220	PZL M28B/PT Bryza	SP 13.eltr/8.BLTr, Kraków/Balice
	0221	PZL M28B/PT Bryza	SP 13.eltr/8.BLTr, Kraków/Balice
	0222	PZL M28B/PT Bryza	SP 13.eltr/8.BLTr, Kraków/Balice
	0223	PZL M28B/PT Bryza	SP 13.eltr/8.BLTr, Kraków/Balice
	0224	PZL M28B/PT Bryza	SP 13.eltr/8.BLTr, Kraków/Balice
	0225	PZL M28B/PT Bryza	SP 13.eltr/8.BLTr, Kraków/Balice
	305	Sukhoi Su-22UM-3K $	SP 8.elt/21.BLT, Swidwin
	308	Sukhoi Su-22UM-3K	SP 40.elt/21.BLT, Swidwin
	310	Sukhoi Su-22UM-3K	SP 40.elt/21.BLT, Swidwin
	0404	PZL M28B-1E Bryza	LMW 30.el/44.BLMW, Cewice/Siemirowice
	0405	PZL M28B-1E Bryza	LMW 30.el/44.BLMW, Cewice/Siemirowice
	508	Sukhoi Su-22UM-3K	SP 8.elt/21.BLT, Swidwin
	509	Sukhoi Su-22UM-3K	SP 40.elt/21.BLT, Swidwin
	707	Sukhoi Su-22UM-3K $	SP 8.elt/21.BLT, Swidwin
	0723	PZL M28B-TD Bryza	LMW 28.el/43.BLMW, Gdynia/Babie Doly
	0810	PZL M28B-1RM Bryza	LMW 30.el/44.BLMW, Cewice/Siemirowice
	1001	Mil Mi-14PL	LMW 29.el/44.BLMW, Darlowo
	1002	Mil Mi-14PL	LMW 29.el/44.BLMW, Darlowo
	1003	Mil Mi-14PL	LMW 29.el/44.BLMW, Darlowo
	1003	PZL M28B-TD Bryza	LMW 28.el/43.BLMW, Gdynia/Babie Doly
	1005	Mil Mi-14PL	LMW 29.el/44.BLMW, Darlowo
	1006	PZL M28B-1R Bryza	LMW 30.el/44.BLMW, Cewice/Siemirowice
	1007	Mil Mi-14PL	LMW 29.el/44.BLMW, Darlowo
	1008	Mil Mi-14PL	LMW 29.el/44.BLMW, Darlowo
	1008	PZL M28B-1R Bryza	LMW 30.el/44.BLMW, Cewice/Siemirowice
	1009	Mil Mi-14PL	LMW 29.el/44.BLMW, Darlowo
	1010	Mil Mi-14PL	LMW 29.el/44.BLMW, Darlowo
	1011	Mil Mi-14PL	LMW 29.el/44.BLMW, Darlowo

Serial	Type (code/other identity)	Owner/operator, location or fate	Notes
1012	Mil Mi-14PL/R	LMW 29.el/44.BLMW, Darlowo	
1017	PZL M28B-1R Bryza $	LMW 30.el/44.BLMW, Cewice/Siemirowice	
1022	PZL M28B-1R Bryza	LMW 30.el/44.BLMW, Cewice/Siemirowice	
1114	PZL M28B-1R Bryza	LMW 30.el/44.BLMW, Cewice/Siemirowice	
1115	PZL M28B-1R Bryza	LMW 30.el/44.BLMW, Cewice/Siemirowice	
1116	PZL M28B-1R Bryza	LMW 30.el/44.BLMW, Cewice/Siemirowice	
1117	PZL M28B-1 Bryza	LMW 28.el/43.BLMW, Gydnia/Babie Doly	
1118	PZL M28B-1 Bryza	LMW 28.el/43.BLMW, Gydnia/Babie Doly	
1501	Lockheed C-130E Hercules	SP 14.eltr/33.BLTr, Powidz	
1502	Lockheed C-130E Hercules	SP 14.eltr/33.BLTr, Powidz	
1503	Lockheed C-130E Hercules	SP 14.eltr/33.BLTr, Powidz	
1504	Lockheed C-130E Hercules	SP 14.eltr/33.BLTr, Powidz	
1505	Lockheed C-130E Hercules $	SP 14.eltr/33.BLTr, Powidz	
3201	Sukhoi Su-22M-4	SP 8.elt/21.BLT, Swidwin	
3304	Sukhoi Su-22M-4	SP 8.elt/21.BLT, Swidwin	
3612	Sukhoi Su-22M-4	SP 40.elt/21.BLT, Swidwin	
3713	Sukhoi Su-22M-4 $	SP 40.elt/21.BLT, Swidwin	
3715	Sukhoi Su-22M-4	SP 40.elt/21.BLT, Swidwin	
3816	Sukhoi Su-22M-4	SP 40.elt/21.BLT, Swidwin	
3817	Sukhoi Su-22M-4	SP 40.elt/21.BLT, Swidwin	
3819	Sukhoi Su-22M-4	SP 8.elt/21.BLT, Swidwin	
3920	Sukhoi Su-22M-4	SP 40.elt/21.BLT, Swidwin	
4040	Lockheed Martin F-16C-52 Fighting Falcon	SP/USAF 416th FTS/412th TW, Edwards AFB, USA	
4041	Lockheed Martin F-16C-52 Fighting Falcon	SP 6.elt/31.BLT, Poznan/Krzesiny	
4042	Lockheed Martin F-16C-52 Fighting Falcon	SP 3.elt/31.BLT, Poznan/Krzesiny	
4043	Lockheed Martin F-16C-52 Fighting Falcon	SP 3.elt/31.BLT, Poznan/Krzesiny	
4044	Lockheed Martin F-16C-52 Fighting Falcon	SP 3.elt/31.BLT, Poznan/Krzesiny	
4045	Lockheed Martin F-16C-52 Fighting Falcon	SP 3.elt/31.BLT, Poznan/Krzesiny	
4046	Lockheed Martin F-16C-52 Fighting Falcon	SP 3.elt/31.BLT, Poznan/Krzesiny	
4047	Lockheed Martin F-16C-52 Fighting Falcon	SP 3.elt/31.BLT, Poznan/Krzesiny	
4048	Lockheed Martin F-16C-52 Fighting Falcon	SP 3.elt/31.BLT, Poznan/Krzesiny	
4049	Lockheed Martin F-16C-52 Fighting Falcon	SP 3.elt/31.BLT, Poznan/Krzesiny	
4050	Lockheed Martin F-16C-52 Fighting Falcon	SP 3.elt/31.BLT, Poznan/Krzesiny	
4051	Lockheed Martin F-16C-52 Fighting Falcon	SP 3.elt/31.BLT, Poznan/Krzesiny	
4052	Lockheed Martin F-16C-52 Fighting Falcon $	SP 6.elt/31.BLT, Poznan/Krzesiny	
4053	Lockheed Martin F-16C-52 Fighting Falcon	SP 6.elt/31.BLT, Poznan/Krzesiny	
4054	Lockheed Martin F-16C-52 Fighting Falcon	SP 6.elt/31.BLT, Poznan/Krzesiny	
4055	Lockheed Martin F-16C-52 Fighting Falcon $	SP 6.elt/31.BLT, Poznan/Krzesiny	
4056	Lockheed Martin F-16C-52 Fighting Falcon	SP 6.elt/31.BLT, Poznan/Krzesiny	
4057	Lockheed Martin F-16C-52 Fighting Falcon	SP 6.elt/31.BLT, Poznan/Krzesiny	
4058	Lockheed Martin F-16C-52 Fighting Falcon $	SP 6.elt/31.BLT, Poznan/Krzesiny	
4059	Lockheed Martin F-16C-52 Fighting Falcon	SP 6.elt/31.BLT, Poznan/Krzesiny	
4060	Lockheed Martin F-16C-52 Fighting Falcon	SP 6.elt/31.BLT, Poznan/Krzesiny	
4061	Lockheed Martin F-16C-52 Fighting Falcon	SP 6.elt/31.BLT, Poznan/Krzesiny	
4062	Lockheed Martin F-16C-52 Fighting Falcon $	SP 6.elt/31.BLT, Poznan/Krzesiny	
4063	Lockheed Martin F-16C-52 Fighting Falcon	SP 10.elt/32.BLT, Lask	
4064	Lockheed Martin F-16C-52 Fighting Falcon	SP 10.elt/32.BLT, Lask	
4065	Lockheed Martin F-16C-52 Fighting Falcon	SP 10.elt/32.BLT, Lask	
4066	Lockheed Martin F-16C-52 Fighting Falcon	SP 10.elt/32.BLT, Lask	
4067	Lockheed Martin F-16C-52 Fighting Falcon	SP 10.elt/32.BLT, Lask	
4068	Lockheed Martin F-16C-52 Fighting Falcon	SP 10.elt/32.BLT, Lask	
4069	Lockheed Martin F-16C-52 Fighting Falcon	SP 10.elt/32.BLT, Lask	
4070	Lockheed Martin F-16C-52 Fighting Falcon	SP 10.elt/32.BLT, Lask	
4071	Lockheed Martin F-16C-52 Fighting Falcon	SP 10.elt/32.BLT, Lask	
4072	Lockheed Martin F-16C-52 Fighting Falcon	SP 10.elt/32.BLT, Lask	
4073	Lockheed Martin F-16C-52 Fighting Falcon	SP 10.elt/32.BLT, Lask	
4074	Lockheed Martin F-16C-52 Fighting Falcon	SP 10.elt/32.BLT, Lask	
4075	Lockheed Martin F-16C-52 Fighting Falcon	SP 10.elt/32.BLT, Lask	
4076	Lockheed Martin F-16D-52 Fighting Falcon	SP 3.elt/31.BLT, Poznan/Krzesiny	
4077	Lockheed Martin F-16D-52 Fighting Falcon	SP 3.elt/31.BLT, Poznan/Krzesiny	
4078	Lockheed Martin F-16D-52 Fighting Falcon	SP 3.elt/31.BLT, Poznan/Krzesiny	
4079	Lockheed Martin F-16D-52 Fighting Falcon	SP 3.elt/31.BLT, Poznan/Krzesiny	

Notes	Serial	Type (code/other identity)	Owner/operator, location or fate
	4080	Lockheed Martin F-16D-52 Fighting Falcon	SP 3.elt/31.BLT, Poznan/Krzesiny
	4081	Lockheed Martin F-16D-52 Fighting Falcon	SP 3.elt/31.BLT, Poznan/Krzesiny
	4082	Lockheed Martin F-16D-52 Fighting Falcon $	SP 6.elt/31.BLT, Poznan/Krzesiny
	4083	Lockheed Martin F-16D-52 Fighting Falcon	SP 6.elt/31.BLT, Poznan/Krzesiny
	4084	Lockheed Martin F-16D-52 Fighting Falcon $	SP 6.elt/31.BLT, Poznan/Krzesiny
	4085	Lockheed Martin F-16D-52 Fighting Falcon	SP 10.elt/32.BLT, Lask
	4086	Lockheed Martin F-16D-52 Fighting Falcon	SP 10.elt/32.BLT, Lask
	4087	Lockheed Martin F-16D-52 Fighting Falcon	SP 10.elt/32.BLT, Lask
	4101	Mikoyan MiG-29A	SP 41.elt/22.BLT, Malbork
	4103	Mikoyan MiG-29A	Crashed 6 July 2018, Paslek
	4104	Mikoyan MiG-29A	SP 41.elt/22.BLT, Malbork
	4105	Mikoyan MiG-29A	SP 1.elt/23.BLT, Minsk/Mazowiecki
	4110	Mikoyan MiG-29UB	SP 41.elt/22.BLT, Malbork
	4113	Mikoyan MiG-29A	SP 41.elt/22.BLT, Malbork
	4116	Mikoyan MiG-29A	SP 41.elt/22.BLT, Malbork
	4120	Mikoyan MiG-29A	SP 41.elt/22.BLT, Malbork
	4121	Mikoyan MiG-29A	SP 41.elt/22.BLT, Malbork
	4122	Mikoyan MiG-29A	SP 41.elt/22.BLT, Malbork
	4123	Mikoyan MiG-29UB	SP 41.elt/22.BLT, Malbork
	7701	Aermacchi M-346 Master (CSX55209)	SP 1.OSzL/41.BLSz, Deblin
	7702	Aermacchi M-346 Master (CSX55210)	SP 1.OSzL/41.BLSz, Deblin
	7703	Aermacchi M-346 Master (CSX55211)	SP 1.OSzL/41.BLSz, Deblin
	7704	Aermacchi M-346 Master (CSX55212)	SP 1.OSzL/41.BLSz, Deblin
	7705	Aermacchi M-346 Master (MM55225)	SP 1.OSzL/41.BLSz, Deblin
	7706	Aermacchi M-346 Master (MM55226)	SP 1.OSzL/41.BLSz, Deblin
	7707	Aermacchi M-346 Master (MT55227)	SP 1.OSzL/41.BLSz, Deblin
	7708	Aermacchi M-346 Master (CSX55228)	SP 1.OSzL/41.BLSz, Deblin
	8101	Sukhoi Su-22M-4	SP 40.elt/21.BLT, Swidwin
	8205	Sukhoi Su-22M-4	SP 40.elt/21.BLT, Swidwin
	8309	Sukhoi Su-22M-4	SP 40.elt/21.BLT, Swidwin
	...	Boeing 737-800 (N785BJ)	SP (on order)
	...	Boeing 737-800	SP (on order)
	Straz Graniczna (Polish Border Guard)		
	SN-50YG	PZL M28-05 Skytruck	Straz Graniczna, Gdansk/Rebiechowo
	SN-60YG	PZL M28-05 Skytruck	Straz Graniczna, Gdansk/Rebiechowo
	Polish Government		
	SP-LIG	Embraer EMB.175-200LR	Polish Government, Warszawa
	SP-LIH	Embraer EMB.175-200LR	Polish Government, Warszawa
	PORTUGAL		
	Força Aérea Portuguesa (FAP)/Marinha		
	11401	Aérospatiale TB-30 Epsilon	FAP Esq 101, Sintra
	11402	Aérospatiale TB-30 Epsilon	FAP Esq 101, Sintra
	11403	Aérospatiale TB-30 Epsilon	FAP Esq 101, Sintra
	11404	Aérospatiale TB-30 Epsilon	FAP Esq 101, Sintra
	11405	Aérospatiale TB-30 Epsilon $	FAP Esq 101, Sintra
	11406	Aérospatiale TB-30 Epsilon	FAP Esq 101, Sintra
	11407	Aérospatiale TB-30 Epsilon	FAP Esq 101, Sintra
	11409	Aérospatiale TB-30 Epsilon	Crashed, 31 March 2015, Monte Real
	11410	Aérospatiale TB-30 Epsilon $	FAP Esq 101, Sintra
	11411	Aérospatiale TB-30 Epsilon	FAP Esq 101, Sintra
	11413	Aérospatiale TB-30 Epsilon	FAP Esq 101, Sintra
	11414	Aérospatiale TB-30 Epsilon	FAP Esq 101, Sintra
	11415	Aérospatiale TB-30 Epsilon	FAP Esq 101, Sintra
	11416	Aérospatiale TB-30 Epsilon $	FAP Esq 101, Sintra
	11417	Aérospatiale TB-30 Epsilon	FAP Esq 101, Sintra
	11418	Aérospatiale TB-30 Epsilon	FAP Esq 101, Sintra
	14807	Lockheed P-3C CUP+ Orion	FAP Esq 601, Beja
	14808	Lockheed P-3C CUP+ Orion $	FAP Esq 601, Beja
	14809	Lockheed P-3C CUP+ Orion	FAP Esq 601, Beja
	14810	Lockheed P-3C CUP+ Orion	FAP, stored Beja
	14811	Lockheed P-3C CUP+ Orion	FAP Esq 601, Beja

Serial	Type (code/other identity)	Owner/operator, location or fate	Notes
15101	Lockheed Martin F-16A MLU Fighting Falcon	FAP Esq 201/Esq 301, Monte Real	
15102	Lockheed Martin F-16A MLU Fighting Falcon	FAP Esq 201/Esq 301, Monte Real	
15103	Lockheed Martin F-16A MLU Fighting Falcon $	FAP Esq 201/Esq 301, Monte Real	
15104	Lockheed Martin F-16A MLU Fighting Falcon	FAP Esq 201/Esq 301, Monte Real	
15105	Lockheed Martin F-16A MLU Fighting Falcon $	FAP Esq 201/Esq 301, Monte Real	
15106	Lockheed Martin F-16A MLU Fighting Falcon $	FAP Esq 201/Esq 301, Monte Real	
15107	Lockheed Martin F-16A MLU Fighting Falcon	FAP Esq 201/Esq 301, Monte Real	
15108	Lockheed Martin F-16A MLU Fighting Falcon	FAP Esq 201/Esq 301, Monte Real	
15109	Lockheed Martin F-16A MLU Fighting Falcon	FAP Esq 201/Esq 301, Monte Real	
15110	Lockheed Martin F-16A MLU Fighting Falcon	FAP Esq 201/Esq 301, Monte Real	
15112	Lockheed Martin F-16A MLU Fighting Falcon	FAP Esq 201/Esq 301, Monte Real	
15113	Lockheed Martin F-16A MLU Fighting Falcon	FAP Esq 201/Esq 301, Monte Real	
15114	Lockheed Martin F-16A MLU Fighting Falcon	FAP Esq 201/Esq 301, Monte Real	
15115	Lockheed Martin F-16A MLU Fighting Falcon	FAP Esq 201/Esq 301, Monte Real	
15116	Lockheed Martin F-16A MLU Fighting Falcon	FAP Esq 201/Esq 301, Monte Real	
15117	Lockheed Martin F-16A MLU Fighting Falcon	FAP Esq 201/Esq 301, Monte Real	
15118	Lockheed Martin F-16B MLU Fighting Falcon	FAP Esq 201/Esq 301, Monte Real	
15119	Lockheed Martin F-16B MLU Fighting Falcon	FAP Esq 201/Esq 301, Monte Real	
15120	Lockheed Martin F-16B MLU Fighting Falcon	FAP Esq 201/Esq 301, Monte Real	
15122	Lockheed Martin F-16A MLU Fighting Falcon	FAP Esq 201/Esq 301, Monte Real	
15131	Lockheed Martin F-16A MLU Fighting Falcon	FAP Esq 201/Esq 301, Monte Real	
15132	Lockheed Martin F-16A MLU Fighting Falcon	FAP Esq 201/Esq 301, Monte Real	
15133	Lockheed Martin F-16A MLU Fighting Falcon	FAP Esq 201/Esq 301, Monte Real	
15134	Lockheed Martin F-16A MLU Fighting Falcon	FAP Esq 201/Esq 301, Monte Real	
15135	Lockheed Martin F-16A MLU Fighting Falcon	FAP Esq 201/Esq 301, Monte Real	
15136	Lockheed Martin F-16A MLU Fighting Falcon	FAP Esq 201/Esq 301, Monte Real	
15141	Lockheed Martin F-16A MLU Fighting Falcon	FAP Esq 201/Esq 301, Monte Real	
16701	CASA C-295M	FAP Esq 502, Lisbon/Montijo & Lajes	
16702	CASA C-295M	FAP Esq 502, Lisbon/Montijo & Lajes	
16703	CASA C-295M	FAP Esq 502, Lisbon/Montijo & Lajes	
16704	CASA C-295M	FAP Esq 502, Lisbon/Montijo & Lajes	
16705	CASA C-295M	FAP Esq 502, Lisbon/Montijo & Lajes	
16706	CASA C-295M	FAP Esq 502, Lisbon/Montijo & Lajes	
16707	CASA C-295M	FAP Esq 502, Lisbon/Montijo & Lajes	
16708	CASA C-295MPA	FAP Esq 502, Lisbon/Montijo & Lajes	
16709	CASA C-295MPA	FAP Esq 502, Lisbon/Montijo & Lajes	
16710	CASA C-295MPA	FAP Esq 502, Lisbon/Montijo & Lajes	
16711	CASA C-295MPA	FAP Esq 502, Lisbon/Montijo & Lajes	
16712	CASA C-295MPA	FAP Esq 502, Lisbon/Montijo & Lajes	
16801	Lockheed C-130H-30 Hercules	FAP Esq 501, Lisbon/Montijo	
16802	Lockheed C-130H-30 Hercules	FAP, stored Lisbon/Montijo	
16803	Lockheed C-130H Hercules	FAP Esq 501, Lisbon/Montijo	
16805	Lockheed C-130H Hercules	FAP Esq 501, Lisbon/Montijo	
16806	Lockheed C-130H-30 Hercules $	FAP Esq 501, Lisbon/Montijo	
17401	Dassault Falcon 50	FAP Esq 504, Lisbon/Montijo	
17402	Dassault Falcon 50	FAP Esq 504, Lisbon/Montijo	
17403	Dassault Falcon 50	FAP Esq 504, Lisbon/Montijo	
19201	Westland Super Lynx Mk.95	Marinha Esq de Helicopteros, Lisbon/Montijo	
19202	Westland Super Lynx Mk.95	Marinha Esq de Helicopteros, Lisbon/Montijo	
19203	Westland Super Lynx Mk.95	Marinha Esq de Helicopteros, Lisbon/Montijo	
19204	Westland Super Lynx Mk.95	Leonardo MW, Yeovil, UK (update)	
19205	Westland Super Lynx Mk.95	Marinha Esq de Helicopteros, Lisbon/Montijo	
19601	EHI EH-101 Mk.514	FAP Esq 751, Lisbon/Montijo	
19602	EHI EH-101 Mk.514	FAP Esq 751, Lisbon/Montijo	
19603	EHI EH-101 Mk.514	FAP Esq 751, Lisbon/Montijo	
19604	EHI EH-101 Mk.514	FAP Esq 751, Lisbon/Montijo	
19605	EHI EH-101 Mk.514	FAP Esq 751, Lisbon/Montijo	
19606	EHI EH-101 Mk.514	FAP Esq 751, Lisbon/Montijo	
19607	EHI EH-101 Mk.515	FAP Esq 751, Lisbon/Montijo	
19608	EHI EH-101 Mk.515	FAP Esq 751, Lisbon/Montijo	
19609	EHI EH-101 Mk.516	FAP Esq 751, Lisbon/Montijo	
19610	EHI EH-101 Mk.516	FAP Esq 751, Lisbon/Montijo	

Notes	Serial	Type (code/other identity)	Owner/operator, location or fate
	19611	EHI EH-101 Mk.516	FAP Esq 751, Lisbon/Montijo
	19612	EHI EH-101 Mk.516	FAP Lisbon/Montijo (damaged)

QATAR

Qatar Emiri Air Force (QEAF)

	211	Lockheed C-130J-30 Hercules II (08-0211) [MAH]	QEAF 12 Transport Sqn, Al-Udeid
	212	Lockheed C-130J-30 Hercules II (08-0212) [MAI]	QEAF 12 Transport Sqn, Al-Udeid
	213	Lockheed C-130J-30 Hercules II (08-0213) [MAJ]	QEAF 12 Transport Sqn, Al-Udeid
	214	Lockheed C-130J-30 Hercules II (08-0214) [MAK]	QEAF 12 Transport Sqn, Al-Udeid
	MAA	Boeing C-17A Globemaster III (08-0201)	QEAF 12 Transport Sqn, Al-Udeid
	MAB	Boeing C-17A Globemaster III (08-0202)	QEAF 12 Transport Sqn, Al-Udeid
	MAC	Boeing C-17A Globemaster III (12-0203)	QEAF 12 Transport Sqn, Al-Udeid
	MAE	Boeing C-17A Globemaster III (12-0204)	QEAF 12 Transport Sqn, Al-Udeid
	MAM	Boeing C-17A Globemaster III (14-0005)	QEAF 12 Transport Sqn, Al-Udeid
	MAN	Boeing C-17A Globemaster III (14-0006)	QEAF 12 Transport Sqn, Al-Udeid
	MAO	Boeing C-17A Globemaster III (14-0009)	QEAF 12 Transport Sqn, Al-Udeid
	MAP	Boeing C-17A Globemaster III (14-0010)	QEAF 12 Transport Sqn, Al-Udeid

Qatari Government

	A7-AAG	Airbus A.320-232	Qatari Amiri Flight, Doha
	A7-AAH	Airbus A.340-313X	Qatari Amiri Flight, Doha
	A7-AAM	Bombardier Global Express	Qatari Amiri Flight/Qatar Airways, Doha
	A7-AFE	Airbus A.310-308	Qatari Amiri Flight, Doha
	A7-HBJ	Boeing 747-8KB	Qatari Amiri Flight, Doha
	A7-HHE	Boeing 747-8KJ	Qatari Amiri Flight, Doha
	A7-HHF	Boeing 747-8Z5	Qatari Amiri Flight, Doha
	A7-HHH	Airbus A.340-541	Qatari Amiri Flight, Doha
	A7-HHJ	Airbus A.319CJ-133	Qatari Amiri Flight, Doha
	A7-HHK	Airbus A.340-211	Qatari Amiri Flight, Doha
	A7-HHM	Airbus A.330-203	Qatari Amiri Flight, Doha
	A7-HJJ	Airbus A.330-202	Qatari Amiri Flight, Doha
	A7-HSJ	Airbus A.320-232	Qatari Amiri Flight, Doha
	A7-MBK	Airbus A.320-232CJ	Qatari Amiri Flight, Doha
	A7-MED	Airbus A.319CJ-133	Qatari Amiri Flight, Doha
	A7-MHH	Airbus A.319CJ-115	Qatari Amiri Flight, Doha

ROMANIA

Fortele Aeriene Romania (FAR)

	2701	Alenia C-27J Spartan	FAR Escadrilla 902, Bucharest/Otopeni
	2702	Alenia C-27J Spartan	FAR Escadrilla 902, Bucharest/Otopeni
	2703	Alenia C-27J Spartan	FAR Escadrilla 902, Bucharest/Otopeni
	2704	Alenia C-27J Spartan	FAR Escadrilla 902, Bucharest/Otopeni
	2705	Alenia C-27J Spartan	FAR Escadrilla 902, Bucharest/Otopeni
	2706	Alenia C-27J Spartan	FAR Escadrilla 902, Bucharest/Otopeni
	2707	Alenia C-27J Spartan	FAR Escadrilla 902, Bucharest/Otopeni
	5930	Lockheed C-130B Hercules	FAR Escadrilla 901, Bucharest/Otopeni
	6166	Lockheed C-130H Hercules	FAR Escadrilla 901, Bucharest/Otopeni
	6191	Lockheed C-130H Hercules	FAR Escadrilla 901, Bucharest/Otopeni

RUSSIA

Voenno-Vozdushniye Sily Rossioki Federatsii (VVS) (Russian Air Force)/Russian Government

	595 w	Sukhoi Su-27P(LL) (36911037511)	VVS, Gromov Research Institute, Zhukhovsky
	597 w	Sukhoi Su-30LL (79371010102)	VVS, Gromov Research Institute, Zhukhovsky
	598 w	Sukhoi Su-27P(LL) (36911037820)	VVS, Gromov Research Institute, Zhukhovsky
	RA-09007	Dassault Falcon 7X	Rossiya Special Flight Det, Moscow/Vnukovo
	RA-26226	Antonov An-30	VVS (Open Skies), Moscow/Kubinka
	RA-30078	Antonov An-30	VVS (Open Skies), Moscow/Kubinka
	RA-64053	Tupolev Tu-204-300	Rossiya Special Flight Det, Moscow/Vnukovo
	RA-64057	Tupolev Tu-204-300	Rossiya Special Flight Det, Moscow/Vnukovo
	RA-64058	Tupolev Tu-204-300	Rossiya Special Flight Det, Moscow/Vnukovo
	RA-64059	Tupolev Tu-204-300	Rossiya Special Flight Det, Moscow/Vnukovo
	RA-64504	Tupolev Tu-214	Rossiya Special Flight Det, Moscow/Vnukovo
	RA-64505	Tupolev Tu-214	Rossiya Special Flight Det, Moscow/Vnukovo

Serial	Type (code/other identity)	Owner/operator, location or fate	Notes
RA-64506	Tupolev Tu-214	Rossiya Special Flight Det, Moscow/Vnukovo	
RA-64515	Tupolev Tu-214SR	Rossiya Special Flight Det, Moscow/Vnukovo	
RA-64516	Tupolev Tu-214SR	Rossiya Special Flight Det, Moscow/Vnukovo	
RA-64517	Tupolev Tu-214PU	Rossiya Special Flight Det, Moscow/Vnukovo	
RA-64520	Tupolev Tu-214PU	Rossiya Special Flight Det, Moscow/Vnukovo	
RA-64521	Tupolev Tu-214	Rossiya Special Flight Det, Ulyanovsk	
RA-64522	Tupolev Tu-214SUS	Rossiya Special Flight Det, Moscow/Vnukovo	
RA-64524	Tupolev Tu-214SUS	Rossiya Special Flight Det, Moscow/Vnukovo	
RA-64526	Tupolev Tu-214SR	Rossiya Special Flight Det, Moscow/Vnukovo	
RA-64527	Tupolev Tu-214SR	Rossiya Special Flight Det, Moscow/Vnukovo	
RA-64528	Tupolev Tu-214SR	Rossiya Special Flight Det, Moscow/Vnukovo	
RA-64531	Tupolev Tu-214PU	Rossiya Special Flight Det (on order)	
RA-65904	Tupolev Tu-134AK-3	Rossiya Special Flight Det, Moscow/Vnukovo	
RA-65905	Tupolev Tu-134AK-3	Rossiya Special Flight Det, Moscow/Vnukovo	
RA-65911	Tupolev Tu-134AK-3	Rossiya Special Flight Det, Moscow/Vnukovo	
RA-73026	Airbus A.319-115CJ	Rossiya Special Flight Det, Moscow/Vnukovo	
RA-73026	Airbus A.319-115CJ	Rossiya Special Flight Det, Moscow/Vnukovo	
RA-82035	Antonov An-124-100	VVS 224th Transport Regiment, Seshcha/Bryansk	
RA-82038	Antonov An-124-100	VVS 224th Transport Regiment, Seshcha/Bryansk	
RA-82039	Antonov An-124-100	VVS 224th Transport Regiment, Seshcha/Bryansk	
RA-85041	Tupolev Tu-154M	VVS 6991 AvB, Chalovskiy	
RA-85155	Tupolev Tu-154M	VVS 8 oae, Chalovskiy	
RA-96012	Ilyushin Il-96-300PU	Rossiya Special Flight Det, Moscow/Vnukovo	
RA-96016	Ilyushin Il-96-300PU	Rossiya Special Flight Det, Moscow/Vnukovo	
RA-96017	Ilyushin Il-96-300S	Rossiya Special Flight Det, Moscow/Vnukovo	
RA-96018	Ilyushin Il-96-300	Rossiya Special Flight Det, Moscow/Vnukovo	
RA-96019	Ilyushin Il-96-300	Rossiya Special Flight Det, Moscow/Vnukovo	
RA-96020	Ilyushin Il-96-300PU	Rossiya Special Flight Det, Moscow/Vnukovo	
RA-96021	Ilyushin Il-96-300PU	Rossiya Special Flight Det, Moscow/Vnukovo	
RA-96022	Ilyushin Il-96-300PU	Rossiya Special Flight Det, Moscow/Vnukovo	
RA-96023	Ilyushin Il-96-300	Rossiya Special Flight Det, Moscow/Vnukovo	
RA-96102	Ilyushin Il-96-400T	Rossiya Special Flight Det, Moscow/Vnukovo	
RA-96104	Ilyushin Il-96-400T	Rossiya Special Flight Det, Moscow/Vnukovo	
RF-36052	Antonov An-30B (87 bk)	VVS (Open Skies), Moscow/Kubinka	
RF-64519	Tupolev Tu-214ON	VVS (Open Skies), Moscow/Kubinka	
RF-82011	Antonov An-124-100	VVS 224th Transport Regiment, Seshcha/Bryansk	
RF-82041	Antonov An-124-100	VVS 224th Transport Regiment, Seshcha/Bryansk	
RF-85655	Tupolev Tu-154M-LK1	VVS (Open Skies), Moscow/Kubinka	

SAUDI ARABIA

Al Quwwat al Jawwiya as Sa'udiya/Royal Saudi Air Force (RSAF) & Saudi Government

111	Lockheed VC-130H Hercules	RSAF 1 Sqn, Riyadh	
112	Lockheed VC-130H Hercules	RSAF 1 Sqn, Riyadh	
464	Lockheed C-130H Hercules	RSAF 4 Sqn, Jeddah	
465	Lockheed C-130H Hercules	RSAF 4 Sqn, Jeddah	
466	Lockheed C-130H Hercules	RSAF 4 Sqn, Jeddah	
467	Lockheed C-130H Hercules	RSAF 4 Sqn, Jeddah	
468	Lockheed C-130H Hercules	RSAF 4 Sqn, Jeddah	
472	Lockheed C-130H Hercules	RSAF 4 Sqn, Jeddah	
473	Lockheed C-130H Hercules	RSAF 4 Sqn, Jeddah	
474	Lockheed C-130H Hercules	RSAF 4 Sqn, Jeddah	
475	Lockheed C-130H Hercules	RSAF 4 Sqn, Jeddah	
477	Lockheed C-130H Hercules	RSAF 4 Sqn, Jeddah	
478	Lockheed C-130H Hercules	RSAF 4 Sqn, Jeddah	
482	Lockheed C-130H Hercules	RSAF 4 Sqn, Jeddah	
483	Lockheed C-130H Hercules	RSAF 4 Sqn, Jeddah	
484	Lockheed C-130H Hercules	RSAF 4 Sqn, Jeddah	
485	Lockheed C-130H Hercules	RSAF 4 Sqn, Jeddah	
486	Lockheed C-130H Hercules	RSAF 4 Sqn, Jeddah	
1601	Lockheed C-130H Hercules	RSAF 4 Sqn, Jeddah	
1602	Lockheed C-130H Hercules	RSAF 16 Sqn, Jeddah	
1604	Lockheed C-130H Hercules	RSAF 16 Sqn, Jeddah	

Notes	Serial	Type (code/other identity)	Owner/operator, location or fate
	1605	Lockheed C-130H Hercules	RSAF 16 Sqn, Jeddah
	1615	Lockheed C-130H Hercules	RSAF 16 Sqn, Jeddah
	1622	Lockheed C-130H-30 Hercules	RSAF 16 Sqn, Jeddah
	1623	Lockheed C-130H Hercules	RSAF 16 Sqn, Jeddah
	1624	Lockheed C-130H Hercules	RSAF 16 Sqn, Jeddah
	1625	Lockheed C-130H Hercules	RSAF 16 Sqn, Jeddah
	1626	Lockheed C-130H Hercules	RSAF 16 Sqn, Jeddah
	1627	Lockheed C-130H Hercules	RSAF 16 Sqn, Jeddah
	1628	Lockheed C-130H Hercules	RSAF 16 Sqn, Jeddah
	1629	Lockheed C-130H Hercules	RSAF 16 Sqn, Jeddah
	1630	Lockheed C-130H-30 Hercules	RSAF 16 Sqn, Jeddah
	1631	Lockheed C-130H-30 Hercules	RSAF 16 Sqn, Jeddah
	1632	Lockheed L.100-30 Hercules	RSAF 16 Sqn, Jeddah
	1801	Boeing E-3A Sentry	RSAF 18 Sqn, Al Kharj
	1802	Boeing E-3A Sentry	RSAF 18 Sqn, Al Kharj
	1803	Boeing E-3A Sentry	RSAF 18 Sqn, Al Kharj
	1804	Boeing E-3A Sentry	RSAF 18 Sqn, Al Kharj
	1805	Boeing E-3A Sentry	RSAF 18 Sqn, Al Kharj
	1901	Boeing RE-3A Sentry	RSAF 19 Sqn, Al Kharj
	1902	Boeing RE-3A Sentry	RSAF 19 Sqn, Al Kharj
	2301	Boeing KE-3A Sentry (1811)	RSAF 23 Sqn, Al Kharj
	2302	Boeing KE-3A Sentry (1812)	RSAF 23 Sqn, Al Kharj
	2303	Boeing KE-3A Sentry (1813)	RSAF 23 Sqn, Al Kharj
	2304	Boeing KE-3A Sentry (1814)	RSAF 23 Sqn, Al Kharj
	2305	Boeing KE-3A Sentry (1815)	RSAF 23 Sqn, Al Kharj
	2306	Boeing KE-3A Sentry (1816)	RSAF 23 Sqn, Al Kharj
	2307	Boeing KE-3A Sentry (1818)	RSAF 23 Sqn, Al Kharj
	2401	Airbus A.330-203 MRTT	RSAF 24 Sqn, Al Kharj
	2402	Airbus A.330-203 MRTT $	RSAF 24 Sqn, Al Kharj
	2403	Airbus A.330-203 MRTT	RSAF 24 Sqn, Al Kharj
	2404	Airbus A.330-203 MRTT	RSAF 24 Sqn, Al Kharj
	2405	Airbus A.330-203 MRTT	RSAF 24 Sqn, Al Kharj
	2406	Airbus A.330-203 MRTT	RSAF 24 Sqn, Al Kharj
	3201	Lockheed KC-130H Hercules	RSAF 32 Sqn, Al Kharj
	3202	Lockheed KC-130H Hercules	RSAF 32 Sqn, Al Kharj
	3203	Lockheed KC-130H Hercules	RSAF 32 Sqn, Al Kharj
	3204	Lockheed KC-130H Hercules	RSAF 32 Sqn, Al Kharj
	3205	Lockheed KC-130H Hercules	RSAF 32 Sqn, Al Kharj
	3206	Lockheed KC-130H Hercules	RSAF 32 Sqn, Al Kharj
	3207	Lockheed KC-130H Hercules	RSAF 32 Sqn, Al Kharj
	3208	Lockheed KC-130J Hercules II	RSAF 32 Sqn, Al Kharj
	3209	Lockheed KC-130J Hercules II	RSAF 32 Sqn, Al Kharj
	8805	BAe Hawk 65A	RSAF 88 Sqn, *Saudi Hawks*, Tabuk
	8806	BAe Hawk 65A	RSAF 88 Sqn, *Saudi Hawks*, Tabuk
	8807	BAe Hawk 65	RSAF 88 Sqn, *Saudi Hawks*, Tabuk
	8808	BAe Hawk 65	RSAF 88 Sqn, *Saudi Hawks*, Tabuk
	8810	BAe Hawk 65	RSAF 88 Sqn, *Saudi Hawks*, Tabuk
	8811	BAe Hawk 65A	RSAF 88 Sqn, *Saudi Hawks*, Tabuk
	8812	BAe Hawk 65A	RSAF 88 Sqn, *Saudi Hawks*, Tabuk
	8813	BAe Hawk 65	RSAF 88 Sqn, *Saudi Hawks*, Tabuk
	8814	BAe Hawk 65	RSAF 88 Sqn, *Saudi Hawks*, Tabuk
	8816	BAe Hawk 65	RSAF 88 Sqn, *Saudi Hawks*, Tabuk
	8817	BAe Hawk 65	RSAF 88 Sqn, *Saudi Hawks*, Tabuk
	8818	BAe Hawk 65A	RSAF 88 Sqn, *Saudi Hawks*, Tabuk
	8819	BAe Hawk 65	RSAF 88 Sqn, *Saudi Hawks*, Tabuk
	8820	BAe Hawk 65	RSAF 88 Sqn, *Saudi Hawks*, Tabuk
	8821	BAe Hawk 65	RSAF 88 Sqn, *Saudi Hawks*, Tabuk
	HZ-101	Boeing 737-7DP	RSAF 1 Sqn, Riyadh
	HZ-102	Boeing 737-8DP	RSAF 1 Sqn, Riyadh
	HZ-103	Grumman G.1159C Gulfstream IV	RSAF 1 Sqn, Riyadh
	HZ-105	BAe 125-800	RSAF 1 Sqn, Riyadh
	HZ-109	BAe 125-800B	RSAF 1 Sqn, Riyadh

Serial	Type (code/other identity)	Owner/operator, location or fate	Notes
HZ-110	BAe 125-800B	RSAF 1 Sqn, Riyadh	
HZ-117	Lockheed L.100-30 Hercules	RSAF 1 Sqn, Riyadh	
HZ-124	Airbus A.340-211	RSAF 1 Sqn, Riyadh	
HZ-128	Lockheed L.100-30 Hercules	RSAF 1 Sqn, Riyadh	
HZ-129	Lockheed L.100-30 Hercules	RSAF 1 Sqn, Riyadh	
HZ-130	BAe 125-800B	RSAF 1 Sqn, Riyadh	
HZ-132	Lockheed L.100-30 Hercules	RSAF 1 Sqn, Riyadh	
HZ-133	Cessna 550 Citation II	RSAF 1 Sqn, Riyadh	
HZ-134	Cessna 550 Citation II	RSAF 1 Sqn, Riyadh	
HZ-135	Cessna 550 Citation II	RSAF 1 Sqn, Riyadh	
HZ-136	Cessna 550 Citation II	RSAF 1 Sqn, Riyadh	
HZ-AFN	Grumman G.1159A Gulfstream III	Saudi Special Flight Services, Jeddah	
HZ-AFR	Grumman G.1159A Gulfstream III	Saudi Special Flight Services, Jeddah	
HZ-AFT	Dassault Falcon 900	Saudi Special Flight Services, Jeddah	
HZ-AFZ	Dassault Falcon 900	Saudi Special Flight Services, Jeddah	
HZ-AS99	Airbus A.318-112CJ	Saudi Royal Flight, Jeddah	
HZ-HM1	Boeing 747-468	Saudi Royal Flight, Jeddah	
HZ-HM1A	Boeing 747-3G1	Saudi Royal Flight, Jeddah	
HZ-HM1B	Boeing 747SP-68	Saudi Royal Flight, Jeddah	
HZ-HM1C	Boeing 747SP-68	Saudi Royal Flight, Jeddah	
HZ-HMED	Boeing 757-23A	Saudi Royal Flight, Riyadh	
HZ-HMS2	Airbus A.340-213X	RSAF, Riyadh	
HZ-MS1A	Bombardier Lear 60	Saudi Armed Forces Medical Services, Riyadh	
HZ-MS1B	Bombardier Lear 60	Saudi Armed Forces Medical Services, Riyadh	
HZ-MS02	Lockheed C-130H Hercules	Saudi Armed Forces Medical Services, Riyadh	
HZ-MS4	Grumman G.1159C Gulfstream IV-SP	Saudi Armed Forces Medical Services, Riyadh	
HZ-MS4A	Gulfstream Aerospace G.450	Saudi Armed Forces Medical Services, Riyadh	
HZ-MS4B	Gulfstream Aerospace G.450	Saudi Armed Forces Medical Services, Riyadh	
HZ-MS4C	Gulfstream Aerospace G.450	Saudi Armed Forces Medical Services, Riyadh	
HZ-MS5A	Gulfstream Aerospace Gulfstream V	Saudi Armed Forces Medical Services, Riyadh	
HZ-MS5B	Gulfstream Aerospace Gulfstream V	Saudi Armed Forces Medical Services, Riyadh	
HZ-MS06	Lockheed L.100-30 Hercules	Saudi Armed Forces Medical Services, Riyadh	
HZ-MS07	Lockheed C-130H Hercules	Saudi Armed Forces Medical Services, Riyadh	
HZ-MS09	Lockheed L.100-30 Hercules	Saudi Armed Forces Medical Services, Riyadh	

SENEGAL

6V-ONE	Airbus A.319CJ-115X	Government of Senegal, Dakar	

SERBIA

YU-BNA	Dassault Falcon 50	Government of Serbia, Belgrade	
YU-SRB	Embraer ERJ.135BJ Legacy 600	Government of Serbia, Belgrade	

SINGAPORE
Republic of Singapore Air Force (RSAF)

720	Lockheed KC-130B Hercules	RSAF 122 Sqn, Paya Labar	
721	Lockheed KC-130B Hercules	RSAF 122 Sqn, Paya Labar	
724	Lockheed KC-130B Hercules	RSAF 122 Sqn, Paya Labar	
725	Lockheed KC-130B Hercules	RSAF 122 Sqn, Paya Labar	
730	Lockheed C-130H Hercules	RSAF 122 Sqn, Paya Labar	
731	Lockheed C-130H Hercules	RSAF 122 Sqn, Paya Labar	
732	Lockheed C-130H Hercules	RSAF 122 Sqn, Paya Labar	
733	Lockheed C-130H Hercules	RSAF 122 Sqn, Paya Labar	
734	Lockheed KC-130H Hercules	RSAF 122 Sqn, Paya Labar	
735	Lockheed C-130H Hercules	RSAF 122 Sqn, Paya Labar	
750	Boeing KC-135R Stratotanker	RSAF 112 Sqn, Changi	
751	Boeing KC-135R Stratotanker	RSAF 112 Sqn, Changi	
752	Boeing KC-135R Stratotanker	RSAF 112 Sqn, Changi	
753	Boeing KC-135R Stratotanker	RSAF 112 Sqn, Changi	
760	Airbus A.330-203 MRTT (EC-333/MRTT033)	RSAF 112 Sqn, Changi	
761	Airbus A.330-203 MRTT (EC-332/MRTT034) $	RSAF 112 Sqn, Changi	
762	Airbus A.330-203 MRTT (EC-336/MRTT035)	RSAF 112 Sqn, Changi (on order)	
763	Airbus A.330-203 MRTT (EC-337/MRTT036)	RSAF 112 Sqn, Changi (on order)	

Notes	Serial	Type (code/other identity)	Owner/operator, location or fate
	764	Airbus A.330-203 MRTT (F-WWYR/EC-335)	RSAF 112 Sqn, Changi (on order)
	765	Airbus A.330-203 MRTT (F-WWYX)	RSAF 112 Sqn, Changi (on order)
	SLOVAKIA		
	Slovenské Vojenske Letectvo (SVL)		
	0619	Mikoyan MiG-29AS	SVL 1.Blt/Zmiešané Letecké Kridlo, Sliač
	0807	Mil Mi-17	SVL 2.Dvlt/Vrtulnikové Letcecké Kridlo, Prešov
	0808	Mil Mi-17	SVL 2.Dvlt/Vrtulnikové Letcecké Kridlo, Prešov
	0820	Mil Mi-17	SVL 2.Dvlt/Vrtulnikové Letcecké Kridlo, Prešov
	0821	Mil Mi-17	SVL 2.Dvlt/Vrtulnikové Letcecké Kridlo, Prešov
	0823	Mil Mi-17M	SVL 2.Dvlt/Vrtulnikové Letcecké Kridlo, Prešov
	0824	Mil Mi-17	SVL 2.Dvlt/Vrtulnikové Letcecké Kridlo, Prešov
	0826	Mil Mi-17	SVL 2.Dvlt/Vrtulnikové Letcecké Kridlo, Prešov
	0841	Mil Mi-17	SVL 2.Dvlt/Vrtulnikové Letcecké Kridlo, Prešov
	0844	Mil Mi-17	SVL 2.Dvlt/Vrtulnikové Letcecké Kridlo, Prešov
	0845	Mil Mi-17	SVL 2.Dvlt/Vrtulnikové Letcecké Kridlo, Prešov
	0846	Mil Mi-17	SVL 2.Dvlt/Vrtulnikové Letcecké Kridlo, Prešov
	0847	Mil Mi-17	SVL 2.Dvlt/Vrtulnikové Letcecké Kridlo, Prešov
	0921	Mikoyan MiG-29AS	SVL 1.Blt/Zmiešané Letecké Kridlo, Sliač
	1133	LET L-410T Turbolet	SVL 1.Dopravná Letka/Dopravné Kridlo, Malacky
	1303	Mikoyan MiG-29UBS $	SVL 1.Blt/Zmiešané Letecké Kridlo, Sliač
	1521	LET L-410FG Turbolet	SVL 1.Dopravná Letka/Dopravné Kridlo, Malacky
	1931	Aeritalia C-27J Spartan (CSX62302)	SVL 1.Dopravná Letka/Dopravné Kridlo, Malacky
	1962	Aeritalia C-27J Spartan (CSX62306)	SVL 1.Dopravná Letka/Dopravné Kridlo, Malacky
	2123	Mikoyan MiG-29AS	SVL 1.Blt/Zmiešané Letecké Kridlo, Sliač
	2311	LET L-410UVP Turbolet	SVL 1.Dopravná Letka/Dopravné Kridlo, Malacky
	2421	LET L-410UVP Turbolet	SVL 1.Dopravná Letka/Dopravné Kridlo, Malacky
	2718	LET L-401UVP-E Turbolet	SVL 1.Dopravná Letka/Dopravné Kridlo, Malacky
	2721	LET L-401UVP-E Turbolet	SVL 1.Dopravná Letka/Dopravné Kridlo, Malacky
	2818	LET L-401UVP-20 Turbolet	SVL 1.Dopravná Letka/Dopravné Kridlo, Malacky
	2901	LET L-401UVP-20 Turbolet	SVL 1.Dopravná Letka/Dopravné Kridlo, Malacky
	3709	Mikoyan MiG-29AS	SVL 1.Blt/Zmiešané Letecké Kridlo, Sliač
	3911	Mikoyan MiG-29AS	SVL 1.Blt/Zmiešané Letecké Kridlo, Sliač
	4701	Aero L-39ZAM Albatros	SVL 2.vlt/Zmiešané Letecké Kridlo, Sliač
	4703	Aero L-39ZAM Albatros	SVL 2.vlt/Zmiešané Letecké Kridlo, Sliač
	4707	Aero L-39ZAM Albatros	SVL, stored Sliač
	4711	Aero L-39ZAM Albatros	*Crashed 10 October 2018, Zvolen*
	5252	Aero L-39CM Albatros	SVL 2.vlt/Zmiešané Letecké Kridlo, Sliač
	5253	Aero L-39CM Albatros	SVL 2.vlt/Zmiešané Letecké Kridlo, Sliač
	5301	Aero L-39CM Albatros $	SVL 2.vlt/Zmiešané Letecké Kridlo, Sliač
	5302	Aero L-39CM Albatros	SVL 2.vlt/Zmiešané Letecké Kridlo, Sliač
	5304	Mikoyan MiG-29UBS $	SVL 1.Blt/Zmiešané Letecké Kridlo, Sliač
	6124	Mikoyan MiG-29AS	SVL 1.Blt/Zmiešané Letecké Kridlo, Sliač
	6526	Mikoyan MiG-29AS	SVL 1.Blt/Zmiešané Letecké Kridlo, Sliač
	6627	Mikoyan MiG-29AS	SVL 1.Blt/Zmiešané Letecké Kridlo, Sliač
	6728	Mikoyan MiG-29AS	SVL 1.Blt/Zmiešané Letecké Kridlo, Sliač
	7639	Sikorsky UH-60M Black Hawk	SVL 2.Dvlt/Vrtulnikové Letcecké Kridlo, Prešov
	7640	Sikorsky UH-60M Black Hawk	SVL 2.Dvlt/Vrtulnikové Letcecké Kridlo, Prešov
	7641	Sikorsky UH-60M Black Hawk	SVL 2.Dvlt/Vrtulnikové Letcecké Kridlo, Prešov
	7642	Sikorsky UH-60M Black Hawk	SVL 2.Dvlt/Vrtulnikové Letcecké Kridlo, Prešov
	....	Sikorsky UH-60M Black Hawk	SVL (on order)
	....	Sikorsky UH-60M Black Hawk	SVL (on order)
	....	Sikorsky UH-60M Black Hawk	SVL (on order)
	....	Sikorsky UH-60M Black Hawk	SVL (on order)
	....	Sikorsky UH-60M Black Hawk	SVL (on order)
	Slovak Government		
	OM-BYA	Airbus A.319-115	Slovak Government, Bratislava/Ivanka
	OM-BYB	Fokker 100	Slovak Government, Bratislava/Ivanka
	OM-BYC	Fokker 100	Slovak Government, Bratislava/Ivanka
	OM-BYK	Airbus A.319-115XCJ	Slovak Government, Bratislava/Ivanka

Serial	Type (code/other identity)	Owner/operator, location or fate	Notes
SLOVENIA			
Slovenska Vojska (SV)/Slovenian Armed Forces			
L1-01	Dassault Falcon 2000EX	Government of Slovenia, Ljubljana	
L4-01	LET 410UVP-E Turbolet	SV 107.Letalska Baza, Cerklje ob Krki	
L9-61	Pilatus PC-9M	SV Letalska Šola, Cerklje ob Krki	
L9-62	Pilatus PC-9M	SV Letalska Šola, Cerklje ob Krki	
L9-63	Pilatus PC-9M	SV Letalska Šola, Cerklje ob Krki	
L9-64	Pilatus PC-9M	SV Letalska Šola, Cerklje ob Krki	
L9-65	Pilatus PC-9M	SV Letalska Šola, Cerklje ob Krki	
L9-66	Pilatus PC-9M	SV Letalska Šola, Cerklje ob Krki	
L9-67	Pilatus PC-9M	SV Letalska Šola, Cerklje ob Krki	
L9-68	Pilatus PC-9M	SV Letalska Šola, Cerklje ob Krki	
L9-69	Pilatus PC-9M	SV Letalska Šola, Cerklje ob Krki	
SOUTH AFRICA			
Suid Afrikaanse Lugmag/South African Air Force (SAAF)			
401	Lockheed C-130BZ Hercules	SAAF 28 Sqn, Waterkloof	
402	Lockheed C-130BZ Hercules	SAAF 28 Sqn, Waterkloof	
403	Lockheed C-130BZ Hercules	SAAF 28 Sqn, Waterkloof	
404	Lockheed C-130BZ Hercules	SAAF 28 Sqn, Waterkloof	
405	Lockheed C-130BZ Hercules $	SAAF 28 Sqn, Waterkloof	
406	Lockheed C-130BZ Hercules	SAAF 28 Sqn, Waterkloof	
409	Lockheed C-130BZ Hercules	SAAF 28 Sqn, Waterkloof	
ZS-NAN	Dassault Falcon 900	SAAF 21 Sqn, Waterkloof	
ZS-RSA	Boeing 737-7ED	SAAF 21 Sqn, Waterkloof	
SOUTH KOREA			
Han Guk Gong Gun/Republic of Korea Air Force			
10001	Boeing 747-4B5	RoKAF 296 Sqn/35 Combined Group, Seoul AB	
SPAIN			
Arma Aérea de l'Armada Española, Ejército del Aire (EdA)/Spanish Air Force & Guardia Civil			
CE.15-01	McDonnell Douglas EF-18BM Hornet [15-70] $	EdA 151 Esc/152 Esc/153 Esc/Ala 15, Zaragoza	
CE.15-2	McDonnell Douglas EF-18BM Hornet [15-71]	EdA 151 Esc/152 Esc/153 Esc/Ala 15, Zaragoza	
CE.15-03	McDonnell Douglas EF-18BM Hornet [15-72]	EdA 151 Esc/152 Esc/153 Esc/Ala 15, Zaragoza	
CE.15-04	McDonnell Douglas EF-18BM Hornet [15-73]	EdA 151 Esc/152 Esc/153 Esc/Ala 15, Zaragoza	
CE.15-5	McDonnell Douglas EF-18BM Hornet [15-74]	EdA 151 Esc/152 Esc/153 Esc/Ala 15, Zaragoza	
CE.15-06	McDonnell Douglas EF-18BM Hornet [15-75]	EdA 151 Esc/152 Esc/153 Esc/Ala 15, Zaragoza	
CE.15-07	McDonnell Douglas EF-18BM Hornet [15-76]	EdA 151 Esc/152 Esc/153 Esc/Ala 15, Zaragoza	
CE.15-08	McDonnell Douglas EF-18BM Hornet [12-71]	EdA 121 Esc/122 Esc/Ala 12, Madrid/Torrejón	
CE.15-09	McDonnell Douglas EF-18BM Hornet [15-77]	EdA 151 Esc/152 Esc/153 Esc/Ala 15, Zaragoza	
CE.15-10	McDonnell Douglas EF-18BM Hornet [12-73] $	EdA 121 Esc/122 Esc/Ala 12, Madrid/Torrejón	
CE.15-11	McDonnell Douglas EF-18BM Hornet [12-74]	EdA 121 Esc/122 Esc/Ala 12, Madrid/Torrejón	
CE.15-12	McDonnell Douglas EF-18BM Hornet [12-75]	EdA 121 Esc/122 Esc/Ala 12, Madrid/Torrejón	
C.15-13	McDonnell Douglas EF-18M Hornet [12-01]	EdA 121 Esc/122 Esc/Ala 12, Madrid/Torrejón	
C.15-14	McDonnell Douglas EF-18M Hornet [15-01] $	EdA 151 Esc/152 Esc/153 Esc/Ala 15, Zaragoza	
C.15-15	McDonnell Douglas EF-18M Hornet [15-02]	EdA 151 Esc/152 Esc/153 Esc/Ala 15, Zaragoza	
C.15-16	McDonnell Douglas EF-18M Hornet [15-03]	EdA 151 Esc/152 Esc/153 Esc/Ala 15, Zaragoza	
C.15-18	McDonnell Douglas EF-18M Hornet [15-05]	EdA 151 Esc/152 Esc/153 Esc/Ala 15, Zaragoza	
C.15-20	McDonnell Douglas EF-18M Hornet [15-07]	EdA 151 Esc/152 Esc/153 Esc/Ala 15, Zaragoza	
C.15-21	McDonnell Douglas EF-18M Hornet [15-08]	EdA 151 Esc/152 Esc/153 Esc/Ala 15, Zaragoza	
C.15-22	McDonnell Douglas EF-18M Hornet [15-09]	EdA 151 Esc/152 Esc/153 Esc/Ala 15, Zaragoza	
C.15-23	McDonnell Douglas EF-18M Hornet [15-10]	EdA 151 Esc/152 Esc/153 Esc/Ala 15, Zaragoza	
C.15-24	McDonnell Douglas EF-18M Hornet [15-11]	EdA 151 Esc/152 Esc/153 Esc/Ala 15, Zaragoza	
C.15-25	McDonnell Douglas EF-18M Hornet [15-12]	EdA 151 Esc/152 Esc/153 Esc/Ala 15, Zaragoza	
C.15-26	McDonnell Douglas EF-18M Hornet [15-13] $	EdA 151 Esc/152 Esc/153 Esc/Ala 15, Zaragoza	
C.15-27	McDonnell Douglas EF-18M Hornet [15-14]	EdA 151 Esc/152 Esc/153 Esc/Ala 15, Zaragoza	
C.15-28	McDonnell Douglas EF-18M Hornet [15-15]	EdA 151 Esc/152 Esc/153 Esc/Ala 15, Zaragoza	
C.15-29	McDonnell Douglas EF-18M Hornet [15-16]	EdA 151 Esc/152 Esc/153 Esc/Ala 15, Zaragoza	
C.15-30	McDonnell Douglas EF-18M Hornet [15-17]	EdA 151 Esc/152 Esc/153 Esc/Ala 15, Zaragoza	
C.15-31	McDonnell Douglas EF-18M Hornet [15-18]	EdA 151 Esc/152 Esc/153 Esc/Ala 15, Zaragoza	
C.15-32	McDonnell Douglas EF-18M Hornet [15-19]	EdA 151 Esc/152 Esc/153 Esc/Ala 15, Zaragoza	

Notes	Serial	Type (code/other identity)	Owner/operator, location or fate
	C.15-33	McDonnell Douglas EF-18M Hornet [15-20]	EdA 151 Esc/152 Esc/153 Esc/Ala 15, Zaragoza
	C.15-34	McDonnell Douglas EF-18M Hornet [12-50] $	EdA 121 Esc/122 Esc/Ala 12, Madrid/Torrejón
	C.15-35	McDonnell Douglas EF-18M Hornet [15-22]	EdA 151 Esc/152 Esc/153 Esc/Ala 15, Zaragoza
	C.15-36	McDonnell Douglas EF-18M Hornet [15-23]	EdA 151 Esc/152 Esc/153 Esc/Ala 15, Zaragoza
	C.15-37	McDonnell Douglas EF-18M Hornet [15-24]	EdA 151 Esc/152 Esc/153 Esc/Ala 15, Zaragoza
	C.15-38	McDonnell Douglas EF-18M Hornet [15-25]	EdA, stored Zaragoza
	C.15-39	McDonnell Douglas EF-18M Hornet [15-26]	EdA 151 Esc/152 Esc/153 Esc/Ala 15, Zaragoza
	C.15-40	McDonnell Douglas EF-18M Hornet [15-27]	EdA 151 Esc/152 Esc/153 Esc/Ala 15, Zaragoza
	C.15-41	McDonnell Douglas EF-18M Hornet [15-28] $	EdA 151 Esc/152 Esc/153 Esc/Ala 15, Zaragoza
	C.15-43	McDonnell Douglas EF-18M Hornet [15-30]	EdA 151 Esc/152 Esc/153 Esc/Ala 15, Zaragoza
	C.15-44	McDonnell Douglas EF-18M Hornet [12-02]	EdA 121 Esc/122 Esc/Ala 12, Madrid/Torrejón
	C.15-45	McDonnell Douglas EF-18M Hornet [12-03]	EdA 121 Esc/122 Esc/Ala 12, Madrid/Torrejón
	C.15-46	McDonnell Douglas EF-18M Hornet [12-04]	EdA 121 Esc/122 Esc/Ala 12, Madrid/Torrejón
	C.15-47	McDonnell Douglas EF-18M Hornet [15-31]	EdA 151 Esc/152 Esc/153 Esc/Ala 15, Zaragoza
	C.15-48	McDonnell Douglas EF-18M Hornet [12-06]	EdA 121 Esc/122 Esc/Ala 12, Madrid/Torrejón
	C.15-49	McDonnell Douglas EF-18M Hornet [12-07]	EdA 121 Esc/122 Esc/Ala 12, Madrid/Torrejón
	C.15-50	McDonnell Douglas EF-18M Hornet [12-08]	EdA 121 Esc/122 Esc/Ala 12, Madrid/Torrejón
	C.15-51	McDonnell Douglas EF-18M Hornet [12-09]	EdA 121 Esc/122 Esc/Ala 12, Madrid/Torrejón
	C.15-53	McDonnell Douglas EF-18M Hornet [12-11]	EdA 121 Esc/122 Esc/Ala 12, Madrid/Torrejón
	C.15-54	McDonnell Douglas EF-18M Hornet [12-12]	EdA 121 Esc/122 Esc/Ala 12, Madrid/Torrejón
	C.15-55	McDonnell Douglas EF-18M Hornet [12-13]	EdA 121 Esc/122 Esc/Ala 12, Madrid/Torrejón
	C.15-56	McDonnell Douglas EF-18M Hornet [12-14]	EdA 121 Esc/122 Esc/Ala 12, Madrid/Torrejón
	C.15-57	McDonnell Douglas EF-18M Hornet [12-15]	EdA 121 Esc/122 Esc/Ala 12, Madrid/Torrejón
	C.15-59	McDonnell Douglas EF-18M Hornet [12-17]	EdA 121 Esc/122 Esc/Ala 12, Madrid/Torrejón
	C.15-60	McDonnell Douglas EF-18M Hornet [12-18]	EdA 121 Esc/122 Esc/Ala 12, Madrid/Torrejón
	C.15-61	McDonnell Douglas EF-18M Hornet [12-19]	EdA 121 Esc/122 Esc/Ala 12, Madrid/Torrejón
	C.15-62	McDonnell Douglas EF-18M Hornet [12-20]	EdA 121 Esc/122 Esc/Ala 12, Madrid/Torrejón
	C.15-64	McDonnell Douglas EF-18M Hornet [15-34]	EdA 151 Esc/152 Esc/153 Esc/Ala 15, Zaragoza
	C.15-65	McDonnell Douglas EF-18M Hornet [12-23]	EdA 121 Esc/122 Esc/Ala 12, Madrid/Torrejón
	C.15-66	McDonnell Douglas EF-18M Hornet [12-24]	EdA 121 Esc/122 Esc/Ala 12, Madrid/Torrejón
	C.15-67	McDonnell Douglas EF-18M Hornet [15-33]	EdA 151 Esc/152 Esc/153 Esc/Ala 15, Zaragoza
	C.15-68	McDonnell Douglas EF-18M Hornet [12-26] $	EdA 121 Esc/122 Esc/Ala 12, Madrid/Torrejón
	C.15-69	McDonnell Douglas EF-18M Hornet [12-27]	EdA 121 Esc/122 Esc/Ala 12, Madrid/Torrejón
	C.15-70	McDonnell Douglas EF-18M Hornet [12-28]	EdA 121 Esc/122 Esc/Ala 12, Madrid/Torrejón
	C.15-72	McDonnell Douglas EF-18M Hornet [12-30]	EdA 121 Esc/122 Esc/Ala 12, Madrid/Torrejón
	C.15-73	McDonnell Douglas F/A-18A+ Hornet [46-01] $	EdA 462 Esc/Ala 46, Gran Canaria
	C.15-75	McDonnell Douglas F/A-18A+ Hornet [46-03]	EdA 462 Esc/Ala 46, Gran Canaria
	C.15-77	McDonnell Douglas F/A-18A+ Hornet [46-05]	EdA 462 Esc/Ala 46, Gran Canaria
	C.15-79	McDonnell Douglas F/A-18A+ Hornet [46-07]	EdA 462 Esc/Ala 46, Gran Canaria
	C.15-80	McDonnell Douglas F/A-18A+ Hornet [46-08]	EdA 462 Esc/Ala 46, Gran Canaria
	C.15-81	McDonnell Douglas F/A-18A+ Hornet [46-09]	EdA 462 Esc/Ala 46, Gran Canaria
	C.15-82	McDonnell Douglas F/A-18A+ Hornet [46-10]	EdA 462 Esc/Ala 46, Gran Canaria
	C.15-83	McDonnell Douglas F/A-18A+ Hornet [46-11]	EdA 462 Esc/Ala 46, Gran Canaria
	C.15-84	McDonnell Douglas F/A-18A+ Hornet [46-12]	EdA 462 Esc/Ala 46, Gran Canaria
	C.15-85	McDonnell Douglas F/A-18A+ Hornet [46-13]	EdA 462 Esc/Ala 46, Gran Canaria
	C.15-86	McDonnell Douglas F/A-18A+ Hornet [46-14]	EdA 462 Esc/Ala 46, Gran Canaria
	C.15-87	McDonnell Douglas F/A-18A+ Hornet [46-15]	EdA 462 Esc/Ala 46, Gran Canaria
	C.15-88	McDonnell Douglas F/A-18A+ Hornet [46-16] $	EdA 462 Esc/Ala 46, Gran Canaria
	C.15-89	McDonnell Douglas F/A-18A+ Hornet [46-17]	EdA 462 Esc/Ala 46, Gran Canaria
	C.15-90	McDonnell Douglas F/A-18A+ Hornet [46-18]	EdA 462 Esc/Ala 46, Gran Canaria
	C.15-92	McDonnell Douglas F/A-18A+ Hornet [46-20]	EdA 462 Esc/Ala 46, Gran Canaria
	C.15-93	McDonnell Douglas F/A-18A+ Hornet [46-21]	EdA 462 Esc/Ala 46, Gran Canaria
	C.15-94	McDonnell Douglas F/A-18A+ Hornet [46-22]	EdA 462 Esc/Ala 46, Gran Canaria
	C.15-95	McDonnell Douglas F/A-18A+ Hornet [46-23]	EdA 462 Esc/Ala 46, Gran Canaria
	C.15-96	McDonnell Douglas F/A-18A+ Hornet [46-24]	EdA 462 Esc/Ala 46, Gran Canaria
	CE.16-01	Eurofighter EF.2000(T) Tifón [11-70]	EdA 111 Esc/113 Esc/Ala 11, Sevilla/Morón
	CE.16-02	Eurofighter EF.2000(T) Tifón [11-71]	EdA 111 Esc/113 Esc/Ala 11, Sevilla/Morón
	CE.16-03	Eurofighter EF.2000(T) Tifón [11-72]	EdA 111 Esc/113 Esc/Ala 11, Sevilla/Morón
	CE.16-04	Eurofighter EF.2000(T) Tifón [11-73]	EdA 111 Esc/113 Esc/Ala 11, Sevilla/Morón
	CE.16-05	Eurofighter EF.2000(T) Tifón [11-74]	EdA 111 Esc/113 Esc/Ala 11, Sevilla/Morón
	CE.16-06	Eurofighter EF.2000(T) Tifón [11-75]	EdA 111 Esc/113 Esc/Ala 11, Sevilla/Morón
	CE.16-07	Eurofighter EF.2000(T) Tifón [11-76]	EdA 111 Esc/113 Esc/Ala 11, Sevilla/Morón

Serial	Type (code/other identity)	Owner/operator, location or fate	Notes
CE.16-09	Eurofighter EF.2000(T) Tifón [11-78]	EdA 111 Esc/113 Esc/Ala 11, Sevilla/Morón	
CE.16-10	Eurofighter EF.2000(T) Tifón [11-79]	EdA 111 Esc/113 Esc/Ala 11, Sevilla/Morón	
CE.16-11	Eurofighter EF.2000(T) Tifón [14-70]	EdA 142 Esc/Ala 14, Albacete/Los Llanos	
CE.16-12	Eurofighter EF.2000(T) Tifón (10000) [14-71]	EdA 142 Esc/Ala 14, Albacete/Los Llanos	
CE.16-13	Eurofighter EF.2000(T) Tifón (10005) [11-80]	EdA 111 Esc/113 Esc/Ala 11, Sevilla/Morón	
CE.16-14	Eurofighter EF.2000(T) Tifón (10015) [11-81]	EdA 111 Esc/113 Esc/Ala 11, Sevilla/Morón	
C.16-20	Eurofighter EF.2000 Tifón [11-91]	EdA 111 Esc/113 Esc/Ala 11, Sevilla/Morón	
C.16-21	Eurofighter EF.2000 Tifón [11-01]	EdA 111 Esc/113 Esc/Ala 11, Sevilla/Morón	
C.16-22	Eurofighter EF.2000 Tifón [11-02]	EdA 111 Esc/113 Esc/Ala 11, Sevilla/Morón	
C.16-23	Eurofighter EF.2000 Tifón [11-03]	EdA 111 Esc/113 Esc/Ala 11, Sevilla/Morón	
C.16-24	Eurofighter EF.2000 Tifón [11-04]	EdA 111 Esc/113 Esc/Ala 11, Sevilla/Morón	
C.16-25	Eurofighter EF.2000 Tifón [11-05]	EdA 111 Esc/113 Esc/Ala 11, Sevilla/Morón	
C.16-26	Eurofighter EF.2000 Tifón [11-06]	EdA 111 Esc/113 Esc/Ala 11, Sevilla/Morón	
C.16-27	Eurofighter EF.2000 Tifón [11-07]	EdA 111 Esc/113 Esc/Ala 11, Sevilla/Morón	
C.16-28	Eurofighter EF.2000 Tifón [11-08]	EdA 111 Esc/113 Esc/Ala 11, Sevilla/Morón	
C.16-29	Eurofighter EF.2000 Tifón [11-09]	EdA 111 Esc/113 Esc/Ala 11, Sevilla/Morón	
C.16-30	Eurofighter EF.2000 Tifón [11-10]	EdA 111 Esc/113 Esc/Ala 11, Sevilla/Morón	
C.16-31	Eurofighter EF.2000 Tifón [14-01]	EdA 142 Esc/Ala 14, Albacete/Los Llanos	
C.16-32	Eurofighter EF.2000 Tifón [11-11]	EdA 111 Esc/113 Esc/Ala 11, Sevilla/Morón	
C.16-33	Eurofighter EF.2000 Tifón [11-12]	EdA 111 Esc/113 Esc/Ala 11, Sevilla/Morón	
C.16-35	Eurofighter EF.2000 Tifón [11-14]	EdA 111 Esc/113 Esc/Ala 11, Sevilla/Morón	
C.16-36	Eurofighter EF.2000 Tifón [14-03]	EdA 142 Esc/Ala 14, Albacete/Los Llanos	
C.16-37	Eurofighter EF.2000 Tifón [14-04]	EdA 142 Esc/Ala 14, Albacete/Los Llanos	
C.16-38	Eurofighter EF.2000 Tifón [14-05]	EdA 142 Esc/Ala 14, Albacete/Los Llanos	
C.16-39	Eurofighter EF.2000 Tifón [14-06]	EdA 142 Esc/Ala 14, Albacete/Los Llanos	
C.16-40	Eurofighter EF.2000 Tifón [11-16]	EdA 111 Esc/113 Esc/Ala 11, Sevilla/Morón	
C.16-41	Eurofighter EF.2000 Tifón [11-17]	EdA 111 Esc/113 Esc/Ala 11, Sevilla/Morón	
C.16-42	Eurofighter EF.2000 Tifón [14-08]	EdA 142 Esc/Ala 14, Albacete/Los Llanos	
C.16-43	Eurofighter EF.2000 Tifón [11-43]	EdA 111 Esc/113 Esc/Ala 11, Sevilla/Morón	
C.16-44	Eurofighter EF.2000 Tifón [14-09]	EdA 142 Esc/Ala 14, Albacete/Los Llanos	
C.16-45	Eurofighter EF.2000 Tifón [14-10]	EdA 142 Esc/Ala 14, Albacete/Los Llanos	
C.16-46	Eurofighter EF.2000 Tifón [11-20]	EdA 111 Esc/113 Esc/Ala 11, Sevilla/Morón	
C.16-47	Eurofighter EF.2000 Tifón [14-11]	EdA 142 Esc/Ala 14, Albacete/Los Llanos	
C.16-48	Eurofighter EF.2000 Tifón [14-12]	EdA 142 Esc/Ala 14, Albacete/Los Llanos	
C.16-49	Eurofighter EF.2000 Tifón [14-13]	EdA 142 Esc/Ala 14, Albacete/Los Llanos	
C.16-50	Eurofighter EF.2000 Tifón [14-14]	EdA 142 Esc/Ala 14, Albacete/Los Llanos	
C.16-51	Eurofighter EF.2000 Tifón [11-21]	EdA 111 Esc/113 Esc/Ala 11, Sevilla/Morón	
C.16-52	Eurofighter EF.2000 Tifón (C.16-10001) [11-52]	EdA 111 Esc/113 Esc/Ala 11, Sevilla/Morón	
C.16-53	Eurofighter EF.2000 Tifón (C.16-10002) [11-53]	EdA 111 Esc/113 Esc/Ala 11, Sevilla/Morón	
C.16-54	Eurofighter EF.2000 Tifón (C.16-10003) [11-24] $	EdA 111 Esc/113 Esc/Ala 11, Sevilla/Morón	
C.16-55	Eurofighter EF.2000 Tifón (C.16-10004) [11-55]	EdA 111 Esc/113 Esc/Ala 11, Sevilla/Morón	
C.16-56	Eurofighter EF.2000 Tifón (10007)	EdA 142 Esc/Ala 14, Albacete/Los Llanos	
C.16-57	Eurofighter EF.2000 Tifón (10012) [11-57]	EdA 111 Esc/113 Esc/Ala 11, Sevilla/Morón	
C.16-58	Eurofighter EF.2000 Tifón (10019) [14-17]	EdA 142 Esc/Ala 14, Albacete/Los Llanos	
C.16-59	Eurofighter EF.2000 Tifón (10020) [14-18]	EdA 142 Esc/Ala 14, Albacete/Los Llanos	
C.16-60	Eurofighter EF.2000 Tifón (10040) [14-19]	EdA 142 Esc/Ala 14, Albacete/Los Llanos	
C.16-61	Eurofighter EF.2000 Tifón (10046) [14-20]	EdA 142 Esc/Ala 14, Albacete/Los Llanos	
C.16-62	Eurofighter EF.2000 Tifón (10047) [14-21]	EdA 142 Esc/Ala 14, Albacete/Los Llanos	
C.16-63	Eurofighter EF.2000 Tifón (10048) [11-63]	EdA 111 Esc/113 Esc/Ala 11, Sevilla/Morón	
C.16-64	Eurofighter EF.2000 Tifón (10053) [14-22]	EdA 142 Esc/Ala 14, Albacete/Los Llanos	
C.16-65	Eurofighter EF.2000 Tifón (10054) [14-23]	EdA 142 Esc/Ala 14, Albacete/Los Llanos	
C.16-66	Eurofighter EF.2000 Tifón (10064) [14-24]	EdA 142 Esc/Ala 14, Albacete/Los Llanos	
C.16-67	Eurofighter EF.2000 Tifón (10090) [14-25]	EdA 142 Esc/Ala 14, Albacete/Los Llanos	
C.16-68	Eurofighter EF.2000 Tifón (10091) [14-26]	EdA 142 Esc/Ala 14, Albacete/Los Llanos	
C.16-70	Eurofighter EF.2000 Tifón	EdA	
C.16-71	Eurofighter EF.2000 Tifón (10146)	EdA 142 Esc/Ala 14, Albacete/Los Llanos	
C.16-72	Eurofighter EF.2000 Tifón (10147) [14-30]	EdA 142 Esc/Ala 14, Albacete/Los Llanos	
C.16-73	Eurofighter EF.2000 Tifón (10155) [14-31]	EdA 142 Esc/Ala 14, Albacete/Los Llanos	
C.16-74	Eurofighter EF.2000 Tifón (10202)	EdA (on order)	
C.16-75	Eurofighter EF.2000 Tifón (10205)	EdA (on order)	
C.16-76	Eurofighter EF.2000 Tifón	EdA (on order)	
D.4-01	Airtech CN.235M-100(MPA) [T.19B-12]	EdA 801 Esc/Ala 49, Palma/Son San Juan	

Notes	Serial	Type (code/other identity)	Owner/operator, location or fate
	D.4-02	Airtech CN.235M-100(MPA) [T.19B-09]	EdA 801 Esc/Ala 49, Palma/Son San Juan
	D.4-03	Airtech CN.235M-100(MPA) [T.19B-10]	EdA 801 Esc/Ala 49, Palma/Son San Juan
	D.4-04	Airtech CN.235M-100(MPA) [T.19B-08]	EdA 802 Esc/Ala 46, Gran Canaria
	D.4-05	Airtech CN.235M-100(MPA) [T.19B-06]	EdA 801 Esc/Ala 49, Palma/Son San Juan
	D.4-06	Airtech CN.235M-100(MPA) [T.19B-05]	EdA 801 Esc/Ala 49, Palma/Son San Juan
	D.4-07	Airtech CN.235M-100(MPA) [T.19B-15]	EdA 803 Esc/Ala 48, Madrid/Getafe
	D.4-08	Airtech CN.235M-100(MPA) [T.19B-14]	EdA 802 Esc/Ala 46, Gran Canaria
	E.25-05	CASA 101EB Aviojet [79-05]	EdA 793 Esc/794 Esc/AGA, Murcia/San Javier
	E.25-06	CASA 101EB Aviojet [79-06]	EdA 793 Esc/794 Esc/AGA, Murcia/San Javier
	E.25-08	CASA 101EB Aviojet [79-08]	EdA 793 Esc/794 Esc/AGA, Murcia/San Javier
	E.25-09	CASA 101EB Aviojet [79-09]	EdA 793 Esc/794 Esc/AGA, Murcia/San Javier
	E.25-11	CASA 101EB Aviojet [79-11]	EdA 793 Esc/794 Esc/AGA, Murcia/San Javier
	E.25-12	CASA 101EB Aviojet [79-12]	EdA 793 Esc/794 Esc/AGA, Murcia/San Javier
	E.25-13	CASA 101EB Aviojet [79-13,5]	EdA Patrulla Aguila/AGA, Murcia/San Javier
	E.25-14	CASA 101EB Aviojet [79-14]	EdA 793 Esc/794 Esc/AGA, Murcia/San Javier
	E.25-15	CASA 101EB Aviojet [79-15]	EdA 793 Esc/794 Esc/AGA, Murcia/San Javier
	E.25-16	CASA 101EB Aviojet [79-16]	EdA 793 Esc/794 Esc/AGA, Murcia/San Javier
	E.25-17	CASA 101EB Aviojet [74-40]	EdA 741 Esc/GEM, Salamanca/Matacán
	E.25-18	CASA 101EB Aviojet [74-42] $	EdA 741 Esc/GEM, Salamanca/Matacán
	E.25-19	CASA 101EB Aviojet [79-19]	EdA 793 Esc/794 Esc/AGA, Murcia/San Javier
	E.25-20	CASA 101EB Aviojet [79-20]	EdA 793 Esc/794 Esc/AGA, Murcia/San Javier
	E.25-21	CASA 101EB Aviojet [79-21]	EdA 793 Esc/794 Esc/AGA, Murcia/San Javier
	E.25-22	CASA 101EB Aviojet [79-22]	EdA 793 Esc/794 Esc/AGA, Murcia/San Javier
	E.25-23	CASA 101EB Aviojet [79-23]	EdA 793 Esc/794 Esc/AGA, Murcia/San Javier
	E.25-24	CASA 101EB Aviojet [79-24]	EdA 793 Esc/794 Esc/AGA, Murcia/San Javier
	E.25-25	CASA 101EB Aviojet [79-25]	EdA 793 Esc/794 Esc/AGA, Murcia/San Javier
	E.25-26	CASA 101EB Aviojet [79-26]	EdA 793 Esc/794 Esc/AGA, Murcia/San Javier
	E.25-27	CASA 101EB Aviojet [79-27,7]	EdA Patrulla Aguila/AGA, Murcia/San Javier
	E.25-28	CASA 101EB Aviojet [79-28]	EdA 793 Esc/794 Esc/AGA, Murcia/San Javier
	E.25-29	CASA 101EB Aviojet [74-45]	EdA 741 Esc/GEM, Salamanca/Matacán
	E.25-31	CASA 101EB Aviojet [79-31,1]	EdA Patrulla Aguila/AGA, Murcia/San Javier
	E.25-33	CASA 101EB Aviojet [74-02]	EdA 741 Esc/GEM, Salamanca/Matacán
	E.25-34	CASA 101EB Aviojet [74-44]	EdA 741 Esc/GEM, Salamanca/Matacán
	E.25-35	CASA 101EB Aviojet [54-20] $	EdA 541 Esc/CLAEX/Grupo 54, Madrid/Torrejón
	E.25-37	CASA 101EB Aviojet [79-37]	EdA 793 Esc/794 Esc/AGA, Murcia/San Javier
	E.25-38	CASA 101EB Aviojet [79-38,2]	EdA Patrulla Aguila/AGA, Murcia/San Javier
	E.25-40	CASA 101EB Aviojet [79-40]	EdA 793 Esc/794 Esc/AGA, Murcia/San Javier
	E.25-41	CASA 101EB Aviojet [74-41]	EdA 741 Esc/GEM, Salamanca/Matacán
	E.25-43	CASA 101EB Aviojet [74-43]	EdA 741 Esc/GEM, Salamanca/Matacán
	E.25-44	CASA 101EB Aviojet [79-44]	EdA 793 Esc/794 Esc/AGA, Murcia/San Javier
	E.25-46	CASA 101EB Aviojet [79-46]	*Withdrawn from use, November 2018*
	E.25-50	CASA 101EB Aviojet [79-33]	EdA 793 Esc/794 Esc/AGA, Murcia/San Javier
	E.25-51	CASA 101EB Aviojet [74-07]	EdA 741 Esc/GEM, Salamanca/Matacán
	E.25-52	CASA 101EB Aviojet [79-34,3]	EdA Patrulla Aguila/AGA, Murcia/San Javier
	E.25-53	CASA 101EB Aviojet [74-09]	EdA 741 Esc/GEM, Salamanca/Matacán
	E.25-54	CASA 101EB Aviojet [79-35]	EdA 793 Esc/794 Esc/AGA, Murcia/San Javier
	E.25-55	CASA 101EB Aviojet [54-21]	EdA 541 Esc/CLAEX/Grupo 54, Madrid/Torrejón
	E.25-56	CASA 101EB Aviojet [74-11]	EdA 741 Esc/GEM, Salamanca/Matacán
	E.25-57	CASA 101EB Aviojet [74-12]	EdA 741 Esc/GEM, Salamanca/Matacán
	E.25-59	CASA 101EB Aviojet [74-13]	EdA 741 Esc/GEM, Salamanca/Matacán
	E.25-61	CASA 101EB Aviojet [54-22]	EdA 541 Esc/CLAEX/Grupo 54, Madrid/Torrejón
	E.25-62	CASA 101EB Aviojet [79-17]	EdA 793 Esc/794 Esc/AGA, Murcia/San Javier
	E.25-63	CASA 101EB Aviojet [74-17,5]	EdA Patrulla Aguila/AGA, Murcia/San Javier
	E.25-65	CASA 101EB Aviojet [79-95]	EdA 793 Esc/794 Esc/AGA, Murcia/San Javier
	E.25-66	CASA 101EB Aviojet [74-20]	EdA 741 Esc/GEM, Salamanca/Matacán
	E.25-67	CASA 101EB Aviojet [74-21]	EdA 741 Esc/GEM, Salamanca/Matacán
	E.25-68	CASA 101EB Aviojet [74-22]	EdA 741 Esc/GEM, Salamanca/Matacán
	E.25-69	CASA 101EB Aviojet [79-97,8]	EdA Patrulla Aguila/AGA, Murcia/San Javier
	E.25-71	CASA 101EB Aviojet [74-25]	EdA 741 Esc/GEM, Salamanca/Matacán
	E.25-72	CASA 101EB Aviojet [74-26]	EdA 741 Esc/GEM, Salamanca/Matacán
	E.25-73	CASA 101EB Aviojet [79-98]	EdA 793 Esc/794 Esc/AGA, Murcia/San Javier
	E.25-74	CASA 101EB Aviojet [74-28]	EdA 741 Esc/GEM, Salamanca/Matacán

Serial	Type (code/other identity)	Owner/operator, location or fate	Notes
E.25-76	CASA 101EB Aviojet [74-30]	EdA 741 Esc/GEM, Salamanca/Matacán	
E.25-78	CASA 101EB Aviojet [79-02,4]	EdA *Patrulla Aguila*/AGA, Murcia/San Javier	
E.25-79	CASA 101EB Aviojet [79-39]	EdA 793 Esc/794 Esc/AGA, Murcia/San Javier	
E.25-80	CASA 101EB Aviojet [79-03]	EdA 793 Esc/794 Esc/AGA, Murcia/San Javier	
E.25-81	CASA 101EB Aviojet [74-34]	EdA 741 Esc/GEM, Salamanca/Matacán	
E.25-83	CASA 101EB Aviojet [74-35]	EdA 741 Esc/GEM, Salamanca/Matacán	
E.25-84	CASA 101EB Aviojet [79-04]	EdA 793 Esc/794 Esc/AGA, Murcia/San Javier	
E.25-86	CASA 101EB Aviojet [79-32]	EdA 793 Esc/794 Esc/AGA, Murcia/San Javier	
E.25-87	CASA 101EB Aviojet [79-29]	EdA 793 Esc/794 Esc/AGA, Murcia/San Javier	
E.25-88	CASA 101EB Aviojet [74-39]	EdA 741 Esc/GEM, Salamanca/Matacán	
HS.23-01	Sikorsky SH-60B Seahawk [01-1001]	Armada 10 Esc, Rota	
HS.23-02	Sikorsky SH-60B Seahawk [01-1002]	Armada 10 Esc, Rota	
HS.23-03	Sikorsky SH-60B Seahawk [01-1003]	Armada 10 Esc, Rota	
HS.23-04	Sikorsky SH-60B Seahawk [01-1004]	Armada 10 Esc, Rota	
HS.23-05	Sikorsky SH-60B Seahawk [01-1005]	Armada 10 Esc, Rota	
HS.23-06	Sikorsky SH-60B Seahawk [01-1006]	Armada 10 Esc, Rota	
HS.23-07	Sikorsky SH-60B Seahawk [01-1007]	Armada 10 Esc, Rota	
HS.23-08	Sikorsky SH-60B Seahawk [01-1008]	Armada 10 Esc, Rota	
HS.23-09	Sikorsky SH-60B Seahawk [01-1009]	Armada 10 Esc, Rota	
HS.23-10	Sikorsky SH-60B Seahawk [01-1010]	Armada 10 Esc, Rota	
HS.23-11	Sikorsky SH-60B Seahawk [01-1011]	Armada 10 Esc, Rota	
HS.23-12	Sikorsky SH-60B Seahawk [01-1012]	Armada 10 Esc, Rota	
HT.23-13	Sikorsky SH-60F Seahawk (10013) [01-1014]	Armada 10 Esc, Rota	
HT.23-14	Sikorsky SH-60F Seahawk (10014) [01-1015]	Armada 10 Esc, Rota	
HT.23-15	Sikorsky SH-60F Seahawk	Armada (on order)	
HT.23-16	Sikorsky SH-60F Seahawk	Armada (on order)	
HT.23-17	Sikorsky SH-60F Seahawk	Armada (on order)	
HT.23-18	Sikorsky SH-60F Seahawk	Armada (on order)	
HE.25-1	Eurocopter EC.120B Colibri [78-20]	EdA *Patrulla Aspa*/Ala 78, Granada/Armilla	
HE.25-2	Eurocopter EC.120B Colibri [78-21]	EdA *Patrulla Aspa*/Ala 78, Granada/Armilla	
HE.25-3	Eurocopter EC.120B Colibri [78-22]	EdA *Patrulla Aspa*/Ala 78, Granada/Armilla	
HE.25-4	Eurocopter EC.120B Colibri [78-23]	EdA *Patrulla Aspa*/Ala 78, Granada/Armilla	
HE.25-5	Eurocopter EC.120B Colibri [78-24]	EdA *Patrulla Aspa*/Ala 78, Granada/Armilla	
HE.25-6	Eurocopter EC.120B Colibri [78-25]	EdA *Patrulla Aspa*/Ala 78, Granada/Armilla	
HE.25-7	Eurocopter EC.120B Colibri [78-26]	EdA *Patrulla Aspa*/Ala 78, Granada/Armilla	
HE.25-8	Eurocopter EC.120B Colibri [78-27]	EdA *Patrulla Aspa*/Ala 78, Granada/Armilla	
HE.25-9	Eurocopter EC.120B Colibri [78-28]	EdA *Patrulla Aspa*/Ala 78, Granada/Armilla	
HE.25-10	Eurocopter EC.120B Colibri [78-29]	EdA 782 Esc/Ala 78, Granada/Armilla	
HE.25-11	Eurocopter EC.120B Colibri [78-30]	EdA 782 Esc/Ala 78, Granada/Armilla	
HE.25-12	Eurocopter EC.120B Colibri [78-31]	EdA *Patrulla Aspa*/Ala 78, Granada/Armilla	
HE.25-13	Eurocopter EC.120B Colibri [78-32]	EdA *Patrulla Aspa*/Ala 78, Granada/Armilla	
HE.25-14	Eurocopter EC.120B Colibri [78-33]	EdA *Patrulla Aspa*/Ala 78, Granada/Armilla	
HE.25-15	Eurocopter EC.120B Colibri [78-34]	EdA *Patrulla Aspa*/Ala 78, Granada/Armilla	
P.3M-08	Lockheed P-3M Orion [22-31]	EdA 221 Esc/Grupo 22, Sevilla/Morón	
P.3M-09	Lockheed P-3M Orion [22-32]	EdA 221 Esc/Grupo 22, Sevilla/Morón	
P.3M-12	Lockheed P-3M Orion [22-35]	EdA 221 Esc/Grupo 22, Sevilla/Morón	
TL.10-01	Lockheed C-130H-30 Hercules [31-01]	EdA 311 Esc/312 Esc/Ala 31, Zaragoza	
T.10-03	Lockheed C-130H Hercules [31-03]	EdA 311 Esc/312 Esc/Ala 31, Zaragoza	
T.10-04	Lockheed C-130H Hercules [31-04]	EdA, stored Sevilla/Morón	
TK.10-05	Lockheed KC-130H Hercules [31-50]	EdA 311 Esc/312 Esc/Ala 31, Zaragoza	
TK.10-06	Lockheed KC-130H Hercules [31-51]	EdA 311 Esc/312 Esc/Ala 31, Zaragoza	
TK.10-07	Lockheed KC-130H Hercules [31-52]	EdA 311 Esc/312 Esc/Ala 31, Zaragoza	
T.10-08	Lockheed C-130H Hercules [31-05]	EdA 311 Esc/312 Esc/Ala 31, Zaragoza	
T.10-09	Lockheed C-130H Hercules [31-06]	EdA 311 Esc/312 Esc/Ala 31, Zaragoza	
T.10-10	Lockheed C-130H Hercules [31-07]	EdA 311 Esc/312 Esc/Ala 31, Zaragoza	
TK.10-11	Lockheed KC-130H Hercules [31-53]	EdA 311 Esc/312 Esc/Ala 31, Zaragoza	
TK.10-12	Lockheed KC-130H Hercules [31-54]	EdA 311 Esc/312 Esc/Ala 31, Zaragoza	
TM.11-3	Dassault Falcon 20D [47-23]	EdA 472 Esc/Grupo Mixto 47, Madrid/Torrejón	
TM.11-4	Dassault Falcon 20E [472-04]	EdA 472 Esc/Grupo Mixto 47, Madrid/Torrejón	
T.12B-13	CASA 212A Aviocar [72-01]	EdA 721 Esc/Ala 72, Murcia/Alcantarilla	
T.12B-49	CASA 212A Aviocar [72-07]	EdA 721 Esc/Ala 72, Murcia/Alcantarilla	
T.12B-55	CASA 212A Aviocar [72-08]	*Withdrawn from use, 2018*	

Notes	Serial	Type (code/other identity)	Owner/operator, location or fate
	T.12B-63	CASA 212A Aviocar [72-14]	EdA 721 Esc/Ala 72, Murcia/Alcantarilla
	T.12B-65	CASA 212A Aviocar [72-11]	EdA 721 Esc/Ala 72, Murcia/Alcantarilla
	T.12B-67	CASA 212A Aviocar [72-12]	EdA 721 Esc/Ala 72, Murcia/Alcantarilla
	T.12B-70	CASA 212A Aviocar [72-17]	EdA 721 Esc/Ala 72, Murcia/Alcantarilla
	T.12B-71	CASA 212A Aviocar [72-10]	EdA 721 Esc/Ala 72, Murcia/Alcantarilla
	TM.12D-72	CASA 212-200ECM Aviocar [47-12]	EdA 472 Esc/Grupo Mixto 47, Madrid/Torrejón
	T.12D-75	CASA 212-200 Aviocar [47-14]	EdA 472 Esc/Grupo Mixto 47, Madrid/Torrejón
	TR.12D-76	CASA 212-200 Aviocar [72-21]	EdA 721 Esc/Ala 72, Murcia/Alcantarilla
	TR.12D-77	CASA 212-200 Aviocar [72-22]	EdA 721 Esc/Ala 72, Murcia/Alcantarilla
	TR.12D-79	CASA 212-200 Aviocar [72-23]	EdA 721 Esc/Ala 72, Murcia/Alcantarilla
	TR.12D-81	CASA 212-200 Aviocar [72-24]	EdA 721 Esc/Ala 72, Murcia/Alcantarilla
	T.18-1	Dassault Falcon 900 [45-40]	EdA 451 Esc/Grupo 45, Madrid/Torrejón
	T.18-2	Dassault Falcon 900 [45-41]	EdA 451 Esc/Grupo 45, Madrid/Torrejón
	T.18-3	Dassault Falcon 900B [45-42]	EdA 451 Esc/Grupo 45, Madrid/Torrejón
	T.18-4	Dassault Falcon 900B [45-43]	EdA 451 Esc/Grupo 45, Madrid/Torrejón
	T.18-5	Dassault Falcon 900B [45-44]	EdA 451 Esc/Grupo 45, Madrid/Torrejón
	T.19A-01	Airtech CN.235M-10 [403-01]	EdA 403 Esc, Madrid/Getafe
	T.19A-02	Airtech CN.235M-10 [403-02]	EdA 403 Esc, Madrid/Getafe
	T.19B-07	Airtech CN.235M-100 [74-07]	EdA 744 Esc/GEM, Salamanca/Matacán
	T.19B-11	Airtech CN.235M-100 [74-11]	EdA 744 Esc/GEM, Salamanca/Matacán
	T.19B-13	Airtech CN.235M-100 [74-13]	EdA 744 Esc/GEM, Salamanca/Matacán
	T.19B-16	Airtech CN.235M-100 [74-16]	EdA 744 Esc/GEM, Salamanca/Matacán
	T.19B-17	Airtech CN.235M-100 [74-17]	EdA 744 Esc/GEM, Salamanca/Matacán
	T.19B-18	Airtech CN.235M-100 [74-18]	EdA 744 Esc/GEM, Salamanca/Matacán
	T.19B-19	Airtech CN.235M-100 [74-19]	EdA 744 Esc/GEM, Salamanca/Matacán
	T.19B-20	Airtech CN.235M-100 [74-20]	EdA 744 Esc/GEM, Salamanca/Matacán
	T.19B-21	Airtech CN.235M VIGMA [09-501]	Guardia Civil Servicio Aéreo, Gran Canaria
	T.19B-22	Airtech CN.235M VIGMA [09-502]	Guardia Civil Servicio Aéreo, Gran Canaria
	TR.20-01	Cessna 560 Citation VI [403-11]	EdA 403 Esc, Madrid/Getafe
	TR.20-02	Cessna 560 Citation VI [403-12]	EdA 403 Esc, Madrid/Getafe
	TR.20-03	Cessna 560 Citation VI [403-21]	EdA 403 Esc, Madrid/Getafe
	T.21-01	CASA C-295M [35-39]	EdA 353 Esc/Ala 35, Madrid/Getafe
	T.21-02	CASA C-295M [35-40]	EdA 353 Esc/Ala 35, Madrid/Getafe
	T.21-03	CASA C-295M [35-41]	EdA 353 Esc/Ala 35, Madrid/Getafe
	T.21-04	CASA C-295M [35-42]	EdA 353 Esc/Ala 35, Madrid/Getafe
	T.21-05	CASA C-295M [35-43]	EdA 353 Esc/Ala 35, Madrid/Getafe
	T.21-06	CASA C-295M [35-44]	EdA 353 Esc/Ala 35, Madrid/Getafe
	T.21-07	CASA C-295M [35-45]	EdA 353 Esc/Ala 35, Madrid/Getafe
	T.21-08	CASA C-295M [35-46]	EdA 353 Esc/Ala 35, Madrid/Getafe
	T.21-09	CASA C-295M [35-47]	EdA 353 Esc/Ala 35, Madrid/Getafe
	T.21-10	CASA C-295M [35-48]	EdA 353 Esc/Ala 35, Madrid/Getafe
	T.21-11	CASA C-295M [35-49]	EdA 353 Esc/Ala 35, Madrid/Getafe
	T.21-12	CASA C-295M [35-50]	EdA 353 Esc/Ala 35, Madrid/Getafe
	T.21-13	CASA C-295M [35-51]	EdA 353 Esc/Ala 35, Madrid/Getafe
	T.22-1	Airbus A.310-304 [45-50]	EdA 451 Esc/Grupo 45, Madrid/Torrejón
	T.22-2	Airbus A.310-304 [45-51]	EdA 451 Esc/Grupo 45, Madrid/Torrejón
	T.23-01	Airbus Military A.400M (10074) [31-21]	EdA 311 Esc/312 Esc/Ala 31, Zaragoza
	TK.23-02	Airbus Military A.400M (10075) [31-22]	EdA 311 Esc/312 Esc/Ala 31, Zaragoza
	TK.23-03	Airbus Military A.400M (10076) [31-23]	EdA 311 Esc/312 Esc/Ala 31, Zaragoza
	T.23-04	Airbus Military A.400M (10174) [31-24]	EdA (on order)
	T.23-05	Airbus Military A.400M	EdA (on order)
	T.23-06	Airbus Military A.400M	EdA (on order)
	T.23-07	Airbus Military A.400M	EdA (on order)
	U.20-1	Cessna 550 Citation II [01-405]	Armada 4 Esc, Rota
	U.20-2	Cessna 550 Citation II [01-406]	Armada 4 Esc, Rota
	U.20-3	Cessna 550 Citation II [01-407]	Armada 4 Esc, Rota
	U.21-01	Cessna 650 Citation VII [01-408]	Armada 4 Esc, Rota
	VA.1B-24	McDonnell Douglas EAV-8B+ Matador [01-914]	Armada 9 Esc, Rota
	VA.1B-25	McDonnell Douglas EAV-8B+ Matador [01-915]	Armada, stored Rota
	VA.1B-26	McDonnell Douglas EAV-8B+ Matador [01-916]	Armada 9 Esc, Rota
	VA.1B-27	McDonnell Douglas EAV-8B+ Matador [01-917]	Armada 9 Esc, Rota
	VA.1B-28	McDonnell Douglas EAV-8B+ Matador [01-918]	Armada, stored Rota

Serial	Type (code/other identity)	Owner/operator, location or fate	Notes
VA.1B-29	McDonnell Douglas EAV-8B+ Matador [01-919]	Armada 9 Esc, Rota	
VA.1B-30	McDonnell Douglas EAV-8B+ Matador [01-920]	Armada 9 Esc, Rota	
VA.1B-33	McDonnell Douglas TAV-8B Matador [01-922]	Armada 9 Esc, Rota	
VA.1B-35	McDonnell Douglas EAV-8B+ Matador [01-923]	Armada 9 Esc, Rota	
VA.1B-36	McDonnell Douglas EAV-8B+ Matador [01-924]	Armada 9 Esc, Rota	
VA.1B-37	McDonnell Douglas EAV-8B+ Matador [01-925]	Armada 9 Esc, Rota	
VA.1B-38	McDonnell Douglas EAV-8B+ Matador [01-926]	Armada 9 Esc, Rota	
VA.1B-39	McDonnell Douglas EAV-8B+ Matador [01-927]	Armada 9 Esc, Rota	
SUDAN			
ST-PSA	Dassault Falcon 900B	Sudanese Government, Khartoum	
ST-PSR	Dassault Falcon 50	Sudanese Government, Khartoum	
SWAZILAND			
3DC-SDF	Airbus A.340-213X	Government of Swaziland, Manzini/Sikhupe	

SWEDEN

Försvarsmakten/Swedish Armed Forces: Försvarsmaktens Helikopterflottilj (Hkpflj)/Armed Forces Helicopter Wing & Svenska Flygvapnet/Swedish Air Force

Serial	Type (code/other identity)	Owner/operator, location or fate	Notes
39-6	SAAB JAS 39C Gripen [6]	SAAB, Linköping/Malmen	
39-7	SAAB JAS 39NG Gripen	SAAB, Linköping/Malmen	
39-8	SAAB JAS 39E Gripen	SAAB, Linköping/Malmen	
39-9	SAAB JAS 39E Gripen	SAAB, Linköping/Malmen	
39-10	SAAB JAS 39E Gripen	SAAB, Linköping/Malmen	
39208	SAAB JAS 39C Gripen [208]	Flygvapnet Flottiljer 17, Ronneby/Kallinge	
39209	SAAB JAS 39C Gripen [209]	Flygvapnet Flottiljer 7, Såtenäs	
39210	SAAB JAS 39C Gripen [210]	Flygvapnet Flottiljer 7, Ronneby/Kallinge	
39211	SAAB JAS 39C Gripen [211]	Flygvapnet Flottiljer 7, Såtenäs	
39212	SAAB JAS 39C Gripen [212]	Flygvapnet Flottiljer 17, Ronneby/Kallinge	
39213	SAAB JAS 39C Gripen [213]	Flygvapnet Flottiljer 7, Såtenäs	
39214	SAAB JAS 39C Gripen [214]	Flygvapnet Flottiljer 7, Såtenäs	
39215	SAAB JAS 39C Gripen [215]	Flygvapnet Flottiljer 7, Såtenäs	
39216	SAAB JAS 39C Gripen [216]	Flygvapnet Flottiljer 17, Ronneby/Kallinge	
39217	SAAB JAS 39C Gripen [217]	Flygvapnet Flottiljer 7, Såtenäs	
39218	SAAB JAS 39C Gripen [218]	Flygvapnet Flottiljer 21, Luleå/Kallax	
39219	SAAB JAS 39C Gripen [219]	Flygvapnet Flottiljer 21, Luleå/Kallax	
39220	SAAB JAS 39C Gripen [220]	Flygvapnet Flottiljer 7, Såtenäs	
39221	SAAB JAS 39C Gripen [221]	Flygvapnet Flottiljer 17, Ronneby/Kallinge	
39222	SAAB JAS 39C Gripen [222]	Flygvapnet Flottiljer 17, Ronneby/Kallinge	
39223	SAAB JAS 39C Gripen [223]	Flygvapnet Flottiljer 21, Luleå/Kallax	
39224	SAAB JAS 39C Gripen [224]	Flygvapnet Flottiljer 17, Ronneby/Kallinge	
39225	SAAB JAS 39C Gripen [225]	Flygvapnet Flottiljer 7, Såtenäs	
39226	SAAB JAS 39C Gripen [226]	Flygvapnet Flottiljer 7, Såtenäs	
39227	SAAB JAS 39C Gripen [227]	Flygvapnet Flottiljer 7, Såtenäs	
39228	SAAB JAS 39C Gripen [228]	Flygvapnet Flottiljer 17, Ronneby/Kallinge	
39229	SAAB JAS 39C Gripen [229]	Flygvapnet Flottiljer 21, Luleå/Kallax	
39230	SAAB JAS 39C Gripen [230]	Flygvapnet Flottiljer 21, Luleå/Kallax	
39231	SAAB JAS 39C Gripen [231]	Flygvapnet Flottiljer 7, Såtenäs	
39232	SAAB JAS 39C Gripen [232]	Flygvapnet Flottiljer 21, Luleå/Kallax	
39233	SAAB JAS 39C Gripen [233]	Flygvapnet Flottiljer 17, Ronneby/Kallinge	
39246	SAAB JAS 39C Gripen [246]	Flygvapnet Flottiljer 21, Luleå/Kallax	
39247	SAAB JAS 39C Gripen [247]	Flygvapnet Flottiljer 17, Ronneby/Kallinge	
39248	SAAB JAS 39C Gripen [248]	Flygvapnet Flottiljer 21, Luleå/Kallax	
39249	SAAB JAS 39C Gripen [249]	Flygvapnet Flottiljer 17, Ronneby/Kallinge	
39250	SAAB JAS 39C Gripen [250]	Flygvapnet FC, Linköping/Malmen	
39251	SAAB JAS 39C Gripen [251]	Flygvapnet FC, Linköping/Malmen	
39252	SAAB JAS 39C Gripen [252]	Flygvapnet Flottiljer 17, Ronneby/Kallinge	
39253	SAAB JAS 39C Gripen [253]	Flygvapnet Flottiljer 7, Såtenäs	
39254	SAAB JAS 39C Gripen [254]	Flygvapnet Flottiljer 17, Ronneby/Kallinge	
39255	SAAB JAS 39C Gripen [255]	Flygvapnet Flottiljer 17, Ronneby/Kallinge	
39256	SAAB JAS 39C Gripen [256]	Flygvapnet Flottiljer 17, Ronneby/Kallinge	
39257	SAAB JAS 39C Gripen [257]	Flygvapnet Flottiljer 21, Luleå/Kallax	

Notes	Serial	Type (code/other identity)	Owner/operator, location or fate
	39258	SAAB JAS 39C Gripen [258]	Flygvapnet Flottiljer 21, Luleå/Kallax
	39260	SAAB JAS 39C Gripen [260]	Flygvapnet Flottiljer 21, Luleå/Kallax
	39261	SAAB JAS 39C Gripen [261]	Flygvapnet Flottiljer 21, Luleå/Kallax
	39262	SAAB JAS 39C Gripen [262]	SAAB, Linköping/Malmen
	39263	SAAB JAS 39C Gripen [263]	Flygvapnet Flottiljer 21, Luleå/Kallax
	39264	SAAB JAS 39C Gripen [264]	Flygvapnet Flottiljer 17, Ronneby/Kallinge
	39265	SAAB JAS 39C Gripen [265]	Flygvapnet Flottiljer 21, Luleå/Kallax
	39266	SAAB JAS 39C Gripen [266]	Flygvapnet Flottiljer 7, Såtenäs
	39267	SAAB JAS 39C Gripen [267]	Flygvapnet Flottiljer 21, Luleå/Kallax
	39268	SAAB JAS 39C Gripen [268]	Flygvapnet Flottiljer 7, Såtenäs
	39269	SAAB JAS 39C Gripen [269]	Flygvapnet Flottiljer 17, Ronneby/Kallinge
	39270	SAAB JAS 39C Gripen [270]	Flygvapnet Flottiljer 7, Såtenäs
	39271	SAAB JAS 39C Gripen [271]	Flygvapnet Flottiljer 21, Luleå/Kallax
	39272	SAAB JAS 39C Gripen [272]	Flygvapnet Flottiljer 21, Luleå/Kallax
	39273	SAAB JAS 39C Gripen [273]	Flygvapnet Flottiljer 17, Ronneby/Kallinge
	39274	SAAB JAS 39C Gripen [274]	Flygvapnet Flottiljer 21, Luleå/Kallax
	39275	SAAB JAS 39C Gripen [275]	Flygvapnet Flottiljer 7, Såtenäs
	39276	SAAB JAS 39C Gripen [276]	Flygvapnet Flottiljer 21, Luleå/Kallax
	39277	SAAB JAS 39C Gripen [277]	Flygvapnet Flottiljer 7, Såtenäs
	39278	SAAB JAS 39C Gripen [278]	Flygvapnet Flottiljer 7, Såtenäs
	39279	SAAB JAS 39C Gripen [279]	Flygvapnet Flottiljer 21, Luleå/Kallax
	39280	SAAB JAS 39C Gripen [280]	Flygvapnet Flottiljer 21, Luleå/Kallax
	39281	SAAB JAS 39C Gripen [281]	Flygvapnet Flottiljer 17, Ronneby/Kallinge
	39282	SAAB JAS 39C Gripen [282]	Flygvapnet Flottiljer 17, Ronneby/Kallinge
	39283	SAAB JAS 39C Gripen [283]	Flygvapnet Flottiljer 21, Luleå/Kallax
	39284	SAAB JAS 39C Gripen [284]	Flygvapnet Flottiljer 17, Ronneby/Kallinge
	39285	SAAB JAS 39C Gripen [285]	Flygvapnet Flottiljer 21, Luleå/Kallax
	39286	SAAB JAS 39C Gripen [286]	Flygvapnet Flottiljer 21, Luleå/Kallax
	39287	SAAB JAS 39C Gripen [287]	Flygvapnet Flottiljer 17, Ronneby/Kallinge
	39288	SAAB JAS 39C Gripen [288]	Flygvapnet Flottiljer 21, Luleå/Kallax
	39289	SAAB JAS 39C Gripen [289]	Flygvapnet Flottiljer 7, Såtenäs
	39290	SAAB JAS 39C Gripen [290]	Flygvapnet Flottiljer 21, Luleå/Kallax
	39291	SAAB JAS 39C Gripen [291]	Flygvapnet Flottiljer 7, Såtenäs
	39292	SAAB JAS 39C Gripen [292]	Flygvapnet Flottiljer 17, Ronneby/Kallinge
	39293	SAAB JAS 39C Gripen [293]	Flygvapnet Flottiljer 7, Såtenäs
	39294	SAAB JAS 39C Gripen [294]	Flygvapnet Flottiljer 17, Ronneby/Kallinge
	39815	SAAB JAS 39D Gripen [815]	Flygvapnet Flottiljer 7, Såtenäs
	39816	SAAB JAS 39D Gripen [816]	Flygvapnet Flottiljer 7, Såtenäs
	39817	SAAB JAS 39D Gripen [817]	Flygvapnet Flottiljer 21, Luleå/Kallax
	39821	SAAB JAS 39D Gripen [821]	Flygvapnet Flottiljer 7, Såtenäs
	39822	SAAB JAS 39D Gripen [822]	Flygvapnet Flottiljer 21, Luleå/Kallax
	39823	SAAB JAS 39D Gripen [823]	Flygvapnet Flottiljer 21, Luleå/Kallax
	39824	SAAB JAS 39D Gripen [824]	Flygvapnet Flottiljer 21, Luleå/Kallax
	39825	SAAB JAS 39D Gripen [825]	Flygvapnet Flottiljer 7, Såtenäs
	39826	SAAB JAS 39D Gripen [826]	Flygvapnet Flottiljer 17, Ronneby/Kallinge
	39827	SAAB JAS 39D Gripen [827]	Flygvapnet Flottiljer 7, Såtenäs
	39829	SAAB JAS 39D Gripen [829]	Flygvapnet Flottiljer 17, Ronneby/Kallinge
	39830	SAAB JAS 39D Gripen [830]	SAAB, Linköping/Malmen
	39831	SAAB JAS 39D Gripen [831]	Flygvapnet Flottiljer 17, Ronneby/Kallinge
	39832	SAAB JAS 39D Gripen [832]	SAAB, Linköping/Malmen
	39833	SAAB JAS 39D Gripen [833]	Flygvapnet Flottiljer 21, Luleå/Kallax
	39834	SAAB JAS 39D Gripen [834]	Flygvapnet Flottiljer 7, Såtenäs
	39835	SAAB JAS 39D Gripen [835]	Flygvapnet Flottiljer 7, Såtenäs
	39836	SAAB JAS 39D Gripen [836]	Flygvapnet Flottiljer 17, Ronneby/Kallinge
	39837	SAAB JAS 39D Gripen [837]	SAAB, Linköping/Malmen
	39838	SAAB JAS 39D Gripen [838]	Flygvapnet Flottiljer 21, Luleå/Kallax
	39839	SAAB JAS 39D Gripen [839]	Flygvapnet Flottiljer 7, Såtenäs
	39840	SAAB JAS 39D Gripen [840]	Flygvapnet Flottiljer 21, Luleå/Kallax
	39841	SAAB JAS 39D Gripen [841]	Flygvapnet Flottiljer 7, Såtenäs
	84004	Lockheed C-130H Hercules (Tp.84) [844]	Flygvapnet TSFE, Såtenäs
	84005	Lockheed C-130H Hercules (Tp.84) [845]	Flygvapnet TSFE, Såtenäs
	84006	Lockheed C-130H Hercules (Tp.84) [846]	Flygvapnet TSFE, Såtenäs

Serial	Type (code/other identity)	Owner/operator, location or fate	Notes
84007	Lockheed C-130H Hercules (Tp.84) [847]	Flygvapnet TSFE, Såtenäs	
84008	Lockheed C-130H Hercules (Tp.84) [848]	Flygvapnet TSFE, Såtenäs	
86001	Rockwell Sabreliner-40 (Tp.86) [861]	Flygvapnet FC, Linköping/Malmen	
100001	SAAB SF.340 (OS.100) [001]	Flygvapnet TSFE, Linköping/Malmen	
100003	SAAB SF.340AEW&C (S.100D Argus) [003]	Flygvapnet TSFE, Linköping/Malmen	
100004	SAAB SF.340AEW&C (S.100D Argus) [004]	Flygvapnet TSFE, Linköping/Malmen	
100008	SAAB SF.340 (Tp.100C) [008]	Flygvapnet TSFE, Linköping/Malmen	
102002	Grumman G.1159C Gulfstream IV (S.102B Korpen)[022]	Flygvapnet TSFE, Linköping/Malmen	
102003	Grumman G.1159C Gulfstream IV (S.102B Korpen)[023]	Flygvapnet TSFE, Linköping/Malmen	
102004	Grumman G.1159C Gulfstream IV-SP (Tp.102C) [024]	Flygvapnet TSFE, Linköping/Malmen	
102005	Gulfstream Aerospace G.550 (Tp.102D) [025]	Flygvapnet TSFE, Linköping/Malmen	
141041	NH Industries NH.90-TTH (Hkp.14A) [41]	Airbus Helicopters, Marignane, France	
141047	NH Industries NH.90-TTH (Hkp.14A) [47]	Hkpflj 1.HkpSkv, Luleå/Kallax	
142042	NH Industries NH.90-TTH (Hkp.14B) [42]	Hkpflj 3.HkpSkv, Ronneby/Kallinge	
142043	NH Industries NH.90-TTH (Hkp.14B) [43]	Hkpflj 3.HkpSkv, Ronneby/Kallinge	
142044	NH Industries NH.90-TTH (Hkp.14B) [44]	Hkpflj 3.HkpSkv, Ronneby/Kallinge	
142045	NH Industries NH.90-TTH (Hkp.14B) [45]	Hkpflj 1.HkpSkv, Luleå/Kallax	
144048	NH Industries NH.90-TTH (Hkp.14D) [48]	Hkpflj 1.HkpSkv, Luleå/Kallax	
144049	NH Industries NH.90-TTH (Hkp.14D) [49]	Hkpflj 1.HkpSkv, Luleå/Kallax	
144050	NH Industries NH.90-TTH (Hkp.14D) [50]	Hkpflj 1.HkpSkv, Luleå/Kallax	
144051	NH Industries NH.90-TTH (Hkp.14D) [51]	Hkpflj 1.HkpSkv, Luleå/Kallax	
144052	NH Industries NH.90-TTH (Hkp.14D) [52]	Hkpflj 1.HkpSkv, Luleå/Kallax	
144053	NH Industries NH.90-TTH (Hkp.14D) [53]	Hkpflj 1.HkpSkv, Luleå/Kallax	
144054	NH Industries NH.90-TTH (Hkp.14D) [54]	Hkpflj 3.HkpSkv, Ronneby/Kallinge	
142055	NH Industries NH.90-SAR (Hkp.14B) [55]	Hkpflj 3.HkpSkv, Ronneby/Kallinge	
145046	NH Industries NH.90-TTH (Hkp.14E) [46]	Hkpflj 1.HkpSkv, Luleå/Kallax	
146056	NH Industries NH.90-SAR (Hkp.14F) [56]	Hkpflj 3.HkpSkv, Ronneby/Kallinge	
146057	NH Industries NH.90-SAR (Hkp.14F) [57]	Hkpflj (on order)	
146058	NH Industries NH.90-SAR (Hkp.14F) [58]	Hkpflj (on order)	
146059	NH Industries NH.90-SAR (Hkp.14F) [59]	Hkpflj (on order)	
151751	Agusta A109LUH Power (Hkp.15A) [21]	Hkpflj 2.HkpSkv, Linköping/Malmen	
151752	Agusta A109LUH Power (Hkp.15A) [22]	Hkpflj 2.HkpSkv, Linköping/Malmen	
151753	Agusta A109LUH Power (Hkp.15A) [23]	Hkpflj 2.HkpSkv, Linköping/Malmen	
151754	Agusta A109LUH Power (Hkp.15A) [24]	Hkpflj 2.HkpSkv, Linköping/Malmen	
151755	Agusta A109LUH Power (Hkp.15A) [25]	Hkpflj 2.HkpSkv, Linköping/Malmen	
151756	Agusta A109LUH Power (Hkp.15A) [26]	Hkpflj 2.HkpSkv, Linköping/Malmen	
151757	Agusta A109LUH Power (Hkp.15A) [27]	Hkpflj 2.HkpSkv, Linköping/Malmen	
151758	Agusta A109LUH Power (Hkp.15A) [28]	Hkpflj 2.HkpSkv, Linköping/Malmen	
151759	Agusta A109LUH Power (Hkp.15A) [29]	Hkpflj 2.HkpSkv, Linköping/Malmen	
152760	Agusta A109LUH Power (Hkp.15B) [30]	Hkpflj 3.HkpSkv, Ronneby/Kallinge	
151761	Agusta A109LUH Power (Hkp.15A) [31]	Hkpflj 2.HkpSkv, Linköping/Malmen	
151762	Agusta A109LUH Power (Hkp.15A) [32]	Hkpflj 2.HkpSkv, Linköping/Malmen	
152763	Agusta A109LUH Power (Hkp.15B) [33]	Hkpflj 3.HkpSkv, Ronneby/Kallinge	
151764	Agusta A109LUH Power (Hkp.15A) [34]	Hkpflj 2.HkpSkv, Linköping/Malmen	
152765	Agusta A109LUH Power (Hkp.15B) [35]	Hkpflj 3.HkpSkv, Ronneby/Kallinge	
152766	Agusta A109LUH Power (Hkp.15B) [36]	Hkpflj 3.HkpSkv, Ronneby/Kallinge	
152767	Agusta A109LUH Power (Hkp.15B) [37]	Hkpflj 3.HkpSkv, Ronneby/Kallinge	
152768	Agusta A109LUH Power (Hkp.15B) [38]	Hkpflj 3.HkpSkv, Ronneby/Kallinge	
152769	Agusta A109LUH Power (Hkp.15B) [39]	Hkpflj 3.HkpSkv, Ronneby/Kallinge	
152770	Agusta A109LUH Power (Hkp.15B) [40]	Hkpflj 3.HkpSkv, Ronneby/Kallinge	
161226	Sikorsky UH-60M Black Hawk (Hkp.16A) [01]	Hkpflj 2.HkpSkv, Linköping/Malmen	
161227	Sikorsky UH-60M Black Hawk (Hkp.16A) [02]	Hkpflj 2.HkpSkv, Linköping/Malmen	
161228	Sikorsky UH-60M Black Hawk (Hkp.16A) [03]	Hkpflj 2.HkpSkv, Linköping/Malmen	
161229	Sikorsky UH-60M Black Hawk (Hkp.16A) [04]	Hkpflj 2.HkpSkv, Linköping/Malmen	
161230	Sikorsky UH-60M Black Hawk (Hkp.16A) [05]	Hkpflj 2.HkpSkv, Linköping/Malmen	
161231	Sikorsky UH-60M Black Hawk (Hkp.16A) [06]	Hkpflj 2.HkpSkv, Linköping/Malmen	
161232	Sikorsky UH-60M Black Hawk (Hkp.16A) [07]	Hkpflj 2.HkpSkv, Linköping/Malmen	
161233	Sikorsky UH-60M Black Hawk (Hkp.16A) [08]	Hkpflj 2.HkpSkv, Linköping/Malmen	
161234	Sikorsky UH-60M Black Hawk (Hkp.16A) [09]	Hkpflj 2.HkpSkv, Linköping/Malmen	
161235	Sikorsky UH-60M Black Hawk (Hkp.16A) [10]	Hkpflj 2.HkpSkv, Linköping/Malmen	
161236	Sikorsky UH-60M Black Hawk (Hkp.16A) [11]	Hkpflj 2.HkpSkv, Linköping/Malmen	
161237	Sikorsky UH-60M Black Hawk (Hkp.16A) [12]	Hkpflj 2.HkpSkv, Linköping/Malmen	

Notes	Serial	Type (code/other identity)	Owner/operator, location or fate
	161238	Sikorsky UH-60M Black Hawk (Hkp.16A) [13]	Hkpflj 2.HkpSkv, Linköping/Malmen
	161239	Sikorsky UH-60M Black Hawk (Hkp.16A) [14]	Hkpflj 2.HkpSkv, Linköping/Malmen
	161240	Sikorsky UH-60M Black Hawk (Hkp.16A) [15]	Hkpflj 2.HkpSkv, Linköping/Malmen
	Kustbevakning/Swedish Coast Guard		
	SE-MAA	Bombardier DHC-8Q-311 [501]	Kustbevakning, Nykoping
	SE-MAB	Bombardier DHC-8Q-311 [502]	Kustbevakning, Nykoping
	SE-MAC	Bombardier DHC-8Q-311 [503]	Kustbevakning, Nykoping
	SWITZERLAND		
	Schweizer Luftwaffe/Swiss Air Force		
	(Most aircraft are pooled centrally. Some carry unit badges but these rarely indicate actual operators.)		
	A-101	Pilatus PC-21	Swiss AF Pilotenschule, Emmen
	A-102	Pilatus PC-21	Swiss AF Pilotenschule, Emmen
	A-103	Pilatus PC-21	Swiss AF Pilotenschule, Emmen
	A-104	Pilatus PC-21	Swiss AF Pilotenschule, Emmen
	A-105	Pilatus PC-21	Swiss AF Pilotenschule, Emmen
	A-106	Pilatus PC-21	Swiss AF Pilotenschule, Emmen
	A-107	Pilatus PC-21	Swiss AF Pilotenschule, Emmen
	A-108	Pilatus PC-21	Swiss AF Pilotenschule, Emmen
	A-912	Pilatus NCPC-7 Turbo Trainer	Swiss AF Instrumentenflugstaffel 14, Emmen
	A-913	Pilatus NCPC-7 Turbo Trainer	Swiss AF Instrumentenflugstaffel 14, Emmen
	A-914	Pilatus NCPC-7 Turbo Trainer	Swiss AF Instrumentenflugstaffel 14, Emmen
	A-915	Pilatus NCPC-7 Turbo Trainer	Swiss AF Instrumentenflugstaffel 14, Emmen
	A-916	Pilatus NCPC-7 Turbo Trainer	Swiss AF Instrumentenflugstaffel 14, Emmen
	A-917	Pilatus NCPC-7 Turbo Trainer	Swiss AF Instrumentenflugstaffel 14, Emmen
	A-918	Pilatus NCPC-7 Turbo Trainer	Swiss AF Instrumentenflugstaffel 14, Emmen
	A-919	Pilatus NCPC-7 Turbo Trainer	Swiss AF Instrumentenflugstaffel 14, Emmen
	A-922	Pilatus NCPC-7 Turbo Trainer	Swiss AF Instrumentenflugstaffel 14, Emmen
	A-923	Pilatus NCPC-7 Turbo Trainer	Swiss AF Instrumentenflugstaffel 14, Emmen
	A-924	Pilatus NCPC-7 Turbo Trainer	Swiss AF Instrumentenflugstaffel 14, Emmen
	A-925	Pilatus NCPC-7 Turbo Trainer	Swiss AF Instrumentenflugstaffel 14, Emmen
	A-926	Pilatus NCPC-7 Turbo Trainer	Swiss AF Instrumentenflugstaffel 14, Emmen
	A-927	Pilatus NCPC-7 Turbo Trainer	Swiss AF Instrumentenflugstaffel 14, Emmen
	A-928	Pilatus NCPC-7 Turbo Trainer	Swiss AF Instrumentenflugstaffel 14, Emmen
	A-929	Pilatus NCPC-7 Turbo Trainer	Swiss AF Instrumentenflugstaffel 14, Emmen
	A-930	Pilatus NCPC-7 Turbo Trainer	Swiss AF Instrumentenflugstaffel 14, Emmen
	A-931	Pilatus NCPC-7 Turbo Trainer	Swiss AF Instrumentenflugstaffel 14, Emmen
	A-932	Pilatus NCPC-7 Turbo Trainer	Swiss AF Instrumentenflugstaffel 14, Emmen
	A-933	Pilatus NCPC-7 Turbo Trainer	Swiss AF Instrumentenflugstaffel 14, Emmen
	A-934	Pilatus NCPC-7 Turbo Trainer	Swiss AF Instrumentenflugstaffel 14, Emmen
	A-935	Pilatus NCPC-7 Turbo Trainer	Swiss AF Instrumentenflugstaffel 14, Emmen
	A-936	Pilatus NCPC-7 Turbo Trainer	Swiss AF Instrumentenflugstaffel 14, Emmen
	A-938	Pilatus NCPC-7 Turbo Trainer	Swiss AF Instrumentenflugstaffel 14, Emmen
	A-939	Pilatus NCPC-7 Turbo Trainer	Swiss AF Instrumentenflugstaffel 14, Emmen
	A-940	Pilatus NCPC-7 Turbo Trainer	Swiss AF Instrumentenflugstaffel 14, Emmen
	A-941	Pilatus NCPC-7 Turbo Trainer	Swiss AF Instrumentenflugstaffel 14, Emmen
	C-405	Pilatus PC-9	Swiss AF Zielflugstaffel 12, Emmen
	C-406	Pilatus PC-9	Swiss AF Zielflugstaffel 12, Emmen
	C-407	Pilatus PC-9	Swiss AF Zielflugstaffel 12, Emmen
	C-408	Pilatus PC-9	Swiss AF Zielflugstaffel 12, Emmen
	C-409	Pilatus PC-9	Swiss AF Zielflugstaffel 12, Emmen
	C-410	Pilatus PC-9	Preserved at Wildegg, March 2018
	C-411	Pilatus PC-9	Swiss AF Zielflugstaffel 12, Emmen
	C-412	Pilatus PC-9	Swiss AF Zielflugstaffel 12, Emmen
	J-3005	Northrop F-5E Tiger II	Withdrawn from use at Emmen, April 2018
	J-3015	Northrop F-5E Tiger II	Swiss AF FlSt 6 & 19, Payerne
	J-3030	Northrop F-5E Tiger II	Swiss AF FlSt 6 & 19, Payerne
	J-3033	Northrop F-5E Tiger II $	Swiss AF FlSt 6 & 19, Payerne
	J-3036	Northrop F-5E Tiger II $	Swiss AF, stored Sion
	J-3038	Northrop F-5E Tiger II $	Swiss AF FlSt 6 & 19, Payerne
	J-3041	Northrop F-5E Tiger II	Swiss AF, stored Sion
	J-3044	Northrop F-5E Tiger II	Swiss AF, stored Emmen

Serial	Type (code/other identity)	Owner/operator, location or fate	Notes
J-3056	Northrop F-5E Tiger II	*Preserved at Lucerne, 2018*	
J-3062	Northrop F-5E Tiger II	Swiss AF, stored Sion	
J-3063	Northrop F-5E Tiger II	Swiss AF, stored Sion	
J-3065	Northrop F-5E Tiger II	Swiss AF FISt 6 & 19, Payerne	
J-3067	Northrop F-5E Tiger II	Swiss AF FISt 6 & 19, Payerne	
J-3068	Northrop F-5E Tiger II	Swiss AF FISt 6 & 19, Payerne	
J-3069	Northrop F-5E Tiger II	*Swiss AF, Payerne, GI use*	
J-3070	Northrop F-5E Tiger II	Swiss AF FISt 6 & 19, Payerne	
J-3072	Northrop F-5E Tiger II	Swiss AF FISt 6 & 19, Payerne	
J-3073	Northrop F-5E Tiger II $	Swiss AF FISt 6 & 19, Payerne	
J-3074	Northrop F-5E Tiger II $	Swiss AF FISt 6 & 19, Payerne	
J-3076	Northrop F-5E Tiger II	Swiss AF FISt 6 & 19, Payerne	
J-3077	Northrop F-5E Tiger II	Swiss AF FISt 6 & 19, Payerne	
J-3079	Northrop F-5E Tiger II	Swiss AF, stored Sion	
J-3080	Northrop F-5E Tiger II	RUAG, Emmen	
J-3081	Northrop F-5E Tiger II	Swiss AF *Patrouille Suisse*, Emmen	
J-3082	Northrop F-5E Tiger II	Swiss AF *Patrouille Suisse*, Emmen	
J-3083	Northrop F-5E Tiger II	Swiss AF *Patrouille Suisse*, Emmen	
J-3084	Northrop F-5E Tiger II	Swiss AF *Patrouille Suisse*, Emmen	
J-3085	Northrop F-5E Tiger II	Swiss AF *Patrouille Suisse*, Emmen	
J-3087	Northrop F-5E Tiger II	Swiss AF *Patrouille Suisse*, Emmen	
J-3088	Northrop F-5E Tiger II	Swiss AF *Patrouille Suisse*, Emmen	
J-3089	Northrop F-5E Tiger II	Swiss AF *Patrouille Suisse*, Emmen	
J-3090	Northrop F-5E Tiger II	Swiss AF *Patrouille Suisse*, Emmen	
J-3091	Northrop F-5E Tiger II	Swiss AF *Patrouille Suisse*, Emmen	
J-3092	Northrop F-5E Tiger II	Swiss AF FISt 6 & 19, Payerne	
J-3093	Northrop F-5E Tiger II	Swiss AF FISt 6 & 19, Payerne	
J-3094	Northrop F-5E Tiger II	Swiss AF FISt 6 & 19, Payerne	
J-3095	Northrop F-5E Tiger II	Swiss AF FISt 6 & 19, Payerne	
J-3097	Northrop F-5E Tiger II	Swiss AF FISt 6 & 19, Payerne	
J-3201	Northrop F-5F Tiger II	Swiss AF, stored Emmen	
J-3203	Northrop F-5F Tiger II	Swiss AF FISt 6 & 19, Payerne	
J-3204	Northrop F-5F Tiger II	Swiss AF FISt 6 & 19, Payerne	
J-3206	Northrop F-5F Tiger II	Swiss AF, stored Emmen	
J-3210	Northrop F-5F Tiger II	Swiss AF FISt 6 & 19, Payerne	
J-3211	Northrop F-5F Tiger II	Swiss AF FISt 6 & 19, Payerne	
J-3212	Northrop F-5F Tiger II	Swiss AF FISt 6 & 19, Payerne	
J-5001	McDonnell Douglas F/A-18C Hornet	Swiss AF FISt 11, Meiringen/FISt 17 & 18 Payerne	
J-5002	McDonnell Douglas F/A-18C Hornet	Swiss AF FISt 11, Meiringen/FISt 17 & 18 Payerne	
J-5003	McDonnell Douglas F/A-18C Hornet	Swiss AF FISt 11, Meiringen/FISt 17 & 18 Payerne	
J-5004	McDonnell Douglas F/A-18C Hornet	Swiss AF FISt 11, Meiringen/FISt 17 & 18 Payerne	
J-5005	McDonnell Douglas F/A-18C Hornet	Swiss AF FISt 11, Meiringen/FISt 17 & 18 Payerne	
J-5006	McDonnell Douglas F/A-18C Hornet	Swiss AF FISt 11, Meiringen/FISt 17 & 18 Payerne	
J-5007	McDonnell Douglas F/A-18C Hornet	Swiss AF FISt 11, Meiringen/FISt 17 & 18 Payerne	
J-5008	McDonnell Douglas F/A-18C Hornet	Swiss AF FISt 11, Meiringen/FISt 17 & 18 Payerne	
J-5009	McDonnell Douglas F/A-18C Hornet	Swiss AF FISt 11, Meiringen/FISt 17 & 18 Payerne	
J-5010	McDonnell Douglas F/A-18C Hornet	Swiss AF FISt 11, Meiringen/FISt 17 & 18 Payerne	
J-5011	McDonnell Douglas F/A-18C Hornet $	Swiss AF FISt 11, Meiringen/FISt 17 & 18 Payerne	
J-5012	McDonnell Douglas F/A-18C Hornet	Swiss AF FISt 11, Meiringen/FISt 17 & 18 Payerne	
J-5013	McDonnell Douglas F/A-18C Hornet	Swiss AF FISt 11, Meiringen/FISt 17 & 18 Payerne	
J-5014	McDonnell Douglas F/A-18C Hornet	Swiss AF FISt 11, Meiringen/FISt 17 & 18 Payerne	
J-5015	McDonnell Douglas F/A-18C Hornet	Swiss AF FISt 11, Meiringen/FISt 17 & 18 Payerne	
J-5016	McDonnell Douglas F/A-18C Hornet	Swiss AF FISt 11, Meiringen/FISt 17 & 18 Payerne	
J-5017	McDonnell Douglas F/A-18C Hornet $	Swiss AF FISt 11, Meiringen/FISt 17 & 18 Payerne	
J-5018	McDonnell Douglas F/A-18C Hornet $	Swiss AF FISt 11, Meiringen/FISt 17 & 18 Payerne	
J-5019	McDonnell Douglas F/A-18C Hornet	Swiss AF FISt 11, Meiringen/FISt 17 & 18 Payerne	
J-5020	McDonnell Douglas F/A-18C Hornet	Swiss AF FISt 11, Meiringen/FISt 17 & 18 Payerne	
J-5021	McDonnell Douglas F/A-18C Hornet	Swiss AF FISt 11, Meiringen/FISt 17 & 18 Payerne	
J-5022	McDonnell Douglas F/A-18C Hornet	Swiss AF FISt 11, Meiringen/FISt 17 & 18 Payerne	
J-5023	McDonnell Douglas F/A-18C Hornet	Swiss AF FISt 11, Meiringen/FISt 17 & 18 Payerne	
J-5024	McDonnell Douglas F/A-18C Hornet	Swiss AF FISt 11, Meiringen/FISt 17 & 18 Payerne	
J-5025	McDonnell Douglas F/A-18C Hornet	Swiss AF FISt 11, Meiringen/FISt 17 & 18 Payerne	
J-5026	McDonnell Douglas F/A-18C Hornet	Swiss AF FISt 11, Meiringen/FISt 17 & 18 Payerne	

Notes	Serial	Type (code/other identity)	Owner/operator, location or fate
	J-5232	McDonnell Douglas F/A-18D Hornet	Swiss AF FlSt 11, Meiringen/FlSt 17 & 18 Payerne
	J-5233	McDonnell Douglas F/A-18D Hornet	Swiss AF FlSt 11, Meiringen/FlSt 17 & 18 Payerne
	J-5234	McDonnell Douglas F/A-18D Hornet	Swiss AF FlSt 11, Meiringen/FlSt 17 & 18 Payerne
	J-5236	McDonnell Douglas F/A-18D Hornet	Swiss AF FlSt 11, Meiringen/FlSt 17 & 18 Payerne
	J-5238	McDonnell Douglas F/A-18D Hornet	Swiss AF FlSt 11, Meiringen/FlSt 17 & 18 Payerne
	R-711	Aurora Flight Services Centaur OPA	Armasuisse, Emmen
	T-311	Aérospatiale AS.332M-1 Super Puma (TH 89)	Swiss AF LtSt 6 & 8, Alpnach/ LtSt 3 & 4, Dübendorf/LtSt 1 & 5, Payerne
	T-312	Aérospatiale AS.332M-1 Super Puma (TH 89)	Swiss AF LtSt 6 & 8, Alpnach/ LtSt 3 & 4, Dübendorf/LtSt 1 & 5, Payerne
	T-313	Aérospatiale AS.332M-1 Super Puma (TH 89)	Swiss AF LtSt 6 & 8, Alpnach/ LtSt 3 & 4, Dübendorf/LtSt 1 & 5, Payerne
	T-314	Aérospatiale AS.332M-1 Super Puma (TH 89)	Swiss AF LtSt 6 & 8, Alpnach/ LtSt 3 & 4, Dübendorf/LtSt 1 & 5, Payerne
	T-315	Aérospatiale AS.332M-1 Super Puma (TH 89)	Swiss AF LtSt 6 & 8, Alpnach/ LtSt 3 & 4, Dübendorf/LtSt 1 & 5, Payerne
	T-316	Aérospatiale AS.332M-1 Super Puma (TH 89) $	Swiss AF LtSt 6 & 8, Alpnach/ LtSt 3 & 4, Dübendorf/LtSt 1 & 5, Payerne
	T-317	Aérospatiale AS.332M-1 Super Puma (TH 89)	Swiss AF LtSt 6 & 8, Alpnach/ LtSt 3 & 4, Dübendorf/LtSt 1 & 5, Payerne
	T-318	Aérospatiale AS.332M-1 Super Puma (TH 89)	Swiss AF LtSt 6 & 8, Alpnach/ LtSt 3 & 4, Dübendorf/LtSt 1 & 5, Payerne
	T-319	Aérospatiale AS.332M-1 Super Puma (TH 89)	Swiss AF LtSt 6 & 8, Alpnach/ LtSt 3 & 4, Dübendorf/LtSt 1 & 5, Payerne
	T-320	Aérospatiale AS.332M-1 Super Puma (TH 89)	Swiss AF LtSt 6 & 8, Alpnach/ LtSt 3 & 4, Dübendorf/LtSt 1 & 5, Payerne
	T-321	Aérospatiale AS.332M-1 Super Puma (TH 89)	Swiss AF LtSt 6 & 8, Alpnach/ LtSt 3 & 4, Dübendorf/LtSt 1 & 5, Payerne
	T-322	Aérospatiale AS.332M-1 Super Puma (TH 89)	Swiss AF LtSt 6 & 8, Alpnach/ LtSt 3 & 4, Dübendorf/LtSt 1 & 5, Payerne
	T-323	Aérospatiale AS.332M-1 Super Puma (TH 89)	Swiss AF LtSt 6 & 8, Alpnach/ LtSt 3 & 4, Dübendorf/LtSt 1 & 5, Payerne
	T-324	Aérospatiale AS.332M-1 Super Puma (TH 89)	Swiss AF LtSt 6 & 8, Alpnach/ LtSt 3 & 4, Dübendorf/LtSt 1 & 5, Payerne
	T-325	Aérospatiale AS.332M-1 Super Puma (TH 89)	Swiss AF LtSt 6 & 8, Alpnach/ LtSt 3 & 4, Dübendorf/LtSt 1 & 5, Payerne
	T-331	Aérospatiale AS.532UL Super Puma (TH 98)	Swiss AF LtSt 6 & 8, Alpnach/ LtSt 3 & 4, Dübendorf/LtSt 1 & 5, Payerne
	T-332	Aérospatiale AS.532UL Super Puma (TH 98)	Swiss AF LtSt 6 & 8, Alpnach/ LtSt 3 & 4, Dübendorf/LtSt 1 & 5, Payerne
	T-333	Aérospatiale AS.532UL Super Puma (TH 98)	Swiss AF LtSt 6 & 8, Alpnach/ LtSt 3 & 4, Dübendorf/LtSt 1 & 5, Payerne
	T-334	Aérospatiale AS.532UL Super Puma (TH 98)	Swiss AF LtSt 6 & 8, Alpnach/ LtSt 3 & 4, Dübendorf/LtSt 1 & 5, Payerne
	T-335	Aérospatiale AS.532UL Super Puma (TH 98)	Swiss AF LtSt 6 & 8, Alpnach/ LtSt 3 & 4, Dübendorf/LtSt 1 & 5, Payerne
	T-336	Aérospatiale AS.532UL Super Puma (TH 98)	Swiss AF LtSt 6 & 8, Alpnach/ LtSt 3 & 4, Dübendorf/LtSt 1 & 5, Payerne
	T-337	Aérospatiale AS.532UL Super Puma (TH 98)	Swiss AF LtSt 6 & 8, Alpnach/ LtSt 3 & 4, Dübendorf/LtSt 1 & 5, Payerne
	T-339	Aérospatiale AS.532UL Super Puma (TH 98)	Swiss AF LtSt 6 & 8, Alpnach/ LtSt 3 & 4, Dübendorf/LtSt 1 & 5, Payerne
	T-340	Aérospatiale AS.532UL Super Puma (TH 98)	Swiss AF LtSt 6 & 8, Alpnach/ LtSt 3 & 4, Dübendorf/LtSt 1 & 5, Payerne
	T-342	Aérospatiale AS.532UL Super Puma (TH 98)	Swiss AF LtSt 6 & 8, Alpnach/ LtSt 3 & 4, Dübendorf/LtSt 1 & 5, Payerne
	T-351	Eurocopter EC.135P-2	Swiss AF LTDB, Dübendorf
	T-352	Eurocopter EC.135P-2	Swiss AF LTDB, Dübendorf
	T-353	Eurocopter EC.635P-2	Swiss AF LtSt 6 & 8, Alpnach/ LtSt 3 & 4, Dübendorf/LtSt 1 & 5, Payerne
	T-354	Eurocopter EC.635P-2	Swiss AF LtSt 6 & 8, Alpnach/ LtSt 3 & 4, Dübendorf/LtSt 1 & 5, Payerne

Serial	Type (code/other identity)	Owner/operator, location or fate	Notes
T-355	Eurocopter EC.635P-2	Swiss AF LtSt 6 & 8, Alpnach/ LtSt 3 & 4, Dübendorf/LtSt 1 & 5, Payerne	
T-356	Eurocopter EC.635P-2	Swiss AF LtSt 6 & 8, Alpnach/ LtSt 3 & 4, Dübendorf/LtSt 1 & 5, Payerne	
T-357	Eurocopter EC.635P-2	Swiss AF LtSt 6 & 8, Alpnach/ LtSt 3 & 4, Dübendorf/LtSt 1 & 5, Payerne	
T-358	Eurocopter EC.635P-2	Swiss AF LtSt 6 & 8, Alpnach/ LtSt 3 & 4, Dübendorf/LtSt 1 & 5, Payerne	
T-359	Eurocopter EC.635P-2	Swiss AF LtSt 6 & 8, Alpnach/ LtSt 3 & 4, Dübendorf/LtSt 1 & 5, Payerne	
T-360	Eurocopter EC.635P-2	Swiss AF LtSt 6 & 8, Alpnach/ LtSt 3 & 4, Dübendorf/LtSt 1 & 5, Payerne	
T-361	Eurocopter EC.635P-2	Swiss AF LtSt 6 & 8, Alpnach/ LtSt 3 & 4, Dübendorf/LtSt 1 & 5, Payerne	
T-362	Eurocopter EC.635P-2	Swiss AF LtSt 6 & 8, Alpnach/ LtSt 3 & 4, Dübendorf/LtSt 1 & 5, Payerne	
T-363	Eurocopter EC.635P-2	Swiss AF LtSt 6 & 8, Alpnach/ LtSt 3 & 4, Dübendorf/LtSt 1 & 5, Payerne	
T-364	Eurocopter EC.635P-2	Swiss AF LtSt 6 & 8, Alpnach/ LtSt 3 & 4, Dübendorf/LtSt 1 & 5, Payerne	
T-365	Eurocopter EC.635P-2	Swiss AF LtSt 6 & 8, Alpnach/ LtSt 3 & 4, Dübendorf/LtSt 1 & 5, Payerne	
T-366	Eurocopter EC.635P-2	Swiss AF LtSt 6 & 8, Alpnach/ LtSt 3 & 4, Dübendorf/LtSt 1 & 5, Payerne	
T-367	Eurocopter EC.635P-2	Swiss AF LtSt 6 & 8, Alpnach/ LtSt 3 & 4, Dübendorf/LtSt 1 & 5, Payerne	
T-368	Eurocopter EC.635P-2	Swiss AF LtSt 6 & 8, Alpnach/ LtSt 3 & 4, Dübendorf/LtSt 1 & 5, Payerne	
T-369	Eurocopter EC.635P-2	Swiss AF LtSt 6 & 8, Alpnach/ LtSt 3 & 4, Dübendorf/LtSt 1 & 5, Payerne	
T-370	Eurocopter EC.635P-2	Swiss AF LtSt 6 & 8, Alpnach/ LtSt 3 & 4, Dübendorf/LtSt 1 & 5, Payerne	
T-721	Beech King Air 350C	Swiss AF LTDB, Dübendorf	
T-729	Beech 1900D	Swiss AF LTDB, Dübendorf	
T-784	Cessna 560XL Citation Excel	Swiss AF LTDB, Bern/Belp	
T-785	Dassault Falcon 900EX EASy II	Swiss AF LTDB, Bern/Belp	
T-786	Pilatus PC-24	Swiss AF LTDB, Bern/Belp	
V-612	Pilatus PC-6B/B2-H2 Turbo Porter	Swiss AF LtSt 7, Emmen	
V-613	Pilatus PC-6B/B2-H2 Turbo Porter	Swiss AF LtSt 7, Emmen	
V-614	Pilatus PC-6B/B2-H2 Turbo Porter	Swiss AF LtSt 7, Emmen	
V-616	Pilatus PC-6B/B2-H2 Turbo Porter	Swiss AF LtSt 7, Emmen	
V-617	Pilatus PC-6B/B2-H2 Turbo Porter	Swiss AF LtSt 7, Emmen	
V-618	Pilatus PC-6B/B2-H2 Turbo Porter	Swiss AF LtSt 7, Emmen	
V-619	Pilatus PC-6B/B2-H2 Turbo Porter	Swiss AF LtSt 7, Emmen	
V-620	Pilatus PC-6B/B2-H2 Turbo Porter	Swiss AF LtSt 7, Emmen	
V-622	Pilatus PC-6B/B2-H2 Turbo Porter $	Swiss AF LtSt 7, Emmen	
V-623	Pilatus PC-6B/B2-H2 Turbo Porter	Swiss AF LtSt 7, Emmen	
V-631	Pilatus PC-6B/B2-H2 Turbo Porter	Swiss AF LtSt 7, Emmen	
V-632	Pilatus PC-6B/B2-H2 Turbo Porter	Swiss AF LtSt 7, Emmen	
V-633	Pilatus PC-6B/B2-H2 Turbo Porter	Swiss AF LtSt 7, Emmen	
V-634	Pilatus PC-6B/B2-H2 Turbo Porter	Swiss AF LtSt 7, Emmen	
V-635	Pilatus PC-6B/B2-H2 Turbo Porter	Swiss AF LtSt 7, Emmen	

Swiss Government

HB-FOG	Pilatus PC-12/45	Armasuisse, Emmen	

SYRIA

YK-ASC	Dassault Falcon 900	Government of Syria, Damascus	

TANZANIA

5H-ONE	Gulfstream Aerospace G.550	Tanzanian Government, Dar-es-Salaam	

Notes	Serial	Type (code/other identity)	Owner/operator, location or fate
	THAILAND		
	HS-CMV	Boeing 737-4Z6 (L11Kh.MWK-01/38) [11-111, 90401]	Royal Thai AF 904 Sqn/6 Wing, Bangkok/Don Muang
	HS-HRH	Boeing 737-448 (L11Kh.MWK-02/47) [99-999, 90409]	Royal Thai AF 904 Sqn/6 Wing, Bangkok/Don Muang
	HS-MVS	Boeing 737-8Z6 (L11Kh2-1/50) [99-904, 90411]	Royal Thai AF 904 Sqn/6 Wing, Bangkok/Don Muang
	HS-TYR	Airbus A.319CJ-133 (B.L15-1/47) [60202]	Royal Thai AF 602 Sqn/6 Wing, Bangkok/Don Muang
	HS-TYT	Airbus A.320CJ-214 (L15K-1/58) [60203]	Royal Thai AF 602 Sqn/6 Wing, Bangkok/Don Muang
	HS-TYV	Airbus A.340-541 (L19-1/59) [60204]	Royal Thai AF 602 Sqn/6 Wing, Bangkok/Don Muang
	L18-1/59	Sukhoi SSJ100-95LR Superjet [60317]	Royal Thai AF 603 Sqn/6 Wing, Bangkok/Don Muang
	L18-2/60	Sukhoi SSJ100-95LR Superjet [60318]	Royal Thai AF 603 Sqn/6 Wing, Bangkok/Don Muang
	L18-3/61	Sukhoi SSJ100-95LR Superjet [60319]	Royal Thai AF 603 Sqn/6 Wing, Bangkok/Don Muang
	TUNISIA		
	Tunisian Air Force/Al Quwwat al-Jawwiya al-Jamahiriyah At'Tunisia & Tunisian Government		
	Z21012	Lockheed C-130H Hercules (TS-MTB)	Tunisian AF 21 Sqn, Bizerte/Sidi Ahmed
	Z21121	Lockheed C-130J-30 Hercules II (TS-MTK)	Tunisian AF 21 Sqn, Bizerte/Sidi Ahmed
	Z21122	Lockheed C-130J-30 Hercules II (TS-MTL)	Tunisian AF 21 Sqn, Bizerte/Sidi Ahmed
	TS-IOO	Boeing 737-7HJ	Government of Tunisia, Tunis
	TURKEY		
	Türk Hava Kuvvetleri (THK)/Turkish Air Force & Turkish Government		
	004	Cessna 650 Citation VII	THK 212 Filo/11 HUAÜK, Ankara/Etimesgut
	3004	Canadair NF-5A-2000 Freedom Fighter	THK 134 Filo, *Turkish Stars*/3 AJEÜ, Konya
	3023	Canadair NF-5A-2000 Freedom Fighter	THK 134 Filo, *Turkish Stars*/3 AJEÜ, Konya
	3025	Canadair NF-5A-2000 Freedom Fighter	THK 134 Filo, *Turkish Stars*/3 AJEÜ, Konya
	3027	Canadair NF-5A-2000 Freedom Fighter	THK 134 Filo, *Turkish Stars*/3 AJEÜ, Konya
	3032	Canadair NF-5A-2000 Freedom Fighter	THK 134 Filo, *Turkish Stars*/3 AJEÜ, Konya
	3036	Canadair NF-5A-2000 Freedom Fighter	THK 134 Filo, *Turkish Stars*/3 AJEÜ, Konya
	3039	Canadair NF-5A-2000 Freedom Fighter	THK 134 Filo, *Turkish Stars*/3 AJEÜ, Konya
	3046	Canadair NF-5A-2000 Freedom Fighter [7]	THK 134 Filo, *Turkish Stars*/3 AJEÜ, Konya
	3048	Canadair NF-5A-2000 Freedom Fighter [5]	THK 134 Filo, *Turkish Stars*/3 AJEÜ, Konya
	3049	Canadair NF-5A-2000 Freedom Fighter [6]	THK 134 Filo, *Turkish Stars*/3 AJEÜ, Konya
	3052	Canadair NF-5A-2000 Freedom Fighter [2]	THK 134 Filo, *Turkish Stars*/3 AJEÜ, Konya
	3058	Canadair NF-5A-2000 Freedom Fighter [3]	THK 134 Filo, *Turkish Stars*/3 AJEÜ, Konya
	3066	Canadair NF-5A-2000 Freedom Fighter	THK 134 Filo, *Turkish Stars*/3 AJEÜ, Konya
	3072	Canadair NF-5A-2000 Freedom Fighter	THK 134 Filo, *Turkish Stars*/3 AJEÜ, Konya
	4001	Canadair NF-5B-2000 Freedom Fighter [4]	THK 134 Filo, *Turkish Stars*/3 AJEÜ, Konya
	4005	Canadair NF-5B-2000 Freedom Fighter	THK 134 Filo, *Turkish Stars*/3 AJEÜ, Konya
	4009	Canadair NF-5B-2000 Freedom Fighter	THK 134 Filo, *Turkish Stars*/3 AJEÜ, Konya
	4013	Canadair NF-5B-2000 Freedom Fighter	THK 134 Filo, *Turkish Stars*/3 AJEÜ, Konya
	4020	Canadair NF-5B-2000 Freedom Fighter	THK 134 Filo, *Turkish Stars*/3 AJEÜ, Konya
	4021	Canadair NF-5B-2000 Freedom Fighter	THK 134 Filo, *Turkish Stars*/3 AJEÜ, Konya
	4026	Canadair NF-5B-2000 Freedom Fighter [1]	THK 134 Filo, *Turkish Stars*/3 AJEÜ, Konya
	57-2609	Boeing KC-135R Stratotanker	THK 101 Filo/10 TÜK, Incirlik
	58-0110	Boeing KC-135R Stratotanker	THK 101 Filo/10 TÜK, Incirlik
	60-0325	Boeing KC-135R Stratotanker	THK 101 Filo/10 TÜK, Incirlik
	60-0326	Boeing KC-135R Stratotanker	THK 101 Filo/10 TÜK, Incirlik
	62-3539	Boeing KC-135R Stratotanker	THK 101 Filo/10 TÜK, Incirlik
	62-3563	Boeing KC-135R Stratotanker	THK 101 Filo/10 TÜK, Incirlik
	62-3567	Boeing KC-135R Stratotanker	THK 101 Filo/10 TÜK, Incirlik
	63-3186	Lockheed C-130E Hercules (63-13186)	THK 222 Filo/12 HUAÜ, Erkilet
	63-13187	Lockheed C-130E Hercules $	THK 222 Filo/12 HUAÜ, Erkilet
	63-3188	Lockheed C-130E Hercules (63-13188)	THK 222 Filo/12 HUAÜ, Erkilet
	63-13189	Lockheed C-130E Hercules $	THK 222 Filo/12 HUAÜ, Erkilet

Serial	Type (code/other identity)	Owner/operator, location or fate	Notes
65-0451	Lockheed C-130E Hercules	THK 222 Filo/12 HUAÜ, Erkilet	
67-0455	Lockheed C-130E Hercules	THK 222 Filo/12 HUAÜ, Erkilet	
68-020	Transall C-160D	THK 221 Filo/12 HUAÜ, Erkilet	
68-023	Transall C-160D	THK 221 Filo/12 HUAÜ, Erkilet	
68-01606	Lockheed C-130E Hercules	THK 222 Filo/12 HUAÜ, Erkilet	
68-01608	Lockheed C-130E Hercules	THK 222 Filo/12 HUAÜ, Erkilet	
68-01609	Lockheed C-130E Hercules	THK 222 Filo/12 HUAÜ, Erkilet	
69-019	Transall C-160D	THK 221 Filo/12 HUAÜ, Erkilet	
69-021	Transall C-160D	THK 221 Filo/12 HUAÜ, Erkilet	
69-024	Transall C-160D	THK 221 Filo/12 HUAÜ, Erkilet	
69-026	Transall C-160D	THK 221 Filo/12 HUAÜ, Erkilet	
69-027	Transall C-160D	THK 221 Filo/12 HUAÜ, Erkilet	
69-029	Transall C-160D	THK 221 Filo/12 HUAÜ, Erkilet	
69-031	Transall C-160D	THK 221 Filo/12 HUAÜ, Erkilet	
69-032	Transall C-160D	THK 221 Filo/12 HUAÜ, Erkilet	
69-033	Transall C-160D $	THK 221 Filo/12 HUAÜ, Erkilet	
69-034	Transall C-160D	THK 221 Filo/12 HUAÜ, Erkilet	
69-036	Transall C-160D	THK 221 Filo/12 HUAÜ, Erkilet	
69-040	Transall C-160D $	THK 221 Filo/12 HUAÜ, Erkilet	
70-01610	Lockheed C-130E Hercules	THK 222 Filo/12 HUAÜ, Erkilet	
70-01947	Lockheed C-130E Hercules	THK 222 Filo/12 HUAÜ, Erkilet	
71-01468	Lockheed C-130E Hercules	THK 222 Filo/12 HUAÜ, Erkilet	
73-0991	Lockheed C-130E Hercules $	THK 222 Filo/12 HUAÜ, Erkilet	
86-0066	TUSAS (GD) F-16C-30 Fighting Falcon	THK 132 Filo/3 AJEÜ, Konya	
86-0068	TUSAS (GD) F-16C-30 Fighting Falcon	THK 132 Filo/3 AJEÜ, Konya	
86-0069	TUSAS (GD) F-16C-30 Fighting Falcon	THK 132 Filo/3 AJEÜ, Konya	
86-0070	TUSAS (GD) F-16C-30 Fighting Falcon	THK 152 Filo/5 AJÜ, Merzifon	
86-0071	TUSAS (GD) F-16C-30 Fighting Falcon	THK 152 Filo/5 AJÜ, Merzifon	
86-0072	TUSAS (GD) F-16C-30 Fighting Falcon	THK 152 Filo/5 AJÜ, Merzifon	
86-0192	TUSAS (GD) F-16D-30 Fighting Falcon	THK 132 Filo/3 AJEÜ, Konya	
86-0193	TUSAS (GD) F-16D-30 Fighting Falcon	THK 132 Filo/3 AJEÜ, Konya	
86-0194	TUSAS (GD) F-16D-30 Fighting Falcon	THK 132 Filo/3 AJEÜ, Konya	
86-0195	TUSAS (GD) F-16D-30 Fighting Falcon	THK 132 Filo/3 AJEÜ, Konya	
86-0196	TUSAS (GD) F-16D-30 Fighting Falcon	THK 132 Filo/3 AJEÜ, Konya	
87-0002	TUSAS (GD) F-16D-30 Fighting Falcon	THK 113 Filo/1 AJÜ, Eskisehir	
87-0003	TUSAS (GD) F-16D-30 Fighting Falcon	THK 401 Filo/1 AJÜ, Eskisehir	
87-0009	TUSAS (GD) F-16C-30 Fighting Falcon	THK 113 Filo/1 AJÜ, Eskisehir	
87-0010	TUSAS (GD) F-16C-30 Fighting Falcon	THK 132 Filo/3 AJEÜ, Konya	
87-0011	TUSAS (GD) F-16C-30 Fighting Falcon	THK 132 Filo/3 AJEÜ, Konya	
87-0013	TUSAS (GD) F-16C-30 Fighting Falcon	THK 152 Filo/5 AJÜ, Merzifon	
87-0014	TUSAS (GD) F-16C-30 Fighting Falcon	THK 113 Filo/1 AJÜ, Eskisehir	
87-0015	TUSAS (GD) F-16C-30 Fighting Falcon	THK 113 Filo/1 AJÜ, Eskisehir	
87-0016	TUSAS (GD) F-16C-30 Fighting Falcon	THK 132 Filo/3 AJEÜ, Konya	
87-0017	TUSAS (GD) F-16C-30 Fighting Falcon	THK 152 Filo/5 AJÜ, Merzifon	
87-0018	TUSAS (GD) F-16C-30 Fighting Falcon	THK 152 Filo/5 AJÜ, Merzifon	
87-0019	TUSAS (GD) F-16C-30 Fighting Falcon	THK 132 Filo/3 AJEÜ, Konya	
87-0020	TUSAS (GD) F-16C-30 Fighting Falcon	THK 152 Filo/5 AJÜ, Merzifon	
87-0021	TUSAS (GD) F-16C-30 Fighting Falcon	THK 132 Filo/3 AJEÜ, Konya	
88-0013	TUSAS (GD) F-16D-30 Fighting Falcon	THK 152 Filo/5 AJÜ, Merzifon	
88-0014	TUSAS (GD) F-16D-40 Fighting Falcon	THK 192 Filo/9 AJÜ, Balikesir	
88-0015	TUSAS (GD) F-16D-40 Fighting Falcon	THK 191 Filo/9 AJÜ, Balikesir	
88-0019	TUSAS (GD) F-16C-30 Fighting Falcon	THK 132 Filo/3 AJEÜ, Konya	
88-0020	TUSAS (GD) F-16C-30 Fighting Falcon	THK 132 Filo/3 AJEÜ, Konya	
88-0021	TUSAS (GD) F-16C-30 Fighting Falcon	THK 152 Filo/5 AJÜ, Merzifon	
88-0024	TUSAS (GD) F-16C-30 Fighting Falcon	THK 152 Filo/5 AJÜ, Merzifon	
88-0025	TUSAS (GD) F-16C-30 Fighting Falcon	THK 152 Filo/5 AJÜ, Merzifon	
88-0026	TUSAS (GD) F-16C-30 Fighting Falcon	THK 152 Filo/5 AJÜ, Merzifon	
88-0027	TUSAS (GD) F-16C-30 Fighting Falcon	THK 152 Filo/5 AJÜ, Merzifon	
88-0028	TUSAS (GD) F-16C-30 Fighting Falcon	THK 191 Filo/9 AJÜ, Balikesir	
88-0029	TUSAS (GD) F-16C-30 Fighting Falcon $	THK 141 Filo/4 AJÜ, Akinci	
88-0030	TUSAS (GD) F-16C-30 Fighting Falcon	THK 152 Filo/5 AJÜ, Merzifon	
88-0031	TUSAS (GD) F-16C-30 Fighting Falcon	THK 401 Filo/1 AJÜ, Eskisehir	

Notes	Serial	Type (code/other identity)	Owner/operator, location or fate
	88-0032	TUSAS (GD) F-16C-30 Fighting Falcon $	THK 141 Filo/4 AJÜ, Akinci
	88-0033	TUSAS (GD) F-16C-40 Fighting Falcon	THK 152 Filo/5 AJÜ, Merzifon
	88-0034	TUSAS (GD) F-16C-40 Fighting Falcon	THK 191 Filo/9 AJÜ, Balikesir
	88-0035	TUSAS (GD) F-16C-40 Fighting Falcon	THK 152 Filo/5 AJÜ, Merzifon
	88-0036	TUSAS (GD) F-16C-40 Fighting Falcon	THK 191 Filo/9 AJÜ, Balikesir
	88-0037	TUSAS (GD) F-16C-40 Fighting Falcon	THK 182 Filo/8 AJÜ, Diyarbakir
	89-0022	TUSAS (GD) F-16C-40 Fighting Falcon	THK
	89-0023	TUSAS (GD) F-16C-40 Fighting Falcon	THK 192 Filo/9 AJÜ, Balikesir
	89-0024	TUSAS (GD) F-16C-40 Fighting Falcon	THK 192 Filo/9 AJÜ, Balikesir
	89-0025	TUSAS (GD) F-16C-40 Fighting Falcon	THK 191 Filo/9 AJÜ, Balikesir
	89-0026	TUSAS (GD) F-16C-40 Fighting Falcon	THK
	89-0027	TUSAS (GD) F-16C-40 Fighting Falcon	THK
	89-0028	TUSAS (GD) F-16C-40 Fighting Falcon	THK
	89-0030	TUSAS (GD) F-16C-40 Fighting Falcon	THK
	89-0031	TUSAS (GD) F-16C-40 Fighting Falcon	*Crashed 22 March 2018, near Ovaören, Turkey*
	89-0034	TUSAS (GD) F-16C-40 Fighting Falcon	THK
	89-0035	TUSAS (GD) F-16C-40 Fighting Falcon	THK 152 Filo/5 AJÜ, Merzifon
	89-0036	TUSAS (GD) F-16C-40 Fighting Falcon	THK
	89-0037	TUSAS (GD) F-16C-40 Fighting Falcon	THK
	89-0038	TUSAS (GD) F-16C-40 Fighting Falcon	THK
	89-0039	TUSAS (GD) F-16C-40 Fighting Falcon	THK 152 Filo/5 AJÜ, Merzifon
	89-0040	TUSAS (GD) F-16C-40 Fighting Falcon	THK 192 Filo/9 AJÜ, Balikesir
	89-0041	TUSAS (GD) F-16C-40 Fighting Falcon	THK 152 Filo/5 AJÜ, Merzifon
	89-0042	TUSAS (GD) F-16D-40 Fighting Falcon	THK 191 Filo/9 AJÜ, Balikesir
	89-0043	TUSAS (GD) F-16D-40 Fighting Falcon	THK 192 Filo/9 AJÜ, Balikesir
	89-0044	TUSAS (GD) F-16D-40 Fighting Falcon	THK 132 Filo/3 AJEÜ, Konya
	89-0045	TUSAS (GD) F-16D-40 Fighting Falcon	THK 152 Filo/5 AJÜ, Merzifon
	90-0004	TUSAS (GD) F-16C-40 Fighting Falcon	THK 152 Filo/5 AJÜ, Merzifon
	90-0005	TUSAS (GD) F-16C-40 Fighting Falcon	THK 191 Filo/9 AJÜ, Balikesir
	90-0006	TUSAS (GD) F-16C-40 Fighting Falcon	THK 182 Filo/8 AJÜ, Diyarbakir
	90-0007	TUSAS (GD) F-16C-40 Fighting Falcon	THK
	90-0008	TUSAS (GD) F-16C-40 Fighting Falcon	THK
	90-0009	TUSAS (GD) F-16C-40 Fighting Falcon	THK
	90-0010	TUSAS (GD) F-16C-40 Fighting Falcon	THK
	90-0011	TUSAS (GD) F-16C-40 Fighting Falcon $	THK
	90-0012	TUSAS (GD) F-16C-40 Fighting Falcon	THK 191 Filo/9 AJÜ, Balikesir
	90-0013	TUSAS (GD) F-16C-40 Fighting Falcon	THK 182 Filo/8 AJÜ, Diyarbakir
	90-0014	TUSAS (GD) F-16C-40 Fighting Falcon $	THK
	90-0016	TUSAS (GD) F-16C-40 Fighting Falcon	THK 182 Filo/8 AJÜ, Diyarbakir
	90-0017	TUSAS (GD) F-16C-40 Fighting Falcon	THK 191 Filo/9 AJÜ, Balikesir
	90-0018	TUSAS (GD) F-16C-40 Fighting Falcon	THK 191 Filo/9 AJÜ, Balikesir
	90-0019	TUSAS (GD) F-16C-40 Fighting Falcon	THK
	90-0020	TUSAS (GD) F-16C-40 Fighting Falcon	THK
	90-0021	TUSAS (GD) F-16C-40 Fighting Falcon	THK
	90-0022	TUSAS (GD) F-16D-40 Fighting Falcon	THK 182 Filo/8 AJÜ, Diyarbakir
	90-0023	TUSAS (GD) F-16D-40 Fighting Falcon	THK 152 Filo/5 AJÜ, Merzifon
	90-0024	TUSAS (GD) F-16D-40 Fighting Falcon	THK 182 Filo/8 AJÜ, Diyarbakir
	91-003	Grumman G.1159C Gulfstream IV	THK 212 Filo/11 HUAÜK, Ankara/Etimesgut
	91-0001	TUSAS (GD) F-16C-40 Fighting Falcon	THK
	91-0002	TUSAS (GD) F-16C-40 Fighting Falcon	THK 401 Filo/1 AJÜ, Eskisehir
	91-0003	TUSAS (GD) F-16C-40 Fighting Falcon	THK 182 Filo/8 AJÜ, Diyarbakir
	91-0004	TUSAS (GD) F-16C-40 Fighting Falcon	THK
	91-0005	TUSAS (GD) F-16C-40 Fighting Falcon	THK 182 Filo/8 AJÜ, Diyarbakir
	91-0006	TUSAS (GD) F-16C-40 Fighting Falcon	THK
	91-0007	TUSAS (GD) F-16C-40 Fighting Falcon	THK
	91-0008	TUSAS (GD) F-16C-40 Fighting Falcon	THK 192 Filo/9 AJÜ, Balikesir
	91-0010	TUSAS (GD) F-16C-40 Fighting Falcon	THK
	91-0011	TUSAS (GD) F-16C-40 Fighting Falcon $	THK
	91-0012	TUSAS (GD) F-16C-40 Fighting Falcon	THK
	91-0013	TUSAS (GD) F-16C-40 Fighting Falcon	THK 192 Filo/9 AJÜ, Balikesir
	91-0014	TUSAS (GD) F-16C-40 Fighting Falcon	THK
	91-0015	TUSAS (GD) F-16C-40 Fighting Falcon	THK 401 Filo/1 AJÜ, Eskisehir

Serial	Type (code/other identity)	Owner/operator, location or fate	Notes
91-0016	TUSAS (GD) F-16C-40 Fighting Falcon	THK 182 Filo/8 AJÜ, Diyarbakir	
91-0017	TUSAS (GD) F-16C-40 Fighting Falcon	THK 182 Filo/8 AJÜ, Diyarbakir	
91-0018	TUSAS (GD) F-16C-40 Fighting Falcon	THK 191 Filo/9 AJÜ, Balikesir	
91-0020	TUSAS (GD) F-16C-40 Fighting Falcon	THK	
91-0022	TUSAS (GD) F-16D-40 Fighting Falcon	THK 191 Filo/9 AJÜ, Balikesir	
91-0024	TUSAS (GD) F-16D-40 Fighting Falcon	THK	
92-0001	TUSAS (GD) F-16C-40 Fighting Falcon	THK 182 Filo/8 AJÜ, Diyarbakir	
92-0002	TUSAS (GD) F-16C-40 Fighting Falcon	THK 182 Filo/8 AJÜ, Diyarbakir	
92-0003	TUSAS (GD) F-16C-40 Fighting Falcon	THK 191 Filo/9 AJÜ, Balikesir	
92-0004	TUSAS (GD) F-16C-40 Fighting Falcon	THK	
92-0005	TUSAS (GD) F-16C-40 Fighting Falcon	THK 192 Filo/9 AJÜ, Balikesir	
92-0006	TUSAS (GD) F-16C-40 Fighting Falcon	THK 182 Filo/8 AJÜ, Diyarbakir	
92-0007	TUSAS (GD) F-16C-40 Fighting Falcon	THK 192 Filo/9 AJÜ, Balikesir	
92-0008	TUSAS (GD) F-16C-40 Fighting Falcon	THK 152 Filo/5 AJÜ, Merzifon	
92-0009	TUSAS (GD) F-16C-40 Fighting Falcon	THK 191 Filo/9 AJÜ, Balikesir	
92-0010	TUSAS (GD) F-16C-40 Fighting Falcon	THK 191 Filo/9 AJÜ, Balikesir	
92-0011	TUSAS (GD) F-16C-40 Fighting Falcon	THK 182 Filo/8 AJÜ, Diyarbakir	
92-0012	TUSAS (GD) F-16C-40 Fighting Falcon	THK 182 Filo/8 AJÜ, Diyarbakir	
92-0013	TUSAS (GD) F-16C-40 Fighting Falcon	THK 132 Filo/3 AJEÜ, Konya	
92-0014	TUSAS (GD) F-16C-40 Fighting Falcon $	THK 192 Filo/9 AJÜ, Balikesir	
92-0015	TUSAS (GD) F-16C-40 Fighting Falcon	THK	
92-0016	TUSAS (GD) F-16C-40 Fighting Falcon	THK	
92-0017	TUSAS (GD) F-16C-40 Fighting Falcon	THK 152 Filo/5 AJÜ, Merzifon	
92-0018	TUSAS (GD) F-16C-40 Fighting Falcon	THK	
92-0019	TUSAS (GD) F-16C-40 Fighting Falcon	THK 181 Filo/8 AJÜ, Diyarbakir	
92-0020	TUSAS (GD) F-16C-40 Fighting Falcon	THK 181 Filo/8 AJÜ, Diyarbakir	
92-0021	TUSAS (GD) F-16C-40 Fighting Falcon	THK 191 Filo/9 AJÜ, Balikesir	
92-0022	TUSAS (GD) F-16D-40 Fighting Falcon	THK	
92-0023	TUSAS (GD) F-16D-40 Fighting Falcon	THK 132 Filo/3 AJEÜ, Konya	
92-0024	TUSAS (GD) F-16D-40 Fighting Falcon	THK 191 Filo/9 AJÜ, Balikesir	
93-005	Cessna 650 Citation VII	THK 212 Filo/11 HUAÜK, Ankara/Etimesgut	
93-0001	TUSAS (GD) F-16C-40 Fighting Falcon	THK 401 Filo/1 AJÜ, Eskisehir	
93-0003	TUSAS (GD) F-16C-40 Fighting Falcon	THK 192 Filo/9 AJÜ, Balikesir	
93-0004	TUSAS (GD) F-16C-40 Fighting Falcon	THK 181 Filo/8 AJÜ, Diyarbakir	
93-0005	TUSAS (GD) F-16C-40 Fighting Falcon	THK 181 Filo/8 AJÜ, Diyarbakir	
93-0006	TUSAS (GD) F-16C-40 Fighting Falcon	THK 181 Filo/8 AJÜ, Diyarbakir	
93-0007	TUSAS (GD) F-16C-40 Fighting Falcon	THK 182 Filo/8 AJÜ, Diyarbakir	
93-0008	TUSAS (GD) F-16C-40 Fighting Falcon	THK 181 Filo/8 AJÜ, Diyarbakir	
93-0009	TUSAS (GD) F-16C-40 Fighting Falcon	THK 182 Filo/8 AJÜ, Diyarbakir	
93-0010	TUSAS (GD) F-16C-40 Fighting Falcon	THK 132 Filo/3 AJEÜ, Konya	
93-0011	TUSAS (GD) F-16C-40 Fighting Falcon	THK 181 Filo/8 AJÜ, Diyarbakir	
93-0012	TUSAS (GD) F-16C-40 Fighting Falcon	THK 181 Filo/8 AJÜ, Diyarbakir	
93-0013	TUSAS (GD) F-16C-40 Fighting Falcon	THK 181 Filo/8 AJÜ, Diyarbakir	
93-0658	TUSAS (GD) F-16C-50 Fighting Falcon	THK 132 Filo/3 AJEÜ, Konya	
93-0659	TUSAS (GD) F-16C-50 Fighting Falcon	THK 191 Filo/9 AJÜ, Balikesir	
93-0660	TUSAS (GD) F-16C-50 Fighting Falcon	THK 152 Filo/5 AJÜ, Merzifon	
93-0661	TUSAS (GD) F-16C-50 Fighting Falcon	THK 132 Filo/3 AJEÜ, Konya	
93-0663	TUSAS (GD) F-16C-50 Fighting Falcon	THK 401 Filo/1 AJÜ, Eskisehir	
93-0664	TUSAS (GD) F-16C-50 Fighting Falcon	THK 132 Filo/3 AJEÜ, Konya	
93-0665	TUSAS (GD) F-16C-50 Fighting Falcon	THK 191 Filo/9 AJÜ, Balikesir	
93-0667	TUSAS (GD) F-16C-50 Fighting Falcon	THK 151 Filo/5 AJÜ, Merzifon	
93-0668	TUSAS (GD) F-16C-50 Fighting Falcon	THK	
93-0669	TUSAS (GD) F-16C-50 Fighting Falcon	THK 151 Filo/5 AJÜ, Merzifon	
93-0670	TUSAS (GD) F-16C-50 Fighting Falcon	THK 191 Filo/9 AJÜ, Balikesir	
93-0671	TUSAS (GD) F-16C-50 Fighting Falcon	THK	
93-0672	TUSAS (GD) F-16C-50 Fighting Falcon	THK 132 Filo/3 AJEÜ, Konya	
93-0673	TUSAS (GD) F-16C-50 Fighting Falcon	THK 132 Filo/3 AJEÜ, Konya	
93-0674	TUSAS (GD) F-16C-50 Fighting Falcon	THK 132 Filo/3 AJEÜ, Konya	
93-0675	TUSAS (GD) F-16C-50 Fighting Falcon	THK 191 Filo/9 AJÜ, Balikesir	
93-0676	TUSAS (GD) F-16C-50 Fighting Falcon	THK 192 Filo/9 AJÜ, Balikesir	
93-0677	TUSAS (GD) F-16C-50 Fighting Falcon $	THK 141 Filo/4 AJÜ, Akinci	
93-0678	TUSAS (GD) F-16C-50 Fighting Falcon	THK 152 Filo/5 AJÜ, Merzifon	

Notes	Serial	Type (code/other identity)	Owner/operator, location or fate
	93-0679	TUSAS (GD) F-16C-50 Fighting Falcon	THK 192 Filo/9 AJÜ, Balikesir
	93-0680	TUSAS (GD) F-16C-50 Fighting Falcon $	THK 192 Filo/9 AJÜ, Balikesir
	93-0681	TUSAS (GD) F-16C-50 Fighting Falcon	THK 192 Filo/9 AJÜ, Balikesir
	93-0682	TUSAS (GD) F-16C-50 Fighting Falcon $	THK 192 Filo/9 AJÜ, Balikesir
	93-0683	TUSAS (GD) F-16C-50 Fighting Falcon	THK 192 Filo/9 AJÜ, Balikesir
	93-0684	TUSAS (GD) F-16C-50 Fighting Falcon	THK
	93-0685	TUSAS (GD) F-16C-50 Fighting Falcon	THK
	93-0687	TUSAS (GD) F-16C-50 Fighting Falcon	THK 132 Filo/3 AJEÜ, Konya
	93-0688	TUSAS (GD) F-16C-50 Fighting Falcon	THK 151 Filo/5 AJÜ, Merzifon
	93-0689	TUSAS (GD) F-16C-50 Fighting Falcon	THK 192 Filo/9 AJÜ, Balikesir
	93-0690	TUSAS (GD) F-16C-50 Fighting Falcon	THK 141 Filo/4 AJÜ, Akinci
	93-0691	TUSAS (GD) F-16D-50 Fighting Falcon $	THK 192 Filo/9 AJÜ, Balikesir
	93-0692	TUSAS (GD) F-16D-50 Fighting Falcon	THK 151 Filo/5 AJÜ, Merzifon
	93-0693	TUSAS (GD) F-16D-50 Fighting Falcon	THK 152 Filo/5 AJÜ, Merzifon
	93-0694	TUSAS (GD) F-16D-50 Fighting Falcon	THK 151 Filo/5 AJÜ, Merzifon
	93-0695	TUSAS (GD) F-16D-50 Fighting Falcon	THK 141 Filo/4 AJÜ, Akinci
	93-0696	TUSAS (GD) F-16D-50 Fighting Falcon $	THK 151 Filo/5 AJÜ, Merzifon
	94-0071	TUSAS (GD) F-16C-50 Fighting Falcon	THK 192 Filo/9 AJÜ, Balikesir
	94-0072	TUSAS (GD) F-16C-50 Fighting Falcon	THK 151 Filo/5 AJÜ, Merzifon
	94-0073	TUSAS (GD) F-16C-50 Fighting Falcon	THK 151 Filo/5 AJÜ, Merzifon
	94-0074	TUSAS (GD) F-16C-50 Fighting Falcon	THK 191 Filo/9 AJÜ, Balikesir
	94-0075	TUSAS (GD) F-16C-50 Fighting Falcon	THK 151 Filo/5 AJÜ, Merzifon
	94-0076	TUSAS (GD) F-16C-50 Fighting Falcon	THK 151 Filo/5 AJÜ, Merzifon
	94-0077	TUSAS (GD) F-16C-50 Fighting Falcon	THK 141 Filo/4 AJÜ, Akinci
	94-0078	TUSAS (GD) F-16C-50 Fighting Falcon	THK 151 Filo/5 AJÜ, Merzifon
	94-0079	TUSAS (GD) F-16C-50 Fighting Falcon	THK 191 Filo/9 AJÜ, Balikesir
	94-0080	TUSAS (GD) F-16C-50 Fighting Falcon	THK 191 Filo/9 AJÜ, Balikesir
	94-0082	TUSAS (GD) F-16C-50 Fighting Falcon	THK 151 Filo/5 AJÜ, Merzifon
	94-0083	TUSAS (GD) F-16C-50 Fighting Falcon	THK 151 Filo/5 AJÜ, Merzifon
	94-0084	TUSAS (GD) F-16C-50 Fighting Falcon	THK 141 Filo/4 AJÜ, Akinci
	94-0085	TUSAS (GD) F-16C-50 Fighting Falcon	THK 191 Filo/9 AJÜ, Balikesir
	94-0086	TUSAS (GD) F-16C-50 Fighting Falcon	THK 191 Filo/9 AJÜ, Balikesir
	94-0088	TUSAS (GD) F-16C-50 Fighting Falcon	THK 151 Filo/5 AJÜ, Merzifon
	94-0089	TUSAS (GD) F-16C-50 Fighting Falcon	THK 152 Filo/5 AJÜ, Merzifon
	94-0090	TUSAS (GD) F-16C-50 Fighting Falcon $	THK 192 Filo/9 AJÜ, Balikesir
	94-0091	TUSAS (GD) F-16C-50 Fighting Falcon	THK 132 Filo/3 AJEÜ, Konya
	94-0092	TUSAS (GD) F-16C-50 Fighting Falcon	THK 132 Filo/3 AJEÜ, Konya
	94-0093	TUSAS (GD) F-16C-50 Fighting Falcon	THK 141 Filo/4 AJÜ, Akinci
	94-0094	TUSAS (GD) F-16C-50 Fighting Falcon	THK 141 Filo/4 AJÜ, Akinci
	94-0095	TUSAS (GD) F-16C-50 Fighting Falcon	THK 192 Filo/9 AJÜ, Balikesir
	94-0096	TUSAS (GD) F-16C-50 Fighting Falcon	THK 141 Filo/4 AJÜ, Akinci
	94-0105	TUSAS (GD) F-16D-50 Fighting Falcon	THK 141 Filo/4 AJÜ, Akinci
	94-0106	TUSAS (GD) F-16D-50 Fighting Falcon	THK 401 Filo/1 AJÜ, Eskisehir
	94-0108	TUSAS (GD) F-16D-50 Fighting Falcon	THK 191 Filo/9 AJÜ, Balikesir
	94-0109	TUSAS (GD) F-16D-50 Fighting Falcon	THK 132 Filo/3 AJEÜ, Konya
	94-0110	TUSAS (GD) F-16D-50 Fighting Falcon	THK 401 Filo/1 AJÜ, Eskisehir
	94-1557	TUSAS (GD) F-16D-50 Fighting Falcon	THK 152 Filo/5 AJÜ, Merzifon
	94-1558	TUSAS (GD) F-16D-50 Fighting Falcon	THK 132 Filo/3 AJEÜ, Konya
	94-1559	TUSAS (GD) F-16D-50 Fighting Falcon	THK 152 Filo/5 AJÜ, Merzifon
	94-1560	TUSAS (GD) F-16D-50 Fighting Falcon	THK 192 Filo/9 AJÜ, Balikesir
	94-1561	TUSAS (GD) F-16D-50 Fighting Falcon	THK 192 Filo/9 AJÜ, Balikesir
	94-1562	TUSAS (GD) F-16D-50 Fighting Falcon	THK 192 Filo/9 AJÜ, Balikesir
	94-1563	TUSAS (GD) F-16D-50 Fighting Falcon	THK 192 Filo/9 AJÜ, Balikesir
	94-1564	TUSAS (GD) F-16D-50 Fighting Falcon	THK 192 Filo/9 AJÜ, Balikesir
	07-1001	TUSAS (GD) F-16C-50 Fighting Falcon	THK
	07-1002	TUSAS (GD) F-16C-50 Fighting Falcon	THK 181 Filo/8 AJÜ, Diyarbakir
	07-1003	TUSAS (GD) F-16C-50 Fighting Falcon	THK 181 Filo/8 AJÜ, Diyarbakir
	07-1004	TUSAS (GD) F-16C-50 Fighting Falcon	THK
	07-1005	TUSAS (GD) F-16C-50 Fighting Falcon	THK 181 Filo/8 AJÜ, Diyarbakir
	07-1006	TUSAS (GD) F-16C-50 Fighting Falcon	THK 181 Filo/8 AJÜ, Diyarbakir
	07-1007	TUSAS (GD) F-16C-50 Fighting Falcon	THK
	07-1008	TUSAS (GD) F-16C-50 Fighting Falcon	THK

Serial	Type (code/other identity)	Owner/operator, location or fate	Notes
07-1009	TUSAS (GD) F-16C-50 Fighting Falcon	THK 152 Filo/5 AJÜ, Merzifon	
07-1010	TUSAS (GD) F-16C-50 Fighting Falcon	THK 152 Filo/5 AJÜ, Merzifon	
07-1011	TUSAS (GD) F-16C-50 Fighting Falcon	THK	
07-1012	TUSAS (GD) F-16C-50 Fighting Falcon	THK	
07-1013	TUSAS (GD) F-16C-50 Fighting Falcon	THK 181 Filo/8 AJÜ, Diyarbakir	
07-1014	TUSAS (GD) F-16C-50 Fighting Falcon	THK	
07-1015	TUSAS (GD) F-16D-50 Fighting Falcon	THK	
07-1016	TUSAS (GD) F-16D-50 Fighting Falcon	THK 181 Filo/8 AJÜ, Diyarbakir	
07-1017	TUSAS (GD) F-16D-50 Fighting Falcon	THK 181 Filo/8 AJÜ, Diyarbakir	
07-1018	TUSAS (GD) F-16D-50 Fighting Falcon	THK 181 Filo/8 AJÜ, Diyarbakir	
07-1019	TUSAS (GD) F-16D-50 Fighting Falcon	THK	
07-1020	TUSAS (GD) F-16D-50 Fighting Falcon	THK 182 Filo/8 AJÜ, Diyarbakir	
07-1021	TUSAS (GD) F-16D-50 Fighting Falcon	THK 181 Filo/8 AJÜ, Diyarbakir	
07-1022	TUSAS (GD) F-16D-50 Fighting Falcon	THK 181 Filo/8 AJÜ, Diyarbakir	
07-1023	TUSAS (GD) F-16D-50 Fighting Falcon	THK 152 Filo/5 AJÜ, Merzifon	
07-1024	TUSAS (GD) F-16D-50 Fighting Falcon	THK 181 Filo/8 AJÜ, Diyarbakir	
07-1025	TUSAS (GD) F-16D-50 Fighting Falcon	THK 181 Filo/8 AJÜ, Diyarbakir	
07-1026	TUSAS (GD) F-16D-50 Fighting Falcon	THK 181 Filo/8 AJÜ, Diyarbakir	
07-1027	TUSAS (GD) F-16D-50 Fighting Falcon	THK	
07-1028	TUSAS (GD) F-16D-50 Fighting Falcon	THK	
07-1029	TUSAS (GD) F-16D-50 Fighting Falcon	THK	
07-1030	TUSAS (GD) F-16D-50 Fighting Falcon	THK	
09-001	Gulfstream Aerospace G.550	THK 212 Filo/11 HUAÜK, Ankara/Etimesgut	
13-001	Boeing 737-7FS AEW&C (E-7T)	THK 131 Filo/3 AJEÜ, Konya	
13-002	Boeing 737-7FS AEW&C (E-7T)	THK 131 Filo/3 AJEÜ, Konya	
13-003	Boeing 737-7FS AEW&C (E-7T)	THK 131 Filo/3 AJEÜ, Konya	
13-0009	Airbus Military A.400M	THK 221 Filo/12 HUAÜ, Erkilet	
13-004	Boeing 737-7FS AEW&C (E-7T)	THK 131 Filo/3 AJEÜ, Konya	
14-0013	Airbus Military A.400M	THK 221 Filo/12 HUAÜ, Erkilet	
14-0028	Airbus Military A.400M	THK 221 Filo/12 HUAÜ, Erkilet	
15-0051	Airbus Military A.400M	THK 221 Filo/12 HUAÜ, Erkilet	
16-0055	Airbus Military A.400M	THK 221 Filo/12 HUAÜ, Erkilet	
17-0075	Airbus Military A.400M	THK 221 Filo/12 HUAÜ, Erkilet	
17-0078	Airbus Military A.400M	THK 221 Filo/12 HUAÜ, Erkilet	
17-0080	Airbus Military A.400M	THK 221 Filo/12 HUAÜ, Erkilet	
1.-0093	Airbus Military A.400M	THK (on order)	
1.-0094	Airbus Military A.400M	THK (on order)	
TC-ANA	Airbus A.319CJ-115X	Turkish Government, Istanbul/Ataturk	
TC-CAN	Airbus A.340-541 (TC-TRK)	Turkish Government, Istanbul/Ataturk	
TC-CBK	Gulfstream Aerospace G.550	THK 212 Filo/11 HUAÜK, Ankara/Etimesgut	
TC-DAP	Gulfstream Aerospace G.550	Turkish Government, Ankara	
TC-GVA	Gulfstream Aerospace G.550 (TC-ATA)	Turkish Government, Ankara	
TC-GVB	Gulfstream Aerospace G.450 (TC-GAP)	Turkish Government, Ankara	
TC-IST	Airbus A.319CJ-133	Turkish Government, Istanbul/Ataturk	
TC-TRK	Boeing 747-8ZV (VQ-BSK)	Turkish Government, Istanbul/Ataturk	
TC-TUR	Airbus A.330-243	Turkish Government, Istanbul/Ataturk	

TURKMENISTAN

EZ-A777	Boeing 777-22KLR	Government of Turkmenistan, Ashkhabad	
EZ-B021	BAe 1000B	Government of Turkmenistan, Ashkhabad	
EZ-B024	Canadair Challenger 870CS	Government of Turkmenistan, Ashkhabad	

UGANDA

5X-UGF	Gulfstream Aerospace G.550	Government of Uganda, Entebbe	

UKRAINE
Ukrainian Air Force

81 y	Antonov An-30	Ukrainian AF 15 Tr AB, Kiev/Boryspil	
76321	Ilyushin Il-76MD	Ukrainian AF 25 Tr AB, Melitopol	
76322	Ilyushin Il-76MD	Ukrainian AF 25 Tr AB, Melitopol	
76323	Ilyushin Il-76MD	Ukrainian AF 25 Tr AB, Melitopol	
76413	Ilyushin Il-76MD	Ukrainian AF 25 Tr AB, Melitopol	

Notes	Serial	Type (code/other identity)	Owner/operator, location or fate
	76423	Ilyushin Il-76MD	Ukrainian AF 25 Tr AB, Melitopol
	76531	Ilyushin Il-76MD	Ukrainian AF 25 Tr AB, Melitopol
	76559	Ilyushin Il-76MD	Ukrainian AF 25 Tr AB, Melitopol
	76564	Ilyushin Il-76MD	Ukrainian AF 25 Tr AB, Melitopol
	76566	Ilyushin Il-76MD	Ukrainian AF 25 Tr AB, Melitopol
	76585	Ilyushin Il-76MD	Ukrainian AF 25 Tr AB, Melitopol
	76631	Ilyushin Il-76MD	Ukrainian AF 25 Tr AB, Melitopol
	76637	Ilyushin Il-76MD	Ukrainian AF 25 Tr AB, Melitopol
	76645	Ilyushin Il-76MD	Ukrainian AF 25 Tr AB, Melitopol
	76647	Ilyushin Il-76MD	Ukrainian AF 25 Tr AB, Melitopol
	76654	Ilyushin Il-76MD	Ukrainian AF 25 Tr AB, Melitopol
	76660	Ilyushin Il-76MD	Ukrainian AF 25 Tr AB, Melitopol
	76661	Ilyushin Il-76MD	Ukrainian AF 25 Tr AB, Melitopol
	76680	Ilyushin Il-76MD	Ukrainian AF 25 Tr AB, Melitopol
	76683	Ilyushin Il-76MD	Ukrainian AF 25 Tr AB, Melitopol
	76697	Ilyushin Il-76MD	Ukrainian AF 25 Tr AB, Melitopol
	76698	Ilyushin Il-76MD	Ukrainian AF 25 Tr AB, Melitopol
	76699	Ilyushin Il-76MD	Ukrainian AF 25 Tr AB, Melitopol
	76732	Ilyushin Il-76MD	Ukrainian AF 25 Tr AB, Melitopol
	78820	Ilyushin Il-76MD	Ukrainian AF 25 Tr AB, Melitopol
	86915	Ilyushin Il-76MD	Ukrainian AF 25 Tr AB, Melitopol
	86922	Ilyushin Il-76MD	Ukrainian AF 25 Tr AB, Melitopol

Government of Ukraine

	UR-ABA	Airbus A.319CJ-115X	Government of Ukraine, Kiev/Boryspil

UNITED ARAB EMIRATES

United Arab Emirates Air Force (UAEAF)

	311	Lockheed L.100-30 Hercules (A6-QFY)	UAEAF 4 Sqn/Transport Wing, Abu Dhabi/Bateen
	312	Lockheed C-130H-30 Hercules	UAEAF 4 Sqn/Transport Wing, Abu Dhabi/Bateen
	430	Aermacchi MB339NAT	UAEAF Al Fursan, Al Ain
	431	Aermacchi MB339NAT	UAEAF Al Fursan, Al Ain
	432	Aermacchi MB339NAT	UAEAF Al Fursan, Al Ain
	433	Aermacchi MB339NAT	UAEAF Al Fursan, Al Ain
	434	Aermacchi MB339NAT	UAEAF Al Fursan, Al Ain
	435	Aermacchi MB339NAT	UAEAF Al Fursan, Al Ain
	436	Aermacchi MB339NAT	UAEAF Al Fursan, Al Ain
	437	Aermacchi MB339NAT	UAEAF Al Fursan, Al Ain
	438	Aermacchi MB339NAT	UAEAF Al Fursan, Al Ain
	439	Aermacchi MB339NAT	UAEAF Al Fursan, Al Ain
	440	Aermacchi MB339NAT	UAEAF Al Fursan, Al Ain
	441	Aermacchi MB339NAT	UAEAF Al Fursan, Al Ain
	442	Aermacchi MB339NAT	UAEAF Al Fursan, Al Ain
	1211	Lockheed C-130H Hercules	UAEAF 4 Sqn/Transport Wing, Abu Dhabi/Bateen
	1212	Lockheed C-130H Hercules	UAEAF 4 Sqn/Transport Wing, Abu Dhabi/Bateen
	1213	Lockheed C-130H Hercules	UAEAF 4 Sqn/Transport Wing, Abu Dhabi/Bateen
	1214	Lockheed C-130H Hercules	UAEAF 4 Sqn/Transport Wing, Abu Dhabi/Bateen
	1215	Lockheed L.100-30 Hercules	UAEAF 4 Sqn/Transport Wing, Abu Dhabi/Bateen
	1216	Lockheed L.100-30 Hercules	UAEAF 4 Sqn/Transport Wing, Abu Dhabi/Bateen
	1217	Lockheed L.100-30 Hercules	UAEAF 4 Sqn/Transport Wing, Abu Dhabi/Bateen
	1223	Boeing C-17A Globemaster III (10-0401)	UAEAF Heavy Transport Sqn, Abu Dhabi/Bateen
	1224	Boeing C-17A Globemaster III (10-0402)	UAEAF Heavy Transport Sqn, Abu Dhabi/Bateen
	1225	Boeing C-17A Globemaster III (10-0403)	UAEAF Heavy Transport Sqn, Abu Dhabi/Bateen
	1226	Boeing C-17A Globemaster III (10-0404)	UAEAF Heavy Transport Sqn, Abu Dhabi/Bateen
	1227	Boeing C-17A Globemaster III (10-0405)	UAEAF Heavy Transport Sqn, Abu Dhabi/Bateen
	1228	Boeing C-17A Globemaster III (10-0406)	UAEAF Heavy Transport Sqn, Abu Dhabi/Bateen
	1229	Boeing C-17A Globemaster III (14-0007)	UAEAF Heavy Transport Sqn, Abu Dhabi/Bateen
	1230	Boeing C-17A Globemaster III (14-0008)	UAEAF Heavy Transport Sqn, Abu Dhabi/Bateen
	1300	Airbus A.330-243 MRTT (EC-339)	UAEAF MRTT Sqn, Al Ain
	1301	Airbus A.330-243 MRTT (EC-334)	UAEAF MRTT Sqn, Al Ain
	1302	Airbus A.330-243 MRTT (EC-332)	UAEAF MRTT Sqn, Al Ain
	1303	Airbus A.330-243 MRTT	UAEAF (on order)
	1325	Bombardier Global 6000	UAEAF (on order)

Serial	Type (code/other identity)	Owner/operator, location or fate	Notes
1326	Bombardier Global 6000	UAEAF (on order)	
UAE Government			
A6-ALN	Boeing 777-2ANER	Amiri Flight, Abu Dhabi	
A6-AUH	Boeing 737-8EX	Amiri Flight, Abu Dhabi	
A6-COM	Boeing 747-433	Dubai Air Wing	
A6-DAW	Boeing 747-48E	Dubai Air Wing	
A6-DFR	Boeing 737-7BC	Amiri Flight, Abu Dhabi	
A6-DLM	Airbus A.320-232	Amiri Flight, Abu Dhabi	
A6-ESH	Airbus A.319-113X	Amiri Flight, Abu Dhabi	
A6-FZZ	Boeing 737-8KN	Dubai Air Wing	
A6-GGP	Boeing 747-412F	Dubai Air Wing	
A6-HEH	Boeing 737-8AJ	Dubai Air Wing	
A6-HHH	Gulfstream Aerospace G.400	*Sold as N516MC, 2018*	
A6-HHH	Gulfstream Aerospace G.650	Dubai Air Wing	
A6-HMS	Airbus A.320-232	Dubai Air Wing	
A6-HRM	Boeing 747-422	Dubai Air Wing	
A6-HRS	Boeing 737-7F0	Dubai Air Wing	
A6-MMM	Boeing 747-422	Dubai Air Wing	
A6-MRM	Boeing 737-8EC	Dubai Air Wing	
A6-MRS	Boeing 737-8EO	Dubai Air Wing	
A6-PFA	Boeing 747-8Z5	*Sold as CN-MBH, October 2017*	
A6-PFC	Boeing 787-8	Amiri Flight, Abu Dhabi	
A6-PFE	Boeing 787-9	Amiri Flight, Abu Dhabi	
A6-RJ1	BAE RJ.85	Dubai Air Wing	
A6-RJ2	BAE RJ.85	Dubai Air Wing	
A6-SHJ	Airbus A.320-232X	Ruler of Sharjah Air Wing	
A6-SIL	Boeing 777-35RER	Amiri Flight, Abu Dhabi	
A6-YAS	Boeing 747-4F6	*Sold as A9C-HAK, 2015*	
DU-141	AgustaWestland AW.139	Dubai Air Wing, Fairoaks, UK (Summer)	
DU-142	AgustaWestland AW.139	Dubai Air Wing, Fairoaks, UK (Summer)	

In 2018 Slovakia acquired two Aeritalia C-27J Spartans, including this one, 1962, of the 1.Dopravn· Letka, based at Malacky.

This section lists the codes worn by some overseas air forces and, alongside, the serial of the aircraft currently wearing this code. This list will be updated occasionally and those with Internet access can download the latest version via the 'Military Aircraft Markings' Web Site, www.militaryaircraftmarkings.co.uk and via the MAM2009 Yahoo! Group.

FRANCE		705-LG	E120	2-EL	58	3-XN	652
FRENCH AIR FORCE		705-LJ	E137	2-EM	63	3-XO	629
D-BD Alpha Jet		705-LK	E125	2-EN	46	3-XP	645
1 [PDF]	E44	705-LP	E129	2-EO	66	3-XT	648
2 [PDF]	E45	705-LU	E148	2-EP	47	3-XV	672
3 [PDF]	E85	705-MA	E35	2-EQ	44	3-XY	649
4 [PDF]	E152	705-MF	E98	2-ET	57	3-XZ	685
5 [PDF]	E146	705-MN	E167	2-EU	55	30-IE	642
6 [PDF]	E139	705-MR	E115	2-EV	59	30-IP	604
7 [PDF]	E113	705-MS	E20	2-EW	48	30-IR	674
8 [PDF]	E127	705-ND	E26	2-EX	40	30-JO	627
9 [PDF]	E68	705-NL	E37	2-EY	42	30-XQ	637
8-AE	E75	705-NP	E155	2-EZ	54	115-AM	525
8-AF	E108	705-RB	E163	2-FZ	41	115-KC	120
8-AG	E109	705-RF	E58	2-ME	61	115-KD	123
8-AK	E144	705-RH	E94	2-MG	65	115-KE	101
8-AO	E112	705-RI	E117	2-MH	67	115-KF	111
8-FD	E151	705-RK	E31	2-MK	74	115-KG	104
8-FM	E105	705-RM	E134	3-AG	681	115-KI	96
8-FN	E116	705-RR	E114	3-AS	635	115-KJ	523
8-FO	E81	705-RS	E149	3-AU	653	115-KL	106
8-FP	E168	705-RT	E152	3-IA	650	115-KN	121
8-LN	E118	705-RU	E153	3-ID	654	115-KR	102
8-LO	E142	705-RW	E166	3-IF	609	115-KS	528
8-LS	E22	705-RY	E170	3-IG	668	115-KV	88
8-LW	E82	705-RZ	E171	3-IJ	638	115-LB	87
8-MA	E173	705-TA	E42	3-IL	622	115-LC	108
8-MH	E48	705-TB	E67	3-IN	640	115-LE	79
8-NF	E141	705-TG	E104	3-IO	647	115-LJ	105
8-RM	E123	705-TM	E128	3-IS	617	115-LK	85
8-RN	E124	705-TU	E7	3-IT	624	115-OA	524
8-RP	E130	705-TZ	E83	3-IU	620	115-OC	529
8-RQ	E138	705-UD	E107	3-IV	683	115-OL	530
8-RX	E135	F-TELC	E87	3-JC	606	115-OR	527
8-TH	E90	F-TEMF	E98	3-JD	643	115-YA	93
8-TJ	E25	F-TEMO	E68	3-JF	660	115-YB	99
8-TX	E93	F-TENE	E73	3-JI	675	115-YC	85
8-UB	E11	F-TERI	E117	3-JJ	639	115-YD	107
8-UC	E157	F-TERJ	E162	3-JM	657	115-YE	122
8-UH	E160	F-TERK	E31	3-JN	658	115-YF	100
102-FA	E140	F-TERN	E46	3-JP	611	115-YG	118
102-FB	E86	F-TETD	E113	3-JR	682	115-YH	109
102-FI	E32	F-TETF	E45	3-JT	677	115-YL	82
102-LI	E53	F-UGFC	E139	3-JU	614	115-YO	113
102-MB	E97	F-UGFE	E119	3-JW	641	115-YT	124
102-NA	E79	F-UHRE	E44	3-JX	679	116-EE	71
102-NB	E29	F-UHRF	E46	3-JY	615	116-EI	38
102-RJ	E76	F-UHRR	E146	3-LH	655	116-ER	68
120-AL	E154	F-UHRT	E152	3-MO	613	118-EB	76
120-FM	E105			3-MQ	646	118-JK	612
120-LT	E147	**Dassault Mirage 2000**		3-XA	662	118-KQ	112
120-LX	E89	2-AX	77	3-XC	618	118-XH	616
120-RO	E131	2-EA	49	3-XD	630	133-AL	669
120-RV	E164	2-EC	78	3-XF	670	133-IC	626
120-TT	E101	2-ED	62	3-XG	625	133-IH	631
705-AB	E28	2-EF	45	3-XJ	602	133-IQ	666
705-AD	E51	2-EG	56	3-XK	671	133-IW	664
705-FJ	E33	2-EH	52	3-XL	603	133-JB	678
705-LC	E87	2-EJ	43	3-XM	680	133-JE	634

Code	No.	Code	No.	Code	No.	Code	No.
133-JG	601	4-IL	337	code)		DBR	5682
133-JH	686	4-IO	338	709 FC	01	DCA	1005
133-JL	628	30-EF	102	709 FD	02	DCB	1052
133-JV	636	30-GB	123	709 FE	03	DCC	1056
133-LF	605	30-GD	125	709 FF	04	DCD	1057
133-MP	623	30-GE	126	709 FG	05	DCE	1071
133-XE	632	30-GF	127	709 FH	06	DCF	1073
133-XI	661	30-GG	128	709 FI	07	DCG	1093
133-XR	659	30-GH	129	709 FJ	08	DCH	1114
133-XX	610	30-GK	132	709 FK	09	DCI	1122
188-XJ	602	30-GM	134	709 FL	10	DCJ	1122
188-YR	91	30-GN	135	709 FM	11	DCK	1130
		30-GQ	138	709 FN	12	DCL	1135
Dassault Rafale		30-GR	139	709 FO	13	DCM	1136
4-EA	303	30-GS	140	709 FP	14	DCN	1142
4-EB	304	30-GT	141	709 FQ	15	DCO	1145
4-EC	305	30-GV	143	709 FR	16	DCP	1150
4-FF	339	30-GW	144	709 FS	17	DCQ	1155
4-FG	340	30-GX	145			DCR	1163
4-FH	341	30-GY	146	**FRENCH ARMY**		DCS	1164
4-FI	342	30-GZ	147	**SA.330 Puma**		DCT	1165
4-FJ	343	30-HE	105	DAA	1006	DCU	1171
4-FK	344	30-HH	104	DAB	1020	DCV	1172
4-FL	345	30-HK	315	DAC	1036	DCW	1177
4-FM	346	30-HM	318	DAD	1037	DCX	1179
4-FN	347	30-HR	103	DAE	1049	DCY	1182
4-FO	348	30-HT	323	DAF	1055	DCZ	1186
4-FP	349	30-HW	324	DAG	1069	DDA	1190
4-FR	351	30-IB	306	DAH	1078	DDB	1192
4-FS	352	30-IF	331	DAI	1092	DDC	1196
4-FT	353	30-IM	109	DAJ	1100	DDD	1198
4-FU	354	30-IN	110	DAK	1102	DDE	1206
4-FV	355	30-IP	111	DAL	1107	DDF	1213
4-FW	356	30-IQ	112	DAM	1109	DDG	1222
4-FX	357	30-IR	113	DAN	1128	DDH	1223
4-GA	122	30-IS	114	DAO	1143	DDI	1228
4-GI	130	30-IT	115	DAP	1149	DDJ	1229
4-GJ	131	30-IU	116	DAQ	1156	DDK	1231
4-GL	133	30-IW	118	DAR	1173	DDL	1235
4-GU	142	30-IX	119	DAS	1176	DDM	1236
4-HA	308	30-IY	120	DAU	1197	DDN	1239
4-HB	309	30-VA	148	DAV	1204	DDO	1244
4-HC	310	104-GC	124	DAW	1211	DDP	1252
4-HD	311	104-GI	130	DAX	1214	DDQ	1255
4-HF	312	104-GO	136	DAY	1217	DDR	1256
4-HI	313	104-GP	137	DAZ	1219	DDS	1260
4-HN	319	104-HR	103	DBA	1232	DDT	1269
4-HO	317	113-FQ	350	DBB	1243	DDU	1411
4-HP	314	113-GC	124	DBC	1248	DDV	1419
4-HQ	321	113-HG	106	DBD	1262	DDW	1447
4-HU	322	113-HJ	107	DBE	1277	DDX	1662
4-HV	320	113-HS	108	DBF	1417		
4-HX	325	113-HY	326	DBG	1438	**SA.342 Gazelle**	
4-HZ	327	113-IV	117	DBH	1451	GAA	3459
4-IA	307	113-IZ	121	DBI	1507	GAB	3476
4-IC	328	118-FQ	350	DBJ	1510	GAC	3512
4-ID	329	118-FR	351	DBK	1512	GAD	3530
4-IE	330	118-GP	137	DBL	1519	GAE	3548
4-IG	332	118-IR	113	DBM	1617	GAF	3664
4-IH	333			DBN	1632	GAG	3848
4-II	334	**Pilatus PC-21**		DBO	1634	GAH	3849
4-IJ	335	(NB: So far none have been		DBP	1654	GAI	3850
4-IK	336	seen with a hyphen in the		DBQ	1663	GAJ	3856

Code	No.	Code	No.	Code	No.	Code	No.
GAK	3859	GEI	4214	GNF	3853	BHD	2015
GAL	3862	GEJ	4215	GNG	3858	BHE	2018
GAM	3863	GEK	4216	GNJ	3896	BHF	2019
GAN	3865	GEL	4217	GNK	3956	BHG	2022
GAO	3868	GEM	4218	GNM	3992	BHH	2001
GAP	3911	GEN	4219	GNN	4008	BHI	2002
GAQ	3921	GEO	4220	GNO	4032	BHJ	2003
GAR	3938	GEP	4221	GNP	4049	BHK	2004
GAS	3947	GEQ	4222	GNQ	4060	BHL	2006
GAT	3948	GER	4223	GNR	4065	BHM	2011
GAU	3957	GES	4224	GNS	4071	BHN	2021
GAV	3964	GET	4225	GNT	4083	BHO	2024
GAW	3996	GEU	4226	GNU	4096	BHP	2023
GAX	4018	GEV	4227	GNV	4118	BHQ	2025
GAY	4019	GEW	4228	GNW	4135	BHR	2026
GAZ	4020	GEX	4229	GNX	4143	BHS	2027
GBA	4026	GEY	4230	GNY	4146	BHT	2012
GBB	4034	GEZ	4231	GNZ	4159	BHU	2028
GBC	4039	GFA	4231	GOA	4178	BHV	2029
GBD	4048	GFB	4233	GOB	4183	BHW	2030
GBE	4053	GFC	4234	GOC	4184	BHX	2031
GBF	4059	GJA	1732	GOD	4192	BHZ	2033
GBG	4061	GJC	3511			BIA	2016
GBH	4066	GJD	3529	**AS.532UL/EC.725AP Cougar**		BIB	2034
GBI	4072	GJF	3546	CAA	2611	BIC	2035
GBJ	4084	GJI	3851	CAB	2628	BIE	2037
GBL	4095	GJJ	3855	CAC	2630	BIG	2039
GBM	4108	GJK	3857	CAD	2631	BIH	2040
GBN	4109	GJL	3864	CAE	2633	BII	2041
GBO	4114	GJM	3867	CAF	2638	BIJ	2042
GBP	4115	GJN	3929	CAG	2640	BIK	2043
GBQ	4119	GJO	3965	CAH	2642	BIL	2044
GBR	4120	GJP	4014	CGA	2252	BIM	2045
GBS	4124	GJQ	4022	CGB	2266	BIN	2046
GBT	4136	GJR	4038	CGC	2267	BIO	2047
GBU	4140	GJS	4047	CGD	2271	BIP	2048
GBV	4141	GJU	4067	CGE	2272	BIQ	2049
GBW	4142	GJV	4078	CGF	2273	BIR	2050
GBX	4144	GJW	4102	CGG	2282	BIS	2051
GBY	4145	GJX	4103	CGH	2285	BIT	2052
GBZ	4151	GJY	4123	CGI	2290	BJA	6001
GCA	4155	GJZ	4166	CGJ	2292	BJB	6002
GCC	4160	GKA	4176	CGK	2299	BJC	6003
GCD	4161	GKB	4177	CGL	2300	BJD	6004
GCE	4162	GKC	4182	CGM	2301	BJE	6005
GCF	4164	GKD	4185	CGN	2303	BJF	6006
GCG	4168	GKE	4187	CGO	2316	BJG	6007
GCH	4172	GMA	3567	CGQ	2323	BJH	6008
GCI	4175	GMB	4042	CGR	2324	BJI	6009
GCJ	4179	GMC	4079	CGS	2325	BJJ	6010
GCK	4180	GMD	4194	CGT	2327	BJK	6011
GCL	4181	GME	3870	CGU	2331	BJL	6012
GCM	4186	GMF	3930	CGV	2336	BJM	6013
GCN	4189	GMG	3939	CGW	2443	BJN	6014
GCO	4191	GMH	4023	CGX	2446	BJO	6015
GCP	4195	GMI	4171	CHA	2342	BJP	6016
GCQ	4198	GMJ	4190	CHB	2369	BJQ	6017
GEA	4204	GMK	4201	CHC	2375	BJR	6018
GEB	4206	GNA	3458			BJS	6019
GEC	4207	GNB	3513	**EC.665 Tigre**		BJT	6020
GED	4208	GNC	3549	BHA	2010	BJU	6021
GEF	4210	GND	3617	BHB	2009	BJV	6022
GEG	4211	GNE	3852	BHC	2013	BJW	6023

Code	Serial	Code	Serial	Code	Serial	Code	Serial
BJX	6024	51-41	MM7183	61-62	MM54512	4-7	MM7290
BJY	6025	51-42	MM7177	61-64	MM54514	4-9	MM7351
BJZ	6026	51-43	MM7178	61-65	MM54515	4-11	MM7291
BKA	6027	51-44	MM7198	61-66	MM54516	4-12	MM7284
BKB	6028	51-45	MM7175	61-70	MM54518	4-13	MM7235
BKC	6029	51-46	MM7197	61-72	MM54533	4-15	MM7271
BKD	6030	51-50	MM7186	61-74	MM54535	4-18	MM7272
BKE	6031	51-51	MM7151	61-106	MM54548	4-20	MM7279
		51-52	MM7171	61-107	MM54549	4-21	MM7304
NH.90-TTH		51-53	MM7180	61-121	MM54458	4-22	MM7309
EAA	1239	51-55	MM7168	61-126	MM55062	4-24	MM55097
EAB	1256	51-56	MM7167	61-127	MM55063	4-26	MM55128
EAC	1271	51-57	MM7190	61-130	MM55064	4-30	MM55096
EAD	1273	51-60	MM7174	61-131	MM55065	4-31	MM55093
EAE	1290	51-61	MM7126	61-132	MM55066	4-32	MM55129
EAF	1291	51-62	MM7182	61-133	MM55067	4-33	MM55130
EAG	1292	51-64	MM7179	61-135	MM55069	4-34	MM55131
EAH	1293	51-65	MM7184	61-136	MM55070	4-35	MM55132
EAI	1294	51-66	MM7169	61-140	MM55072	4-36	MM54133
EAJ	1295	51-67	MM7194	61-141	MM55073	4-37	MM55168
EAK	1306	51-70	MM7192	61-143	MM55075	4-41	MM7299
EAL	1307	51-71	MM7189	61-144	MM55076	4-44	MM7300
EAM	1308	51-72	MM7163	61-145	MM55077	4-45	MM7320
EAN	1309	51-80	MM55037	61-146	MM55078	4-46	MM7326
EAO	1310	51-81	MM55043	61-147	MM55079	4-47	MM7327
EAP	1311	51-82	MM55044	61-150	MM55080	4-50	MM7306
EAQ	1312	51-83	MM55049	61-151	MM55081	4-51	MM7295
EAR	1313	51-84	MM55051	61-152	MM55082	4-52	MM7294
EAS	1332	RS-14	MM7177	61-154	MM55084	4-60	MM7338
EAT	1333	RS-20	MM55034	61-155	MM55085	4-61	MM7339
EAU	1334			61-156	MM55086	36-02	MM7286
EAV	1335	**Aermacchi MB339**		61-157	MM55087	36-03	MM7281
EAW	1336	0 [FT]	MM54534	61-160	MM55088	36-05	MM7276
EAX	1337	1 [FT]		61-162	MM55090	36-10	MM7341
EAY	1338	2 [FT]	MM54517	RS-32	MM55091	36-12	MM7318
EAZ	1386	3 [FT]	MM55058	RS-33	MM55068	36-14	MM7277
EBA	1390	4 [FT]	MM55053			36-15	MM7282
EBB	1391	5 [FT]	MM54505	**Aermacchi T-346A Master**		36-21	MM7292
EBC	1387	6 [FT]	MM54538	61-01	MM55143	36-22	MM7296
EBD	1392	7 [FT]	MM55053	61-02	MM55144	36-23	MM7297
EBE	1...	8 [FT]	MM54514	61-04	MM55155	36-24	MM7298
EBF	1...	9 [FT]	MM54539	61-05	MM55153	36-25	MM7302
EBG	1...	10 [FT]	MM54505	61-06	MM55213	36-30	MM7280
EBH	1404	11 [FT]	MM55052	61-07	MM55214	36-31	MM7308
EBI	1405	12 [FT]	MM54551	61-10	MM55215	36-32	MM7310
EBJ	1432	32-161	MM55089	61-11	MT55152	36-34	MM7312
		36-06	MM55074	61-12	MM55216	36-35	MM7313
ITALY		61-11	MM54457	61-13	MM55217	36-37	MM7314
Aeritalia-EMB AMX		61-15	MM55054	61-14	MM55218	36-40	MM7322
32-47	MM55046	61-20	MM55055	61-15	MM55221	36-41	MM7324
32-51	MM55036	61-21	MM54465	61-16	MM55220	36-42	MM7288
32-53	MM55047	61-24	MM54468	61-20	MT55219	36-44	MM7325
32-56	MM55042	61-26	MM55059	61-21	MT55222	36-46	MM7315
51-10	MM7159	61-32	MM54488	61-22	MT55223	36-50	MM7341
51-26	MM7149	61-36	MM54492	61-23	MM55224	36-51	MM7342
51-27	MM7114	61-37	MM54493			36-52	MM7343
51-30	MM7170	61-42	MM54496	**Eurofighter Typhoon**		36-53	MM7347
51-31	MM7161	61-45	MM54499	4-1	MM7270	36-54	MM7349
51-32	MM7166	61-52	MM54504	4-2	MM7303	36-55	MM7350
51-33	MM7162	61-55	MM54507	4-3	MM7287	36-60	MM55094
51-34	MM7191	61-57	MM54509	4-4	MM7274	36-62	MM55092
51-35	MM7196	61-60	MM54510	4-5	MM7289	36-65	MM55095
51-36	MM7185	61-61	MM54511	4-6	MM7323	37-01	MM7307

Code	Serial
37-05	MM7319
37-07	MM7316
37-10	MM7311
37-11	MM7294
37-12	MM7321
37-14	MM7328
37-15	MM7329
37-16	MM7331
37-21	MM7330
37-22	MM7293
37-24	MM7348
37-37	MM7346
37-45	MM7345
RMV-01	MMX603
RS-01	MMX602

**Lockheed Martin F-35A/
F-35B Lightning II**

Code	Serial
4-01	MM7451
32-01	MM7332
32-02	MM7333
32-03	MM7334
32-04	MM7335
32-05	MM7336
32-07	MM7357
32-08	MM7358
32-09	MM7359
32-10	MM7360
32-11	MM7361
32-13	MM7337

Panavia Tornado

Code	Serial
6-01	MM7007
6-02	MM7019
6-03	MM7084
6-04	MM7057
6-05	MM7025
6-06	MM7036
6-07	MM7075
6-10	MM7088
6-11	MM7058
6-12	MM7071
6-13	MM7014
6-15	MM55006
6-16	MM7037
6-20	MM7021
6-21	MM7040
6-22	MM7029
6-25	MM7043
6-26	MM7063
6-27	MM7035
6-30	MM7072
6-31	MM7006
6-32	MM7015
6-33	MM7039
6-34	MM7073
6-35	MM7026
6-37	MM7038
6-41	MM7067
6-42	MM55010
6-44	MM55009
6-45	MM55008
6-50	MM7024

Code	Serial
6-51	MM55007
6-52	MM55001
6-53	MM55004
6-55	MM7004
6-57	MM7081
6-60	MM7086
6-61	MM7047
6-62	MM7082
6-63	MM7023
6-64	MM7052
6-65	MM7055
6-66	MM7059
6-67	MM7068
6-71	MM7070
6-72	MM7051
6-74	MM7062
6-75	MM7013
6-77	MM7020
6-100	MM7054
6-101	MM7053
36-50	CSX7085
50-01	MM7021
50-04	MM7030
50-53	MM7008
50-57	MM7067
RS-01	CSX7041
RS-05	CSX7047

SPAIN
CASA 101EB Aviojet

Code	Serial
54-20	E.25-35
54-21	E.25-55
54-22	E.25-61
74-02	E.25-33
74-07	E.25-51
74-09	E.25-53
74-11	E.25-56
74-12	E.25-57
74-13	E.25-59
74-17	E.25-63
74-20	E.25-66
74-21	E.25-67
74-22	E.25-68
74-25	E.25-71
74-26	E.25-72
74-28	E.25-74
74-30	E.25-76
74-34	E.25-81
74-35	E.25-83
74-39	E.25-88
74-40	E.25-17
74-41	E.25-41
74-42	E.25-18
74-43	E.25-43
74-44	E.25-34
74-45	E.25-29
79-02	E.25-78
79-03	E.25-80
79-04	E.25-84
79-05	E.25-05
79-06	E.25-06
79-08	E.25-08
79-09	E.25-09

Code	Serial
79-11	E.25-11
79-12	E.25-12
79-13	E.25-13
79-14	E.25-14
79-15	E.25-15
79-16	E.25-16
79-17	E.25-62
79-20	E.25-20
79-21	E.25-21
79-22	E.25-22
79-23	E.25-23
79-24	E.25-24
79-25	E.25-25
79-27	E.25-27
79-28	E.25-28
79-29	E.25-87
79-31	E.25-31
79-32	E.25-86
79-33	E.25-50
79-34	E.25-52
79-35	E.25-54
79-37	E.25-37
79-38	E.25-38
79-39	E.25-79
79-40	E.25-40
79-44	E.25-44
79-49	E.25-49
79-95	E.25-65
79-97	E.25-69
79-98	E.25-73

CASA 212 Aviocar

Code	Serial
47-12	TM.12D-72
47-14	T.12D-75
72-01	T.12B-13
72-07	T.12B-49
72-09	T.12B-66
72-11	T.12B-65
72-12	T.12B-67
72-14	T.12B-63
72-15	T.12B-69
72-17	T.12B-70
72-21	TR.12D-76
72-22	TR.12D-77
72-23	TR.12D-79
72-24	TR.12D-81

Eurofighter Tifón

Code	Serial
11-01	C.16-21
11-02	C.16-22
11-03	C.16-23
11-04	C.16-24
11-05	C.16-25
11-06	C.16-26
11-07	C.16-27
11-08	C.16-28
11-09	C.16-29
11-10	C.16-30
11-11	C.16-32
11-12	C.16-33
11-14	C.16-35
11-16	C.16-40
11-17	C.16-41

Code	Serial
11-20	C.16-46
11-21	C.16-51
11-24	C.16-54
11-43	C.16-43
11-52	C.16-52
11-53	C.16-53
11-55	C.16-55
11-57	C.16-57
11-63	C.16-63
11-70	CE.16-01
11-71	CE.16-02
11-72	CE.16-03
11-73	CE.16-04
11-74	CE.16-05
11-75	CE.16-06
11-76	CE.16-07
11-78	CE.16-09
11-79	CE.16-10
11-80	CE.16-13
11-81	CE.16-14
11-91	C.16-20
14-01	C.16-31
14-03	C.16-36
14-04	C.16-37
14-05	C.16-38
14-06	C.16-39
14-07	C.16-41
14-08	C.16-42
14-09	C.16-44
14-10	C.16-45
14-11	C.16-47
14-12	C.16-48
14-13	C.16-49
14-14	C.16-50
14-17	C.16-58
14-18	C.16-59
14-19	C.16-60
14-20	C.16-61
14-21	C.16-62
14-22	C.16-64
14-23	C.16-65
14-24	C.16-66
14-25	C.16-67
14-26	C.16-68
14-30	C.16-72
14-31	C.16-73
14-70	CE.16-11
14-71	CE.16-12

US MILITARY AIRCRAFT MARKINGS

All USAF and US Army aircraft have been allocated a fiscal year (FY) number since 1921. Individual aircraft are given a serial according to the fiscal year in which they are ordered. The numbers commence at 0001 and are prefixed with the year of allocation. For example F-15C Eagle 84-0001 was the first aircraft ordered in 1984. The fiscal year (FY) serial is carried on the technical data block which is usually stencilled on the left-hand side of the aircraft just below the cockpit. The number displayed on the fin is a corruption of the FY serial. Most tactical aircraft carry the fiscal year in small figures followed by the last three or four digits of the serial in large figures. Large transport and tanker aircraft such as C-130s and KC-135s sometimes display a five-figure number commencing with the last digit of the appropriate fiscal year and four figures of the production number. An example of this is Boeing KC-135R Stratotanker 58-0128 which displays 80128 on its fin.

US Army serials have been allocated in a similar way to USAF serials although in recent years an additional zero has been added so that all US Army serials now have the two-figure fiscal year part followed by five digits. This means that, for example C-20E 70140 is officially 87-00140 although as yet this has not led to any alterations to serials painted on aircraft.

USN and USMC serials follow a straightforward numerical sequence which commenced, for the present series, with the allocation of 00001 to an SB2C Helldiver by the Bureau of Aeronautics in 1940. Numbers in the 168000 series are presently being issued. They are usually carried in full on the rear fuselage of the aircraft.

US Coast Guard serials began with the allocation of the serial 1 to a Loening OL-5 in 1927.

UK-BASED USAF AIRCRAFT

The following aircraft are normally based in the UK. They are listed in numerical order of type with individual aircraft in serial number order, as depicted on the aircraft. The number in brackets is either the alternative presentation of the five-figure number commencing with the last digit of the fiscal year, or the fiscal year where a five-figure serial is presented on the aircraft. Where it is possible to identify the allocation of aircraft to individual squadrons by means of colours carried on fin or cockpit edge, this is also provided.

Notes	Serial	Type (code/other identity)	Owner/operator, location or fate
	McDonnell Douglas F-15C Eagle/F-15D Eagle/F-15E Strike Eagle		
	84-0001	McD F-15C Eagle [LN] *bk/y*	USAF 493rd FS/48th FW, Lakenheath
	84-0010	McD F-15C Eagle [LN] *bk/y* $	USAF 493rd FS/48th FW, Lakenheath
	84-0015	McD F-15C Eagle [LN] *bk/y*	USAF 493rd FS/48th FW, Lakenheath
	84-0019	McD F-15C Eagle [LN] *bk/y*	USAF 493rd FS/48th FW, Lakenheath
	84-0027	McD F-15C Eagle [LN] *bk/y* [493 FS]	USAF 493rd FS/48th FW, Lakenheath
	84-0044	McD F-15D Eagle [LN] *bk/y*	USAF 493rd FS/48th FW, Lakenheath
	84-0046	McD F-15D Eagle [LN] *bk/y*	USAF 493rd FS/48th FW, Lakenheath
	86-0154	McD F-15C Eagle [LN] *bk/y*	USAF 493rd FS/48th FW, Lakenheath
	86-0156	McD F-15C Eagle [LN] *bk/y*	USAF 493rd FS/48th FW, Lakenheath
	86-0159	McD F-15C Eagle [LN] *m* [48 OG]	USAF 493rd FS/48th FW, Lakenheath
	86-0160	McD F-15C Eagle [LN] *bk/y*	USAF 493rd FS/48th FW, Lakenheath
	86-0163	McD F-15C Eagle [LN] *bk/y*	USAF 493rd FS/48th FW, Lakenheath
	86-0164	McD F-15C Eagle [LN] *bk/y*	USAF 493rd FS/48th FW, Lakenheath
	86-0165	McD F-15C Eagle [LN] *bk/y*	USAF 493rd FS/48th FW, Lakenheath
	86-0166	McD F-15C Eagle [LN] *bk/y*	USAF 493rd FS/48th FW, Lakenheath
	86-0171	McD F-15C Eagle [LN] *bk/y*	USAF 493rd FS/48th FW, Lakenheath
	86-0172	McD F-15C Eagle [LN] *bk/y*	USAF 493rd FS/48th FW, Lakenheath
	86-0174	McD F-15C Eagle [LN] *bk/y*	USAF 493rd FS/48th FW, Lakenheath
	86-0175	McD F-15C Eagle [LN] *bk/y*	USAF 493rd FS/48th FW, Lakenheath
	86-0176	McD F-15C Eagle [LN] *bk/y*	USAF 493rd FS/48th FW, Lakenheath
	86-0178	McD F-15C Eagle [LN] *bk/y*	USAF 493rd FS/48th FW, Lakenheath
	91-0301	McD F-15E Strike Eagle [LN] *bl/w*	USAF 492nd FS/48th FW, Lakenheath
	91-0302	McD F-15E Strike Eagle [LN] *bl/w*	USAF 492nd FS/48th FW, Lakenheath
	91-0303	McD F-15E Strike Eagle [LN] *bl/w*	USAF 492nd FS/48th FW, Lakenheath
	91-0306	McD F-15E Strike Eagle [LN] *bl/w*	USAF 492nd FS/48th FW, Lakenheath
	91-0307	McD F-15E Strike Eagle [LN] *bl/w*	USAF 492nd FS/48th FW, Lakenheath
	91-0308	McD F-15E Strike Eagle [LN] *bl/w*	USAF 492nd FS/48th FW, Lakenheath
	91-0309	McD F-15E Strike Eagle [LN] *r/w*	USAF 494th FS/48th FW, Lakenheath
	91-0310	McD F-15E Strike Eagle [LN] *r/w*	USAF 494th FS/48th FW, Lakenheath
	91-0311	McD F-15E Strike Eagle [LN] *m* [48 FW]	USAF 494th FS/48th FW, Lakenheath
	91-0312	McD F-15E Strike Eagle [LN] *bl/w*	USAF 492nd FS/48th FW, Lakenheath
	91-0313	McD F-15E Strike Eagle [LN] *r/w*	USAF 494th FS/48th FW, Lakenheath
	91-0314	McD F-15E Strike Eagle [LN] *r/w* [494 FS]	USAF 494th FS/48th FW, Lakenheath
	91-0315	McD F-15E Strike Eagle [LN] *bl/w*	USAF 492nd FS/48th FW, Lakenheath
	91-0316	McD F-15E Strike Eagle [LN] *bl/w*	USAF 492nd FS/48th FW, Lakenheath

Notes	Serial	Type (code/other identity)	Owner/operator, location or fate
	91-0317	McD F-15E Strike Eagle [LN] *bl/w*	USAF 492nd FS/48th FW, Lakenheath
	91-0318	McD F-15E Strike Eagle [LN] *r/w*	USAF 494th FS/48th FW, Lakenheath
	91-0320	McD F-15E Strike Eagle [LN] *r/w*	USAF 494th FS/48th FW, Lakenheath
	91-0321	McD F-15E Strike Eagle [LN] *bl/w*	USAF 492nd FS/48th FW, Lakenheath
	91-0324	McD F-15E Strike Eagle [LN] *r/w*	USAF 494th FS/48th FW, Lakenheath
	91-0326	McD F-15E Strike Eagle [LN] *r/w*	USAF 494th FS/48th FW, Lakenheath
	91-0327	McD F-15E Strike Eagle [LN] *bl/w*	USAF 492nd FS/48th FW, Lakenheath
	91-0329	McD F-15E Strike Eagle [LN] *r/w*	USAF 494th FS/48th FW, Lakenheath
	91-0331	McD F-15E Strike Eagle [LN] *bl/w*	USAF 492nd FS/48th FW, Lakenheath
	91-0332	McD F-15E Strike Eagle [LN] *bl/w*	USAF 492nd FS/48th FW, Lakenheath
	91-0334	McD F-15E Strike Eagle [LN] *r/w*	USAF 494th FS/48th FW, Lakenheath
	91-0335	McD F-15E Strike Eagle [LN] *r/w*	USAF 494th FS/48th FW, Lakenheath
	91-0602	McD F-15E Strike Eagle [LN] *r/w*	USAF 494th FS/48th FW, Lakenheath
	91-0603	McD F-15E Strike Eagle [LN] *r/w*	USAF 494th FS/48th FW, Lakenheath
	91-0604	McD F-15E Strike Eagle [LN] *r/w*	USAF 494th FS/48th FW, Lakenheath
	91-0605	McD F-15E Strike Eagle [LN] *bl/w*	USAF 492nd FS/48th FW, Lakenheath
	92-0364	McD F-15E Strike Eagle [LN] *r/w*	USAF 494th FS/48th FW, Lakenheath
	96-0201	McD F-15E Strike Eagle [LN] *r/w*	USAF 494th FS/48th FW, Lakenheath
	96-0202	McD F-15E Strike Eagle [LN] *bl/w*	USAF 492nd FS/48th FW, Lakenheath
	96-0204	McD F-15E Strike Eagle [LN] *r/w*	USAF 494th FS/48th FW, Lakenheath
	96-0205	McD F-15E Strike Eagle [LN] *bl/w*	USAF 492nd FS/48th FW, Lakenheath
	97-0218	McD F-15E Strike Eagle [LN] *bl/w*	USAF 492nd FS/48th FW, Lakenheath
	97-0219	McD F-15E Strike Eagle [LN] *bl/w* $	USAF 492nd FS/48th FW, Lakenheath
	97-0220	McD F-15E Strike Eagle [LN] *bl/w*	USAF 492nd FS/48th FW, Lakenheath
	97-0221	McD F-15E Strike Eagle [LN] *bl/w* [492 FS]	USAF 492nd FS/48th FW, Lakenheath
	97-0222	McD F-15E Strike Eagle [LN] *bl/w*	USAF 492nd FS/48th FW, Lakenheath
	98-0131	McD F-15E Strike Eagle [LN] *bl/w*	USAF 492nd FS/48th FW, Lakenheath
	98-0133	McD F-15E Strike Eagle [LN] *bl/w*	USAF 492nd FS/48th FW, Lakenheath
	98-0134	McD F-15E Strike Eagle [LN] *bl/w*	USAF 492nd FS/48th FW, Lakenheath
	98-0135	McD F-15E Strike Eagle [LN] *bl/w*	USAF 492nd FS/48th FW, Lakenheath
	00-3000	McD F-15E Strike Eagle [LN] *r/w*	USAF 494th FS/48th FW, Lakenheath
	00-3001	McD F-15E Strike Eagle [LN] *r/w*	USAF 494th FS/48th FW, Lakenheath
	00-3002	McD F-15E Strike Eagle [LN] *r/w*	USAF 494th FS/48th FW, Lakenheath
	00-3003	McD F-15E Strike Eagle [LN] *r/w*	USAF 494th FS/48th FW, Lakenheath
	00-3004	McD F-15E Strike Eagle [LN] *r/w*	USAF 494th FS/48th FW, Lakenheath
	01-2000	McD F-15E Strike Eagle [LN] *r/w*	USAF 494th FS/48th FW, Lakenheath
	01-2001	McD F-15E Strike Eagle [LN] *r/w*	USAF 494th FS/48th FW, Lakenheath
	01-2002	McD F-15E Strike Eagle [LN] *r/w*	USAF 494th FS/48th FW, Lakenheath
	01-2003	McD F-15E Strike Eagle [LN] *r/w*	USAF 494th FS/48th FW, Lakenheath
	01-2004	McD F-15E Strike Eagle [LN] *r/w*	USAF 494th FS/48th FW, Lakenheath

Bell-Boeing CV-22B Osprey

Notes	Serial	Type (code/other identity)	Owner/operator, location or fate
	0033	Bell-Boeing CV-22B Osprey (07-0033)	USAF 7th SOS/352nd SOW, Mildenhall
	0050	Bell-Boeing CV-22B Osprey (08-0050)	USAF 7th SOS/352nd SOW, Mildenhall
	0051	Bell-Boeing CV-22B Osprey (08-0051)	USAF 7th SOS/352nd SOW, Mildenhall
	0052	Bell-Boeing CV-22B Osprey (10-0052)	USAF 7th SOS/352nd SOW, Mildenhall
	0057	Bell-Boeing CV-22B Osprey (11-0057)	*Returned to the USA, 9 December 2018*
	0058	Bell-Boeing CV-22B Osprey (11-0058)	*Returned to the USA, 9 December 2018*
	0059	Bell-Boeing CV-22B Osprey (11-0059)	USAF 7th SOS/352nd SOW, Mildenhall
	0060	Bell-Boeing CV-22B Osprey (11-0060)	USAF 7th SOS/352nd SOW, Mildenhall
	0061	Bell-Boeing CV-22B Osprey (11-0061)	*Returned to the USA, 9 December 2018*
	0063	Bell-Boeing CV-22B Osprey (12-0063)	USAF 7th SOS/352nd SOW, Mildenhall
	0064	Bell-Boeing CV-22B Osprey (12-0064)	USAF 7th SOS/352nd SOW, Mildenhall
	0065	Bell-Boeing CV-22B Osprey (12-0065)	USAF 7th SOS/352nd SOW, Mildenhall

Lockheed MC-130J Commando II

Notes	Serial	Type (code/other identity)	Owner/operator, location or fate
	05714	Lockheed MC-130J Commando II (10-5714)	USAF 67th SOS/352nd SOW, RAF Mildenhall
	15731	Lockheed MC-130J Commando II (11-5731)	USAF 67th SOS/352nd SOW, RAF Mildenhall
	15737	Lockheed MC-130J Commando II (11-5737)	USAF 67th SOS/352nd SOW, RAF Mildenhall
	25757	Lockheed MC-130J Commando II (12-5757)	USAF 67th SOS/352nd SOW, RAF Mildenhall
	25759	Lockheed MC-130J Commando II (12-5759)	USAF 67th SOS/352nd SOW, RAF Mildenhall
	25760	Lockheed MC-130J Commando II (12-5760)	USAF 67th SOS/352nd SOW, RAF Mildenhall

Serial	Type (code/other identity)	Owner/operator, location or fate	Notes
35778	Lockheed MC-130J Commando II (13-5778)	USAF 67th SOS/352nd SOW, RAF Mildenhall	
35786	Lockheed MC-130J Commando II (13-5786)	USAF 67th SOS/352nd SOW, RAF Mildenhall	
Boeing KC-135R Stratotanker/Boeing KC-135T Stratotanker			
00324	Boeing KC-135R Stratotanker (60-0324) [D] *r/w/bl*	USAF 351st ARS/100th ARW, RAF Mildenhall	
00333	Boeing KC-135R Stratotanker (60-0333) [D] *r/w/bl*	*Returned to the USA, 10 August 2018*	
00344	Boeing KC-135T Stratotanker (60-0344) [D] *r/w/bl*	USAF 351st ARS/100th ARW, RAF Mildenhall	
00355	Boeing KC-135R Stratotanker (60-0355) [D] *r/w/bl*	USAF 351st ARS/100th ARW, RAF Mildenhall	
10288	Boeing KC-135R Stratotanker (61-0288) [D] *r/w/bl*	USAF 351st ARS/100th ARW, RAF Mildenhall	
10292	Boeing KC-135R Stratotanker (61-0292) [D] *r/w/bl*	USAF 351st ARS/100th ARW, RAF Mildenhall	
10299	Boeing KC-135R Stratotanker (61-0299) [D] *r/w/bl*	*Returned to the USA, 23 August 2018*	
10321	Boeing KC-135R Stratotanker (61-0321) [D] *r/w/bl*	*Returned to the USA, 27 September 2018*	
23551	Boeing KC-135R Stratotanker (62-3551) [D] *r/w/bl*	USAF 351st ARS/100th ARW, RAF Mildenhall	
23559	Boeing KC-135R Stratotanker (62-3559) [D] *r/w/bl*	*Returned to the USA, 7 June 2018*	
37999	Boeing KC-135R Stratotanker (63-7999) [D] *r/w/bl*	USAF 351st ARS/100th ARW, RAF Mildenhall	
38871	Boeing KC-135R Stratotanker (63-8871) [D] *r/w/bl*	*Returned to the USA, 25 June 2018*	
71440	Boeing KC-135R Stratotanker (57-1440) [D] *r/w/bl*	USAF 351st ARS/100th ARW, RAF Mildenhall	
71474	Boeing KC-135R Stratotanker (57-1474) [D] *r/w/bl*	USAF 351st ARS/100th ARW, RAF Mildenhall	
71493	Boeing KC-135R Stratotanker (57-1493) [D] *r/w/bl*	USAF 351st ARS/100th ARW, RAF Mildenhall	
72605	Boeing KC-135R Stratotanker (57-2605) [D] *r/w/bl*	USAF 351st ARS/100th ARW, RAF Mildenhall	
80001	Boeing KC-135T Stratotanker (58-0001) [D] *r/w/bl*	USAF 351st ARS/100th ARW, RAF Mildenhall	
80094	Boeing KC-135T Stratotanker (58-0094) [D] *r/w/bl*	*Returned to the USA, 29 January 2019*	
80100	Boeing KC-135R Stratotanker (58-0100) [D] *r/w/bl*	USAF 351st ARS/100th ARW, RAF Mildenhall	
80113	Boeing KC-135R Stratotanker (58-0113) [D] *r/w/bl*	USAF 351st ARS/100th ARW, RAF Mildenhall	
91511	Boeing KC-135R Stratotanker (59-1511) [D] *r/w/bl*	*Returned to the USA, 16 June 2018*	
91513	Boeing KC-135T Stratotanker (59-1513) [D] *r/w/bl*	USAF 351st ARS/100th ARW, RAF Mildenhall	

The 351st Air Refuelling Squadron of the 100th Air Refuelling Wing operates a fleet of KC-135R and KC-135T Stratotankers from RAF Mildenhall. For heavy maintenance the aircraft return to the US and are replaced by others in the fleet and this one, 61-0321, was on strength until 27 September 2018, when it returned to the USA.

These aircraft are normally based in Western Europe with the USAFE. They are shown in numerical order of type designation, with individual aircraft in serial number order as carried on the aircraft. Fiscal year (FY) details are also provided if necessary. The unit allocation and operating bases are given for most aircraft.

Notes	Serial	Type (code/other identity)	Owner/operator, location or fate
	Beech C-12 Huron		
	30497	Beech C-12D Huron (83-0497)	*To US Embassy, Accra, January 2018*
	31217	Beech C-12C Huron (73-1217)	USAF US Embassy Flight, Taszár, Hungary
	63239	Beech C-12C Huron (76-3239)	*To US Embassy, Ankara, December 2018*
	Lockheed (GD) F-16CM/F-16DM Fighting Falcon		
	87-0350	Lockheed (GD) F-16CM-40 Fighting Falcon [AV] gn/y	USAF 555th FS/31st FW, Aviano, Italy
	87-0351	Lockheed (GD) F-16CM-40 Fighting Falcon [AV] gn/y	USAF 555th FS/31st FW, Aviano, Italy
	87-0355	Lockheed (GD) F-16CM-40 Fighting Falcon [AV] pr/w	USAF 510th FS/31st FW, Aviano, Italy
	87-0359	Lockheed (GD) F-16CM-40 Fighting Falcon [AV] gn/y	USAF 555th FS/31st FW, Aviano, Italy
	88-0413	Lockheed (GD) F-16CM-40 Fighting Falcon [AV] pr/w	USAF 510th FS/31st FW, Aviano, Italy
	88-0425	Lockheed (GD) F-16CM-40 Fighting Falcon [AV] gn/y	USAF 555th FS/31st FW, Aviano, Italy
	88-0435	Lockheed (GD) F-16CM-40 Fighting Falcon [AV] gn/y	USAF 555th FS/31st FW, Aviano, Italy
	88-0443	Lockheed (GD) F-16CM-40 Fighting Falcon [AV] pr/w	USAF 510th FS/31st FW, Aviano, Italy
	88-0444	Lockheed (GD) F-16CM-40 Fighting Falcon [AV] pr/w	USAF 510th FS/31st FW, Aviano, Italy
	88-0446	Lockheed (GD) F-16CM-40 Fighting Falcon [AV] gn/y	USAF 555th FS/31st FW, Aviano, Italy
	88-0460	Lockheed (GD) F-16CM-40 Fighting Falcon [AV] pr/w	USAF 510th FS/31st FW, Aviano, Italy
	88-0462	Lockheed (GD) F-16CM-40 Fighting Falcon [AV] pr/w	USAF 510th FS/31st FW, Aviano, Italy
	88-0491	Lockheed (GD) F-16CM-40 Fighting Falcon [AV] pr/w	USAF 510th FS/31st FW, Aviano, Italy
	88-0516	Lockheed (GD) F-16CM-40 Fighting Falcon [AV] pr/w	USAF 510th FS/31st FW, Aviano, Italy
	88-0521	Lockheed (GD) F-16CM-40 Fighting Falcon [AV] pr/w	USAF 510th FS/31st FW, Aviano, Italy
	88-0525	Lockheed (GD) F-16CM-40 Fighting Falcon [AV] pr/w	USAF 510th FS/31st FW, Aviano, Italy
	88-0526	Lockheed (GD) F-16CM-40 Fighting Falcon [AV] gn/y	USAF 555th FS/31st FW, Aviano, Italy
	88-0532	Lockheed (GD) F-16CM-40 Fighting Falcon [AV] gn/y	USAF 555th FS/31st FW, Aviano, Italy
	88-0535	Lockheed (GD) F-16CM-40 Fighting Falcon [AV] gn/y	USAF 555th FS/31st FW, Aviano, Italy
	88-0541	Lockheed (GD) F-16CM-40 Fighting Falcon [AV] pr/w	USAF 510th FS/31st FW, Aviano, Italy
	89-2001	Lockheed (GD) F-16CM-40 Fighting Falcon [AV] m [31 FW]	USAF 31st FW, Aviano, Italy
	89-2008	Lockheed (GD) F-16CM-40 Fighting Falcon [AV] pr/w	USAF 510th FS/31st FW, Aviano, Italy
	89-2009	Lockheed (GD) F-16CM-40 Fighting Falcon [AV] pr/w	USAF 510th FS/31st FW, Aviano, Italy
	89-2011	Lockheed (GD) F-16CM-40 Fighting Falcon [AV] pr/w	USAF 510th FS/31st FW, Aviano, Italy
	89-2016	Lockheed (GD) F-16CM-40 Fighting Falcon [AV] gn/y	USAF 555th FS/31st FW, Aviano, Italy
	89-2018	Lockheed (GD) F-16CM-40 Fighting Falcon [AV] gn/y	USAF 555th FS/31st FW, Aviano, Italy
	89-2023	Lockheed (GD) F-16CM-40 Fighting Falcon [AV] gn/y	USAF 555th FS/31st FW, Aviano, Italy
	89-2024	Lockheed (GD) F-16CM-40 Fighting Falcon [AV] gn/y	USAF 555th FS/31st FW, Aviano, Italy
	89-2026	Lockheed (GD) F-16CM-40 Fighting Falcon [AV] pr/w	USAF 510th FS/31st FW, Aviano, Italy
	89-2029	Lockheed (GD) F-16CM-40 Fighting Falcon [AV] pr/w	USAF 510th FS/31st FW, Aviano, Italy
	89-2030	Lockheed (GD) F-16CM-40 Fighting Falcon [AV] pr/w [510 FS]	USAF 510th FS/31st FW, Aviano, Italy
	89-2035	Lockheed (GD) F-16CM-40 Fighting Falcon [AV] gn/y [555 FS]	USAF 555th FS/31st FW, Aviano, Italy
	89-2038	Lockheed (GD) F-16CM-40 Fighting Falcon [AV] pr/w	USAF 510th FS/31st FW, Aviano, Italy
	89-2039	Lockheed (GD) F-16CM-40 Fighting Falcon [AV] gn/y	USAF 555th FS/31st FW, Aviano, Italy
	89-2041	Lockheed (GD) F-16CM-40 Fighting Falcon [AV] gn/y	USAF 555th FS/31st FW, Aviano, Italy
	89-2044	Lockheed (GD) F-16CM-40 Fighting Falcon [AV] gn/y	USAF 555th FS/31st FW, Aviano, Italy
	89-2046	Lockheed (GD) F-16CM-40 Fighting Falcon [AV] pr/w	USAF 510th FS/31st FW, Aviano, Italy
	89-2047	Lockheed (GD) F-16CM-40 Fighting Falcon [AV] pr/w	USAF 510th FS/31st FW, Aviano, Italy
	89-2049	Lockheed (GD) F-16CM-40 Fighting Falcon [AV] pr/w [USAFE]	USAF 510th FS/31st FW, Aviano, Italy
	89-2057	Lockheed (GD) F-16CM-40 Fighting Falcon [AV] pr/w	USAF 510th FS/31st FW, Aviano, Italy
	89-2068	Lockheed (GD) F-16CM-40 Fighting Falcon [AV] gn/y	USAF 555th FS/31st FW, Aviano, Italy
	89-2096	Lockheed (GD) F-16CM-40 Fighting Falcon [AV] pr/w	USAF 510th FS/31st FW, Aviano, Italy
	89-2102	Lockheed (GD) F-16CM-40 Fighting Falcon [AV] pr/w	USAF 510th FS/31st FW, Aviano, Italy
	89-2118	Lockheed (GD) F-16CM-40 Fighting Falcon [AV] gn/y	USAF 555th FS/31st FW, Aviano, Italy
	89-2137	Lockheed (GD) F-16CM-40 Fighting Falcon [AV] pr/w [31 OG]	USAF 510th FS/31st FW, Aviano, Italy
	89-2152	Lockheed (GD) F-16CM-40 Fighting Falcon [AV] gn/y	USAF 555th FS/31st FW, Aviano, Italy
	89-2178	Lockheed (GD) F-16DM-40 Fighting Falcon [AV] gn/y	USAF 555th FS/31st FW, Aviano, Italy

Serial	Type (code/other identity)	Owner/operator, location or fate	Notes
90-0709	Lockheed (GD) F-16CM-40 Fighting Falcon [AV] pr/w	USAF 510th FS/31st FW, Aviano, Italy	
90-0772	Lockheed (GD) F-16DM-40 Fighting Falcon [AV] gn/y	USAF 555th FS/31st FW, Aviano, Italy	
90-0773	Lockheed (GD) F-16DM-40 Fighting Falcon [AV] gn/y	USAF 555th FS/31st FW, Aviano, Italy	
90-0777	Lockheed (GD) F-16DM-40 Fighting Falcon [AV] pr/w	USAF 510th FS/31st FW, Aviano, Italy	
90-0795	Lockheed (GD) F-16DM-40 Fighting Falcon [AV] gn/y	USAF 555th FS/31st FW, Aviano, Italy	
90-0796	Lockheed (GD) F-16DM-40 Fighting Falcon [AV] gn/y	USAF 555th FS/31st FW, Aviano, Italy	
90-0800	Lockheed (GD) F-16DM-40 Fighting Falcon [AV] gn/y	USAF 555th FS/31st FW, Aviano, Italy	
90-0813	Lockheed (GD) F-16CM-50 Fighting Falcon [SP] r/w	USAF 480th FS/52d FW, Spangdahlem, Germany	
90-0818	Lockheed (GD) F-16CM-50 Fighting Falcon [SP] r/w	USAF 480th FS/52nd FW, Spangdahlem, Germany	
90-0827	Lockheed (GD) F-16CM-50 Fighting Falcon [SP] r/w	USAF 480th FS/52nd FW, Spangdahlem, Germany	
90-0828	Lockheed (GD) F-16CM-50 Fighting Falcon [SP] r/w	USAF 480th FS/52nd FW, Spangdahlem, Germany	
90-0829	Lockheed (GD) F-16CM-50 Fighting Falcon [SP] r/w [52 OG]	USAF 480th FS/52nd FW, Spangdahlem, Germany	
90-0833	Lockheed (GD) F-16CM-50 Fighting Falcon [SP] r/w	USAF 480th FS/52nd FW, Spangdahlem, Germany	
91-0338	Lockheed (GD) F-16CM-50 Fighting Falcon [SP] r/w	USAF 480th FS/52nd FW, Spangdahlem, Germany	
91-0340	Lockheed (GD) F-16CM-50 Fighting Falcon [SP] r/w	USAF 480th FS/52nd FW, Spangdahlem, Germany	
91-0342	Lockheed (GD) F-16CM-50 Fighting Falcon [SP] r/w	USAF 480th FS/52nd FW, Spangdahlem, Germany	
91-0343	Lockheed (GD) F-16CM-50 Fighting Falcon [SP] r/w	USAF 480th FS/52nd FW, Spangdahlem, Germany	
91-0344	Lockheed (GD) F-16CM-50 Fighting Falcon [SP] r/w	USAF 480th FS/52nd FW, Spangdahlem, Germany	
91-0351	Lockheed (GD) F-16CM-50 Fighting Falcon [SP] r/w	USAF 480th FS/52nd FW, Spangdahlem, Germany	
91-0352	Lockheed (GD) F-16CM-50 Fighting Falcon [SP] m [52 FW]	USAF 480th FS/52nd FW, Spangdahlem, Germany	
91-0358	Lockheed (GD) F-16CM-50 Fighting Falcon [SP] r/w	USAF 480th FS/52nd FW, Spangdahlem, Germany	
91-0360	Lockheed (GD) F-16CM-50 Fighting Falcon [SP] r/w	USAF 480th FS/52nd FW, Spangdahlem, Germany	
91-0361	Lockheed (GD) F-16CM-50 Fighting Falcon [SP] r/w	USAF 480th FS/52nd FW, Spangdahlem, Germany	
91-0368	Lockheed (GD) F-16CM-50 Fighting Falcon [SP]	USAF 480th FS/52nd FW, Spangdahlem, Germany	
91-0402	Lockheed (GD) F-16CM-50 Fighting Falcon [SP] r/w	USAF 480th FS/52nd FW, Spangdahlem, Germany	
91-0403	Lockheed (GD) F-16CM-50 Fighting Falcon [SP] r/w	USAF 480th FS/52nd FW, Spangdahlem, Germany	
91-0407	Lockheed (GD) F-16CM-50 Fighting Falcon [SP] r/w	USAF 480th FS/52nd FW, Spangdahlem, Germany	
91-0412	Lockheed (GD) F-16CM-50 Fighting Falcon [SP] r/w	USAF 480th FS/52nd FW, Spangdahlem, Germany	
91-0416	Lockheed (GD) F-16CM-50 Fighting Falcon [SP] r/w	USAF 480th FS/52nd FW, Spangdahlem, Germany	
91-0417	Lockheed (GD) F-16CM-50 Fighting Falcon [SP] r/w	USAF 480th FS/52nd FW, Spangdahlem, Germany	
91-0418	Lockheed (GD) F-16CM-50 Fighting Falcon [SP] r/w	USAF 480th FS/52nd FW, Spangdahlem, Germany	
91-0472	Lockheed (GD) F-16DM-50 Fighting Falcon [SP] r/w	USAF 480th FS/52nd FW, Spangdahlem, Germany	
91-0481	Lockheed (GD) F-16DM-50 Fighting Falcon [SP] r/w	USAF 480th FS/52nd FW, Spangdahlem, Germany	
92-3918	Lockheed (GD) F-16CM-50 Fighting Falcon [SP] r/w	USAF 480th FS/52nd FW, Spangdahlem, Germany	
96-0080	Lockheed (GD) F-16CM-50 Fighting Falcon [SP] r/w [480 FS]	USAF 480th FS/52nd FW, Spangdahlem, Germany	
96-0083	Lockheed (GD) F-16CM-50 Fighting Falcon [SP] r/w	USAF 480th FS/52nd FW, Spangdahlem, Germany	

Gates C-21A

40083	Gates C-21A (84-0083)	USAF 76th AS/86th AW, Ramstein, Germany	
40085	Gates C-21A (84-0085)	USAF 76th AS/86th AW, Ramstein, Germany	
40087	Gates C-21A (84-0087)	USAF 76th AS/86th AW, Ramstein, Germany	
40096	Gates C-21A (84-0096)	USAF 76th AS/86th AW, Ramstein, Germany	
40126	Gates C-21A (84-0126)	USAF 76th AS/86th AW, Ramstein, Germany	

Gulfstream Aerospace C-37A Gulfstream V

10076	Gulfstream Aerospace C-37A Gulfstream V (01-0076)	USAF 309th AS/86th AW, Chièvres, Belgium	
90402	Gulfstream Aerospace C-37A Gulfstream V (99-0402)	USAF 309th AS/86th AW, Chièvres, Belgium	

Boeing C-40B

20042	Boeing C-40B (02-0042)	USAF 76th AS/86th AW, Ramstein, Germany	

Sikorsky HH-60G Pave Hawk

26205	Sikorsky HH-60G Pave Hawk (89-26205) [AV]	USAF 56th RQS/31st FW, Aviano, Italy	
26206	Sikorsky HH-60G Pave Hawk (89-26206) [AV]	USAF 56th RQS/31st FW, Aviano, Italy	
26208	Sikorsky HH-60G Pave Hawk (89-26208) [AV]	USAF 56th RQS/31st FW, Aviano, Italy	
26212	Sikorsky HH-60G Pave Hawk (89-26212) [AV]	USAF 56th RQS/31st FW, Aviano, Italy	
26353	Sikorsky HH-60G Pave Hawk (91-26353) [AV]	USAF 56th RQS/31st FW, Aviano, Italy	

EUROPEAN-BASED USAF AIRCRAFT

Notes	Serial	Type (code/other identity)	Owner/operator, location or fate
	Lockheed C-130J-30 Hercules II		
	15736	Lockheed C-130J-30 Hercules II (11-5736)[RS] *bl/w*	USAF 37th AS/86th AW, Ramstein, Germany
	43142	Lockheed C-130J-30 Hercules II (04-3142)[RS] *bl/w*	USAF 37th AS/86th AW, Ramstein, Germany
	55822	Lockheed C-130J-30 Hercules II (15-5822)[RS] *bl/w*	USAF 37th AS/86th AW, Ramstein, Germany
	55831	Lockheed C-130J-30 Hercules II (15-5831)[RS] *bl/w*	USAF 37th AS/86th AW, Ramstein, Germany
	65840	Lockheed C-130J-30 Hercules II (16-5840)[RS] *bl/w*	USAF 37th AS/86th AW, Ramstein, Germany
	68610	Lockheed C-130J-30 Hercules II (06-8610)[RS] *bl/w*	*Transferred to the 374th AW, 2018*
	68611	Lockheed C-130J-30 Hercules II (06-8611)[RS] *bl/w*	USAF 37th AS/86th AW, Ramstein, Germany
	68612	Lockheed C-130J-30 Hercules II (06-8612)[RS] *bl/w*	*Returned to the USA, 2018*
	74635	Lockheed C-130J-30 Hercules II (07-4635)[RS] *bl/w*	USAF 37th AS/86th AW, Ramstein, Germany
	78608	Lockheed C-130J-30 Hercules II (07-8608)[RS] *bl/w*	USAF 37th AS/86th AW, Ramstein, Germany
	78609	Lockheed C-130J-30 Hercules II (07-8609)[RS] *bl/w*	USAF 37th AS/86th AW, Ramstein, Germany
	78613	Lockheed C-130J-30 Hercules II (07-8613)[RS] *bl/w*	*Transferred to the 19th AW, October 2018*
	78614	Lockheed C-130J-30 Hercules II (07-8614)[RS] *bl/w*	USAF 37th AS/86th AW, Ramstein, Germany
	83176	Lockheed C-130J-30 Hercules II (08-3176)[RS] *bl/w*	USAF 37th AS/86th AW, Ramstein, Germany
	88601	Lockheed C-130J-30 Hercules II (08-8601)[RS] *bl/w* [86 AW]	USAF 37th AS/86th AW, Ramstein, Germany
	88602	Lockheed C-130J-30 Hercules II (08-8602)[RS] *bl/w* [86 OG]	USAF 37th AS/86th AW, Ramstein, Germany
	88603	Lockheed C-130J-30 Hercules II (08-8603)[RS] *bl/w* [37 AS]	USAF 37th AS/86th AW, Ramstein, Germany
	88607	Lockheed C-130J-30 Hercules II (08-8607)[RS] *bl/w*	*Transferred to the 374th AW, 2018*

EUROPEAN-BASED US NAVY AIRCRAFT

Notes	Serial	Type (code/other identity)	Owner/operator, location or fate
	Fairchild C-26D		
	900528	Fairchild C-26D	USN NAF Sigonella, Italy
	900530	Fairchild C-26D	USN NAF Sigonella, Italy
	900531	Fairchild C-26D	USN NAF Naples, Italy
	910502	Fairchild C-26D	USN NAF Naples, Italy

Wearing the blue and white tail bands of the 492nd Fighter Squadron, F-15E Strike Eagle 96-0205 is operated by the 48th Fighter Wing at RAF Lakenheath.

Serial	Type (code/other identity)	Owner/operator, location or fate	Notes
Beech C-12 Huron			
40156	Beech C-12U-3 Huron (84-00156)	US Army E/1-214th AVN, Wiesbaden, Germany	
40157	Beech C-12U-3 Huron (84-00157)	US Army E/1-214th AVN, Wiesbaden, Germany	
40160	Beech C-12U-3 Huron (84-00160)	US Army E/1-214th AVN, Wiesbaden, Germany	
40162	Beech C-12U-3 Huron (84-00162)	US Army E/1-214th AVN, Wiesbaden, Germany	
40165	Beech C-12U-3 Huron (84-00165)	US Army E/1-214th AVN, Wiesbaden, Germany	
40173	Beech C-12U-3 Huron (84-00173)	US Army E/1-214th AVN, Wiesbaden, Germany	
Cessna UC-35A Citation V			
50123	Cessna UC-35A Citation V (95-00123)	US Army E/1-214th AVN, Wiesbaden, Germany	
70102	Cessna UC-35A Citation V (97-00102)	US Army E/1-214th AVN, Wiesbaden, Germany	
70105	Cessna UC-35A Citation V (97-00105)	US Army E/1-214th AVN, Wiesbaden, Germany	
90102	Cessna UC-35A Citation V (99-00102)	US Army E/1-214th AVN, Wiesbaden, Germany	
Boeing-Vertol CH-47F Chinook			
13-08132	Boeing-Vertol CH-47F Chinook	US Army B/1-214th AVN, Ansbach, Germany	
13-08133	Boeing-Vertol CH-47F Chinook	US Army B/1-214th AVN, Ansbach, Germany	
13-08134	Boeing-Vertol CH-47F Chinook	US Army B/1-214th AVN, Ansbach, Germany	
13-08135	Boeing-Vertol CH-47F Chinook	US Army B/1-214th AVN, Ansbach, Germany	
13-08432	Boeing-Vertol CH-47F Chinook	US Army B/1-214th AVN, Ansbach, Germany	
13-08434	Boeing-Vertol CH-47F Chinook	US Army B/1-214th AVN, Ansbach, Germany	
13-08435	Boeing-Vertol CH-47F Chinook	US Army B/1-214th AVN, Ansbach, Germany	
13-08436	Boeing-Vertol CH-47F Chinook	US Army B/1-214th AVN, Ansbach, Germany	
13-08437	Boeing-Vertol CH-47F Chinook	US Army B/1-214th AVN, Ansbach, Germany	
15-08176	Boeing-Vertol CH-47F Chinook	US Army B/1-214th AVN, Ansbach, Germany	
15-08178	Boeing-Vertol CH-47F Chinook	US Army B/1-214th AVN, Ansbach, Germany	
Sikorsky H-60 Black Hawk			
23936	Sikorsky UH-60A+ Black Hawk (84-23936)	US Army C/1-214th AVN, Grafenwöhr, Germany	
24397	Sikorsky UH-60A+ Black Hawk (85-24397)	US Army C/1-214th AVN, Grafenwöhr, Germany	
24437	Sikorsky UH-60A+ Black Hawk (85-24437)	US Army C/1-214th AVN, Grafenwöhr, Germany	
24446	Sikorsky UH-60A+ Black Hawk (85-24446)	US Army C/1-214th AVN, Grafenwöhr, Germany	
24538	Sikorsky UH-60A Black Hawk (86-24538)	*Returned to the USA, March 2018*	
24583	Sikorsky UH-60A Black Hawk (87-24583)	*Returned to the USA, March 2018*	
24584	Sikorsky UH-60A Black Hawk (87-24584)	*Returned to the USA, April 2018*	
24589	Sikorsky UH-60A Black Hawk (87-24589)	*Returned to the USA, April 2018*	
24614	Sikorsky UH-60A+ Black Hawk (87-24614)	US Army C/1-214th AVN, Grafenwöhr, Germany	
24642	Sikorsky UH-60A Black Hawk (87-24642)	*Returned to the USA, March 2018*	
24643	Sikorsky UH-60A Black Hawk (87-24643)	*Returned to the USA, April 2018*	
26004	Sikorsky UH-60A+ Black Hawk (87-26004)	US Army C/1-214th AVN, Grafenwöhr, Germany	
26027	Sikorsky UH-60A Black Hawk (88-26027)	*Returned to the USA, March 2018*	
26071	Sikorsky UH-60A Black Hawk (88-26071)	*Returned to the USA, March 2018*	
26163	Sikorsky UH-60A+ Black Hawk (89-26163)	US Army C/1-214th AVN, Grafenwöhr, Germany	
26485	Sikorsky UH-60L Black Hawk (93-26485)	*Returned to the USA, March 2018*	
20245	Sikorsky UH-60L Black Hawk (10-20245)	US Army A/1-214th AVN, Wiesbaden, Germany	
20272	Sikorsky UH-60L Black Hawk (10-20272)	US Army A/1-214th AVN, Wiesbaden, Germany	
20276	Sikorsky UH-60L Black Hawk (10-20276)	US Army A/1-214th AVN, Wiesbaden, Germany	
20311	Sikorsky UH-60L Black Hawk (10-20311)	US Army A/1-214th AVN, Wiesbaden, Germany	
20314	Sikorsky UH-60L Black Hawk (15-20314)	US Army A/1-214th AVN, Wiesbaden, Germany	
20741	Sikorsky UH-60L Black Hawk (15-20741)	US Army A/1-214th AVN, Wiesbaden, Germany	
20742	Sikorsky UH-60L Black Hawk (15-20742)	US Army A/1-214th AVN, Wiesbaden, Germany	
20743	Sikorsky UH-60L Black Hawk (15-20743)	US Army A/1-214th AVN, Wiesbaden, Germany	
20744	Sikorsky UH-60L Black Hawk (15-20744)	US Army A/1-214th AVN, Wiesbaden, Germany	
20745	Sikorsky UH-60L Black Hawk (15-20745)	US Army A/1-214th AVN, Wiesbaden, Germany	
20754	Sikorsky UH-60L Black Hawk (15-20754)	US Army A/1-214th AVN, Wiesbaden, Germany	
MDH AH-64D Apache			
05316	MDH AH-64D Apache (02-05316)	US Army 1-3rd AVN, Ansbach, Germany	
05321	MDH AH-64D Apache (02-05321)	US Army 1-3rd AVN, Ansbach, Germany	
05327	MDH AH-64D Apache (02-05327)	US Army 1-3rd AVN, Ansbach, Germany	
05381	MDH AH-64D Apache (03-05381)	US Army 1-3rd AVN, Ansbach, Germany	
05384	MDH AH-64D Apache (03-05384)	US Army 1-3rd AVN, Ansbach, Germany	

Notes	Serial	Type (code/other identity)	Owner/operator, location or fate
	05419	MDH AH-64D Apache (04-05419)	US Army 1-3rd AVN, Ansbach, Germany
	05426	MDH AH-64D Apache (04-05426)	US Army 1-3rd AVN, Ansbach, Germany
	05429	MDH AH-64D Apache (04-05429)	US Army 1-3rd AVN, Ansbach, Germany
	05431	MDH AH-64D Apache (04-05431)	US Army 1-3rd AVN, Ansbach, Germany
	05437	MDH AH-64D Apache (04-05437)	US Army 1-3rd AVN, Ansbach, Germany
	05439	MDH AH-64D Apache (04-05439)	US Army 1-3rd AVN, Ansbach, Germany
	05444	MDH AH-64D Apache (04-05444)	US Army 1-3rd AVN, Ansbach, Germany
	05453	MDH AH-64D Apache (04-05453)	US Army 1-3rd AVN, Ansbach, Germany
	05467	MDH AH-64D Apache (04-05467)	US Army 1-3rd AVN, Ansbach, Germany
	05535	MDH AH-64D Apache (07-05535)	US Army 1-3rd AVN, Ansbach, Germany
	05543	MDH AH-64D Apache (08-05543)	US Army 1-3rd AVN, Ansbach, Germany
	05550	MDH AH-64D Apache (08-05550)	US Army 1-3rd AVN, Ansbach, Germany
	05580	MDH AH-64D Apache (09-05580)	US Army 1-3rd AVN, Ansbach, Germany
	05581	MDH AH-64D Apache (09-05581)	US Army 1-3rd AVN, Ansbach, Germany
	05587	MDH AH-64D Apache (09-05587)	US Army 1-3rd AVN, Ansbach, Germany
	05589	MDH AH-64D Apache (09-05589)	US Army 1-3rd AVN, Ansbach, Germany
	05620	MDH AH-64D Apache (10-05620)	US Army 1-3rd AVN, Ansbach, Germany
	07010	MDH AH-64D Apache (05-07010)	US Army 1-3rd AVN, Ansbach, Germany
	07014	MDH AH-64D Apache (06-07014)	US Army 1-3rd AVN, Ansbach, Germany
	Eurocopter UH-72A Lakota		
	72097	Eurocopter UH-72A Lakota (09-72097)	US Army JMRC, Hohenfels
	72098	Eurocopter UH-72A Lakota (09-72098)	US Army JMRC, Hohenfels
	72100	Eurocopter UH-72A Lakota (09-72100)	US Army JMRC, Hohenfels
	72105	Eurocopter UH-72A Lakota (09-72105)	US Army JMRC, Hohenfels
	72106	Eurocopter UH-72A Lakota (09-72106)	US Army JMRC, Hohenfels
	72107	Eurocopter UH-72A Lakota (09-72107)	US Army JMRC, Hohenfels
	72108	Eurocopter UH-72A Lakota (09-72108)	US Army JMRC, Hohenfels

This Aeritalia C-27J Spartan is unusual from most Italian Air Force machines, which reside at Pisa. CSX62219/RS-50 is operated by the Reparto Sperimentale Volo (Experimental Flight School) at Pratica di Mare.

The following aircraft are normally based in the USA but are likely to be seen visiting the UK from time to time. The presentation is in numerical order of the type, commencing with the B-**1B** and concluding with the C-**135**. The aircraft are listed in numerical progression by the serial actually carried externally. Fiscal year information is provided, together with details of mark variations and in some cases operating units. Where base-code letter information is carried on the aircrafts' tails, this is detailed with the squadron/base data; for example the 7th Wing's B-1B 60105 carries the letters DY on its tail, thus identifying the Wing's home base as Dyess AFB, Texas.

Serial	Type (code/other identity)	Owner/operator, location or fate	Notes
Rockwell B-1B Lancer			
50059	Rockwell B-1B Lancer (85-0059) [DY] *bk/w* $	USAF 9th BS/7th BW, Dyess AFB, TX	
50060	Rockwell B-1B Lancer (85-0060) [EL] *bk/r*	USAF 34th BS/28th BW, Ellsworth AFB, SD	
50061	Rockwell B-1B Lancer (85-0061) [DY] *bl/w*	USAF 28th BS/7th BW, Dyess AFB, TX	
50064	Rockwell B-1B Lancer (85-0064) [OT] *bk/gy*	USAF 337th TES/53rd Wg, Dyess AFB, TX	
50066	Rockwell B-1B Lancer (85-0066) [EL] *bk/y* $	USAF 37th BS/28th BW, Ellsworth AFB, SD	
50068	Rockwell B-1B Lancer (85-0068) [ED]	USAF 419th FLTS/412th TW, Edwards AFB	
50069	Rockwell B-1B Lancer (85-0069) [EL] *bk/r*	USAF 34th BS/28th BW, Ellsworth AFB, SD	
50072	Rockwell B-1B Lancer (85-0072) [EL] *bk/r*	USAF 34th BS/28th BW, Ellsworth AFB, SD	
50073	Rockwell B-1B Lancer (85-0073) [DY] *bl/w* [7 OG]	USAF 28th BS/7th BW, Dyess AFB, TX	
50074	Rockwell B-1B Lancer (85-0074) [DY] *bk/w*	USAF 9th BS/7th BW, Dyess AFB, TX	
50075	Rockwell B-1B Lancer (85-0075) [ED]	USAF 419th FLTS/412th TW, Edwards AFB	
50077	Rockwell B-1B Lancer (85-0077) [WA] *y/bk* [77 WPS]	USAF 77th WPS/57th Wg, Dyess AFB, TX	
50079	Rockwell B-1B Lancer (85-0079) [EL] *bk/y*	USAF 37th BS/28th BW, Ellsworth AFB, SD	
50080	Rockwell B-1B Lancer (85-0080) [DY] *bk/w*	USAF 9th BS/7th BW, Dyess AFB, TX	
50081	Rockwell B-1B Lancer (85-0081) [EL] *bk/r*	USAF 34th BS/28th BW, Ellsworth AFB, SD	
50083	Rockwell B-1B Lancer (85-0083) [EL] *bk/r*	USAF 34th BS/28th BW, Ellsworth AFB, SD	
50084	Rockwell B-1B Lancer (85-0084) [EL] *bk/r*	USAF 34th BS/28th BW, Ellsworth AFB, SD	
50085	Rockwell B-1B Lancer (85-0085) [EL] *bk/y*	USAF 37th BS/28th BW, Ellsworth AFB, SD	
50087	Rockwell B-1B Lancer (85-0087) [DY] *bk/w*	USAF 9th BS/7th BW, Dyess AFB, TX	
50088	Rockwell B-1B Lancer (85-0088) [DY] *bk/w*	USAF 9th BS/7th BW, Dyess AFB, TX	
50089	Rockwell B-1B Lancer (85-0089) [DY] *bk/w*	USAF 9th BS/7th BW, Dyess AFB, TX	
50090	Rockwell B-1B Lancer (85-0090) [DY] *bl/w*	USAF 28th BS/7th BW, Dyess AFB, TX	
60094	Rockwell B-1B Lancer (86-0094) [EL] *bk/y* $	USAF 37th BS/28th BW, Ellsworth AFB, SD	
60095	Rockwell B-1B Lancer (86-0095) [EL] *bk/r*	USAF 34th BS/28th BW, Ellsworth AFB, SD	
60097	Rockwell B-1B Lancer (86-0097) [DY] *bk/w*	USAF 9th BS/7th BW, Dyess AFB, TX	
60098	Rockwell B-1B Lancer (86-0098) [DY] *bl/w*	USAF 28th BS/7th BW, Dyess AFB, TX	
60099	Rockwell B-1B Lancer (86-0099) [EL] *bk/y* [28 OG]	USAF 37th BS/28th BW, Ellsworth AFB, SD	
60101	Rockwell B-1B Lancer (86-0101) [DY] *bl/w*	USAF 28th BS/7th BW, Dyess AFB, TX	
60102	Rockwell B-1B Lancer (86-0102) [EL] *bk/y*	USAF 37th BS/28th BW, Ellsworth AFB, SD	
60103	Rockwell B-1B Lancer (86-0103) [DY] *bl/w*	USAF 28th BS/7th BW, Dyess AFB, TX	
60104	Rockwell B-1B Lancer (86-0104) [EL] *bk/y*	USAF 37th BS/28th BW, Ellsworth AFB, SD	
60105	Rockwell B-1B Lancer (86-0105) [DY] *bl/w*	USAF 28th BS/7th BW, Dyess AFB, TX	
60107	Rockwell B-1B Lancer (86-0107) [DY] *bk/w*	USAF 9th BS/7th BW, Dyess AFB, TX	
60108	Rockwell B-1B Lancer (86-0108) [EL] *bk/y*	USAF 37th BS/28th BW, Ellsworth AFB, SD	
60109	Rockwell B-1B Lancer (86-0109) [DY] *bl/w*	USAF 289th BS/7th BW, Dyess AFB, TX	
60110	Rockwell B-1B Lancer (86-0110) [DY] *bl/w*	USAF 28th BS/7th BW, Dyess AFB, TX	
60111	Rockwell B-1B Lancer (86-0111) [EL] *bk/r*	USAF 34th BS/28th BW, Ellsworth AFB, SD	
60112	Rockwell B-1B Lancer (86-0112) [DY] *bl/w*	USAF 28th BS/7th BW, Dyess AFB, TX	
60113	Rockwell B-1B Lancer (86-0113) [EL] *bk/y*	USAF 37th BS/28th BW, Ellsworth AFB, SD	
60115	Rockwell B-1B Lancer (86-0115) [EL] *bk/r*	USAF 34th BS/28th BW, Ellsworth AFB, SD	
60117	Rockwell B-1B Lancer (86-0117) [DY] *bk/y* [7th BW]	USAF 9th BS/7th BW, Dyess AFB, TX	
60118	Rockwell B-1B Lancer (86-0118) [EL] *bk/y*	USAF 37th BS/28th BW, Ellsworth AFB, SD	
60119	Rockwell B-1B Lancer (86-0119) [DY] *bl/w*	USAF 28th BS/7th BW, Dyess AFB, TX	
60120	Rockwell B-1B Lancer (86-0120) [EL] *bk/y*	USAF 37th BS/28th BW, Ellsworth AFB, SD	
60121	Rockwell B-1B Lancer (86-0121) [EL] *bk/y*	USAF 37th BS/28th BW, Ellsworth AFB, SD	
60122	Rockwell B-1B Lancer (86-0122) [DY] *bk/w*	USAF 9th BS/7th BW, Dyess AFB, TX	
60123	Rockwell B-1B Lancer (86-0123) [DY] *bk/w*	USAF 9th BS/7th BW, Dyess AFB, TX	
60124	Rockwell B-1B Lancer (86-0124) [DY] *bk/w*	USAF 9th BS/7th BW, Dyess AFB, TX	
60125	Rockwell B-1B Lancer (86-0125) [DY] *bl/w*	USAF 28th BS/7th BW, Dyess AFB, TX	
60126	Rockwell B-1B Lancer (86-0126) [DY] *bl/w*	USAF 28th BS/7th BW, Dyess AFB, TX	
60127	Rockwell B-1B Lancer (86-0127) [DY] *bk/w*	USAF 9th BS/7th BW, Dyess AFB, TX	
60129	Rockwell B-1B Lancer (86-0129) [EL] *bk/r*	USAF 34th BS/28th BW, Ellsworth AFB, SD	
60132	Rockwell B-1B Lancer (86-0132) [DY] *bl/w*	USAF 28th BS/7th BW, Dyess AFB, TX	

Notes	Serial	Type (code/other identity)	Owner/operator, location or fate
	60133	Rockwell B-1B Lancer (86-0133) [DY] *bl/w*	USAF 28th BS/7th BW, Dyess AFB, TX
	60134	Rockwell B-1B Lancer (86-0134) [EL] *bk/r* [34 BS]	USAF 34th BS/28th BW, Ellsworth AFB, SD
	60135	Rockwell B-1B Lancer (86-0135) [DY] *bl/w*	USAF 28th BS/7th BW, Dyess AFB, TX
	60136	Rockwell B-1B Lancer (86-0136) [DY] *bl/w*	USAF 28th BS/7th BW, Dyess AFB, TX
	60138	Rockwell B-1B Lancer (86-0138) [EL] *bk/y*	USAF 37th BS/28th BW, Ellsworth AFB, SD
	60139	Rockwell B-1B Lancer (86-0139) [EL] *bl/y* [34 BS]	USAF 34th BS/28th BW, Ellsworth AFB, SD
	60140	Rockwell B-1B Lancer (86-0140) [DY] *bk/r* [345 BS]	USAF 28th BS/7th BW, Dyess AFB, TX

Northrop B-2 Spirit
(Names are given where known. Each begins *Spirit of ...*)

Notes	Serial	Type (code/other identity)	Owner/operator, location or fate
	00040	Northrop B-2 Spirit (90-0040) [WM] *Alaska*	USAF 509th BW, Whiteman AFB, MO
	00041	Northrop B-2 Spirit (90-0041) [WM] *Hawaii*	USAF 509th BW, Whiteman AFB, MO
	20700	Northrop B-2 Spirit (92-0700) [WM] *Florida*	USAF 509th BW, Whiteman AFB, MO
	21066	Northrop B-2 Spirit (82-1066) [WM] *America*	USAF 509th BW, Whiteman AFB, MO
	21067	Northrop B-2 Spirit (82-1067) [WM] *Arizona*	USAF 509th BW, Whiteman AFB, MO
	21068	Northrop B-2 Spirit (82-1068) [WM] *New York*	USAF 509th BW, Whiteman AFB, MO
	21069	Northrop B-2 Spirit (82-1069) [WM] *Indiana*	USAF 509th BW, Whiteman AFB, MO
	21070	Northrop B-2 Spirit (82-1070) [WM] *Ohio*	USAF 509th BW, Whiteman AFB, MO
	21071	Northrop B-2 Spirit (82-1071) [WM] *Mississippi*	USAF 509th BW, Whiteman AFB, MO
	31085	Northrop B-2 Spirit (93-1085) [ED] *Oklahoma*	USAF 419th FLTS/412th TW, Edwards AFB,CA
	31086	Northrop B-2 Spirit (93-1086) [WM] *Kitty Hawk*	USAF 509th BW, Whiteman AFB, MO
	31087	Northrop B-2 Spirit (93-1087) [WM] *Pennsylvania*	USAF 509th BW, Whiteman AFB, MO
	31088	Northrop B-2 Spirit (93-1088) [WM] *Louisiana*	USAF 509th BW, Whiteman AFB, MO
	80328	Northrop B-2 Spirit (88-0328) [WM] *Texas*	USAF 509th BW, Whiteman AFB, MO
	80329	Northrop B-2 Spirit (88-0329) [WM] *Missouri*	USAF 509th BW, Whiteman AFB, MO
	80330	Northrop B-2 Spirit (88-0330) [WM] *California*	USAF 509th BW, Whiteman AFB, MO
	80331	Northrop B-2 Spirit (88-0331) [WM] *South Carolina*	USAF 509th BW, Whiteman AFB, MO
	80332	Northrop B-2 Spirit (88-0332) [WM] *Washington*	USAF 509th BW, Whiteman AFB, MO
	90128	Northrop B-2 Spirit (89-0128) [WM] *Nebraska*	USAF 509th BW, Whiteman AFB, MO
	90129	Northrop B-2 Spirit (89-0129) [WM] *Georgia*	USAF 509th BW, Whiteman AFB, MO

Lockheed U-2

Notes	Serial	Type (code/other identity)	Owner/operator, location or fate
	68-10329	Lockheed U-2S [BB]	USAF 9th RW, Beale AFB, CA
	68-10331	Lockheed U-2S [BB]	USAF 9th RW, Beale AFB, CA
	68-10336	Lockheed U-2S [BB]	USAF 9th RW, Beale AFB, CA
	68-10337	Lockheed U-2S [BB] [9 OG]	USAF 9th RW, Beale AFB, CA
	80-1064	Lockheed TU-2S [BB]	USAF 9th RW, Beale AFB, CA
	80-1065	Lockheed TU-2S [BB]	USAF 9th RW, Beale AFB, CA
	80-1066	Lockheed U-2S [BB]	USAF 9th RW, Beale AFB, CA
	80-1067	Lockheed U-2S [BB]	USAF 9th RW, Beale AFB, CA
	80-1069	Lockheed U-2S [BB]	USAF 9th RW, Beale AFB, CA
	80-1070	Lockheed U-2S [BB]	USAF 9th RW, Beale AFB, CA
	80-1071	Lockheed U-2S [BB]	USAF 9th RW, Beale AFB, CA
	80-1073	Lockheed U-2S [BB]	USAF 9th RW, Beale AFB, CA
	80-1074	Lockheed U-2S [BB]	USAF 9th RW, Beale AFB, CA
	80-1076	Lockheed U-2S [BB]	USAF 9th RW, Beale AFB, CA
	80-1077	Lockheed U-2S [BB]	USAF 9th RW, Beale AFB, CA
	80-1078	Lockheed TU-2S [BB]	USAF 9th RW, Beale AFB, CA
	80-1079	Lockheed U-2S [BB]	USAF 9th RW, Beale AFB, CA
	80-1080	Lockheed U-2S [BB]	USAF 9th RW, Beale AFB, CA
	80-1081	Lockheed U-2S [BB]	USAF 9th RW, Beale AFB, CA
	80-1083	Lockheed U-2S [BB]	USAF 9th RW, Beale AFB, CA
	80-1084	Lockheed U-2S [BB]	USAF 9th RW, Beale AFB, CA
	80-1085	Lockheed U-2S [BB]	USAF 9th RW, Beale AFB, CA
	80-1086	Lockheed U-2S [BB]	USAF 9th RW, Beale AFB, CA
	80-1087	Lockheed U-2S [BB]	USAF 9th RW, Beale AFB, CA
	80-1089	Lockheed U-2S [BB]	USAF 9th RW, Beale AFB, CA
	80-1090	Lockheed U-2S [BB]	USAF 9th RW, Beale AFB, CA
	80-1091	Lockheed TU-2S [BB]	USAF 9th RW, Beale AFB, CA
	80-1092	Lockheed U-2S [BB]	USAF 9th RW, Beale AFB, CA
	80-1093	Lockheed U-2S [BB]	USAF 9th RW, Beale AFB, CA
	80-1094	Lockheed U-2S [BB]	USAF 9th RW, Beale AFB, CA

Serial	Type (code/other identity)	Owner/operator, location or fate	Notes
80-1096	Lockheed U-2S [BB]	USAF 9th RW, Beale AFB, CA	
80-1099	Lockheed U-2S [BB]	USAF 9th RW, Beale AFB, CA	

Boeing E-3 Sentry

00137	Boeing E-3B(mod) Sentry (80-0137) [OK] w	USAF 960th AACS/552nd ACW, Tinker AFB, OK	
00138	Boeing E-3G Sentry (80-0138) [OK] r	USAF 964th AACS/552nd ACW, Tinker AFB, OK	
00139	Boeing E-3G Sentry (80-0139) [OK] w	USAF 960th AACS/552nd ACW, Tinker AFB, OK	
10004	Boeing E-3C Sentry (81-0004) [AK] gn	USAF 962nd AACS/3rd Wg, Elmendorf, AK	
10005	Boeing E-3G Sentry (81-0005) [OK] w	USAF 963rd ACCS/552nd ACW, Tinker AFB, OK	
11407	Boeing E-3B Sentry (71-1407) [ZZ] or	USAF 961st AACS/18th Wg, Kadena AB, Japan	
11408	Boeing E-3B Sentry (71-1408) [ZZ] or	USAF 961st AACS/18th Wg, Kadena AB, Japan	
20006	Boeing E-3G Sentry (82-0006) [OK] r	USAF 964th AACS/552nd ACW, Tinker AFB, OK	
20007	Boeing E-3G Sentry (82-0007) [OK]	USAF 960th AACS/552nd ACW, Tinker AFB, OK	
30009	Boeing E-3C Sentry (83-0009) [OK]	USAF 960th AACS/552nd ACW, Tinker AFB, OK	
31675	Boeing E-3G Sentry (73-1675) [OK] r	USAF 964th AACS/552nd ACW, Tinker AFB, OK	
50556	Boeing E-3B Sentry (75-0556) [OK] w	USAF 960th AACS/552nd ACW, Tinker AFB, OK	
50557	Boeing E-3B Sentry (75-0557) [OK] r	USAF 964th AACS/552nd ACW, Tinker AFB, OK	
50558	Boeing E-3G Sentry (75-0558) [OK] r	USAF 964th AACS/552nd ACW, Tinker AFB, OK	
50559	Boeing E-3G Sentry (75-0559) [ZZ] or	USAF 961st AACS/18th Wg, Kadena AB, Japan	
50560	Boeing E-3B Sentry (75-0560) [AK] gn	USAF 962nd AACS/3rd Wg, Elmendorf, AK	
61604	Boeing E-3G Sentry (76-1604) [OK] w	USAF 963rd ACCS/552nd ACW, Tinker AFB, OK	
61605	Boeing E-3G Sentry (76-1605) [OK] r/w	USAF 960th AACS/552nd ACW, Tinker AFB, OK	
61606	Boeing E-3B Sentry (76-1606) [OK] w	USAF 960th AACS/552nd ACW, Tinker AFB, OK	
61607	Boeing E-3G Sentry (76-1607) [OK] w	USAF 960th AACS/552nd ACW, Tinker AFB, OK	
70351	Boeing E-3G Sentry (77-0351) [OK] w	USAF 960th AACS/552nd ACW, Tinker AFB, OK	
70352	Boeing E-3B Sentry (77-0352) [OK] w	USAF 960th AACS/552nd ACW, Tinker AFB, OK	
70353	Boeing E-3G Sentry (77-0353) [OK] r	USAF 964th AACS/552nd ACW, Tinker AFB, OK	
70355	Boeing E-3B Sentry (77-0355) [OK] r	USAF 964th AACS/552nd ACW, Tinker AFB, OK	
70356	Boeing E-3G Sentry (77-0356) [OK] w	USAF 960th AACS/552nd ACW, Tinker AFB, OK	
80576	Boeing E-3G Sentry (78-0576) [OK] r	USAF 964th AACS/552nd ACW, Tinker AFB, OK	
80577	Boeing E-3G Sentry (78-0577) [OK] r	USAF 964th AACS/552nd ACW, Tinker AFB, OK	
80578	Boeing E-3G Sentry (78-0578) [OK] w	USAF 960th AACS/552nd ACW, Tinker AFB, OK	
90001	Boeing E-3G Sentry (79-0001) [OK] w	USAF 960th AACS/552nd ACW, Tinker AFB, OK	
90002	Boeing E-3B Sentry (79-0002) [OK] w	USAF 960th AACS/552nd ACW, Tinker AFB, OK	
90003	Boeing E-3B Sentry (79-0003) [OK] m	USAF 552nd ACW, Tinker AFB, OK	

Boeing E-4B

31676	Boeing E-4B (73-1676)	USAF 1st ACCS/595th CACG, Offutt AFB, NE	
31677	Boeing E-4B (73-1677)	USAF 1st ACCS/595th CACG, Offutt AFB, NE	
40787	Boeing E-4B (74-0787)	USAF 1st ACCS/595th CACG, Offutt AFB, NE	
50125	Boeing E-4B (75-0125)	USAF 1st ACCS/595th CACG, Offutt AFB, NE	

Lockheed C-5M Super Galaxy

31285	Lockheed C-5M Super Galaxy (83-1285) bl/y	USAF 9th AS/436th AW, Dover AFB, DE	
40060	Lockheed C-5M Super Galaxy (84-0060) w/bk	USAF 22nd AS/60th AMW, Travis AFB, CA	
40061	Lockheed C-5M Super Galaxy (84-0061) bl/y	USAF 9th AS/436th AW, Dover AFB, DE	
40062	Lockheed C-5M Super Galaxy (84-0062) w/bk	USAF 22nd AS/60th AMW, Travis AFB, CA	
50001	Lockheed C-5M Super Galaxy (85-0001) bl/y	USAF 9th AS/436th AW, Dover AFB, DE	
50002	Lockheed C-5M Super Galaxy (85-0002) bl/y	USAF 9th AS/436th AW, Dover AFB, DE	
50003	Lockheed C-5M Super Galaxy (85-0003) bl/y	USAF 9th AS/436th AW, Dover AFB, DE	
50004	Lockheed C-5M Super Galaxy (85-0004) bl/y	USAF 9th AS/436th AW, Dover AFB, DE	
50005	Lockheed C-5M Super Galaxy (85-0005) bl/y	USAF 9th AS/436th AW, Dover AFB, DE	
50006	Lockheed C-5M Super Galaxy (85-0006)	USAF 68th AS/433rd AW Kelly AFB, TX	
50007	Lockheed C-5M Super Galaxy (85-0007) bl/y	USAF 9th AS/436th AW, Dover AFB, DE	
50008	Lockheed C-5M Super Galaxy (85-0008) bl/y	USAF 9th AS/436th AW, Dover AFB, DE	
50009	Lockheed C-5M Super Galaxy (85-0009)	USAF 68th AS/433rd AW Kelly AFB, TX	
50010	Lockheed C-5M Super Galaxy (85-0010) w/bk	USAF 22nd AS/60th AMW, Travis AFB, CA	
60011	Lockheed C-5M Super Galaxy (86-0011) w/bk	USAF 22nd AS/60th AMW, Travis AFB, CA	
60012	Lockheed C-5M Super Galaxy (86-0012) bl/r	USAF 337th AS/439th AW, Westover ARB, MA	
60013	Lockheed C-5M Super Galaxy (86-0013) bl/y	USAF 9th AS/436th AW, Dover AFB, DE	
60014	Lockheed C-5M Super Galaxy (86-0014) bl/r	USAF 337th AS/439th AW, Westover ARB, MA	
60015	Lockheed C-5M Super Galaxy (86-0015) w/bk	USAF 22nd AS/60th AMW, Travis AFB, CA	

Notes	Serial	Type (code/other identity)	Owner/operator, location or fate
	60016	Lockheed C-5M Super Galaxy (86-0016) w/bk	USAF 22nd AS/60th AMW, Travis AFB, CA
	60017	Lockheed C-5M Super Galaxy (86-0017) bl/y	USAF 9th AS/436th AW, Dover AFB, DE
	60018	Lockheed C-5M Super Galaxy (86-0018) bl/r	USAF 337th AS/439th AW, Westover ARB, MA
	60019	Lockheed C-5M Super Galaxy (86-0019)	USAF 68th AS/433rd AW Kelly AFB, TX
	60020	Lockheed C-5M Super Galaxy (86-0020) bl/y	USAF 9th AS/436th AW, Dover AFB, DE
	60021	Lockheed C-5M Super Galaxy (86-0021)	USAF 68th AS/433rd AW Kelly AFB, TX
	60022	Lockheed C-5M Super Galaxy (86-0022) w/bk	USAF 22nd AS/60th AMW, Travis AFB, CA
	60023	Lockheed C-5M Super Galaxy (86-0023)	USAF 68th AS/433rd AW Kelly AFB, TX
	60024	Lockheed C-5M Super Galaxy (86-0024) w/bk	USAF 22nd AS/60th AMW, Travis AFB, CA
	60025	Lockheed C-5M Super Galaxy (86-0025) bl/y	USAF 9th AS/436th AW, Dover AFB, DE
	60026	Lockheed C-5M Super Galaxy (86-0026) w/bk	USAF 22nd AS/60th AMW, Travis AFB, CA
	70027	Lockheed C-5M Super Galaxy (87-0027)	USAF 68th AS/433rd AW Kelly AFB, TX
	70028	Lockheed C-5M Super Galaxy (87-0028) w/bk	USAF 22nd AS/60th AMW, Travis AFB, CA
	70029	Lockheed C-5M Super Galaxy (87-0029) w/bk	USAF 22nd AS/60th AMW, Travis AFB, CA
	70030	Lockheed C-5M Super Galaxy (87-0030) w/bk	USAF 22nd AS/60th AMW, Travis AFB, CA
	70031	Lockheed C-5M Super Galaxy (87-0031) bl/r	USAF 337th AS/439th AW, Westover ARB, MA
	70032	Lockheed C-5M Super Galaxy (87-0032) w/bk	USAF 22nd AS/60th AMW, Travis AFB, CA
	70033	Lockheed C-5M Super Galaxy (87-0033)	USAF 68th AS/433rd AW Kelly AFB, TX
	70034	Lockheed C-5M Super Galaxy (87-0034) w/bk	USAF 22nd AS/60th AMW, Travis AFB, CA
	70035	Lockheed C-5M Super Galaxy (87-0035) bl/y	USAF 9th AS/436th AW, Dover AFB, DE
	70036	Lockheed C-5M Super Galaxy (87-0036) bl/y	USAF 9th AS/436th AW, Dover AFB, DE
	70037	Lockheed C-5M Super Galaxy (87-0037) bl/r	USAF 337th AS/439th AW, Westover ARB, MA
	70038	Lockheed C-5M Super Galaxy (87-0038)	USAF 68th AS/433rd AW Kelly AFB, TX
	70039	Lockheed C-5M Super Galaxy (87-0039) bl/r	USAF 337th AS/439th AW, Westover ARB, MA
	70040	Lockheed C-5M Super Galaxy (87-0040) bl/y	USAF 9th AS/436th AW, Dover AFB, DE
	70041	Lockheed C-5M Super Galaxy (87-0041) bl/r	USAF 337th AS/439th AW, Westover ARB, MA
	70042	Lockheed C-5M Super Galaxy (87-0042) w/bk	USAF 22nd AS/60th AMW, Travis AFB, CA
	70043	Lockheed C-5M Super Galaxy (87-0043) bl/r	USAF 337th AS/439th AW, Westover ARB, MA
	70044	Lockheed C-5M Super Galaxy (87-0044) w/bk	USAF 22nd AS/60th AMW, Travis AFB, CA
	70045	Lockheed C-5M Super Galaxy (87-0045) bl/y	USAF 9th AS/436th AW, Dover AFB, DE
	80213	Lockheed C-5M Super Galaxy (68-0213) w/bk	USAF 22nd AS/60th AMW, Travis AFB, CA
	80216	Lockheed C-5M Super Galaxy (68-0216) w/bk	USAF 22nd AS/60th AMW, Travis AFB, CA
	90024	Lockheed C-5M Super Galaxy (69-0024) bl/y	USAF 9th AS/436th AW, Dover AFB, DE

Boeing E-8C J-STARS

	02000	Boeing E-8C J-STARS (00-2000) [GA] r/bk	USAF 116th ACW GA ANG, Robins AFB
	12005	Boeing E-8C J-STARS (01-2005) [GA] r/bk	USAF 116th ACW GA ANG, Robins AFB
	29111	Boeing E-8C J-STARS (02-9111) [GA] r/bk	USAF 116th ACW GA ANG, Robins AFB
	23289	Boeing E-8C J-STARS (92-3289) [GA] r/bk	USAF 116th ACW GA ANG, Robins AFB
	23290	Boeing E-8C J-STARS (92-3290) [GA] r/bk	USAF 116th ACW GA ANG, Robins AFB
	31097	Boeing E-8C J-STARS (93-1097) [GA] r/bk	USAF 116th ACW GA ANG, Robins AFB
	40284	Boeing E-8C J-STARS (94-0284) [GA] r/bk	USAF 116th ACW GA ANG, Robins AFB
	40285	Boeing E-8C J-STARS (94-0285) [GA] r/bk	USAF 116th ACW GA ANG, Robins AFB
	50121	Boeing E-8C J-STARS (95-0121) [GA] r/bk	USAF 116th ACW GA ANG, Robins AFB
	50122	Boeing E-8C J-STARS (95-0122) [GA] r/bk	USAF 116th ACW GA ANG, Robins AFB
	60042	Boeing E-8C J-STARS (96-0042) [GA] r/bk	USAF 116th ACW GA ANG, Robins AFB
	60043	Boeing E-8C J-STARS (96-0043) [GA] r/bk	USAF 116th ACW GA ANG, Robins AFB
	70100	Boeing E-8C J-STARS (97-0100) [GA] r/bk	USAF 116th ACW GA ANG, Robins AFB
	70200	Boeing E-8C J-STARS (97-0200) [GA] r/bk	USAF 116th ACW GA ANG, Robins AFB
	70201	Boeing E-8C J-STARS (97-0201) [GA] r/bk	USAF 116th ACW GA ANG, Robins AFB
	90006	Boeing E-8C J-STARS (99-0006) [GA] r/bk	USAF 116th ACW GA ANG, Robins AFB

McDonnell Douglas KC-10A Extender

	20191	McDonnell Douglas KC-10A Extender (82-0191) w/bk	USAF 60th AMW, Travis AFB, CA
	20192	McDonnell Douglas KC-10A Extender (82-0192) w/bk	USAF 60th AMW, Travis AFB, CA
	20193	McDonnell Douglas KC-10A Extender (82-0193) w/bk	USAF 60th AMW, Travis AFB, CA
	30075	McDonnell Douglas KC-10A Extender (83-0075) w/bk	USAF 60th AMW, Travis AFB, CA
	30076	McDonnell Douglas KC-10A Extender (83-0076) w/bk	USAF 60th AMW, Travis AFB, CA
	30077	McDonnell Douglas KC-10A Extender (83-0077) w/bk	USAF 60th AMW, Travis AFB, CA
	30078	McDonnell Douglas KC-10A Extender (83-0078) w/bk	USAF 60th AMW, Travis AFB, CA
	30079	McDonnell Douglas KC-10A Extender (83-0079) bl	USAF 305th AMW, McGuire AFB, NJ
	30080	McDonnell Douglas KC-10A Extender (83-0080) w/bk	USAF 60th AMW, Travis AFB, CA

Serial	Type (code/other identity)	Owner/operator, location or fate	Notes
30081	McDonnell Douglas KC-10A Extender (83-0081) *bl*	USAF 305th AMW, McGuire AFB, NJ	
30082	McDonnell Douglas KC-10A Extender (83-0082) *bl*	USAF 305th AMW, McGuire AFB, NJ	
40185	McDonnell Douglas KC-10A Extender (84-0185) *w/bk*	USAF 60th AMW, Travis AFB, CA	
40186	McDonnell Douglas KC-10A Extender (84-0186) *bl*	USAF 305th AMW, McGuire AFB, NJ	
40187	McDonnell Douglas KC-10A Extender (84-0187) *w/bk*	USAF 60th AMW, Travis AFB, CA	
40188	McDonnell Douglas KC-10A Extender (84-0188) *bl*	USAF 305th AMW, McGuire AFB, NJ	
40189	McDonnell Douglas KC-10A Extender (84-0189) *bl*	USAF 305th AMW, McGuire AFB, NJ	
40190	McDonnell Douglas KC-10A Extender (84-0190) *bl*	USAF 305th AMW, McGuire AFB, NJ	
40191	McDonnell Douglas KC-10A Extender (84-0191) *w/bk*	USAF 60th AMW, Travis AFB, CA	
40192	McDonnell Douglas KC-10A Extender (84-0192) *bl*	USAF 305th AMW, McGuire AFB, NJ	
50027	McDonnell Douglas KC-10A Extender (85-0027) *bl*	USAF 305th AMW, McGuire AFB, NJ	
50028	McDonnell Douglas KC-10A Extender (85-0028) *bl*	USAF 305th AMW, McGuire AFB, NJ	
50029	McDonnell Douglas KC-10A Extender (85-0029) *w/bk*	USAF 60th AMW, Travis AFB, CA	
50030	McDonnell Douglas KC-10A Extender (85-0030) *bl*	USAF 305th AMW, McGuire AFB, NJ	
50031	McDonnell Douglas KC-10A Extender (85-0031) *bl*	USAF 305th AMW, McGuire AFB, NJ	
50032	McDonnell Douglas KC-10A Extender (85-0032) *bl*	USAF 305th AMW, McGuire AFB, NJ	
50033	McDonnell Douglas KC-10A Extender (85-0033) *w/bk*	USAF 60th AMW, Travis AFB, CA	
50034	McDonnell Douglas KC-10A Extender (85-0034) *bl*	USAF 305th AMW, McGuire AFB, NJ	
60027	McDonnell Douglas KC-10A Extender (86-0027) *bl*	USAF 305th AMW, McGuire AFB, NJ	
60028	McDonnell Douglas KC-10A Extender (86-0028) *bl*	USAF 305th AMW, McGuire AFB, NJ	
60029	McDonnell Douglas KC-10A Extender (86-0029) *w/bk*	USAF 60th AMW, Travis AFB, CA	
60030	McDonnell Douglas KC-10A Extender (86-0030) *bl*	USAF 305th AMW, McGuire AFB, NJ	
60031	McDonnell Douglas KC-10A Extender (86-0031) *w/bk*	USAF 60th AMW, Travis AFB, CA	
60032	McDonnell Douglas KC-10A Extender (86-0032) *bl*	USAF 305th AMW, McGuire AFB, NJ	
60033	McDonnell Douglas KC-10A Extender (86-0033) *w/bk*	USAF 60th AMW, Travis AFB, CA	
60034	McDonnell Douglas KC-10A Extender (86-0034) *w/bk*	USAF 60th AMW, Travis AFB, CA	
60035	McDonnell Douglas KC-10A Extender (86-0035) *bl*	USAF 305th AMW, McGuire AFB, NJ	
60036	McDonnell Douglas KC-10A Extender (86-0036) *bl*	USAF 305th AMW, McGuire AFB, NJ	
60037	McDonnell Douglas KC-10A Extender (86-0037) *w/bk*	USAF 60th AMW, Travis AFB, CA	
60038	McDonnell Douglas KC-10A Extender (86-0038) *w/bk*	USAF 60th AMW, Travis AFB, CA	
70117	McDonnell Douglas KC-10A Extender (87-0117) *w/bk*	USAF 60th AMW, Travis AFB, CA	
70118	McDonnell Douglas KC-10A Extender (87-0118) *bl*	USAF 305th AMW, McGuire AFB, NJ	
70119	McDonnell Douglas KC-10A Extender (87-0119) *w/bk*	USAF 60th AMW, Travis AFB, CA	
70120	McDonnell Douglas KC-10A Extender (87-0120) *bl*	USAF 305th AMW, McGuire AFB, NJ	
70121	McDonnell Douglas KC-10A Extender (87-0121) *bl*	USAF 305th AMW, McGuire AFB, NJ	
70122	McDonnell Douglas KC-10A Extender (87-0122) *bl*	USAF 305th AMW, McGuire AFB, NJ	
70123	McDonnell Douglas KC-10A Extender (87-0123) *w/bk*	USAF 60th AMW, Travis AFB, CA	
70124	McDonnell Douglas KC-10A Extender (87-0124) *bl*	USAF 305th AMW, McGuire AFB, NJ	
90433	McDonnell Douglas KC-10A Extender (79-0433) *bl*	USAF 305th AMW, McGuire AFB, NJ	
90434	McDonnell Douglas KC-10A Extender (79-0434) *bl*	USAF 305th AMW, McGuire AFB, NJ	
91710	McDonnell Douglas KC-10A Extender (79-1710) *bl*	USAF 305th AMW, McGuire AFB, NJ	
91711	McDonnell Douglas KC-10A Extender (79-1711) *bl*	USAF 305th AMW, McGuire AFB, NJ	
91712	McDonnell Douglas KC-10A Extender (79-1712) *bl*	USAF 305th AMW, McGuire AFB, NJ	
91713	McDonnell Douglas KC-10A Extender (79-1713) *w/bk*	USAF 60th AMW, Travis AFB, CA	
91946	McDonnell Douglas KC-10A Extender (79-1946) *w/bk*	USAF 60th AMW, Travis AFB, CA	
91947	McDonnell Douglas KC-10A Extender (79-1947) *bl*	USAF 305th AMW, McGuire AFB, NJ	
91948	McDonnell Douglas KC-10A Extender (79-1948) *w/bk*	USAF 60th AMW, Travis AFB, CA	
91949	McDonnell Douglas KC-10A Extender (79-1949) *bl*	USAF 305th AMW, McGuire AFB, NJ	
91950	McDonnell Douglas KC-10A Extender (79-1950) *w/bk*	USAF 60th AMW, Travis AFB, CA	
91951	McDonnell Douglas KC-10A Extender (79-1951) *w/bk*	USAF 60th AMW, Travis AFB, CA	

Bombardier E-11A Global Express

Serial	Type (code/other identity)	Owner/operator, location or fate	Notes
19001	Bombardier E-11A Global Express (11-9001)	USAF 430th EECS/653rd ELSW, Hanscom MA	
19355	Bombardier E-11A Global Express (11-9355)	USAF 430th EECS/653rd ELSW, Hanscom MA	
19358	Bombardier E-11A Global Express (11-9358)	USAF 430th EECS/653rd ELSW, Hanscom MA	
29506	Bombardier E-11A Global Express (12-9506)	USAF 430th EECS/653rd ELSW, Hanscom MA	

Boeing C-17A Globemaster III

Serial	Type (code/other identity)	Owner/operator, location or fate	Notes
00171	Boeing C-17A Globemaster III (00-0171) [AK] *bl/y*	USAF 144th AS/176th Wg, Elmendorf AFB, AK ANG	
00172	Boeing C-17A Globemaster III (00-0172) *y/bl*	USAF 437th AW, Charleston AFB, SC	
00174	Boeing C-17A Globemaster III (00-0174) [AK] *bl/y*	USAF 144th AS/176th Wg, Elmendorf AFB, AK ANG	
00175	Boeing C-17A Globemaster III (00-0175) *bl*	USAF 6th AS/305th AMW, McGuire AFB, NJ	

Notes	Serial	Type (code/other identity)	Owner/operator, location or fate
	00176	Boeing C-17A Globemaster III (00-0176) r/w	USAF 155th AS/164th AW, Memphis, TN ANG
	00177	Boeing C-17A Globemaster III (00-0177) bl	USAF 137th AS/105th AW, Stewart AFB, NY ANG
	00178	Boeing C-17A Globemaster III (00-0178) r/w	USAF 89th AS/445th AW AFRC, Wright-Patterson AFB, OH
	00179	Boeing C-17A Globemaster III (00-0179) r/y	USAF 58th AS/97th AMW, Altus AFB, OK
	00180	Boeing C-17A Globemaster III (00-0180) gn	USAF 62nd AW, McChord AFB, WA
	00181	Boeing C-17A Globemaster III (00-0181) r/w	USAF 167th AS/167th AW, Martinsburg, WV ANG
	00182	Boeing C-17A Globemaster III (00-0182) r/w	USAF 167th AS/167th AW, Martinsburg, WV ANG
	00183	Boeing C-17A Globemaster III (00-0183) bk	USAF 156th AS/145th AW, Charlotte-Douglas, NC ANG
	00184	Boeing C-17A Globemaster III (00-0184) gn	USAF 62nd AW, McChord AFB, WA
	00185	Boeing C-17A Globemaster III (00-0185) [AK] bl/y	USAF 144th AS/176th Wg, Elmendorf AFB, AK ANG
	00213	Boeing C-17A Globemaster III (10-0213) y/bl	USAF 437th AW, Charleston AFB, SC
	00214	Boeing C-17A Globemaster III (10-0214) y/bl	USAF 437th AW, Charleston AFB, SC
	00215	Boeing C-17A Globemaster III (10-0215) y/bl	USAF 437th AW, Charleston AFB, SC
	00216	Boeing C-17A Globemaster III (10-0216) gn	USAF 62nd AW, McChord AFB, WA
	00217	Boeing C-17A Globemaster III (10-0217) gn	USAF 62nd AW, McChord AFB, WA
	00218	Boeing C-17A Globemaster III (10-0218) gn	USAF 62nd AW, McChord AFB, WA
	00219	Boeing C-17A Globemaster III (10-0219) gn	USAF 62nd AW, McChord AFB, WA
	00220	Boeing C-17A Globemaster III (10-0220) gn	USAF 62nd AW, McChord AFB, WA
	00221	Boeing C-17A Globemaster III (10-0221) y/bl	USAF 437th AW, Charleston AFB, SC
	00222	Boeing C-17A Globemaster III (10-0222) y/bl	USAF 437th AW, Charleston AFB, SC
	00223	Boeing C-17A Globemaster III (10-0223) y/bl	USAF 437th AW, Charleston AFB, SC
	00532	Boeing C-17A Globemaster III (90-0532) bk	USAF 156th AS/145th AW, Charlotte-Douglas, NC ANG
	00533	Boeing C-17A Globemaster III (90-0533) [HH] r/y	USAF 535th AS/15th Wg, Hickam AFB, HI
	00534	Boeing C-17A Globemaster III (90-0534) y/bl	USAF 437th AW, Charleston AFB, SC
	00535	Boeing C-17A Globemaster III (90-0535) r/w	USAF 89th AS/445th AW AFRC, Wright-Patterson AFB, OH
	10186	Boeing C-17A Globemaster III (01-0186) bl/y	USAF 3rd AS/436th AW, Dover AFB, DE
	10187	Boeing C-17A Globemaster III (01-0187) gn	USAF 62nd AW, McChord AFB, WA
	10188	Boeing C-17A Globemaster III (01-0188) bl	USAF 137th AS/105th AW, Stewart AFB, NY ANG
	10189	Boeing C-17A Globemaster III (01-0189) r/w	USAF 155th AS/164th AW, Memphis, TN ANG
	10190	Boeing C-17A Globemaster III (01-0190) r/y	USAF 58th AS/97th AMW, Altus AFB, OK
	10191	Boeing C-17A Globemaster III (01-0191) bl/y	USAF 3rd AS/436th AW, Dover AFB, DE
	10192	Boeing C-17A Globemaster III (01-0192) bl	USAF 137th AS/105th AW, Stewart AFB, NY ANG
	10193	Boeing C-17A Globemaster III (01-0193) y/bl	USAF 437th AW, Charleston AFB, SC
	10194	Boeing C-17A Globemaster III (01-0194) r/w	USAF 89th AS/445th AW AFRC, Wright-Patterson AFB, OH
	10195	Boeing C-17A Globemaster III (01-0195) r/y	USAF 58th AS/97th AMW, Altus AFB, OK
	10196	Boeing C-17A Globemaster III (01-0196) r/w	USAF 167th AS/167th AW, Martinsburg, WV ANG
	10197	Boeing C-17A Globemaster III (01-0197) bk	USAF 156th AS/145th AW, Charlotte-Douglas, NC ANG
	21098	Boeing C-17A Globemaster III (02-1098) bl	USAF 6th AS/305th AMW, McGuire AFB, NJ
	21099	Boeing C-17A Globemaster III (02-1099) bk/y	USAF 758th AS/911th AMW AFRC, Greater Pittsburgh, PA
	21100	Boeing C-17A Globemaster III (02-1100) r/w	USAF 155th AS/164th AW, Memphis, TN ANG
	21101	Boeing C-17A Globemaster III (02-1101) bk/y	USAF 758th AS/911th AMW AFRC, Greater Pittsburgh, PA
	21102	Boeing C-17A Globemaster III (02-1102) r/y	USAF 58th AS/97th AMW, Altus AFB, OK
	21103	Boeing C-17A Globemaster III (02-1103) r/y	USAF 58th AS/97th AMW, Altus AFB, OK
	21104	Boeing C-17A Globemaster III (02-1104) r/y [97 OG]	USAF 58th AS/97th AMW, Altus AFB, OK
	21105	Boeing C-17A Globemaster III (02-1105) gn	USAF 62nd AW, McChord AFB, WA
	21106	Boeing C-17A Globemaster III (02-1106) gn	USAF 62nd AW, McChord AFB, WA
	21107	Boeing C-17A Globemaster III (02-1107) gn	USAF 62nd AW, McChord AFB, WA
	21108	Boeing C-17A Globemaster III (02-1108) gn	USAF 62nd AW, McChord AFB, WA
	21109	Boeing C-17A Globemaster III (02-1109) gn	USAF 62nd AW, McChord AFB, WA
	21110	Boeing C-17A Globemaster III (02-1110) r/w	USAF 155th AS/164th AW, Memphis, TN ANG
	21111	Boeing C-17A Globemaster III (02-1111) gn	USAF 62nd AW, McChord AFB, WA
	21112	Boeing C-17A Globemaster III (02-1112) bl/gd	USAF 183rd AS/172nd AW, Jackson Int'l Airport, MS ANG
	23291	Boeing C-17A Globemaster III (92-3291) r/w	USAF 155th AS/164th AW, Memphis, TN ANG

Serial	Type (code/other identity)	Owner/operator, location or fate	Notes
23292	Boeing C-17A Globemaster III (92-3292) *y/bl*	USAF 437th AW, Charleston AFB, SC	
23293	Boeing C-17A Globemaster III (92-3293) *y/bl*	USAF 437th AW, Charleston AFB, SC	
23294	Boeing C-17A Globemaster III (92-3294) *gn*	USAF 62nd AW, McChord AFB, WA	
30599	Boeing C-17A Globemaster III (93-0599) [AK] *bl/y*	USAF 144th AS/176th Wg, Elmendorf AFB, AK ANG	
30600	Boeing C-17A Globemaster III (93-0600) *r/w*	USAF 155th AS/164th AW, Memphis, TN ANG	
30601	Boeing C-17A Globemaster III (93-0601) *bk/y*	USAF 758th AS/911th AMW AFRC, Greater Pittsburgh, PA	
30602	Boeing C-17A Globemaster III (93-0602) $	USAF 156th AS/145th AW, Charlotte-Douglas, NC ANG	
30603	Boeing C-17A Globemaster III (93-0603) *r/w*	USAF 89th AS/445th AW AFRC, Wright-Patterson AFB, OH	
30604	Boeing C-17A Globemaster III (93-0604) *r/w*	USAF 89th AS/445th AW AFRC, Wright-Patterson AFB, OH	
33113	Boeing C-17A Globemaster III (03-3113) *bl/gd*	USAF 183rd AS/172nd AW, Jackson Int'l Airport, MS ANG	
33114	Boeing C-17A Globemaster III (03-3114) *bl/gd*	USAF 183rd AS/172nd AW, Jackson Int'l Airport, MS ANG	
33115	Boeing C-17A Globemaster III (03-3115) *bl/gd*	USAF 183rd AS/172nd AW, Jackson Int'l Airport, MS ANG	
33116	Boeing C-17A Globemaster III (03-3116) *bl/gd*	USAF 183rd AS/172nd AW, Jackson Int'l Airport, MS ANG	
33117	Boeing C-17A Globemaster III (03-3117) *bl/gd*	USAF 183rd AS/172nd AW, Jackson Int'l Airport, MS ANG	
33118	Boeing C-17A Globemaster III (03-3118) *bl/gd*	USAF 183rd AS/172nd AW, Jackson Int'l Airport, MS ANG	
33119	Boeing C-17A Globemaster III (03-3119) *bl/gd*	USAF 183rd AS/172nd AW, Jackson Int'l Airport, MS ANG	
33120	Boeing C-17A Globemaster III (03-3120) *gn*	USAF 62nd AW, McChord AFB, WA	
33121	Boeing C-17A Globemaster III (03-3121) [ED]	USAF 418th FLTS/412th TW, Edwards AFB, CA	
33122	Boeing C-17A Globemaster III (03-3122) *r/y*	USAF 58th AS/97th AMW, Altus AFB, OK	
33123	Boeing C-17A Globemaster III (03-3123) *r/w*	USAF 167th AS/167th AW, Martinsburg, WV ANG	
33124	Boeing C-17A Globemaster III (03-3124) *y/bl*	USAF 437th AW, Charleston AFB, SC	
33125	Boeing C-17A Globemaster III (03-3125) *bl*	USAF 6th AS/305th AMW, McGuire AFB, NJ	
33126	Boeing C-17A Globemaster III (03-3126) *bl*	USAF 6th AS/305th AMW, McGuire AFB, NJ	
33127	Boeing C-17A Globemaster III (03-3127) *gn*	USAF 62nd AW, McChord AFB, WA	
40065	Boeing C-17A Globemaster III (94-0065) *r/w*	USAF 155th AS/164th AW, Memphis, TN ANG	
40066	Boeing C-17A Globemaster III (94-0066) *gn*	USAF 62nd AW, McChord AFB, WA	
40067	Boeing C-17A Globemaster III (94-0067) *bl*	USAF 137th AS/105th AW, Stewart AFB, NY ANG	
40068	Boeing C-17A Globemaster III (94-0068) *or/y*	USAF 729th AS/452nd AMW AFRC, March ARB, CA	
40069	Boeing C-17A Globemaster III (94-0069) *r/w*	USAF 167th AS/167th AW, Martinsburg, WV ANG	
40070	Boeing C-17A Globemaster III (94-0070) *r/w*	USAF 167th AS/167th AW, Martinsburg, WV ANG	
44128	Boeing C-17A Globemaster III (04-4128) *bl*	USAF 6th AS/305th AMW, McGuire AFB, NJ	
44129	Boeing C-17A Globemaster III (04-4129) *r/y*	USAF 58th AS/97th AMW, Altus AFB, OK	
44130	Boeing C-17A Globemaster III (04-4130) *bl*	USAF 6th AS/305th AMW, McGuire AFB, NJ	
44131	Boeing C-17A Globemaster III (04-4131) *bl*	USAF 6th AS/305th AMW, McGuire AFB, NJ	
44132	Boeing C-17A Globemaster III (04-4132) *bl*	USAF 6th AS/305th AMW, McGuire AFB, NJ	
44133	Boeing C-17A Globemaster III (04-4133) *bl*	USAF 6th AS/305th AMW, McGuire AFB, NJ	
44134	Boeing C-17A Globemaster III (04-4134) *bl*	USAF 6th AS/305th AMW, McGuire AFB, NJ	
44135	Boeing C-17A Globemaster III (04-4135) *r/y*	USAF 58th AS/97th AMW, Altus AFB, OK	
44136	Boeing C-17A Globemaster III (04-4136) *bl*	USAF 6th AS/305th AMW, McGuire AFB, NJ	
44137	Boeing C-17A Globemaster III (04-4137) *bl*	USAF 6th AS/305th AMW, McGuire AFB, NJ	
44138	Boeing C-17A Globemaster III (04-4138) *or/y*	USAF 729th AS/452nd AMW AFRC, March ARB, CA	
50102	Boeing C-17A Globemaster III (95-0102) *y/bl*	USAF 437th AW, Charleston AFB, SC	
50103	Boeing C-17A Globemaster III (95-0103) *gn*	USAF 62nd AW, McChord AFB, WA	
50104	Boeing C-17A Globemaster III (95-0104) *r/w*	USAF 155th AS/164th AW, Memphis, TN ANG	
50105	Boeing C-17A Globemaster III (95-0105) *bl*	USAF 137th AS/105th AW, Stewart AFB, NY ANG	
50106	Boeing C-17A Globemaster III (95-0106) *gn*	USAF 62nd AW, McChord AFB, WA	
50107	Boeing C-17A Globemaster III (95-0107) *y/bl*	USAF 437th AW, Charleston AFB, SC	
55139	Boeing C-17A Globemaster III (05-5139) *or/y*	USAF 729th AS/452nd AMW AFRC, March ARB, CA	

Notes	Serial	Type (code/other identity)	Owner/operator, location or fate
	55140	Boeing C-17A Globemaster III (05-5140) *or/y*	USAF 729th AS/452nd AMW AFRC, March ARB, CA
	55141	Boeing C-17A Globemaster III (05-5141) *or/y*	USAF 729th AS/452nd AMW AFRC, March ARB, CA
	55142	Boeing C-17A Globemaster III (05-5142) *or/y*	USAF 729th AS/452nd AMW AFRC, March ARB, CA
	55143	Boeing C-17A Globemaster III (05-5143) *r/w*	USAF 89th AS/445th AW AFRC, Wright-Patterson AFB, OH
	55144	Boeing C-17A Globemaster III (05-5144) *or/y*	USAF 729th AS/452nd AMW AFRC, March ARB, CA
	55145	Boeing C-17A Globemaster III (05-5145) *or/y*	USAF 729th AS/452nd AMW AFRC, March ARB, CA
	55146	Boeing C-17A Globemaster III (05-5146) [HH] *r/y*	USAF 535th AS/15th Wg, Hickam AFB, HI
	55147	Boeing C-17A Globemaster III (05-5147) [HH] *r/y*	USAF 535th AS/15th Wg, Hickam AFB, HI
	55148	Boeing C-17A Globemaster III (05-5148) [HH] *r/y*	USAF 535th AS/15th Wg, Hickam AFB, HI
	55149	Boeing C-17A Globemaster III (05-5149) [HH] *r/y*	USAF 535th AS/15th Wg, Hickam AFB, HI
	55150	Boeing C-17A Globemaster III (05-5150) [HH] *r/y*	USAF 535th AS/15th Wg, Hickam AFB, HI
	55151	Boeing C-17A Globemaster III (05-5151) [HH] *r/y*	USAF 535th AS/15th Wg, Hickam AFB, HI
	55152	Boeing C-17A Globemaster III (05-5152) [HH] *r/y*	USAF 535th AS/15th Wg, Hickam AFB, HI
	55153	Boeing C-17A Globemaster III (05-5153) [HH] *r/y*]	USAF 758th AS/15th Wg, Hickam AFB, HI
	60001	Boeing C-17A Globemaster III (96-0001) *bk/y*	USAF 758th AS/911th AMW AFRC, Greater Pittsburgh, PA
	60002	Boeing C-17A Globemaster III (96-0002) *y/bl*	USAF 437th AW, Charleston AFB, SC
	60003	Boeing C-17A Globemaster III (96-0003) *gn*	USAF 62nd AW, McChord AFB, WA
	60004	Boeing C-17A Globemaster III (96-0004) *gn*	USAF 62nd AW, McChord AFB, WA
	60005	Boeing C-17A Globemaster III (96-0005) *bl*	USAF 137th AS/105th AW, Stewart AFB, NY ANG
	60006	Boeing C-17A Globemaster III (96-0006) *r/w*	USAF 167th AS/167th AW, Martinsburg, WV ANG
	60007	Boeing C-17A Globemaster III (96-0007) *bl/gd*	USAF 183rd AS/172nd AW, Jackson Int'l Airport, MS ANG
	60008	Boeing C-17A Globemaster III (96-0008) *r/y*	USAF 58th AS/97th AMW, Altus AFB, OK
	66154	Boeing C-17A Globemaster III (06-6154) *w/bk*	USAF 21st AS/60th AMW, Travis AFB, CA
	66155	Boeing C-17A Globemaster III (06-6155) *w/bk*	USAF 21st AS/60th AMW, Travis AFB, CA
	66156	Boeing C-17A Globemaster III (06-6156) *w/bk*	USAF 21st AS/60th AMW, Travis AFB, CA
	66157	Boeing C-17A Globemaster III (06-6157) *w/bk*	USAF 21st AS/60th AMW, Travis AFB, CA
	66158	Boeing C-17A Globemaster III (06-6158) *w/bk*	USAF 21st AS/60th AMW, Travis AFB, CA
	66159	Boeing C-17A Globemaster III (06-6159) *w/bk*	USAF 21st AS/60th AMW, Travis AFB, CA
	66160	Boeing C-17A Globemaster III (06-6160) *w/bk*	USAF 21st AS/60th AMW, Travis AFB, CA
	66161	Boeing C-17A Globemaster III (06-6161) *w/bk*	USAF 21st AS/60th AMW, Travis AFB, CA
	66162	Boeing C-17A Globemaster III (06-6162) *w/bk*	USAF 21st AS/60th AMW, Travis AFB, CA
	66163	Boeing C-17A Globemaster III (06-6163) *w/bk*	USAF 21st AS/60th AMW, Travis AFB, CA
	66164	Boeing C-17A Globemaster III (06-6164) *w/bk*	USAF 21st AS/60th AMW, Travis AFB, CA
	66165	Boeing C-17A Globemaster III (06-6165) *bl/y*	USAF 3rd AS/436th AW, Dover AFB, DE
	66166	Boeing C-17A Globemaster III (06-6166) *bl/y*	USAF 3rd AS/436th AW, Dover AFB, DE
	66167	Boeing C-17A Globemaster III (06-6167) *bl/y*	USAF 3rd AS/436th AW, Dover AFB, DE
	66168	Boeing C-17A Globemaster III (06-6168) *bl/y*	USAF 3rd AS/436th AW, Dover AFB, DE
	70041	Boeing C-17A Globemaster III (97-0041) *y/bl*	USAF 437th AW, Charleston AFB, SC
	70042	Boeing C-17A Globemaster III (97-0042) *r/w*	USAF 155th AS/164th AW, Memphis, TN ANG
	70043	Boeing C-17A Globemaster III (97-0043) *or/y*	USAF 729th AS/452nd AMW AFRC, March ARB, CA
	70044	Boeing C-17A Globemaster III (97-0044) *r/w*	USAF 89th AS/445th AW AFRC, Wright-Patterson AFB, OH
	70045	Boeing C-17A Globemaster III (97-0045) *bl*	USAF 137th AS/105th AW, Stewart AFB, NY ANG
	70046	Boeing C-17A Globemaster III (97-0046) *y/bl*	USAF 437th AW, Charleston AFB, SC
	70047	Boeing C-17A Globemaster III (97-0047) *y/bl*	USAF 437th AW, Charleston AFB, SC
	70048	Boeing C-17A Globemaster III (97-0048) *r/w*	USAF 89th AS/445th AW AFRC, Wright-Patterson AFB, OH
	77169	Boeing C-17A Globemaster III (07-7169) *bl/y*	USAF 3rd AS/436th AW, Dover AFB, DE
	77170	Boeing C-17A Globemaster III (07-7170) *bl/y*	USAF 3rd AS/436th AW, Dover AFB, DE
	77171	Boeing C-17A Globemaster III (07-7171) *bl*	USAF 6th AS/305th AMW, McGuire AFB, NJ
	77172	Boeing C-17A Globemaster III (07-7172) *w/bk*	USAF 21st AS/60th AMW, Travis AFB, CA
	77173	Boeing C-17A Globemaster III (07-7173) *bl/y*	USAF 3rd AS/436th AW, Dover AFB, DE

Serial	Type (code/other identity)	Owner/operator, location or fate	Notes
77174	Boeing C-17A Globemaster III (07-7174) bl/y	USAF 3rd AS/436th AW, Dover AFB, DE	
77175	Boeing C-17A Globemaster III (07-7175) bl/y	USAF 3rd AS/436th AW, Dover AFB, DE	
77176	Boeing C-17A Globemaster III (07-7176) bl/y	USAF 3rd AS/436th AW, Dover AFB, DE	
77177	Boeing C-17A Globemaster III (07-7177) bl/y	USAF 3rd AS/436th AW, Dover AFB, DE	
77178	Boeing C-17A Globemaster III (07-7178) bl	USAF 6th AS/305th AMW, McGuire AFB, NJ	
77179	Boeing C-17A Globemaster III (07-7179) w/bk	USAF 21st AS/60th AMW, Travis AFB, CA	
77180	Boeing C-17A Globemaster III (07-7180) y/bl	USAF 437th AW, Charleston AFB, SC	
77181	Boeing C-17A Globemaster III (07-7181) y/bl	USAF 437th AW, Charleston AFB, SC	
77182	Boeing C-17A Globemaster III (07-7182) y/bl	USAF 437th AW, Charleston AFB, SC	
77183	Boeing C-17A Globemaster III (07-7183) y/bl	USAF 437th AW, Charleston AFB, SC	
77184	Boeing C-17A Globemaster III (07-7184) y/bl	USAF 437th AW, Charleston AFB, SC	
77185	Boeing C-17A Globemaster III (07-7185) y/bl	USAF 437th AW, Charleston AFB, SC	
77186	Boeing C-17A Globemaster III (07-7186) y/bl	USAF 437th AW, Charleston AFB, SC	
77187	Boeing C-17A Globemaster III (07-7187) y/bl	USAF 437th AW, Charleston AFB, SC	
77188	Boeing C-17A Globemaster III (07-7188) y/bl	USAF 437th AW, Charleston AFB, SC	
77189	Boeing C-17A Globemaster III (07-7189) y/bl	USAF 437th AW, Charleston AFB, SC	
80049	Boeing C-17A Globemaster III (98-0049) r/y	USAF 58th AS/97th AMW, Altus AFB, OK	
80050	Boeing C-17A Globemaster III (98-0050) r/y	USAF 58th AS/97th AMW, Altus AFB, OK	
80051	Boeing C-17A Globemaster III (98-0051) [AK] bl/y	USAF 144th AS/176th Wg, Elmendorf AFB, AK ANG	
80052	Boeing C-17A Globemaster III (98-0052) gn	USAF 62nd AW, McChord AFB, WA	
80053	Boeing C-17A Globemaster III (98-0053) gn	USAF 62nd AW, McChord AFB, WA	
80054	Boeing C-17A Globemaster III (98-0054) y/bl	USAF 437th AW, Charleston AFB, SC	
80055	Boeing C-17A Globemaster III (98-0055) r/y $	USAF 58th AS/97th AMW, Altus AFB, OK	
80056	Boeing C-17A Globemaster III (98-0056) [AK] bl/y	USAF 144th AS/176th Wg, Elmendorf AFB, AK ANG	
80057	Boeing C-17A Globemaster III (98-0057) bl	USAF 137th AS/105th AW, Stewart AFB, NY ANG	
80265	Boeing C-17A Globemaster III (88-0265) gn	USAF 62nd AW, McChord AFB, WA	
80266	Boeing C-17A Globemaster III (88-0266) y/bl	USAF 437th AW, Charleston AFB, SC	
88190	Boeing C-17A Globemaster III (08-8190) y/bl	USAF 437th AW, Charleston AFB, SC	
88191	Boeing C-17A Globemaster III (08-8191) y/bl	USAF 437th AW, Charleston AFB, SC	
88192	Boeing C-17A Globemaster III (08-8192) gn	USAF 62nd AW, McChord AFB, WA	
88193	Boeing C-17A Globemaster III (08-8193) gn	USAF 62nd AW, McChord AFB, WA	
88194	Boeing C-17A Globemaster III (08-8194) gn	USAF 62nd AW, McChord AFB, WA	
88195	Boeing C-17A Globemaster III (08-8195) gn	USAF 62nd AW, McChord AFB, WA	
88196	Boeing C-17A Globemaster III (08-8196) gn	USAF 62nd AW, McChord AFB, WA	
88197	Boeing C-17A Globemaster III (08-8197) gn	USAF 62nd AW, McChord AFB, WA	
88198	Boeing C-17A Globemaster III (08-8198) y/bl	USAF 437th AW, Charleston AFB, SC	
88199	Boeing C-17A Globemaster III (08-8199) gn	USAF 62nd AW, McChord AFB, WA	
88200	Boeing C-17A Globemaster III (08-8200) gn	USAF 62nd AW, McChord AFB, WA	
88201	Boeing C-17A Globemaster III (08-8201) gn	USAF 62nd AW, McChord AFB, WA	
88202	Boeing C-17A Globemaster III (08-8202) gn	USAF 62nd AW, McChord AFB, WA	
88203	Boeing C-17A Globemaster III (08-8203) gn	USAF 62nd AW, McChord AFB, WA	
88204	Boeing C-17A Globemaster III (08-8204) y/bl	USAF 437th AW, Charleston AFB, SC	
90058	Boeing C-17A Globemaster III (99-0058) gn	USAF 62nd AW, McChord AFB, WA	
90059	Boeing C-17A Globemaster III (99-0059) gn	USAF 62nd AW, McChord AFB, WA	
90060	Boeing C-17A Globemaster III (99-0060) gn	USAF 62nd AW, McChord AFB, WA	
90061	Boeing C-17A Globemaster III (99-0061) r/y	USAF 58th AS/97th AMW, Altus AFB, OK	
90062	Boeing C-17A Globemaster III (99-0062) y/bl	USAF 437th AW, Charleston AFB, SC	
90063	Boeing C-17A Globemaster III (99-0063) r/y	USAF 58th AS/97th AMW, Altus AFB, OK	
90064	Boeing C-17A Globemaster III (99-0064) r/y	USAF 58th AS/97th AMW, Altus AFB, OK	
90165	Boeing C-17A Globemaster III (99-0165) r/w	USAF 89th AS/445th AW AFRC, Wright-Patterson AFB, OH	
90166	Boeing C-17A Globemaster III (99-0166) gn	USAF 62nd AW, McChord AFB, WA	
90167	Boeing C-17A Globemaster III (99-0167) [AK] bl/y	USAF 144th AS/176th Wg, Elmendorf AFB, AK ANG	
90168	Boeing C-17A Globemaster III (99-0168) [AK] bl/y	USAF 144th AS/176th Wg, Elmendorf AFB, AK ANG	
90169	Boeing C-17A Globemaster III (99-0169) y/bl	USAF 437th AW, Charleston AFB, SC	
90170	Boeing C-17A Globemaster III (99-0170) [AK] bl/y	USAF 144th AS/176th Wg, Elmendorf AFB, AK ANG	

US-BASED USAF AIRCRAFT

Notes	Serial	Type (code/other identity)	Owner/operator, location or fate
	91189	Boeing C-17A Globemaster III (89-1189) *bk/y*	USAF 758th AS/911th AMW AFRC, Greater Pittsburgh, PA
	91190	Boeing C-17A Globemaster III (89-1190) *r/w*	USAF 167th AS/167th AW, Martinsburg, WV ANG
	91191	Boeing C-17A Globemaster III (89-1191) *bl*	USAF 137th AS/105th AW, Stewart AFB, NY ANG
	91192	Boeing C-17A Globemaster III (89-1192) *y/bl*	USAF 437th AW, Charleston AFB, SC
	99205	Boeing C-17A Globemaster III (09-9205) *y/bl*	USAF 437th AW, Charleston AFB, SC
	99206	Boeing C-17A Globemaster III (09-9206) *y/bl*	USAF 437th AW, Charleston AFB, SC
	99207	Boeing C-17A Globemaster III (09-9207) *y/bl*	USAF 437th AW, Charleston AFB, SC
	99208	Boeing C-17A Globemaster III (09-9208) *y/bl*	USAF 437th AW, Charleston AFB, SC
	99209	Boeing C-17A Globemaster III (09-9209) *gn*	USAF 62nd AW, McChord AFB, WA
	99210	Boeing C-17A Globemaster III (09-9210) *gn*	USAF 62nd AW, McChord AFB, WA
	99211	Boeing C-17A Globemaster III (09-9211) *gn*	USAF 62nd AW, McChord AFB, WA
	99212	Boeing C-17A Globemaster III (09-9212) *y/bl*	USAF 437th AW, Charleston AFB, SC

Grumman C-20F Gulfstream IV

	10108	Grumman C-20F Gulfstream IV (91-00108)	To 309th AMARG, July 2018

Lockheed Martin F-22A Raptor

NB: Following the hurricane damage to Tyndall AFB in October 2018, 2nd FS & 43rd FS have moved to Eglin AFB and 95th FS to Langley AFB. At the time of going to press it isn't clear if this is permanent or temporary but we have tried to keep track of bases in the interim, as detailed below.

	91-4004	Lockheed Martin F-22A Raptor [ED]	USAF 411th FLTS/412th TW, Edwards AFB, CA
	91-4006	Lockheed Martin F-22A Raptor [ED]	USAF 411th FLTS/412th TW, Edwards AFB, CA
	91-4007	Lockheed Martin F-22A Raptor [ED] [412 TW]	USAF 411th FLTS/412th TW, Edwards AFB, CA
	91-4009	Lockheed Martin F-22A Raptor [ED]	USAF 411th FLTS/412th TW, Edwards AFB, CA
	99-4010	Lockheed Martin F-22A Raptor [OT] [422 TES]	USAF 422nd TES/53rd Wg, Nellis AFB, NV
	99-4011	Lockheed Martin F-22A Raptor [WA]	USAF 433rd WPS/57th Wg, Nellis AFB, NV
	00-4012	Lockheed Martin F-22A Raptor [TY]	USAF 43rd FS/325th FW, Eglin AFB, FL
	00-4015	Lockheed Martin F-22A Raptor [TY]	USAF 43rd FS/325th FW, Eglin AFB, FL
	00-4016	Lockheed Martin F-22A Raptor [TY]	USAF 43rd FS/325th FW, Eglin AFB, FL
	00-4017	Lockheed Martin F-22A Raptor [TY]	USAF 43rd FS/325th FW, Eglin AFB, FL
	01-4018	Lockheed Martin F-22A Raptor [TY]	USAF 43rd FS/325th FW, Eglin AFB, FL
	01-4019	Lockheed Martin F-22A Raptor [TY]	USAF 95th FS/325th FW, Langley AFB, FL
	01-4020	Lockheed Martin F-22A Raptor [TY]	USAF 43rd FS/325th FW, Eglin AFB, FL
	01-4021	Lockheed Martin F-22A Raptor [TY]	USAF 95th FS/325th FW, Langley AFB, FL
	01-4022	Lockheed Martin F-22A Raptor [TY]	USAF 95th FS/325th FW, Langley AFB, FL
	01-4023	Lockheed Martin F-22A Raptor [TY]	USAF 95th FS/325th FW, Langley AFB, FL
	01-4024	Lockheed Martin F-22A Raptor [TY]	USAF 95th FS/325th FW, Langley AFB, FL
	01-4025	Lockheed Martin F-22A Raptor [TY]	USAF 43rd FS/325th FW, Eglin AFB, FL
	01-4026	Lockheed Martin F-22A Raptor [TY]	USAF 43rd FS/325th FW, Eglin AFB, FL
	01-4027	Lockheed Martin F-22A Raptor [TY]	USAF 43rd FS/325th FW, Eglin AFB, FL
	02-4028	Lockheed Martin F-22A Raptor [TY]	USAF 95th FS/325th FW, Langley AFB, FL
	02-4029	Lockheed Martin F-22A Raptor [TY]	USAF 43rd FS/325th FW, Eglin AFB, FL
	02-4030	Lockheed Martin F-22A Raptor [TY]	USAF 43rd FS/325th FW, Eglin AFB, FL
	02-4031	Lockheed Martin F-22A Raptor [TY]	USAF 95th FS/325th FW, Langley AFB, FL
	02-4032	Lockheed Martin F-22A Raptor [TY]	USAF 43rd FS/325th FW, Eglin AFB, FL
	02-4033	Lockheed Martin F-22A Raptor [TY]	USAF 43rd FS/325th FW, Eglin AFB, FL
	02-4034	Lockheed Martin F-22A Raptor [TY]	USAF 43rd FS/325th FW, Eglin AFB, FL
	02-4035	Lockheed Martin F-22A Raptor [TY] [325 OG]	USAF 43rd FS/325th FW, Eglin AFB, FL
	02-4036	Lockheed Martin F-22A Raptor [TY]	USAF 95th FS/325th FW, Langley AFB, FL
	02-4037	Lockheed Martin F-22A Raptor	USAF
	02-4038	Lockheed Martin F-22A Raptor [TY]	USAF 43rd FS/325th FW, Eglin AFB, FL
	02-4039	Lockheed Martin F-22A Raptor [TY]	USAF 95th FS/325th FW, Langley AFB, FL
	02-4040	Lockheed Martin F-22A Raptor [TY] [325 FW]	USAF 95th FS/325th FW, Langley AFB, FL
	03-4041	Lockheed Martin F-22A Raptor [TY]	USAF 43rd FS/325th FW, Eglin AFB, FL
	03-4042	Lockheed Martin F-22A Raptor [TY]	USAF 43rd FS/325th FW, Eglin AFB, FL
	03-4043	Lockheed Martin F-22A Raptor [TY] [43 FS]	USAF 43rd FS/325th FW, Eglin AFB, FL
	03-4044	Lockheed Martin F-22A Raptor [TY]	USAF 95th FS/325th FW, Langley AFB, FL
	03-4045	Lockheed Martin F-22A Raptor [HH]	USAF 199th FS/154th Wg, Hickam AFB, HI ANG

Serial	Type (code/other identity)	Owner/operator, location or fate	Notes
03-4046	Lockheed Martin F-22A Raptor [HH] [199 FS]	USAF 199th FS/154th Wg, Hickam AFB, HI ANG	
03-4047	Lockheed Martin F-22A Raptor [HH]	USAF 199th FS/154th Wg, Hickam AFB, HI ANG	
03-4048	Lockheed Martin F-22A Raptor [HH]	USAF 199th FS/154th Wg, Hickam AFB, HI ANG	
03-4049	Lockheed Martin F-22A Raptor [HH]	USAF 199th FS/154th Wg, Hickam AFB, HI ANG	
03-4050	Lockheed Martin F-22A Raptor [HH]	USAF 199th FS/154th Wg, Hickam AFB, HI ANG	
03-4051	Lockheed Martin F-22A Raptor [HH]	USAF 199th FS/154th Wg, Hickam AFB, HI ANG	
03-4052	Lockheed Martin F-22A Raptor [HH]	USAF 199th FS/154th Wg, Hickam AFB, HI ANG	
03-4053	Lockheed Martin F-22A Raptor [HH]	USAF 199th FS/154th Wg, Hickam AFB, HI ANG	
03-4054	Lockheed Martin F-22A Raptor [HH] [154 Wg]	USAF 199th FS/154th Wg, Hickam AFB, HI ANG	
03-4055	Lockheed Martin F-22A Raptor [HH]	USAF 199th FS/154th Wg, Hickam AFB, HI ANG	
03-4056	Lockheed Martin F-22A Raptor [HH]	USAF 199th FS/154th Wg, Hickam AFB, HI ANG	
03-4057	Lockheed Martin F-22A Raptor [HH]	USAF 199th FS/154th Wg, Hickam AFB, HI ANG	
03-4058	Lockheed Martin F-22A Raptor [HH]	USAF 199th FS/154th Wg, Hickam AFB, HI ANG	
03-4059	Lockheed Martin F-22A Raptor [HH]	USAF 199th FS/154th Wg, Hickam AFB, HI ANG	
03-4060	Lockheed Martin F-22A Raptor [HH]	USAF 199th FS/154th Wg, Hickam AFB, HI ANG	
03-4061	Lockheed Martin F-22A Raptor [HH]	USAF 199th FS/154th Wg, Hickam AFB, HI ANG	
04-4062	Lockheed Martin F-22A Raptor [HH]	USAF 199th FS/154th Wg, Hickam AFB, HI ANG	
04-4063	Lockheed Martin F-22A Raptor [HH]	USAF 199th FS/154th Wg, Hickam AFB, HI ANG	
04-4064	Lockheed Martin F-22A Raptor [HH]	USAF 199th FS/154th Wg, Hickam AFB, HI ANG	
04-4065	Lockheed Martin F-22A Raptor [FF]	USAF 94th FS/1st FW, Langley AFB, VA	
04-4066	Lockheed Martin F-22A Raptor [OT]	USAF 422nd TES/53rd Wg, Nellis AFB, NV	
04-4067	Lockheed Martin F-22A Raptor [FF]	USAF 94th FS/1st FW, Langley AFB, VA	
04-4068	Lockheed Martin F-22A Raptor [OT]	USAF 422nd TES/53rd Wg, Nellis AFB, NV	
04-4069	Lockheed Martin F-22A Raptor [OT]	USAF 422nd TES/53rd Wg, Nellis AFB, NV	
04-4070	Lockheed Martin F-22A Raptor [FF]	USAF 94th FS/1st FW, Langley AFB, VA	
04-4071	Lockheed Martin F-22A Raptor [WA]	USAF 433rd WPS/57th Wg, Nellis AFB, NV	
04-4072	Lockheed Martin F-22A Raptor [TY]	USAF 95th FS/325th FW, Langley AFB, FL	
04-4073	Lockheed Martin F-22A Raptor [FF]	USAF 27th FS/1st FW, Langley AFB, VA	
04-4074	Lockheed Martin F-22A Raptor [AK]	USAF 90th FS/3rd Wg, Elmendorf AFB, AK	
04-4075	Lockheed Martin F-22A Raptor [AK]	USAF 90th FS/3rd Wg, Elmendorf AFB, AK	
04-4076	Lockheed Martin F-22A Raptor [TY]	USAF 95th FS/325th FW, Langley AFB, FL	
04-4077	Lockheed Martin F-22A Raptor [AK]	USAF 525th FS/3rd Wg, Elmendorf AFB, AK	
04-4078	Lockheed Martin F-22A Raptor [TY]	USAF 95th FS/325th FW, Langley AFB, FL	
04-4079	Lockheed Martin F-22A Raptor [TY]	USAF 95th FS/325th FW, Langley AFB, FL	
04-4080	Lockheed Martin F-22A Raptor [TY]	USAF 95th FS/325th FW, Langley AFB, FL	
04-4082	Lockheed Martin F-22A Raptor [FF] [149 FS]	USAF 149th FS/192nd FW/1st FW, Langley AFB, VA ANG	
04-4083	Lockheed Martin F-22A Raptor [TY] [301 FS]	USAF 301st FS/44th FG AFRES/325th FW, Eglin AFB, FL	
05-4081	Lockheed Martin F-22A Raptor (04-4081) [TY]	USAF 95th FS/325th FW, Langley AFB, FL	
05-4084	Lockheed Martin F-22A Raptor [TY]	USAF 95th FS/325th FW, Langley AFB, FL	
05-4085	Lockheed Martin F-22A Raptor [FF]	USAF 94th FS/1st FW, Langley AFB, VA	
05-4086	Lockheed Martin F-22A Raptor [TY]	USAF 95th FS/325th FW, Langley AFB, FL	
05-4087	Lockheed Martin F-22A Raptor [AK]	USAF 90th FS/3rd Wg, Elmendorf AFB, AK	
05-4088	Lockheed Martin F-22A Raptor [TY]	USAF 95th FS/325th FW, Langley AFB, FL	
05-4089	Lockheed Martin F-22A Raptor [TY]	USAF 95th FS/325th FW, Langley AFB, FL	
05-4090	Lockheed Martin F-22A Raptor [AK]	USAF 90th FS/3rd Wg, Elmendorf AFB, AK	
05-4091	Lockheed Martin F-22A Raptor [TY]	USAF 95th FS/325th FW, Langley AFB, FL	
05-4092	Lockheed Martin F-22A Raptor [AK]	USAF 525th FS/3rd Wg, Elmendorf AFB, AK	
05-4093	Lockheed Martin F-22A Raptor [TY]	USAF 95th FS/325th FW, Langley AFB, FL	
05-4094	Lockheed Martin F-22A Raptor [TY]	USAF 95th FS/325th FW, Langley AFB, FL	
05-4095	Lockheed Martin F-22A Raptor [TY] [95 FS]	USAF 95th FS/325th FW, Langley AFB, FL	
05-4096	Lockheed Martin F-22A Raptor [WA]	USAF 433rd WPS/57th Wg, Nellis AFB, NV	
05-4097	Lockheed Martin F-22A Raptor [TY]	USAF 95th FS/325th FW, Langley AFB, FL	
05-4098	Lockheed Martin F-22A Raptor [TY]	USAF 95th FS/325th FW, Langley AFB, FL	
05-4099	Lockheed Martin F-22A Raptor [TY]	USAF 95th FS/325th FW, Langley AFB, FL	
05-4100	Lockheed Martin F-22A Raptor [TY]	USAF 95th FS/325th FW, Langley AFB, FL	
05-4101	Lockheed Martin F-22A Raptor [TY]	USAF 95th FS/325th FW, Langley AFB, FL	
05-4102	Lockheed Martin F-22A Raptor [AK] [302 FS]	USAF 302nd FS/477th FG AFRES/3rd Wg, Elmendorf AFB, AK	
05-4103	Lockheed Martin F-22A Raptor [AK] [3 Wg]	USAF 90th FS/3rd Wg, Elmendorf AFB, AK	
05-4104	Lockheed Martin F-22A Raptor [TY]	USAF 95th FS/325th FW, Langley AFB, FL	

Notes	Serial	Type (code/other identity)	Owner/operator, location or fate
	05-4105	Lockheed Martin F-22A Raptor [TY] [44 FG]	USAF 95th FS/325th FW, Langley AFB, FL
	05-4106	Lockheed Martin F-22A Raptor [TY]	USAF 95th FS/325th FW, Langley AFB, FL
	05-4107	Lockheed Martin F-22A Raptor [TY]	USAF 95th FS/325th FW, Langley AFB, FL
	06-4108	Lockheed Martin F-22A Raptor [AK]	USAF 525th FS/3rd Wg, Elmendorf AFB, AK
	06-4109	Lockheed Martin F-22A Raptor [WA]	USAF 433rd WPS/57th Wg, Nellis AFB, NV
	06-4110	Lockheed Martin F-22A Raptor [AK] [11 AF]	USAF 525th FS/3rd Wg, Elmendorf AFB, AK
	06-4111	Lockheed Martin F-22A Raptor [OT]	USAF 422nd TES/53rd Wg, Nellis AFB, NV
	06-4112	Lockheed Martin F-22A Raptor [AK]	USAF 525th FS/3rd Wg, Elmendorf AFB, AK
	06-4113	Lockheed Martin F-22A Raptor [AK] [3 OG]	USAF 525th FS/3rd Wg, Elmendorf AFB, AK
	06-4114	Lockheed Martin F-22A Raptor [AK]	USAF 525th FS/3rd Wg, Elmendorf AFB, AK
	06-4115	Lockheed Martin F-22A Raptor [AK] [525 FS]	USAF 525th FS/3rd Wg, Elmendorf AFB, AK
	06-4116	Lockheed Martin F-22A Raptor [WA] [433 WPS]	USAF 433rd WPS/57th Wg, Nellis AFB, NV
	06-4117	Lockheed Martin F-22A Raptor [AK]	USAF 525th FS/3rd Wg, Elmendorf AFB, AK
	06-4118	Lockheed Martin F-22A Raptor [AK]	USAF 525th FS/3rd Wg, Elmendorf AFB, AK
	06-4119	Lockheed Martin F-22A Raptor [AK]	USAF 525th FS/3rd Wg, Elmendorf AFB, AK
	06-4120	Lockheed Martin F-22A Raptor [OT]	USAF 422nd TES/53rd Wg, Nellis AFB, NV
	06-4121	Lockheed Martin F-22A Raptor [AK]	USAF 525th FS/3rd Wg, Elmendorf AFB, AK
	06-4122	Lockheed Martin F-22A Raptor [AK]	USAF 525th FS/3rd Wg, Elmendorf AFB, AK
	06-4123	Lockheed Martin F-22A Raptor [AK]	USAF 525th FS/3rd Wg, Elmendorf AFB, AK
	06-4124	Lockheed Martin F-22A Raptor [OT]	USAF 422nd TES/53rd Wg, Nellis AFB, NV
	06-4126	Lockheed Martin F-22A Raptor [AK]	USAF 525th FS/3rd Wg, Elmendorf AFB, AK
	06-4127	Lockheed Martin F-22A Raptor [AK]	USAF 525th FS/3rd Wg, Elmendorf AFB, AK
	06-4128	Lockheed Martin F-22A Raptor [OT]	USAF 422nd TES/53rd Wg, Nellis AFB, NV
	06-4129	Lockheed Martin F-22A Raptor [AK]	USAF 525th FS/3rd Wg, Elmendorf AFB, AK
	06-4130	Lockheed Martin F-22A Raptor [AK]	USAF 525th FS/3rd Wg, Elmendorf AFB, AK
	07-4131	Lockheed Martin F-22A Raptor [AK]	USAF 525th FS/3rd Wg, Elmendorf AFB, AK
	07-4132	Lockheed Martin F-22A Raptor [ED] [411 FLTS]	USAF 411th FLTS/412th TW, Edwards AFB, CA
	07-4133	Lockheed Martin F-22A Raptor [AK]	USAF 525th FS/3rd Wg, Elmendorf AFB, AK
	07-4134	Lockheed Martin F-22A Raptor [AK]	USAF 525th FS/3rd Wg, Elmendorf AFB, AK
	07-4135	Lockheed Martin F-22A Raptor [AK]	USAF 90th FS/3rd Wg, Elmendorf AFB, AK
	07-4136	Lockheed Martin F-22A Raptor [AK]	USAF 90th FS/3rd Wg, Elmendorf AFB, AK
	07-4137	Lockheed Martin F-22A Raptor [AK]	USAF 90th FS/3rd Wg, Elmendorf AFB, AK
	07-4138	Lockheed Martin F-22A Raptor [AK]	USAF 90th FS/3rd Wg, Elmendorf AFB, AK
	07-4139	Lockheed Martin F-22A Raptor [AK]	USAF 90th FS/3rd Wg, Elmendorf AFB, AK
	07-4140	Lockheed Martin F-22A Raptor [AK]	USAF 90th FS/3rd Wg, Elmendorf AFB, AK
	07-4141	Lockheed Martin F-22A Raptor [AK]	USAF 90th FS/3rd Wg, Elmendorf AFB, AK
	07-4142	Lockheed Martin F-22A Raptor [AK]	USAF 90th FS/3rd Wg, Elmendorf AFB, AK
	07-4143	Lockheed Martin F-22A Raptor [AK]	USAF 90th FS/3rd Wg, Elmendorf AFB, AK
	07-4144	Lockheed Martin F-22A Raptor [AK]	USAF 90th FS/3rd Wg, Elmendorf AFB, AK
	07-4145	Lockheed Martin F-22A Raptor [AK]	USAF 90th FS/3rd Wg, Elmendorf AFB, AK
	07-4146	Lockheed Martin F-22A Raptor [AK]	*Damaged at Fallon AFB, 13 April 2018*
	07-4147	Lockheed Martin F-22A Raptor [AK]	USAF 90th FS/3rd Wg, Elmendorf AFB, AK
	07-4148	Lockheed Martin F-22A Raptor [AK]	USAF 90th FS/3rd Wg, Elmendorf AFB, AK
	07-4149	Lockheed Martin F-22A Raptor [AK]	USAF 90th FS/3rd Wg, Elmendorf AFB, AK
	07-4150	Lockheed Martin F-22A Raptor [AK]	USAF 90th FS/3rd Wg, Elmendorf AFB, AK
	07-4151	Lockheed Martin F-22A Raptor [AK]	USAF 90th FS/3rd Wg, Elmendorf AFB, AK
	08-4152	Lockheed Martin F-22A Raptor [FF]	USAF 94th FS/1st FW, Langley AFB, VA
	08-4153	Lockheed Martin F-22A Raptor [FF]	USAF 94th FS/1st FW, Langley AFB, VA
	08-4154	Lockheed Martin F-22A Raptor [FF]	USAF 94th FS/1st FW, Langley AFB, VA
	08-4155	Lockheed Martin F-22A Raptor [FF]	USAF 27th FS/1st FW, Langley AFB, VA
	08-4156	Lockheed Martin F-22A Raptor [FF]	USAF 94th FS/1st FW, Langley AFB, VA
	08-4157	Lockheed Martin F-22A Raptor [FF]	USAF 27th FS/1st FW, Langley AFB, VA
	08-4158	Lockheed Martin F-22A Raptor [FF]	USAF 27th FS/1st FW, Langley AFB, VA
	08-4159	Lockheed Martin F-22A Raptor [FF]	USAF 27th FS/1st FW, Langley AFB, VA
	08-4160	Lockheed Martin F-22A Raptor [FF]	USAF 94th FS/1st FW, Langley AFB, VA
	08-4161	Lockheed Martin F-22A Raptor [FF]	USAF 27th FS/1st FW, Langley AFB, VA
	08-4162	Lockheed Martin F-22A Raptor [FF] [1 FW]	USAF 94th FS/1st FW, Langley AFB, VA
	08-4163	Lockheed Martin F-22A Raptor [FF]	USAF 27th FS/1st FW, Langley AFB, VA
	08-4164	Lockheed Martin F-22A Raptor [FF]	USAF 94th FS/1st FW, Langley AFB, VA
	08-4165	Lockheed Martin F-22A Raptor [FF]	USAF 27th FS/1st FW, Langley AFB, VA
	08-4166	Lockheed Martin F-22A Raptor [FF]	USAF 94th FS/1st FW, Langley AFB, VA
	08-4167	Lockheed Martin F-22A Raptor [FF]	USAF 27th FS/1st FW, Langley AFB, VA

Serial	Type (code/other identity)	Owner/operator, location or fate	Notes
08-4168	Lockheed Martin F-22A Raptor [FF]	USAF 94th FS/1st FW, Langley AFB, VA	
08-4169	Lockheed Martin F-22A Raptor [FF]	USAF 27th FS/1st FW, Langley AFB, VA	
08-4170	Lockheed Martin F-22A Raptor [FF]	USAF 27th FS/1st FW, Langley AFB, VA	
08-4171	Lockheed Martin F-22A Raptor [FF]	USAF 27th FS/1st FW, Langley AFB, VA	
09-4172	Lockheed Martin F-22A Raptor [FF] [27 FS]	USAF 27th FS/1st FW, Langley AFB, VA	
09-4173	Lockheed Martin F-22A Raptor [FF]	USAF 27th FS/1st FW, Langley AFB, VA	
09-4174	Lockheed Martin F-22A Raptor [FF]	USAF 27th FS/1st FW, Langley AFB, VA	
09-4175	Lockheed Martin F-22A Raptor [FF]	USAF 94th FS/1st FW, Langley AFB, VA	
09-4176	Lockheed Martin F-22A Raptor [FF]	USAF 27th FS/1st FW, Langley AFB, VA	
09-4177	Lockheed Martin F-22A Raptor [FF]	USAF 27th FS/1st FW, Langley AFB, VA	
09-4178	Lockheed Martin F-22A Raptor [FF]	USAF 27th FS/1st FW, Langley AFB, VA	
09-4179	Lockheed Martin F-22A Raptor [FF]	USAF 94th FS/1st FW, Langley AFB, VA	
09-4180	Lockheed Martin F-22A Raptor [FF]	USAF 27th FS/1st FW, Langley AFB, VA	
09-4181	Lockheed Martin F-22A Raptor [FF]	USAF 94th FS/1st FW, Langley AFB, VA	
09-4182	Lockheed Martin F-22A Raptor [FF]	USAF 27th FS/1st FW, Langley AFB, VA	
09-4183	Lockheed Martin F-22A Raptor [FF]	USAF 94th FS/1st FW, Langley AFB, VA	
09-4184	Lockheed Martin F-22A Raptor [FF]	USAF 27th FS/1st FW, Langley AFB, VA	
09-4185	Lockheed Martin F-22A Raptor [FF] [1 OG]	USAF 27th FS/1st FW, Langley AFB, VA	
09-4186	Lockheed Martin F-22A Raptor [FF]	USAF 27th FS/1st FW, Langley AFB, VA	
09-4187	Lockheed Martin F-22A Raptor [FF]	USAF 94th FS/1st FW, Langley AFB, VA	
09-4188	Lockheed Martin F-22A Raptor [OT]	USAF 422nd TES/53rd Wg, Nellis AFB, NV	
09-4189	Lockheed Martin F-22A Raptor [FF]	USAF 27th FS/1st FW, Langley AFB, VA	
09-4190	Lockheed Martin F-22A Raptor [AK]	USAF 90th FS/3rd Wg, Elmendorf AFB, AK	
09-4191	Lockheed Martin F-22A Raptor [FF]	USAF 94th FS/1st FW, Langley AFB, VA	
10-4192	Lockheed Martin F-22A Raptor [FF] [192 FW]	USAF 149th FS/192nd FW/1st FW, Langley AFB, VA ANG	
10-4193	Lockheed Martin F-22A Raptor [AK] [3 Wg]	USAF 525th FS/3rd Wg, Elmendorf AFB, AK	
10-4194	Lockheed Martin F-22A Raptor [FF] [94 FS]	USAF 94th FS/1st FW, Langley AFB, VA	
10-4195	Lockheed Martin F-22A Raptor [AK] [525 FS]	USAF 525th FS/3rd Wg, Elmendorf AFB, AK	
	Boeing VC-25A/VC-25B		
28000	Boeing VC-25A (82-8000)	USAF PAS/89th AW, Andrews AFB, MD	
29000	Boeing VC-25A (92-9000)	USAF PAS/89th AW, Andrews AFB, MD	
N894BA	Boeing VC-25B	USAF (on order)	
N895BA	Boeing VC-25B	USAF (on order)	
	Pilatus U-28A		
10415	Pilatus U-28A (N415PB/01-0415)	USAF 318th SOS/27th SOW, Cannon AFB, NM	
40688	Pilatus U-28A (N707KH/04-0688)	USAF 318th SOS/27th SOW, Cannon AFB, NM	
50409	Pilatus U-28A (N922RG/05-0409)	USAF 319th SOS/1st SOW, Hurlburt Field, FL	
50419	Pilatus U-28A (N419WA/05-0419)	USAF 319th SOS/1st SOW, Hurlburt Field, FL	
50424	Pilatus U-28A (N424PB/05-0424)	USAF 318th SOS/27th SOW, Cannon AFB, NM	
50446	Pilatus U-28A (N131JN/05-0446)	USAF 318th SOS/27th SOW, Cannon AFB, NM	
50447	Pilatus U-28A (N447PC/05-0447)	USAF 319th SOS/1st SOW, Hurlburt Field, FL	
50482	Pilatus U-28A (N482WA/05-0482)	USAF 319th SOS/1st SOW, Hurlburt Field, FL	
50556	Pilatus U-28A (N556HL/05-0556)	USAF 318th SOS/27th SOW, Cannon AFB, NM	
50573	Pilatus U-28A (N666GT/05-0573)	USAF 319th SOS/1st SOW, Hurlburt Field, FL	
50597	Pilatus U-28A (N597CH/05-0597)	USAF 318th SOS/27th SOW, Cannon AFB, NM	
60692	Pilatus U-28A (N692BC/06-0692)	USAF 318th SOS/27th SOW, Cannon AFB, NM	
60740	Pilatus U-28A (N740AF/06-0740)	USAF 318th SOS/27th SOW, Cannon AFB, NM	
70488	Pilatus U-28A (N56EZ/07-0488)	USAF 319th SOS/1st SOW, Hurlburt Field, FL	
70691	Pilatus U-28A (N691PC/07-0691)	USAF 319th SOS/1st SOW, Hurlburt Field, FL	
70711	Pilatus U-28A (N711PN/07-0711)	USAF 319th SOS/1st SOW, Hurlburt Field, FL	
70712	Pilatus U-28A (N609TW/07-0712)	USAF 319th SOS/1st SOW, Hurlburt Field, FL	
70777	Pilatus U-28A (N72DZ/07-0777)	USAF 318th SOS/27th SOW, Cannon AFB, NM	
70779	Pilatus U-28A (N779PC/07-0779)	USAF 319th SOS/1st SOW, Hurlburt Field, FL	
70793	Pilatus U-28A (N96MV/07-0793)	USAF 319th SOS/1st SOW, Hurlburt Field, FL	
70808	Pilatus U-28A (N531MP/07-0808)	USAF 318th SOS/27th SOW, Cannon AFB, NM	
70821	Pilatus U-28A (N821PE/07-0821)	USAF 319th SOS/1st SOW, Hurlburt Field, FL	
70829	Pilatus U-28A (N829PE/07-0829)	USAF 319th SOS/1st SOW, Hurlburt Field, FL	
70838	Pilatus U-28A (N838PE/07-0838)	USAF 319th SOS/1st SOW, Hurlburt Field, FL	
70840	Pilatus U-28A (N840PE/07-0840)	USAF 319th SOS/1st SOW, Hurlburt Field, FL	

Notes	Serial	Type (code/other identity)	Owner/operator, location or fate
	80519	Pilatus U-28A (N519PC/08-0519)	USAF 319th SOS/1st SOW, Hurlburt Field, FL
	80581	Pilatus U-28A (N581PC/08-0581)	USAF 319th SOS/1st SOW, Hurlburt Field, FL
	80646	Pilatus U-28A (N875RJ/08-0646)	USAF 319th SOS/1st SOW, Hurlburt Field, FL
	80700	Pilatus U-28A (N600KP/08-0700)	USAF 319th SOS/1st SOW, Hurlburt Field, FL
	80718	Pilatus U-28A (N824BK/08-0718)	USAF 319th SOS/1st SOW, Hurlburt Field, FL
	80790	Pilatus U-28A (N757ED/08-0790)	USAF 319th SOS/1st SOW, Hurlburt Field, FL
	80809	Pilatus U-28A (N36EG/08-0809)	USAF 319th SOS/1st SOW, Hurlburt Field, FL
	80822	Pilatus U-28A (N822BM/08-0822)	USAF 319th SOS/1st SOW, Hurlburt Field, FL
	80835	Pilatus U-28A (N100MS/08-0835)	USAF 318th SOS/27th SOW, Cannon AFB, NM
	80850	Pilatus U-28A (N850CB/08-0850)	USAF 319th SOS/1st SOW, Hurlburt Field, FL

Boeing C-32

* Please note that there is evidence to suggest that the serials 25001, 86001, 86006 and 96143 are used by more than one airframe.

	09001	Boeing C-32B (00-9001)	USAF 150th SOS/108th Wg, McGuire AFB, NJ
	24452	Boeing C-32B (02-4452)	USAF 150th SOS/108th Wg, McGuire AFB, NJ
	25001	Boeing C-32B (N226G or N610G/02-5001)*	USAF 486th FLTS/46th TW, Eglin AFB, FL
	80001	Boeing C-32A (98-0001)	USAF 1st AS/89th AW, Andrews AFB, MD
	80002	Boeing C-32A (98-0002)	USAF 1st AS/89th AW, Andrews AFB, MD
	86006	Boeing C-32B (N226G or N610G/98-6006)*	USAF 486th FLTS/46th TW, Eglin AFB, FL
	90003	Boeing C-32A (99-0003)	USAF 1st AS/89th AW, Andrews AFB, MD
	90004	Boeing C-32A (99-0004)	USAF 1st AS/89th AW, Andrews AFB, MD
	90015	Boeing C-32A (09-0015)	USAF 1st AS/89th AW, Andrews AFB, MD
	90016	Boeing C-32A (09-0016)	USAF 1st AS/89th AW, Andrews AFB, MD
	90017	Boeing C-32A (09-0017)	USAF 1st AS/89th AW, Andrews AFB, MD
	96143	Boeing C-32B (N226G or N610G/99-6143)*	USAF 486th FLTS/46th TW, Eglin AFB, FL

Gulfstream Aerospace C-37 Gulfstream V

	1778	Gulfstream Aerospace C-37A Gulfstream V (04-01778)	US Army OSAC/PAT, Andrews AFB, MD
	1863	Gulfstream Aerospace C-37A Gulfstream V (02-01863)	US Army OSAC/PAT, Andrews AFB, MD
	1944	Gulfstream Aerospace C-37A Gulfstream V (97-01944)	US Army OSAC/PAT, Andrews AFB, MD
	10028	Gulfstream Aerospace C-37A Gulfstream V (01-0028)	USAF 310th AS/6th AMW, MacDill AFB, FL
	10029	Gulfstream Aerospace C-37A Gulfstream V (01-0029)	USAF 310th AS/6th AMW, MacDill AFB, FL
	10030	Gulfstream Aerospace C-37A Gulfstream V (01-0030)	USAF 310th AS/6th AMW, MacDill AFB, FL
	10065	Gulfstream Aerospace C-37A Gulfstream V (01-0065)	USAF 65th AS/15th Wg, Hickam AFB, HI
	10550	Gulfstream Aerospace C-37B Gulfstream V (11-0550)	USAF 99th AS/89th AW, Andrews AFB, MD
	60500	Gulfstream Aerospace C-37B Gulfstream V (06-0500)	USAF 99th AS/89th AW, Andrews AFB, MD
	70400	Gulfstream Aerospace C-37A Gulfstream V (97-0400)	USAF 99th AS/89th AW, Andrews AFB, MD
	70401	Gulfstream Aerospace C-37A Gulfstream V (97-0401)	USAF 99th AS/89th AW, Andrews AFB, MD
	90404	Gulfstream Aerospace C-37A Gulfstream V (99-0404)	USAF 99th AS/89th AW, Andrews AFB, MD
	90525	Gulfstream Aerospace C-37B Gulfstream V (09-0525)	USAF 99th AS/89th AW, Andrews AFB, MD

Boeing C-40

	10015	Boeing C-40B (N378BJ/01-0015)	USAF 65th AS/15th Wg, Hickam AFB, HI
	10040	Boeing C-40B (N371BJ/01-0040)	USAF 1st AS/89th AW, Andrews AFB, MD
	10041	Boeing C-40B (N374BC/01-0041)	USAF 1st AS/89th AW, Andrews AFB, MD
	20201	Boeing C-40C (N752BC/02-0201)	USAF 201st AS/113th FW DC ANG, Andrews AFB, MD
	20202	Boeing C-40C (N754BC/02-0202)	USAF 201st AS/113th FW DC ANG, Andrews AFB, MD
	20203	Boeing C-40C (N236BA/02-0203)	USAF 201st AS/113th FW DC ANG, Andrews AFB, MD
	50730	Boeing C-40C (N365BJ/05-0730)	USAF 73rd AS/932nd AW AFRC, Scott AFB, IL
	50932	Boeing C-40C (N366BJ/05-0932)	USAF 73rd AS/932nd AW AFRC, Scott AFB, IL
	54613	Boeing C-40C (N368BJ/05-4613)	USAF 73rd AS/932nd AW AFRC, Scott AFB, IL
	90540	Boeing C-40C (N736JS/09-0540)	USAF 73rd AS/932nd AW AFRC, Scott AFB, IL

Boeing 767-2C/KC-46A Pegasus

	46001	Boeing 767-2LKC (N461FT/11-46001)	Boeing, Everett, for USAF
	46002	Boeing KC-46A Pegasus (N462KC/11-46002)	Boeing, Seattle, for USAF
	46003	Boeing 767-2LKC (N463FT/11-46003)	Boeing, Everett, for USAF
	46004	Boeing KC-46A Pegasus (N464KC/11-46004)	Boeing, Seattle, for USAF

Serial	Type (code/other identity)	Owner/operator, location or fate	Notes
56005	Boeing KC-46A Pegasus (N842BA/15-46005)	USAF 418th FLTS/412th TW, Edwards AFB, CA	
56006	Boeing 767-2LKC (N884BA/15-46006)	Boeing, Seattle, for USAF	
56007	Boeing KC-46A Pegasus (15-46007)	Boeing, Everett, for USAF	
56008	Boeing KC-46A Pegasus (15-46008)	Boeing, Everett, for USAF	
56009	Boeing KC-46A Pegasus (N50217/15-46009)	USAF 22nd ARW, McConnell AFB, KS	
56010	Boeing KC-46A Pegasus (15-46010)	Boeing, Everett, for USAF	
56011	Boeing KC-46A Pegasus (15-46011)	Boeing, Everett, for USAF	
66012	Boeing KC-46A Pegasus (16-46012)	Boeing, Everett, for USAF	
66013	Boeing KC-46A Pegasus (16-46013)	Boeing, Everett, for USAF	
66014	Boeing KC-46A Pegasus (16-46014)	Boeing, Everett, for USAF	
66015	Boeing KC-46A Pegasus (16-46015)	Boeing, Everett, for USAF	
66016	Boeing KC-46A Pegasus (16-46016)	Boeing, Seattle, for USAF	
66017	Boeing KC-46A Pegasus (16-46017)	Boeing, Seattle, for USAF	
66018	Boeing KC-46A Pegasus (N5514J/16-46018)	Boeing, Everett, for USAF	
66019	Boeing KC-46A Pegasus (N5514K/16-46019)	Boeing, Everett, for USAF	
66020	Boeing KC-46A Pegasus (N5514V/16-46020)	Boeing, Everett, for USAF	
66021	Boeing KC-46A Pegasus (N5514X/16-46021)	Boeing, Everett, for USAF	
66022	Boeing KC-46A Pegasus (N5573S/16-46022)	USAF 22nd ARW, McConnell AFB, KS	
66023	Boeing KC-46A Pegasus (16-46023)	Boeing, Seattle, for USAF	
76024	Boeing KC-46A Pegasus (17-46024)	Boeing, Everett, for USAF	
76025	Boeing KC-46A Pegasus (17-46025)	Boeing, Seattle, for USAF	
76026	Boeing KC-46A Pegasus (17-46026)	Boeing, Seattle, for USAF	
76027	Boeing KC-46A Pegasus (17-46027)	USAF 56th ARS/97th AMW, Altus AFB, OK	
76028	Boeing KC-46A Pegasus (17-46028)	Boeing, Everett, for USAF	
76029	Boeing KC-46A Pegasus (17-46029)	Boeing, Everett, for USAF	
76030	Boeing KC-46A Pegasus (N6009F/17-46030)	USAF 22nd ARW, McConnell AFB, KS	
76031	Boeing KC-46A Pegasus (N5513X/17-46031)	USAF 22nd ARW, McConnell AFB, KS	
76032	Boeing KC-46A Pegasus (17-46032)	Boeing, Everett, for USAF	
76033	Boeing KC-46A Pegasus (17-46033)	Boeing, Everett, for USAF	
76034	Boeing KC-46A Pegasus (17-46034)	Boeing, Everett, for USAF	
76035	Boeing KC-46A Pegasus (17-46035)	Boeing, Everett, for USAF	
76036	Boeing KC-46A Pegasus (17-46036)	Boeing, Everett, for USAF	
76037	Boeing KC-46A Pegasus (17-46037)	USAF (on order)	
76038	Boeing KC-46A Pegasus (17-46038)	Boeing, Everett, for USAF	
86039	Boeing KC-46A Pegasus (18-46039)	Boeing, Everett, for USAF	
86040	Boeing KC-46A Pegasus (18-46040)	Boeing, Everett, for USAF	
86041	Boeing KC-46A Pegasus (18-46041)	Boeing, Everett, for USAF	
86042	Boeing KC-46A Pegasus (18-46042)	USAF (on order)	
86043	Boeing KC-46A Pegasus (18-46043)	USAF (on order)	
86044	Boeing KC-46A Pegasus (18-46044)	USAF (on order)	
86045	Boeing KC-46A Pegasus (18-46045)	USAF (on order)	
86046	Boeing KC-46A Pegasus (18-46046)	USAF (on order)	
86047	Boeing KC-46A Pegasus (18-46047)	USAF (on order)	
86048	Boeing KC-46A Pegasus (18-46048)	USAF (on order)	
86049	Boeing KC-46A Pegasus (18-46049)	USAF (on order)	
86050	Boeing KC-46A Pegasus (18-46050)	USAF (on order)	
86051	Boeing KC-46A Pegasus (18-46051)	USAF (on order)	
86052	Boeing KC-46A Pegasus (18-46052)	USAF (on order)	
86053	Boeing KC-46A Pegasus (18-46053)	USAF (on order)	
96054	Boeing KC-46A Pegasus (19-46054)	USAF (on order)	
96055	Boeing KC-46A Pegasus (19-46055)	USAF (on order)	
96056	Boeing KC-46A Pegasus (19-46056)	USAF (on order)	
96057	Boeing KC-46A Pegasus (19-46057)	USAF (on order)	
96058	Boeing KC-46A Pegasus (19-46058)	USAF (on order)	
96059	Boeing KC-46A Pegasus (19-46059)	USAF (on order)	
96060	Boeing KC-46A Pegasus (19-46060)	USAF (on order)	
96061	Boeing KC-46A Pegasus (19-46061)	USAF (on order)	
96062	Boeing KC-46A Pegasus (19-46062)	USAF (on order)	
96063	Boeing KC-46A Pegasus (19-46063)	USAF (on order)	
96064	Boeing KC-46A Pegasus (19-46064)	USAF (on order)	
96065	Boeing KC-46A Pegasus (19-46065)	USAF (on order)	
96066	Boeing KC-46A Pegasus (19-46066)	USAF (on order)	

Notes	Serial	Type (code/other identity)	Owner/operator, location or fate
	96067	Boeing KC-46A Pegasus (19-46067)	USAF (on order)
	96068	Boeing KC-46A Pegasus (19-46068)	USAF (on order)
	Boeing B-52H Stratofortress		
	00001	Boeing B-52H Stratofortress (60-0001) [LA] *r*	USAF 96th BS/2nd BW, Barksdale AFB, LA
	00002	Boeing B-52H Stratofortress (60-0002) [LA] *gn* [2 BW]	USAF 96th BS/2nd BW, Barksdale AFB, LA
	00003	Boeing B-52H Stratofortress (60-0003) [BD] *or/bl*	USAF 93rd BS/307th BW AFRC, Barksdale AFB, LA
	00004	Boeing B-52H Stratofortress (60-0004) [MT] *r/y*	USAF 23rd BS/5th BW, Minot AFB, ND
	00005	Boeing B-52H Stratofortress (60-0005) [MT] *r/y* $	USAF 23rd BS/5th BW, Minot AFB, ND
	00007	Boeing B-52H Stratofortress (60-0007) [MT] *r/y*	USAF 23rd BS/5th BW, Minot AFB, ND
	00008	Boeing B-52H Stratofortress (60-0008) [LA] *bl* [8th AF]	USAF 20th BS/2nd BW, Barksdale AFB, LA
	00009	Boeing B-52H Stratofortress (60-0009) [MT] *y/bk* $	USAF 69th BS/5th BW, Minot AFB, ND
	00011	Boeing B-52H Stratofortress (60-0011) [BD] *or/bl* [11 BS]	USAF 93rd BS/307th BW AFRC, Barksdale AFB, LA
	00012	Boeing B-52H Stratofortress (60-0012) [MT] *y/bk*	USAF 69th BS/5th BW, Minot AFB, ND
	00013	Boeing B-52H Stratofortress (60-0013) [LA] *bl*	USAF 20th BS/2nd BW, Barksdale AFB, LA
	00015	Boeing B-52H Stratofortress (60-0015) [BD] *or/bl*	USAF 93rd BS/307th BW AFRC, Barksdale AFB, LA
	00017	Boeing B-52H Stratofortress (60-0017) [MT] *y/bk*	USAF 69th BS/5th BW, Minot AFB, ND
	00018	Boeing B-52H Stratofortress (60-0018) [MT] *y/bk*	USAF 69th BS/5th BW, Minot AFB, ND
	00021	Boeing B-52H Stratofortress (60-0021) [LA] *r*	USAF 96th BS/2nd BW, Barksdale AFB, LA
	00022	Boeing B-52H Stratofortress (60-0022) [LA] *r*	USAF 96th BS/2nd BW, Barksdale AFB, LA
	00023	Boeing B-52H Stratofortress (60-0023) [MT] *r/y*	USAF 23rd BS/5th BW, Minot AFB, ND
	00024	Boeing B-52H Stratofortress (60-0024) [LA] *bl*	USAF 20th BS/2nd BW, Barksdale AFB, LA
	00025	Boeing B-52H Stratofortress (60-0025) [LA] *bl*	USAF 20th BS/2nd BW, Barksdale AFB, LA
	00026	Boeing B-52H Stratofortress (60-0026) [MT] *r/y*	USAF 23rd BS/5th BW, Minot AFB, ND
	00028	Boeing B-52H Stratofortress (60-0028) [LA] *r*	USAF 96th BS/2nd BW, Barksdale AFB, LA
	00029	Boeing B-52H Stratofortress (60-0029) [BD] *or/bl* [93 BS]	USAF 93rd BS/307th BW AFRC, Barksdale AFB, LA
	00031	Boeing B-52H Stratofortress (60-0031) [OT] *or/w*	USAF 49th TES/53rd TEG, Barksdale AFB, LA
	00032	Boeing B-52H Stratofortress (60-0032) [MT] *y/bk*	USAF 69th BS/5th BW, Minot AFB, ND
	00033	Boeing B-52H Stratofortress (60-0033) [MT] *r/y*	USAF 23rd BS/5th BW, Minot AFB, ND
	00035	Boeing B-52H Stratofortress (60-0035) [BD] *or/bl*	USAF 93rd BS/307th BW AFRC, Barksdale AFB, LA
	00036	Boeing B-52H Stratofortress (60-0036) [ED]	USAF 419th FLTS/412th TW, Edwards AFB, CA
	00037	Boeing B-52H Stratofortress (60-0037) [MT] *r/y*	USAF 23rd BS/5th BW, Minot AFB, ND
	00038	Boeing B-52H Stratofortress (60-0038) [BD] *or/bl*	USAF 93rd BS/307th BW AFRC, Barksdale AFB, LA
	00041	Boeing B-52H Stratofortress (60-0041) [BD] *or/bl*	USAF 93rd BS/307th BW AFRC, Barksdale AFB, LA
	00042	Boeing B-52H Stratofortress (60-0042) [BD] *or/bl*	USAF 93rd BS/307th BW AFRC, Barksdale AFB, LA
	00044	Boeing B-52H Stratofortress (60-0044) [MT] *r/y*	USAF 23rd BS/5th BW, Minot AFB, ND
	00045	Boeing B-52H Stratofortress (60-0045) [BD] *or/bl* [307 BG]	USAF 93rd BS/307th BW AFRC, Barksdale AFB, LA
	00048	Boeing B-52H Stratofortress (60-0048) [LA] *bl*	USAF 20th BS/2nd BW, Barksdale AFB, LA
	00050	Boeing B-52H Stratofortress (60-0050) [ED]	USAF 419th FLTS/412th TW, Edwards AFB, CA
	00051	Boeing B-52H Stratofortress (60-0051) [OT] *or/w* [49 TES]	USAF 49th TES/53rd TEG, Barksdale AFB, LA
	00052	Boeing B-52H Stratofortress (60-0052) [LA] *r*	USAF 96th BS/2nd BW, Barksdale AFB, LA
	00054	Boeing B-52H Stratofortress (60-0054) [LA] *r*	USAF 96th BS/2nd BW, Barksdale AFB, LA
	00055	Boeing B-52H Stratofortress (60-0055) [MT] *r/y* [5 OG]	USAF 23rd BS/5th BW, Minot AFB, ND
	00056	Boeing B-52H Stratofortress (60-0056) [MT] *r/y*	USAF 23rd BS/5th BW, Minot AFB, ND
	00057	Boeing B-52H Stratofortress (60-0057) [BD] *or/bl* [340 WPS]	USAF 93rd BS/307th BW AFRC, Barksdale AFB, LA
	00058	Boeing B-52H Stratofortress (60-0058) [LA] *bl*	USAF 20th BS/2nd BW, Barksdale AFB, LA
	00059	Boeing B-52H Stratofortress (60-0059) [LA] *r* [96 BS]	USAF 96th BS/2nd BW, Barksdale AFB, LA
	00060	Boeing B-52H Stratofortress (60-0060) [MT] *r/y*	USAF 23rd BS/5th BW, Minot AFB, ND
	00061	Boeing B-52H Stratofortress (60-0061) [BD] *or/bl* [307 BW]	USAF 93rd BS/307th BW AFRC, Barksdale AFB, LA
	00062	Boeing B-52H Stratofortress (60-0062) [LA] *bl*	USAF 20th BS/2nd BW, Barksdale AFB, LA

Serial	Type (code/other identity)	Owner/operator, location or fate	Notes
10001	Boeing B-52H Stratofortress (61-0001) [MT] y/bk	USAF 69th BS/5th BW, Minot AFB, ND	
10002	Boeing B-52H Stratofortress (61-0002) [LA] gn [2D OG]	USAF 96th BS/2nd BW, Barksdale AFB, LA	
10003	Boeing B-52H Stratofortress (61-0003) [MT] y/bk	USAF 69th BS/5th BW, Minot AFB, ND	
10004	Boeing B-52H Stratofortress (61-0004) [LA] r	USAF 96th BS/2nd BW, Barksdale AFB, LA	
10005	Boeing B-52H Stratofortress (61-0005) [MT] y/bk	USAF 69th BS/5th BW, Minot AFB, ND	
10006	Boeing B-52H Stratofortress (61-0006) [LA] r	USAF 96th BS/2nd BW, Barksdale AFB, LA	
10007	Boeing B-52H Stratofortress (61-0007) [MT] y/bk	USAF 69th BS/5th BW, Minot AFB, ND	
10008	Boeing B-52H Stratofortress (61-0008) [BD] or/bl	USAF 93rd BS/307th BW AFRC, Barksdale AFB, LA	
10010	Boeing B-52H Stratofortress (61-0010) [LA] or/bl [343 BS]	USAF 93rd BS/307th BW AFRC, Barksdale AFB, LA	
10011	Boeing B-52H Stratofortress (61-0011) [BD] or/bl	USAF 93rd BS/307th BW AFRC, Barksdale AFB, LA	
10012	Boeing B-52H Stratofortress (61-0012) [LA] r	USAF 96th BS/2nd BW, Barksdale AFB, LA	
10013	Boeing B-52H Stratofortress (61-0013) [LA] bl	USAF 20th BS/2nd BW, Barksdale AFB, LA	
10014	Boeing B-52H Stratofortress (61-0014) [MT] y/bk	USAF 69th BS/5th BW, Minot AFB, ND	
10015	Boeing B-52H Stratofortress (61-0015) [BD] or/bl	USAF 93rd BS/307th BW AFRC, Barksdale AFB, LA	
10016	Boeing B-52H Stratofortress (61-0016) [LA] r	USAF 96th BS/2nd BW, Barksdale AFB, LA	
10017	Boeing B-52H Stratofortress (61-0017) [BD] or/bl	USAF 93rd BS/307th BW AFRC, Barksdale AFB, LA	
10018	Boeing B-52H Stratofortress (61-0018) [MT] y/bk	USAF 69th BS/5th BW, Minot AFB, ND	
10019	Boeing B-52H Stratofortress (61-0019) [LA] r	USAF 96th BS/2nd BW, Barksdale AFB, LA	
10020	Boeing B-52H Stratofortress (61-0020) [LA] bl [20 BS]	USAF 20th BS/2nd BW, Barksdale AFB, LA	
10021	Boeing B-52H Stratofortress (61-0021) [BD] or/bl	USAF 93rd BS/307th BW AFRC, Barksdale AFB, LA	
10028	Boeing B-52H Stratofortress (61-0028) [OT] y/w [49 TES]	USAF 49th TES/53rd TEG, Barksdale AFB, LA	
10029	Boeing B-52H Stratofortress (61-0029) [BD] or/bl [93 BS]	USAF 93rd BS/307th BW AFRC, Barksdale AFB, LA	
10031	Boeing B-52H Stratofortress (61-0031) [BD] or/bl	USAF 93rd BS/307th BW AFRC, Barksdale AFB, LA	
10032	Boeing B-52H Stratofortress (61-0032) [MT] r/y	USAF 23rd BS/5th BW, Minot AFB, ND	
10034	Boeing B-52H Stratofortress (61-0034) [MT] r/y	USAF 23rd BS/5th BW, Minot AFB, ND	
10035	Boeing B-52H Stratofortress (61-0035) [MT] r/y	USAF 23rd BS/5th BW, Minot AFB, ND	
10036	Boeing B-52H Stratofortress (61-0036) [LA] r	USAF 96th BS/2nd BW, Barksdale AFB, LA	
10038	Boeing B-52H Stratofortress (61-0038) [BD] or/bl	USAF 93rd BS/307th BW AFRC, Barksdale AFB, LA	
10039	Boeing B-52H Stratofortress (61-0039) [MT] y/bk	USAF 69th BS/5th BW, Minot AFB, ND	
10040	Boeing B-52H Stratofortress (61-0040) [MT] r/y	USAF 23rd BS/5th BW, Minot AFB, ND	

Lockheed C-130

Serial	Type (code/other identity)	Owner/operator, location or fate	Notes
00162	Lockheed MC-130H Combat Talon II (90-0162)	USAF 15th SOS/1st SOW, Hurlburt Field, FL	
00164	Lockheed AC-130U Spooky (90-0164)	USAF 4th SOS/1st SOW, Hurlburt Field, FL	
00165	Lockheed AC-130U Spooky (90-0165)	USAF 4th SOS/1st SOW, Hurlburt Field, FL	
00166	Lockheed AC-130U Spooky (90-0166)	USAF 4th SOS/1st SOW, Hurlburt Field, FL	
00167	Lockheed AC-130U Spooky (90-0167)	USAF 4th SOS/1st SOW, Hurlburt Field, FL	
00322	Lockheed C-130H Hercules (80-0322) y/bk	USAF 118th AS/103rd AW, Bradley ANGB, CT ANG	
00324	Lockheed C-130H Hercules (80-0324)	USAF 186th AS/120th AW, Great Falls, MT ANG	
00326	Lockheed C-130H Hercules (80-0326) y/bk	USAF 118th AS/103rd AW, Bradley ANGB, CT ANG	
01057	Lockheed C-130H Hercules (90-1057) bl	USAF 142nd AS/166th AW, New Castle County, DE ANG	
01058	Lockheed AC-130W Stinger II (90-1058)	USAF 16th SOS/27th SOW, Cannon AFB, NM	
01791	Lockheed C-130H Hercules (90-1791)	USAF 180th AS/139th AW, Rosencrans Memorial, MO ANG	
01792	Lockheed C-130H Hercules (90-1792)	USAF 180th AS/139th AW, Rosencrans Memorial, MO ANG	
01793	Lockheed C-130H Hercules (90-1793)	USAF 180th AS/139th AW, Rosencrans Memorial, MO ANG	
01794	Lockheed C-130H Hercules (90-1794)	USAF 180th AS/139th AW, Rosencrans Memorial, MO ANG	
01795	Lockheed C-130H Hercules (90-1795)	USAF 180th AS/139th AW, Rosencrans Memorial, MO ANG	
01796	Lockheed C-130H Hercules (90-1796)	USAF 180th AS/139th AW, Rosencrans Memorial, MO ANG	
01797	Lockheed C-130H Hercules (90-1797)	USAF 180th AS/139th AW, Rosencrans Memorial, MO ANG	

Notes	Serial	Type (code/other identity)	Owner/operator, location or fate
	01798	Lockheed C-130J Hercules (90-1798)	USAF 180th AS/139th AW, Rosencrans Memorial, MO ANG
	01934	Lockheed EC-130J Commando Solo III (00-1934)	USAF 193rd SOS/193rd SOW, Harrisburg, PA ANG
	02103	Lockheed HC-130N Combat King (90-2103)	USAF 39th RQS/920th RQW AFRC, Patrick AFB, FL
	05700	Lockheed C-130J-30 Hercules II (10-5700) r	USAF 39th AS/317th AW, Dyess AFB, TX
	05701	Lockheed C-130J-30 Hercules II (10-5701) r [317 AG]	USAF 39th AS/317th AW, Dyess AFB, TX
	05714	Lockheed MC-130J Commando II (10-5714)	USAF 67th SOS/352nd SOG, RAF Mildenhall, UK
	05716	Lockheed HC-130J Combat King II (10-5716) [FT]	USAF 79th RQS/563rd RQG, Davis-Monthan AFB, AZ
	05717	Lockheed HC-130J Combat King II (10-5717) [FT]	USAF 79th RQS/563rd RQG, Davis-Monthan AFB, AZ
	05728	Lockheed C-130J-30 Hercules II (10-5728) y	USAF 48th AS/314th AW, Little Rock AFB, AR
	05771	Lockheed C-130J-30 Hercules II (10-5771) w/bk	USAF 61st AS/19th AW Little Rock AFB, AR
	09107	Lockheed C-130H Hercules (90-9107) bl/r	USAF 757th AS/910th AW AFRC, Youngstown ARS, OH
	09108	Lockheed C-130H Hercules (90-9108) bl/r	USAF 757th AS/910th AW AFRC, Youngstown ARS, OH
	10626	Lockheed C-130H Hercules (81-0626) r	USAF 164th AS/179th AW, Mansfield, OH ANG
	10629	Lockheed C-130H Hercules (81-0629) r $	USAF 154th TS/189th AW, Little Rock, AR ANG
	11231	Lockheed C-130H Hercules (91-1231) w/bk	USAF 165th AS/123rd AW, Standiford Field, KY ANG
	11232	Lockheed C-130H Hercules (91-1232) w/bk	USAF 165th AS/123rd AW, Standiford Field, KY ANG
	11233	Lockheed C-130H Hercules (91-1233) w/bk	USAF 165th AS/123rd AW, Standiford Field, KY ANG
	11234	Lockheed C-130H Hercules (91-1234) w/bk	USAF 165th AS/123rd AW, Standiford Field, KY ANG
	11235	Lockheed C-130H Hercules (91-1235) w/bk	USAF 165th AS/123rd AW, Standiford Field, KY ANG
	11236	Lockheed C-130H Hercules (91-1236) w/bk	USAF 165th AS/123rd AW, Standiford Field, KY ANG
	11237	Lockheed C-130H Hercules (91-1237) w/bk	USAF 165th AS/123rd AW, Standiford Field, KY ANG
	11238	Lockheed C-130H Hercules (91-1238) w/bk	USAF 165th AS/123rd AW, Standiford Field, KY ANG
	11461	Lockheed C-130J-30 Hercules II (01-1461) gn	USAF 115th AS/146th AW, Channel Island ANGS, CA ANG
	11462	Lockheed C-130J-30 Hercules II (01-1462) gn	USAF 115th AS/146th AW, Channel Island ANGS, CA ANG
	11652	Lockheed C-130H Hercules (91-1652)	USAF 180th AS/139th AW, Rosencrans Memorial, MO ANG
	11653	Lockheed C-130H Hercules (91-1653)	USAF 180th AS/139th AW, Rosencrans Memorial, MO ANG
	11935	Lockheed EC-130J Commando Solo III (01-1935)	USAF 193rd SOS/193rd SOW, Harrisburg, PA ANG
	14862	Lockheed EC-130H Compass Call (64-14862) [DM]	USAF 43rd ECS/55th ECG, Davis-Monthan AFB, AZ
	14866	Lockheed C-130H Hercules (64-14866)	USAF 198th AS/156th AW, San Juan, PR ANG
	15719	Lockheed HC-130J Combat King II (11-5719) [FT]	USAF 79th RQS/563rd RQG, Davis-Monthan AFB, AZ
	15725	Lockheed HC-130J Combat King II (11-5725) [FT]	USAF 71st RQS/347th RG, Moody AFB, GA
	15727	Lockheed HC-130J Combat King II (11-5727) [FT]	USAF 71st RQS/347th RG, Moody AFB, GA
	15729	Lockheed MC-130J Commando II (11-5729)	USAF 522nd SOS/27th SOW, Cannon AFB, NM
	15731	Lockheed MC-130J Commando II (11-5731)	USAF 67th SOS/352nd SOG, RAF Mildenhall, UK
	15732	Lockheed C-130J-30 Hercules II (11-5732)	USAF 317th AW, Dyess AFB, TX
	15733	Lockheed MC-130J Commando II (11-5733)	LMTAS, Marietta, GA
	15734	Lockheed C-130J-30 Hercules II (11-5734) w/bk	USAF 61st AS/19th AW Little Rock AFB, AR
	15735	Lockheed MC-130J Commando II (11-5735)	USAF 522nd SOS/27th SOW, Cannon AFB, NM
	15736	Lockheed C-130J-30 Hercules II (11-5736) [RS] bl/w	USAF 37th AS/86th AW, Ramstein AB, Germany
	15737	Lockheed MC-130J Commando II (11-5737)	USAF 67th SOS/352nd SOG, RAF Mildenhall, UK
	15738	Lockheed C-130J-30 Hercules II (11-5738) w/bk	USAF 61st AS/19th AW Little Rock AFB, AR

Serial	Type (code/other identity)	Owner/operator, location or fate	Notes
15740	Lockheed C-130J-30 Hercules II (11-5740)	USAF 317th AW, Dyess AFB, TX	
15745	Lockheed C-130J-30 Hercules II (11-5745) *w/bk*	USAF 41st AS/19th AW Little Rock AFB, AR	
15748	Lockheed C-130J-30 Hercules II (11-5748) *w/bk*	USAF 61st AS/19th AW Little Rock AFB, AR	
15752	Lockheed C-130J-30 Hercules II (11-5752) *w/bk*	USAF 61st AS/19th AW Little Rock AFB, AR	
15765	Lockheed HC-130J Combat King II (11-5765) [FT]	USAF 71st RQS/347th RG, Moody AFB, GA	
19141	Lockheed C-130H Hercules (91-9141) *bl/w*	USAF 357th AS/908th AW AFRC, Maxwell AFB, AL	
19142	Lockheed C-130H Hercules (91-9142) *bl/w*	USAF 357th AS/908th AW AFRC, Maxwell AFB, AL	
19143	Lockheed C-130H Hercules (91-9143) *bl/w*	USAF 357th AS/908th AW AFRC, Maxwell AFB, AL	
19144	Lockheed C-130H Hercules (91-9144) *bl/w*	USAF 357th AS/908th AW AFRC, Maxwell AFB, AL	
20055	Lockheed C-130H Hercules (82-0055) *r*	USAF 164th AS/179th AW, Mansfield, OH ANG	
20056	Lockheed C-130H Hercules (82-0056)	USAF 16th SOS/27th SOW, Cannon AFB, NM	
20061	Lockheed C-130H Hercules (82-0061)	USAF	
20253	Lockheed AC-130U Spooky (92-0253)	*Withdrawn from use, September 2018*	
20314	Lockheed C-130J-30 Hercules II (02-0314) *y $*	USAF 48th AS/314th AW, Little Rock AFB, AR	
20547	Lockheed C-130H Hercules (92-0547) *bl/w*	USAF 192nd AS/152nd AW, Reno, NV ANG	
20548	Lockheed C-130H Hercules (92-0548) *bl/w*	USAF 192nd AS/152nd AW, Reno, NV ANG	
20549	Lockheed C-130H Hercules (92-0549) *bl/w*	USAF 192nd AS/152nd AW, Reno, NV ANG	
20550	Lockheed C-130H Hercules (92-0550) *bl*	USAF 700th AS/94th AW AFRC, Dobbins ARB, GA	
20551	Lockheed C-130H Hercules (92-0551) *bl*	USAF 700th AS/94th AW AFRC, Dobbins ARB, GA	
20552	Lockheed C-130H Hercules (92-0552) *bl*	USAF 700th AS/94th AW AFRC, Dobbins ARB, GA	
20553	Lockheed C-130H Hercules (92-0553) *bl/w*	USAF 192nd AS/152nd AW, Reno, NV ANG	
20554	Lockheed C-130H Hercules (92-0554) *bl/w*	USAF 192nd AS/152nd AW, Reno, NV ANG	
21094	Lockheed LC-130H Hercules (92-1094)	USAF 139th AS/109th AW, Schenectady, NY ANG	
21095	Lockheed LC-130H Hercules (92-1095)	USAF 139th AS/109th AW, Schenectady, NY ANG	
21434	Lockheed C-130J-30 Hercules II (02-1434) *r*	USAF 143rd AS/143rd AW, Quonset, RI ANG	
21451	Lockheed C-130H Hercules (92-1451) *or/bk*	USAF 169th AS/182nd AW, Peoria, IL ANG	
21452	Lockheed C-130H Hercules (92-1452) *or/bk*	USAF 169th AS/182nd AW, Peoria, IL ANG	
21453	Lockheed C-130H-3 Hercules (92-1453) *bl/w*	USAF 181st AS/136th AW, NAS Dallas, TX ANG	
21454	Lockheed C-130H-3 Hercules (92-1454) *bl/w*	USAF 181st AS/136th AW, NAS Dallas, TX ANG	
21463	Lockheed C-130J Hercules II (02-1463) *gn*	USAF 115th AS/146th AW, Channel Island ANGS, CA ANG	
21464	Lockheed C-130J Hercules II (02-1464) *gn*	USAF 115th AS/146th AW, Channel Island ANGS, CA ANG	
21531	Lockheed C-130H-3 Hercules (92-1531) *y/bk*	USAF 187th AS/153rd AW, Cheyenne, WY ANG	
21532	Lockheed C-130H-3 Hercules (92-1532) *y/bk*	USAF 187th AS/153rd AW, Cheyenne, WY ANG	
21533	Lockheed C-130H-3 Hercules (92-1533) *y/bk*	USAF 187th AS/153rd AW, Cheyenne, WY ANG	
21534	Lockheed C-130H-3 Hercules (92-1534) *y/bk*	USAF 187th AS/153rd AW, Cheyenne, WY ANG	
21535	Lockheed C-130H-3 Hercules (92-1535) *y/bk*	USAF 187th AS/153rd AW, Cheyenne, WY ANG	
21536	Lockheed C-130H-3 Hercules (92-1536) *y/bk*	USAF 187th AS/153rd AW, Cheyenne, WY ANG	
21537	Lockheed C-130H-3 Hercules (92-1537) *y/bk*	USAF 187th AS/153rd AW, Cheyenne, WY ANG	
21538	Lockheed C-130H-3 Hercules (92-1538) *y/bk*	USAF 187th AS/153rd AW, Cheyenne, WY ANG	
22104	Lockheed HC-130N Combat King (92-2104)	USAF 39th RQS/920th RQW AFRC, Patrick AFB, FL	
23021	Lockheed C-130H Hercules (92-3021) *bl/r*	USAF 757th AS/910th AW AFRC, Youngstown ARS, OH	
23022	Lockheed C-130H Hercules (92-3022) *bl/r*	USAF 757th AS/910th AW AFRC, Youngstown ARS, OH	
23023	Lockheed C-130H Hercules (92-3023) *bl/r*	USAF 757th AS/910th AW AFRC, Youngstown ARS, OH	
23024	Lockheed C-130H Hercules (92-3024) *bl/r*	USAF 757th AS/910th AW AFRC, Youngstown ARS, OH	
23281	Lockheed C-130H-3 Hercules (92-3281) *pr/w*	USAF 96th AS/934th AW AFRC, Minneapolis/St Paul, MN	
23282	Lockheed C-130H-3 Hercules (92-3282) *pr/w*	USAF 96th AS/934th AW AFRC, Minneapolis/St Paul, MN	
23283	Lockheed C-130H-3 Hercules (92-3283) *pr/w*	USAF 96th AS/934th AW AFRC, Minneapolis/St Paul, MN	
23284	Lockheed C-130H-3 Hercules (92-3284) *pr/w $*	USAF 96th AS/934th AW AFRC, Minneapolis/St Paul, MN	
23285	Lockheed C-130H-3 Hercules (92-3285) *pr/w*	USAF 96th AS/934th AW AFRC, Minneapolis/St Paul, MN	

C-130

Notes	Serial	Type (code/other identity)	Owner/operator, location or fate
	23286	Lockheed C-130H-3 Hercules (92-3286) pr/w	USAF 96th AS/934th AW AFRC, Minneapolis/ St Paul, MN
	23287	Lockheed C-130H-3 Hercules (92-3287) pr/w	USAF 96th AS/934th AW AFRC, Minneapolis/ St Paul, MN
	23288	Lockheed C-130H-3 Hercules (92-3288) pr/w	USAF 96th AS/934th AW AFRC, Minneapolis/ St Paul, MN
	25753	Lockheed AC-130J Ghostrider (12-5753)	USAF 73rd SOS/1st SOW, Hurlburt Field, FL
	25754	Lockheed AC-130J Ghostrider (12-5754)	LMTAS, Marietta, GA
	25755	Lockheed HC-130J Combat King II (12-5755)	USAF 415th SOS/58th SOW, Kirtland AFB, NM
	25756	Lockheed C-130J-30 Hercules II (12-5756) w/bk	USAF 61st AS/19th AW Little Rock AFB, AR
	25757	Lockheed MC-130J Commando II (12-5757)	USAF 67th SOS/352nd SOG, RAF Mildenhall, UK
	25759	Lockheed MC-130J Commando II (12-5759)	USAF 67th SOS/352nd SOG, RAF Mildenhall, UK
	25760	Lockheed MC-130J Commando II (12-5760)	USAF 67th SOS/352nd SOG, RAF Mildenhall, UK
	25761	Lockheed MC-130J Commando II (12-5761)	USAF 17th SOS/353rd SOG, Kadena AB, Japan
	25762	Lockheed MC-130J Commando II (12-5762)	USAF 17th SOS/353rd SOG, Kadena AB, Japan
	25763	Lockheed MC-130J Commando II (12-5763)	USAF 17th SOS/353rd SOG, Kadena AB, Japan
	25768	Lockheed HC-130J Combat King II (12-5768) [FT]	USAF 71st RQS/347th RG, Moody AFB, GA
	25769	Lockheed HC-130J Combat King II (12-5769) [FT]	USAF 71st RQS/347th RG, Moody AFB, GA
	25772	Lockheed AC-130J Ghostrider (12-5772)	USAF 73rd SOS/1st SOW, Hurlburt Field, FL
	25773	Lockheed HC-130J Combat King II (12-5773) [FT]	USAF 71st RQS/347th RG, Moody AFB, GA
	28155	Lockheed C-130J-30 Hercules II (02-8155) r	USAF 815th AS/403rd AW AFRC, Keesler AFB, MO
	30487	Lockheed C-130H Hercules (83-0487)	USAF 139th AS/109th AW, Schenectady, NY ANG
	30489	Lockheed C-130H Hercules (83-0489)	USAF 139th AS/109th AW, Schenectady, NY ANG
	30490	Lockheed LC-130H Hercules (83-0490)	USAF 139th AS/109th AW, Schenectady, NY ANG
	30491	Lockheed LC-130H Hercules (83-0491)	USAF 139th AS/109th AW, Schenectady, NY ANG
	30492	Lockheed LC-130H Hercules (83-0492)	USAF 139th AS/109th AW, Schenectady, NY ANG
	30493	Lockheed C-130H Hercules (83-0493)	USAF 139th AS/109th AW, Schenectady, NY ANG
	31036	Lockheed C-130H Hercules (93-1036) bl	USAF 700th AS/94th AW AFRC, Dobbins ARB, GA
	31037	Lockheed C-130H Hercules (93-1037) bl	USAF 700th AS/94th AW AFRC, Dobbins ARB, GA
	31038	Lockheed C-130H Hercules (93-1038) bl	USAF 700th AS/94th AW AFRC, Dobbins ARB, GA
	31039	Lockheed C-130H Hercules (93-1039) bl	USAF 700th AS/94th AW AFRC, Dobbins ARB, GA
	31040	Lockheed C-130H Hercules (93-1040) bl	USAF 700th AS/94th AW AFRC, Dobbins ARB, GA
	31041	Lockheed C-130H Hercules (93-1041) pr/w	USAF 731st AS/302nd AW AFRC, Peterson AFB, CO
	31096	Lockheed LC-130H Hercules (93-1096)	USAF 139th AS/109th AW, Schenectady, NY ANG
	31455	Lockheed C-130H-3 Hercules (93-1455) bl/w	USAF 181st AS/136th AW, NAS Dallas, TX ANG
	31456	Lockheed C-130H-3 Hercules (93-1456) bl/w	USAF 181st AS/136th AW, NAS Dallas, TX ANG
	31457	Lockheed C-130H-3 Hercules (93-1457) bl/w	USAF 181st AS/136th AW, NAS Dallas, TX ANG
	31459	Lockheed C-130H-3 Hercules (93-1459) bl/w	USAF 181st AS/136th AW, NAS Dallas, TX ANG
	31561	Lockheed C-130H-3 Hercules (93-1561) r/bk	USAF 158th AS/165th AW, Savannah, GA ANG
	31562	Lockheed C-130H-3 Hercules (93-1562) r/bk	USAF 158th AS/165th AW, Savannah, GA ANG
	31563	Lockheed C-130H-3 Hercules (93-1563) r/bk	USAF 158th AS/165th AW, Savannah, GA ANG
	31580	Lockheed EC-130H Compass Call (73-1580) [DM]	USAF 43rd ECS/55th ECG, Davis-MonthanAFB, AZ
	31581	Lockheed EC-130H Compass Call (73-1581) [DM] $	USAF 43rd ECS/55th ECG, Davis-MonthanAFB, AZ
	31583	Lockheed EC-130H Compass Call (73-1583) [DM] r	USAF 43rd ECS/55th ECG, Davis-MonthanAFB, AZ
	31584	Lockheed EC-130H Compass Call (73-1584) [DM]	USAF 43rd ECS/55th ECG, Davis-MonthanAFB, AZ
	31585	Lockheed EC-130H Compass Call (73-1585) [DM]	USAF 43rd ECS/55th ECG, Davis-MonthanAFB, AZ
	31586	Lockheed EC-130H Compass Call (73-1586) [DM] bl	USAF 43rd ECS/55th ECG, Davis-MonthanAFB, AZ
	31587	Lockheed EC-130H Compass Call (73-1587) [DM]	USAF 43rd ECS/55th ECG, Davis-MonthanAFB, AZ
	31588	Lockheed EC-130H Compass Call (73-1588) [DM]	USAF 43rd ECS/55th ECG, Davis-MonthanAFB, AZ
	31590	Lockheed EC-130H Compass Call (73-1590) [DM]	USAF 43rd ECS/55th ECG, Davis-MonthanAFB, AZ
	31592	Lockheed EC-130H Compass Call (73-1592) [DM] bl	USAF 41st ECS/55th ECG, Davis-Monthan AFB, AZ
	31594	Lockheed EC-130H Compass Call (73-1594) [DM]	USAF 41st ECS/55th ECG, Davis-Monthan AFB, AZ
	31595	Lockheed EC-130H Compass Call (73-1595) [DM]	USAF 43rd ECS/55th ECG, Davis-MonthanAFB, AZ
	32041	Lockheed C-130H-3 Hercules (93-2041) or/bk	USAF 169th AS/182nd AW, Peoria, IL ANG
	32042	Lockheed C-130H-3 Hercules (93-2042) or/bk	USAF 169th AS/182nd AW, Peoria, IL ANG
	32105	Lockheed HC-130N Combat King (93-2105)	USAF 39th RQS/920th RQW AFRC, Patrick AFB, FL
	32106	Lockheed HC-130N Combat King (93-2106)	USAF 39th RQS/920th RQW AFRC, Patrick AFB, FL
	33300	Lockheed LC-130H Hercules (73-3300)	USAF 139th AS/109th AW, Schenectady, NY ANG
	35770	Lockheed MC-130J Commando II (13-5770)	USAF 522nd SOS/27th SOW, Cannon AFB, NM

Serial	Type (code/other identity)	Owner/operator, location or fate	Notes
35775	Lockheed MC-130J Commando II (13-5775)	USAF 17th SOS/353rd SOG, Kadena AB, Japan	
35776	Lockheed MC-130J Commando II (13-5776)	USAF 17th SOS/353rd SOG, Kadena AB, Japan	
35777	Lockheed MC-130J Commando II (13-5777)	USAF 17th SOS/353rd SOG, Kadena AB, Japan	
35778	Lockheed MC-130J Commando II (13-5778)	USAF 67th SOS/352nd SOG, RAF Mildenhall, UK	
35782	Lockheed HC-130J Combat King II (13-5782) [FT]	USAF 71st RQS/347th RG, Moody AFB, GA	
35783	Lockheed AC-130J Ghostrider (13-5783)	USAF 73rd SOS/1st SOW, Hurlburt Field, FL	
35784	Lockheed HC-130J Combat King II (13-5784) [FT]	USAF 71st RQS/347th RG, Moody AFB, GA	
35785	Lockheed HC-130J Combat King II (13-5785) [FT]	USAF 71st RQS/347th RG, Moody AFB, GA	
35786	Lockheed MC-130J Commando II (13-5786)	USAF 67th SOS/352nd SOG, RAF Mildenhall, UK	
35790	Lockheed HC-130J Combat King II (13-5790) [FT]	USAF 71st RQS/347th RG, Moody AFB, GA	
37311	Lockheed C-130H-3 Hercules (93-7311) *bl/w*	USAF 192nd AS/152nd AW, Reno, NV ANG	
37312	Lockheed C-130H-3 Hercules (93-7312) *or/bk*	USAF 169th AS/182nd AW, Peoria, IL ANG	
37313	Lockheed C-130H-3 Hercules (93-7313) *bl/w*	USAF 192nd AS/152nd AW, Reno, NV ANG	
37314	Lockheed C-130H-3 Hercules (93-7314) *bl/w*	USAF 192nd AS/152nd AW, Reno, NV ANG	
38154	Lockheed C-130J-30 Hercules II (03-8154) *r*	USAF 815th AS/403rd AW AFRC, Keesler AFB, MO	
40206	Lockheed C-130H Hercules (84-0206) *bl*	USAF 142nd AS/166th AW, New Castle County, DE ANG	
40207	Lockheed C-130H Hercules (84-0207) *bl*	USAF 142nd AS/166th AW, New Castle County, DE ANG	
40208	Lockheed C-130H Hercules (84-0208) *bl*	USAF 142nd AS/166th AW, New Castle County, DE ANG	
40209	Lockheed C-130H Hercules (84-0209) *bl*	USAF 142nd AS/166th AW, New Castle County, DE ANG	
40210	Lockheed C-130H Hercules (84-0210) *bl*	USAF 142nd AS/166th AW, New Castle County, DE ANG	
40212	Lockheed C-130H Hercules (84-0212) *bl*	USAF 142nd AS/166th AW, New Castle County, DE ANG	
40213	Lockheed C-130H Hercules (84-0213) *bl*	USAF 142nd AS/166th AW, New Castle County, DE ANG	
40476	Lockheed MC-130H Combat Talon II (84-0476)	*To 309th AMARG, August 2018*	
41659	Lockheed C-130H Hercules (74-1659) *r*	USAF 164th AS/179th AW, Mansfield, OH ANG	
41660	Lockheed C-130H Hercules (74-1660) *r*	USAF 164th AS/179th AW, Mansfield, OH ANG	
41661	Lockheed C-130H Hercules (74-1661)	USAF 186th AS/120th AW, Great Falls, MT ANG	
41663	Lockheed C-130H Hercules (74-1663) *r*	USAF 164th AS/179th AW, Mansfield, OH ANG	
41664	Lockheed C-130H Hercules (74-1664) *y/bk*	USAF 118th AS/103rd AW, Bradley ANGB, CT ANG	
41666	Lockheed C-130H Hercules (74-1666) *r*	USAF 164th AS/179th AW, Mansfield, OH ANG	
41669	Lockheed C-130H Hercules (74-1669) *y/bk*	USAF 118th AS/103rd AW, Bradley ANGB, CT ANG	
41670	Lockheed C-130H Hercules (74-1670)	USAF 186th AS/120th AW, Great Falls, MT ANG	
41671	Lockheed C-130H Hercules (74-1671)	USAF 186th AS/120th AW, Great Falls, MT ANG	
41674	Lockheed C-130H Hercules (74-1674)	USAF 186th AS/120th AW, Great Falls, MT ANG	
41679	Lockheed C-130H Hercules (74-1679)	USAF 186th AS/120th AW, Great Falls, MT ANG	
41680	Lockheed C-130H Hercules (74-1680) *y/bk*	USAF 118th AS/103rd AW, Bradley ANGB, CT ANG	
41682	Lockheed C-130H Hercules (74-1682)	USAF	
41685	Lockheed C-130H Hercules (74-1685) *y/bk*	USAF 118th AS/103rd AW, Bradley ANGB, CT ANG	
41687	Lockheed C-130H Hercules (74-1687) *y/bk*	USAF 118th AS/103rd AW, Bradley ANGB, CT ANG	
41688	Lockheed C-130H Hercules (74-1688)	USAF 186th AS/120th AW, Great Falls, MT ANG	
41691	Lockheed C-130H Hercules (74-1691)	USAF 186th AS/120th AW, Great Falls, MT ANG	
41692	Lockheed C-130H Hercules (74-1692) *r*	USAF 164th AS/179th AW, Mansfield, OH ANG	
42061	Lockheed C-130H Hercules (74-2061)	USAF 198th AS/156th AW, San Juan, PR ANG	
42065	Lockheed C-130H Hercules (74-2065)	USAF 186th AS/120th AW, Great Falls, MT ANG	
42067	Lockheed C-130H Hercules (74-2067) *r*	USAF 164th AS/179th AW, Mansfield, OH ANG	
42069	Lockheed C-130H Hercules (74-2069) *y/bk*	USAF 118th AS/103rd AW, Bradley ANGB, CT ANG	
42132	Lockheed C-130H Hercules (74-2132)	USAF 186th AS/120th AW, Great Falls, MT ANG	
42134	Lockheed C-130H Hercules (74-2134) *y/bk*	USAF 118th AS/103rd AW, Bradley ANGB, CT ANG	
43142	Lockheed C-130J-30 Hercules II (04-3142) [RS] *bl/w*	USAF 37th AS/86th AW, Ramstein AB, Germany	
43143	Lockheed C-130J-30 Hercules II (04-3143) *r*	USAF 39th AS/317th AW, Dyess AFB, TX	
45787	Lockheed AC-130J Ghostrider (14-5787)	USAF 73rd SOS/1st SOW, Hurlburt Field, FL	
45788	Lockheed C-130J-30 Hercules II (14-5788) *w/bk*	USAF 61st AS/19th AW Little Rock AFB, AR	
45789	Lockheed AC-130J Ghostrider (14-5789)	USAF 15th SOS/1st SOW, Hurlburt Field, FL	
45791	Lockheed C-130J-30 Hercules II (14-5791) *w/bk*	USAF 61st AS/19th AW Little Rock AFB, AR	
45793	Lockheed MC-130J Commando II (14-5793)	USAF 9th SOS/27th SOW, Cannon AFB, NM	
45795	Lockheed MC-130J Commando II (14-5795)	USAF 9th SOS/27th SOW, Cannon AFB, NM	

Notes	Serial	Type (code/other identity)	Owner/operator, location or fate
	45796	Lockheed C-130J-30 Hercules II (14-5796) w/bk	USAF 61st AS/19th AW Little Rock AFB, AR
	45797	Lockheed AC-130J Ghostrider (14-5797)	USAF 73rd SOS/1st SOW, Hurlburt Field, FL
	45800	Lockheed MC-130J Commando II (14-5800)	USAF 9th SOS/27th SOW, Cannon AFB, NM
	45802	Lockheed C-130J-30 Hercules II (14-5802) y $	USAF 48th AS/314th AW, Little Rock AFB, AR
	45803	Lockheed AC-130J Ghostrider (14-5803)	USAF 73rd SOS/1st SOW, Hurlburt Field, FL
	45804	Lockheed C-130J-30 Hercules II (14-5804) y	USAF 48th AS/314th AW, Little Rock AFB, AR
	45805	Lockheed MC-130J Commando II (14-5805)	USAF 9th SOS/27th SOW, Cannon AFB, NM
	45807	Lockheed C-130J-30 Hercules II (14-5807) [YJ] r [374 AW]	USAF 36th AS/374th AW, Yokota AB, Japan
	45809	Lockheed AC-130J Ghostrider (14-5809)	USAF 73rd SOS/1st SOW, Hurlburt Field, FL
	45815	Lockheed HC-130J Combat King II (14-5815) [AK]	USAF 211th RQS/176th Wg, Elmendorf AFB, AK ANG
	46701	Lockheed C-130H-3 Hercules (94-6701) or/bk	USAF 169th AS/182nd AW, Peoria, IL ANG
	46702	Lockheed C-130H-3 Hercules (94-6702) or/bk	USAF 169th AS/182nd AW, Peoria, IL ANG
	46703	Lockheed C-130H-3 Hercules (94-6703) or/bk	USAF 169th AS/182nd AW, Peoria, IL ANG
	46705	Lockheed C-130H-3 Hercules (94-6705) r/bk	USAF 158th AS/165th AW, Savannah, GA ANG
	46706	Lockheed C-130H-3 Hercules (94-6706) r/bk	USAF 158th AS/165th AW, Savannah, GA ANG
	46707	Lockheed C-130H-3 Hercules (94-6707) r/bk	USAF 158th AS/165th AW, Savannah, GA ANG
	46708	Lockheed C-130H-3 Hercules (94-6708) r/bk	USAF 158th AS/165th AW, Savannah, GA ANG
	47310	Lockheed C-130H-3 Hercules (94-7310) pr/w	USAF 731st AS/302nd AW AFRC, Peterson AFB, CO
	47315	Lockheed C-130H-3 Hercules (94-7315) pr/w	USAF 731st AS/302nd AW AFRC, Peterson AFB, CO
	47316	Lockheed C-130H-3 Hercules (94-7316) pr/w	USAF 731st AS/302nd AW AFRC, PetersonAFB, CO
	47317	Lockheed C-130H-3 Hercules (94-7317) pr/w	USAF 731st AS/302nd AW AFRC, PetersonAFB, CO
	47318	Lockheed C-130H-3 Hercules (94-7318) pr/w	USAF 731st AS/302nd AW AFRC, PetersonAFB, CO
	47319	Lockheed C-130H-3 Hercules (94-7319) pr/w	USAF 731st AS/302nd AW AFRC, PetersonAFB, CO
	47320	Lockheed C-130H-3 Hercules (94-7320) pr/w	USAF 731st AS/302nd AW AFRC, PetersonAFB, CO
	47321	Lockheed C-130H-3 Hercules (94-7321) r/bk	USAF 158th AS/165th AW, Savannah, GA ANG
	48151	Lockheed C-130J Hercules II (94-8151) r	USAF 815th AS/403rd AW AFRC, Keesler AFB, MO
	48152	Lockheed C-130J Hercules II (94-8152) r	USAF 815th AS/403rd AW AFRC, Keesler AFB, MO
	48153	Lockheed C-130J-30 Hercules II (04-8153) r	USAF 815th AS/403rd AW AFRC, Keesler AFB, MO
	50011	Lockheed MC-130H Combat Talon II (85-0011)	USAF 15th SOS/1st SOW, Hurlburt Field, FL
	50963	Lockheed C-130H Hercules (65-0963)	USAF 198th AS/156th AW, San Juan, PR ANG
	50966	Lockheed C-130H Hercules (65-0966)	USAF 198th AS/156th AW, San Juan, PR ANG
	50967	Lockheed EC-130H Compass Call (65-0967) [DM]	USAF 43rd ECS/55th ECG, Davis-Monthan AFB, AZ
	50968	Lockheed C-130H Hercules (65-0968)	*Crashed 2 May 2018, Savannah, GA*
	50974	Lockheed HC-130P Combat King (65-0974)	USAF 102nd RQS/106th RQW, Suffolk Field, NY ANG
	50978	Lockheed HC-130P Combat King (65-0978)	USAF 102nd RQS/106th RQW, Suffolk Field, NY ANG
	50980	Lockheed WC-130H Hercules (65-0980)	USAF 198th AS/156th AW, San Juan, PR ANG
	50984	Lockheed WC-130H Hercules (65-0984)	USAF 198th AS/156th AW, San Juan, PR ANG
	50985	Lockheed WC-130H Hercules (65-0985)	USAF 198th AS/156th AW, San Juan, PR ANG
	50989	Lockheed EC-130H Compass Call (65-0989)	*To 309th AMARG, August 2018*
	51001	Lockheed C-130H Hercules (95-1001) pr/bk	USAF 109th AS/133rd AW, Minneapolis, MN ANG
	51002	Lockheed C-130H Hercules (95-1002) pr/bk	USAF 109th AS/133rd AW, Minneapolis, MN ANG
	51363	Lockheed C-130H Hercules (85-1363) bl/w	USAF 181st AS/136th AW, NAS Dallas, TX ANG
	51364	Lockheed C-130H Hercules (85-1364) bl/w	USAF 181st AS/136th AW, NAS Dallas, TX ANG
	51365	Lockheed C-130H Hercules (85-1365) bl/w	USAF 181st AS/136th AW, NAS Dallas, TX ANG
	51366	Lockheed C-130H Hercules (85-1366) bl/w	USAF 181st AS/136th AW, NAS Dallas, TX ANG
	51367	Lockheed C-130H Hercules (85-1367) bl/w	USAF 181st AS/136th AW, NAS Dallas, TX ANG
	51435	Lockheed C-130J-30 Hercules II (05-1435)	USAF 19th AW Little Rock AFB, AR
	51436	Lockheed C-130J-30 Hercules II (05-1436) r	USAF 143rd AS/143rd AW, Quonset, RI ANG
	51465	Lockheed C-130J-30 Hercules II (05-1465) gn	USAF 115th AS/146th AW, Channel Island ANGS, CA ANG

Serial	Type (code/other identity)	Owner/operator, location or fate	Notes
51466	Lockheed C-130J-30 Hercules II (05-1466) *gn*	USAF 115th AS/146th AW, Channel Island ANGS, CA ANG	
53145	Lockheed C-130J-30 Hercules II (05-3145) *w/bk*	USAF 53rd AS/19th AW Little Rock AFB, AR	
53146	Lockheed C-130J-30 Hercules II (05-3146) *y*	USAF 48th AS/314th AW, Little Rock AFB, AR	
53147	Lockheed C-130J-30 Hercules II (05-3147) *gn*	USAF 41st AS/19th AW Little Rock AFB, AR	
55810	Lockheed C-130J-30 Hercules II (15-5810) [YJ] *r* [374 OG]	USAF 36th AS/374th AW, Yokota AB, Japan	
55811	Lockheed AC-130J Ghostrider (15-5811)	USAF 73rd SOS/1st SOW, Hurlburt Field, FL	
55813	Lockheed C-130J-30 Hercules II (15-5813) [YJ] *r* [36 AS]	USAF 36th AS/374th AW, Yokota AB, Japan	
55817	Lockheed C-130J-30 Hercules II (15-5817) [YJ] *r*	USAF 36th AS/374th AW, Yokota AB, Japan	
55822	Lockheed C-130J-30 Hercules II (15-5822) [RS] *bl/w*	USAF 37th AS/86th AW, Ramstein AB, Germany	
55825	Lockheed MC-130J Commando II (15-5825)	USAF 15th SOS/1st SOW, Hurlburt Field, FL	
55826	Lockheed C-130J-30 Hercules II (15-5826)	USAF 40th AS/317th AW, Dyess AFB, TX	
55827	Lockheed HC-130J Combat King II (15-5827) [AK]	USAF 211th RQS/176th Wg, Elmendorf AFB, AK ANG	
55828	Lockheed C-130J-30 Hercules II (15-5828) *w/bk*	USAF 41st AS/19th AW Little Rock AFB, AR	
55829	Lockheed HC-130J Combat King II (15-5829) [AK]	USAF 211th RQS/176th Wg, Elmendorf AFB, AK ANG	
55831	Lockheed C-130J-30 Hercules II (15-5831) [RS] *bl/w*	USAF 37th AS/86th AW, Ramstein AB, Germany	
55832	Lockheed HC-130J Combat King II (15-5832) [AK]	USAF 211th RQS/176th Wg, Elmendorf AFB, AK ANG	
55833	Lockheed C-130J-30 Hercules II (15-5833) [YJ] *r* [5 AF]	USAF 36th AS/374th AW, Yokota AB, Japan	
55842	Lockheed HC-130J Combat King II (15-5842) [CA]	USAF 130th RQS/129th RQW, Moffett Field CA ANG	
56709	Lockheed C-130H-3 Hercules (95-6709)	USAF	
56710	Lockheed C-130H-3 Hercules (95-6710) *pr/y*	USAF 130th AS/130th AW, Yeager Int'l, Charleston, WV ANG	
56711	Lockheed C-130H-3 Hercules (95-6711) *pr/y*	USAF 130th AS/130th AW, Yeager Int'l, Charleston, WV ANG	
56712	Lockheed C-130H-3 Hercules (95-6712) *pr/y*	USAF 130th AS/130th AW, Yeager Int'l, Charleston, WV ANG	
58152	Lockheed C-130J-30 Hercules II (05-8152) *r*	USAF 815th AS/403rd AW AFRC, Keesler AFB, MO	
58156	Lockheed C-130J-30 Hercules II (05-8156) *r*	USAF 815th AS/403rd AW AFRC, Keesler AFB, MO	
58157	Lockheed C-130J-30 Hercules II (05-8157) *r*	USAF 815th AS/403rd AW AFRC, Keesler AFB, MO	
58158	Lockheed C-130J-30 Hercules II (05-8158) *r*	USAF 815th AS/403rd AW AFRC, Keesler AFB, MO	
60212	Lockheed MC-130P Combat Shadow (66-0212) *bl*	USAF 130th RQS/129th RQW, Moffett Field CA ANG	
60216	Lockheed MC-130P Combat Shadow (66-0216) *bl*	*Withdrawn from use, November 2018*	
60219	Lockheed MC-130P Combat Shadow (66-0219)	*To 309th AMARG, May 2018*	
60222	Lockheed HC-130P Combat King (66-0222)	USAF 102nd RQS/106th RQW, Suffolk Field, NY ANG	
60223	Lockheed MC-130P Combat Shadow (66-0223)	*Withdrawn from use at Sheppard AFB, March 2018*	
60410	Lockheed C-130H Hercules (86-0410)	*To 309th AMARG, March 2018*	
60411	Lockheed C-130H Hercules (86-0411)	USAF 198th AS/156th AW, San Juan, PR ANG	
60414	Lockheed C-130H Hercules (86-0414)	*To 309th AMARG, February 2018*	
60418	Lockheed C-130H Hercules (86-0418)	USAF 198th AS/156th AW, San Juan, PR ANG	
60419	Lockheed C-130H Hercules (86-0419)	USAF 198th AS/156th AW, San Juan, PR ANG	
61003	Lockheed C-130H Hercules (96-1003) *pr/bk*	USAF 109th AS/133rd AW, Minneapolis, MN ANG	
61004	Lockheed C-130H Hercules (96-1004) *pr/bk*	USAF 109th AS/133rd AW, Minneapolis, MN ANG	
61005	Lockheed C-130H Hercules (96-1005) *pr/bk*	USAF 109th AS/133rd AW, Minneapolis, MN ANG	
61006	Lockheed C-130H Hercules (96-1006) *pr/bk*	USAF 109th AS/133rd AW, Minneapolis, MN ANG	
61007	Lockheed C-130H Hercules (96-1007) *pr/bk*	USAF 109th AS/133rd AW, Minneapolis, MN ANG	
61008	Lockheed C-130H Hercules (96-1008) *pr/bk*	USAF 109th AS/133rd AW, Minneapolis, MN ANG	
61391	Lockheed C-130H Hercules (86-1391)	*Withdrawn from use, 2018*	
61437	Lockheed C-130J-30 Hercules II (06-1437) *r*	USAF 143rd AS/143rd AW, Quonset, RI ANG	
61438	Lockheed C-130J-30 Hercules II (06-1438) *r*	USAF 143rd AS/143rd AW, Quonset, RI ANG	
61467	Lockheed C-130J-30 Hercules II (06-1467) *gn*	USAF 115th AS/146th AW, Channel Island ANGS, CA ANG	
61699	Lockheed MC-130H Combat Talon II (86-1699)	USAF 15th SOS/1st SOW, Hurlburt Field, FL	
63171	Lockheed C-130J-30 Hercules II (06-3171) *bl*	USAF 40th AS/317th AW, Dyess AFB, TX	

US-BASED USAF AIRCRAFT

Notes	Serial	Type (code/other identity)	Owner/operator, location or fate
	63301	Lockheed LC-130H Hercules (76-3301)	USAF 139th AS/109th AW, Schenectady, NY ANG
	63302	Lockheed LC-130H Hercules (76-3302)	USAF 139th AS/109th AW, Schenectady, NY ANG
	64631	Lockheed C-130J-30 Hercules II (06-4631) w/bk	USAF 41st AS/19th AW Little Rock AFB, AR
	64632	Lockheed C-130J-30 Hercules II (06-4632) y/bk	USAF 41st AS/19th AW Little Rock AFB, AR
	64633	Lockheed C-130J-30 Hercules II (06-4633) [YJ] r	USAF 36th AS/374th AW, Yokota AB, Japan
	64634	Lockheed C-130J-30 Hercules II (06-4634) w/bk	USAF 41st AS/19th AW Little Rock AFB, AR
	65300	Lockheed WC-130J Hercules II (96-5300)	USAF 53rd WRS/403rd AW AFRC, Keesler AFB, MO
	65301	Lockheed WC-130J Hercules II (96-5301)	USAF 53rd WRS/403rd AW AFRC, Keesler AFB, MO
	65302	Lockheed WC-130J Hercules II (96-5302)	USAF 53rd WRS/403rd AW AFRC, Keesler AFB, MO
	65834	Lockheed C-130J-30 Hercules II (16-5834)	USAF 40th AS/317th AW, Dyess AFB, TX
	65835	Lockheed AC-130J Ghostrider (16-5835)	USAF 73rd SOS/1st SOW, Hurlburt Field, FL
	65638	Lockheed C-130J-30 Hercules II (16-5858) [YJ] r	USAF 36th AS/374th AW, Yokota AB, Japan
	65839	Lockheed MC-130J Commando II (16-5839)	LMTAS, Marietta, GA
	65840	Lockheed C-130J-30 Hercules II (16-5840) [RS] bl/w	USAF 37th AS/86th AW, Ramstein AB, Germany
	65641	Lockheed C-130J-30 Hercules II (16-5841) [YJ] r	USAF 36th AS/374th AW, Yokota AB, Japan
	65843	Lockheed C-130J-30 Hercules II (16-5843) [YJ] r	USAF 36th AS/374th AW, Yokota AB, Japan
	65844	Lockheed AC-130J Ghostrider (16-5844)	LMTAS, Marietta, GA
	65846	Lockheed HC-130J Combat King II (16-5846)	LMTAS, Marietta, GA
	65849	Lockheed C-130J-30 Hercules II (16-5849)	USAF 40th AS/317th AW, Dyess AFB, TX
	65851	Lockheed C-130J-30 Hercules II (16-5851)	USAF 19th AW Little Rock AFB, AR
	65853	Lockheed C-130J-30 Hercules II (16-5853)	USAF 40th AS/317th AW, Dyess AFB, TX
	65855	Lockheed C-130J-30 Hercules II (16-5855)	USAF 19th AW Little Rock AFB, AR
	65857	Lockheed HC-130J Combat King II (16-5857)	LMTAS, Marietta, GA
	65858	Lockheed HC-130J Combat King II (16-5858) [CA]	USAF 130th RQS/129th RQW, Moffett Field CA ANG
	65859	Lockheed C-130J-30 Hercules II (05-3146) w/bk	USAF 41st AS/19th AW Little Rock AFB, AR
	65861	Lockheed C-130J-30 Hercules II (16-5861)	LMTAS, Marietta, GA
	65862	Lockheed HC-130J Combat King II (16-5862) [CA]	USAF 130th RQS/129th RQW, Moffett Field CA ANG
	65864	Lockheed C-130J-30 Hercules II (16-5864)	LMTAS, Marietta, GA
	67322	Lockheed C-130H-3 Hercules (96-7322) pr/y	USAF 130th AS/130th AW, Yeager Int'l, Charleston, WV ANG
	67323	Lockheed C-130H-3 Hercules (96-7323) pr/y	USAF 130th AS/130th AW, Yeager Int'l, Charleston, WV ANG
	67324	Lockheed C-130H-3 Hercules (96-7324) pr/y	USAF 130th AS/130th AW, Yeager Int'l, Charleston, WV ANG
	67325	Lockheed C-130H-3 Hercules (96-7325) pr/w	USAF 731st AS/302nd AW AFRC, Peterson AFB, CO
	68153	Lockheed EC-130J Commando Solo III (96-8153)	USAF 193rd SOS/193rd SOW, Harrisburg, PA ANG
	68154	Lockheed EC-130J Commando Solo III (96-8154)	USAF 193rd SOS/193rd SOW, Harrisburg, PA ANG
	68159	Lockheed C-130J Hercules II (06-8159) r	USAF 815th AS/403rd AW AFRC, Keesler AFB, MO
	68610	Lockheed C-130J-30 Hercules II (06-8610)[YJ] r	USAF 36th AS/374th AW, Yokota AB, Japan
	68611	Lockheed C-130J-30 Hercules II (06-8611) [RS] bl/w	USAF 37th AS/86th AW, Ramstein AB, Germany
	68612	Lockheed C-130J-30 Hercules II (06-8612) w/bk	USAF 61st AS/19th AW Little Rock AFB, AR
	70023	Lockheed MC-130H Combat Talon II (87-0023)	USAF 17th SOS/353rd SOG, Kadena AB, Japan
	70024	Lockheed MC-130H Combat Talon II (87-0024)	USAF 17th SOS/353rd SOG, Kadena AB, Japan
	70125	Lockheed MC-130H Combat Talon II (87-0125)	USAF 15th SOS/1st SOW, Hurlburt Field, FL
	70126	Lockheed MC-130H Combat Talon II (87-0126)	USAF 15th SOS/1st SOW, Hurlburt Field, FL
	70128	Lockheed AC-130U Spooky (87-0128)	USAF 4th SOS/1st SOW, Hurlburt Field, FL
	71351	Lockheed C-130J Hercules II (97-1351) y	USAF 48th AS/314th AW, Little Rock AFB, AR
	71352	Lockheed C-130J Hercules II (97-1352)	USAF 19th AW Little Rock AFB, AR
	71353	Lockheed C-130J Hercules II (97-1353) y	USAF 48th AS/314th AW, Little Rock AFB, AR
	71354	Lockheed C-130J Hercules II (97-1354) y	USAF 48th AS/314th AW, Little Rock AFB, AR
	71468	Lockheed C-130J-30 Hercules II (07-1468) gn	USAF 115th AS/146th AW, Channel Island ANGS, CA ANG
	71931	Lockheed EC-130J Commando Solo III (97-1931)	USAF 193rd SOS/193rd SOW, Harrisburg, PA ANG
	73170	Lockheed C-130J-30 Hercules II (07-3170) bl	USAF 40th AS/317th AW, Dyess AFB, TX
	74635	Lockheed C-130J-30 Hercules II (07-4635) [RS] bl/w	USAF 37th AS/86th AW, Ramstein AB, Germany
	74636	Lockheed C-130J-30 Hercules II (07-4636) w/bk	USAF 41st AS/19th AW Little Rock AFB, AR

Serial	Type (code/other identity)	Owner/operator, location or fate	Notes
74637	Lockheed C-130J-30 Hercules II (07-4637) w/bk	USAF 41st AS/19th AW Little Rock AFB, AR	
74638	Lockheed C-130J-30 Hercules II (07-4638)	USAF 317th AW, Dyess AFB, TX	
74639	Lockheed C-130J-30 Hercules II (07-4639) w/bk	USAF 41st AS/19th AW Little Rock AFB, AR	
746310	Lockheed C-130J-30 Hercules II (07-46310) w/bk	USAF 41st AS/19th AW Little Rock AFB, AR	
746311	Lockheed C-130J-30 Hercules II (07-46311) w/bk	USAF 41st AS/19th AW Little Rock AFB, AR	
746312	Lockheed C-130J-30 Hercules II (07-46312) w/bk	USAF 41st AS/19th AW Little Rock AFB, AR	
75303	Lockheed WC-130J Hercules II (97-5303)	USAF 53rd WRS/403rd AW AFRC, Keesler AFB, MO	
75304	Lockheed WC-130J Hercules II (97-5304)	USAF 53rd WRS/403rd AW AFRC, KeeslerAFB, MO	
75305	Lockheed WC-130J Hercules II (97-5305)	USAF 53rd WRS/403rd AW AFRC, KeeslerAFB, MO	
75306	Lockheed WC-130J Hercules II (97-5306)	USAF 53rd WRS/403rd AW AFRC, KeeslerAFB, MO	
78608	Lockheed C-130J-30 Hercules II (07-8608) [RS] bl/w	USAF 37th AS/86th AW, Ramstein AB, Germany	
78609	Lockheed C-130J-30 Hercules II (07-8609) [RS] bl/w	USAF 37th AS/86th AW, Ramstein AB, Germany	
78613	Lockheed C-130J-30 Hercules II (07-8613) w/bk	USAF 41st AS/19th AW Little Rock AFB, AR	
78614	Lockheed C-130J-30 Hercules II (07-8614) [RS] bl/w	USAF 37th AS/86th AW, Ramstein AB, Germany	
79281	Lockheed C-130H Hercules (87-9281)	USAF	
79282	Lockheed C-130H Hercules (87-9282)	USAF	
79283	Lockheed C-130H Hercules (87-9283) bl/r	USAF 757th AS/910th AW AFRC, Youngstown ARS, OH	
79285	Lockheed C-130H Hercules (87-9285)	USAF	
79286	Lockheed AC-130W Stinger II (87-9286)	USAF 16th SOS/27th SOW, Cannon AFB, NM	
79287	Lockheed C-130H Hercules (87-9287)	USAF	
79288	Lockheed AC-130W Stinger II (87-9288)	USAF 16th SOS/27th SOW, Cannon AFB, NM	
80191	Lockheed MC-130H Combat Talon II (88-0191)	USAF 1st SOS/353rd SOG, Kadena AB, Japan	
80193	Lockheed MC-130H Combat Talon II (88-0193)	USAF 15th SOS/1st SOW, Hurlburt Field, FL	
80194	Lockheed MC-130H Combat Talon II (88-0194)	USAF 15th SOS/1st SOW, Hurlburt Field, FL	
80195	Lockheed MC-130H Combat Talon II (88-0195)	USAF 15th SOS/1st SOW, Hurlburt Field, FL	
80264	Lockheed MC-130H Combat Talon II (88-0264)	USAF 15th SOS/1st SOW, Hurlburt Field, FL	
81301	Lockheed AC-130W Stinger II (88-1301)	USAF 16th SOS/27th SOW, Cannon AFB, NM	
81302	Lockheed AC-130W Stinger II (88-1302)	USAF 16th SOS/27th SOW, Cannon AFB, NM	
81303	Lockheed AC-130W Stinger II (88-1303)	USAF 16th SOS/27th SOW, Cannon AFB, NM	
81304	Lockheed AC-130W Stinger II (88-1304)	USAF 16th SOS/27th SOW, Cannon AFB, NM	
81305	Lockheed AC-130W Stinger II (88-1305)	USAF 16th SOS/27th SOW, Cannon AFB, NM	
81306	Lockheed AC-130W Stinger II (88-1306)	USAF 16th SOS/27th SOW, Cannon AFB, NM	
81307	Lockheed AC-130W Stinger II (88-1307)	USAF 16th SOS/27th SOW, Cannon AFB, NM	
81308	Lockheed AC-130W Stinger II (88-1308)	USAF 16th SOS/27th SOW, Cannon AFB, NM	
81355	Lockheed C-130J Hercules II (98-1355) y	USAF 48th AS/314th AW, Little Rock AFB, AR	
81356	Lockheed C-130J Hercules II (98-1356) y	USAF 48th AS/314th AW, Little Rock AFB, AR	
81357	Lockheed C-130J Hercules II (98-1357) y	USAF 48th AS/314th AW, Little Rock AFB, AR	
81358	Lockheed C-130J Hercules II (98-1358) y	USAF 48th AS/314th AW, Little Rock AFB, AR	
81803	Lockheed MC-130H Combat Talon II (88-1803)	USAF 1st SOS/353rd SOG, Kadena AB, Japan	
81932	Lockheed EC-130J Commando Solo III (98-1932)	USAF 193rd SOS/193rd SOW, Harrisburg, PA ANG	
82101	Lockheed HC-130N Combat King (88-2101)	*To 309th AMARG, November 2018*	
82102	Lockheed HC-130P Combat King (88-2102)	*To 309th AMARG, November 2018*	
83172	Lockheed C-130J-30 Hercules II (08-3172) bl	USAF 40th AS/317th AW, Dyess AFB, TX	
83173	Lockheed C-130J-30 Hercules II (08-3173) bl	USAF 40th AS/317th AW, Dyess AFB, TX	
83175	Lockheed C-130J-30 Hercules II (08-3175) bl	USAF 40th AS/317th AW, Dyess AFB, TX	
83176	Lockheed C-130J-30 Hercules II (08-3176) [RS] bl/w	USAF 37th AS/86th AW, Ramstein AB, Germany	
83177	Lockheed C-130J-30 Hercules II (08-3177) [YJ] r	USAF 36th AS/374th AW, Yokota AB, Japan	
83178	Lockheed C-130J-30 Hercules II (08-3178) bl	USAF 40th AS/317th AW, Dyess AFB, TX	
83179	Lockheed C-130J-30 Hercules II (08-3179) bl	USAF 40th AS/317th AW, Dyess AFB, TX	
84401	Lockheed C-130H Hercules (88-4401)	USAF 39th RQS/920th RQW AFRC, Patrick AFB, FL	
84402	Lockheed C-130H Hercules (88-4402) r	USAF 154th TS/189th AW, Little Rock, AR ANG	
84403	Lockheed C-130H Hercules (88-4403) r	USAF 154th TS/189th AW, Little Rock, AR ANG	
84405	Lockheed C-130H Hercules (88-4405)	USAF	
84406	Lockheed C-130H Hercules (88-4406) bl/w	USAF 357th AS/908th AW AFRC, Maxwell AFB, AL	
85307	Lockheed WC-130J Hercules II (98-5307)	USAF 53rd WRS/403rd AW AFRC, Keesler AFB, MO	

Notes	Serial	Type (code/other identity)	Owner/operator, location or fate
	85308	Lockheed WC-130J Hercules II (98-5308)	USAF 53rd WRS/403rd AW AFRC, Keesler AFB, MO
	85675	Lockheed C-130J-30 Hercules II (08-5675) bl	USAF 40th AS/317th AW, Dyess AFB, TX
	85678	Lockheed C-130J-30 Hercules II (08-5678) bl	USAF 40th AS/317th AW, Dyess AFB, TX
	85679	Lockheed C-130J-30 Hercules II (08-5679) bl	USAF 40th AS/317th AW, Dyess AFB, TX
	85683	Lockheed C-130J-30 Hercules II (08-5683) r	USAF 39th AS/317th AW, Dyess AFB, TX
	85684	Lockheed C-130J-30 Hercules II (08-5684) r	USAF 39th AS/317th AW, Dyess AFB, TX
	85685	Lockheed C-130J-30 Hercules II (08-5685) r	USAF 39th AS/317th AW, Dyess AFB, TX
	85686	Lockheed C-130J-30 Hercules II (08-5686) r	USAF 39th AS/317th AW, Dyess AFB, TX
	85691	Lockheed C-130J-30 Hercules II (08-5691) r	USAF 39th AS/317th AW, Dyess AFB, TX
	85692	Lockheed C-130J-30 Hercules II (08-5692) [YJ] r	USAF 36th AS/374th AW, Yokota AB, Japan
	85693	Lockheed C-130J-30 Hercules II (08-5693) r	USAF 39th AS/317th AW, Dyess AFB, TX
	85697	Lockheed MC-130J Commando II (08-5697)	USAF 522nd SOS/27th SOW, Cannon AFB, NM
	85705	Lockheed C-130J-30 Hercules II (08-5705) r	USAF 39th AS/317th AW, Dyess AFB, TX
	85712	Lockheed C-130J-30 Hercules II (08-5712) r	USAF 39th AS/317th AW, Dyess AFB, TX
	85715	Lockheed C-130J-30 Hercules II (08-5715) r	USAF 39th AS/317th AW, Dyess AFB, TX
	85724	Lockheed C-130J-30 Hercules II (08-5724) r	USAF 39th AS/317th AW, Dyess AFB, TX
	85726	Lockheed C-130J-30 Hercules II (08-5726) r	USAF 39th AS/317th AW, Dyess AFB, TX
	86201	Lockheed MC-130J Commando II (08-6201)	USAF 522nd SOS/27th SOW, Cannon AFB, NM
	86202	Lockheed MC-130J Commando II (08-6202)	USAF 522nd SOS/27th SOW, Cannon AFB, NM
	86203	Lockheed MC-130J Commando II (08-6203) [58 OG]	USAF 415th SOS/58th SOW, Kirtland AFB, NM
	86204	Lockheed MC-130J Commando II (08-6204)	USAF 522nd SOS/27th SOW, Cannon AFB, NM
	86205	Lockheed MC-130J Commando II (08-6205)	USAF 415th SOS/58th SOW, Kirtland AFB, NM
	86206	Lockheed MC-130J Commando II (08-6206)	USAF 415th SOS/58th SOW, Kirtland AFB, NM
	88601	Lockheed C-130J-30 Hercules II (08-8601) [RS] bl/w $	USAF 37th AS/86th AW, Ramstein AB, Germany
	88602	Lockheed C-130J-30 Hercules II (08-8602) [RS] bl/w $	USAF 37th AS/86th AW, Ramstein AB, Germany
	88603	Lockheed C-130J-30 Hercules II (08-8603) [RS] bl/w $	USAF 37th AS/86th AW, Ramstein AB, Germany
	88604	Lockheed C-130J-30 Hercules II (08-8604) [YJ] r	USAF 36th AS/374th AW, Yokota AB, Japan
	88605	Lockheed C-130J-30 Hercules II (08-8605) [YJ] r	USAF 36th AS/374th AW, Yokota AB, Japan
	88606	Lockheed C-130J-30 Hercules II (08-8606) w/bk	USAF 41st AS/19th AW Little Rock AFB, AR
	88607	Lockheed C-130J-30 Hercules II (08-8607) r	USAF 39th AS/317th AW, Dyess AFB, TX
	90108	Lockheed HC-130J Combat King II (09-0108) [OT]	USAF 85th TES/53rd Wg, Eglin AFB, FL
	90109	Lockheed HC-130J Combat King II (09-0109)	USAF 415th SOS/58th SOW, Kirtland AFB, NM
	90280	Lockheed MC-130H Combat Talon II (89-0280)	USAF 1st SOS/353rd SOG, Kadena AB, Japan
	90282	Lockheed MC-130H Combat Talon II (89-0282)	USAF 15th SOS/1st SOW, Hurlburt Field, FL
	90283	Lockheed MC-130H Combat Talon II (89-0283)	USAF 1st SOS/353rd SOG, Kadena AB, Japan
	90509	Lockheed AC-130U Spooky (89-0509)	*To 309th AMARG, August 2018*
	90510	Lockheed AC-130U Spooky (89-0510)	USAF 4th SOS/1st SOW, Hurlburt Field, FL
	90511	Lockheed AC-130U Spooky (89-0511)	*To 309th AMARG, May 2018*
	90512	Lockheed AC-130U Spooky (89-0512)	*To 309th AMARG, January 2018*
	90513	Lockheed AC-130U Spooky (89-0513)	USAF 4th SOS/1st SOW, Hurlburt Field, FL
	91051	Lockheed AC-130W Stinger II (89-1051)	USAF 16th SOS/27th SOW, Cannon AFB, NM
	91052	Lockheed AC-130U Spooky (89-1052)	USAF 4th SOS/1st SOW, Hurlburt Field, FL
	91053	Lockheed AC-130U Spooky (89-1053)	USAF 4th SOS/1st SOW, Hurlburt Field, FL
	91054	Lockheed AC-130U Spooky (89-1054)	USAF 4th SOS/1st SOW, Hurlburt Field, FL
	91055	Lockheed C-130H Hercules (89-1055) bl/w	USAF 357th AS/908th AW AFRC, Maxwell AFB, AL
	91056	Lockheed AC-130U Spooky (89-1056)	USAF 4th SOS/1st SOW, Hurlburt Field, FL
	91181	Lockheed C-130H Hercules (89-1181) r/bk	USAF 158th AS/165th AW, Savannah, GA ANG
	91182	Lockheed C-130H Hercules (89-1182) bl/w	USAF 181st AS/136th AW, NAS Dallas, TX ANG
	91183	Lockheed C-130H Hercules (89-1183) r	USAF 154th TS/189th AW, Little Rock, AR ANG
	91184	Lockheed C-130H Hercules (89-1184) r $	USAF 154th TS/189th AW, Little Rock, AR ANG
	91185	Lockheed C-130H Hercules (89-1185) bl/w	USAF 181st AS/136th AW, NAS Dallas, TX ANG
	91186	Lockheed C-130H Hercules (89-1186) r	USAF 154th TS/189th AW, Little Rock, AR ANG
	91187	Lockheed C-130H Hercules (89-1187) bl/w	USAF 357th AS/908th AW AFRC, Maxwell AFB, AL
	91188	Lockheed C-130H Hercules (89-1188) bl/w	USAF 357th AS/908th AW AFRC, Maxwell AFB, AL
	91431	Lockheed C-130J-30 Hercules II (99-1431) r	USAF 143rd AS/143rd AW, Quonset, RI ANG
	91432	Lockheed C-130J-30 Hercules II (99-1432) r	USAF 143rd AS/143rd AW, Quonset, RI ANG
	91433	Lockheed C-130J-30 Hercules II (99-1433) r	USAF 143rd AS/143rd AW, Quonset, RI ANG
	91933	Lockheed EC-130J Commando Solo III (99-1933)	USAF 193rd SOS/193rd SOW, Harrisburg, PA ANG
	95309	Lockheed WC-130J Hercules II (99-5309)	USAF 53rd WRS/403rd AW AFRC, Keesler AFB, MO
	95706	Lockheed HC-130J Combat King II (09-5706)	USAF 415th SOS/58th SOW, Kirtland AFB, NM

Serial	Type (code/other identity)	Owner/operator, location or fate	Notes
95707	Lockheed HC-130J Combat King II (09-5707) [FT]	USAF 79th RQS/563rd RQG, Davis-Monthan AFB, AZ	
95708	Lockheed HC-130J Combat King II (09-5708) [FT]	USAF 79th RQS/563rd RQG, Davis-Monthan AFB, AZ	
95709	Lockheed HC-130J Combat King II (09-5709) [FT]	USAF 79th RQS/563rd RQG, Davis-Monthan AFB, AZ	
95711	Lockheed MC-130J Commando II (09-5711)	USAF 17th SOS/353rd SOG, Kadena AB, Japan	
95713	Lockheed MC-130J Commando II (09-5713)	USAF 9th SOS/27th SOW, Cannon AFB, NM	
95829	Lockheed HC-130N Combat King (69-5829)	USAF 39th RQS/920th RQW AFRC, Patrick AFB, FL	
96207	Lockheed MC-130J Commando II (09-6207)	USAF 415th SOS/58th SOW, Kirtland AFB, NM	
96208	Lockheed MC-130J Commando II (09-6208)	USAF 415th SOS/58th SOW, Kirtland AFB, NM	
96209	Lockheed MC-130J Commando II (09-6209) [58 SOW]	USAF 415th SOS/58th SOW, Kirtland AFB, NM	
96210	Lockheed MC-130J Commando II (09-6210)	USAF 15th SOS/1st SOW, Hurlburt Field, FL	
99102	Lockheed C-130H Hercules (89-9102) r	USAF 154th TS/189th AW, Little Rock, AR ANG	
99103	Lockheed C-130H Hercules (89-9103) bl/w	USAF 357th AS/908th AW AFRC, Maxwell AFB, AL	
99104	Lockheed C-130H Hercules (89-9104) bl/r	USAF 757th AS/910th AW AFRC, Youngstown ARS, OH	
99105	Lockheed C-130H Hercules (89-9105) bl/r	USAF 757th AS/910th AW AFRC, Youngstown ARS, OH	
99106	Lockheed C-130H Hercules (89-9106) bl/r	USAF 757th AS/910th AW AFRC, Youngstown ARS, OH	

Boeing C-135

Serial	Type (code/other identity)	Owner/operator, location or fate	Notes
00313	Boeing KC-135R Stratotanker (60-0313)	USAF 22nd ARW, McConnell AFB, KS	
00314	Boeing KC-135R Stratotanker (60-0314) r/w	USAF 74th ARS/434th ARW AFRC, Grissom AFB, IN	
00315	Boeing KC-135R Stratotanker (60-0315) w/bl	USAF 126th ARS/128th ARW, Mitchell Field, WI ANG	
00316	Boeing KC-135R Stratotanker (60-0316) bl/bk	USAF 191st ARS/151st ARW, Salt Lake City, UT ANG	
00318	Boeing KC-135R Stratotanker (60-0318)	USAF 314th ARS/940th ARW, Beale AFB, CA	
00320	Boeing KC-135R Stratotanker (60-0320)	USAF 22nd ARW, McConnell AFB, KS	
00322	Boeing KC-135R Stratotanker (60-0322) bl	USAF 72nd ARS/434th ARW AFRC, Grissom AFB, IN	
00323	Boeing KC-135R Stratotanker (60-0323) [HH] y/bk	USAF 203rd ARS/15th Wg, Hickam AFB, HI ANG	
00324	Boeing KC-135R Stratotanker (60-0324) [D] r/w/bl	USAF 351st ARS/100th ARW, RAF Mildenhall, UK	
00328	Boeing KC-135R Stratotanker (60-0328) [ZZ] or/bk	USAF 909th ARS/18th Wg, Kadena AB, Japan	
00329	Boeing KC-135R Stratotanker (60-0329) [HH] y/bk	USAF 203rd ARS/15th Wg, Hickam AFB, HI ANG	
00331	Boeing KC-135R Stratotanker (60-0331)	USAF 314th ARS/940th ARW, Beale AFB, CA	
00332	Boeing KC-135R Stratotanker (60-0332) [AK] bl/y	USAF 168th ARS/168th ARW, Eielson AFB, AK ANG	
00333	Boeing KC-135R Stratotanker (60-0333)	USAF	
00334	Boeing KC-135R Stratotanker (60-0334) y/bl	USAF 6th AMW, MacDill AFB, FL	
00335	Boeing KC-135T Stratotanker (60-0335)	USAF 22nd ARW, McConnell AFB, KS	
00336	Boeing KC-135T Stratotanker (60-0336)	USAF 22nd ARW, McConnell AFB, KS	
00337	Boeing KC-135T Stratotanker (60-0337)	USAF 22nd ARW, McConnell AFB, KS	
00339	Boeing KC-135T Stratotanker (60-0339)	USAF 92nd ARW, Fairchild AFB, WA	
00341	Boeing KC-135T Stratotanker (60-0341)	USAF 153rd ARS/186th AW, Meridian, MS ANG	
00342	Boeing KC-135T Stratotanker (60-0342)	USAF 92nd ARW, Fairchild AFB, WA	
00343	Boeing KC-135T Stratotanker (60-0343)	USAF 22nd ARW, McConnell AFB, KS	
00344	Boeing KC-135T Stratotanker (60-0344) [D] r/w/bl	USAF 351st ARS/100th ARW, RAF Mildenhall, UK	
00345	Boeing KC-135T Stratotanker (60-0345) bk/y $	USAF 171st ARS/127th Wg, Selfridge ANGB, MI ANG	
00346	Boeing KC-135T Stratotanker (60-0346) bk/y	USAF 171st ARS/127th Wg, Selfridge ANGB, MI ANG	
00347	Boeing KC-135R Stratotanker (60-0347) r/w	USAF 166th ARS/121st ARW, Rickenbacker ANGB, OH ANG	
00348	Boeing KC-135R Stratotanker (60-0348) y/r	USAF 54th ARS/97th AMW, Altus AFB, OK	
00349	Boeing KC-135R Stratotanker (60-0349) gn/y	USAF 77th ARS/916th ARW AFRC, Seymour Johnson AFB, NC	
00350	Boeing KC-135R Stratotanker (60-0350) y/r	USAF 54th ARS/97th AMW, Altus AFB, OK	

Notes	Serial	Type (code/other identity)	Owner/operator, location or fate
	00351	Boeing KC-135R Stratotanker (60-0351)	USAF 22nd ARW, McConnell AFB, KS
	00353	Boeing KC-135R Stratotanker (60-0353) y/bl	USAF 6th AMW, MacDill AFB, FL
	00355	Boeing KC-135R Stratotanker (60-0355) [D] r/w/bl	USAF 351st ARS/100th ARW, RAF Mildenhall, UK
	00356	Boeing KC-135R(RT) Stratotanker (60-0356)	USAF 22nd ARW, McConnell AFB, KS
	00357	Boeing KC-135R(RT) Stratotanker (60-0357)	USAF 22nd ARW, McConnell AFB, KS
	00358	Boeing KC-135R Stratotanker (60-0358) w/bl	USAF 108th ARS/126th AMW, Scott AFB, IL ANG
	00359	Boeing KC-135R Stratotanker (60-0359) r/w	USAF 74th ARS/434th ARW AFRC, Grissom AFB, IN
	00360	Boeing KC-135R Stratotanker (60-0360) y/r	USAF 54th ARS/97th AMW, Altus AFB, OK
	00362	Boeing KC-135R(RT) Stratotanker (60-0362)	USAF 22nd ARW, McConnell AFB, KS
	00363	Boeing KC-135R Stratotanker (60-0363) bl	USAF 72nd ARS/434th ARW AFRC, Grissom AFB, IN
	00364	Boeing KC-135R Stratotanker (60-0364) r/w	USAF 74th ARS/434th ARW AFRC, Grissom AFB, IN
	00365	Boeing KC-135R Stratotanker (60-0365) bl/y	USAF 117th ARS/190th ARW, Forbes Field, KS ANG
	00366	Boeing KC-135R Stratotanker (60-0366) r	USAF 141st ARS/108th ARW, McGuire AFB, NJ ANG
	00367	Boeing KC-135R Stratotanker (60-0367) r/w	USAF 166th ARS/121st ARW, Rickenbacker ANGB, OH ANG
	10264	Boeing KC-135R Stratotanker (61-0264) r/w	USAF 166th ARS/121st ARW, Rickenbacker ANGB, OH ANG
	10266	Boeing KC-135R Stratotanker (61-0266) bl/y	USAF 117th ARS/190th ARW, Forbes Field, KS ANG
	10267	Boeing KC-135R Stratotanker (61-0267)	USAF
	10272	Boeing KC-135R Stratotanker (61-0272) r/w	USAF 74th ARS/434th ARW AFRC, Grissom AFB, IN
	10275	Boeing KC-135R Stratotanker (61-0275) bl/bk	USAF 191st ARS/151st ARW, Salt Lake City, UT ANG
	10276	Boeing KC-135R Stratotanker (61-0276) r/w	USAF 173rd ARS/155th ARW, Lincoln, NE ANG
	10277	Boeing KC-135R Stratotanker (61-0277) bl/y	USAF 117th ARS/190th ARW, Forbes Field, KS ANG
	10280	Boeing KC-135R Stratotanker (61-0280) or/y	USAF 336th ARS/452nd AMW AFRC, March ARB, CA
	10284	Boeing KC-135R Stratotanker (61-0284)	USAF 197th ARS/161st ARW, Phoenix, AZ ANG
	10288	Boeing KC-135R Stratotanker (61-0288) [D] r/w/bl	USAF 351st ARS/100th ARW, RAF Mildenhall, UK
	10290	Boeing KC-135R Stratotanker (61-0290) [HH] y/bk	USAF 203rd ARS/15th Wg, Hickam AFB, HI ANG
	10292	Boeing KC-135R Stratotanker (61-0292) [D] r/w/bl	USAF 351st ARS/100th ARW, RAF Mildenhall, UK
	10293	Boeing KC-135R(RT) Stratotanker (61-0293)	USAF 22nd ARW, McConnell AFB, KS
	10294	Boeing KC-135R Stratotanker (61-0294) gn/y	USAF 77th ARS/916th ARW AFRC, Seymour Johnson AFB, NC
	10295	Boeing KC-135R Stratotanker (61-0295) y/r	USAF 54th ARS/97th AMW, Altus AFB, OK
	10298	Boeing KC-135R Stratotanker (61-0298) w/bl	USAF 126th ARS/128th ARW, Mitchell Field, WI ANG
	10299	Boeing KC-135R Stratotanker (61-0299)	USAF
	10300	Boeing KC-135R Stratotanker (61-0300) w/bl	USAF 108th ARS/126th ARW, Scott AFB, IL ANG
	10305	Boeing KC-135R Stratotanker (61-0305) y/bl	USAF 6th AMW, MacDill AFB, FL
	10307	Boeing KC-135R Stratotanker (61-0307) y/bk	USAF 756th ARS/459th ARW AFRC, Andrews AFB, MD
	10308	Boeing KC-135R Stratotanker (61-0308)	USAF 22nd ARW, McConnell AFB, KS
	10309	Boeing KC-135R Stratotanker (61-0309) w/bl	USAF 126th ARS/128th ARW, Mitchell Field, WI ANG
	10310	Boeing KC-135R Stratotanker (61-0310) w/bl	USAF 126th ARS/128th ARW, Mitchell Field, WI ANG
	10311	Boeing KC-135R Stratotanker (61-0311)	USAF 92nd ARW, Fairchild AFB, WA
	10313	Boeing KC-135R Stratotanker (61-0313) gn/y	USAF 77th ARS/916th ARW AFRC, Seymour Johnson AFB, NC
	10314	Boeing KC-135R Stratotanker (61-0314)	USAF 92nd ARW, Fairchild AFB, WA
	10315	Boeing KC-135R Stratotanker (61-0315) y/bl	USAF 6th AMW, MacDill AFB, FL
	10317	Boeing KC-135R Stratotanker (61-0317) bl	USAF 133rd ARS/157th ARW, Pease ANGB, NH ANG

Serial	Type (code/other identity)	Owner/operator, location or fate	Notes
10318	Boeing KC-135R Stratotanker (61-0318) *bl/y*	USAF 117th ARS/190th ARW, Forbes Field, KS ANG	
10320	Boeing KC-135R Stratotanker (61-0320) [ED]	USAF 418th FLTS/412th TW, Edwards AFB, CA	
10321	Boeing KC-135R Stratotanker (61-0321)	USAF	
10323	Boeing KC-135R Stratotanker (61-0323) *y/bl*	USAF 6th AMW, MacDill AFB, FL	
10324	Boeing KC-135R Stratotanker (61-0324) *or/y*	USAF 336th ARS/452nd AMW AFRC, March ARB, CA	
12662	Boeing RC-135S Cobra Ball (61-2662) [OF] *bk*	USAF 45th RS/55th Wg, Offutt AFB, NE	
12663	Boeing RC-135S Cobra Ball (61-2663) [OF] *bk*	USAF 45th RS/55th Wg, Offutt AFB, NE	
12666	Boeing NC-135W (61-2666)	USAF 645th Materiel Sqn, Greenville, TX	
12667	Boeing WC-135W Constant Phoenix (61-2667) [OF] *bk*	USAF 45th RS/55th Wg, Offutt AFB, NE	
12670	Boeing OC-135B Open Skies (61-2670) [OF] *bk*	USAF 45th RS/55th Wg, Offutt AFB, NE	
12672	Boeing OC-135B Open Skies (61-2672) [OF] *bk*	USAF 45th RS/55th Wg, Offutt AFB, NE	
14828	Boeing KC-135R Stratotanker (64-14828) *bl/bk*	USAF 191st ARS/151st ARW, Salt Lake City, UT ANG	
14829	Boeing KC-135R Stratotanker (64-14829)	USAF 197th ARS/161st ARW, Phoenix, AZ ANG	
14830	Boeing KC-135R Stratotanker (64-14830)	USAF	
14831	Boeing KC-135R Stratotanker (64-14831)	USAF 197th ARS/161st ARW, Phoenix, AZ ANG	
14832	Boeing KC-135R Stratotanker (64-14832) *w/or*	USAF 151st ARS/134th ARW, Knoxville, TN ANG	
14834	Boeing KC-135R Stratotanker (64-14834) *r/w*	USAF 74th ARS/434th ARW AFRC, Grissom AFB, IN	
14835	Boeing KC-135R Stratotanker (64-14835) *or/y*	USAF 336th ARS/452nd AMW AFRC, March ARB, CA	
14836	Boeing KC-135R Stratotanker (64-14836) *bl*	USAF 133rd ARS/157th ARW, Pease ANGB, NH ANG	
14837	Boeing KC-135R Stratotanker (64-14837) *y/bl*	USAF 6th AMW, MacDill AFB, FL	
14839	Boeing KC-135R Stratotanker (64-14839) *w/bl*	USAF 108th ARS/126th ARW, Scott AFB, IL ANG	
14840	Boeing KC-135R Stratotanker (64-14840) *r/w*	USAF 166th ARS/121st ARW, Rickenbacker ANGB, OH ANG	
14841	Boeing RC-135V Rivet Joint (64-14841) [OF] *gn*	USAF 38th RS/55th Wg, Offutt AFB, NE	
14842	Boeing RC-135V Rivet Joint (64-14842) *r*	USAF 38th RS/55th Wg, Offutt AFB, NE	
14843	Boeing RC-135V Rivet Joint (64-14843) *gn*	USAF 38th RS/55th Wg, Offutt AFB, NE	
14844	Boeing RC-135V Rivet Joint (64-14844) *gn*	USAF 38th RS/55th Wg, Offutt AFB, NE	
14845	Boeing RC-135V Rivet Joint (64-14845) [OF] *gn*	USAF 38th RS/55th Wg, Offutt AFB, NE	
14846	Boeing RC-135V Rivet Joint (64-14846) *gn*	USAF 38th RS/55th Wg, Offutt AFB, NE	
14847	Boeing RC-135U Combat Sent (64-14847) [OF] *bk*	USAF 45th RS/55th Wg, Offutt AFB, NE	
14848	Boeing RC-135V Rivet Joint (64-14848) *gn*	USAF 343rd RS/55th Wg, Offutt AFB, NE	
14849	Boeing RC-135U Combat Sent (64-14849) [OF] *bk*	USAF 45th RS/55th Wg, Offutt AFB, NE	
23498	Boeing KC-135R Stratotanker (62-3498) [ZZ] *or/bk*	USAF 909th ARS/18th Wg, Kadena AB, Japan	
23499	Boeing KC-135R Stratotanker (62-3499)	USAF 92nd ARW, Fairchild AFB, WA	
23500	Boeing KC-135R Stratotanker (62-3500) *bl*	USAF 133rd ARS/157th ARW, Pease ANGB, NH ANG	
23502	Boeing KC-135R Stratotanker (62-3502) *y/bl*	USAF 6th AMW, MacDill AFB, FL	
23503	Boeing KC-135R Stratotanker (62-3503) *bl/y*	USAF 465th ARS/507th ARW AFRC, Tinker AFB, OK	
23505	Boeing KC-135R Stratotanker (62-3505)	USAF 92nd ARW, Fairchild AFB, WA	
23506	Boeing KC-135R Stratotanker (62-3506) *bl/y*	USAF 117th ARS/190th ARW, Forbes Field, KS ANG	
23507	Boeing KC-135R Stratotanker (62-3507)	USAF 22nd ARW, McConnell AFB, KS	
23508	Boeing KC-135R Stratotanker (62-3508) *r* $	USAF 141st ARS/108th ARW, McGuire AFB, NJ ANG	
23509	Boeing KC-135R Stratotanker (62-3509) *gn/y*	USAF 77th ARS/916th ARW AFRC, Seymour Johnson AFB, NC	
23510	Boeing KC-135R Stratotanker (62-3510) *r/w*	USAF 74th ARS/434th ARW AFRC, Grissom AFB, IN	
23511	Boeing KC-135R Stratotanker (62-3511) *r/w*	USAF 166th ARS/121st ARW, Rickenbacker ANGB, OH ANG	
23512	Boeing KC-135R Stratotanker (62-3512) *w/bl*	USAF 126th ARS/128th ARW, Mitchell Field, WI ANG	
23513	Boeing KC-135R Stratotanker (62-3513) *w/gn*	USAF 132nd ARS/101st ARW, Bangor, MN ANG	
23514	Boeing KC-135R Stratotanker (62-3514) *r*	USAF 141st ARS/108th ARW, McGuire AFB, NJ ANG	

Notes	Serial	Type (code/other identity)	Owner/operator, location or fate
	23515	Boeing KC-135R Stratotanker (62-3515) w/bl	USAF 108th ARS/126th ARW, Scott AFB, IL ANG
	23516	Boeing KC-135R Stratotanker (62-3516) $	USAF 197th ARS/161st ARW, Phoenix, AZ ANG
	23517	Boeing KC-135R Stratotanker (62-3517)	USAF 92nd ARW, Fairchild AFB, WA
	23518	Boeing KC-135R Stratotanker (62-3518) bl	USAF 72nd ARS/434th ARW AFRC, Grissom AFB, IN
	23519	Boeing KC-135R Stratotanker (62-3519)	USAF 22nd ARW, McConnell AFB, KS
	23521	Boeing KC-135R Stratotanker (62-3521) bl	USAF 72nd ARS/434th ARW AFRC, Grissom AFB, IN
	23523	Boeing KC-135R Stratotanker (62-3523)	USAF 22nd ARW, McConnell AFB, KS
	23524	Boeing KC-135R Stratotanker (62-3524) [AK] bl/y	USAF 168th ARS/168th ARW, Eielson AFB, AK ANG
	23526	Boeing KC-135R Stratotanker (62-3526) r/w	USAF 173rd ARS/155th ARW, Lincoln, NE ANG
	23528	Boeing KC-135R Stratotanker (62-3528) gn/y	USAF 77th ARS/916th ARW AFRC, Seymour Johnson AFB, NC
	23529	Boeing KC-135R Stratotanker (62-3529)	USAF 314th ARS/940th ARW, Beale AFB, CA
	23530	Boeing KC-135R Stratotanker (62-3530) bl	USAF 72nd ARS/434th ARW AFRC, Grissom AFB, IN
	23531	Boeing KC-135R Stratotanker (62-3531) r/w	USAF 166th ARS/121st ARW, Rickenbacker ANGB, OH ANG
	23533	Boeing KC-135R Stratotanker (62-3533)	USAF 328th ARS/914th ARW AFRC, Niagara Falls NY
	23534	Boeing KC-135R Stratotanker (62-3534)	USAF 22nd ARW, McConnell AFB, KS
	23537	Boeing KC-135R Stratotanker (62-3537) gn/y	USAF 77th ARS/916th ARW AFRC, Seymour Johnson AFB, NC
	23538	Boeing KC-135R Stratotanker (62-3538)	USAF 92nd ARW, Fairchild AFB, WA
	23540	Boeing KC-135R Stratotanker (62-3540) y/r	USAF 54th ARS/97th AMW, Altus AFB, OK
	23541	Boeing KC-135R Stratotanker (62-3541)	USAF 92nd ARW, Fairchild AFB, WA
	23542	Boeing KC-135R Stratotanker (62-3542) gn/y	USAF 77th ARS/916th ARW AFRC, Seymour Johnson AFB, NC
	23543	Boeing KC-135R Stratotanker (62-3543) y/bk	USAF 756th ARS/459th ARW AFRC, Andrews AFB, MD
	23544	Boeing KC-135R Stratotanker (62-3544) r $	USAF 141st ARS/108th ARW, McGuire AFB, NJ ANG
	23545	Boeing KC-135R Stratotanker (62-3545)	USAF 22nd ARW, McConnell AFB, KS
	23547	Boeing KC-135R Stratotanker (62-3547) bl/y	USAF 117th ARS/190th ARW, Forbes Field, KS ANG
	23549	Boeing KC-135R Stratotanker (62-3549) y/r	USAF 54th ARS/97th AMW, Altus AFB, OK
	23550	Boeing KC-135R Stratotanker (62-3550)	USAF 197th ARS/161st ARW, Phoenix, AZ ANG
	23551	Boeing KC-135R Stratotanker (62-3551) [D] r/w/bl	USAF 351st ARS/100th ARW, RAF Mildenhall, UK
	23552	Boeing KC-135R Stratotanker (62-3552)	USAF 22nd ARW, McConnell AFB, KS
	23553	Boeing KC-135R Stratotanker (62-3553)	USAF 92nd ARW, Fairchild AFB, WA
	23554	Boeing KC-135R Stratotanker (62-3554)	USAF 22nd ARW, McConnell AFB, KS
	23556	Boeing KC-135R Stratotanker (62-3556) y/bk	USAF 756th ARS/459th ARW AFRC, Andrews AFB, MD
	23557	Boeing KC-135R Stratotanker (62-3557)	USAF 328th ARS/914th ARW AFRC, Niagara Falls NY
	23558	Boeing KC-135R Stratotanker (62-3558) or/y	USAF 336th ARS/452nd AMW AFRC, March ARB, CA
	23559	Boeing KC-135R Stratotanker (62-3559)	USAF 22nd ARW, McConnell AFB, KS
	23561	Boeing KC-135R Stratotanker (62-3561) [ZZ] or/bk	USAF 909th ARS/18th Wg, Kadena AB, Japan
	23562	Boeing KC-135R Stratotanker (62-3562) [ZZ] or/bk	USAF 909th ARS/18th Wg, Kadena AB, Japan
	23564	Boeing KC-135R Stratotanker (62-3564) [ZZ] or/bk	USAF 909th ARS/18th Wg, Kadena AB, Japan
	23565	Boeing KC-135R Stratotanker (62-3565) [ZZ] or/bk	USAF 909th ARS/18th Wg, Kadena AB, Japan
	23566	Boeing KC-135R Stratotanker (62-3566) y/bk	USAF 174th ARS/185th ARW, Sioux City, IA ANG
	23568	Boeing KC-135R Stratotanker (62-3568) y/bl	USAF 6th AMW, MacDill AFB, FL
	23569	Boeing KC-135R Stratotanker (62-3569)	USAF 22nd ARW, McConnell AFB, KS
	23571	Boeing KC-135R Stratotanker (62-3571) [AK] bl/y	USAF 168th ARS/168th ARW, Eielson AFB, AK ANG
	23572	Boeing KC-135R Stratotanker (62-3572) bl/y	USAF 117th ARS/190th ARW, Forbes Field, KS ANG
	23573	Boeing KC-135R Stratotanker (62-3573)	USAF 22nd ARW, McConnell AFB, KS

Serial	Type (code/other identity)	Owner/operator, location or fate	Notes
23575	Boeing KC-135R Stratotanker (62-3575) *y/bl*	USAF 6th AMW, MacDill AFB, FL	
23576	Boeing KC-135R Stratotanker (62-3576) *w/bl*	USAF 108th ARS/126th ARW, Scott AFB, IL ANG	
23577	Boeing KC-135R Stratotanker (62-3577) *gn/y*	USAF 77th ARS/916th ARW AFRC, Seymour Johnson AFB, NC	
23578	Boeing KC-135R Stratotanker (62-3578) *r*	USAF 141st ARS/108th ARW, McGuire AFB, NJ ANG	
23580	Boeing KC-135R Stratotanker (62-3580)	USAF 328th ARS/914th ARW AFRC, Niagara Falls NY	
23582	Boeing WC-135C Constant Phoenix (62-3582) [OF] *bk*	USAF 45th RS/55th Wg, Offutt AFB, NE	
24125	Boeing RC-135W Rivet Joint (62-4125) *gn*	USAF 38th RS/55th Wg, Offutt AFB, NE	
24126	Boeing RC-135W Rivet Joint (62-4126) *bl*	USAF 343rd RS/55th Wg, Offutt AFB, NE	
24127	Boeing TC-135W (62-4127) *gn*	USAF 38th RS/55th Wg, Offutt AFB, NE	
24128	Boeing RC-135S Cobra Ball (62-4128) [OF] *bk*	USAF 45th RS/55th Wg, Offutt AFB, NE	
24129	Boeing TC-135W (62-4129) *gn*	USAF 38th RS/55th Wg, Offutt AFB, NE	
24130	Boeing RC-135W Rivet Joint (62-4130) *gn*	USAF 38th RS/55th Wg, Offutt AFB, NE	
24131	Boeing RC-135W Rivet Joint (62-4131) [OF] *bl*	USAF 343rd RS/55th Wg, Offutt AFB, NE	
24132	Boeing RC-135W Rivet Joint (62-4132) *gn*	USAF 38th RS/55th Wg, Offutt AFB, NE	
24133	Boeing TC-135W (62-4133) *gn*	USAF 38th RS/55th Wg, Offutt AFB, NE	
24134	Boeing RC-135W Rivet Joint (62-4134) *bl*	USAF 343rd RS/55th Wg, Offutt AFB, NE	
24135	Boeing RC-135W Rivet Joint (62-4135) *gn*	USAF 38th RS/55th Wg, Offutt AFB, NE	
24138	Boeing RC-135W Rivet Joint (62-4138) *bl*	USAF 343rd RS/55th Wg, Offutt AFB, NE	
24139	Boeing RC-135W Rivet Joint (62-4139) *gn*	USAF 38th RS/55th Wg, Offutt AFB, NE	
37976	Boeing KC-135R Stratotanker (63-7976) *y/r*	USAF 54th ARS/97th AMW, Altus AFB, OK	
37977	Boeing KC-135R Stratotanker (63-7977) [ZZ] *or/bk*	USAF 909th ARS/18th Wg, Kadena AB, Japan	
37978	Boeing KC-135R Stratotanker (63-7978) [ZZ] *or/bk*	USAF 909th ARS/18th Wg, Kadena AB, Japan	
37979	Boeing KC-135R Stratotanker (63-7979)	USAF 22nd ARW, McConnell AFB, KS	
37980	Boeing KC-135R Stratotanker (63-7980) [ED]	USAF 418th FLTS/412th TW, Edwards AFB, CA	
37981	Boeing KC-135R Stratotanker (63-7981) *w/bl*	USAF 108th ARS/126th ARW, Scott AFB, IL ANG	
37982	Boeing KC-135R Stratotanker (63-7982)	USAF 92nd ARW, Fairchild AFB, WA	
37984	Boeing KC-135R Stratotanker (63-7984) *w/r*	USAF 106th ARS/117th ARW, Birmingham, AL ANG	
37985	Boeing KC-135R Stratotanker (63-7985) *bl/y*	USAF 465th ARS/507th ARW AFRC, Tinker AFB, OK	
37987	Boeing KC-135R Stratotanker (63-7987)	USAF 22nd ARW, McConnell AFB, KS	
37988	Boeing KC-135R Stratotanker (63-7988) *r/w*	USAF 173rd ARS/155th ARW, Lincoln, NE ANG	
37991	Boeing KC-135R Stratotanker (63-7991) *r/w*	USAF 173rd ARS/155th ARW, Lincoln, NE ANG	
37992	Boeing KC-135R Stratotanker (63-7992)	USAF 153rd ARS/186th AW, Meridian, MS ANG	
37993	Boeing KC-135R Stratotanker (63-7993) *m*	USAF 166th ARS/121st ARW, Rickenbacker ANGB, OH ANG	
37995	Boeing KC-135R Stratotanker (63-7995)	USAF 22nd ARW, McConnell AFB, KS	
37996	Boeing KC-135R Stratotanker (63-7996) *bl*	USAF 72nd ARS/434th ARW AFRC, Grissom AFB, IN	
37997	Boeing KC-135R Stratotanker (63-7997) [ZZ] *or/bk*	USAF 909th ARS/18th Wg, Kadena AB, Japan	
37999	Boeing KC-135R Stratotanker (63-7999) [D] *r/w/bl*	USAF 351st ARS/100th ARW, RAF Mildenhall, UK	
38000	Boeing KC-135R Stratotanker (63-8000)	USAF 92nd ARW, Fairchild AFB, WA	
38002	Boeing KC-135R Stratotanker (63-8002)	USAF 22nd ARW, McConnell AFB, KS	
38003	Boeing KC-135R Stratotanker (63-8003) *r*	USAF 141st ARS/108th ARW, McGuire AFB, NJ ANG	
38004	Boeing KC-135R Stratotanker (63-8004) *bl/y*	USAF 117th ARS/190th ARW, Forbes Field, KS ANG	
38006	Boeing KC-135R Stratotanker (63-8006) *y/r*	USAF 54th ARS/97th AMW, Altus AFB, OK	
38007	Boeing KC-135R Stratotanker (63-8007) *w/r*	USAF 106th ARS/117th ARW, Birmingham, AL ANG	
38008	Boeing KC-135R Stratotanker (63-8008)	USAF 92nd ARW, Fairchild AFB, WA	
38011	Boeing KC-135R Stratotanker (63-8011) *y/bl*	USAF 6th AMW, MacDill AFB, FL	
38012	Boeing KC-135R Stratotanker (63-8012)	USAF 314th ARS/940th ARW, Beale AFB, CA	
38013	Boeing KC-135R Stratotanker (63-8013) *r/w*	USAF 166th ARS/121st ARW, Rickenbacker ANGB, OH ANG	
38014	Boeing KC-135R Stratotanker (63-8014) *gn/y*	USAF 77th ARS/916th ARW AFRC, Seymour Johnson AFB, NC	
38015	Boeing KC-135R Stratotanker (63-8015) [AK] *bl/y*	USAF 168th ARS/168th ARW, Eielson AFB, AK ANG	

Notes	Serial	Type (code/other identity)	Owner/operator, location or fate
	38017	Boeing KC-135R Stratotanker (63-8017)	USAF 328th ARS/914th ARW AFRC, Niagara Falls NY
	38018	Boeing KC-135R Stratotanker (63-8018) r/w	USAF 173rd ARS/155th ARW, Lincoln, NE ANG
	38019	Boeing KC-135R Stratotanker (63-8019)	USAF 22nd ARW, McConnell AFB, KS
	38020	Boeing KC-135R Stratotanker (63-8020) y/r	USAF 54th ARS/97th AMW, Altus AFB, OK
	38021	Boeing KC-135R Stratotanker (63-8021)	USAF 92nd ARW, Fairchild AFB, WA
	38022	Boeing KC-135R Stratotanker (63-8022) [ZZ] or/bk	USAF 909th ARS/18th Wg, Kadena AB, Japan
	38023	Boeing KC-135R Stratotanker (63-8023) w/bl	USAF 126th ARS/128th ARW, Mitchell Field, WI ANG
	38024	Boeing KC-135R Stratotanker (63-8024) or/y	USAF 336th ARS/452nd AMW AFRC, March ARB, CA
	38025	Boeing KC-135R Stratotanker (63-8025)	USAF 22nd ARW, McConnell AFB, KS
	38026	Boeing KC-135R Stratotanker (63-8026) bl/bk	USAF 191st ARS/151st ARW, Salt Lake City, UT ANG
	38027	Boeing KC-135R Stratotanker (63-8027) y/bl	USAF 6th AMW, MacDill AFB, FL
	38028	Boeing KC-135R Stratotanker (63-8028) [AK] bl/y	USAF 168th ARS/168th ARW, Eielson AFB, AK ANG
	38029	Boeing KC-135R Stratotanker (63-8029) r	USAF 141st ARS/108th ARW, McGuire AFB, NJ ANG
	38030	Boeing KC-135R Stratotanker (63-8030) [HH] y/bk	USAF 203rd ARS/15th Wg, Hickam AFB, HI ANG
	38031	Boeing KC-135R Stratotanker (63-8031)	USAF 22nd ARW, McConnell AFB, KS
	38032	Boeing KC-135R Stratotanker (63-8032) bl	USAF 72nd ARS/434th ARW AFRC, Grissom AFB, IN
	38033	Boeing KC-135R Stratotanker (63-8033) y/r	USAF 54th ARS/97th AMW, Altus AFB, OK
	38034	Boeing KC-135R Stratotanker (63-8034)	USAF 92nd ARW, Fairchild AFB, WA
	38035	Boeing KC-135R Stratotanker (63-8035) w/r	USAF 106th ARS/117th ARW, Birmingham, AL ANG
	38036	Boeing KC-135R Stratotanker (63-8036)	USAF 197th ARS/161st ARW, Phoenix, AZ ANG
	38038	Boeing KC-135R Stratotanker (63-8038) [HH] y/bk	USAF 203rd ARS/15th Wg, Hickam AFB, HI ANG
	38039	Boeing KC-135R Stratotanker (63-8039) bl/y	USAF 465th ARS/507th ARW AFRC, Tinker AFB, OK
	38040	Boeing KC-135R Stratotanker (63-8040) r	USAF 141st ARS/108th ARW, McGuire AFB, NJ ANG
	38041	Boeing KC-135R Stratotanker (63-8041) bl	USAF 72nd ARS/434th ARW AFRC, Grissom AFB, IN
	38043	Boeing KC-135R Stratotanker (63-8043) [AK] bl/y	USAF 168th ARS/168th ARW, Eielson AFB, AK ANG
	38044	Boeing KC-135R Stratotanker (63-8044)	USAF 328th ARS/914th ARW AFRC, Niagara Falls NY
	38045	Boeing KC-135R Stratotanker (63-8045) y/bl	USAF 6th AMW, MacDill AFB, FL
	38871	Boeing KC-135R Stratotanker (63-8871)	USAF
	38872	Boeing KC-135R Stratotanker (63-8872) w/gn	USAF 132nd ARS/101st ARW, Bangor, MN ANG
	38873	Boeing KC-135R Stratotanker (63-8873) w/gn	USAF 132nd ARS/101st ARW, Bangor, MN ANG
	38874	Boeing KC-135R Stratotanker (63-8874)	USAF 92nd ARW, Fairchild AFB, WA
	38875	Boeing KC-135R Stratotanker (63-8875) bl/y	USAF 117th ARS/190th ARW, Forbes Field, KS ANG
	38876	Boeing KC-135R Stratotanker (63-8876) [AK] bl/y	USAF 168th ARS/168th ARW, Eielson AFB, AK ANG
	38878	Boeing KC-135R Stratotanker (63-8878)	USAF 22nd ARW, McConnell AFB, KS
	38879	Boeing KC-135R Stratotanker (63-8879)	USAF 314th ARS/940th ARW, Beale AFB, CA
	38880	Boeing KC-135R Stratotanker (63-8880) [HH] y/bk	USAF 203rd ARS/15th Wg, Hickam AFB, HI ANG
	38881	Boeing KC-135R Stratotanker (63-8881) bl/bk	USAF 191st ARS/151st ARW, Salt Lake City, UT ANG
	38883	Boeing KC-135R Stratotanker (63-8883)	USAF 22nd ARW, McConnell AFB, KS
	38884	Boeing KC-135R Stratotanker (63-8884)	USAF
	38885	Boeing KC-135R Stratotanker (63-8885) y/bl	USAF 6th AMW, MacDill AFB, FL
	38887	Boeing KC-135R Stratotanker (63-8887) y/bl	USAF 6th AMW, MacDill AFB, FL
	38888	Boeing KC-135R Stratotanker (63-8888) [ZZ] or/bk	USAF 909th ARS/18th Wg, Kadena AB, Japan
	39792	Boeing RC-135V Rivet Joint (63-9792) gn $	USAF 38th RS/55th Wg, Offutt AFB, NE
	71419	Boeing KC-135R Stratotanker (57-1419) bl	USAF 133rd ARS/157th ARW, Pease ANGB, NH ANG

Serial	Type (code/other identity)	Owner/operator, location or fate	Notes
71427	Boeing KC-135R Stratotanker (57-1427) *bl/y*	USAF 117th ARS/190th ARW, Forbes Field, KS ANG	
71428	Boeing KC-135R Stratotanker (57-1428) *w/or*	USAF 151st ARS/134th ARW, Knoxville, TN ANG	
71430	Boeing KC-135R Stratotanker (57-1430) *bl* $	USAF 133rd ARS/157th ARW, Pease ANGB, NH ANG	
71432	Boeing KC-135R Stratotanker (57-1432) *bl/bk*	USAF 191st ARS/151st ARW, Salt Lake City, UT ANG	
71435	Boeing KC-135R Stratotanker (57-1435) *bl/bk*	USAF 191st ARS/151st ARW, Salt Lake City, UT ANG	
71436	Boeing KC-135R Stratotanker (57-1436) *w/or*	USAF 151st ARS/134th ARW, Knoxville, TN ANG	
71437	Boeing KC-135R Stratotanker (57-1437) *gn/y*	USAF 77th ARS/916th ARW AFRC, Seymour Johnson AFB, NC	
71438	Boeing KC-135R Stratotanker (57-1438) *or/y*	USAF 336th ARS/452nd AMW AFRC, March ARB, CA	
71439	Boeing KC-135R Stratotanker (57-1439) *y/bl*	USAF 6th AMW, MacDill AFB, FL	
71440	Boeing KC-135R Stratotanker (57-1440) [D] *r/w/bl*	USAF 351st ARS/100th ARW, RAF Mildenhall, UK	
71441	Boeing KC-135R Stratotanker (57-1441) *y/bk*	USAF 174th ARS/185th ARW, Sioux City, IA ANG	
71451	Boeing KC-135R Stratotanker (57-1451) *w/or*	USAF 151st ARS/134th ARW, Knoxville, TN ANG	
71453	Boeing KC-135R Stratotanker (57-1453) *w/r*	USAF 106th ARS/117th ARW, Birmingham, AL ANG	
71454	Boeing KC-135R Stratotanker (57-1454) [ZZ] *or/bk*	USAF 909th ARS/18th Wg, Kadena AB, Japan	
71456	Boeing KC-135R Stratotanker (57-1456) *gn/y*	USAF 77th ARS/916th ARW AFRC, Seymour Johnson AFB, NC	
71459	Boeing KC-135R Stratotanker (57-1459) *or/y*	USAF 336th ARS/452nd AMW AFRC, March ARB, CA	
71461	Boeing KC-135R Stratotanker (57-1461) *r/w*	USAF 173rd ARS/155th ARW, Lincoln, NE ANG	
71462	Boeing KC-135R Stratotanker (57-1462)	USAF 153rd ARS/186th AW, Meridian, MS ANG	
71468	Boeing KC-135R Stratotanker (57-1468) *or/y*	USAF 336th ARS/452nd AMW AFRC, March ARB, CA	
71469	Boeing KC-135R Stratotanker (57-1469) $	USAF 197th ARS/161st ARW, Phoenix, AZ ANG	
71472	Boeing KC-135R Stratotanker (57-1472) *bl*	USAF 72nd ARS/434th ARW AFRC, Grissom AFB, IN	
71473	Boeing KC-135R Stratotanker (57-1473) *w/r*	USAF 106th ARS/117th ARW, Birmingham, AL ANG	
71474	Boeing KC-135R Stratotanker (57-1474) [D] *r/w/bl*	USAF 351st ARS/100th ARW, RAF Mildenhall, UK	
71479	Boeing KC-135R Stratotanker (57-1479) *y/bk*	USAF 756th ARS/459th ARW AFRC, Andrews AFB, MD	
71483	Boeing KC-135R Stratotanker (57-1483)	USAF 92nd ARW, Fairchild AFB, WA	
71486	Boeing KC-135R Stratotanker (57-1486)	USAF 153rd ARS/186th AW, Meridian, MS ANG	
71487	Boeing KC-135R Stratotanker (57-1487) *y/bk*	USAF 756th ARS/459th ARW AFRC, Andrews AFB, MD	
71488	Boeing KC-135R Stratotanker (57-1488) [ZZ] *or/bk*	USAF 909th ARS/18th Wg, Kadena AB, Japan	
71493	Boeing KC-135R Stratotanker (57-1493) [D] *r/w/bl*	USAF 351st ARS/100th ARW, RAF Mildenhall, UK	
71499	Boeing KC-135R Stratotanker (57-1499) *bl/bk*	USAF 191st ARS/151st ARW, Salt Lake City, UT ANG	
71502	Boeing KC-135R Stratotanker (57-1502) [ZZ] *or/bk*	USAF 909th ARS/18th Wg, Kadena AB, Japan	
71506	Boeing KC-135R Stratotanker (57-1506) *y/r*	USAF 54th ARS/97th AMW, Altus AFB, OK	
71508	Boeing KC-135R Stratotanker (57-1508)	USAF 314th ARS/940th ARW, Beale AFB, CA	
71512	Boeing KC-135R Stratotanker (57-1512) *y/bk*	USAF 756th ARS/459th ARW AFRC, Andrews AFB, MD	
71514	Boeing KC-135R Stratotanker (57-1514) *w/bl*	USAF 126th ARS/128th ARW, Mitchell Field, WI ANG	
72597	Boeing KC-135R Stratotanker (57-2597) *w/or*	USAF 151st ARS/134th ARW, Knoxville, TN ANG	
72598	Boeing KC-135R Stratotanker (57-2598) *or/y*	USAF 336th ARS/452nd AMW AFRC, March ARB, CA	
72599	Boeing KC-135R Stratotanker (57-2599) *gn/y*	USAF 77th ARS/916th ARW AFRC, Seymour Johnson AFB, NC	
72603	Boeing KC-135R Stratotanker (57-2603) *or/y*	USAF 336th ARS/452nd AMW AFRC, March ARB, CA	
72605	Boeing KC-135R Stratotanker (57-2605) [D] *r/w/bl*	USAF 351st ARS/100th ARW, RAF Mildenhall, UK	
72606	Boeing KC-135R Stratotanker (57-2606) *y/bk*	USAF 174th ARS/185th ARW, Sioux City, IA ANG	
80001	Boeing KC-135R Stratotanker (58-0001) [D] *r/w/bl*	USAF 351st ARS/100th ARW, RAF Mildenhall, UK	

Notes	Serial	Type (code/other identity)	Owner/operator, location or fate
	80004	Boeing KC-135R Stratotanker (58-0004) w/r	USAF 106th ARS/117th ARW, Birmingham, AL ANG
	80009	Boeing KC-135R Stratotanker (58-0009) w/bl	USAF 126th ARS/128th ARW, Mitchell Field, WI ANG
	80010	Boeing KC-135R Stratotanker (58-0010) r	USAF 141st ARS/108th ARW, McGuire AFB, NJ ANG
	80011	Boeing KC-135R(RT) Stratotanker (58-0011)	USAF 22nd ARW, McConnell AFB, KS
	80015	Boeing KC-135R Stratotanker (58-0015) bl/y	USAF 465th ARS/507th ARW AFRC, Tinker AFB, OK
	80016	Boeing KC-135R Stratotanker (58-0016)	USAF 92nd ARW, Fairchild AFB, WA
	80018	Boeing KC-135R(RT) Stratotanker (58-0018)	USAF 22nd ARW, McConnell AFB, KS
	80021	Boeing KC-135R Stratotanker (58-0021) w/gn	USAF 132nd ARS/101st ARW, Bangor, MN ANG
	80023	Boeing KC-135R Stratotanker (58-0023) bl/bk	USAF 191st ARS/151st ARW, Salt Lake City, UT ANG
	80027	Boeing KC-135R Stratotanker (58-0027) bl/bk	USAF 191st ARS/151st ARW, Salt Lake City, UT ANG
	80030	Boeing KC-135R Stratotanker (58-0030) w/gn	USAF 132nd ARS/101st ARW, Bangor, MN ANG
	80034	Boeing KC-135R Stratotanker (58-0034) y/bl	USAF 6th AMW, MacDill AFB, FL
	80035	Boeing KC-135R Stratotanker (58-0035)	USAF 92nd ARW, Fairchild AFB, WA
	80036	Boeing KC-135R Stratotanker (58-0036) y/r	USAF 54th ARS/97th AMW, Altus AFB, OK
	80038	Boeing KC-135R Stratotanker (58-0038) gn/y	USAF 77th ARS/916th ARW AFRC, Seymour Johnson AFB, NC
	80042	Boeing KC-135T Stratotanker (58-0042)	USAF 22nd ARW, McConnell AFB, KS
	80045	Boeing KC-135T Stratotanker (58-0045)	USAF 171st ARW, Greater Pittsburgh, PA ANG
	80046	Boeing KC-135T Stratotanker (58-0046) y/bl	USAF 6th AMW, MacDill AFB, FL
	80047	Boeing KC-135T Stratotanker (58-0047)	USAF 22nd ARW, McConnell AFB, KS
	80049	Boeing KC-135T Stratotanker (58-0049) bk/y	USAF 171st ARS/127th Wg, Selfridge ANGB, MI ANG
	80050	Boeing KC-135T Stratotanker (58-0050) y/bl	USAF 6th AMW, MacDill AFB, FL
	80051	Boeing KC-135R Stratotanker (58-0051) bl/y	USAF 465th ARS/507th ARW AFRC, Tinker AFB, OK
	80052	Boeing KC-135R Stratotanker (58-0052) or/y	USAF 336th ARS/452nd AMW AFRC, March ARB, CA
	80054	Boeing KC-135T Stratotanker (58-0054) y/bk	USAF 171st ARW, Greater Pittsburgh, PA ANG
	80055	Boeing KC-135T Stratotanker (58-0055)	USAF 92nd ARW, Fairchild AFB, WA
	80056	Boeing KC-135R Stratotanker (58-0056) [HH] y/bk	USAF 203rd ARS/15th Wg, Hickam AFB, HI ANG
	80057	Boeing KC-135R Stratotanker (58-0057) y/bk	USAF 174th ARS/185th ARW, Sioux City, IA ANG
	80058	Boeing KC-135R Stratotanker (58-0058) bl/y	USAF 465th ARS/507th ARW AFRC, Tinker AFB, OK
	80059	Boeing KC-135R Stratotanker (58-0059) bl/y	USAF 117th ARS/190th ARW, Forbes Field, KS ANG
	80060	Boeing KC-135T Stratotanker (58-0060) y/bk	USAF 171st ARW, Greater Pittsburgh, PA ANG
	80061	Boeing KC-135T Stratotanker (58-0061)	USAF 22nd ARW, McConnell AFB, KS
	80062	Boeing KC-135T Stratotanker (58-0062) bk/y	USAF 171st ARS/127th Wg, Selfridge ANGB, MI ANG
	80063	Boeing KC-135R Stratotanker (58-0063)	USAF 328th ARS/914th ARW AFRC, Niagara Falls NY
	80065	Boeing KC-135T Stratotanker (58-0065)	USAF 22nd ARW, McConnell AFB, KS
	80066	Boeing KC-135R Stratotanker (58-0066) bl	USAF 133rd ARS/157th ARW, Pease ANGB, NH ANG
	80067	Boeing KC-135R Stratotanker (58-0067) y/bk	USAF 174th ARS/185th ARW, Sioux City, IA ANG
	80069	Boeing KC-135T Stratotanker (58-0069)	USAF 92nd ARW, Fairchild AFB, WA
	80071	Boeing KC-135T Stratotanker (58-0071) y/bl	USAF 6th AMW, MacDill AFB, FL
	80072	Boeing KC-135T Stratotanker (58-0072) y/bk	USAF 171st ARW, Greater Pittsburgh, PA ANG
	80073	Boeing KC-135R Stratotanker (58-0073) w/r	USAF 106th ARS/117th ARW, Birmingham, AL ANG
	80074	Boeing KC-135T Stratotanker (58-0074) y/bk	USAF 171st ARW, Greater Pittsburgh, PA ANG
	80075	Boeing KC-135R Stratotanker (58-0075) y/bk	USAF 756th ARS/459th ARW AFRC, Andrews AFB, MD
	80076	Boeing KC-135R Stratotanker (58-0076) r/w	USAF 74th ARS/434th ARW AFRC, Grissom AFB, IN
	80077	Boeing KC-135T Stratotanker (58-0077) y/bk	USAF 171st ARW, Greater Pittsburgh, PA ANG

Serial	Type (code/other identity)	Owner/operator, location or fate	Notes
80079	Boeing KC-135R Stratotanker (58-0079)	USAF 153rd ARS/186th AW, Meridian, MS ANG	
80083	Boeing KC-135R Stratotanker (58-0083) r/w	USAF 166th ARS/121st ARW, Rickenbacker ANGB, OH ANG	
80084	Boeing KC-135T Stratotanker (58-0084) y/bk	USAF 171st ARW, Greater Pittsburgh, PA ANG	
80085	Boeing KC-135R Stratotanker (58-0085) or/y	USAF 336th ARS/452nd AMW AFRC, March ARB, CA	
80086	Boeing KC-135T Stratotanker (58-0086)	USAF 92nd ARW, Fairchild AFB, WA	
80088	Boeing KC-135T Stratotanker (58-0088) bk/y	USAF 171st ARS/127th Wg, Selfridge ANGB, MI ANG	
80089	Boeing KC-135T Stratotanker (58-0089) y/bl	USAF 6th AMW, MacDill AFB, FL	
80092	Boeing KC-135R Stratotanker (58-0092)	USAF 22nd ARW, McConnell AFB, KS	
80093	Boeing KC-135R Stratotanker (58-0093) y/r	USAF 54th ARS/97th AMW, Altus AFB, OK	
80094	Boeing KC-135T Stratotanker (58-0094)	USAF	
80095	Boeing KC-135T Stratotanker (58-0095)	USAF 92nd ARW, Fairchild AFB, WA	
80098	Boeing KC-135R Stratotanker (58-0098) w/gn	USAF 132nd ARS/101st ARW, Bangor, MN ANG	
80099	Boeing KC-135R Stratotanker (58-0099) y/bk	USAF 171st ARW, Greater Pittsburgh, PA ANG	
80100	Boeing KC-135R Stratotanker (58-0100) [D] r/w/bl	USAF 351st ARS/100th ARW, RAF Mildenhall, UK	
80102	Boeing KC-135R Stratotanker (58-0102) bl/y	USAF 465th ARS/507th ARW AFRC, Tinker AFB, OK	
80103	Boeing KC-135T Stratotanker (58-0103) y/bl	USAF 6th AMW, MacDill AFB, FL	
80104	Boeing KC-135R Stratotanker (58-0104) bl	USAF 133rd ARS/157th ARW, Pease ANGB, NH ANG	
80106	Boeing KC-135R Stratotanker (58-0106) w/r	USAF 106th ARS/117th ARW, Birmingham, AL ANG	
80107	Boeing KC-135R Stratotanker (58-0107) w/gn	USAF 132nd ARS/101st ARW, Bangor, MN ANG	
80109	Boeing KC-135R Stratotanker (58-0109) y/bk	USAF 174th ARS/185th ARW, Sioux City, IA ANG	
80112	Boeing KC-135T Stratotanker (58-0112) y/bk	USAF 171st ARW, Greater Pittsburgh, PA ANG	
80113	Boeing KC-135R Stratotanker (58-0113) [D] r/w/bl	USAF 351st ARS/100th ARW, RAF Mildenhall, UK	
80117	Boeing KC-135T Stratotanker (58-0117) y/bk	USAF 171st ARW, Greater Pittsburgh, PA ANG	
80118	Boeing KC-135R Stratotanker (58-0118)	USAF	
80119	Boeing KC-135R Stratotanker (58-0119) w/or	USAF 151st ARS/134th ARW, Knoxville, TN ANG	
80120	Boeing KC-135R Stratotanker (58-0120)	USAF 153rd ARS/186th AW, Meridian, MS ANG	
80121	Boeing KC-135R Stratotanker (58-0121) bl/y	USAF 465th ARS/507th ARW AFRC, Tinker AFB, OK	
80122	Boeing KC-135R Stratotanker (58-0122) bl/y	USAF 117th ARS/190th ARW, Forbes Field, KS ANG	
80123	Boeing KC-135R Stratotanker (58-0123)	USAF 22nd ARW, McConnell AFB, KS	
80124	Boeing KC-135R(RT) Stratotanker (58-0124)	USAF 22nd ARW, McConnell AFB, KS	
80125	Boeing KC-135T Stratotanker (58-0125) y/bl	USAF 6th AMW, MacDill AFB, FL	
80126	Boeing KC-135R(RT) Stratotanker (58-0126)	USAF 22nd ARW, McConnell AFB, KS	
80128	Boeing KC-135R Stratotanker (58-0128) [ZZ] or/bk	USAF 909th ARS/18th Wg, Kadena AB, Japan	
80129	Boeing KC-135T Stratotanker (58-0129) bk/y	USAF 171st ARS/127th Wg, Selfridge ANGB, MI ANG	
91444	Boeing KC-135R Stratotanker (59-1444) r/w	USAF 166th ARS/121st ARW, Rickenbacker ANGB, OH ANG	
91446	Boeing KC-135R Stratotanker (59-1446) w/gn	USAF 132nd ARS/101st ARW, Bangor, MN ANG	
91448	Boeing KC-135R Stratotanker (59-1448)	USAF 153rd ARS/186th AW, Meridian, MS ANG	
91450	Boeing KC-135R Stratotanker (59-1450)	USAF 197th ARS/161st ARW, Phoenix, AZ ANG	
91453	Boeing KC-135R Stratotanker (59-1453)	USAF 153rd ARS/186th AW, Meridian, MS ANG	
91455	Boeing KC-135R Stratotanker (59-1455) [HH] y/bk	USAF 203rd ARS/15th Wg, Hickam AFB, HI ANG	
91458	Boeing KC-135R Stratotanker (59-1458) r/w	USAF 166th ARS/121st ARW, Rickenbacker ANGB, OH ANG	
91459	Boeing KC-135R Stratotanker (59-1459) [ZZ] or/bk	USAF 909th ARS/18th Wg, Kadena AB, Japan	
91460	Boeing KC-135T Stratotanker (59-1460) y/bk	USAF 171st ARW, Greater Pittsburgh, PA ANG	
91461	Boeing KC-135R Stratotanker (59-1461) w/bl	USAF 126th ARS/128th ARW, Mitchell Field, WI ANG	
91462	Boeing KC-135T Stratotanker (59-1462)	USAF 22nd ARW, McConnell AFB, KS	
91463	Boeing KC-135R Stratotanker (59-1463) w/r	USAF 106th ARS/117th ARW, Birmingham, AL ANG	
91464	Boeing KC-135T Stratotanker (59-1464)	USAF 92nd ARW, Fairchild AFB, WA	
91466	Boeing KC-135R Stratotanker (59-1466) w/bl	USAF 108th ARS/126th ARW, Scott AFB, IL ANG	
91467	Boeing KC-135T Stratotanker (59-1467) y/bk	USAF 171st ARW, Greater Pittsburgh, PA ANG	

Notes	Serial	Type (code/other identity)	Owner/operator, location or fate
	91468	Boeing KC-135R Stratotanker (59-1468) *y/bk*	USAF 171st ARW, Greater Pittsburgh, PA ANG
	91469	Boeing KC-135R Stratotanker (59-1469) *y/bk*	USAF 756th ARS/459th ARW AFRC, Andrews AFB, MD
	91470	Boeing KC-135T Stratotanker (59-1470)	USAF 92nd ARW, Fairchild AFB, WA
	91471	Boeing KC-135T Stratotanker (59-1471)	USAF 92nd ARW, Fairchild AFB, WA
	91472	Boeing KC-135R Stratotanker (59-1472)	USAF 314th ARS/940th ARW, Beale AFB, CA
	91474	Boeing KC-135R Stratotanker (59-1474) *bk/y*	USAF 171st ARS/127th Wg, Selfridge ANGB, MI ANG
	91475	Boeing KC-135R Stratotanker (59-1475) [ZZ] *or/bk*	USAF 909th ARS/18th Wg, Kadena AB, Japan
	91476	Boeing KC-135R Stratotanker (59-1476)	USAF 92nd ARW, Fairchild AFB, WA
	91478	Boeing KC-135R Stratotanker (59-1478) *w/or*	USAF 151st ARS/134th ARW, Knoxville, TN ANG
	91480	Boeing KC-135T Stratotanker (59-1480) *y/bl*	USAF 6th AMW, MacDill AFB, FL
	91482	Boeing KC-135R Stratotanker (59-1482)	USAF 328th ARS/914th ARW AFRC, Niagara Falls NY
	91483	Boeing KC-135R Stratotanker (59-1483) *r/w*	USAF 166th ARS/121st ARW, Rickenbacker ANGB, OH ANG
	91486	Boeing KC-135R Stratotanker (59-1486)	USAF 92nd ARW, Fairchild AFB, WA
	91488	Boeing KC-135R Stratotanker (59-1488) *w/gn*	USAF 132nd ARS/101st ARW, Bangor, MN ANG
	91490	Boeing KC-135T Stratotanker (59-1490) *y/bk*	USAF 171st ARW, Greater Pittsburgh, PA ANG
	91492	Boeing KC-135R Stratotanker (59-1492) [ZZ] *or/bk*	USAF 909th ARS/18th Wg, Kadena AB, Japan
	91495	Boeing KC-135R Stratotanker (59-1495) *r/w*	USAF 173rd ARS/155th ARW, Lincoln, NE ANG
	91498	Boeing KC-135R Stratotanker (59-1498) *w/gn*	USAF 132nd ARS/101st ARW, Bangor, MN ANG
	91499	Boeing KC-135R Stratotanker (59-1499) [HH] *y/bk*	USAF 203rd ARS/15th Wg, Hickam AFB, HI ANG
	91500	Boeing KC-135R Stratotanker (59-1500) *w/bl*	USAF 108th ARS/126th ARW, Scott AFB, IL ANG
	91501	Boeing KC-135R Stratotanker (59-1501)	USAF 92nd ARW, Fairchild AFB, WA
	91502	Boeing KC-135R Stratotanker (59-1502)	USAF 22nd ARW, McConnell AFB, KS
	91504	Boeing KC-135T Stratotanker (59-1504) *y/bk*	USAF 171st ARW, Greater Pittsburgh, PA ANG
	91505	Boeing KC-135R Stratotanker (59-1505) *w/or*	USAF 151st ARS/134th ARW, Knoxville, TN ANG
	91506	Boeing KC-135R Stratotanker (59-1506) *y/bk*	USAF 174th ARS/185th ARW, Sioux City, IA ANG
	91507	Boeing KC-135R Stratotanker (59-1507) *bl/y*	USAF 117th ARS/190th ARW, Forbes Field, KS ANG
	91508	Boeing KC-135R Stratotanker (59-1508)	USAF 92nd ARW, Fairchild AFB, WA
	91509	Boeing KC-135R Stratotanker (59-1509) *w/or*	USAF 151st ARS/134th ARW, Knoxville, TN ANG
	91510	Boeing KC-135T Stratotanker (59-1510) *y/bl*	USAF 6th AMW, MacDill AFB, FL
	91511	Boeing KC-135R Stratotanker (59-1511)	USAF 92nd ARW, Fairchild AFB, WA
	91512	Boeing KC-135T Stratotanker (59-1512) *bk/y*	USAF 171st ARS/127th Wg, Selfridge ANGB, MI ANG
	91513	Boeing KC-135T Stratotanker (59-1513) [D] *r/w/bl*	USAF 351st ARS/100th ARW, RAF Mildenhall, UK
	91515	Boeing KC-135R Stratotanker (59-1515)	USAF 92nd ARW, Fairchild AFB, WA
	91516	Boeing KC-135R Stratotanker (59-1516) *w/bl*	USAF 126th ARS/128th ARW, Mitchell Field, WI ANG
	91517	Boeing KC-135R Stratotanker (59-1517) *w/or*	USAF 151st ARS/134th ARW, Knoxville, TN ANG
	91519	Boeing KC-135R Stratotanker (59-1519) *y/bk*	USAF 174th ARS/185th ARW, Sioux City, IA ANG
	91520	Boeing KC-135T Stratotanker (59-1520)	USAF 92nd ARW, Fairchild AFB, WA
	91521	Boeing KC-135R Stratotanker (59-1521) [AK] *bl/y*	USAF 168th ARS/168th ARW, Eielson AFB, AK ANG
	91522	Boeing KC-135R Stratotanker (59-1522) *w/bl*	USAF 108th ARS/126th ARW, Scott AFB, IL ANG
	91523	Boeing KC-135T Stratotanker (59-1523) *y/bk*	USAF 171st ARW, Greater Pittsburgh, PA ANG

PZL-Mielec C-145A Combat Coyote

Notes	Serial	Type (code/other identity)	Owner/operator, location or fate
	20331	PZL-Mielec C-145A Combat Coyote (N331MF/12-0331)	USAF 6th SOS/919th SOW, Duke Field, FL
	20335	PZL-Mielec C-145A Combat Coyote (N335RH/12-0335)	USAF 6th SOS/919th SOW, Duke Field, FL
	20336	PZL-Mielec C-145A Combat Coyote (N336MJ/12-0336)	USAF 6th SOS/919th SOW, Duke Field, FL
	20337	PZL-Mielec C-145A Combat Coyote (N337GU/12-0337)	USAF 6th SOS/919th SOW, Duke Field, FL
	20338	PZL-Mielec C-145A Combat Coyote (N338CH/12-0338)	USAF 6th SOS/919th SOW, Duke Field, FL

Dornier C-146A Wolfhound

Notes	Serial	Type (code/other identity)	Owner/operator, location or fate
	03026	Dornier C-146A Wolfhound (N929EF/10-3026)	USAF 524th SOS/27th SOW, Cannon AFB, NM
	03068	Dornier C-146A Wolfhound (N565EF/10-3068)	USAF 524th SOS/27th SOW, Cannon AFB, NM
	03077	Dornier C-146A Wolfhound (N577EF/10-3077)	USAF 524th SOS/27th SOW, Cannon AFB, NM
	13016	Dornier C-146A Wolfhound (N941EF/11-3016)	USAF 524th SOS/27th SOW, Cannon AFB, NM
	13031	Dornier C-146A Wolfhound (N975EF/11-3031)	USAF 524th SOS/27th SOW, Cannon AFB, NM

Serial	Type (code/other identity)	Owner/operator, location or fate	Notes
13075	Dornier C-146A Wolfhound (N953EF/11-3075)	USAF 524th SOS/27th SOW, Cannon AFB, NM	
13097	Dornier C-146A Wolfhound (N307EF/11-3097)	USAF 524th SOS/27th SOW, Cannon AFB, NM	
13104	Dornier C-146A Wolfhound (N907EF/11-3104)	USAF 524th SOS/27th SOW, Cannon AFB, NM	
23040	Dornier C-146A Wolfhound (N340LS/12-3040)	USAF 524th SOS/27th SOW, Cannon AFB, NM	
23047	Dornier C-146A Wolfhound (N347EF/12-3047)	USAF 524th SOS/27th SOW, Cannon AFB, NM	
23050	Dornier C-146A Wolfhound (N355EF/12-3050)	USAF 524th SOS/27th SOW, Cannon AFB, NM	
23060	Dornier C-146A Wolfhound (N360EF/12-3060)	USAF 524th SOS/27th SOW, Cannon AFB, NM	
23085	Dornier C-146A Wolfhound (N385EF/12-3085)	USAF 49th SOS/919th SOW, Duke Field, FL	
53058	Dornier C-146A Wolfhound (N570EF/95-3058)	USAF 524th SOS/27th SOW, Cannon AFB, NM	
53086	Dornier C-146A Wolfhound (N328ST/15-3086)	USAF 524th SOS/27th SOW, Cannon AFB, NM	
63020	Dornier C-146A Wolfhound (N524AW/16-3020)	USAF 49th SOS/919th SOW, Duke Field, FL	
63025	Dornier C-146A Wolfhound (N250BG/16-3025)	USAF 859th SOS/919th SOW, Duke Field, FL	
73091	Dornier C-146A Wolfhound (N391EF/97-3091)	USAF 524th SOS/27th SOW, Cannon AFB, NM	
73093	Dornier C-146A Wolfhound (N545EF/97-3093)	USAF 859th SOS/919th SOW, Duke Field, FL	
93106	Dornier C-146A Wolfhound (N525EF/99-3106)	USAF 524th SOS/27th SOW, Cannon AFB, NM	

Mirage 2000D 624 wears these special markings to commemorate 75 years of Escadre de Chasse (Fighter Wing) 01.003 'Navarre', based at Nancy. Close inspection reveals that some of the art work had already come off during this photo taken in July 2018, possibly as a result of the spectacular displays it performed with another of the type as part of the superb 'Couteau Delta' team.

Coded FZ, this Eurocopter AS.332L-1 Super Puma, 2235, belongs to the French Air Force's Escadron díHelicoptÈres (Helicopter Squadron) 03.067 'Parisis', based Villacoublay on the outskirts of Paris.

Notes	Serial	Type (code/other identity)	Owner/operator, location or fate
	150521	Lockheed NP-3D Orion [521]	USN VX-30, NAS Point Mugu, CA
	156511	Lockheed EP-3E ARIES II [511]	USN VQ-1, NAS Whidbey Island, WA
	156517	Lockheed EP-3E ARIES II [517]	USN VQ-1, NAS Whidbey Island, WA
	156528	Lockheed EP-3E ARIES II [528]	USN VQ-1, NAS Whidbey Island, WA
	156529	Lockheed EP-3E ARIES II [529]	USN VQ-1, NAS Whidbey Island, WA
	157316	Lockheed EP-3E ARIES II [316]	USN VQ-1, NAS Whidbey Island, WA
	157318	Lockheed EP-3E ARIES II [318]	USN VQ-1, NAS Whidbey Island, WA
	157325	Lockheed EP-3E ARIES II [325]	USN VQ-1, NAS Whidbey Island, WA
	157326	Lockheed EP-3E ARIES II [326]	USN VQ-1, NAS Whidbey Island, WA
	158210	Lockheed P-3C AIP+ Orion [PJ-210]	USN VP-69, NAS Whidbey Island, WA
	158215	Lockheed P-3C AIP Orion [215]	*To 309th AMARG, July 2018*
	158222	Lockheed P-3C AIP+ Orion [222]	USN VP-1, NAS Whidbey Island, WA
	158224	Lockheed P-3C AIP+ Orion [224]	USN VP-40, NAS Whidbey Island, WA
	158225	Lockheed P-3C AIP Orion [225]	*To 309th AMARG, September 2018*
	158564	Lockheed P-3C AIP+ Orion [564]	USN VP-62, NAS Jacksonville, FL
	158567	Lockheed P-3C AIP+ Orion [PD-567]	*Scrapped 2018*
	158570	Lockheed P-3C-IIIR Orion [RL-570]	USN VXS-1, Patuxent River, MD
	158574	Lockheed P-3C-IIIR Orion	USN NASC-FS, Point Mugu, CA
	158912	Lockheed NP-3C Orion [RL-912]	USN VXS-1, Patuxent River, MD
	158922	Lockheed P-3C AIP Orion [922]	*Scrapped November 2018*
	158934	Lockheed P-3C AIP+ Orion [302]	USN VX-30, NAS Point Mugu, CA
	159326	Lockheed P-3C AIP+ Orion [RC-326]	USN VP-46, NAS Whidbey Island, WA
	159504	Lockheed P-3CSPA Orion	USN VPU-2, NAS Whidbey Island, WA
	159887	Lockheed EP-3E ARIES II [887]	USN VQ-1, NAS Whidbey Island, WA
	159893	Lockheed EP-3E ARIES II [893]	USN VQ-1, NAS Whidbey Island, WA
	160287	Lockheed P-3C AIP+ Orion [287]	USN VP-46, NAS Whidbey Island, WA
	160290	Lockheed P-3CSPA Orion [LL-290]	USN VP-30, NAS Jacksonville, FL
	160292	Lockheed P-3CSPA Orion [292]	USN VPU-2, NAS Whidbey Island, WA
	160293	Lockheed P-3C BMUP Orion [LL-293]	USN VP-30, NAS Jacksonville, FL
	160610	Lockheed P-3C AIP+ Orion [610]	USN VQ-1, NAS Whidbey Island, WA
	160627	Lockheed KC-130R Hercules [627]	USN VX-20, Patuxent River, MD
	160764	Lockheed EP-3E ARIES II [764]	USN VQ-1, NAS Whidbey Island, WA
	161012	Lockheed P-3C AIP+ Orion [012]	USN VP-69, NAS Whidbey Island, WA
	161121	Lockheed P-3C BMUP+ Orion [121]	USN VP-62, NAS Jacksonville, FL
	161122	Lockheed P-3CSPA Orion [226]	USN VPU-2, NAS Whidbey Island, WA
	161127	Lockheed P-3C BMUP Orion [127]	USN VP-69, NAS Whidbey Island, WA
	161129	Lockheed P-3C BMUP+ Orion [129]	USN VXS-1, Patuxent River, MD
	161132	Lockheed P-3C BMUP+ Orion [132]	USN VP-46, NAS Whidbey Island, WA
	161333	Lockheed P-3C AIP+ Orion [333]	*To 309th AMARG, December 2018*
	161337	Lockheed P-3C-II½ Orion [337]	USN NASC-FS, Dallas/Love Field, TX
	161339	Lockheed P-3C BMUP Orion [RC-339]	USN VP-46, NAS Whidbey Island, WA
	161404	Lockheed P-3C BMUP+ Orion [YB-404]	USN VP-1, NAS Whidbey Island, WA
	161405	Lockheed P-3C BMUP+ Orion [405]	USN VP-69, NAS Whidbey Island, WA
	161406	Lockheed P-3C AIP+ Orion [RC-406]	USN VP-46, NAS Whidbey Island, WA
	161407	Lockheed P-3C AIP+ Orion [407]	USN VP-1, NAS Whidbey Island, WA
	161408	Lockheed P-3C BMUP+ Orion [408]	USN VP-40, NAS Whidbey Island, WA
	161410	Lockheed EP-3E ARIES II [410]	USN VQ-1, NAS Whidbey Island, WA
	161411	Lockheed P-3C BMUP+ Orion [411]	USN VP-1, NAS Whidbey Island, WA
	161413	Lockheed P-3C AIP+ Orion [413]	USN VPU-2, NAS Whidbey Island, WA
	161414	Lockheed P-3C BMUP+ Orion [RC-414]	USN VP-46, NAS Whidbey Island, WA
	161415	Lockheed P-3C BMUP+ Orion [415]	USN VP-62, NAS Jacksonville, FL
	161586	Lockheed P-3C BMUP+ Orion [QE-586]	USN VP-40, NAS Whidbey Island, WA
	161587	Lockheed P-3C BMUP+ Orion [587]	USN VP-1, NAS Whidbey Island, WA
	161588	Lockheed P-3C BMUP+ Orion [RC-588]	USN VP-46, NAS Whidbey Island, WA
	161589	Lockheed P-3C BMUP+ Orion [589]	USN VP-40, NAS Whidbey Island, WA
	161590	Lockheed P-3C BMUP+ Orion [590]	USN VP-30, NAS Jacksonville, FL
	161593	Lockheed P-3C BMUP+ Orion [593]	USN VP-46, NAS Whidbey Island, WA
	161594	Lockheed P-3C AIP+ Orion [594]	*Withdrawn from use, April 2018*
	161596	Lockheed P-3C BMUP+ Orion [596]	USN VP-1, NAS Whidbey Island, WA
	161766	Lockheed P-3C AIP Orion [RC-766]	*To 309th AMARG, April 2018*
	162308	Lockheed KC-130T Hercules [308]	USN, stored Patuxent River, MD
	162309	Lockheed KC-130T Hercules [406]	USN VX-30, NAS Point Mugu, CA

Serial	Type (code/other identity)	Owner/operator, location or fate	Notes
162310	Lockheed KC-130T Hercules [WB-2310]	USN	
162311	Lockheed KC-130T Hercules [405]	USN VX-30, NAS Point Mugu, CA	
162316	Lockheed P-3C AIP+ Orion [316]	*To 309th AMARG, September 2018*	
162317	Lockheed P-3C AIP+ Orion [317]	USN VQ-1, NAS Whidbey Island, WA	
162318	Lockheed P-3C AIP+ Orion [318]	USN VP-69, NAS Whidbey Island, WA	
162770	Lockheed P-3C AIP+ Orion [770]	USN VP-30, NAS Jacksonville, FL	
162771	Lockheed P-3C AIP+ Orion [771]	*Scrapped*	
162772	Lockheed P-3C AIP+ Orion [772]	USN VP-40, NAS Whidbey Island, WA	
162773	Lockheed P-3C AIP+ Orion [773]	USN VP-40, NAS Whidbey Island, WA	
162776	Lockheed P-3C AIP+ Orion [776]	USN VP-40, NAS Whidbey Island, WA	
162777	Lockheed P-3C AIP+ Orion [777]	USN VP-69, NAS Whidbey Island, WA	
162778	Lockheed P-3C AIP+ Orion [304]	USN VP-30, NAS Jacksonville, FL	
162782	Boeing E-6B Mercury	USN VQ-3/SCW-1, Tinker AFB, OK	
162783	Boeing E-6B Mercury	USN VQ-3/SCW-1, Tinker AFB, OK	
162784	Boeing E-6B Mercury	USN VQ-4/SCW-1, Tinker AFB, OK	
162998	Lockheed P-3C AIP+ Orion [RC-998]	USN VP-46, NAS Whidbey Island, WA	
162999	Lockheed P-3C AIP+ Orion [999]	USN VX-30, NAS Point Mugu, CA	
163000	Lockheed P-3C AIP+ Orion [000]	USN VP-30, NAS Jacksonville, FL	
163001	Lockheed P-3C AIP+ Orion [001]	USN VP-69, NAS Whidbey Island, WA	
163004	Lockheed P-3C AIP+ Orion [004]	USN VP-69, NAS Whidbey Island, WA	
163023	Lockheed KC-130T Hercules [404]	USN VX-30, NAS Point Mugu, CA	
163290	Lockheed P-3C AIP+ Orion [LL-290]	USN VP-30, NAS Jacksonville, FL	
163291	Lockheed P-3C AIP+ Orion [291]	USN VP-46, NAS Whidbey Island, WA	
163293	Lockheed P-3C AIP+ Orion [LL-293]	USN VP-30, NAS Jacksonville, FL	
163294	Lockheed P-3C AIP+ Orion [303]	USN VX-30, NAS Point Mugu, CA	
163295	Lockheed P-3C AIP+ Orion [295]	USN VP-1, NAS Whidbey Island, WA	
163310	Lockheed KC-130T Hercules [3310]	USN, stored Patuxent River, MD	
163311	Lockheed KC-130T Hercules [RU-311]	USN VR-55, NAS Point Mugu, CA	
163591	Lockheed KC-130T Hercules [RU-591]	USN VR-55, NAS Point Mugu, CA	
163691	Grumman C-20D Gulfstream III	USN VR-1, NAF Washington, MD	
163692	Grumman C-20D Gulfstream III	USN VR-1, NAF Washington, MD	
163918	Boeing E-6B Mercury	USN VQ-3/SCW-1, Tinker AFB, OK	
163919	Boeing E-6B Mercury	USN VQ-3/SCW-1, Tinker AFB, OK	
163920	Boeing E-6B Mercury	USN VQ-3/SCW-1, Tinker AFB, OK	
164105	Lockheed KC-130T Hercules [NY-105]	USMC VMGR-452, Stewart Field, NY	
164106	Lockheed KC-130T Hercules [RU-106]	USN VR-55, NAS Point Mugu, CA	
164180	Lockheed KC-130T Hercules [NY-180]	USMC VMGR-452, Stewart Field, NY	
164181	Lockheed KC-130T Hercules [NY-181]	USMC VMGR-452, Stewart Field, NY	
164386	Boeing E-6B Mercury	USN VQ-4/SCW-1, Tinker AFB, OK	
164387	Boeing E-6B Mercury	USN VQ-3/SCW-1, Tinker AFB, OK	
164388	Boeing E-6B Mercury	USN VQ-4/SCW-1, Tinker AFB, OK	
164404	Boeing E-6B Mercury	USN VQ-4/SCW-1, Tinker AFB, OK	
164405	Boeing E-6B Mercury	USN VQ-4/SCW-1, Tinker AFB, OK	
164406	Boeing E-6B Mercury	USN VQ-3/SCW-1, Tinker AFB, OK	
164407	Boeing E-6B Mercury	USN VQ-4/SCW-1, Tinker AFB, OK	
164408	Boeing E-6B Mercury	USN VQ-4/SCW-1, Tinker AFB, OK	
164409	Boeing E-6B Mercury	USN VQ-4/SCW-1, Tinker AFB, OK	
164410	Boeing E-6B Mercury	USN VQ-4/SCW-1, Tinker AFB, OK	
164441	Lockheed KC-130T Hercules [NY-441]	USN, stored Patuxent River, MD	
164442	Lockheed KC-130T Hercules [NY-442]	USMC VMGR-452, Stewart Field, NY	
164597	Lockheed KC-130T-30 Hercules [RU-597]	USN VR-55, NAS Point Mugu, CA	
164598	Lockheed KC-130T-30 Hercules [RU-598]	USN VR-55, NAS Point Mugu, CA	
164762	Lockheed C-130T Hercules [CW-762]	USN VR-54, NAS New Orleans, LA	
164763	Lockheed C-130T Hercules	USN *Blue Angels*, Pensacola NAS, FL	
164993	Lockheed C-130T Hercules [BD-993]	USN VR-64, NAS Willow Grove, PA	
164994	Lockheed C-130T Hercules [CW-994]	USN VR-54, NAS New Orleans, LA	
164995	Lockheed C-130T Hercules [AX-995]	USN VR-53, NAF Washington, MD	
164996	Lockheed C-130T Hercules [BD-996]	USN VR-64, NAS Willow Grove, PA	
164997	Lockheed C-130T Hercules [AX-997]	USN, stored Patuxent River, MD	
164998	Lockheed C-130T Hercules [BD-998]	USN VR-64, NAS Willow Grove, PA	
164999	Lockheed KC-130T Hercules [NY-999]	USMC VMGR-452, Stewart Field, NY	
165093	Grumman C-20G Gulfstream IV	*To 309th AMARG, March 2018*	

Notes	Serial	Type (code/other identity)	Owner/operator, location or fate
	165094	Grumman C-20G Gulfstream IV	USN VR-51, MCBH Kaneohe Bay, Hawaii
	165151	Grumman C-20G Gulfstream IV	USN CFLSW Det., Sigonella, Italy
	165152	Grumman C-20G Gulfstream IV	USMC VMR-Det, MCBH Kaneohe Bay, HI
	165153	Grumman C-20G Gulfstream IV	USMC VMR-Det, MCBH Kaneohe Bay, HI
	165158	Lockheed C-130T Hercules [CW-158]	USN VR-54, NAS New Orleans, LA
	165159	Lockheed C-130T Hercules [CW-159]	USN VR-54, NAS New Orleans, LA
	165160	Lockheed C-130T Hercules [CW-160]	USN VR-54, NAS New Orleans, LA
	165161	Lockheed C-130T Hercules [BD-161]	USN VR-64, NAS Willow Grove, PA
	165162	Lockheed KC-130T Hercules [NY-162]	USMC VMGR-452, Stewart Field, NY
	165163	Lockheed KC-130T Hercules [NY-163]	USMC VMGR-452, Stewart Field, NY
	165313	Lockheed C-130T Hercules [JW-313]	USN VR-62, NAS Jacksonville, FL
	165314	Lockheed C-130T Hercules [JW-314]	USN VR-62, NAS Jacksonville, FL
	165315	Lockheed KC-130T Hercules [NY-315]	USMC VMGR-452, Stewart Field, NY
	165316	Lockheed KC-130T Hercules [NY-316]	USMC VMGR-452, Stewart Field, NY
	165348	Lockheed C-130T Hercules [AX-348]	USN VR-53, NAF Washington, MD
	165349	Lockheed C-130T Hercules [JW-349]	USN VR-62, NAS Jacksonville, FL
	165350	Lockheed C-130T Hercules [350]	USN VX-20, Patuxent River, MD
	165351	Lockheed C-130T Hercules [AX-351]	USN VR-53, NAF Washington, MD
	165352	Lockheed KC-130T Hercules [NY-352]	USMC VMGR-452, Stewart Field, NY
	165353	Lockheed KC-130T Hercules [NY-353]	USMC VMGR-452, Stewart Field, NY
	165378	Lockheed C-130T Hercules [RU-378]	USN VR-55, NAS Point Mugu, CA
	165379	Lockheed C-130T Hercules [BD-379]	USN VR-64, NAS Willow Grove, PA
	165735	Lockheed KC-130J Hercules II [QB-735]	USMC VMGR-352, Miramar MCAS, CA
	165736	Lockheed KC-130J Hercules II [QB-736]	USMC VMGR-352, Miramar MCAS, CA
	165737	Lockheed KC-130J Hercules II [BH-737]	USMC VMGR-252, Cherry Point MCAS, NC
	165738	Lockheed KC-130J Hercules II [BH-738]	USMC VMGR-252, Cherry Point MCAS, NC
	165739	Lockheed KC-130J Hercules II [QH-739]	USMC VMGR-234, Fort Worth JRB, TX
	165740	Cessna UC-35C Citation V [EZ]	USMC MWHS-4, NAS New Orleans, LA
	165741	Cessna UC-35C Citation V [EZ]	USMC MWHS-4, NAS New Orleans, LA
	165809	Lockheed KC-130J Hercules II [BH-809]	USMC VMGR-252, Cherry Point MCAS, NC
	165810	Lockheed KC-130J Hercules II [BH-810]	USMC VMGR-252, Cherry Point MCAS, NC
	165829	Boeing C-40A Clipper (N1003N) [829]	USN VR-58, NAS Jacksonville, FL
	165830	Boeing C-40A Clipper (N1003M) [830]	USN VR-59, Fort Worth JRB, TX
	165831	Boeing C-40A Clipper (N1786B) [831]	USN VR-59, Fort Worth JRB, TX
	165832	Boeing C-40A Clipper (N1787B) [832]	USN VR-61, Fort Worth JRB, TX
	165833	Boeing C-40A Clipper [833]	USN VR-59, Fort Worth JRB, TX
	165834	Boeing C-40A Clipper [834]	USN VR-58, NAS Jacksonville, FL
	165835	Boeing C-40A Clipper (N543BA) [835]	USN VR-57, NAS North Island, CA
	165836	Boeing C-40A Clipper [836]	USN VR-57, NAS North Island, CA
	165939	Cessna UC-35D Citation V	USMC MAW-4, Miramar MCAS, CA
	165957	Lockheed KC-130J Hercules II [QD-957] $	USMC VMGR-152, Iwakuni MCAS, Japan
	166374	Cessna UC-35D Citation V	USMC VMR-2, NAF Washington, MD
	166375	Gulfstream Aerospace C-37A Gulfstream V [365]	USN CFLSW Det, MCBH Kaneohe Bay, HI
	166376	Gulfstream Aerospace C-37B Gulfstream V [376]	USN VR-1, NAF Washington, MD
	166377	Gulfstream Aerospace C-37B Gulfstream V [377]	USN VR-1, NAF Washington, MD
	165378	Lockheed C-130T Hercules [JW-378]	USN VR-62, NAS Jacksonville, FL
	166379	Gulfstream Aerospace NC-37B Gulfstream V [BH-100]	USN VX-30, NAS Point Mugu, CA
	166380	Lockheed KC-130J Hercules II [BH-380]	USMC VMGR-252, Cherry Point MCAS, NC
	166381	Lockheed KC-130J Hercules II [BH-381]	USMC VMGR-252, Cherry Point MCAS, NC
	166382	Lockheed KC-130J Hercules II [QB-382]	USMC VMGR-352, Miramar MCAS, CA
	166472	Lockheed KC-130J Hercules II [BH-472]	USMC VMGR-252, Cherry Point MCAS, NC
	166473	Lockheed KC-130J Hercules II [QH-473]	USMC VMGR-234, Fort Worth JRB, TX
	166474	Cessna UC-35D Citation V	USMC MAW-4, Miramar MCAS, CA
	166500	Cessna UC-35D Citation V	USMC MAW-4, Miramar MCAS, CA
	166511	Lockheed KC-130J Hercules II [511]	USN VX-20, Patuxent River, MD
	166512	Lockheed KC-130J Hercules II [QB-512]	USMC VMGR-352, Miramar MCAS, CA
	166513	Lockheed KC-130J Hercules II [BH-513]	USMC VMGR-252, Cherry Point MCAS, NC
	166514	Lockheed KC-130J Hercules II [BH-514]	USMC VMGR-252, Cherry Point MCAS, NC
	166693	Boeing C-40A Clipper [693]	USN VR-57, NAS North Island, CA
	166694	Boeing C-40A Clipper [694]	USN VR-59, Fort Worth JRB, TX
	166695	Boeing C-40A Clipper (N1787B) [695]	USN VR-56, NAS Oceana, VA
	166696	Boeing C-40A Clipper [696]	USN VR-56, NAS Oceana, VA

Serial	Type (code/other identity)	Owner/operator, location or fate	Notes
166712	Cessna UC-35D Citation V	USMC MWHS-1, Futenma MCAS, Japan	
166713	Cessna UC-35D Citation V	USMC MWHS-1, Futenma MCAS, Japan	
166714	Cessna UC-35D Citation V [VM]	USMC VMR-2, NAF Washington, MD	
166715	Cessna UC-35D Citation V	USMC MAW-4, Miramar MCAS, CA	
166762	Lockheed KC-130J Hercules II [QB-762]	USMC VMGR-352, Miramar MCAS, CA	
166763	Lockheed KC-130J Hercules II [QD-763]	USMC VMGR-152, Iwakuni MCAS, Japan	
166764	Lockheed KC-130J Hercules II [BH-764]	USMC VMGR-252, Cherry Point MCAS, NC	
166765	Lockheed KC-130J Hercules II [QB-765]	USMC VMGR-352, Miramar MCAS, CA	
166766	Cessna UC-35D Citation V	USMC MWHS-1, Futenma MCAS, Japan	
166767	Cessna UC-35D Citation V [VM]	USMC VMR-2, NAF Washington, MD	
167108	Lockheed KC-130J Hercules II [QB-108]	USMC VMGR-352, Miramar MCAS, CA	
167109	Lockheed KC-130J Hercules II [QD-109]	USN VX-20, Patuxent River, MD	
167110	Lockheed KC-130J Hercules II [QB-110]	USMC VMGR-352, Miramar MCAS, CA	
167111	Lockheed KC-130J Hercules II [QH-111]	USMC VMGR-234, Fort Worth JRB, TX	
167112	Lockheed KC-130J Hercules II [BH-112]	USMC VMGR-252, Cherry Point MCAS, NC	
167923	Lockheed KC-130J Hercules II [QD-923]	USMC VMGR-152, Iwakuni MCAS, Japan	
167924	Lockheed KC-130J Hercules II [QB-924]	USMC VMGR-352, Miramar MCAS, CA	
167925	Lockheed KC-130J Hercules II [QD-925]	USMC VMGR-152, Iwakuni MCAS, Japan	
167926	Lockheed KC-130J Hercules II [QD-926]	USMC VMGR-152, Iwakuni MCAS, Japan	
167927	Lockheed KC-130J Hercules II [QD-927]	USMC VMGR-152, Iwakuni MCAS, Japan	
167951	Boeing P-8A Poseidon (N541BA) [951]	USN VX-20, Patuxent River, MD	
167952	Boeing P-8A Poseidon (N398DS) [952]	USN NASC-FS, Dallas/Love Field, TX	
167953	Boeing P-8A Poseidon (N441BA) [953]	USN VX-20, Patuxent River, MD	
167954	Boeing P-8A Poseidon (N397DS)	USN VX-20, Patuxent River, MD	
167955	Boeing P-8A Poseidon (N328DS) [JA-955]	USN VX-1, NAS Patuxent River, MD	
167956	Boeing P-8A Poseidon (N391DS) [JA-956]	USN VX-1, NAS Patuxent River, MD	
167981	Lockheed KC-130J Hercules II [QD-981]	*Crashed 6 December 2018, off Muroto Cape, Japan*	
167982	Lockheed KC-130J Hercules II [QD-982]	USMC VMGR-152, Iwakuni MCAS, Japan	
167983	Lockheed KC-130J Hercules II [QD-983]	USMC VMGR-152, Iwakuni MCAS, Japan	
167984	Lockheed KC-130J Hercules II [QB-984]	USMC VMGR-352, Miramar MCAS, CA	
167985	Lockheed KC-130J Hercules II [QB-985]	USMC VMGR-352, Miramar MCAS, CA	
168065	Lockheed KC-130J Hercules II [QB-065]	USMC VMGR-352, Miramar MCAS, CA	
168066	Lockheed KC-130J Hercules II [QD-066]	USMC VMGR-152, Iwakuni MCAS, Japan	
168067	Lockheed KC-130J Hercules II [QB-067]	USMC VMGR-352, Miramar MCAS, CA	
168068	Lockheed KC-130J Hercules II [QB-068]	USMC VMGR-352, Miramar MCAS, CA	
168069	Lockheed KC-130J Hercules II [BH-069]	USMC VMGR-252, Cherry Point MCAS, NC	
168070	Lockheed KC-130J Hercules II [BH-070]	USMC VMGR-252, Cherry Point MCAS, NC	
168071	Lockheed KC-130J Hercules II [BH-071]	USMC VMGR-252, Cherry Point MCAS, NC	
168072	Lockheed KC-130J Hercules II [QB-072]	USMC VMGR-352, Miramar MCAS, CA	
168073	Lockheed KC-130J Hercules II [QH-073]	USMC VMGR-234, Fort Worth JRB, TX	
168074	Lockheed KC-130J Hercules II [QD-074]	USMC VMGR-152, Iwakuni MCAS, Japan	
168075	Lockheed KC-130J Hercules II [QD-075]	USMC VMGR-152, Iwakuni MCAS, Japan	
168428	Boeing P-8A Poseidon (N392DS) [LA-428]	USN VP-5, NAS Jacksonville, FL	
168429	Boeing P-8A Poseidon (N397DS) [429]	USN VP-30, NAS Jacksonville, FL	
168430	Boeing P-8A Poseidon (N398DS) [LK-430]	USN VP-26, NAS Jacksonville, FL	
168431	Boeing P-8A Poseidon (N507DS) [431]	USN VP-10, NAS Jacksonville, FL	
168432	Boeing P-8A Poseidon (N516DS) [LA-432]	USN VP-5, NAS Jacksonville, FL	
168433	Boeing P-8A Poseidon (N530DS) [LD-433]	USN VP-10, NAS Jacksonville, FL	
168434	Boeing P-8A Poseidon (N532DS) [LN-434]	USN VP-45, NAS Jacksonville, FL	
168435	Boeing P-8A Poseidon (N533DS) [435]	USN VP-45, NAS Jacksonville, FL	
168436	Boeing P-8A Poseidon (N536DS) [436]	USN VP-16, NAS Jacksonville, FL	
168437	Boeing P-8A Poseidon (N537DS) [LF-437]	USN VP-16, NAS Jacksonville, FL	
168438	Boeing P-8A Poseidon (N327DS) [LK-438]	USN VP-26, NAS Jacksonville, FL	
168439	Boeing P-8A Poseidon (N539DS) [LD-439]	USN VP-10, NAS Jacksonville, FL	
168440	Boeing P-8A Poseidon (N708DS) [440]	USN VP-45, NAS Jacksonville, FL	
168754	Boeing P-8A Poseidon (N736DS) [LC-754]	USN VP-8, NAS Jacksonville, FL	
168755	Boeing P-8A Poseidon (N740DS) [755]	USN VP-4, NAS Whidbey Island, WA	
168756	Boeing P-8A Poseidon (N753DS) [756]	USN VP-45, NAS Jacksonville, FL	
168757	Boeing P-8A Poseidon (N755DS) [YD-757]	USN VP-4, NAS Whidbey Island, WA	
168758	Boeing P-8A Poseidon (N758DS) [RD-758]	USN VP-47, NAS Whidbey Island, WA	
168759	Boeing P-8A Poseidon (N762DS) [759]	USN VP-16, NAS Jacksonville, FL	
168760	Boeing P-8A Poseidon (N768DS) [RD-760]	USN VP-47, NAS Whidbey Island, WA	

Notes	Serial	Type (code/other identity)	Owner/operator, location or fate
	168761	Boeing P-8A Poseidon (N771DS) [LN-761]	USN VP-45, NAS Jacksonville, FL
	168762	Boeing P-8A Poseidon (N780DS) [762]	USN VP-16, NAS Jacksonville, FL
	168763	Boeing P-8A Poseidon (N781DS) [LK-763]	USN VP-26, NAS Jacksonville, FL
	168764	Boeing P-8A Poseidon (N783DS) [764]	USN VP-26, NAS Jacksonville, FL
	168848	Boeing P-8A Poseidon (N784DS) [LK-848]	USN VP-26, NAS Jacksonville, FL
	168849	Boeing P-8A Poseidon (N785DS) [849]	USN VP-10, NAS Jacksonville, FL
	168850	Boeing P-8A Poseidon (N789DS) [YD-850]	USN VP-4, NAS Whidbey Island, WA
	168851	Boeing P-8A Poseidon (N790DS) [YD-851]	USN VP-4, NAS Whidbey Island, WA
	168852	Boeing P-8A Poseidon (N715DS) [852]	USN VP-30, NAS Jacksonville, FL
	168853	Boeing P-8A Poseidon (N717DS) [RD-853]	USN VP-47, NAS Whidbey Island, WA
	168854	Boeing P-8A Poseidon (N722DS) [LC-854]	USN VP-8, NAS Jacksonville, FL
	168855	Boeing P-8A Poseidon (N729DS) [855]	USN VP-45, NAS Jacksonville, FL
	168856	Boeing P-8A Poseidon (N805DS) [856]	USN VP-30, NAS Jacksonville, FL
	168857	Boeing P-8A Poseidon (N590DS) [LK-857]	USN VP-26, NAS Jacksonville, FL
	168858	Boeing P-8A Poseidon (N591DS) [LD-858]	USN VP-10, NAS Jacksonville, FL
	168859	Boeing P-8A Poseidon (N592DS) [859]	USN VP-26, NAS Jacksonville, FL
	168860	Boeing P-8A Poseidon (N593DS) [860]	USN VP-16, NAS Jacksonville, FL
	168980	Boeing C-40A Clipper (N513NV) [980]	USN VR-61, Fort Worth JRB, TX
	168981	Boeing C-40A Clipper (N514NV) [981]	USN VR-61, Fort Worth JRB, TX
	168996	Boeing P-8A Poseidon (N595DS) [996]	USN NASC-FS, NAS Jacksonville, FL
	168997	Boeing P-8A Poseidon (N597DS) [RD-997]	USN VP-47, NAS Whidbey Island, WA
	168998	Boeing P-8A Poseidon (N598DS) [LD-998]	USN VP-10, NAS Jacksonville, FL
	168999	Boeing P-8A Poseidon (N910DS) [999]	USN VP-30, NAS Jacksonville, FL
	169000	Boeing P-8A Poseidon (N914DS) [000]	USN VP-16, NAS Jacksonville, FL
	169001	Boeing P-8A Poseidon (N931DS) [001]	USN VP-30, NAS Jacksonville, FL
	169002	Boeing P-8A Poseidon (N934DS) [PD-002]	USN VP-9, NAS Whidbey Island, WA
	169003	Boeing P-8A Poseidon (N935DS) [LK-003]	USN VP-26, NAS Jacksonville, FL
	169004	Boeing P-8A Poseidon (N936DS) [YD-004]	USN VP-4, NAS Whidbey Island, WA
	169005	Boeing P-8A Poseidon (N941DS) [LC-005]	USN VP-8, NAS Jacksonville, FL
	169006	Boeing P-8A Poseidon (N942DS) [006]	USN VP-45, NAS Jacksonville, FL
	169007	Boeing P-8A Poseidon (N943DS) [LC-007]	USN VP-8, NAS Jacksonville, FL
	169008	Boeing P-8A Poseidon (N944DS) [YD-008]	USN VP-4, NAS Whidbey Island, WA
	169009	Boeing P-8A Poseidon (N949DS) [YD-009]	USN VP-4, NAS Whidbey Island, WA
	169010	Boeing P-8A Poseidon (N957DS) [010]	USN NASC-FS, Dallas/Love Field, TX
	169011	Boeing P-8A Poseidon (N958DS) [LA-011]	USN VP-5, NAS Jacksonville, FL
	169018	Lockheed KC-130J Hercules II [QH-018]	USMC VMGR-234, Fort Worth JRB, TX
	169036	Boeing C-40A Clipper (N515NV) [036]	USN VR-61, Fort Worth JRB, TX
	169225	Lockheed KC-130J Hercules II [BH-225]	USMC VMGR-252, Cherry Point MCAS, NC
	169226	Lockheed KC-130J Hercules II [QB-226]	USMC VMGR-352, Miramar MCAS, CA
	169227	Lockheed KC-130J Hercules II [QD-227]	USMC VMGR-152, Iwakuni MCAS, Japan
	169228	Lockheed KC-130J Hercules II [QH-228]	USMC VMGR-234, Fort Worth JRB, TX
	169229	Lockheed KC-130J Hercules II [QH-229]	USMC VMGR-234, Fort Worth JRB, TX
	169230	Lockheed KC-130J Hercules II [QB-230]	USMC VMGR-352, Miramar MCAS, CA
	169324	Boeing P-8A Poseidon (N960DS) [LK-324]	USN VP-26, NAS Jacksonville, FL
	169325	Boeing P-8A Poseidon (N962DS) [RD-325]	USN VP-47, NAS Whidbey Island, WA
	169326	Boeing P-8A Poseidon (N969DS) [326]	USN VP-30, NAS Jacksonville, FL
	169327	Boeing P-8A Poseidon (N963DS) [RD-327]	USN VP-47, NAS Whidbey Island, WA
	169328	Boeing P-8A Poseidon (N964DS) [328]	USN VP-30, NAS Jacksonville, FL
	169329	Boeing P-8A Poseidon (N968DS) [PD-329]	USN VP-9, NAS Whidbey Island, WA
	169330	Boeing P-8A Poseidon (N843DS) [330]	USN VP-30, NAS Jacksonville, FL
	169331	Boeing P-8A Poseidon (N852DS) [RD-331]	USN VP-47, NAS Whidbey Island, WA
	169332	Boeing P-8A Poseidon (N848DS) [PD-332]	USN VP-9, NAS Whidbey Island, WA
	169333	Boeing P-8A Poseidon (N838DS) [333]	USN VX-1/VX-20, NAS Patuxent River, MD
	169334	Boeing P-8A Poseidon (N839DS) [LC-334]	USN VP-8, NAS Jacksonville, FL
	169335	Boeing P-8A Poseidon (N854DS) [335]	USN VP-30, NAS Jacksonville, FL
	169336	Boeing P-8A Poseidon (N857DS) [LC-336]	USN VP-8, NAS Jacksonville, FL
	169337	Boeing P-8A Poseidon (N858DS) [LA-337]	USN VP-5, NAS Jacksonville, FL
	169338	Boeing P-8A Poseidon (N860DS) [338]	USN VP-30, NAS Jacksonville, FL
	169339	Boeing P-8A Poseidon (N863DS) [LA-339]	USN VP-5, NAS Jacksonville, FL
	169340	Boeing P-8A Poseidon (N864DS) [LA-340]	USN VP-5, NAS Jacksonville, FL
	169341	Boeing P-8A Poseidon (N869DS) [LC-341]	USN VP-8, NAS Jacksonville, FL
	169342	Boeing P-8A Poseidon (N874DS) [LC-342]	USN VP-8, NAS Jacksonville, FL

Serial	Type (code/other identity)	Owner/operator, location or fate	Notes
169343	Boeing P-8A Poseidon (N873DS) [343]	USN VP-30, NAS Jacksonville, FL	
169344	Boeing P-8A Poseidon (N304DS) [344]	USN VP-30, NAS Jacksonville, FL	
169345	Boeing P-8A Poseidon (N308DS) [345]	USN VP-30, NAS Jacksonville, FL	
169346	Boeing P-8A Poseidon (N318DS) [346]	USN VP-30, NAS Jacksonville, FL	
169347	Boeing P-8A Poseidon (N322DS) [347]	USN VP-30, NAS Jacksonville, FL	
169348	Boeing P-8A Poseidon (N323DS) [348]	USN VP-30, NAS Jacksonville, FL	
169349	Boeing P-8A Poseidon (N328DS) [349]	USN VP-10, NAS Jacksonville, FL	
169426	Boeing P-8A Poseidon (N332DS) [426]	USN (on order)	
169542	Boeing P-8A Poseidon (N348DS) [542]	USN (on order)	
169543	Boeing P-8A Poseidon (N347DS) [543]	USN (on order)	
169544	Boeing P-8A Poseidon (N360DS) [544]	USN (on order)	
169545	Boeing P-8A Poseidon (N364DS) [545]	USN (on order)	
169546	Boeing P-8A Poseidon (N368DS) [546]	USN (on order)	
169547	Boeing P-8A Poseidon (N383DS) [547]	USN (on order)	
169548	Boeing P-8A Poseidon (N374DS) [548]	USN (on order)	
169...	Boeing P-8A Poseidon (N391DS)	USN (on order)	
169...	Boeing P-8A Poseidon (N392DS)	USN (on order)	
169...	Boeing P-8A Poseidon (N397DS)	USN (on order)	
169...	Boeing P-8A Poseidon (N398DS)	USN (on order)	
169...	Boeing P-8A Poseidon (N410DS)	USN (on order)	
169...	Boeing P-8A Poseidon	USN (on order)	
169...	Boeing P-8A Poseidon	USN (on order)	
169...	Boeing P-8A Poseidon	USN (on order)	

Based on the popular Boeing 737-800, Boeing's P-8A Poseidon is rapidly replacing the P-3A Orion in US Navy service. This one, 168849, is operated by VP-10 from NAS Jacksonville in Florida.

US-BASED US COAST GUARD AIRCRAFT

Notes	Serial	Type (code/other identity)	Owner/operator, location or fate
	01	Gulfstream Aerospace C-37A Gulfstream V (N527GA)	USCG, Commandants Flt, Washington DC
	02	Gulfstream Aerospace C-37B Gulfstream V (N640W)	USCG, Commandants Flt, Washington DC
	1503	Lockheed HC-130H Hercules	USCG, USCGS Clearwater, FL
	1701	Lockheed HC-130H Hercules	USCG, USCGS Barbers Point, HI
	1702	Lockheed HC-130H Hercules	USCG, USCGS Kodiak, AK
	1703	Lockheed HC-130H Hercules	USCG, USCGS Barbers Point, HI
	1704	Lockheed HC-130H Hercules	USCG, USCGS Clearwater, FL
	1706	Lockheed HC-130H Hercules	USCG, USCGS Clearwater, FL
	1707	Lockheed HC-130H Hercules	USCG, USCGS Barbers Point, HI
	1709	Lockheed HC-130H Hercules	USCG, USCGS Sacramento, CA
	1711	Lockheed HC-130H Hercules	USCG, USCGS Clearwater, FL
	1712	Lockheed HC-130H Hercules	USCG, USCGS Clearwater, FL
	1715	Lockheed HC-130H Hercules	USCG, USCGS Clearwater, FL
	1716	Lockheed HC-130H Hercules	USCG, USCGS Barbers Point, HI
	1718	Lockheed HC-130H Hercules	USCG, USCGS Clearwater, FL
	1720	Lockheed HC-130H Hercules	USCG, USCGS Barbers Point, HI
	1790	Lockheed HC-130H Hercules	USCG, USCGS Barbers Point, HI
	2001	Lockheed HC-130J Hercules II	USCG, USCGS Elizabeth City, NC
	2002	Lockheed HC-130J Hercules II	USCG, USCGS Elizabeth City, NC
	2003	Lockheed HC-130J Hercules II	USCG, USCGS Elizabeth City, NC
	2004	Lockheed HC-130J Hercules II	USCG, USCGS Elizabeth City, NC
	2005	Lockheed HC-130J Hercules II	USCG, USCGS Elizabeth City, NC
	2006	Lockheed HC-130J Hercules II	USCG, USCGS Elizabeth City, NC
	2007	Lockheed HC-130J Hercules II	USCG, USCGS Elizabeth City, NC
	2008	Lockheed HC-130J Hercules II	USCG, USCGS Elizabeth City, NC
	2009	Lockheed HC-130J Hercules II	USCG, USCGS Kodiak, AK
	2010	Lockheed HC-130J Hercules II	USCG, USCGS Elizabeth City, NC
	2011	Lockheed HC-130J Hercules II	USCG, Waco, TX
	2012	Lockheed HC-130J Hercules II	USCG, Waco, TX
	2013	Lockheed HC-130J Hercules II	USCG (on order)
	2014	Lockheed HC-130J Hercules II	USCG (on order)

Aircraft in US Government or Military Service with Civil Registrations

Notes	Serial	Type (code/other identity)	Owner/operator, location or fate
	N85	Canadair CL.601 Challenger	Federal Aviation Administration, Oklahoma City, OK
	N86	Canadair CL.601 Challenger	Federal Aviation Administration, Oklahoma City, OK
	N87	Canadair CL.601 Challenger	Federal Aviation Administration, Oklahoma City, OK
	N88	Canadair CL.604 Challenger	Federal Aviation Administration, Oklahoma City, OK
	N89	Canadair CL.605 Challenger	Federal Aviation Administration, Oklahoma City, OK
	N90	Canadair CL.605 Challenger	Federal Aviation Administration, Oklahoma City, OK

The list below is not intended to be a complete list of military aviation sites on the Internet. The sites listed cover Museums, Locations, Air Forces, Companies and Organisations that are mentioned elsewhere in 'Military Aircraft Markings'. Sites listed are in English or contain sufficient English to be reasonably easily understood. Each site address was correct at the time of going to press. Additions are welcome, via the usual address found at the front of the book, or via e-mail to admin@aviation-links.co.uk. An up to date copy of this list is to be found at The 'Military Aircraft Markings' Web Site, http://www.militaryaircraftmarkings.co.uk/.

Name of Site	Web Address All prefixed 'http://')
MILITARY SITES-UK	
No 1 Sqn	www.raf.mod.uk/our-organisation/squadrons/1-f-squadron/
No 2 Sqn	www.raf.mod.uk/our-organisation/squadrons/ii-ac-squadron/
No 3 Sqn	www.raf.mod.uk/our-organisation/squadrons/3-f-squadron/
No 4 Sqn	www.raf.mod.uk/our-organisation/squadrons/iv-squadron/
No 5 Sqn	www.raf.mod.uk/our-organisation/squadrons/v-ac-squadron/
No 6 Sqn	www.raf.mod.uk/our-organisation/squadrons/6-squadron/
No 7 Sqn	www.raf.mod.uk/our-organisation/squadrons/7-squadron/
No 8 Sqn	www.raf.mod.uk/our-organisation/squadrons/8-squadron/
No 9 Sqn	www.raf.mod.uk/our-organisation/squadrons/ix-b-squadron/
No 10 Sqn	www.raf.mod.uk/our-organisation/squadrons/10-squadron/
No 11 Sqn	www.raf.mod.uk/our-organisation/squadrons/xi-f-squadron/
No 12 Sqn	www.raf.mod.uk/our-organisation/squadrons/12-squadron/
No 13 Sqn	www.raf.mod.uk/our-organisation/squadrons/13-squadron/
No 14 Sqn	www.raf.mod.uk/our-organisation/squadrons/14-squadron/
No 16 Sqn	www.raf.mod.uk/our-organisation/squadrons/16-squadron/
No 17 Sqn	www.raf.mod.uk/our-organisation/squadrons/17-squadron/
No 18 Sqn	www.raf.mod.uk/our-organisation/squadrons/18-squadron/
No 24 Sqn	www.raf.mod.uk/our-organisation/squadrons/xxiv-squadron/
No 27 Sqn	www.raf.mod.uk/our-organisation/squadrons/27-squadron/
No 28 Sqn	www.raf.mod.uk/our-organisation/squadrons/28-squadron/
No 29 Sqn	www.raf.mod.uk/our-organisation/squadrons/29-squadron/
No 31 Sqn	www.raf.mod.uk/our-organisation/squadrons/31-squadron/
No 32(The Royal) Sqn	www.raf.mod.uk/our-organisation/squadrons/32-squadron/
No 33 Sqn	www.raf.mod.uk/our-organisation/squadrons/33-squadron/
No 39 Sqn	www.raf.mod.uk/our-organisation/squadrons/39-squadron/
No 41 Sqn	www.raf.mod.uk/our-organisation/squadrons/41-squadron/
No 45 Sqn	www.raf.mod.uk/our-organisation/squadrons/45-squadron/
No 47 Sqn	www.raf.mod.uk/our-organisation/squadrons/47-squadron/
No 51 Sqn	www.raf.mod.uk/our-organisation/squadrons/51-squadron/
No 54 Sqn	www.raf.mod.uk/our-organisation/squadrons/54-squadron/
No 56 Sqn	www.raf.mod.uk/our-organisation/squadrons/56-squadron/
No 57 Sqn	www.raf.mod.uk/our-organisation/squadrons/lvii-squadron/
No 60 Sqn	www.raf.mod.uk/our-organisation/squadrons/60-squadron/
No 70 Sqn	www.raf.mod.uk/our-organisation/squadrons/lxx-squadron/
No 72 Sqn	www.raf.mod.uk/our-organisation/squadrons/72-squadron/
No 84 Sqn	www.raf.mod.uk/our-organisation/squadrons/84-squadron/
No 92 Sqn	www.raf.mod.uk/our-organisation/squadrons/92-squadron/
No 99 Sqn	www.raf.mod.uk/our-organisation/squadrons/99-squadron/
No 100 Sqn	www.raf.mod.uk/our-organisation/squadrons/100-squadron/
No 101 Sqn	www.raf.mod.uk/our-organisation/squadrons/101-squadron/
No 115 Sqn	www.raf.mod.uk/our-organisation/squadrons/115-squadron/
No 202 Sqn	www.raf.mod.uk/our-organisation/squadrons/202-squadron/
No 206 Sqn	www.raf.mod.uk/our-organisation/squadrons/206-squadron/
No 230 Sqn	www.raf.mod.uk/our-organisation/squadrons/230-squadron/
No 617 Sqn	www.raf.mod.uk/our-organisation/squadrons/617-squadron/
No 703 NAS	www.royalnavy.mod.uk/our-organisation/the-fighting-arms/fleet-air-arm/support-and-training/703-naval-air-squadron
No 705 NAS	www.royalnavy.mod.uk/our-organisation/the-fighting-arms/fleet-air-arm/support-and-training/705-naval-air-squadron
No 727 NAS	www.royalnavy.mod.uk/our-organisation/the-fighting-arms/fleet-air-arm/support-and-training/727-naval-air-squadron
No 736 NAS	www.royalnavy.mod.uk/our-organisation/the-fighting-arms/fleet-air-arm/hawk-jets/736-naval-air-squadron

Name of Site	Web Address All prefixed 'http://'
No 750 NAS	www.royalnavy.mod.uk/our-organisation/the-fighting-arms/fleet-air-arm/support-and-training/750-naval-air-squadron
No 809 NAS	www.royalnavy.mod.uk/our-organisation/the-fighting-arms/fleet-air-arm/future-aircraft/809-naval-air-squadron
No 814 NAS	www.royalnavy.mod.uk/our-organisation/the-fighting-arms/fleet-air-arm/helicopter-squadrons/merlin-mk2/814-naval-air-squadron
No 815 NAS	www.royalnavy.mod.uk/our-organisation/the-fighting-arms/fleet-air-arm/helicopter-squadrons/wildcat/815-naval-air-squadron
No 820 NAS	www.royalnavy.mod.uk/our-organisation/the-fighting-arms/fleet-air-arm/helicopter-squadrons/merlin-mk2/820-naval-air-squadron
No 824 NAS	www.royalnavy.mod.uk/our-organisation/the-fighting-arms/fleet-air-arm/helicopter-squadrons/merlin-mk2/824-naval-air-squadron
No 825 NAS	www.royalnavy.mod.uk/our-organisation/the-fighting-arms/fleet-air-arm/helicopter-squadrons/wildcat/825-naval-air-squadron
No 845 NAS	www.royalnavy.mod.uk/our-organisation/the-fighting-arms/fleet-air-arm/helicopter-squadrons/merlin-mk-3/845-naval-air-squadron
No 846 NAS	www.royalnavy.mod.uk/our-organisation/the-fighting-arms/fleet-air-arm/helicopter-squadrons/merlin-mk-3/846-naval-air-squadron
No 847 NAS	www.royalnavy.mod.uk/our-organisation/the-fighting-arms/fleet-air-arm/helicopter-squadrons/wildcat/847-naval-air-squadron
No 849 NAS	www.royalnavy.mod.uk/our-organisation/the-fighting-arms/fleet-air-arm/helicopter-squadrons/sea-king-asac-mk7/849-naval-air-squadron
The Army Air Corps	www.army.mod.uk/who-we-are/corps-regiments-and-units/army-air-corps/
Fleet Air Arm	www.royalnavy.mod.uk/our-organisation/the-fighting-arms/fleet-air-arm
Ministry of Defence	www.gov.uk/government/organisations/ministry-of-defence
QinetiQ	www.qinetiq.com/
RAF Akrotiri	www.raf.mod.uk/our-organisation/stations/raf-akrotiri/
RAF Benson	www.raf.mod.uk/our-organisation/stations/raf-benson/
RAF Brize Norton	www.raf.mod.uk/our-organisation/stations/raf-brize-norton/
RAF College Cranwell	www.raf.mod.uk/our-organisation/stations/raf-college-cranwell/
RAF Coningsby	www.raf.mod.uk/our-organisation/stations/raf-coningsby/
Coningsby Aviation Site (unofficial)	milky01.co.uk/
RAF Cosford	www.raf.mod.uk/our-organisation/stations/raf-cosford/
RAF Leeming	www.raf.mod.uk/our-organisation/stations/raf-leeming/
RAF Linton-on-Ouse	www.raf.mod.uk/our-organisation/stations/raf-linton-on-ouse/
RAF Lossiemouth	www.raf.mod.uk/our-organisation/stations/raf-lossiemouth/
RAF Marham	www.raf.mod.uk/our-organisation/stations/raf-marham/
RAF Mount Pleasant	www.raf.mod.uk/our-organisation/stations/raf-mount-pleasant/
RAF Northolt	www.raf.mod.uk/our-organisation/stations/raf-northolt/
RAF Odiham	www.raf.mod.uk/our-organisation/stations/raf-odiham/
RAF Scampton	www.raf.mod.uk/our-organisation/stations/raf-scampton/
RAF Shawbury	www.raf.mod.uk/our-organisation/stations/raf-shawbury/
RAF Syerston	www.raf.mod.uk/our-organisation/stations/raf-syerston/
RAF Valley	www.raf.mod.uk/our-organisation/stations/raf-valley/
RAF Waddington	www.raf.mod.uk/our-organisation/stations/raf-waddington/
RAF Wittering	www.raf.mod.uk/our-organisation/stations/raf-wittering/
RAF Woodvale	www.raf.mod.uk/our-organisation/stations/raf-woodvale/
RAF Wyton	www.raf.mod.uk/our-organisation/stations/raf-wyton/
Red Arrows	www.raf.mod.uk/display-teams/red-arrows/
Royal Air Force	www.raf.mod.uk/
University Air Squadrons	www.raf.mod.uk/our-organisation/university-air-squadrons/
MILITARY SITES-US	
Air Combat Command	www.acc.af.mil/
Air Force Reserve Command	www.afrc.af.mil/
Air National Guard	www.ang.af.mil/
Aviano Air Base	www.aviano.af.mil/
Liberty Wing Home Page (48th FW)	www.lakenheath.af.mil/
NASA	www.nasa.gov/
Mildenhall	www.mildenhall.af.mil/
Ramstein Air Base	www.ramstein.af.mil/
Spangdahlem Air Base	www.spangdahlem.af.mil/

Name of Site	Web Address All prefixed 'http://')
USAF	www.af.mil/
USAF Europe	www.usafe.af.mil/
USAF World Wide Web Sites	www.af.mil/AF-Sites/
US Army	www.army.mil/
US Marine Corps	www.marines.mil/
US Navy	www.navy.mil/
US Navy Patrol Squadrons (unofficial)	www.vpnavy.com/

MILITARY SITES-ELSEWHERE

Armée de l'Air	www.defense.gouv.fr/air/
Aeronautica Militare	www.aeronautica.difesa.it
Austrian Armed Forces (in German)	www.bundesheer.at/
Finnish Defence Force	puolustusvoimat.fi/en/frontpage
Forca Aerea Portuguesa	www.emfa.pt/
German Marine	www.deutschemarine.de/
Greek Air Force	www.haf.gr/en/
Irish Air Corps	www.military.ie/air-corps
Luftforsvaret	forsvaret.no/en/
Luftwaffe	www.luftwaffe.de/
NATO	www.nato.int/
Royal Australian Air Force	www.airforce.gov.au/
Royal Canadian Air Force	www.airforce.forces.gc.ca/
Royal Danish Air Force (in Danish)	www2.forsvaret.dk/Pages/forside.aspx
Royal Netherlands AF	www.defensie.nl/organisatie/luchtmacht
Royal New Zealand AF	www.airforce.mil.nz/
Singapore Air Force	www.mindef.gov.sg/web/portal/rsaf/home/
South African AF Site (unofficial)	www.saairforce.co.za/
Swedish Air Force	www.forsvarsmakten.se/sv/var-verksamhet/verksamhetsomraden/flygvapnet/
Turkish Air Force	www.hvkk.tsk.tr/en-us/

AIRCRAFT & AERO ENGINE MANUFACTURERS

Airbus Defence & Security	www.airbus.com/defence.html
BAE Systems	www.baesystems.com/
Beechcraft	beechcraft.txtav.com/
Bell	www.bellflight.com/
Boeing	www.boeing.com/
Bombardier	www.bombardier.com/
Britten-Norman	www.britten-norman.com/
Dassault	www.dassault-aviation.com/
Embraer	www.embraer.com/
General Electric	www.ge.com/
Grob Aircraft AG	grob-aircraft.com/en/
Gulfstream Aerospace	www.gulfstream.com/
Kaman Aerospace	www.kaman.com/
Leonardo	www.leonardocompany.com/
Lockheed Martin	www.lockheedmartin.com/
Rolls-Royce	www.rolls-royce.com/
Sikorsky	www.lockheedmartin.com/en-us/capabilities/sikorsky.html

UK AVIATION MUSEUMS

Boscombe Down Aviation Collection, Old Sarum	www.boscombedownaviationcollection.co.uk/
Bournemouth Aviation Museum	www.aviation-museum.co.uk/
Brooklands Museum	www.brooklandsmuseum.com/
City of Norwich Aviation Museum	www.cnam.org.uk/
de Havilland Aircraft Museum	www.dehavillandmuseum.co.uk/
Dumfries & Galloway Aviation Museum	www.dumfriesaviationmuseum.com/
Fleet Air Arm Museum	www.fleetairarm.com/
Gatwick Aviation Museum	www.gatwick-aviation-museum.co.uk/
IWM, Duxford	iwm.org.uk/visits/iwm-duxford
Imperial War Museum, Duxford (unofficial)	abetheaviator.wixsite.com/website/about
The Jet Age Museum	www.jetagemuseum.org/
Lincs Aviation Heritage Centre	www.lincsaviation.co.uk/

Name of Site	Web Address All prefixed 'http://'
Midland Air Museum	www.midlandairmuseum.co.uk/
Museum of Army Flying	www.armyflying.com/
Museum of Berkshire Aviation	www.museumofberkshireaviation.co.uk/
Museum of Science & Industry, Manchester	www.scienceandindustrymuseum.org.uk/
National Museum of Flight, East Fortune	www.nms.ac.uk/national-museum-of-flight?item_id=
Newark Air Museum	www.newarkairmuseum.org/
North East Aircraft Museum	www.nelsam.org.uk/NEAM/NEAM.htm
RAF Museum, Cosford & Hendon	www.rafmuseum.org.uk/
Science Museum, South Kensington	www.sciencemuseum.org.uk/
South Yorkshire Aircraft Museum	www.southyorkshireaircraftmuseum.org.uk/
Yorkshire Air Museum, Elvington	www.yorkshireairmuseum.org/

AVIATION SOCIETIES

Air Britain	www.air-britain.com/
Air Yorkshire	www.airyorkshire.org.uk/
Aviation Heritage UK (was BAPC)	aviationheritageuk.org/
LAAS International	www.laasdata.com/
Military Aviation Review	militaryaviationreview.com/
Royal Aeronautical Society	www.aerosociety.com/
Scramble (Dutch Aviation Society)	www.scramble.nl/
Solent Aviation Society	www.solent-aviation-society.co.uk/
Spitfire Society	www.spitfiresociety.org/
The Aviation Society Manchester	www.tasmanchester.com/
Ulster Aviation Society	www.ulsteraviationsociety.org/
Wolverhampton Aviation Group	www.wolverhamptonaviationgroup.co.uk/

OPERATORS OF HISTORIC AIRCRAFT

The Aircraft Restoration Company	www.aircraftrestorationcompany.com/
Battle of Britain Memorial Flight	www.raf.mod.uk/display-teams/battle-of-britain-memorial-flight/
The Catalina Society	www.catalina.org.uk/
Hangar 11 Collection	www.hangar11.co.uk/
Horizon Aircraft Services	www.horizonaircraftservices.com/
Navy Wings	www.navywings.org.uk/
The Fighter Collection	www.fighter-collection.com/
The Real Aeroplane Company	www.realaero.com/
The Shuttleworth Collection	www.shuttleworth.org/

SITES RELATING TO SPECIFIC TYPES OF MILITARY AIRCRAFT

The 655 Maintenance & Preservation Society	www.xm655.com/
B-24 Liberator	www.b24bestweb.com/
C-130 Hercules	www.c-130hercules.net/
EE Canberra	www.bywat.co.uk/
English Electric Lightning - Vertical Reality	www.aviation-picture-hangar.co.uk/Lightning.html
The Eurofighter site	www.eurofighter.com/
The ex FRADU Canberra Site	www.fradu-canberras.co.uk/
The ex FRADU Hunter Site	www.fradu-hunters.co.uk/
F-4 Phantom II Society	www.f4phantom.com/
F-16: The Complete Reference	www.f-16.net/
The Gripen	saab.com/gripen/
Jet Provost Heaven	www.jetprovosts.com
K5083 - Home Page (Hawker Hurricane)	www.k5083.mistral.co.uk/
Lockheed SR-71 Blackbird	www.wvi.com/~lelandh/sr-71~1.htm
The MiG-21 Page	www.topedge.com/panels/aircraft/sites/kraft/mig.htm
P-3 Orion Research Group	www.p3orion.nl/
Thunder & Lightnings (Postwar British Aircraft)	www.thunder-and-lightnings.co.uk/
UK Apache Resource Centre	www.ukapache.com/

Name of Site	Web Address All prefixed 'http://')
MISCELLANEOUS	
Aerodata Software Ltd.	www.aerodata.org/
AeroResource	www.aeroresource.co.uk/
The AirNet Web Site	www.aviation-links.co.uk/
Aviation Databases	www.aviationdatabases.com/
Delta Reflex	www.deltareflex.com/forum
Demobbed - Out of Service British Military Aircraft	demobbed.org.uk/
Euro Demobbed	www.eurodemobbed.org.uk/
Fighter Control	fightercontrol.co.uk/
Freebird Aviation Database	www.freebirddb.com/
Iconic Aircraft	www.iconicaircraft.co.uk/
Joseph F. Baugher's US Military Serials Site	www.joebaugher.com/
The 'Military Aircraft Markings' Web Site	www.militaryaircraftmarkings.co.uk/
Pacific Aviation Database Organisation	www.gfiapac.com/
PlaneBaseNG	www.planebase.biz/
Thunder & Lightnings: Airfield Viewing Guides	www.thunder-and-lightnings.co.uk/spotting/
UK Airshow Review	www.airshows.co.uk/
UK Military Aircraft Serials Resource Centre	www.ukserials.com/

1115 is a PZL M28B-1R Bryza of the Polish Navy. it belongs to 30 Eskadra Lotnicza (Air Sqn) of 44 Baza Lotnictwa Morskiego at Cewice/Siemirowice.

23 blue is one of just five Mil Mi-8Ts operated by the Lithuanian Air Force's Sraigtasparniu Eskadrile at Siauliai/Zokniai for Search & Rescue (SAR).

NEW MILITARY SERIALS LOG

Serial	Type	Operator

Serial	Type	Operator

Serial	Type	Operator

NEW MILITARY SERIALS LOG

Serial	Type	Operator

Serial	Type	Operator